MW01709818

Microsoft® Official Academic Course

Configuring Windows 8
Exam 70-687

Craig Zacker

With Ed Baker, Steven Fullmer, Garrett Stevens, and Richard Watson

WILEY

Credits

VP & PUBLISHER	Don Fowley
EXECUTIVE EDITOR	John Kane
DIRECTOR OF SALES	Mitchell Beaton
EXECUTIVE MARKETING MANAGER	Chris Ruel
MICROSOFT PRODUCT MANAGER	Gene R. Longo of Microsoft Learning
EDITORIAL PROGRAM ASSISTANT	Allison Winkle
TECHNICAL EDITOR	Brian Svidergol
ASSISTANT MARKETING MANAGER	Debbie Martin
SENIOR PRODUCTION & MANUFACTURING MANAGER	Janis Soo
ASSOCIATE PRODUCTION MANAGER	Joel Balbin
PRODUCTION EDITOR	Eugenia Lee
CREATIVE DIRECTOR	Harry Nolan
COVER DESIGNER	Georgina Smith
SENIOR PRODUCT DESIGNER	Thomas Kulesa
CONTENT EDITOR	Wendy Ashenberg

This book was set in Garamond by Aptara, Inc. and printed and bound by Bind Rite Graphics. The covers were printed by Bind Rite Graphics.

ISBN 978-1-118-51108-4

Printed in the United States of America

10 9 8 7 6 5 4 3

Foreword from the Publisher

Wiley's publishing vision for the Microsoft Official Academic Course series is to provide students and instructors with the skills and knowledge they need to use Microsoft technology effectively in all aspects of their personal and professional lives. Quality instruction is required to help both educators and students get the most from Microsoft's software tools and to become more productive. Thus, our mission is to make our instructional programs trusted educational companions for life.

To accomplish this mission, Wiley and Microsoft have partnered to develop the highest-quality educational programs for information workers, IT professionals, and developers. Materials created by this partnership carry the brand name "Microsoft Official Academic Course," assuring instructors and students alike that the content of these textbooks is fully endorsed by Microsoft, and that they provide the highest-quality information and instruction on Microsoft products. The Microsoft Official Academic Course textbooks are "Official" in still one more way—they are the officially sanctioned courseware for Microsoft IT Academy members.

The Microsoft Official Academic Course series focuses on *workforce development.* These programs are aimed at those students seeking to enter the workforce, change jobs, or embark on new careers as information workers, IT professionals, and developers. Microsoft Official Academic Course programs address their needs by emphasizing authentic workplace scenarios with an abundance of projects, exercises, cases, and assessments.

The Microsoft Official Academic Courses are mapped to Microsoft's extensive research and job-task analysis, the same research and analysis used to create the Microsoft Certified Solutions Associate (MCSA) exam. The textbooks focus on real skills for real jobs. As students work through the projects and exercises in the textbooks and labs, they enhance their level of knowledge and their ability to apply the latest Microsoft technology to everyday tasks. These students also gain resume-building credentials that can assist them in finding a job, keeping their current job, or in furthering their education.

The concept of life-long learning is today an utmost necessity. Job roles, and even whole job categories, are changing so quickly that none of us can stay competitive and productive without continuously updating our skills and capabilities. The Microsoft Official Academic Course offerings, and their focus on Microsoft certification exam preparation, provide a means for people to acquire and effectively update their skills and knowledge. Wiley supports students in this endeavor through the development and distribution of these courses as Microsoft's official academic publisher.

Today educational publishing requires attention to providing quality print and robust electronic content. By integrating Microsoft Official Academic Course products, MOAC Labs Online, and Microsoft certifications, we are better able to deliver efficient learning solutions for students and teachers alike.

Joseph Heider

General Manager and Senior Vice President

Preface

Welcome to the Microsoft Official Academic Course (MOAC) program for becoming a Microsoft Certified Solutions Associate for Windows 8. MOAC represents the collaboration between Microsoft Learning and John Wiley & Sons, Inc. Microsoft and Wiley teamed up to produce a series of textbooks that deliver compelling and innovative teaching solutions to instructors and superior learning experiences for students. Infused and informed by in-depth knowledge from the creators of Windows 8, and crafted by a publisher known worldwide for the pedagogical quality of its products, these textbooks maximize skills transfer in minimum time. Students are challenged to reach their potential by using their new technical skills as highly productive members of the workforce.

Because this knowledgebase comes directly from Microsoft, architect of Windows 8 and creator of the Microsoft Certified Solutions Associate exams, you are sure to receive the topical coverage that is most relevant to students' personal and professional success. Microsoft's direct participation not only assures you that MOAC textbook content is accurate and current; it also means that students will receive the best instruction possible to enable their success on certification exams and in the workplace.

■ The Microsoft Official Academic Course Program

The Microsoft Official Academic Course series is a complete program for instructors and institutions to prepare and deliver great courses on Microsoft software technologies. With MOAC, we recognize that because of the rapid pace of change in the technology and curriculum developed by Microsoft, there is an ongoing set of needs beyond classroom instruction tools for an instructor to be ready to teach the course. The MOAC program endeavors to provide solutions for all these needs in a systematic manner in order to ensure a successful and rewarding course experience for both instructor and student—including technical and curriculum training for instructor readiness with new software releases; the software itself for student use at home for building hands-on skills, assessment, and validation of skill development; and a great set of tools for delivering instruction in the classroom and lab. All are important to the smooth delivery of an interesting course on Microsoft software, and all are provided with the MOAC program. We think about the model below as a gauge for ensuring that we completely support you in your goal of teaching a great course. As you evaluate your instructional materials options, you may wish to use the model for comparison purposes with available products.

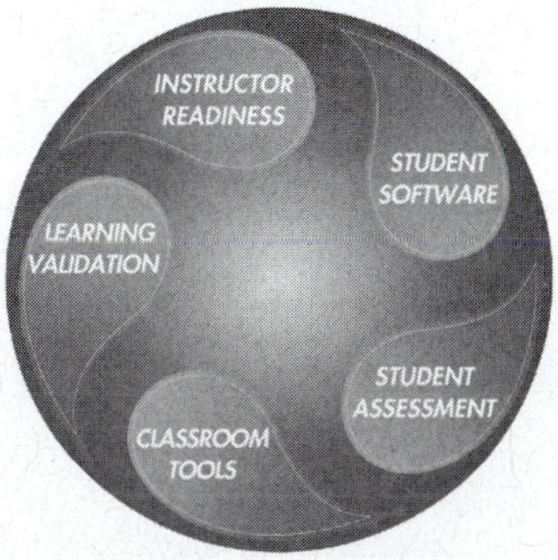

Illustrated Book Tour

▪ Textbook Organization

This textbook is organized in twenty-six lessons, with each lesson corresponding to a particular exam objective for the 70-687 Configuring Windows 8 exam. This MOAC textbook covers all the learning objectives for the 70-687 certification exam, which is the first of two exams needed in order to obtain a Microsoft Certified Solutions Associate (MCSA) certification. The exam objectives are highlighted throughout the textbook.

▪ Pedagogical Features

Many pedagogical features have been developed specifically for Microsoft Official Academic Course programs.

Presenting the extensive procedural information and technical concepts woven throughout the textbook raises challenges for the student and instructor alike. The Illustrated Book Tour that follows provides a guide to the rich features contributing to Microsoft Official Academic Course program's pedagogical plan. Following is a list of key features in each lesson designed to prepare students for success on the certification exams and in the workplace:

- Each lesson begins with an overview of the skills covered in the lesson. More than a standard list of learning objectives, the overview correlates skills to the certification exam objective.
- Illustrations: Screen images provide visual feedback as students work through the exercises. The images reinforce key concepts, provide visual clues about the steps, and allow students to check their progress.
- Key Terms: Important technical vocabulary is listed at the beginning of the lesson. When these terms are used later in the lesson, they appear in bold italic type and are defined.
- Engaging point-of-use reader aids, located throughout the lessons, tell students why this topic is relevant (*The Bottom Line*), provide students with helpful hints (*Take Note*), or show cross-references to where content is covered in greater detail (*X Ref*). Reader aids also provide additional relevant or background information that adds value to the lesson.
- Certification Ready features throughout the text signal students where a specific certification objective is covered. They provide students with a chance to check their understanding of that particular exam objective and, if necessary, review the section of the lesson where it is covered.
- Knowledge Assessments provide lesson-ending activities that test students' comprehension and retention of the material taught, presented using some of the question types that they'll see on the certification exam.
- An important supplement to this textbook is the accompanying lab work. Labs are available via a Lab Manual, and also by MOAC Labs Online. MOAC Labs Online provides students with the ability to work on the actual software simply by connecting through their Internet Explorer web browser. Either way, the labs use real-world scenarios to help students learn workplace skills associated with configuring Windows 8 in an enterprise environment.

■ Lesson Features

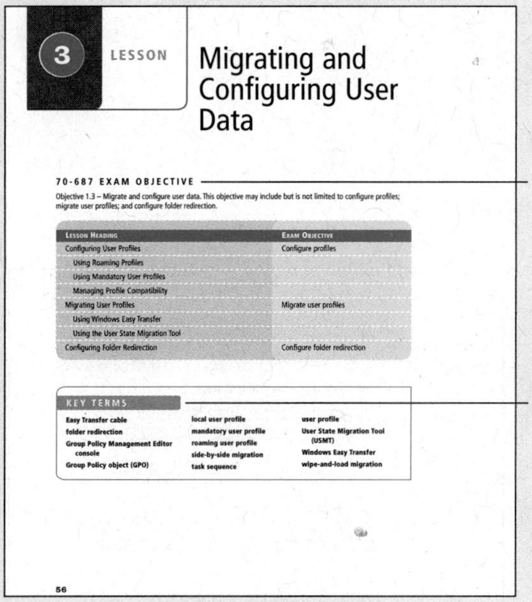
3 LESSON

Migrating and Configuring User Data

70-687 EXAM OBJECTIVE

Objective 1.3 – Migrate and configure user data. This objective may include but is not limited to configure profiles; migrate user profiles; and configure folder redirection.

Lesson Heading	Exam Objective
Configuring User Profiles	Configure profiles
Using Roaming Profiles	
Using Mandatory User Profiles	
Managing Profile Compatibility	
Migrating User Profiles	Migrate user profiles
Using Windows Easy Transfer	
Using the User State Migration Tool	
Configuring Folder Redirection	Configure folder redirection

KEY TERMS

Easy Transfer cable	local user profile	user profile
folder redirection	mandatory user profile	User State Migration Tool (USMT)
Group Policy Management Editor console	roaming user profile	Windows Easy Transfer
Group Policy object (GPO)	side-by-side migration	wipe-and-load migration
	task sequence	

56

Exam Objective

Key Terms

Bottom Line Reader Aid

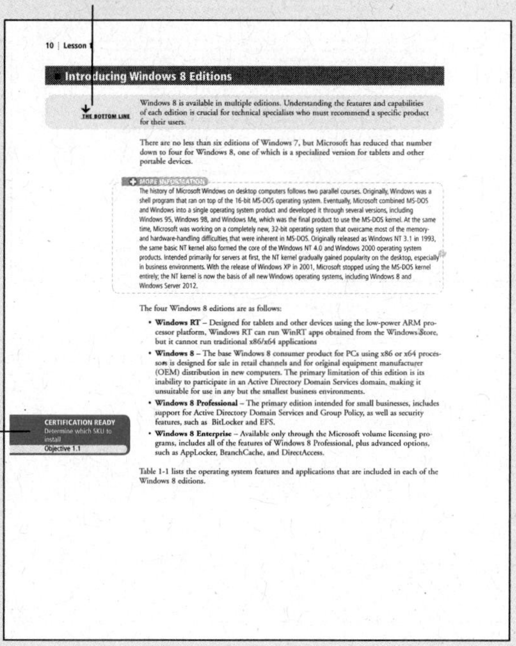
10 | Lesson 1

Introducing Windows 8 Editions

THE BOTTOM LINE Windows 8 is available in multiple editions. Understanding the features and capabilities of each edition is crucial for technical specialists who must recommend a specific product for their users.

There are no less than six editions of Windows 7, but Microsoft has reduced that number down to four for Windows 8, one of which is a specialized version for tablets and other portable devices.

MORE INFORMATION The history of Microsoft Windows on desktop computers follows two parallel courses. Originally, Windows was a shell program that ran on top of the 16-bit MS-DOS operating system. Eventually, Microsoft combined MS-DOS and Windows into a single operating system product and developed it through several versions, including Windows 95, Windows 98, and Windows Me, which was the final product to use the MS-DOS kernel. At the same time, Microsoft was working on a completely new, 32-bit operating system that overcame most of the memory- and hardware-handling difficulties that were inherent in MS-DOS. Originally released as Windows NT 3.1 in 1993, the same basic NT kernel also formed the core of the Windows NT 4.0 and Windows 2000 operating system products. Intended primarily for servers at first, the NT kernel gradually gained popularity on the desktop, especially in business environments. With the release of Windows XP in 2001, Microsoft stopped using the MS-DOS kernel entirely; the NT kernel is now the basis of all new Windows operating systems, including Windows 8 and Windows Server 2012.

The four Windows 8 editions are as follows:

- **Windows RT** – Designed for tablets and other devices using the low-power ARM processor platform, Windows RT can run WinRT apps obtained from the Windows Store, but it cannot run traditional x86/x64 applications
- **Windows 8** – The base Windows 8 consumer product for PCs using x86 or x64 processors is designed for sale in retail channels and for original equipment manufacturer (OEM) distribution in new computers. The primary limitation of this edition is its inability to participate in an Active Directory Domain Services domain, making it unsuitable for use in any but the smallest business environments.
- **Windows 8 Professional** – The primary edition intended for small businesses, includes support for Active Directory Domain Services and Group Policy, as well as security features, such as BitLocker and EFS.
- **Windows 8 Enterprise** – Available only through the Microsoft volume licensing programs, includes all of the features of Windows 8 Professional, plus advanced options, such as AppLocker, BranchCache, and DirectAccess.

CERTIFICATION READY Determine which SKU to install Objective 1.1

Table 1-1 lists the operating system features and applications that are included in each of the Windows 8 editions.

Certification Ready Alert

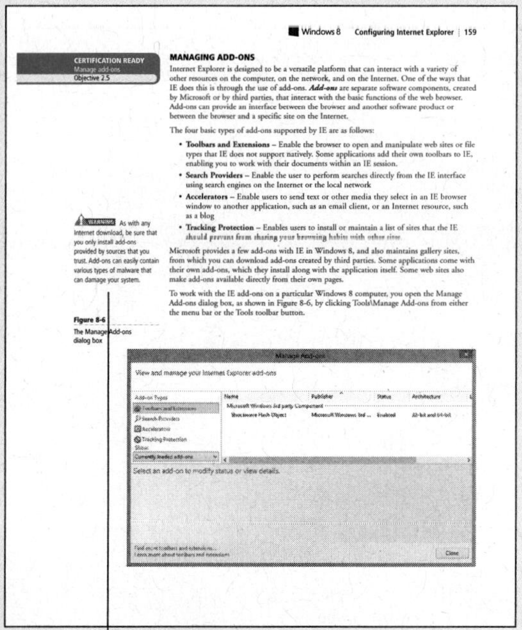
Windows 8 Configuring Internet Explorer | 159

CERTIFICATION READY Manage add-ons Objective 2.5

MANAGING ADD-ONS

Internet Explorer is designed to be a versatile platform that can interact with a variety of other resources on the computer, on the network, and on the Internet. One of the ways that IE does this is through the use of add-ons. ***Add-ons*** are separate software components, created by Microsoft or by third parties, that interact with the basic functions of the web browser. Add-ons can provide an interface between the browser and another software product or between the browser and a specific site on the Internet.

The four basic types of add-ons supported by IE are as follows:

- **Toolbars and Extensions** – Enable the browser to open and manipulate web sites or file types that IE does not support natively. Some applications add their own toolbars to IE, enabling you to work with their documents within an IE session.
- **Search Providers** – Enable the user to perform searches directly from the IE interface using search engines on the Internet or the local network
- **Accelerators** – Enable users to send text or other media they select in an IE browser window to another application, such as an email client, or an Internet resource, such as a blog
- **Tracking Protection** – Enables users to install or maintain a list of sites that the IE should prevent from sharing your browsing habits with other sites.

WARNING As with any Internet download, be sure that you only install add-ons provided by sources that you trust. Add-ons can easily contain various types of malware that can damage your system.

Microsoft provides a few add-ons with IE in Windows 8, and also maintains gallery sites, from which you can download add-ons created by third parties. Some applications come with their own add-ons, which they install along with the application itself. Some web sites also make add-ons available directly from their own pages.

To work with the IE add-ons on a particular Windows 8 computer, you open the Manage Add-ons dialog box, as shown in Figure 8-6, by clicking Tools\Manage Add-ons from either the menu bar or the Tools toolbar button.

Figure 8-6 The Manage Add-ons dialog box

Warning Reader Aid

www.wiley.com/college/microsoft *or*
call the MOAC Toll-Free Number: 1+(888) 764-7001 (U.S. & Canada only)

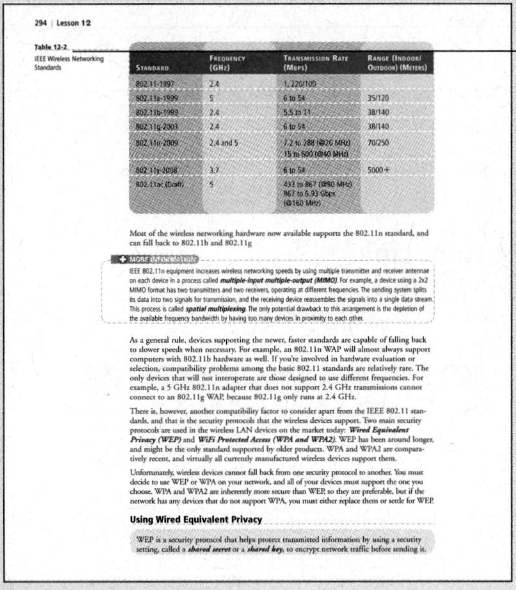
294 | Lesson 12

Table 12-2

IEEE Wireless Networking Standards

Standard	Frequency (GHz)	Transmission Rate (Mbps)	Range (Indoor/Outdoor) (Meters)
802.11-1997	2.4	1, 2 20/100	
802.11a-1999	5	6 to 54	35/120
802.11b-1999	2.4	5.5 to 11	38/140
802.11g-2003	2.4	6 to 54	38/140
802.11n-2009	2.4 and 5	7.2 to 288 (@20 MHz) 15 to 600 (@40 MHz)	70/250
802.11y-2008	3.7	6 to 54	5000+
802.11ac (Draft)	5	433 to 867 (@80 MHz) 867 to 6.93 Gbps (@160 MHz)	

Most of the wireless networking hardware now available supports the 802.11n standard, and can fall back to 802.11b and 802.11g

MORE INFORMATION

IEEE 802.11n equipment increases wireless networking speeds by using multiple transmitter and receiver antennae on each device in a process called ***multiple-input multiple-output (MIMO)***. For example, a device using a 2x2 MIMO format has two transmitters and two receivers, operating at different frequencies. The sending system splits its data into two signals for transmission, and the receiving device reassembles the signals into a single data stream. This process is called ***spatial multiplexing***. The only potential drawback to this arrangement is the depletion of the available frequency bandwidth by having too many devices in proximity to each other.

As a general rule, devices supporting the newer, faster standards are capable of falling back to slower speeds when necessary. For example, an 802.11n WAP will almost always support computers with 802.11b hardware as well. If you're involved in hardware evaluation or selection, compatibility problems among the basic 802.11 standards are relatively rare. The only devices that will not interoperate are those designed to use different frequencies. For example, a 5 GHz 802.11n adapter that does not support 2.4 GHz transmissions cannot connect to an 802.11g WAP, because 802.11g only runs at 2.4 GHz.

There is, however, another compatibility factor to consider apart from the IEEE 802.11 standards, and that is the security protocols that the wireless devices support. Two main security protocols are used in the wireless LAN devices on the market today: ***Wired Equivalent Privacy (WEP)*** and ***WiFi Protected Access (WPA and WPA2)***. WEP has been around longer, and might be the only standard supported by older products. WPA and WPA2 are comparatively recent, and virtually all currently manufactured wireless devices support them.

Unfortunately, wireless devices cannot fall back from one security protocol to another. You must decide to use WEP or WPA on your network, and all of your devices must support the one you choose. WPA and WPA2 are inherently more secure than WEP, so they are preferable, but if the network has any devices that do not support WPA, you must either replace them or settle for WEP.

Using Wired Equivalent Privacy

WEP is a security protocol that helps protect transmitted information by using a security setting, called a ***shared secret*** or a ***shared key***, to encrypt network traffic before sending it.

Easy-to-Read Tables

Take Note Reader Aid

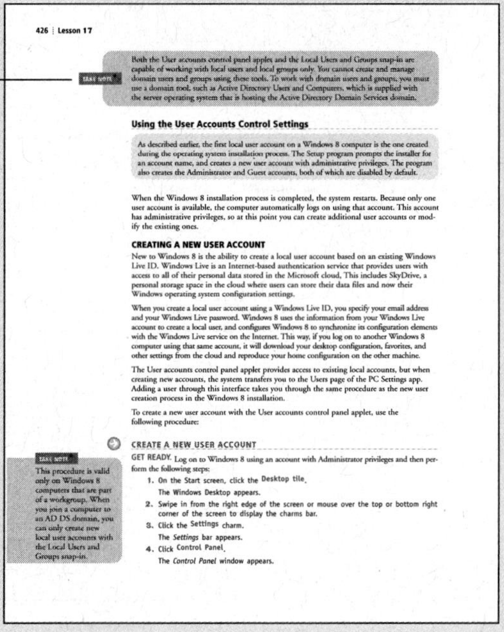
426 | Lesson 17

TAKE NOTE: Both the User accounts control panel applet and the Local Users and Groups snap-in are capable of working with local users and local groups only. You cannot create and manage domain users and groups using these tools. To work with domain users and groups, you must use a domain tool, such as Active Directory Users and Computers, which is supplied with the server operating system that is hosting the Active Directory Domain Services domain.

Using the User Accounts Control Settings

As described earlier, the first local user account on a Windows 8 computer is the one created during the operating system installation process. The Setup program prompts the installer for an account name, and creates a new user account with administrative privileges. The program also creates the Administrator and Guest accounts, both of which are disabled by default.

When the Windows 8 installation process is completed, the system restarts. Because only one user account is available, the computer automatically logs on using that account. This account has administrative privileges, so at this point you can create additional user accounts or modify the existing ones.

CREATING A NEW USER ACCOUNT

New to Windows 8 is the ability to create a local user account based on an existing Windows Live ID. Windows Live is an Internet-based authentication service that provides users with access to all of their personal data stored in the Microsoft cloud, This includes SkyDrive, a personal storage space in the cloud where users can store their data files and now their Windows operating system configuration settings.

When you create a local user account using a Windows Live ID, you specify your email address and your Windows Live password. Windows 8 uses the information from your Windows Live account to create a local user, and configures Windows 8 to synchronize its configuration elements with the Windows Live service on the Internet. This way, if you log on to another Windows 8 computer using that same account, it will download your desktop configuration, favorites, and other settings from the cloud and reproduce your home configuration on the other machine.

The User accounts control panel applet provides access to existing local accounts, but when creating new accounts, the system transfers you to the Users page of the PC Settings app. Adding a user through this interface takes you through the same procedure as the new user creation process in the Windows 8 installation.

To create a new user account with the User accounts control panel applet, use the following procedure:

CREATE A NEW USER ACCOUNT

TAKE NOTE: This procedure is valid only on Windows 8 computers that are part of a workgroup. When you join a computer to an AD DS domain, you can only create new local user accounts with the Local Users and Groups snap-in.

GET READY. Log on to Windows 8 using an account with Administrator privileges and then perform the following steps:

1. On the Start screen, click the **Desktop tile**.
   The Windows Desktop appears.
2. Swipe in from the right edge of the screen or mouse over the top or bottom right corner of the screen to display the charms bar.
3. Click the **Settings** charm.
   The *Settings* bar appears.
4. Click **Control Panel**.
   The *Control Panel* window appears.

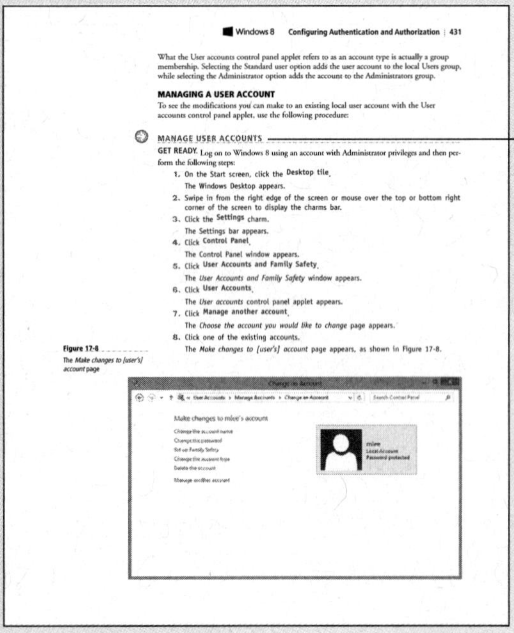
Windows 8 Configuring Authentication and Authorization | 431

What the User accounts control panel applet refers to as an account type is actually a group membership. Selecting the Standard user option adds the user account to the local Users group, while selecting the Administrator option adds the account to the Administrators group.

MANAGING A USER ACCOUNT

To see the modifications you can make to an existing local user account with the User accounts control panel applet, use the following procedure:

MANAGE USER ACCOUNTS

GET READY. Log on to Windows 8 using an account with Administrator privileges and then perform the following steps:

1. On the Start screen, click the **Desktop tile**.
   The Windows Desktop appears.
2. Swipe in from the right edge of the screen or mouse over the top or bottom right corner of the screen to display the charms bar.
3. Click the **Settings** charm.
   The Settings bar appears.
4. Click **Control Panel**.
   The Control Panel window appears.
5. Click **User Accounts and Family Safety**.
   The *User Accounts and Family Safety* window appears.
6. Click **User Accounts**.
   The *User accounts* control panel applet appears.
7. Click **Manage another account**.
   The *Choose the account you would like to change* page appears.
8. Click one of the existing accounts.
   The *Make changes to [user's] account* page appears, as shown in Figure 17-8.

Figure 17-8

The *Make changes to [user's] account* page

Step-by-Step Exercises

www.wiley.com/college/microsoft *or*
call the MOAC Toll-Free Number: 1+(888) 764-7001 (U.S. & Canada only)

Screen Images

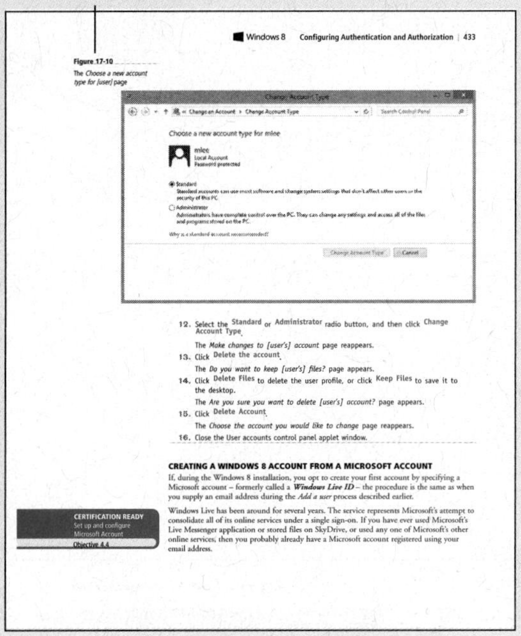
Windows 8 Configuring Authentication and Authorization | 433

Figure 17-10
The *Choose a new account type for [user]* page

12. Select the Standard or Administrator radio button, and then click Change Account Type.
    The *Make changes to [user's] account* page reappears.
13. Click Delete the account.
    The *Do you want to keep [user's] files?* page appears.
14. Click Delete Files to delete the user profile, or click Keep Files to save it to the desktop.
    The *Are you sure you want to delete [user's] account?* page appears.
15. Click Delete Account.
    The *Choose the account you would like to change* page reappears.
16. Close the User accounts control panel applet window.

CREATING A WINDOWS 8 ACCOUNT FROM A MICROSOFT ACCOUNT

If, during the Windows 8 installation, you opt to create your first account by specifying a Microsoft account – formerly called a ***Windows Live ID*** – the procedure is the same as when you supply an email address during the *Add a user* process described earlier.

CERTIFICATION READY
Set up and configure Microsoft Account
Objective 4.4

Windows Live has been around for several years. The service represents Microsoft's attempt to consolidate all of its online services under a single sign-on. If you have ever used Microsoft's Live Messenger application or stored files on SkyDrive, or used any one of Microsoft's other online services, then you probably already have a Microsoft account registered using your email address.

Informative Diagrams

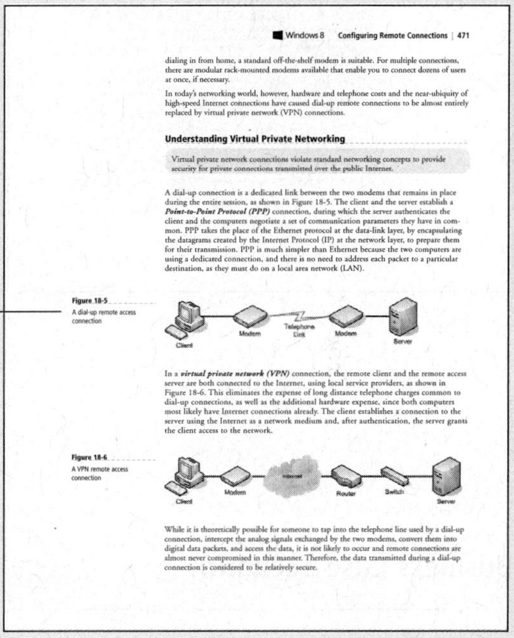
Windows 8 Configuring Remote Connections | 471

dialing in from home, a standard off-the-shelf modem is suitable. For multiple connections, there are modular rack-mounted modems available that enable you to connect dozens of users at once, if necessary.

In today's networking world, however, hardware and telephone costs and the near-ubiquity of high-speed Internet connections have caused dial-up remote connections to be almost entirely replaced by virtual private network (VPN) connections.

Understanding Virtual Private Networking

Virtual private network connections violate standard networking concepts to provide security for private connections transmitted over the public Internet.

A dial-up connection is a dedicated link between the two modems that remains in place during the entire session, as shown in Figure 18-5. The client and the server establish a ***Point-to-Point Protocol (PPP)*** connection, during which the server authenticates the client and the computers negotiate a set of communication parameters they have in common. PPP takes the place of the Ethernet protocol at the data-link layer, by encapsulating the datagrams created by the Internet Protocol (IP) at the network layer, to prepare them for their transmission. PPP is much simpler than Ethernet because the two computers are using a dedicated connection, and there is no need to address each packet to a particular destination, as they must do on a local area network (LAN).

Figure 18-5
A dial-up remote access connection

Client — Modem — Telephone Link — Modem — Server

In a ***virtual private network (VPN)*** connection, the remote client and the remote access server are both connected to the Internet, using local service providers, as shown in Figure 18-6. This eliminates the expense of long distance telephone charges common to dial-up connections, as well as the additional hardware expense, since both computers most likely have Internet connections already. The client establishes a connection to the server using the Internet as a network medium and, after authentication, the server grants the client access to the network.

Figure 18-6
A VPN remote access connection

Client — Modem — Internet — Router — Switch — Server

While it is theoretically possible for someone to tap into the telephone line used by a dial-up connection, intercept the analog signals exchanged by the two modems, convert them into digital data packets, and access the data, it is not likely to occur and remote connections are almost never compromised in this manner. Therefore, the data transmitted during a dial-up connection is considered to be relatively secure.

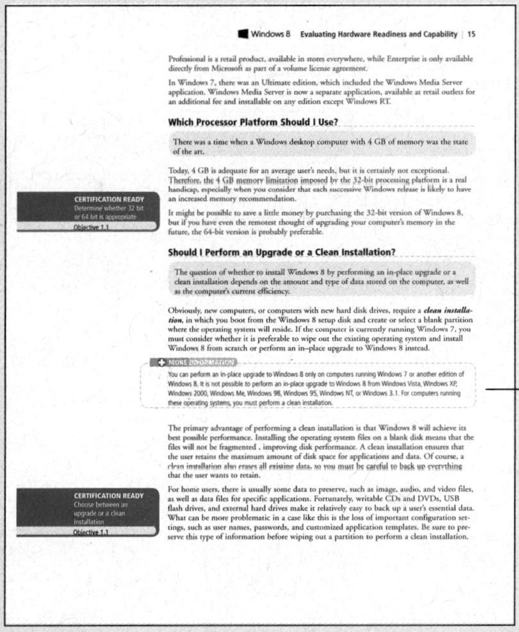
Windows 8 Evaluating Hardware Readiness and Capability | 15

Professional is a retail product, available in stores everywhere, while Enterprise is only available directly from Microsoft as part of a volume license agreement.

In Windows 7, there was an Ultimate edition, which included the Windows Media Server application. Windows Media Server is now a separate application, available at retail outlets for an additional fee and installable on any edition except Windows RT.

Which Processor Platform Should I Use?

There was a time when a Windows desktop computer with 4 GB of memory was the state of the art.

Today, 4 GB is adequate for an average user's needs, but it is certainly not exceptional. Therefore, the 4 GB memory limitation imposed by the 32-bit processing platform is a real handicap, especially when you consider that each successive Windows release is likely to have an increased memory recommendation.

CERTIFICATION READY
Determine whether 32 bit or 64 bit is appropriate
Objective 1.1

It might be possible to save a little money by purchasing the 32-bit version of Windows 8, but if you have even the remotest thought of upgrading your computer's memory in the future, the 64-bit version is probably preferable.

Should I Perform an Upgrade or a Clean Installation?

The question of whether to install Windows 8 by performing an in-place upgrade or a clean installation depends on the amount and type of data stored on the computer, as well as the computer's current efficiency.

Obviously, new computers, or computers with new hard disk drives, require a ***clean installation***, in which you boot from the Windows 8 setup disk and create or select a blank partition where the operating system will reside. If the computer is currently running Windows 7, you must consider whether it is preferable to wipe out the existing operating system and install Windows 8 from scratch or perform an in–place upgrade to Windows 8 instead.

MORE INFORMATION
You can perform an in-place upgrade to Windows 8 only on computers running Windows 7 or another edition of Windows 8. It is not possible to perform an in-place upgrade to Windows 8 from Windows Vista, Windows XP, Windows 2000, Windows Me, Windows 98, Windows 95, Windows NT, or Windows 3.1. For computers running these operating systems, you must perform a clean installation.

The primary advantage of performing a clean installation is that Windows 8 will achieve its best possible performance. Installing the operating system files on a blank disk means that the files will not be fragmented , improving disk performance. A clean installation ensures that the user retains the maximum amount of disk space for applications and data. Of course, a clean installation also erases all existing data, so you must be careful to back up everything that the user wants to retain.

CERTIFICATION READY
Choose between an upgrade or a clean installation
Objective 1.1

For home users, there is usually some data to preserve, such as image, audio, and video files, as well as data files for specific applications. Fortunately, writable CDs and DVDs, USB flash drives, and external hard drives make it relatively easy to back up a user's essential data. What can be more problematic in a case like this is the loss of important configuration settings, such as user names, passwords, and customized application templates. Be sure to preserve this type of information before wiping out a partition to perform a clean installation.

More Information Reader Aid

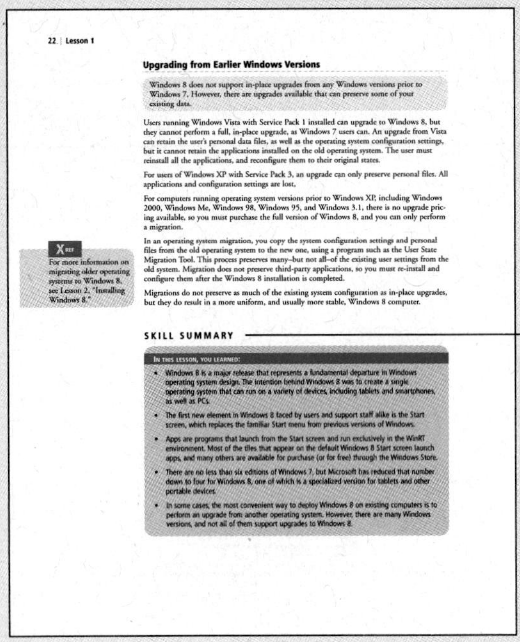

22 | Lesson 1

Upgrading from Earlier Windows Versions

Windows 8 does not support in-place upgrades from any Windows versions prior to Windows 7. However, there are upgrades available that can preserve some of your existing data.

Users running Windows Vista with Service Pack 1 installed can upgrade to Windows 8, but they cannot perform a full, in-place upgrade, as Windows 7 users can. An upgrade from Vista can retain the user's personal data files, as well as the operating system configuration settings, but it cannot retain the applications installed on the old operating system. The user must reinstall all the applications, and reconfigure them to their original states.

For users of Windows XP with Service Pack 3, an upgrade can only preserve personal files. All applications and configuration settings are lost,

For computers running operating system versions prior to Windows XP, including Windows 2000, Windows Me, Windows 98, Windows 95, and Windows 3.1, there is no upgrade pricing available, so you must purchase the full version of Windows 8, and you can only perform a migration.

X REF
For more information on migrating older operating systems to Windows 8, see Lesson 2, "Installing Windows 8."

In an operating system migration, you copy the system configuration settings and personal files from the old operating system to the new one, using a program such as the User State Migration Tool. This process preserves many–but not all–of the existing user settings from the old system. Migration does not preserve third-party applications, so you must re-install and configure them after the Windows 8 installation is completed.

Migrations do not preserve as much of the existing system configuration as in-place upgrades, but they do result in a more uniform, and usually more stable, Windows 8 computer.

SKILL SUMMARY

IN THIS LESSON, YOU LEARNED:

- Windows 8 is a major release that represents a fundamental departure in Windows operating system design. The intention behind Windows 8 was to create a single operating system that can run on a variety of devices, including tablets and smartphones, as well as PCs.
- The first new element in Windows 8 faced by users and support staff alike is the Start screen, which replaces the familiar Start menu from previous versions of Windows.
- Apps are programs that launch from the Start screen and run exclusively in the WinRT environment. Most of the tiles that appear on the default Windows 8 Start screen launch apps, and many others are available for purchase (or for free) through the Windows Store.
- There are no less than six editions of Windows 7, but Microsoft has reduced that number down to four for Windows 8, one of which is a specialized version for tablets and other portable devices.
- In some cases, the most convenient way to deploy Windows 8 on existing computers is to perform an upgrade from another operating system. However, there are many Windows versions, and not all of them support upgrades to Windows 8.

Skill Summary

Knowledge Assessment

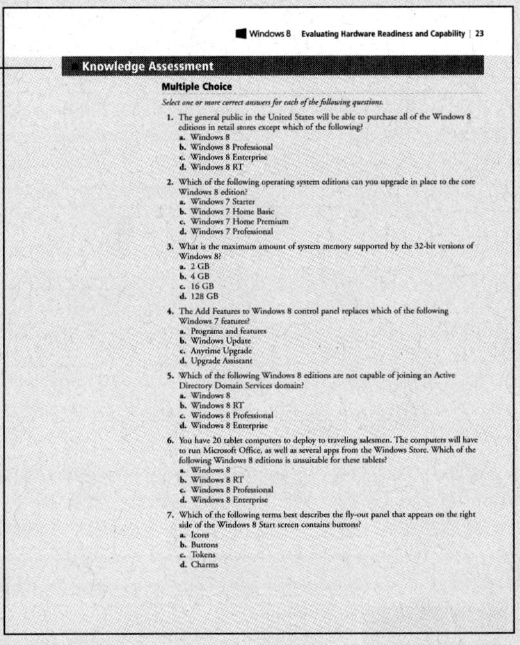

Windows 8 Evaluating Hardware Readiness and Capability | 23

Knowledge Assessment

Multiple Choice

Select one or more correct answers for each of the following questions.

1. The general public in the United States will be able to purchase all of the Windows 8 editions in retail stores except which of the following?
   a. Windows 8
   b. Windows 8 Professional
   c. Windows 8 Enterprise
   d. Windows 8 RT
2. Which of the following operating system editions can you upgrade in place to the core Windows 8 edition?
   a. Windows 7 Starter
   b. Windows 7 Home Basic
   c. Windows 7 Home Premium
   d. Windows 7 Professional
3. What is the maximum amount of system memory supported by the 32-bit versions of Windows 8?
   a. 2 GB
   b. 4 GB
   c. 16 GB
   d. 128 GB
4. The Add Features to Windows 8 control panel replaces which of the following Windows 7 features?
   a. Programs and features
   b. Windows Update
   c. Anytime Upgrade
   d. Upgrade Assistant
5. Which of the following Windows 8 editions are not capable of joining an Active Directory Domain Services domain?
   a. Windows 8
   b. Windows 8 RT
   c. Windows 8 Professional
   d. Windows 8 Enterprise
6. You have 20 tablet computers to deploy to traveling salesmen. The computers will have to run Microsoft Office, as well as several apps from the Windows Store. Which of the following Windows 8 editions is unsuitable for these tablets?
   a. Windows 8
   b. Windows 8 RT
   c. Windows 8 Professional
   d. Windows 8 Enterprise
7. Which of the following terms best describes the fly-out panel that appears on the right side of the Windows 8 Start screen contains buttons?
   a. Icons
   b. Buttons
   c. Tokens
   d. Charms

Business Case Scenarios

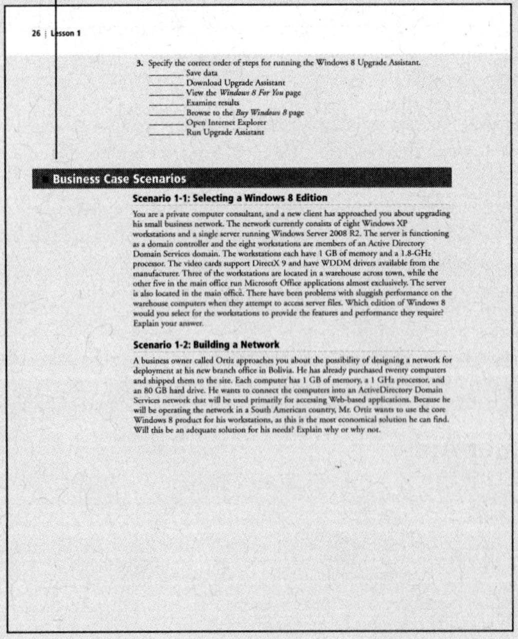

26 | Lesson 1

3. Specify the correct order of steps for running the Windows 8 Upgrade Assistant.
   ________ Save data
   ________ Download Upgrade Assistant
   ________ View the *Windows 8 For You* page
   ________ Examine results
   ________ Browse to the *Buy Windows 8* page
   ________ Open Internet Explorer
   ________ Run Upgrade Assistant

Business Case Scenarios

Scenario 1-1: Selecting a Windows 8 Edition

You are a private computer consultant, and a new client has approached you about upgrading his small business network. The network currently consists of eight Windows XP workstations and a single server running Windows Server 2008 R2. The server is functioning as a domain controller and the eight workstations are members of an Active Directory Domain Services domain. The workstations each have 1 GB of memory and a 1.8-GHz processor. The video cards support DirectX 9 and have WDDM drivers available from the manufacturer. Three of the workstations are located in a warehouse across town, while the other five in the main office run Microsoft Office applications almost exclusively. The server is also located in the main office. There have been problems with sluggish performance on the warehouse computers when they attempt to access server files. Which edition of Windows 8 would you select for the workstations to provide the features and performance they require? Explain your answer.

Scenario 1-2: Building a Network

A business owner called Ortiz approaches you about the possibility of designing a network for deployment at his new branch office in Bolivia. He has already purchased twenty computers and shipped them to the site. Each computer has 1 GB of memory, a 1 GHz processor, and an 80 GB hard drive. He wants to connect the computers into an ActiveDirectory Domain Services network that will be used primarily for accessing Web-based applications. Because he will be operating the network in a South American country, Mr. Ortiz wants to use the core Windows 8 product for his workstations, as this is the most economical solution he can find. Will this be an adequate solution for his needs? Explain why or why not.

www.wiley.com/college/microsoft ***or***
call the MOAC Toll-Free Number: 1+(888) 764-7001 (U.S. & Canada only)

Conventions and Features Used in This Book

This book uses particular fonts, symbols, and heading conventions to highlight important information or to call your attention to special steps. For more information about the features in each lesson, refer to the Illustrated Book Tour section.

CONVENTION	MEANING
THE BOTTOM LINE	This feature provides a brief summary of the material to be covered in the section that follows.
CERTIFICATION READY	This feature signals the point in the text where a specific certification objective is covered. It provides you with a chance to check your understanding of that particular exam objective and, if necessary, review the section of the lesson where it is covered.
TAKE NOTE* MORE INFORMATION	Reader aids appear in shaded boxes found in your text. *Take Note and More Information* provide helpful hints related to particular tasks or topics.
WARNING	*Warning* points out instances when error or misuse could cause damage to the computer or network.
X REF	These *X Ref* notes provide pointers to information discussed elsewhere in the textbook or describe interesting features of Windows 8 that are not directly addressed in the current topic or exercise.
A ***shared printer*** can be used by many individuals on a network.	Key terms appear in bold italic.
`cd\windows\system32\ServerMigrationTools`	Commands that are to be typed are shown in a special font.
Click **Install Now**.	Any button on the screen you are supposed to click on or select will appear bold in blue.

Instructor Support Program

The Microsoft Official Academic Course programs are accompanied by a rich array of resources that incorporate the extensive textbook visuals to form a pedagogically cohesive package. These resources provide all the materials instructors need to deploy and deliver their courses. Resource information available at www.wiley.com/college/microsoft includes:

- **DreamSpark Premium.** The DreamSpark Premium is designed to provide the easiest and most inexpensive developer tools, products, and technologies available to faculty and students in labs, classrooms, and on student PCs. A free three-year membership is available to qualified MOAC adopters.

  Note: Windows 8 can be downloaded from DreamSpark Premium for use in this course.
- **Instructor's Guide.** The Instructor's Guide contains solutions to all the textbook exercises as well as chapter summaries and lecture notes. The Instructor's Guide and Syllabi for various term lengths are available from the Instructor's Book Companion site.
- **Test Bank.** The Test Bank contains hundreds of questions organized by lesson in multiple-choice, best answer, build list, and essay formats and is available to download from the Instructor's Book Companion site. A complete answer key is provided.
- **PowerPoint Presentations.** A complete set of PowerPoint presentations is available on the Instructor's Book Companion site to enhance classroom presentations. Tailored to the text's topical coverage, these presentations are designed to convey key Windows 8 concepts addressed in the text.
- **Available Textbook Figures.** All figures from the text are on the Instructor's Book Companion site. By using these visuals in class discussions, you can help focus students' attention on key elements of Windows 8 and help them understand how to use it effectively in the workplace.
- **MOAC Labs Online.** MOAC Labs Online is a cloud-based environment that enables students to conduct exercises using real Microsoft products. These are not simulations but instead are live virtual machines where faculty and students can perform any activities they would on a local virtual machine. MOAC Labs Online relieves the need for local setup, configuration, and most troubleshooting tasks. This represents an opportunity to lower costs, eliminate the hassle of lab setup, and support and improve student access and portability. Contact your Wiley rep about including MOAC Labs Online with your course offering.
- **Lab Answer Keys.** Answer keys for review questions found in the lab manuals and MOAC Labs Online are available on the Instructor's Book Companion site.
- **Lab Worksheets.** The review questions found in the lab manuals and MOAC Labs Online are gathered in Microsoft Word documents for students to use. These are available on the Instructor's Book Companion site.
- **Sharing with Fellow Faculty Members.** When it comes to improving the classroom experience, there is no better source of ideas and inspiration than your colleagues teaching the same material. The Wiley Faculty Network connects instructors with technology, facilitates the exchange of best practices, and helps to enhance instructional efficiency and effectiveness. Faculty Network activities include technology training and tutorials, virtual seminars, peer-to-peer exchanges of experiences and ideas, personal consulting, and sharing of resources. For details visit www.WhereFacultyConnect.com.

Wiley Faculty Network

DREAMSPARK PREMIUM—FREE 3-YEAR MEMBERSHIP AVAILABLE TO QUALIFIED ADOPTERS!

DreamSpark Premium is designed to provide the easiest and most inexpensive way for institutions to make the latest Microsoft developer tools, products, and technologies available in labs, classrooms, and on student PCs. DreamSpark Premium is an annual membership program for departments teaching Science, Technology, Engineering, and Mathematics (STEM) courses. The membership provides a complete solution to keep academic labs, faculty, and students on the leading edge of technology.

Software available through the DreamSpark Premium program is provided at no charge to adopting departments through the Wiley and Microsoft publishing partnership.

Contact your Wiley rep for details.

For more information about the DreamSpark Premium program, go to Microsoft's DreamSpark website.

Note: Windows 8 can be downloaded from DreamSpark Premium for use by students in this course.

■ Important Web Addresses and Phone Numbers

To locate the Wiley Higher Education Rep in your area, go to http://www.wiley.com/college and click on the "*Contact Us*" link at the top of the page, or call the MOAC Toll Free Number: 1 + (888) 764-7001 (U.S. & Canada only).

To learn more about becoming a Microsoft Certified Solutions Associate and exam availability, visit Microsoft's Training & Certification website. Try www.microsoft.com/learning.

Student Support Program

Book Companion Website (www.wiley.com/college/microsoft)

The students' book companion site for the MOAC series includes any resources, exercise files, and web links that will be used in conjunction with this course.

Wiley E-Text: Powered by VitalSource

Wiley E-Texts: Powered by VitalSource, are innovative, electronic versions of printed textbooks. Students can buy Wiley E-Texts for around 50% off the U.S. price of the printed text and get the added value of permanence and portability. Wiley E-Texts provide students with numerous additional benefits that are not available with other e-text solutions.

Once a Wiley E-Text is downloaded to the computer desktop, students have instant access to all of the content without being online. Students can also print the sections they prefer to read in hard copy. Students also have access to fully integrated resources within their Wiley E-Text. From highlighting their e-text to taking and sharing notes, students can easily personalize their Wiley E-Text as they are reading or following along in class.

Microsoft Software

Various Microsoft software is available through a DreamSpark student membership. DreamSpark is a Microsoft program that provides students with free access to Microsoft software for learning, teaching, and research purposes. Students can download full versions of Microsoft software at no cost by visiting Microsoft's DreamSpark website.

■ Microsoft Certification

Microsoft Certification has many benefits and enables you to keep your skills relevant, applicable, and competitive. In addition, Microsoft Certification is an industry standard that is recognized worldwide—which helps open doors to potential job opportunities. After you earn your Microsoft Certification, you have access to a number of benefits, which can be found on the Microsoft Certified Professional member site.

Microsoft Learning has reinvented the Microsoft Certification Program by building cloud-related skills validation into the industry's most recognized certification program. Microsoft Certified Solutions Expert (MCSE) and Microsoft Certified Solutions Developer (MCSD) are Microsoft's flagship certifications for professionals who want to lead their IT organization's journey to the cloud. These certifications recognize IT professionals with broad and deep skill sets across Microsoft solutions. The Microsoft Certified Solutions Associate (MCSA) is the certification for aspiring IT professionals and is also the prerequisite certification necessary to earn an MCSE. These new certifications integrate cloud-related and on-premise skills validation in order to support organizations and recognize individuals who have the skills required to be productive using Microsoft technologies.

On-premise or in the cloud, Microsoft training and certification empowers technology professionals to expand their skills and gain knowledge directly from the source. Securing these essential skills will allow you to grow your career and make yourself indispensable as the industry shifts to the cloud. Cloud computing ultimately enables IT to focus on more mission-critical activities, raising the bar of required expertise for IT professionals and developers. These reinvented certifications test on a deeper set of skills that map to real-world business context. Rather than testing only on a feature of a technology, Microsoft Certifications now validate more advanced skills and a deeper understanding of the platform.

Microsoft Certified Solutions Associate (MCSA)

The Microsoft Certified Solutions Associate (MCSA) certification is for students preparing to get their first jobs in Microsoft technology. Whether in the cloud or on-premise, this certification validates the core platform skills needed in an IT environment. The MCSA certifications are a requirement to achieve Microsoft's flagship Microsoft Certified Solutions Expert (MCSE) and Microsoft Certified Solutions Developer (MCSD) certifications.

The MCSA Windows 8 certification shows that you have the primary set of Windows 8 skills that are relevant across multiple solution areas in a business environment. Candidates for the 70-687 exam will show their knowledge in configuring and supporting Windows 8 computers, devices, users, and associated network and security resources. These networks are typically configured as a domain-based or peer-to-peer environment with access to the Internet and cloud services. These IT professional could be a consultant, full-time desktop support technician, or an IT generalist who administers Windows 8-based computers and devices as a portion of their broader technical responsibilities.

If you are a student new to IT who may not yet be ready for MCSA, the Microsoft Technology Associate (MTA) certification is an optional starting point that may be available through your institution.

You can learn more about the MCSA certification at the Microsoft Training & Certification website.

Preparing to Take an Exam

Unless you are a very experienced user, you will need to use test preparation materials to prepare to complete the test correctly and within the time allowed. The Microsoft Official Academic Course series is designed to prepare you with a strong knowledge of all exam topics, and with some additional review and practice on your own, you should feel confident in your ability to pass the appropriate exam.

After you decide which exam to take, review the list of objectives for the exam. You can easily identify tasks that are included in the objective list by locating the exam objective overview at the start of each lesson and the Certification Ready sidebars in the margin of the lessons in this book.

To register for the 70-687 exam, visit Microsoft Training & Certifications Registration webpage for directions on how to register with Prometric, the company that delivers the MCSA exams. Keep in mind these following important items about the testing procedure:

- **What to expect.** Microsoft Certification testing labs typically have multiple workstations, which may or may not be occupied by other candidates. Test center administrators strive to provide a quiet and comfortable environment for all test takers.
- **Plan to arrive early.** It is recommended that you arrive at the test center at least 30 minutes before the test is scheduled to begin.
- **Bring your identification.** To take your exam, you must bring the identification (ID) that was specified when you registered for the exam. If you are unclear about which forms of ID are required, contact the exam sponsor identified in your registration information. Although requirements vary, you typically must show two valid forms of ID, one with a photo, both with your signature.
- **Leave personal items at home.** The only item allowed into the testing area is your identification, so leave any backpacks, laptops, briefcases, and other personal items at home. If you have items that cannot be left behind (such as purses), the testing center might have small lockers available for use.
- **Nondisclosure agreement.** At the testing center, Microsoft requires that you accept the terms of a nondisclosure agreement (NDA) and complete a brief demographic survey before taking your certification exam.

About the Author

Craig Zacker is an instructor, writer, editor, and networker whose computing experience began in the days of teletypes and paper tape. After making the move from minicomputers to PCs, he worked as a network administrator and PC support technician while operating a freelance desktop publishing business. After earning a Master's Degree in English and American Literature from New York University, Craig worked extensively on the integration of Microsoft Windows operating systems into existing internetworks, supported fleets of Windows workstations, and was employed as a technical writer, content provider, and webmaster for the online services group of a large software company. Since devoting himself to writing and editing full-time, Craig has authored or contributed to dozens of books on operating systems, networking topics, and PC hardware. He has also published articles with top industry publications, developed online training courses for the various firms, and authored the following Microsoft Official Academic Course (MOAC), Academic Learning Series (ALS), and Self-Paced Training Kit titles:

MOAC: Windows Server 2012, Installing and Configuring Windows Server (Exam 70-410)

MOAC: Windows Server 2008, Enterprise Administrator (Exam 70-647)

MOAC: Windows 7 Configuration (Exam 70-680)

MOAC: Windows Server Administrator (Exam 70-646)

MOAC: Configuring Windows Server 2008 Application Services (Exam 70-643)

MOAC: Configuring Microsoft Windows Vista (Exam 70-620)

MOAC: Implementing & Administering Security in a Windows Server 2003 Network (Exam 70-299)

MOAC: Managing & Maintaining a Microsoft Windows Server 2003 Environment (Exam 70-290)

ALS: Network+ Certification, Second, Third, and Fourth Editions

ALS: Planning & Maintaining a Windows Server 2003 Network Infrastructure (Exam 70-293)

ALS: Microsoft Windows 2000 Network Infrastructure Administration, Second Edition (2002)

MCSE Self-Paced Training Kit (Exam 70-293): Planning & Maintaining a Microsoft Windows Server 2003 Network Infrastructure (2003)

MCSA/MCSE Self-Paced Training Kit: Microsoft Windows 2000 Network Infrastructure Administration, Exam 70-216, Second Edition (2002)

MCSA Training Kit: Managing a Windows 2000 Network Environment (2002)

Network+ Certification Training Kit, First and Second Editions (2001)

Network+ Certification Readiness Review (2001)

About the Contributors

Ed Baker, Microsoft Certified Trainer (MCT), Microsoft Certified Solutions Associate (MCSA) and a Microsoft Certified Solutions Expert (MCSE), has 20 years of experience in the IT industry as a consultant, trainer, author, and project manager. Ed has experience in many of Microsoft's key technologies including Windows Server, Windows Client, Exchange Server, System Center, and SQL Server. Ed also teaches in Microsoft's IT Academy program in the United Kingdom. When not teaching or writing, you will no doubt find Ed either blogging (as a guest blogger for UK Technet and other IT sites) or riding his motorcycle.

Steven Fullmer, MCT, PMP, MBA, ITIL, MCTS/MCITP/MCSA, CTT+/A+, CDP/CCP, is a Staff Instructor for Interface Technical Training. He has more than 32 years of architecture and development experience in the supercomputer, financial, security, telecommunication, and Internet industries with Honeywell Large Computer Products, NEC Supercomputers, First Interstate Bank, Wells Fargo Bank, AG Communication Systems, and Lucent Technologies. Steven is an internationally published author including CIO.com, InformIT, Dr. Dobbs Journal, and One Planet Magazine.

Garrett Stevens is a Systems Software Specialist for Black Hills State University (BHSU). He currently designs, tests, implements, and manages solutions to efficiently meet and excel above the University's needs of virtualization, messaging, storage, backup, server operations, and client support. Garrett has earned the following certifications: Microsoft Certified Trainer (MCT), Microsoft Certified Solutions Associate (MCSA): Server 2012, MCSA: Server 2008, Microsoft Certified IT Professional (MCITP): Enterprise Administrator on Windows Server 2008, MCITP: Enterprise Messaging Administrator on Exchange 2010, and HP Accredited Platform Specialist. In his free time, Garrett enjoys spending time with his wife and children, hiking in the Black Hills, disk golf, writing, and trap shooting.

Richard Watson has over 20 years of industry experience in the technology and training fields. He has worked in the biotech, manufacturing, healthcare, and telecommunications industries as a Microsoft Certified Systems Engineer. Over the years, he has brought his real-world experience to the classroom by creating and teaching courses on network administration and security fundamentals. These courses were delivered to public universities, community colleges, and private businesses across the country. He is currently the President of Bridgehill Learning Solutions, LLC, which provides technical training/writing, content development, and content conversion services.

Acknowledgements

We thank the MOAC faculty and instructors who have assisted us in building the Microsoft Official Academic Course courseware. These elite educators have acted as our sounding board on key pedagogical and design decisions leading to the development of the MOAC courseware for future Information Technology workers. They have provided invaluable advice in the service of quality instructional materials, and we truly appreciate their dedication to technology education.

Brian Bridson, Baker College of Flint

David Chaulk, Baker College Online

Ron Handlon, Remington College—Tampa Campus

Katherine James, Seneca College of Applied Arts & Technology

Wen Liu, ITT Educational Services

Zeshan Sattar, Pearson in Practice

Jared Spencer, Westwood College Online

David Vallerga, MTI College

Bonny Willy, Ivy Tech State College

We also thank Microsoft Learning's Alison Cunard, Zubair Murtaza, Tim Sneath, Keith Loeber, Rob Linsky, Anne Hamilton, Shelby Grieve, Gene Longo, Mike Mulcare, Paul Schmitt, Martin DelRe, Colin Klein, Julia Stasio, and Josh Barnhill for their encouragement and support in making the Microsoft Official Academic Course programs the finest academic materials for mastering the newest Microsoft technologies for both students and instructors.

Brief Contents

Contents

Evaluating Hardware Readiness and Capability

LESSON 1

70-687 EXAM OBJECTIVE

Objective 1.1 – Evaluate hardware readiness and compatibility. This objective may include but is not limited to determine whether 32 bit or 64 bit is appropriate; determine screen resolution; choose between an upgrade or a clean installation; and determine which SKU to install.

Lesson Heading	Exam Objective
Introducing Windows 8	
Using the Start Screen	
Using the Windows Desktop	
Accessing Configuration Settings	
Introducing Windows 8 Editions	Determine which SKU to install Determine whether 32 bit or 64 bit is appropriate
Understanding Windows 8 System Requirements	Determine screen resolution
Selecting Installation Options	
Will the Hardware Support the New Operating System?	
Will the New Operating System Support the Existing Applications?	
Which Windows 8 Edition Should I Install?	
Which Processor Platform Should I Use?	Determine whether 32 bit or 64 bit is appropriate
Should I Perform an Upgrade or a Clean Installation?	Choose between an upgrade or a clean installation
Do I Have to Install Multiple Languages?	
Running Windows 8 Upgrade Assistant	
Identifying Upgrade Paths	
Upgrading Windows 8 Editions	
Upgrading from Windows 7	
Upgrading from Earlier Windows Versions	

KEY TERMS

apps	edge UI	multilingual user interface (MUI)
charms	in-place upgrade	Start screen
clean installation	live tiles	Upgrade Assistant

■ Introducing Windows 8

THE BOTTOM LINE

Windows 8 is a major release that represents a fundamental departure in Windows operating system design. The intention behind Windows 8 was to create a single operating system that can run on a variety of devices, including tablets and smartphones, as well as PCs.

For users, Windows 8 provides a new way of looking at the software running on the computer. Many of the familiar Windows components are gone or substantially changed, and there are new ways of doing almost everything.

For IT specialists responsible for installing, configuring, and maintaining Windows 8 computers, many of the familiar configuration tools are still there, such as Control Panel and Administrative Tools; you just have to become accustomed to accessing them in different ways.

Using the Start Screen

The first new element in Windows 8 faced by users and support staff alike is the ***Start screen***, which replaces the familiar Start menu from previous versions of Windows.

Designed to support both touch-based screens and the traditional mouse, the Start screen contains a series of tiles that provide access to the various operating system elements, as shown in Figure 1-1.

Figure 1-1

The Windows 8 Start screen

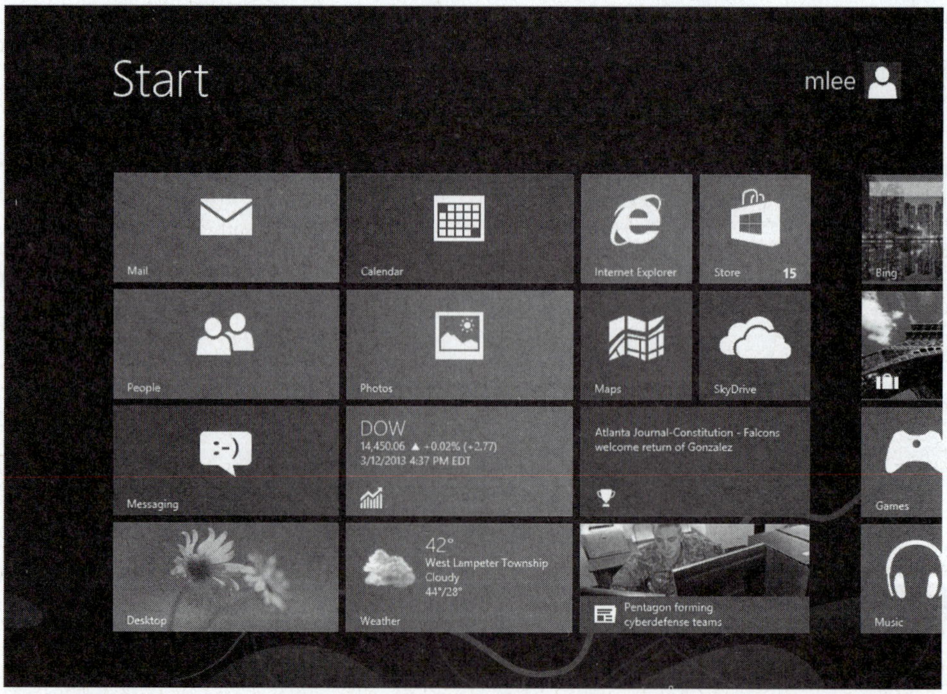

Tiles are larger than the icons found on the Windows desktop, and unlike the static icons, they can contain dynamic content provided by the software they represent. For example, the tile for a Web browser can contain a thumbnail of the currently open Web site, while the Messaging tile can display part of your latest incoming email. Icons in Windows 8 that contain this type of dynamic content are called ***live tiles***.

ACCESSING START SCREEN CONTROLS

The Start screen has no visible controls on it, initially. By touching the screen in specific ways or by mousing over certain areas designated as hot spots, you can navigate around the screen or make controls appear. For example, swiping a finger from right to left on a touch screen scrolls the Smart screen display to one side, displaying any tiles that were previously hidden. The mouse equivalent is a standard scroll bar.

However, when you swipe a finger from the right edge of a touch screen towards the center, a fly-out panel with icons on it called the ***edge UI*** appears, as shown in Figure 1-2. The mouse equivalent to this gesture is to place your cursor in the right-side top or bottom corner of the screen.

Figure 1-2

The Windows 8 charm bar

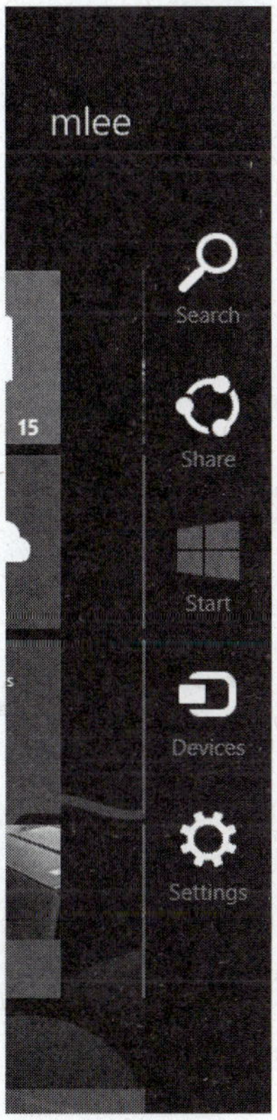

This UI (user interface) contains a series of buttons called ***charms***, which provide access to common operating system functions, including the following:

- **Search** – Enables you to perform a system-wide search for apps, settings, or files, based on a word or phrase appearing in the element's name or in its content, as shown in Figure 1-3
- **Share** – Provides access to the bidirectional sharing options for the currently selected app
- **Start** – Toggles between the Start screen and the Windows Desktop
- **Devices** – Provides quick access to hardware devices, such as printers, which you can use with the currently selected app
- **Settings** – Provides access to a Settings bar containing operating system controls specific to the current screen, as shown in Figure 1-4

Figure 1-3

The Windows 8 search bar

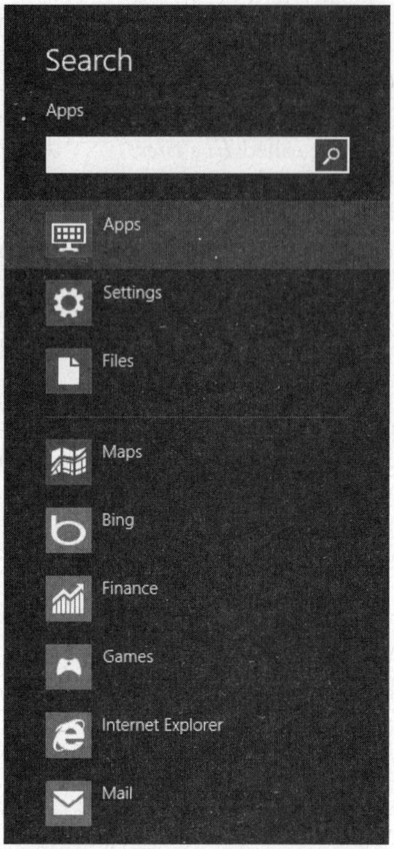

Figure 1-4

The Windows 8 settings bar

The same swiping gesture from the left edge of the screen, or mousing over the lower left corner and dragging up, displays a thumbnail bar containing your currently open apps, as shown in Figure 1-5.

Figure 1-5

The Windows 8 thumbnail bar

Swiping up from the bottom of the screen, or right-clicking on the Start screen background, displays an All Apps button, which leads to an Apps screen full of small tiles representing all of the applications installed on the computer, as shown in Figure 1-6. This is the closest equivalent to the Start menu of previous versions in Windows 8.

Figure 1-6

The Windows 8 Apps screen

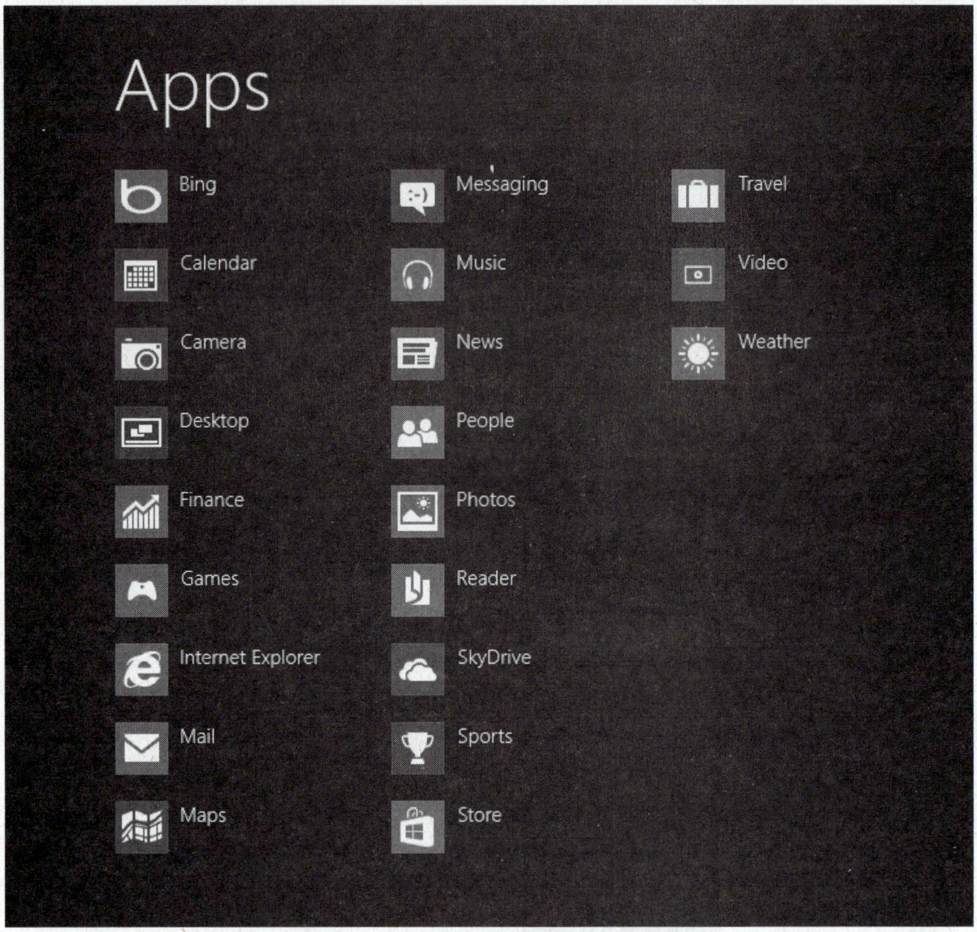

MORE INFORMATION

The Windows 8 Start screen is the primary element of the user interface intended for use on tablets and smartphones. All of the Start screen's features and capabilities are accessible using the mouse and the keyboard, but it is only with a touch screen that it takes on a certain ergonomic elegance. Operating a touch screen requires a familiarity with certain finger gestures, such as the following:

- **Tap** – Press a fingertip to the screen and release it. The function is identical to that of a mouse click.
- **Double-tap** – Press a fingertip to the screen twice in quick succession on the same spot. The function is identical to that of a double mouse click.
- **Press and hold** – Tap a point on the screen and press down for approximately two seconds. The function is the same as that of mousing over a designated spot and hovering.
- **Slide** – Press a point on the screen and draw your finger across it without pausing. The function is the same as clicking and dragging a mouse.
- **Swipe** – Draw a finger across the screen in the indicated direction.

The tiles on the Start screen are configurable in a number of ways. Users can move the tiles around, change their size, and control whether they display live content. It is also possible to remove seldom-used tiles and add new tiles for applications, files, and shortcuts on the computer.

RUNNING START SCREEN APPS

The Windows 8 Start screen is not just a new way of launching your applications, however. The screen also provides a runtime environment called WinRT, which is designed to run a new class of software components called apps.

TAKE NOTE* In the past, for many computer users, the term app was simply an abbreviation for the term application. Today, the term app is typically used to refer to a small, inexpensive program designed to perform a few specialized tasks. The term application is more commonly reserved for large, commercial, multipurpose software products.

Apps are programs that launch from the Start screen and run exclusively in the WinRT environment. Most of the tiles that appear on the default Windows 8 Start screen launch apps, and many others are available for purchase (or for free) through the Windows Store.

MORE INFORMATION

For more information on the Windows Store and on obtaining new apps, see Lesson 6, "Installing and Configuring Windows Store Applications."

CLOSING START SCREEN APPS

One of the more frequent complaints made by new users of Windows 8 concerns the difficulty they have in closing applications. When you open an app on the Start menu, there are no window controls, such as the X button in the upper right corner.

Experienced Windows users are accustomed to closing unneeded applications, to free up system resources for other purposes. Windows 8 handles system memory in quite a different manner from previous Windows versions, however. When an application remains idle for a period of time, the operating system suspends it and reassigns its memory automatically, so there is really is no reason to close applications, from a performance standpoint.

However, having a thumbnail bar with a dozen or more apps on it can be unwieldy, so users still might want to close their unused apps, which you can do in any of the following ways:

- On the thumbnail bar, drag a thumbnail to the bottom of the screen or right-click a thumbnail and select Close from the context menu,
- On a full screen app, tap or mouse over the top of the screen and, when the cursor changes to a hand, drag it down to the bottom of the screen.
- Press Alt+F4 on the keyboard.

Using the Windows Desktop

Although the Start screen appears by default when you boot a Windows 8 computer, the familiar Windows Desktop is still there, and it still functions in much the same way as previous Windows versions.

To access the Desktop from the Start screen, you tap or click the bottom left tile, which as a photograph of daisies on it by default. The Desktop appears, along with the standard Taskbar and the Recycle Bin icon. Users accustomed to launching applications from desktop icons or pinning them to the Taskbar can continue to do so. You cannot, however, run WinRT apps from the Desktop; they require the Start screen for their operating environment.

Once on the Desktop, you can return to the Start screen by mousing over the lower left corner of the screen, selecting the Start charm on the charm bar, or tapping the Win key.

Many users and administrators have expressed a desire to boot Windows 8 directly to the desktop, bypassing the Start screen entirely, but Windows 8 unfortunately provides no such option. There are third-party utilities available that can do this, as well as restore the Windows 7-style Start menu.

However, the easiest workaround at this time is to use the Windows Task Scheduler to load the Desktop every time you log on to Windows. Explorer.exe (in the C:\Windows folder) has been the executable for the Desktop ever since the earliest days of Windows, and running that file will make the Desktop appear immediately after the logon sequence completes.

Accessing Configuration Settings

For the IT professional working with Windows 8 for the first time, accessing the operating system's configuration settings will be a top priority.

As mentioned earlier, many of the familiar Windows configuration tools are still there in Windows 8; it's just a matter of finding them.

USING THE SETTINGS BARS

As mentioned earlier, clicking or tapping the Settings charm displays a Settings bar, the contents of which differ slightly, depending on whether you are accessing it from the Start screen or the Desktop.

The Start screen version enables you to modify the behavior of the screen tiles, while the Desktop version provides access to the main Windows Control Panel and the Personalization and System control panels. Both versions also include tiles that provide access to network, audio, display, notifications, power, and keyboard settings. Finally, when you click Change PC Settings at the bottom of the bar, the PC Settings screen appears, with a multitude of configuration settings on eleven separate pages, as shown in Figure 1-7.

Figure 1-7

The PC Settings screen

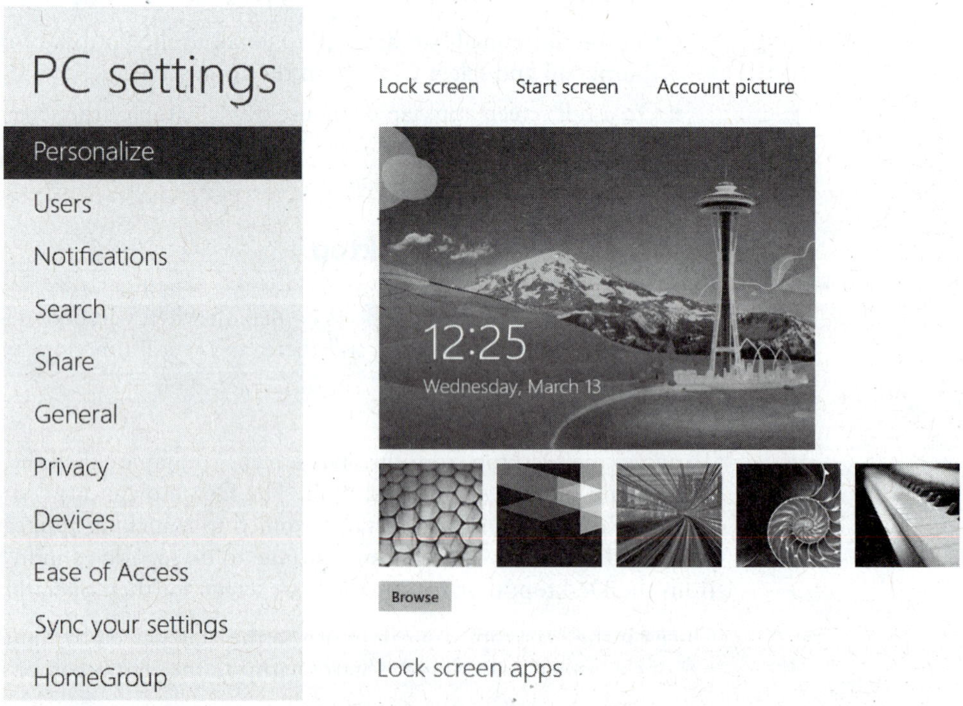

USING THE WINDOWS TOOLS MENU

When you mouse over the lower left corner of the screen and right-click the resulting thumbnail, or press the Win+X key combination, a Windows tools context menu appears that provides access to most of the tools an administrator is likely to need, including the following:

- Programs and Features
- Power Options
- Event Viewer
- System control panel
- Device Manager
- Disk Management
- Computer Management
- Command Prompt
- Command Prompt (Admin)
- Task Manager/
- Control Panel
- File Explorer
- Search
- Run
- Desktop

USING KEYBOARD SHORTCUTS

Because Windows 8 tends to hide administrative controls beneath multiple layers of user action, keyboard shortcuts–always a handy tool for Windows power users–are even more valuable. For any Windows 8 administrator, and more most users as well, memorizing some of the more common key combinations is a worthwhile activity.

In addition to supporting the keyboard shortcuts from previous versions of Windows, Windows 8 adds several new ones, many of which use the Windows key, typically found between the Ctrl and Alt keys on most modern keyboards.

Some of the most useful Win key combinations in Windows 8 are as follows:

- **Win+X** – Displays the Windows tools menu, which contains links to the Event Viewer, Control Panel, Command Prompt, Task Manager, Device Manager, Computer Management, and File Explorer windows
- **Win+Tab** – Displays the task switcher
- **Win** – Displays the Start screen
- **Win+D** – Displays the Windows Desktop
- **Win+C** – Displays the charms bar
- **Win+Q** – Displays the apps search bar
- **Win+F** – Displays the files search bar
- **Win+H** – Displays the Share menu for the currently running app
- **Win+W** – Displays the settings search bar
- **Win+I** – Displays the Settings bar for the currently running app
- **Win+E** – Displays a File Explorer window
- **Win+R** – Displays the Run dialog box

Introducing Windows 8 Editions

THE BOTTOM LINE

Windows 8 is available in multiple editions. Understanding the features and capabilities of each edition is crucial for technical specialists who must recommend a specific product for their users.

There are no less than six editions of Windows 7, but Microsoft has reduced that number down to four for Windows 8, one of which is a specialized version for tablets and other portable devices.

MORE INFORMATION

The history of Microsoft Windows on desktop computers follows two parallel courses. Originally, Windows was a shell program that ran on top of the 16-bit MS-DOS operating system. Eventually, Microsoft combined MS-DOS and Windows into a single operating system product and developed it through several versions, including Windows 95, Windows 98, and Windows Me, which was the final product to use the MS-DOS kernel. At the same time, Microsoft was working on a completely new, 32-bit operating system that overcame most of the memory- and hardware-handling difficulties that were inherent in MS-DOS. Originally released as Windows NT 3.1 in 1993, the same basic NT kernel also formed the core of the Windows NT 4.0 and Windows 2000 operating system products. Intended primarily for servers at first, the NT kernel gradually gained popularity on the desktop, especially in business environments. With the release of Windows XP in 2001, Microsoft stopped using the MS-DOS kernel entirely; the NT kernel is now the basis of all new Windows operating systems, including Windows 8 and Windows Server 2012.

The four Windows 8 editions are as follows:

- **Windows RT** – Designed for tablets and other devices using the low-power ARM processor platform, Windows RT can run WinRT apps obtained from the Windows Store, but it cannot run traditional x86/x64 applications
- **Windows 8** – The base Windows 8 consumer product for PCs using x86 or x64 processors is designed for sale in retail channels and for original equipment manufacturer (OEM) distribution in new computers. The primary limitation of this edition is its inability to participate in an Active Directory Domain Services domain, making it unsuitable for use in any but the smallest business environments.
- **Windows 8 Professional** – The primary edition intended for small businesses, includes support for Active Directory Domain Services and Group Policy, as well as security features, such as BitLocker and EFS.
- **Windows 8 Enterprise** – Available only through the Microsoft volume licensing programs, includes all of the features of Windows 8 Professional, plus advanced options, such as AppLocker, BranchCache, and DirectAccess.

CERTIFICATION READY
Determine which SKU to install
Objective 1.1

Table 1-1 lists the operating system features and applications that are included in each of the Windows 8 editions.

Table 1-1

Feature Support in Windows 8 Editions

	Windows 8 RT	Windows 8	Windows 8 Professional	Windows 8 Enterprise
Platform	ARM	X86/x64	X86/x64	X86/x64
Max Number of Processors	2	1	2	2
Licensing	OEM only	Retail / OEM	Retail / OEM	Volume only
AD DS Domain Support	No	No	Yes	Yes
AppLocker	No	No	No	Yes
Boot from VHD		No	Yes	Yes
BitLocker / BitLocker To Go	No	No	Yes	Yes
BranchCache	No	No	No	Yes
DirectAccess	No	No	No	Yes
Encrypting file System (EFS)	No	No	Yes	Yes
Group Policy	No	No	Yes	Yes
Hyper-V Client	No	No	Yes	Yes
Install x86/x64 desktop apps	No	Yes	Yes	Yes
Microsoft Office	Yes	No	No	No
Remote Desktop	Client only	Client only	Client and host	Client and host
Storage Spaces	No	Yes	Yes	Yes
Windows Media Player	No	Yes	Yes	Yes
Windows To Go	No	No	No	Yes

CERTIFICATION READY
Determine whether 32 bit or 64 bit is appropriate
Objective 1.1

For the Windows 8, Windows 8 Professional, and Windows 8 Enterprise editions, you also have a choice between running the 32-bit or 64-bit version. The main difference between the two is the amount of system memory each can address.

Table 1-2 lists the differences between the two platforms.

Table 1-2

Differences Between Windows 8 32-bit and 64-bit Platforms

	32-bit	64-bit
Maximum addressable memory	4 GB	192 GB
Hyper-V support	No	Yes

Understanding Windows 8 System Requirements

THE BOTTOM LINE

Windows 8 has the same hardware requirements as Windows 7, making the upgrade process relatively painless. However, an upgrade to Windows 8 from Windows XP is likely to require hardware upgrades, and a thorough understanding of the Windows 8 system requirements is essential for the technical specialist.

Because the various Windows 8 editions differ primarily in the number and type of applications included with each product, the basic minimum system requirements are the same for all of the editions. Table 1-3 shows the minimum hardware requirements for each of these designations.

Table 1-3

Minimum System Requirements for Windows 8

	32-BIT (x86)	64-BIT (x64)
Processor speed	1 gigahertz (GHz) or faster	1 GHz or faster
System memory	1 gigabyte (GB)	2 GB
Available hard disk space	16 GB	20 GB
Graphics adapter	DirectX 9 graphics adapter with WDDM driver	DirectX 9 graphics adapter with WDDM driver

While the official system requirements that Microsoft provides are a useful starting point, they do not provide the whole picture. Upgrading to Windows 8 is a subject that is sure to be on the minds of many Windows users, ranging from home users with a single computer to corporate managers responsible for thousands of workstations. For these users, simply falling within the system requirements is not enough. They want to be sure that Windows 8 will be an improvement over their previous OS, and that requires them to consider the individual system components more carefully.

- **Processor** – Of the major computer components, the processor is likely to have the least effect on overall system performance. The 1 GHz processor called for in the Windows 8 system requirements is relatively outdated by today's desktop standards. Most of the PCs in use today have processors much faster than 1 GHz, and even computers that are four or five years old will most likely meet the required speeds. The benefits derived from a faster processor depend largely on the applications the computer is running. Hardcore gamers are the users most intent on wringing every last GHz from their systems, but for general computer use, the requirements are not so heavy. For the purposes of upgrading to Windows 8, it is probably not worthwhile to purchase a new computer just to get a faster processor.
- **System memory** – The memory requirements of the Windows operating systems have risen precipitously in recent years. The 512 megabyte (MB) minimum required for a Vista Capable PC was pushing the lower limit, and often resulted in disappointing performance levels. Microsoft now treats the 1 GB minimum previously cited for a Windows Vista Premium Ready PC as the minimum for Windows 8. Memory is easy and inexpensive to upgrade, however; no other hardware upgrade will yield a more immediately detectable performance increase. The Windows 8 one GB memory minimum is barely sufficient for a general-purpose workstation, but memory-intensive applications such as video and image editing, as well as high-end games, will benefit from

more. Be sure to check the system documentation to determine what memory upgrades are possible for your computers.

- **Hard disk space** – Windows 8 requires much more hard disk space than earlier versions of Windows, but with the low prices and high capacities of today's hard disk drives, it is not difficult to meet or exceed the system requirements. For most users, the real disk space hog is not operating system files or even applications, but rather the collections of audio and video files that users all seem to accumulate. Another aspect to consider, however, is the performance level of the hard drive(s) in the computer. Older drives that spin at 5400 RPM can lead to palpably poorer performance than drives running at 7200 RPM or faster. For even better performance, solid state drives (SSDs) up to 256 GB and more are now available, providing fast access with no moving parts.

CERTIFICATION READY
Determine screen resolution
Objective 1.1

- **Screen resolution** – Windows Store applications require a minimum screen resolution of 1024x768. Below that, they fail to run. For snap functionality, the screen resolution must be at least 1366x768.

For businesses running hundreds or thousands of workstations, the cost of hardware upgrades can be enormous, so you should carefully consider the current state of your computers and what new hardware your organization will need to make a Windows 8 deployment practical and productive.

Selecting Installation Options

THE BOTTOM LINE

Before installing Windows 8, or any operating system, whether on a single computer or a fleet of machines, you must first answer a number of questions to determine what type of installation to perform.

Every Windows 8 installation should begin with a planning phase, which varies depending on the complexity of the installation you are contemplating. For standalone home users, installing Windows 8 might mean thinking about what data to preserve, determining whether the existing hardware will work with the new operating system (OS), and finally purchasing the right Windows 8 edition. For enterprise administrators responsible for hundreds or thousands of computers, an operating system deployment requires a huge amount of testing and preparation, and can represent a massive expense. However, the technicians supporting home users and enterprise technical specialists ask themselves essentially the same questions, just on a different scale.

The following sections examine some of the most important of these questions.

Will the Hardware Support the New Operating System?

Later in this lesson, you learn about the various Windows 8 editions and their hardware requirements. The first question to ask yourself when contemplating an operating system upgrade is whether the computer's current hardware can run the new software effectively.

In many cases, this question is not just a matter of whether the computer meets the Windows 8 minimum hardware requirements. After all, the user expects the new operating system to run better than the old one, not worse. If the computer does not meet the Windows 8 hardware specifications, you should consider a hardware upgrade.

For the home user, a hardware upgrade might mean purchasing and installing a new memory module or two, or perhaps a graphics adapter. Experienced users might install the hardware themselves, while less savvy users might have a professional do it. Either way, the cost and the time involved are relatively small.

However, to perform hardware upgrades like these, enterprise administrators must multiply the cost and the installation time by hundreds or thousands of workstations, and factor in other elements such as lost productivity and overtime costs. Therefore, as with all aspects of a large-scale deployment, administrators in an enterprise environment must plan and test carefully before even considering an upgrade to Windows 8. For example, you might want to perform a series of test installations on differently configured computers to determine exactly what hardware upgrade provides the best performance at the lowest cost.

Will the New Operating System Support the Existing Applications?

The second major consideration for a client contemplating a Windows 8 installation is whether the applications the client already owns will run on the new operating system. The last thing clients want to hear after the successful installation of a new operating system is that they need to purchase additional new software.

As with hardware upgrades, the prospect of upgrading or changing applications is far more daunting in the enterprise environment than for the home user. Home users typically run commercial, off-the-shelf applications, and prices for upgrades supporting new operating systems typically fall soon after the release of the OS.

At the enterprise level, however, you are more likely to find special-purpose or customized applications; these present greater difficulties. It might take time for developers to produce updates for special-purpose applications; for customized applications, it might be necessary to commission additional work from a programmer. Commercial applications can be extremely costly to upgrade, especially when you have to purchase hundreds or thousands of licenses.

In enterprise environments, application testing is as important as hardware testing. Even if an updated version of an application is available, you must test it carefully with the new operating system to ensure that it functions properly. The alternative could be the failure of a mission-critical application across the entire enterprise, resulting in extended down time and lost productivity.

X REF

To aid in evaluating and testing applications in the Windows 8 environment, Microsoft provides a free Application Compatibility Toolkit. For more information on using this and deploying applications on Windows 8, see Lesson 5, "Installing and Configuring Desktop Applications."

Which Windows 8 Edition Should I Install?

You should select a Windows 8 edition based on several factors, including the tasks the user will be performing and, of course, your budget.

For home and small business users, the choice between Windows 8 and Windows 8 Professional should be based primarily on networking requirements. If you are running an AD DS domain, then you must have Professional installed on your computers to join that domain.

Most enterprise installations require their workstations to log on to an Active Directory Domain Services domain, which eliminates the base Windows 8 edition as a possible choice because it lacks domain support. In most cases, the organization's relationship with Microsoft is the deciding factor in the choice between Windows 8 Professional and Enterprise. Windows 8

Professional is a retail product, available in stores everywhere, while Enterprise is only available directly from Microsoft as part of a volume license agreement.

In Windows 7, there was an Ultimate edition, which included the Windows Media Server application. Windows Media Server is now a separate application, available at retail outlets for an additional fee and installable on any edition except Windows RT.

Which Processor Platform Should I Use?

There was a time when a Windows desktop computer with 4 GB of memory was the state of the art.

Today, 4 GB is adequate for an average user's needs, but it is certainly not exceptional. Therefore, the 4 GB memory limitation imposed by the 32-bit processing platform is a real handicap, especially when you consider that each successive Windows release is likely to have an increased memory recommendation.

CERTIFICATION READY
Determine whether 32 bit or 64 bit is appropriate
Objective 1.1

It might be possible to save a little money by purchasing the 32-bit version of Windows 8, but if you have even the remotest thought of upgrading your computer's memory in the future, the 64-bit version is probably preferable.

Should I Perform an Upgrade or a Clean Installation?

The question of whether to install Windows 8 by performing an in-place upgrade or a clean installation depends on the amount and type of data stored on the computer, as well as the computer's current efficiency.

Obviously, new computers, or computers with new hard disk drives, require a ***clean installation***, in which you boot from the Windows 8 setup disk and create or select a blank partition where the operating system will reside. If the computer is currently running Windows 7, you must consider whether it is preferable to wipe out the existing operating system and install Windows 8 from scratch or perform an in–place upgrade to Windows 8 instead.

MORE INFORMATION

You can perform an in-place upgrade to Windows 8 only on computers running Windows 7 or another edition of Windows 8. It is not possible to perform an in-place upgrade to Windows 8 from Windows Vista, Windows XP, Windows 2000, Windows Me, Windows 98, Windows 95, Windows NT, or Windows 3.1. For computers running these operating systems, you must perform a clean installation.

The primary advantage of performing a clean installation is that Windows 8 will achieve its best possible performance. Installing the operating system files on a blank disk means that the files will not be fragmented , improving disk performance. A clean installation ensures that the user retains the maximum amount of disk space for applications and data. Of course, a clean installation also erases all existing data, so you must be careful to back up everything that the user wants to retain.

CERTIFICATION READY
Choose between an upgrade or a clean installation
Objective 1.1

For home users, there is usually some data to preserve, such as image, audio, and video files, as well as data files for specific applications. Fortunately, writable CDs and DVDs, USB flash drives, and external hard drives make it relatively easy to back up a user's essential data. What can be more problematic in a case like this is the loss of important configuration settings, such as user names, passwords, and customized application templates. Be sure to preserve this type of information before wiping out a partition to perform a clean installation.

WARNING If you decide to perform a clean installation of Windows 8 on a home user's computer, be sure to question the user carefully about all possible data that might need to be backed up first. Many less experienced users are unaware, for example, that accessing their email involves a server logon. Another technician might have set up the user name and password long ago, and all the user knows is to click the email icon.

Performing an ***in-place upgrade*** to Windows 8 means that whatever disk and registry clutter is present under the previous operating system will remain in place. Files might be extensively fragmented, even to the point of executing poorly, and outdated applications and data files could occupy significant amounts of disk space.

The advantage to performing an in-place upgrade is that all of the user's applications, data files, and configuration settings remain intact, but even this could be a problem. Upgrades can generate incompatibilities with drivers or applications that you must rectify before the computer can run properly.

In an enterprise environment, it is more typical for users to store their data files on servers, as opposed to local drives. Also, a properly maintained enterprise network should document all configuration settings and logon credentials. This minimizes the problem of potential data loss when performing a clean installation.

Clean installations are generally preferable in an enterprise environment because they ensure that all of the computers are running an identical system configuration. This eliminates many of the technical support problems that can occur when computers are running different configurations.

Do I Have to Install Multiple Languages?

Before Windows Vista, each language-specific version of a Windows operating system had to be developed, maintained, and distributed separately. Starting with Vista, however, and now with Windows 8, it is possible to install multiple language packs on a single computer so that individuals can work in multiple languages.

The main problems for multilingual users in the past have been the availability of the languages they need and the complex procedure for implementing multiple languages on a single computer. To use multiple languages on a Windows XP computer, you must begin with an installation of the English language Windows XP version. Then you install the ***multilingual user interface (MUI)*** pack and whatever additional language packs you need. Unfortunately, some of the language packs provide more complete support than others.

Windows 8 contains an MUI architecture that makes it easier to install multilingual support on a computer. In Windows 8, the binary code that makes up the operating system is entirely language-neutral. During the operating system installation process, the Setup program installs the operating system and then applies a language pack containing the information needed to provide the localized user interface.

Because the language packs for Windows 8 contain no binary code, they are interchangeable. Therefore, it is no longer necessary for technicians to consider localization issues before installing the operating system. You can change a Windows 8 installation from one language to another at any time, or install multiple language packs that utilize the same binary code.

MORE INFORMATION

Because the Windows 8 binaries are language-neutral there is no need for language-specific service packs or other updates. Microsoft is therefore able to release each update in one generic version suitable for all Windows 8 computers around the world, regardless of the language they use.

Running Windows 8 Upgrade Assistant

THE BOTTOM LINE All administrators should be familiar with the Windows 8 Upgrade Assistant application, as it is the surest way of determining whether a computer is capable of running Windows 8.

Upgrade Assistant is a Windows application that scans an individual computer's hardware and software to determine whether it is capable of running Windows 8 at peak efficiency.

To run Windows 8 Upgrade Assistant, perform the steps in the following section.

RUN UPGRADE ASSISTANT

GET READY. Before you run Upgrade Assistant, be sure to plug in and turn on any USB devices or other devices such as printers, external hard drives, or scanners that you regularly use with the PC you are evaluating. Then perform the following steps:

1. Open Internet Explorer or another Web browser and then browse to the *Buy Windows 8* page (try http://windows.microsoft.com/en-us/windows/buy).

   The Buy Windows 8 page appears, as shown in Figure 1-8.

Figure 1-8

The *Buy Windows 8* page

2. Click **Get Started**.

   The *Do you want to run or save Windows8-UpgradeAssistant.exe* bar appears at the bottom of the screen.

   An Internet Explorer – Security Warning message box appears, asking if you want to run the software.

3. Click **Run**.

   The Windows 8 Upgrade Assistant Wizard appears, displaying the *Here's what we found* page, as shown in Figure 1-9.

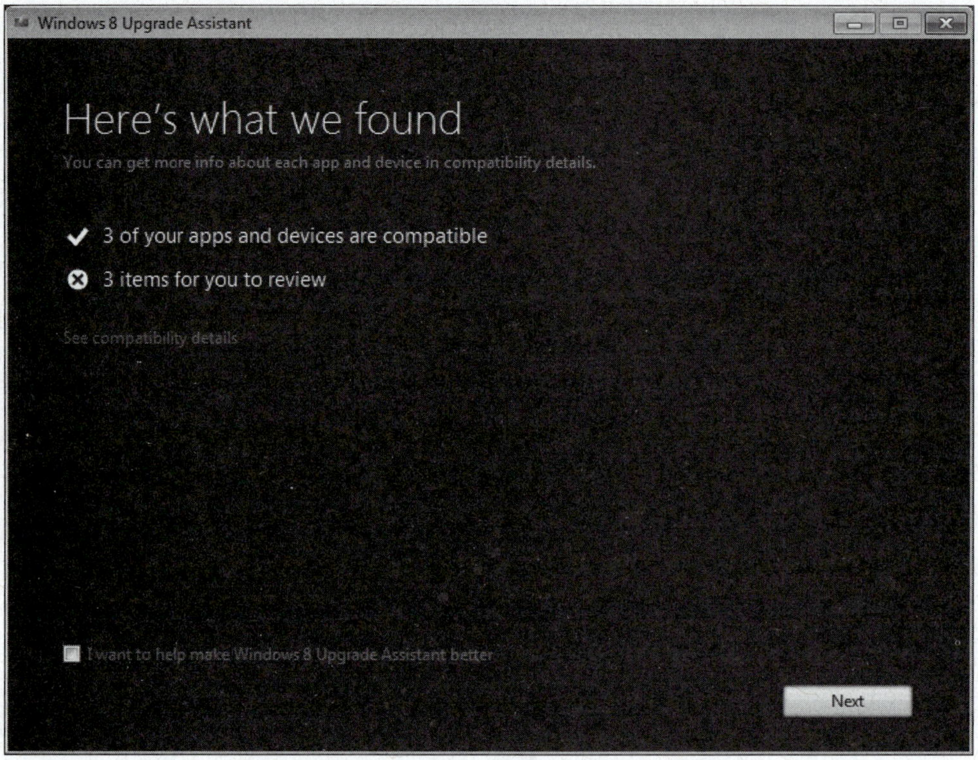

Figure 1-9
The *Here's what we found* page in the Windows 8 Upgrade Assistant

4. Examine the results and click **Next**.

   The *Choose what to keep* page appears as shown in Figure 1-10.

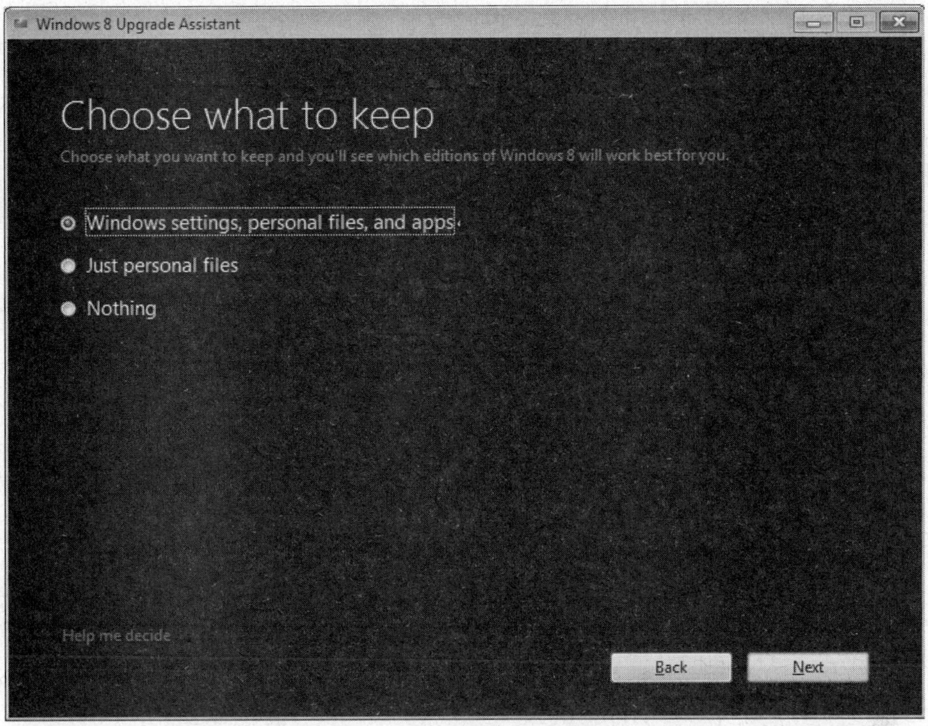

Figure 1-10

The *Choose what to keep* page in the Windows 8 Upgrade Assistant

5. Select the option corresponding to the data you want to preserve from your existing installation and then click Next.

   A *Windows 8 for you* page appears listing the Windows editions available for immediate purchase as shown in Figure 1-11.

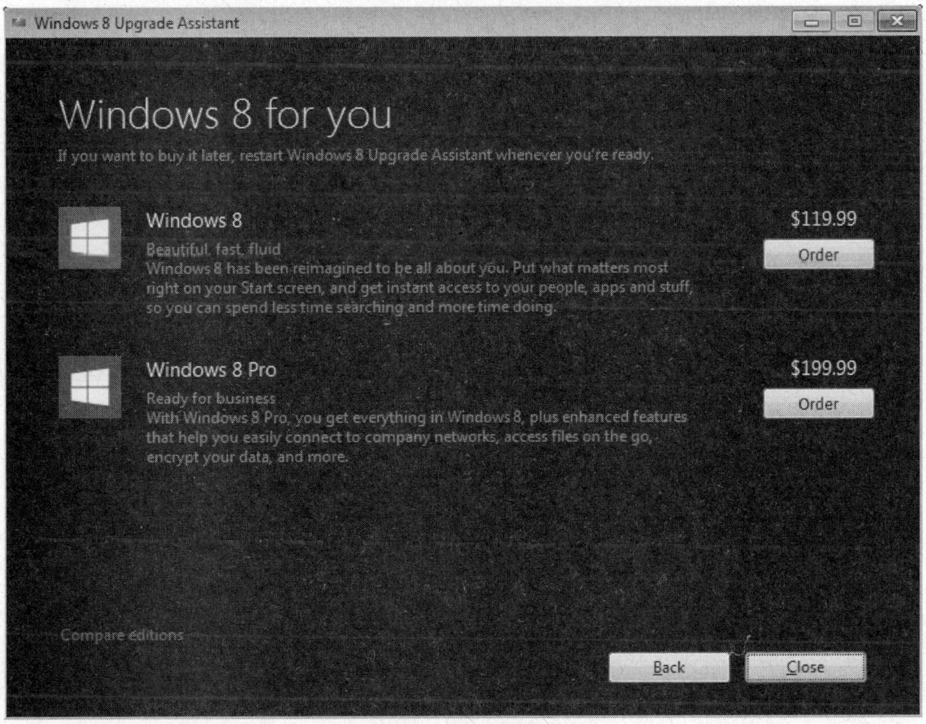

Figure 1-11

The *Windows 8 for you* page in the Windows 8 Upgrade Assistant

6. Click Close.

The Windows 8 Upgrade Assistant is designed to provide retail users with immediate access to operating system upgrades. Enterprise customers using one of the Microsoft volume licensing programs should use their regular contact to discuss upgrades and pricing.

Identifying Upgrade Paths

THE BOTTOM LINE

In some cases, the most convenient way to deploy Windows 8 on existing computers is to perform an upgrade from another operating system. However, there are a multitude of Windows versions, and not all of them support upgrades to Windows 8.

The term upgrade usually refers to an in-place upgrade, in which you install a new operating system over an old one, leaving the existing applications, configuration settings, and personal files intact. Windows 8 actually only supports in-place upgrades from Windows 7 and other editions of Windows 8.

TAKE NOTE*

When discussing operating system upgrades, it is important to distinguish between the purchase of an upgraded operating system license and the actual installation of the upgraded operating system. The term *in-place upgrade* refers to an installation of Windows 8 on an existing computer, retaining all applications, files, and settings. Some users, however, might be eligible for an upgrade to Windows 8, but can't perform an in-place upgrade. For example, Microsoft allows all licensed Windows XP and Windows Vista users to purchase an upgrade version of Windows 8 at a reduced price, but this does not necessarily mean that they can install Windows 8 with Windows XP or Windows Vista in place. In fact, Windows XP systems always require a clean installation to run Windows 8.

Performing an in-place upgrade from Windows 7 to Windows 8 is a quick and convenient way to provide user with the new operating system without sacrificing the personal files and configuration settings that the users have built up over the years. If you choose to install Windows 8 to the partition that contains the old operating system, the Setup program renames the existing Windows folder to Windows.old, so that the old operating system is still recoverable.

For computers running versions earlier than Windows 7, the types of data you can retain from your old installation vary.

Upgrading Windows 8 Editions

In Windows 8, the Anytime Upgrade feature from Windows 7 and Windows Vista is replaced by an Add Features to Windows 8 control panel, which enables retail users to purchase and install upgrades.

The fairly complicated Anytime Upgrade matrix from Windows 7 and Vista is now reduced to a few basic options. If you are running the core Windows 8 product, you can purchase an upgrade to Windows 8 Professional and, if desired, add Windows Media Center as well. Users already running the Professional edition can add Windows Media Center for a small fee.

In all of these cases, the existing operating system installation remains in place, and all applications, settings, and data files are unchanged. The Add Features to Windows 8 control panel enables you to purchase upgrades online and download them immediately, or if you already have a product key for an upgraded version, you can apply the upgrade immediately.

Windows 8 Enterprise is excluded from this feature, as it is only available to volume licensing customers.

Upgrading from Windows 7

Windows 7 is the only down-level operating system from which you can perform a true in-place upgrade to Windows 8.

To perform an in-place upgrade from Windows 7 to Windows 8, you run the Windows 8 Setup.exe program from within Windows 7 and select the Upgrade option. Users can purchase a Windows 8 upgrade disk or download the operating system after purchasing it at an upgrade price.

Generally speaking, you can upgrade any Windows 7 edition to the same or higher version of Windows 8, as shown in Table 1-4. The distinction between home and business versions in Windows 7 is essentially gone in Windows 8, so you can now upgrade Windows 7 Home Basic or Home Premium to Windows 8 Professional, something you could not do when upgrading Windows Vista to Windows 7.

Table 1-4

In-place Upgrade Paths from Windows 7 to Windows 8

	To Windows 8	To Windows 8 Professional	To Windows 8 Enterprise
From Windows 7 Starter	Yes	Yes	
From Windows 7 Home Basic	Yes	Yes	
From Windows 7 Home Premium	Yes	Yes	
From Windows 7 Professional		Yes	Yes (volume license only)
From Windows 7 Enterprise			Yes (volume license only)
From Windows 7 Ultimate		Yes	

TAKE NOTE*

Windows 8 does not support in-place upgrades of 32-bit to 64-bit operating systems under any circumstances, or vice versa.

In theory, an in-place upgrade from Windows 7 to Windows 8 preserves everything you might want to retain on the system, substituting only the new operating system. However, in reality, this is not always the case. Not every application can run properly after an upgrade, and not every customized setting is retained. When planning an in-place upgrade, you should always run the Upgrade Assistant application, and pay particular attention to the compatibility report it provides.

For administrators in an enterprise environment, in-place upgrades take much more time to complete and are often unreliable or inconsistent in their results. Generally speaking, a migration of settings to a clean Windows 8 installation is a much better solution.

Upgrading from Earlier Windows Versions

Windows 8 does not support in-place upgrades from any Windows versions prior to Windows 7. However, there are upgrades available that can preserve some of your existing data.

Users running Windows Vista with Service Pack 1 installed can upgrade to Windows 8, but they cannot perform a full, in-place upgrade, as Windows 7 users can. An upgrade from Vista can retain the user's personal data files, as well as the operating system configuration settings, but it cannot retain the applications installed on the old operating system. The user must reinstall all the applications, and reconfigure them to their original states.

For users of Windows XP with Service Pack 3, an upgrade can only preserve personal files. All applications and configuration settings are lost,

For computers running operating system versions prior to Windows XP, including Windows 2000, Windows Me, Windows 98, Windows 95, and Windows 3.1, there is no upgrade pricing available, so you must purchase the full version of Windows 8, and you can only perform a migration.

X REF

For more information on migrating older operating systems to Windows 8, see Lesson 2, "Installing Windows 8."

In an operating system migration, you copy the system configuration settings and personal files from the old operating system to the new one, using a program such as the User State Migration Tool. This process preserves many–but not all–of the existing user settings from the old system. Migration does not preserve third-party applications, so you must re-install and configure them after the Windows 8 installation is completed.

Migrations do not preserve as much of the existing system configuration as in-place upgrades, but they do result in a more uniform, and usually more stable, Windows 8 computer.

SKILL SUMMARY

In this lesson, you learned:

- Windows 8 is a major release that represents a fundamental departure in Windows operating system design. The intention behind Windows 8 was to create a single operating system that can run on a variety of devices, including tablets and smartphones, as well as PCs.
- The first new element in Windows 8 faced by users and support staff alike is the Start screen, which replaces the familiar Start menu from previous versions of Windows.
- Apps are programs that launch from the Start screen and run exclusively in the WinRT environment. Most of the tiles that appear on the default Windows 8 Start screen launch apps, and many others are available for purchase (or for free) through the Windows Store.
- There are no less than six editions of Windows 7, but Microsoft has reduced that number down to four for Windows 8, one of which is a specialized version for tablets and other portable devices.
- In some cases, the most convenient way to deploy Windows 8 on existing computers is to perform an upgrade from another operating system. However, there are many Windows versions, and not all of them support upgrades to Windows 8.

Knowledge Assessment

Multiple Choice

Select one or more correct answers for each of the following questions.

1. The general public in the United States will be able to purchase all of the Windows 8 editions in retail stores except which of the following?
   a. Windows 8
   b. Windows 8 Professional
   c. Windows 8 Enterprise
   d. Windows 8 RT

2. Which of the following operating system editions can you upgrade in place to the core Windows 8 edition?
   a. Windows 7 Starter
   b. Windows 7 Home Basic
   c. Windows 7 Home Premium
   d. Windows 7 Professional

3. What is the maximum amount of system memory supported by the 32-bit versions of Windows 8?
   a. 2 GB
   b. 4 GB
   c. 16 GB
   d. 128 GB

4. The Add Features to Windows 8 control panel replaces which of the following Windows 7 features?
   a. Programs and features
   b. Windows Update
   c. Anytime Upgrade
   d. Upgrade Assistant

5. Which of the following Windows 8 editions are not capable of joining an Active Directory Domain Services domain?
   a. Windows 8
   b. Windows 8 RT
   c. Windows 8 Professional
   d. Windows 8 Enterprise

6. You have 20 tablet computers to deploy to traveling salesmen. The computers will have to run Microsoft Office, as well as several apps from the Windows Store. Which of the following Windows 8 editions is unsuitable for these tablets?
   a. Windows 8
   b. Windows 8 RT
   c. Windows 8 Professional
   d. Windows 8 Enterprise

7. Which of the following terms best describes the fly-out panel that appears on the right side of the Windows 8 Start screen contains buttons?
   a. Icons
   b. Buttons
   c. Tokens
   d. Charms

8. Which of the following operating systems can you upgrade in place to Windows 8?
   a. Windows 7
   b. Windows Vista
   c. Windows XP
   d. Windows Me

9. Which of the following elements can be retained when you upgrade a computer running Windows Vista with Service Pack 1 to Windows 8?
   a. Operating system configuration settings
   b. Applications installed on the Vista computer
   c. The user's personal data files
   d. Application configuration settings

10. Which of the following Windows operating system versions required Microsoft to develop and maintain separate SKUs for each language?
    a. Windows 8
    b. Windows 7
    c. Windows Vista
    d. Windows XP

Best Answer

Choose the letter that corresponds to the best answer. More than one answer choice may achieve the goal. Select the BEST answer.

1. Which product or combination of products would provide the closest experience to the Windows 7 Ultimate Edition product?
   a. Windows 8
   b. Windows 8 RT
   c. Windows 8 Professional
   d. Windows 8 Enterprise
   e. Windows Media Server

2. Which of the following represents the best way to deploy a bilingual French-English version of Windows 8?
   a. Purchase separate French and English versions of Windows 8 and install them one after the other on the same computer.
   b. Purchase separate French and English versions of Windows 8 , install the English version, and then change the installed product key to the one from the French version.
   c. Purchase Windows 8, select one of the desired languages during the operating system installation, and then download and install the language pack for the other language.
   d. Install Windows 8 with one of the desired languages, and then change to the other language in Contriol Panel, as needed.

3. Which of the following is the best way to display the All Apps icon on a Windows 8 computer with a touch screen?
   a. Swipe a finger up from the bottom edge of the screen.
   b. Press the WIN key.
   c. Swipe a finger from the right side to the center of the screen.
   d. Right-click the background of the Start screen.

4. Which of the following is the best way to determine whether you can upgrade your computer to Windows 8?
   a. Boot the system from a Windows 8 installation disk.
   b. Start the Windows 8 Setup program from an installation disk while the old operating system is running.

c. Run the Microsoft Upgrade Assistant application.
d. Run Windows Update to determine whether the new operating system is available for download.

5. For which of the following operating systems is there no upgrade pricing to Windows 8?
   a. Windows 7
   b. Windows Vista
   c. Windows XP
   d. Windows 2000
   e. Windows Me
   f. Windows 98
   g. Windows 95
   h. Windows 3.1

Matching and Identification

Match the following terms with their corresponding definitions.

_______ a) Windows 8 RT
_______ b) Upgrade Assistant
_______ c) In-place upgrade
_______ d) Windows 8 Enterprise
_______ e) Windows 8 Pro
_______ f) Windows 8 32-bit
_______ g) Multilingual user interface
_______ h) Edge UI
_______ i) Charms
_______ j) Live tiles

1. Supports no more than 4 GB of memory
2. Available as a retail product
3. Runs on an ARM processor
4. Icons that display information supplied by the applications they run
5. Supported fully only from Windows 7
6. Integrated into the language neutral Windows 8 operating system
7. Appears when you swipe a finger from the side of a touch screen to the center
8. Specifies possibility of performing an in-place upgrade
9. Available only through volume licensing programs
10. Icons on fly-out screens

Build a List

1. Place the following charms in the order in which they appear in the Windows 8 edge UI, from top to bottom.
   _______ Share
   _______ Devices
   _______ Search
   _______ Settings
   _______ Start

2. Arrange the following Windows 8 operating systems in order from most capable to least capable.
   _______ Windows 8 RT
   _______ Windows 8 Enterprise
   _______ Windows 8
   _______ Windows 8 Pro

3. Specify the correct order of steps for running the Windows 8 Upgrade Assistant.
   _________ Save data
   _________ Download Upgrade Assistant
   _________ View the *Windows 8 For You* page
   _________ Examine results
   _________ Browse to the *Buy Windows 8* page
   _________ Open Internet Explorer
   _________ Run Upgrade Assistant

■ Business Case Scenarios

Scenario 1-1: Selecting a Windows 8 Edition

You are a private computer consultant, and a new client has approached you about upgrading his small business network. The network currently consists of eight Windows XP workstations and a single server running Windows Server 2008 R2. The server is functioning as a domain controller and the eight workstations are members of an Active Directory Domain Services domain. The workstations each have 1 GB of memory and a 1.8-GHz processor. The video cards support DirectX 9 and have WDDM drivers available from the manufacturer. Three of the workstations are located in a warehouse across town, while the other five in the main office run Microsoft Office applications almost exclusively. The server is also located in the main office. There have been problems with sluggish performance on the warehouse computers when they attempt to access server files. Which edition of Windows 8 would you select for the workstations to provide the features and performance they require? Explain your answer.

Scenario 1-2: Building a Network

A business owner called Ortiz approaches you about the possibility of designing a network for deployment at his new branch office in Bolivia. He has already purchased twenty computers and shipped them to the site. Each computer has 1 GB of memory, a 1 GHz processor, and an 80 GB hard drive. He wants to connect the computers into an ActiveDirectory Domain Services network that will be used primarily for accessing Web-based applications. Because he will be operating the network in a South American country, Mr. Ortiz wants to use the core Windows 8 product for his workstations, as this is the most economical solution he can find. Will this be an adequate solution for his needs? Explain why or why not.

Installing Windows 8

LESSON 2

70-687 EXAM OBJECTIVE

Objective 1.2 – Install Windows 8. This objective may include but is not limited to install as Windows to Go; migrate from Windows XP or Windows Vista; upgrade from Windows 7 to Windows 8 or from one edition of Windows 8 and to another edition of Windows 8; install VHD

LESSON HEADING	EXAM OBJECTIVE
Understanding the Windows 8 Boot Environment	
Introducing Windows PE	
What's New in Windows PE	
Understanding Windows PE Limitations	
Using Windows PE	
Understanding the Windows 8 Startup Process	
Performing a Clean Installation	
Installing Third-Party Device Drivers	
Working with Installation Partitions	
Installing to a VHD	Install VHD
Upgrading to Windows 8	Upgrade from Windows 7 to Windows 8 or from one edition of Windows 8 to another edition of Windows 8
Preparing to Upgrade	
Upgrading from Windows 7 to Windows 8	
Upgrading Windows 8 Editions	
Migrating from Windows XP or Windows Vista	Migrate from Windows XP or Windows Vista
Installing Windows to Go	Install as Windows to Go

KEY TERMS

- **Application Compatibility Toolkit (ACT)**
- **clean installation**
- **system recovery disk**
- **Upgrade Assistant program**
- **User State Migration Tool (USMT)**
- **virtual hard disk (VHD)**
- **Volume Activation Management Tool (VAMT)**
- **Windows 8 Assessment and Deployment Kit (ADK)**
- **Windows Easy Transfer**
- **Windows PE 4.0**
- **Windows Recovery Environment**
- **Windows To Go**

■ Understanding the Windows 8 Boot Environment

THE BOTTOM LINE Windows 8 eliminates DOS from the installation process and provides a new boot environment.

Those who have performed clean installations of standalone Windows XP systems should recall that the very beginning of the process, immediately after the system boots from the installation disk, consists of several character-based (that is, non-graphical) screens, like that shown in Figure 2-1. On these screens, you opt to perform the installation, agree to the terms of the End User License Agreement (EULA), select the drive partition on which you want to install Windows XP, and then watch as the program copies the installation files from the CD-ROM to a temporary folder on the hard disk.

Figure 2-1

A character-based screen from the MS-DOS phase of a Windows XP installation

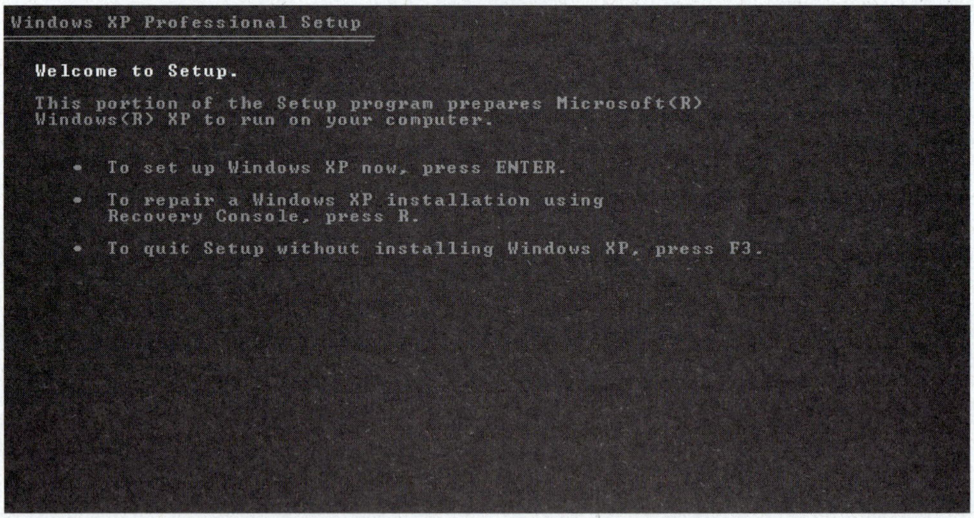

These screens are character-based because all of the Windows operating systems up to and including Windows XP required an MS-DOS boot at the beginning of the installation process. The MS-DOS boot was necessary because the computer required an operating system to run the installation program and to gain access to the disk drives.

For original equipment manufacturers (OEMs) and enterprise installations, deploying Windows on a large number of computers typically required a boot from an MS-DOS system disk to provide access to the computer's drives and to provide access to a network share where the Windows installation files or a disk image was located.

This need for an MS-DOS boot became increasingly problematic over the years for several reasons, including the following:

- **Limited disk support** – MS-DOS can provide access only to disk drives formatted using one of the File Allocation Table (FAT) formats. MS-DOS cannot provide access to the NTFS drives that most of today's Windows computers use.
- **No internal networking support** – MS-DOS has no internal networking support, and because it is a 16-bit operating system administrators had to obtain and load 16-bit real mode network adapter drivers (as compared to the 32-bit drivers that current Windows versions use), as well as a TCP/IP client, before they can access a share containing Windows installation files.
- **Limited script support** – MS-DOS has no internal support for any scripting languages other than rudimentary batch files.
- **Boot device limitations** – Many computers today, especially those in corporate environments, do not have floppy disk drives, and creating bootable MS-DOS CD-ROMs can be problematic.

Introducing Windows PE

Ever since Windows Me was retired, Microsoft has eliminated the need for MS-DOS as an underlying operating system for Windows, but Windows 8 is only the third workstation OS (after Windows Vista and Windows 7) to completely eliminate MS-DOS from the installation process. To replace the MS-DOS boot, Windows 8 includes Windows Preinstallation Environment 4.0 (Windows PE).

Windows PE 4.0 is a stripped-down operating system, based on the Windows 8 kernel, that enables system administrators to boot a computer that has no operating system installed and initiate the operating system setup process. When compared to MS-DOS, Windows PE has a number of distinct advantages, including the following:

- **Native 32-bit or 64-bit support** – Windows PE is a native 32-bit or 64-bit operating system that enables the computer to address memory just as the full Windows 8 operating system does. MS-DOS is a 16-bit OS and is relatively limited in its memory addressing capabilities.
- **Native 32-bit or 64-bit driver support** – Because Windows PE is a 32-bit or 64-bit OS, it can use the same drivers as a full Windows 8 installation. System administrators therefore do not have to search for antiquated 16-bit real mode network drivers as they did with MS-DOS.
- **Internal networking support** – Windows PE includes its own internal TCP/IP networking stack and is capable of functioning as a Windows file sharing client. This means that after booting Windows PE, an administrator only has to supply a driver for the network adapter and the networking stack is complete.
- **Internal NTFS support** – Windows PE includes internal support for the NTFS file system used by Windows 8, as well as the FAT file systems that MS-DOS supports. This means that when you boot a system using Windows PE, you can read from and write to existing NTFS drives in the computer, as well as create and format new NTFS partitions. It is even possible to create and manage dynamic volumes using Windows PE.
- **Scripting language support** – Windows PE includes internal support for a subset of the Win32 application programming interface (API), meaning that it is possible to run some Windows programs in the preinstallation environment. Windows PE also includes support for Windows Management Instrumentation (WMI) and Windows Script Host, which makes it possible for administrators to create scripts that are far more powerful than MS-DOS batch files.

- **Flexible boot options** – Windows PE can boot from a variety of media, including CD-ROMs, DVD-ROMs, USB devices, such as flash disks and floppy drives, or a Windows Deployment Services (WDS) server. The computer can then run the Windows PE operating system from a variety of media, including the DVD, a temporary folder on a hard disk, a USB flash drive, a RAM disk, or a network share.

MORE INFORMATION

Windows PE 4.0 is available in both 32-bit and 64-bit versions. You must use the 32-bit version of Windows PE to install the 32-bit version of Windows 8 and the 64-bit version of Windows PE to install the 64-bit version of Windows 8.

What's New in Windows PE

The latest versions of Windows PE, versions 3.0 and 4.0, are more readily available than previous versions, and are packages with a variety of tools you can use to customize the Windows PE environment.

The most important development in the latest versions of Windows PE (3.0 and 4.0) is that anyone can obtain them. Prior to Windows 7, Microsoft made Windows PE available only to customers with service agreements. Now, it's available for free in a standalone version as part of the ***Windows 8 Assessment and Deployment Kit (ADK).***

TAKE NOTE*

Windows 8 ADK, including Windows PE 4.0, is available free of charge from the Microsoft Download Center.

The Windows 8 ADK includes the following components:

- ***Application Compatibility Toolkit (ACT)*** – Enables administrators to test, detect, and prioritize application compatibility issues
- **Deployment Tools** – Includes tools that enable administrators to capture, manage, and deploy system images
- ***User State Migration Tool (USMT)*** – Scriptable command line tools that enable administrators to migrate user profile information to newly installed Windows 8 workstations
- ***Volume Activation Management Tool (VAMT)*** – Enables administrators to manage the activation of product keys for Microsoft products, obtained through retail and volume channels
- **Windows Assessment Toolkit** – Includes tools that enable\administrators to capture and evaluate performance data on Windows 8 workstations
- **Windows Assessment Services** – Includes tools that enable administrators to remotely manage computers in a laboratory environment
- **Windows Preinstallation Environment (Windows PE)** – Provides a minimized version of the Windows operating system for installation and maintenance purposes

Understanding Windows PE Limitations

Microsoft intends Windows PE to be a reduced subset of the Windows 8 operating system, only providing sufficient capability to perform certain installation, diagnostic, and recovery functions while running from a minimized hardware environment, such as a RAM drive.

Because there was never any intention for Windows PE to function as a full-time operating system, and to facilitate its rapid deployment and execution, there are certain inherent limitations in the product, such as the following:

- Windows PE does not support the entire collection of Win32 APIs as a full installation of Windows 8 does. Microsoft limits the APIs in Windows PE primarily to those providing disk and network input/output functions, as well as certain APIs that make it possible to run basic programs. Reducing the API support enables Windows PE to run in a smaller memory space than Windows 8.

TAKE NOTE*

Because Windows PE requires a relatively small memory space, the entire operating system can run from a RAM disk. A RAM disk is a driver that allocates a section of active memory for use as a virtual disk drive, complete with drive letter. Because the RAM disk is based in memory it is much faster than a hard disk drive, but it is also volatile; all of its contents are lost when the computer restarts. Running the Windows 8 Setup program from a RAM disk enables all of the operating system file handles to remain open throughout the installation process, allowing you to remove the boot device, if necessary. By contrast, running the Setup program directly from a DVD makes it impossible to remove the disk (to load third-party drivers, for example) without interrupting the installation procedure. In the same way, running the Setup program from a temporary folder on a hard disk interferes with partition creation and management functions that might be needed during the installation.

- Windows PE automatically stops and reboots the computer after 72 hours of continuous operation. This deliberate limitation prevents individuals from using the product as a permanent operating environment.
- Windows PE will not fit on a floppy disk, but it is possible to create bootable Windows PE CD-ROMs, DVD-ROMs, and USB flash drives.
- You must use the 32-bit version of Windows PE to install the 32-bit version of Windows 8, and the 64-bit version of Windows PE to install the 64-bit Windows 8.
- While it is possible to modify the Windows PE registry when the operating system is running, all registry keys are reset to their default values each time the operating system restarts. It is possible to make permanent changes to the registry, but to do so you must make the changes offline by manually editing the registry while Windows PE is not running.
- While you can create drive letter assignments in a Windows PE session, these assignments are not persistent between sessions.
- Windows PE does not have file server or Remote Desktop capabilities, nor does it support the Microsoft .NET framework or the Common Language Runtime (CLR), Windows on Windows 32 (WOW32), Windows on Windows 64 (WOW64), Virtual DOS Machine (VDM), OS/2, or POSIX subsystems.
- Windows PE does not support the installation of Windows Installer package (.msi) files.
- Windows PE can access Distributed File System (DFS) folders, but only those in standalone DFS roots.

Using Windows PE

In addition to functioning as a platform for individual installations of Windows 8, Windows PE is useful for other scenarios that require a basic operating system with minimal resource usage.

Some of the other scenarios that can make use of Windows PE are as follows:

- **Custom deployments** – Windows 8 uses Windows PE during the default installation procedure, but it is possible for administrators to build their own unattended installation routines using Windows PE as a platform to run scripts and deploy customized disk images on fleets of workstations. You can even use Windows PE to deploy operating systems other than Windows 8.
- **System troubleshooting** – If a Windows 8 computer fails to start, or if it crashes repeatedly, a technician can launch the ***Windows Recovery Environment*** (Windows RE), which is simply another name given to Windows PE on a computer with Windows 8 already installed. In the Windows RE environment, the technician can use Windows' built-in troubleshooting utilities or run third-party or custom diagnostic tools.
- **System recovery** – OEMs who build their own computers typically supply their customers with a ***system recovery disk*** rather than an operating system installation disk. A system recovery disk contains image files that can restore the computer to its original state, just as it was when it left the factory. OEMs can use Windows PE to build recovery solutions that automate the process of setting up Windows 8, installing specific drivers, installing applications, and configuring the entire system to create a standardized environment.

Understanding the Windows 8 Startup Process

Windows 8 uses a startup process that is substantially different from those of Windows XP and previous versions, and technical specialists should be familiar with the changes.

The Windows 8 startup procedure is vastly different from those of Windows XP and other NT-based Windows versions. Table 2-1 lists the new components found in Windows 8, and the Windows XP components they replace.

Table 2-1

Windows XP and Windows 8 Startup Components

Windows 8 Component	Function	Windows XP Component
Windows Boot Manager Windows Boot Loader	Displays the boot menu and loads the kernel	NTLDR
Boot Configuration Data (BCD) registry file	Contains the boot options displayed on the boot menu	Boot.ini
Merged into the kernel, as hardware profiles are no longer needed	Detects hardware and loads the appropriate hardware profile	Ntdetect.com
Windows Recovery Environment (Windows RE)	Provides limited access to operating system tools	Recovery Console

The Windows 8 startup process consists of the following steps:

1. *Power-on self test (POST)* phase – When you first turn the computer on, it loads the BIOS or Extensible Firmware Interface (EFI) and runs a hardware self-test procedure that detects the devices installed in the system and configures them using settings stored in non-volatile memory. After the main POST, any devices with their own BIOS firmware (such as video display adapters) can run their own self-test procedures.
2. Initial startup phase – On BIOS-equipped computers, the system reads the BIOS settings to determine which hardware device it should use to boot the computer. When booting from a hard disk, the system loads the master boot record (MBR) from the disk and locates the active (bootable) partition. The system then loads and runs a stub

program called Bootmgr, which switches the processor from real mode to protected mode and loads the Windows Boot Manager application. EFI computers have their own built-in boot manager, which Windows 8 configures to run the same Windows Boot Manager application, eliminating the need for the interim disk location steps.

3. Windows Boot Manager phase – The system reads the Boot Configuration Data (BCD) registry file, which contains the system's boot menu information, and provides the user with access to the boot menu. If there is only one operating system installed on the computer, the boot menu only appears when the user presses the a key just after the POST, or presses the F8 key to display the Advanced Boot Options menu. If there are multiple operating systems installed, the boot menu appears, providing the user with 30 seconds to select one of the operating systems before it loads the default.
4. Windows Boot Loader phase – The system initiates the memory paging process and loads various operating system elements into memory, such as the Windows kernel, the hardware abstraction layer (HAL), the system registry hive, and boot class device drivers, but it does not actually run them.
5. Kernel loading phase – The system runs the Windows Executive (consisting of the Windows kernel and the HAL), which processes the registry hive and initializes the drivers and services specified there. The kernel then starts the Session Manager, which loads the kernel-mode part of the Win32 subsystem, causing the system to switch from text mode to graphics mode. Then the kernel loads the user-mode portion of Win32, which provides applications with indirect, protected access to the system hardware. At this time, the system also performs delayed rename operations resulting from system updates that must replace files that were in use when the update was installed. Finally, the kernel creates additional virtual memory paging files and starts the Logon Manager.
6. Logon phase – The system loads the Service Control Manager (SCM) and the Local Security Authority (LSA), and then presents the logon user interface (LogonUI). The interface passes the credentials supplied by the user to the LSA for authentication, and the SCM loads the Plug and Play services and drivers that are configured for autoloading. If the authentication is successful, the Logon Manager launches Userinit.exe, which is responsible for applying group policy settings and running the programs in the Startup group, and then loads the Windows Explorer shell, which provides the Windows desktop.

■ Performing a Clean Installation

THE BOTTOM LINE

A ***clean installation*** is the simplest way to deploy Windows 8 on a new computer or a computer with a partition that you are willing to reformat (losing all of the data on the partition in the process).

If a computer is brand new and has no operating system installed on it, then it cannot start until you supply a boot disk, such as the Windows 8 installation disk. During the installation you will select the disk partition on which you want to install Windows, and the Setup program will copy the operating system files there.

If the computer has an operating system installed on it, and you have already backed up all of the data that you want to preserve, then you are ready to boot the computer from the Windows 8 installation disk. During the setup process you can erase a partition on the disk in preparation for installing Windows there.

TAKE NOTE*

The following procedure is for an installation of Windows 8 Professional Edition. Although the installation procedure for the other editions is nearly identical, you might see minor differences in the procedure.

PERFORM A CLEAN INSTALLATION

GET READY. Prepare the computer for the Windows 8 installation by making sure that all of its external peripheral devices are connected and powered on.

1. Turn on the computer and insert the Windows 8 installation disk into the DVD drive.
2. Press any key to boot from the DVD (if necessary).

   A progress indicator screen appears as Windows is loading files.

TAKE NOTE*

The device that a PC uses to boot is specified in its system (or BIOS) settings. In some cases, you might have to modify these settings to enable the computer to boot from the Windows 8 DVD. If you are not familiar with the operation of a particular computer, watch the screen carefully as the system starts and look for an instruction specifying what key to press to access the system settings.

3. The computer switches to the Windows graphical interface and the Windows Setup screen appears, as shown in Figure 2-2.

Figure 2-2

The *Windows Setup* page

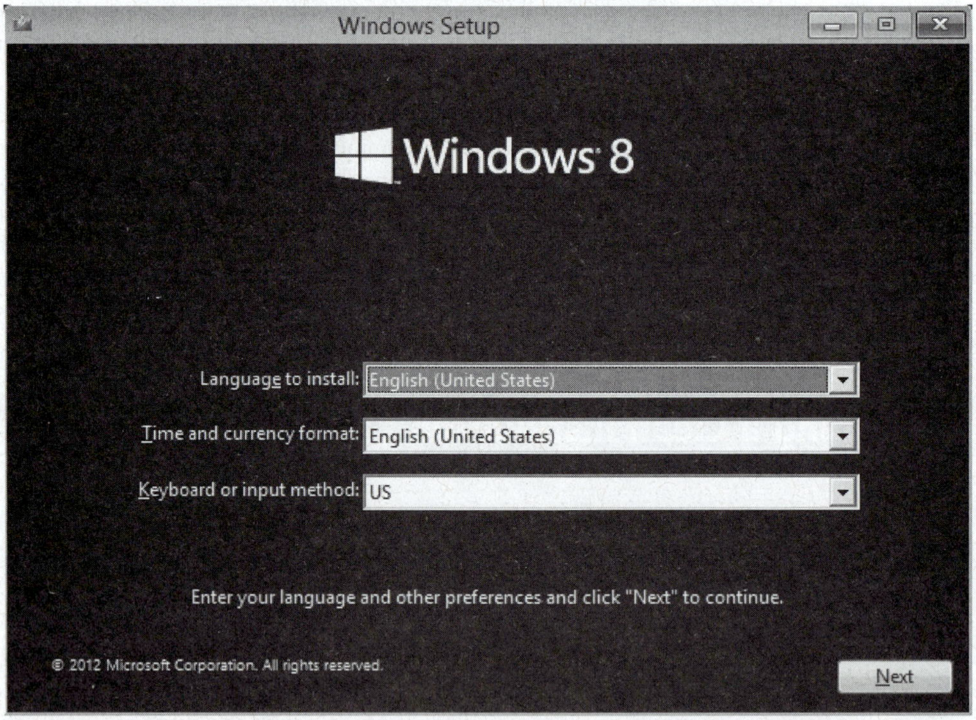

TAKE NOTE*

At this point, the computer is running Windows PE as its operating system, providing it with the means to execute the Setup program and to load drivers providing access to the disk drives and other hardware resources.

4. Using the drop-down lists provided, select the appropriate Language to install, Time and currency format, and Keyboard or input method and then click **Next**.

The *Windows 8 Install now* page appears, as shown in Figure 2-3.

Figure 2-3

The *Windows 8 Install now* page

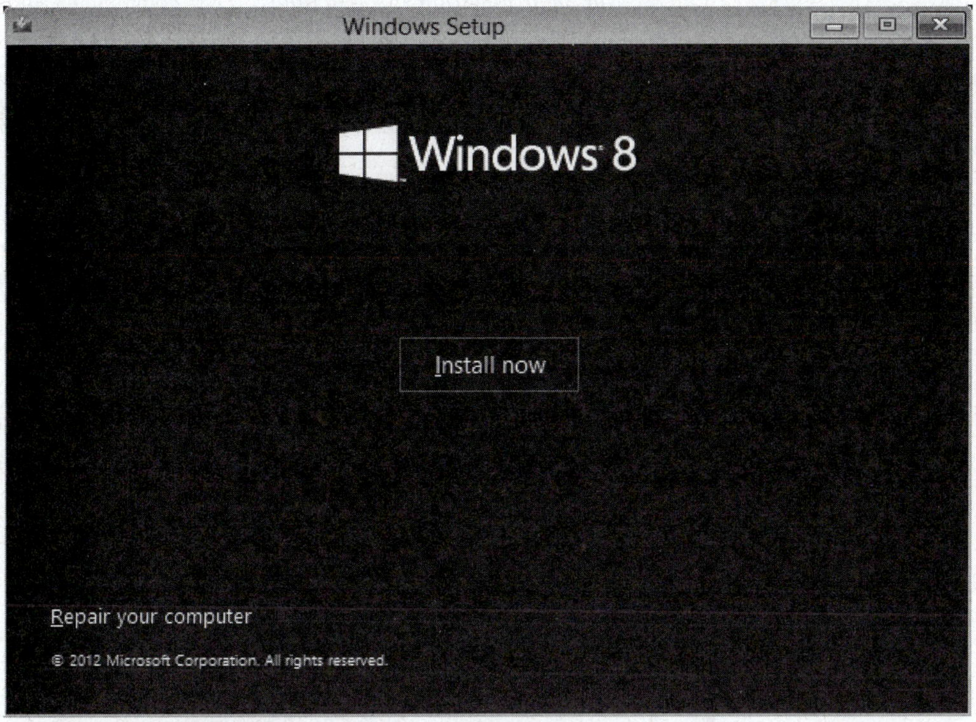

5. Click the **Install now** button.

   The *License terms* page appears, as shown in Figure 2-4.

TAKE NOTE*

Depending on the Windows 8 edition you are installing and the type of license, you might be required to type in a product key at this time.

Figure 2-4

The *License terms* page

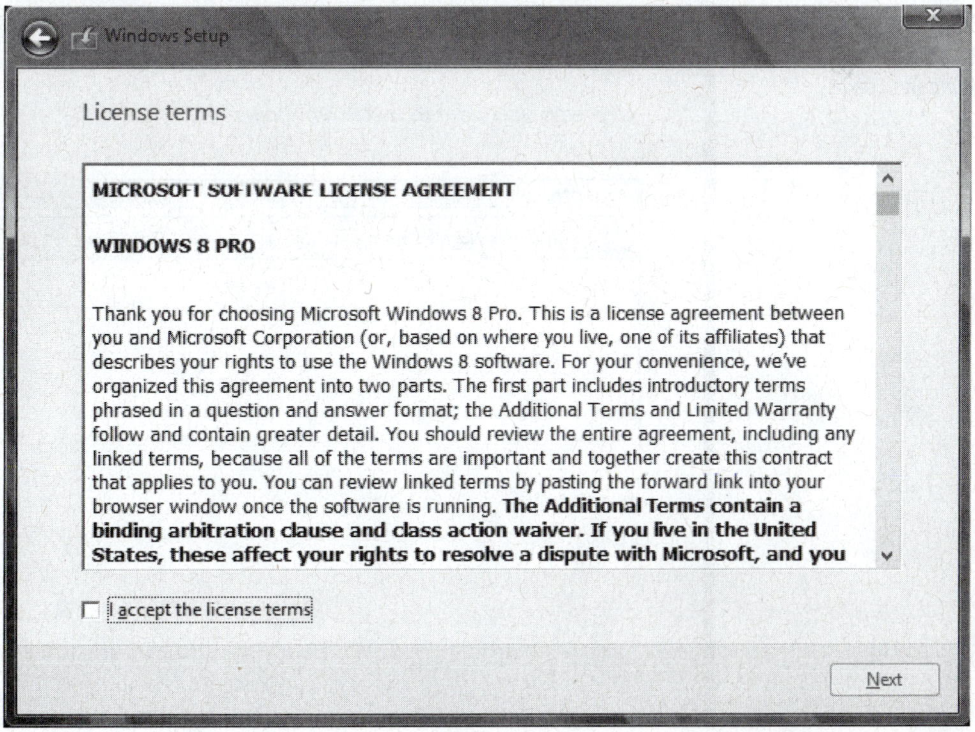

6. Select the **I accept the license terms** checkbox and then click **Next**. The *Which type of installation do you want?* page appears, as shown in Figure 2-5.

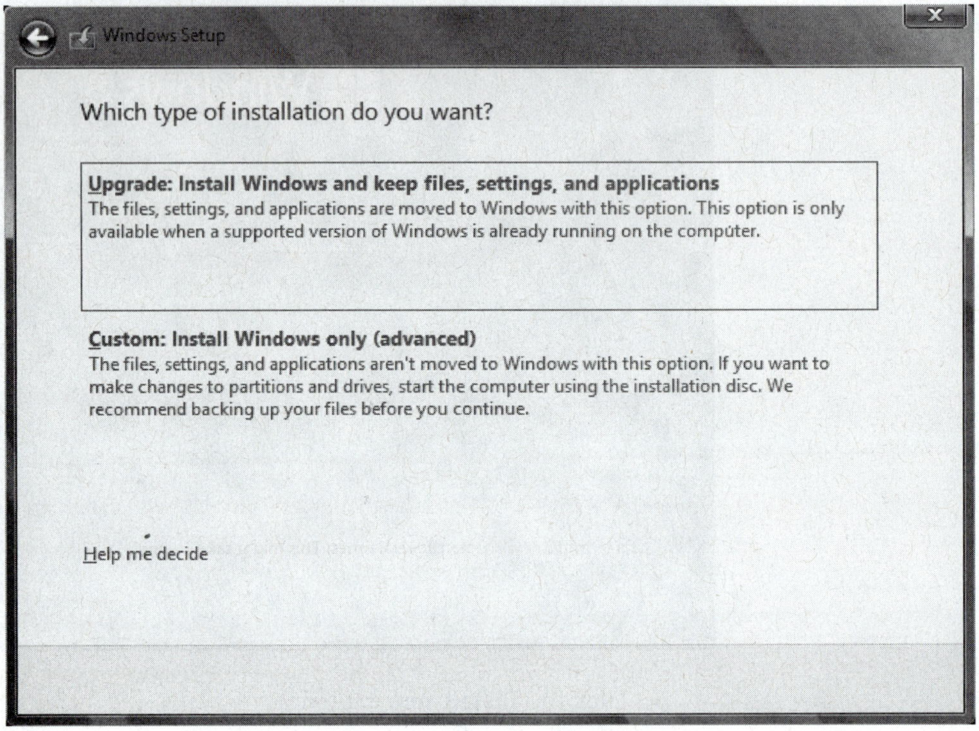

Figure 2-5

The *Which type of installation do you want?* page

7. Click the **Custom: Install Windows only (advanced)** option.

   The *Where do you want to install Windows?* page appears, as shown in Figure 2-6.

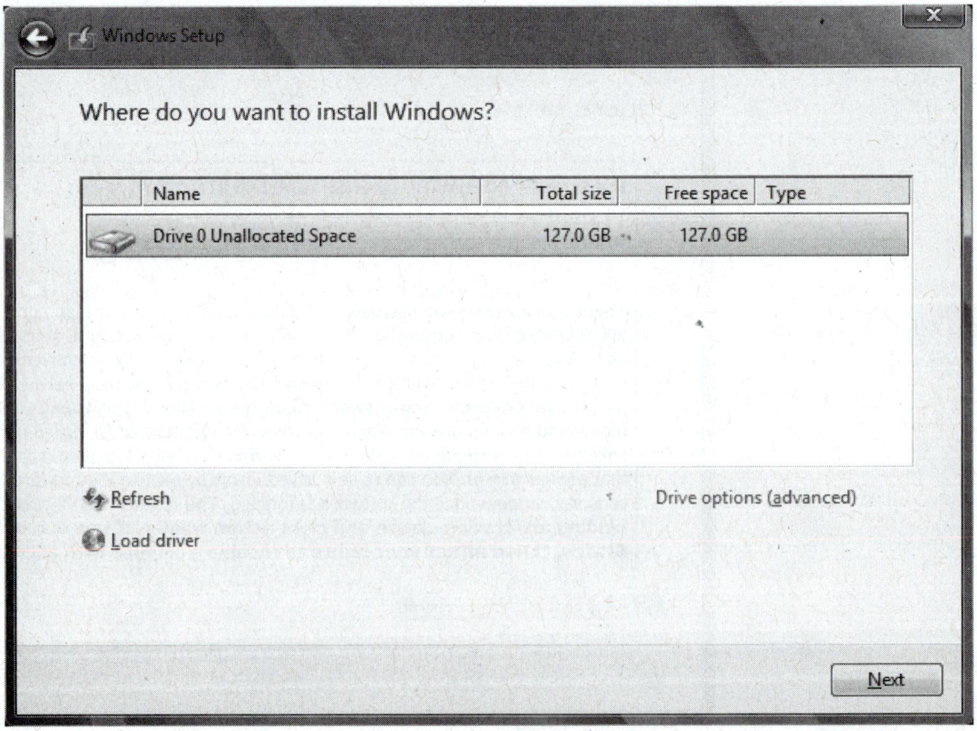

Figure 2-6

The *Where do you want to install Windows?* page

TAKE NOTE* The Upgrade option is currently disabled because you booted the computer using the Windows 8 installation disk. For the Upgrade option to function, you must boot an existing Windows 7 operating system and start the Windows 8 installation program from there. See "Upgrading to Windows 8" later in this lesson for more information.

8. From the list provided, select the partition on which you want to install Windows 8, or select an area of unallocated disk space where the Setup program can create a new partition. Then click **Next**.

   The Installing Windows page appears, as shown in Figure 2-7.

Figure 2-7

The *Installing Windows* page

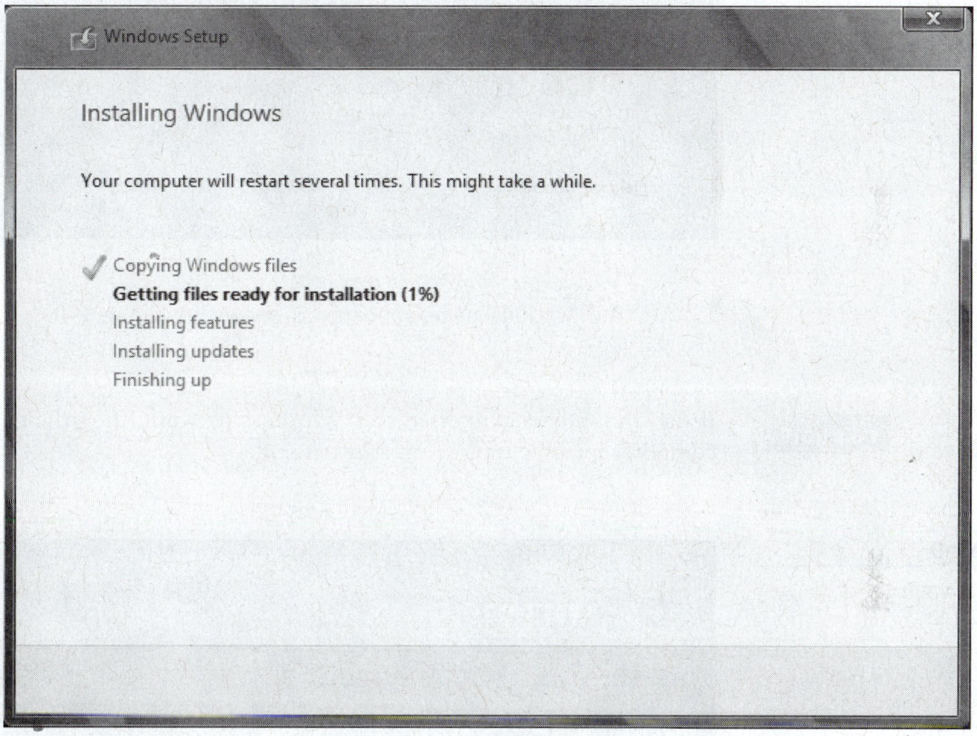

9. After several minutes, during which the Setup program installs Windows 8, the computer reboots and the Personalize page appears, as shown in Figure 2-8.
10. Select a color for your screen background and in the PC name text box, type a name for the computer, and then click **Next**.

Figure 2-8

The *Personalize* page

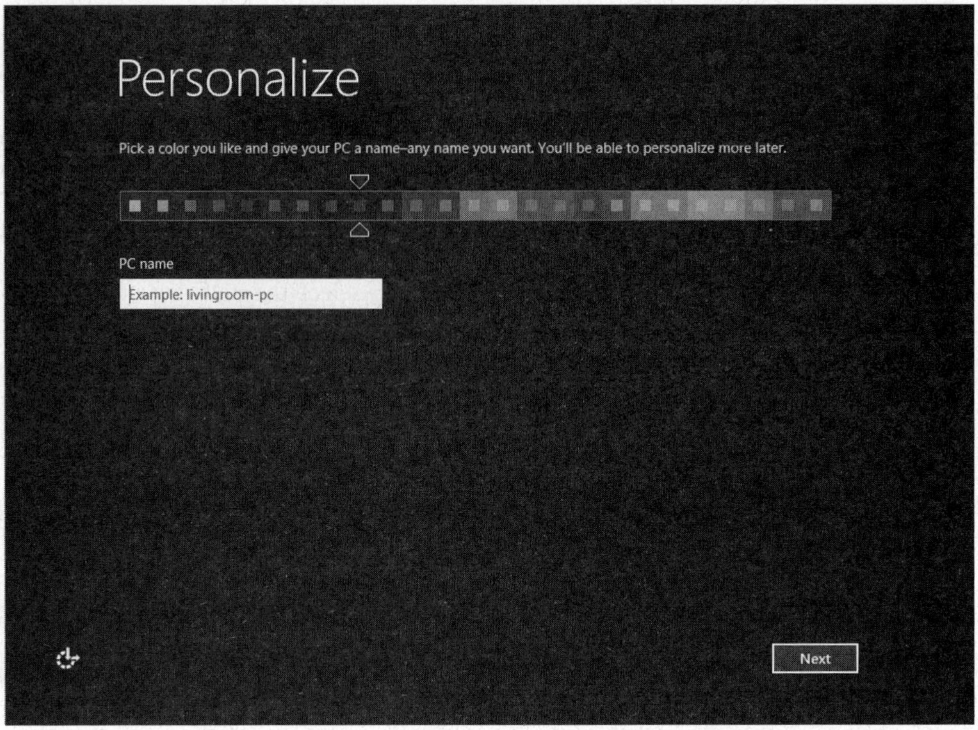

The Settings page appears, as shown in Figure 2-9.

TAKE NOTE* If the computer is connected to a Windows network, then the name you specify for the computer must be unique on that network.

Figure 2-9

The *Settings* page

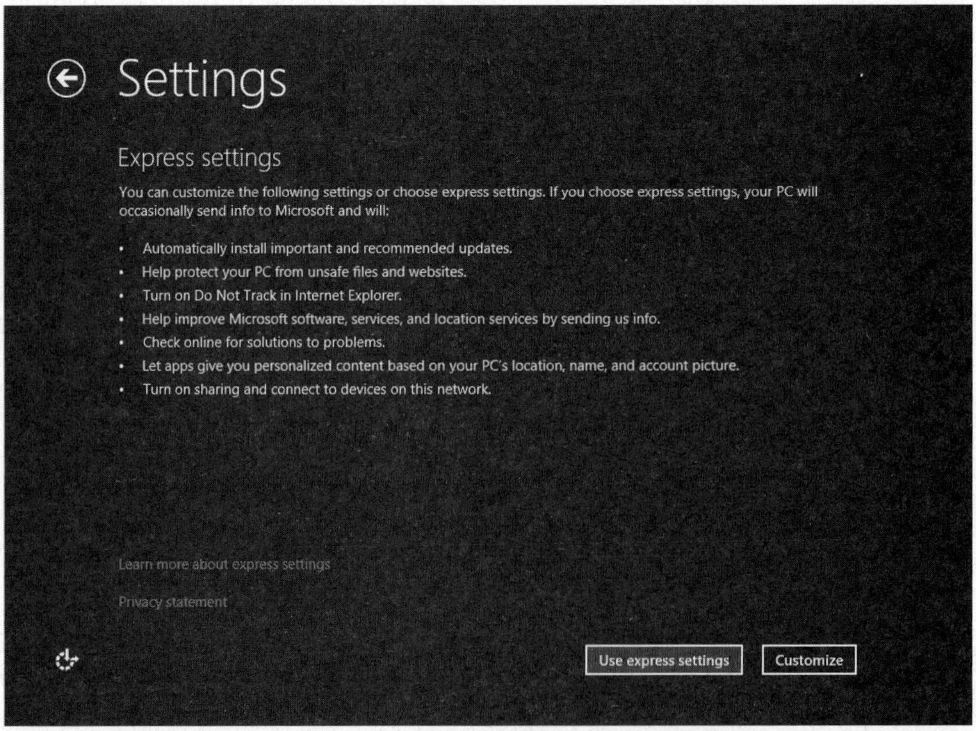

11. Click **Use Express Settings**. The *Sign in to your PC* page appears, as shown in Figure 2-10.

Figure 2-10

The *Sign in to your PC* page

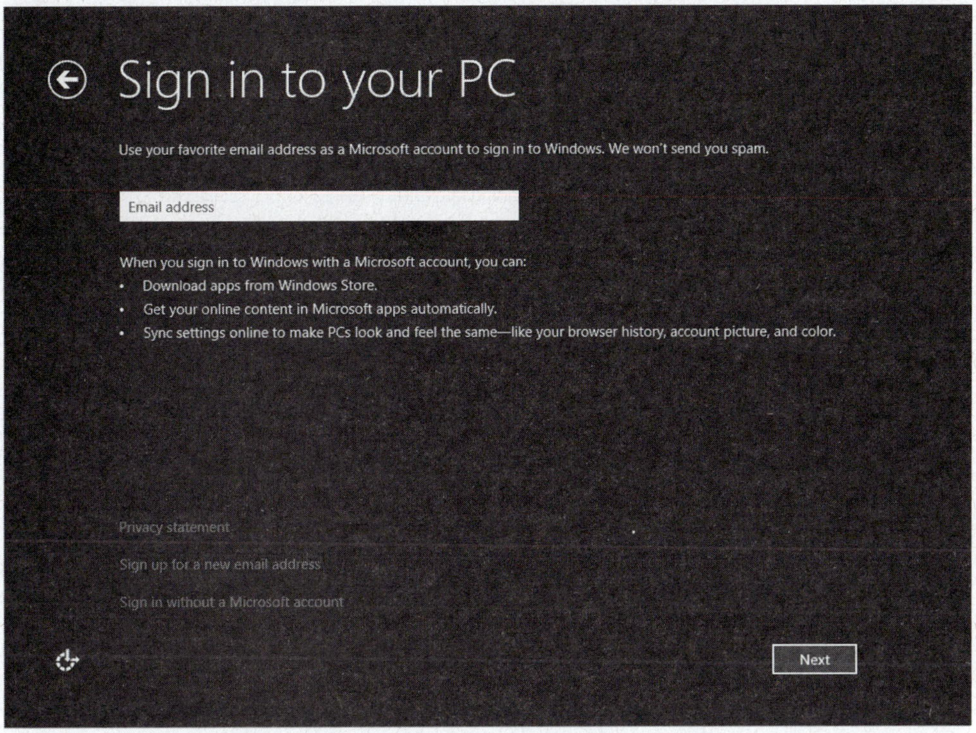

12. In the *Email address* text box, type the address associated with a Microsoft account and then click Next.

    The *Enter your Microsoft account password* page appears, as shown in Figure 2-11.

Figure 2-11

The *Enter your Microsoft account password* page

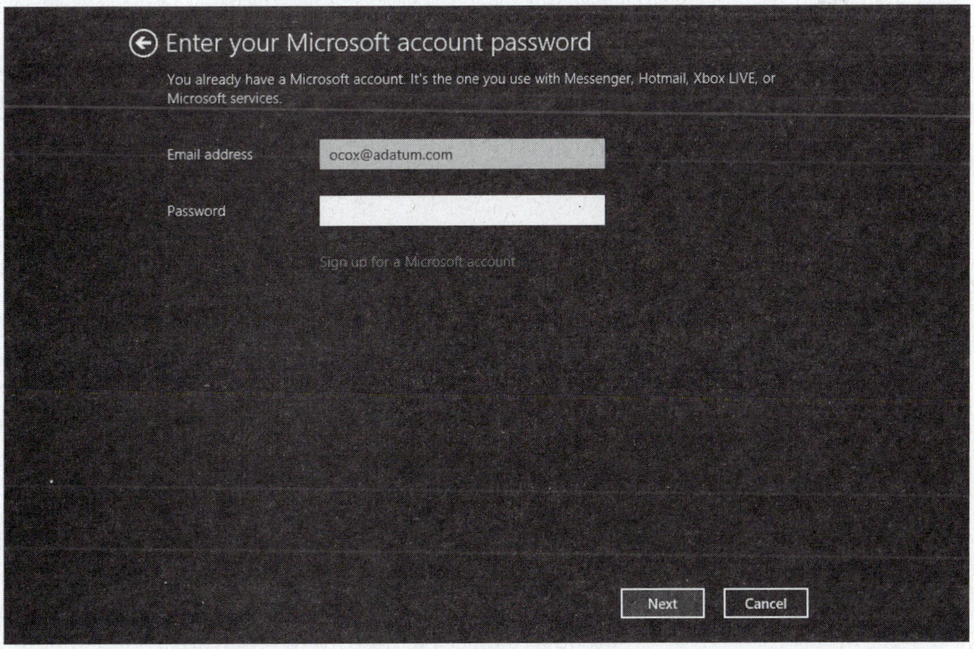

TAKE NOTE* If you do not have a Microsoft account, you can click the *Sign up for a new email address* link to obtain one or click *Sign in without a Microsoft account* to create a traditional local Windows account without an email address.

13. In the Password text box, type the password associated with your Microsoft account and then click **Next**.

    A series of screens introducing Windows 8 functions appear, followed by the Windows 8 Start screen.

At this point, you can remove the installation disk from the drive.

Installing Third-Party Device Drivers

During the Windows 8 installation procedure, the Setup program enables you to select a disk partition or an area of unallocated disk space where you want to install the operating system.

The *Where do you want to install Windows?* page lists the partitions on all of the hard disks that the Setup program can detect with its default drivers. In most cases, all of the computer's hard disks will appear in the list; If they do not, it is probably because Windows PE does not include a driver for the computer's drive controller.

If the hard disk drives in the computer are connected to a third-party controller, rather than the one integrated into the motherboard, the list of partitions might appear empty, and you will have to supply a driver before the Setup program can see the disks. Check the controller manufacturer's website for a driver supporting Windows 8. If none is available, use the most recent Windows 7 driver.

MORE INFORMATION

There are several reasons why a computer might employ a third-party disk controller, rather than the one integrated into the motherboard. The computer might have a relatively old motherboard and more modern drives whose capabilities are not supported by the older controller. The computer might also be using SCSI (Small Computer Systems Interface) or SAS (Serial Attached SCSI) rather than SATA (Serial ATA) or IDE (Integrated Drive Electronics) hard drives, and a SCSI or SAS host adapter that is not supported by Windows PE. Finally, the computer might be using a specialized controller that provides advanced disk management technologies, such as RAID (Redundant Array of Independent Disks).

To install a third-party disk driver, use the following procedure:

INSTALL A THIRD-PARTY DISK DRIVER

GET READY. If, during a Windows 8 installation, no disk partitions or unallocated space appear on the *Where do you want to install Windows?* page, you must install the appropriate driver for your disk controller using the following procedure before the installation can continue.

1. On the *Where do you want to install Windows?* page, click the **Load Driver** button.

   A *Load Driver* message box appears, as shown in Figure 2-12.

2. Insert the storage medium containing the driver into the computer. You can supply drivers on a CD, DVD, USB flash drive, or floppy disk.

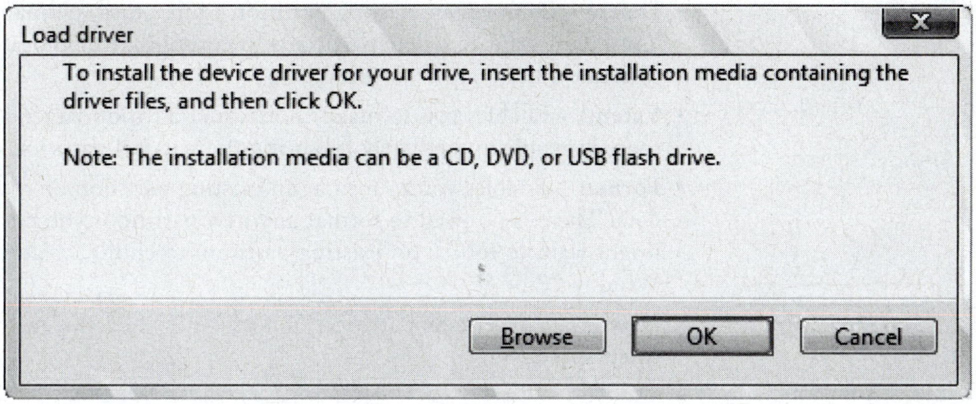

Figure 2-12

The *Load Driver* message box

TAKE NOTE*

Because Windows PE is running on a RAM drive, it is possible to remove the Windows 8 installation disk from the DVD drive and insert another disk containing drivers. You will later have to re-insert the Windows 8 disk to complete the installation.

3. Click **OK** if the driver is in the root directory of the storage medium or click **Browse** if it is necessary to locate the driver in the directory structure of the disk. When the driver loads, the partitions and unallocated space on the associated disks appear in the list on the *Where do you want to install Windows?* page.
4. Select the partition or area of unallocated space where you want to install Windows 8 and then continue with the rest of the installation procedure, as covered earlier in this lesson.

Working with Installation Partitions

In addition to installing disk drivers, the *Where do you want to install Windows?* page enables you to create, manage, and delete the partitions on your disks.

Clicking the *Drive options (advanced)* button on the page causes four additional buttons to appear, as shown in Figure 2-13. These buttons have the following functions:

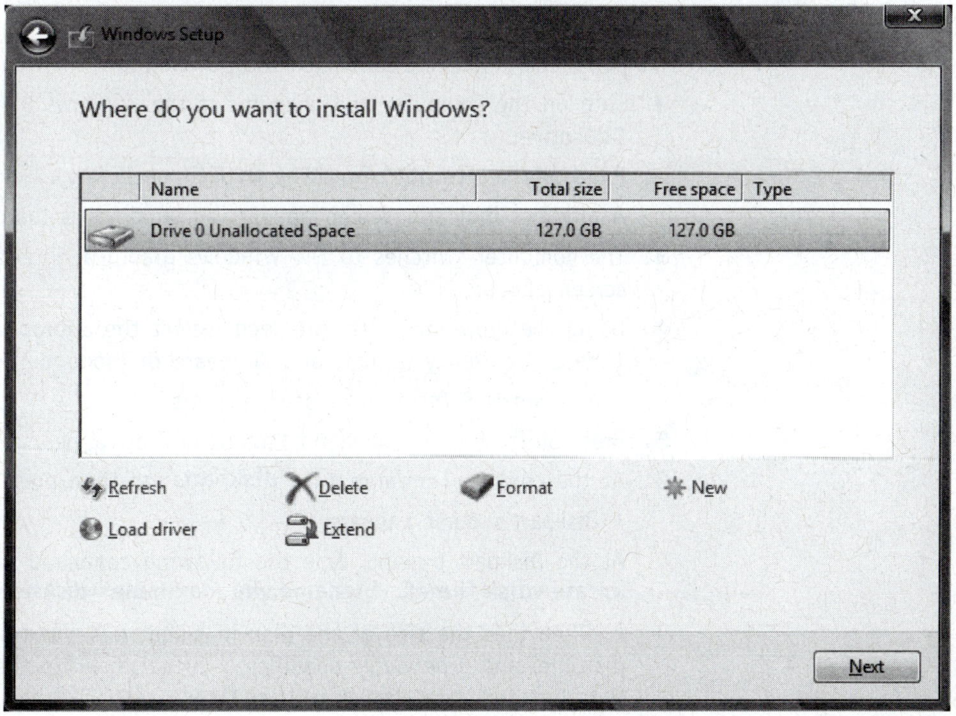

Figure 2-13

Additional buttons on the *Where do you want to install Windows?* page

- **Delete** – Removes an existing partition from a disk, permanently erasing all of its data. You might want to delete partitions to consolidate unallocated disk space, enabling you to create a new, larger partition.
- **Extend** – Enables you to make an existing partition larger, as long as there is unallocated space available immediately following the selected partition on the disk.
- **Format** – Enables you to format an existing partition on a disk, thereby erasing all of its data. There is no need to format any new partitions you create for the install, but you might want to format an existing partition to eliminate unwanted files prior to installing Windows 8 on it.
- **New** – Creates a new partition of a user-specified size in the selected area of unallocated space.

Installing to a VHD

During a clean installation of Windows 8, the *Where do you want to install Windows?* page enables you to select any partition on any physical disk as the destination for the Windows system files. However, it is also possible to install Windows 8 on a ***virtual hard disk (VHD)*** file stored on any one of the computer's physical disks.

When you install Windows 8 on a VHD, it becomes an alternative boot device to the standard disk partition installation. The boot loader that appears when you start the computer lists the VHD installation as well as the standard disk installation, enabling you to select either one. When you boot from the VHD installation, the entire operating systems loads from the VHD file, and the main installation becomes inaccessible.

CERTIFICATION READY
Install VHD
Objective 1.2

This ability makes it possible to maintain any number of independent Windows 8 installations on a single computer and boot into any one as needed.

To install Windows 8 to a VHD file, use the following procedure.

INSTALL WINDOWS 8 TO A VHD

GET READY. Prepare the computer for the Windows 8 installation by making sure that all of its external peripheral devices are connected and powered on.

1. Turn on the computer and then insert the Windows 8 installation disk into the DVD drive.
2. Press any key to boot from the DVD (if necessary).

   A progress indicator screen appears as Windows is loading files.
3. The computer switches to the Windows graphical interface and the Windows Setup screen appears.
4. Using the drop-down lists provided, select the appropriate Language to install, Time and currency format, and Keyboard or input method and then click **Next**.

   The *Windows 8 Install now* page appears.
5. Press Shift+F10. A Command Prompt window appears.
6. At the command prompt, type **diskpart** and then press **Enter**.

   A Diskpart prompt appears.
7. At the Diskpart prompt, type the following command and then press **Enter**.
   create vdisk file=C:\filename.vhd maximum=*disksize* type=fixed|expandable

   size specifies the size of the disk in megabytes, *fixed* specifies a fixed size virtual disk file, and *expandable* specifies a virtual disk file that resizes to accommodate the allocated data. The default is **fixed**.

8. Type **select vdisk file=C:\filename.vhd** and then press **Enter**.
9. Type **attach vdisk** and then press **Enter**.
10. Type **exit** and then press **Enter** to close the Diskpart prompt.
11. Type **exit** and then press **Enter** to close the Command Prompt window.
12. Click the ***Install now*** button.

    The *License terms* page appears.
13. Select the **I accept the license terms** checkbox and then click **Next**.

    The *Which type of installation do you want?* page appears.
14. Click the **Custom: Install Windows only (advanced)** option.

    The *Where do you want to install Windows?* page appears, with the new VHD you created appearing as one of the disks available for selection.
15. From the list provided, select the partition representing the VHD you just created, and then click **Next**.

    The *Installing Windows* page appears.
16. Proceed with the rest of the installation in the normal manner.

Once you have completed the installation, you can select the VHD installation from the boot loader each time you start the computer.

Upgrading to Windows 8

THE BOTTOM LINE

To the workstation user, performing an in-place upgrade to Windows 8 is a relatively simple procedure, but the activities the Setup program performs behind the scenes are highly complex.

During the upgrade process, the Setup program creates a new Windows folder and installs the Windows 8 operating system files into it. This is only half of the process, however. The program must then migrate the applications, files, and settings from the old OS. This calls for a variety of procedures, such as importing the user profiles, copying all pertinent settings from the old registry to the new one, locating applications and data files, and updating device drivers with new versions.

While in-place upgrades often proceed smoothly, the complexity of the upgrade process and the large number of variables involved means that there are many things that can potentially go wrong. To minimize the risks involved, it is important for an administrator to take the upgrade process seriously, prepare the system beforehand, and have the ability to troubleshoot any problems that might arise. The following sections discuss these subjects in greater detail.

TAKE NOTE*

An in-place upgrade from Windows 7 to Windows 8 is much more complex than an upgrade from one Windows 8 edition to another. All of the Windows 8 editions use the same basic core files and architecture. Upgrades are primarily a matter of activating additional applications, which is not as invasive or dangerous.

Preparing to Upgrade

Before you begin an in-place upgrade to Windows 8, you should perform a number of preliminary procedures to ensure that the process goes smoothly and that the user data is protected.

Consider the following before you perform any upgrade to Windows 8:

- **Run Upgrade Assistant** – To be sure that the computer is capable of running the Windows 8 edition you plan on installing, run Upgrade Assistant and take note of its advisories regarding the computer's hardware and software. If it is necessary to perform hardware upgrades, do so before installing Windows 8, making sure that the new hardware is operational before proceeding.

X REF

For more information on Windows 8's hardware requirements, and on running the Upgrade Assistant program, see Lesson 1, "Evaluating Hardware Readiness and Capability."

- **Check hardware compatibility** – The ***Upgrade Assistant program*** can point out hardware inadequacies in the computer, especially in regard to the Windows 8 system requirements. If it is necessary to upgrade hardware, make certain that the products you purchase are certified for use with Windows 8. The Upgrade Assistant program can also identify devices that might not function under Windows 8. However, it is sometimes possible to make such devices run properly with a driver or firmware upgrade. It is a good idea to perform an inventory of the computer's primary components before you perform the upgrade, and consider the age and capabilities of each one. It is always best to locate potential hardware incompatibilities before you perform the upgrade procedure.
- **Search for updated drivers** – As part of your hardware inventory, be sure to consider the age of the device drivers installed on the computer. Check hardware manufacturers' websites for driver updates, especially those that are specifically intended to provide support for Windows 8. In some cases it might be preferable to install the new drivers while Vista or Windows 7 is still running, but if the manufacturer provides separate Vista, Windows 7, and Windows 8 drivers, wait until you have installed Windows 8. Even if no updates are available, it is a good idea to gather all of the drivers for the computer's hardware together and copy them to a removable storage medium, such as a writable CD or flash drive. This way, if the Setup program requires a driver during the upgrade process, you have it available.
- **Check application compatibility** – Upgrade Assistant can point out possible application compatibility problems, but you can sometimes solve these problems by updating or upgrading the application. Create an inventory of the software products installed on the computer and check the manufacturers' websites for updates, availability of upgrades, and announcements regarding support for Windows 8. For example, if the computer is running Microsoft Office, use the Office Online website to download the latest updates. Check the applications' system requirements as well. Install any free updates that are available and consider the need for paid upgrades. In an enterprise environment, you should test all applications for Windows 8 compatibility, no matter what the manufacturer says, before you perform any operating system upgrades. However, for standalone clients, testing usually isn't practical. The best you can do is to inform the user that there might be problems with specific applications and warn them that there might be additional costs involved for new versions or different products.
- **Check disk space** – Make sure that there is at least 20 gigabytes of disk space free on the partition where the old operating system is installed. During the upgrade procedure, sufficient disk space is needed to hold both operating systems simultaneously. After the upgrade is complete, you can remove the old Windows files, freeing up some additional space.
- **Ensure computer functionality** – Make sure that Windows 7 is running properly on the computer before you begin the upgrade process. You must start an in-place upgrade

from within Windows 7, so you cannot count on Windows 8 to correct any problems that prevent the computer from starting or running the Setup program.

- **Perform a full backup** – Before you perform any upgrade procedure you should back up the entire system, or at the very least the essential user files. You can use Windows Easy Transfer if no other tool is available. Removable hard drives make this a simple process, even if the client does not have a suitable backup device in the computer.
- **Purchase Windows 8** – Be sure to purchase the appropriate Windows 8 edition for the upgrade, and have the installation disk and product key handy. For more information on the allowed upgrade paths to Windows 8, see Lesson 1.

Upgrading from Windows 7 to Windows 8

CERTIFICATION READY
Upgrading from Windows 7 to Windows 8
Objective 1.2

Once you complete the steps in the previous section, you are ready to perform an in-place upgrade from Windows 7 to Windows 8.

To upgrade a computer running Windows 7 to Windows 8 while preserving all files and settings, use the following procedure:

UPGRADE WINDOWS 7 TO WINDOWS 8

GET READY. Turn on the computer running Windows 7 and make sure you have the Windows 8 installation disk and product key ready.

1. Insert the Windows 8 installation disk into the DVD drive.
   An Autoplay dialog box appears.
2. Click **Run setup.exe**.
   A User Account Control message box appears.
3. Click **Yes**.
   The Windows Setup screen appears.
4. Click **Install now.**
   The Get *important updates for Windows Setup* page appears.
5. Click **No thanks**.
   The *License terms* page appears.

TAKE NOTE* If the computer is connected to the Internet, you might want to click *Go online to get the latest updates for installation* to ensure that the computer's drivers and other software are up to date.

6. Select the **I accept the license terms** checkbox and then click **Next**.
   The *Which type of installation do you want?* page appears, as shown in Figure 2-14.
7. Click **Upgrade: Install Windows and keep files, settings, and applications**.
   The *Compatibility report* page appears.
8. Read the contents of the compatibility report and, if possible, click **Next**.
   The *Upgrading Windows* page appears.

TAKE NOTE* Note that unlike the previous Windows 8 installation procedure in this Lesson, the Upgrade option is activated.

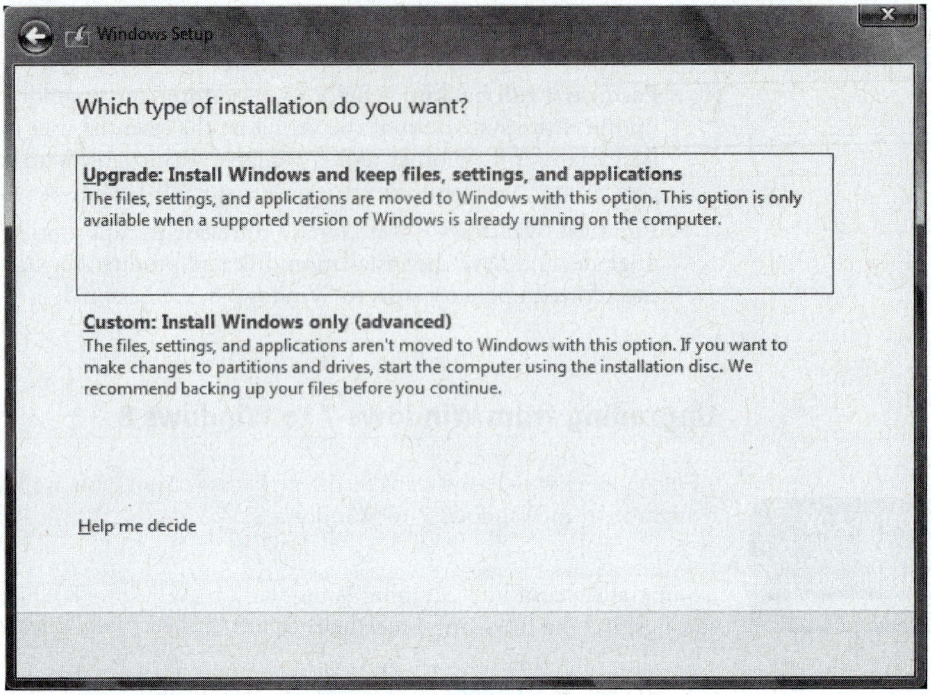

Figure 2-14
The *Which type of installation do you want?* page

9. After a delay, during which the Setup program installs Windows 8, the computer reboots and the *Personalize* page appears.

TAKE NOTE* Depending on the applications installed and the complexity of the system configuration, an in-place upgrade can take anywhere from several minutes to several hours.

10. Select a color for your screen background and then click **Next**.

    The *Settings* page appears.

11. Click **Use Express Settings**.

    The *Windows Lock* screen appears.

Upgrading Windows 8 Editions

One of the main advantages of the new architecture that Microsoft devised for Windows 8 is that it makes upgrades to other editions incredibly simple.

CERTIFICATION READY
Upgrading from one edition of Windows 8 to another edition of Windows 8
Objective 1.2

There are basically two scenarios in which an end user might be in a position to upgrade Windows 8 from one edition to another. If you are running the core Windows 8 product, you might want to upgrade to Windows 8 Professional. Among other things, this provides the ability to join the computer to an Active Directory Domain Services domain. This is likely to be a frequently encountered situation, as many computers sold by original equipment manufacturers (OEMs) have the core version of Windows 8 already installed on them.

The other possibility is that of a Windows 8 Professional user who wants to add the Windows 8 Media Center Pack. Both the Windows 8 Professional upgrade and the Windows 8 Media Center Pack are available directly through the operating system, using the Add features to Windows 8 control panel.

To upgrade a Windows 8 installation to another edition, use the following procedure.

USE THE ADD FEATURES TO WINDOWS 8 CONTROL PANEL

GET READY. Start the Windows 8 computer and log on using an account with administrative privileges.

1. On the Windows 8 computer, open the charms bar and then click **Search**.

   The Search bar appears.
2. With the Settings option selected, type **add features** in the text box.

   The *Add features to Windows 8* application appears in the results display.
3. Click **Add features to Windows 8**.

   A User Account Control message box appears.
4. Click **Yes**.

   The *Add features to Windows 8* control panel appears, displaying the *How do you want to get started?* page, which specifies the currently installed Windows 8 version.
5. Click **I want to buy a product key online**.

   A *Here's what we found* page appears, displaying the product options available for the computer.
6. Click the **Choose** button for the upgrade that you want to purchase.

   A Microsoft Store Wizard appears to step you through the process of purchasing the upgrade.
7. Follow the instructions to purchase and then install the upgrade.

Migrating from Windows XP or Windows Vista

> There is no direct upgrade path from Windows Vista or Windows XP to Windows 8. The only way to retain any of your system information from these earlier operating systems while installing Windows 8 is to perform a migration, either side-by-side or wipe-and-load, as described in Lesson 3, "Migrating and Configuring User Data."

Migrating from Windows 7 to Windows 8 is relatively simple, because both operating systems have versions of ***Windows Easy Transfer*** that are compatible with each other. You simply run the utility on each computer and the wizards guide you through the process of migrating user profile information from the old computer to the new one, using a direct link, a removable storage medium, or a network share.

CERTIFICATION READY
Migrate from Windows XP or Windows Vista
Objective 1.2

If your existing computer is running Windows Vista or Windows XP, you must install the correct version of Windows Easy Transfer on the source computer before you can perform the migration. To extract the installation files from Windows 8 and transfer them to the source computer, use the following procedure.

CREATING WINDOWS EASY TRANSFER INSTALLATION FILES

GET READY. Log on to your Windows 8 computer using an account with administrative privileges.

1. On the Windows 8 computer, open the charms bar and then click **Search**.

   The Search bar appears.
2. With the Apps option selected, type **easy** in the text box.

   The Windows Easy Transfer application appears in the results display.

3. Click **Windows Easy Transfer**.

   The *Windows Easy Transfer Wizard* appears, displaying the *Welcome* page.

4. Click **Next**.

   The *What do you want to use to transfer items to your new PC?* page appears.

5. Click ***A network***.

   The *Which PC are you using now?* page appears.

6. Click ***This is my new PC***.

   The *Has Windows Easy Transfer already saved your files from your old PC to an external hard disk or USB flash drive?* page appears.

7. Click **No**.

   The *Do you need to install Windows Easy Transfer on your old PC?* page appears.

8. Click ***My old PC is running Windows XP or Windows Vista***.

   The *How do you want to install Windows Easy Transfer on your old PC?* page appears.

9. Select one of the following options:

   - **External hard disk or shared network folder** – Enables you to select a folder on the computer or the network where the wizard will copy the Windows Easy Transfer installation files.
   - **USB flash drive** – Enables you to selected a mounted USB flash drive, where the wizard will copy the Windows Easy Transfer installation files.

10. Select a destination for the Windows Easy Transfer files. The wizard copies the files to the selected location and the *Install Windows Easy Transfer on your old PC* page appears.

11. Follow the instructions to run Windows Easy Transfer on your source computer running Windows XP or Windows Vista.

Once you have installed Windows Easy Transfer on your source computer, the process is nearly identical to that of a migration from Windows 7, as described in Lesson 3. The difference is that when migrating from Windows Vista to Windows 8, the systems transfer user accounts and files, as well as Windows settings, but you must reinstall all of your applications. When migrating from Windows XP to Windows 8, the systems transfer only your user accounts and settings. You must reconfigure your Windows settings and reinstall your applications.

Installing Windows To Go

THE BOTTOM LINE

Windows To Go is a new feature in Windows 8 that enables administrators to deploy system images on removable USB drives.

When a user plugs a Windows To Go drive into a remote computer, the system loads the complete Windows 8 environment from the removable medium, including applications and any other data incorporated into the image file. The user can therefore access a familiar environment on any computer with hardware sufficient to run Windows 8.

CERTIFICATION READY
Installing Windows to Go
Objective 1.2

Once Windows 8 is loaded from the Windows To Go drive, the storage subsystem on the host computer is disabled, so that no remnants of the Windows To Go environment are left on that computer. Users can therefore load Windows To Go on any computer, without worrying about leaving any confidential information behind, and enterprise administrators can permit temporary visitors to use their own computers.

For security purposes, Windows To Go supports the use of BitLocker, bypassing the Trusted Platform Module (TPM) because the feature is designed for use on different computers.

To create a Windows To Go drive, use the following procedure.

CREATE A WINDOWS TO GO DRIVE

GET READY. Start the Windows 8 computer and log on using an account with administrative privileges.

1. Plug the USB drive into an available port.
2. Insert a Windows 8 Enterprise installation disk into a drive.
3. On the Windows 8 computer, open the charms bar and then click **Search**.

   The Search bar appears.
4. With the Settings option selected, type **windows to go** in the text box.

   The *Windows To Go* application appears in the results display.
5. Click **Windows To Go**.

   The *Create a Windows To Go Workspace Wizard* appears, displaying the *Choose the drive you want to use* page, as shown in Figure 2-15.

Figure 2-15

The *Choose the drive you want to use* page

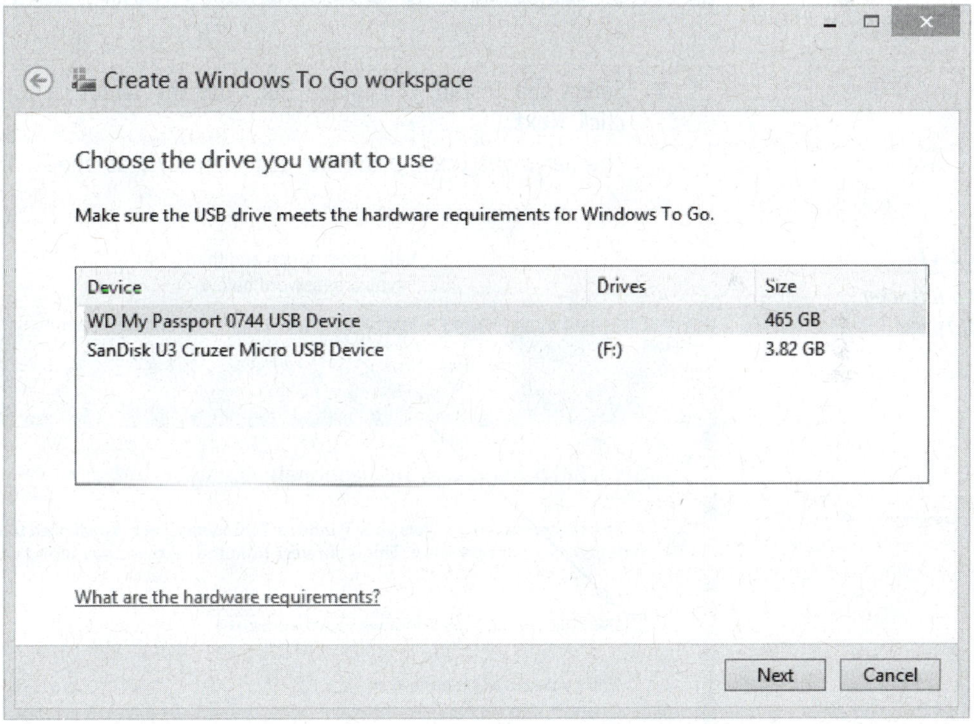

6. Select the USB device you want to convert to a Windows To Go drive from the device list and then click **Next**.

   The *Choose a Windows 8 Image* page appears, as shown in Figure 2-16.

Figure 2-16

The *Choose a Windows 8 image* page

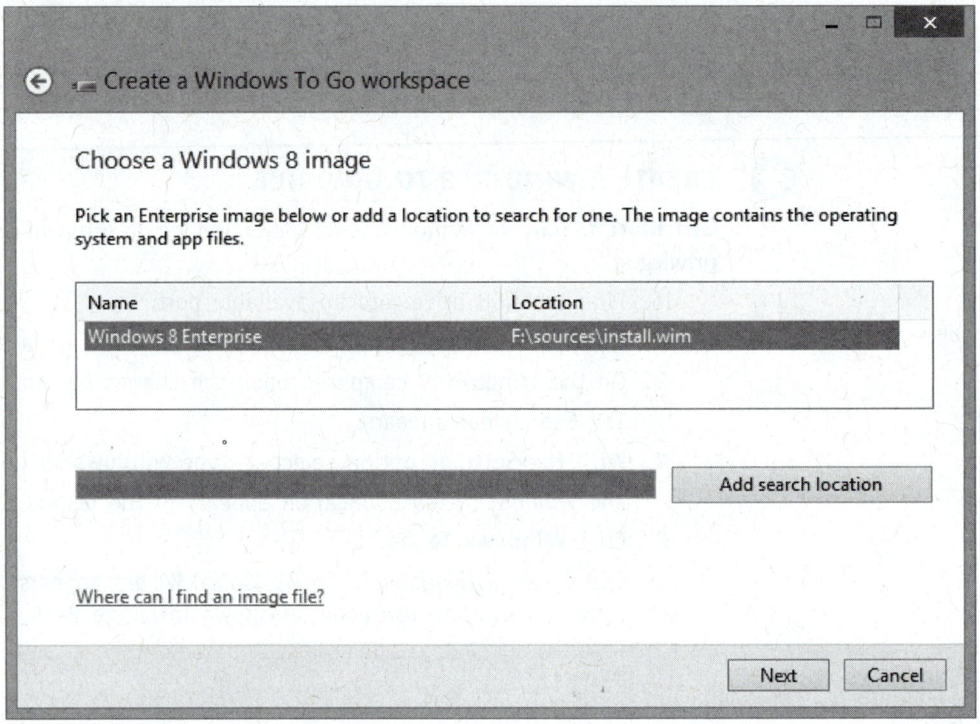

7. Select the Install.wim image file from the Windows 8 installation disk and then click **Next**.

   The *Set a BitLocker password* page appears, as shown in Figure 2-17.

Figure 2-17

The *Set a BitLocker password* page

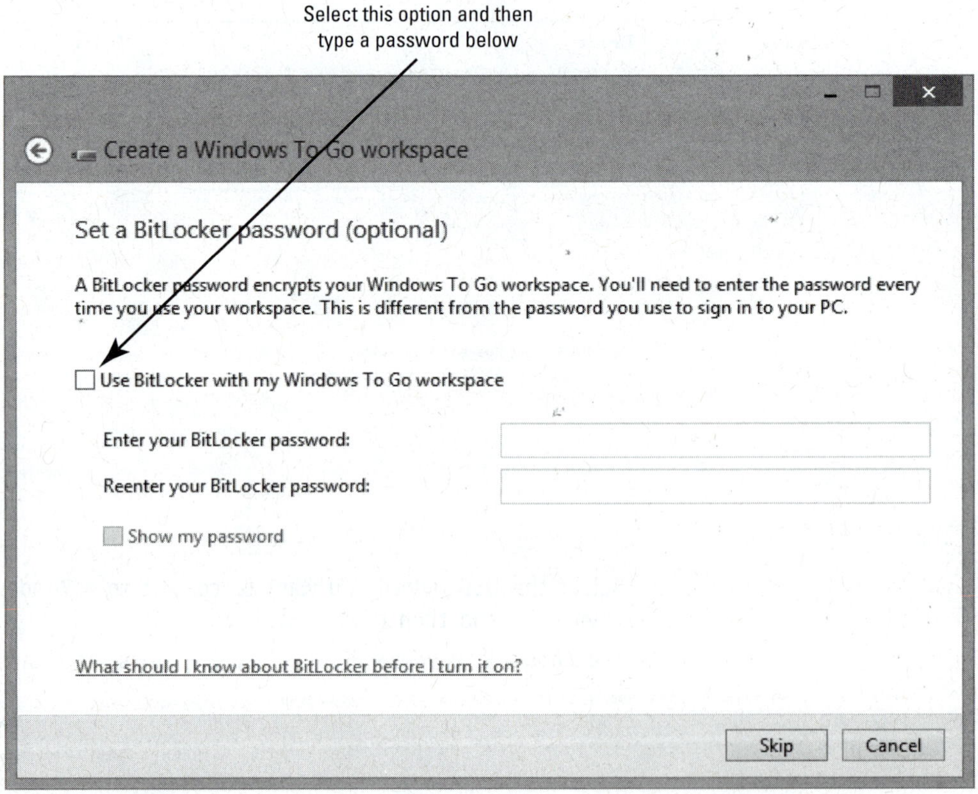

TAKE NOTE*

You can use any system image file to create a Windows To Go workspace, including an image that you have customized with drivers, applications, configuration settings, and data files.

8. Optionally, select the **Use BitLocker with my Windows To Go workspace** check-box and specify a password in the two text boxes provided. Then click **Next**.

   The *Ready to create your Windows To Go workspace* page appears.

9. Click **Create**. The Creating your Windows To Go workspace page appears as the wizard prepares the drive.

   After an interval, the *Choose a boot option* page appears, as shown in Figure 2-18.

Figure 2-18

The *Choose a boot option* page

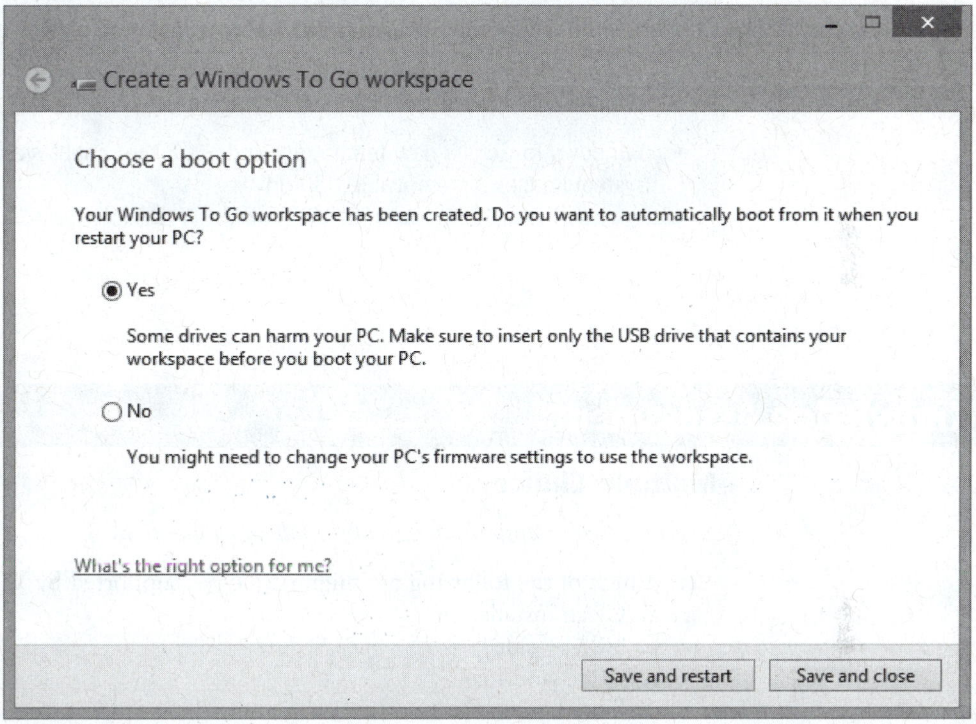

TAKE NOTE*

The process of creating a Windows To Go workspace can be a lengthy one, as long as 30 minutes or more, depending on the size of the image file you select.

10. Select **Yes** and then click **Save and close**.
11. Remove the USB device from computer.

You can now use the USB device to a boot any computer with hardware sufficient to run Windows 8 into the Windows To Go workspace.

TAKE NOTE*

Converting a USB drive to a Windows To Go workspace modifies its volume attributes. To decommission the device so that it becomes usable as a standard USB storage drive again, you must use the Diskpart utility to run the clean command on the drive, which removes all data, formatting, and initialization information.

SKILL SUMMARY

IN THIS LESSON, YOU LEARNED:

- Windows 8 includes a new preinstallation environment called Windows PE.
- In a clean installation, you boot from the Windows 8 Setup disk and create or select a blank partition where Windows 8 will reside.
- It is possible to migrate files and settings from an existing Windows installation to a newly installed Windows 8 installation using either Windows Easy Transfer or User State Migration Tool.
- Windows 8 supports in-place upgrades only from Windows 7 or another Windows 8 edition.
- To perform an in-place upgrade, you must launch the Windows 8 Setup program from within Windows 7.
- To upgrade from one Windows 8 edition to another, you can use the Add features to Windows 8 found in the Windows 8 Control Panel.
- Windows To Go is a new feature in Windows 8 that enables administrators to deploy system images on removable USB drives

Knowledge Assessment

Multiple Choice

Select the correct answer for each of the following questions.

1. Which of the following are migration types supported by Windows Easy Transfer?
   - **a.** Clean installation
   - **b.** Side-by-side
   - **c.** Wipe–and-load
   - **d.** Single sideload
2. A computer running Windows PE will automatically reboot after how long?
   - **a.** 24 hours
   - **b.** 48 hours
   - **c.** 72 hours
   - **d.** 96 hours
3. When a serious problem occurs with Windows 8, you might be able to repair it by starting the Windows PE operating system and running diagnostic tools. In this scenario, Windows PE is called by which of the following names?
   - **a.** Windows RT
   - **b.** Windows RE
   - **c.** Windows ARM
   - **d.** Windows Repair ________.
4. It is possible to remove the Windows 8 installation disk to supply the Setup program with drivers because Windows PE runs on which of the following?
   - **a.** USB disk
   - **b.** Ramdisk

c. Scratch disk
d. DVD

5. Which of the following upgrades can you purchase through the *Add features to Windows 8* control panel?
   a. Windows 7 Professional to Windows 8 Professional
   b. Windows 8 to Windows 8 Professional
   c. Windows 8 to Windows 8 Enterprise
   d. Windows 8 Professional to Windows 8 Enterprise

6. Which of the following mechanisms provides security in Windows To Go?
   a. IPsec
   b. Trusted Platform Module (TPM)
   c. BitLocker
   d. Kerberos

7. Which of the following tools must you use while installing Windows 8 to a virtual hard disk (VHD) file?
   a. Scanstate.exe
   b. Loadstate.exe
   c. Vdisk.exe
   d. Diskpart.exe

8. Which of the following media can you not use to transfer the Windows Easy Transfer installation files from a Windows 8 computer to a Windows XP computer?
   a. A network share
   b. A USB flash drive
   c. An Easy Transfer cable
   d. An external hard disk

9. As a preinstallation environment, Windows PE is a vast improvement over MS-DOS because it includes internal support for which of the following?
   a. Networking
   b. scripts
   c. NTFS
   d. 64-bit drivers

10. Which of the following is not included in the Windows Assessment and Deployment Kit?
    a. Activation Management Tool (VAMT)
    b. User State Migration Tool (USMT)
    c. Application Compatibility Toolkit (ACT)
    d. Windows Easy Transfer
    e. Windows Assessment Services

Best Answer

Choose the letter that corresponds to the best answer. More than one answer choice may achieve the goal. Select the BEST answer.

1. Which of the following tools is the best choice when you are performing a scripted migration in an enterprise environment?
   a. Windows Easy Transfer
   b. User State Migration Tool
   c. Update Assistant
   d. AppLocker

2. Which of the following operating systems provides the easiest migration to Windows 8?
   a. Windows 2000
   b. Windows XP
   c. Windows Vista
   d. Windows 7

3. Which of the following is the worst choice of removable storage medium for migrating data with Windows Easy Transfer?
   a. Floppy disk
   b. USB flash drive
   c. Network share
   d. Removable hard drive

4. Which of the following are the two best reasons why Windows PE is a better installation environment for Windows 8 than MS-DOS?
   a. Windows PE boots faster than MS-DOS.
   b. Windows PE includes internal networking support
   c. Windows PE supports the NTFS file system
   d. Windows PE boots from floppy drives

Matching and Identification

1. Match the following terms with their corresponding definitions.
   _______ a) wipe-and-load migration
   _______ b) Windows PE
   _______ c) Upgrade Assistant
   _______ d) side-by-side migration
   _______ e) Windows To Go
   _______ f) Windows Easy Transfer
   _______ g) Windows 8 Assessment and Deployment Kit
   _______ h) Virtual hard disk
   _______ i) system recovery disk
   _______ j) Windows RE
   1. Environment similar to Windows PE, used for troubleshooting
   2. Image of an entire hard disk stored as a single file
   3. Transfers user profiles data using two computers
   4. Replaces MS-DOS as system boot medium
   5. Determines whether an in-place upgrade is possible
   6. Contains an image of a computer in its newly installed state
   7. Transfers user profile data using one computer
   8. Installs a system image to a removable drive
   9. Wizard-based user profile migration utility
   10. Includes Windows PE and the User State Migration Tool

Build a List

1. Place the following steps for installing Windows 8 with a third party disk driver in the correct order.
   _______ a) Click Custom: Install Windows Only.
   _______ b) Accept the license terms for the installation.
   _______ c) Boot the computer from a Windows 8 installation disk.
   _______ d) Select the partition where you want to install Windows.
   _______ e) Click Install now.
   _______ f) Personalize the installation.

_________ **g)** Click the Load Driver button.
_________ **h)** Insert the disk containing the third party driver.
_________ **i)** Select appropriate language, time and currency, and keyboard settings.

2. Place the following steps for installing Windows To Go in the correct order.
_________ **a)** Launch the Windows To Go application.
_________ **b)** Plug a removable drive into the computer's USB port.
_________ **c)** Specify a password for BitLocker security.
_________ **d)** Launch the Create a Windows To Go Workspace Wizard.
_________ **e)** Insert a Windows 8 installation DVD into the disk drive.
_________ **f)** Close the Create a Windows To Go Workspace Wizard.
_________ **g)** Click Create.
_________ **h)** Select the removable drive as the target for the Windows To Go image.
_________ **i)** Choose Yes for the automatic boot option.
_________ **j)** Select the Install.wim image from the installation disk as the source image.

Business Case Scenarios

Scenario 2-1: Upgrading Windows 8 Editions

You are working as a desktop support technician at a computer store, and a customer approaches you with a laptop computer he purchased three years ago. The computer came with Windows XP Home Basic installed on it, and the customer has already purchased a copy of Windows 8 core edition. He now wants to upgrade the computer to Windows 8 without affecting his files and also use the computer to log on to the Active Directory Domain Services domain at his office. Explain in detail the procedure you would have to use to fulfill the customer's request.

Scenario 2-2: Understanding the Difference Between a Side-by-Side Migration and a Wipe-and-Load Migration

You have been assigned the task of migrating 50 older workstations running Windows XP to Windows 8 Pro. However, your supervisor does not understand the difference between a side-by-side migration and a wipe-and-load migration. Explain the difference between the two migration types.

3 LESSON

Migrating and Configuring User Data

70-687 EXAM OBJECTIVE

Objective 1.3 – Migrate and configure user data. This objective may include but is not limited to configure profiles; migrate user profiles; and configure folder redirection.

Lesson Heading	Exam Objective
Configuring User Profiles	Configure profiles
Using Roaming Profiles	
Using Mandatory User Profiles	
Managing Profile Compatibility	
Migrating User Profiles	Migrate user profiles
Using Windows Easy Transfer	
Using the User State Migration Tool	
Configuring Folder Redirection	Configure folder redirection

KEY TERMS

Easy Transfer cable
folder redirection
Group Policy Management Editor console
Group Policy object (GPO)
local user profile
mandatory user profile
roaming user profile
side-by-side migration
task sequence
user profile
User State Migration Tool (USMT)
Windows Easy Transfer
wipe-and-load migration

Configuring User Profiles

THE BOTTOM LINE

As discussed in Lesson 2, "Installing Windows 8," a ***user profile*** is a series of folders, associated with a specific user account, that contain personal documents, user-specific registry settings, Internet favorites, and other personalized information—everything that provides a user's familiar working environment. On a Windows 8 computer, user profiles are stored in the Users folder, in subfolders named for the user accounts.

CERTIFICATION READY
Configure profiles
Objective 1.3

On computers running Windows 8, user profiles automatically create and maintain the desktop settings for each user's work environment on the local computer in a folder beneath C:\Users. The system creates a new user profile for each user logging on at the computer for the first time.

Each of these user folders contains a separate user profile for that person. A typical user profile consists of the following folders, some of which are hidden, plus a hidden registry file.

- AppData
- Contacts
- Desktop
- Downloads
- Favorites
- Links
- My Documents
- My Music
- My Pictures
- My Videos
- Saved Games
- Searches

When a user logs on at the workstation using a local or domain account, the system loads that individual's profile and uses it throughout the session until the user logs off. During the session, the My Documents folder in the user's profile becomes the operative My Documents folder for the system, as do all the other folders in the profile.

There are three main types of user profiles, as follows:

- ***Local user profile*** – A profile that Windows 8 automatically creates when each user logs on at the computer for the first time. The local user profile is stored on the computer's local hard disk.
- ***Roaming user profile*** – A copy of a local user profile that is stored on a shared folder on the network, making it accessible from anywhere on the network. A roaming user profile merges any changes with the local user profile to the server during the log off process.
- ***Mandatory user profile*** – A roaming profile that users cannot change. Administrators use mandatory user profiles to enforce particular desktop settings for individuals or for a group of users. A fourth variation, called a super-mandatory profile, requires the user to access the server-based profile or the logon fails.

Using Roaming Profiles

To support users who work at multiple computers on the same network, administrators can create roaming user profiles.

A ***roaming user profile*** is simply a copy of a local user profile that is stored on a network share (to which the user has appropriate permissions), so that the user can access it from any computer on the network. No matter which computer a user logs on from, he or she always receives the files and desktop settings from the profile stored on the server.

To enable a user to access a roaming user profile, rather than a local profile, you must open the user's *Properties* sheet to the Profile tab, as shown in Figure 3-1, and specify the location of the roaming profile in the Profile Path field.

Figure 3-1

The *Profile* tab of a domain user's *Properties* sheet

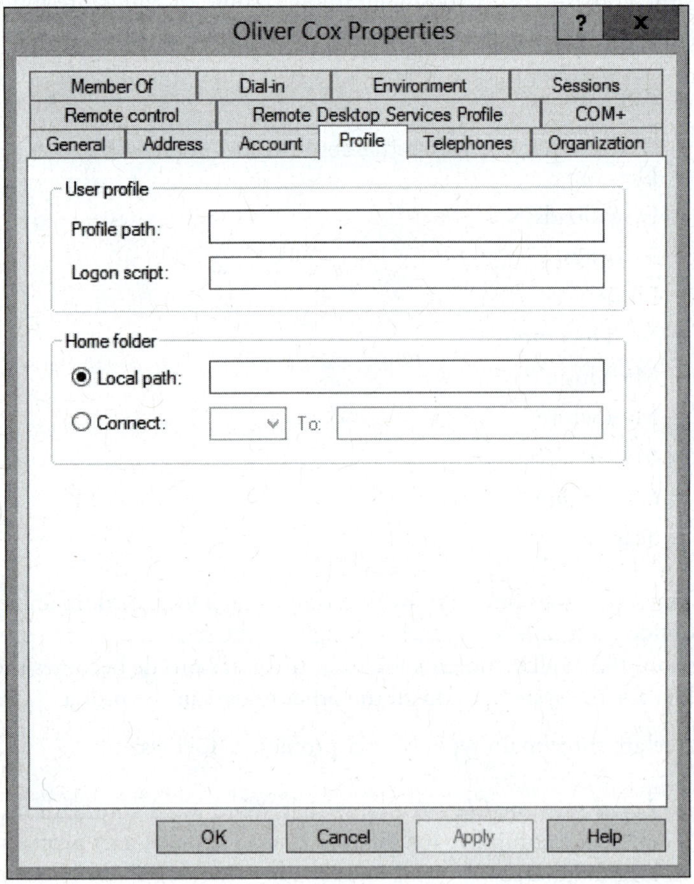

Then, the next time the user logs on, Windows 8 accesses the roaming user profile in the following manner:

1. During the user's first logon, the computer copies the entire contents of the roaming profile to the appropriate subfolder in the Users folder on the local drive. Having the roaming user profile contents stored on the local drive enables the user access to the profile during later logons, even if the server containing the roaming profile is unavailable.

2. The computer applies the roaming user profile settings to the computer, making it the active profile.
3. As the user works, the system saves any changes he or she makes to the user profile to the copy on the local drive.
4. When the user logs off, the computer replicates any changes made to the local copy of the user profile back to the server where the roaming profile is stored.
5. The next time the user logs on at the same computer, the system compares the contents of the locally stored profile with the roaming profile stored on the server. The computer copies only the roaming profile components that have changed to the copy on the local drive, which makes the logon process shorter and more efficient.

You should create roaming user profiles on a file server that you back up frequently, so that you always have copies of your users' most recent profiles. To improve logon performance for a busy network, place the users' roaming profiles folder on a member server (in the same site) instead of a domain controller.

Using Mandatory User Profiles

A ***mandatory user profile*** is simply a read-only roaming user profile.

Users receive files and desktop settings from a server-based profile, just as they would with any roaming profile, and they can modify their desktop environments while they are logged on. However, because the profile is read-only, the system cannot save any profile changes back to the server when the users log off. The next time the user logs on, the server-based profile will be the same as during the previous logon.

Windows 8 downloads the mandatory profile settings to the local computer each time the user logs on. You can assign one mandatory profile to multiple users who require the same desktop settings, such as a group of users who all do the same job. Because the profile never changes, you do not have to worry about one user making changes that affect all of the other users. Also, a mandatory profile makes it possible to modify the desktop environment for multiple users by changing only one profile.

To create a mandatory user profile, you rename the Ntuser.dat file in the folder containing the roaming profile to Ntuser.man. The Ntuser.dat file consists of the Windows 8 system registry settings that apply to the individual user account and contains the user environment settings, such as those controlling the appearance of the desktop. Renaming this file with a .man extension makes it read-only, preventing the client computers from saving changes to the profile when a user logs off.

Managing Profile Compatibility

User profiles created with Windows 8 are not compatible with Windows 7 or earlier versions. If you use a computer running Windows 8 to access a roaming profile created with Windows 7, Windows 8 automatically upgrades the profile to its new format, rendering it unusable with Windows 7.

In an environment where users might log on to workstations running different versions of Windows, you must create and maintain separate profiles for each version. To control which profile a workstation uses based on the operating system version, you can use a Group Policy setting called *Set roaming profile path for all users logging onto this computer.*

Located in the Computer Configuration\Policies\Administrative Templates\System\User Profiles folder of a ***Group Policy object (GPO)***, this policy, shown in Figure 3-2, overrides any profile specified in a user's account properties.

Figure 3-2

The *Set roaming profile path for all users logging onto this computer* dialog box

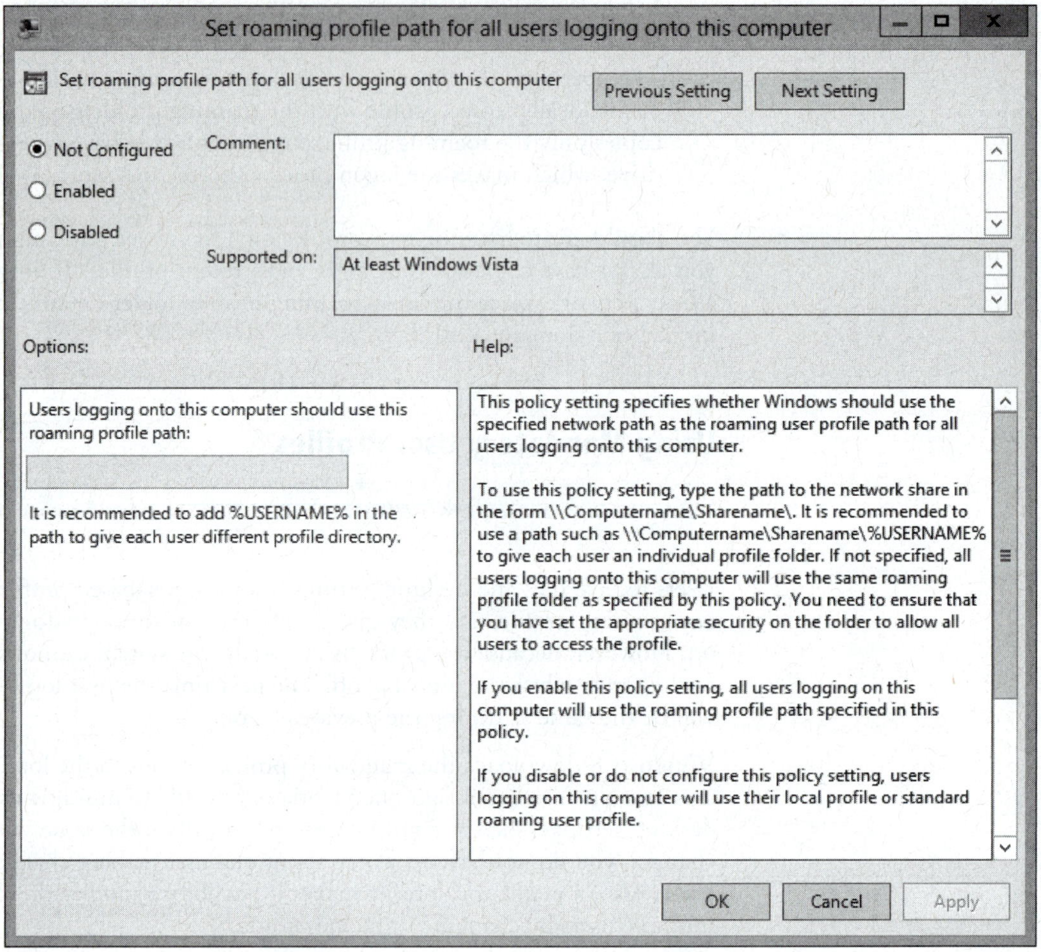

When you specify a path for the roaming profiles the computer will use, you must add the %USERNAME% variable to the Universal Naming Convention path, as in the following example: \\Server\share\%USERNAME%. This appends a folder named for each user to the path, so every user still maintains a unique profile.

To support profiles for multiple Windows versions, you must create a separate GPO for each version and configure each GPO to be applied only to the computers running that version.

Migrating User Profiles

THE BOTTOM LINE

Performing a clean installation of Windows 8 on a user's workstation does not necessarily mean that the user has to lose his or her personal files and folders, operating system and application settings, and Internet favorites. Using tools supplied with Windows 8 or the Windows Assessment and Deployment Kit (ADK), you can migrate these elements from one operating system to another.

CERTIFICATION READY
Migrate user profiles
Objective 1.3

In some cases, performing a clean installation of Windows 8 is a perfectly adequate solution. You might be working with a brand new computer, or the user might not have any important data to carry over from the previous operating system. However, most experienced computer users have settings and data they want to keep, data that is typically stored in a Windows user profile.

A user profile is a series of folders, associated with a specific user account, that contain personal documents, user-specific registry settings, Internet favorites, and other personalized information—everything that provides a user's familiar working environment. On a standalone Windows XP workstation, user profiles are stored in the Documents and Settings folder, in subfolders named for the user accounts. Starting in Windows Vista and continuing through Windows 8 workstations, the subfolders are found in the Users folder. On a workstation that is joined to an Active Directory Domain Services (AD DS) domain, the user profiles are also stored on a network server.

MORE INFORMATION

User profiles consist of files, such as a user's personal documents and Internet favorites, stored in appropriate profile folders, and settings stored in a registry file. The registry settings include basic display parameters, such as the colors, themes, and images you have designated for your Windows desktop, as well as configuration parameters for specific applications. Windows loads the profile information into memory each time that particular user logs on to Windows, and saves any changes the user has made to the profile when logging off. User profiles make it possible for different users to maintain their own individual settings on one Windows computer.

There are two basic methods for deploying Windows 8 to a client while retaining the user profile settings: upgrade and migration. In an upgrade, you install Windows 8 on the computer running an earlier operating system. If you install Windows over a previous Windows installation, all previous Windows files and directories are moved to a Windows.old folder, including the contents of the Users, Program Files, and Windows directories. In a migration, you copy the user profile information from the old operating system to some temporary medium and transfer it to a new, clean installation of Windows 8.

Microsoft has created two different tools for migrating files and settings to new computers, which are as follows:

- **Windows Easy Transfer** – Designed for the migration of a single computer, Easy Transfer is a wizard-based utility that makes it possible to migrate user profile information for multiple users from one computer to another.
- **User State Migration Tool** – Designed for large-scale enterprise deployments, User State Migration Tool is a command line utility that can migrate profile information for multiple users on multiple computers.

In the following sections, you learn the procedure for using Windows Easy Transfer to migrate user profile settings from an existing Windows 7 workstation to a new Windows 8 workstation. You also learn some basic facts about using the User State Migration Tool.

Using Windows Easy Transfer

Windows Easy Transfer is a tool that migrates user profile information from an existing Windows computer to a new computer with a clean installation of Windows 8.

Windows Easy Transfer migrates user profile data from one computer to another in a variety of scenarios. As long as you are working with the user accounts from one single computer, Windows Easy Transfer can function in virtually any hardware configuration. Some of the options you can select are as follows:

- **Number of computers** – Windows Easy Transfer supports both side-by-side and wipe-and-load migrations. In a ***side-by-side migration***, you have two computers running simultaneously; one is the source computer containing the user profile information you want to transfer, and the other is the destination computer running Windows 8 to which you want to transfer the profile information. In a ***wipe-and-load migration***, you have only one computer, which initially contains the user profile settings you want to transfer. After saving the profile information to a removable storage medium, you perform a clean Windows 8 installation, wiping out all data on the computer's hard disk, and then transfer the profile data from the removable medium back to the computer.

- **Direct or indirect** – When you are performing a side-by-side migration, you can use Windows Easy Transfer with the computers connected together directly, using a cable or a network, or connected indirectly, using a removable storage medium.
- **Storage medium** – Windows Easy Transfer can use virtually any storage medium to transfer profile data between computers, as long as it provides sufficient storage space and is accessible by both machines. You can use a writable CD or DVD, a USB flash drive, an external hard drive, or a network share. Floppy disks are not supported because they have insufficient capacity.

The procedure for migrating files consists of two basic elements: saving the user profile information on the existing computer and transferring the information to the new computer. Using the capabilities of Windows Easy Transfer, you should be able to satisfy the requirements of virtually any standalone user that wants to move to Windows 8 without performing an upgrade. The most common scenarios are likely to be the following:

- **Scenario 1** – A user purchases a new computer on which he wants to run Windows 8, but he also wants to retain the files and settings from his existing Windows computer.
- **Scenario 2** – A user wants to install Windows 8 on her existing Windows computer and retain all of her files and settings, but she wants to avoid performing an upgrade to maximize her Windows 8 performance.

The following sections describe the Windows Easy Transfer procedures for each of these scenarios.

PERFORMING MIGRATION SCENARIO 1

Ed is a longtime Windows 7 user with a small network in his home. He has just purchased a new computer with Windows 8 preinstalled on it, and wants to migrate his files and settings from his Windows 7 computer to the Windows 8 computer. The new computer came with recovery disks, but no Windows 8 installation disk.

In this scenario, you perform a side-to-side migration with both computers connected to the user's home network. Because the source computer is running Windows 7, which has its own compatible version of Windows Easy Transfer, no special software installation is necessary.

If the source computer is running Windows Vista or Windows XP, then you must install an appropriate version of Windows Easy Transfer. Windows Easy Transfer versions for Windows Vista and Windows XP, in 32- and 64-bit iterations, are available from the Microsoft Download Center.

PERFORM MIGRATION SCENARIO 1

GET READY. Both computers must be powered on and connected to the network.

1. On the Windows 8 computer, open the charms bar and then click **Search**.

   The Search bar appears.

2. With the Apps option selected, type **easy** in the text box.

   The Windows Easy Transfer application appears in the results display.

3. Click **Windows Easy Transfer**.

   The Windows Easy Transfer Wizard appears, displaying the *Welcome* page, as shown in Figure 3-3.

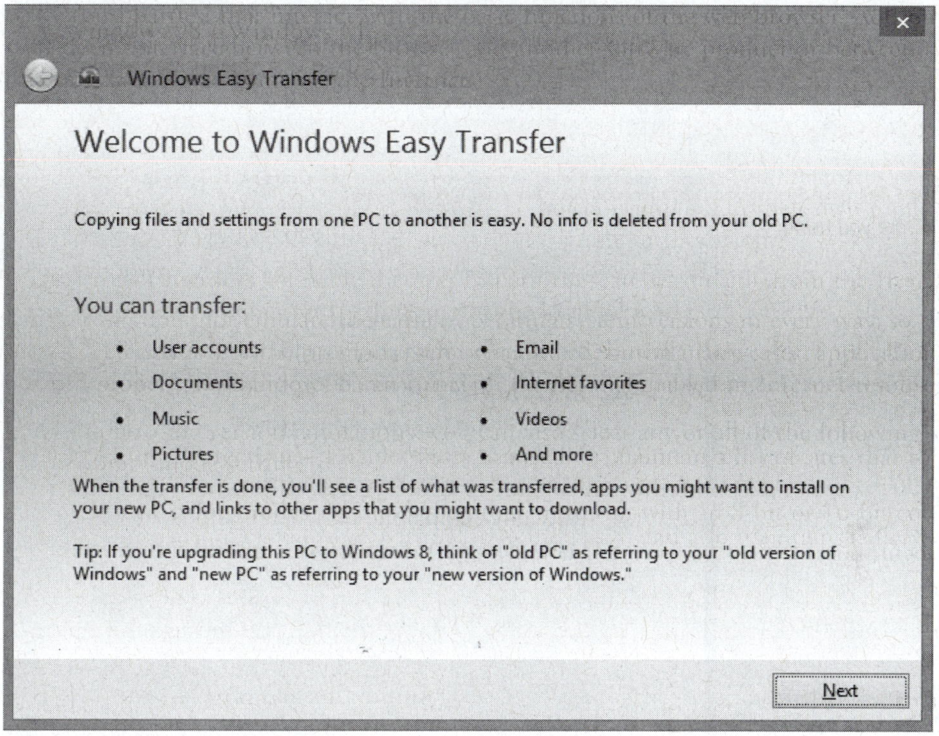

Figure 3-3

The *Welcome to Windows Easy Transfer* page

4. Click **Next**.

   The *What do you want to use to transfer items to your new PC?* page appears, as shown in Figure 3-4.

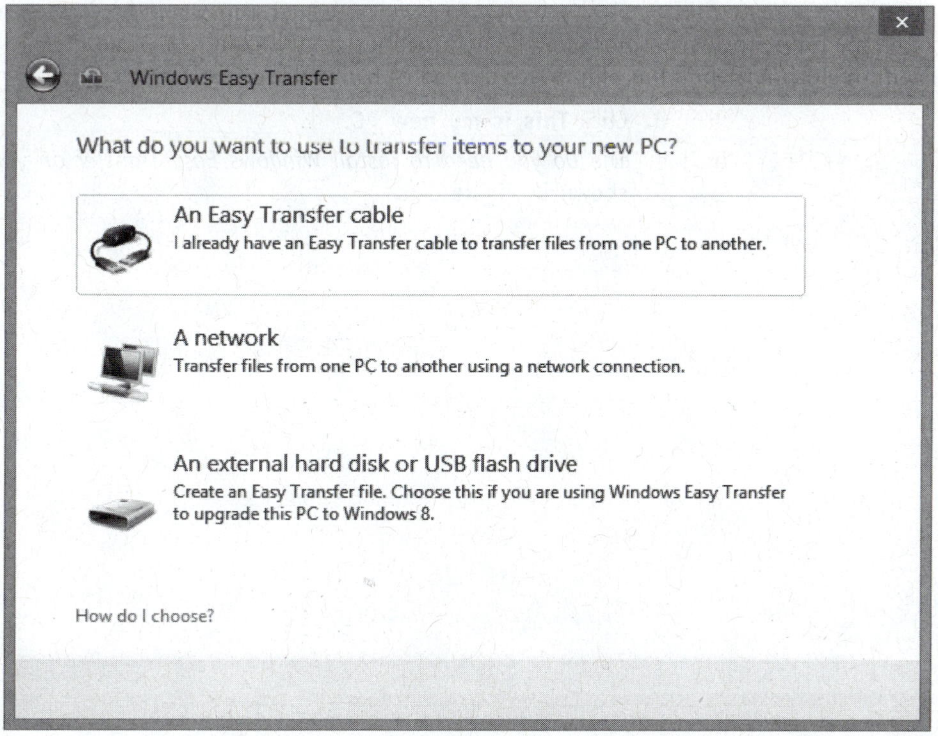

Figure 3-4

The *What do you want to use to transfer items to your new PC?* page

MORE INFORMATION

An ***Easy Transfer cable*** is a special USB cable that you can use to connect two Windows computers together solely for the purpose of using the Windows Easy Transfer utility. In this particular scenario, the user has a network available, which performs the same function.

5. Click **A network**.

   The *Which PC are you using now?* page appears, as shown in Figure 3-5.

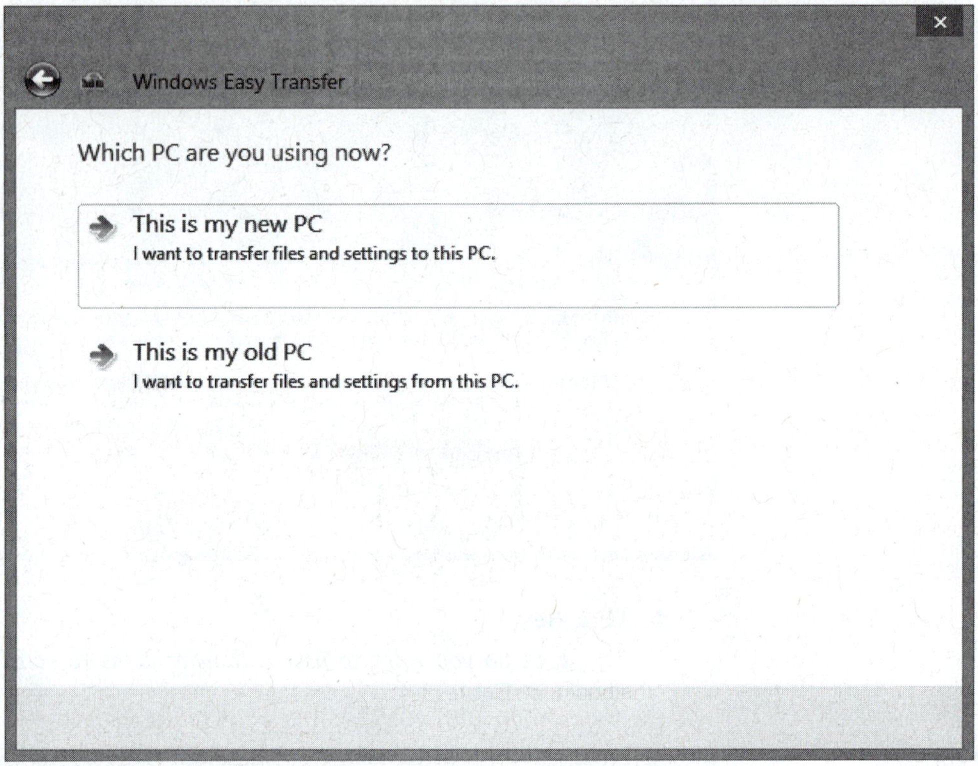

Figure 3-5

The *Which PC are you using now?* page

6. Click **This is my new PC**.

   The *Do you need to install Windows Easy Transfer on your old PC?* page appears, as shown in Figure 3-6.

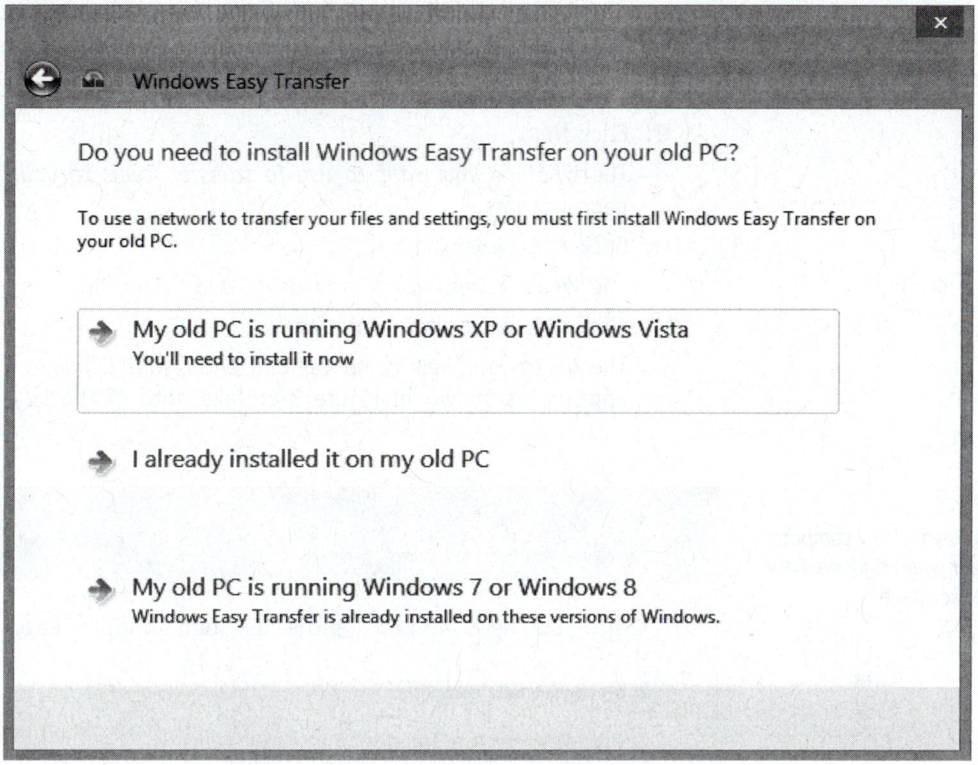

Figure 3-6

The *Do you need to install Windows Easy Transfer on your old PC?* page

7. Click **My old PC is running Windows 7 or Windows 8**.

   The *Open Windows Easy Transfer on your old PC and get a Windows Easy Transfer key* page appears, as shown in Figure 3-7.

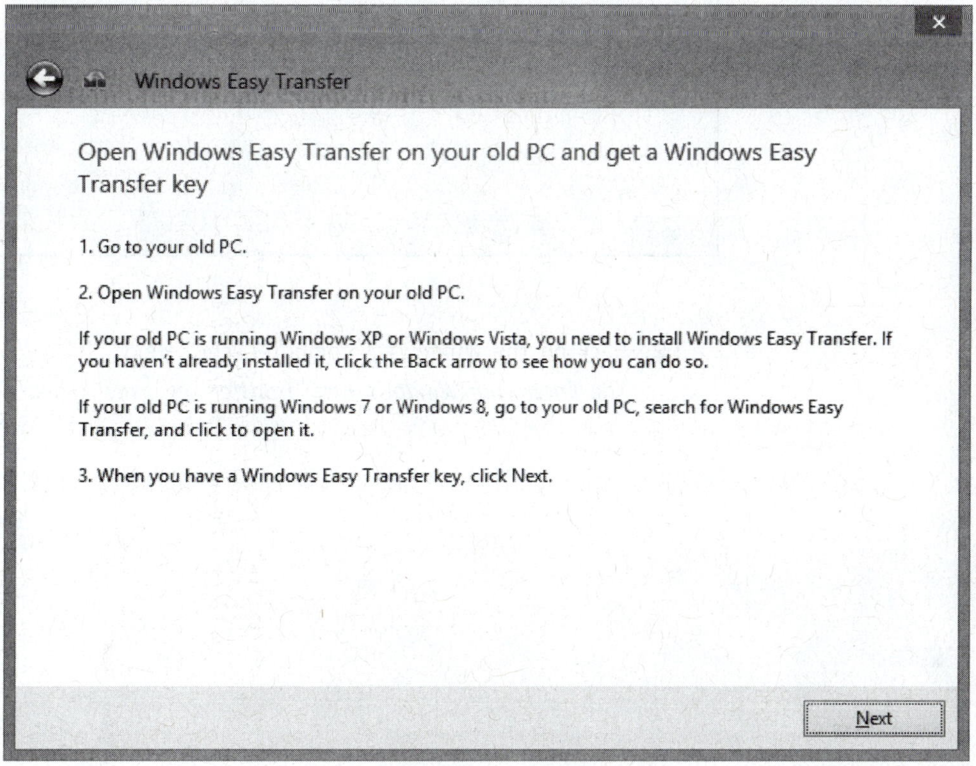

Figure 3-7

The *Open Windows Easy Transfer on your old PC and get a Windows Easy Transfer key* page

8. On the Windows 7 computer, click **Start > All Programs > Accessories > System Tools** and then select **Windows Easy Transfer**.

   The Windows Easy Transfer Wizard appears.

9. Click **Next**.

   The *What do you want to use to transfer items to your new computer?* page appears.

10. Click ***A network***.

    The *Which computer are you using now?* page appears.

11. Click ***This is my old computer***.

    The *Go to your new computer and enter your Windows Easy Transfer key* page appears, as shown in Figure 3-8. Take note of the key number that appears.

Figure 3-8

The *Go to your new computer and enter your Windows Easy Transfer key* page

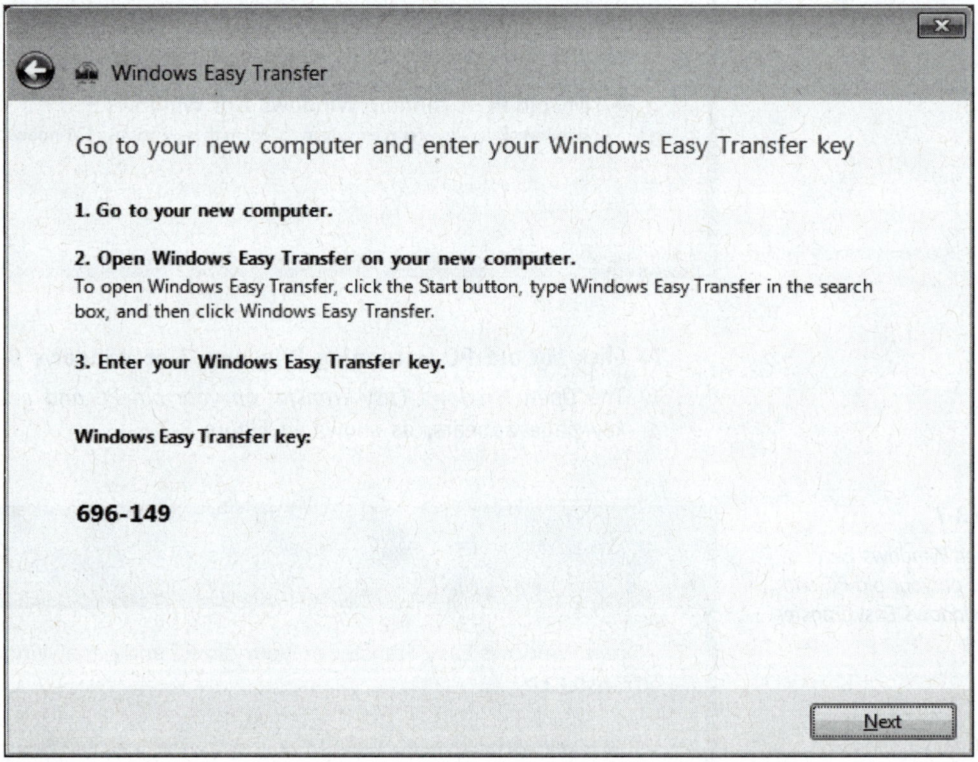

12. Back on the Windows 8 computer, click **Next**.

    The *Enter your Windows Easy Transfer key* page appears, as shown in Figure 3-9.

Figure 3-9

The *Enter your Windows Easy Transfer key* page

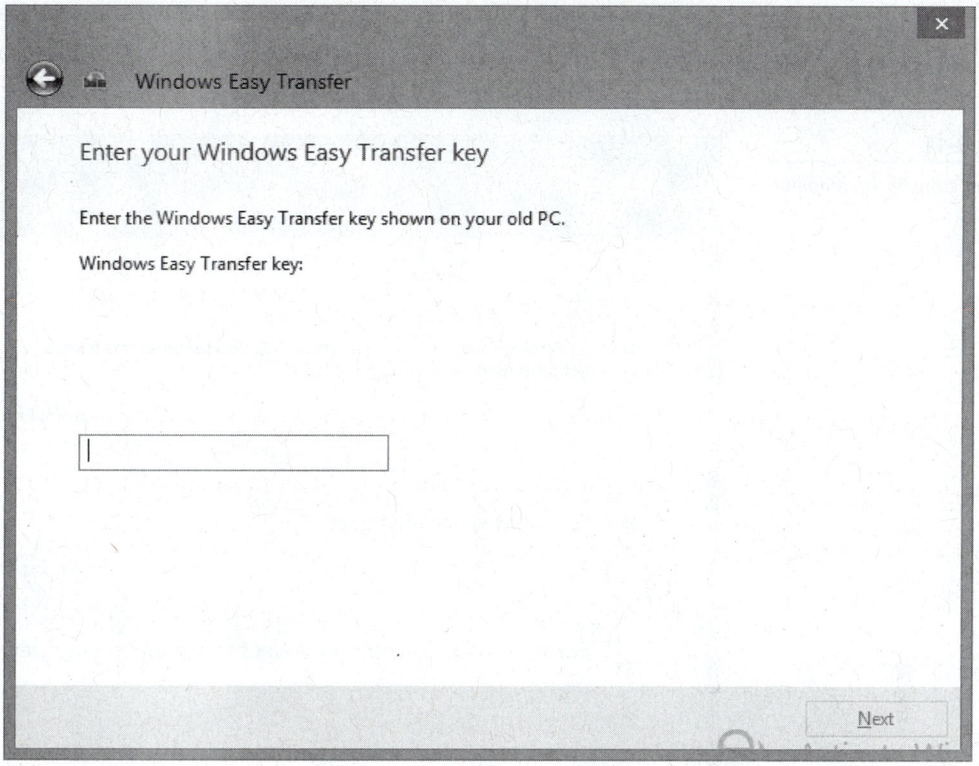

13. In the Windows Easy Transfer Key text box, type the key that appeared on your Windows 7 computer (see step 11) and click **Next**.

    The Windows 8 computer establishes a connection with the Windows 7 computer, scans it for files and settings it can transfer, and displays the results in the *Choose what to transfer* page, as shown in Figure 3-10.

Figure 3-10

The *Choose what to transfer* page

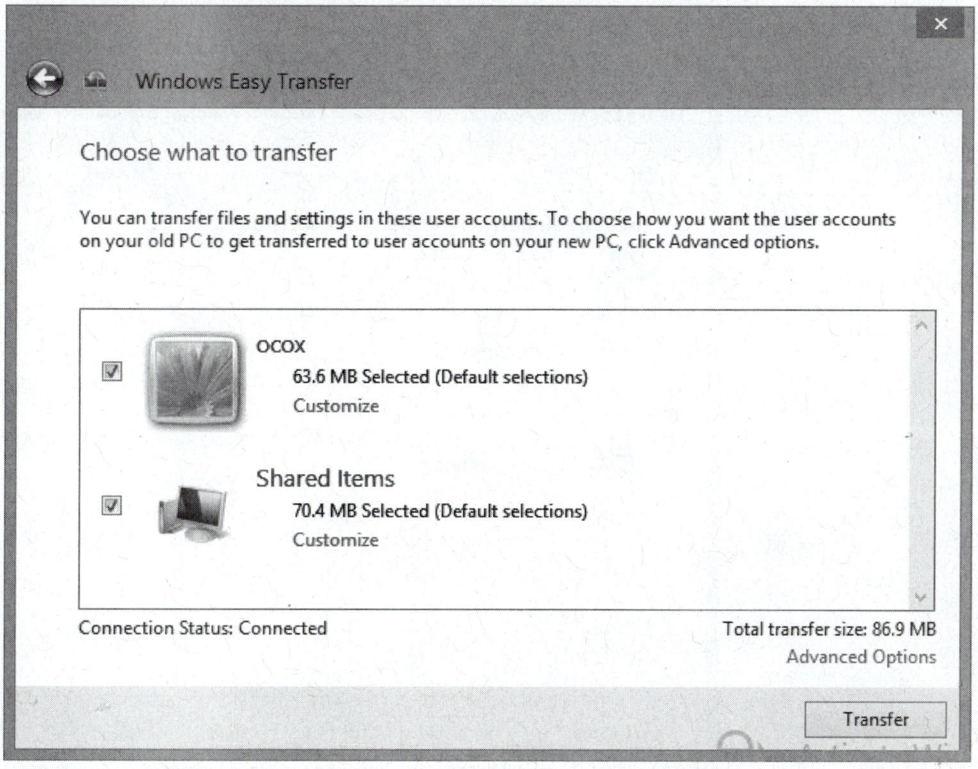

14. Select the items you want to copy to the new computer and click **Transfer**.

    The program transfers the selected items to the new computer, and then the *Your transfer is complete* page appears, as shown in Figure 3-11.

Figure 3-11

The *Your transfer is complete* page

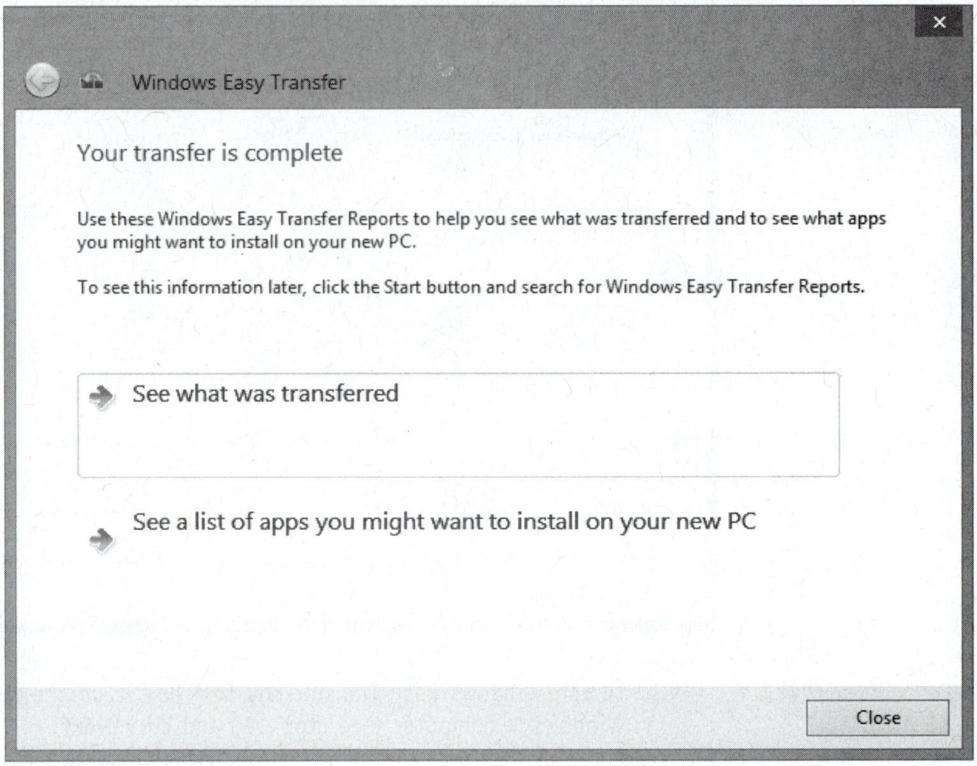

15. Click ***See what was transferred***.

    A Windows Easy Transfer Reports window appears, as shown in Figure 3-12.

Figure 3-12

A *Windows Easy Transfer Reports* window

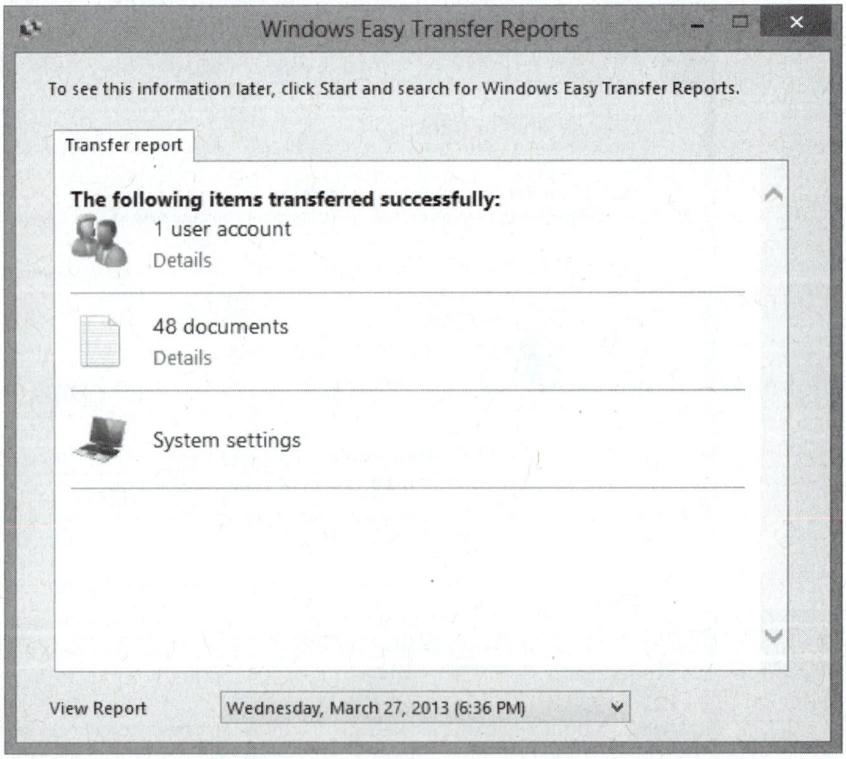

16. Close the Windows Easy Transfer Reports window and, on the *Your transfer is complete* page, click **Close**.
17. On the Windows 7 computer, on the *The transfer is complete* page, click **Close**.

PERFORMING MIGRATION SCENARIO 2

Alice has a Windows 7 computer that she has been sharing with her roommates for several years. She recently purchased the retail version of Windows 8, which came bundled with a free external hard drive. Alice wants to install Windows 8, retaining the files and settings she has accrued and omitting the files and settings created by her roommates. However, she does not want to perform an upgrade, because she has recently noticed that the computer's performance has degraded, possibly due to file fragmentation and registry clutter.

In this scenario, you perform a wipe-and-load migration using the external hard drive to temporarily store the files and settings from the Windows 7 operating system. Then, after performing a clean installation of Windows 8, you transfer the files and settings from the external drive back to the computer.

PERFORM MIGRATION SCENARIO 2

GET READY. Plug the external hard drive into a USB port on the source Windows 7 computer and make sure that it is connected and operating. Then make a secondary backup of the client's important files as a safety measure, in case there is a problem with the migration procedure.

1. Click **Start** > **All Programs** > **Accessories** > **System Tools** > **Windows Easy Transfer**.

   The *Windows Easy Transfer Wizard* appears, displaying the *Welcome* page.
2. Click **Next**.

   The *What do you want to use to transfer items to your new computer?* page appears.
3. Click **An external hard disk or USB flash drive**.

   The *Which computer are you using now?* page appears.
4. Click **This is my old computer**.

   The program displays a *Checking what can be transferred* page and scans the computer for files and settings it can transfer. The program then displays the results in the *Choose what to transfer from this computer* page.
5. Select the items you want to copy to the new computer and click **Next**.

   The *Save your files and settings for transfer* page appears, as shown in Figure 3-13.
6. In the *Password* and *Confirm Password* text boxes, type a password to protect the data to be transferred and click **Save**.

   The *Save Your Easy Transfer File* combo box appears.

Figure 3-13

The *Save your files and settings for transfer* page

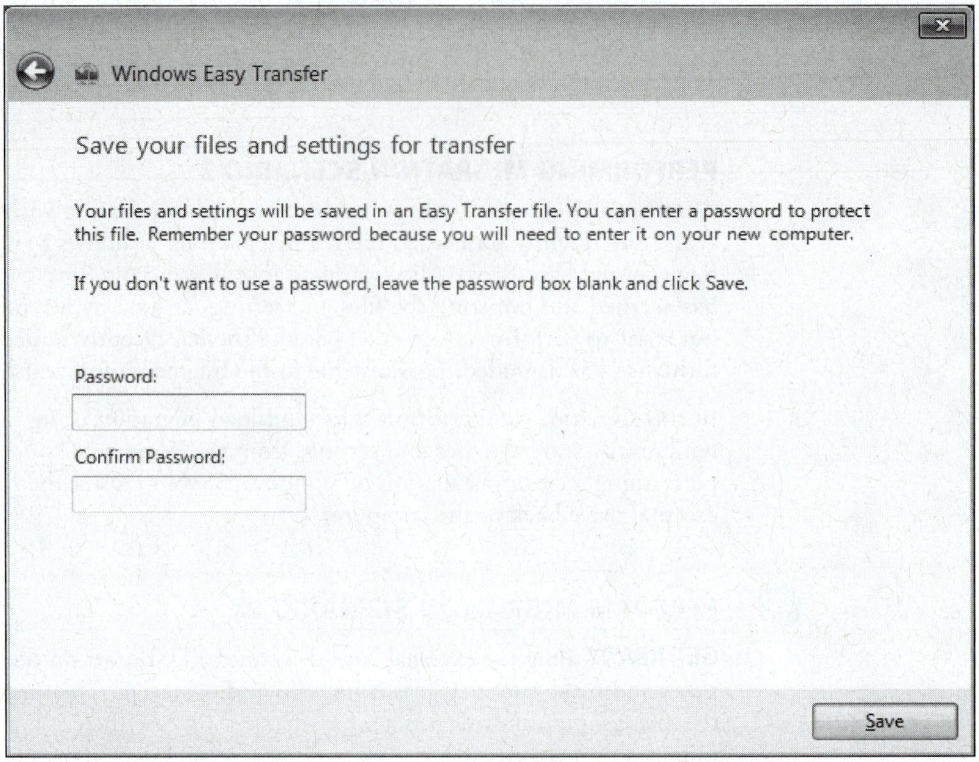

7. Browse to the external hard drive and click **Save**.

   The program transfers the selected items to the external drive and the *These files and settings have been saved for your transfer* page appears, as shown in Figure 3-14.

Figure 3-14

The *These files and settings have been saved for your transfer* page

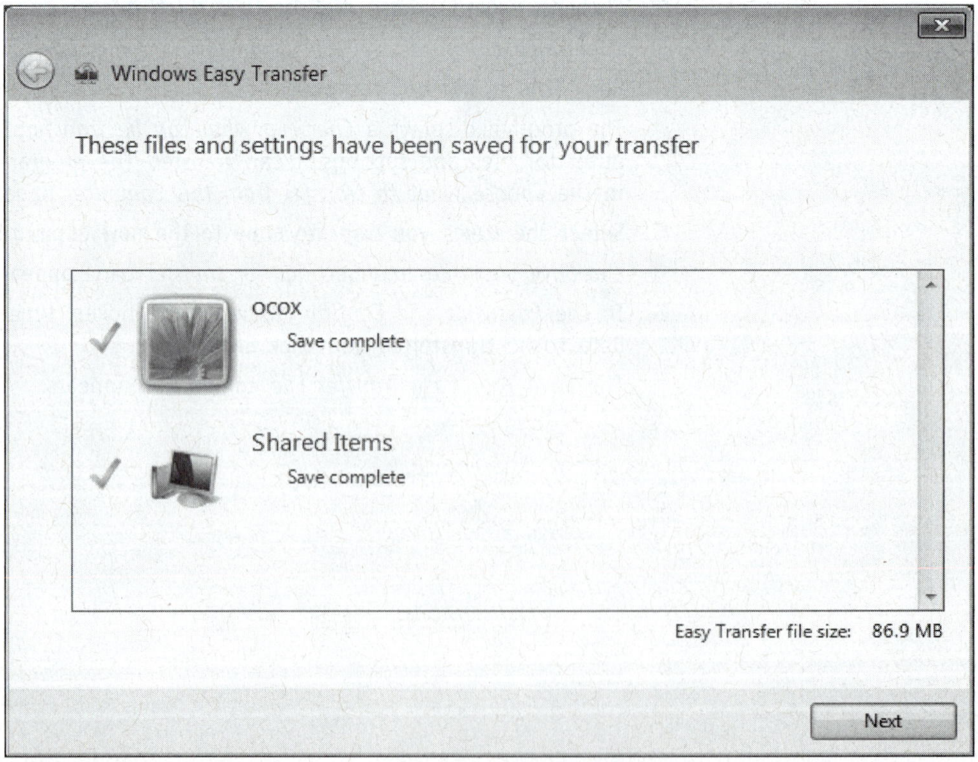

8. Click **Next**.

   The *Your transfer file is complete* page appears, specifying the name and location of the file containing the transferred data.

9. Click **Next**.

   The *Your Transfer file is complete* page appears.

10. Click **Next**.

    The *Windows Easy Transfer is complete on this computer* page appears.

11. Click **Close**.
12. Disconnect the external hard drive from the computer.
13. Perform a clean installation of Windows 8 on the computer, as detailed in Lesson 2, "Installing Windows 8," erasing the partition on which Windows 7 was installed.
14. Reconnect the external hard drive to the computer and make sure that it is functioning.
15. On the Windows 8 computer, open the charms bar and then click **Search**.

    The Search bar appears.

16. With the Apps option selected, type **easy** in the text box.

    The Windows Easy Transfer application appears in the results display.

17. Click **Windows Easy Transfer**. The Windows Easy Transfer Wizard appears, displaying the *Welcome* page.
18. Click **Next**. The *What do you want to use to transfer items to your new PC?* page appears.
19. Click **An external hard disk or USB flash drive**.

    The *Which PC are you using now?* page appears.

20. Click **This is my new computer**.

    The *Has Windows Easy Transfer already saved your files from your old computer to an external hard disk or USB flash drive?* page appears.

21. Click **Yes**.

    The Open an Easy Transfer File combo box appears.

22. Browse to the external hard drive, select the Windows Easy Transfer–Items From Old Computer file and click **Open**.

    The *Enter the password you used to help protect your transfer file and start the transfer* page appears, as shown in Figure 3-15.

Figure 3-15

The *Enter the password you used to help protect your transfer file and start the transfer* page

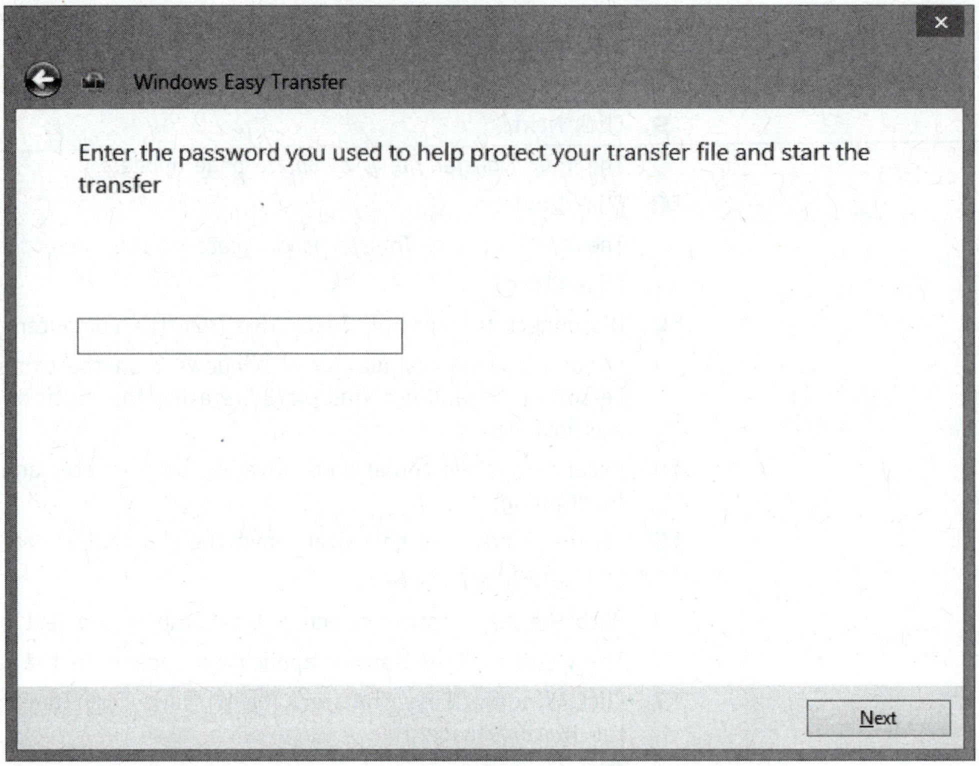

23. Type the password you specified earlier and click **Next**.

The *Choose what to transfer to this PC* page appears, as shown in Figure 3-16.

Figure 3-16

The *Choose what to transfer to this PC* page

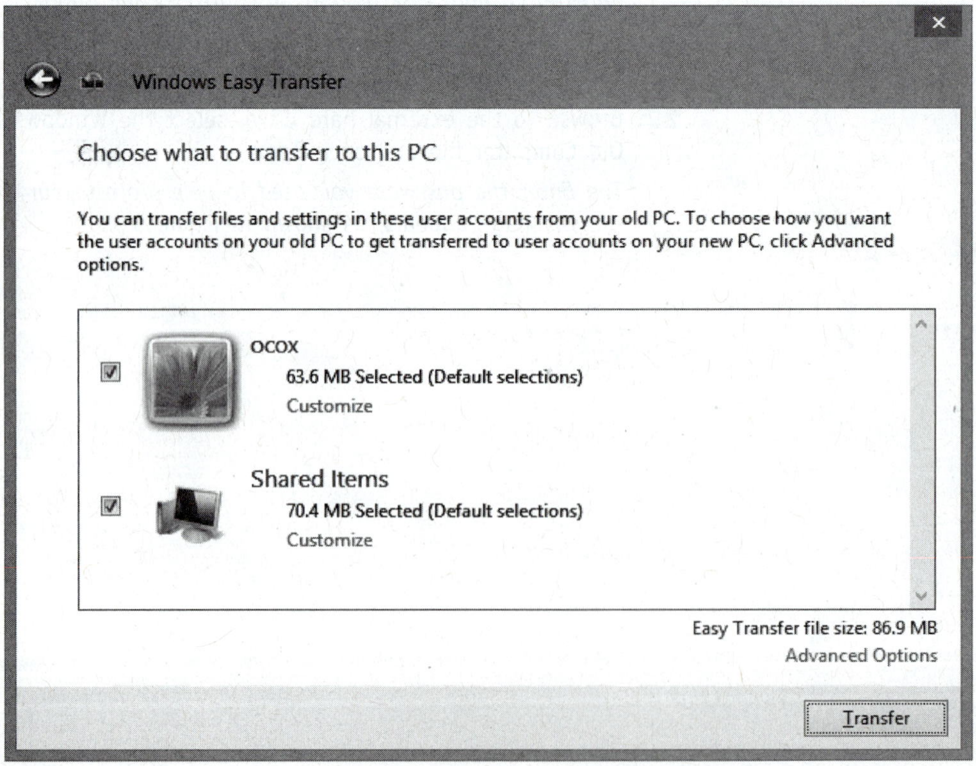

24. Select the items you want to copy and click **Transfer**.

    The program transfers the selected items to the computer, and then the *Your transfer is complete* page appears.

25. Click **See what was transferred**.

    A Windows Easy Transfer Reports window appears

26. Close the Windows Easy Transfer Reports window and, on the *Your transfer is complete* page, click **Close**.

Using the User State Migration Tool

The ***User State Migration Tool (USMT)*** has the same basic capabilities as Windows Easy Transfer. The primary difference between the two is that USMT is a command line program that lacks a graphical interface.

USMT's command line interface is not a disadvantage, although individuals that prefer graphical utilities might perceive it as such. The command line interface enables administrators to incorporate USMT tasks into scripts, making it more suitable for large-scale deployments than Windows Easy Transfer.

For example, Microsoft Deployment Toolkit 2010 enables administrators to incorporate migration tasks into an installation script called a ***task sequence***. A properly configured task sequence can save the user data on a workstation to a network share, perform a clean Windows 8 installation on the workstation, and then load the saved user data, all with little or no user interaction required.

USMT includes two separate command line programs: ScanState.exe, which saves user profile data; and LoadState.exe, which restores previously-saved user profile data. Each program supports a variety of command line parameters that enable you to specify a storage location and control what data the programs save and restore.

In addition to the command line interface, the other big advantage to using USMT for large scale deployments is the ability to customize the migration process. USMT uses XML (Extensible Markup Language) files to control the migration process. The default XML files supplied with the program enable it to migrate the most common user data sources, but it is also possible to create your own XML files to migrate specific application settings and data.

Configuring Folder Redirection

THE BOTTOM LINE

It is preferable to store user data on a network share rather than the local workstation for several reasons, including the following:

- **Backups** – Backing up one or two servers is much faster, easier, and often cheaper than backing up multiple workstations.
- **Mobility** – With all data files stored on a network shared folder, users can work from any computer and move to another location as needed.
- **Replacement** – Deploying new client computers in the place of older ones is a simple matter of replacing the hardware; no migration of data files is necessary.

Folder redirection is simply a means of storing a copy of certain user profile folders on another computer, usually a file server. The process is completely invisible to the workstation user. Once the folders are redirected to the server, that user can log on at any workstation and the system copies the redirected folders to the user's local profile on that computer.

CERTIFICATION READY
Configure folder redirection
Objective 1.3

To implement folder redirection on Windows 8, you must join the workstation to an Active Directory Domain Services domain and create a Group Policy object that specifies which folders to redirect and where to store them.

The Group Policy settings for folder redirection are located in the following path: User Configuration\Policies\Windows Settings\Folder Redirection, as shown in Figure 3-17.

Figure 3-17

The Folder Redirection policies in a GPO

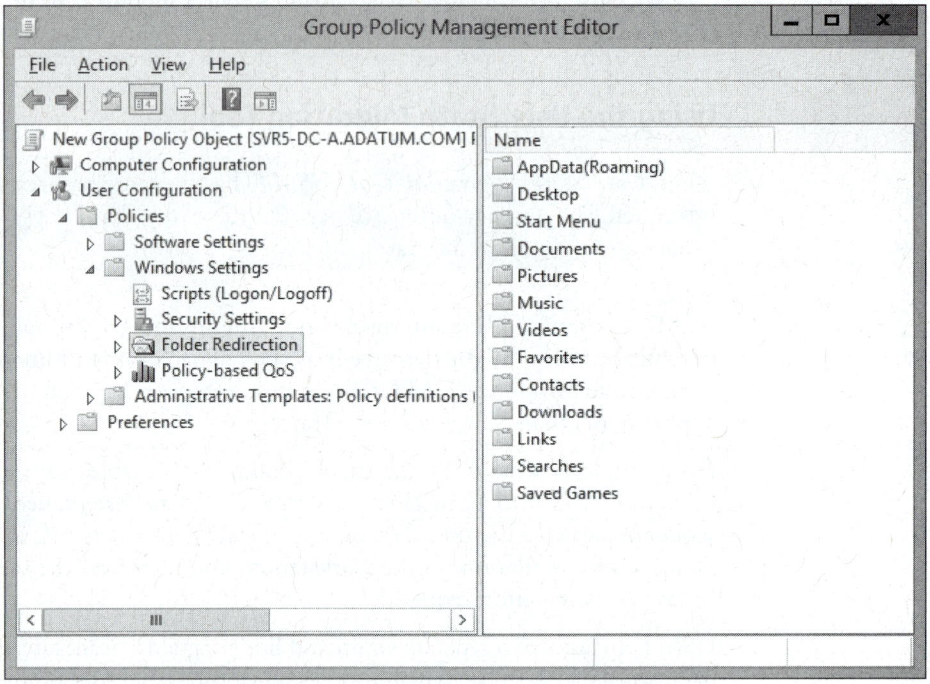

You can use the ***Group Policy Management Editor console*** to modify the Folder Redirection settings in a GPO by right-clicking one of the folders under the Folder Redirection node and opening its *Properties* sheet, as shown in Figure 3-18.

Figure 3-18

The *Properties* sheet for a Folder Redirection policy

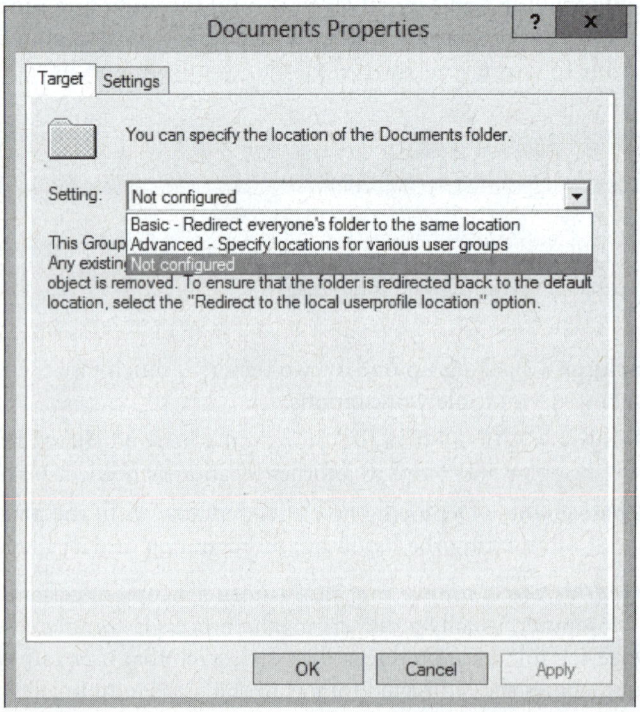

Table 3-1 lists the settings for the Folder Redirection folders and explains their functions.

Table 3-1

Folder Redirection Group Policy Settings

SETTING	FUNCTION
Setting	• Basic – Redirect Everyone's Folder To The Same Location – Causes workstations to redirect the folder for all users to the same server share • Advanced – Specify locations for various user groups – Causes workstations to redirect the folders to different locations based on group memberships • Follow the Documents folder – Allows the Pictures, Music, and Videos folders to be redirected as subfolders of the Documents folder
Target Folder Location	• Create A Folder For Each User Under The Root Path – Causes workstations to create a separate folder for each user on the server share • Redirect to the following location – Causes workstations to redirect the folder to a single location for all users • Redirect to the local userprofile location – Causes work-stations to redirect the folder to the user's local userprofile location
Root Path	Specifies the server share where you want to store the redirected folders.
Grant The User Exclusive Rights To [the folder]	Prevents anyone except the user from receiving permission to access the redirected folder.
Move The Contents Of [the folder] To The New Location	Causes the workstation to copy the contents of the redirected folders on its local drive to the target folder on the server share.
Also Apply Redirection Policy To Windows 2000, Windows 2000 Server, Windows XP, And Windows Server 2003 Operating Systems	Provides compatibility with earlier operating systems that use different folder names in their user profiles, such as My Documents.
Policy Removal	• Leave the folder in the new location when policy is removed – Causes the workstation to direct the folders back to the local drives without copying their contents from the server, thus rendering those contents inaccessible • Redirect The Folder Back To The Local Userprofile Location When Policy Is Removed – Causes the workstation to copy the contents of the redirected folders back to the local drive in the event that an administrator disables the Folder Redirection Group Policy settings

SKILL SUMMARY

IN THIS LESSON, YOU LEARNED:

- A user profile is a series of folders, associated with a specific user account, that contain personal documents, user-specific registry settings, Internet favorites, and other personalized information—everything that provides a user's familiar working environment.
- A roaming user profile is simply a copy of a local user profile that is stored on a network share (to which the user has appropriate permissions), so that the user can access it from any computer on the network.
- A mandatory user profile is simply a read-only roaming user profile.
- Windows Easy Transfer is a tool that migrates user profile information from an existing Windows computer to a new computer with a clean installation of Windows 8.
- The User State Migration Tool (USMT) has the same basic capabilities as Windows Easy Transfer. The primary difference between the two is that USMT is a command line program that lacks a graphical interface.
- Folder redirection is a Windows 8 feature that is simply a means of storing a copy of certain user profile folders on another computer, usually a file server.

■ Knowledge Assessment

Multiple Choice

Select one or more correct answers for each of the following questions.

1. What is the term used to describe a read-only copy of a user profile stored on a network share?
- **a.** mandatory profile
- **b.** super-mandatory profile
- **c.** roaming profile
- **d.** search profile

2. Which of the following are the two types of migration supported by Windows Easy Transfer?
- **a.** wipe-and-load
- **b.** side-by-side
- **c.** preview-and-wipe
- **d.** copy-and-redirect

3. Which of the following are command line programs? (Choose two.)
- **a.** Windows Easy Transfer
- **b.** Scanstate
- **c.** Folder Redirection
- **d.** Loadstate

4. Which of the following tools do you use to configure folder redirection?
- **a.** File Explorer
- **b.** Computer Management
- **c.** Active Directory Users and Computers
- **d.** Group Policy Management Editor

5. Which of the following storage media can you not use for a Windows Easy Transfer migration?
   a. RAM disk
   b. Network share
   c. USB flash drive
   d. CD-ROM
6. Which of the following Setting values in Folder Redirection creates a folder for each user beneath a single parent folder?
   a. Redirect
   b. Basic
   c. Advanced
   d. Not configured
7. How many computers are required for a wipe-and-load migration?
   a. 1
   b. 2
   c. 3
   d. 4
8. Which of the following user profile types can only be stored on server drives?
   a. Local
   b. Mandatory
   c. Roaming
   d. Super-mandatory
9. On a computer running Windows 8, local user profiles are located in which of the following folders?
   a. C:\Windows
   b. C:\Users
   c. C:\Documents and Settings
   d. C:\Profiles
10. How does the Windows Easy Transfer program establish a connection between two computers during a network-based side-by-side migration?
    a. You must specify the IP address of the other computer on the destination computer.
    b. The program creates a dedicated network connection between the two computers.
    c. You must connect the two computers togewther using a special Easy Transfer cable.
    d. The source computer supplies a Windows Easy Transfer key, which you must enter on the destination computer.

Best Answer

1. Which of the following are valid reasons why redirecting users' folders to server drives is a good idea?
   a. Because backing up servers is faster and easier than backing up workstations.
   b. Replacing workstations is easier when they do not hold any user data.
   c. Users can log on from any workstation and access their data.
   d. Files take up less storage space on server drives.
2. Which is the best type of profile to use if you want to prevent users from logging on if the profile is not available?
   a. Local
   b. Roaming
   c. Mandatory
   d. Super-mandatory

3. Which of the following is the best explanation for why it is necessary to include %USERNAME% in the path for roaming profiles?
   a. Because Windows servers automatically create a folder called %USERNAME%, where it stores profiles.
   b. Because %USERNAME% is a variable replaced by the system with the user's account name.
   c. Because the inclusion of %USERNAME% causes the profile to roam.
   d. Because including %USERNAME% enables the system to create a separate profile for each user.

Matching and Identification

1. Match the following terms with their corresponding definitions.

   ________ a) Folder redirection
   ________ b) User State Migration Tool
   ________ c) Windows Easy Transfer
   ________ d) Mandatory user profile
   ________ e) Wipe-and-load migration
   ________ f) Roaming profile
   ________ g) Side-by-side migration
   ________ h) Super-mandatory profile
   ________ i) Task sequence
   ________ j) Group Policy object

   1. Wizard-based utility
   2. Enables Windows 8 to store profile folders on server drives
   3. Command line utility
   4. Transfers profile data to a newly installed computer
   5. Denied logon if profile is not available
   6. Saves profile data to an external storage device
   7. Server-based user profile
   8. Container for Folder Redirection and other settings
   9. Read-only profile
   10. Script containing Scanstate and Loadstate commands

Build a List

1. Place the steps of the following process by which Windows 8 accesses and updates roaming profiles in the correct order.

   ________ The workstation applies the roaming profile settings.
   ________ The workstation copies the roaming profile to the local drive.
   ________ As the user works, the workstation makes changes to the profile on the local drive.
   ________ The workstation copies the changes from the local profile to the roaming profile.
   ________ The user logs on.
   ________ The user logs off.

2. Place the steps of the following procedure for configuring Folder Redirection in the correct order.
   _________ Close the Group Policy Object Editor console.
   _________ Log on to a domain controller.
   _________ Open the GPO in the Group Policy Object Editor console.
   _________ Close the Group Policy Management console.
   _________ Create a new Group Policy object.
   _________ Log off of the domain controller.
   _________ Configure the Folder Redirection policies.
   _________ Browse to the Folder Redirection folder in User Configuration node.
   _________ Open the Group Policy Management Console.

Business Case Scenario

Scenario 3-1: Deploying Windows 8

Alice has been assigned the task of deploying Windows 8 on her department's existing workstations. To facilitate future support efforts, she wants to perform clean Windows 8 installations on all of the computers now running Windows XP. When presenting her action plan to her superiors, Alice states that there is no need to perform any type of upgrade or data migration from the existing computers before wiping their drives and installing Windows 8.

Which of the following could combine to explain why this is so?

a. The computers already have all of their data folders redirected to server drives.
b. Folder redirection is configured using Group Policy objects stored in Active Directory.
c. The users all have roaming profiles stored on network servers.
d. Windows 8 automatically creates a new profile for each user.
e. It is not possible to upgrade or migrate computers running Windows XP to Windows 8.

4 LESSON

Working with Disks and Devices

70-687 EXAM OBJECTIVE

Objective 2.1 – Configure devices and device drivers. This objective may include but is not limited to install, update, disable, and roll back drivers; resolve driver issues; and configure driver settings.

LESSON HEADING	EXAM OBJECTIVE
Working with Devices and Drivers	
Understanding Device Drivers	
Working with Devices	Install drivers Update drivers
Using Device Manager	Disable drivers Configure driver settings Roll back drivers Resolve driver issues

KEY TERMS

device driver
Device Manager
digital signature
protected checksum
public key cryptography

Working with Devices and Drivers

THE BOTTOM LINE

A computer is a collection of hardware devices, each of which requires a software component called a device driver to function. Windows 8 includes a large library of device drivers, but it is still sometimes necessary to obtain them yourself.

As most people know, a PC is a collection of hardware devices, all of which are connected together and installed inside or connected to a single case. Disk drives, keyboards, mice, cameras, and printers are all types of devices. To communicate with the operating system running on the computer, each device also requires a software element called a ***device driver***. The device driver provides the operating system with information about a specific device.

For example, when you use a word processing application to save a file to a hard disk, the application issues a generic WriteFile function call to the operating system. The application knows nothing specific about the disk drive hardware; it just issues an instruction to store a particular file there. When the operating system processes the function call, it accesses the device driver for the hard disk drive, which provides detailed information about how to communicate with the drive. If the user selects a different target location for the file, the operating system accesses the device driver for that location, whether it's a hard drive, a floppy drive, or USB flash drive.

In most cases the information the device driver provides is integrated into the Windows interface. For example, the Properties sheet for a printer includes generic system information, such as which port the printer is connected to and who is permitted to use it. Other tabs, and particularly the Device Settings tab, as shown in Figure 4-1, are based on hardware-specific information provided by the device driver.

Figure 4-1

The *Device Settings* tab of a printer's *Properties* sheet

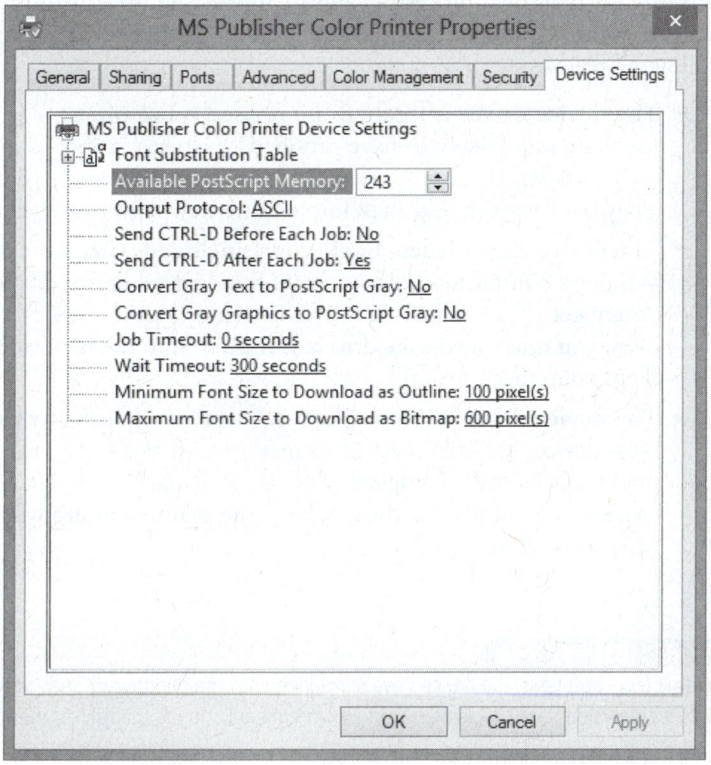

In addition to providing information about a device, drivers also permit the operating system to modify the hardware configuration settings of the device. For example, when you configure a printer to print a document in landscape mode instead of portrait mode, the printer device driver generates the appropriate command and sends it to the hardware.

Understanding Device Drivers

The process of installing a hardware device consists primarily of identifying the device and installing a device driver for it. This process can occur during the operating system installation or at a later time, but the steps are fundamentally the same.

A major part of the Windows 8 installation process consists of identifying the devices in the computer and installing the appropriate drivers for them. The Windows 8 installation package includes hundreds of drivers for many different devices, which is why many installations finish without any user intervention. Sometimes, however, you might have to supply device drivers yourself.

UNDERSTANDING DRIVER COMPLEXITY

Virtually every component in a PC requires a device driver, but they can vary greatly in complexity. Many of the standard computer devices are so standardized that their drivers operate virtually invisibly. When was the last time you had a problem with a keyboard driver, for example? Nearly every computer has a keyboard and the generic keyboard driver included with Windows 8 functions properly in almost every case. If you have a keyboard with special features, you might need a special driver to access them, but the basic keyboard functions will still function even without it.

At the other end of the scale are more complex drivers, such as those for graphics adapters. Many of the graphics adapters on the market are really self-contained computers in themselves, with their own processors and memory. The drivers for these complex devices are equally complex, and are often much more problematic than simple keyboard drivers, for the following reasons:

- **The device driver is likely to be revised more often** – Drivers that are required to do more are more likely to have problems. Generic keyboard drivers can go for years without upgrades, because keyboards rarely change. Manufacturers often release new graphics adapters, however, and therefore require new drivers as well.
- **The device driver is less likely to be included with the operating system** – The Windows 8 installation disk includes hundreds of device drivers, but the older the operating system gets, the less likely it is to include the latest drivers for the newest devices. In these cases, you must obtain the drivers you need from the hardware manufacturer and install them yourself.
- **The device driver is more likely to cause compatibility or functionality problems** – New devices are often rushed to market, and as a result, the drivers that ship with them might not be fully debugged. This is particularly true, again, with graphic adapter drivers. It is a good idea to always check the manufacturer's web site for the latest drivers before installing new hardware.

+ MORE INFORMATION

With a few exceptions, the device drivers included with the Windows 8 operating system, as well as all other Windows versions, are supplied by the hardware manufacturers themselves, not by Microsoft. Therefore, if you experience driver problems for a specific device, you are much more likely to get help from the hardware manufacturer than from Microsoft.

CREATING A DRIVER UPDATE POLICY

As an IT Professional, you are likely to be working with many different computers, each containing many devices. Keeping up with the drivers for all of these devices can be difficult, and you also must consider whether installing each driver update is necessary and, above all, safe.

There are two basic schools of thought when it comes to updating drivers. The "latest is the greatest" school advocates downloading and installing every new driver that is released, while the "if it ain't broken, don't fix it" school prefers to leave things as they are until it experiences a problem. Both of these philosophies have their advantages and disadvantages, and unfortunately, this is not likely to be a question that is best answered with a hard and fast rule or a company policy.

Other than supporting new hardware, there are three main reasons why hardware manufacturers release new driver updates:

- To address problems with the previous driver release(s)
- To implement new features
- To enhance performance of the device

The question of whether to update a Windows 8 driver is most easily answered for the first of these reasons. If you are experiencing the problem that the update is designed to address, then you should install it. Otherwise, you probably should not. As to the other two reasons, new features and enhanced performance are certainly desirable, but you should be sure that the driver update does not introduce new problems at the same time.

As a general rule, it is a good idea to test all driver updates before deploying them, especially in an enterprise environment. A comprehensive testing program will apply a new update to all of the workstation environments currently in use on production networks and run them through a realistic program of everyday tasks under typical operating conditions.

Another good safety measure is to avoid installing driver updates as soon as they are released. Waiting at least a week or so gives the manufacturer time to address any major issues that arise.

Above all, the question of whether to install driver updates should depend on the hardware devices involved and the policies and reputation of the hardware manufacturer. Some manufacturers release driver updates frequently and haphazardly, while others are more careful. Examining the manufacturer's support web site is a good way to ascertain how they deal with hardware problems and how often they release driver updates.

UNDERSTANDING DRIVER SIGNING

As with any other software component, device drivers have the potential to damage a computer configuration. Unscrupulous programmers can conceivably alter device drivers by adding their own malware, and the average user, downloading the driver from the Internet, would never know the difference. For that reason, Microsoft has instituted the practice of digitally signing the device drivers they have tested and approved.

A signed driver is a device driver that includes a ***digital signature***. The signer uses a cryptographic algorithm to compute the digital signature value and then appends that value to the device driver. A signer is an organization, or publisher, that uses a private key to create the digital signature for the device driver. This process ensures that the device driver does come from the authentic publisher and that someone has not maliciously altered it.

MORE INFORMATION

Public key cryptography is an encryption method based on a pair of keys, called the public key and the private key. As the names imply, the public key is freely available to anyone and the private key is kept secret by its owner. Any code that is digitally encrypted using the public key can only be decrypted by the holder of the private key. In the same way, any code that is encrypted using the private key, can only be decrypted by the public key. It is the latter example that publishers use for driver signing. The signer encrypts the device driver using its private key. The fact that the user can decrypt the driver using that signer's public key confirms that owner of the private key has signed it, and that the software has not been modified.

Generally, the process the publisher uses to create the digital signature starts by running the device driver files through a hash algorithm and then using the publisher's private key to transform the hash result cryptographically. The resulting value is the digital signature of the device driver.

The digital signature value is a ***protected checksum.*** A protected checksum is the value of an algorithmic function that is dependent on the contents of the data object and that is stored together with the data object. Its purpose is to protect the data object against active attacks that attempt to change the checksum to match changes that a malicious individual has made to the data object. Thus, the properties of a cryptographic hash ensure that when a malicious individual attempts to change the data object, the digital signature no longer matches the object.

If Windows 8 perceives a problem with a digital signature of a device driver, it alerts you with one of the following messages during the installation attempt:

- **Windows can't verify the publisher of this driver** – Either a certification authority has not verified the digital signature or the driver does not contain a digital signature. Only install this driver if you obtained it from the original manufacturer's disk.
- **This driver has been altered** – Someone has altered this driver after the verified publisher has digitally signed it, possibly with malicious intent. The driver package may now include malware that could harm your system or steal information. Only install this driver if you obtained it from the original manufacturer's disk.
- **Windows cannot install this driver** – x64-based versions of Windows 8 cannot install a device driver that someone has altered after the verified publisher has digitally signed it or one that that lack a valid digital signature altogether.

As with earlier 64-bit versions of Windows, Windows 8 requires device drivers to be digitally signed, or it will not install them. Also, new to Windows 8 is a check to see if a driver has been modified. If it has, Windows 8 will again refuse to install it.

BYPASSING DIGITAL SIGNATURE REQUIREMENTS

Also different in Windows 8 is the procedure to bypass the digital signature requirements. In Windows 7 and earlier versions, you can interrupt the boot process by pressing the F8 key, which displays an advanced boot options menu. One of the options in this menu is Disable Driver Signing, which enables the system to load drivers regardless of their signatures.

However, one of the design imperatives in Windows 8 is faster booting, and the designers were successful to the point at which, depending on the system hardware, the interval during which a user can press the F8 key can be as small as 200 ms. Windows 8 therefore has a different method for modifying the boot options, as described in the following procedure.

ACCESS ADVANCED BOOT OPTIONS

GET READY. Log on to Windows 8 using an account with Administrator privileges.

1. Mouse over the lower-right corner of the screen, and when the fly-out menu appears, click the Settings charm.

   The Settings menu appears.

2. Select **Change PC Settings**.

   The *PC Settings* menu appears, as shown in Figure 4-2.

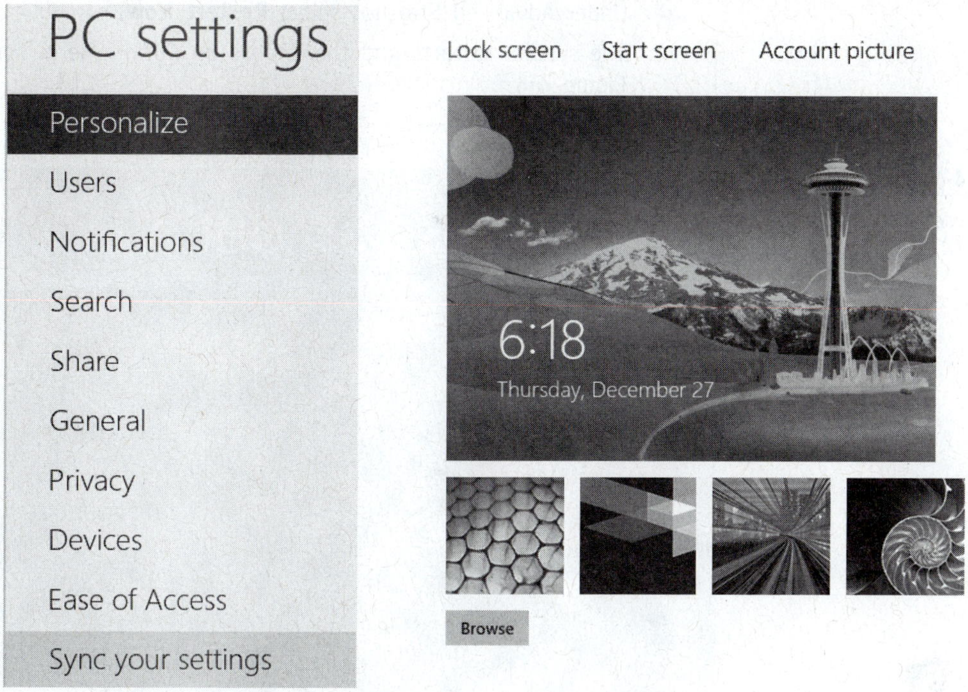

Figure 4-2

The *PC Settings* menu

3. Select **General**.

   The *General* menu appears, as shown in Figure 4-3.

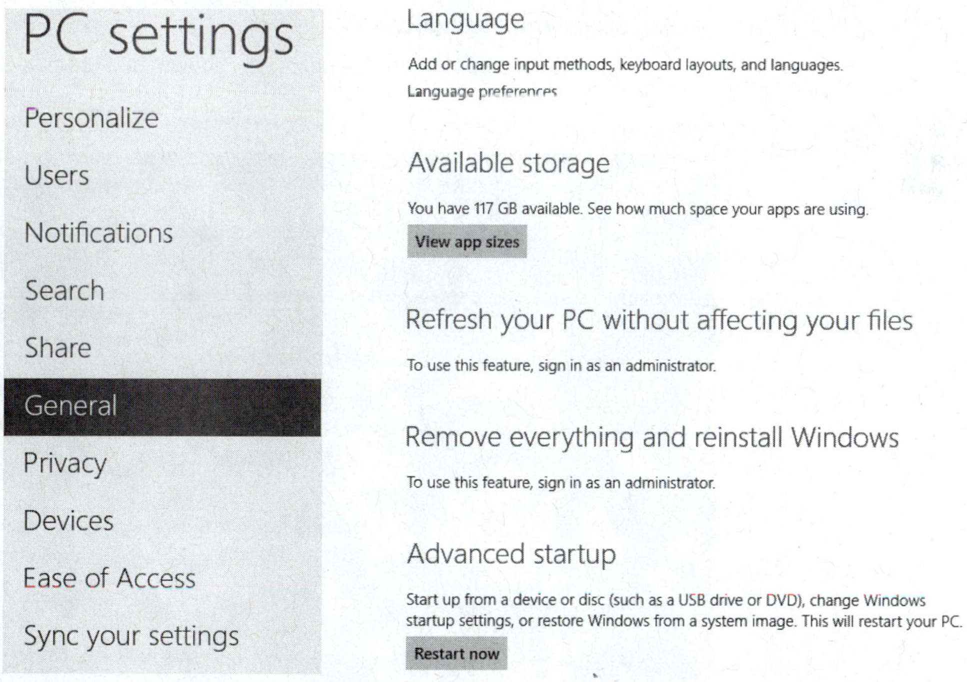

Figure 4-3

The *General* menu

4. Under Advanced Startup, select **Restart Now**.

   The system restarts and the *Choose an Option* menu appears, as shown in Figure 4-4.

Figure 4-4

The *Choose an Option* menu

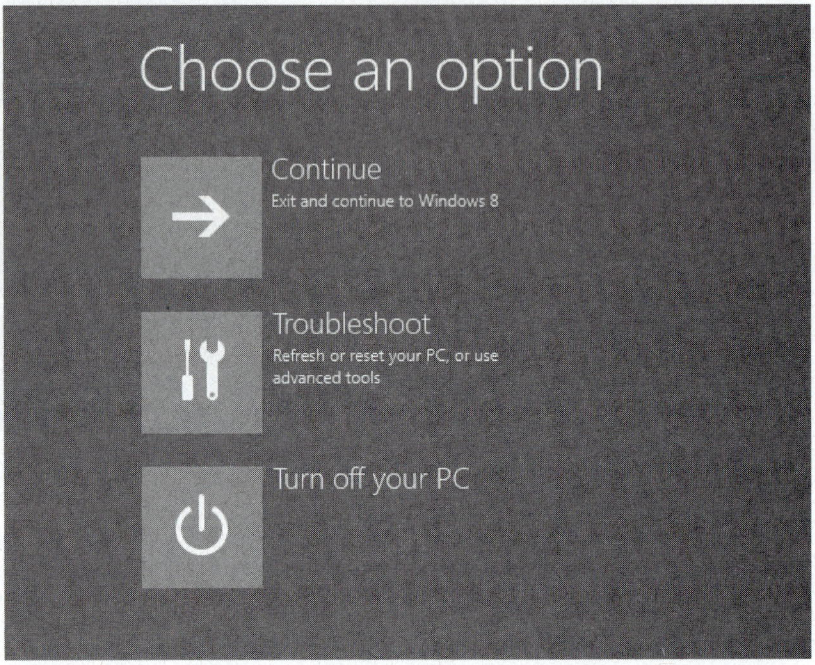

5. Select **Troubleshoot**.

   The *Troubleshoot* menu appears, as shown in Figure 4-5.

Figure 4-5

The *Troubleshoot* menu

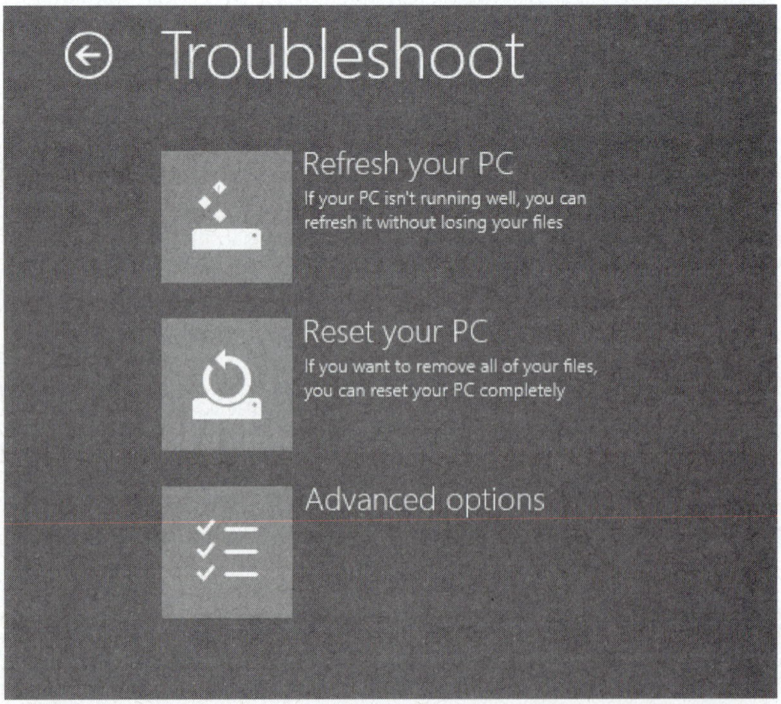

6. Select **Advanced Options**.

   The *Advanced Options* menu appears, as shown in Figure 4-6.

Figure 4-6

The *Advanced Options* menu

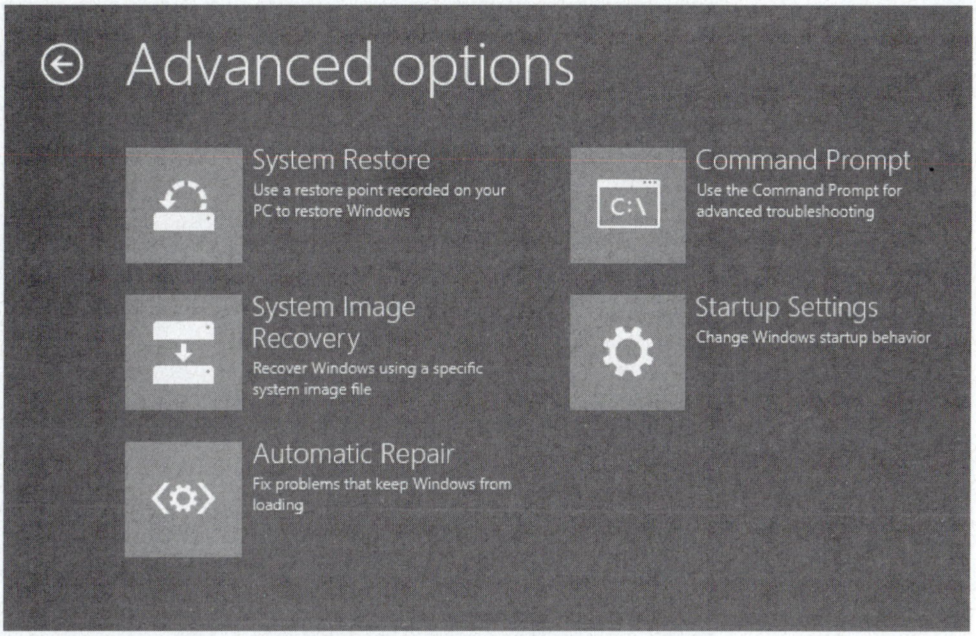

7. Select **Startup Settings**.

   The *Startup Settings* page appears, as shown in Figure 4-7.

Figure 4-7

The *Startup Settings* page

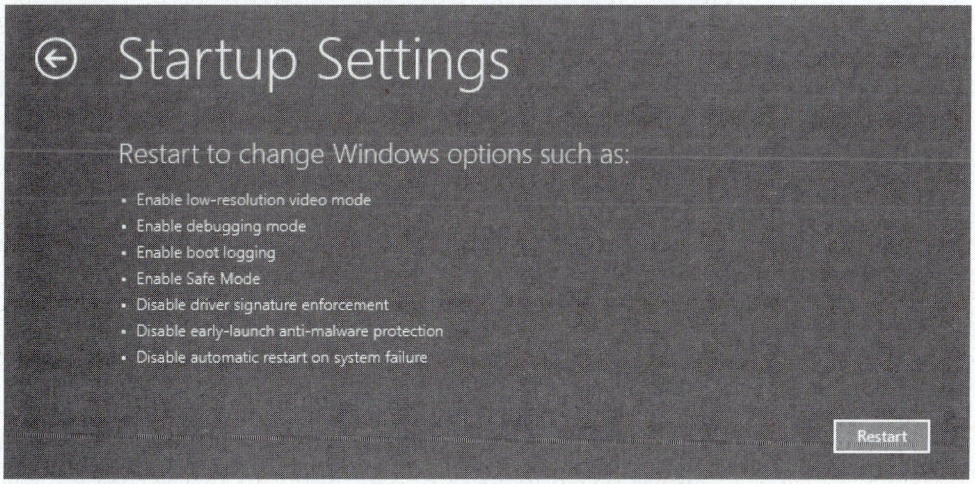

8. Click **Restart**.

   The *Startup Settings* menu appears, as shown in Figure 4-8.

Figure 4-8

The *Startup Settings* menu

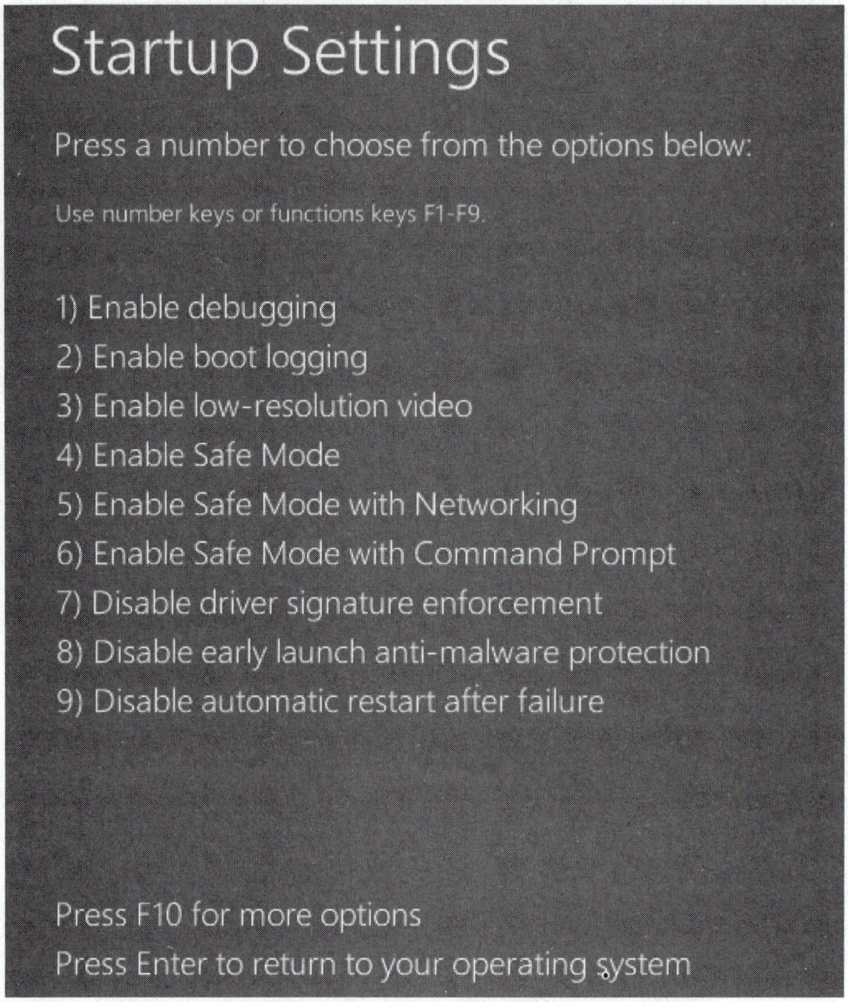

9. Press **7** to disable driver signature enforcement.

   The system starts, loading all drivers, whether signed or not, or altered or not.
10. Log on to Windows 8 in the normal manner.

Working with Devices

Windows 8 is, in most cases, able to detect the devices connected to a computer when you install the operating system, as well as any new devices you attach later.

Most PCs use USB (Universal Serial Bus) connections for peripheral devices, and Plug and Play is an integral part of the USB standard. When you connect a printer, a camera, a scanner, or another type of device to a computer running Windows 8 using a USB port, the system usually detects it, adds it to the *Devices and Printers* control panel, as shown in Figure 4-9, and installs the appropriate device driver for it.

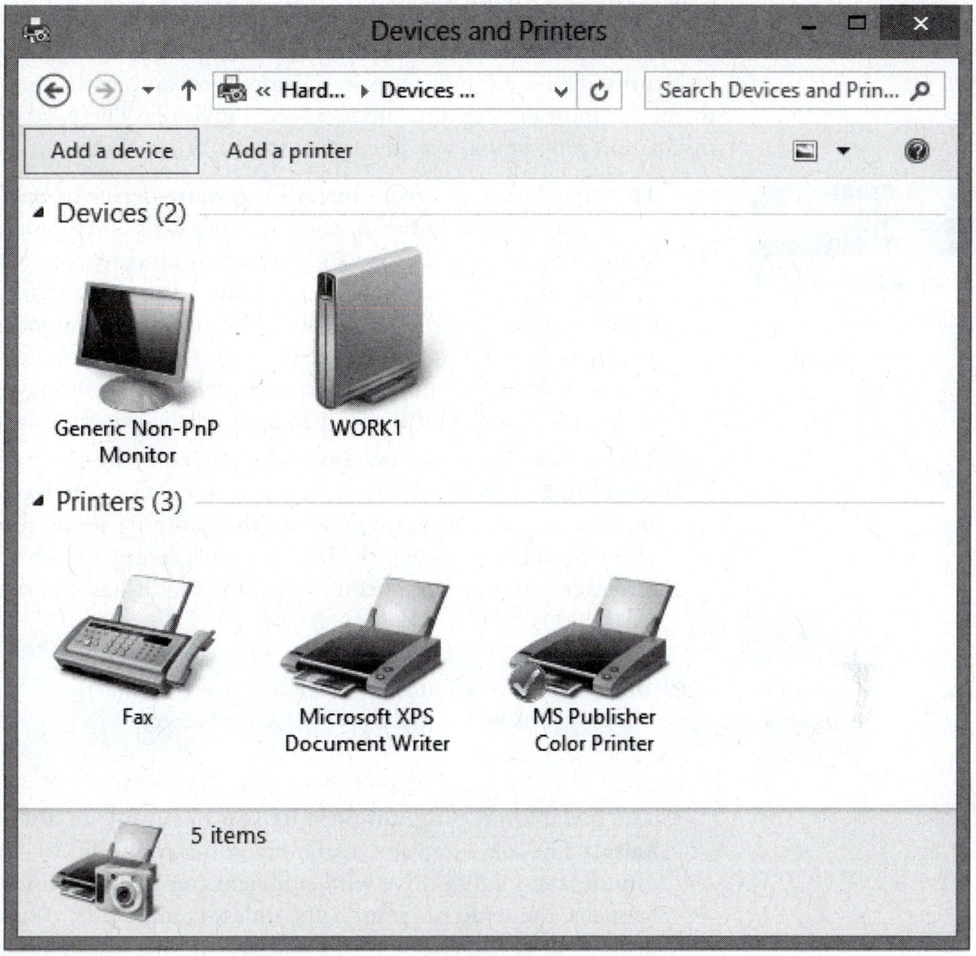

Figure 4-9
The *Devices and Printers* control panel

CERTIFICATION READY
Install drivers
Objective 2.1

You can also manually install a device by selecting *Add a device*, to display the *Choose a device or a printer to add to this PC* page, as shown in Figure 4-10.

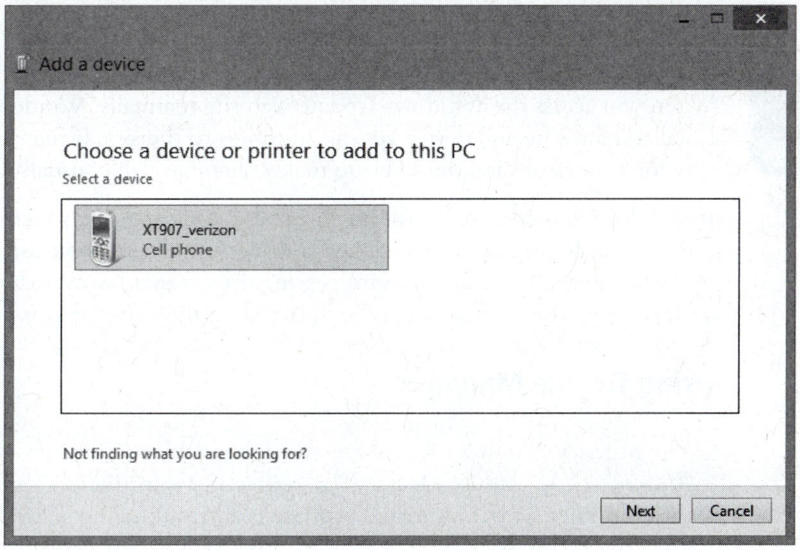

Figure 4-10
The *Choose a device or a printer to add to this PC* page

SUPPLYING DRIVERS DURING WINDOWS 8 INSTALLATION

As mentioned earlier, one of the primary functions of the Windows 8 installation program is to identify the hardware devices in the computer and install the appropriate device drivers for them. For most devices, this process occurs invisibly. There are occasions, however, when the installation program fails to identify a device. When this occurs, one of three things happens:

CERTIFICATION READY
Install drivers
Objective 2.1

- **The installation program installs a generic driver instead** – For devices that are essential to system operation, such as keyboards and graphics adapters. Windows 8 includes generic drivers that support nearly all hardware devices. If Windows 8 does not include a driver for your specific graphics adapter, for example, it installs a generic VGA (video graphics array) driver. This VGA driver won't support the esoteric features of your graphics adapter, but it will at least display an image on your screen, albeit a low-resolution one. After the operating system installation is completed, you can obtain a driver for your hardware and install it in place of the generic driver.
- **The installation program leaves the device without a driver and completes the installation** – If the hardware device is not essential to basic system operation, such as an audio adapter, Windows 8 leaves the hardware uninstalled and proceeds with the rest of the installation. When the installation is completed, the hardware appears in Device Manager with a warning icon, indicating that it has no driver.

X REF

To install a device driver after the Windows 8 installation is complete, you must use the Device Manager utility, as described later in this lesson in "Using Device Manager."

- **The installation program permits you to supply an alternate driver or, failing that, halts** – The sole exception to the preceding condition is when the installation program cannot access a disk drive with sufficient free space to install Windows 8. When this happens, the setup program halts, unless you are able to supply the device driver for an unrecognized mass storage hardware device. For example, if your hard drives are connected to an interface adapter that Windows 8 does not recognize, you can click Load Driver on the installation program's *Where do you want to install windows?* page, and specify the location of a driver for the adapter.

UPDATING DRIVERS WITH WINDOWS UPDATE

The Windows Update web site was originally designed to provide users with operating system updates, but it now includes a large library of device driver updates as well. The drivers distributed through Windows Update have all undergone Windows Hardware Quality Labs (WHQL) testing and have received the Windows logo.

CERTIFICATION READY
Update drivers
Objective 2.1

When you access the Windows Update web site manually, Windows 8 transmits a list of installed hardware and device version numbers to the site. If there are any updated drivers available for your hardware, the web site makes them available, usually as an optional download.

If Windows 8 is configured to use automatic updating, the system will download device drivers only for hardware that does not have a driver installed. If you use Device Manager to search for updated drivers, Windows 8 examines the drivers that are available and only downloads a new driver if it is a better match for the device than the driver that is currently installed.

Using Device Manager

The primary Windows 8 tool for managing devices and their drivers is called ***Device Manager***. You can use Device Manager to get information about the devices installed in the computer, as well as install, update, and troubleshoot device drivers.

Although it is not immediately apparent, Device Manager is a snap-in for the Microsoft Management Console (MMC). This means that there are many ways that you can access Device Manager, including the following:

- On the Windows 8 desktop, right-click the lower left corner of the taskbar and, from the context menu that appears, select Device Manager.
- Open the Windows 8 Control Panel and select Hardware and Sound and, under devices and printers, click Device Manager.
- Open the Computer Management console from the Administrative Tools program group in the System and Security control panel and click Device Manager in the left pane.
- Run the Microsoft Management Console shell application (Mmc.exe), select File , Add/ Remove Snap-in, and select Device Manager from the list of snap-ins provided.
- Open the Run dialog box and type the file name of the Device Manager snap-in (Devmgmt.msc) in the Open text box, and then click OK.

TAKE NOTE* To access the Run dialog box, right-click the lower left corner of the taskbar on the Windows 8 desktop and, from the context menu that appears, select Run.

Each of these procedures launches the Device Manager and displays a window with an interface like that shown in Figure 4-11.

Figure 4-11

The *Windows 8 Device Manager* display

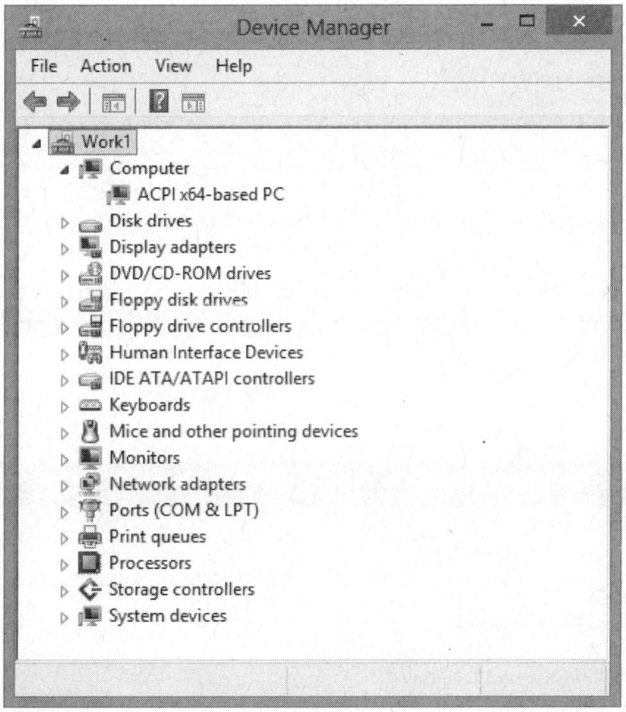

When you launch Device Manager while logged on with a standard user account, a message box appears, warning you that you can only view the settings in the console. To modify settings in Device Manager, you must log on with an account that has Administrative privileges.

VIEWING DEVICE PROPERTIES

Device Manager is capable of displaying information in the following four modes:

- **Devices by type** – Displays a list of device categories, which you can expand to show the devices in each category. This is the default Device Manager view, as shown in Figure 4-12.

Figure 4-12

Device Manager's *Devices By Type* display

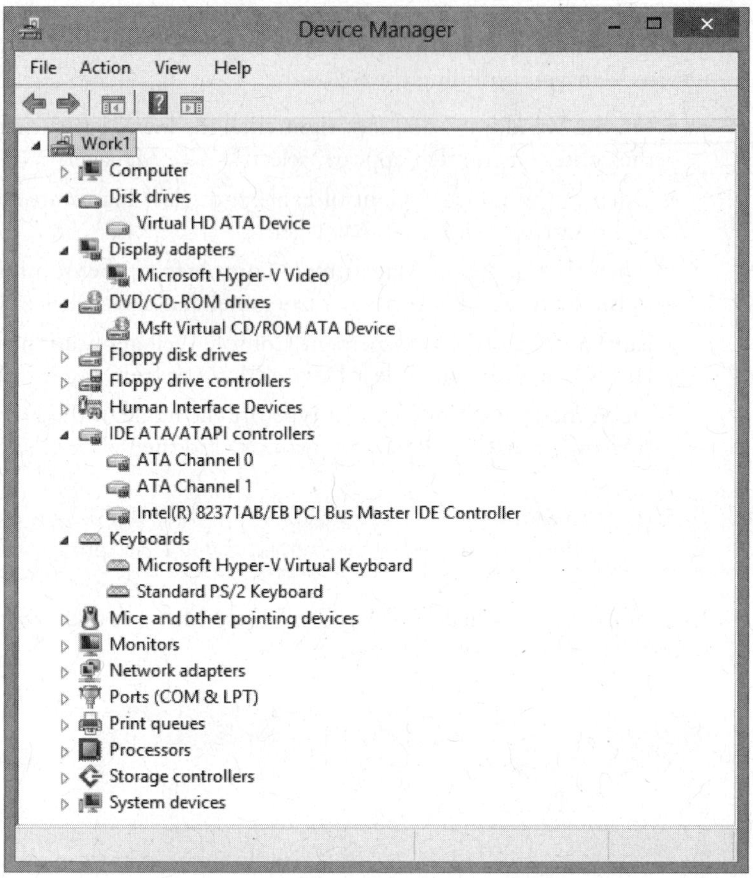

- **Devices by connection** – Displays a list of the interfaces that hardware devices use to communicate with the computer. Expanding a connection shows the devices using that connection, as shown in Figure 4-13.

Figure 4-13

Device Manager's *Devices By Connection* display

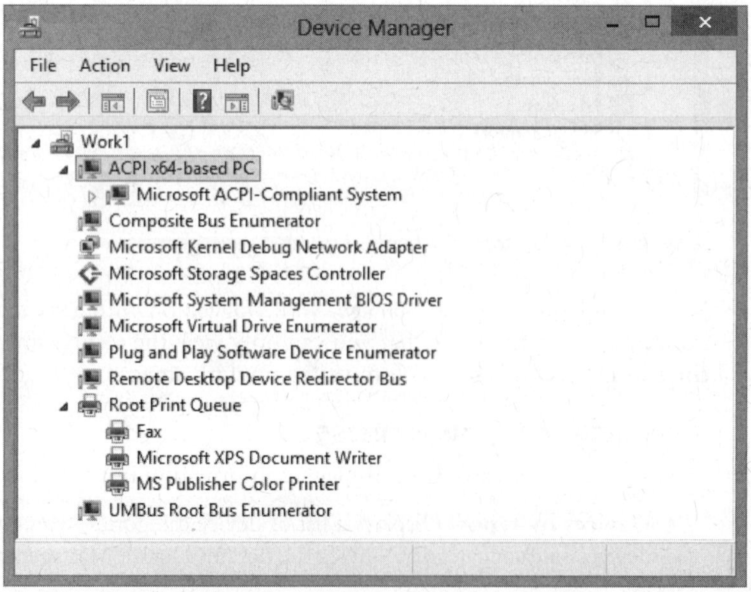

- **Resources by type** – Displays a list of resource types, including Direct Memory Access (DMA), Input/Output (I/O), Interrupt Request (IRQ), and Memory, which you can expand to show the resources of each type and the devices that are using them, as shown in Figure 4-14.

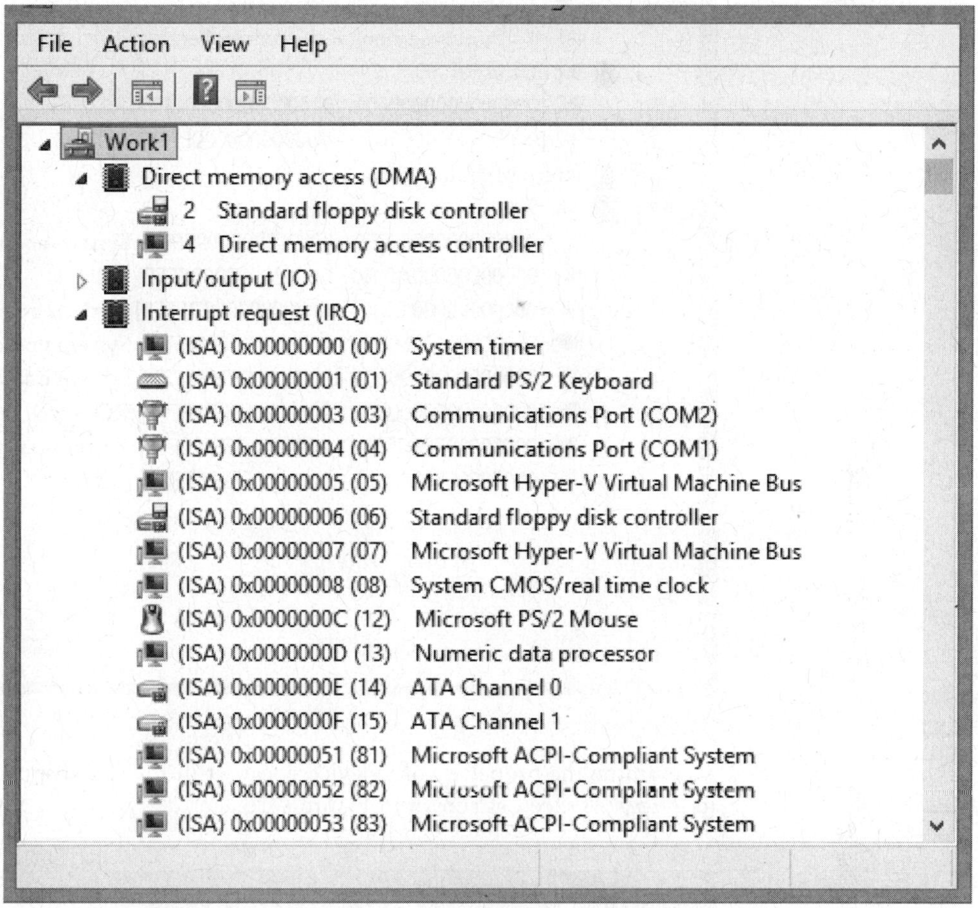

Figure 4-14

Device Manager's *Resources by Type* display

- **Resources by connection** – Displays a list of resource types, including Direct Memory Access (DMA), Input/Output (I/O), Interrupt Request (IRQ), and Memory, which you can expand to show the connection associated with each individual resource and the device using each connection, as shown in Figure 4-15.

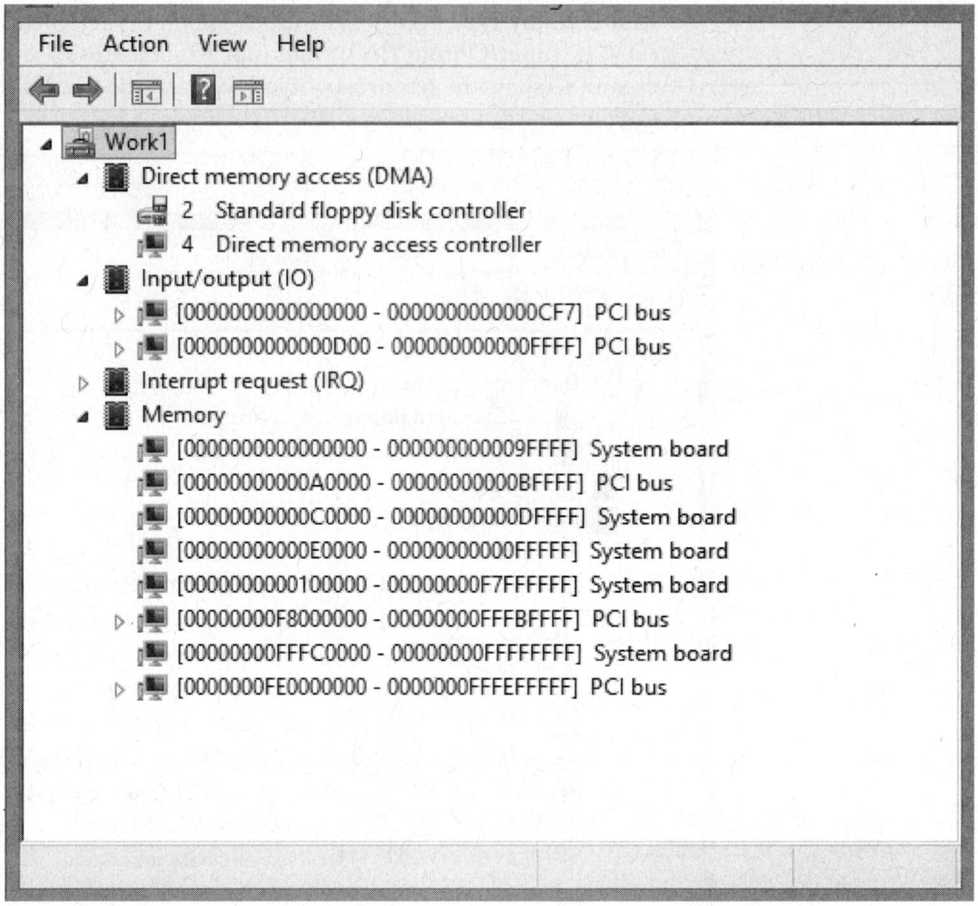

Figure 4-15

Device Manager's *Resources by Connection* display

To examine the properties of a device, locate it in the tree display and double-click it to open its *Properties* sheet, as shown in Figure 4-16.

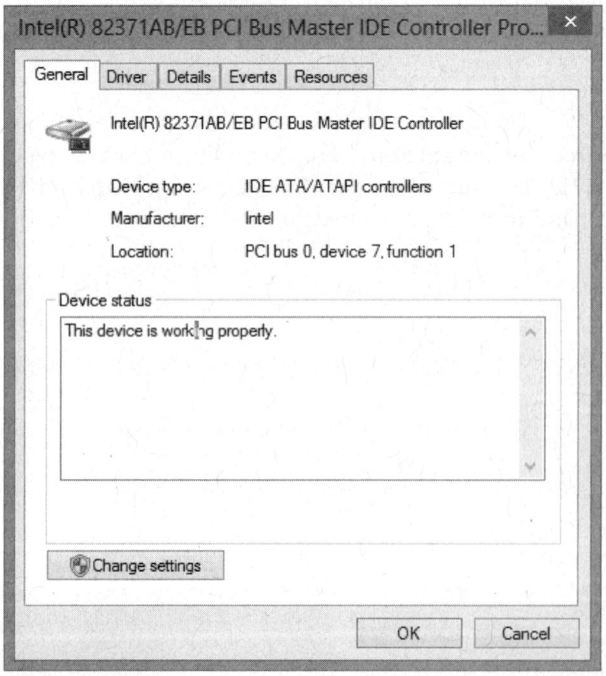

Figure 4-16

A Device Manager *Properties* sheet

The tabs on the Properties sheet vary depending on the nature of the device you select, but virtually all devices have the following four tabs:

- **General** – Displays the name of the device, its type, manufacturer, and location in the system. The Device Status box indicates whether the device is functioning and, if not, provides troubleshooting help.
- **Driver** – Displays the device driver's provider, date, version, and digital signer. The tab also provides buttons you can use to display driver details, update, roll back, or uninstall the driver, and enable or disable the device.
- **Details** – Displays extensive information about the driver and its properties.
- **Events** – Displays events associated with the driver.
- **Resources** – Displays the hardware resources being used by the device and indicates whether there are any conflicts with other devices in the computer.

CERTIFICATION READY
Configure driver settings
Objective 2.1

ENABLING AND DISABLING DEVICES

With Device Manager, you can disable any device in the computer, using any of the following procedures:

- Select the device and then choose Disable from the Action menu
- Right-click the device and then choose Disable from the context menu
- Open the device's Properties sheet and then click the Disable button on the Driver tab

CERTIFICATION READY
Disable drivers
Objective 2.1

Disabling a device does not affect the hardware in any way or uninstall the device driver, it simply renders the device inoperative until you enable it again. Obviously, you cannot disable devices that are necessary for the system to function, such as the processor, and some devices that are currently in use require you to restart the system before they can be disabled.

TAKE NOTE* Disabling a device releases the hardware resources it was using back to the operating system. If you restart the computer with the device disabled, Windows might reassign those hardware resources to other devices. If you then re-enable the device, the computer might allocate different hardware resources to it than it had originally.

UPDATING DRIVERS

CERTIFICATION READY
Update drivers
Objective 2.1

When you update a driver using Device Manager, you can point to a location on your computer where you have already saved the new driver, or you can run a search of your computer and the Internet. To update a device driver, use the following procedure.

UPDATE A DEVICE DRIVER

GET READY. Log on to Windows 8 using an account with Administrator privileges.

1. Open Device Manager and locate the device that you want to update.
2. Double-click the device you want to update, so that its Properties sheet appears.
3. Click the *Driver* tab and then click the **Update Driver** button.

   The *How do you want to search for driver software?* page appears, as shown in Figure 4-17.

Figure 4-17

The *How do you want to search for driver software?* page

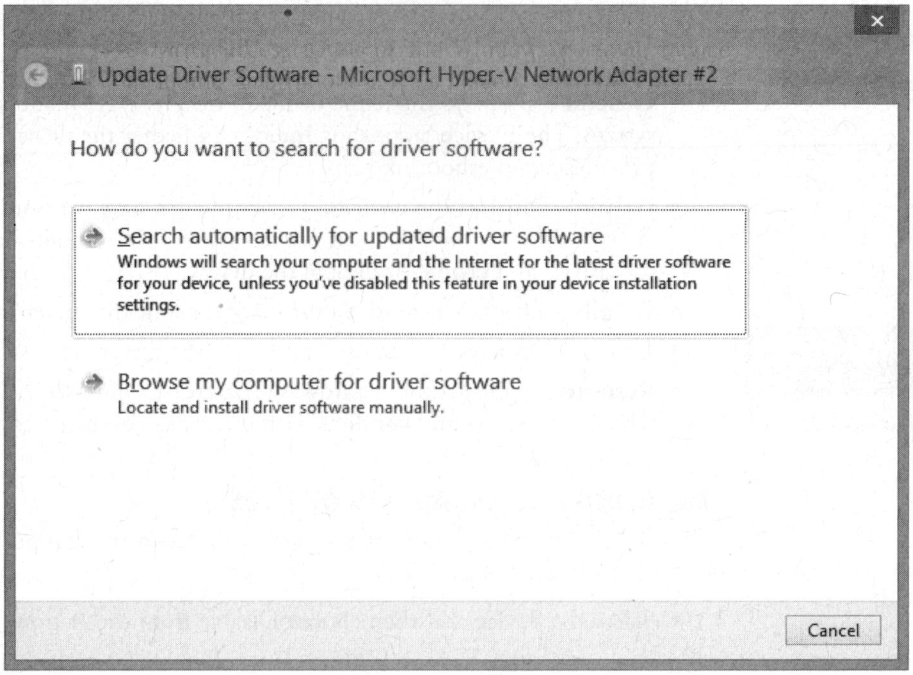

4. Click *Browse my computer for driver software* to specify a location for the driver or to select from a list of installed drivers, as shown in Figure 4-18. Or click *Search automatically for updated driver software* to initiate a search for a driver.

Figure 4-18

The *Browse for driver software on your computer* page

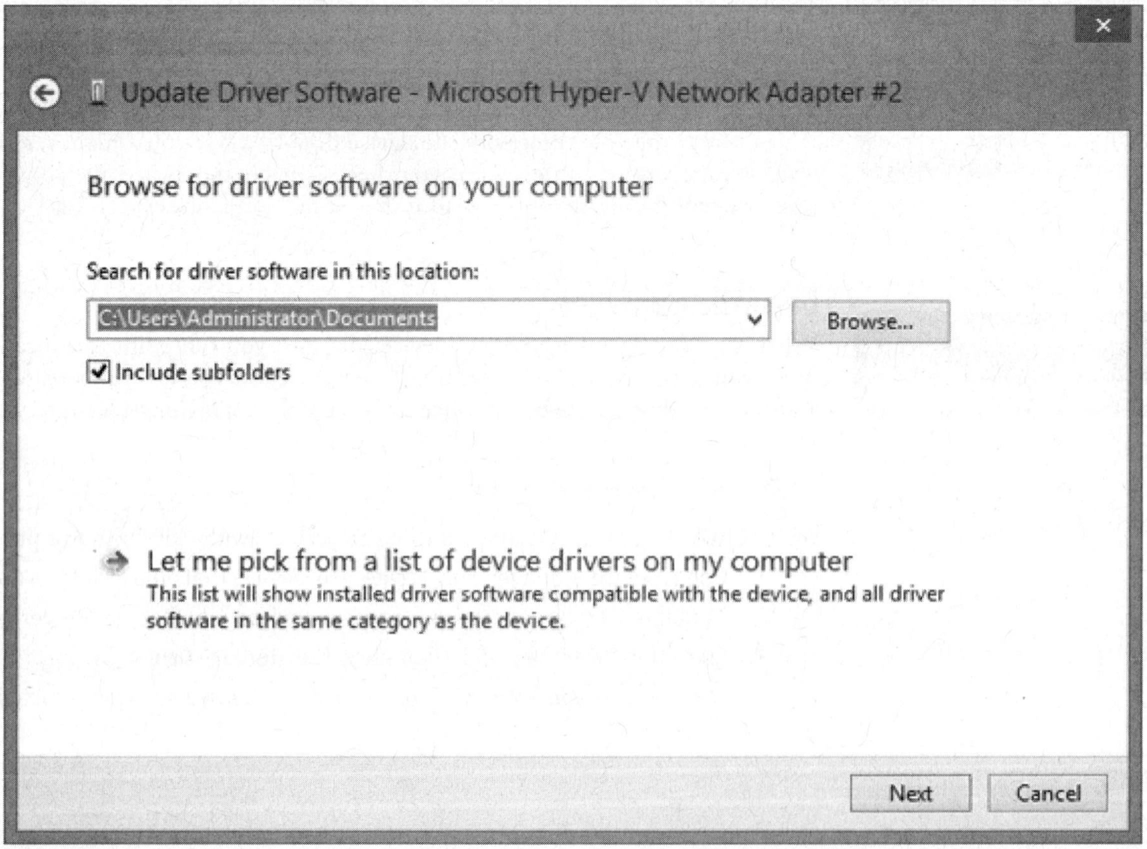

5. Locate the driver you want to install and then click **Next**.

   The *Windows has successfully updated your driver software* page appears.

6. Click **Close**.

7. Close the *Device Manager* console.

ROLLING BACK DRIVERS

When you update a device driver in Windows 8, the operating system does not discard the old driver completely. It is not uncommon for new drivers to cause more problems than they solve, and many users find that they would prefer to go back to the old version. Windows 8 makes this possible with the Roll Back feature, which you initiate by clicking the Roll Back Driver button on the Driver tab of the device's Properties sheet. This procedure uninstalls the current driver and reinstalls the previous version, returning the device to the state before you performed the most recent driver update.

CERTIFICATION READY
Roll back drivers
Objective 2.1

TAKE NOTE* The Roll Back Driver button is active only when there is a previous version of the current driver available on the system. Otherwise, the button is grayed out.

TROUBLESHOOTING DRIVERS

Installing a new hardware device or a new device driver is a risky undertaking. There is always the possibility of a problem that, depending on the devices involved, could be trivial or catastrophic. For a peripheral device, such as a printer, a hardware misconfiguration or faulty driver would probably just cause the new device to malfunction. However, if the device involved is a graphics adapter, a bad driver could prevent the system from functioning.

CERTIFICATION READY
Resolve driver issues.
Objective 2.1

To troubleshoot hardware or driver problems, consider some of the following techniques:

- Open the Properties sheet for the device and check the Device Status box on the General tab. If the device is malfunctioning, this tab informs you of its status and enables you to launch a troubleshooter.
- Open the Device Manager and delete the device entirely. Then restart the system and allow Windows 8 to detect and install the device over again. This process will cause Windows to re-allocate hardware resources to the device, which could resolve the problem if it was caused by a hardware resource conflict.
- If the device or driver malfunction prevents the system from running properly, as in the case of a bad graphics driver that prevents an image from appearing on the screen, you can start the computer in Safe Mode by using the Advanced Boot Options procedure described earlier in this lesson. Safe Mode loads the operating system with a minimal set of generic devices drivers, bypassing the troublesome ones, so you can uninstall or troubleshoot them.

SKILL SUMMARY

IN THIS LESSON, YOU LEARNED:

- Device drivers are software components that enable applications and operating systems to communicate with specific hardware devices. Every hardware device you install in a computer must have a corresponding driver.
- Plug and Play is a standard that enables computers to detect and identify hardware devices, and then install and configure drivers for those devices. PnP dynamically assigns

(continued)

hardware resources to each device, and can reconfigure devices at will to accommodate each component's special needs.

- The drivers included with Windows 8 have all been digitally signed to ensure that they have not been modified since they were published.
- Device Manager is an MMC snap-in that lists all hardware devices in the computer and indicates problems with hardware identification or driver configuration. Using Device Manager, you can enable and disable devices, update and roll back drivers, and manage device and device driver properties.

Knowledge Assessment

Multiple Choice

Select one or more correct answers for each of the following questions.

1. Which of the following are the three main reasons why manufacturers release driver updates?
a. To address problems with previous driver versions
b. To enhance device performance
c. To add new driver features
d. To fulfill Microsoft testing requirements

2. Under which of the following conditions will Windows 8 fail to load an unsigned device driver?
a. When you modify the Windows startup settings by disabling driver signature enforcement
b. When you are running the 32-bit version of Windows 8
c. When you are running the 64-bit version of Windows 8
d. When you are running the Windows 8 Enterprise edition

3. All digitally signed device drivers included with Windows 8 have undergone testing by which of the following bodies?
a. The manufacturer
b. Windows Hardware Quality Lab
c. American National Standards Institute (ANSI)
d. Internet Engineering Task Force (IETF)

4. What does the Windows 8 installation program do when it does not have a device driver for the specific model of graphics adapter installed in the computer?
a. The installation program prompts the user to supply an appropriate driver for the adapter.
b. The installation program searches the Internet for an appropriate driver for the adapter.
c. The installation program installs a generic driver for the adapter.
d. The installation program halts, because it is unable to supply an appropriate driver.

5. Which of the following tasks are you unable to perform using the Windows 8 Device Manager application?
a. Install a new hardware device
b. Update an existing device driver
c. Roll back an installed device driver to a previous version
d. Disable a device driver

6. Which of the following is not a tab found on Properties sheets in Device Manager?
   a. General
   b. Driver
   c. Details
   d. Events
   e. Advanced

7. Which of the following statements about public key cryptography are true?
   a. Data encrypted with a user's public key can only be decrypted with that same public key.
   b. Data encrypted with a user's private key can only be decrypted with that same private key.
   c. Data encrypted with a user's public key can only be decrypted with that same user's private key.
   d. Data encrypted with a user's private key can only be decrypted with that same user's public key.

8. What typically happens after you delete a device using Device Manager?
   a. Device Manager immediately reinstalls the device
   b. The system reinstalls the device during the next restart
   c. You must reinstall the device manually
   d. The device is permanently removed from the system

9. Which of the following is the default view of the Device Manager?
   a. Resources by connection
   b. Resources by type
   c. Devices by connection
   d. Devices by type

Best Answer

1. Which of the following is the best reason for rolling back a driver?
   a. Because a newly installed device fails to function
   b. Because a newly released driver update is buggy
   c. Because the installed driver is not digitally signed
   d. Because there is no Windows 8 driver available for the device

2. Which of the following devices is most likely to have drivers that cause problems with Windows 8?
   a. A new ergonomic keyboard
   b. A five year old serial mouse
   c. The latest high performance graphics adapter
   d. The network adapter integrated into your motherboard

Build a List

1. Place the following steps of the procedure for disabling driver signature enforcement in the proper order.
   _________ Select General.
   _________ Open the fly-out menu and click the Settings charm.
   _________ Click Advanced Options.
   _________ Press 7 to disable driver signature enforcement
   _________ Log on to Windows 8 with Administrator privileges.
   _________ Click Troubleshooting
   _________ Click Restart
   _________ Click Change PC Settings.
   _________ Scroll down and under Advanced Startup, click Restart Now
   _________ Click Startup Settings

■ Business Case Scenario

Scenario 4-1: Troubleshooting Graphics Drivers

A user asks you to troubleshoot his Windows 8 workstation, which is behaving erratically. He has recently purchased and installed a new graphics adapter, and ever since then, he sees occasional wavy lines in the display. You run Device Manager on the system and note the manufacturer, model, and version number of the device driver for the graphics adapter. Then, you check the adapter manufacturer's web site and discover that there is a new driver available for the adapter. After downloading and installing the driver update, you restart the system. The system appears to start normally, except that the graphical interface has been replaced by incomprehensible noise. Because you can't see the display, you can't work with the system. What should you do return the computer to an operational state?

Installing and Configuring Desktop Applications

LESSON 5

70-687 EXAM OBJECTIVE

Objective 2.2 – Install and configure desktop applications. This objective may include but is not limited to: configure default program settings; modify file associations; install and repair applications by using Windows Installer; set compatibility mode; and manage App-V applications.

Lesson Heading	Exam Objective
Configuring Program Defaults	
Setting Default Programs	Configure default program settings
Modifying File Associations	Modify file associations
Modifying Autoplay Settings	
Setting Program Access Defaults	
Using Windows Installer	Install and repair applications by using Windows Installer
Configuring Application Compatibility	
Troubleshooting Program Compatibility	
Setting Compatibility Modes	Set compatibility mode
Configuring Application Compatibility Policies	
Virtualizing Applications Using App-V	Manage App-V applications

KEY TERMS

Application Virtualization Client
Application Virtualization Management Console
Application Virtualization Sequencer
compatibility mode
Microsoft Application Virtualization (App-V)
Program Compatibility Assistant (PCA)
Program Compatibility Troubleshooter
Virtual Application Server

Configuring Program Defaults

THE BOTTOM LINE

Windows 8 is, above all, a platform for running applications, and the operating system includes many controls that facilitate that function.

Administrators must often work with applications that are technically outdated, and Windows 8 provides compatibility settings that help those applications to run efficiently. Administrators might also need to control which applications are associated with specific file types and specific user activities, such as sending an email message or inserting a DVD. The Default Programs control panel in Windows 8, as shown in Figure 5-1, contains controls for all of these functions.

Figure 5-1

The *Default Programs* control panel

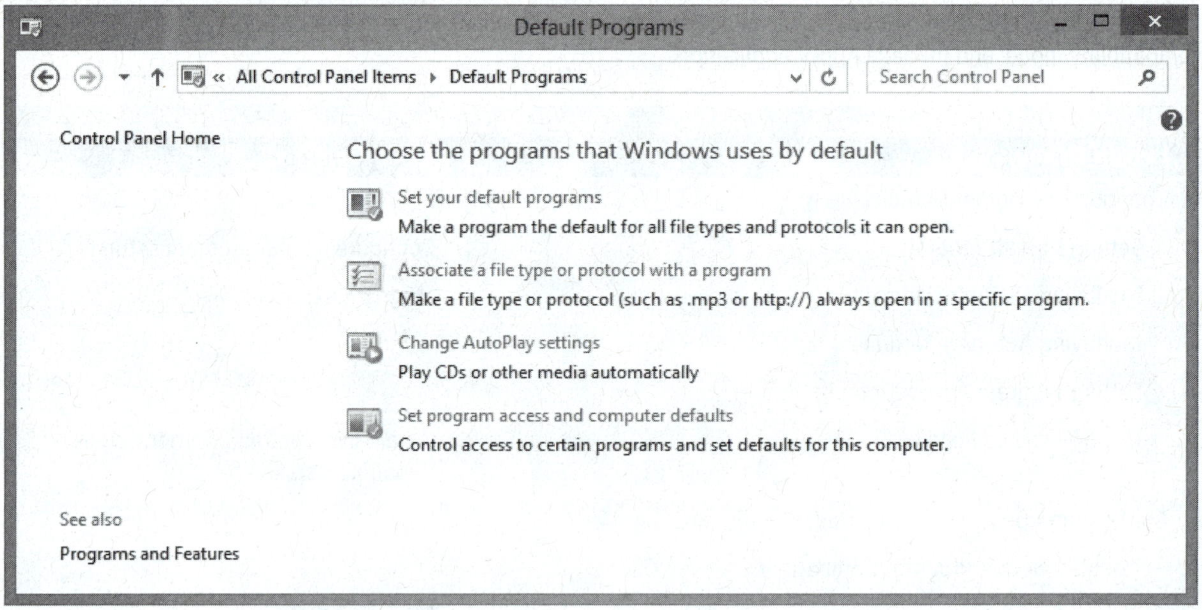

Setting Default Programs

The Set Default Programs interface enables you to specify which file types are associated with an application. With these associations in place, a user can simply double-click a file, and the application will launch itself and load that file.

Many applications have their own file types, and those types are associated with the application when you install it. For example, Microsoft Word is associated with the Microsoft Word Document (.docx) file type, and there is rarely any reason for an administrator or user to change it.

CERTIFICATION READY
Configure default program settings
Objective 2.2

Other file types, however, can be opened by multiple applications, and administrators and users can use program defaults to select their favorite applications for particular file types. For example, you might want to change the default program for MP3 music files to your favorite music player application. For image files, such as Windows Bitmaps, you might want to select either an image viewer or an image editor.

Many applications reset their own defaults, to take control over certain file types. This can occur when you install the application, or in some cases, every time you launch the application. In some instances, you might have two or more applications competing for the same file types, each of which resets the program defaults in its favor each time you run it. Most well-behaved programs let you control this behavior, but in the event that one does not, you can use the control to change the program defaults.

When you click the *Set your default programs* link in the Default Programs control panel, the *Set your default programs* page appears, as shown in Figure 5-2. On this page, the Programs box contains a list of all the applications on the system, those installed by default with the Windows 8 operating system and those that you installed afterwards, either through the desktop or the Windows Store.

Figure 5-2

The *Set Your Default Programs* page

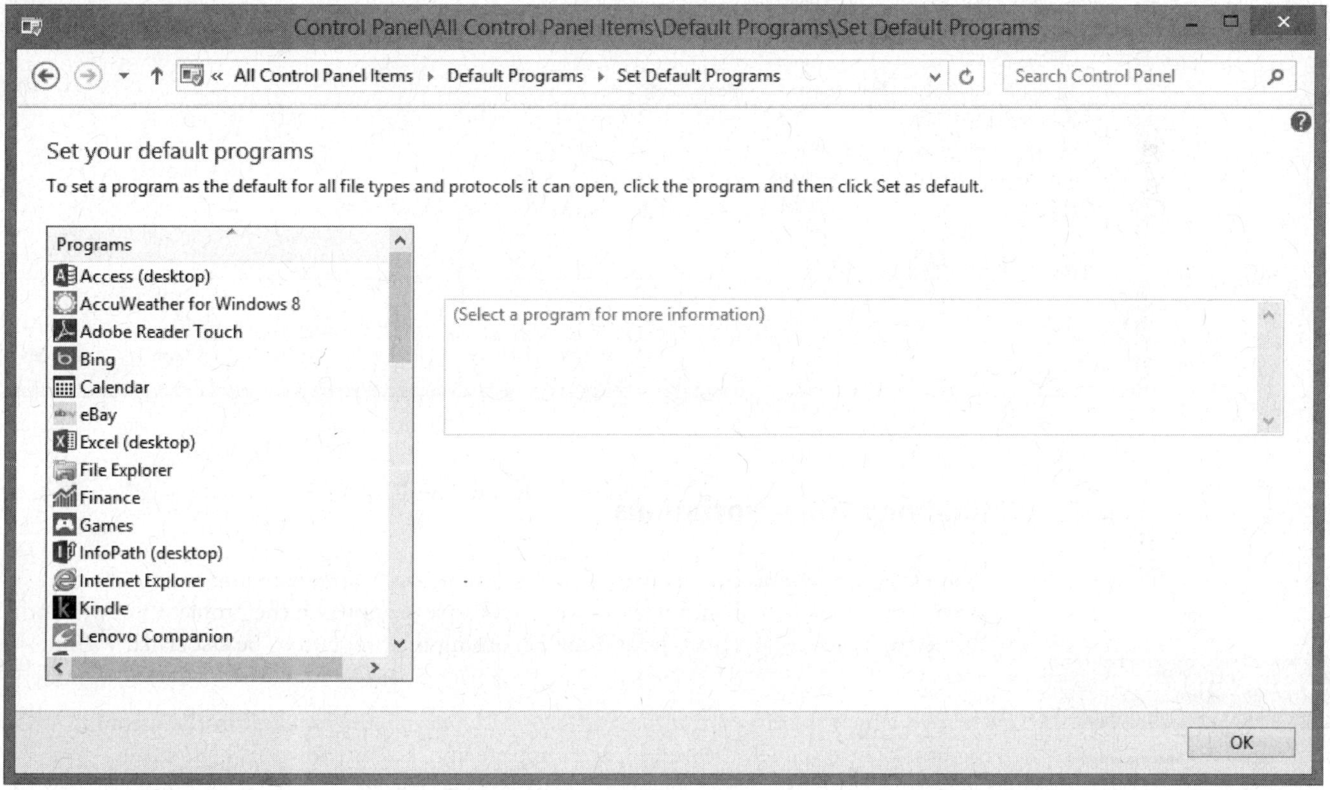

When you select a program from the list, the rest of the page contains information about the program, and about the current status of its default file types. In addition, there are two links at the bottom of the page, as follows:

- **Set this program as default** – If the program is not currently associated with all of its default file types, this link resets those defaults.
- **Choose defaults for this program** – Opens the *Set program associations* page, as shown in Figure 5-3, in which you can select the file types that you want to associate with the program.

Figure 5-3

The *Set Program Associations* page

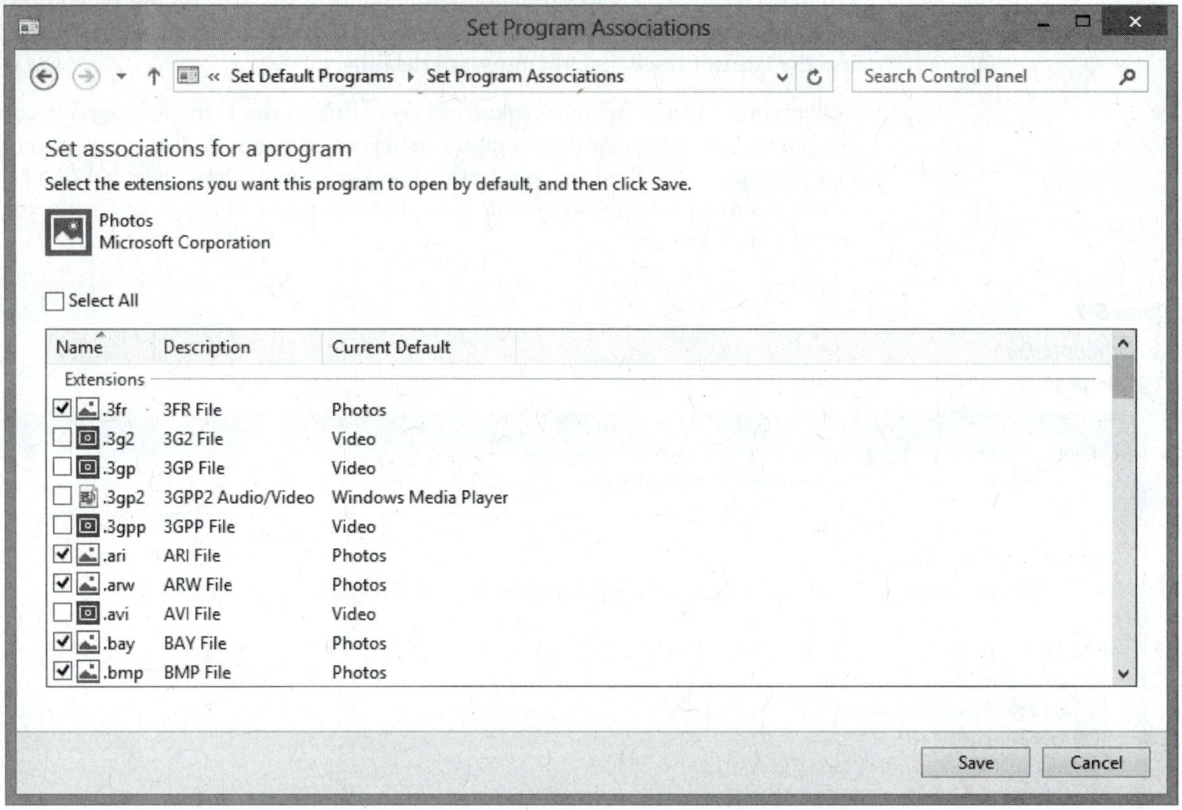

Modifying File Associations

The Default Programs control panel enables you to select a program and choose the file types that are associated with it. However, you can also approach the problem from the other direction, by selecting a file type and then choosing the program to be associated with it.

CERTIFICATION READY
Modify file associations
Objective 2.2

When you click the *Associate a file type or protocol with a program* link in the Default Programs control panel, the *Set Associations* page appears, as shown in Figure 5-4.

Figure 5-4

The *Set Associations* page

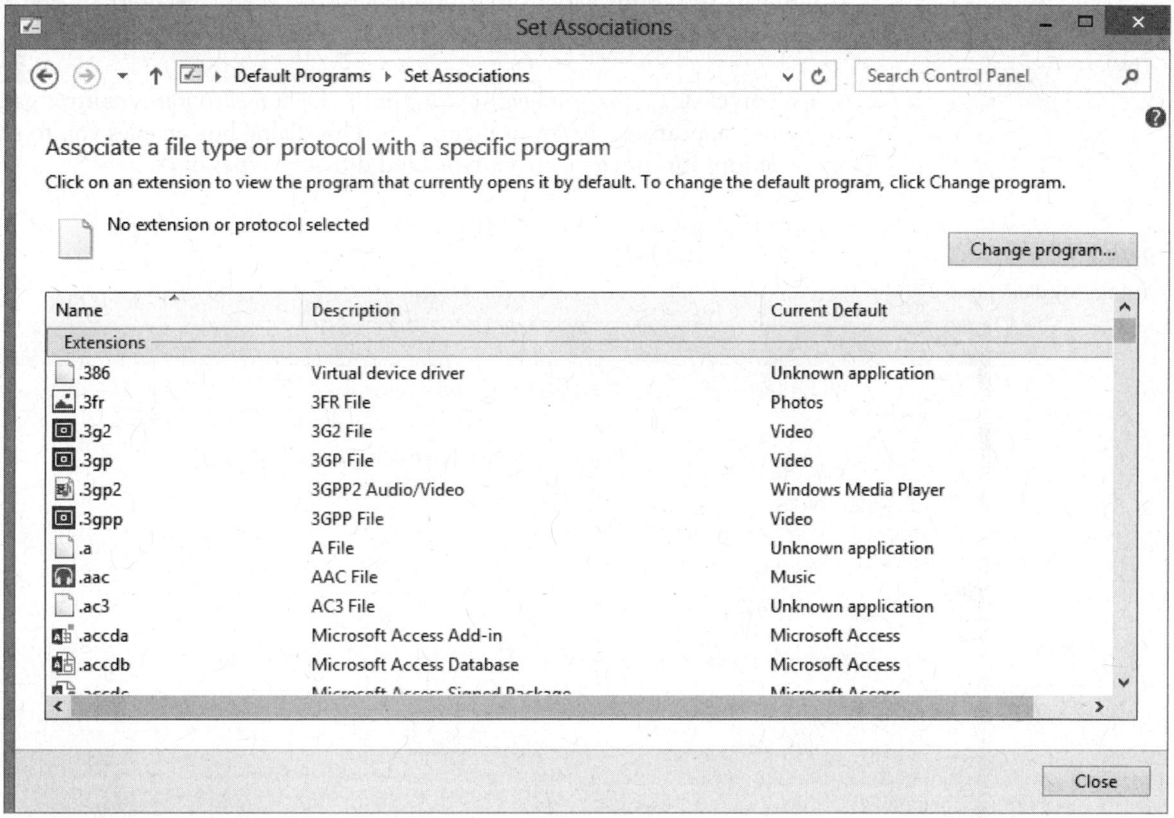

Scrolling down in the list, you can select any of the file extensions registered on the system and click Change Program to open the *How do you want to open this type of file* box, as shown in Figure 5-5. By selecting another application, you change the association between the file type and the application.

Figure 5-5

The *How do you want to open this type of file* box

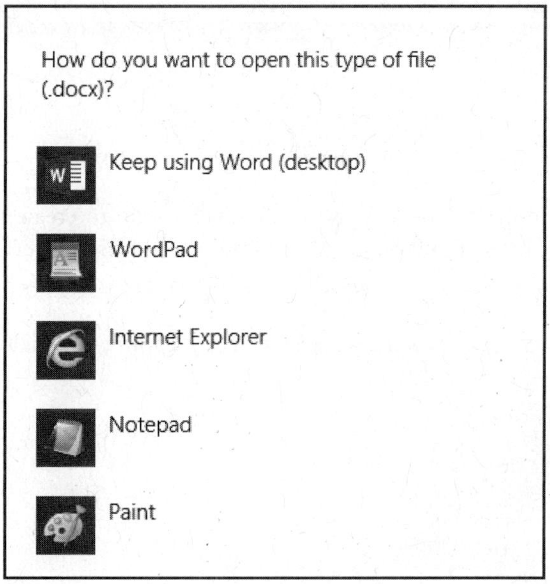

Modifying Autoplay Settings

Autoplay defines the actions that Windows takes when you insert a new removable medium, such as a CD, DVD, or USB flash drive, in to the computer.

When you click *Change Autoplay settings* in the Default Programs control panel, the *AutoPlay* dialog box appears, as shown in Figure 5-6. This dialog box enables you to select from a variety of actions for different media types and different types of content.

Figure 5-6

The *AutoPlay* dialog box

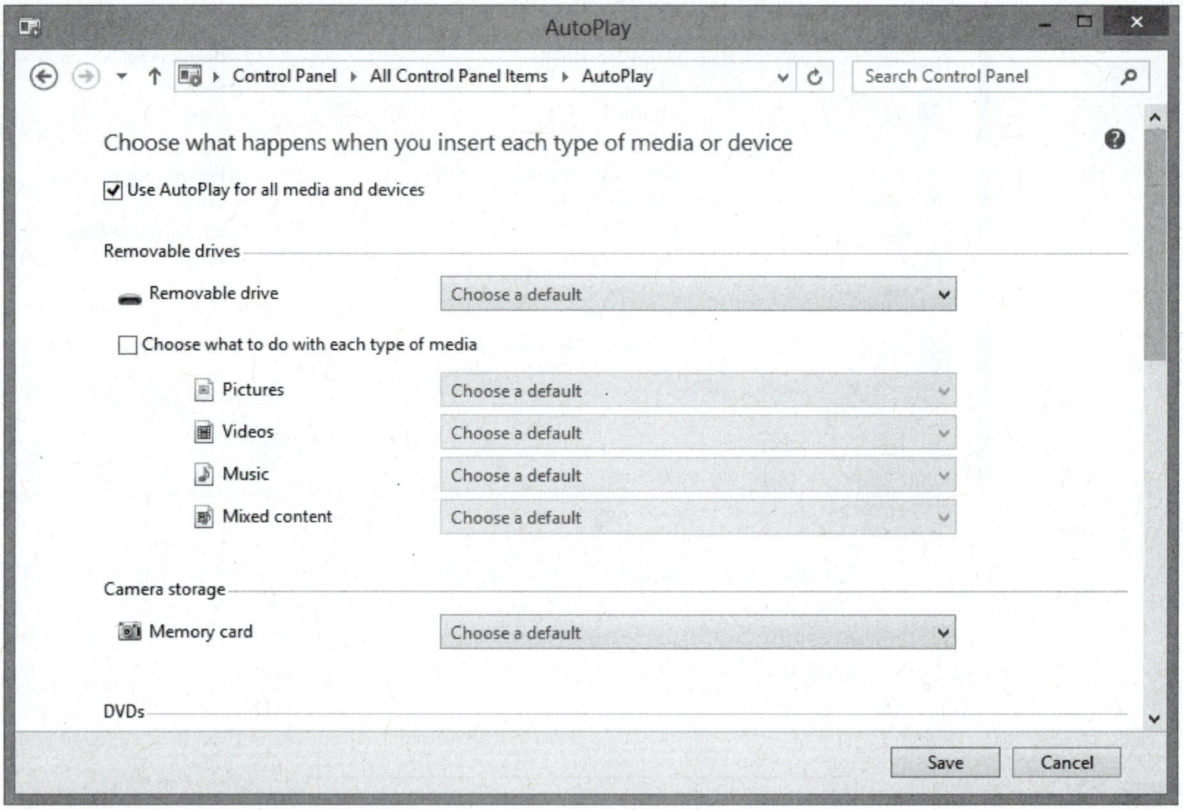

Setting Program Access Defaults

The Default Programs control panel also enables you to create a program configuration that specifies which applications Windows 8 should use to perform specific tasks, such as browse the Web, send email, and play media files.

When you click *Set program access and computer defaults*, the dialog box shown in Figure 5-7 appears.

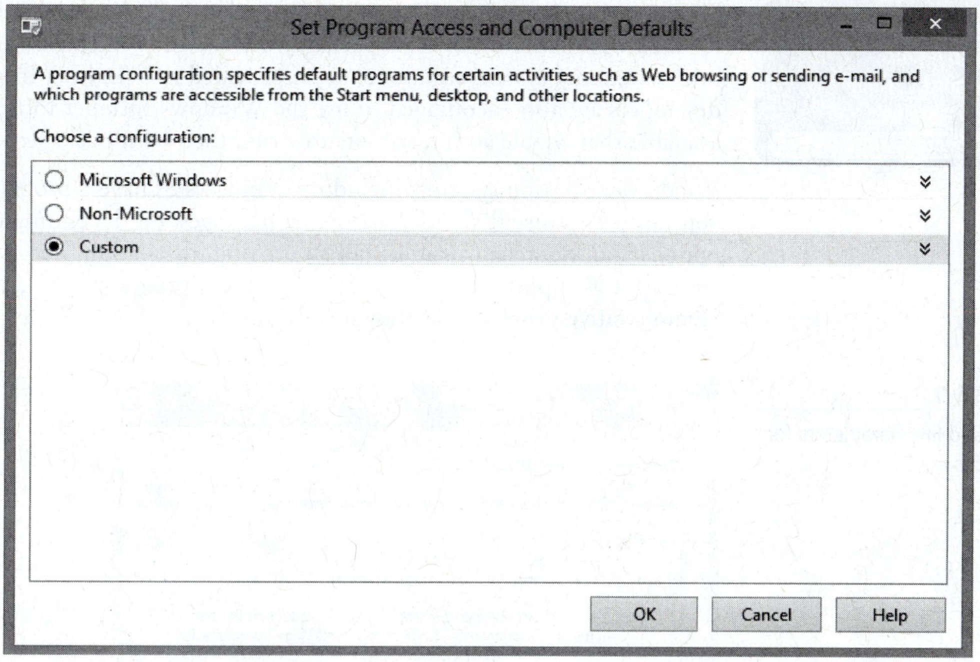

Figure 5-7

The *Set Program Access and Computer Defaults* dialog box

The three options on this page enable you to select an all-Microsoft solution, stick with the applications your system is currently using, or select a combination of the two, as shown in Figure 5-8.

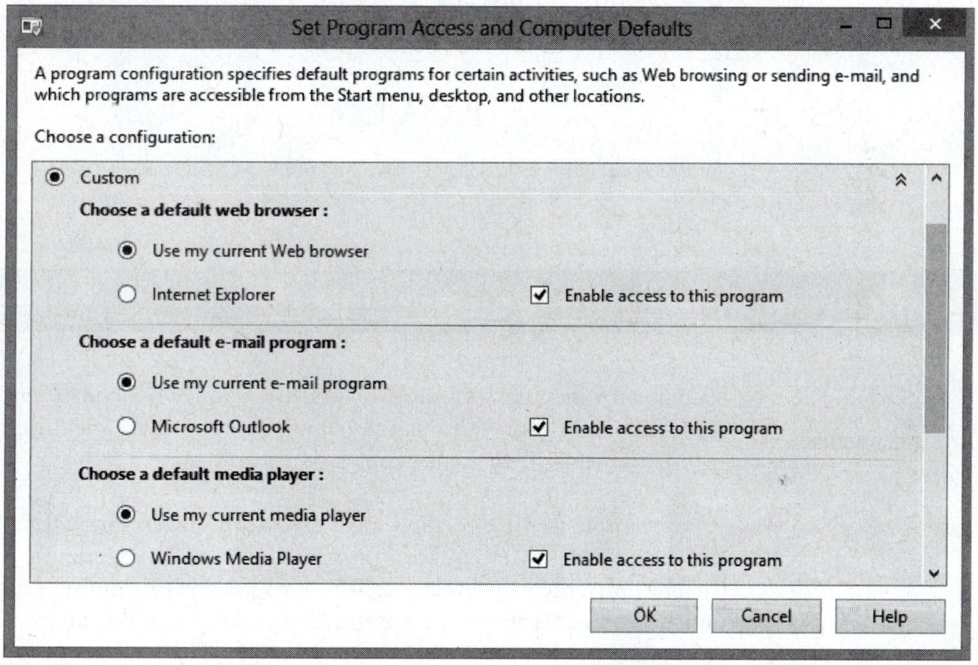

Figure 5-8

The Custom option in the *Set Program Access* and *Computer Defaults* dialog box

Using Windows Installer

Windows Installer is a software installation, repair, and removal engine that can simplify the process of deploying applications on Windows computers.

CERTIFICATION READY
Install and repair applications by using Windows Installer
Objective 2.2

Windows Installer is based on a file format that includes the application files and instructions for their installation in a single package, with an .msi extension. Many Windows updates and other operating system components are provided as Windows Installer packages. Third-party developers are also encouraged to use the Windows Installer format, and there are utilities available that enable administrators to create their own packages.

Windows operating systems, including Windows 8, have a program called Msiexec.exe, which you can use to install Windows Installer packages, or, depending on the command line options you use, repair or uninstall an existing installation. To view the command line parameters options supported by Msiexec.exe, run the program from a command prompt with administrative privileges, as shown in Figure 5-9.

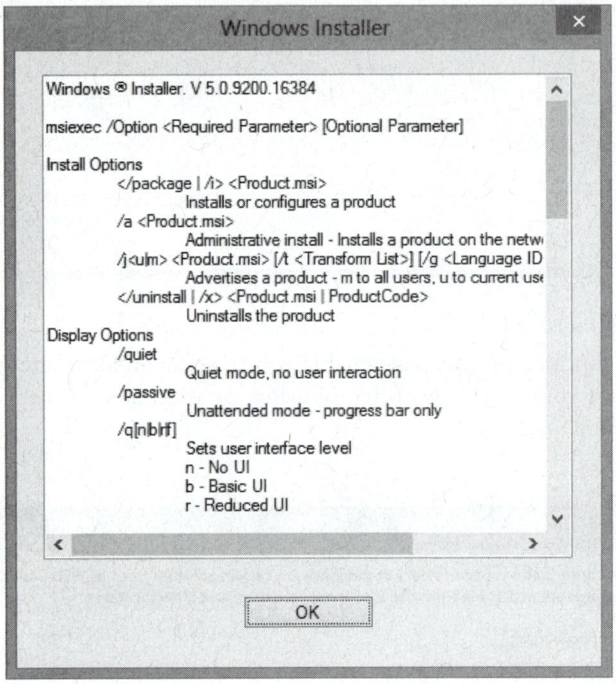

Figure 5-9
Command line parameters for qsiexec.exe

Configuring Application Compatibility

THE BOTTOM LINE

Windows 8 includes a number of security features that can alter the ability of certain applications to run. Administrators must therefore take measures to ensure the compatibility of their legacy applications.

One example of these features, data execution prevention (DEP), prevents applications from executing code in certain areas of memory. Another, mandatory integrity control (MIC), defines four integrity levels that Windows assigns to running processes, which specify the amount of access that the processes receive to system resources.

As a result of features like these, some programs that run perfectly well in older versions of Windows, particularly Windows XP and earlier, cannot run on Windows 8. For enterprise network administrators, deploying Windows 8 can be a massive undertaking in itself. The prospect of upgrading all of their applications as well can be reason enough to delay or even cancel the project.

Fortunately, Windows 8 includes a number of compatibility tools and features that can provide administrators with several ways to run their applications successfully. These tools and features are discussed in the following sections.

Troubleshooting Program Compatibility

The simplest method of coping with an application compatibility issue in Windows 8 is to run the Program Compatibility Troubleshooter.

The ***Program Compatibility Troubleshooter*** is a wizard-based solution that users or administrators can use to automatically configure an executable file to use an appropriate Windows 8 compatibility mechanism. Thus, the troubleshooter is not a compatibility mechanism in itself; it is just a method for applying other mechanisms.

To run the Program Compatibility Troubleshooter, you right-click an executable file or a shortcut to an executable file and select Troubleshoot Compatibility from the context menu. When the troubleshooter launches, it attempts to determine what is preventing the program from running properly. The troubleshooter then gives you two options, as shown in Figure 5-10.

Figure 5-10

The *Select troubleshooting option* page in the Program Compatibility Troubleshooter

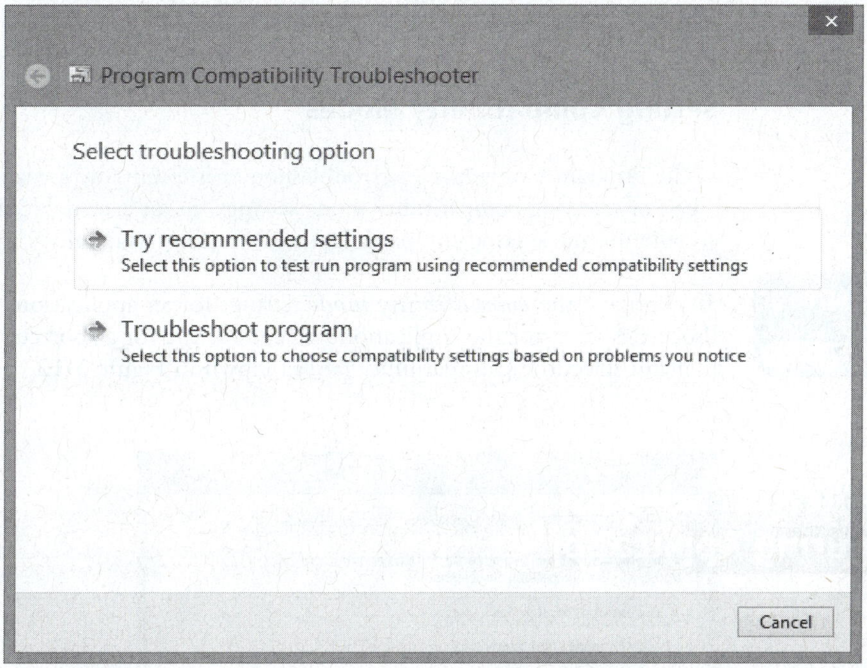

- **Try recommended settings** – implements the compatibility settings that the troubleshooter has determined will resolve the problem and configures the executable to use those settings whenever you run it.
- **Troubleshoot program** – Displays a *What problems do you notice?* page, shown in Figure 5-11, on which you can select the problems you have experienced. The troubleshooter then leads you through a series of pages that further identify the problem and configure the executable with specific compatibility settings.

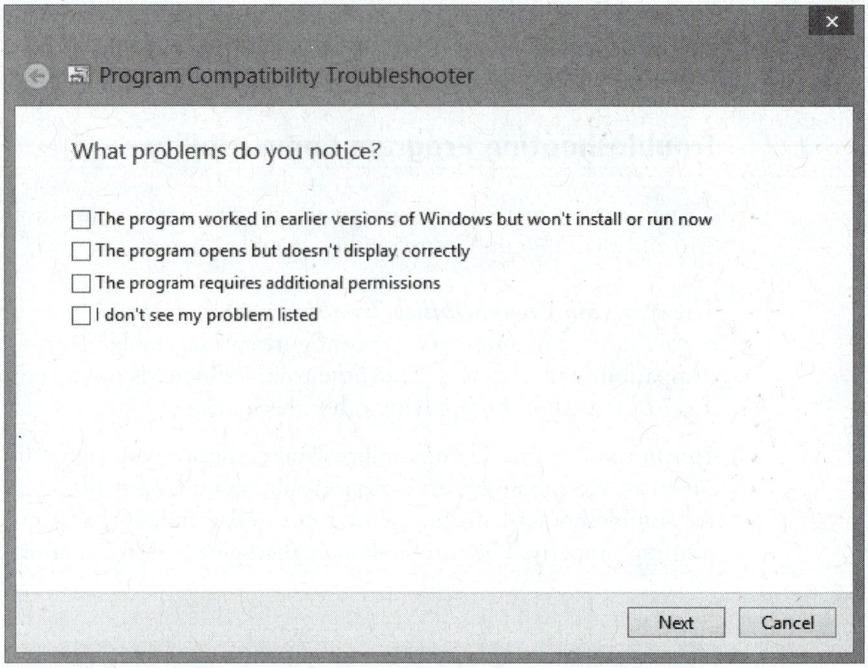

Figure 5-11

The *What problems do you notice?* page in the Program Compatibility Troubleshooter

Setting Compatibility Modes

The Program Compatibility Troubleshooter is essentially a wizard that simplifies the process of selecting compatibility mode settings for an executable. However, you can also configure those same compatibility mode settings manually.

CERTIFICATION READY
Set compatibility mode
Objective 2.2

To configure the ***compatibility mode*** settings for an application, you must open the Properties sheet for the application's executable file (or a shortcut pointing to that executable file) and select the Compatibility tab, as shown in Figure 5-12.

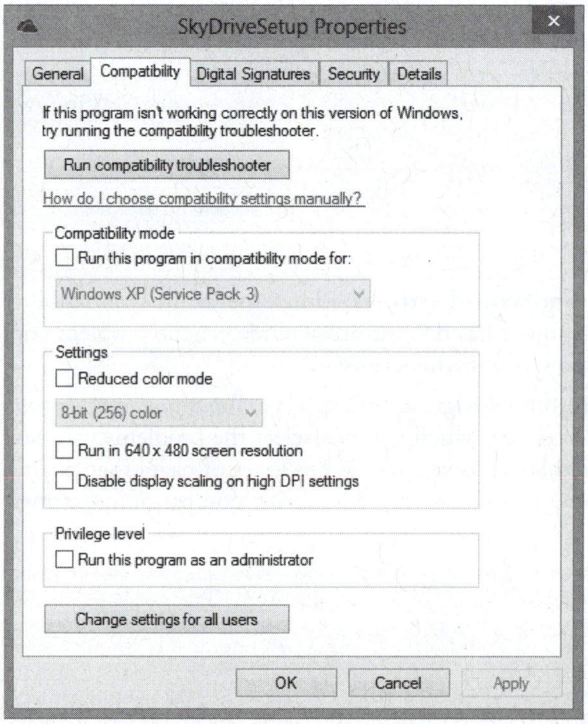

Figure 5-12

The *Compatibility* tab of an executable's Properties sheet

Selecting the *Run the program in compatibility mode for* checkbox, you can select a previous version of Windows from the drop-down list, under which you were able to run the program successfully. The Windows emulation modes are as follows:

- Windows 95
- Windows 98 / Windows Me
- Windows XP (Service Pack 2)
- Windows XP (Service Pack 3)
- Windows Vista
- Windows Vista (Service Pack 1)
- Windows Vista (Service Pack 2)
- Windows 7

This setting does not emulate the earlier operating system versions in every way, so the successful execution of the program is not guaranteed, but in many cases, applications that do not run properly in Windows 8 can run with this setting enabled.

In addition to the version emulations, you can also select any or all of the following compatibility mode settings:

- **Reduced color modes** – Causes the program to run with an 8-bit or 16-bit color depth
- **Run in 640 x 480 screen resolution** – Causes the program to run at a limited screen resolution
- **Disable display scaling on high DPI images** – Disables application resizing due to large font sizes
- **Run this program as an administrator** – Executes the program with elevated privileges

By default, the executable or shortcut you select retains the compatibility mode settings for the user currently logged on. You can also click *Change settings for all users* to apply the same settings to all of the computers users.

Configuring Application Compatibility Policies

The Program Compatibility Troubleshooter, and to some extent the compatibility mode settings themselves, are designed to be easily accessible and understandable to the end user. However, in some enterprise network environments, administrators manage compatibility issues themselves, and would prefer that users not see Windows 8 compatibility warnings.

To suppress application compatibility warnings, administrators can use the Group Policy settings located in a GPO at Computer Configuration\Administrative Templates\System\Troubleshooting and Diagnostics\Application Compatibility Diagnostics, as shown in Figure 5-13.

Figure 5-13

The *Application Compatibility Diagnostics* Group Policy settings

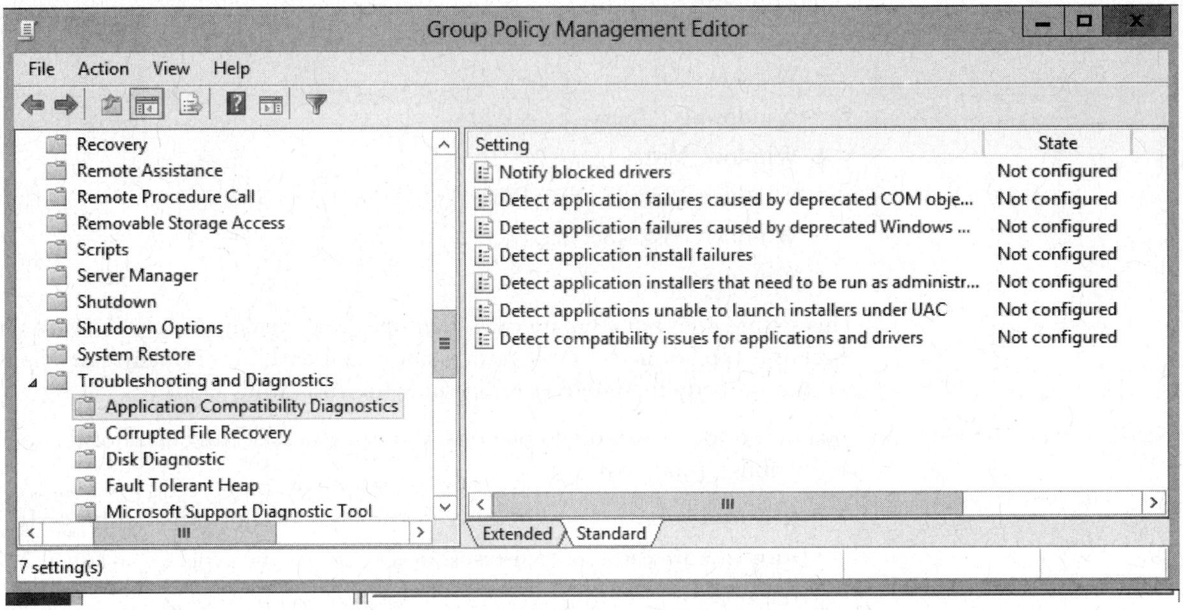

The Application Compatibility Diagnostics settings are as follows:

- **Notify blocked drivers** – Specifies whether the ***Program Compatibility Assistant (PCA)*** should notify users when drivers are blocked for compatibility reasons
- **Detect application failures caused by deprecated com objects** – Specifies whether the PCA should attempt to detect the creation of COM objects that no longer exist in Windows 8
- **Detect application failures caused by deprecated windows DLLs** – Specifies whether the PCA should detect attempts to load DLLs that no longer exist in Windows 8
- **Detect application install failures** – Specifies whether the PCA should attempt to detect application installation failures and prompt to restart the installation in compatibility mode
- **Detect application installers that need to be run as administrator** – Specifies whether the PCA should detect application installations that fail due to a lack of administrative privileges and prompt to restart the installation as an administrator
- **Detect applications unable to launch installers under UAC** – Specifies whether the PCA should detect the failure of child installer processes to launch due to the lack of elevated privileges
- **Detect compatibility issues for applications and drivers** – Specifies whether the PCA should detect failures during application installation and runtime, and drivers blocked due to compatibility issues

Administrators can also limit users' access to compatibility mode controls using Group Policy. These settings are located in Computer Configuration\Administrative Templates\Windows Components\Application Compatibility, as shown in Figure 5-14.

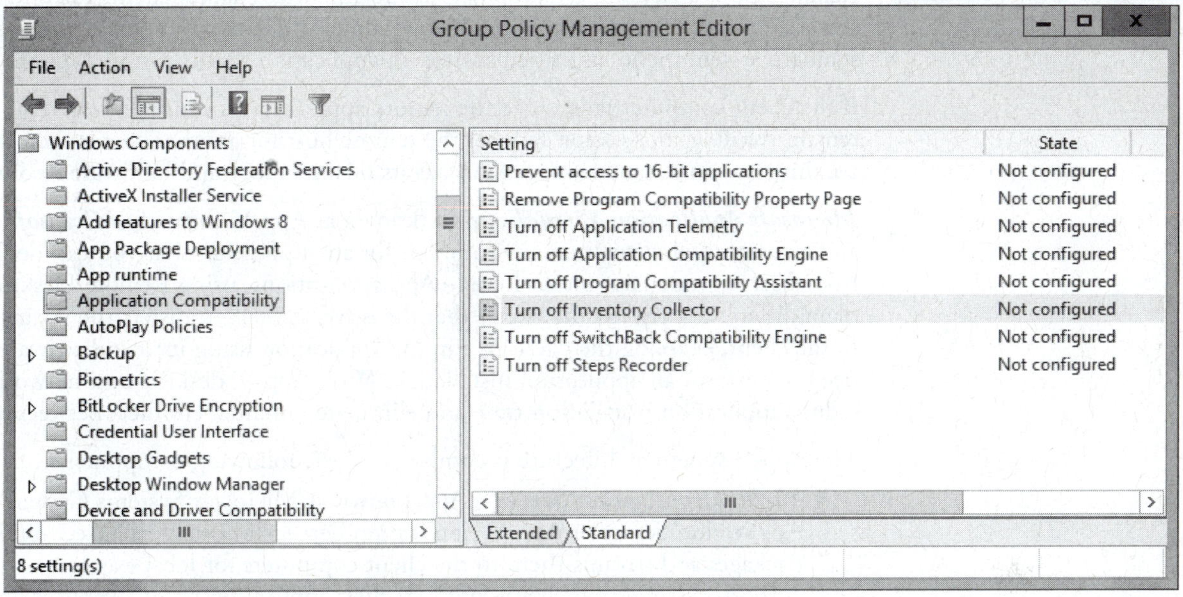

Figure 5-14

The *Application Compatibility* Group Policy settings

- **Prevent access to 16-bit applications** – Disables the MS-DOS subsystem on the computer, preventing 16-bit applications from running.
- **Remove Program Compatibility Property Page** – Removes the Compatibility tab from the Properties sheets of executables and shortcuts.
- **Turn off Application Telemetry** – Disables the application telemetry engine, which tracks anonymous usage of Windows system components by applications.
- **Turn off Application Compatibility Engine** – Prevents the computer from looking up applications in the compatibility database, boosting system performance but possible affecting the execution of legacy applications.
- **Turn off Program Compatibility Assistant** – Disables the PCA, preventing the system from displaying compatibility warnings during application installations and start-ups.
- **Turn off Inventory Collector** – Prevents the system from inventorying applications, files, devices, and drivers on the system and sending the resulting information to Microsoft.
- **Turn off Switchback Compatibility Engine** – Prevents the computer from providing generic compatibility mitigations to older applications, thus boosting performance.
- **Turn off Steps Recorder** – Prevents the computer from capturing the steps taken by the user.

Virtualizing Applications Using App-V

THE BOTTOM LINE

Windows Server 2012 and Windows 8 both can use Hyper-V to virtualize entire operating systems, but it is also possible to virtualize individual applications.

When you ***virtualize*** an operating system, you create a separate partitioned space with virtual resources that appear just like physical ones to users and applications. You can run as many applications as you need on a single virtual machine, depending on the resources available to it.

CERTIFICATION READY
Manage App-V applications
Objective 2.2

Virtualizing an application is roughly the same thing, except that you are allocating a set of virtual resources to a single application.

RemoteApp is a Remote Desktop Services feature that enables clients to run Remote Desktop server applications within an individual window. While the Windows is resizable and has a standard system menu and title bar, it is an application that is running on another computer.

If the client computer fails, since the remote application is running on a remote host, it will remain running. If a session fails on the remote host for another client, the other sessions continue to run because each session has its own memory and hardware resources.

Microsoft Application Virtualization (known as App-V, formerly ***Microsoft SoftGrid***) creates a customized virtualized environment for an application that you can deploy to clients from a server, much as you do RemoteApp applications, using Remote Desktop servers. The main difference between the two is that the server actually transfers the virtual environment to the client, enabling the client to run the application using its own hardware, without the need to perform an application installation. With App-V, desktop and network users can reduce application installation time and eliminate potential conflicts between applications.

The App-V system architecture is composed of the following components:

- ***Virtual Application Server*** – Also known as Microsoft Systems Center Virtual Application Server or App-V Application Server. It hosts virtualized application packages and streams them to the client computers for local execution. It also authorizes requesting clients and logs their application usage. Applications are converted to virtualized packages using the App-V Sequencer.
- ***Application Virtualization Client*** – Also known as Microsoft Application Virtualization Client for Windows Desktops or Microsoft Application Virtualization Client for Remote Session Hosts, as shown in Figure 5-15. It is the client side runtime that requests the application server to stream some application, receives the streamed virtual application packages, sets up the runtime environment and executes the applications locally.

Figure 5-15

The *Application Virtualization Client*

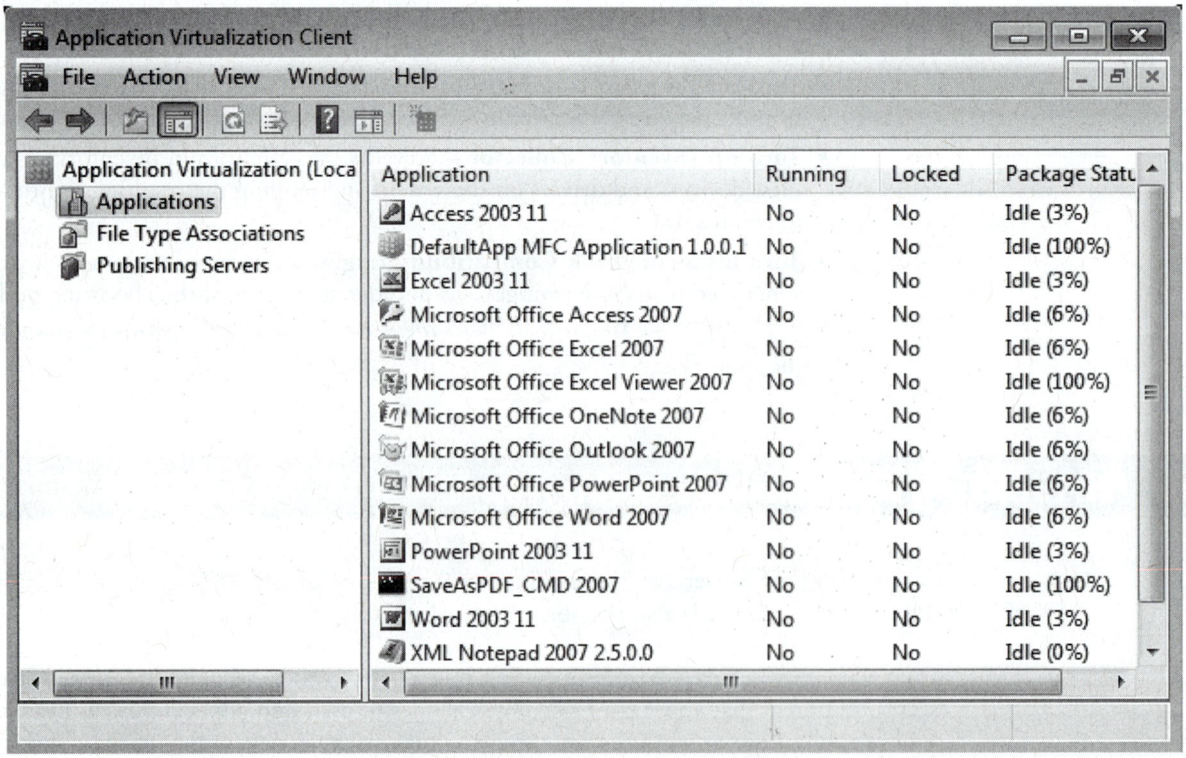

- ***Application Virtualization Management Console*** – The management console to set up, administer and manage App-V servers, as shown in Figure 5-16. It can also be used to create, manage, update and replicate virtualized application packages.

Figure 5-16

The *Application Virtualization Management Console*

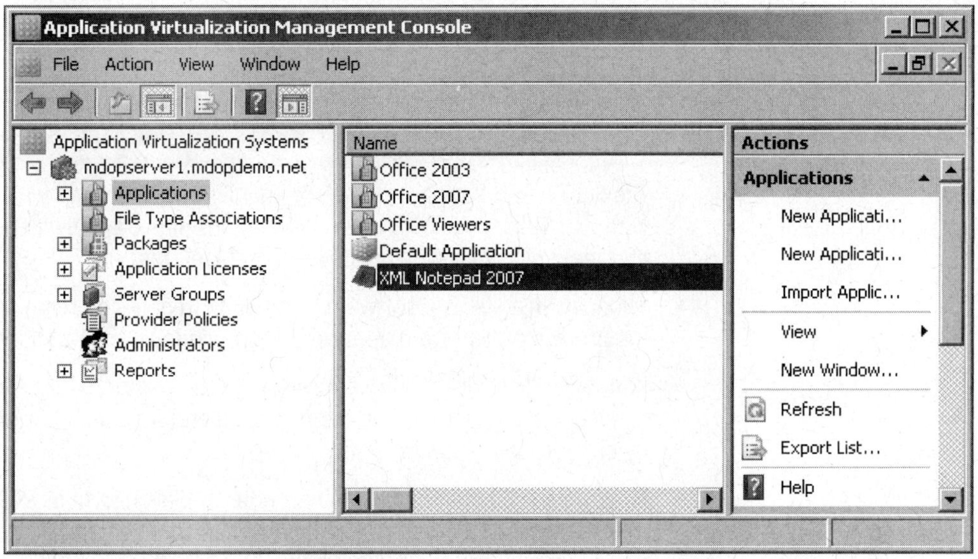

- ***Application Virtualization Sequencer*** – A tool for preparing applications for virtualization, as shown in Figure 5-17.

Figure 5-17

The *Microsoft Application Virtualization Sequencer*

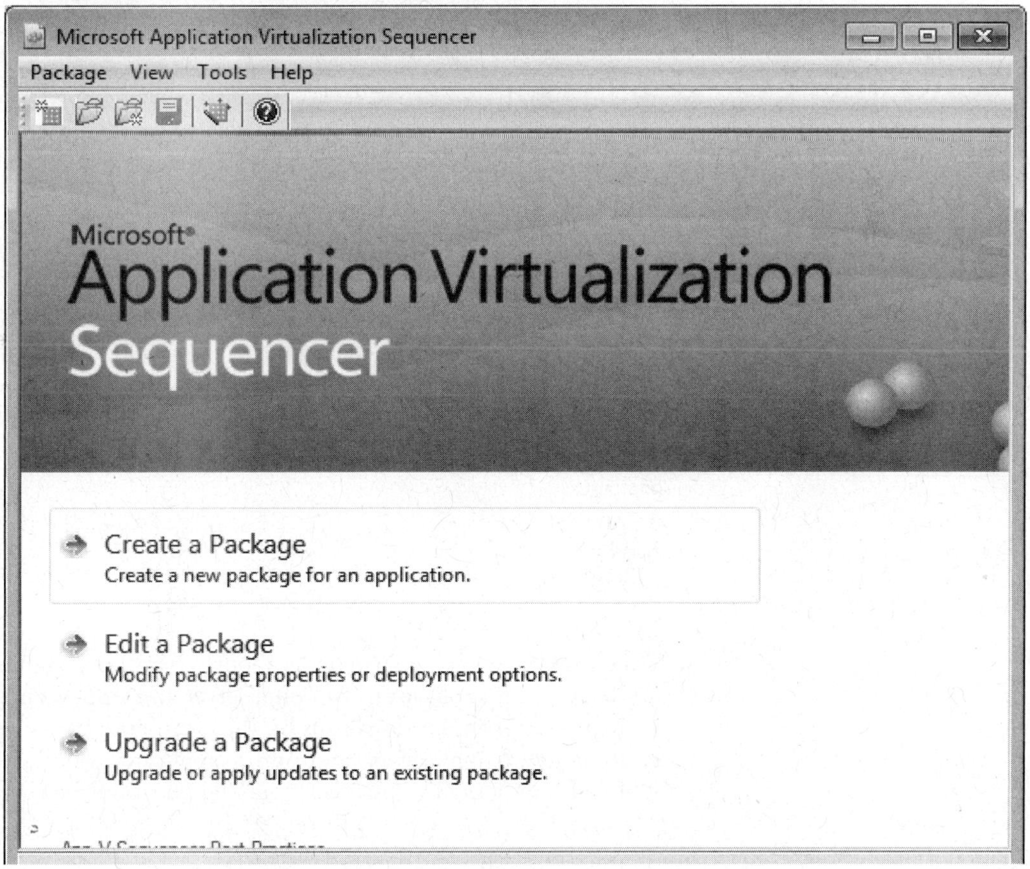

- **Application Virtualization Datastore** – Maintains application information in a SQL Server database.

When planning the deployment of App-V, since WAN links are generally too slow, you should ensure that each branch office has its own Virtual Application server.

SKILL SUMMARY

IN THIS LESSON, YOU LEARNED:

- The Set Default Programs interface enables you to specify which file types are associated with an application. With these associations in place, a user can simply double-click a file, and the application will launch itself and load that file.
- Windows Installer is a software installation, repair, and removal engine that can simplify the process of deploying applications on Windows computers.
- Windows 8 includes a number of new security features that can alter the ability of certain applications to run. Administrators must therefore take measures to ensure the compatibility of their legacy applications.
- The Program Compatibility Troubleshooter is designed to be easily accessible and understandable to the end user. However, in some enterprise network environments, administrators manage compatibility issues themselves.
- App-V creates a customized virtualized environment for an application that you can deploy to clients from a server, much as you do RemoteApp applications, using Remote Desktop servers.

■ Knowledge Assessment

Multiple Choice

Select one or more correct answers for each of the following questions.

1. Which of the following is not an emulation mode supported by Windows 8?
   a. Windows 2000
   b. Windows 95
   c. Windows 98
   d. Windows XP SP2
   e. Windows Vista
2. Which of the following is the file name extension associated with Windows Installer packages?
   a. exe
   b. com
   c. msi
   d. win
3. Which of the following statements about server-based application deployment is true?
   a. RemoteApp applications run on a server and App-V applications run on the client.
   b. RemoteApp applications runs on the client and App-V applications run on the server.
   c. RemoteApp applications and App-V applications both run on the server.
   d. RemoteApp applications and App-V applications both run on the client.

4. Which of the following controls are intended for use by the Windows 8 end user? (Choose all that apply.)
   a. Program Compatibility Troubleshooter
   b. Application Compatibility Policies
   c. Application Virtualization Sequencer
   d. Compatibility mode

5. Which of the following is not one of the links in the Default Programs control panel?
   a. Set your default programs
   b. Associate a file type or protocol with a program
   c. Change Autoplay settings
   d. Set program access and computer defaults
   e. Change Windows Installer Properties

6. Which of the following tasks is Windows Installer not capable of performing? (Choose all that apply.)
   a. Installing an application on the local system
   b. Deploying an application on multiple remote systems
   c. Repairing an application the local system
   d. Uninstalling an application on a remote system

7. Which of the following are Windows 8 mechanisms that can prevent older applications from running properly? (Choose all that apply.)
   a. Data execution prevention
   b. Security zones
   c. Mandatory integrity control
   d. Microsoft Application Virtualization

Matching and Identification

Complete the following exercise by matching the terms with their corresponding definitions.

_______ a) Application Virtualization Sequencer
_______ b) Compatibility mode
_______ c) File association
_______ d) Autoplay default
_______ e) Program access default
_______ f) Windows Installer
_______ g) Application Virtualization Datastore
_______ h) Virtual Application Server
_______ i) Application Compatibility Policies
_______ j) Program Compatibility Troubleshooter

1. Packages applications and installation instructions
2. Launches applications based on file name extensions
3. Can prevent users from seeing compatibility warnings
4. A SQL Server
5. Packages applications for deployment to clients
6. Associates an application with a specific task
7. Supports applications designed for older operating systems
8. Streams applications to clients
9. Controls what happens when you insert a removable medium
10. Wizard-based solution for outdated applications

Best Answer

1. Which of the following is the most likely situation in which an administrator might want to modify the file associations on Windows 8 workstations?
   a. When he has just deployed an application with a unique file name extension
   b. When the workstations have two or more applications installed that can open the same file type
   c. When there are two applications with different file types that use the same file name extension
   d. When an application can open multiple file types

2. Which of the following is the most logical reason for changing the default Autoplay settings?
   a. To prevent a media sharing system from automatically playing movie DVDs when you insert them
   b. To prevent burner software from writing to a DVD using a CD format
   c. To enforce DVD-ROM burning standards.
   d. To use Windows Installer to install the application on the removable medium.

3. Which of the following is the best command to use to deploy a Windows Installer package and restart the workstation without any interaction from the user?
   a. Msiexec.exe app.msi /n
   b. Msiexec.exe app.msi /passive /n
   c. Msiexec.exe app.msi /quiet /restart
   d. Msiexec.exe app.msi /quiet /n /forcerestart

4. Which of the following Program Compatibility Troubleshooter problems could most likely be resolved by changing the application's compatibility mode?
   a. The program worked in earlier versions of Windows but won't install or run now.
   b. The program opens but doesn't display correctly
   c. The program requires additional permissions
   d. I don't see my problem listed

Build a List

1. Place the following steps of an App-V application deployment in the correct order.
   _______ **a)** Create an App-V package using the Application Virtualization Sequencer
   _______ **b)** Execute the App-V package using the Application Virtualization Client
   _______ **c)** Use the Virtual Application Server to stream the App-V package to the client
   _______ **d)** Save the App-V package to the Application Virtualization Datastore

2. Place the following steps of a Windows 7 File Recovery backup procedure in the correct order.
   _______ **a)** Click Save on a network
   _______ **b)** Supply the path to the network share
   _______ **c)** Select what you want to back up
   _______ **d)** Specify the time of day that you want the job to run.
   _______ **e)** Click Set up backup.
   _______ **f)** Click Save settings and run backup
   _______ **g)** Launch Windows 7 File Recovery
   _______ **h)** Click change schedule.
   _______ **i)** Supply credentials to access the share
   _______ **j)** Specify whether you want the job to run daily, weekly, or monthly
   _______ **k)** Specify the day of the week or the monthly date that you want the job to run.

Business Case Scenario

Scenario 5-1: Application Errors

Alice is the help desk supervisor at Wingtip Toys, Ltd. and she has noticed an increasing number of similar help calls from users in the company's main office. The users are all running Windows 8 on their workstations, and many of the complaints involve errors writing data to specific memory addresses, the type of errors not often seen in Windows 8. After examining the errors in Event Viewer and looking a one of the computers involved, Alice determines that a group of users in the main office are running old games that were designed on MS-DOS and Windows 95. All of the authorized applications on the workstations are designed to run on Windows 8.

How can Alice prevent all of the main office users from running this downlevel software without having to create rules excluding each game individually?

Alice should create a Group Policy object containing the following policies in the Computer Configuration\Administrative Templates\Windows Components\Application Compatibility folder, and then link the GPO to the domain containing the offending users and their computers.

- Prevent access to 16-bit applications: Enable
- Remove Program Compatibility Property Page: Enable
- Turn off Switchback Compatibility Engine: Enable

6 LESSON

Installing and Configuring Windows Store Applications

70-687 EXAM OBJECTIVE

Objective 2.3 – Install and configure Windows Store applications. This objective may include but is not limited to Store applications; install, reinstall, and update Windows; restrict Windows Store content; add internal content (side loading); and disable Windows Store.

LESSON HEADING	EXAM OBJECTIVE
Installing and Configuring Windows Store Apps	
Installing, Reinstalling, and Updating Windows Store Apps	Install, reinstall, and update Windows Store applications
Restricting Access to the Windows Store Content	Restrict Windows Store content
Adding Internal Content (Side Loading)	Add internal content (side loading)
Disabling the Windows Store	Disable Windows Store

KEY TERMS

Application Identity service
app listing page
AppLocker
Bring Your Own Device (BYOD) policy
Deployment Imaging Servicing and Management (DISM.exe)
Group Policy Management console (gpmc.msc)
Group Policy object (GPO)
line of business (LOB) apps
Local Group Policy editor (gpedit.msc)
Local Security Policy editor (secpol.msc)
Microsoft account
provisioned apps
purchase page
Remote Server Administration Tools (RSAT) for Windows 8
rule collections
side loading
Windows apps
Windows Store

Installing and Configuring Windows Store Apps

THE BOTTOM LINE

The Windows Store is a central location for purchasing and downloading thousands of new apps for Windows 8 devices. Understanding the process for installing, updating, and configuring apps as well as managing access to the Windows Store is critical when it comes to not only supporting your users but aligning their needs with your company's policies.

The ***Windows Store*** is Microsoft's central location for distributing and purchasing apps. It provides access to both traditional apps as well as Windows apps (e.g., packaged apps). ***Windows apps*** use the new Windows user interface (UI) designed to display and work across Windows 8 devices with different form factors and display sizes.

There are currently thousands of Windows 8 apps available within the store, and the number is continuing to grow on a daily basis. Each of these apps must meet a certain benchmark for quality and functionality to be placed in the store.

With so many apps to choose from, why not just open them up to everyone? If you're using a Windows 8 device for personal use at home, there might be no reason to restrict access to the Store or the apps. On the other hand, if you bring that same device or use additional company-supplied devices in your work environment, your company most likely has a ***Bring Your Own Device (BYOD) policy***. A BYOD policy defines the standards, restrictions, and procedures for end users who have authorized access to company data from their personal device (such as tablet, laptop, and smartphone). The policy also includes hardware and related software not approved, owned, or supplied by the company.

As an administrator, it is your responsibility to configure and manage access to the Windows Store to align with these policies.

In this lesson, you learn about the process for installing, uninstalling, reinstalling, and updating your Windows Store apps, explore the options for restricting access to Windows Store content, learn how to install apps directly to a device without going through the Windows Store (for example, side loading), and discover the steps you can use to disable the Windows Store.

Installing, Reinstalling, and Updating Windows Store Apps

To install, reinstall, and update Windows Store apps, you need a Microsoft account and an Internet connection. Using a Microsoft User account allows you to not only access Windows Store apps but synchronize key files and settings in the cloud and across multiple Windows 8 devices providing a consistent look/feel and access to the same content on all your devices.

Before you can install an app from the Windows Store, you need a Microsoft account and an Internet connection. A ***Microsoft account*** (formerly called *Windows Live ID*) includes an email address and a password that allows you to sign in to all Microsoft sites and services. If you don't have one, you can either create a new Microsoft account or use an existing email address you already have.

CERTIFICATION READY
Install, reinstall, and update Windows Store applications
Objective 2.3

Setting up a Microsoft account allows you to download apps from the Windows Store and sync settings across your other Windows 8 devices.

The process for setting up a Microsoft is as follows:

1. Move your mouse to the upper-right corner of your desktop and click *Settings*.
2. Click *Change PC Settings*.

3. Select *Users.*
4. Click *Add a user.*
5. Type the email address you want use or sign up for a new email address.
6. Click *Finish.*

You can also set up a Microsoft account by visiting the Microsoft website and enter the search phrase "Microsoft account sign up."

Once your account is created, you're ready to browse, download, and install apps from the Windows Store.

INSTALLING AND UNINSTALLING WINDOWS STORE APPS

You can visit the Windows Store landing page by clicking the Store tile on the Windows 8 *Start* screen (see Figure 6-1). It should be noted that the Windows Store tile is not installed on a graphical user interface (GUI) installation of Windows Server 2012 by default but can be added via Server Manager > Add Roles and Features.

Figure 6-1

Accessing the Windows Store

Once on the Store landing page, you find free and paid apps grouped into categories such as Spotlight, Games, Social, Photo, Books & Reference, Productivity Tools, Business, and News & Weather. These categories are visible across the top of the screen with each category featuring selected apps of interest. Each group is further divided into the subcategories: paid, free, and new releases.

If you're not looking for a specific app, you can simply browse through the categories to find a program that interests you. If you know the type of app you want or the name of the app, start typing the word while inside the Store. For example, if you type *calculator,* the Charms bar automatically opens and provides you with several apps that match your search criteria (see Figure 6-2).

Figure 6-2

Searching the Windows Store

Another approach is to select the Windows logo key + Q to open the Search function while working in Windows 8 to search for apps.

Searching within the Windows Store automatically sets the context to Store; searching from outside the store requires that you set the context to Store to limit your query to that location.

Each app is represented by a tile that once selected, takes you to a ***purchase page*** (also called an ***app listing page***). From there you can gather information such as the app's download size, its publisher, and a detailed description of its features (see Figure 6-3).

Figure 6-3

Viewing an app's purchase page

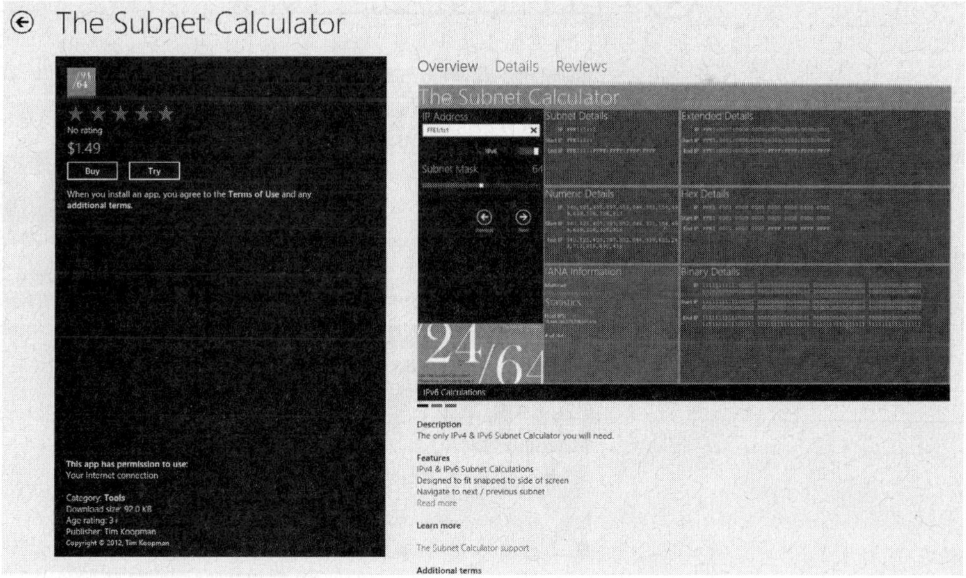

After reviewing the details on the app listing page, you are ready to start the installation. For free apps, it's pretty simple… click *Install.* For paid apps, you select either the *Try* link or the *Buy* link. Selecting *Buy* asks that you confirm the purchase. Enter your Microsoft account password and then prompt you for a payment method. After selecting the app, you're automatically taken back to the previous page to explore others. Selecting a free app also starts the installation and returns you to the previous page.

Once the installation completes, you receive a notification message. If you click the message, you can use the app immediately; otherwise, you will find a tile for the app on your Windows 8 *Start* screen.

If you decide after using the app that you no longer need it, you can right-click the app's tile and choose Uninstall from the menu that appears along the bottom of the Windows *Start* screen.

REINSTALLING WINDOWS STORE APPS

Each time you install a Windows app on a device, it's saved to your Microsoft account and the device is added to the list of devices allowed to run it. This provides you with two capabilities. First, you can install the app on up to five Windows 8 devices using the same account. Second, if you uninstall a Windows App, you can reinstall it quickly. The steps you use to install an app on additional Windows 8 devices and reinstall the app you removed on your existing device are the same.

INSTALL OR REINSTALL AN APP

GET READY. To install or reinstall an app, perform the following steps:

1. Press the Windows logo key to open the Windows 8 Start menu and click the **Store** tile to browse to the Windows Store.
2. Right-click and choose **Your Apps**.
3. Click **Apps not installed on this PC** (see Figure 6-4).

Figure 6-4

Identifying *Apps not installed on this PC*

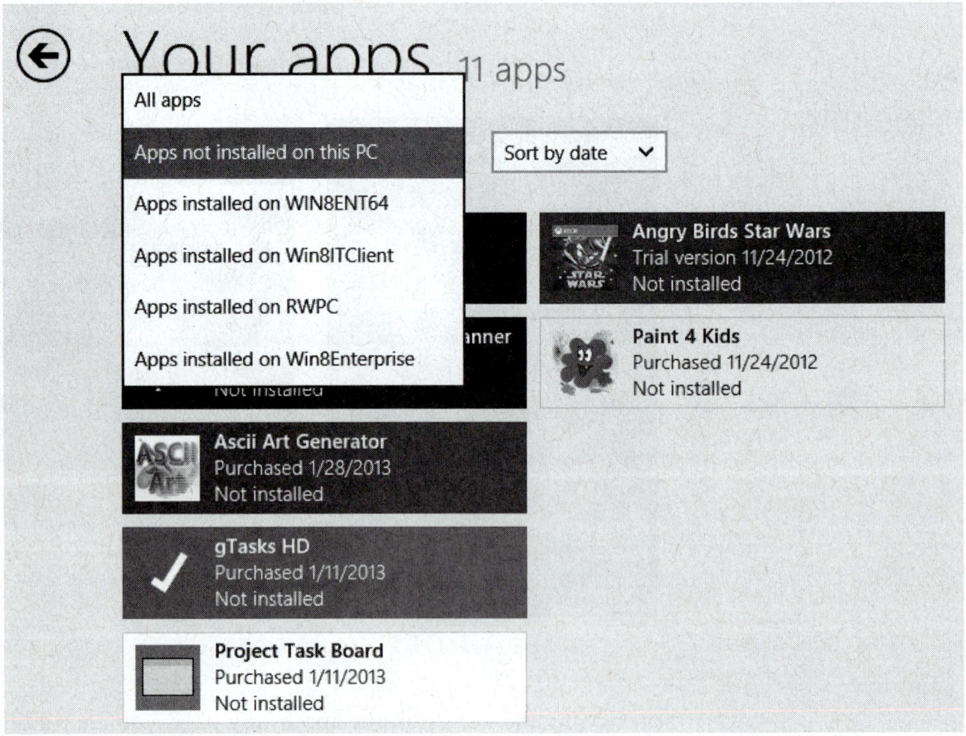

4. Select the app(s) you want to install.
5. Click **Install**.

If you reach the maximum number of devices, you will need to remove one of them to add the app to a new device. You can do this by performing the steps in the next exercise.

REMOVE AN APP

GET READY. To remove an app, perform the following steps:

1. Press the **Windows logo key** to open the Windows 8 Start menu and then click the **Store** tile to browse to the Windows Store.
2. Move your mouse to the upper-right corner and click **Settings**.
3. Click **Your Account**.
4. Select the PC you want to remove from your Microsoft account.
5. Click **Remove**.

UPDATING WINDOWS STORE APPS

On a daily basis, Microsoft checks to see whether there are any updates for the apps you've previously downloaded from the Windows Store. If any are found, a number indicator appears on the Store tile as shown in Figure 6-5. In this example, there are three updates ready to be installed.

Figure 6-5

Reviewing the notification of Store Updates

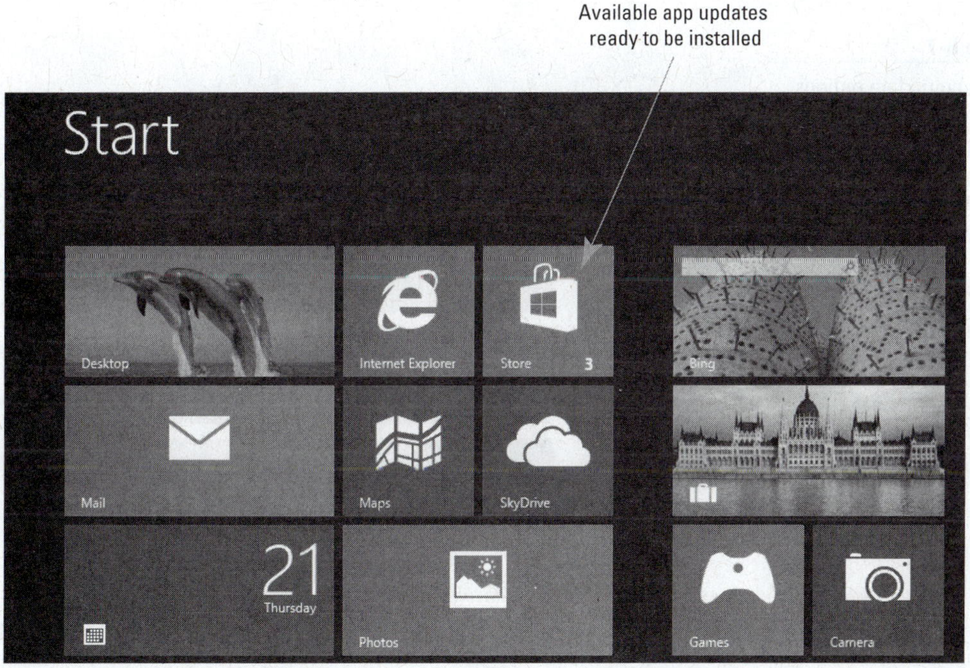

To see the actual apps requiring updates, click the *Store* tile. After you're connected to the Store, locate the updates by selecting the *Updates* link (see Figure 6-6).

Figure 6-6
Selecting the Updates link

By default, all updates are selected automatically and clicking *Install* starts the update process (see Figure 6-7). If for some reason you don't want to update all your apps at one time, you can click or touch each app to exclude it.

Figure 6-7
Managing update options

By default, Windows 8 is configured to download Windows app updates (but not install them) automatically in the background when your device is idle. If you don't want this to occur, you need to either change the appropriate setting on the Windows 8 device or use Group Policy to control the setting.

On a Windows 8 device, you can turn off the automatic download updates for apps by performing the steps in the following exercise.

DISABLE AUTOMATIC DOWNLOAD UPDATES FROM WITHIN THE WINDOWS STORE APP

GET READY. To disable the automatic download updates for apps, perform the following steps:

1. Press the **Windows logo key** to open the Windows 8 Start menu and then click the **Store** tile to browse to the Windows Store.
2. Move your mouse to the upper-right corner and then click **Settings**.
3. Click **App Updates**.
4. Move the slider all the way to the left to set it to **No** (see Figure 6-8).

Figure 6-8

Turning off *Apps updates* on Windows 8

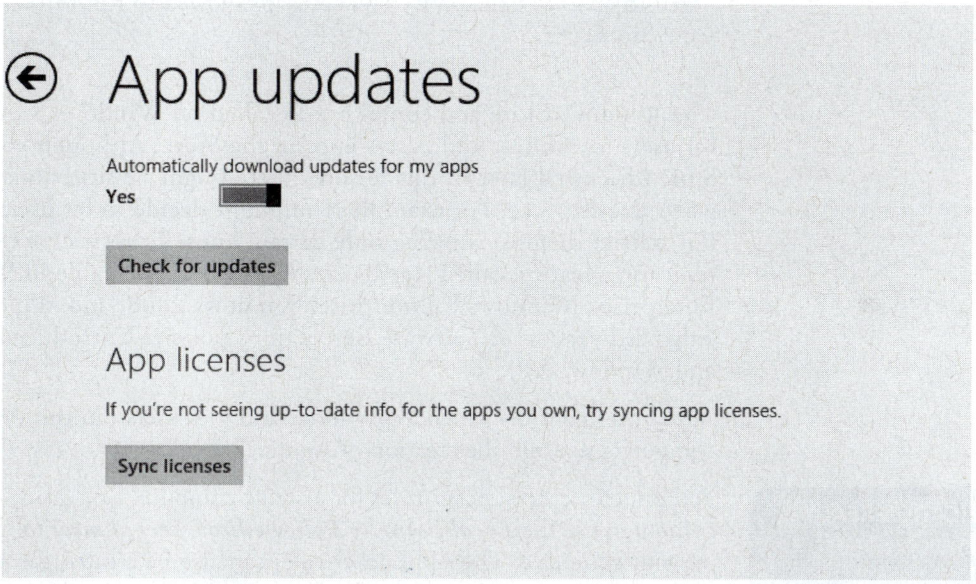

To change the setting through Group Policy, you can use either the ***Local Group Policy editor (gpedit.msc)*** or the ***Group Policy Management console (gpmc.msc)***. Both are Microsoft Management consoles but differ in their overall scope. The Local Group Policy configures Group Policy settings on a local computer whereas the Group Policy Management console provides you with a single administrative interface that can be used to configure Group Policy across your entire enterprise.

DISABLE AUTOMATIC DOWNLOAD UPDATES USING THE LOCAL GROUP POLICY EDITOR

GET READY. To disable automatic updates by using the Local Group Policy editor (gpedit.msc), perform the following steps:

1. Press the **Windows logo key + r**.
2. In the *Run* dialog box, type **gpedit.msc**.
3. Click **Computer Configuration > Administrative Templates > Windows Components > Store**.
4. Double-click **Turn off Automatic Download of updates**.
5. For the policy setting, select **Enabled**.

To disable the same setting for multiple Windows 8 client computers across your entire enterprise, use the Group Policy Management console (gpmc.msc), create a new GPO, and access the policy setting located at *Computer Configuration > Administrative Templates > Windows Components > Store*.

TAKE NOTE*

The Group Policy Management tool is available through the ***Remote Server Administration Tools (RSAT) for Windows 8***. RSAT allows you to remotely manage roles and features in Windows Server 2012. Some of the tools can be used to manage Windows Server 2008/2008R2 and 2003 from a computer running Windows 8.

Restricting Access to the Windows Store Content

You can restrict access to the Windows Store content by using AppLocker, which can be used to control which Windows apps are allowed to run through the configuration of rules and properties.

The Windows Store app comes pre-installed on Windows 8 devices, which makes it easy for users to connect and access apps in the Store. Although you can disable access to the Store (discussed later in this lesson), there might be situations where you don't want to go to that extreme. For example, you might decide to let users access the Windows Store but restrict them to running only certain apps. To restrict access to Windows Store content, use a feature called *AppLocker*. AppLocker (available in Windows 7 (Ultimate/Enterprise), Windows 8 Enterprise, Windows 2008, and Windows Server 2012) is an enhanced version of Software Restrictions policies (introduced in Windows Server 2003 and Windows XP).

AppLocker controls which applications and files users can run on their Windows 8 client computers through the creation of AppLocker rules.

CERTIFICATION READY
Restrict Windows Store content
Objective 2.3

You can create AppLocker rules for a single computer or a group of computers. For a single computer, use the ***Local Security Policy editor (secpol.msc)*** to modify local security settings on your computer. The AppLocker rules can also be created through the Local Group Policy editor (gpedit.msc) because the AppLocker rules are accessible through the Windows Settings > Security settings folder.

You create AppLocker rules for a group of computers by using the Group Policy Management console (GPMC) within a ***Group Policy object (GPO)***. A GPO is a group of settings that define how a computer will behave for a group of users. The GPO can then be associated with a selected Active Directory container (for example, site, domain, and organizational unit) that includes the users and/or computers you want to apply it to. If you are in an enterprise environment, you can use GPMC to create and apply the policy to a single computer. This allows you to easily expand the rules to more computers as they are purchased in the future.

TAKE NOTE*

AppLocker requires the ***Application Identity service***, which is used to determine and verify the identity of an application. This service should be configured to start automatically.

The AppLocker Microsoft Management console is organized into four areas (executable files, scripts, Windows installer files, and packaged apps) called ***rule collections***. These rule collections allow you to differentiate the rules for different types of applications. AppLocker uses rules and a file's properties to determine whether applications are allowed to run. A traditional app consists of several components (such as exe, dll's, and scripts) that might not share the same publisher, product, or product version attribute. To manage the traditional app, AppLocker needs to control them using different rule collections. On the other hand, a Windows app (packaged app) shares the same attributes; therefore, you can create a single rule to control the entire application.

Rule collections include the following:

- Executable files (.exe, .com)
- Scripts (.ps2, .bat, .js, .cmd, vbs)
- Windows Installer files (.msi, .mst, .msp)
- Appx (Packaged apps and Packaged app installers) (.appx)—This includes Windows apps and sideloaded line of business (LOB) apps.

By default, there are no rules in any of the rule collections; therefore, AppLocker allows every file covered in each collection to run.

TAKE NOTE*

When working with packaged apps, you are limited to applying the AppLocker policies to Windows Server 2012/Windows 8. Rules created for traditional apps can be used to control Windows Server 2012/2008/2008R2 and Windows 7.

When creating rules with AppLocker, you have the following options:

- **Create New Rule:** This wizard walks you through the process of creating one AppLocker rule at a time. You set permissions, publishers, and exceptions, and provide a name for the rule.
- **Automatically Generate Rules:** This wizard allows you to create rules for multiple packaged apps in a single step. You can select a folder and let the wizard create the applicable rules for the files in the folder, or for packaged apps create rules for all Windows apps on your computer.
- **Create Default Rules:** This wizard creates a single rule that allows the Everyone group to run packaged apps that are signed. You can then use the Exception tab to deny access to specific apps.

The Create Default Rules option is meant to ensure that some key Windows paths are allowed for execution (c:\Windows or c:\Program files). If you create a rule and don't have the default rules created yet, Windows will prompt to you create the default rules.

When configuring exceptions for apps, you can also set the exceptions so that one or more Active Directory groups are allowed to run a specific app.

BLOCK A WINDOWS APP BY USING APP-LOCKER RULE

GET READY. To block specific Windows apps using the Automatically Generate Rules Wizard, log on to a Windows 8 system and then perform the following steps:

1. Press the **Windows logo key + r**.
2. In the *Run* box, type **compmgmt.msc** and then click **OK**.
3. In the left pane, expand **Services and Applications**.
4. Click **Services** and then double-click the **Application Identity service**.
5. Set the *Startup type* to **Automatic** and then click **OK**.
6. Close the *Computer Management* console.
7. Press the **Windows logo key + r**.
8. In the *Run* box, type **secpolicy.msc** and then click **OK**.
9. Click **Application Control Policies > AppLocker**.

10. Right-click **Packaged app Rules** and choose **Automatically Generate Rules**.
11. Select **Generate rules for all packaged apps installed on this computer** and then click **Next**.
12. On the *Rule Preference* screen, click **Next** and then click **Create**.

    AppLocker rules are created based on the apps that are installed on your PC (see Figure 6-9).

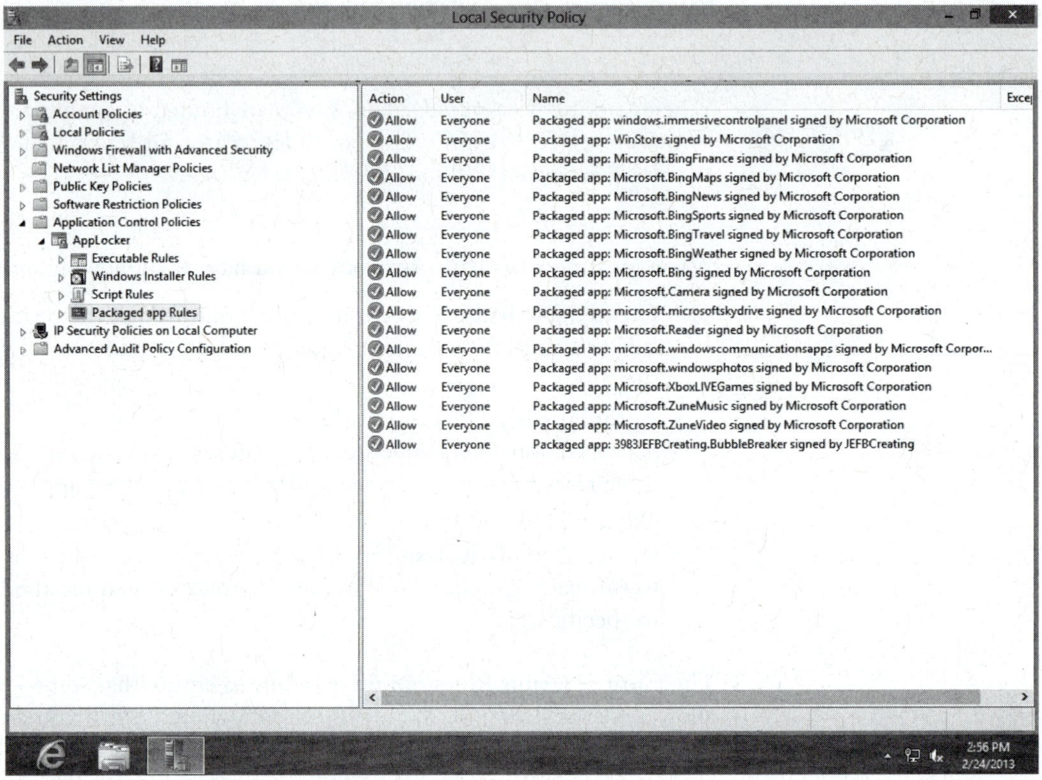

Figure 6-9

Reviewing AppLocker rules

13. Double-click the **Packaged app: Microsoft.BingSports signed by Microsoft Corporation** rule.
14. On the *General* tab, in the *Action* section, select **Deny** and then click **OK**.
15. Press the **Windows logo key** to toggle to the Windows 8 *Start* screen.
16. Click the **Sports** tile. The message shown in Figure 6-10 is displayed.

Figure 6-10

Blocking the Sports app

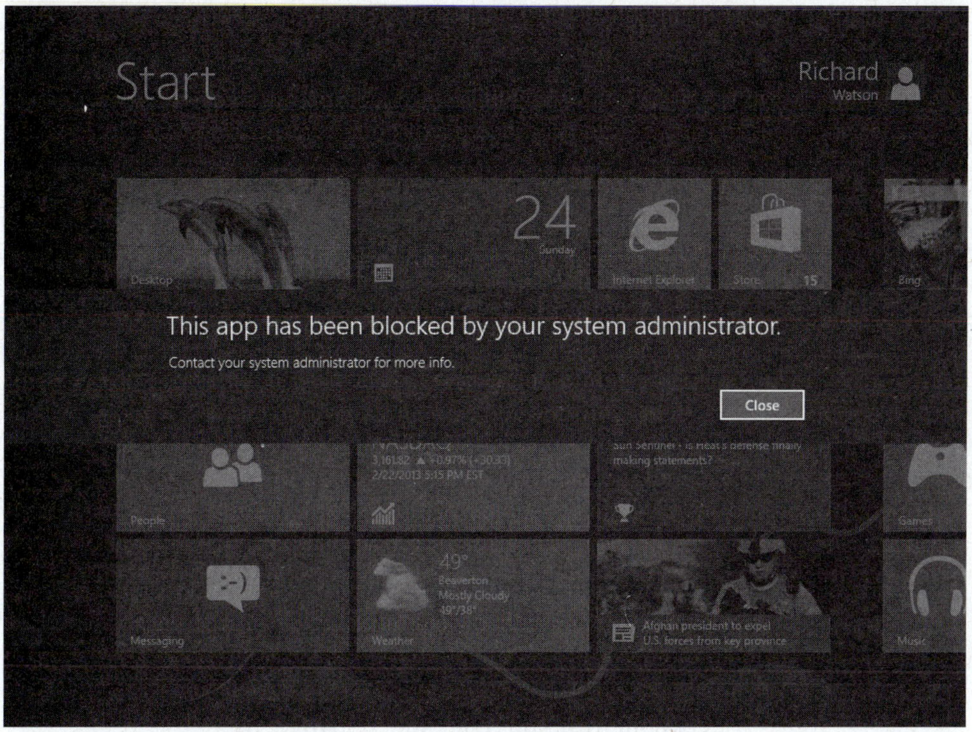

17. Click **Close**.

Adding Internal Content (Side Loading)

THE BOTTOM LINE

Side loading an app allows you to install a Windows app directly without publishing it to and downloading it from the Windows Store. Publishing an app to the Windows Store makes it available to the public.

Line of business (LOB) apps include apps that are critical to running the business of the company as well as apps that are unique to the main business of the company. If your organization has its own LOB apps, you have two options for installing them on devices running Windows RT, Windows 8 (Enterprise/Pro) and Windows Server 2012:

CERTIFICATION READY
Add internal content (side loading)
Objective 2.3

- Access the app through the Windows Store
- Side loading

To make the app available via the Windows Store, you need to adhere to certification policies and processes used by Microsoft to ensure the app is compatible and meets the criteria for apps deployed in the Store. By distributing your LOB app via the Windows Store, you also make it available publically to others outside your company.

To bypass the Store requirements and make your Windows app(s) available only to internal users, you can use a process called ***side loading***. Side loaded apps do not have to be certified by or installed through the Windows Store.

The following describes the basic steps for side loading an LOB app:

1. Create the Windows Store app using a tool such as Microsoft Visual Studio Express 2012 for Windows 8. This requires that you obtain a developer license.
2. Sign the app with a certificate that is chained to a trusted root certificate.

3. Confirm computers that will have the app side loaded on them are running Windows 8 Enterprise, they are joined to a domain, and the "Allow all trusted apps to install" Group Policy setting is enabled. For Windows 8 Enterprise and Windows 8 Professional computers not joined to the domain, you install a side loading product activation key. The side loading product activation key can be obtained from Microsoft's Volume Licensing Service Center (VLSC).
4. Side load the app using the `add-appxpackage "name of app"` command if you want it to be available for the current user or use the ***Deployment Imaging Servicing and Management (DISM.exe)*** tool. DISM is a command-line tool used to service an online or offline Windows image. Windows Apps installed via a Windows image are called ***provisioned apps***.

You can set Group Policy for a single Windows 8 computer by opening the Local Group Policy Editor and enabling the *Allow all trusted apps to install* group policy setting. It is located in the following location:

```
Computer Configuration\Administrative Templates\Windows Components\App
Package Deployment
```

To apply the policy to multiple computers, you can use the Group Policy Management console (GPMC). The *Allow all trusted apps to install* group policy setting is located in the following location:

```
Computer Configuration\Policies\Administrative Templates\Windows
Components\App Package Deployment
```

If you obtained a product activation key from the VLSC, you can add it by using the following commands from a command prompt while logged on as a local administrator. You need to run this command from an elevated command prompt.

To add the key:

```
Slmgr /ipk <sideloading product key>
```

To activate the key:

```
Slmgr /ato ec67814b-30e6-4a50-bf7b-d55daf729d1e
```

Once the computer is prepared, you can install the package on a per-user basis using the following Windows PowerShell command:

```
Add-Appxpackage -Path C:\<directory>\<Winappv1.appx>
```

To update the package at a later date, manually update the Windows App by using the following command:

```
Add-appxpackage -Path \\<servername>
<share>\<Winappv2.appx>
```

Disabling the Windows Store

THE BOTTOM LINE

To maintain control over the apps installed on Windows 8 computers, you can disable access to the Windows Store completely. This is common in corporate environments where you want to maintain consistency between computers in the domain and reduce the time and complexity of having to troubleshoot multiple configurations.

If your company policy dictates that access to the Windows Store should be disabled, you can easily configure it through the Local Group Policy editor (gpedit.msc) for a single computer or use GPMC if you are working in a domain-based environment.

CERTIFICATION READY
Disable Windows Store
Objective 2.3

When you create a Group Policy object, you see a User Configuration section and a Computer configuration section of the policy. Use the User Configuration section to set policies that apply to users, regardless of which computer they log on to. Use the Computer Configuration section to set policies that apply to computers regardless of who logs on to the computers.

Group Policy settings are processed in the following order

1. Local Group Policy object.
2. Group Policies linked to the Site container.
3. Group Policies linked to the Domain container.
4. Group Policies linked to the Organizational Unit that is highest in the OU hierarchy are processed first, followed by GPOs linked to the child OU, and so on. If there are multiple GPOs linked to the same OU, they are processed in the order specified by the administrator.

A shortcut to help you remember the order of precedence is LSDO. This stands for **L**ocal, **S**ite, **D**omain, and **O**rganizational Unit.

In the previous example, you can see that local Group Policies are processed first. Group Policies linked to the OU that contains the user/computer is processed last, which overwrites the earlier GPOs. In situations where you create a GPO and set it to Enforced (No Override) with respect to the site, domain, or OU, its setting will not be overwritten by any GPOs that follow it in the order of precedence. If you have two GPOs that are both set to Enforced (No Override), the one that is highest in the Active Directory hierarchy takes precedence.

DISABLE STORE ACCESS FOR ALL USERS

GET READY. To disable access to the Store for all users working on a specific Windows 8 client computer, perform the following steps using the Local Group Policy editor:

1. Press the **Windows logo key + r**.
2. In the *Run* dialog box, type **gpedit.msc**.
3. Click **Computer Configuration > Administrative Templates > Windows Components > Store**.
4. Double-click **Turn off the Store application**.
5. Select **Enabled** and then click **OK**.

USE GMPC TO DISABLE STORE ACCESS FOR MULTIPLE WINDOWS 8 CLIENT COMPUTERS

GET READY. To disable access to the Store for multiple Windows 8 client computers that are members of a domain, use a Windows 8 client computer to perform the following steps using the GPMC:

TAKE NOTE*

To use the GPMC, the Windows 8 computer must be a member of the domain and have Remote Server Administration Tools (RSAT) installed.

1. Select the **Windows logo key + r**.
2. In the *Run* dialog box, type **gpmc.msc** and then press **Enter**.
3. Right-click **Group Policy Objects** and click **New**.
4. Type a name for the policy and click **OK**.
5. Right-click the GPO you created in step 4 and choose **Edit**.

6. Click **Computer Configuration > Policies > Administrative Templates > Windows Components > Store**.
7. Double-click **Turn off the Store application**.
8. Select **Enabled** and then click **OK**.
9. Close the *Group Policy Management* editor.
10. Right-click the Active Directory domain container (for example, contoso.com) and choose **Link an Existing GPO**.
11. Click the Group Policy object you created in step 4 and then click **OK**.
12. Press the **Windows logo key + r**.
13. Type **gpupdate /force** and click **Enter**.
14. Attempt to access the Windows Store. It will be blocked.

DISABLE ACCESS TO THE WINDOWS STORE USING THE LOCAL GROUP POLICY EDITOR (GPEDIT.MSC)

GET READY. To disable access to the Windows Store on a Windows 8 computer using the Local Group Policy editor (gpedit.msc), log on to Windows 8 system and then perform the following steps:

1. Press the **Windows logo key + r**.
2. In the *Run* dialog box, type **gpedit.msc** and then click **OK**.
3. Click **Computer Configuration > Administrative Templates > Windows Components**.
4. Click the **Store** folder.
5. Double-click **Turn off the Store application** (see Figure 6-11).

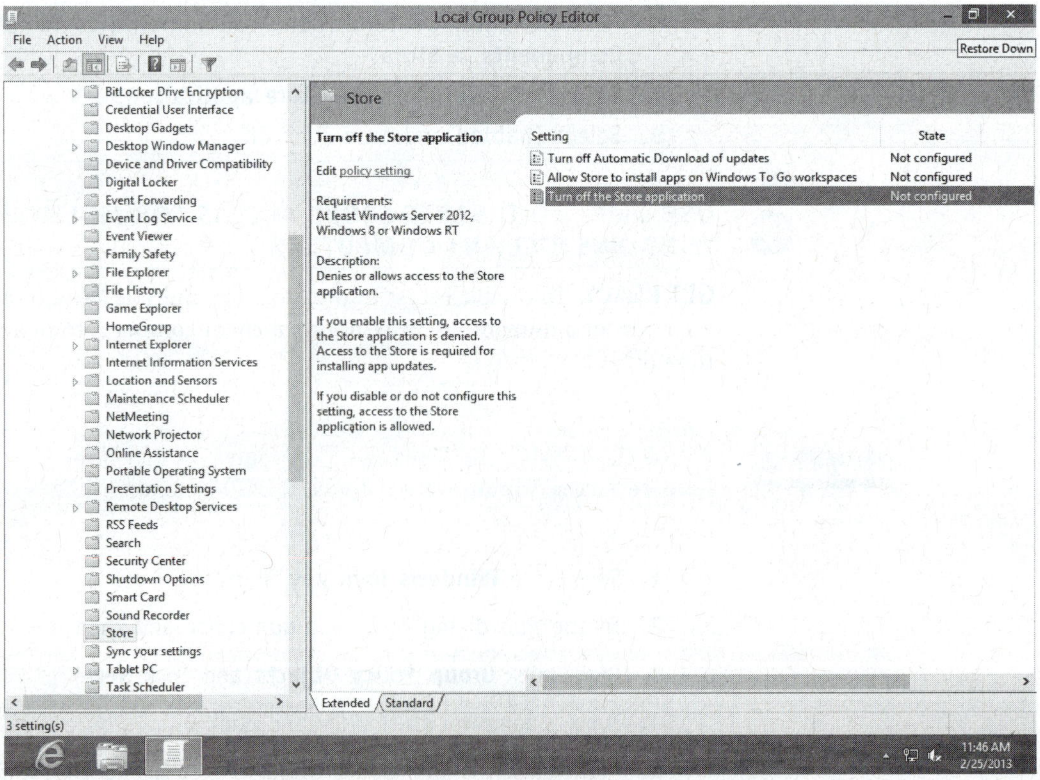

Figure 6-11

Turning off the Store application

6. Select **Enabled** and then click **OK**.
7. Select the **Windows logo key** to toggle to the Windows *Start* screen.
8. Click the **Windows Store** tile. The message shown in Figure 6-12 is displayed.

Figure 6-12

Blocking access to the Windows Store

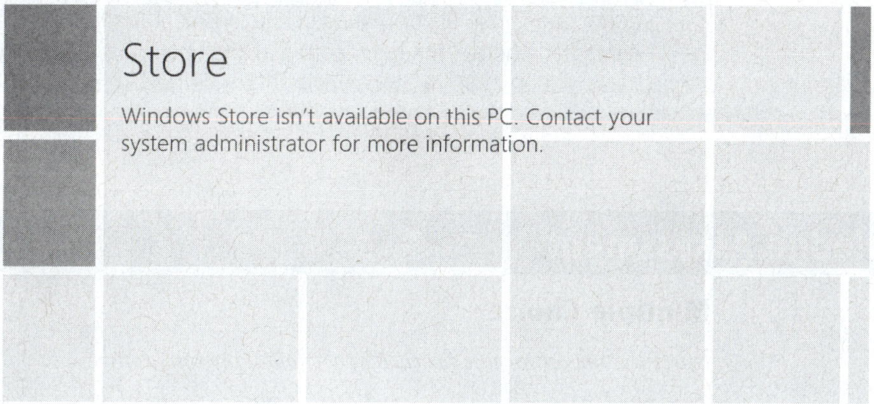

9. To regain access to the Windows Store, return to the Local Group Policy editor and set the policy to **Not Configured**.

SKILL SUMMARY

IN THIS LESSON, YOU LEARNED:

- The Windows Store is Microsoft's central location for distributing and purchasing Windows apps (also called *Packaged apps*).
- To access the store, you need a Microsoft account and an Internet connection.
- Each Windows app is represented by a tile in the Windows Store. Selecting the tile takes you to a purchase page where you can find additional information and install the app. Once installed, the app appears on your Windows 8 *Start* screen as a tile.
- You can delete an app by right-clicking it and selecting uninstall.
- You can install Windows apps on up to five Windows 8 devices. Because the apps are saved to your Microsoft account, you can access them from any device using the Your Apps menu.
- When updates are ready for Windows Apps, a number indicator appears on the Store tile. By default, updates are only downloaded; the user must initiate the actual update process.
- You can turn off automatic updates through App Updates and by using Group Policy, which can be configured using the Local Group Policy editor and Group Policy Management console.
- You can use AppLocker to control which applications and files users can run on their Windows 8 client computer through the creation of AppLocker rules. These rules are based on rule collections: executable files, scripts, windows installer files, and Appx (Packaged apps and Packaged app installers).
- You can bypass the Store certification requirements and make your Windows apps available to internal users through a process called *side loading*.

(continued)

- You can enable side loading of an app by joining Windows 8 Enterprise and Windows Server 2012 machines to an Active Directory domain. For systems not joined to a domain, or running Windows 8 Professional or Windows 8 RT, you need a side loading product activation key.
- Disabling access to the Windows Store can be accomplished via the Local Group Policy editor and Group Policy Management console. The former configures the policy on a single computer whereas the latter configures the policy for the entire enterprise.

Knowledge Assessment

Multiple Choice

Select the correct answer for each of the following questions.

1. What is the maximum number of Windows 8 devices on you can install a Windows app?
 a. 1
 b. 3
 c. 5
 d. 10

2. Which of the following can be used to turn off automatic download of updates from the Windows store on a Windows 8 computer? (Select all that apply.)
 a. Windows Store > Settings > App Updates > Move slider to No
 b. gpedit.msc
 c. gpmc.msc
 d. AppLocker

3. Which of the following rule collections is used to configure an AppLocker rule for a packaged app?
 a. Executable files
 b. Scripts
 c. Appx
 d. Windows Installer files

4. To create rules for multiple packaged apps in a single step, which wizard would you use with AppLocker?
 a. Create New Rule
 b. Create Default Rules
 c. Automatically Generate Rules
 d. Create Multiple Rules

5. Where can you obtain a side loading product activation key to side load an app on a Windows 8 Professional computer?
 a. Microsoft TechNet
 b. Volume Service Center
 c. Volume Licensing Service Center
 d. Running sideloadkey.exe from a command prompt

6. Which option represents the order of precedence for GPOs starting from first to last?
 a. Local Group Policy, Site GPO, Domain GPO, Organizational Unit GPO
 b. Site GPO, Domain GPO, Organizational Unit GPO, Local Group Policy.
 c. Site GPO, Domain GPO, Local Group Policy, Organizational Unit GPO
 d. Organizational Unit, Site GPO, Domain GPO, Local Group Policy

7. Which represents the correct path for disabling the *Turn off the Store application* using the Local Group Policy editor?
   a. Computer Configuration > Windows Components > Store
   b. Computer Configuration > Administrative Templates > Windows Store
   c. Computer Configuration > Administrative Templates > Windows Components > Store
   d. Computer Configuration > Administrator Templates > Windows Components > Windows Store

8. Which command can be used to add a side loading product activation key?
   a. slmgr /ipk <sideloading product key>
   b. slmgr /pk <sideloading product key>
   c. slmgr /ato <sideloading product key>
   d. slmgr /ato ec67814b-30e6-4a50-bf7b-d55daf729d1e

9. To create a single rule that allows the Everyone group to run packaged apps that are signed, which wizard would you use in AppLocker?
   a. Automatically Generate Rules
   b. Create Default Rules
   c. Create New Rule
   d. Create Default Rule

10. Which of the following are true regarding updating Windows apps from the Windows Store?
    a. Only the user can update the apps, but they can be downloaded automatically in the background.
    b. A number indicator appears on the Store icon that will inform you of the number of updates available.
    c. Free Windows apps cannot be updated.
    d. The updates are downloaded and installed in the background.

Best Answer

Choose the letter that corresponds to the best answer. More than one answer choice may achieve the goal. Select the BEST answer.

1. You have 25 Windows 8 computers in a Windows Active Directory domain named *contoso.com*. Which of the following tools should be used to disable the automatic download of updates from the Windows Store on all of them with the least amount of administrative effort?
   a. Local Group Policy editor
   b. Group Policy Management console
   c. Turn off via App Updates in the Windows Store
   d. Delete the automatic updates registry key

2. To set up an AppLocker rule that disables access to Windows apps, which of the following rule collections would you create the rule from?
   a. Scripts
   b. Windows Installer files
   c. Executable files
   d. Appx

3. To uninstall a Windows app that you recently purchased on one of your Windows 8 devices last week but now would like to reinstall it, which of the following options best describes the process to reinstall it?
   a. Visit the Windows Store, browse through the categories to find the app, and reinstall it at no charge.
   b. Visit the Windows Store, browse through the categories to find the app, and pay for the app to reinstall it.

c. Visit the Windows Store, access Your Apps, and click Apps not installed on this PC. Select and install.
d. Remove the app from one of your other Windows 8 devices, access Your Apps, and click Apps not installed on this PC. Select and install.

4. As the administrator for a network that has 50 Windows 8 client computers, which of the following approaches can be used to initiate Windows app updates on the users' machines?
   a. Configure a Group Policy.
   b. Configure a Local Policy.
   c. Turn on automatic download/install of Windows Apps.
   d. Ask users to perform updates when they see the indicator on their Store tile.
5. You have a Windows 8 computer set up with the 20 Windows Apps that you want everyone to have access to. Which of the following AppLocker wizards will create all the rules in a single step?
   a. Create New Rule
   b. Create Default Rules
   c. Automatically Generate Rules
   d. Create Custom Rule

Matching and Identification

1. Match the following terms with their corresponding definitions.

   _______ a) Application Identity service
   _______ b) Group Policy Management console
   _______ c) Line of Business apps
   _______ d) AppLocker
   _______ e) Local Security Policy editor
   _______ f) side loading
   _______ g) Windows Apps
   _______ h) Windows Store
   _______ i) rule collections
   _______ j) Group Policy object

   1. Apps that are unique to the main business of the company.
   2. Used to bypass the Windows Store and load LOB apps.
   3. A service that is required by AppLocker to verify the identity of an app.
   4. Central location for distributing and purchasing apps.
   5. Can be associated with a selected Active Directory container.
   6. Controls which applications and files users can run on their Windows 8 computer.
   7. Also known as *packaged apps.*
   8. Used to configure Group Policy across your entire enterprise.
   9. Includes executable files, scripts, Windows installer files, and Appx.
   10. Used to modify local security settings on your computer (secpol.msc).

Build a List

1. In order of first to last, specify the order of precedence for processing Group Policy objects.

   _______ Group Policies linked to the Site container
   _______ Group Policies linked to the Organizational Unit
   _______ Local Group Policy object
   _______ Group Policies linked to the Domain container

2. After deleting a Windows App that is installed on four other Windows 8 devices, specify the correct order of steps required to reinstall the Windows app.
   _______ Click Apps not installed on this PC.
   _______ Select the Windows logo key to open the Windows Start menu and select the Store tile.
   _______ Select the app you want to install.
   _______ Right-click and select Your Apps.
   _______ Click Install.

3. In order of first to last, specify the tasks that must be completed to disable access to the Windows Store using the Local Group Policy editor.
   _______ Click Computer Configuration > Administrative Templates > Windows Components > Store.
   _______ Click Enabled and then click OK.
   _______ Press the Windows logo key + r.
   _______ Double-click *Turn off the Store application.*
   _______ In the Run dialog box, type gpedit.msc.

■ Business Case Scenarios

Scenario 6-1: Distributing a Line of Business App

Lee Jensen, owner of a large manufacturing company on the West Coast, recently approved the purchase and installation of 50 Windows 8 Enterprise desktops for his organization. A month earlier, the company installed 25 Windows 8 Professional client computers. All the computers are part of the Windows 2012 Active Directory domain named *jensenmfg.com.*

The company has a Line of Business app called *jenMax* it would like to make available to its internal employees via the Windows Store. He has asked you to research the process and requirements and report back. What are the potential issues/recommendations you should bring to his attention?

Scenario 6-2: Disabling Windows Store Auto-Update

You have 50 Windows 8 Enterprise client computers on your network that are joined to the company's Active Directory domain. You have several Group Policy objects linked to the domain including one GPO that has the "Turn off Automatic Download of updates" option set to Enabled. You open the Local Group Policy editor on one of the Windows 8 Enterprise client computers, navigate to the "Turn off Automatic Download of updates" option, and set it to Disabled. What would happen if you made this change?

7 LESSON

Controlling Access to Local Hardware and Applications

70-687 EXAM OBJECTIVE

Objective 2.4 – Control access to local hardware and applications. This objective may include but is not limited to manage installation of removable devices; configure access through Group Policy or Local Security Policy; and configure AppLocker.

Lesson Heading	Exam Objective
Configuring Hardware Restrictions	
Controlling Device Installation	
Controlling Removable Storage Access	Manage installation of removable devices
Configuring Application Restrictions	
Using Software Restriction Policies	Configure access through Group Policy or Local Security Policy
Using AppLocker	Configure AppLocker

KEY TERMS

application control policies
AppLocker
certificate rules
default rule
executable rules
hash rules
network zone rules
packaged app rules
path rules
script rules
software restriction policies
Windows Installer rules

■ Configuring Hardware Restrictions

THE BOTTOM LINE

Data storage technology has advanced to the point at which anyone can carry enormous amounts of information in a device no larger than a postage stamp. The storage capacities of flash memory cards, USB flash drives, and portable hard drives are increasing at an exponential rate, and for many administrators, this represents a critical threat.

High-capacity removable disks and drives are dangerous to enterprise networks in that they can allow data in, as well as carry it out. Users can easily introduce unauthorized software into the environment, and they can also copy corporate data and carry it out. One way to minimize these threats is to limit the ability to use these devices on enterprise workstations.

Windows Server 2012 and Windows 8 both support Group Policy settings that enable administrators to limit user access to specific types of removable storage devices. As with most Group Policy settings, administrators can deploy them on Windows 8 computers individually by modifying the Local Security Policy settings, but in an enterprise environment, it is usually more practical to create a Group Policy object (GPO) with the appropriate settings and link it to an Active Directory Domain Services (AD DS) object.

Controlling Device Installation

> The Device Installation Restrictions folder in a GPO contains policy settings that enable you to prevent Windows computers from installing and updating device drivers under specific conditions.

The policies in the Computer Configuration/Policies/Administrative Templates/System/Device Installation/Device Installation Restrictions folder, shown in Figure 7-1, enable you to specify if or when the computers on your network can install drivers for hardware devices.

Figure 7-1

The Device Installation Restrictions policies

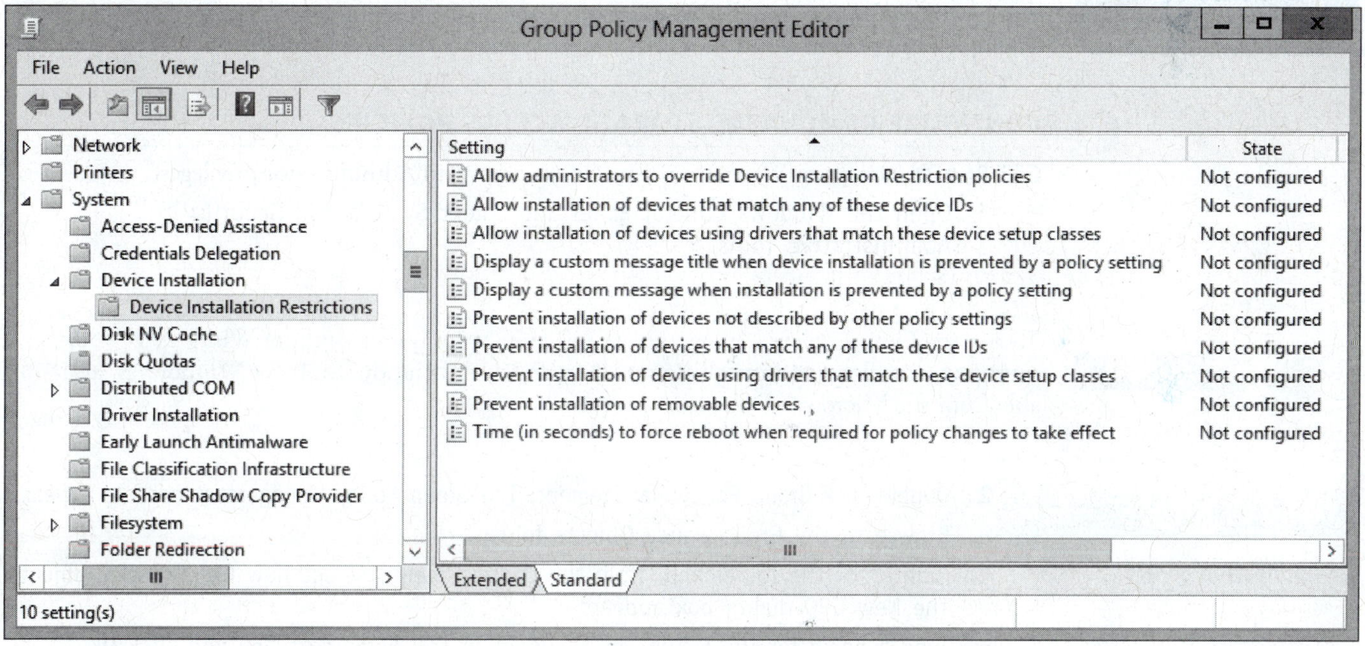

For example, the *Prevent installation of removable devices* setting enables you to prevent computers from installing any devices which the drivers identify as removable. This would therefore prevent users from inserting USB flash drives or portable hard drives for the first time.

The policy also prevents any drivers for removable devices already installed on the system from being updated. However, the policy does nothing to inhibit the functionality of drivers that are already installed.

For more granular control over device installation, you can use any of the following additional policies:

- **Allow/Prevent installation of devices that match any of these device IDs** – Enables you to allow or prevent installation or update of device drivers based on their Plug and Play hardware IDs. Use this *Allow* setting only when the *Prevent installation of devices not described by other policy settings* is also enabled.

- **Allow/Prevent installation of devices using drivers that match these device setup classes** – Enables you to allow or prevent installation or update of device drivers based on the globally unique identifiers (GUIDs) of their setup classes. Use this *Allow* setting only when the *Prevent installation of devices not described by other policy settings* is also enabled.
- **Prevent installation of devices not described by other policy settings** – Provides a prohibition against the installation or update of all devices not named in the *Allow installation of devices that match any of these device IDs* and/or *Allow installation of devices using drivers that match these To device setup classes* policies.
- **Allow administrators to override Device Installation Restriction policies** – Provides members of the Administrators group with the ability to install and update device drivers regardless of all other policy settings.

Controlling Removable Storage Access

In many enterprise situations, administrators might want to prevent people from using some or all removable storage devices, both to protect company data and prevent the introduction of malware.

CERTIFICATION READY
Manage installation of removable devices
Objective 2.4

To implement policies controlling removable storage access, use the following procedure.

CONFIGURE REMOVABLE STORAGE ACCESS POLICIES

GET READY. Log on to Windows 8 using an account with Administrator privileges.

1. Open the Windows Control Panel and select System and Security > Administrative Tools.

TAKE NOTE* To run the Group Policy Management console on a computer running Windows 8, you must first download and install Remote Server Administration Tools for Windows 8, available from the Microsoft Download Center.

2. Double-click Group Policy Management. The Group Policy Management console appears.
3. Browse to the Group Policy Objects folder.
4. Right-click the folder and, from the context menu, select New Group Policy object. The New GPO dialog box appears.
5. Type a name for the Group Policy object in the Name text box and click OK.
6. Right-click the GPO you created and, in the context menu, select Edit. The Group Policy Management Editor appears.
7. Browse to the Computer Configuration/Policies/Administrative Templates/System/ Device Installation/ Removable Storage Access folder, as shown in Figure 7-2.

Figure 7-2

The Removable Storage Access policies

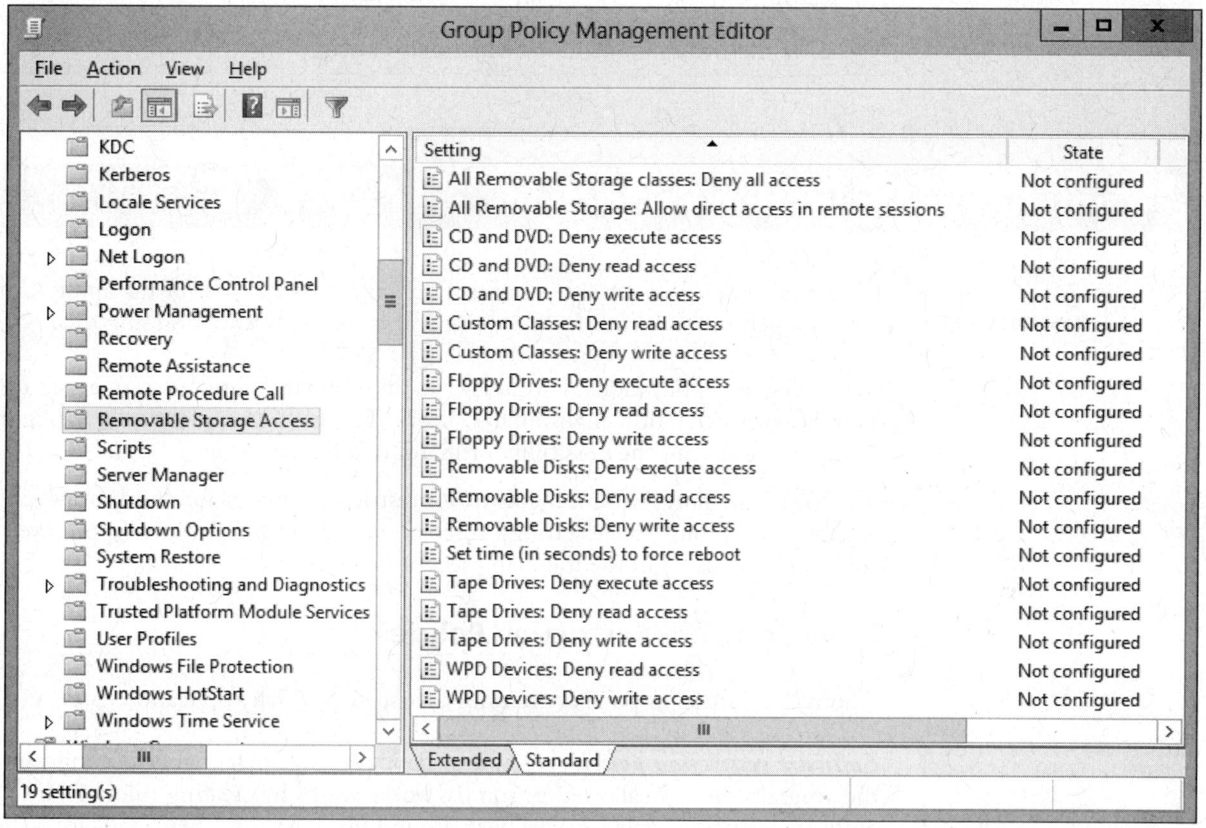

8. For control over access to specific types of removable storage, configure any of the following policy settings:
   - **All Removable Storage classes: Deny all access** – Enables you to block access to all classes of removable storage device. This policy takes precedence over all of the policy settings for individual classes.
   - **All Removable Storage: Allow direct access in remote sessions** – Enables users to access removable storage devices directly during remote sessions.
   - **CD and DVD: Deny read/write/execute access** – Enables you to deny users read, write, and/or execute access to all of the CD or DVD drives in the computer.
   - **Custom Classes: Deny read/write access** – Enables you to deny users read and/or write access to custom device classes identified by their GUIDs.
   - **Floppy Drives: Deny read/write/execute access** – Enables you to deny users read, write, and/or execute access to all of the floppy drives in the computer, including USB floppy drives.
   - **Removable Disks: Deny read/write/execute access** – Enables you to deny users read, write, and/or execute access to all of the removable disks in the computer.
   - **Tape Drives: Deny read/write/execute access** – Enables you to deny users read, write, and/or execute access to all of the tape drives in the computer.

TAKE NOTE*

For control at the user level, the same policies appear in the User Configuration/Policies/Administrative Templates/System/Removable Storage Access folder.

- **WPD Devices: Deny read/write access** – Enables you to deny users read and/or write access to all of the Windows Portable Devices in the computer, including smartphones, MP3 players, and cameras.

9. Close the Group Policy Management Editor console.
10. Close the Group Policy Management console.

Configuring Application Restrictions

THE BOTTOM LINE

In an enterprise environment, administrators often prefer to limit the applications their users are permitted to run. In Windows 8, there are two ways of doing this.

Restricting the applications that users can run on their computers is one step towards creating a consistent workstation environment. Workstations that are identically configured are easier to support and limit the possibility of malware infiltration.

Windows 8 supports two mechanisms for restricting application, both of which you can deploy using Group Policy settings: software restriction policies and AppLocker. These mechanisms are discussed in the following sections.

Using Software Restriction Policies

Software restriction policies are rules that specify which applications users can run.

Software restriction policies are Group Policy settings that enable administrators to specify the programs that are allowed to run on workstations by creating rules of various types. Software restriction policies have been around for years, and their main advantage is that you can create one set of policies that apply to Windows XP, Windows Vista, and Windows 7 workstations, as well as Windows 8. The disadvantage of software restriction policies is that, unlike the newer AppLocker feature, you can only create rules manually and individually.

CREATING RULES

The software restriction policy rules that you can create include the following:

- ***Certificate rules*** – Identify applications based on the inclusion of a certificate signed by the software publisher. An application can continue to match this type of rule, even if the executable file is updated, as long as the certificate remains valid.
- ***Hash rules*** – Identify applications based on a digital fingerprint that remains valid even when the name or location of the executable file changes.
- ***Network zone rules*** – Identify Windows Installer (.msi) packages downloaded with Internet Explorer based on the security zone of the site from which they are downloaded.
- ***Path rules*** – Identify applications by specifying a file or folder name or a registry key. The potential vulnerability of this type of rule is that any file can match the rule, as long as it is the correct name or location.

To create rules, use the following procedure.

CREATE SOFTWARE RESTRICTION POLICY RULES

GET READY. Log on to Windows 8 using an account with Administrator privileges.

1. Open the Windows Control Panel and select System and Security > Administrative Tools.

TAKE NOTE* To run the Group Policy Management console on a computer running Windows 8, you must first download and install Remote Server Administration Tools for Windows 8, available from the Microsoft Download Center.

2. Double-click Group Policy Management. The Group Policy Management console appears.
3. Browse to the Group Policy Objects folder.
4. Right-click the folder and, from the context menu, select New Group Policy object. The New GPO dialog box appears.
5. Type a name for the Group Policy object in the Name text box and click OK.
6. Right-click the GPO you created and, in the context menu, select Edit. The Group Policy Management Editor appears.
7. Browse to the Computer Configuration\Policies\Windows Settings\Security Settings\Software Restriction Policies folder.
8. Right-click the Software Restriction Polices object and, from the context menu, select New Software Restriction Policies. The policies appear, as shown in Figure 7-3.

Figure 7-3
Software Restriction Policies

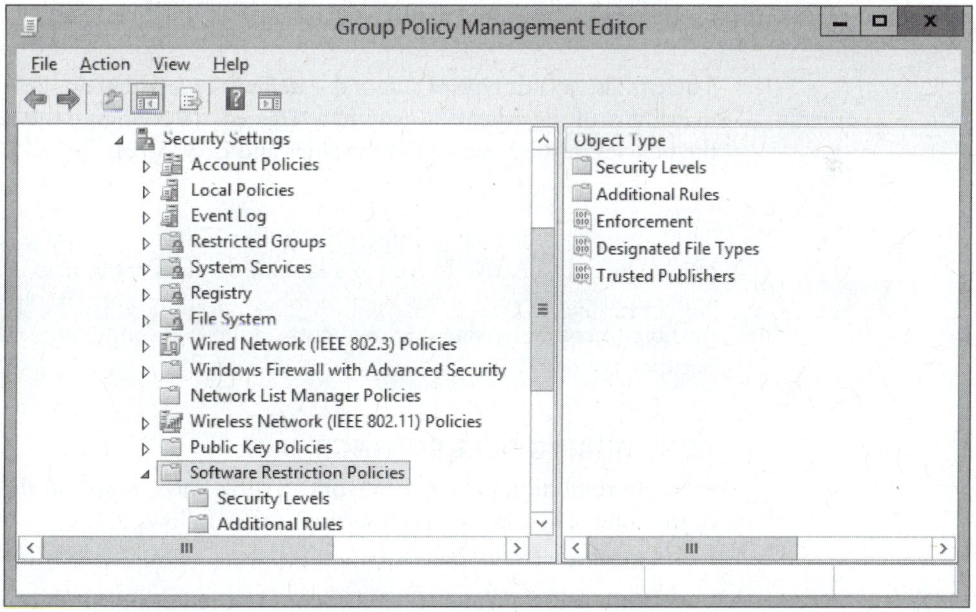

CERTIFICATION READY
Configure access through Group Policy or local security policy
Objective 2.4

9. Right-click the Additional Rules folder and, from the context menu, select New Path Rule. The *New Path Rule* dialog box appears, as shown in Figure 7-4.

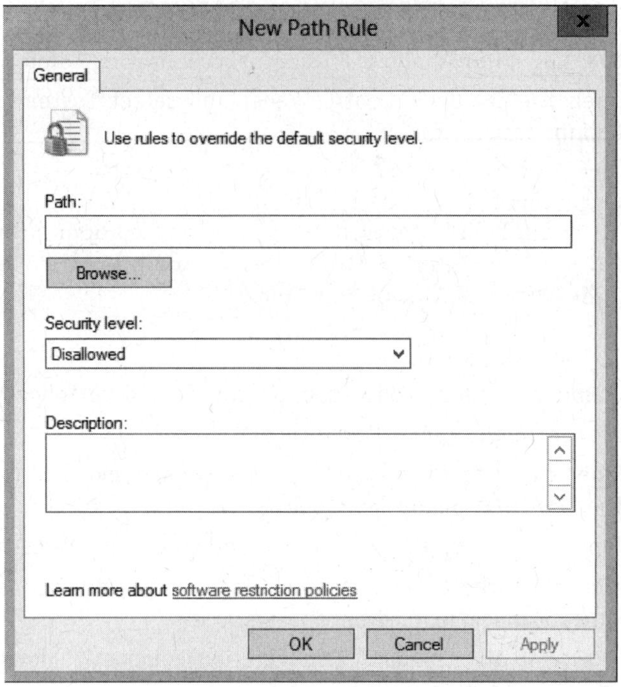

Figure 7-4
The *New Path Rule* dialog box

10. In the *Path* text box, type the path to the file you want to restrict.
11. In the *Security level* drop-down list, select an appropriate value and click OK.
12. Close the Group Policy Management Editor console.
13. Close the Group Policy Management console.

There is also a fifth type of rule – the ***default rule*** – that applies when an application does not match any of the other rules you have created. To configure the default rule, you select one of the policies in the Security Levels folder and click *Set As Default* on its *Properties* sheet.

TAKE NOTE*

The most common way to implement software restriction policies is through Group Policy objects linked to Active Directory Domain Services containers, so that administrators can apply their policy settings to large numbers of computers simultaneously. However, it is also possible to configure software restriction policies on individual computers using Local Security Policy.

CONFIGURING RULE SETTINGS

Software restriction policies can work in three ways, based on the settings you choose for each of the rules. The three possible settings are as follows:

- **Disallowed** – Prevents an application matching a rule from running.
- **Basic user** – Allows all applications not requiring administrative privileges to run. Allows applications that do require administrative privileges to run only if they match a rule.
- **Unrestricted** – Allows an application matching a rule to run

The most restrictive – and the most secure – way to use the settings is to set the default rule to Disallowed and then create additional Unrestricted rules for the applications you want your users to be able to run. This prevents them from launching any applications other than the ones you specify. The reverse of this method is to set the default rule to Unrestricted and use additional Disallowed rules to specify applications that you want to prevent users from running.

Although the most obvious way of using these settings is to creates rules for individual applications, there are other alternatives also. You can, for example, create rules that prevent users from running applications from anywhere other than the Program Files folder, and then use NTFS permissions to prevent them from installing new application to Program Files.

RESOLVING CONFLICTS

It is possible to create rules in such a way that conflicts occur because more than one rule applies to a single application. When this is the case, the more specific rule takes precedence over the less specific. Thus, the order of precedence is as follows:

1. Hash rules
2. Certificate rules
3. Path rules
4. Zone rules
5. Default rule

Using AppLocker

AppLocker is a feature first introduced in Windows 7 that enables administrators to create application restriction rules much more easily than software restriction policies.

CERTIFICATION READY
Configure AppLocker
Objective 2.4

Software restriction policies can be a powerful tool, but they can also require a great deal of administrative overhead. If you elect to disallow all applications except those matching the rules you create, there are a great many programs in Windows 8 itself that need rules, in addition to the applications you want to install. Administrators must also create the rules manually, which can be an onerous chore.

AppLocker, also known as ***application control policies***, is essentially an updated version of the concept implemented in software restriction policies. AppLocker also uses rules, which administrators must manage, but the process of creating the rules is much easier, thanks to a wizard-based interface.

AppLocker is also more flexible than software restriction policies. You can apply AppLocker rules to specific users and groups and also create rules that support all future versions of an application. The primary disadvantage of AppLocker is that you can only apply the policies to computers running Windows 7, Windows 8, Windows Server 2008 R2, and Windows Server 2012.

UNDERSTANDING RULE TYPES

The AppLocker settings are located in Group Policy objects in the Computer Configuration\Policies\Windows Settings\Security Settings\Application Control Policies\AppLocker container, as shown in Figure 7-5.

Figure 7-5
AppLocker settings

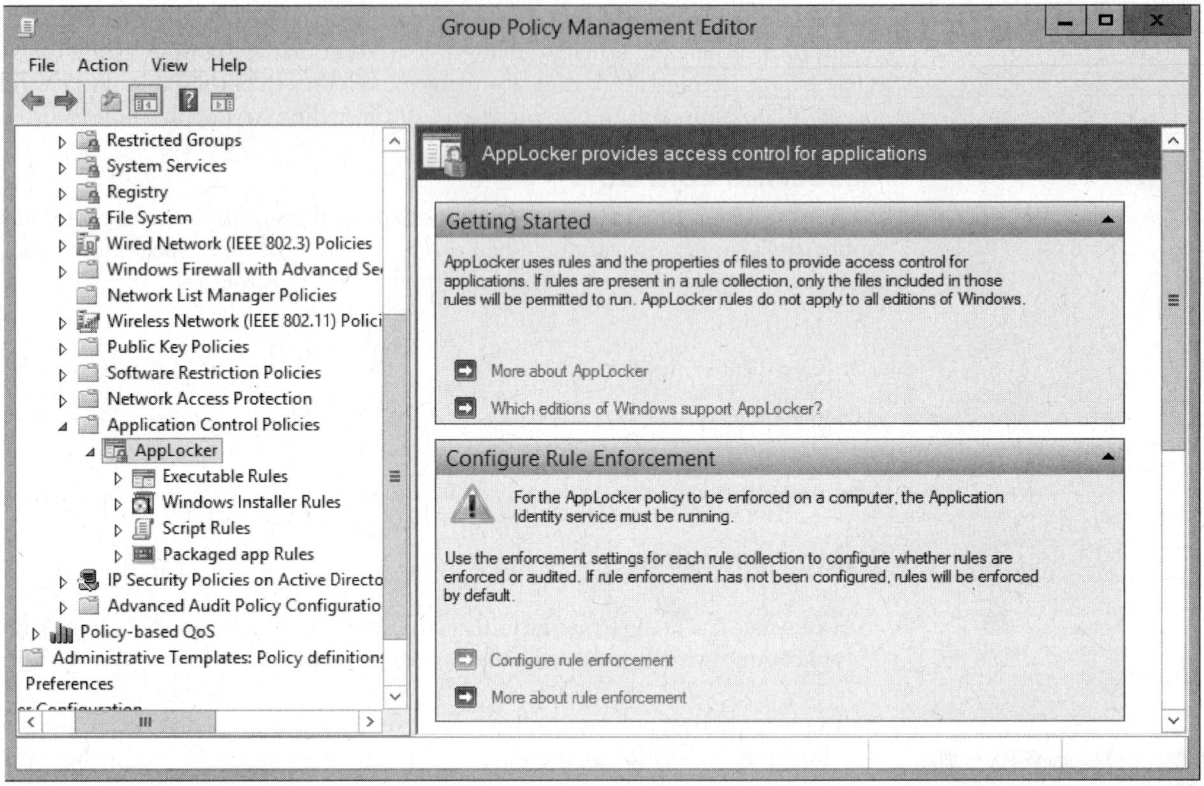

The AppLocker container in a GPOIn the AppLocker container, there are four nodes that contain the basic rule types, as follows:

- ***Executable Rules*** – Contains rules that apply to files with .exe and .com extensions.
- ***Windows Installer Rules*** – Contains rules that apply to Windows Installer packages with .msi and .msp extensions.
- ***Script Rules*** – Contains rules that apply to script files with .ps1, .bat, .cmd, .vbs, and .js extensions.
- ***Packaged app Rules*** – Contains rules that apply to applications purchased through the Windows Store.

TAKE NOTE*

You can also configure AppLocker to use DLL rules, which require administrators to create rules that provide users with access to all of the dynamic link libraries (DLLs) in an application, as well as the executables. This option, while more secure, can incur a significant performance penalty, because AppLocker must confirm access to each of an application's DLLs before it can load. To configure this option, open the *Properties* sheet for the AppLocker container, click the *Advanced* tab, and select the *Enable the DLL rule collection* checkbox.

Each of the rules you create in each of these containers can allow or block access to specific resources, based on one of the following criteria:

- **Publisher** – Identifies code-signed applications by means of a digital signature extracted from an application file. You can also create publisher rules that apply to all future versions of an application.

- **Path** – Identifies applications by specifying a file or folder name. The potential vulnerability of this type of rule is that any file can match the rule, as long as it is the correct name or location.
- **File Hash** – Identifies applications based on a digital fingerprint that remains valid even when the name or location of the executable file changes. This type of rules functions much like its equivalent in software restriction policies; in AppLocker, however, the process of creating the rules and generating file hashes is much easier.

CREATING DEFAULT RULES

By default, AppLocker blocks all executables, installer packages, and scripts, except for those specified in *Allow* rules. Therefore, to use AppLocker, you must create rules that enable users to access the files needed for Windows and the system's installed applications to run. The simplest way to do this is to right-click each of the three rules containers and select *Create Default Rules* from the context menu.

The default rules for each container, as shown in Figure 7-6, are standard rules that you can replicate, modify, or delete as necessary. You can also create your own rules instead, as long as you are careful to provide access to all the resources the computer needs to run Windows.

Figure 7-6

The default AppLocker executable rules

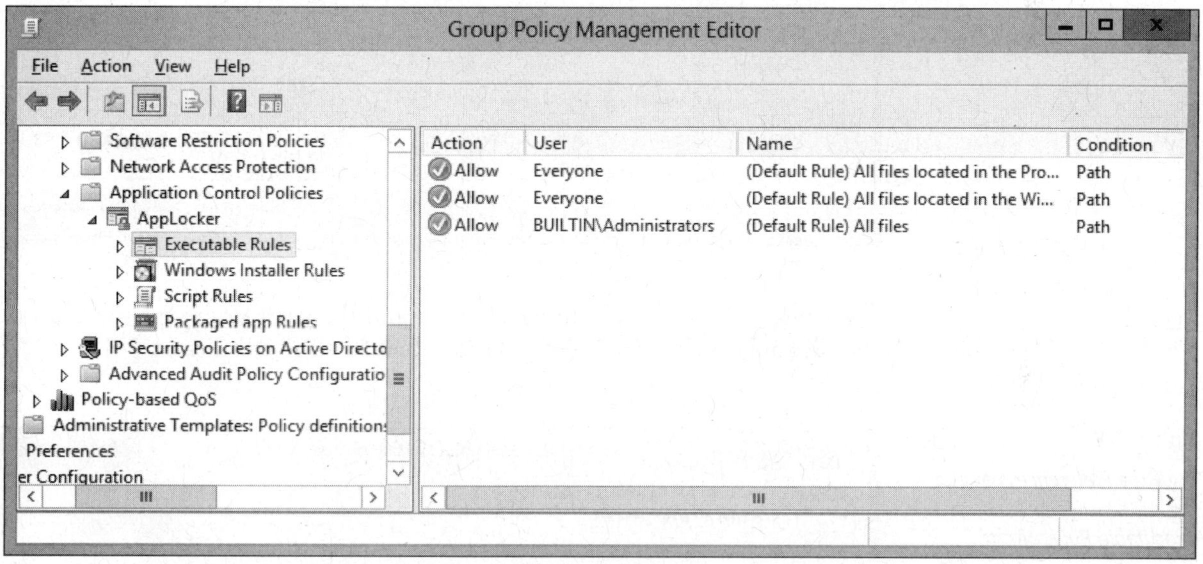

TAKE NOTE*

To use AppLocker, Windows 8 requires the Application Identity service to be running. By default, this service uses the manual startup type, so you must start it yourself in the Services console before Windows 8 can apply the AppLocker policies. This behavior is deliberate. With AppLocker, it is relatively easy to inadvertently create a set of rules that omits access to executables or other files that Windows needs to run, thus disabling the operating system. If this should occur, simply restarting the computer will cause the operating system to load without the Application Identity service, preventing AppLocker from loading. Only when you are certain that you have configured your rules properly should you change the startup type for the Application Identity service to automatic.

CREATING RULES AUTOMATICALLY

The greatest advantage of AppLocker over software restriction policies is the ability to create rules automatically. When you right-click one of the three rules containers and select *Create Rules Automatically* from the context menu, an *Automatically Generate Rules* wizard appears, as shown in Figure 7-7.

Figure 7-7

The *Automatically Generate Executable Rules* wizard

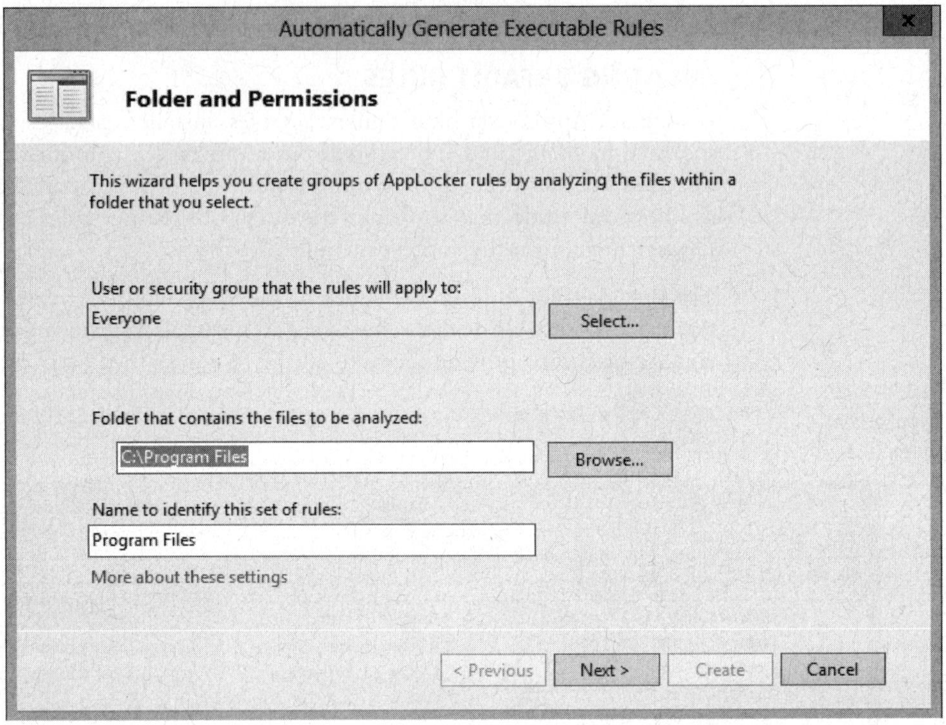

After specifying the folder to be analyzed and the users or groups to which the rules should apply, a *Rule Preferences* page appears, as shown in Figure 7-8.

Figure 7-8

The *Rule Preferences* page of the *Automatically Generate Executable Rules* wizard

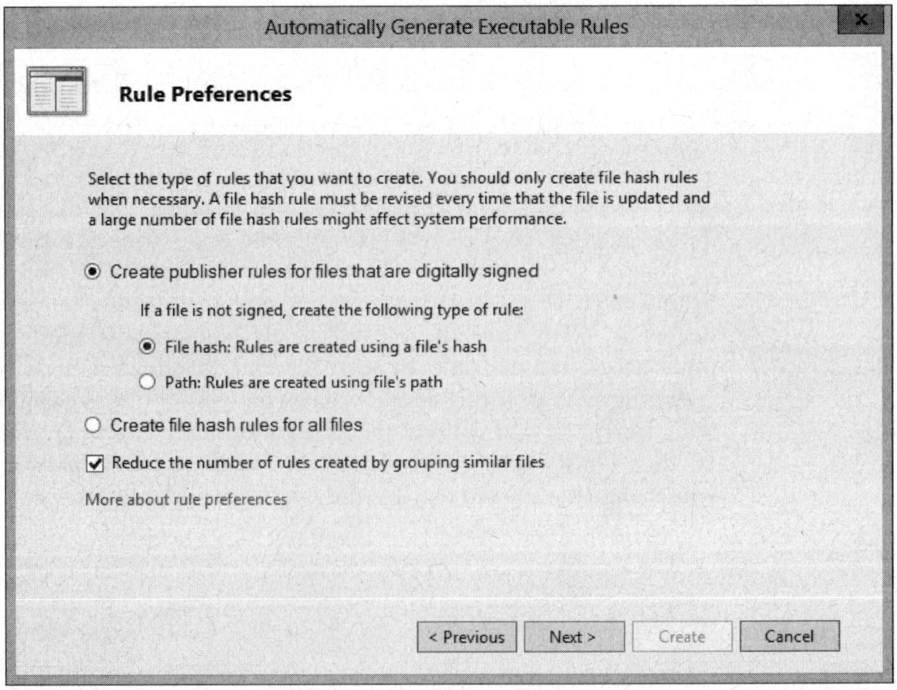

The wizard then displays a summary of its results in the *Review Rules* page, as shown in Figure 7-9, and adds the rules to the container.

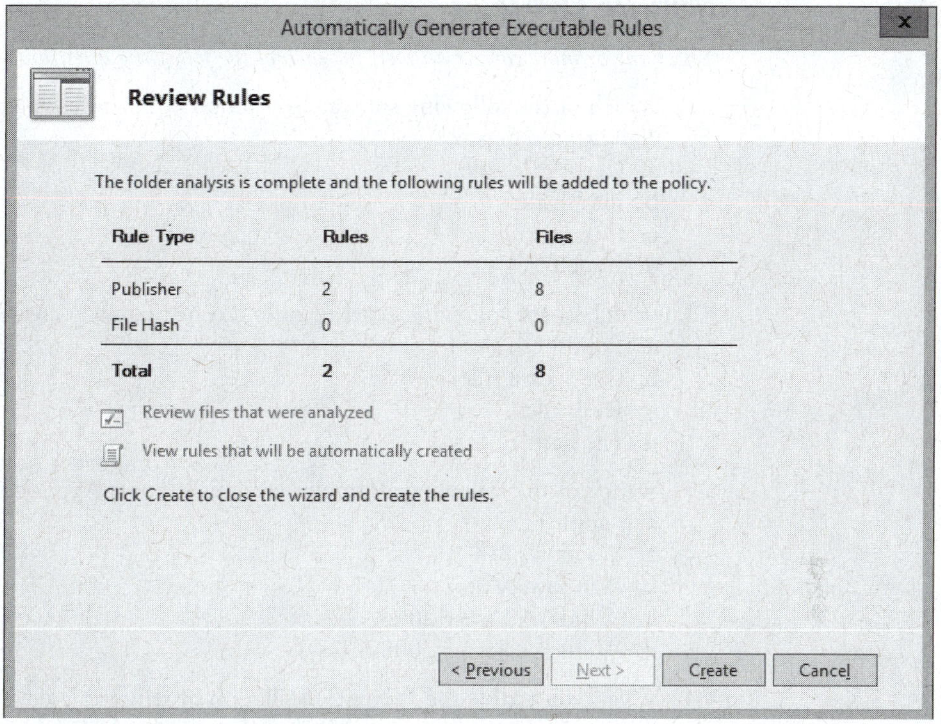

Figure 7-9

The *Review Rules* page of the *Automatically Generate Executable Rules* wizard

CREATING RULES MANUALLY

In addition to creating rules automatically, you can also do it manually, using a wizard-based interface you activate by selecting Create New Rule from the context menu for one of the three rule containers. The wizard prompts you for the following information:

- **Action** – Specifies whether you want to allow or deny the user or group access to the resource. In AppLocker, explicit deny rules always override allow rules.
- **User or group** – Specifies the name of the user or group to which the policy should apply.
- **Conditions** – Specifies whether you want to create a publisher, path, or file hash rule. The wizard generates an additional page for whichever option you select, enabling you to configure its parameters.
- **Exceptions** – Enables you to specify exceptions to the rule you are creating, using any of the three conditions: publisher, path, or file hash.

SKILL SUMMARY

IN THIS LESSON, YOU LEARNED:

- Using Group Policy, you can restrict user access to removable storage devices on their workstations.
- Software restriction policies are Group Policy settings that enable administrators to specify the programs that are allowed to run on workstations by creating rules of various types.
- AppLocker is a new feature in the Windows 8 Enterprise and Ultimate editions that enables administrators to create application restriction rules much more easily.

Knowledge Assessment

Multiple Choice

Select one or more correct answers for each of the following questions.

1. Which of the following software restriction policy rule types takes the highest precedence?
   a. Certificate rules
   b. Hash rules
   c. Default rules
   d. Zone rules
2. Which of the following types of rules can be manually created in AppLocker?
   a. Publisher rules
   b. Certificate rules
   c. Path rules
   d. File hash rules
3. Which of the following Windows versions support AppLocker policies? (Choose all that apply.)
   a. Windows 8
   b. Windows Vista
   c. Windows Server 2003
   d. Windows Server 2008 SP2
4. When you enable the Prevent installation of removable devices policy in a GPO and link that GPO to a domain, what is the effect on the devices already installed on computers in that domain?
   a. The policy has no effect on removable devices that have already been installed.
   b. The policy causes already-installed removable devices to be uninstalled.
   c. The policy allows already-installed removable devices to function, but prevents their drivers from being updated.
   d. The policy disables already-installed removable devices, but does not uninstall them.
5. Which of the following rule types can *not* be used to create software restriction policies?
   a. Hash rules
   b. Certificate rules
   c. Path rules
   d. Code rules
6. When creating an AppLocker rules manually, which of the following is *not* information the wizard prompts you to supply?
   a. Conditions
   b. User or group
   c. Function
   d. Action
7. Which of the following is *not* a setting for software restriction policies?
   a. Basic user
   b. Disallowed
   c. Advanced user
   d. Unrestricted

Best Answer

1. Which of the following statements is the primary reason why AppLocker is an improvement over software restriction policies?
   a. AppLocker has more rule types than software restriction policies.
   b. AppLocker can generate its own rules automatically.

c. AppLocker can be deployed in Group Policy objects in Active Directory.
d. AppLocker requires the Application Identity service to be running.

2. Which of the following statements is the primary reason why you must start the Application Identity service manually before using AppLocker?
   a. Because AppLocker needs the Application Identity service to be running in order to function.
   b. Because the Application Identity service will hang the system if it starts with Windows.
   c. Because requiring the manual start prevents improperly configured AppLocker rules from permanently hanging the system.
   d. Because Windows 8 does not support starting the Application Identity service automatically.

Matching and Identification

Complete the following exercise by matching the terms with their corresponding definitions.

_______ a) Path rules
_______ b) Windows Installer Rules
_______ c) Certificate rules
_______ d) Executable Rules
_______ e) Hash rules
_______ f) Packaged app Rules
_______ g) Default rule
_______ h) Network zone rules
_______ i) Script Rules
_______ j) DLL rules

1. Applies to files with .exe and .com extensions
2. Applies to packages with .msi and .msp extensions
3. Applies to files with .ps1, .bat, .cmd, .vbs, and .js extensions
4. Applies to Windows Store purchases
5. Applies to digitally signed applications
6. Applies to applications with a digital fingerprint
7. Applies to packages downloaded with Internet Explorer
8. Applies to applications with a specific file or folder name
9. Applies to libraries, as well as executables
10. Applies to applications that do not match any other rule type

Business Case Scenario

Scenario 7-1: Using AppLocker

Sophie is planning on using AppLocker to control access to applications on a new network she has constructed for the Research and Development department at a major aerospace firm. The software developers in the department have recently deployed a new application called Virtual Wind Tunnel, which is based on government project research and is therefore classified. All of the full-time personnel have sufficient clearance to use the application, but the interns in the department do not. Sophie has placed the user accounts for everyone in the department into a security group called ResDev. The interns are also members of a group called RDint.

How can Sophie use AppLocker to provide everyone in the department with access to the Virtual Wind Tunnel application without changing the group memberships and without having to apply policies to individual users?

8 LESSON

Configuring Internet Explorer

70-687 EXAM OBJECTIVE

Objective 2.5 – Configure Internet Explorer. This objective may include but is not limited to: configure compatibility view; manage add-ons; configure Download Manager; configure WebSockets; and configure security settings.

Lesson Heading	Exam Objective
Administering Internet Explorer	
Configuring Internet Explorer	Configure compatibility view Manage add-ons Configure Download Manager
Introducing WebSockets	Configure WebSockets
Securing Internet Explorer	Configure security settings
Understanding Protected Mode	
Configuring Security Zones	
Configuring the SmartScreen Filter	
Using InPrivate Mode	
Browsing with Certificates	

KEY TERMS

accelerators
add-ons
certification authority (CA)
compatibility logging
Compatibility View
InPrivate Filtering
InPrivate Mode
Mandatory Integrity Control (MIC)
phishing
podcasts
protected mode
public key infrastructure (PKI)
RSS feeds
Secure Sockets Layer (SSL)
security zones
SmartScreen Filter
social engineering
Trusted Sites zone
WebSockets

Administering Internet Explorer

THE BOTTOM LINE Administrators must be familiar with the administrative controls in Internet Explorer (IE) to protect users from Internet predators.

Windows 8 includes the latest version of the Internet Explorer web browser, Version 10, which enhances the features introduced in earlier versions and includes some important upgrades of its own. For administrators , these changes are likely to result in an increasing number of "user error" calls as users become accustomed to the new tools and the changes to the interface. Internet Explorer 10 also includes security tools that you must know how to configure for maximum effectiveness.

The chief innovation in IE10 is that the browser now has two distinct interfaces. When you launch IE from the desktop, you see the same familiar screen arrangement as in previous versions, with a menu bar and tabs across the top. When you launch IE by clicking the tile on the Start screen, however, you initially see a screen with a dark-colored address bar along the bottom, as shown in Figure 8-1, but that soon disappears, leaving the entire screen filled with the webpage content.

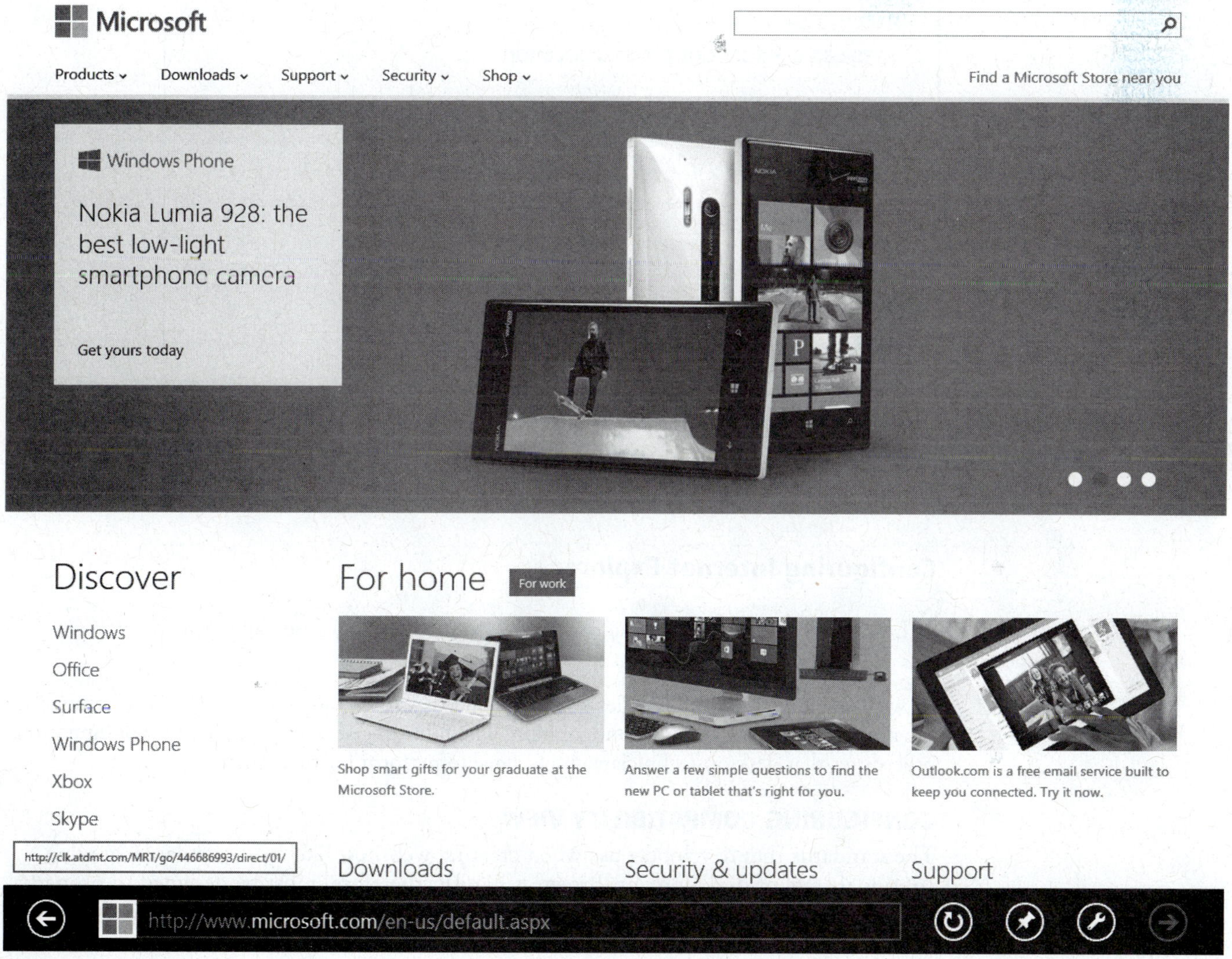

Figure 8-1
The IE Start screen interface

TAKE NOTE*

The controls described in the following sections pertain to the desktop version of IE. The *Start* screen version does not include all of the features and controls found in the desktop version.

This *Start* screen version of IE is equipped with an interface designed specifically for touch screens and is based on the full-screen paradigm found in other *Start* screen applications. Browser controls appear when you right-click the mouse or swipe in from an edge of the screen, but for the most part, the entire screen is occupied by content.

Although the look of this *Start* screen version of IE is different from the desktop version, they are in fact the same application. As with many other apps, the basic controls for the *Start* screen IE appear in an *Internet Explorer Settings* fly-out panel, as shown in Figure 8-2. The desktop version of IE retains the Internet Options tabbed dialog box familiar from previous *versions.*

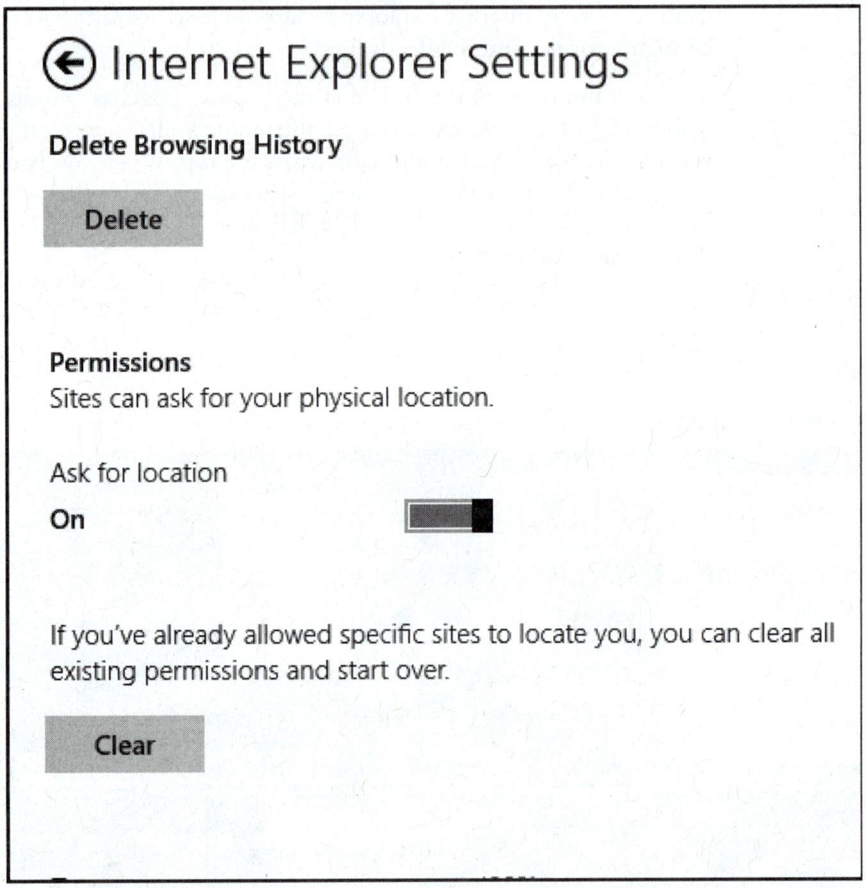

Figure 8-2

The *Internet Explorer Settings* panel

Configuring Internet Explorer

IE includes new features that administrators must be able to use and *configure.*

As with earlier versions, IE satisfies most users' needs with no adjustment. However, some of the new features in IE require configuration. The following sections examine the configuration procedures that desktop technicians might have to perform for their clients.

CONFIGURING COMPATIBILITY VIEW

The standards that developers use when creating websites, like most standards, are in a continual state of development. Browsers like IE, therefore, must be designed to properly display pages that conform to the latest version standards. IE10 operates in a default standards mode that enables it to display pages created using Cascading Style Sheets 3, Hypertext Markup Language version 5 (HTML5), Web Sockets, and other standards.

CERTIFICATION READY
Configure compatibility view
Objective 2.5

The problem with this regular development is that many of the pages on the Internet still conform to older versions of the standards, and IE10 might not display them properly. To accommodate these older pages, IE10 includes a feature called ***Compatibility View***, which enables the browser to display older pages properly.

From the user's perspective, the most easily visible indication of Compatibility View is the broken window icon that appears at the right end of the IE address box, as shown in Figure 8-3. When a website designed to earlier standards does not display properly, clicking this icon switches IE into Compatibility View mode, which can sometimes improve the appearance of the site. You can also enable Compatibility View by selecting Tools/Compatibility View from the Tools menu.

Figure 8-3
The IE *Compatibility View* icon

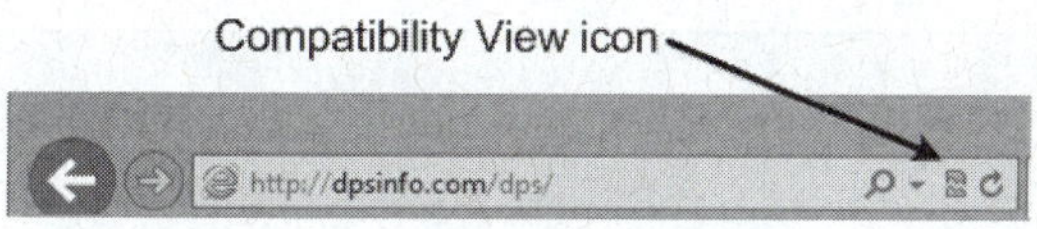

When you select Tools/Compatibility View Settings from the Tools menu, the *Compatibility View Settings* dialog box appears, as shown in Figure 8-4. In this dialog box, you can maintain a list of websites for which you want to use *Compatibility View* all of the time.

Figure 8-4
The IE *Compatibility View Settings* dialog box

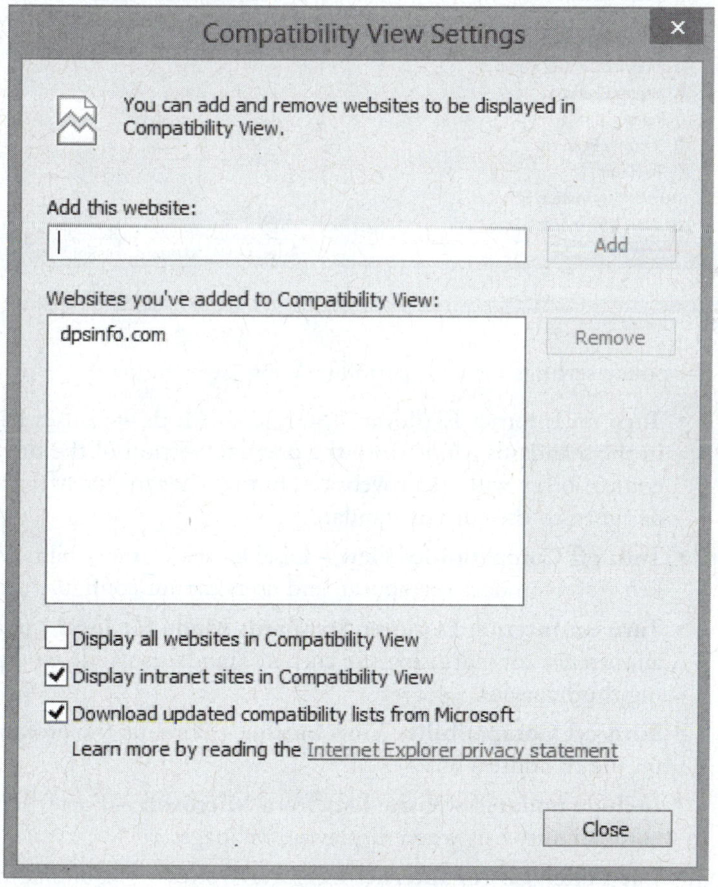

In addition to maintaining individual lists on each computer, Microsoft also maintains its own list of sites that can benefit from Compatibility View. When you select the *Download*

updated compatibility lists from Microsoft checkbox on the Compatibility View Settings dialog box, IE includes the Microsoft-supplied sites in the computer's list.

TAKE NOTE*

Any META tags in a webpage's code specifying a rendering standard override the presence of the site in the computer's Compatibility View list.

For website developers, it is possible to include tags in HTML files that cause IE to view the page in Compatibility View mode. For example, to render a page using the IE Version 7 standards, you can include the following code in the page's HEAD section:

```
<meta http-equiv="X-UA-Compatible" content="IE=7" />
```

For workstations on an Active Directory Domain Services (AD DS) network, administrators can configure Compatibility View settings using Group Policy, as shown in Figure 8-5. The settings are located in the Computer Configuration\Policies\Administrative Templates\Windows Components\Internet Explorer\Compatibility View container.

Figure 8-5

Compatibility View settings in a Group Policy object

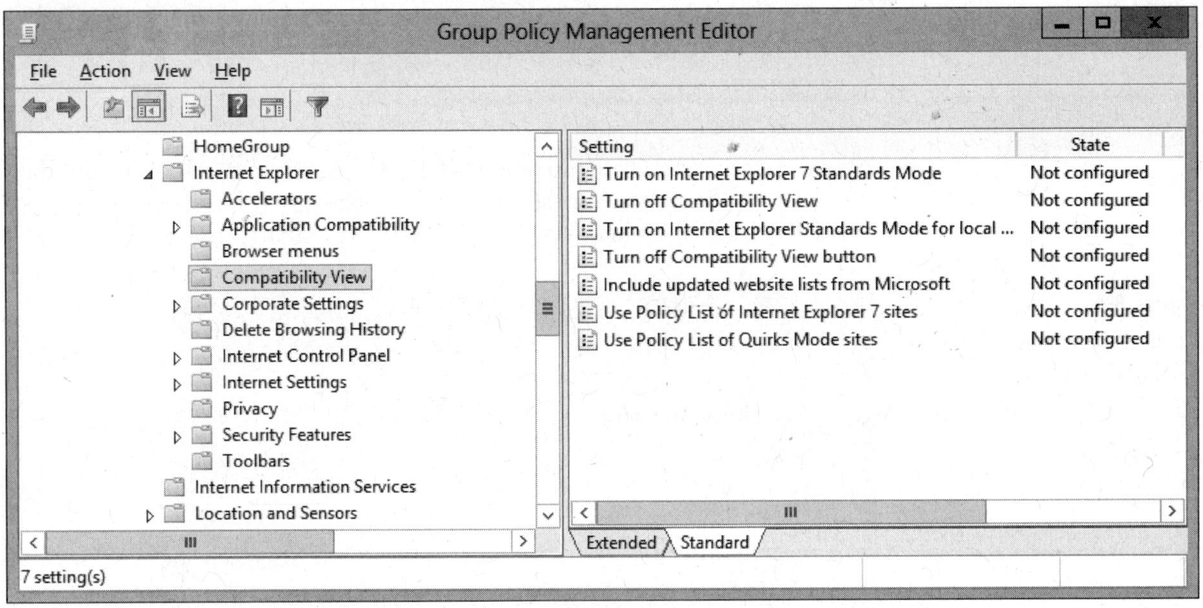

The policy settings for Compatibility View are as follows:

- **Turn on Internet Explorer 7 Standards Mode** – Causes IE to render all webpages in the Standards Mode from the previous version of the browser. This improves compatibility with older websites, but can negatively affect the appearance of sites designed to the current standard.
- **Turn off Compatibility View** – Disables the Compatibility View feature in IE. The broken view icon does not appear, and users cannot configure the Compatibility View settings.
- **Turn on Internet Explorer Standards Mode for local intranet** – Causes IE to display all intranet content using the current Standards Mode, and prevents users from modifying this behavior.
- **Turn off Compatibility View button** – Prevents the broken page icon from appearing on the IE address box.
- **Include updated website lists from Microsoft** – Forces IE to use the Microsoft site compatibility lists when displaying webpages.
- **Use Policy List of Internet Explorer 7 sites** – Enables administrators to create a common list of sites that IE should display using Compatibility View mode.
- **Use policy List of Quirks Mode sites** – Enables IE to identify itself to servers with an IE7 user agent string and operate in quirks mode, which supports incomplete standards, as opposed to standard mode.

CERTIFICATION READY
Manage add-ons
Objective 2.5

MANAGING ADD-ONS

IE is designed to be a versatile platform that can interact with a variety of other resources on the computer, on the network, and on the Internet. One of the ways that IE does this is through the use of add-ons. ***Add-ons*** are separate software components, created by Microsoft or by third parties, that interact with the basic functions of the web browser. Add-ons can provide an interface between the browser and another software product or between the browser and a specific site on the Internet.

The four basic types of add-ons supported by IE are as follows:

- **Toolbars and Extensions** – Enable the browser to open and manipulate websites or file types that IE does not support natively. Some applications add their own toolbars to IE, enabling you to work with their documents within an IE session.
- **Search Providers** – Enable the user to perform searches directly from the IE interface using search engines on the Internet or the local network
- **Accelerators** – Enable users to send text or other media they select in an IE browser window to another application, such as an email client, or an Internet resource, such as a blog.
- **Tracking Protection** – Enables users to install or maintain a list of sites that the IE should prevent from sharing your browsing habits with other sites.

WARNING As with any Internet download, be sure that you install add-ons provided only by sources that you trust. Add-ons can easily contain various types of malware that can damage your system.

Microsoft provides a few add-ons with IE in Windows 8, and also maintains gallery sites, from which you can download add-ons created by third parties. Some applications come with their own add-ons, which they install along with the application itself. Some websites also make add-ons available directly from their own pages.

To work with the IE add-ons on a particular Windows 8 computer, you open the *Manage Add-ons* dialog box, as shown in Figure 8-6, by clicking Tools\Manage Add-ons from either the menu bar or the Tools toolbar button.

Figure 8-6

The *Manage Add-ons* dialog box

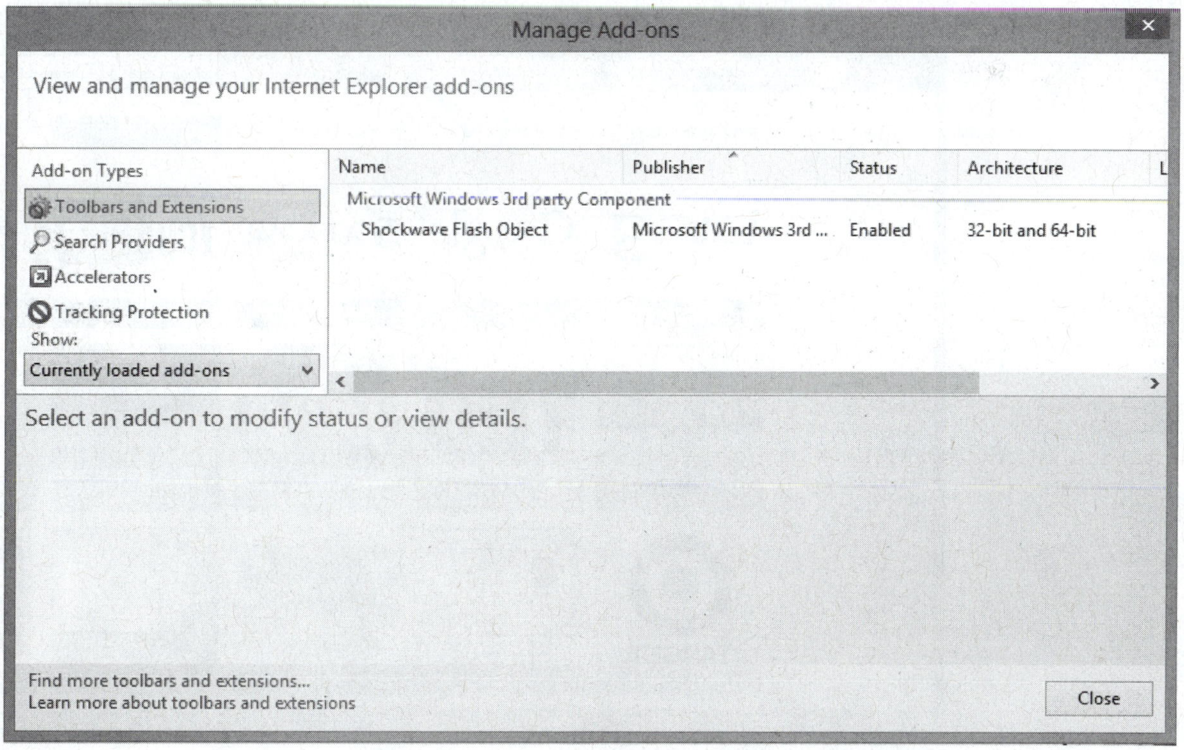

TAKE NOTE*

Only the desktop version of IE10 supports the use of add-ons. The *Start* screen version does not.

When you select one of the categories in the *Add-on Types* list, you see a list of the computer's currently-installed add-ons. With the controls that appear on the bottom pane of the dialog box, you can temporarily disable an add-on, remove it permanently, or select it as the default add-on of that type.

CONFIGURING SEARCH OPTIONS

Search providers are one of the most useful types of IE add-on. By default, the *Instant Search* box found in IE enables users to perform searches using Microsoft's Bing engine. To use other search engines, you must first install them to the list of search providers. Search providers are add-ons specifically designed to conform to the syntax required by other search engines.

IE supports virtually any type of search provider, not just the well-known web search engines such as Google. You can also add search providers for specific topics or sites, such as *Wikipedia* and *The New York Times*. Finally, you can add internal search engines of your own design, so that users can search your corporate intranet.

Adding Search Providers

To add search providers to the *Instant Search* list, use the following procedure:

ADD A SEARCH PROVIDER

GET READY. Log on to Windows 8 and then perform the following steps:

1. On the **Start** screen, click the **Desktop** tile.
   The Windows desktop appears.
2. In the taskbar, click the **Internet Explorer icon**.
   The IE window appears.
3. Click the down arrow on the right side of the search icon and then, from the context menu, select **Add**.
   The *Add-ons* page of the IE gallery appears, as shown in Figure 8-7.

Figure 8-7

The *Add-ons* page of the IE gallery

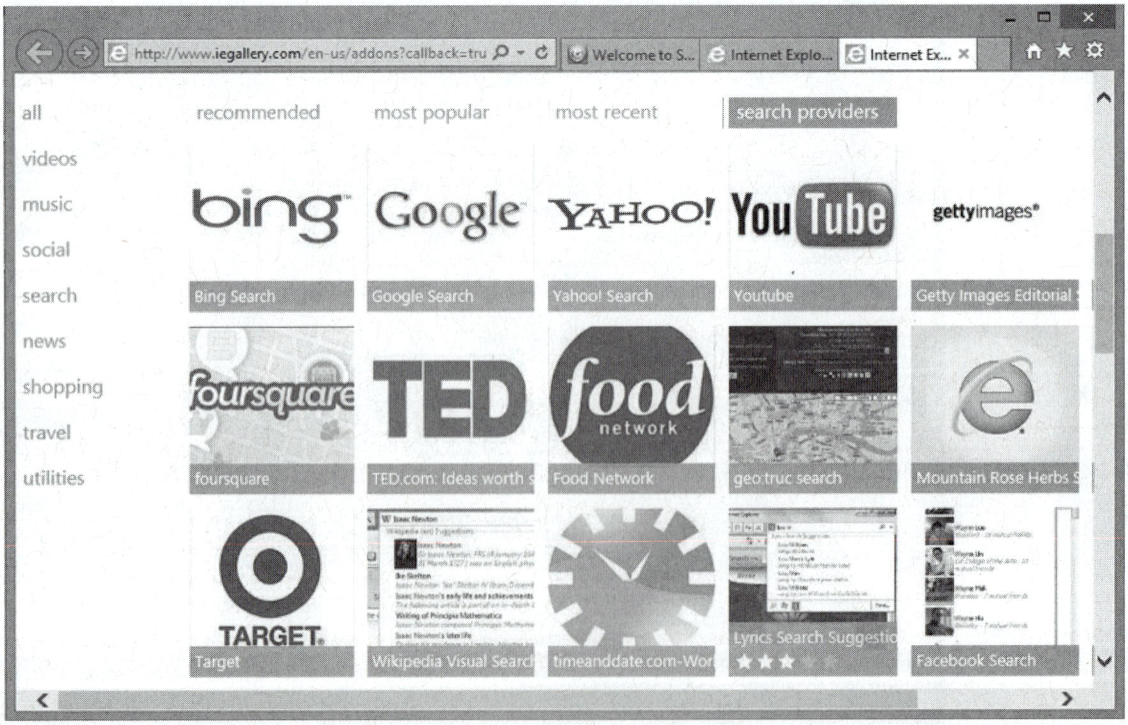

4. Click the tile for one of the web search or topic search providers.

   A page dedicated to that provider appears, as shown in Figure 8-8.

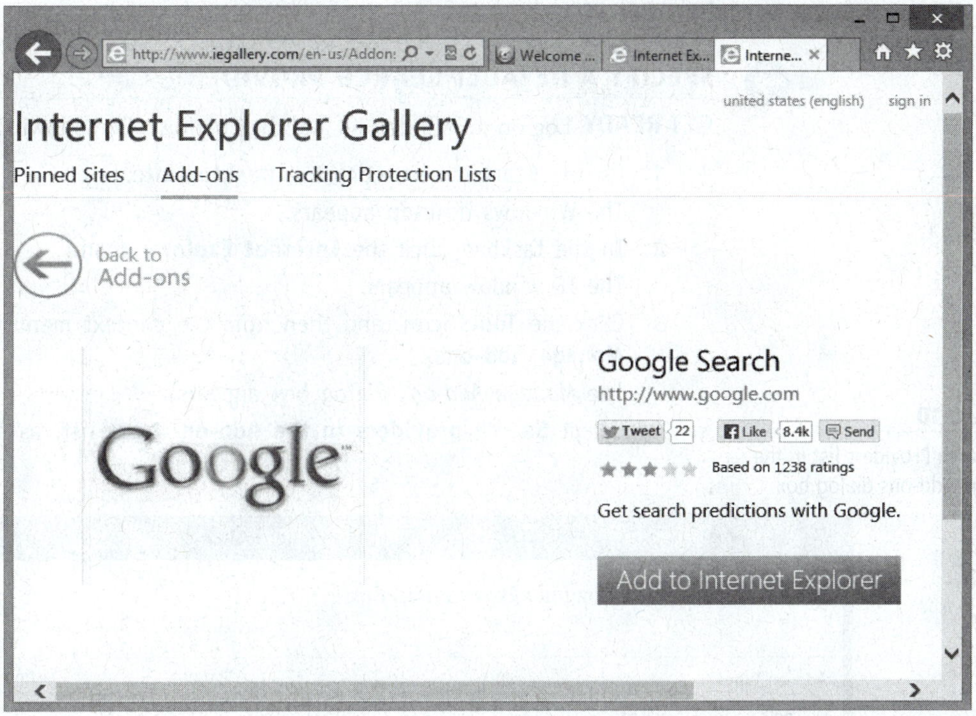

Figure 8-8

A search provider page

5. Click **Add to Internet Explorer**.

   An *Add Search Provider* dialog box appears, as shown in Figure 8-9.

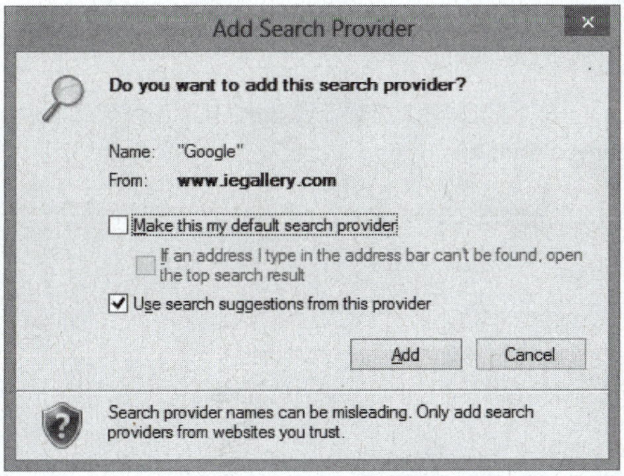

Figure 8-9

The *Add Search Provider* dialog box

6. If you want the selected provider to replace Bing as the IE default, select the *Make this my default search provider* checkbox. If you want the provider to provide suggestions as you type searches, select the *Use search suggestions from this provider* checkbox. Then, click **Add** to add the selected provider to the *Instant Search* list.

Once you configure IE with multiple search providers, you can click the down arrow on the right side of the *Search* icon to select the provider you want to use for a particular search.

Specifying a Default Search Provider

When you first open an IE window, the default search providers *Bing*. Once you have added other search providers , you can specify a different default provider, using the following procedure:

SPECIFY A DEFAULT SEARCH PROVIDER

GET READY. Log on to Windows 8 and then perform the following steps:

1. On the **Start** screen, click the **Desktop tile**.
   The Windows desktop appears.
2. In the taskbar, click the **Internet Explorer icon**.
   The IE window appears.
3. Click the **Tools** icon, and then from the context menu that appears, select **Manage Add-ons**.
   The *Manage Add-ons* dialog box appears.
4. Select **Search providers in the Add-on types** list, as shown in Figure 8-10.

Figure 8-10

The Search Providers list in the Manage Add-ons dialog box

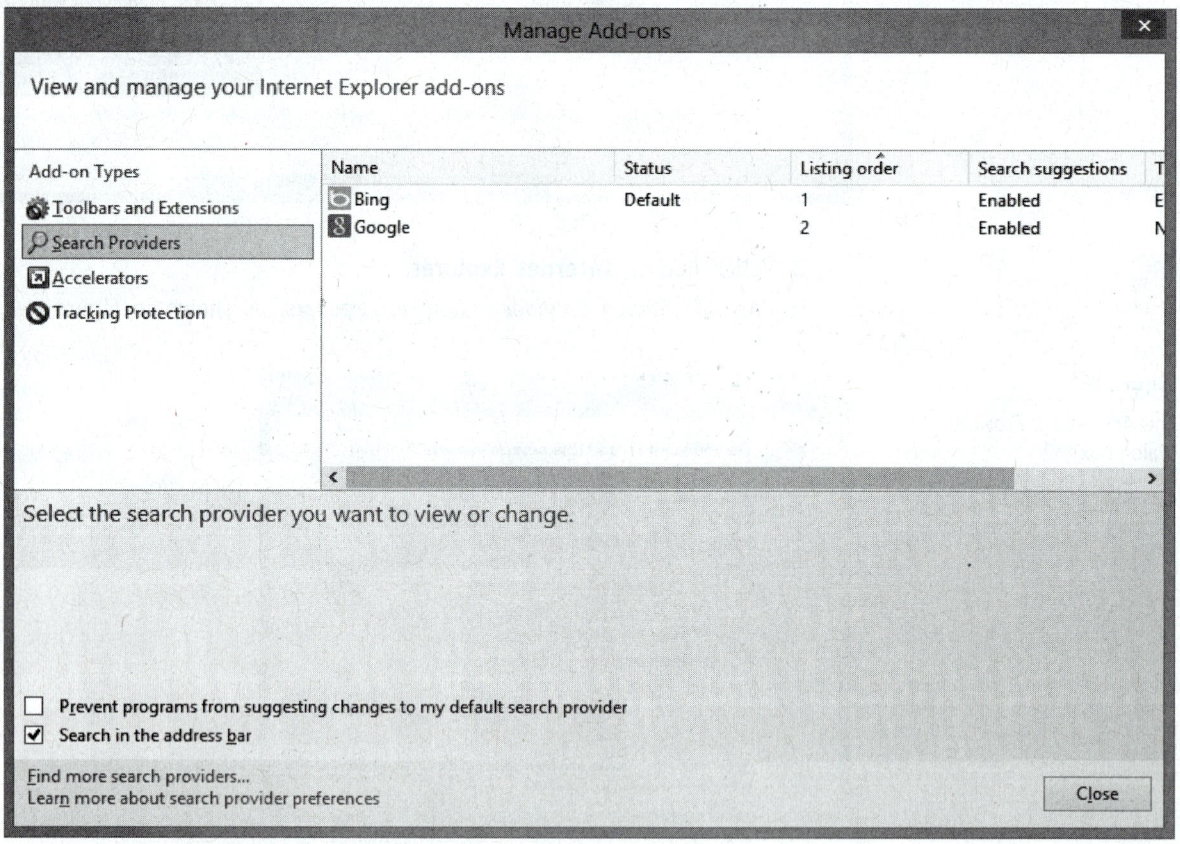

5. Select one of the search providers you installed earlier and click **Set as default**.
   The *Status* indicator changes to show the selected provider as the default.
6. Click **Close**.

CONFIGURING ACCELERATORS

Like search providers, ***accelerators*** enable users to send content to other resources, in the form of applications running on the computer or other sites on the Internet. However, instead of the user typing content into a search box, accelerators enable you to highlight content in a browser window and select the accelerator for the resource you want to receive that content.

By default, IE includes accelerators that enable users to email content, find it on a map, or translate it to another language. By clicking the *Find more accelerators* link on the *Manage Add-ons* dialog box, you can install new accelerators from the Microsoft Add-ons Gallery, as shown in Figure 8-11, using them to replace or augment the default ones.

Figure 8-11

Accelerators in the *Manage Add-ons* gallery

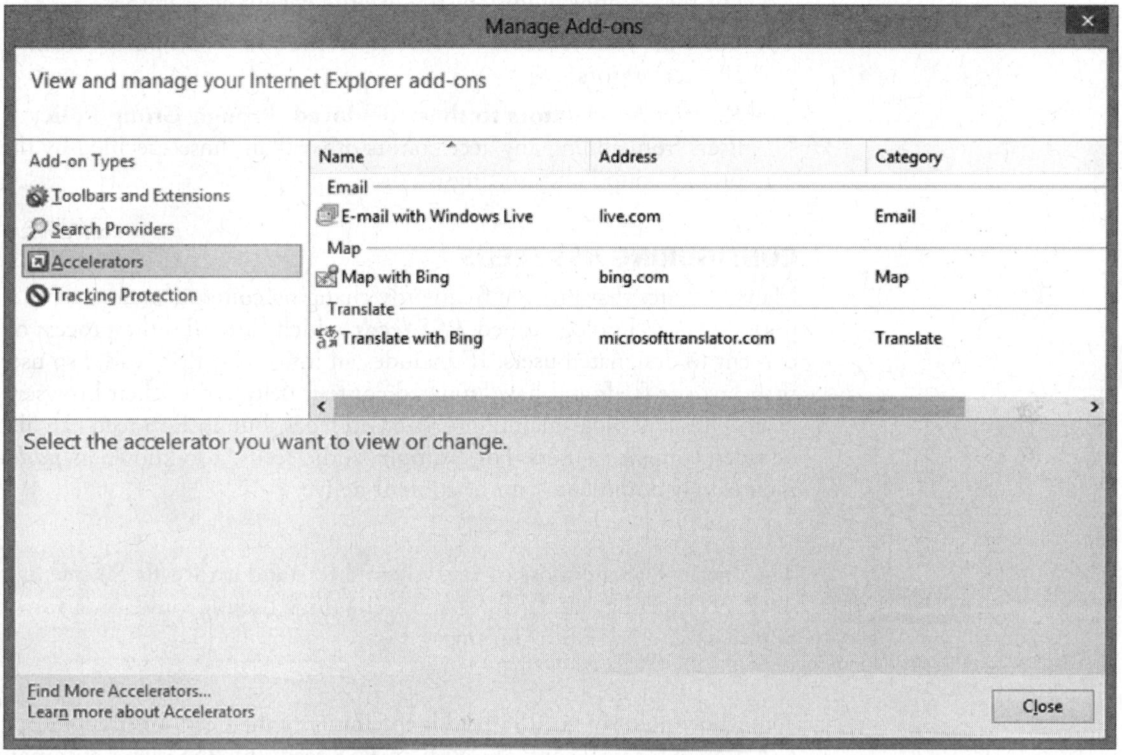

Administrators can control the use of accelerators on Windows 8 computers using Group Policy, as shown in Figure 8-12. The settings are located in the Computer Configuration\Policies\Administrative Templates\Windows Components\Internet Explorer\Accelerators container.

Figure 8-12

Accelerators settings in a Group Policy object

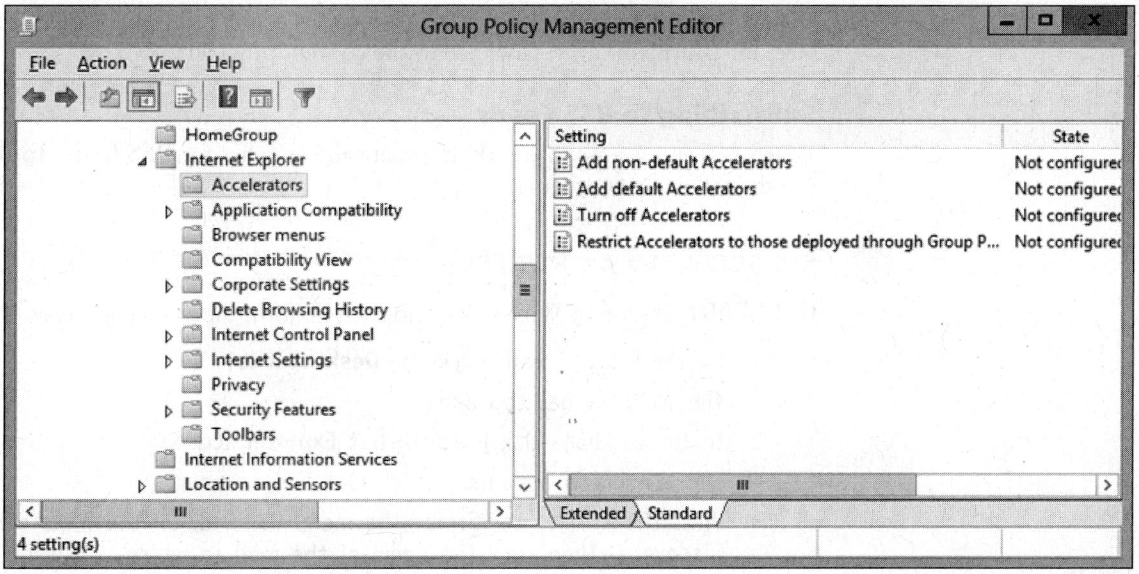

The Accelerators Group Policy settings are as follows:

- **Add non-default Accelerators** – Enables administrators to specify additional accelerators to be installed on Windows 8 computers. Users can also add their own non-default accelerators at will, but they cannot modify or remove the accelerators specified by the administrator.
- **Add default Accelerators** – Causes Windows 8 computers to deploy the accelerators included with IE by default. Default. Users can also add their own accelerators at will, but they cannot modify or remove the default accelerators.
- **Turn off Accelerators** – Prevents Windows 8 computers from running any IE accelerators.
- **Restrict Accelerators to those deployed through Group Policy** – Prevents Windows 8 users from adding any accelerators other than those specified by the administrator in other Group Policy settings.

CONFIGURING RSS FEEDS

Many websites that provide frequently changing content, such as news sites and blogs, support a push technology called ***RSS feeds***, which simplifies the process of delivering updated content to designated users. IE includes an integrated RSS reader so users can subscribe to their favorite feeds and have updated content delivered to their browsers on a regular basis. Many sites and blogs maintain text-based feeds, but an RSS feed can also push images, audio, or video content to users. For example, audio feeds, also known as ***podcasts***, have become an increasingly dominant form of content delivery.

TAKE NOTE* The initials RSS are most commonly said to stand for Really Simple Syndication, but several competing standards for the technology use the same initials, including Rich Site Summary and RDF Site Summary.

The whole point of an RSS feed is to eliminate the need for users to open multiple websites and browse for new content. With an RSS feed, the RSS client automatically retrieves new content from the content provider, enabling users to browse only the new information from their favorite sites.

Before you can receive RSS feeds with IE, however, you must subscribe to them. "Subscription" is the term used to refer to the process of configuring the RSS client to receive transmissions from a particular site. At the present time, most RSS feeds are available for subscription free of charge, but it is possible that future incarnations of the technology will take the form of services for which you must pay a fee to the content provider.

Subscribing to RSS Feeds

When you access a webpage, IE automatically searches for RSS feeds. To subscribe to a feed, use the following procedure.

SUBSCRIBE TO AN RSS FEED

GET READY. Log on to Windows 8 and then perform the following steps:

1. On the **Start** screen, click the **Desktop tile**.

   The Windows desktop appears.
2. In the taskbar, click the **Internet Explorer icon**.

   The IE window appears.
3. Press the **Alt** key to display the menu bar and, on the *Tools* menu, click **Feed Discovery**. Then click the name of the feed to which you want to subscribe.

A home page for the feed appears, as shown in Figure 8-13. You can always read the current contents of the feed on this page, whether you are subscribed or not.

Figure 8-13

An RSS feed page in IE

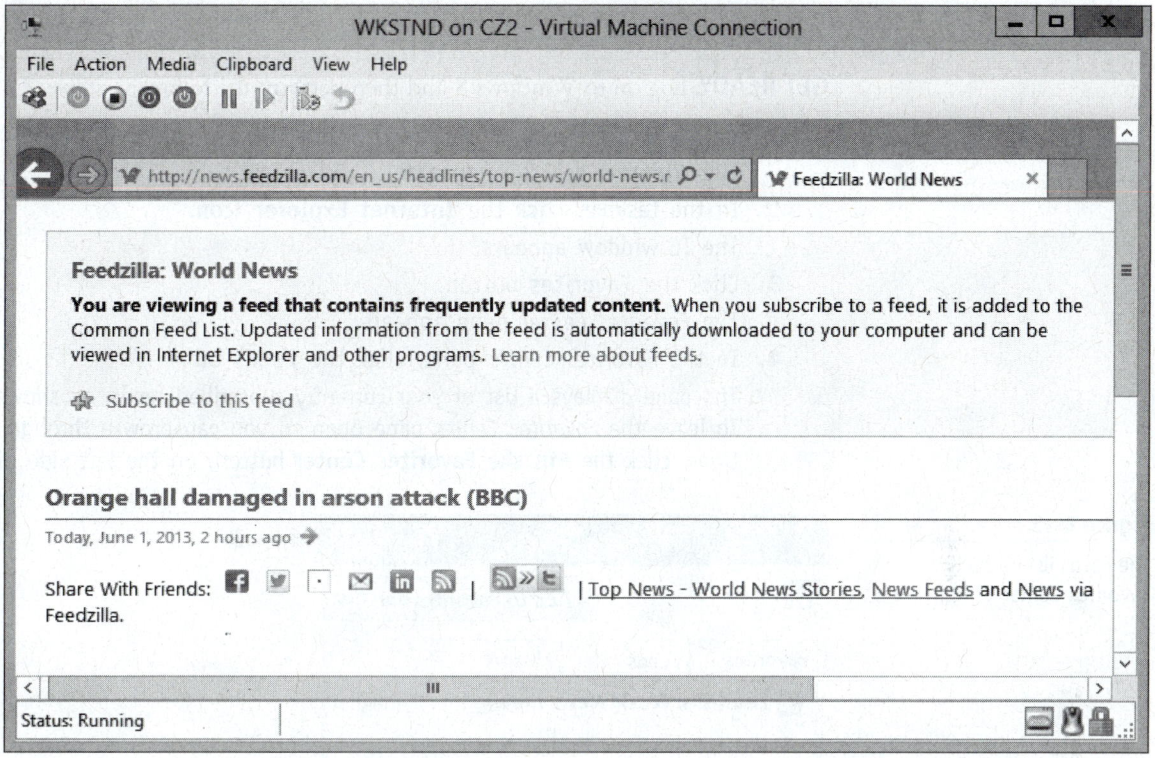

4. Click the **Subscribe to this feed** link.

   A *Subscribe to this Feed* dialog box appears, as shown in Figure 8-14.

Figure 8-14

An IE *Subscribe to this Feed* dialog box

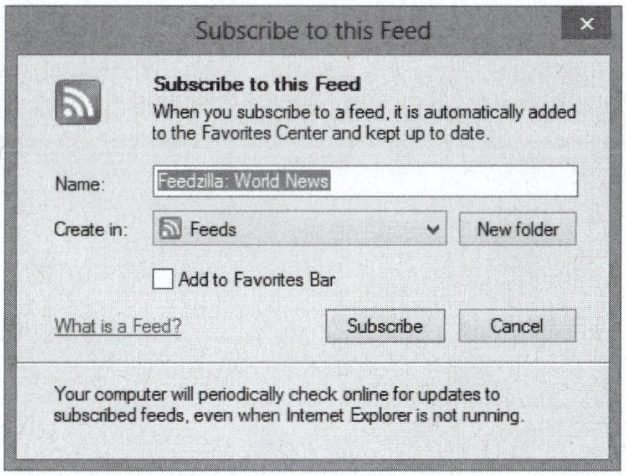

5. In the *Name* text box, type a name you want to assign to the feed (if it differs from the default).
6. Select the folder to which you want to add the feed, or click **New folder** to create one. Then click **Subscribe**.

   The feed page changes to indicate that you have successfully subscribed to the feed.

Viewing RSS Feeds

Once you have subscribed to RSS feeds, you can view their contents at any time by using the following procedure:

VIEW RSS FEEDS

GET READY. Log on to Windows 8 and then perform the following steps:

1. On the **Start** screen, click the **Desktop tile**.
   The Windows desktop appears.
2. In the taskbar, click the **Internet Explorer icon**.
   The IE window appears.
3. Click the **Favorites** button.
   The *Favorites Center* pane appears.
4. In the *Favorites Center* pane, click the **Feeds** tab.
   The pane displays a list of your currently subscribed feeds, as shown in Figure 8-15. To leave the *Favorites Center* pane open so you can browse through a list of subscriptions, click the **Pin the Favorites Center** button, on the left side of the menu bar.

Figure 8-15

The Feeds list in the IE Favorites Center

5. Click one of your subscribed feeds to display its contents in the main IE window.

Configuring Feed Settings

When you subscribe to an RSS feed using IE, the content is updated once every day, by default. You can modify the default update setting for all feeds or for individual feeds. To update the default setting for all feeds, use the following procedure:

CONFIGURE DEFAULT FEED SETTINGS

GET READY. Log on to Windows 8 and then perform the following steps:

1. On the **Start** screen, click the **Desktop tile**.

   The Windows desktop appears.

2. In the taskbar, click the **Internet Explorer icon**.

   The IE window appears.

3. Click the **Tools** button and then select **Internet Options**.

   The Internet Options dialog box appears, as shown in Figure 8-16.

Figure 8-16

The *Internet Options* dialog box

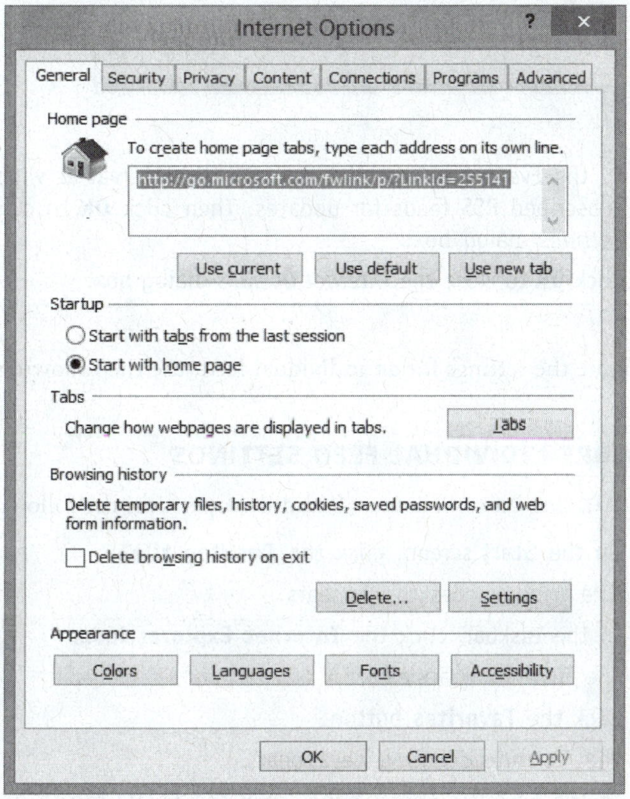

4. Click the **Content** tab and then, in the *Feeds* section, click **Settings**.

   The Feed and Web Slice Settings dialog box appears, as shown in Figure 8-17.

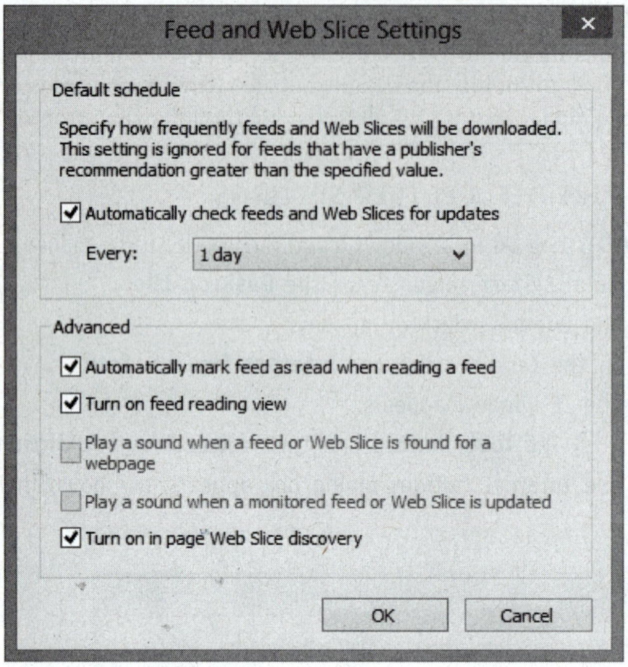

Figure 8-17
The *Feed and Web Slice Settings* dialog box

5. In the *Every* dropdown list, specify the interval at which IE should check the subscribed RSS feeds for updates. Then click **OK** to close the *Feed and Web Slice Settings* dialog box.
6. Click **OK** to close the *Internet Options* dialog box.

To configure the settings for an individual feed, use the following procedure.

CONFIGURE INDIVIDUAL FEED SETTINGS

GET READY. Log on to Windows 8 and then perform the following steps:

1. On the **Start** screen, click the **Desktop tile**.
   The Windows desktop appears.
2. In the taskbar, click the **Internet Explorer icon**.
   The IE window appears.
3. Click the **Favorites** button.
   The *Favorites Center* pane appears.
4. In the *Favorites Center* pane, click the **Feeds** tab.
   The pane displays a list of your currently subscribed feeds.
5. Right-click one of your feed subscriptions and then, from the context menu, select **Properties**.
   The Feed Properties dialog box appears, as shown in Figure 8-18.

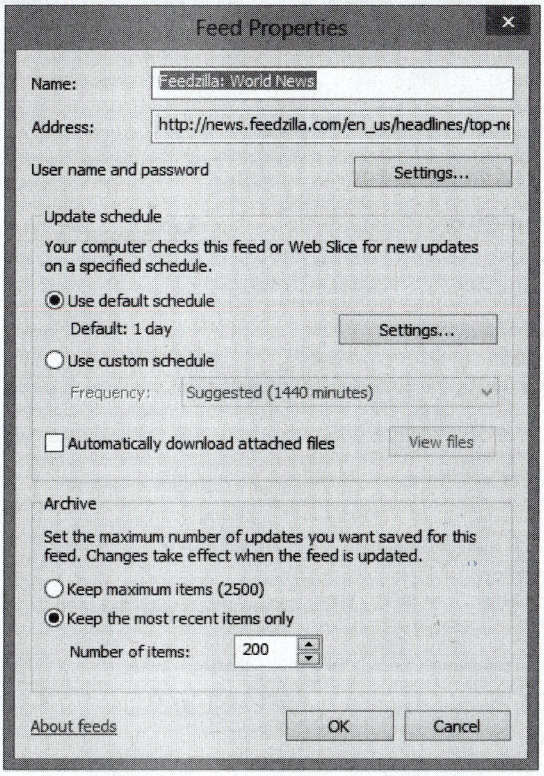

Figure 8-18

The *Feed Properties* dialog box

6. To change the update schedule, select the **Use custom schedule** radio button and then, in the *Frequency* dropdown list, select the desired interval.
7. When subscribing to an RSS feed that includes podcasts, you must also select the **Automatically download attached files** checkbox.
8. To change the *Archive* settings for the feed, change the *Number of items* spin box to specify the number of new content items you want to retain in the feed window, or select the **Keep maximum items** radio button.
9. Click **OK** to close the *Feed Properties* dialog box.

PRINTING WITH IE

Prior to version 7, IE had some long-standing problems with the printing of webpages that are now addressed in the current release. At one time, it was common for webpages to print with some text cut off in portrait mode. The only workaround was to switch to landscape mode, which printed all of the text but wasted a lot of paper and provided an awkward reading experience.

IE now has a *Print Preview* page, as shown in Figure 8-19, that provides users with greater flexibility, both in viewing and formatting the pages to be printed. For example, the default *Shrink To Fit* setting reduces each webpage to the point that it will fit on a single sheet of paper. No longer is text cut off on the right, and there are no more orphaned lines that print on a second page.

Figure 8-19

The IE Print Preview dialog box

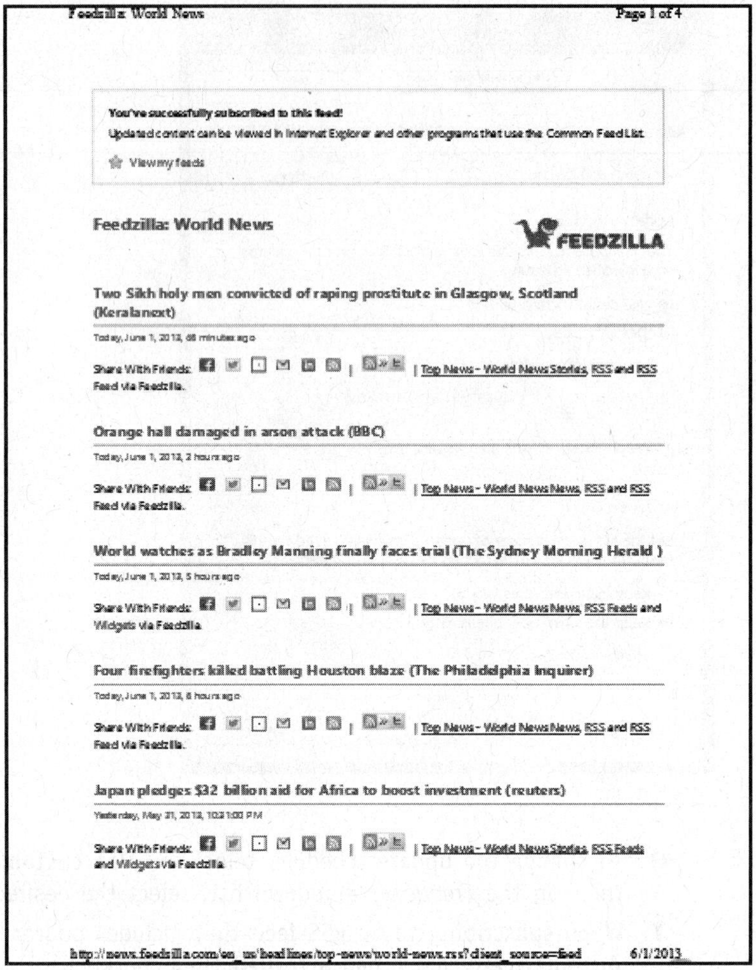

In addition to shrinking webpages to fit the printed page size, you can also make pages larger or smaller by adjusting the sizes using percentages. This enables you to print enlarged pages for easier reading or reduce the size to print multiple webpages on a single sheet of paper.

When you click the down arrow next to the Print button on the toolbar, you can choose from the following options.

- **Print** – The Print dialog box enables you to select a printer, choose the pages you want to print, print multiple copies, and, on the Options tab, print specific frames from a webpage.
- **Print Preview** – The Print Preview window enables you to view the current webpage at various sizes, select the page orientation (portrait or landscape), specify the size at which the webpage should print, and dynamically adjust the margins.
- **Page Setup** – The Page Setup dialog box enables you to select a paper size, source tray, and orientation; modify the default header and footer that will print on each page; and adjust the margins numerically.

CERTIFICATION READY
Configure Download Manager
Objective 2.5

CONFIGURING DOWNLOAD MANAGER

When you download a file from a website in IE10, the browser's built-in download manager takes over, prompting you confirm the download with a dialog box like that shown in Figure 8-20. From this dialog box, you can do any of the following:

- Download and run the selected file.
- Download and save the selected file to the program's default folder.
- Download and save the selected file to another folder.
- Cancel the download.

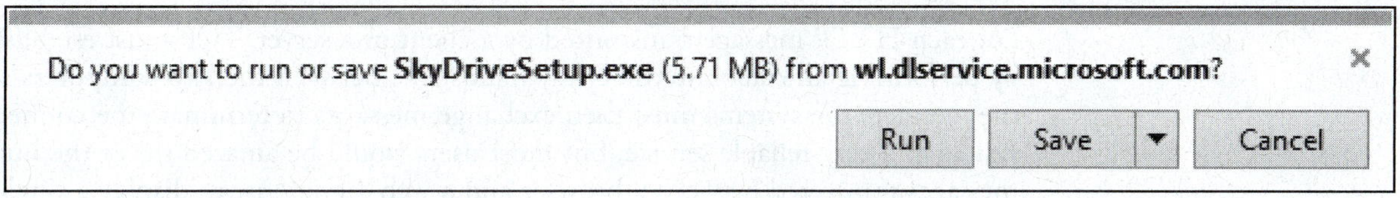

Figure 8-20
IE download options

When you choose an option to proceed with the download, the process begins and control is immediately returned to the browser, so you can continue working as the download proceeds.

When the download finishes, the dialog box shown in Figure 8-21 appears, providing you with the following options:

- Run the selected file.
- Open the folder containing the file in File Explorer.
- Open the Download Manager window.

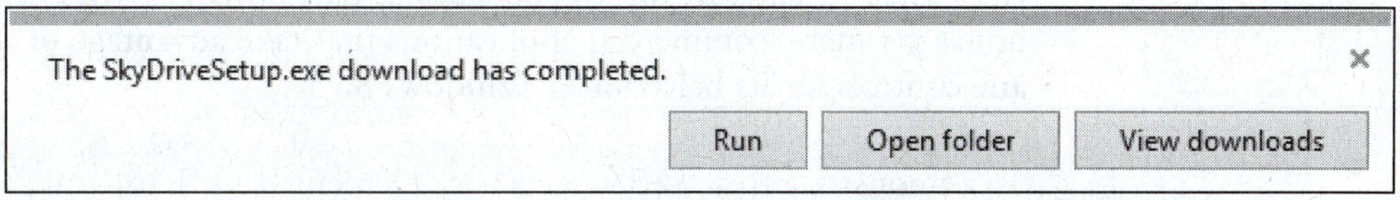

Figure 8-21
IE downloaded file options

The *View Downloads* window, shown in Figure 8-22, provides you with access to all of your previous downloads. You can also click Options to change the default download folder and select whether the manager should notify you when downloads are complete.

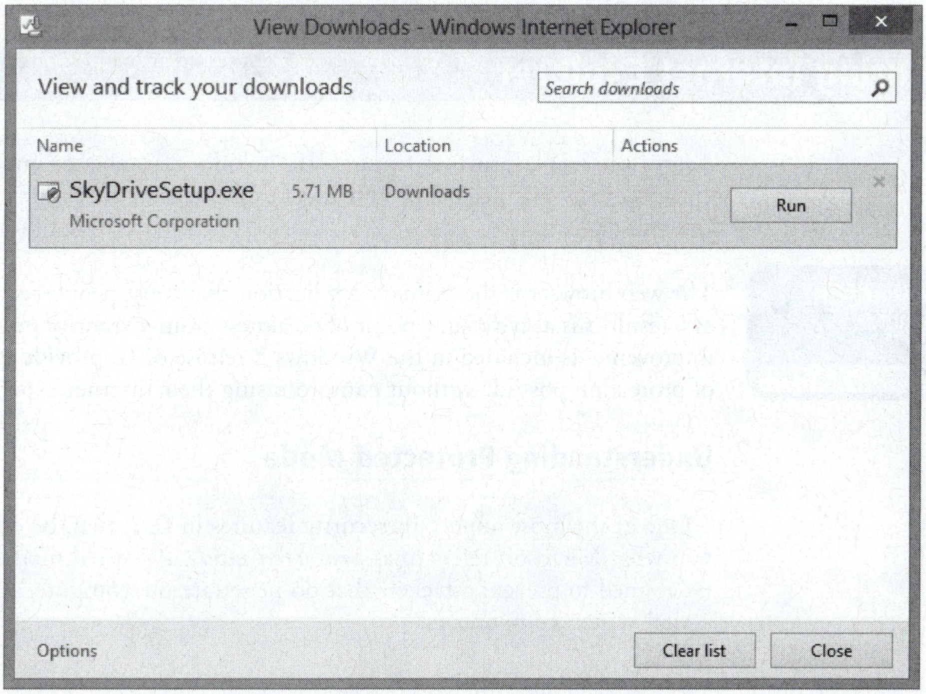

Figure 8-22
The IE View Downloads window

Introducing WebSockets

In traditional web communications, clients and servers use the HyperText Transfer Protocol (HTTP) to exchange messages formatted using the HyperText Markup Language (HTML). This has been a viable solution for many years, but its primary problem is the amount of traffic overhead these exchanges incur.

CERTIFICATION READY
Configure WebSockets
Objective 2.5

Every HTML and image file that makes up a standard webpage requires a separate HTTP transaction. HTTP is an application layer protocol that uses the transport service provided by the Transmission Control Protocol (TCP).

For each HTTP message transmitted by a client or a server, TCP must establish a connection by performing an elaborate three-way handshake between the two computers. After sending the message, the systems must then exchange messages to terminate the connection. This results in a very reliable service, but most users would be amazed to see the hundreds of messages transacted between a browser and a web server, just to display a single webpage.

WebSockets is a standard defining a new protocol that enables Internet clients and servers to exchange data immediately as it becomes available, without the overhead created by HTTP and TCP. A websocket is essentially an open connection between a client and a server that remains open for as long as the systems have data to exchange. For example, in the case of a web-based, real-time, multiplayer game, the latency generated by HTTP communications can easily make rapid-fire play difficult or impossible. Using WebSockets, nearly all of the connection establishment and termination messages required by HTTP and TCP are eliminated. The client establishes a single connection to the server, and the two proceed to exchange data in either direction, with greatly reduced latency.

IE10 includes support for WebSockets, as part of its HTML5 implementation, but there are not as yet many commercial applications that take advantage of the technology, nor are there any controls for its behavior in Windows 8.

TAKE NOTE*

To demonstrate that WebSockets is implemented in IE10, you can open two separate IE10 browser windows on the same computer and type the URL *http://html5demos.com/web-socket* in each one. The page will show a *Socket Open* status and allow you to exchange text messages with the other window. If you try this with any lower version of IE, there will be no socket established.

Securing Internet Explorer

THE BOTTOM LINE

Apart from its performance features, IE includes a number of important security enhancements that help to protect users from malware incursions and other Internet dangers.

CERTIFICATION READY
Configure security settings
Objective 2.5

The web browser is the primary application that most people use to access the Internet, and as a result it is also a major point of weakness from a security perspective. The security improvements included in the Windows 8 release of IE provide users with the highest degree of protection possible without compromising their Internet experiences.

Understanding Protected Mode

One of the most important security features in IE is that, by default, the browser operates in what Microsoft refers to as ***protected mode***. Protected mode is an operational state designed to prevent attackers that do penetrate the computer's defenses from accessing vital system components.

Protected mode is essentially a way to run IE with highly reduced privileges. Windows 8 includes a security feature called ***Mandatory Integrity Control (MIC)***, which assigns various integrity access levels to processes running on the computer. These integrity access levels control what system resources the process is allowed to access. Table 8-1 shows the integrity levels assigned by MIC.

Table 8-1

Mandatory Integrity Control

Integrity Access Level	Privilege Level	Privileges
High	Administrator	The process is granted full access to the system, including write access to the Program Files folder and the HKEY_LOCAL_MACHINE registry key.
Medium	User	The process is granted limited access to the system, including write access to user-specific areas, such as the user's Documents folder and the HKEY_CURRENT_USER registry key. All processes that are not explicitly assigned an integrity access level receive this level of access.
Low	Untrusted	The process is granted minimal access to the system, including write access only to the Temporary Internet Files\Low folder and the HKEY_CURRENT_USER\Software\Microsoft\Internet Explorer/LowRegistry registry key

In Windows 8, IE protected mode means that it runs as a low-integrity procedure. The browser application can therefore write to only low-integrity disk locations, such as the Temporary Internet Files folder and the standard IE storage areas, including the History, Cookies, and Favorites folders.

What this means is that even if attackers manage to gain access to the computer through a web browser connection, there is little they can do to damage the system because they do not have access to vital system areas. For example, even if an attacker manages to upload a destructive application to the system, he or she cannot force it to load each time the system starts by adding it to the Startup group.

Protected mode is not a complete defense against malware in itself. IE10 and Windows 8 have many other security mechanisms that work in combination. Protected mode is designed to limit the damage that attackers can do if they manage to penetrate the other security measures.

DETECTING PROTECTED MODE INCOMPATIBILITIES

Because IE on Windows 8 runs in protected mode by default, it is possible that web-based applications designed to run on earlier versions might not run properly. These applications might be designed to write to a disk area that is inaccessible while in protected mode, or they might not know how to handle the new prompts in IE.

However, you might find that applications that did not run under IE version 7 now do run in IE10, using the default settings. This is because in IE7, websites in the local intranet zone ran in protected mode by default. In IE8 and later, Microsoft changed the defaults, and disabled protected mode for local intranet sites, as shown in Figure 8-23.

Figure 8-23

Protected Mode disabled

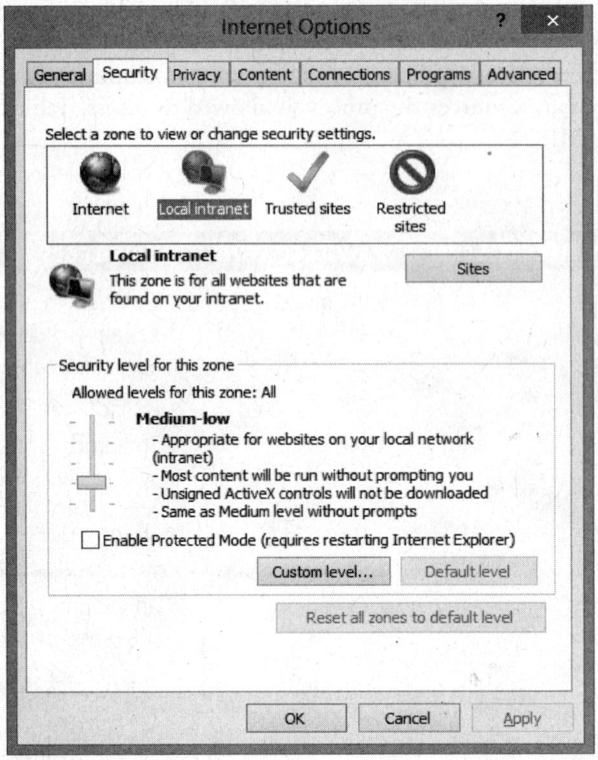

Comprehensive testing of all web-based applications should be an essential part of every Windows 8 or IE deployment. To gather information about application incompatibilities, enable *Turn on* ***compatibility logging*** setting in the Local Group Policy, located in the Computer Configuration\Administrative Templates\Windows Components\Internet Explorer folder or the User Configuration\Administrative Templates\Windows Components\Internet Explorer folder, as shown in Figure 8-24.

Figure 8-24

The *Turn on compatibility logging* policy setting

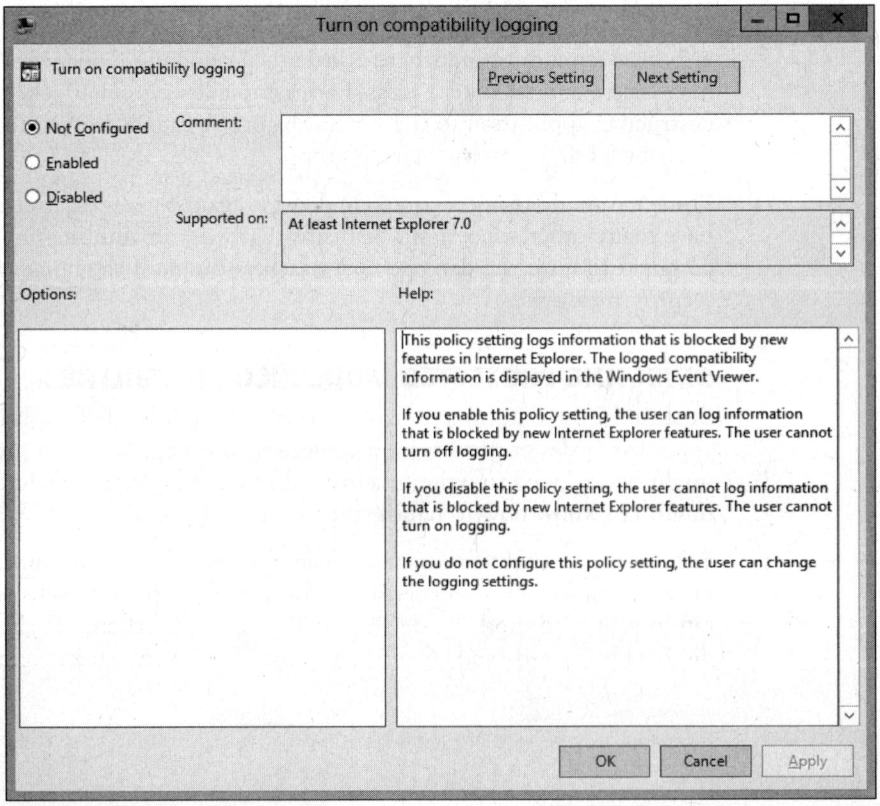

Once you enable the *Turn on compatibility logging* policy, Windows 8 begins logging all information blocked by the IE security settings. The logged data appears in the *Event Viewer* console in the IE application log.

RESOLVING PROTECTED MODE INCOMPATIBILITIES

Once you have determined the exact source of your application's incompatibility, you can use the following techniques to try to resolve the problem.

- **Move the site to the Trusted Sites zone** – IE maintains different security zones that provide applications with different levels of privileges. Sites in the Internet zone run in protected mode, with minimal privileges, but if you move them to the ***Trusted Sites zone***, they do not run in protected mode, and receive elevated privileges.
- **Disable protected mode in IE** – Although Microsoft does not recommend this practice, you can disable protected mode by selecting a zone and clearing the Enable Protected Mode checkbox. Disabling protected mode causes IE to apply the medium integrity access level to the zone.
- **Modify the application** – Probably the most difficult and time-consuming option, you can also modify the application itself so that it can run properly using the minimal privileges provided by protected mode.

INTRODUCING ENHANCED PROTECTED MODE

In addition to the protection provided by protected mode, IE10 includes an extension of that feature, called Enhanced Protected Mode. Enhanced Protected Mode uses the same basic philosophy as protected mode to block unauthorized access to addition system resources, such as personal information and corporate network resources,

Enhanced Protected Mode runs by default in the *Start* screen version of IE10, but it is disabled by default in the desktop version because it is incompatible with some of the more popular plug-ins. The *Start* screen version does not support plug-ins, so this is not a problem, but when you check *Enable Enhanced Protected Mode* in the *Advanced* tab of the *Internet Options* dialog box, as shown in Figure 8-25, IE10 disables any installed add-ins that are not compatible.

Figure 8-25
Enabling *Enhanced Protected Mode*

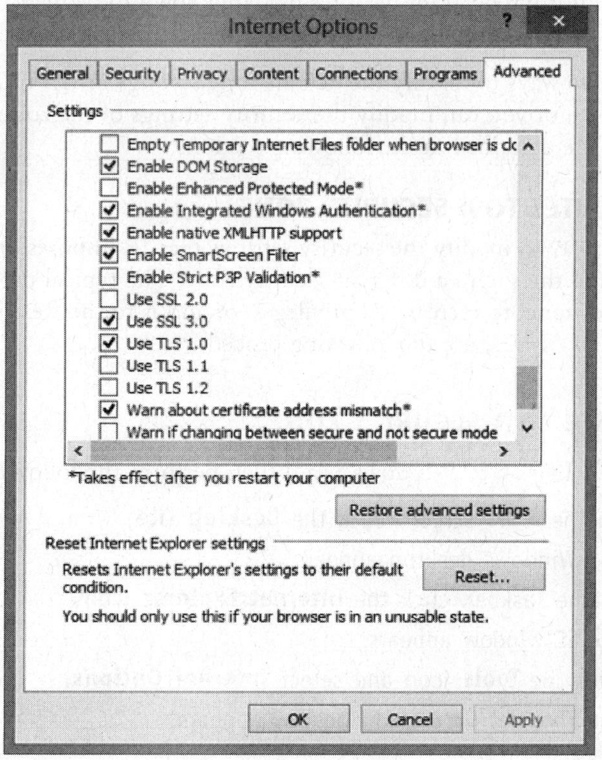

Configuring Security Zones

With the appropriate development tools and programming expertise, web-based applications can do virtually anything that traditional software applications do, which can be either a good or a bad thing.

For companies developing their own in-house software, web browsers provide a stable, proven technological base. However, a web-based intranet application is likely to require extensive access to system resources. An intranet application might have to install software on the computer, for example, or change system configuration settings.

Granting this type of access is acceptable for an internal application, but you could not grant the same privileges to an Internet website. Imagine what it would be like to surf the Internet if every site you accessed had the ability to install any software it wanted on your computer, or modify any of your system configuration settings. Your computer would likely be rendered inoperative within a matter of hours.

To provide different levels of access to specific applications, IE divides the addresses accessible with the web browser into several different ***security zones***, each of which has a different set of privileges. The four zones are as follows:

- **Internet** – All website that are not listed in the other three zones fall into this zone. Sites in the Internet zone run in protected mode and have minimal access to the computer's drives and configuration settings.
- **Local intranet** – IE automatically detects sites that originate from the local intranet and places them in this zone. Sites in this zone do not run in protected mode and have significant access to the system, including the ability to run certain scripts, ActiveX controls, and plug-ins.
- **Trusted sites** – This zone provides the most elevated set of privileges and is intended for sites that you can trust not to damage the computer. By default, there are no sites in this zone; you must add them manually.
- **Restricted sites** – This zone has the most reduced set of privileges and runs in protected mode. It is intended for websites that are known to be malicious, but which users still must access for some reason. As with the Trusted sites zone, this zone is empty by default.

There are two ways to modify the default zone settings in IE. You can assign websites to specific zones, or you can modify the security settings of the zones themselves. These two procedures are described in the following sections.

ADDING SITES TO A SECURITY ZONE

The easiest way to modify the security settings that IE imposes on a specific website is to manually add the site to a different security zone. The typical procedure is to add a site to the Trusted sites zone, to increase its privileges, or add it to the Restricted sites zone, to reduce its privileges. To do this, use the following procedure.

ADD A SITE TO A SECURITY ZONE

GET READY. Log on to Windows 8 and then perform the following steps:

1. On the **Start** screen, click the **Desktop tile**.

   The Windows desktop appears.

2. In the taskbar, click the **Internet Explorer icon**.

   The IE window appears.

3. Click the **Tools** icon and select **Internet Options**.

   The *Internet Options* dialog box appears.

4. Click the **Security** tab, as shown in Figure 8-26.

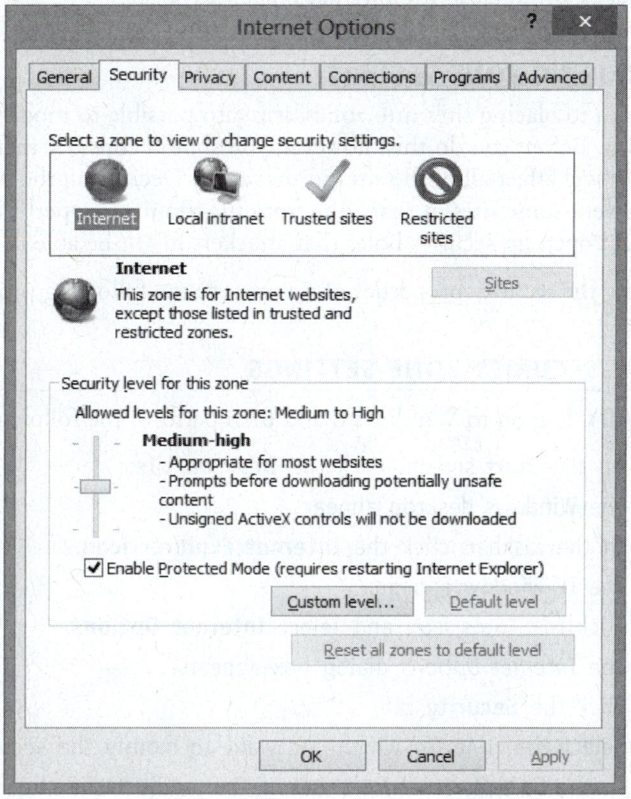

Figure 8-26

The *Security* tab of the *Internet Options* dialog box

5. Select the zone, either **Trusted sites** or **Restricted sites**, to which you want to add a **site**.
6. Click **Sites**.

   The *Trusted sites* or *Restricted sites* dialog box appears, like the one shown in Figure 8-27.

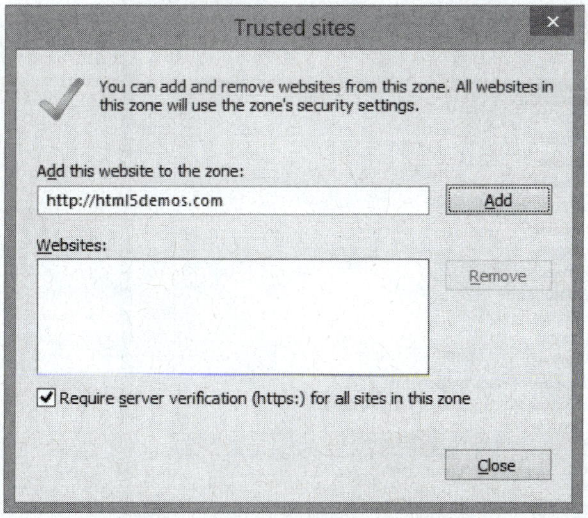

Figure 8-27

The *Trusted sites* dialog box

7. Type the URL of the website you want to add to the zone into the *Add this website to the zone* text box, and then click **Add**.

   The URL appears in the *Websites* list.

8. Click **Close** to close the *Trusted sites* or *Restricted sites* dialog box.
9. Click **OK** to close the *Internet Properties* sheet.

CONFIGURING ZONE SECURITY

In addition to placing sites into zones, it is also possible to modify the properties of the zones themselves. Before you do this, however, you should consider that changing a zone's security properties will affect all of the sites in that zone. Decreasing the privileges allocated to a zone could prevent some sites in that zone from functioning properly. Increasing the privileges of a zone could open up security holes that attackers might be able to exploit.

To modify the security properties of a zone, use the following procedure:

MODIFY SECURITY ZONE SETTINGS

GET READY. Log on to Windows 8 and then perform the following steps:

1. On the **Start** screen, click the **Desktop tile.**
   The Windows desktop appears.
2. In the taskbar, click the **Internet Explorer icon.**
   The IE window appears.
3. Click the **Tools** icon and select **Internet Options.**
   The *Internet Options* dialog box appears.
4. Click the **Security** tab.
5. Select the zone for which you want to modify the security settings.
6. In the *Security level for this zone* box, adjust the slider to increase or decrease the security level for the zone. Moving the slider up increases the protection for the zone and moving the slider down decreases it.
7. Select or clear the **Enable protected mode** checkbox, if desired,
8. To exercise more precise control over the zone's security settings, click **Custom level.**
   The *Security Settings* dialog box for the zone appears, as shown in Figure 8-28.

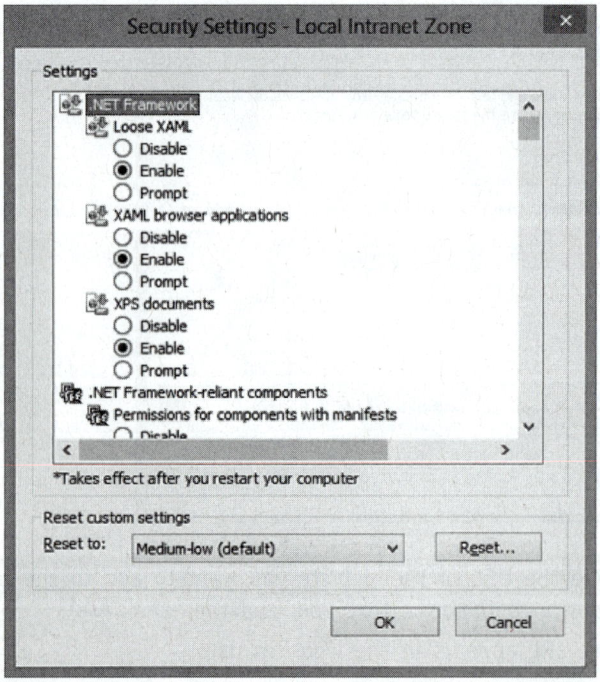

Figure 8-28

The *Security Settings* dialog box for the *Local Intranet Zone*

9. Select radio buttons for the individual settings in each of the security categories. The radio buttons typically make it possible to enable a setting, disable it, or prompt the user before enabling it.
10. Click **OK** to close the *Security Settings* dialog box.
11. Click **OK** to close the *Internet Options* dialog box.

Configuring the SmartScreen Filter

Social engineering is a term that describes any attempt to penetrate the security of a system by convincing people to disclose secret information.

Many would-be attackers have realized that discovering a user's password with an elaborate software procedure is a lot more difficult than simply calling the user on the telephone and asking for it. When asked for information by an authoritative-sounding person saying that they work for the IT department, most people are eager to help and are all too willing to give out information that should be kept confidential.

Phishing is a technique that takes social engineering to a mass scale. Instead of convincing-sounding telephone callers, phishing uses convincing-looking websites that urge users to supply personal information, such as passwords and account numbers.

For example, an attacker might send out thousands of email messages directed at customers of a particular bank, urging them to update their account information or risk having their accounts closed. Unsuspecting users click the hyperlink in the email and are taken to a webpage that looks very much like that of the actual bank site, but it isn't. The page is part of a bogus site set up by the attacker and probably copied from the bank site. This false site proceeds to ask the user for information such as bank account numbers, PINs, and passwords, which the attacker can then use to access the account.

Defending against phishing is more a matter of educating users than competing in a technological arms race, as is the case with viruses and other types of malware. IE10 includes a component called the ***SmartScreen Filter*** that examines traffic for evidence of phishing activity and displays a warning to the user if it finds any. It is up to the user to recognize the warning signs and to refrain from supplying confidential information to unknown parties.

FILTERING FOR PHISHING ATTACKS

The IE SmartScreen Filter uses three techniques to identify potential phishing websites. These techniques are as follows.

- **Online lookup of phishing sites** – Microsoft maintains a list of known phishing sites that it updates several times every hour. When a user attempts to access a websites, IE transmits the URL, along with other nonconfidential system information, to a Microsoft server, which compares it with the phishing site list. If the online lookup process determines that a website is a known phishing site, IE displays a warning. However, the user can continue to the site, if desired.
- **Online lookup of download sites** – When a user attempts to download a file, IE checks the source against Microsoft's list of known malicious software sites. If the source site appears on the list, IE blocks the download and displays a warning.
- **Onsite analysis** – IE examines the code of each webpage as the system downloads it for patterns and phrases indicative of a phishing attempt. This technique provides a means to detect phishing sites that have not yet been positively identified and reported as such. If the scan indicates that the site might include a phishing attempt, IE displays a yellow suspicious site warning in the *Address* bar. Clicking the warning button displays more detail about the suspicion, but the user can also ignore the warning and proceed.

DISABLING SMARTSCREEN FILTER

When you run IE10 for the first time, you can elect to set up the browser by using express settings, or by configuring settings individually.

The express settings option enables the SmartScreen Filter, but you can disable it at any time by clicking the Tools icon and selecting Safety> Turn off SmartScreen Filter, to display the Microsoft SmartScreen Filter dialog box, as shown in Figure 8-29.

Figure 8-29

The *Microsoft SmartScreen Filter* dialog box

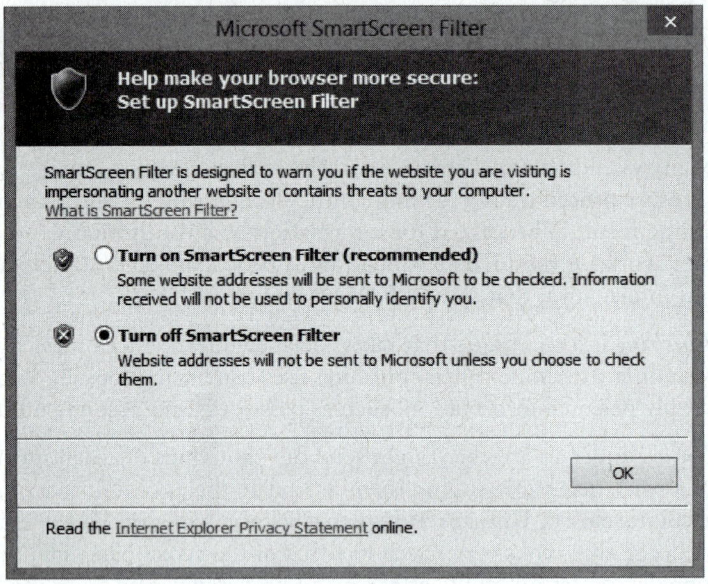

Phishing sites present no danger other than the temptation to reply to requests for confidential information. It is possible to turn the SmartScreen Filter off and remain safe from phishing attempts, as long as you follow one simple rule: Don't trust hyperlinks. Never supply a password or any other confidential information to a website unless you type the URL yourself and you are sure that it is correct.

Most successful phishing attempts occur when a user clicks a hyperlink in an email or another website. It is a simple matter to create a hyperlink that looks like http://www.woodgrovebank.com, but which actually points to a server run by an evil attacker in another domain. However, as long as you yourself type www.woodgrovebank.com in the browser's *Address* bar, you are assured of accessing the true website of Woodgrove Bank.

Using InPrivate Mode

IE has always maintained a record of each user's activities, in the form of temporary files, cookies, and a browsing history.

The user could delete these elements individually after the fact, but there was no easy way to prevent IE from gathering them all in the first place. ***InPrivate Mode*** is a feature in IE10 that enables you to surf the Internet without leaving any record of your activities.

InPrivate Mode consists of the following two technologies:

- **InPrivate Browsing** – Prevents IE from maintaining a permanent record of the user's activities during browsing session.
- ***InPrivate Filtering*** – Prevents third-party websites from compiling information about an IE user's browsing practices.

USING INPRIVATE BROWSING

To use InPrivate Browsing, you click the Safety button on the toolbar and select InPrivate Browsing. A new IE window appears, as shown in Figure 8-30. The InPrivate Browsing policies apply during the entire browsing session, including any additional tabs you create in that IE window.

Figure 8-30

InPrivate Browsing in IE

During the browsing session, IE stores some information temporarily, such as that found in cookies and temporary files, and deletes it when you terminate the session by closing the browser window. However, there is some information that IE does not store at all, including the browsing history, any data you supply in forms, and *Address* bar and AutoComplete data.

USING INPRIVATE FILTERING

Many Internet websites incorporate content from third-party providers, such as advertisements, maps, and videos. As a user browses to various sites that use these same providers, they can build up a profile of the user's browsing habits, and use that information to target them for specific types of ads. InPrivate Filtering enables you to block specific providers – or all providers – from gathering that information.

You can open a browser window that uses InPrivate Filtering by clicking the Tools button in the toolbar and selecting InPrivate Filtering.

CONFIGURING INPRIVATE MODE USING GROUP POLICY

AD DS administrators can configure InPrivate Mode settings for Windows 8 users all over the network using Group Policy. The policy settings are located in the Computer Configuration\Policies\Administrative Templates\Windows Components\Internet Explorer\Privacy container, as shown in Figure 8-31.

Figure 8-31

InPrivate Settings in a Group Policy object

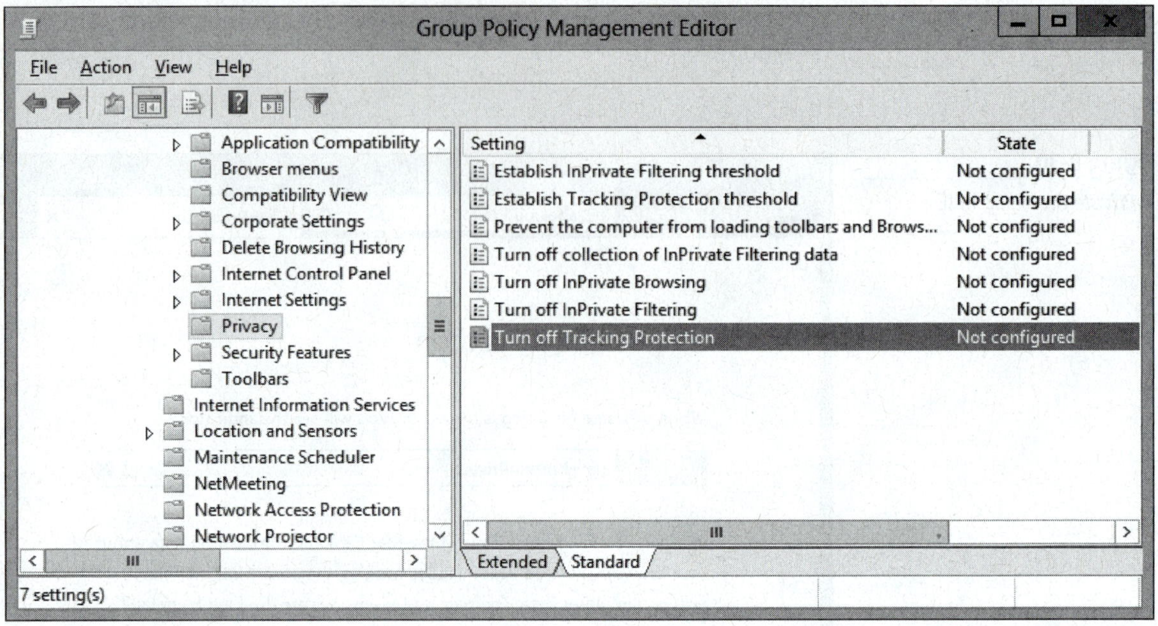

The policy settings for InPrivate Mode are as follows:

- **Establish InPrivate Filtering threshold** – Specifies the number of sites in which a third-party content provider must be found before the site is blocked. The range of allowable values is 3 to 30.
- **Establish Tracking Protection threshold** – Specifies the number of first-party sites that a third-party item can be referenced from before it is blocked. The range of allowable values is 3 to 30.
- **Prevent the computer from loading toolbars and Browser Helper Objects when InPrivate Browsing starts** – Disables all toolbars and browser helper objects (BHOs) during InPrivate Browsing sessions.
- **Turn off collection of InPrivate Filtering data** – Specifies whether Windows 8 computers should collect InPrivate filtering data.
- **Turn off InPrivate Browsing** – Disables InPrivate Browsing for all browsing sessions. When you disable the setting, InPrivate Browsing is available for use
- **Turn off InPrivate Filtering** – Disables InPrivate Filtering for all browsing sessions. When you disable the setting, InPrivate Filtering is available for use.
- **Turn off Tracking Protection** – Disables Tracking Protection for all browsing sessions. When you disable the setting, Tracking Protection is available for use.

Browsing with Certificates

Secure Sockets Layer (SSL) is the protocol that most websites use when establishing secure connections with clients over the Internet.

SSL communication is based on the exchange of digital certificates. A digital certificate is a credential, issued by a trusted party, that confirms the identity of the web server and enables the client and the server to exchange encrypted traffic.

SSL communications are based on a ***public key infrastructure (PKI)***, which requires two encryptions keys, a public one and a private one. Data encrypted using the public key can only be decrypted with the private key, and in the same way, data encrypted with the private key can only be encrypted using the public key. A web server participating in a PKI receives a digital certificate from a ***certification authority (CA)***, which contains its public key. The server also generates a private key, which it stores locally.

When a web server on the Internet establishes an SSL connection with a client, it transmits its certificate. Then, when the server sends data encrypted with its private key to a client, the fact that the client can successfully decrypt the data using the public key from the certificate confirms the identity of the server. When the client transmits data encrypted using the public key, only the possessor of the private key – the server – can decrypt it.

When a Windows 8 IE user connects to a site that is secured using SSL, a lock appears in the address bar, along with the name of the organization to which the CA issued the certificate, as shown in Figure 8-32.

Figure 8-32

A secure connection in IE10

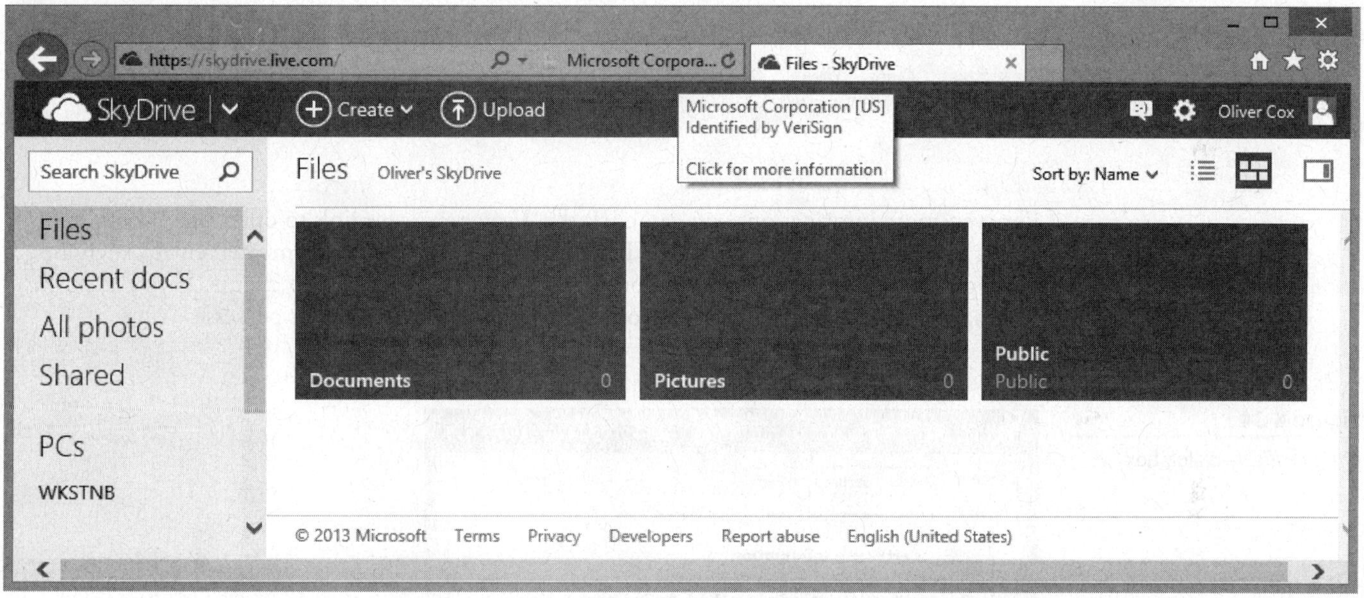

Clicking the lock icon displays more information about the site, including the identity of the CA that issued the certificate, as shown in Figure 8-33.

Figure 8-33

Displaying certificate information in IE10

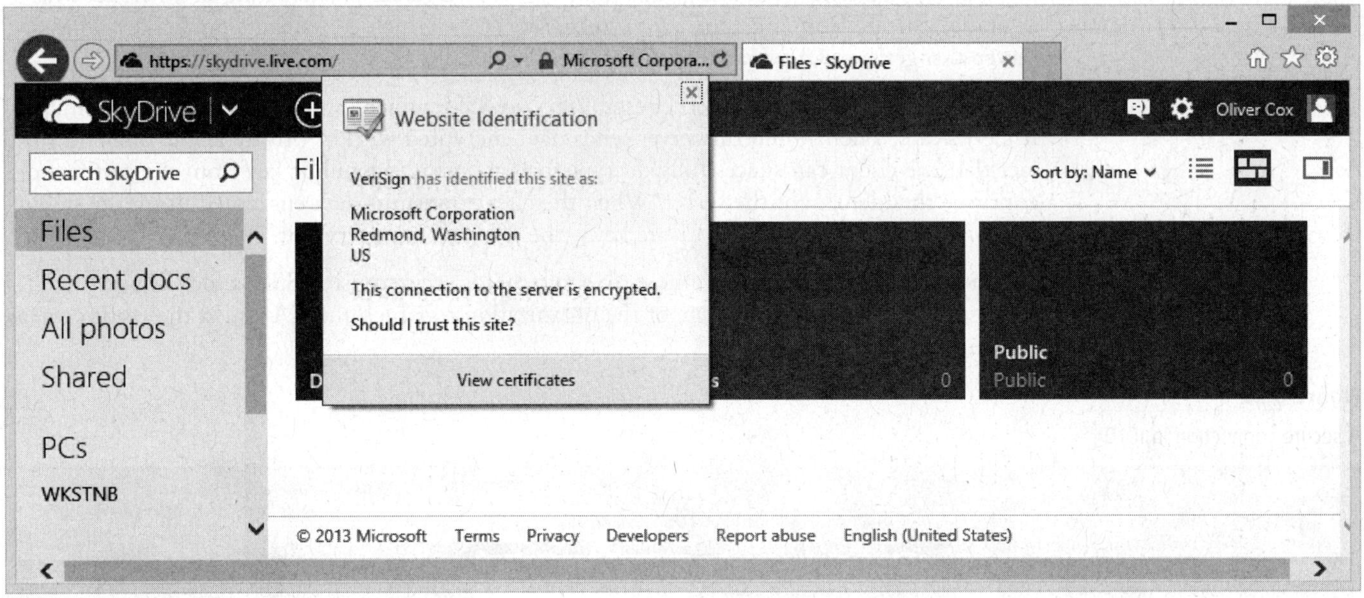

For even more information, you can click the *View certificates* link to open the *Certificate* dialog box, as shown in Figure 8-34. In most cases, the CA is a commercial entity, such as VeriSign or Thawte, which is in the business of issuing certificates to clients. If you trust the CA that issued the certificate, then you should trust the website that possesses it.

Figure 8-34

The *Certificate* dialog box

At times, an IE user might connect to a site that has a certificate that is improper in some way. The certificate might have expired, it might be corrupted, it might have been revoked, or it might have a name that is different from that of the site itself. When this occurs, IE blocks access to the site and displays a warning screen stating that there is a problem with the certificate. The user can then opt to close the browser window or ignore the warning and continue on to the site.

SKILL SUMMARY

IN THIS LESSON, YOU LEARNED:

- Many of the pages on the Internet still conform to old standards, and IE10 might not display them properly. To accommodate these pages, IE10 includes a feature called Compatibility View, which enables the browser to display older pages properly.
- One of the ways that IE interacts with other resources is through the use of add-ons. Add-ons are separate software components, created by Microsoft or by third parties, that interact with the basic functions of the web browser.
- Accelerators enable users to send content to other resources, in the form of applications running on the computer or other sites on the Internet. Accelerators enable you to highlight content in a browser window and select the accelerator for the resource you want to receive that content.
- Many websites that provide frequently changing content, such as news sites and blogs, support a push technology called RSS, which simplifies the process of delivering updated content to designated users.
- Protected mode is a way to run IE with highly reduced privileges. Enhanced protected mode provides more protection, at the cost of compatibility with some add-ons.
- Phishing is a technique that uses convincing-looking websites that urge users to supply personal information, such as passwords and account numbers. IE8 includes a SmartScreen Filter that examines traffic for evidence of phishing activity and displays a warning to the user if it finds any.
- To provide different levels of access to specific applications, IE divides the addresses accessible with the web browser into several different security zones, each of which has a different set of privileges.

Knowledge Assessment

Multiple Choice

Select one or more correct answers for each of the following questions.

1. What are the names of the two security zones in IE that have no sites in them by default? (Choose all that apply.)
   a. Internet
   b. Local intranet
   c. Trusted sites
   d. Restricted sites
2. Which of the following is NOT one of the add-on types supported by IE8?
   a. Toolbars and Extensions
   b. Search Providers

c. Accelerators
d. SmartScreen Filtering

3. What does a broken window icon in the IE8 address bar indicate?
   a. A failure to successfully download a certificate from the website
   b. A webpage that is incompatible with IE8
   c. A failure to update a subscribed RSS feed
   d. A failure to print a document from IE
4. Which of the following can be used to highlight content in a browser window instead of typing content directly into the browser's search box?
   a. Accelerator
   b. Search Provider
   c. RSS Feed
   d. Toolbars and Extensions
5. When you subscribe to an RSS Feed in IE, the content is updated how frequently by default?
   a. Weekly
   b. Daily
   c. Hourly
   d. Monthly
6. When downloading a file from a website in IE10, the browser's built-in download manager manages the process. Which of the following are valid options from within the download manager? (Choose all that apply.)
   a. Download and run the selected file.
   b. Download and save the selected file into the program's default folder.
   c. Download and save the selected file to another folder.
   d. Cancel the download.
7. Which of the following best describes the role of a WebSocket? (Choose all that apply.)
   a. Establishes a three-way handshake between the sending and receiving computer.
   b. Application layer protocol that uses TCP's transport service.
   c. Allows clients and servers to exchange data immediately as it becomes available.
   d. An open connection between client and server that remains open as long as the systems have data to exchange.
8. Which of the following are true regarding IE in Windows 8 and the use of mandatory integrity control? (Choose all that apply.)
   a. IE runs as a low integrity access level.
   b. IE runs at a medium integrity access level.
   c. IE can write to the History, Cookies, and Favorites folders.
   d. IE runs at a high integrity access level.
9. By default, there are no sites included in which of these IE security zones; you must add them manually. (Choose all that apply.)
   a. Trusted sites
   b. Restricted sites
   c. Local intranet
   d. Internet
10. Which of the following represent techniques used by IE to identify potential phishing websites? (Choose all that apply.)
    a. Online lookup of phishing sites
    b. Onsite analysis
    c. Online lookup of download sites
    d. Offline lookup of download sites

Best Answer

Choose the letter that corresponds to the best answer. More than one answer choice may achieve the goal. Select the BEST answer.

1. The company is designing a new web-based application that is likely to require extensive access to system resources. Users will connect to it over their local network segment. To make sure the application works as planned, in which security zone should the website be placed to allow it to function at its full capability?
   a. Trusted sites zone
   b. Internet zone
   c. Local intranet zone
   d. Restricted sites zone
2. A new company has just installed Windows 8 on their computers. They want to be able to protect themselves against phishing attacks. Which combinations below will ensure they are using the best approach to defend against these types of attacks?
   a. Prevent browsing to any sites that are not included in the Trusted sites zone
   b. Educate users on how to recognize phishing attacks and use SmartScreen Filter to display warnings if the site is suspicious.
   c. Prevent browsing to any sites that are not included in the Local intranet zone.
   d. Place a list of known phishing sites into each user's Restricted sites zone
3. Several users on the network do sensitive research for the company using IE on 50 Windows 8 computers. They do not want IE to maintain a permanent record of their activities during their browser sessions? What is the best approach to use to address their need?
   a. Configure InPrivate Browsing on each of the computers.
   b. Configure InPrivate Browsing on a subset of the computers and direct the users to only browse when working at those computers.
   c. Configure InPrivate Browsing using Group Policy and apply it to the users' computers.
   d. Configure InPrivate Browsing using Group Policy and apply it to a subset of the comptuers; ask users to work on those computers only.
4. In Windows 8, IE runs in protected mode. Which of the following best describes the capabilities of IE when running in this mode?
   a. IE can write to the Temporary Internet files folder.
   b. IE can write to the Temporary Internet files and the History folders.
   c. IE can write to the Temporary Internet files, History, and Cookies folders.
   d. IE can write to the Temporary Internet files, History, Cookies, and Favorites folder.
5. The company is considering upgrading to Windows 8 but is concerned that some of their web-based applications may not be compatible. What is the best way to test for incompatibilities?
   a. Upgrade a few computers to Windows 8 and ask users to report any problems they have to the help desk.
   b. Upgrade all computers to Windows 8 and ask users to report any problems they have to the help desk.
   c. Upgrade a subset of computers that use all of the web-based applications and turn on compatibility logging via the Local Group policy.
   d. Upgrade a subset of computers that use all of the web-based applications. Ask users to report any problems. If problems are found, clear the Enable Protected Mode checkbox in the Local Intranet zone.

Matching and Identification

Complete the following exercise by matching the terms with their corresponding definitions.

_________ **a)** Add-ons
_________ **b)** RSS Feeds
_________ **c)** Social engineering
_________ **d)** Security zones
_________ **e)** Accelerators
_________ **f)** SmartScreen Filter
_________ **g)** WebSockets
_________ **h)** Protected mode
_________ **i)** InPrivate Mode
_________ **j)** Compatibility View

1. Describes any attempt to penetrate the security of a system by convincing people to disclose secret information.
2. Enables browser to display older pages properly.
3. Enables clients and servers to exchange data immediately.
4. Enables surfing the Internet without leaving any record of your activities.
5. Enable users to highlight content in a browser window instead of using the search box.
6. A push technology that simplifies the process of delivery updated content to designated users.
7. Examines traffic for evidence of phishing activity.
8. Used by IE to divide websites and assign different sets of privileges to each.
9. Provides a way to run IE with highly reduced privileges.
10. Software components that interact with the basic functions of the web browser.

Build a List

1. In order of first to last, specify the correct order of steps to configure a default Search Provider.

_________ On the Start screen, click the **Desktop tile**.
_________ Click the **Tools** icon, and from the context menu that appears, select **Manage Add-ons**.
_________ Select one of the search providers you installed earlier and click **Set as default**.
_________ Select **Search providers in the Add-on types** list,
_________ Click **Close**.
_________ In the taskbar, click the **Internet Explorer icon**.

2. Specify the correct order of steps to subscribe to an RSS Feed.

_________ Click the **Subscribe to this feed** link.
_________ On the Start screen, click the **Desktop tile**.
_________ In the taskbar, click the **Internet Explorer icon**.
_________ Press the Alt key to display the menu bar and, on the Tools menu, click **Feed Discovery**. Then click the name of the feed to which you want to subscribe.
_________ In the Name text box, type a name you want to assign to the feed (if it differs from the default).
_________ Select the folder to which you want to add the feed, or click **New folder** to create one. Then click **Subscribe**. The feed page changes to indicate that you have successfully subscribed to the feed.

3. Specify the correct order of steps to add a site to a Security Zone.

_________ Click the **Tools** icon and select **Internet Options**.
_________ In the taskbar, click the **Internet Explorer icon**.
_________ Type the URL of the website you want to add to the zone into the *Add this website to the zone* text box, and then click **Add**.
_________ Click **Sites**.
_________ On the Start screen, click the **Desktop tile**.
_________ Click **Close** to close the *Trusted sites* or *Restricted sites* dialog box.
_________ Select the zone, either **Trusted sites** or **Restricted sites**, to which you want to add a site.
_________ Click **OK** to close the Internet Properties sheet.
_________ Click the **Security** tab.

Business Case Scenarios

Scenario 8-1: Using the SmartScreen Filter

Several employees at the company you work for have recently been victims of identity theft. These incidents were the result of emails received by the victims requesting that they supply personal bank account information to a website or risk having their accounts closed. The website was, of course, not legitimate, and attackers used the information collected there to transfer funds from the victims' accounts. The company has recently upgraded all of the company workstations to Windows 8, and you are examining the capabilities of the SmartScreen Filter in the IE8. Your superiors have told you that you can use any of the new IE8 security features for the company workstations, as long as they do not consume any additional Internet bandwidth.

Explain to your supervisor the various methods IE8 uses to protect against phishing attacks, and specify which ones you intend to use for the company workstations.

Scenario 8-2: Resolving Application Compatibility Issues

A web-based site is needed by all users on the company's network in order to perform research on the company's competitors. After installing Windows 8, calls start coming into the help desk indicating there are compatibility problems with the site. What are some techniques that can be tried to address the problem?

9 LESSON

Configuring Client Hyper-V

70-687 EXAM OBJECTIVE

Objective 2.6 – Configure Hyper-V. This objective may include but is not limited to create and configure virtual machines; create and manage snapshots; create and configure virtual switches; and create and configure virtual disks.

Lesson Heading	Exam Objective
Installing Client Hyper-V and Configuring Virtual Machines	
Installing Client Hyper-V	
Exploring Hyper-V Manager	
Creating a Virtual Machine Using Hyper-V Manager	Create and Configure Virtual Machines
Configuring Virtual Machine Settings	
Managing Snapshots	Create and Manage Snapshots
Working with Virtual Switches	Create and Configure Virtual Switches
Creating Virtual Hard Disks	
Understanding Virtual Hard Disk Formats	Create and Configure Virtual Disks
Managing and Configuring Virtual Hard Disks	

KEY TERMS

Client Hyper-V
Dynamic Memory
Hypervisor
Hyper-V Manager
snapshot
VHDX
virtual hard disk (VHD)
virtualization

Installing Client Hyper-V and Configuring Virtual Machine

THE BOTTOM LINE

Hyper-V virtualization technology has been providing virtualized server environments since Windows Server 2008. Windows 8 is the first Windows client version to include Hyper-V. Hyper-V supports a large range of virtualization features, many of which are included in Windows 8 in a new feature called ***Client Hyper-V***. This lesson introduces you to the Client Hyper-V functionality in Windows 8, explains how it differs from Windows Server 2012 Hyper-V, and explains how to effectively configure and manage the features and functions in Client Hyper-V in Windows 8.

Client Hyper-V provides the capability to share a computer's hardware with one or more operating systems that run inside the same computer. The technology that allows this to happen is called a ***Hypervisor***. The Hypervisor keeps the host or parent operating system separate from all the virtual machines installed. This allows for the installation and running of multiple child operating systems as separate and secure virtual machines, all within one physical computer. ***Virtualization*** is the technology that allows for dramatic reductions in power consumption while increasing the utilization of data centers and individual servers, thereby saving money and resources. Microsoft has provided Client Hyper-V in Windows 8 as a free component in 64-bit Windows 8 Pro and Enterprise editions only. Client Hyper-V also has a greater level of machine hardware requirements, which are:

- Windows 8 Pro or Enterprise edition (64-bit)
- Second Level Address Translation (SLAT) processor
- 4GB RAM

MORE INFORMATION

SLAT is a required feature for Client Hyper-V. SLAT leverages AMD-V Rapid Virtualization Indexing (RVI) and Intel VT Extended Page Tables (NPT) technology to allow users to run virtual instances of operating systems on their PC as if they were standard desktop applications. A PC within a PC is a good description of it. SLAT ensures that the end-user experience for all applications is optimized.

Installing Client Hyper-V

Client Hyper-V is available to install in Windows 8 Pro and Enterprise 64-bit editions only.

The Hypervisor requires the 64-bit operating system to be able to act as a host for other 64-bit operating systems such as Windows Server 2012. In the following exercise, you install Client Hyper-V.

INSTALL CLIENT HYPER-V

GET READY. Log on to the Windows 8 computer with administrative privileges. To install the Client Hyper-V feature, perform the following steps:

1. Hold down the **Windows Key** and press the **X** key. In the *Quick Link* menu, click **Control Panel**.

   The *Control Panel* window opens.
2. Click **Programs**, and then in the *Programs* window, click **Turn Windows Features on or off**.

3. In the *Windows Features* window, expand **Hyper-V** and expand **Hyper-V management Tools**, as shown in Figure 9-1.

Figure 9-1

Installing Client Hyper-V—Windows feature disabled

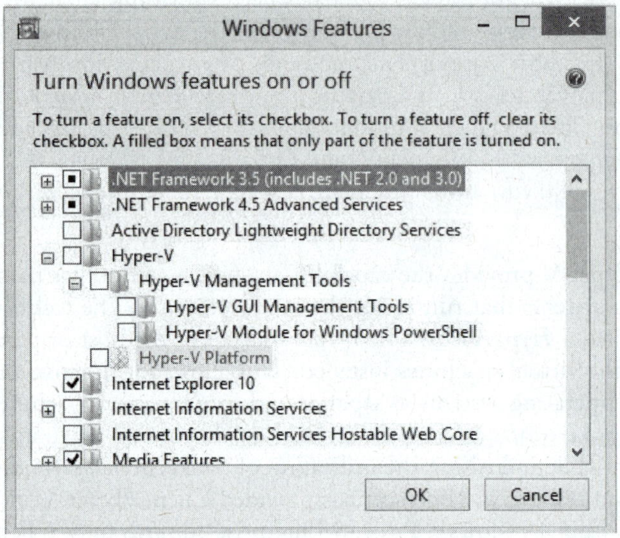

The Hyper-V Platform is grayed out. This is because the PC does not have a SLAT-enabled processor. In this case, only the management tools can be installed to allow the remote management of other Hyper-V host computers. Figure 9-2 shows a similar window, but this time the processor is SLAT-enabled and the feature can be installed as shown by the check marks in each box.

Figure 9-2

Installing Client Hyper-V—SLAT-enabled

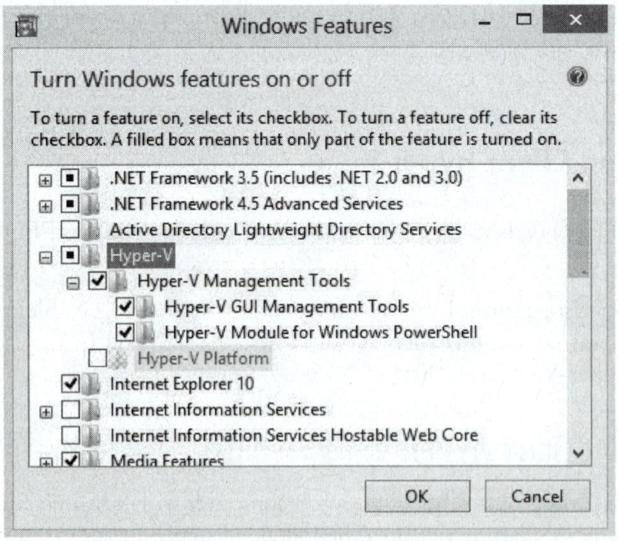

4. Select the Hyper-V platform check box and Hyper-V management Tools check box and click OK.

   Figure 9-3 shows the successful completion of the operation.

Figure 9-3

Installing Client Hyper-V, completed

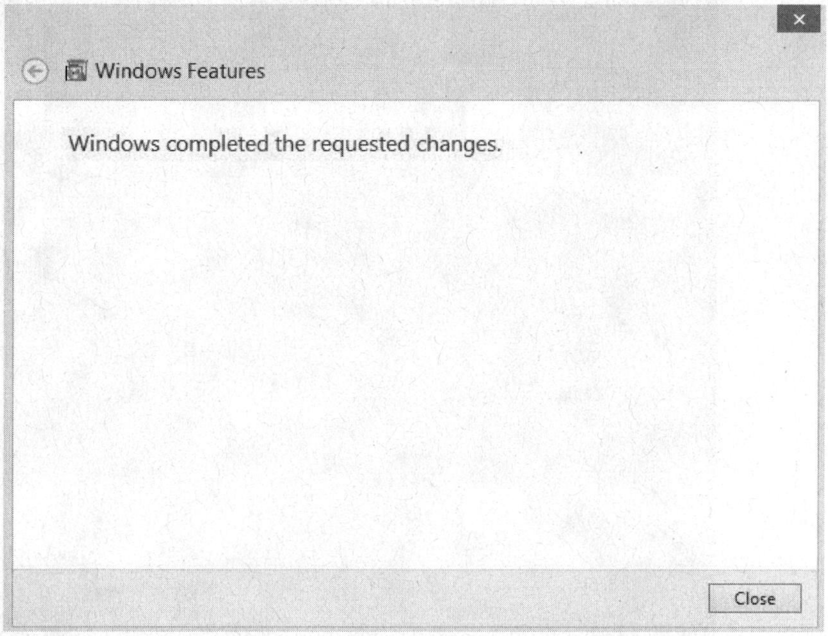

With the Client Hyper-V feature and management tools installed, the Hyper-V Manager and Hyper-V virtual machine connection applications are available from the Windows 8 desktop. These can be seen in Figure 9-4 as part of the desktop, and in Figure 9-5, it is filtered out after typing *hyper* at the desktop.

Figure 9-4

Showing Hyper-V applications

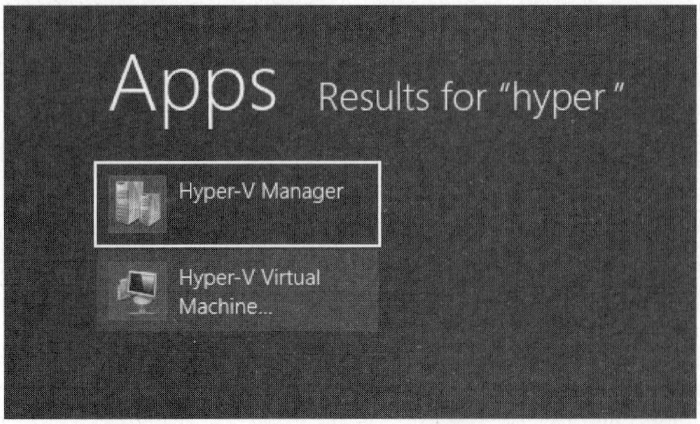

Figure 9-5

Showing Hyper-V desktop applications

The two new tiles you see after logging in with the administrative account are:

- **Hyper-V Manager:** This is the Management Console for creating and managing your virtual machines and setting up your test network.
- **Hyper-V Virtual Machine Connection:** This is used when you want to work with a single virtual machine that you have already created. It's similar to the Remote Desktop Connection utility.

USING WINDOWS POWERSHELL

You can also enable Client Hyper-V using Windows PowerShell from a command line:

```
Enable-WindowsOptionalFeature -online -FeatureName
Microsoft-Hyper-V-all
```

Exploring Hyper-V Manager

> ***Hyper-V Manager*** is a Microsoft Management Console (MMC) 3.0 snap-in application that allows management of the Hypervisor on a local or remote machine.

When you start the Hyper-V Manager from the desktop, the Microsoft Management Console window appears with the Hyper-V snap-in loaded (see Figure 9-6 for an example of a Hyper-V Manager window with several virtual machines).

Figure 9-6

Starting Hyper-V Manager

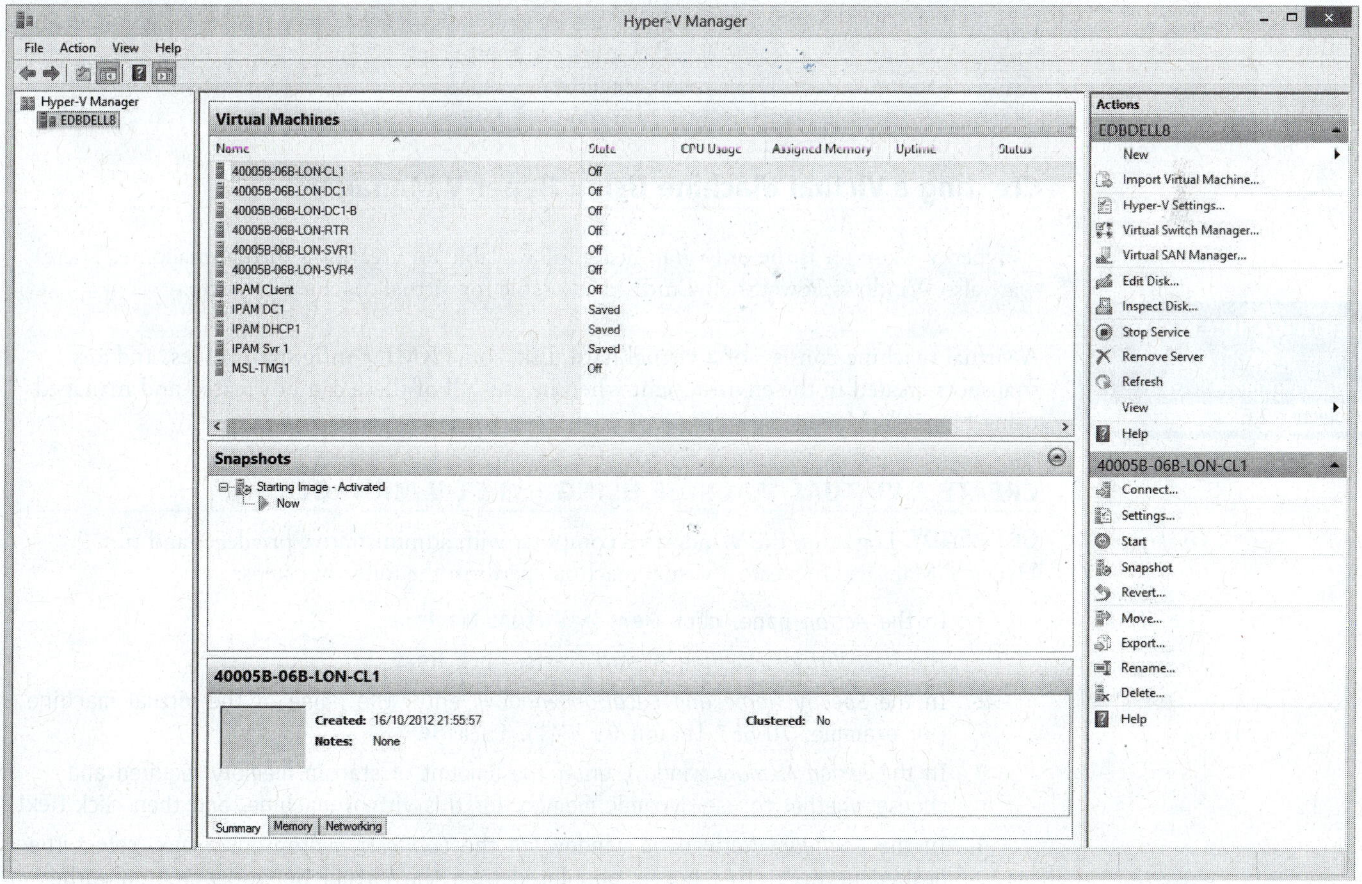

The Hyper V Manager snap-in consists of five areas or panes. These are shown in Figure 9-6 and their names and functions are listed in Table 9-1.

Table 9-1

Hyper-V Manager

No	Pane	Functions	Comments
1	Hyper-V Hosts	This pane allows a local and remote connection to any number of Hyper-V host computers.	The authenticated user must have permissions to connect to the remote hosts as must the computer account.
2	Virtual Machines	This pane lists all virtual machines contained in the currently selected Hyper-V host.	
3	Actions	This pane is split into two sections. The top section relates to the Hyper-V host computer, and the bottom relates to the currently selected virtual machine. It is similar to right-clicking on the virtual machine itself.	All host networking and settings are configured in this pane.
4	Snapshots	This pane contains all saved snapshots of the currently selected virtual machine.	
5	VM tabs	The VM tabs pane is a "window" into the currently selected virtual machine and each tab shows a different area of functionality. The Replication tab appears only if the Hyper-V host and the virtual machine are enabled for replication using Hyper-V replica.	Summary, Memory, and Networking tabs are always available. Double clicking on the Virtual Machine image "connects" the user to the VM.

Creating a Virtual Machine Using Hyper-V Manager

Hyper-V Manager is the only graphical tool available for creating a virtual machine. There are also Windows PowerShell CmdLets available for virtual machine creation.

CERTIFICATION READY
Create and configure virtual machines
Objective 2.6

A virtual machine consists of a virtual hard disk, some XML configuration files, and any snapshots created in the environment when in use. All of these can be created and managed using Hyper-V Manager.

CREATE A VIRTUAL MACHINE USING HYPER-V MANAGER

GET READY. Log on to the Windows 8 computer with administrative privileges and run Hyper-V Manager. To create a virtual machine, perform the following steps:

1. In the *Action* pane, click **New > Virtual Machine**.

   The *New Virtual Machine Wizard* starts. Click **Next**.
2. In the *Specify Name and Location* window, enter the name of the virtual machine (for example, 70-687 Lesson 09 VM1). Click **Next**.
3. In the *Assign Memory* window, enter the amount of startup memory required and choose whether to use dynamic memory for this virtual machine, and then click **Next**.
4. In the *Configure Networking* window, in the *Connection* drop-down box, select the desired network. This box is populated from the Virtual Networks created earlier in the Virtual Network Switch settings. Click **Next**.

5. In the *Connect Virtual Hard Disk* window, select **Create a virtual hard disk**, choose the location, and then click **Next**.
6. In the installation options, select **Install an operating system later**, and then click **Next**.
7. In the *Completing the New Virtual Machine Wizard* window, check the settings for the new VM and click **Finish**. Once completed, the new virtual machine appears in the Virtual Machines list of the Hyper-V Manager.

In the *Actions* pane, if you click *Start* for the virtual machine (or right-click on the virtual machine and click *Start*), the machine starts successfully. In the *Action* pane, if click *Connect*, a window opens (similar to a remote connection to the virtual machine) and you can see that the virtual machine has indeed started but that because there is no operating system installed on the hard disk, the error message *Boot Failure* appears on the screen. The next stage is of creating a usable virtual machine to configure the necessary settings and to add an operating system.

MORE INFORMATION

Dynamic Memory is a Hyper-V feature that helps you use physical memory more efficiently. With Dynamic Memory, Hyper-V treats memory as a shared resource that can be reallocated automatically among running virtual machines. Dynamic Memory adjusts the amount of memory available to a virtual machine, based on changes in memory demand and values that you specify. The Dynamic Memory feature allows memory to be adjusted between VM's even when they are switched on. As a result, Hyper-V can distribute memory more efficiently among the running virtual machines configured with Dynamic Memory. Depending on factors such as workload, this efficiency can make it possible to run more virtual machines at the same time on one physical computer.

TAKE NOTE*

Windows 8 does not come with any virtualization rights. This is different than Hyper-V on Windows Server. Every virtual machine you create using a Windows 8 Client Hyper-V environment needs a valid end user license for the operating system you install on it.

Configuring Virtual Machine Settings

An empty virtual machine is of little practical use, the next stage is to work through the Virtual Machine Settings to ensure the virtual machine has the correct operating system and hardware characteristics for your desired purpose.

The virtual machine created in the previous section is of no practical use until an operating system is installed on the virtual hard disk. In this section, you configure all of the required settings to create a fully functional Windows 8 virtual machine.

CONFIGURE VIRTUAL MACHINE SETTINGS

GET READY. Log on to the Windows 8 computer with administrative privileges and run Hyper-V Manager. To configure a virtual machine, perform the following steps:

1. In the *Virtual Machines* pane, click the newly created virtual machine **(70-687 Lesson 09 VM1)**, and then in the *Action* pane, for the virtual machine, click **Settings**.
2. The *Settings for 70-687 Lesson 09 VM1* dialog box opens and presents you with a number of options.

   You have already created an empty virtual machine and all you need to do is provide this machine with an operating system disc or image.

3. In the *Hardware* pane, under the *IDE Controller 1* section, click **DVD Drive**.

   This screen provides the option to connect the VM directly to the Host machines' DVD drives, or to use an image file (*.iso, for example), or to have no media at all. In this instance, place your Windows 8 DVD disc into the host machine DVD drive and click **Physical CD/DVD drive**. (The drop-down box allows you to choose which drive letter to use if the host has more than one optical drive.)

4. Click **OK**.

   By placing a DVD into the host DVD drive, the virtual machine also has access to the inserted DVD.

5. In the *Virtual Machines* pane of Server Manager, click **70-687 Lesson 09 VM1**. Right-click and click **Start**, and then right-click and click **Connect**.

   The virtual machine starts, and the remote connection window opens. The boot process commences and because there is no operating system on the VHD, the VM boots from the DVD drive or DVD image.

6. Complete the Windows 8 setup process as normal.

There are many more Virtual Machine settings, as shown in Figure 9-7 and described in Table 9-2.

Figure 9-7

Viewing Virtual Machine settings

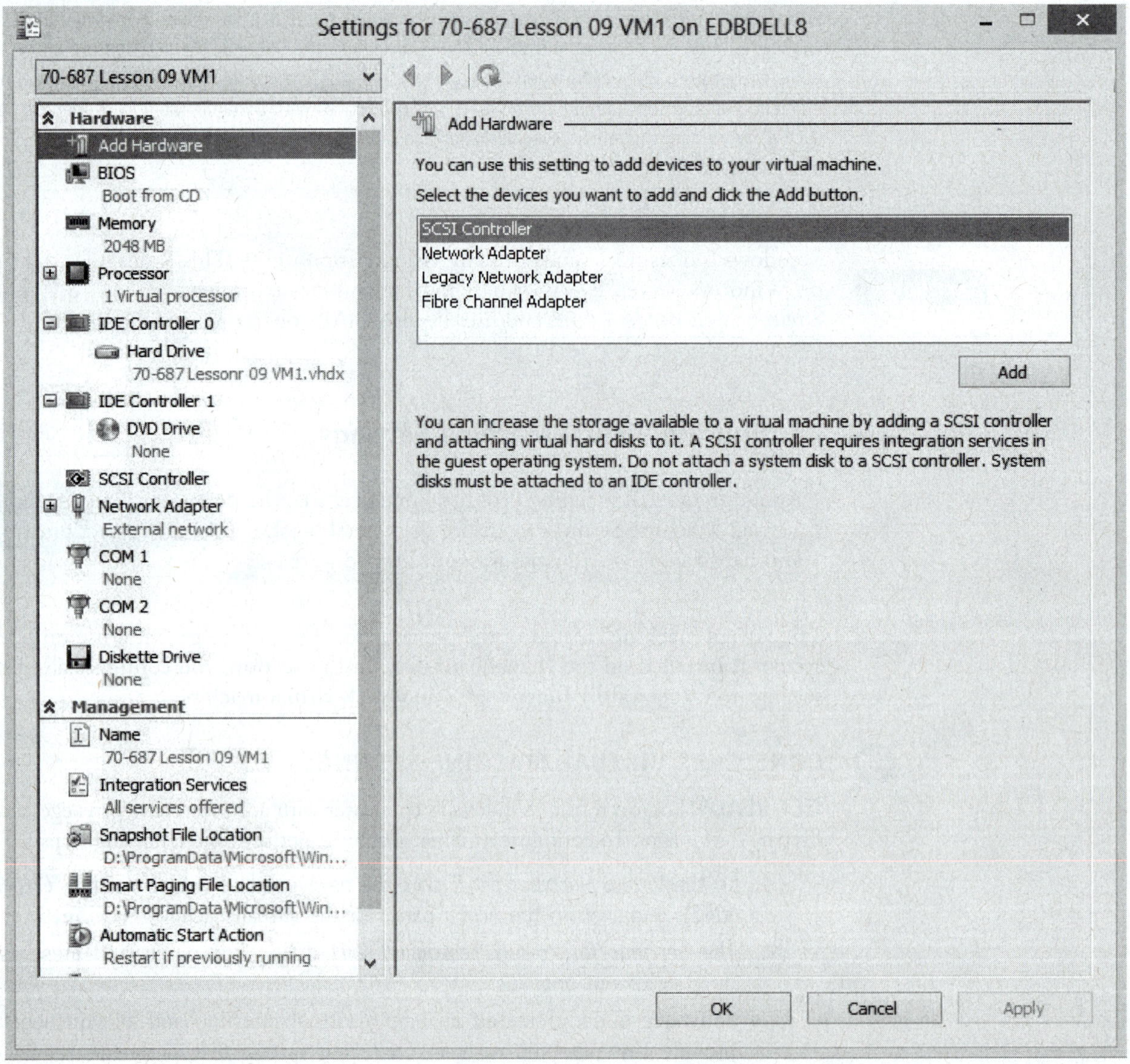

Table 9-2

Virtual Machine Settings

Title	Functions	Comments
Add Hardware	Allows the addition of SCSI controllers, network adaptors, and Fibre Channel adaptors to the virtual machine architecture.	
BIOS	Allows the boot order of the virtual machine to be changed and the Num Lock to be preset at startup.	Legacy NIC is required for network installation of an operating system.
Memory	Allows the startup Ram, Dynamic RAM, memory buffer, and memory weighting to be set for each virtual machine.	
Processor	Allows the number of Virtual Processors allocated to the virtual machine to be set, along with resource control settings to balance virtual machine usage of physical resources across the whole host.	As many virtual processors are available as cores in the host machine.
IDE Controller	Allows two IDE controllers that can each have two devices, either a hard drive and / or a DVD drive.	
SCSI Controller	Allows the addition of a number of SCSI controllers each of which can have a number of hard drives added (these can be added even if the virtual machine runs).	
Legacy Network Adaptor	Allows connection of the virtual machine to a network at 100Mbps and allows PXE network booting for operating system installation. Allows dynamic or static MAC addresses and other advanced security and redundancy features.	
Network Adaptor	Allows connection of the virtual machine to a network at 10Gbps, allows all the features of a legacy NIC but also allows bandwidth management and hardware acceleration features.	
Com Ports	There are two virtual serial ports for communication with legacy devices.	
Diskette Drive	There is one virtual floppy drive to allow the use of .vfd virtual floppy drive files.	
Name	Allows the virtual machine name to be created and changed.	
Integration Services	Allows the host machine to interact with the virtual machine and provide certain services to the guest operating systems. (Note limited number of OS's are compatible with Hyper-V integration services)	Services OS Shutdown Time Sync Data Exchange Heartbeat VSS backups
Snapshot File Location	Allows the VM snapshot to be stored in a different location to the VM (once a snapshot has been created, this cannot be changed)	

(continued)

Table 9-2
(continued)

Title	Functions	Comments
Smart Paging File Location	Allows the smart-paging file to be stored in a specific location for speed or redundancy. Provides a reliable way to keep virtual machines running when there is not enough physical memory available.	If a virtual machine is configured with a lower minimum memory than its startup memory and Hyper-V needs additional memory to restart it, Hyper-V smart paging is used to bridge the gap between minimum and startup memory.
Automatic Start Action	Allows automatic start of a virtual machine when the host starts (or starts only if it was running when the host shut down, or, does not start).	
Automatic Stop Action	Allows the virtual machine state to be saved when the host shuts down, or the virtual machine is to be turned off (equivalent to the power button being switched off), or the guest operating system is to be shut down.	

USING WINDOWS POWERSHELL

A large number of Hyper-V Windows PowerShell 3.0 Cmdlets allow you to configure virtual machines that also work in Client Hyper-V examples, such as `Get-VMMemory` and `Set-VMMemory`, which allow the administrator to access and configure the memory settings on a particular virtual machine. The example enables dynamic memory on virtual machine 70-687 Lesson 9 VM1, sets its minimum, startup, and maximum memory, its memory priority, and sets its buffer:

```
Set-VMMemory 70-687 Lesson 9 VM1 -DynamicMemoryEnabled $true
-MinimumBytes 64MB -StartupBytes 256MB -MaximumBytes 2GB -Priority
80 -Buffer 25
```

Managing Snapshots

THE BOTTOM LINE

Client Hyper-V provides a feature that enables a user to take a point-in-time image of the current settings and configuration and even the system state of a virtual machine. This image is called a ***snapshot*** and is useful in testing changes to a setup or installation of software. If the changes fail, there is no need to uninstall or redo the actions; the ability to apply any snapshot at any time enables quick and easy testing and reverting.

CERTIFICATION READY
Create and manage snapshots
Objective 2.6

Client Hyper-V is a perfect tool for testing software development platforms and deployment of changes to production environments. It is normal for these changes to lead to errors and system failures. The use of snapshots to recover from these errors and to reset the VM to a previous point in time can save a considerable amount of time and effort when testing systems.

Snapshot data files are stored as .avhd files. Taking multiple snapshots can quickly consume storage space. Snapshot data files usually are located in the same folder as the virtual hard disk by default. Snapshots are not recommended for use in production environments.

MORE INFORMATION

The following exceptions affect the location of the snapshot data files: If the virtual machine was imported with snapshots, they are stored in their own folder. If the virtual machine has no snapshots and you configure the virtual machine snapshot setting, all snapshots you take afterwards will be stored in the folder you specify.

CONFIGURE SNAPSHOTS

GET READY. Log on to the Windows 8 computer with administrative privileges and run Hyper-V Manager. To configure a Virtual Machine Snapshot, perform the following steps:

1. In the *Virtual Machines* pane, click the newly created and installed virtual machine **70-687 Lesson 09 VM1**. In the *Action* pane for the virtual machine, click **Start**.
2. In the *Virtual Machines* pane, click the newly created and installed virtual machine **70-687 Lesson 09 VM1**, and then in the *Action* pane for the virtual machine, click **Connect**.
3. In Hyper-V Manager, in the key *Virtual Machines* pane, right-click the **70-687 Lesson 09 VM1** virtual machine and click **Snapshot**.

   A snapshot is created and appears in the Snapshot pane for this virtual machine. The default snapshot name is the name of the virtual machine with the date and time of the snapshot in parentheses.
4. Right-click the snapshot and click **Rename**, type **Post Install,** and press **Enter**.
5. In the virtual machine on the *Windows 8 Start* screen, type **Notepad** and press **Enter**. Type some words and save the document as aftersnapshot.txt in the default documents library.
6. In Hyper-V Manager in the *Virtual Machines* pane, right-click the **70-687 Lesson 09 VM1** virtual machine and click **Revert**.

You will see that the virtual machine shuts down and the previous version (snapshot) starts up. The document you just saved is not in the library. This snapshot was taken before the file was created. Because you did not take another snapshot after the document was created and before you reverted, the document is lost (unless you backed up the files).

It is possible to create a number of snapshots and switch between them at will. It is also possible to create trees of snapshots (see Figure 9-8). The Snapshot pane clearly shows two different trees, one for Office 2013 and one for Office 2010. This clearly shows the principle of separate trees of snapshot images.

Figure 9-8

Showing snapshot trees

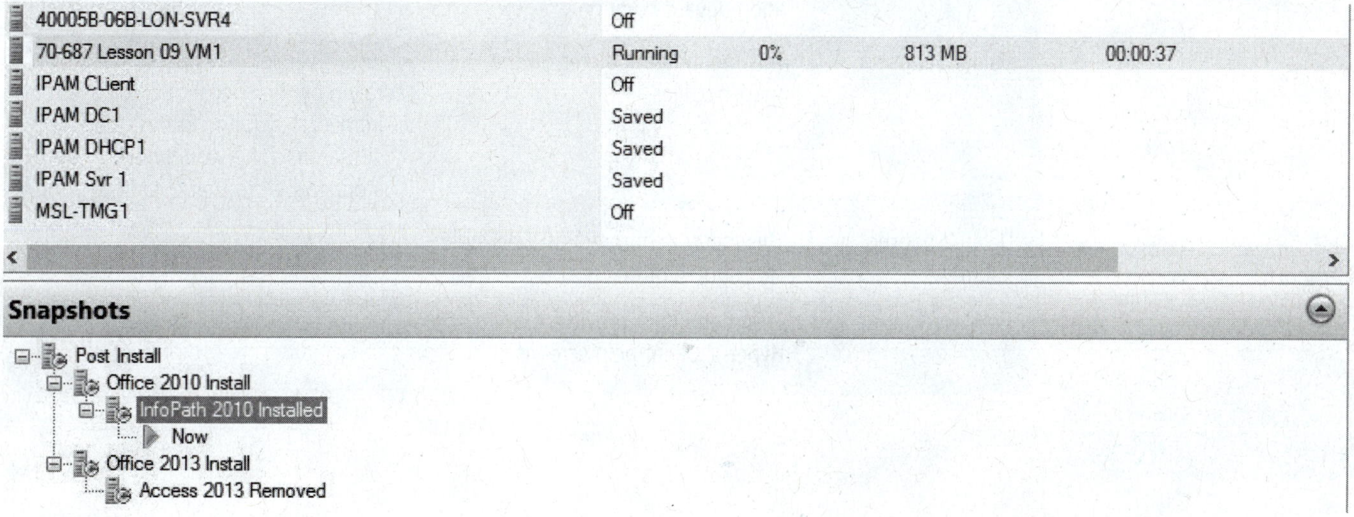

MANAGE SNAPSHOTS

GET READY. Log on to the Windows 8 computer with administrative privileges and run Hyper-V Manager. To configure a Virtual Machine Snapshot, perform the following steps:

1. In the *Virtual Machines* pane, click the newly created and installed virtual machine (**70-687 Lesson 09 VM1**. In the *Action* pane for the virtual machine, click **Start**, and then in the *Action* pane for the virtual machine, click **Connect**.

   Once the virtual machine has started, follow the steps in the previous section and create a number of snapshots with different machine hardware characteristics and files created and saved. Ensure that the snapshots are in two or three different trees.
2. To revert to the previous snapshot in a tree, right-click the virtual machine and click **Revert**. To apply a specific snapshot in a different tree or in the same tree but not the immediately preceding the snapshot, right-click on the chosen snapshot and then click **Apply**.

There are several other functions that can be performed on a snapshot; these are performed by right-clicking an individual snapshot. The options are listed in Table 9-3.

Table 9-3

Snapshot Functions

Title	Functions	Comments
Settings	This menu item opens the Virtual Machine Settings dialog for the particular snapshot.	A snapshot file saves the hardware settings for a virtual machine and maintains them separately from the other snapshots.
Apply	This menu item applies the chosen snapshot and loads the virtual machine in the state that was present when it was created.	If the virtual machine was saved or off when the snapshot was taken, that is how the virtual machine will appear once applied. Likewise, if the virtual machine was running when the snapshot was taken, it will reappear as a running virtual machine.
Rename	This menu item allows you to give the chosen snapshot a meaningful and relevant name.	
Delete Snapshot	This menu item deletes all the snapshot files.	In this version of Hyper-V, the space taken by the snapshot is released immediately (prior to this, the virtual machine would have to be stopped before that could happen).
Delete Snapshot Subtree	This menu item removes the whole snapshot subtree.	
Help	This menu item provides basic Hyper-V Client help screens.	

Working with Virtual Switches

THE BOTTOM LINE

Client Hyper-V provides a software-based Layer 2 network switch. This switch allows virtual machines to connect to external networks and virtual networks on Hyper-V hosts. The virtual switch sits between the host Physical NIC and the virtual machine virtual NIC to provide a layer of abstraction as well as additional security for the host and virtual machines.

The Hyper-V Virtual Switch is a software-based layer-2 network switch that is available in Hyper-V Manager when you install the Hyper-V server role. The switch includes the capability to connect virtual machines to both virtual networks and the physical network. In addition, Hyper-V Virtual Switch provides policy enforcement for security, isolation, and service levels.

The Hyper-V Virtual Switch introduces several features and enhanced capabilities for virtual machines and multiple-tenant isolation, traffic shaping, protection against malicious virtual machines, and simplified troubleshooting.

The Hyper-V Virtual Switch enables independent software vendors (ISVs) to create extensible plug-ins (known as Virtual Switch Extensions) that can provide enhanced networking and security capabilities. Virtual Switch Extensions that you add to the Hyper-V Virtual Switch are listed in the Virtual Switch Manager feature of Hyper-V Manager.

The virtual switch has a number of important features. These are listed in Table 9-4.

Table 9-4

Client Hyper-V – Virtual switch features

Title	Functions
ARP/ND Poisoning (spoofing) protection	Provides protection against a malicious virtual machine using Address Resolution Protocol (ARP) spoofing to steal IP addresses from other virtual machines. Provides protection against attacks that can be launched for IPv6 using Neighbor Discovery (ND) spoofing.
DHCP Guard protection	Protects against a malicious virtual machine representing itself as a Dynamic Host Configuration Protocol (DHCP) server for man-in-the-middle attacks.
Port Access Control Lists (ACLs)	Provides traffic filtering based on Media Access Control (MAC) or Internet Protocol (IP) addresses/ranges, which enables you to set up virtual network isolation.
Trunk mode to a Virtual Machine	Enables administrators to set up a specific VM as a virtual appliance, and then direct traffic from various VLANs to that virtual machine.
Network traffic monitoring	Enables administrators to review traffic that is traversing the network switch.
Isolated (private) VLAN	Enables administrators to segregate traffic on multiple VLANs to more easily establish isolated tenant communities.

There are three different types of virtual switches:

- **External:** This type of switch connects directly to a physical NIC and the virtual machines can communicate with the external network as well as the host computer (if configured to allow that option). Note that a physical NIC can be part of only one external network.
- **Internal:** This type of switch allows the virtual machines to communicate together and with the host computer.
- **Private:** This type of switch allows the virtual machines to communicate together but not to communicate with the host computer.

CREATE AND CONFIGURE A VIRTUAL SWITCH

CERTIFICATION READY
Create and configure virtual switches
Objective 2.6

GET READY. Log on to the Windows 8 computer with administrative privileges and run Hyper-V Manager. To create and configure a virtual switch, perform the following steps:

1. In the *Action* pane, click **Virtual Switch Manager**.

   The *Virtual Switch Manager* dialog box opens (see Figure 9-9).

Figure 9-9

The *Virtual Switch Manager* dialog box

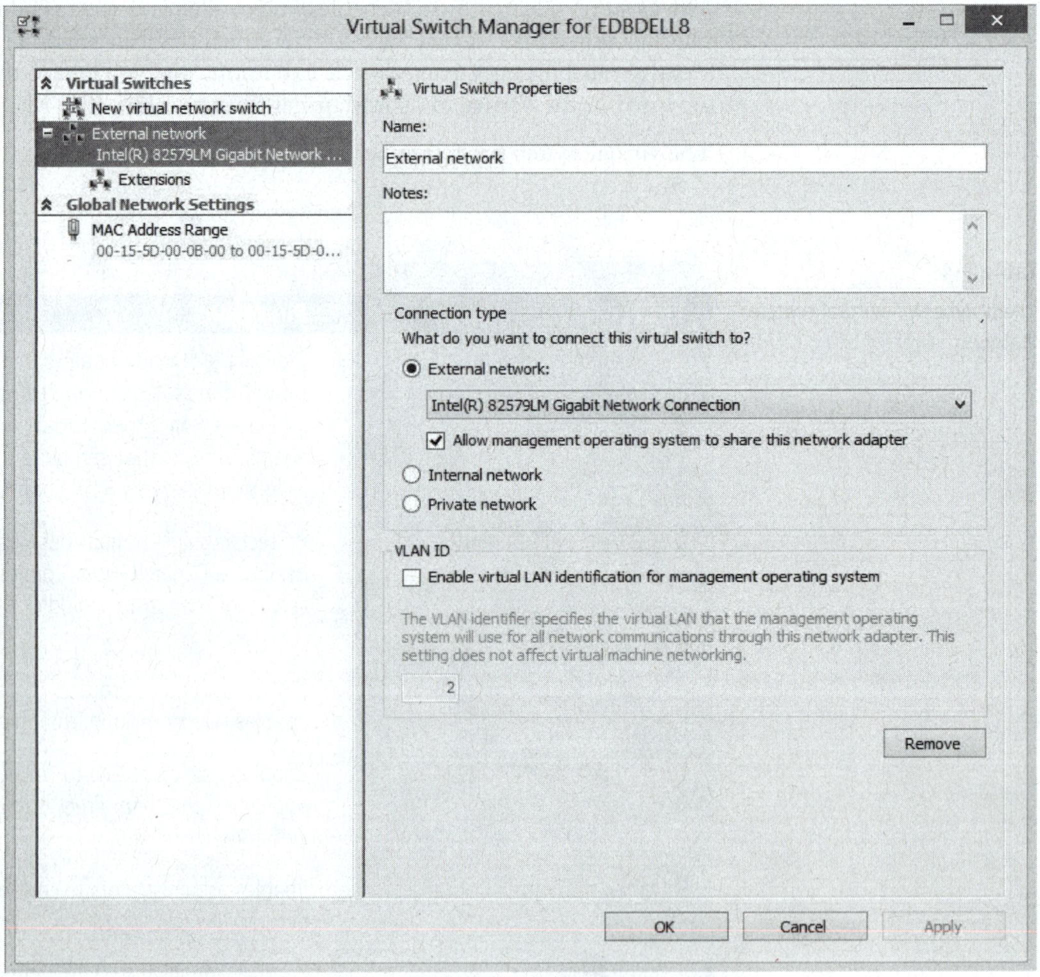

2. Select which type of virtual switch you would like to create; in this instance, select **External**. Click **New virtual network Switch**.

   The *Virtual Switch Properties* page opens and you then have several choices (see Figure 9-10).

Figure 9-10

Displaying *Virtual Switch Properties*

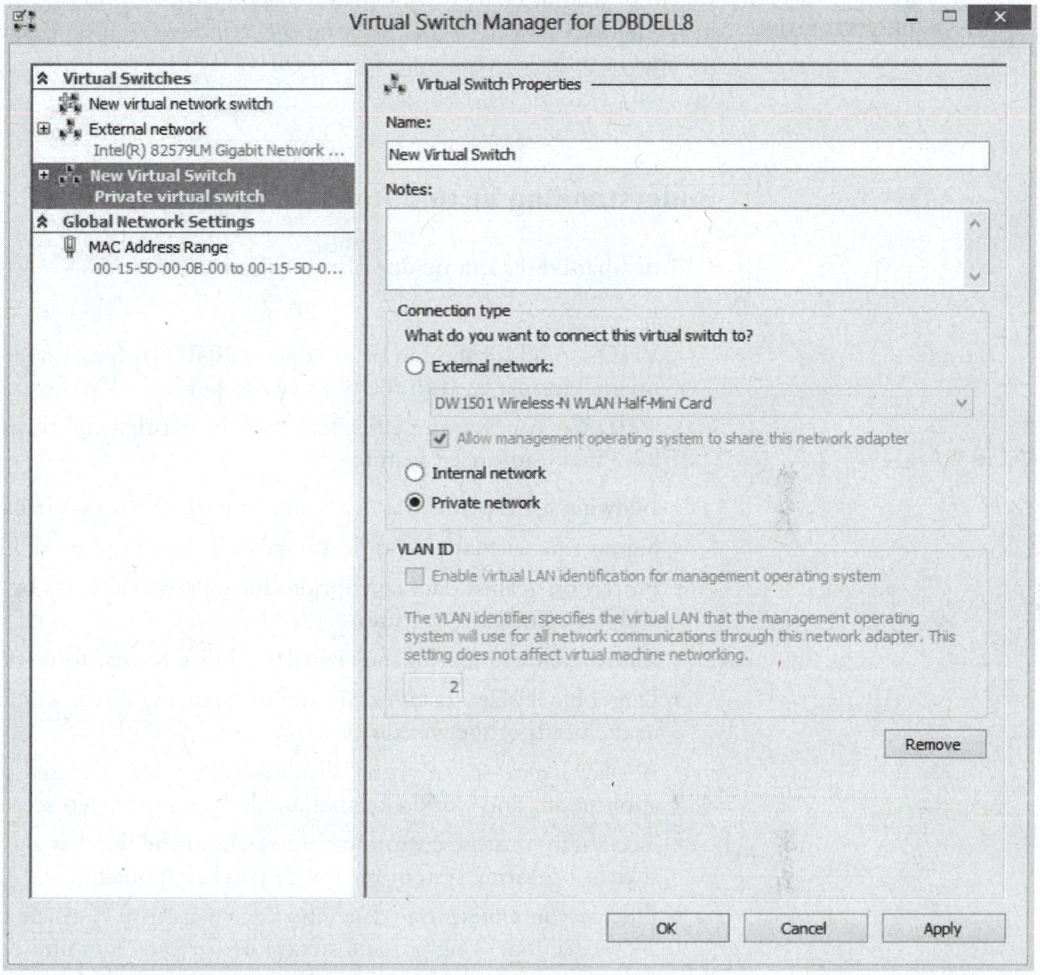

3. From the drop-down, select which external network you would like to choose (if there is more than one physical NIC in the host computer). You also have the opportunity to set a VLAN ID if this network switch is to be part of a specific VLAN number. Click **OK**.

   The new virtual switch has now been created and you can connect any of your virtual machines to it. Because this is an external switch, the virtual machine can also connect to networked devices outside the host computer.

TAKE NOTE*

During the creation of the virtual switch, you can name the switch and add notes to identify the purpose and function of the switch. This helps prevent accidentally joining virtual machines to the wrong network.

Creating Virtual Hard Disks

THE BOTTOM LINE

In order for a virtual machine to function, it must have one or more ***virtual hard disks (VHDs)***. VHDs are files that reside on the host computer and contain either an operating system or data to be used by a virtual machine. In addition, it is possible to boot a physical machine from a VHD if it is running the Windows 7 or 8 operating system. There are a number of different types and formats of VHD that can be used in a Client Hyper-V solution.

Understanding Virtual Hard Disk Formats

Virtual hard disks can be one of two different formats:

- **VHD**—A VHD file can be as large as 2040 GB (just under 2TB) in size and was the original format used in the predecessor to Hyper-V (Virtual PC).
- ***VHDX***—A new more efficient VHD format that can be as large as 64TB. VHDX disks have many advanced features.

The following list explains the new features in the VHDX Virtual Hard Disk format.

- Support for virtual hard disk storage capacity of up to 64 TB.
- Protection against data corruption during power failures by logging updates to the VHDX metadata structures.
- Improved alignment of the virtual hard disk format to work well on large sector disks.
- Larger block sizes for dynamic and differencing disks, which allows these disks to attune to the needs of the workload.
- A 4-KB logical sector virtual disk that allows for increased performance when used by applications and workloads that are designed for 4-KB sectors.
- The ability to store custom metadata about the file that the user might want to record, such as operating system version or patches applied.
- Efficiency in representing data (also known as "trim"), which results in smaller file size and allows the underlying physical storage device to reclaim unused space. (Trim requires physical disks directly attached to a virtual machine or SCSI disks, and trim-compatible hardware.)

TAKE NOTE*

The VHDX format is not compatible with versions of Hyper-V or operating systems below Windows Server 2012 and Windows 8. If you are creating a VM that is likely to be moved to a Hyper-V host running on Windows Server 2008 or Windows Server 2008, then it is necessary to use the VHD format.

CREATE VIRTUAL HARD DISKS

CERTIFICATION READY
Create and configure virtual disks
Objective 2.6

GET READY. Log on to the Windows 8 computer with administrative privileges and run Hyper-V Manager. To create a virtual hard disk, perform the following steps:

1. In the *Action* pane, click **New > Hard Disk**.

   The *New Virtual Hard Disk Wizard* opens.

2. Click **Next** to choose the virtual hard disk format (see Figure 9-11).

Figure 9-11

Displaying Virtual Hard Disk Format Choice

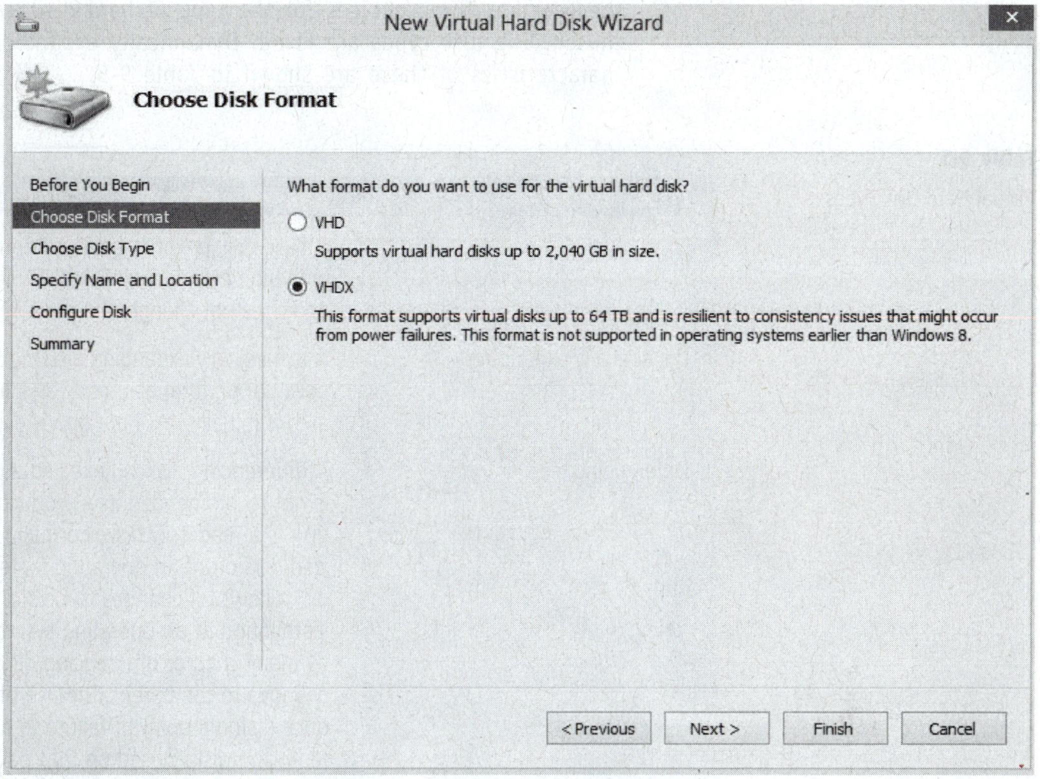

3. Select the **VHDX radio button** and then click **Next**.

   The *Choose Disk* type page is displayed (see Figure 9-12).

Figure 9-12

Displaying Virtual Hard Disk Format Choice

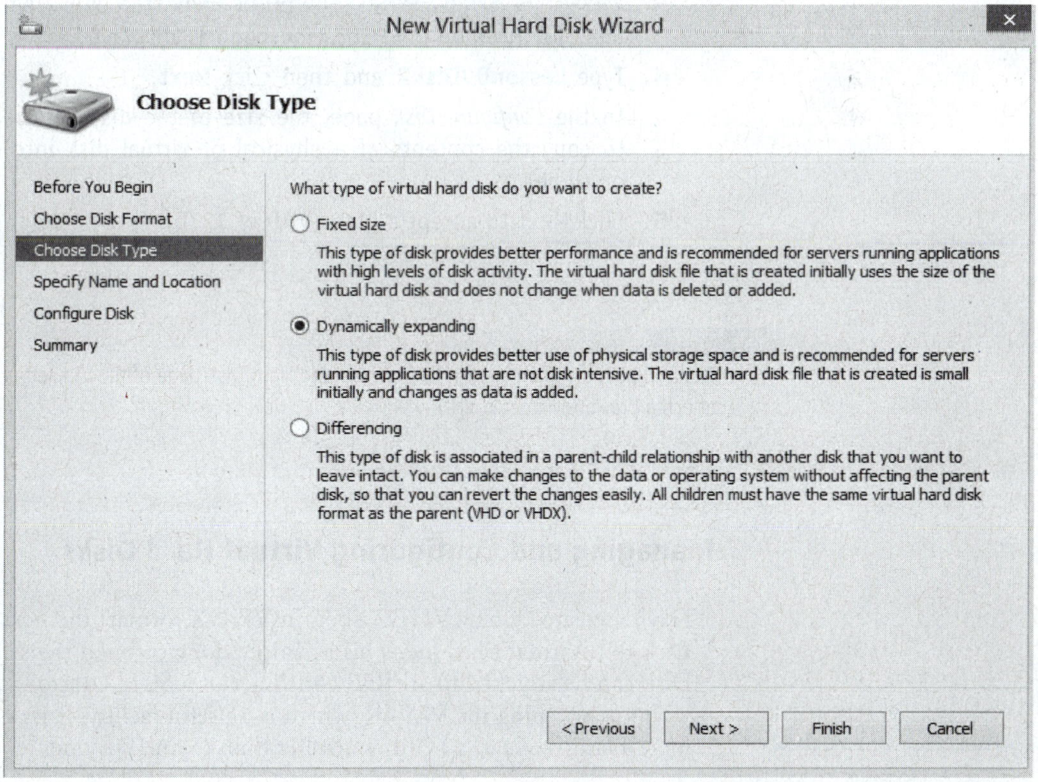

The user has three choices for the type of hard disk, regardless of the format chosen. The disk types are Fixed, Dynamically expanding, and Differencing. The characteristics of these are shown in Table 9-5.

Table 9-5

Virtual Hard Disk Types

Title	Characteristics
Fixed	A fixed disk provides better performance especially on servers with high disk activity. The VHD file is the same size as the disk and does not change.
Dynamically expanding	A dynamically expanding disk makes better use of disk space but does not perform as quickly as a fixed disk type. The VHD file created is initially small but grows as data is added to the disk.
Differencing	A differencing disk is linked to a parent disk. This type of disk is not recommended in a production environment. The parent disk is a read only disk, normally with a prepared and generalized version of an operating system installed. The differencing disk allows all changes to be stored. This system allows one installation of an operating system or parent disk to be used by many child or differencing disks without making any changes to the parent. The use of a single parent does introduce a single point of failure to all Virtual machines using differencing disks based on that parent. All child differencing disks must also have the same format as the parent disk (that is, All VHD or VHDX, no mixing is permitted)

3. Select the **Dynamically expanding disk type** and then click **Next**.

   The *Specify Name and Location* page is displayed.

4. Type **Lesson09Disk2** and then click **Next**.

   In the *Configure Disk* page, the size of the disk can be set. It is also possible to copy the contents of a physical or virtual disk into this new disk (a copy or clone).

5. Click **Next** to accept a blank VHD of 127GB (the default), and then click **Finish**.

MORE INFORMATION

It is also possible to create a VHD from the add Hard Disk page of the VM settings. This is also the place that you attach a previously created VHD.

Managing and Configuring Virtual Hard Disks

Having created a new VHD (albeit in VHDX format) the next step is to attach the Hard Disk to a Virtual Machine. This is simply done through the settings of that VM. A hard Disk can be attached to an IDE controller or a SCSI controller. The latter maybe attached without switching the VM off, which is a useful facility. It is also possible to attach many more Hard Disks to a SCSI controller than to an IDE one.

It is possible that a VHD may require some changes after it has been in use for some time. Using the *Edit Virtual Hard Disk Wizard* from the Hyper-V manager, it is possible to convert the format and type of the original disk. This is actually carried out by copying the contents to a new disk of a different type or format. In addition, the disk may be compacted or expanded in size.

There is one other useful utility available. Inspect a disk. This allows a user to see the size, location, format, type and file size of the disk, as shown in Figure 9-13.

Figure 9-13

Inspecting a virtual hard disk

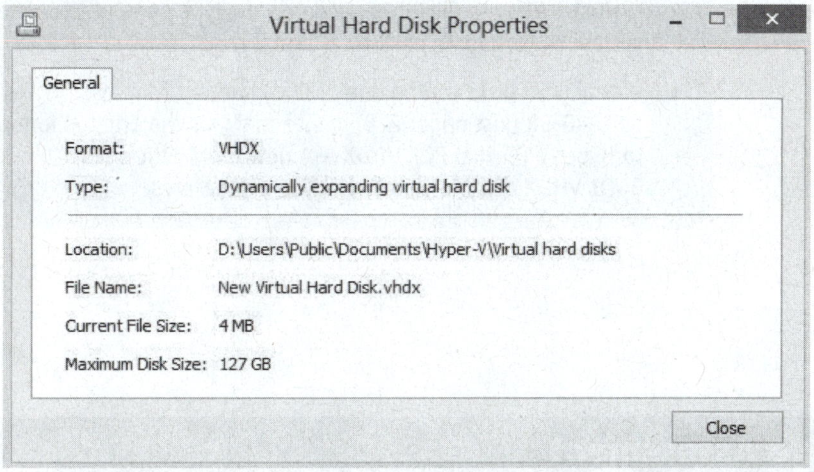

Inspect disk is available from the Hyper-V Manager, from the *Action* pane, or from the *Add disk* page of the Virtual Machine Settings.

SKILL SUMMARY

IN THIS LESSON YOU LEARNED:

- Hyper-V virtualization technology has been providing virtualized server environments since Windows Server 2008. Windows 8 is the first Windows client version to include Hyper-V. Hyper-V supports a large range of virtualization features, many of which are included in Windows 8 in a new feature called Client Hyper-V.
- Client Hyper-V provides the capability to share a computer's hardware with one or more operating systems that run inside the same computer. The technology that allows this to happen is called a Hypervisor. The Hypervisor requires the 64-bit operating system to be able to act as a host for other 64-bit operating systems such as Windows Server 2012.
- Hyper-V Manager is a Microsoft Management Console (MMC) 3.0 snap-in application that allows management of the Hypervisor on a local or remote machine.
- A virtual machine consists of a virtual hard disk, some XML configuration files, and any snapshots created in the environment when in use. All of these can be created and managed using Hyper-V Manager.
- Dynamic Memory is a Hyper-V feature that helps you use physical memory more efficiently. With Dynamic Memory, Hyper-V treats memory as a shared resource that can be reallocated automatically among running virtual machines. Dynamic Memory adjusts the amount of memory available to a virtual machine, based on changes in memory demand and values that you specify.

(continued)

- Client Hyper-V provides a feature that enables a user to take a point-in-time image of the current settings and configuration and even the system state of a virtual machine. This image is called a snapshot and is useful in testing changes to a setup or installation of software.
- Client Hyper-V provides a software-based Layer 2 network switch. This switch allows virtual machines to connect to external networks and virtual networks on Hyper-V hosts.
- In order for a virtual machine to function, it must have one or more virtual hard disks (VHDs). VHDs are files that reside on the host computer and contain either an operating system or data to be used by a virtual machine.
- Virtual hard disks can be one of two different formats: VHD—A VHD file can be as large as 2040 GB (just under 2TB) in size and was the original format used in the predecessor to Hyper-V (Virtual PC). VHDX—A new more efficient VHD format that can be as large as 64TB. VHDX disks have many advanced features.

Knowledge Assessment

Multiple Choice

1. Which of the following virtual hard disk types can be used to reduce physical hard disk storage in a production environment?
 a. Dynamically expanding
 b. Parent
 c. Fixed
 d. Differencing

2. Which of the following allows a virtual hard disk size of up to 64TB?
 a. VHDX
 b. VHD
 c. VFD
 d. VMDK

3. How many IDE controllers can a virtual machine have?
 a. 7
 b. 4
 c. 1
 d. 2

4. Which Hyper-V client utility is used to convert a VHD into a VHDX format?
 a. Create Disk
 b. Inspect Disk
 c. Edit Disk
 d. Add Disk

5. Which of the following is a requirement for using the VHDX format? (Choose all that apply.)
 a. Windows 8
 b. Windows Server 2012
 c. Hard Disk of 4TB in size
 d. Virtual SCSI disk controller

6. Which VHD type is not recommended for use in a production environment? (Choose all that apply.)
   a. Differencing
   b. Fixed
   c. Dynamically expanding
   d. Encrypted

7. What is a requirement for booting a virtual machine from a network to install an operating system?
   a. Legacy Network Adaptor
   b. Network Adaptor
   c. Virtual Switch extension
   d. Bandwidth management

8. Which of the following statements about the Virtual Switch Manager in Hyper-V client is not true?
   a. MAC address ranges can be specified.
   b. An external network may allow the host computer to share the network adaptor.
   c. The Private virtual switch is the default type when creating a new switch.
   d. VLAN IDs are not enabled by default

9. Which of the following is not a valid integration service in Hyper-V client?
   a. Operating system shutdown
   b. Heartbeat
   c. application integration
   d. volume snapshot backups

10. Which of the following is not a virtual network adaptor advanced feature?
    a. DCHP guard
    b. Router guard
    c. NIC teaming
    d. Virtual machine queue

Best Answer

Choose the letter that corresponds to the best answer. More than one answer choice may achieve the goal. Select the BEST answer.

1. Which virtual format provides the capability to create a disk of 1.5TB in a Hyper-V client?
   a. VHD
   b. VHDX
   c. VFD
   d. VMDK

2. Which virtual hard disk type increases performance in a production environment?
   a. Dynamically expanding
   b. Parent
   c. Fixed
   d. Differencing

3. Which type of virtual switch allows communication between a virtual machine and the host computer?
   a. Private
   b. Internal
   c. External
   d. Virtual

4. To provide a host computer with the capability to share a network adaptor, which of the following should be enabled?
   a. An external network
   b. Virtual machine queue
   c. Private network
   d. IPSec task offloading

5. To allow a network adaptor to use a specific MAC address, which of the following should be used?
   a. Virtual Switch Manager
   b. Virtual Machine Settings
   c. Host Network adaptor settings
   d. MAC address spoofing

Matching and Identification

1. Identify which of the following are Hyper-V virtual hard disk format resource records.
   _______ a) `VFD`
   _______ b) `VMDK`
   _______ c) `VHD`
   _______ d) `WIM`
   _______ e) `VHDX`
   _______ f) `UDIF`
   _______ g) `VDI`

Build a list

1. Identify the correct order in which a virtual hard disk is created? Not all steps will be used.
   _______ a) Choose the operating system.
   _______ b) Choose a disk format.
   _______ c) Enable BitLocker Drive Encryption.
   _______ d) Configure the disk.
   _______ e) Choose disk type.
   _______ f) Copy disk data.
   _______ g) Specify a name and location.

■ Business Case Scenarios

Scenario 9-1: Choosing a Suitable VHD Format

When creating multiple virtual machines using Windows 8 Professional, to minimize the host computers use of hard disk space, in a development environment, which implementation of a virtual hard disk format and type for all the virtual hard disks involved is best?

Scenario 9-2: Choosing a Virtual Network Switch

How do you create a small test network using Hyper-V client for which the test network must not be able to communicate with the Internet or with the host computer?

Scenario 9-3: Managing VM disks

A number of test networks run on a Windows 8 Hyper-V client system. One Virtual machine runs out of space on its main VHD. The virtual machine can be powered down to achieve results. Which solution should be implemented to fix the problem?

Configuring IP Settings

LESSON 10

70-687 EXAM OBJECTIVE

Objective 3.1 – Configure IP settings. This objective may include but is not limited to configure name resolution; connect to a network; configure network locations; and resolve connectivity issues.

LESSON HEADING	EXAM OBJECTIVE
Networking Basics	
The Physical Layer	
The Data-Link Layer	
The Network Layer	Configure name resolution
The Transport Layer	
The Upper Layers	
Connecting to a Network	Connect to a network
Installing Network Support	
Using the Network and Sharing Center	Configure network locations
Managing Network Connections	Resolve connectivity issues
Using TCP/IP Tools	
Using Ipconfig.exe	
Using Ping.exe	
Using Tracert.exe	
Using Nslookup.exe	
Using Netstat.exe	

KEY TERMS

8P8C connectors
Automatic Private IP Addressing (APIPA)
classless inter-domain routing (CIDR)
connectionless protocol
connection-oriented protocol
data encapsulation
datagram
firewall
frame
Internet Protocol (IP)
IP addresses
media access control (MAC) addresses
network address translation (NAT)
Open Systems Interconnection OSI reference model
packet-switching networks
ports
protocols
router
socket
stateless address autoconfiguration
subnet mask
unshielded twisted pair (UTP)

Networking Basics

THE BOTTOM LINE

The networking modifications introduced in Windows Vista were the most significant changes to the Windows networking engine since it was first incorporated into the operating system in Windows 95. Windows 8 networking now includes a revamped TCP/IP stack and a variety of new tools that simplify the networking process, for both users and administrators.

Networking is one of the primary functions of Windows 8. Most Windows computers are connected to either a private local area network (LAN) or to the Internet, and many are connected to both. These connections provide users with access to remotely-stored data, shared resources, network-attached hardware, and the virtually unlimited information and services available on the Internet.

Most Windows users are unaware of how computer networks function or even of when they are accessing a network resource, as opposed to a local one. Users expect Windows to provide a seamless network experience, wherever they happen to be located, and Windows 8 includes many networking features that help to provide this experience.

To promote interoperability between hardware manufacturers' products, computer networks are, for the most part, based on independent standards. The networking capabilities built into Windows 8 are implementations of those standards. Before you work directly with the Windows 8 networking tools, it is helpful to have a firm grasp of the underlying principles on which they were designed.

Computer networking is a highly complex process, but most of the technology operates invisibly, both to the user and the administrator. Computers on a network communicate using ***protocols***, which are nothing more than languages that all of the computers understand. These protocols operate on different levels, forming what is commonly known as a networking stack or protocol stack. The most common method for illustrating the operations of the networking stack is the ***Open Systems Interconnection (OSI) reference model***, which consists of seven layers, as shown in Figure 10-1.

Figure 10-1

The OSI reference model

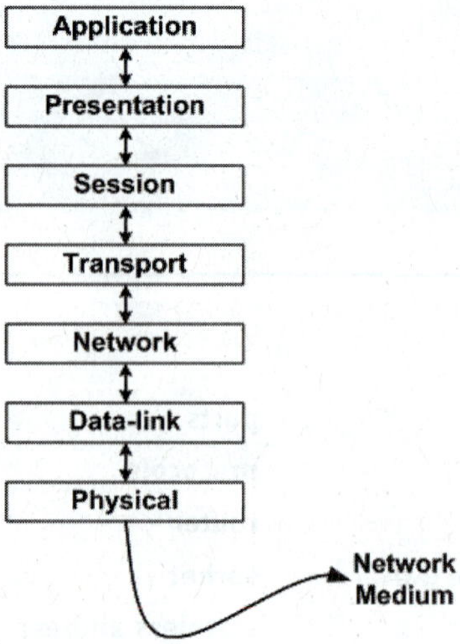

The following sections examine the functions provided by each of the seven model layers and the protocols that implement them.

The Physical Layer

At the bottom of the OSI model is the physical layer, which represents the hardware that forms the network.

The physical layer of the OSI model consists of the cable or the radio signals that carry data from one system to another and the network interface adapters, which are the hardware components in the computers that provide the connection to the physical network.

Most cabled networks use a type of cable called ***unshielded twisted pair (UTP)***, which is similar to the cable used for telephone wiring. UTP cable consists of four pairs of wires, with each pair twisted individually. At either end of each cable run are modular ***8P8C connectors*** (often incorrectly referred to as RJ45 connectors), which are similar to the RJ11 connectors used for telephones.

X REF

For more information on wireless networking, see Lesson 11, "Configuring Network Settings."

A network interface adapter is the component that provides the connection to the network. Most of the computers manufactured today have Ethernet network or wireless interface adapters integrated into their motherboards, but the adapter can also take the form of an expansion card that you install into the computer or an external device that connects to a Universal Serial Bus (USB) port. For wireless networking, the cables and cable connectors are replaced by radio transceivers that transmit the same data using a different kind of signal.

The Data-Link Layer

As you move up beyond the physical layer, the subsequent layers of the OSI model are realized in software, as protocols that provide different types of communications.

Most Windows networks use a protocol called Ethernet at the data-link layer. Local area networks are sometimes described as ***packet-switching networks***, which means that the messages generated by each computer are divided up into small pieces called packets, which the computer transmits individually over the network. A single file might be divided into hundreds or thousands of packets, each of which is transmitted separately. The packets might take different routes to the destination, and might even arrive there in a different order. The receiving computer is responsible for putting the pieces back together to reassemble the file.

MORE INFORMATION

The cable on a packet-switching network, at any given moment, can be carrying packets generated by dozens of different computers. The alternative to a packet-switching network is called a circuit-switching network, in which two systems establish a dedicated connection that they use exclusively until their transaction is completed. The most common example of a circuit-switching network is the public switched telephone network (PSTN), the standard land-based telephone system.

TAKE NOTE*

There are other data-link layer protocols, but the vast majority of LANs today use Ethernet. Two computers must both be running the same data-link layer protocol to communicate.

For the packets to reach their destination, they have to know where they are going. Therefore, they require an address. Just like letters mailed in the post office, each packet needs an address identifying the computer that will be its destination. Ethernet is the protocol responsible for addressing the packets at the data-link layer, which it does by surrounding the data it receives from the network layer just above it with a header and footer, as shown in Figure 10-2. This header and footer and the data they contain are collectively called a ***frame*** and the process of applying it is called ***data encapsulation***. The header and footer perform the same functions as the envelope does to a letter, protecting the contents and displaying the address of the recipient.

Figure 10-2

Data-link layer data encapsulation

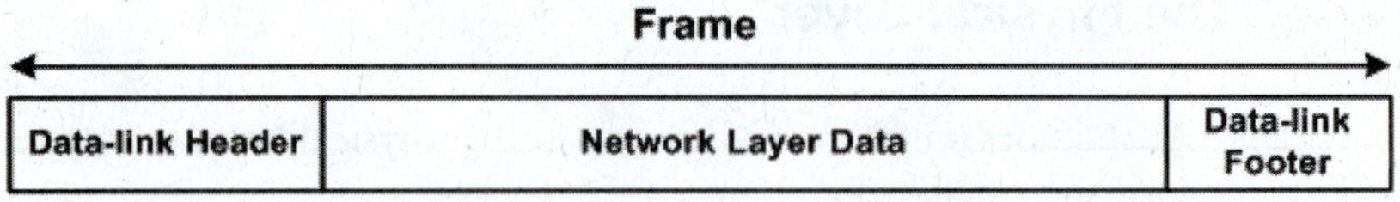

The addresses computers use at the data-link layer are six-byte hexadecimal sequences, hard-coded into each network interface adapter by the manufacturer. These sequences are called hardware addresses or ***media access control (MAC) addresses***. The first three bytes of a hardware address identify the manufacturer of the network interface adapter, and the last three bytes identify the adapter itself.

MORE INFORMATION

The standards on which Ethernet networks are based are published by the Institute of Electrical and Electronics Engineers (IEEE) and are known as IEEE 802.3, which refers to the number of the working group that produced the standards. The IEEE 802.3 standard defines three elements of an Ethernet network: a frame format for the packets transmitted over the network, a media access control mechanism called Carrier Sense Multiple Access with Collision Detection (CSMA/CD), and a series of physical layer specifications that describe the types of cables and other media that can be used to build an Ethernet network. For more information on Ethernet and for access to the standards, go to IEEE 802.3's website.

In addition to addresses, the Ethernet header contains other information that helps to direct and protect the data in the packet. Each Ethernet frame contains a code that identifies the network-layer protocol that generated the data in the packet, and a checksum that the receiving system will use to confirm that the packet has not been altered in transit.

The Network Layer

The protocols that Windows uses by default at the network and transport layers are collectively called TCP/IP. TCP is the Transmission Control Protocol and IP is the ***Internet Protocol***.

Early versions of Windows used a different protocol called NetBIOS, but TCP/IP is the native protocol of the Internet, and the explosive growth in the Internet's popularity eventually led the developers of all network operating systems to adopt TCP/IP as their default protocol.

IP is the network layer protocol that performs many important networking functions. These functions are described in the following sections.

IP ROUTING

The term internet (with a lowercase "i") literally means a network of networks. The Internet as we know it (with a capital "I") is a huge conglomeration of networks, all connected together by devices called routers. A ***router*** is simply a device that connects one network to another. When you install a LAN in a home or office, and connect it to the Internet, you are actually installing a router that connects your network to another network belonging to an Internet service provider (ISP).

MORE INFORMATION

Windows 8 itself can function as a router. When a Windows 8 computer is connected to two networks, such as a LAN and an ISP's network, you can activate the Internet Connection Sharing (ICS) feature, which enables Windows 8 to route packets between the networks. In most cases, however, routers are not general-purpose computers, but rather specialized devices that are dedicated to routing functions.

IP is the primary end-to-end protocol used on most data networks. Data-link layer protocols like Ethernet are actually LAN protocols; they are designed to send packets from one system to another system on the same local network. An *end-to-end protocol* like IP is responsible for the complete transmission of a packet from its source to its final destination on another network.

To get to that final destination, packets must be passed from router to router, through many different networks. A single packet might pass through dozens of routers before it reaches its destination network. The IP protocol is responsible for this routing process. Every TCP/IP system maintains a routing table that functions as the road map to other networks. By examining the destination address on each packet, and comparing it with the information in the routing table, IP decides which router to send the packet to next. The next router to receive the packet does the same thing, and step by step, the packet makes its way to the destination. Actually, each router the packet passes through is called a *hop*, so it is really a hop-by-hop process.

Of course, this process occurs much more quickly than this text can describe it. When you type a URL into your web browser and press the Enter key, in the time it takes for the webpage to begin appearing on your screen, dozens of packets have traveled back and forth through dozens of routers to and from a destination that might be in another city or another country.

MORE INFORMATION

To see how many routers there are between your Windows 8 computer and a destination on the Internet, open a Command Prompt window and type **tracert destination**, where *destination* is the name of a server on the Internet, such as www.microsoft.com. The Tracert.exe program will gradually compile a list of the routers as they process the packets on the way to the destination.

IPv4 ADDRESSING

IP has its own addressing system, which it uses to identify all of the devices on a network. Every network interface in a computer, and every device that is directly connected to a TCP/IP network, must have an IP address. IP addresses are independent of the hardware addresses assigned to network interface adapters. A Windows 8 computer that is connected to a LAN has both a hardware address and an IP address.

As mentioned earlier, data-link layer protocols like Ethernet are LAN protocols; their addresses are only used to transmit packets to other systems on the same local network. The IP address in a given packet, on the other hand, always identifies the packet's final destination, even if it is on another network. This is why IP is called an end-to-end protocol. When you use your web browser to connect to a site on the Internet, the packets your computer generates contain the IP address of the destination site, but at the data-link layer, they carry the hardware address of a router on the local network that they can use to access the Internet. Thus, the data-link layer and the network layer both have their own addressing systems, and the two addresses do not have to point to the same destination.

The current standard for IP is version 4 (IPv4), which defines a 32-bit address space. Each address is split into two parts:

- **Network identifier** – As the name implies, specifies the network on which a particular system is located.
- **Host identifier** – Specifies a particular network interface (also called a *host*) on the network.

Unlike hardware addresses, however, which always use three bytes for the network and three bytes for the interface, IP addresses can have variable numbers of network bits and host bits. To locate the division between the network identifier and the host identifier, TCP/IP systems use a mechanism called a ***subnet mask***.

MORE INFORMATION

The TCP/IP protocols are defined by public domain documents that are published by a body called the Internet Engineering Task Force (IETF). When they are first published, these documents are known as Requests For Comments (RFC). They then proceed through a lengthy ratification process before being declared Internet standards. The original IP standard, published as RFC 791, "Internet Protocol: DARPA Internet Program Protocol Specification" in September 1981, is a relatively short document that concentrates largely on IPv4 addressing. There are numerous other RFCs that define other aspects of the IP protocol, all of which are available from the IETF website at http://www.ietf.org.

Subnet Masking

IPv4 addresses are expressed in dotted decimal notation, that is, four eight-bit numbers, separated by dots (or periods), such as 192.168.3.64. An eight-bit binary number, when expressed in decimal form, can have any value from 0 to 255. A subnet mask is also a 32-bit number, expressed in dotted decimal notation, such as 255.255.255.0. The difference between a subnet mask and an IPv4 address is that a subnet mask consists, in binary form, of a series of consecutive ones followed by a series of consecutive zeroes. When you compare the binary values of the subnet mask to those of the IPv4 address, the one bits in the mask represent the network identifier, while the 0 bits represent the host identifier.

For example, a Windows 8 computer might be configured with the following IPv4 address and subnet mask:

- **IP address:** 192.168.3.64
- **Subnet mask:** 255.255.255.0

The whole concept of the subnet mask is easier to understand if you convert both values from decimal to binary, as follows:

- **IP address:** 11000000 10101000 00000011 100000000
- **Subnet mask:** 11111111 11111111 11111111 00000000

In binary form, you can see that the first 24 bits of the subnet mask are ones. Therefore, the first 24 bits of the IPv4 address form the network identifier. The last eight bits of the mask are zeroes, so the last eight bits of the address are the host identifier. As a result, in decimal form, the network identifier is 192.168.3 and the host identifier is 64.

The original IP standard defines three classes of IP addresses, based on the byte divisions of their subnet masks. These classes, and their characteristics, are shown in Table 10-1.

Table 10-1

IPv4 Address Classes

	Class A	Class B	Class C
Subnet mask	255.0.0.0	255.255.0.0	255.255.255.0
First bit values (binary)	0	10	110
First byte value (decimal)	0–127	128–191	192–223
Number of network identifier bits	8	16	24
Number of host identifier bits	24	16	8
Number of possible networks	126	16,384	2,097,152
Number of possible hosts	16,777,214	65,534	254

Classless Inter-Domain Routing (CIDR)

In practical use, the IP address classes proved to be wasteful, and when the Internet first experienced a massive period of growth in the 1990s, it was feared that there might at some time be a shortage of addresses. To avoid assigning entire addresses of a particular class to networks that didn't have that many hosts, the IETF eventually published a new standard for assigning IP addresses called ***classless inter-domain routing (CIDR)***.

CIDR differs from traditional addressing (now called *classful addressing*) by allowing the division between the network identifier and the host identifier to fall anywhere in an IPv4 address; it does not have to fall on one of the eight-bit boundaries. For example, a subnet mask of 255.255.240.0 translates into a binary value of 11111111 11111111 11110000 00000000, meaning that the network identifier is 20 bits long and the host identifier is 12 bits. This falls between a Class B and a Class C address, and enables ISPs to assign clients only the number of addresses they need, which conserves the IP address space.

CIDR also introduced a new syntax for IP network address references. In classful notation, an address like 172.23.0.0 was assumed to be a Class B address and use the standard 255.255.0.0 Class B subnet mask. In CIDR notation, the network address is followed by a slash and the number of bits in the network identifier. Therefore, 172.23.0.0/16 would be the CIDR equivalent of a Class B address. An address that used the 255.255.240.0 subnet mask described earlier would therefore look something like 172.23.0.0/20.

Private IP Addressing

Computers that are connected directly to the Internet must use IPv4 addresses that are registered with the Internet Assigned Numbers Authority (IANA). This is to prevent the duplication of IP addresses on the Internet. The IANA assigns blocks of network identifiers to ISPs, who assign them in turn to their customers. Once an organization is assigned a network identifier, it is up to the network administrators to assign a unique host identifier to each computer on the network.

Private LANs do not need registered addresses, so they can use network identifiers from three special ranges of private addresses that are reserved for that purpose. The three private address ranges are shown in Table 10-2.

Table 10-2

IPv4 Private Addresses

Address Class	IPv4 Private Address Range	Subnet Mask
Class A	10.0.0.0 through 10.255.255.255	255.0.0.0
Class B	172.16.0.0 through 172.31.255.255	255.255.0.0
Class C	192.168.0.0 through 192.168.255.255	255.255.255.0

Internet routers do not forward these private addresses, so computers that use them are theoretically not accessible from the Internet. However, most networks today that use private IP addresses provide their computers with Internet access using a technology such as ***network address translation (NAT)***.

NAT is a feature built into many routers that takes the packets destined for the Internet that are generated by the computers on a private network, substitutes a registered address for the computer's private address, and then forwards the packets to the Internet destinations. When the Internet servers send replies, the NAT router does the same thing in reverse. As a result, an entire private network can share a single registered address.

Assigning IP Addresses

Windows 8 computers can acquire IP addresses in the following three ways:

- **Manual configuration** – It is possible for administrators to manually assign IP addresses to hosts and configure each computer to use the address assigned to it. However, this method requires much more time and effort than the other alternatives, and is prone to error.
- **Dynamic Host Configuration Protocol (DHCP)** – DHCP is a client/server application and protocol that enables clients to obtain IP addresses from a pool provided by a server, and then return the addresses to the pool when the clients no longer need them. Windows 8 includes a DHCP client, which it uses by default. The Windows server products all include a full-featured DHCP server, which you can configure to assign any range of addresses in a variety of ways.
- ***Automatic Private IP Addressing (APIPA)*** – When a Windows 8 computer with no IP address starts, and it fails to locate a DHCP server on the network, the TCP/IP client automatically configures itself using an address in the 169.254.0.0/16 network. This enables computers on a small network with no DHCP server to communicate without the need for manual configuration.

DNS NAME RESOLUTION

CERTIFICATION READY
Configure name resolution
Objective 3.1

All TCP/IP communication is based on IP addresses, and in TCP/IP parlance, each network interface in a computer is called a host. In addition to IP addresses, hosts can also have names, and the host names are grouped together in units called domains. When users access a website on the Internet, they do so by specifying or selecting a DNS name, which consists of a host name and two or more domain names (such as www.adatum.com), not an IP address. This is because names are far easier to remember and use than IP addresses.

For TCP/IP systems to use these friendly host names, they must have some means of discovering the IP address associated with a specific name. This discovery process is called name resolution, and the application that resolves names into IP addresses is the Domain Name System (DNS).

DNS is a client/server application that is essentially a distributed database. Information about the names and addresses of Internet computers is distributed among thousands of DNS servers, all over the world. Virtually all operating systems have a DNS client, called a resolver, that enables it to send a host name to a DNS server and receive the IP address associated with that name in return.

In its most basic form, the DNS name resolution process consists of a resolver submitting a name resolution request to the DNS server specified in its TCP/IP configuration settings. When the server does not possess information about the requested name, it forwards the request to another DNS server on the network, a process called recursion. The second server generates a response containing the IP address of the requested name and returns it to the first server, which relays the information in turn to the resolver. In actual practice, the DNS name resolution process can be considerably more complex, but the basic message exchanges are essentially the same.

IPv6 ADDRESSING

When the IP protocol was first developed, in the late 1970s, the Internet was an experimental network used only by a few hundred engineers and scientists. At that time, the 32-bit address space defined in the IPv4 standard seemed enormous. No one could have foreseen the explosive growth of the Internet that began in the 1990s, and which soon threatened to deplete the existing supply of IP addresses.

To address this situation, work began in the 1990s on a new revision of the IP protocol, known as Internet Protocol Version 6, or IPv6. IPv6 expands the address space from 32 to 128 bits, which is large enough to provide more than 6.7×10^{23} addresses for each square meter of the Earth's surface.

Because this address space is so huge, IPv6 supports multiple subnet levels, and not just one, as in IPv4. Individual hosts can also have multiple IPv6 addresses for various purposes, with little chance of the address space being depleted in the foreseeable future. IPv6 supports automatic assignment of addresses, in both stateful and stateless configurations.

IPv6 also simplifies the packet header format by moving some of the IPv4 header information to optional fields. This reduces the size of routing tables and decreases the processing burden on routers throughout the IPv6 universe.

IPv6 Address Format

Unlike IPv4 addresses, which use decimal notation, IPv6 addresses use hexadecimal notation, in the form of eight two-byte values, separated by colons, as follows:

```
XX:XX:XX:XX:XX:XX:XX:XX
```

Each X is a hexadecimal value for one byte, resulting in a total of 16 bytes, or 128 bits. An example of an IPv6 address would be as follows:

```
FDC0:0000:0000:02BD:00FF:BECB:FEF4:961D
```

To simplify the address somewhat, you can remove the leading zeroes, leaving you with the following:

```
FDC0:0:0:02BD:FF:BECB:FEF4:961D
```

TAKE NOTE*

In hexadecimal (or base 16) notation, each digit can have a value from 0 to 9 or A to F, for a total of 16 possible values. Remember, an eight-bit (one-byte) number can have 256 possible values. If each hexadecimal digit can have 16 values, two digits are required to express the 256 possible values for each byte of the address ($16^2 = 256$). This is why some of the two-byte values in the sample IPv6 address require four digits.

To simplify the notation further, you can eliminate the zero blocks from an address and replace them with a double colon, as follows:

```
FDC0::02BD:FF:BECB:FEF4:961D
```

Subnetting IPv6

To identify the network bits of an address, IPv6 uses the same type of notation as CIDR, in which the address is followed by a slash and a decimal value specifying the size of the network prefix, as in the following example:

```
FDC0::02BD/64
```

This notation is the only way to identify subnets in IPv6; there are no subnet masks.

Understanding IPv6 Address Types

Much as IPv4 supports unicast, broadcast, and multicast addresses, IPv6 has three address types, as follows:

- **Unicast** – Identifies a single network interface in a computer or other device. Packets addressed to a unicast address are delivered to one node only.
- **Anycast** – Identifies a set of network interfaces. Packets addressed to an anycast address are delivered only to the interface closest to the source (by number of hops).
- **Multicast** – Identifies a group of multiple network interfaces. Packets addressed to a multicast address are delivered to all of the interfaces designated as members of the group. One standard multicast address, known as the "all nodes" multicast group, performs the role of the IPv4 broadcast address, so there is no need for an explicit broadcast address type in IPv6.

IPv6 addresses each have a scope, which defines the area within which the address is unique. The scopes defined in the IPv6 standards are as follows:

- **Node local unicast** – Limited to an individual interface. This is the equivalent to the loopback address in IPv4.
- **Link local unicast** – Limited to systems on the directly-attached network.
- **Unique local unicast** – Routable within an organization. The IPv6 equivalent of the 10.0.0.0/8, 172.16.0.0/12, and 192.168.0.0/16 private network addresses in IPv4.
- **Site local unicast** – Limited to interfaces at a single site. Once intended to be the equivalent of private IPv4 addresses, this scope is now deprecated.
- **Organization local** – Designed to span multiple sites belonging to an individual organization.
- **Global** – Unique throughout the IPv6 universe.

IPv6 Name Resolution

Name resolution for computers with global IPv6 addresses is provided by the Domain Name System (DNS), just as it is in IPv4. For computers with link-local addresses, which might not have access to a DNS server, the system uses the ***Link Local Multicast Name Resolution (LLMNR)*** protocol.

To use LLMNR, systems transmit name query request messages as multicasts to the local network. The request contains the name the computer is trying to resolve. The other computers on the local network, on receiving the messages, compare the requested name with their own names. The computer with the requested name then replies with a message containing its IP address, which it transmits as a unicast to the original requestor.

IPv6 Address Autoconfiguration

At the time IPv4 was conceived, there were some data-link layer implementations that required network administrators to manually assign addresses to the network interface hardware for media access control purposes. The designers of IPv4 therefore decided to design an addressing system that was completely independent from the underlying protocol at the data-link layer.

Today, all network interface adapters have factory-assigned hardware addresses, so IPv6 derives its host identifiers from those hardware addresses. There is therefore no need for APIPA or NAT or DHCP host address assignments.

IPv6 address assignment is much more of an automatic process than in IPv4. A technique called ***stateless address autoconfiguration*** enables computers to configure their own addresses after transmitting router solicitation multicasts to the routers on the network and receiving router advertisement messages in return. For situations where stateless autoconfiguration is not appropriate, Windows 8 workstations can use DHCP for stateful address autoconfiguration instead.

IPv6 Transition

More than ten years after the initial publication of the IPv6 standard, and despite its almost universal operating system and router support, the vast majority of the systems on the Internet still rely on IPv4. However, the inclusion of IPv6 support in Windows 8 and Windows Server 2012 makes the operating systems ready for the transition when it occurs. Windows 8, by default, installs support for both IPv4 and IPv6 addressing when it detects a network interface adapter in the computer, as shown in Figure 10-3. Microsoft refers to this as Windows 8's *dual IP stack*.

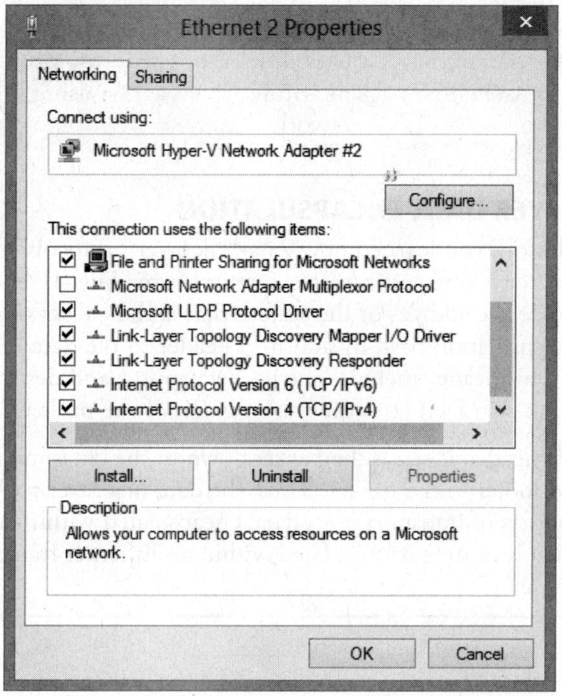

Figure 10-3

Windows 8 support for IPv4 and IPv6

In addition, the DHCP Server application in Windows Server 2012 support both addressing standards, so when a Windows 8 computer requests IP addresses, the DHCP server can supply both IPv4 and IPv6 information. Windows 8 applications that are capable of using IPv6 do so by default; otherwise, applications revert to IPv4.

As the transition from IPv4 to IPv6 proceeds, there are times when it is necessary for computers running IPv6-only applications to exchange messages over an IPv4-only network. For example, computers at different locations cannot communicate over the Internet using IPv6, because as of this writing, the Internet still uses IPv4. However, Windows 8 (and Windows Server 2012) support a number of transition mechanisms that make this communication possible, including the following:

- **IPv4-compatible addresses** – A hybrid IPv6/IPv4 address that enables an IPv6 system to communicate using an IPv4 infrastructure. The address format consists of 96 bits of zeroes, followed by an IPv4 address in its standard dotted decimal notation, as in the following example:
  `::192.168.1.99.`
- **IPv4-mapped addresses** – A hybrid IPv6/IPv4 address that enables an IPv6 system to recognize an IPv4-only system. The address format consists of 80 bits of zeroes, followed by 16 bits of ones, followed by an IPv4 address in its standard dotted decimal notation, as in the following example:
  `::ffff:192.168.1.99.`
- **6to4** – A tunneling technology that enables computers to transmit IPv6 packets over an IPv4 network. The 6to4 address that an IPv6 system uses when connecting to the IPv6 Internet through an intermediate IPv4 network takes the following format: 2002:<first 16 bits of the IPv4 address>:<second 16 bits of the IPv4 address>::/16. For example, the IPv4 address 192.168.1.99 would appear as follows:
  `2002:C0A8:0163::/16.`
- **Teredo** – A tunneling protocol that enables computers to transmit IPv6 packets through NAT routers that do not support IPv6. A Teredo address consists of a 32-bit prefix: 2001:0000, followed by the IPv4 address of the Teredo server, 16 flag bits, and the UDP port number and public IPv4 address of the NAT router. These last 48 bits are obfuscated by having their bit values reversed.

TAKE NOTE*

Tunneling is a networking technique that enables systems to encapsulate packets within other packets, for security or compatibility purposes. In the case of 6to4, for example, a computer encapsulates IPv6 packets within IPv4 packets using UDP, so that the system can transmit them over an IPv4 network.

NETWORK LAYER DATA ENCAPSULATION

Earlier in this lesson, you learned how data-link layer protocols encapsulate data for transmission, much as an envelope encapsulates a letter for mailing. IP encapsulates data as well, so that it can provide the address of the system that is the packet's final destination. In fact, IP performs its encapsulation first, by adding a header to the data it receives from the transport layer protocol. This header includes the packet's source and destination IP addresses, as well as other information that facilitates the transmission of the packet.

After IP adds its header, it sends the packet down to the data-link layer, where Ethernet adds its own header and footer to the packet. Thus, the data-link layer packet that gets transmitted over the network consists of transport layer data, encapsulated within an IP packet, which is called a ***datagram***, which is in turn encapsulated within an Ethernet frame, as shown in Figure 10-4.

Figure 10-4

IP data encapsulation

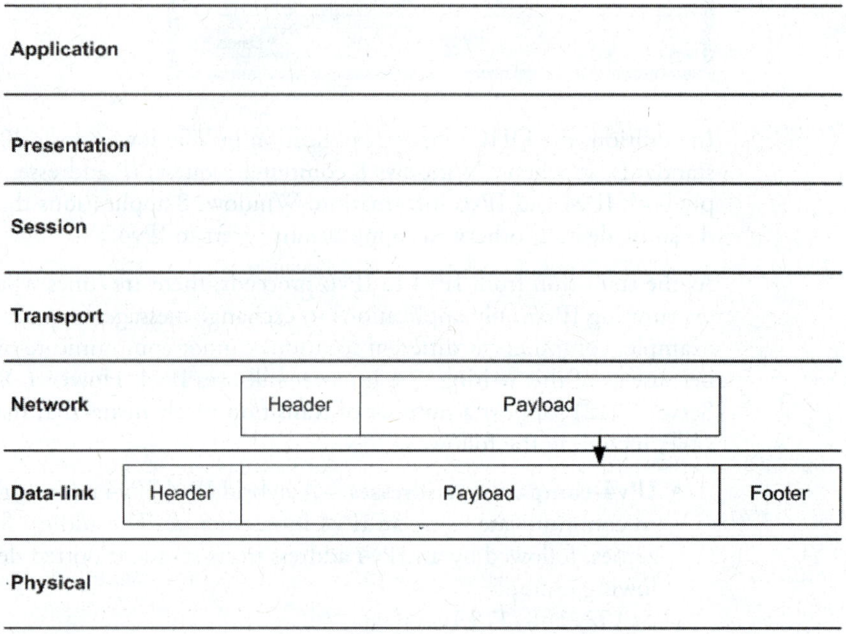

As with Ethernet, one of the functions of the IP header is to identify the protocol that generated the data in the datagram. The Protocol field in the IP header uses codes standardized by the IANA to specify the transport layer protocol that created the packet.

The Transport Layer

The OSI reference model calls for the network and transport layers to provide a flexible quality of service, so that applications can operate at peak efficiency.

There are two types of protocols that operate at the network and transport layers:

- **Connection-oriented** – A ***connection-oriented protocol*** is one in which two communicating systems establish a connection before they transmit any data. Once the connection is established, the computers exchange packets with complex headers designed to provide error detection and correction. A connection-oriented protocol ensures bit-perfect data transmissions, but at the price of greatly increased overhead.

- **Connectionless** – A ***connectionless protocol*** does not require the establishment of a connection, nor does it perform error detection or correction. Systems simply transmit their packets to the destination, without knowing if the destination system is ready to accept data, or if it even exists. Connectionless protocols do not guarantee delivery of their data, but they operate with a very low overhead that conserves network bandwidth.

IP, at the network layer, is a connectionless protocol, and there is no connection-oriented alternative at that layer. At the transport layer, TCP is the connection-oriented protocol, and the connectionless alternative is the User Datagram Protocol (UDP).

CONNECTION-ORIENTED PROTOCOLS

Applications that use TCP require every bit of data they transmit to be received properly at the destination. For example, if you download a service pack from the Microsoft website, a single garbled bit could render the package useless. Using the combination of TCP and IP guarantees that every message eventually arrives intact. If a packet is damaged or lost, the systems retransmit it. However, to use TCP, the systems must exchange extra packets to establish a connection and append a 20-byte header to each packet. This adds up to a lot of extra data that have to be transmitted over the network.

CONNECTIONLESS PROTOCOLS

Applications that use UDP are not terribly concerned if a packet goes astray. There are two reasons why this can be so. Either the messages are so small that the systems can easily retransmit them if they do not receive a response, or the data transmitted by the application is of a type that can tolerate the loss of an occasional packet.

An example of the former reason is the Domain Name System (DNS) communications that are a part of every Internet transaction. When you type a URL into your web browser, the first thing the system does is send a UDP message to a DNS server requesting the IP address corresponding to the domain name in the URL. This is a tiny message that fits in a single packet, so it's not worth transmitting several additional packets to establish a TCP connection. It's more economical just to retransmit the DNS request if no response if forthcoming.

A good example of the latter reason is streaming video. A video stream consists of large amounts of data, but unlike a file transfer, a few missing bits will not cause a catastrophic failure. A few packets lost from a video stream due to damaged UDP packets might mean a few lost frames, but that would hardly be noticeable to the viewer. The alternative, using TCP to transmit all of the packets, would provide a perfect viewing experience for the user, but at the cost of vastly increased bandwidth.

PORTS AND SOCKETS

Just like the network and data-link layers, transport layer protocols encapsulate the data they receive from the layer above by appending a header to each packet, as shown in Figure 10-5. Unlike the lower layers, however, transport layer protocols are not concerned with addressing packets to the correct system. This addressing is performed by IP and Ethernet, so there is no need for it here. However, transport layer protocols are concerned with identifying the applications that created the packet and to which the packet will ultimately be delivered.

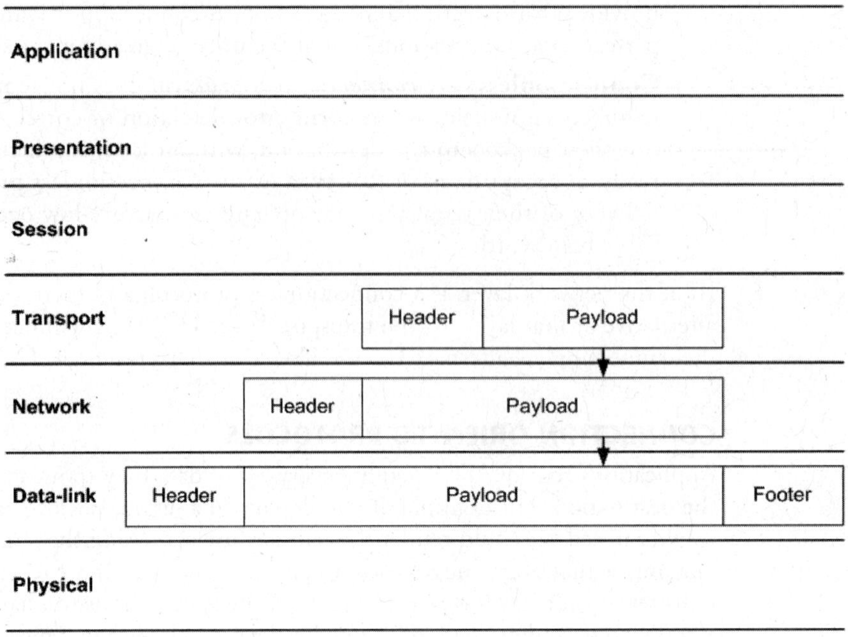

Figure 10-5

Transport layer data encapsulation

As with the protocol codes included in IP headers, the TCP and UDP headers both contain codes that identify specific applications running on the system. The codes, called ***ports***, are again published by the IANA, and the combination of an IP address and a port number is called a ***socket***. For example, the standard port number for the Hypertext Transfer Protocol (HTTP), the application layer protocol used for web communications, is 80. If your web browser is sending an HTTP request to a web server with the IP address 192.168.87.33, the web server application on that computer can be identified by the socket 192.168.87.33:80.

There are two basic types of port numbers: *well-known port numbers*, which are numbers permanently assigned to specific applications, and *ephemeral port numbers*, which are random values created automatically by client applications. In the previous example, the web browser is using the well-known HTTP port 80 as the destination for its packets, but the source port would be an ephemeral port number created by the system running the browser.

This system works because the client is initiating contact with the server. The client has to know the port number to use in its messages to the server, so it uses a well-known port. There is no need for the client to have a well-known port number because the server will be able to discover the client's ephemeral port number from its incoming messages.

Some of the most common well-known port numbers are listed in Table 10-3.

TRANSPORT LAYER DATA ENCAPSULATION

The headers that the TCP and UDP protocols add to the data they receive from the application layer are vastly different in size and complexity. The headers for both protocols contain source and destination port numbers. The UDP header includes little else, except for a checksum used to check for errors in the header. The TCP header, on the other hand, includes a multitude of fields that implement additional services, including the following:

- **Packet acknowledgment** – Informs the sender which packets have been delivered successfully.
- **Error correction** – Informs the sender which packets must be retransmitted.
- **Flow control** – Regulates the rate at which the sending system transmits its data.

Table 10-3

Well-Known Port Numbers Used by TCP and UDP

Service Name	Port Number	Protocol	Function
ftp-data	20	TCP	FTP data channel; used for transmitting files between systems
ftp	21	TCP	FTP control channel; used by FTP-connected systems for exchanging commands and responses
Ssh	22	TCP and UDP	SSH (Secure Shell) Remote Login Protocol; used to security log on to a computer from another computer on the same network and execute commands.
telnet	23	TCP	Telnet; used to execute commands on network-connected systems
Smtp	25	TCP	Simple Mail Transport Protocol (SMTP); used to send email messages
Domain	53	TCP and UDP	DNS; used to receive host name resolution requests from clients
Bootps	67	TCP and UDP	Bootstrap Protocol (BOOTP) and DHCP servers; used to receive TCP/IP configuration requests from clients
Bootpc	68	TCP and UDP	BOOTP and DHCP clients; used to send TCP/IP configuration requests to servers
http	80	TCP	HTTP; used by Web servers to receive requests from client browsers
pop3	110	TCP	Post Office Protocol 3 (POP3); used to retrieve email requests from clients
nntp	119	TCP and UDP	Network News Transfer Protocol; used to post and distribute messages to, and retrieve them from, Usenet servers on the Internet.
ntp	123	TCP and UDP	Network Time Protocol; used to exchange time signals for the purpose of synchronizing the clocks in network computers.
imap	143	TCP and UDP	Internet Message Access Protocol version 4; used by email client programs to retrieve messages from a mail server
snmp	161	TCP and UDP	Simple Network Management Protocol (SNMP); used by SNMP agents to transmit status information to a network management console
https	443	TCP and UDP	Hypertext Transfer Protocol Over TLS/SSL;

The Upper Layers

The application layer is the top of the networking stack, and as such, it provides the entrance point for programs running on a computer.

Windows applications themselves have no networking capabilities. They simply make function calls to application layer protocols, which in turn initiate the entire network communications process.

TAKE NOTE*

In TCP/IP, the session and presentation layers do not have individual protocols dedicated to them. In most cases, application layer protocols include functions attributed to all of the top three layers.

For example, a mail client is a program that enables you to send messages to users on other computers, but the mail program knows nothing about the nature of your network. When you send an email message to someone, the client takes the message and the address of the intended recipient and packages it using an application layer protocol called Simple Mail Transfer Protocol (SMTP). SMTP creates a properly formatted email message and passes it down to the proper protocol at the next lower layer in the networking stack, the transport layer, which for this application is TCP.

TCP then adds its header, passes the packet down to IP at the network layer, which encapsulates it and passes it down to Ethernet at the data-link layer, which adds its frame and transmits it over the network. Thus, by the time the email message reaches the network, it has been encapsulated four times, by SMTP, TCP, IP, and Ethernet, as shown in Figure 10-6.

Figure 10-6

Application layer data encapsulation

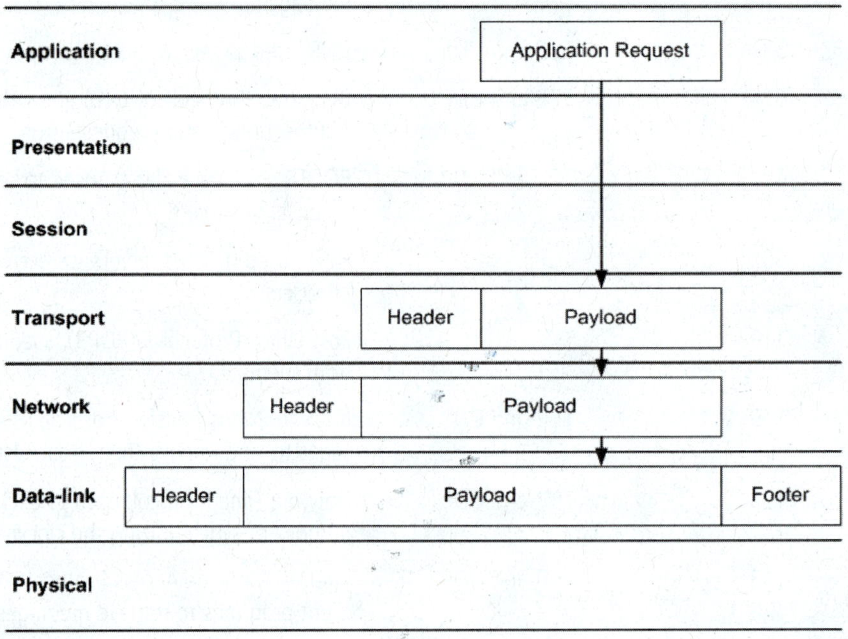

When the packet arrives at its final destination, the networking stack on the receiving computer performs the same steps in reverse. The system passes the incoming packets up through the layers, with each one removing its header and using the header information to pass the contents to the correct protocol at the next higher layer. Finally, the packet arrives at its final terminus, which is an application running on the destination computer, in this case, an email server.

Connecting to a Network

THE BOTTOM LINE

The networking capabilities in Windows 8 have been designed to minimize the threat of intrusion from outside intruders, while providing users with a simple and reliable networking experience. The following sections examine some of the networking tools and concepts in Windows 8.

CERTIFICATION READY
Connect to a network
Objective 3.1

Networking provides Windows 8 with an open door to a virtually unlimited array of resources, but an open door can let things in as easily as it lets things out. This makes security a primary concern for Windows 8 administrators. Windows 8 includes a variety of tools and features that enable users and administrators to manage the operating system's networking capabilities and help to protect it against unauthorized access. Many of these features operate invisibly to both users and administrators.

Some of the tools that desktop technicians must use regularly, and the concepts they support, are discussed in the following sections:

Installing Network Support

Windows 8 usually is able to detect a network interface adapter in a computer and automatically install and configure the networking client.

The installation of Windows 8's networking support is usually automatic. When Windows 8 detects a network interface adapter in the computer, either during the operating system installation or afterwards, it installs a device driver for the adapter, as well as the components of the default networking stack, which are as follows:

- **Client for Microsoft Networks** – Provides application layer services that enable programs to access shared files and printers on the network.
- **QoS Packet Scheduler** – Enables the network client to prioritize network traffic based on bandwidth availability and changing network conditions.
- **File and Printer Sharing for Microsoft Networks** – Enables the computer to share its files and printers with other users on the network.
- **Microsoft Network Adapter Multiplexor Protocol** – Provides support for network adapter load balancing and failover.
- **Microsoft LLDP Protocol Driver** – Provides Link Layer Discovery Protocol support for Microsoft Data Center Networking (DCN).
- **Link Layer Topology Discovery Mapper I/O Driver and Link Layer Topology Discovery Responder** – Implement the protocol that enables Windows 7Windows 8 to compile a map of the computers on the network.
- **Internet Protocol Version 6 (TCP/IPv6)** – Provides support for the IPv6 network layer protocol, including 128-bit IP addresses.
- **Internet Protocol Version 4 (TCP/IPv4)** – Provides support for the IPv4 network layer protocol, including 32-bit IP addresses.

The first time that the computer connects to a network, Windows 8 presents the user with the option to turn on sharing and connect to network devices or not, as shown in Figure 10-7. The settings you can choose from are as follows:

- **No, don't turn on sharing or connect to devices** – Intended for use on public networks, such as coffee shops and airports, this setting prevents the computer from sharing its folders and prevents you from connecting to network devices.
- **Yes, turn on sharing and connect to devices** – For home and small business networks that you trust, this setting enables you to connect to network devices, such as printers and share your folders.

Figure 10-7

Windows 8 Networks controls

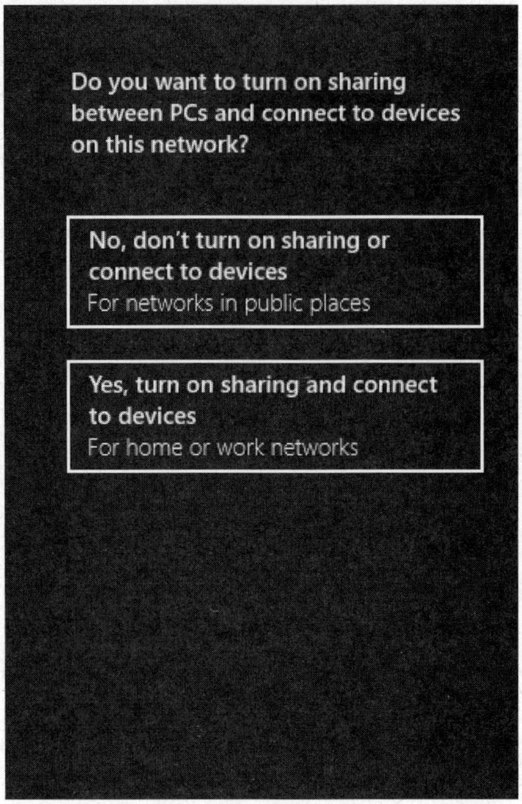

These options do not appear when you connect to an Active Directory Domain Services domain. Depending on your selection, the system configures the computer to use one of three network location designations. These selections are actually combinations of network discovery and file sharing settings, which determine how much access the workstation user will have to the network and how much access network users will have to the workstation.

These three network location options are as follows:

- **Private** – Indicates that the computer is connected to a private workgroup or HomeGroup network and not directly connected to the Internet. This means that it is safe for the computer to share its files and discover other computers.
- **Public** – Indicates that the computer is connected to a network in a public place, such as an airport or coffee shop "hot spot" for wireless computers, or is connected directly to the Internet without an intervening router. This means that the computer and its shares cannot be seen or accessed from the network, nor can the system create or join a HomeGroup network. In addition, some applications might not be able to access the network.
- **Domain** – Indicates that the computer is connected to an Active Directory Domain Services (AD DS) domain. This option is set automatically when you join the computer to the domain.

These Networks controls are accessible through the edge UI by swiping inwards from the right side of the screen, mousing over the right-side top or bottom corner of the screen, or by pressing the Win + I key combination, to display the Charms bar. When you touch or click the Settings charm, a network icon appears at the bottom of the display. Click the icon to display a list of the networks to which the computer is connected.

By right-clicking a network, you can turn file sharing on or off, as shown in Figure 10-8.

In addition to the new Windows 8 controls, users and administrators can also configure the network with the more familiar Network and Sharing Center.

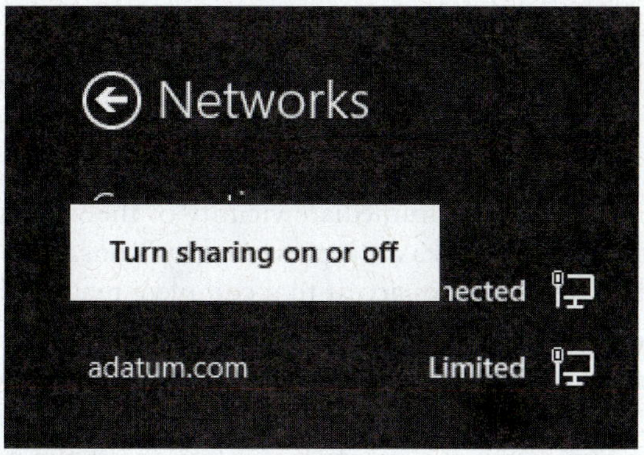

Figure 10-8

Windows 8 Network sharing controls

Using the Network and Sharing Center

> The Network and Sharing Center is a centralized console that provides technical specialists and system administrators with access to most of the major networking tools included with Windows 8.

The Windows 8 Network and Sharing Center provides a central access point for all of the network connections on the computer. Many of the common network configuration and administration tasks that technicians perform on Windows 8 computers start by opening the Network and Sharing Center. As with many Windows tools, there are several ways to open the Network and Sharing Center, two of which are as follows:

- Click the Search charm, select Settings, and search for "Network and Sharing Center."
- From the Desktop, click the Settings charm and click Control Panel. Then click Network and Internet > Network and Sharing Center.

When the Network and Sharing Center appears, you see a window like the one shown in Figure 10-9.

Figure 10-9

The Network and Sharing Center

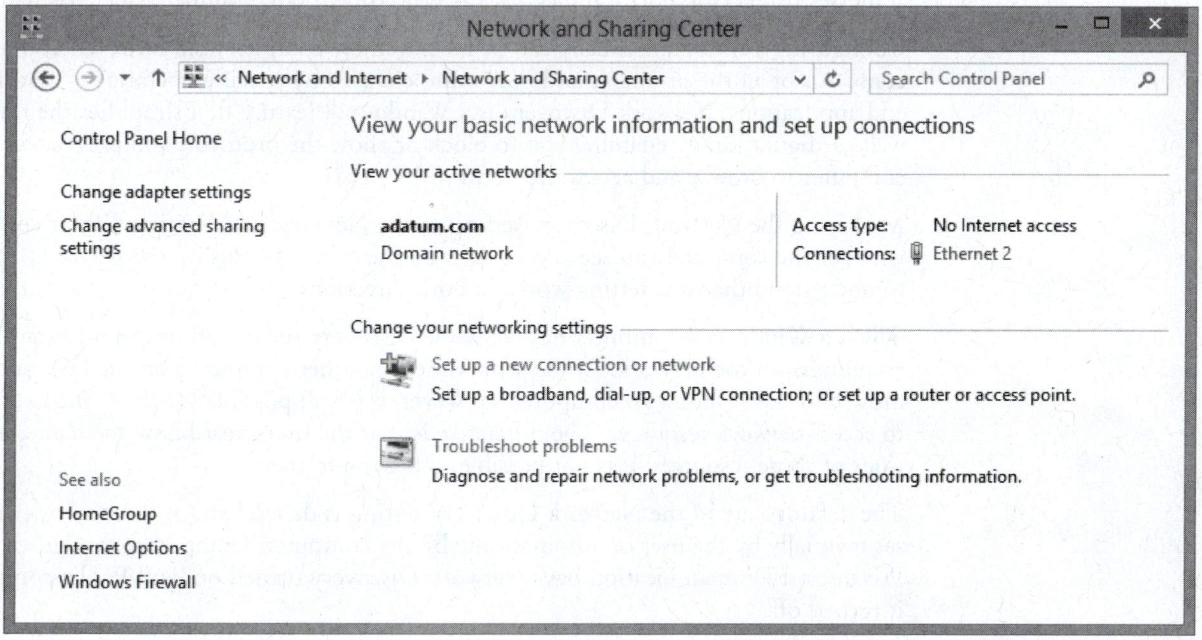

The Network and Sharing Center main window consists of the following elements:

- **Task list (left pane)** – Contains links that enable you to manager network adapter settings and configure sharing parameters.
- **Summary network map (top right)** – Provides a graphical representation of the computers and networks in the immediate vicinity of the workstation and their connections. The computers and networks are represented by icons, with lines representing their connections. A link also provides access to a complete map of the entire network.
- **View your active networks (middle right)** – Displays the name of the network and other information, such as the network location (private, domain, or public), whether the workstation is connected to a local network, the Internet, or both, and the name of the local area connection the system is using to access the network. There are also links the enable you to connect to or disconnect from the network and view the current status of the local area connection.
- **Change your networking settings (bottom right)** – Contains switches that enable you to control the sharing and discovery behavior of the network.

UNDERSTANDING NETWORK DISCOVERY

Network Discovery is an important security concept first introduced in Windows Vista. It enables users to control critical network firewall controls with a single switch. Windows Firewall is a feature that was first introduced in the Windows XP Service Pack 2 release, and is now included in Windows 8 as well.

A ***firewall*** is a software routine that acts as a virtual barrier between a computer and the network to which it is attached. A firewall is essentially a filter that enables certain types of incoming and outgoing traffic to pass through the barrier, while blocking other types.

Firewalls typically base their filtering on the TCP/IP characteristics at the network, transport, and application layers, as follows:

- ***IP addresses*** – which represent specific computers on the network
- **Protocol numbers** – which identify the transport layer protocol being used by the packets
- **Port numbers** – which identify specific applications running on the computer

If, for example, you want to prevent all computers on the network from accessing your system using the Telnet protocol, you would configure the firewall to block the traffic from all IP addresses using TCP port number 23, the well-known port number associated with Telnet.

Configuring a firewall manually can be an extremely complex task, however. You must be conscious of all the protocols and port numbers used by specific operating system functions and applications. Network Discovery is a Windows 8 feature that simplifies the task of firewall configuration by enabling you to block or allow the protocols and ports need for the computer to browse and access the network.

Modifying the Network Discovery setting in the Network and Sharing Center controls whether the computer can see and be seen by the other systems on the network. It is critical to understand that this setting works in both directions.

When a Windows 8 computer has Network Discovery turned off, it cannot browse the other computers on the network. At the same time, the other computers on the network cannot browse to the Windows 8 computer. However, it is still possible for the Windows 8 computer to access network resources. The difference is that the user must know the names and locations of those resources; it is not possible to browse to them.

The default state of the Network Discovery setting is dependent on the network location, as set manually by the user or automatically by the computer. Computers configured with the Private and Domain location have Network Discovery turned on, and Public computers have it turned off.

CHANGING THE NETWORK LOCATION

CERTIFICATION READY
Configure network locations
Objective 3.1

After you select the initial network location during the network interface adapter installation, Windows 8 attempts to detect the type of location whenever you connect to a different network. If, for example, your laptop computer used the Private location when you installed Windows 8 on your home network, and you later take the computer to a coffee shop with a wireless network, Windows 8 will most likely detect the change and alter the network location to Public. This turns the Network Discovery and file sharing options off, for greater security.

Unlike Windows 7, in which you can easily change the network location using the Network and Sharing Center controls, changing the network location is more difficult in Windows 8. In most cases, when Windows 8 is unable to detect the network type for any reason, it errs on the side of caution and sets the network location to Public, which is the safest option.

One method for detecting the problem and changing the Public setting to Private is to use the HomeGroup Troubleshooter, as in the following procedure.

CHANGE THE NETWORK LOCATION USING HOMEGROUP TROUBLESHOOTER

GET READY. Log on to Windows 8 using an account with administrative capabilities and then perform the following steps:

1. Open the **Network and Sharing Center.**

   The *Network and Sharing Center* window appears.
2. Click the **HomeGroup** link.

   The *Share with other home computers* page appears.
3. Click **Start the HomeGroup troubleshooter**.

   The *Troubleshoot and help prevent computer problems* page appears, as shown in Figure 10-10.

Figure 10-10
The *Troubleshoot and help prevent computer problems* page

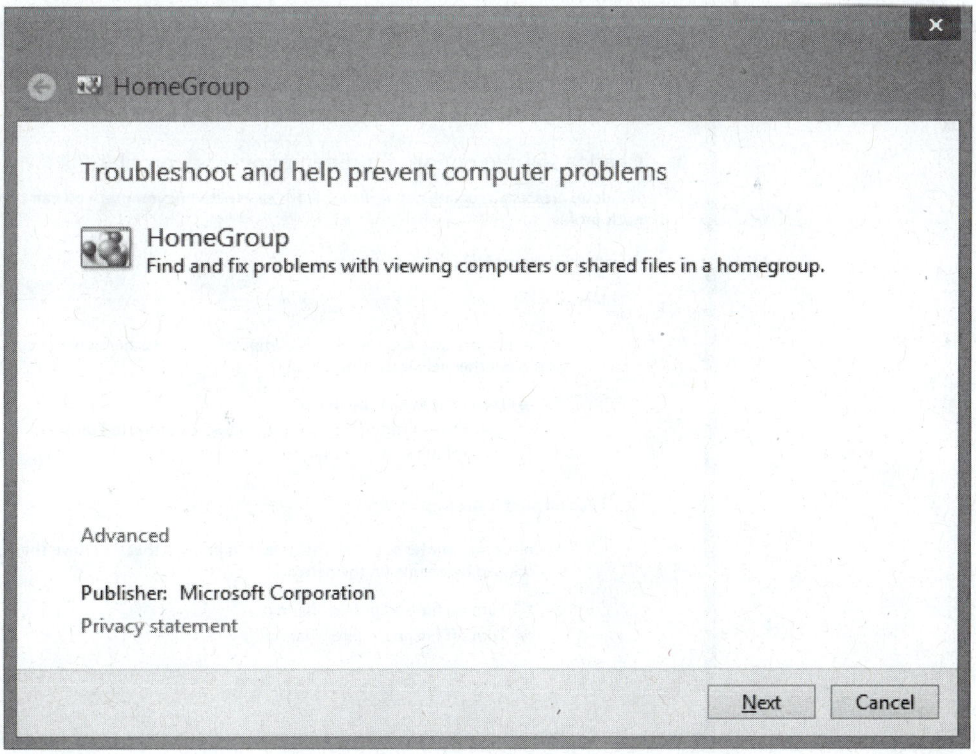

4. Click **Next**. The *Troubleshoot network problems* page appears.
5. Click **Troubleshoot network problems**.

   The troubleshooter should detect the problem and offer to change the network location to Private.
6. Click **Apply this fix**. After the fix is applied, you can select whether you want to join the computer to a homegroup or not.

When you select the option to join a homegroup network, the system searches for existing homegroups on the network. If it fails to find one, the system creates a new homegroup network and supplies a password for it. For more information on homeroup networking, see Lesson 14, "Configuring Shared Resources."

CONFIGURING ADVANCED SHARING SETTINGS

With some limitations, you can manually change the Network Discovery and other sharing settings, whichever network location the system is using, by using the following procedure:

CONFIGURE ADVANCED SHARING

GET READY. Log on to Windows 8 using an account with administrative capabilities and then perform the following steps:

1. Open the **Network and Sharing Center**.

   The *Network and Sharing Center* window appears.
2. In the left pane, click **Change advanced sharing settings**.

   The *Change sharing options for different network profiles* dialog box appears.
3. Click the down arrow for the network location whose settings you want to modify, to produce the display shown in Figure 10-11.

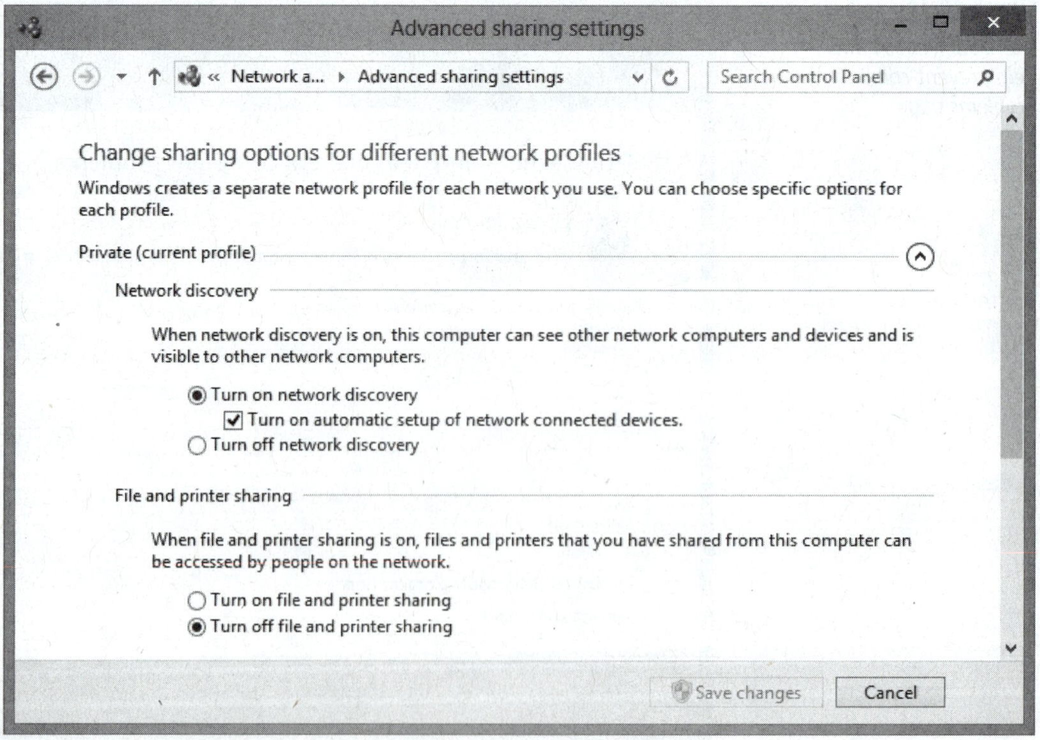

Figure 10-11

The *Change sharing options for different network profiles* dialog box

4. Configure the following settings by selecting from the options provided:
   - **Network Discovery** – Enables the computer to see other devices on the network and renders it visible from the network
   - **Turn on automatic setup of network connected devices** – Enables the system to automatically configure itself to access printers and other network devices.
   - **File and printer sharing** – Enables network users to access the files and printers shared on the computer
   - **Public folder sharing** – Enables network users to access the Public folders on the computer
   - **Media streaming** – Enables network users to access media files on the computer, and enables the computer to locate media files on the network
   - **File sharing connections** – Specifies whether clients accessing the computer's shares must use 128-bit encryption
   - **Password protected sharing** – Specifies whether network users accessing the computer's shares must have local user accounts with passwords
   - **HomeGroup connections** – Specifies whether Windows 8 should manage HomeGroup connections automatically
5. Click **Save Changes**.
   The *Network and Sharing Center* window reappears.

Managing Network Connections

Windows 8 creates and configures local area connections automatically, but you can also manage and modify the properties of the connections manually.

When Windows 8 detects a network interface adapter, it creates a network connection automatically, installs the TCP/IP networking components, and configures it to use DHCP to obtain IP addresses and other network configuration settings. To view and modify the Properties of local area connection, use the procedures in the following sections.

VIEWING A CONNECTION'S STATUS

Each local area connection on a Windows 8 system has a status dialog box that displays real time information about the connection. To view the status of a connection, use the following procedure.

VIEW CONNECTION STATUS

GET READY. Log on to Windows 8 using an account with administrative capabilities and then perform the following steps:

1. Open the **Network and Sharing Center**.
   The *Network and Sharing Center* window appears.
2. In the *View your active networks* section, click **Ethernet** or the name of the connection whose status you want to view.
   The Ethernet Status dialog box appears, as shown in Figure 10-12.

Figure 10-12

The *Ethernet Status* dialog box

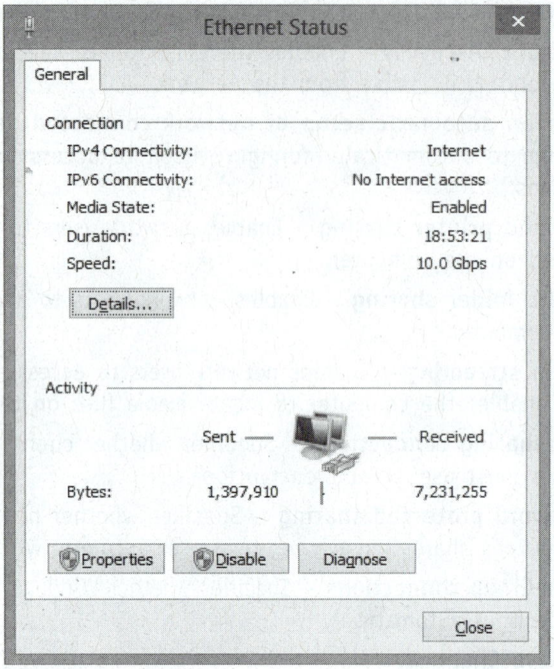

3. Click **Details**. The Network Connection Details dialog box appears, as shown in Figure 10-13.

Figure 10-13

The *Network Connection Details* dialog box

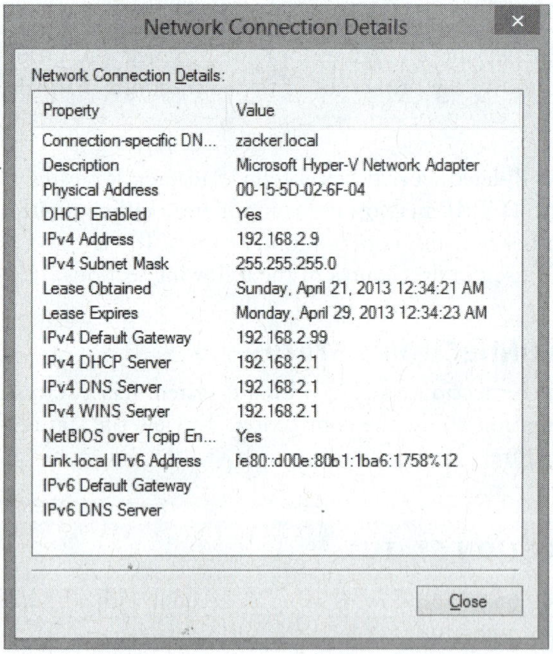

4. Click **Close** to close the *Network Connection Details* dialog box.
5. Click **Close** to close the *Local Area Connection Status* dialog box.

The *Ethernet Status* dialog box displays basic information about the connection, such as its speed, which version(s) of IP it is using, and how long the computer has been connected. In the Activity area, you can see the number of bytes that the computer has sent and received in a real-time display, so you can tell if the network connection is currently functional.

At the bottom of the dialog box are buttons that enable you to perform the following tasks:

- **Properties** – Open the *Properties* sheet for the network connection.
- **Disable/Enable** – Toggle the operational status of the network connection.
- **Diagnose** – Start Windows Network Diagnostics and attempt to detect any problems affecting the network connection.

TAKE NOTE*

Disabling a network connection does not affect its configuration settings in any way. The networking hardware is still installed and configured and the TCP/IP settings remain intact. The connection is simply turned off until you turn it back on again, which renders it immediately operational.

The *Network Connection Details* page displays the configuration settings for the network connection, including the TCP/IP settings obtained using DHCP.

CONFIGURING IPv4 SETTINGS

Most networks today use DHCP to configure the TCP/IP configuration settings of their workstations. DHCP automates the configuration process and prevents the duplication of IP addresses. However, there are still some situations in which it is desirable or necessary to configure the Windows 8 TCP/IP client manually. To do this, use the following procedure:

CONFIGURE IPv4 SETTINGS

GET READY. Log on to Windows 8 using an account with administrative capabilities and then perform the following steps:

1. Open the **Network and Sharing Center**.

   The *Network and Sharing Center* window appears.
2. Click **Change adapter settings**.

   The Network Connections window appears, as shown in Figure 10-14.

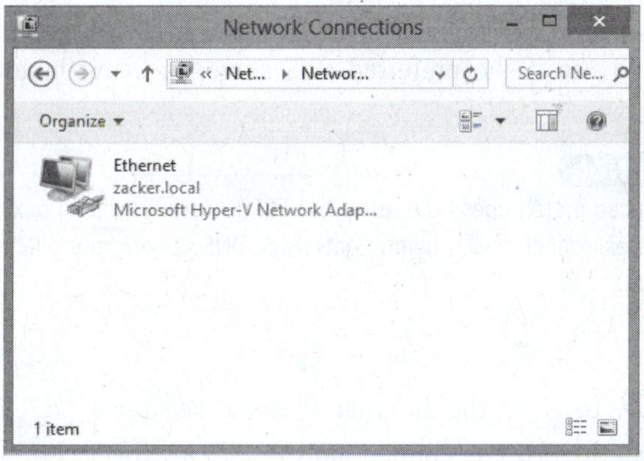

Figure 10-14
The *Network Connections* window

3. Right-click the connection you want to manage and, from the context menu, select **Properties**.

   The connection's *Properties* sheet appears.
4. Select **Internet Protocol Version 4 (TCP/IPv4)** and then click **Properties**.

   The Internet Protocol Version 4 (TCP/IPv4) Properties sheet appears, as shown in Figure 10-15.

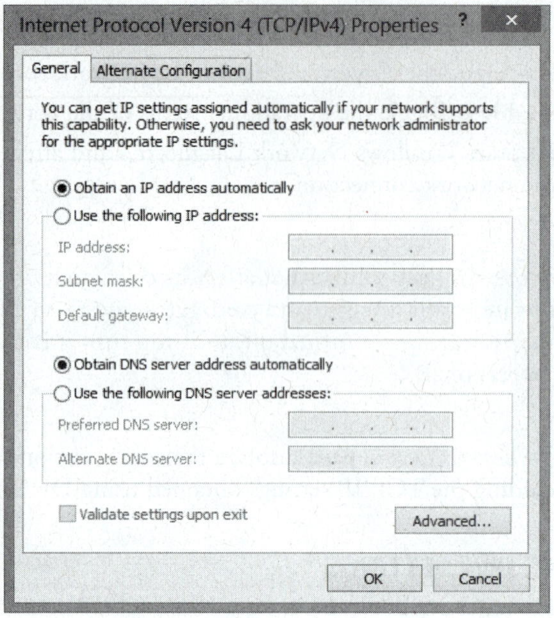

Figure 10-15

The *Internet Protocol Version 4 (TCP/IPv4) Properties* sheet

5. Select the **Use the following IP address** option and then enter appropriate values for the following parameters:
   - **IP address** – A 32-bit IPv4 address, in dotted decimal notation.
   - **Subnet Mask** – An appropriate mask indicating which part of the IP address is the network identifier and which part the host identifier.
   - **Default Gateway** – The IP address of the router on the local network that the computer should use to access other networks and/or the Internet.
6. Select the **Use The Following DNS Server Addresses** option and then enter appropriate values for the following parameters:
   - **Preferred DNS Server** – The IP address of the DNS server the computer should use to resolve host and domain names into IP addresses
   - **Alternate DNS Server** – The IP address of a DNS server that the computer should use if the preferred DNS server is unavailable

MORE INFORMATION

Clicking the Advanced button opens the Advanced TCP/IP Settings dialog box, in which you can configure multiple IP addresses, subnet masks, default gateways, DNS servers, and WINS servers for client computers with special requirements.

7. Click **OK** to close the *Internet Protocol Version 4 (TCP/IPv4) Properties* sheet.
8. Click **OK** to close the connection's *Properties* sheet.

The command line alternative to this graphical interface is a program called Netsh.exe. Netsh.exe is a powerful tool that you can use interactively or with command line parameters to configure virtually any Windows 8 networking setting. To configure the basic IPv4 parameters for a network connection, you use the following syntax:

```
netsh interface ipv4 set address connection_name
static ip_address subnet_mask default_gateway
```

An example of an actual command would be as follows:

```
netsh interface ipv4 set address "Ethernet" static
192.168.1.23 255.255.255.0 192.168.1.1
```

Then, to configure the DNS server address, you would use the following command syntax:

```
netsh interface ipv4 set dnsservers connection_name
static ip_address
```

An example of an actual command would be as follows:

```
netsh interface ipv4 set dnsservers "Ethernet" static
192.168.1.99
```

To configure a connection to obtain its settings from a DHCP server, use the following commands:

```
netsh interface ipv4 set address name="Ethernet"
source=dhcp
```

```
netsh interface ipv4 set dnsservers name="Ethernet"
source=dhcp
```

Prior to Windows 8, configuring IP addresses and other network interface settings with Windows PowerShell was a complicated affair involving scripts and Windows Management Instrumentation (WMI) classes. Windows PowerShell 3.0, however, adds a NetTCPIP module that includes cmdlets that simplify these tasks.

To configure the basic settings for a network interface, including the IP address, the subnet mask, and the default gateway address, you use the `New-NetIPAddress` cmdlet with the following syntax:

```
New-NetIPAddress -InterfaceIndex <number>
-Ipaddress <address> -PrefixLength <number>
-DefaultGateway <address>
```

To determine the index number of the network interface you want to configure, you run the `Get NetIPInterface` cmdlet. Once you have the index number, you can configure the interface, as in the following example:

```
New-NetIPAddress -InterfaceIndex 12 -IPaddress
192.168.4.55 -PrefixLength 24 -DefaultGateway
192.168.4.1
```

The one essential parameter that the `New-NetIPAddress` cmdlet cannot configure is the DNS server address the system will use. To configure this, you must use the `Set-DNSClientServerAddress` cmdlet, with the followng syntax:

```
Set-DNSClientServerAddress -InterfaceIndex <number> -
ServerAddresses ("10.0.0.1","10.0.0.7"]
```

CONFIGURING IPv6 SETTINGS

Because most computers use IPv6 autoconfiguration or DHCP, manual configuration of the Windows 8 IPv6 implementation is rarely necessary, but it is possible.

The procedure for configuring IPv6 using the graphical interface is the same as that for IPv4, except that, in the *Local Area Connection Properties* sheet, you select Internet Protocol Version 6 (TCP/IPv6) and click Properties. The Internet Protocol Version 6 (TCP/IPv6) Properties sheet appears, as shown in Figure 10-16.

Figure 10-16

The *Internet Protocol Version 6 (TCP/IPv6) Properties* sheet

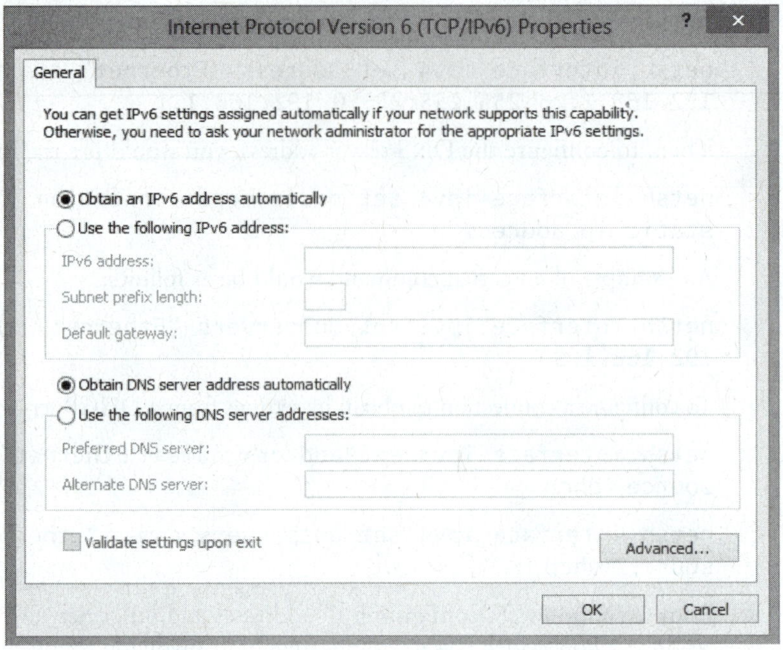

To configure IPv6 from the command prompt, you use Netsh.exe in the same way you would for IPv4, substituting the ipv6 parameter for ipv4 and an IPv6 address for the IPv4 address and subnet mask, as in the following example:

```
netsh interface ipv6 set address "Ethernet" static
FE80::7166:22E6:1D18:BDAA
```

To configure DNS server addresses, use a command like the following:

```
netsh interface ipv6 set dnsservers "Ethernet" static
FE80::7166:22E6:1D18:BD01
```

RUNNING NETWORK DIAGNOSTICS

CERTIFICATION READY
Resolve connectivity issues
Objective 3.1

The Network and Sharing Center shows the devices on the network and their status. Improperly configured devices have yellow warning signs on their icons and non-functioning connections have red X's on them.

When a networking problem exists, clicking a warning icon launches Windows Network Diagnostics. This utility attempts to automatically discover the cause of the problem and displays possible solutions, as shown in Figure 10-17.

Figure 10-17

Running *Windows Network Diagnostics*

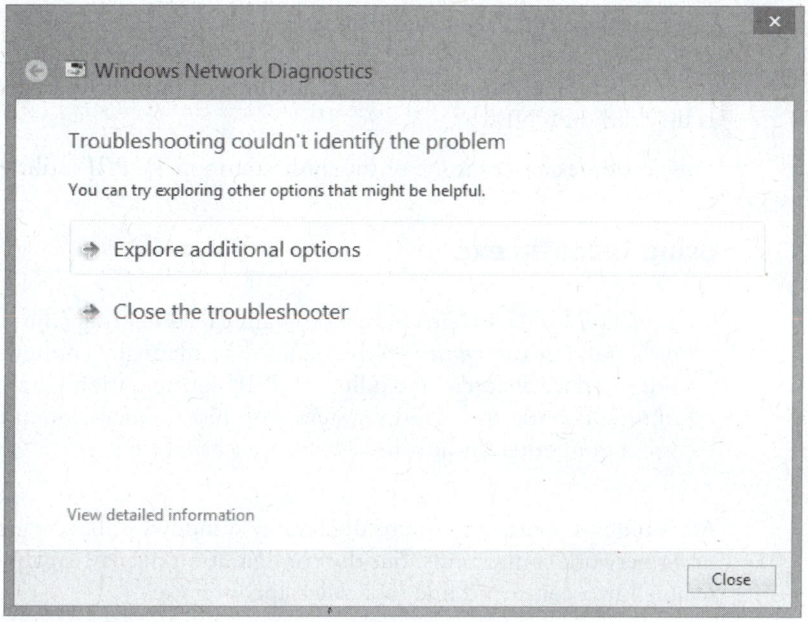

MORE INFORMATION

You can also launch Windows Network Diagnostics by opening the Network Connections window, right-clicking one of the network connections, and selecting Diagnose from the context menu.

Unlike previous troubleshooting tools, Network Diagnostics does not just display error messages, it tells you in clear language what might be wrong and what you have to do to repair the problem. The Network Diagnostics Framework (NDF) includes troubleshooting routines for wireless as well as wired networks. Problems that the system can diagnose include the following:

- Broken or detached cable connections
- IP address and subnet mask problems
- Default gateway problems
- DNS and DHCP configuration problems
- Networking hardware configuration problems
- Internet server addresses and service settings

If, after identifying a networking problem, the system can repair it automatically, it provides a link that you can select to have it do so. Otherwise, it displays a list of manual fixes that you can perform to address the problem.

Using TCP/IP Tools

THE BOTTOM LINE

Virtually all network operating systems today include support for the TCP/IP protocols, and TCP/IP traditionally includes some basic tools that you can use to troubleshoot network connectivity problems yourself.

The traditional TCP/IP troubleshooting tools originated on UNIX systems, and as a result, they are command line tools that you run in Windows 8 by opening a Command Prompt window first. The Windows implementations of these utilities generally use the same syntax as they did on UNIX.

This section examines some of the most common TCP/IP utilities and their purposes.

Using Ipconfig.exe

> UNIX and Linux systems have a program called ifconfig (the name is derived from the words *interface configuration*) that you use to manually configure the properties of network interface adapters, including TCP/IP configuration parameters such as IP addresses. Running ifconfig on a UNIX system with just the name of an interface displays the current configuration information for that interface.

All Windows operating systems, including Windows 8, have a graphical interface for configuring network connections, but the configuration display capabilities of ifconfig have been retained in a command line tool called Ipconfig.exe.

When you run Ipconfig.exe with the/all parameter at the Windows 8 command prompt, you see a display like the one shown in Figure 10-18.

Figure 10-18

The Ipconfig.exe display

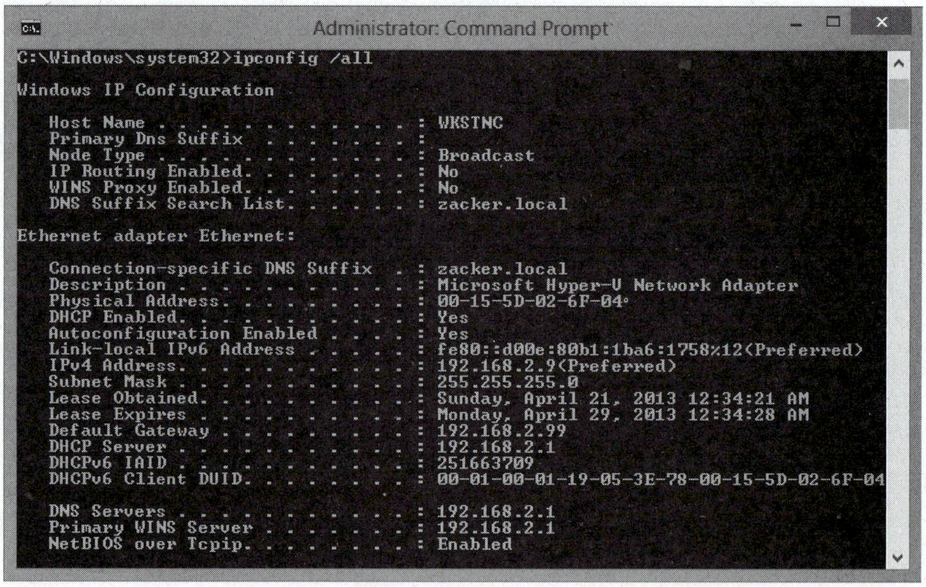

The value of Ipconfig.exe is particularly apparent when a Windows 8 computer autoconfigures its TCP/IP client or uses DHCP to obtain its IP address and other TCP/IP configuration parameters. A DHCP-configured computer does not display any configuration information in the Ethernet Properties sheet; it just shows that the DHCP client is activated. One of the few ways to see what settings the DHCP server has assigned to the computer (without examining the DHCP server itself) is to use Ipconfig.exe.

In addition to displaying the DHCP-obtained configuration settings, Ipconfig.exe also enables you to manually release the IP address the system obtained from the DHCP server and renew existing address leases. By running Ipconfig.exe with the /release and /renew command-line parameters, you can release or renew the IP address assignment of one of the network interfaces in the computer or for all of the interfaces at once.

Using Ping.exe

Ping is the most basic of TCP/IP utilities, and is included in some form with every TCP/IP implementation. On Windows 8 systems, the program is called Ping.exe.

Ping.exe can tell you if the TCP/IP stack of another system on the network is functioning normally. The Ping.exe program generates a series of Echo Request messages using the Internet Control Message Protocol (ICMP) and transmits them to the computer whose name or IP address you specify on the command line. The basic syntax of the Ping program is as follows:

```
ping target
```

The *target* variable contains the IPv4 or IPv6 address or name of any computer on the network. Because Ping.exe is a TCP/IP utility, the target computer can be running any operating system, not just Windows. You can use DNS host and domain names or Windows NetBIOS names in Ping commands. Ping resolves the name into an IP address before sending the Echo Request messages, and it then displays the address in its output.

TCP/IP computers respond to any *Echo Request* messages they receive that are addressed to them by generating Echo Reply messages and transmitting them back to the sender. When the pinging computer receives the Echo Reply messages, it produces a display like the one shown in Figure 10-19.

Figure 10-19

The Ping.exe display

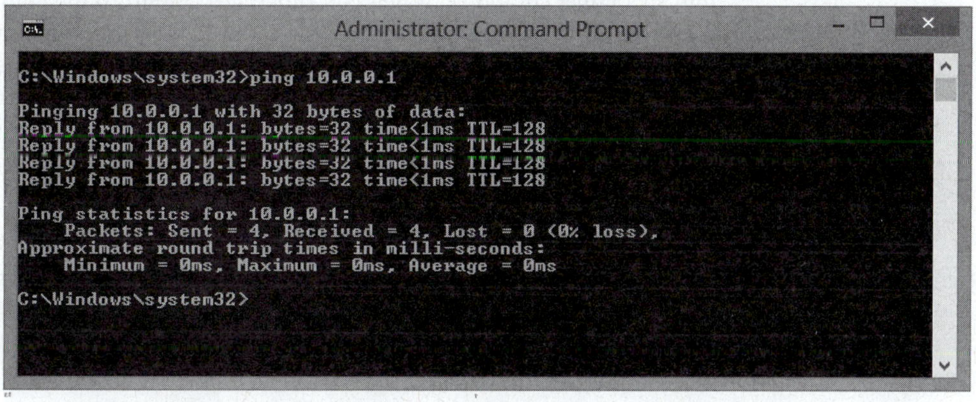

In Windows 8's Ping.exe implementation, the display shows the IP address of the computer receiving the Echo Requests, the number of bytes of data included with each request, the elapsed time between the transmission of each request and the receipt of each reply, and the value of the Time To Live (TTL) field in the IP header.

In this example, the target computer was on the same local area network (LAN), so the time measurement is very short—less than 1 millisecond. When pinging a computer on the Internet, the interval is likely to be longer. A successful Ping result like this one indicates that the target computer's networking hardware is functioning properly, as are its TCP/IP protocols, at least as high as the network layer of the OSI model. If a Ping test fails, there might be a firewall blocking the ICMP traffic between the two systems. If there is no firewall, then the Ping test failure indicates that there is a problem in one or both of the computers or in the network medium connecting them.

Ping.exe also has a series of command-line switches that you can use to modify the operational parameters of the program, such as the number of Echo Request messages it generates and the amount of data in each message. To display the syntax of the program, type `ping /?` at the command prompt.

Using Tracert.exe

> Traceroute is another UNIX program that was designed to display the path that TCP/IP packets take to their final destination. Called traceroute in UNIX, in Windows 8 it is implemented as Tracert.exe. Because of the nature of IP routing, the path from a packet's source to its destination on another network can change from minute to minute, especially on the Internet. Tracert.exe displays a list of the routers that are currently forwarding packets to a particular destination.

Tracert.exe is a variation on Ping.exe. The program uses ICMP Echo Request and Echo Reply messages just like Ping, but it modifies the messages by changing the value of the TTL field in the IP header. The values in the TTL field prevent packets from getting caught in router loops that keep them circulating endlessly around the internetwork. On a Windows 8 computer, the default value for the TTL field is relatively high, 128. Each time a packet passes from one network to another, the router connecting the networks reduces the TTL value by one. If the TTL value ever reaches zero, the router processing the packet discards it and transmits an ICMP error message back to the original sender.

Tracert.exe works by modifying the TTL values in the successive Ping.exe packets that it transmits to a target computer. When you run Tracert.exe from the command prompt with a *target* parameter, the program generates its first set of Echo Request messages with TTL values of 1. When the messages arrive at the first router on their path to the destination, the router decrements the TTL values to 0, discards the packets, and reports the errors to the sender. The error messages contain the router's address, which Tracert.exe displays as the first hop in the path to the destination.

Tracert.exe's second set of Echo Request messages use a TTL value of 2, causing the second router on the path to discard the packets and generate error messages. The Echo Request messages in the third set have a TTL value of 3, and so on. Each set of packets travels one hop farther than the previous set before causing a router to return error messages to the source. The list of routers displayed by the program as the path to the destination is the result of these error messages.

The following is an example of a Tracert.exe display:

```
Tracing route to www.fineartschool.co.uk [173.146.1.1] over a maximum
of 30 hops:

   1   <10 ms   1   ms   <10 ms   192.168.2.99
   2   105 ms   92  ms   98  ms   qrvl-67terminal01.cpandl.com
   3   101 ms   110 ms   98  ms   qrvl.cpandl.com
   4   123 ms   109 ms   118 ms   svcr03-7b.cpandl.com
   5   123 ms   112 ms   114 ms   clsm02-2.cpandl.com
   6   136 ms   130 ms   133 ms   sl-gw19-pen-6-1-0-T3.fabrikam.com
   7   143 ms   126 ms   138 ms   sl-bb10-pen-4-3.fabrikam.com
   8   146 ms   129 ms   133 ms   sl-bb20-pen-12-0.fabrikam.com
```

```
 9    131 ms   128 ms   139 ms   sl-bb20-nyc-13-0.fabrikam.com
 10   130 ms   134 ms   134 ms   sl-gw9-nyc-8-0.fabrikam.com
 11   147 ms   149 ms   152 ms   sl-demon-1-0.fabrikam.com
 12   154 ms   146 ms   145 ms   ny2-backbone-ge021.fabrikam.com
 13   230 ms   225 ms   226 ms   tele-backbone-ge023.adatum.co.uk
 14   233 ms   220 ms   226 ms   tele-core-3-fxp1.adatum.co.uk
 15   223 ms   224 ms   224 ms   tele-access-1-14.adatum.co.uk
 16   236 ms   221 ms   226 ms   tele-service-2-165.adatum.co.uk
 17   220 ms   224 ms   210 ms   www.fineartschool.co.uk
Trace complete.
```

In this example, Tracert.exe displays the path between a computer in Pennsylvania and one in the United Kingdom. Each of the hops contains the elapsed times between the transmission and reception of three sets of Echo Request and Echo Reply packets. In this trace, you can clearly see the point at which the packets begin traveling across the Atlantic Ocean. At hop 13, the elapsed times increase from approximately 150 to 230 milliseconds (ms) and stay in that range for the subsequent hops. This additional delay of only 80 ms is the time it takes the packets to travel the thousands of miles across the Atlantic Ocean.

Ping.exe simply tells you whether two TCP/IP systems are having trouble communicating. It can't pinpoint the location of the problem. A failure to contact a remote computer could be due to a problem in your workstation, in the remote computer, or in any of the routers in between. Tracert.exe can tell you how far your packets are going before they run into the problem.

TAKE NOTE *

Because the configuration of the Internet is constantly changing, there is no guarantee that the route displayed by Tracert.exe is completely accurate. The ICMP messages that execute each step of the Tracert.exe process could conceivably be taking different routes to the same destination, resulting in the display of a composite route between two points that does not actually exist. There is also no way of knowing what path the packets are taking as they return to the source. In addition, routers typically deprioritize ICMP processing in favor of packet forwarding and other more critical router tasks. When a router is busy, it might delay the processing of an Echo Request or Echo Reply packet. The resulting latency numbers will be higher than the delay experienced by actual data packets crossing the network.

Using Nslookup.exe

The ***Nslookup.exe*** command-line utility enables you to generate DNS request messages and transmit them to specific DNS servers on the network. The advantage of Nslookup.exe is that you can test the functionality and the quality of the information on a specific DNS server by specifying it on the command line.

The basic command-line syntax of Nslookup.exe is as follows:

`nslookup` *`DNSname DNSserver`*

- `DNSname` specifies the DNS name that you want to resolve
- `DNSserver` specifies the DNS name or IP address of the DNS server that you want to query for the name specified in the *DNSname* variable

There are also many additional parameters that you can include on the command line to control the server query process. The output generated by Nslookup.exe in Windows 8 looks like the one shown in Figure 10-20.

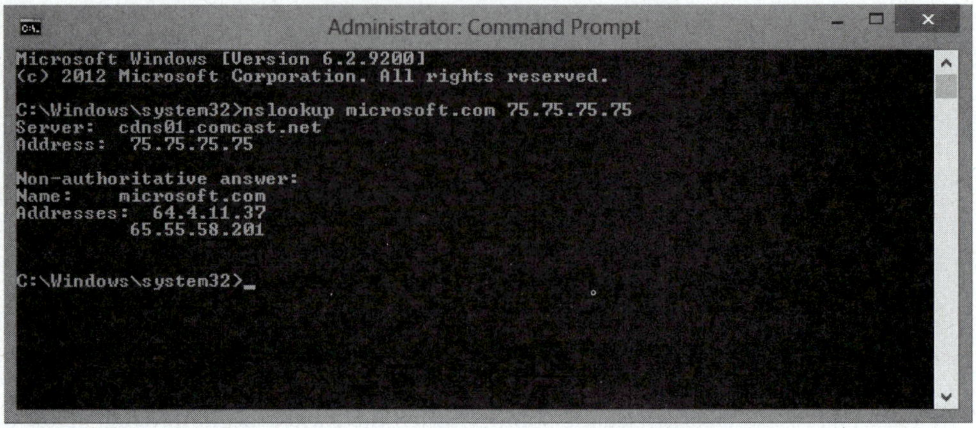

Figure 10-20
The Nslookup.exe display

The Nslookup.exe utility has two operational modes: command-line and interactive. When you run Nslookup.exe with no command-line parameters, the program displays its own prompt from which you can issue commands to specify the default DNS server to query, resolve multiple names, and configure many other aspects of the program's functionality.

Using Netstat.exe

Netstat.exe is a command-line program that displays status information about the current network connections on a computer running Windows 8 and about the traffic generated by the various TCP/IP protocols. In UNIX, the program is called netstat, and in Windows 8, it is called Netstat.exe.

The syntax for the Windows 8 version of Netstat.exe is as follows:

`NETSTAT [interval][-a][-b][-e][-f][-n][-o][-p protocol][-r][-s][-t]`

- *interval* – Specifies the time interval (in seconds) between display refreshes.
- `-a` – Displays the current network connections and the ports that are currently listening for incoming network connections.
- `-b` – Displays the executable associated with each active connection and listening port.
- `-e` – Displays Ethernet traffic statistics for the network interface, broken down into bytes, unicast packets, nonunicast packets, discards, errors, and unknown protocols.
- `-f` – When combined with other parameters, causes the program to display foreign addresses as fully qualified domain names.
- `-n` – When combined with other parameters, causes the program to display addresses and port numbers in numerical, rather than alphabetical, form.
- `-o` – Displays the process ID associated with each active connection and listening port.
- `-p` – *protocol* – Displays the current active connections for the protocol specified by the *protocol* variable.
- `-r` – Displays the computer's IPv4 and IPv6 routing tables.

- `-s` – Displays detailed network traffic statistics for the IP, ICMP, TCP, and UDP protocols, in both v4 and v6 versions.
- `-t` – Displays the offload state of the current connection.

Part of the default network connection listing displayed by Netstat.exe on a computer running Windows 8 appears in Figure 10-21.

Figure 10-21

The network connection listing in Netstat.exe

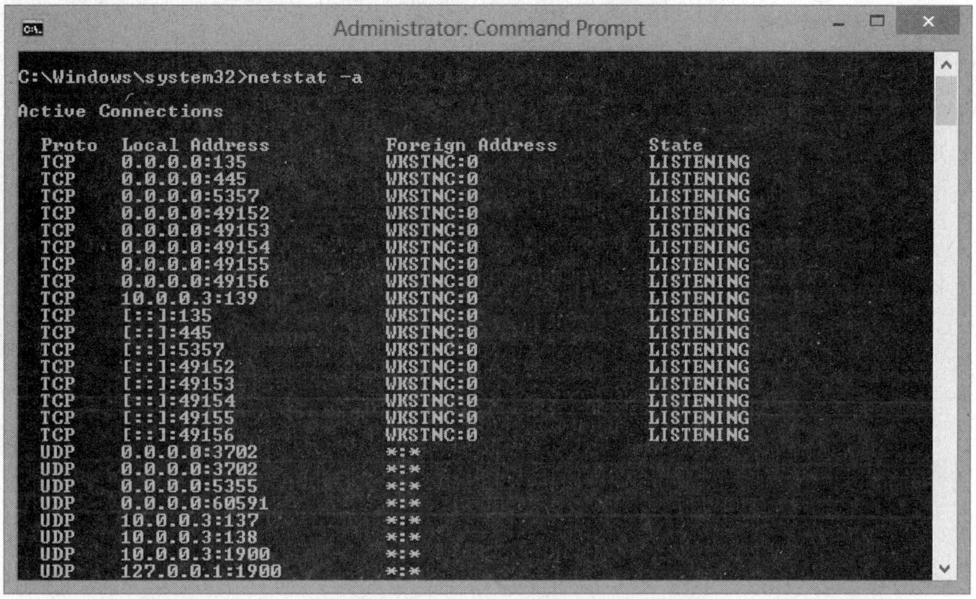

The Ethernet interface statistics, as displayed by netstat.exe, are shown in Figure 10-22.

Figure 10-22

The Ethernet interface statistics in Netstat.exe

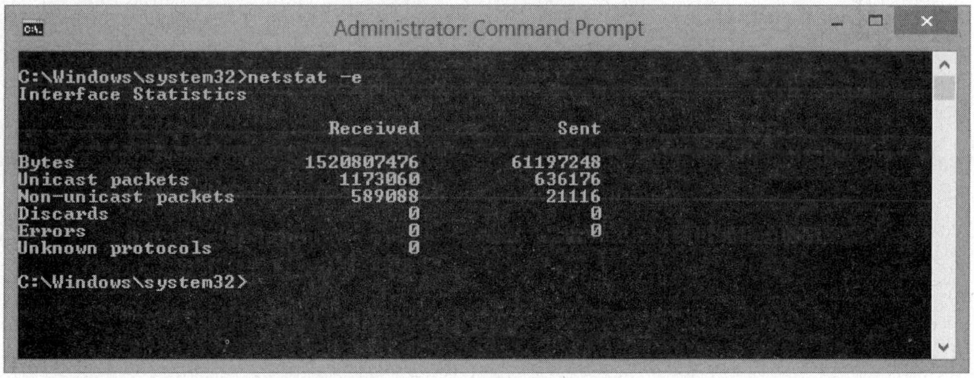

The routing tables for a computer running Windows 8 appear as shown in Figure 10-23.

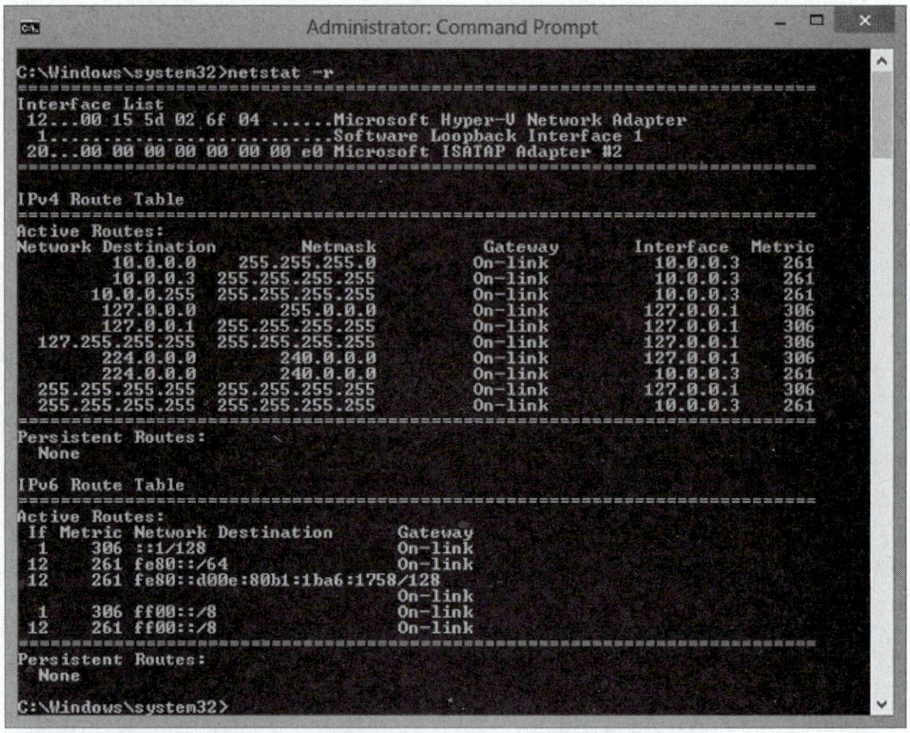

Figure 10-23

The IPv4 and IPv6 routing tables in Netstat.exe

SKILL SUMMARY

IN THIS LESSON, YOU LEARNED:

- The networking stack used on Windows 8 computers corresponds roughly to the seven-layer OSI reference model.
- The OSI (Open Systems Interconnection) reference model consists of seven layers: physical, data-link, network, transport, session, presentation, and application.
- Ethernet, the data-link layer protocol used on most LANs, consists of physical layer specifications, a frame format, and a MAC mechanism.
- The network and transport layer protocols work together to provide an end-to-end communication service that achieves the quality of service required by the application requesting network services.
- The functions of the session, presentation, and application layers are often combined into a single application layer protocol.
- Windows 8 includes support for both the IPv4 and IPv6 protocols. IPv6 increases the IP address space from 32 to 128 bits, simplifies the routing process, and improves address autoconfiguration.
- Network Discovery is a Windows 8 feature that simplifies the task of firewall configuration by enabling you to block or allow the protocols and ports need for the computer to browse and access the network.
- Most networks use DHCP to configure their TCP/IP clients, but it is still possible to configure them manually, using a graphical interface or the Netsh.exe command line utility.
- Windows 8 includes a variety of command line TCP/IP tools, including Ipconfig.exe, Ping.exe, Tracert.exe, Nslookup.exe, and Netstat.exe.

Knowledge Assessment

Multiple Choice

Select one or more correct answers for each of the following questions.

1. Which of the following is the primary method for transmitting IPv6 traffic over an IPv4 network?
   a. Subnetting
   b. Tunneling
   c. Supernetting
   d. Contracting

2. Which of the following is the IPv6 equivalent to a private IPv4 address?
   a. Link-local unicast address
   b. Global unique unicast address
   c. Unique local unicast address
   d. Anycast address

3. Which of the following is an automatic tunneling protocol used by Windows operating systems that are located behind NAT routers?
   a. Teredo
   b. 6to4
   c. ISATAP
   d. APIPA

4. What kind of IP address must a system have to be visible from the Internet?
   a. Registered
   b. Binary
   c. Class B
   d. Subnetted

5. What subnet mask would you use when configuring a TCP/IP client with an IPv4 address on the 172.16.32.0/19 network?
   a. 255.224.0.0
   b. 255.240.0.0
   c. 255.255.224.0
   d. 255.255.240.0
   e. 255.255.255.240

6. This protocol is responsible for addressing packets at the data link layer?
   a. Internet Protocol
   b. Transmission Control Protocol
   c. Ethernet
   d. CIDR

7. Windows 8 computers can acquire IP addresses in which of the following ways? Select all that apply.
   a. APIPA
   b. Manual configuration
   c. DHCP
   d. TCP/IP

8. Which of the following are true statements regarding IPv4 and IPv6 addressing? Select all that apply.
   a. IPv4 addresses are 32 bits in length
   b. IPv4 addresses are 128 bits in length
   c. IPv6 addresses are 128 bits in length
   d. IPv4 and IPv6 support stateful and stateless configuration

9. Computers with link-local addresses, that do not have access to a DNS server, use this protocol?
   a. Link Local Name Resolution
   b. Link Local Multicast Name Resolution
   c. Link Local Unicast Name Resolution
   d. Link Local Anycast Name Resolution

10. In which layer of the OSI model would packet acknowledgment, error correction and flow control services typically be handled.?
   a. Network layer
   b. Physical layer
   c. Transport layer
   d. Data Link layer

Best Answer

Choose the letter that corresponds to the best answer. More than one answer choice may achieve the goal. Select the BEST answer.

1. A computer is currently experiencing connectivity problems. The network administrator is unsure whether the source of the problem is the local computer, the remote computer or one of the routers between the two. Which tool would most likely provide the information needed to answer these questions and pinpoint the location of the problem?
   a. nslookup
   b. ping
   c. netstat
   d. tracert

2. Two computers are configured to communicate on a local network segment 192.168.2.0/24? Computer A is currently assigned 192.168.2.17 and Computer B is assigned 192.168.2.22. A new administrator adds a third computer (Computer C) to the network and forgets to configure its IP address. If the DHCP server were *temporarily* unavailable, which of the following would most likely be the result?
   a. Computer C would be assigned an address automatically
   b. Computer C would be assigned an APIPA address
   c. Computer C would be assigned an APIPA address and not be able to communicate with the other two computers
   d. Computer C would be assigned an APIPA address and not be able to communicate with the other two computers. Once the DHCP server came back online, all computers will be able to communicate.

3. The network administrator is currently having problems connecting and gathering information from a Windows 8 computer using telnet. He wants to use telnet on a very limited basis. Which of the following would represent the best approach to solve this problem?
   a. Turn the Windows Firewall off on the target computer.
   b. Disable the Windows Firewall on the target computer temporarily.
   c. Configure the target computer's Windows Firewall to allow traffic directed to port 23, 20, and 21.
   d. Configure the target computer's Windows Firewall to allow traffic directed to port 23; complete the work and then block the port until he needs to connect at a late date/time.

4. When troubleshooting computers and networks, it's wise to use the OSI model as a guide. If a user is experiencing problems with resolving host names to IP addresses, which layer of the OSI model would you focus on to quickly resolve the problem?
   a. Data Link
   b. Physical Layer
   c. Network Layer
   d. Application Layer

5. A network administrator is trying to locate where packets are being delayed in transit. She uses the tracert command and receives the following information. Which of these hops would be the source of the delay?
   a. <100 ms 103 ms <130 ms
   b. <210 ms 200 ms <205 ms
   c. <250 ms 210 ms <240 ms
   d. <375 ms 300 ms <360 ms

Matching and Identification

Complete the following exercise by matching the terms with their corresponding definitions.

_______ a) ipconfig
_______ b) netstat
_______ c) media access control address
_______ d) network address translation
_______ e) connectionless protocol
_______ f) connection-oriented protocol
_______ g) Transmission Control Protocol
_______ h) Internet Protocol
_______ i) packet switching network
_______ j) Automatic Private IP Addressing (APIPA)

1. Used to view the settings assigned to a DHCP-enabled client
2. Allows computers on network without DHCP to communicate with each other when not assigned manual IP addresses
3. A protocol that does not perform error detection or correction.
4. Used to display ports that are currently listening for incoming network connections
5. Protocol in which two system establish a connection before they transmit any data.
6. A hardware address used at the data link layer
7. Also referred to as a local area network.
8. Feature built into routers; substitutes a registered address for the computer's private address and then forwards to destination
9. A connectionless protocol found at the Network Layer
10. A connection-oriented protocol found at the Transport Layer.

Build a List

1. In order of first to last, specify the correct order of steps to view connection status.
   _______ Open the **Network and Sharing Center**.
   _______ Click **Close** to close the *Network Connection Details* dialog box.
   _______ Click **Close** to close the *Local Area Connection Status* dialog box
   _______ Click **Details**. The *Network Connection Details* dialog box appears.
   _______ In the *View your active networks* section, click **Ethernet** or the name of the connection whose status you want to view.

2. Specify the correct order of steps to configure IPv4 settings.
   ________ Click **Change adapter settings**.
   ________ Select **Internet Protocol Version 4 (TCP/IPv4)** and then click **Properties**.
   ________ Select the **Use The Following DNS Server Addresses** option and then enter appropriate values for the following parameters (preferred DNS Server, alternate DNS server.
   ________ Right-click the connection you want to manage and, from the context menu, select **Properties**.
   ________ Open the **Network and Sharing Center**.
   ________ Click **OK** to close the *Internet Protocol Version 4 (TCP/IPv4) Properties* sheet.
   ________ Select the **Use The Following IP Address** option and then enter appropriate values for IP address, subnet mask, and default gateway).
   ________ Click **OK** to close the connection's *Properties* sheet.

3. Specify the correct order of steps to configure Advanced Sharing settings.
   ________ Open the **Network and Sharing Center**.
   ________ Configure the following settings by selecting from the options provided (Network Discovery, Turn on automatic setup of network connected device, file/printer sharing, public folder sharing, media streaming, file sharing connections, password protected sharing, and HomeGroup connections)
   ________ Click **Save Changes**.
   ________ Click the down arrow for the network location whose settings you want to modify.
   ________ In the left pane, click **Change advanced sharing settings**. The *Change sharing options for different network profiles* dialog box appears.

Business Case Scenarios

Scenario 10-1: Using Port Numbers

While you are installing an Internet web server on your company network, the owner of the company tells you that he also wants to build a web server for internal use by the company's employees. This intranet web server will not contain confidential information, but it should not be accessible from the company's Internet website. To do this, you create a second site on the web server. The Internet site uses the well-known port number for web servers, which is 80. For the intranet site, you select the port number 283. Assuming that the web server's IP address on the internal network is 10.54.3.145, what should the users on the company network do to access the intranet website with Microsoft Internet Explorer?

Scenario 10-2: Configuring TCP/IP Clients

Mark is setting up a small Ethernet network in his home by installing network adapters in three computers running Windows 8 and connecting them to a switch. Mark only uses one of the computers to access the Internet with a dial-up modem, but he wants to be able to access files and his printer from any one of the three systems. After he installs the network interface adapters, he notes that the default networking components have been installed on all three systems, and he sets about configuring their TCP/IP configuration parameters manually. Of the settings on the Internet Protocol Version 4 (TCP/IPv4) Properties sheet, which must Mark configure to provide the network connectivity he desires, and which can he leave blank?

Configuring Network Settings

LESSON 11

70-687 EXAM OBJECTIVE

Objective 3.2 – Configure networking settings. This objective may include but is not limited to connect to a wireless network; manage preferred wireless networks; configure network adapters; and configure location-aware printing.

LESSON HEADING	EXAM OBJECTIVE
Configuring Network Settings	
Connecting to Wireless Networks	Connect to a wireless network
Managing Preferred Wireless Networks	Manage preferred wireless networks
Prioritizing Networks in Windows 8	
Removing Wireless Networks/Profiles	
Configuring Network Adapters	Configure network adapters
Configuring Location-Aware Printing	Configure location-aware printing

KEY TERMS

adhoc mode
infrastructure mode
location-aware printing
mobile broadband networks
Network and Sharing Center
network adapter
Network List Service
Network Location Awareness service
passphrases
service set identifier (SSID)
wireless profile
Wireless Profile Manager

Configuring Network Settings

THE BOTTOM LINE

Configuring, connecting and troubleshooting a computer's network settings is a key skill set that every administrator must have in order to ensure their users can access the resources they need. Administrators must be able to understand how Windows 8 functions in both wired and wireless networks, how it selects a wireless network to connect to, and how it can be configured to locate default printers when users work across multiple networks.

In this lesson, you learn the basics for connecting to wireless networks and the compatibility and security issues you face when configuring your Windows 8 computer. The wireless trend continues to grow and companies need to have someone who can ensure their users are staying connected while still maintaining a secure operating environment.

As employees move between home, work, the local coffee shop, and other public hotspots, Windows 8 must be able to differentiate between the locations while still providing a streamlined approach to connecting and using those networks. As the administrator, you must know how Windows 8 functions in these environments and how to remove connections that are no longer valid.

The setup of your network adapters (wired, wireless) can be accomplished with minimal effort in Windows 8 but you must know how to perform basic configuration of the adapters when you need to troubleshoot connectivity problems or address wireless performance issues.

Finally, with so many users taking advantage of mobile devices, they are looking for you to help them configure their Windows 8 computers so they can easily locate, connect and print to printers located on multiple networks.

Connecting to Wireless Networks

THE BOTTOM LINE

When connecting Windows 8 to a wireless network, the process can differ depending upon whether or not the wireless network is broadcasting its network name.

The process for connecting a Windows 8 computer to a wireless network is very simple when the network is broadcasting its ***service set identifier (SSID)***. The SSID is the name for the wireless network. Any wireless network that is broadcasting its name appears in the list of available networks in Windows 8. If you hold your mouse over the network name without clicking, you can see the security type (e.g., WEP, WPA2) used and the wireless protocol required (e.g., 802.11g, 802.11n).

CERTIFICATION READY
Connect to a wireless network
Objective 3.2

If you click the network, Windows 8 scans for the security settings and then prompts you to type the correct security key. Once you type the correct key, you have the option of enabling sharing on the network. If you are working on a private network (home,work), sharing is recommended. If you are on a public network, make sure you do not turn on sharing. After you are connected, the network icon in the task tray shows a small bar graph indicating the strength of the wireless signal. To disconnect, you simply click the network on the list and choose Disconnect.

CONNECT TO A WIRELESS NETWORK BROADCASTING ITS SSID

GET READY. In order to complete this exercise, you need to have a wireless network in range and know its assigned security key. To connect to a wireless network that is broadcasting its SSID, perform the following steps:

1. From the *Start* menu, press the **Windows logo key + c** to open the *Charms* bar.
2. On the *Charms* bar click **Settings**.
3. In the *Settings* menu, click the **wireless network icon** (see Figure 11-1).
   The word *Available*, shown under the icon, indicates you are currently within range of one or more wireless networks. If you were already connected to a wireless network, you would see its name under the wireless network icon.

Figure 11-1

Selecting the wireless network icon

4. On the *Networks* menu, you see a list of wireless networks that are within range. Move your mouse over the network(s) to see the security type and wireless protocol being used and then click the network you want to connect to.
   If this were a network that you wanted to connect to one time only, you would uncheck the option *Connect automatically*. The default setting causes Windows 8 to always connect to the network automatically when it is within range.
5. Click **Connect**.
6. In the *Enter the network security key* field, type the security key for the network and then click **Next**.
7. When prompted, Do you want to turn on sharing between PCs and connect to devices on this network? Click **Yes, turn on sharing and connect to devices**.

Your computer is now connected to the network you selected in Step 4. The network will now show its status as *Connected* in the *Networks* menu.

If you need to connect to a wireless network that is not broadcasting its SSID, the process is a little more involved. Because the network is not broadcasting, it does not appear in the list of available networks. This means you have to enter information such as the network's SSID (network name), security type, encryption type and security key to connect to it.

Because the network does not appear on your network list, you must connect to it by using the ***Network and Sharing Center***. The Network and Sharing Center provides a central location for network configuration controls (changing settings, managing wireless networks, network sharing settings).

CONNECT TO A HIDDEN WIRELESS NETWORK

GET READY. To connect to a hidden wireless network that is not broadcasting its SSID, perform the following steps:

1. From the *Start* menu, press the **Windows logo key + c** to open the Charms bar.
2. On the *Charms* bar click **Settings**.
3. From the *Settings* menu, click **Control Panel**.
4. In the *Control Panel*, click **Network and Internet > Network and Sharing Center**.
5. From the *Network and Sharing Center*, click **Set up a new connection or network**.
6. Under *Choose a connection option*, choose **Manually connect to a wireless network** and then click **Next**.
7. Type the *Network name*, choose the *Security type* and *Encryption type* and then type the *Security Key* for the wireless network as shown in Figure 11-2.

TAKE NOTE* The information entered is for demonstration purposes only. You must confirm the wireless network information for your specific network.

Figure 11-2
Entering wireless settings manually

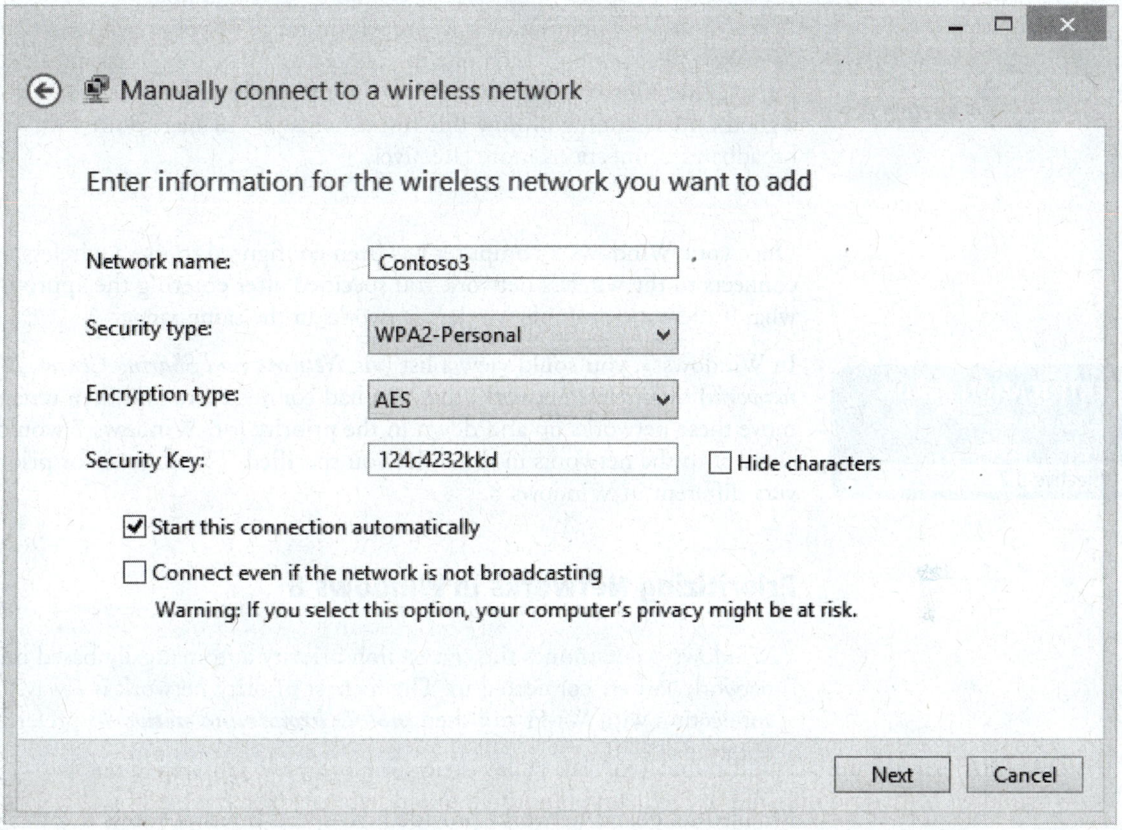

8. Click **Next** to continue.
9. When the message *Successfully added Contoso 3* appears, click **Close**.
10. If the network is within range, you see its signal strength (series of full bars) by checking the network icon in the task tray.

Managing Preferred Wireless Networks

THE BOTTOM LINE

When multiple wireless networks are within range of your Windows 8 computer, it needs to make a decision on which one to connect to. Windows 8 has automated this process for you (meaning that you do not have to manage preferred networks yourself) but having a good understanding of how this works helps you manage both your wireless and mobile broadband connections more effectively.

Once your Windows 8 computer has been configured to use a wireless network adapter, it connects to the wireless network you specified after entering the appropriate security key. But, what if there are multiple wireless networks in the same range?

CERTIFICATION READY
Manage preferred wireless networks
Objective 3.2

In Windows 7, you could view a list (via *Network and Sharing Center*, *Manage wireless networks*) of wireless networks that you had connected to and then rename, remove, or move these networks up and down in the priority list. Windows 7 would then attempt to connect to the networks in the order you specified. The process for prioritizing networks is very different in Windows 8.

Prioritizing Networks in Windows 8

Windows 8 determines the connection priority automatically based on the type of network you are connected to. The highest priority network is always an Ethernet (wired) connection with Wi-Fi and then ***mobile broadband networks*** preferred when Ethernet is not available.

Mobile broadband networks provide high-speed Internet access through portable devices and require a data plan with a mobile broadband provider.

When you connect to a new Wi-Fi network from a Windows 8 computer, Windows adds the new network to the list of wireless networks on your computer. If you connect to another wireless network, while in range of the first one, the second network is now preferred over the first. To see the list of networks, click the wireless network icon in your task tray.

If you connect to a mobile broadband network while a Wi-Fi network is within range, the mobile broadband network is the preferred network for that specific session only. The next time you attempt to connect and both the mobile broadband and the Wi-Fi network are within range, the Wi-Fi network is preferred.

As you can see from the previous examples, Windows 8 is designed to learn your preferences and adjust the list of networks for you. If you want to move a network up in the priority list, you simply have to connect automatically when the network is in range.

SELECT A PREFERRED NETWORK

GET READY. To select a preferred network, perform the following steps:

TAKE NOTE* To complete this activity, your Windows 8 computer must be connected to a wireless network and also have a second wireless network that is within range. In this example, Contoso1 and Contoso2 are used to represent the two wireless networks.

1. From the Windows 8 task tray, click your wireless connection icon.
2. From the *Networks* menu (see Figure 11-3), choose **Contoso2** and then click **Connect**. In Figure 11-3, Windows 8 is currently connected to Contoso1 and is treating it as the preferred network between the two. This means anytime the computer is within range, it automatically connects to Contoso1. Connecting to Contoso2 manually causes Windows 8 to make a note of this and use Contoso2 as the preferred network the next time you are within range of the two networks.

Figure 11-3

Connecting to a preferred network

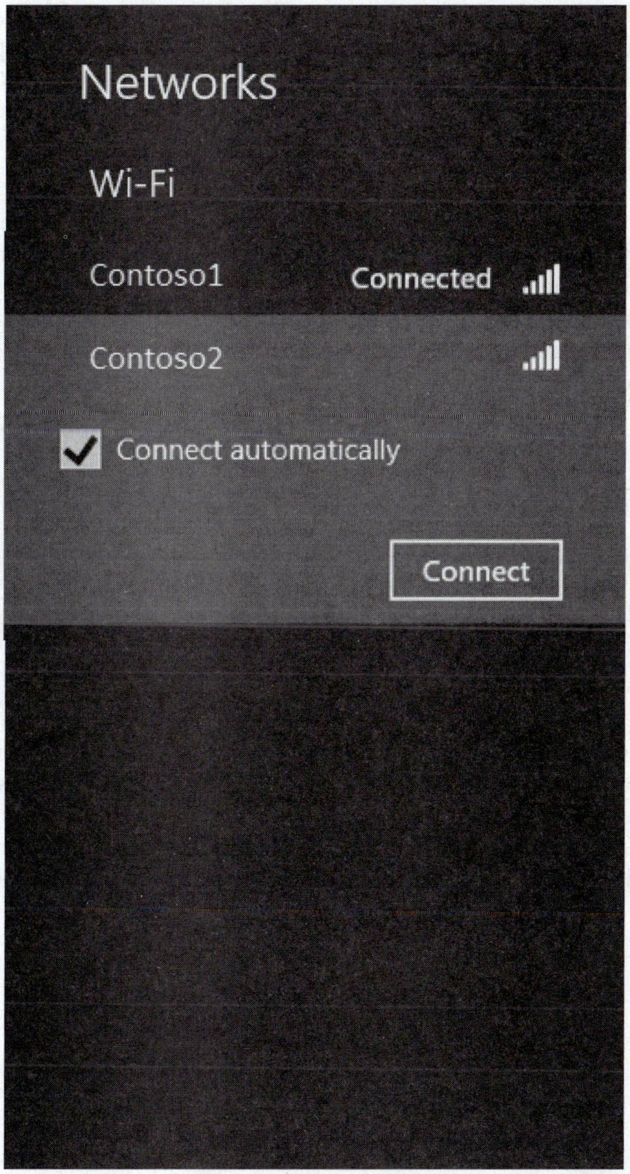

3. In the *Enter the network security key* field, type the security key for the wireless network and then click **Next**.
4. When prompted, Do you want to turn on sharing between PCs and connect to devices on this network? Click **Yes, turn on sharing and connect to devices**.

Your computer is now connected to the preferred network (in this example, Contoso2) and shows its status as *Connected* in the *Networks* menu.

Removing Wireless Networks/Profiles

Wireless profiles contain information that allows you to connect to wireless networks automatically. Understanding how to delete them will help you to maintain an updated list of only valid networks.

Another key difference between Windows 7 and Windows 8 is the absence of a Wireless Profile Manager in Windows 8. In Windows 7, the ***Wireless Profile Manager*** was used to create, delete, and modify wireless profiles. A ***wireless profile*** is a file in Windows 8 that stores information about a wireless network that you use on a repeated basis. The profile includes the wireless network name, the security type, encryption type and any security keys or ***passphrases*** used to connect to the wireless network. The main benefit of the profile is that is allows you to connect to the wireless network automatically when you are within range.

Over time, the list of wireless networks and profiles can become large and you may want to remove them from the list. This is very common when you connect using public Wi-Fi spots (library, coffee shops, fast food restaurants, etc.). Although Windows 8 no longer provides the Wireless Profile Manager, you can use the following commands to first show the wireless profiles on your computer and then delete the profile if the wireless network is no longer in range.

To view all wireless profiles currently stored on your computer, from a command prompt, type the following and then press Enter:

```
netsh wlan show profiles
```

To delete a wireless profile that is no longer within range, from a command prompt, type the following and press Enter. Be sure to replace *<profile name>* with the actual name of the profile you want to remove:

```
netsh wlan delete profile name="<profile name>"
```

If the network is in range, you can click the wireless network icon in your task tray, right-click the network you want to remove from the list and then choose *Forget this network.* This option works well for situations where you connected to a wireless network to perform a one-time task and do not want to automatically connect to it the next time you are within range or if the settings have changed on the wireless access point. When using this option, Windows 8 removes the wireless network and erase the wireless profile from its internal database.

Configuring Network Adapters

THE BOTTOM LINE

In order for Windows 8 to communicate on a network using a wireless or wired network adapter, you must understand the options available for configuring these types of interfaces. These configuration settings can allow you to troubleshoot problems with the adapter.

A ***network adapter*** (network interface card [NIC], ethernet adapter, wireless adapter, Wi-Fi card) is the hardware component used to connect your Windows 8 computer to a wired or wireless network.

The easiest way to access the configuration settings for a network adapter is to use the Network and Sharing Center (Figure 11-4). To configure the network adapter click the *Change adapter settings* link.

Figure 11-4

Reviewing the Network and Sharing Center

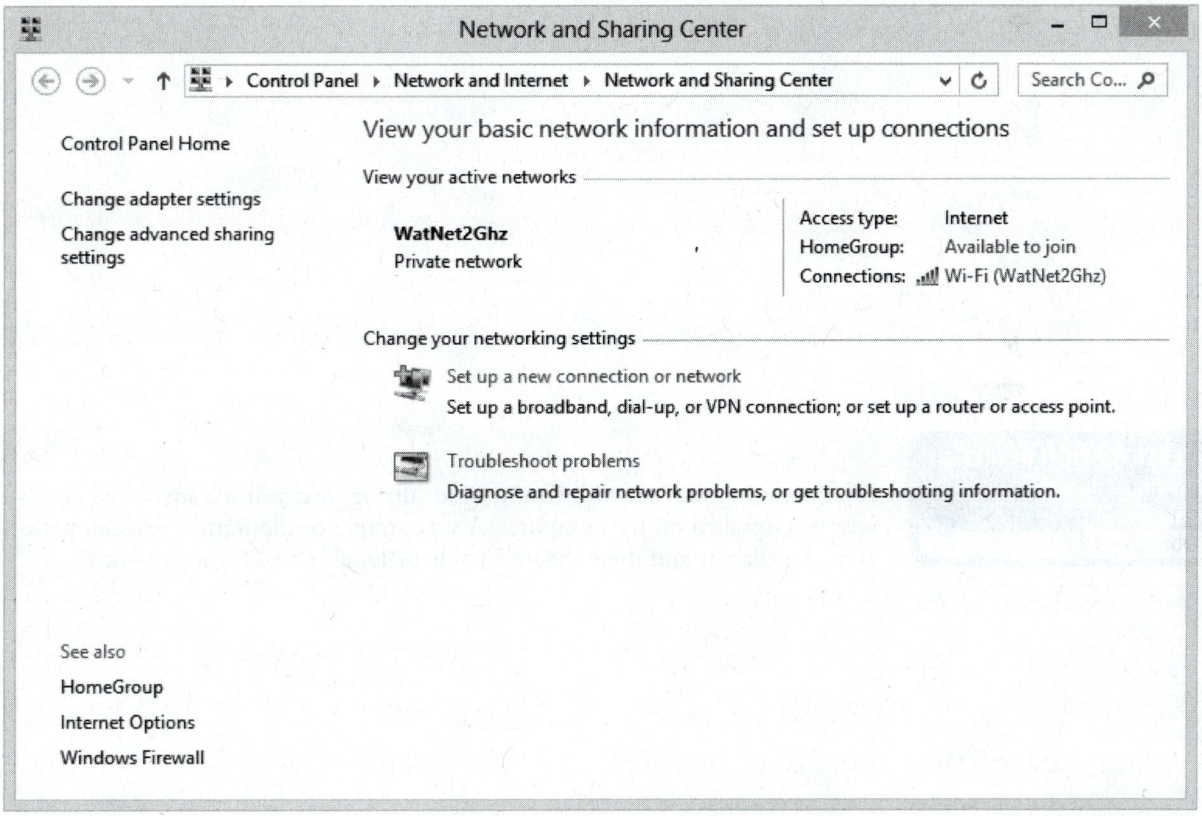

This takes you to the Network Connections dialog box shown in Figure 11-5.

Figure 11-5

Reviewing the Network Connections dialog box

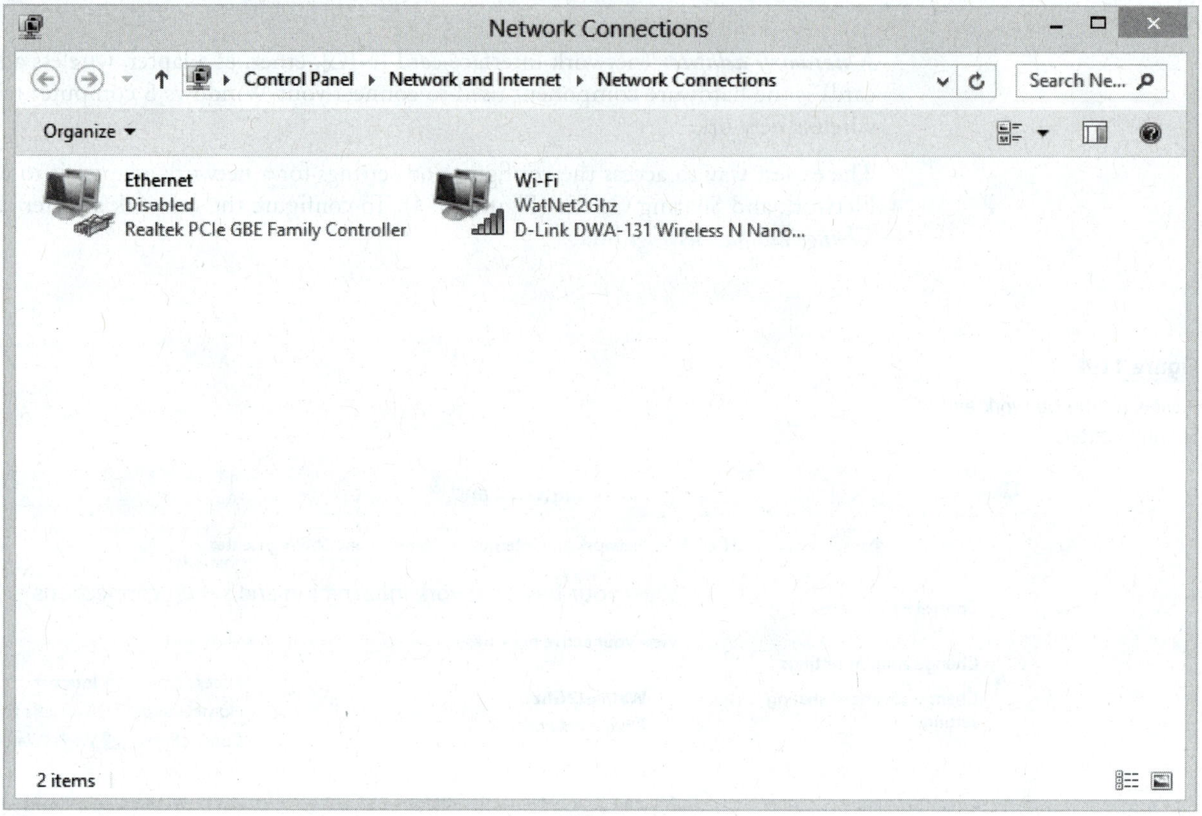

CERTIFICATION READY
Configure network adapters
Objective 3.2

After accessing the Network Connections dialog box, you see any wired and wireless network adapters installed on the computer. A very simple configuration you can perform is to right-click the adapter and then choose Enable or Disable (see Figure 11-6).

Figure 11-6

Enabling a network adapter

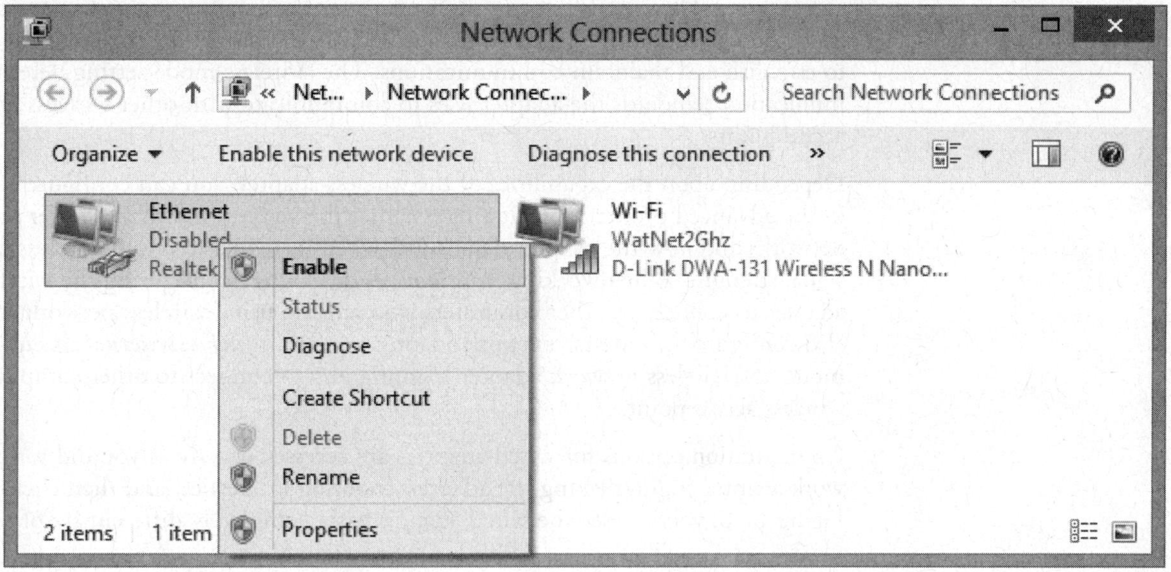

Disabling and enabling a network adapter can sometimes help you to solve connection problems. It can also prevent wireless interference with other devices and improve battery life when you a wireless connection is no longer needed. An alternative approach to disabling and enabling wireless on a laptop is to use the external switch located on the side or front of the laptop.

In addition to enabling and disabling adapters, you can also perform additional configurations by right-clicking the adapter, choosing Properties, and then click Configure. The configuration options that are available differ between network adapter manufacturers as well as between adapter types (wired, wireless).

In Figure 11-7, you can see this wireless network adapter has two property settings that you can configure: Beacon Interval and Wireless Mode.

Figure 11-7

Reviewing the advanced configuration options for wireless network adapter

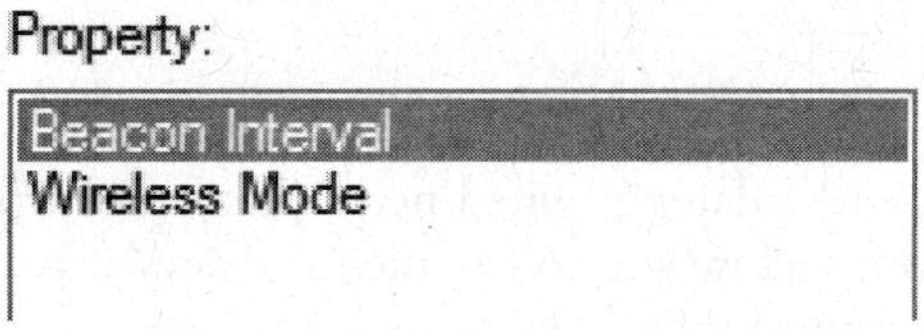

For this wireless network adapter, the Beacon Interval is set to 100 ms. This determines the duration between beacon packets. Beacons are special data transmissions from the wireless access point. These packets carry the wireless network name, channel information, and security protocols. Think of it as a "heartbeat" of the wireless network that allows wireless clients to establish and maintain communications. The Wireless mode setting determines the communication standards the adapter uses to communicate with other wireless clients and wireless access points.

Depending upon the capabilities of the wireless adapter, you can configure additional settings in the advanced properties including whether the wireless network adapter supports adhoc networks and how the adapter determines when to switch to another access point based on signal strength. When working in ***adhoc mode***, you are configuring the wireless network adapter to connect to other computers who are also using wireless network adapters. You can also configure the wireless network adapter to work in ***infrastructure mode***. In infrastructure mode, the wireless network adapter is configured to connect to other computers through a wireless access point.

Configuration options for wired adapters are accessed exactly as you did for the wireless network adapter (right-clicking the adapter, choosing Properties, and then click Configure). In Figure 11-8, you can see the wired adapter has a completely different set of options.

Figure 11-8

Reviewing the advanced configuration options for wired network adapter

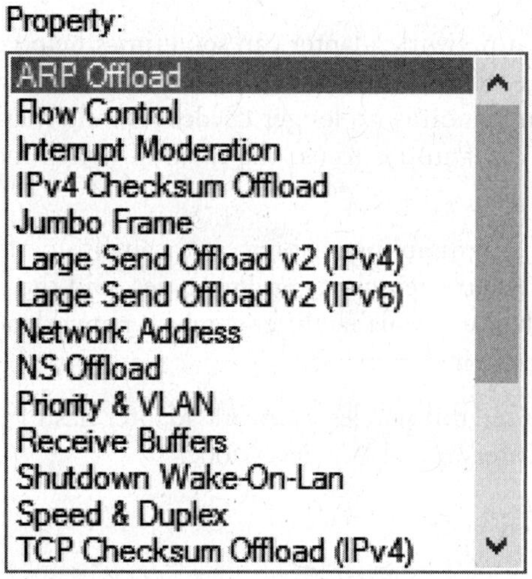

Just as with wireless network adapters, wired network adapter settings can vary between manufacturers. The settings allow you to troubleshoot and/or gain additional performance approvements should you need them.

REVIEW A WIRELESS NETWORK ADAPTER'S CONFIGURATION OPTIONS

GET READY. Review the configuration options for your wireless network adapter by logging in with administrative privileges and performing the following steps:

1. From the *Start* menu, press the **Windows logo key + w**, type **network and sharing**, and then choose **Network and Sharing Center** from *Results*.
2. In the *Network and Sharing* dialog box, click **Change adapter settings**.
3. In the *Network Connections* dialog box, right-click your wireless network adapter and then choose **Properties**.
4. In the *Wi-Fi Properties* dialog box, click **Configure**.
5. Click the **Advanced** tab.
6. Scroll through each property setting to see what is available for your specific wireless network adapter and then click **OK**.
7. Close the *Network Connections* dialog box.
8. Close the *Network and Sharing Center* dialog box.

Configuring Location-Aware Printing

THE BOTTOM LINE

As users become more mobile, they need to be able to easily locate, connect and print to printers located on multiple networks. These printers might be located on a home, office, airport or coffee shop's network.

Users who work from laptop computers often find themselves connecting to different printers depending upon where they are working from at any given point in time. For example, they may have a specific printer they like to use while at work while needing to switch to a different printer when connected to their home network. In either case, when the user connects from work or from home, they often have to set and reset the default printer to ensure their documents go to the right device. Windows 8 has a featured called ***location-aware printing*** that can make the process of moving between networks and connecting to printers much simpler.

MORE INFORMATION

Location-aware printing is only available for computers that run on batteries (e.g., laptops).

CERTIFICATION READY
Configure location-aware printing
Objective 3.2

Location-aware printing, works by telling Windows 8 Professional to update and select the default printer based on the currently connected network. By configuring the default network for each printer, the user's documents are automatically sent to the right printer each time whether working from home or at work.

Location-aware printing depends upon the ***Network Location Awareness service*** and the ***Network List Service*** to determine network information. The Network Location Awareness service collects and stores configuration information for the networks and notifies programs when the information is changed. The Network List Service identifies the networks to which the computer is connected. If either of these services are not running or they are malfunctioning, Windows 8 is not able to detect changes in networks and cannot adjust the default printer accordingly. You can confirm these services are functioning properly by pressing the Windows logo key + r, typing services.msc in the Run dialog box and then reviewing their status in the Services console.

To configure location-aware printing, you must be running a laptop computer with Windows 8 Professional or later and need to connect to printers on at least two different networks.

CONFIGURE LOCATION-AWARE PRINTING

GET READY. Configure location-aware printing on a Windows 8 laptop by logging in with administrative privileges and performing the following steps:

TAKE NOTE* In this lesson, it is assumed that you have two printers available that are located on different networks (home and office)

1. From the *Start* menu, press the **Windows logo key + w,** type **devices**, and then choose **Devices and Printers** from *Results*.
2. Click the printer you want to configure and then in the menu bar, choose **Manage default printers**.
3. In the *Manage Default Printers* dialog box (see Figure 11-9), click **Change my default printer when I change networks**.

Figure 11-9

Changing the default printer when changing networks

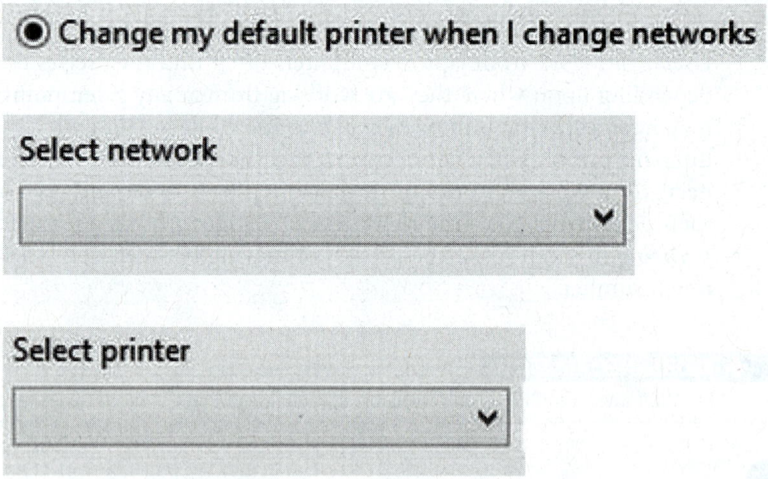

4. Under *Select network* click the down arrow and choose a network and then under *Select printer*, choose the printer that will be used as the default printer for that network.
5. Click **Add**.
6. To close the *Manage Default Printers* dialog box, click **OK**.
7. Close the *Device and Printers* dialog box.

SKILL SUMMARY

IN THIS LESSON, YOU LEARNED:

- If a wireless network is broadcasting its SSID (network name) and it is within range of your Windows 8 computer, it appears in the list of available networks. You can simply click the network and enter the appropriate security key to connect.
- If a wireless network is not broadcasting its SSID, you have to enter information such as the network's SSID, security type, encrypting type and security key manually by going through the Network and Sharing Center.
- Windows 8 automates the process of managing the preferred network when it is within range. Unlike Windows 7 which allowed you to set the priority of one network over another, Windows 8 determines the priority based on the type of network you are connected to and the order in which you connect to the network.
- A wireless profile is a file that contains the wireless SSID, security type and encryption type and security keys. The main benefit of the profile is that is allows you to connect to the wireless network automatically when you are within range. The netsh tool can be used to view and delete these profiles.
- If you do not want Windows 8 to automatically connect to a network, you can use the *Forget this network* option if you are currently in range or the `netsh wlan delete profile name="<profile name>"` command if the network is no longer within range of your computer.
- Adhoc mode is used when you configure a wireless network adapter to bypass a WAP and connect directly to other wireless computers. Infrastructure mode is used when you want the wireless adapter to connect to a WAP.
- Location-aware printing, available on Windows 8 computers that have batteries only (e.g., laptops) allows you to configure a default printer for each network you connect to. This ensures a user's print jobs are directed to the appropriate printer when they are working from home or the office.
- The Network Location Awareness services and the Network List Service are required in order for location-aware print to work. If either of these two services is not functioning, Windows 8 is not able to detect changes in networks and cannot adjust the default printer accordingly.

Knowledge Assessment

Multiple Choice

Select one or more correct answers for each of the following questions.

1. When a wireless network broadcasts this information to potential wireless clients, it appears in the list of available networks in Windows 8.
   a. WPA
   b. WEP
   c. SSID
   d. Beacon

2. Which of the following are included in a wireless profile? Select all that apply.
   a. SSID
   b. Security type
   c. Encryption type
   d. Security keys

3. In which mode would you configure a wireless client to connect through a wireless access point (WAP)?
   a. Ad hoc mode
   b. Infrastructure mode
   c. WAP mode
   d. Implementation mode

4. Which Windows 8 feature would you use to configure a default printer for each network the computer connects to?
   a. WAP
   b. Location-aware processing
   c. Location-aware printing
   d. Beacons

5. You are connected to a wireless network at a local coffee shop and want to make sure the next time you are in range of the network that Windows 8 does not automatically connect to it. What should you do before moving out of range of the network?
   a. Right-click the network and then choose *Forget this network*.
   b. Run the `netsh wlan delete profile "<profile name>"` command.
   c. Run the `netsh delete profile name="<profile name>"` command.
   d. Run the `netsh wlan delete name="<profile name>"` command.

6. Which of the following represents the correct order that Windows 8 uses to prioritize networks?
   a. Ethernet, Wi-Fi and then mobile broadband networks.
   b. Mobile, Wi-Fi and then Ethernet.
   c. Ethernet, mobile broadband and then Wi-Fi.
   d. Windows 8 allows you to set the priority via the *Manage wireless networks* option.
7. Which command would you use to view all wireless profiles currently stored on your Windows 8 computer?
   a. `netsh wlan show wireless profiles`
   b. `netsh wlan show profiles`
   c. `netsh wlan show profiles = all`
   d. `netsh wlan show profiles` *<all profiles>*
8. You are currently connected to a mobile broadband network while a Wi-Fi network is within range. Which of the following statements are true on how Windows 8 manages these connections in regard to priority? Select all that apply.
   a. The mobile broadband network is preferred for this session only.
   b. The mobile broadband network is always the preferred network.
   c. The Wi-Fi network is preferred the next time you are within range of both networks.
   d. The Wi-Fi network forces the mobile broadband network to disconnect and replace it with the Wi-Fi network that is in range.

Best Answer

Choose the letter that corresponds to the best answer. More than one answer choice may achieve the goal. Select the BEST answer.

1. You would like to setup location-aware printing on your Windows 8 computer. After opening *Devices and Printers*, you cannot find the option *Manage Default Printers* on the menu bar. What is the most likely reason?
   a. You do not have administrative privileges.
   b. You are logged in to a Windows 8 Professional desktop computer.
   c. You are logged in to a Windows 8 Enterprise desktop computer.
   d. You are not logged in to a Windows 8 Professional/Enterprise laptop.
2. You would like to prevent wireless interference with other devices and improve battery life on your laptop. What is the best way to disable your wireless connection when it is not in use?
   a. Delete the wireless adapters from the *Network Connections* dialog box.
   b. Right-click the wireless network and choose *Forget this network.*
   c. Right-click the wireless network adapter and choose Disable.
   d. Turn off your laptop when not connecting to the wireless network.

3. You are running a Windows 8 computer that has a wireless adapter installed. What is the easiest way to determine the security type and wireless protocol being used by the network that is currently in range and broadcasting its SSID?
   a. Contact the administrator of the WAP.
   b. Use a third-party tool to scan the network for wireless configurations.
   c. Under the *Networks* menu, move your mouse over the visible network.
   d. Review the properties of the wireless network adapter after you connect.

Matching and Identification

Complete the following exercise by matching the terms with their corresponding definitions.

_______ **a)** Passphrase
_______ **b)** Location-aware printing
_______ **c)** Mobile broadband network
_______ **d)** Ad hoc mode
_______ **e)** Infrastructure mode

1. Configures wireless adapter to connect through a WAP.
2. Words and characters used to authenticate a wireless connection.
3. Feature that allows you to set default printer for each network you connect to.
4. Configures wireless adapter to connect to other wireless computers bypassing the WAP.
5. Provide high-speed access through portable devices; requires data plan.

Build a List

1. In order of first to last, specify the order of steps you would use to connect to a wireless network broadcasting its SSID.
   _______ In the *Settings* menu, click the **Network icon**.
   _______ From the Windows 8 *Start* menu, press the **Windows logo key + c**, to open the *Charms* bar.
   _______ Click **Connect**.
   _______ When prompted, Do *you want to turn on sharing between PCs and connect to devices on this network?* Click **Yes, turn on sharing and connect to devices**.
   _______ In the *Networks* menu, choose the network you want to connect to
   _______ On the *Charms* bar click **Settings**.
   _______ In the *Enter the network security key* field, type the security key for the network and then click **Next**.

2. Specify the correct order of steps required to keep Windows 8 from automatically connecting to a wireless network that used for a one time task while you are still within range of the network.
   ________ From the Windows 8 task tray, click your wireless connection icon.
   ________ Make sure your computer is currently within range of the network you want to remove.
   ________ From the *Networks* menu, locate the network you want to remove.
   ________ Right-click the network and choose **Forget this network.**

3. In order of first to last, specify the steps needed to configure location-aware printing on a Windows 8 laptop.
   ________ Under *Select network* click the down arrow and choose a network and then under *Select printer* choose the printer that will be used as the default printer for that network.
   ________ To close the *Manage Default Printers* dialog box, click **OK**.
   ________ Click the printer you want to configure and then in the menu bar, choose **Manage default printers**.
   ________ Click **Add**.
   ________ Close the *Device and Printers* dialog box.
   ________ In the *Manage Default Printers* dialog box, click **Change my default printer when I change networks**.
   ________ From the Windows 8 Start menu, press the **Windows logo key + w**, type **devices** and then choose **Devices and Printers** from *Results*.

Business Case Scenarios

Scenario 11-1: Troubleshooting Location-Aware Printing

You currently have two users in your company that work from home on Wednesday's. After setting up their Windows 8 laptops to use location-aware printing, you discover the computers are not defaulting to the appropriate printer when they connect to a network. How would you troubleshoot this problem?

Scenario 11-2: Deleting Wireless Networks No Longer in Range

A few of your Windows 8 laptop users recently returned from a convention where they used the local wireless network extensively. They have no intention of every going back to that convention and want to know how to delete the wireless profile from their machines. What would you tell them?

Configuring and Maintaining Network Security

LESSON 12

70-687 EXAM OBJECTIVE

Objective 3.3 – Configure and maintain network security. This objective may include but is not limited to configure Windows Firewall; configure Windows Firewall with Advanced Security; configure connection security rules (IPsec); configure network discovery; configure authenticated exceptions; and manage wireless security.

LESSON HEADING	EXAM OBJECTIVE
Defending Against Malware	
Using Windows 8 Action Center	
Using Windows Firewall	Configure Windows Firewall Configure Windows Firewall with Advanced Security Configure connection security rules (IPsec) Configure network discovery Configure authenticated exceptions
Introducing Windows Defender	
Using the Malicious Software Removal Tool	
Understanding Wireless Security	Manage wireless security
Evaluating Wireless Networking Hardware	
Using Wired Equivalent Privacy	
Selecting an Authentication Method	
Using Wi-Fi Protected Access	

KEY TERMS

Advanced Encryption System (AES)
authenticated exception
filter
firewall
IP Security (IPsec)
Malicious Software Removal Tool
malware
multiple-input multiple-output (MIMO)
rules
shared secret/shared key
spatial multiplexing
spyware
tunneling
Temporal Key Integrity Protocol (TKIP)
Windows Defender
Wi-Fi Protected Access (WPA and WPA2)
Wired Equivalent Privacy (WEP)
WPA-Enterprise
WPA-Personal

Defending Against Malware

THE BOTTOM LINE

Malware is one of the primary threats to Windows 8 security, and the operating system includes a variety of tools that you can use to combat it. The following sections examine these tools and how to implement and configure them.

Windows 8 holds security as one its primary goals. Beginning with the Windows XP Service Pack 2 release, Windows has monitored the state of the security mechanisms included with the operating system and warns the user if any components are misconfigured, outdated, or not functioning.

Chief among the threats to Windows 8 computers is malicious software created specifically for the purpose of infiltrating or damaging a computer system without the user's knowledge or consent. This type of software includes a variety of technologies, including viruses, Trojan horses, worms, spyware, and adware. The term most commonly used to collectively refer to these malicious software technologies is ***malware***.

The types of malware to which Windows 8 is susceptible range from the relatively innocuous to the extremely destructive. The effects they can have on a Windows 8 computer include the following:

- Collect usage information about the computer user and transmit to an Internet server.
- Display advertisements on the user's system.
- Use the system's email address book to send spam.
- Attach code to document files that spreads to other files on any system opening the document.
- Install and run a program that enables a remote user to take control of the system.
- Damage or destroy the files stored on the computer.
- Infiltrate the computer's boot sector and spread to other systems.

Malware is, in most cases, introduced onto a computer by a deliberate action on the part of a user. Someone opens an email attachment, installs an infected program, or accesses a dangerous website, and the malicious code is introduced to the system. Windows 8 includes a variety of tools that try to prevent users from inadvertently infecting their computers and also attempt to block the activities of malicious software programs once they are present.

Security is a pervasive concern throughout the Windows 8 operating system, and as a result there are some Windows 8 security mechanisms that are discussed elsewhere in this text:

- In Lesson 8, "Configuring Internet Explorer," you learn about the security features included in Internet Explorer.
- In Lesson 16, "Configure Local Security Settings," you learn how User Account Control helps to prevent malware from obtaining administrative privileges.
- In Lesson 15, "Configuring File and Folder Access," you learn about the permissions Windows uses to control access to files and other system resources.

Using Windows 8 Action Center

The Windows 8 Action Center ensures that your system is protected from malware intrusion by notifying you if any of the Windows 8 security mechanisms are not running properly.

Like the Network and Sharing Center, the ***Action Center*** is a centralized console that enables users and administrators to access, monitor, and configure the various Windows 8 security mechanisms. The primary function of the Action Center is to provide an automatic notification system that alerts users when the system is vulnerable.

Action Center is a service that starts automatically and runs continuously on Windows 8 computers, by default. The service constantly monitors the different security mechanisms running on the computer. If Action Center detects a mechanism that is not functioning properly for any of several reasons, it displays an icon in the notification area (formerly known as the taskbar tray) to inform the user of the condition, as shown in Figure 12-1.

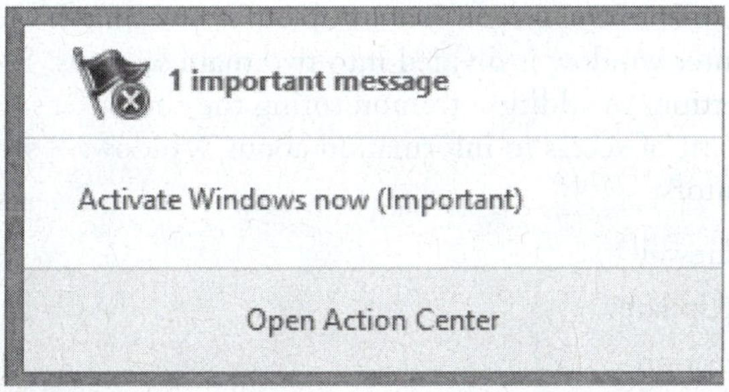

Figure 12-1

The *Action Center* menu in the notification area

TAKE NOTE*

The Windows 8 Action Center is not limited to monitoring Microsoft security solutions. The service can also monitor third-party programs for their currency and operational status.

ACCESSING ACTION CENTER

When a user clicks the notification area icon to open the Action Center window (or opens it from the Control Panel), the system displays information about the problems it has discovered, and links to possible solutions.

For example, the Action Center window shown in Figure 12-2 contains Spyware and unwanted software protection and Virus protection warnings. Clicking *Find an app online to help protect my PC* opens a webpage on Microsoft's site linking to various providers of virus protection software.

Figure 12-2

The *Action Center* window

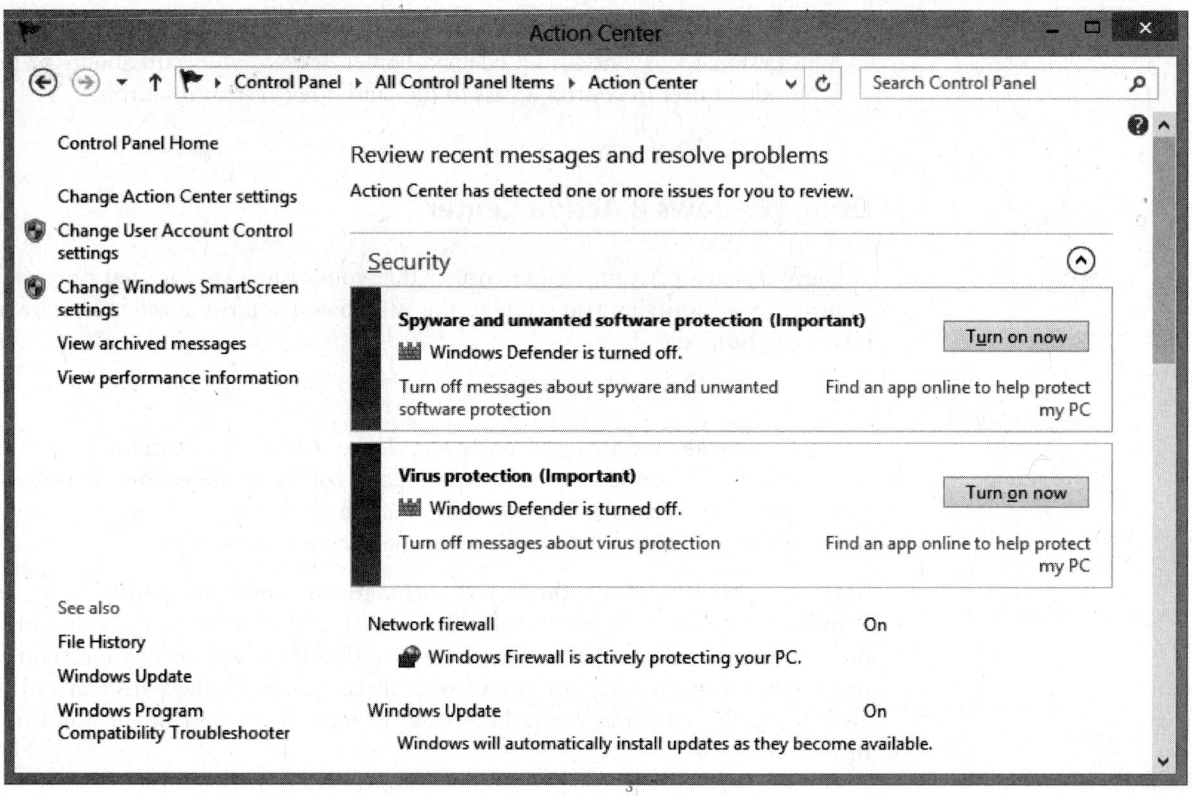

The Action Center window is divided into two main sections: Security and Maintenance. The Security section, in addition to monitoring the computer's security status, provides users with a single point of access to information about Windows 8 security, in the form of the following indicators:

- Network firewall
- Windows Update
- Virus Protection
- Spyware and unwanted software protection
- Internet security settings
- User Account Control
- Windows SmartScreen
- Network Access Protection
- Windows activation

The Maintenance section contains these indicators:

- Check for solutions to problem reports
- Automatic maintenance
- HomeGroup

- File History
- Drive status
- Device software

Each of these indicators displays the current status of the security or maintenance feature and, if appropriate, supplies a link to the controls for that feature.

Links to other related features appear on the left side of the window, including a link to the *Change Action Center Settings* window, as shown in Figure 12-3. From this window, you can control which messages appear in the *Action Center* interface.

Figure 12-3

The *Change Action Center Settings* window

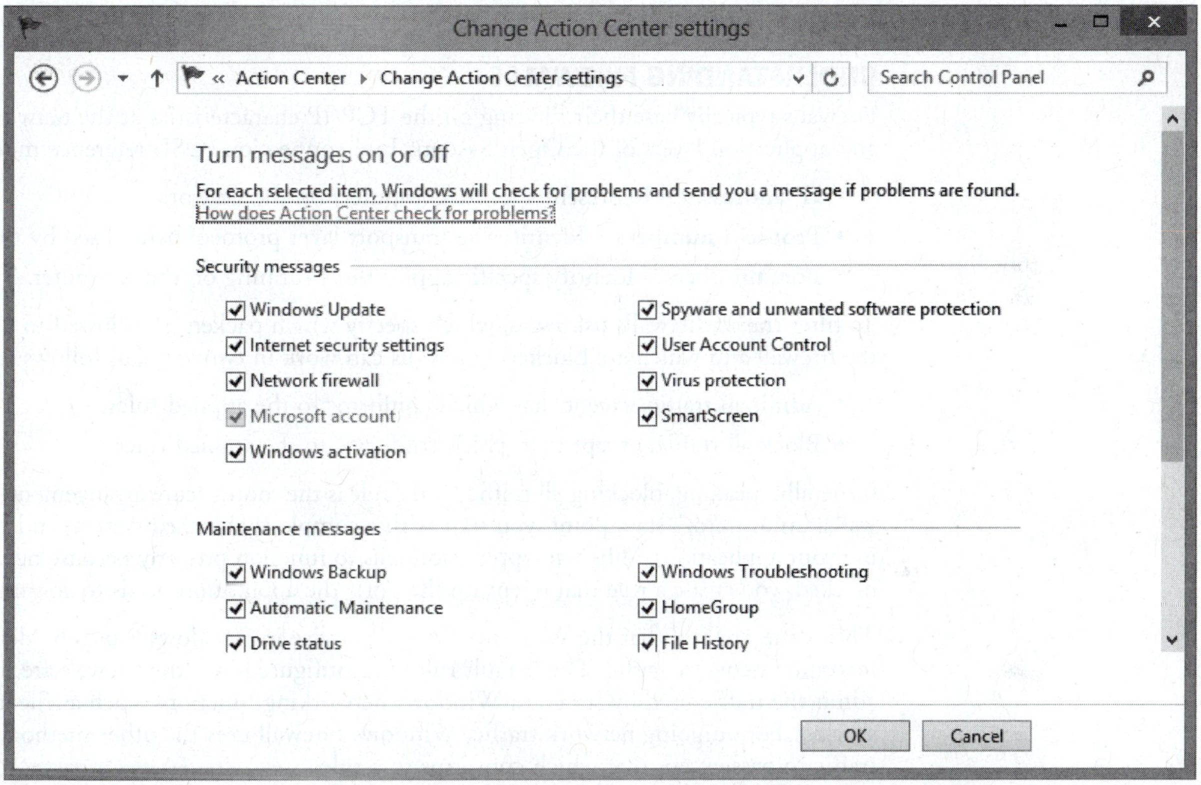

Using Windows Firewall

Windows Firewall protects Windows 8 computers by blocking dangerous traffic, both incoming and outgoing. A ***firewall*** is a software program or hardware device that protects a computer by allowing certain types of network traffic in and out of the system while blocking others.

Firewalls are essentially packet filters that examine the contents of packets and the traffic patterns to and from the network to determine which packets should be allowed passage through the filter.

Network connections are all but ubiquitous in the computing world these days. All business computers are networked, and virtually all home computers have an Internet connection. Many homes have local area networks as well. Network connections provide Windows 8 users with access to virtually unlimited resources, but any door that allows data out can also allow data in. Some of the hazards that firewalls protect against are as follows:

- Trojan horse applications that users inadvertently download and run can open a connection to a computer on the Internet, enabling an attacker on the outside to run programs or store data on the system.
- A mobile computer can be compromised while connected to a public network and then brought onto a private network, compromising the resources there in turn.
- Network scanner applications can probe systems for unguarded ports, which are essentially unlocked doors that attackers can use to gain access to the system.
- Attackers that obtain passwords by illicit means, such as social engineering, can use remote access technologies to log on to a computer from another location and compromise its data and programming.

UNDERSTANDING FIREWALLS

Firewalls typically base their filtering on the TCP/IP characteristics at the network, transport, and application layers of the Open Systems Interconnection (OSI) reference model, as follows:

- **IP addresses** – Represent specific computers on the network.
- **Protocol numbers** – Identify the transport layer protocol being used by the packets.
- **Port numbers** – Identify specific applications running on the computer.

To filter traffic, firewalls use ***rules***, which specify which packets are allowed to pass through the firewall and which are blocked. Firewalls can work in two ways, as follows:

- Admit all traffic, except that which conforms to the applied rules.
- Block all traffic, except that which conforms to the applied rules.

Generally speaking, blocking all traffic by default is the more secure arrangement. From the firewall administrator's standpoint, you start with a completely blocked system, and then start testing your applications. When an application fails to function properly because network access is blocked, you create a rule that opens up the ports the application needs to communicate.

This is the method that the Windows Firewall service in Windows 8 uses by default for incoming network traffic. The default rules preconfigured into the firewall are designed to admit the traffic used by standard Windows networking functions, such as file and printer sharing. For outgoing network traffic, Windows Firewall uses the other method, allowing all traffic to pass except that which conforms to a rule.

MONITORING WINDOWS FIREWALL

Windows Firewall is one of the programs monitored by the Action Center service. The main *Action Center* window indicates whether Windows Firewall is running, and also whether any third-party firewall products are running.

When you open the Windows Control Panel and click System and Security > Windows Firewall, a *Windows Firewall* window appears, displaying the firewall's status in greater detail, as shown in Figure 12-4.

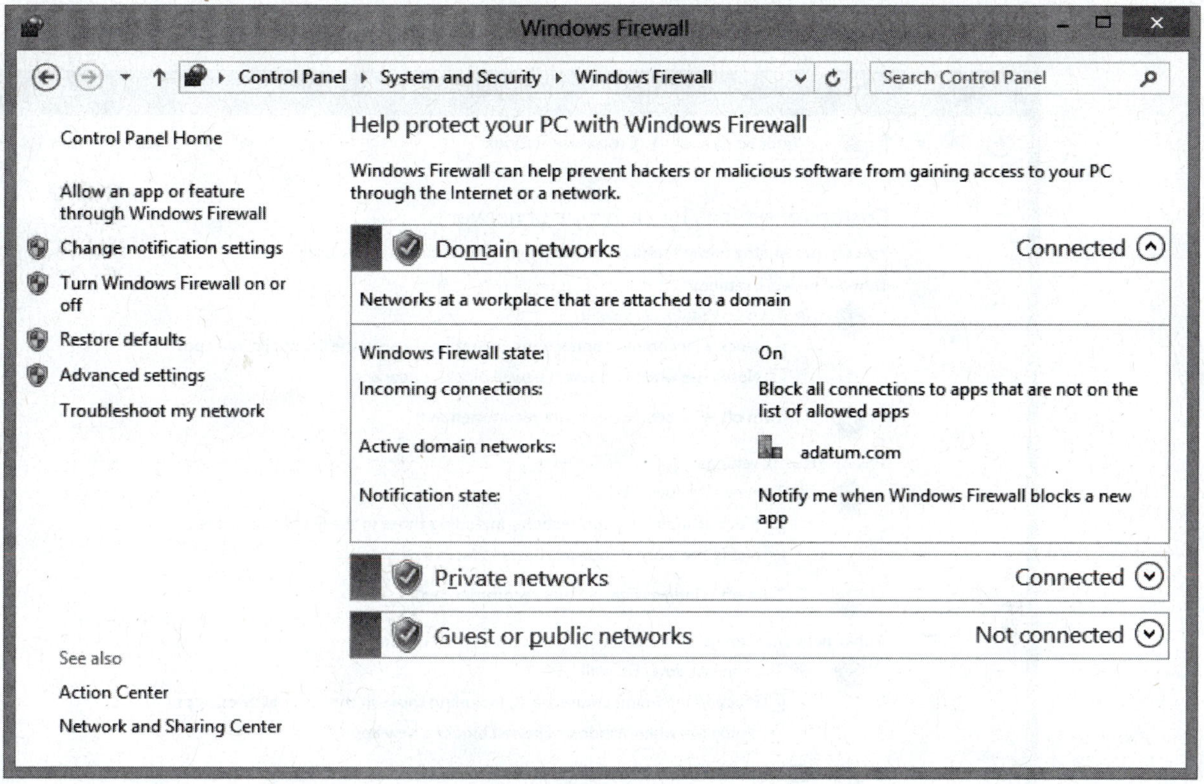

Figure 12-4
The *Windows Firewall* window

The Windows Firewall window contains expandable headings for the computer's network locations: public, guest or private, and domain (if the computer is joined to an Active Directory Domain Services domain). Each of the headings contains information on

- whether the computer is connected to a domain, private, or public network,
- whether the Windows Firewall service is currently turned on or off,
- whether inbound and outbound connections are blocked, or
- whether users are notified when a program is blocked.

Windows Firewall maintains a separate profile for each of the network locations, so you can have a different firewall configuration for each one. Whenever you are working with Windows Firewall settings, you must be conscious of the profile to which the settings apply.

USING THE WINDOWS FIREWALL CONTROL PANEL

On the left side of the Windows Firewall window is a series of links that enable you to configure Windows Firewall to allow a specific app or feature through its barrier, change the firewall notification settings, turn Windows Firewall on and off, restore the default firewall settings, and configure advanced firewall settings.

CERTIFICATION READY
Configure Windows Firewall
Objective 3.3

Clicking *Change notification settings* or *Turn Windows firewall on or off* displays the *Customize settings for each type of network* dialog box, as shown in Figure 12-5. As in the *Windows Firewall* window, controls for the domain profile only appear when the computer is joined to an AD DS domain.

Figure 12-5

The *Customize settings for each type of network* dialog box

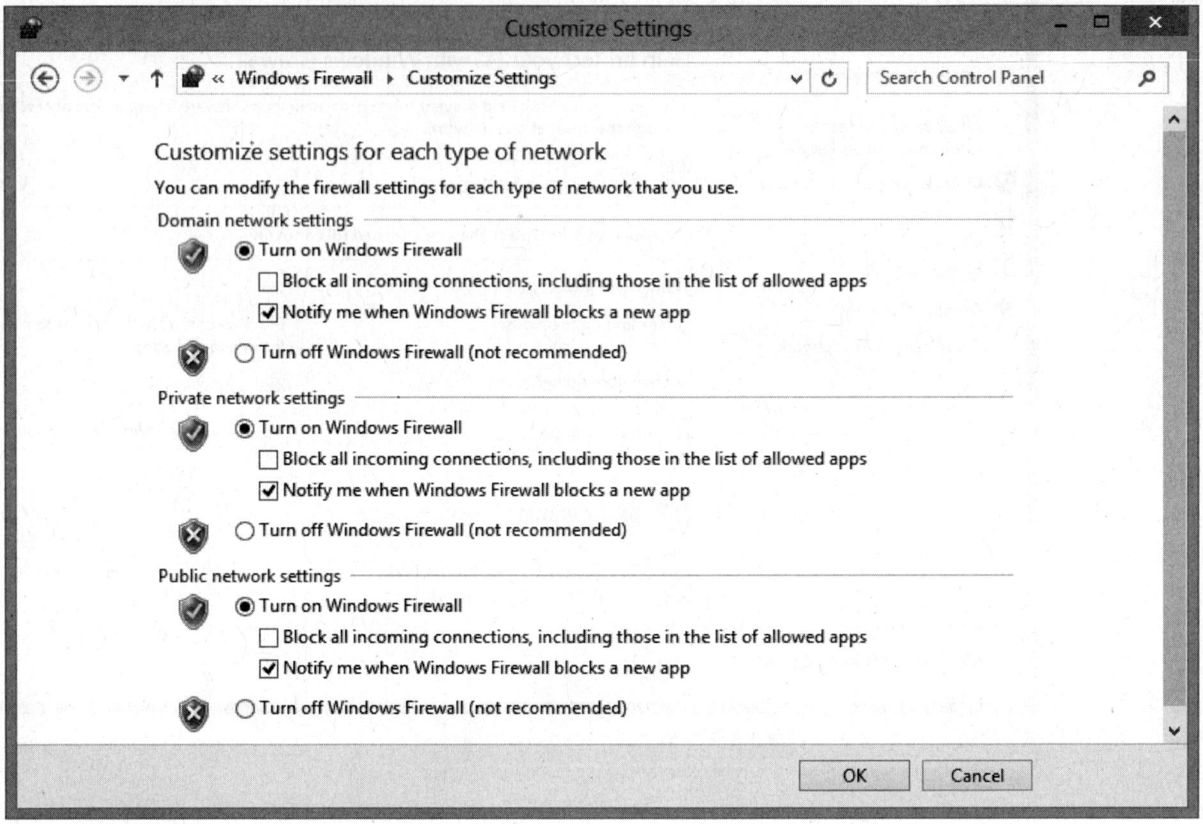

Using this interface, you can turn Windows Firewall completely on or off for each of the network locations and configure each location to block all incoming traffic and notify the user when the firewall blocks a program.

BLOCKING INCOMING CONNECTIONS

Selecting the *Block all incoming connections, including those in the list of allowed apps* checkbox enables you to increase the security of your system by blocking all unsolicited attempts to connect to your computer. Note, however, that this does not prevent you from performing common networking tasks, such as accessing websites and sending or receiving emails. These activities are not unsolicited connection attempts; they begin with the client contacting the server first. When the firewall detects the outgoing traffic from your web browser to a web server on the Internet, for example, it knows that it should admit the incoming response from the server.

ALLOWING PROGRAMS THROUGH THE FIREWALL

Users might want to modify the firewall settings in other ways also, typically because a specific application requires access to a port not anticipated by the firewall's preconfigured rules. Clicking *Allow an app or feature through Windows Firewall* opens the *Allow programs to communicate through Windows Firewall* dialog box, as shown in Figure 12-6. In this dialog box, you can open up a port through the firewall for specific programs and features installed on the computer, simply by selecting the appropriate checkboxes.

Figure 12-6

The *Allow programs to communicate through Windows Firewall* dialog box

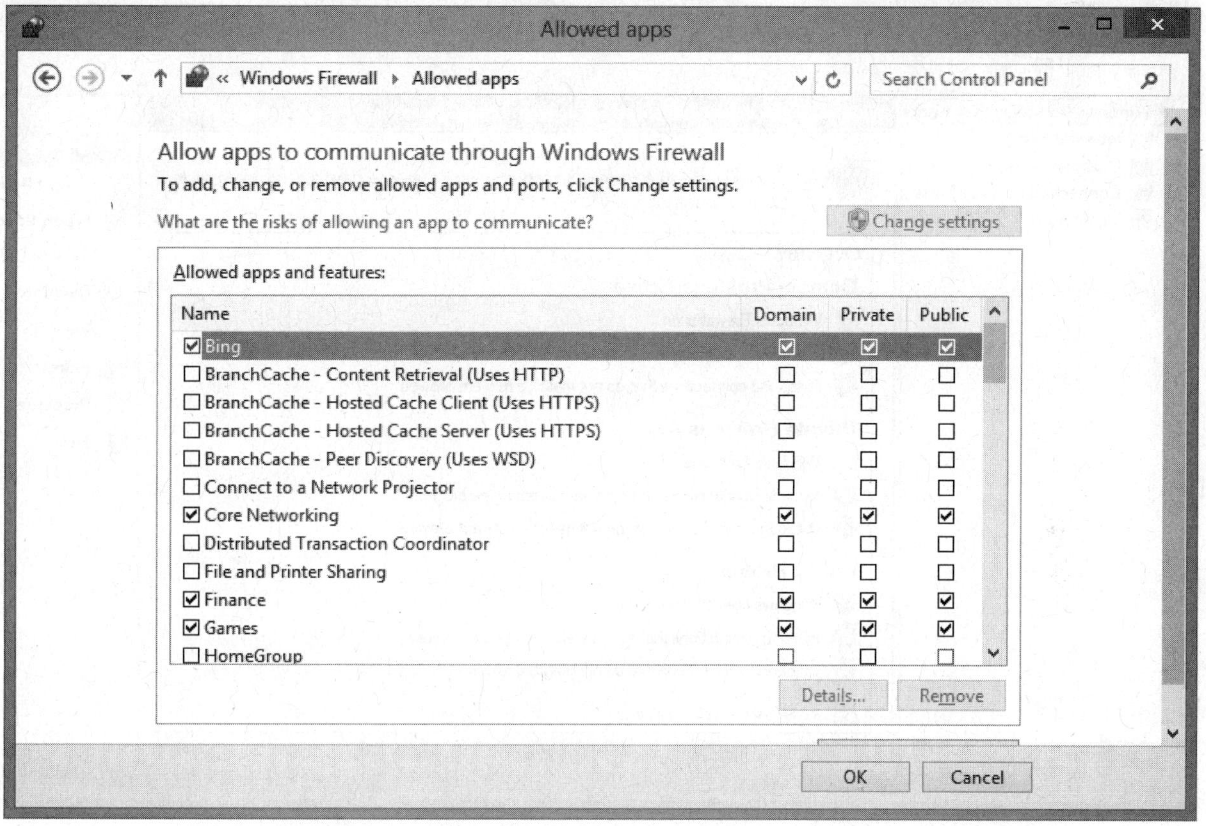

Opening a port in your firewall is an inherently dangerous activity. The more holes you make in a wall, the greater the likelihood that intruders will get in. For this reason, the Windows Firewall controls in the Windows 8 Control Panel are quite limited. In Windows 8, you cannot open up specific port numbers using Control Panel; you can only select from a list of installed applications and features. For full access to Windows Firewall, you must use the Windows Firewall with Advanced Security console, as discussed in the next section.

USING THE WINDOWS FIREWALL WITH ADVANCED SECURITY CONSOLE

The Windows Firewall with Advanced Security snap-in for Microsoft Management Console (MMC) provides direct access to the rules that control the behavior of Windows Firewall. To access the console from the Windows Control Panel, click System and Security > Administrative Tools > Windows Firewall with Advanced Security. The Windows Firewall with Advanced Security console appears, as shown in Figure 12-7.

Figure 12-7

The *Windows Firewall with Advanced Security* snap-in

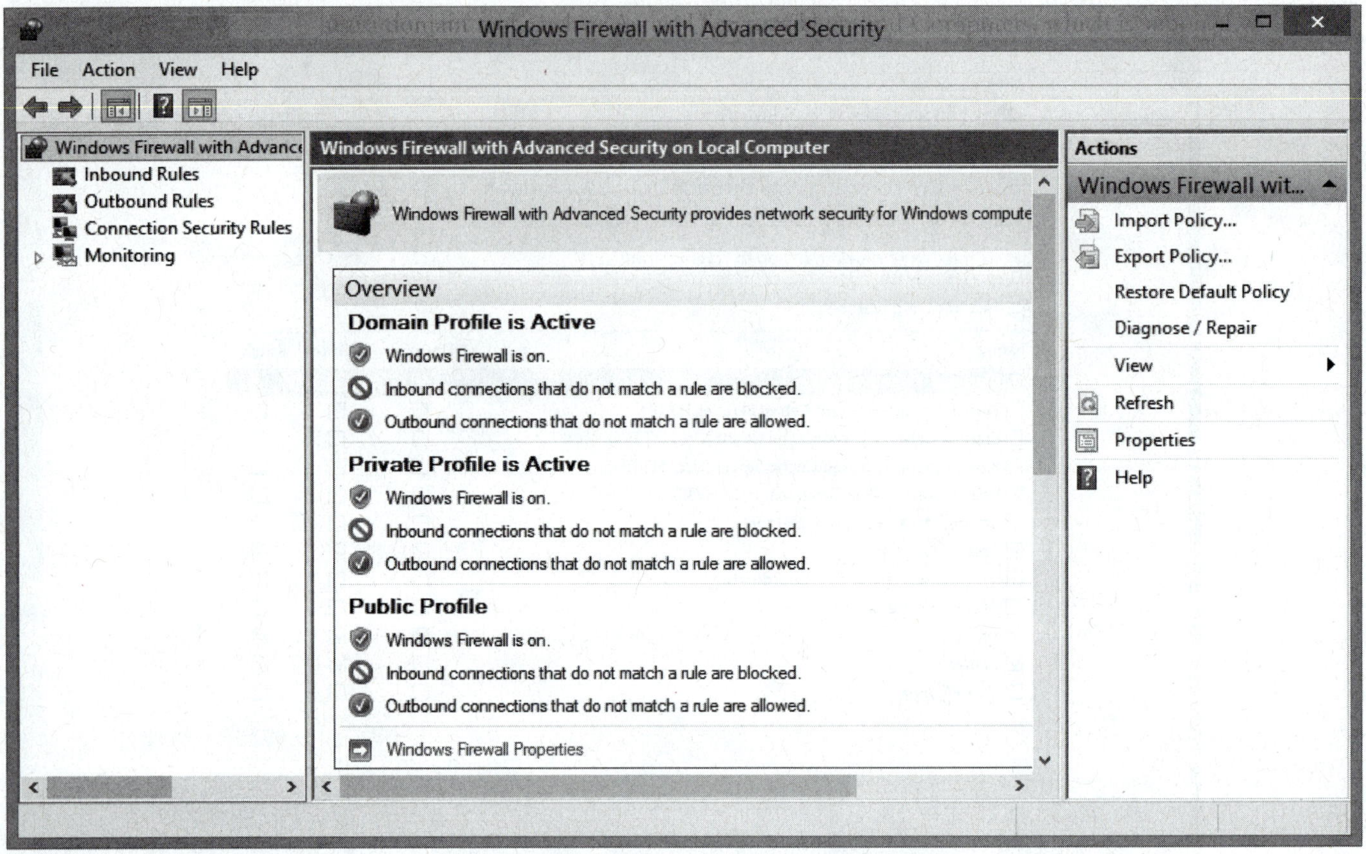

CERTIFICATION READY
Configure Windows Firewall with Advanced Security
Objective 3.3

Configuring Profile Settings

At the top of the center pane, in the Overview section, are status displays for the computer's three possible network locations. Windows Firewall maintains separate profiles for each of the three possible network locations: domain, private, and public. If you connect the computer to a different network, as in the case of a laptop computer that you bring to an Internet "hot spot" in a coffee shop, Windows Firewall loads a different configuration for that profile and a different set of rules.

Unlike the Windows Firewall control panel, the Windows Firewall with Advanced Security console always displays all three network location profiles, even if the computer is not joined to a domain. This enables you to work with the rules in any of the profiles, whether that profile is active or not. As you can tell from the Overview display, the default Windows Firewall settings call for the same basic configuration for all three profiles: the firewall is turned on, incoming traffic is blocked unless it matches a rule, and outgoing traffic is allowed unless it matches a rule. You can change this default behavior by clicking the Windows Firewall Properties link, which displays the *Windows Firewall with Advanced Security on Local Computer Properties* sheet, as shown in Figure 12-8.

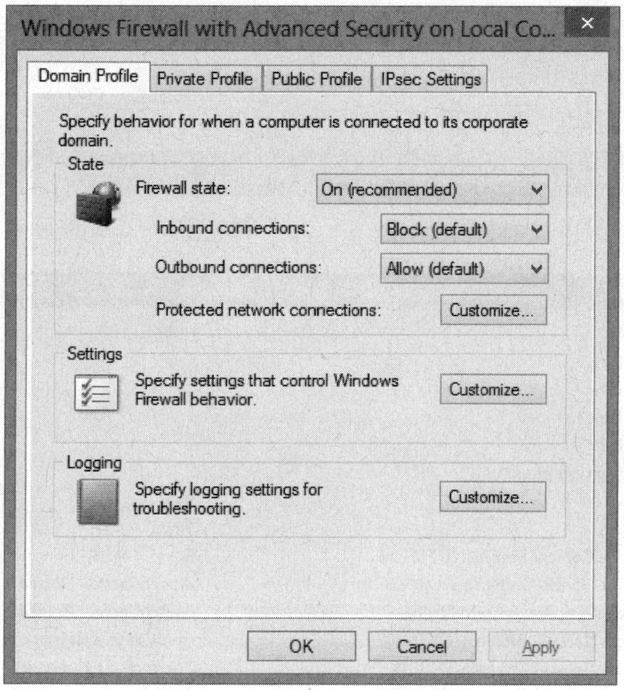

Figure 12-8

The *Windows Firewall with Advanced Security on Local Computer Properties* sheet

On this properties sheet, each of the three location profiles has a tab with identical controls that enables you to modify the default profile settings. You can, for example, configure the firewall to shut down completely when it is connected to a domain network, and turn the firewall on with its most protective settings when you connect the computer to a public network. You can also configure the firewall's notification option, which specifies whether the firewall should display a message to the user when it blocks a program, and its logging behavior.

The most important settings in this properties sheet are those that establish the default behavior for each profile, because these settings determine the nature of the rules that Windows Firewall will use. In the default settings, *Inbound connections* is set to *Block*, so the rules you create must allow certain types of traffic to pass through the firewall. If you change the default to allow inbound connections, then you must create rules that block certain types of traffic. The setting for *Outbound connections* are the opposite, by default.

Creating Rules

Selecting apps and features in the Windows Firewall control panel is a relatively friendly method for working with firewall rules. In the *Windows Firewall with Advanced Security* console, you can work with the rules in their raw form. Selecting either Inbound Rules or Outbound Rules in the left pane displays a list of all the rules operating in that direction, as shown in Figure 12-9. The rules that are currently operational have a checkmark in a green circle, while the rules not in force are grayed out.

Figure 12-9

The *Inbound Rules* list in the *Windows Firewall with Advanced Security* console

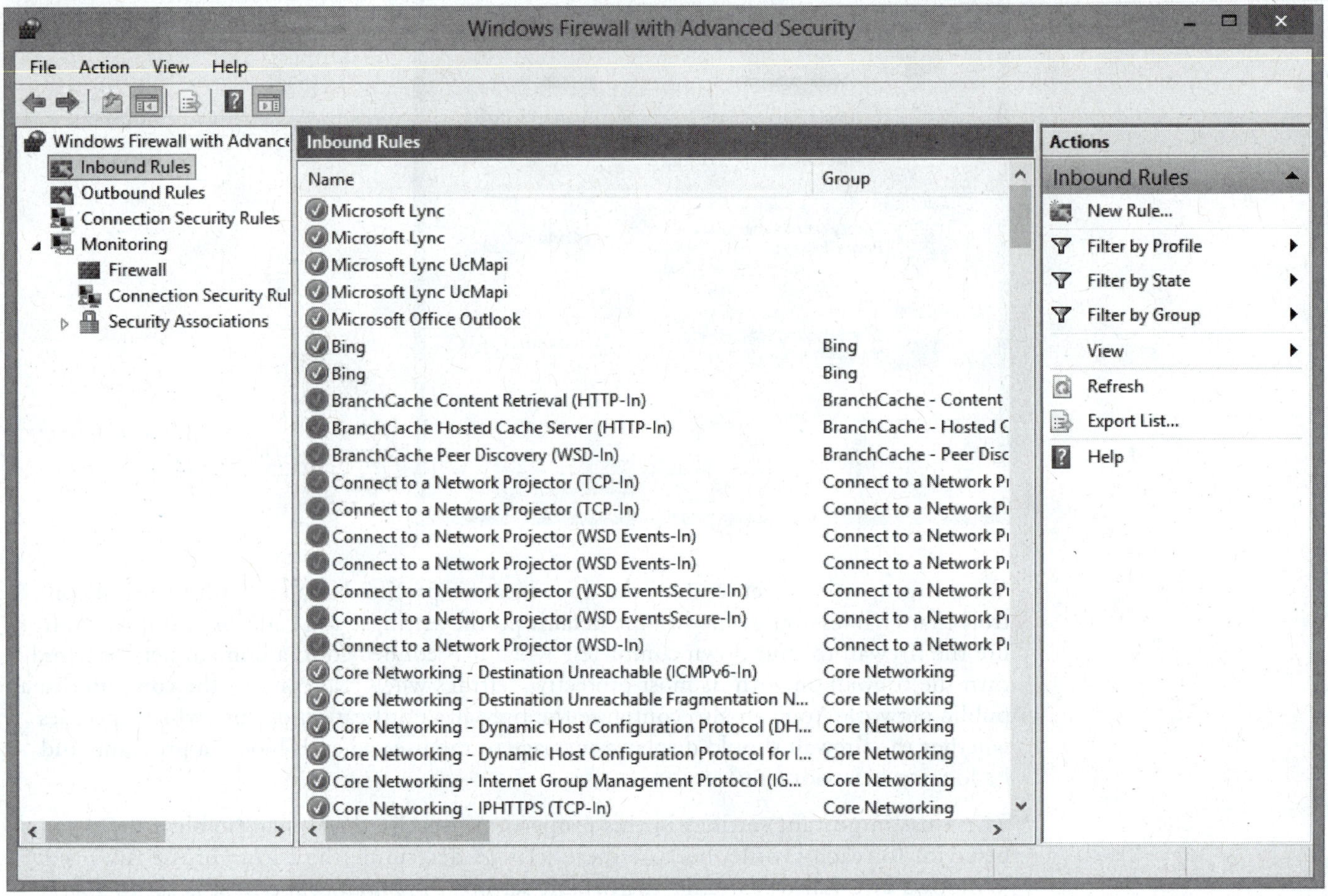

TAKE NOTE*

It is important to remember that in the Windows Firewall with Advanced Security console, you are always working with a complete list of rules for all of the profiles, while in the *Windows Firewall Settings* dialog box, you are working only with the rules that apply to the currently active profile.

CERTIFICATION READY
Configure network discovery
Objective 3.3

The default rules for three profiles differ, with the public profile providing the most secure environment and the private profile the least. Table 12-1 lists some of the primary networking services in Windows 8 and their default firewall settings for each profile. This is a highly simplified list, as most of these services use a variety of protocols that each require their own rules for incoming and outgoing traffic. When you modify the default networking behavior in Windows 8 – such as when you enable Network Discovery in the Advanced Sharing Settings control panel – the controls change the default settings for the Windows Firewall rules.

TAKE NOTE*

For more information on Network Discovery and its relationship to Windows Firewall, see "Understanding Network Discovery" in Lesson 10, "Configuring IP Settings."

Table 12-1

Default Windows Firewall Rules Settings

	Private	Public	Domain
Core Networking	Enabled	Enabled	Enabled
File and Printer Sharing	Enabled	Disabled	Disabled
Homegroup	Disabled	N/A	N/A
Network Discovery	Enabled	Disabled	Disabled
Remote Desktop	Disabled	Disabled	Disabled

TAKE NOTE* Whenever a network service fails to function as expected, checking the rules for that service in the Windows Firewall with Advanced Security console should be one your first troubleshooting steps.

Creating new rules with this interface provides a great deal more flexibility than the Windows Firewall control panel. When you right-click the Inbound Rules or Outbound Rules node and select New Rule from the context menu, the New Rule Wizard, shown in Figure 12-10, takes you through the process of configuring the following sets of parameters:

TAKE NOTE* The New Inbound Rule and New Outbound Rule Wizards are adaptive, meaning that you will not see all of the pages listed here each time you run the wizard. The option you select on the Rule Type page determines what additional pages appear next.

- **Rule Type** – Specifies whether you want to create a program rule, a port rule, a variant on one of the predefined rules, or a custom rule. This selection determines which of the following pages the wizard displays.
- **Program** – Specifies whether the rule applies to all programs, to one specific program, or to a specific service.
- **Protocol and Ports** – Specifies the protocol and the local and remote ports to which the rule applies. This enables you to specify the exact types of traffic that the rule should block or allow.
- **Scope** – Specifies the IP addresses of the local and remote systems to which the rule applies. This enables you to block or allow traffic between specific computers.
- **Action** – Specifies the action the firewall should take when a packet matches the rule. You configure the rule to allow traffic if it is blocked by default, or block traffic if it is allowed by default. You can also configure the rule to allow traffic only when the connection between the communicating computers is secured using IPsec. This is called an ***authenticated exception***.

CERTIFICATION READY
Configure authenticated exceptions
Objective 3.3

- **Profile** – Specifies the profile(s) to which the rule should apply: domain, private, and/or public.
- **Name** – Specifies a name and (optionally) a description for the rule.

Figure 12-10

The New Inbound Rule Wizard

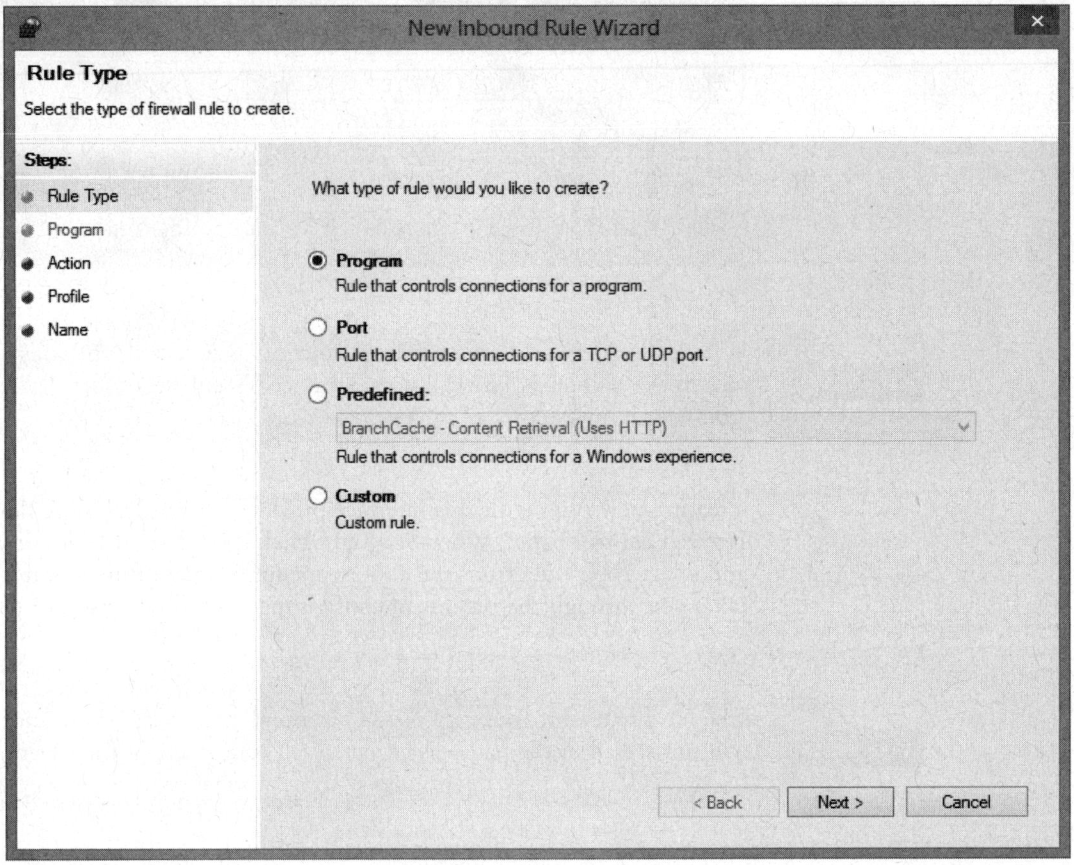

The rules you can create using the New Rule Wizards range from simple program rules to highly complex and specific rules that block or allow only specific types of traffic between specific computers. The more complicated the rules become, however, the more you have to know about TCP/IP communications in general and the specific behavior of your applications. Modifying the default firewall settings to accommodate some special applications is relatively simple, but creating an entirely new firewall configuration is a formidable task.

Importing and Exporting Rules

The process of creating and modifying rules in the Windows Firewall with Advanced Security console can be time-consuming, and repeating the process on multiple computers even more so. Therefore, the console makes it possible for you to save the rules and settings you have created by exporting them to a policy file.

A ***policy file*** is a file with a .wfw extension that contains all of the property settings in a Windows Firewall installation, as well as all of its rules, including the preconfigured rules and the ones you have created or modified yourself. To create a policy file, you select Export Policy from the Action menu in the Windows Firewall with Advanced Security console, and specify a name and location for the file.

You can then duplicate the rules and settings on another computer by copying the file and using the Import Policy function to read in the contents.

TAKE NOTE*

When you import policies from a file, the console warns you that all existing rules and settings will be overwritten. You must therefore be careful not to create custom rules on a computer, and then expect to import other rules using a policy file.

Using Filters

Although what a firewall does is sometimes referred to as packet filtering, in the Windows Firewall with Advanced Security console, the term ***filter*** is used to refer to a feature that enables you to display rules according to the profile they apply to, their current state, or the group to which they belong.

For example, to display only the rules that apply to the public profile, click Action > Filter By Profile > Filter By Public Profile. The display changes to show only the rules that apply to the public profile. In the same way, you can apply a filter that causes the console to display only the rules that are currently turned on, or the rules that belong to a particular group. Click Action > Clear All Filters to return to the default display showing all of the rules.

Configuring Connection Security Rules

Windows 8 includes a feature in Windows Firewall that incorporates IPsec data protection into the Windows Firewall. The ***IP Security (IPsec)*** standards are a collection of documents that define a method for securing data while it is in transit over a TCP/IP network. IPsec includes a connection establishment routine, during which computers authenticate each other before transmitting data, and a technique called ***tunneling***, in which data packets are encapsulated within other packets for their protection.

MORE INFORMATION

Data protection technologies such as the Windows 8 Encrypting File System (EFS) and BitLocker protect data while it is stored on a drive. However, they do nothing to protect data while it is being transmitted over the network, because they both decrypt the data before sending it. IPsec, by contrast, protects data while it is in transit.

In addition to inbound and outbound rules, the Windows Firewall with Advanced Security console enables you to create connection security rules, using the New Connection Security Rule Wizard. Connection security rules defines the type of protection you want to apply to the communications that conform to Windows Firewall rules.

CERTIFICATION READY
Configure connection security rules (IPsec)
Objective 3.3

When you right-click the Connection Security Rules node and select New Rule from the context menu, the New Connection Security Rule Wizard, shown in Figure 12-11, takes you through the process of configuring the following sets of parameters:

- **Rule Type** – Specifies the basic function of the rule, such as to isolate computers based on authentication criteria, to exempt certain computers (such as infrastructure servers) from authentication, to authenticate two specific computers or groups of computers, or to tunnel communications between two computers. You can also create custom rules combining these functions.
- **Endpoints** – Specifies the IP addresses of the computer that will establish a secured connection before transmitting any data.
- **Requirements** – Specifies whether authentication between two computers should be requested or required in each direction.
- **Authentication Method** – Specifies the type of authentication the computers should use when establishing a connection.
- **Profile** – Specifies the profile(s) to which the rule should apply: domain, private, and/or public.
- **Name** – Specifies a name and (optionally) a description for the rule.

Figure 12-11

The New Connection Security Rule Wizard

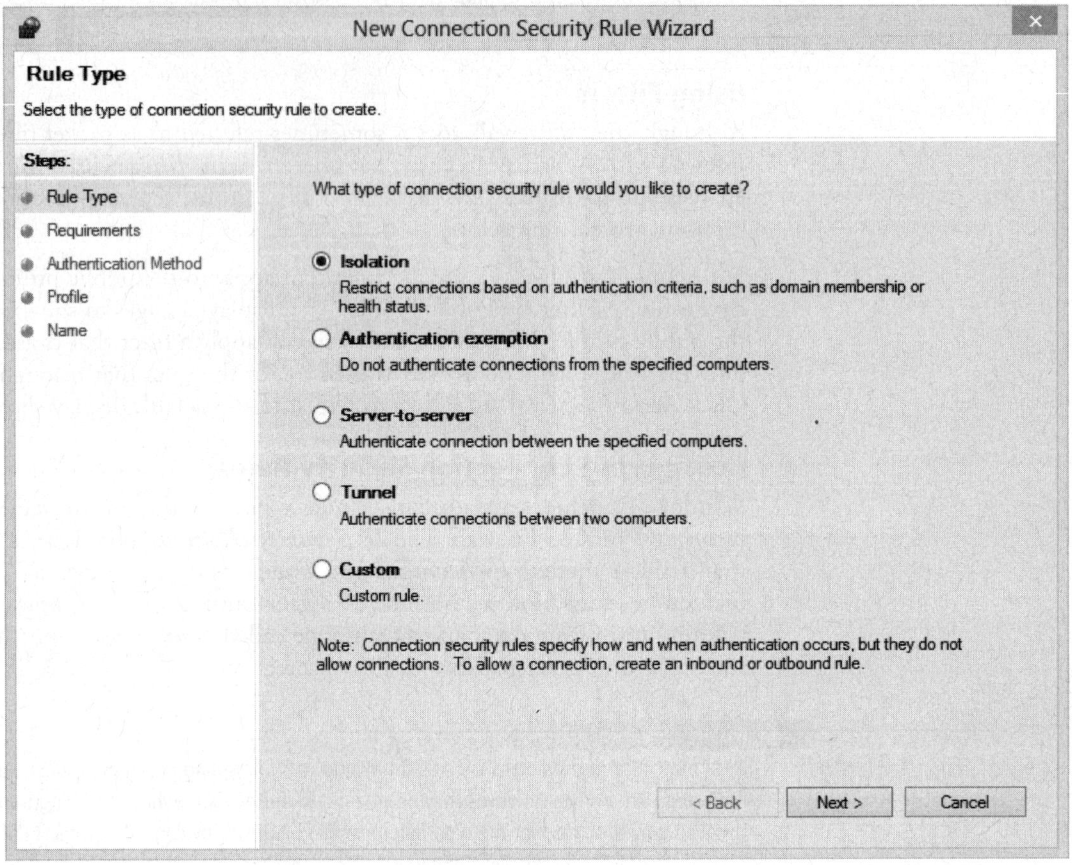

CONFIGURING WINDOWS FIREWALL WITH GROUP POLICY

As with many other Windows 8 features, configuring Windows Firewall on individual computers is not practical in an enterprise network environment. However, it is possible to configure firewall settings on Windows workstations using Group Policy.

When you browse to the Computer Configuration\Policies\Windows Settings\Security Settings\Windows Firewall with Advanced Security node in a GPO, you see the interface shown in Figure 12-12, which is similar to that of the Windows Firewall with Advanced Security console.

Clicking Windows Firewall Properties opens a dialog box with the same controls as the Windows Firewall with Advanced Security on Local Computer Properties sheet and clicking Inbound Rules and Outbound Rules launches the same wizards as the console.

Figure 12-12

The *Windows Firewall with Advanced Security* node in a GPO

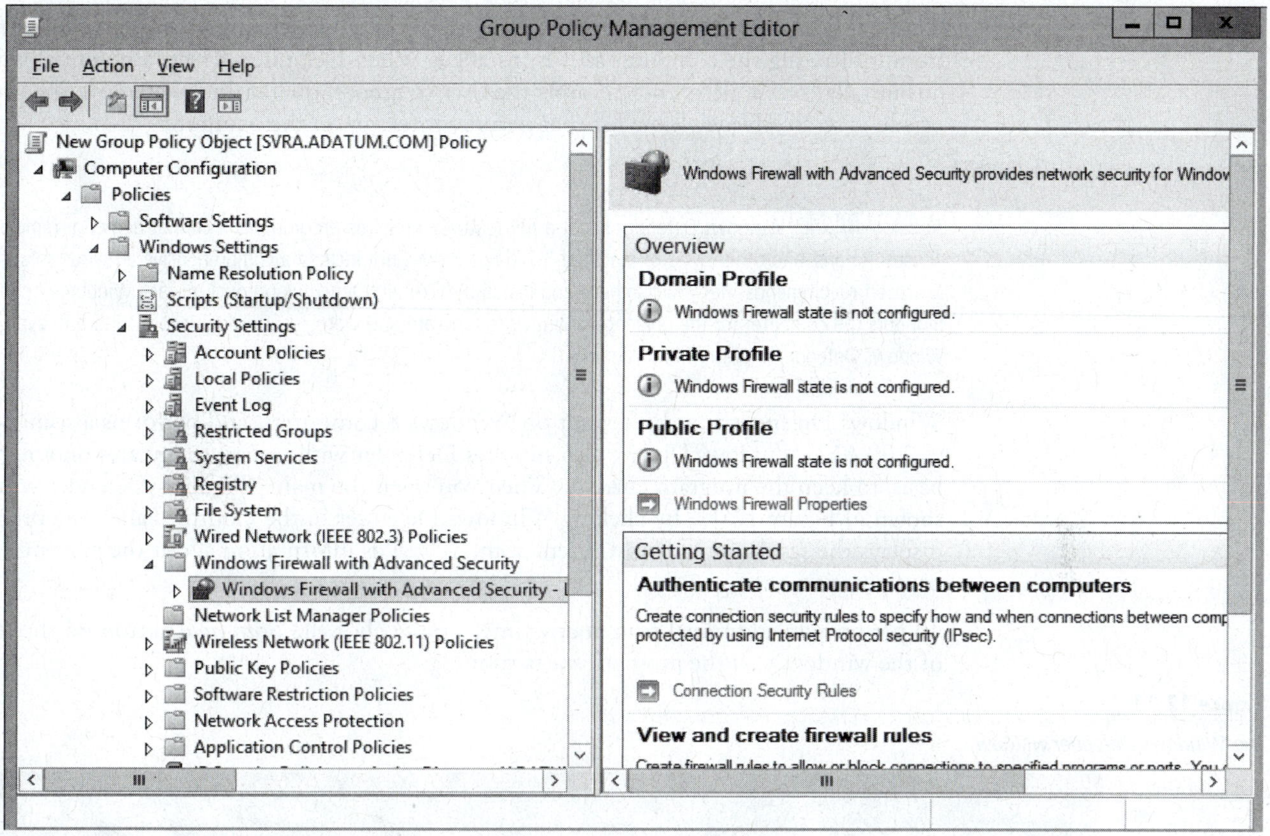

Introducing Windows Defender

> ***Windows Defender*** is a Windows 8 application that prevents the infiltration of spyware into the system.

Originally, the people who created and disseminated viruses and other types of malware did so purely out of gratuitous vandalism. Today, the primary motive is profit, and this has led to the development of new kinds of malware. ***Spyware***, for example, is a type of software that gathers information about computer users and transmits it back to the attacker.

The type of information spyware can gather ranges from the trivial to the critical. Some programs simply collect information about users' web surfing habits, the better to target potential customers with their marketing efforts. Others collect personal and confidential information about the computer's users, including passwords and account numbers, which attackers can use for identity theft and other crimes. In addition to compromising the security of a computer, spyware can also affect its performance by consuming system resources.

Windows 8 includes an application called Windows Defender that helps to defend against spyware by scanning the places where it most commonly infiltrates a computer. Spyware is typically a program that is installed along with other software that the user deliberately downloads and installs. To be effective, spyware has to be running all the time, so the installer typically places the program in one of the standard Windows preloading mechanisms, such as the Startup folder and the Run key in the registry. Windows Defender has a set of predefined definitions that it searches for in these places, which help it to identify specific threats.

Windows Defender also includes real-time monitoring, which attempts to prevent spyware from infiltrating the computer as it is installed. When Defender detects a potentially dangerous installation, it alerts and prompts the user to ignore, quarantine, or remove the program, or add it to an Always Allow list that permits it to run on the computer.

WARNING Windows Defender is not a full-featured antivirus program, as it cannot detect or remove true viruses, Trojans, and other types of malware. Windows 8 does not include a comprehensive antivirus solution, and Microsoft recommends that you purchase and install a third-party antivirus product. In fact, Windows Action Center monitors the computer for the presence of antivirus software and warns users when it fails to find it, even when Windows Defender is present and running.

Windows Defender runs by default on Windows 8 computers, and performs a scan every day at 2:00 AM. Windows Update also supplies Defender with signature updates on a regular basis, to keep the program current. When you open the main Windows Defender window, as shown in Figure 12-13, by clicking Windows Defender in the Control Panel, the program displays the results of the most recent scan, as well as information about the current configuration settings.

To perform an additional scan at any time, simply click the *Scan now* button on the left side of the window, and the program starts running.

Figure 12-13

The *Windows Defender* window

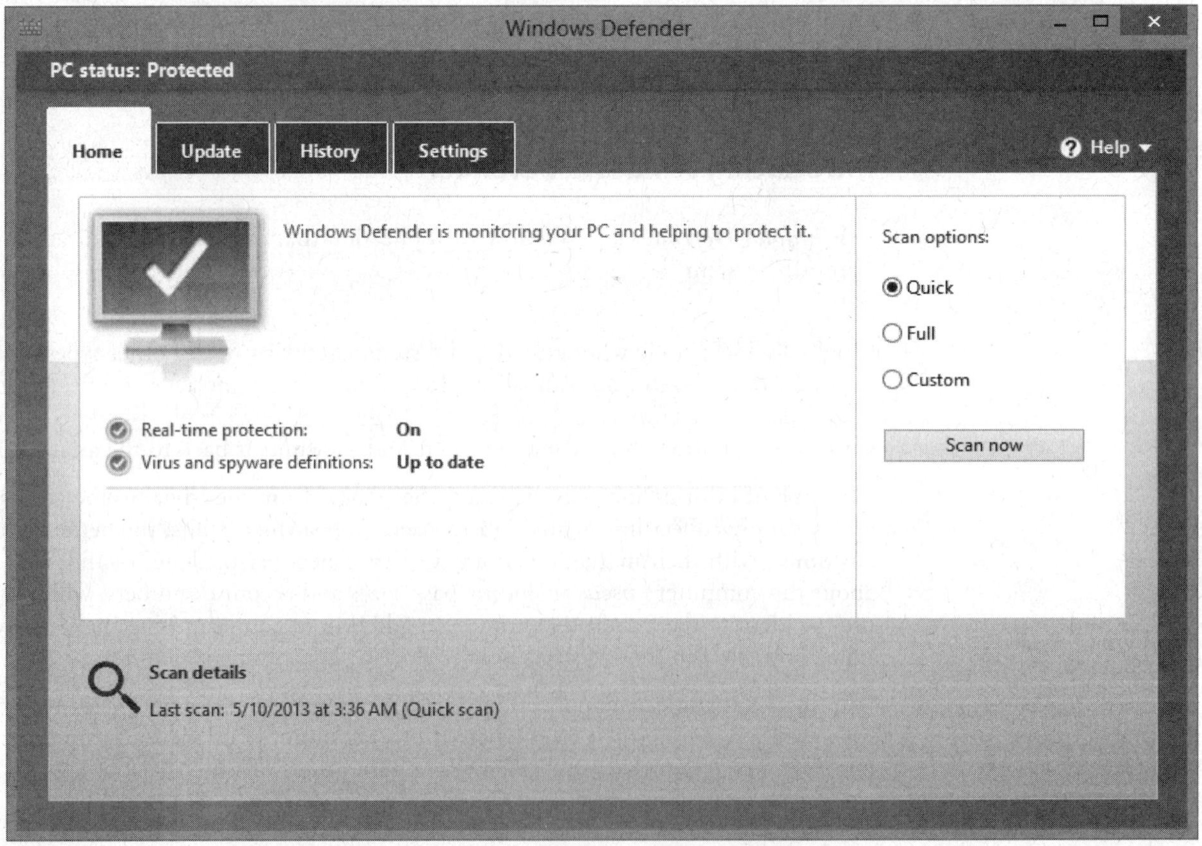

CONFIGURING WINDOWS DEFENDER

You can modify the configuration of Windows Defender by using the following procedure:

CONFIGURE WINDOWS DEFENDER

GET READY. Log on to Windows 8 using an account with administrative capabilities.

1. On the Windows 8 computer, open the charms bar and click **Search**.

   The Search bar appears.

2. With the Apps option selected, type **defender** in the text box.

   The Windows Defender application appears in the results display.

TAKE NOTE* Unlike Windows Vista, Windows Defender is difficult to find in Windows 8. There is no shortcut in the Start menu, and it only appears in the Control Panel when you select the *Large icons* or *Small icons* view.

3. Click **Windows Defender**.

   The Windows Defender window appears. This window shows the current status of Windows Defender, and indicates whether the program has detected any unwanted or harmful software.

4. Click **Settings**.

   The Settings page appears, as shown in Figure 12-14.

Figure 12-14

The *Windows Defender Settings* page

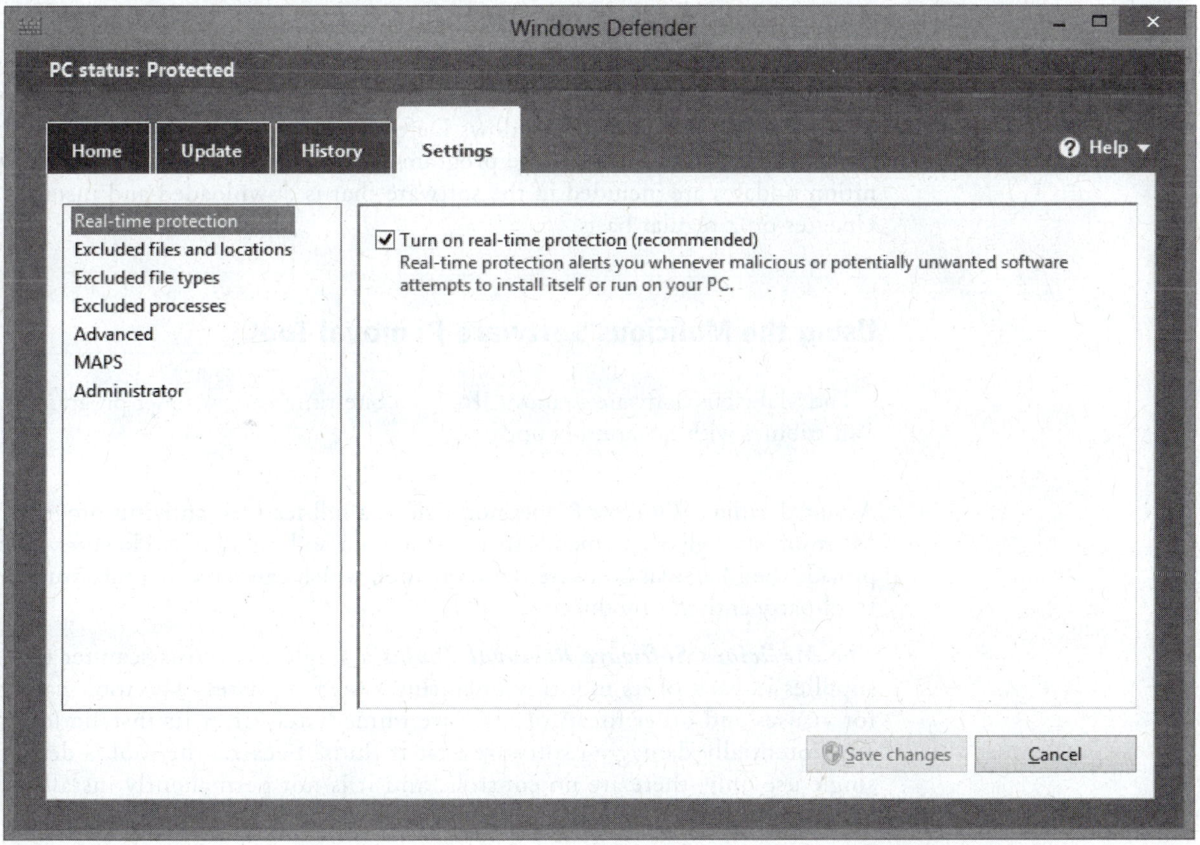

5. Modify the configuration settings for any of the following items and click **Save changes**.
   - **Automatic scanning** – Specifies if, when, and how often Defender should scan the system. You can also configure the program to download updated definitions before scanning.
   - **Default actions** – Specifies what action Defender should take when it detects items at each of the alert levels.
   - **Real-time protection** – Specifies whether Defender should provide real-time protection and enables you to specify which types of real-time protection Defender should provide.
   - **Excluded files and locations** – Specifies the names of files and folders that you do not want Windows Defender to scan
   - **Excluded file types** – Specifies the extensions of file types that you do not want Windows Defender to scan.
   - **Excluded processes** – Specifies the processes that you do not want Windows Defender to scan
   - **Advanced** – Enables you to configure Defender to scan within archives, create a restore point before applying actions, scan email and removable drives, and use heuristics to locate partial signature matches.
   - **MAPS** – Enables you to report malware to the Microsoft Active Protection Service (MAPS), which supports the creation of new signature definitions.
   - **Administrator** – Enables you to configure Defender to alert all users if it detects spyware and to allow all users to initiate Defender scans.
6. Close the **Windows Defender** window.

UPDATING DEFINITIONS

Protecting Windows 8 computers against malware is a constant struggle between the attackers who create the malicious software and the people who design protective software for them. As a result, Windows Defender relies on continual updates to its definitions, which determine what the program should scan and how. Windows Defender definition updates are included in the software that is downloaded and installed by Windows Updates on a regular basis.

Using the Malicious Software Removal Tool

The Malicious Software Removal Tool is a one-time virus scanner program that Microsoft distributes with its monthly updates.

As stated earlier, Windows 8 does not include a full-featured antivirus program, and Microsoft strongly recommends that users obtain and install one. However, Microsoft does provide the Malicious Software Removal Tool, which can serve as a substitute or a backup to third-party antivirus products.

The ***Malicious Software Removal Tool*** is a single user virus scanner that Microsoft supplies in each of its monthly operating system updates. The tool scans the system for viruses and other forms of malware immediately after its installation, and removes any potentially damaging software that it finds. Because the tool is designed for a single use only, there are no controls, and it is not permanently installed in the operating system.

For systems with no other antivirus protection, the Malicious Software Removal Tool can function as a substitute until you obtain one. For systems that already have antivirus software, the tool functions as an effective backup. There are types of malware that are capable of disabling well-known virus scanners, and the Malicious Software Removal Tool can provide an effective scan in the event that the main software is not functioning.

Understanding Wireless Security

THE BOTTOM LINE Wireless networks are subject to many of the same security threats as cabled networks, but the medium they use makes it easier for attackers to penetrate them.

Establishing a wireless connection is not difficult, but establishing a secure one can be. Wired networks typically rely on physical security to protect the privacy of their communications. A potential intruder must have physical access to the network cable to connect to the network. This is not the case with wireless networks. If a wireless network is not properly secured, an intruder in a car parked outside can use a laptop to gain full access to the network's communications.

CERTIFICATION READY
Manage wireless security
Objective 3.3

Connecting to a wireless network can grant an attacker access to resources on an organization's internal network, or it might enable the attacker to access the Internet while hiding his or her identity. Some of the specific types of attacks to which an unsecured wireless network is subject are as follows:

- **Eavesdropping** – Attackers can capture traffic as a wireless computer communicates with a wireless access point (WAP). Depending on the type of antennae the devices use and their transmitting power, an attacker might be able to eavesdrop from hundreds or thousands of feet away.
- **Masquerading** – Attackers might be able to gain access to restricted network resources by impersonating authorized wireless users. This enables the attacker to engage in illegal activities or attack hosts on remote networks while disguised with another identity.
- **Attacks against wireless clients** – Attackers can launch a network-based attack on a wireless computer that is connected to an ad hoc or untrusted wireless network.
- **Denial of service** – Attackers can jam the wireless frequencies by using a transmitter, preventing legitimate users from successfully communicating with a WAP.
- **Data tampering** – Attackers can delete, replay, or modify wireless communications with a man-in-the-middle attack. A man-in-the-middle attack is when an intruder intercepts network communications and modifies the contents of the packets before sending them on to their destination.

The concerns over the abuse of wireless networks are far from theoretical. Intruders have a wide variety of tools available for detecting, connecting to, and abusing wireless networks. As with most aspects of security, technologies are available that you can use to limit the vulnerabilities presented by wireless networks. Specifically, you must configure the network computers so that all wireless communications are authenticated and encrypted. This provides protection similar to that offered by the physical security of wired networks.

Evaluating Wireless Networking Hardware

The 802.11 standards published by the Institute of Electrical and Electronic Engineers (IEEE) dictate the frequencies, transmission speeds, and ranges of wireless networking products.

Table 12-2 lists the IEEE 802.11 standards and their capabilities.

Table 12-2
IEEE Wireless Networking Standards

Standard	Frequency (GHz)	Transmission Rate (Mbps)	Range (Indoor/Outdoor) (Meters)
802.11-1997	2.4	1, 220/100	
802.11a-1999	5	6 to 54	35/120
802.11b-1999	2.4	5.5 to 11	38/140
802.11g-2003	2.4	6 to 54	38/140
802.11n-2009	2.4 and 5	7.2 to 288 (@20 MHz) 15 to 600 (@40 MHz)	70/250
802.11y-2008	3.7	6 to 54	5000+
802.11ac (Draft)	5	433 to 867 (@80 MHz) 867 to 6.93 Gbps (@160 MHz)	

Most of the wireless networking hardware now available supports the 802.11n standard, and can fall back to 802.11b and 802.11g

MORE INFORMATION

IEEE 802.11n equipment increases wireless networking speeds by using multiple transmitter and receiver antennae on each device in a process called ***multiple-input multiple-output (MIMO)***. For example, a device using a 2x2 MIMO format has two transmitters and two receivers, operating at different frequencies. The sending system splits its data into two signals for transmission, and the receiving device reassembles the signals into a single data stream. This process is called ***spatial multiplexing***. The only potential drawback to this arrangement is the depletion of the available frequency bandwidth by having too many devices in proximity to each other.

As a general rule, devices supporting the newer, faster standards are capable of falling back to slower speeds when necessary. For example, an 802.11n WAP will almost always support computers with 802.11b hardware as well. If you're involved in hardware evaluation or selection, compatibility problems among the basic 802.11 standards are relatively rare. The only devices that will not interoperate are those designed to use different frequencies. For example, a 5 GHz 802.11n adapter that does not support 2.4 GHz transmissions cannot connect to an 802.11g WAP, because 802.11g only runs at 2.4 GHz.

There is, however, another compatibility factor to consider apart from the IEEE 802.11 standards, and that is the security protocols that the wireless devices support. Two main security protocols are used in the wireless LAN devices on the market today: ***Wired Equivalent Privacy (WEP)*** and ***WiFi Protected Access (WPA and WPA2)***. WEP has been around longer, and might be the only standard supported by older products. WPA and WPA2 are comparatively recent, and virtually all currently manufactured wireless devices support them.

Unfortunately, wireless devices cannot fall back from one security protocol to another. You must decide to use WEP or WPA on your network, and all of your devices must support the one you choose. WPA and WPA2 are inherently more secure than WEP, so they are preferable, but if the network has any devices that do not support WPA, you must either replace them or settle for WEP.

Using Wired Equivalent Privacy

WEP is a security protocol that helps protect transmitted information by using a security setting, called a ***shared secret*** or a ***shared key***, to encrypt network traffic before sending it.

To use WEP, administrators must configure all of the devices on the wireless network with the same shared secret key. The devices use that key to encrypt all of their transmissions. Any outside party who gains possession of that key can, at the very least, read the contents of the transmitted packets, and at worst, participate on the network.

Unfortunately, the cryptography used by WEP is relatively weak, and programs that can analyze captured traffic and derive the key from it are readily available. These factors have resulted in WEP becoming one of the most easily cracked network encryption protocols today.

In addition to its weak cryptography, another factor contributing to WEP's vulnerability is that the protocol standard doesn't provide any mechanism for automatically changing the shared secret. On wireless networks with hundreds of hosts, manually changing the shared secret on a regular basis is a practical impossibility. Therefore, on most WEP networks, the same shared secret tends to stay in place indefinitely. As with any cryptographic function, the longer a system uses the same code, the more time an attacker has to penetrate that code. A static WEP installation that uses the same permanent key gives attackers sufficient opportunity to crack the shared secret and all the time they need to gain access to the network.

If administrators could change the shared secret on a regular basis, however, they would be able to prevent an attacker from gathering enough data to crack the WEP key, and this would significantly improve WEP's privacy. There are techniques for dynamically and automatically changing the shared secret to dramatically reduce WEP's weaknesses, such as the 802.1X authentication protocol.

Selecting an Authentication Method

The initial WEP standards provided for two types of computer authentication:

- **Open system** – Enables any client to connect without providing a password
- **Shared secret** – Requires wireless clients to authenticate by using a secret key

Fortunately, choosing between open system and shared secret authentication is easy: always use open system authentication. On the surface this might seem illogical, because open system authentication does not require any proof of identity while shared key authentication requires knowledge of a secret key. However, shared secret authentication actually weakens security because most WEP client implementations use the same secret key for both authentication and WEP encryption. If a malicious user captures the authentication key and manages to penetrate its code, then the WEP encryption key is compromised as well.

Therefore, although shared secret authentication is stronger than open system for authentication, it weakens the WEP encryption. If you use open system authentication, any computer can easily join your network. However, without the WEP encryption key the unauthorized clients cannot send or receive wireless communications, and they will not be able to abuse the wireless network.

Using Wi-Fi Protected Access

To address the weaknesses of WEP, the Wi-Fi Alliance, a consortium of the leading wireless network equipment vendors, developed Wi-Fi Protected Access (WPA).

WPA can use the same authentication mechanisms and encryption algorithms as WEP, which enables manufacturers to add support for WPA to existing products with a simple software or firmware upgrade.

There are two encryption options for WPA, as follows:

- ***Temporal Key Integrity Protocol (TKIP)*** – Implemented in the original WPA standard, TKIP encrypts data using the RC4 algorithm with a 128-bit key. This is the same algorithm as WEP, but TKIP virtually eliminates WEP's most exploited vulnerability by using a unique encryption key for each packet.

- ***Advanced Encryption System (AES)*** – Implemented in the WPA2 standard, AES uses a different and more secure encryption algorithm, called CCMP. However, while it is possible to upgrade some legacy WEP equipment to support WPA-TKIP, most equipment cannot be upgraded to support AES. As a result, a wireless network will probably not be able to use AES encryption unless the organization chooses equipment that specifically supports it.

In its current form, WPA has two operational modes, as follows:

- **WPA-Personal** – Also known as WPA-PSK or preshared key mode, an administrator selects a passphrase that is automatically associated with the dynamically generated security settings. This passphrase is stored with the network settings in the WAP and on each of the networked computers. Only wireless devices with the WPA passphrase can join the network and decrypt network transmissions.
- **WPA-Enterprise** – Also known as WPA-802.1X or WPA-RADIUS, requires an authentication server using Remote Authentication Dial-In User Service (RADIUS) and the 802.1X authentication protocol, as implemented in the Network Policy and Access Services role in Windows Server 2008 R2. Although more difficult to implement and configure, the use of RADIUS and 802.1X is more secure. This combination provides centralized administration, auditing, and logging, and eliminates the need for a shared passphrase, which is a potential vulnerability.

SKILL SUMMARY

IN THIS LESSON, YOU LEARNED:

- Malware is malicious software created specifically for the purpose of infiltrating or damaging a computer system without the user's knowledge or consent. This type of software includes a variety of technologies, including viruses, Trojan horses, worms, spyware, and adware.
- Action Center is a centralized console that enables users and administrators to access, monitor, and configure the various Windows 8 security mechanisms.
- Windows Firewall is a software program that protects a computer by allowing certain types of network traffic in and out of the system while blocking others.
- You configure Windows Firewall by creating rules that specify what types of traffic to block and/or allow.
- Windows Defender helps to defend against spyware by scanning the places where it most commonly infiltrates a computer.
- The Malicious Software Removal Tool is a single user virus scanner that Microsoft supplies in each of its monthly operating system updates.
- The 802.11 standards published by the Institute of Electrical and Electronic Engineers (IEEE) dictate the frequencies, transmission speeds, and ranges of wireless networking products.
- WEP is a wireless security protocol that helps protect transmitted information by using a security setting, called a shared secret or a shared key, to encrypt network traffic before sending it.
- To address the weaknesses of WEP, the Wi-Fi Alliance, a consortium of the leading wireless network equipment vendors, developed Wi-Fi Protected Access (WPA).

Knowledge Assessment

Multiple Choice

Select one or more correct answers for each of the following questions.

1. Which of the following mechanisms is used most often used in firewall rules to allow traffic onto the network?
   a. Protocol numbers
   b. IP addresses
   c. Port numbers
   d. Hardware addresses

2. Which of the following actions can you not perform from the Windows Firewall control panel? (Choose all that apply.)
   a. Turn Windows firewall off for all three profiles
   b. Manage firewall exceptions for the domain profile
   c. Allow a program through the firewall in all three profiles
   d. Create firewall exceptions based on port numbers

3. Connection security rules require that network traffic allowed through the firewall use which of the following security mechanisms?
   a. IPsec
   b. EFS
   c. UAC
   d. PIV

4. Windows Firewall uses three profiles to represent the type of network to which the server is connected. What are the three profiles?
   a. Private, Temporary, and Authenticated
   b. Public, DMZ, and Private
   c. Internet, Secure, and Private
   d. Domain, Private, and Public

5. When a user attempts to visit an Internet-based web server, what is the default action of the Windows Firewall?
   a. The firewall will not permit the user to visit a non-corporate website.
   b. The firewall by default will not block client-initiated network traffic.
   c. The firewall will block the web request unless the user is already authenticated.
   d. The firewall will block all outbound traffic.

6. In the Windows Firewall With Advanced Security console, while creating a new rule, the Program page specifies whether the ________.
   a. rule applies to all programs, to one specific program
   b. rule applies to all users, to one specific user
   c. rule applies to all systems, to one specific system
   d. rule applies to all programs, to one specific program, or to a specific service

7. By exporting the Windows Firewall policy, you have a file with a .wfw extension that contains ________.
   a. all the rules you have created or modified
   b. preconfigured rules to be applied to another firewall
   c. all its rules, including the preconfigured rules and the ones you have created or modified
   d. firewall settings as specified by the Group Policy settings

8. Which of the following statements about Windows Defender is true?
   a. Windows Defender uses rules that you create to control its scans.
   b. Windows Defender can detect spyware that is already present on the system, but it cannot prevent the infiltration of new spyware.
   c. Windows Defender eliminates the need for third-party anti-virus software.
   d. Windows Defender requires definition updates that are supplied free with the regularly scheduled Windows Update downloads.

9. Which of the following wireless networking standards uses spatial multiplexing to increase bandwidth?
   a. IEEE 802.11b
   b. IEEE 802.11g
   c. IEEE 802.11n
   d. IEEE 802.1X

10. Which of the following wireless security protocols is the most secure?
    a. WPA-TKIP
    b. WEP (128-bit) with 802.1X authentication
    c. WEP (128-bit)
    d. WPA-AES

Best Answer

Choose the letter that corresponds to the best answer. More than one answer choice may achieve the goal. Select the BEST answer.

1. What is the primary objective of a firewall?
   a. To permit traffic in and out for legitimate users, and to block the rest
   b. To authenticate and authorize users past the network perimeter
   c. To compare traffic information against a list of known valid traffic
   d. To protect a network by allowing certain types of network traffic in and out of the system

2. Windows Firewall Customize Settings contains three profiles (Public, Private and Domain). What differentiates these profiles from each other?
   a. Public is for servers accessible to temporary users. Private is for servers on an internal network. Domain is for servers in which users are all authenticated.
   b. Public is for servers accessible to unauthenticated users. Private is for inaccessible servers. Domain is for servers accessible only to authenticated users.
   c. Public is for servers accessible to temporary users. Private is for servers on an internal network. Domain is for servers across multiple sites.
   d. Public is for servers accessible to unauthenticated users. Private is for servers on a private network. Domain is for servers spanning different domain groups.

3. Windows Firewall allows you to create inbound, outbound, and connection security rules for individual servers or systems. How can you do this for multiple systems?
   a. You can delegate to administrators the task of performing the same configuration to their local servers.
   b. You can create a new Group Policy object (GPO) and create matching rules to match the desired configuration. Then deploy the GPO to other systems on the network.
   c. You can visit individual systems and configure them as you have the initial system.
   d. You can create a new GPO and you can import settings from a policy file created earlier. Then deploy the GPO to other systems on the network.

4. What is the primary benefit of configuring Windows Firewall through the Windows Firewall With Advanced Security snap-in for the Microsoft Management Console?
   a. The Microsoft Management Console offers a more familiar interface than the Windows Firewall control panel.
   b. The Microsoft Management Console snap-in applies the rules faster than the Windows Firewall control panel.
   c. Compared to the Windows Firewall control panel, the Microsoft Management Console can be brought up in fewer clicks.
   d. The Microsoft Management Console snap-in offers full access compared to the Windows Firewall control panel.

5. When creating a firewall exception, what is the difference between opening a port and allowing an application?
   a. Opening a port is permanent, and thus is less risky than allowing an application.
   b. Allowing an application opens the specified port only while the program is running, and thus is less risky.
   c. Both options are available in the Windows Firewall with Advanced Security console.
   d. There is no functional difference between opening a port and allowing an application.

Build a List

1. Specify the order of steps for processing an application in Windows Firewall.
   _______ Click Allow an app or feature through Windows Firewall. The Allowed Apps dialog box appears.
   _______ Scroll down in the Allowed apps and features list and select the check box for the application you want to allow through the firewall.
   _______ Log on to Windows 8, using an account with administrator privileges.
   _______ Click OK to close the Allowed Apps dialog box.
   _______ Open the Control Panel and click System and Security > Windows Firewall. The Windows Firewall window appears.

2. In order of first to last, specify the order of steps for creating Windows Firewall rules.
   _______ From the Action menu, select Export Policy. The Save As combo box appears.
   _______ Log on to Windows 8, using an account with administrator privileges.
   _______ Modify the inbound or outbound firewall rules or create new rules as needed.
   _______ Open the Control Panel and select System & Security > Administrative Tools > Windows Firewall With Advanced Security. The Windows Firewall with Advanced Security console appears.
   _______ In the left pane, select the Windows Firewall with Advanced Security on Local Computer node.
   _______ In the File Name text box, type a name for the policy file and click Save.

Business Case Scenarios

Scenario 12-1: Configuring Windows Firewall

You are a desktop technician in the IT department of a small corporation. Today is the day of the company picnic and, as the junior member of the department, you have been left in charge of the entire corporate network while everyone else is out of the office. Shortly after 2:00 PM, an email arrives from the company's biggest customer, complaining that they can't access the web server they use to place their orders. After checking the web server logs, it seems clear that the server is undergoing a denial-of-service attack, because there are suddenly hundreds of Internet computers repeatedly trying to access it. What temporary modifications could you make to Windows Firewall on the Windows 8 computer that stands between the web server and the Internet that would allow customers to access the web server while blocking the attackers?

Scenario 12-2: Evaluating Wireless Security Risks

Ed is a desktop technician at a large law firm. Ed's firm is a slow adopters of new technologies, and the organization has, to date, not deployed a wireless network. After bringing up the benefits of wireless networks at a recent meeting with the IT staff, Ed was told that the company will not be deploying a wireless network for several years, if ever.

The lack of an IT-configured wireless network has not entirely stopped their adoption, however. Yesterday, Ed noticed a junior attorney surfing the web with his laptop in the lunch room, without a network cable. When Ed asked the attorney how he was connected to the network, he confessed that he plugged a consumer WAP into the network port in his office.

Explain the potential risks of having a rogue wireless network in the office.

Configuring Remote Management

LESSON 13

70-687 EXAM OBJECTIVE

Objective 3.4 – Configure remote management. This objective may include but is not limited to choose the appropriate remote management tools; modify settings remotely by using MMCs or Windows PowerShell; and configure remote management settings.

Lesson Heading	Exam Objective
Using Remote Access Technologies	Choose the appropriate remote management tools
Using Microsoft Management Console	Modify settings remotely by using MMCs or Windows PowerShell
Using Remote Assistance	
Using Remote Desktop	
Using Windows Remote Management	Configure remote management settings
	Modify settings remotely by using MMCs or Windows PowerShell

KEY TERMS

Microsoft Management Console (MMC)
Remote Assistance
Remote Desktop
Remote Desktop Protocol (RDP)
Windows PowerShell
Windows Remote Management
WinRS.exe

Using Remote Access Technologies

THE BOTTOM LINE

Remote access technologies enable a user on one computer to effectively take control of another computer on the network. For desktop administrators, this capability can save many hours of travel time.

A main objective for desktop administrators working on large corporate networks is to minimize the amount of travel from site to site to work on individual computers. Some of the troubleshooting tools included with Windows 8 are capable of managing services on remote

CERTIFICATION READY
Choose the appropriate remote management tools
Objective 3.4

computers as well as on the local system. For example, most MMC snap-ins have this capability, enabling technicians to work on systems throughout the enterprise without traveling. However, most snap-ins are specialized tools used only for certain administration tasks. For comprehensive access to a remote computer, Windows 8 includes two tools that are extremely useful to the desktop technician: Remote Assistance and Remote Desktop.

Using Microsoft Management Console

The shortcuts to various Microsoft Management Console (MMC) tools that appear in Windows 8 are all configured to manage resources on the local system.

CERTIFICATION READY
Modify settings remotely by using MMCs or Windows PowerShell
Objective 3.4

However, many of the snap-ins supplied with Windows 8 enable you to manage other Windows computers on the network as well. There are two ways to access a remote computer using an ***Microsoft Management Console (MMC)*** snap-in.

- Redirect an existing snap-in to another system.
- Create a custom console with snap-ins directed to other systems.

To connect to and manage another system using an MMC snap-in, you must launch the console with an account that has administrative credentials on the remote computer. The exact permissions required depend on the functions performed by the snap-in. If your credentials do not provide the proper permissions on the target computer, you will be able to load the snap-in, but you will not be able to read information from or modify settings on the target computer.

REDIRECTING A SNAP-IN

A snap-in that is directed at a specific system typically has a Connect To Another Computer command in its Action menu. Selecting this command opens a *Select Computer* dialog box, as shown in Figure 13-1, in which you can specify or browse to another computer on the network. Once you select the name of the computer you want to manage and click OK, the snap-in element in the scope pane changes to reflect the name of the computer you selected.

Figure 13-1
The *Select Computer* dialog box in an MMC console

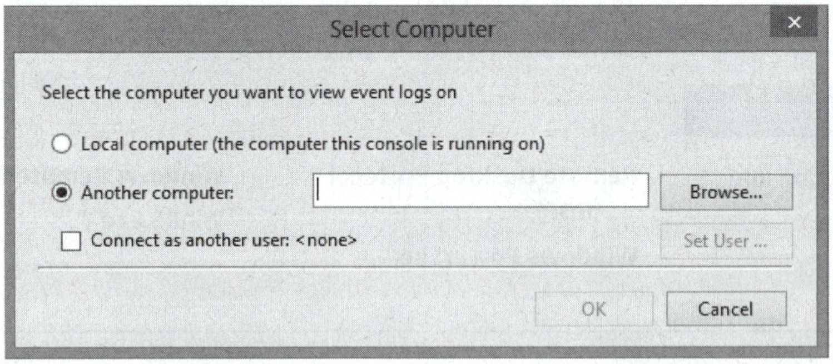

Not every snap-in has the ability to connect to a remote computer, because some do not need it. For example, the Active Directory Domain Services consoles automatically locate a domain controller for the current domain and access the directory service from there. There is no need to specify a computer name. However, you will find Change Domain and Change Domain Controller commands in the Action menu in these consoles, which enable you to manage a different domain or select a specific domain controller in the present domain.

The other factor that can affect the ability of an MMC snap-in to connect to a remote computer is the existence of Windows Firewall rules that block the necessary network traffic between the computers. The traffic that an individual snap-in requires and whether the default Windows Firewall rules restrict it depends on the functions that the snap-in performs.

TAKE NOTE*

For more information on Windows Firewall and how to manipulate its rules, see Lesson 12, "Configuring and Maintaining Network Security."

CREATING A REMOTE CONSOLE

Connecting to a remote computer by redirecting an existing console is convenient for impromptu management tasks, but it is limited by the fact that you can access only one computer at a time. You also have to open the console and redirect it every time you want to access the remote system. A more permanent solution is to create a custom console with snap-ins that are already directed at other computers.

When you add a snap-in to a custom console, you select the computer you want to manage with that snap-in. You can also add multiple copies of the same snap-in to a custom console, with each one pointed at a different computer. This adds a whole new dimension to MMC's functionality. Not only can you create custom consoles containing a variety of tools, you can also create consoles containing tools for a variety of computers. For example, you can create a single console containing multiple instances of the Event Viewer snap-in, with each one pointing to a different computer. This enables you to monitor the event logs for computers all over the network from a single console.

Using Remote Assistance

Remote Assistance is a Windows 8 feature that enables an administrator, trainer, or technical specialist at one location to connect to a distant user's computer, chat with the user, and either view all of the user's activities or take complete control of the system.

Remote Assistance eliminates the need for administrative personnel to travel to a user's location for any of the following reasons:

- **Technical support** – A desktop administrator can use Remote Assistance to connect to a remote computer to modify configuration parameters, install new software, or troubleshoot user problems.
- **Troubleshooting** – By connecting in read-only mode, an expert can observe a remote user's activities and determine whether improper procedures are the source of problems the user is experiencing. The expert can also connect in interactive mode to try to recreate the problem or to modify system settings to resolve it. This is far more efficient than trying to give instructions to inexperienced users over the telephone.
- **Training** – Trainers and help desk personnel can demonstrate procedures to users right on their systems, without having to travel to their locations.

TAKE NOTE*

In Microsoft interfaces and documentation, the person connecting to a client using Remote Assistance is referred to as an expert or a helper.

To receive remote assistance, the computer running Windows 8 must be configured to use the Remote Assistance feature in one of the following ways:

- **Using Control Panel** – Open Control Panel and click System and Security > System > Remote settings. In the System Properties sheet, on the Remote tab, select the *Allow Remote Assistance connections to this computer* checkbox, as shown in Figure 13-2. By clicking the Advanced button, the user can specify whether the expert can take control of the computer or simply view activities on the computer. The user can also specify the amount of time that the invitation for remote assistance remains valid.

Figure 13-2

The Remote tab of the System Properties sheet

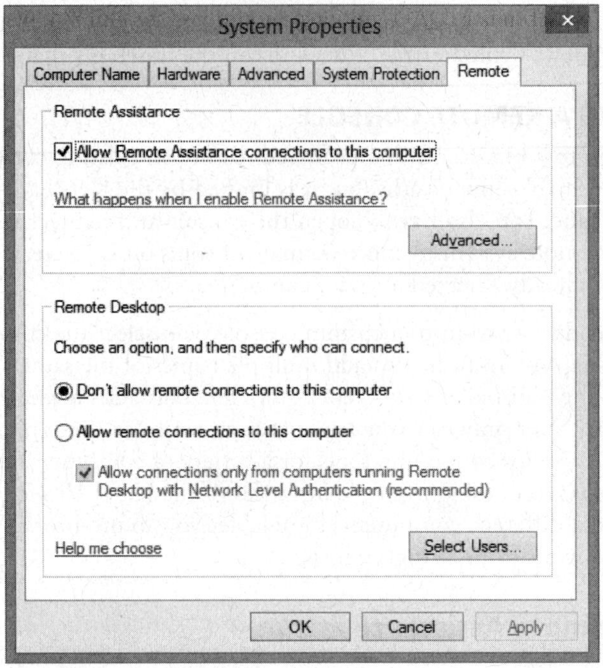

- **Using Group Policy –** Use the Group Policy Object Editor snap-in for MMC to access the computer's Local Computer Policy settings. Browse to the Computer Configuration > Administrative Templates > System > Remote Assistance container and enable the Configure Solicited Remote Assistance policy, as shown in Figure 13-3. The Solicited

Figure 13-3

The Solicited Remote Assistance policy in the Group Policy Object Editor console

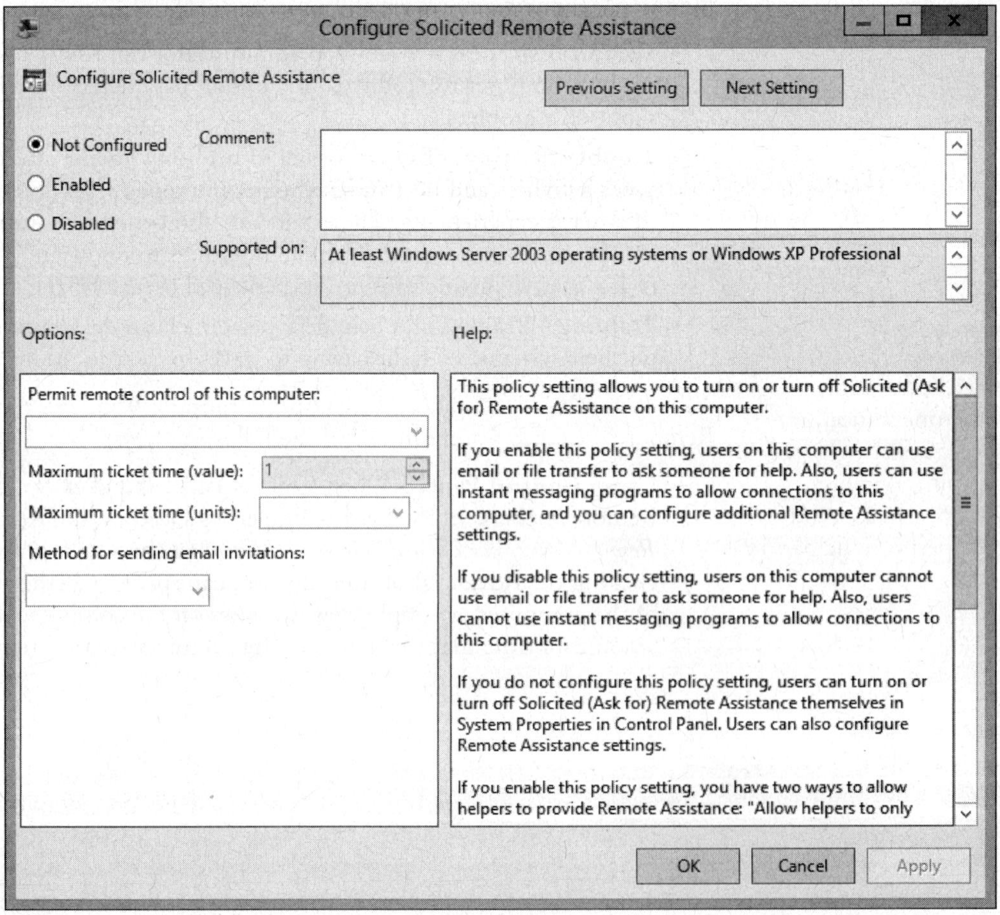

Remote Assistance policy also enables you to specify the degree of control the expert receives over the client computer, the duration of the invitation, and the method for sending email invitations. The Configure Offer Remote Assistance policy enables you to specify the names of users or groups that can function as experts, and whether those experts can perform tasks or just observe. You can also configure these same settings in Group Policy object (GPO) linked to an Active Directory Domain Services (AD DS) domain, site, or organizational unit object.

CREATING AN INVITATION

To request a Remote Assistance session, a client must issue an invitation and send it to a particular expert. The client can send the invitation using email, or save it as a file to be sent to the expert in some other manner. To create an invitation, use the following procedure:

TAKE NOTE* It is also possible for an expert to initiate a Remote Assistance connection to the client by specifying the client's computer name or IP address. However, Windows 8 cannot establish the session unless the client approves the connection.

CREATE AN INVITATION

GET READY. Log on to Windows 8 and then perform the following steps:

1. Open the *Windows Control Panel* and click **System and Security > Action Center > Troubleshooting > Get help from a friend**.

   The *Use Remote Assistance to contact someone you trust for help* page appears, as shown in Figure 13-4.

Figure 13-4

The *Use Remote Assistance to contact someone you trust for help* page in the Windows Remote Assistance wizard

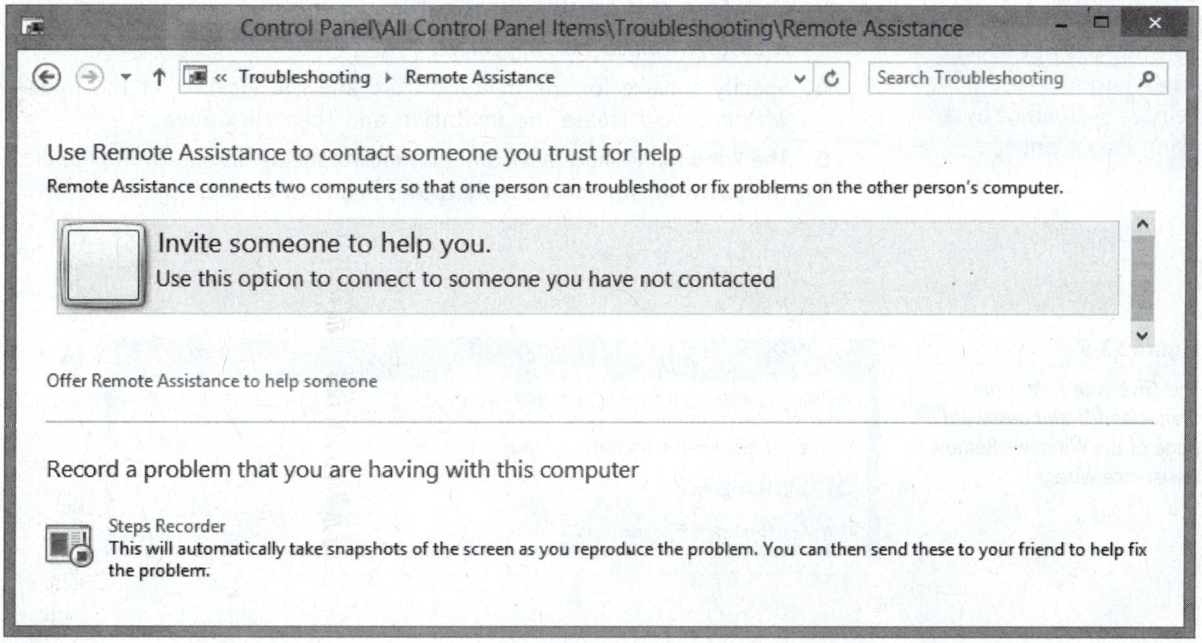

2. Click **Invite someone to help you**.

   The Windows Remote Assistance Wizard appears, displaying the *How do you want to invite your trusted helper?* page, as shown in Figure 13-5.

Figure 13-5

The *How do you want to invite your trusted friend to help you?* page in the Windows Remote Assistance wizard

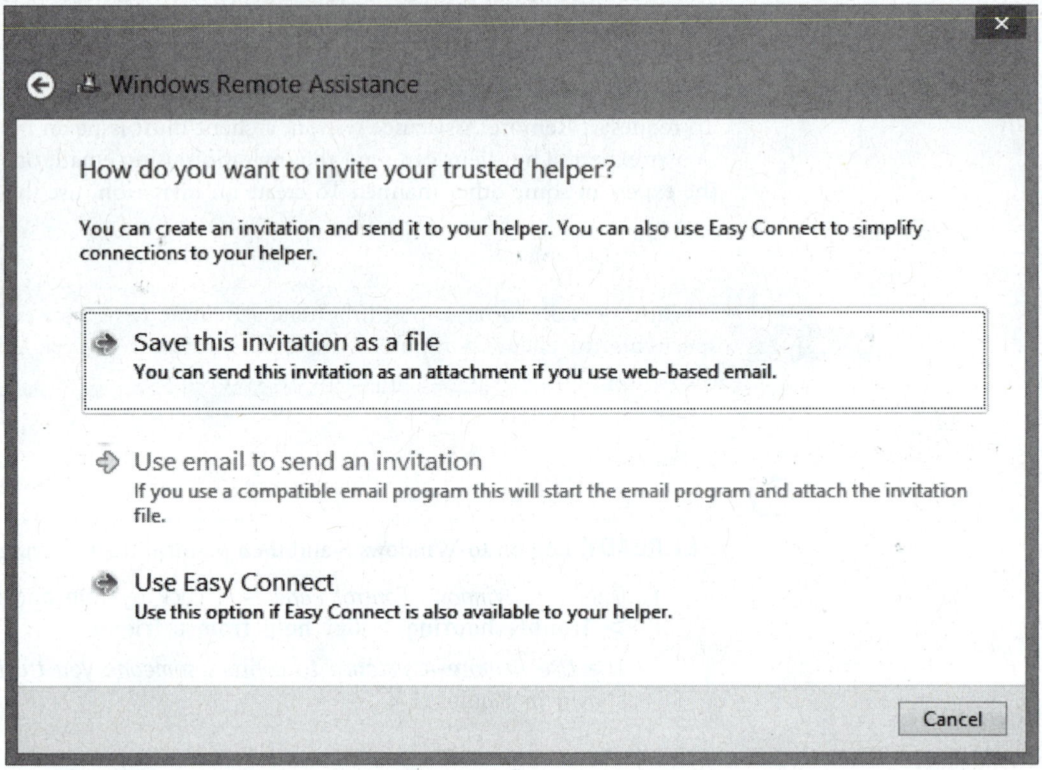

TAKE NOTE*

You can also opt to send an invitation to the helper via email or by using Easy Connect.

3. Click **Save this invitation as a file**.

   A *Save As combo* box appears.

4. Specify a name for the invitation file and the location of the folder in which the wizard should create the invitation and then click **Save**.

5. The Windows Remote Assistance window appears, as shown in Figure 13-6, displaying the password you must supply to the helper or expert.

Figure 13-6

The *Give your helper the invitation file and password* page of the Windows Remote Assistance wizard

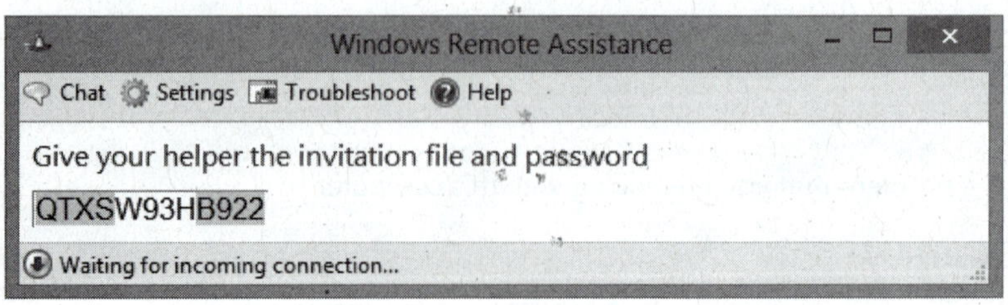

Once the expert receives the invitation, invoking it launches the Remote Assistance application, which enables the expert to connect to the remote computer. Using this interface, the user and the expert can talk or type messages to each other and, by default, the expert can see everything that the user is doing on the computer. If the client computer is configured to allow remote control, the expert can also click the Take Control button and operate the client computer interactively.

SECURING REMOTE ASSISTANCE

Because an expert offering remote assistance to another user can perform virtually any activity on the remote computer that the local user can, this feature can be a significant security hazard. An unauthorized user who takes control of a computer using Remote Assistance can cause almost unlimited damage. However, Remote Assistance is designed to minimize the dangers. Some of the protective features of Remote Assistance are as follows:

- **Invitations** – No person can connect to another computer using Remote Assistance unless that person has received an invitation from the client. Clients can configure the effective lifespan of their invitations in minutes, hours, or days to prevent experts from attempting to connect to the computer later.
- **Interactive connectivity** – When an expert accepts an invitation from a client and attempts to connect to the computer, a user must be present at the client console to grant the expert access. You cannot use Remote Assistance to connect to an unattended computer.
- ***Client-side control*** – The client always has ultimate control over a Remote Assistance connection. The client can terminate the connection at any time, by pressing the Esc key or clicking Stop Control (ESC) in the client-side Remote Assistance page.
- **Remote control configuration** – Using the System Properties sheet or the Remote Assistance Group Policy settings, users and administrators can specify whether experts are permitted to take control of client computers. An expert who has read-only access cannot modify the computer's configuration in any way using Remote Assistance. The group policies also enable administrators to grant specific users expert status, so that no one else can use Remote Assistance to connect to a client computer, even with the client's permission.
- **Firewalls** – Remote Assistance uses Transmission Control Protocol (TCP) port number 3389 for all its network communications. For networks that use Remote Assistance internally and are also connected to the Internet, it is recommended that network administrators block this port in their firewalls to prevent users outside the network from taking control of computers that request remote assistance. However, it is also possible to provide remote assistance to clients over the Internet, which would require leaving port 3389 open.

Using Remote Desktop

While Remote Assistance is intended to enable users to obtain interactive help from other users, ***Remote Desktop*** is an administrative feature that enables users to access computers from remote locations, with no interaction required at the remote site.

Remote Desktop is essentially a remote control program for Windows computers; there are no invitations and no read-only capabilities. When you connect to a computer using Remote Desktop, you can operate the remote computer as though you were sitting at the console and perform most configuration and application tasks.

MORE INFORMATION

One of the most useful application of Remote Desktop is to connect to servers, such as those in a locked closet or data center, that are not otherwise easily accessible. In fact, some administrators run their servers without monitors or input devices once the initial installation and configuration of the computer is complete, relying solely on Remote Desktop access for everyday monitoring and maintenance.

Remote Desktop is essentially an implementation of the Remote Desktop Services (formerly known as Terminal Services) technology built into the Windows server operating systems. When you use Remote Desktop Services on a server to host a large number of clients, you must purchase licenses for them. However, Windows 8 allows a single Remote Desktop connection for administrative purposes, without the need for a separate license.

The Remote Desktop Connection client communicates with a host computer using the ***Remote Desktop Protocol (RDP)***. This protocol essentially transmits screen information, keystrokes, and mouse movements between the two computers. Any applications you launch in the client are still running on the remote computer, using its processor, memory, and storage resources.

When you connect to a computer using Remote Desktop, you must log on, just as you would if you were sitting at the console, meaning that you must have a user account and the appropriate privileges to access the host system. After you log on, the system displays the desktop configuration associated with your user account, and you can then proceed to work as you normally would.

ACTIVATING REMOTE DESKTOP

By default, the Remote Desktop Services service that powers the server side of Remote Desktop is not started on computers running Windows 8. Before you can connect to a distant computer using Remote Desktop, you must start it using the controls on the Remote tab of the System Properties sheet, which you access from the Control Panel. Select the *Allow remote connections to this computer* option and, depending on your security needs, you can select the checkbox requiring Network Level Authentication.

TAKE NOTE*

Because Remote Desktop requires the remote user to perform a standard logon, it is inherently more secure than Remote Assistance, and needs no special security measures such as invitations and session passwords. However, you can also click Select Users in the Remote tab to display a Remote Desktop Users dialog box, in which you can specify the names of the users or groups that are permitted to access the computer using Remote Desktop. All users with Administrator privileges are granted access by default.

USING THE REMOTE DESKTOP CONNECTION CLIENT

In addition to the Remote Desktop Services service, Windows 8 includes the Remote Desktop Connection client program needed to connect to a host computer. To connect to a remote computer with the client, use the following procedure.

RUN THE REMOTE DESKTOP CLIENT

GET READY. Log on to Windows 8 and then perform the following steps:

1. On the Windows 8 computer, open the charms bar and then click **Search**.

   The *Search* bar appears.

2. With the Apps option selected, type **remote** and, in the results display, click **Remote Desktop Connection**.

   The Remote Desktop Connection dialog box appears, as shown in Figure 13-7.

Figure 13-7
The *Remote Desktop Connection* dialog box

3. Click **Show options**.

   The dialog box expands to show additional controls, as shown in Figure 13-8.

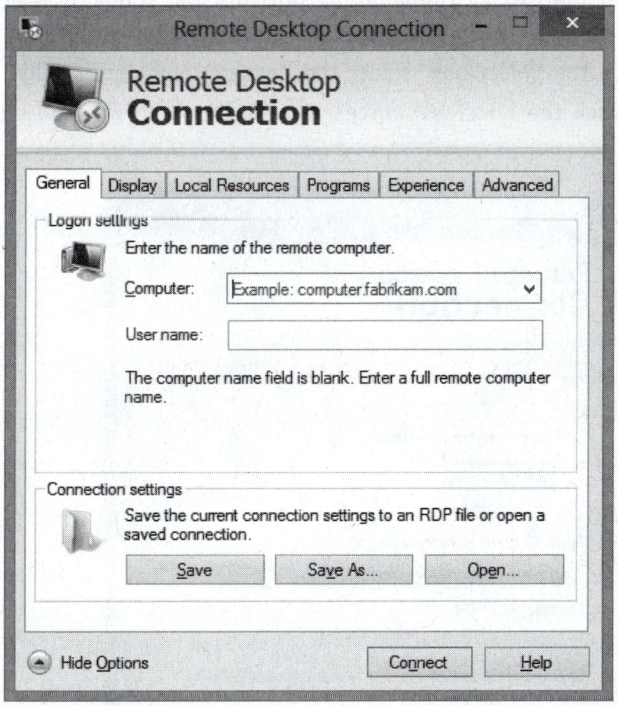

Figure 13-8
The General tab in the expanded *Remote Desktop Connection* dialog box

4. On the *General* tab, type the name of the host computer you want to access in the *Computer* text box. Then click the **Display** tab, as shown in Figure 13-9.

Figure 13-9

The Display tab in the *Remote Desktop Connection* dialog box

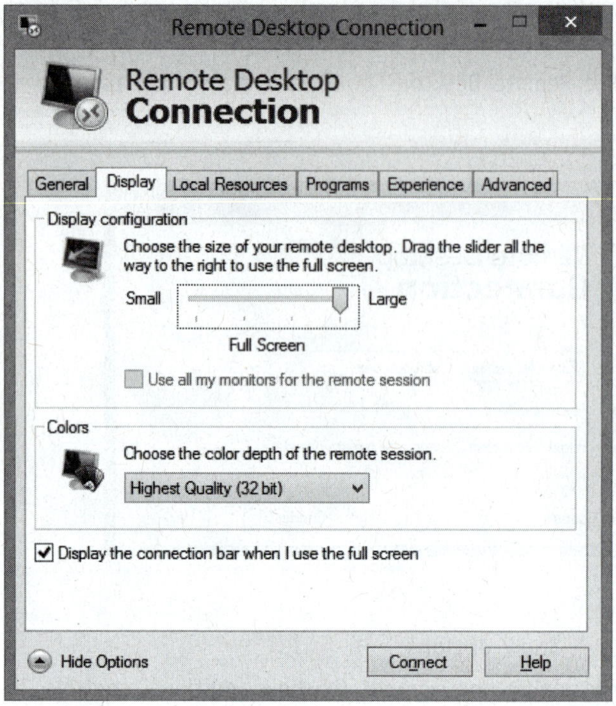

5. In the *Display configuration* box, use the slider to select the desired size for the image of the host computer's desktop that will appear on the client system.
6. In the *Colors* box, select the desired color depth using the dropdown list.
7. Click the **Local Resources** tab, as shown in Figure 13-10.

Figure 13-10

The Local Resources tab in the *Remote Desktop Connection* dialog box

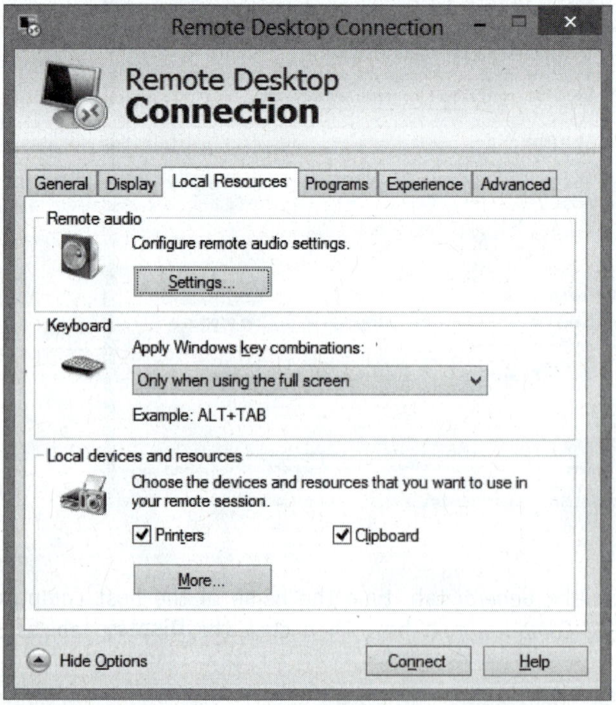

8. Using the controls provided, specify which of the resources on the remote computer you want to bring to your local computer, including sound, printers, clipboard, smart cards, serial ports, drives, and other Plug and Play devices.
9. In the *Keyboard* box, specify how you want the client to handle the Windows key combinations you press on your local computer.
10. Click the **Experience** tab, as shown in Figure 13-11.

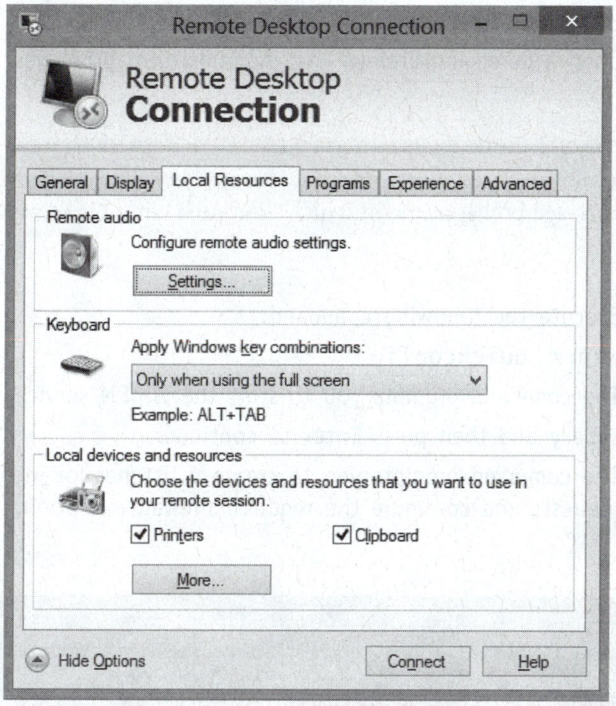

Figure 13-11

The Experience tab in the *Remote Desktop Connection* dialog box

On the *Experience* tab, you can enhance the performance of the Remote Desktop Connection client by eliminating nonessential visual effects from the display information transmitted over the network.

11. Select one of the network connection speeds from the dropdown list or choose the items you want to suppress by clearing their checkboxes.
12. Click **Connect** to initiate the connection process.

    A *Windows Security* dialog box appears.
13. Supply *User Name* and *Password* values to log on to the remote computer, and then click **OK**.

    A *Remote Desktop* window appears containing an image of the remote computer's desktop.

Using Windows Remote Management

Using Windows Remote Management, administrators can execute programs from the command line on remote computers without having to open a Remote Desktop session.

CERTIFICATION READY
Configure remote management settings
Objective 3.4

Windows Remote Management is a Windows 8 service that enables administrators to execute commands on remote computers, using Windows PowerShell or the Windows Remote Shell (WinRS.exe) command line program. However, Windows 8 does not start the service by default or configure the computer to allow remote management communications. To do this, you must complete the following procedure.

CONFIGURE REMOTE MANAGEMENT

GET READY. Log on to Windows 8 using an account with administrative privileges and then perform the following steps:

1. Open a Command Prompt with Administrator privileges.

TAKE NOTE* If you are working on a computer that is a member of a workgroup, a User Account Control message box appears, in which you must click Yes to continue.

2. Execute the following command:

   `winrm quickconfig`

   The command prompts you to start the WinRM service, as shown in Figure 13-12.
3. Type **y** and then press **Enter** to continue.

   The command prompts you to create a listener for incoming remote management requests and configure the required firewall exception.

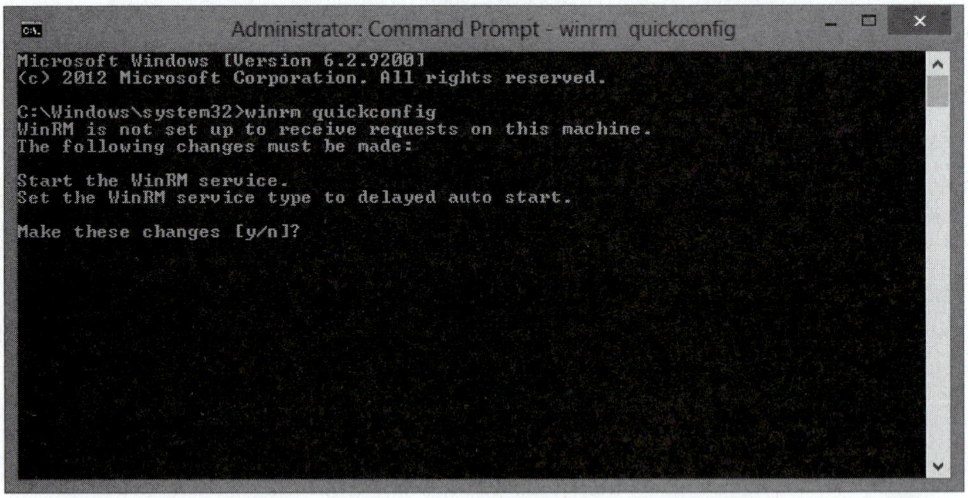

Figure 13-12
Starting the WinRM service

4. Type **y** and then press **Enter** to continue, as shown in Figure 13-13.

Figure 13-13

Configuring a listener and firewall exception

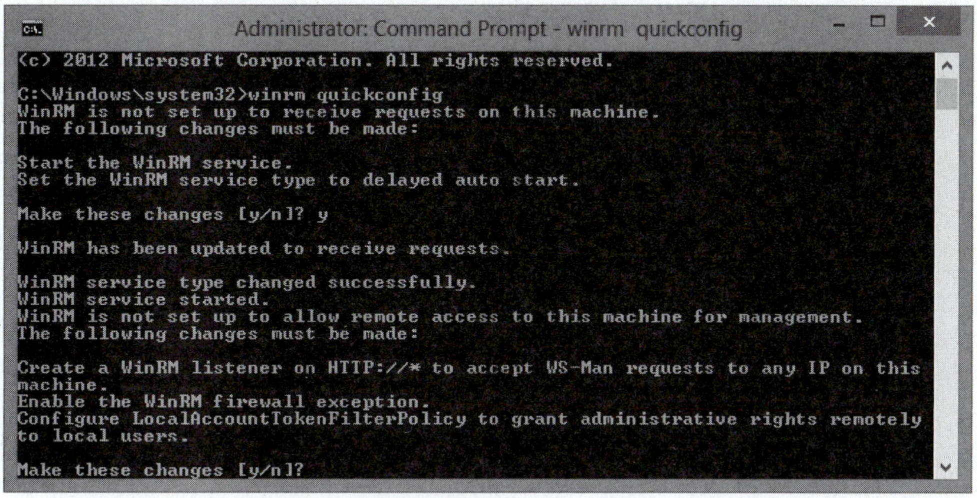

5. **Close** the *Administrator: Command Prompt* window.

TAKE NOTE*

The WinRM.exe program will fail to configure the required firewall exception if the computer's network location is set to Public. The computer must use either the Private or Domain location settings for the remote management configuration process to succeed.

In addition to this manual method, you can also configure Windows Remote Management using the Group Policy settings found in the Computer Configuration\Policies\Administrative Templates\Windows Components\Windows Remote Management (WinRM)\WinRM Service container of every Group Policy object (GPO), as shown in Figure 13-14.

Figure 13-14

Windows Remote Management Group Policy settings

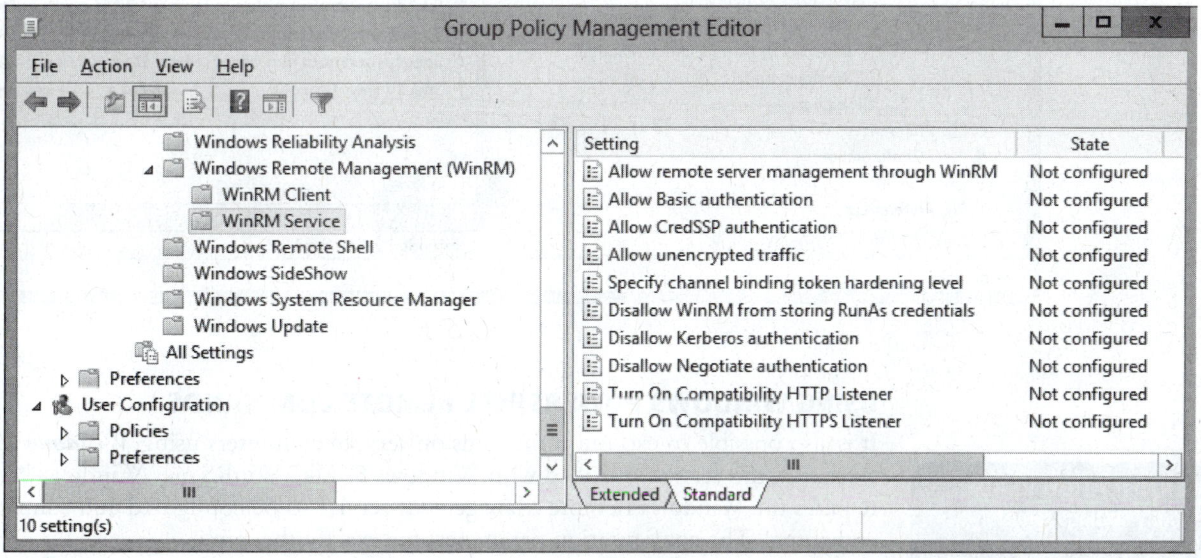

USING WINRS.EXE

Once you have configured the Remote Management service, you can execute commands on other computers that have been similarly configured. To execute a command from the Windows 8 command prompt, you must use the ***WinRS.exe*** program.

To use WinRS.exe, you frame the command you want to execute on the remote computer as follows:

```
winrs -r:computer [-u:user] [-p:password] command
```

- ***–r:computer*** – Specifies the name of the computer on which you want to execute the command, using a NetBIOS name or a fully qualified domain name (FQDN).
- ***-u:user*** – Specifies the account on the remote computer that you want to use to execute the command.
- ***-p:password*** – Specifies the password associated with the account specified in the –u parameter. If you do not specify a password on the command line, WinRS.exe prompts you for one before executing the command.
- ***command*** – Specifies the command (with arguments) that you want to execute on the remote computer.

You can configure the behavior of WinRS.exe using the Group Policy settings found in the Computer Configuration\Policies\Administrative Templates\Windows Components\Windows Remote Shell container of every Group Policy object (GPO), as shown in Figure 13-15.

Figure 13-15

Windows Remote Shell Group Policy settings

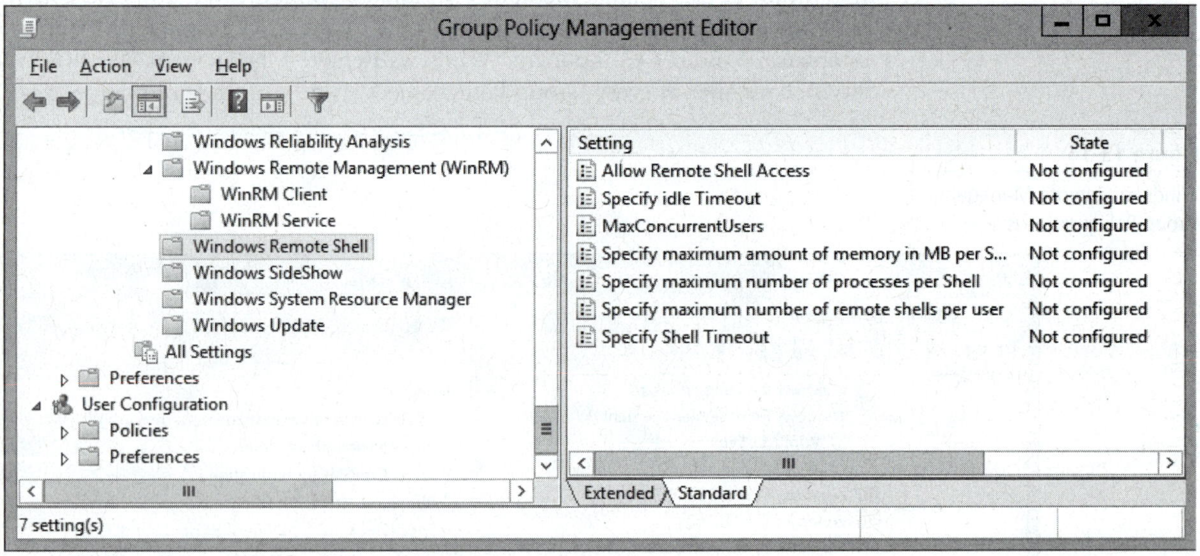

USING WINDOWS POWERSHELL REMOTE COMMANDS

CERTIFICATION READY
Modify settings remotely by using MMCs or Windows PowerShell
Objective 3.4

It is also possible to execute commands on remote computers using ***Windows PowerShell*** version 3, the version included with Windows 8. Like WinRS.exe, Windows PowerShell requires the Windows Remote Management service to be configured and running on both computers. The configuration parameters are exactly the same.

To execute a Windows PowerShell command on a remote computer, you must open an elevated Windows PowerShell session and use the following syntax:

```
icm computer {command}
```

- **computer** – Specifies the name of the computer on which you want to execute the command.
- **{command}** – Specifies the Windows PowerShell command you want to execute of the remote computer. The command must be enclosed in curly brackets.

MORE INFORMATION

The icm command is an alias for the Invoke-Command cmdlet, which you can use in its place, if desired. For information on the other parameters supported by the Invoke-Command cmdlet, see the help screens for the cmdlet.

SKILL SUMMARY

IN THIS LESSON, YOU LEARNED:

- The shortcuts to various Microsoft Management Console (MMC) tools that appear in Windows 8 are all configured to manage resources on the local system. However, many of the snap-ins supplied with Windows 8 enable you to manage other Windows computers on the network as well.
- Remote Assistance is a Windows 8 feature that enables an administrator, trainer, or desktop technician at one location to connect to a distant user's computer, chat with the user, and either view all the user's activities or take complete control of the system.
- Remote Desktop is an administrative feature that enables users to access computers from remote locations, with no interaction required at the remote site.
- Windows Remote Management is a Windows 8 service that enables administrators to execute commands on remote computers, using Windows PowerShell or the Windows Remote Shell (WinRS.exe).

Knowledge Assessment

Multiple Choice

Select one or more correct answers for each of the following questions.

1. Which of the following remote access solutions requires a user to be present at the remote site and allow the connection to be established?
   a. Remote Desktop
   b. Remote Assistance
   c. WinRM
   d. WinRS.exe
2. Which of the following are true statements regarding the capabilities of Remote Desktop connections? Select all that apply.
   a. Allows you to operate the remote computer as if you were sitting at its console.
   b. Requires a separate license for each connection.
   c. Communicates with the host computer over RDP.
   d. Requires that you have an account on the remote computer to access the system.

3. Which of the following use Windows Remote Management to execute commands on remote computers? Select all that apply.
   a. RDP
   b. WinRS.exe
   c. Windows PowerShell
   d. Remote Assistance

4. To receive remote help, the computer running Windows 8 can be configured to use remote assistance. Where can this setting be configured? Select all that apply.
   a. Control Panel > System and Security > System > Remote settings > Remote tab
   b. Using the Group Policy Object Editor snap-in
   c. Control Panel > System > Remote settings > Remote tab
   d. Control Panel > System and Security > Remote settings > Remote tab

5. Which of the following can be used to initiate a Remote Assistance session? Select all that apply.
   a. Create and send invitation via email.
   b. Create and send invitation via file.
   c. Accept an approve a remote assistance connection on the client computer.
   d. Through a chat session.

6. Which of the following are true statements regarding the use of snap-ins? Select all that apply.
   a. Not all snap-ins have the ability to connect to a remote computer.
   b. The Windows Firewall can block a snap-in's functionality.
   c. A single console can only manage one instance of each snap-in.
   d. A single console can be created that contains multiple instances of the same snap-in (e.g., Event Viewer).

7. Remote Assistance can provide which of the following benefits to administrative personnel?
   a. Installing of software.
   b. Observing a remote user's activities.
   c. Assisting a remote user who has lost connectivity to the Internet.
   d. Training end users on their local system.

8. Which of the following names are used to describe the person connecting to a client using Remote Assistance? Select all that apply.
   a. Remote Expert
   b. Expert
   c. Assistant
   d. Helper

9. Remote Assistance provides which of the following protective features? Select all that apply.
   a. Invitations
   b. Interactive connectivity
   c. Client-side control
   d. A valid user account on the client computer

10. Which command is used to start the Windows Remote Management service from a command prompt?
   a. `winrm quickconfig`
   b. `winrm startconfig`
   c. `win quickconfig`
   d. `winrm quickconfig/start`

Best Answer

Choose the letter that corresponds to the best answer. More than one answer choice may achieve the goal. Select the BEST answer.

1. Which tool would work best when it comes to passively observing and assisting a remote user as they attempt to learn a new program while still providing interactive assistance when necessary?
   a. Remote Desktop
   b. Remote Assistance
   c. Windows PowerShell
   d. WinRS.exe

2. An administrator has setup a remote computer for one of the company's employees. She knows the IP address and the computer's name. Which option would allow her to remotely assist the employee with the least amount of effort assuming the employee is currently sitting in front of their computer?
   a. Have the remote employee send an invitation via email.
   b. Have the remote employee send an invitation via chat.
   c. Have the remote employee call the administrator and then walk them through the setup of a Remote Assistance connection.
   d. Initiate a Remote Assistance connection to the remote employee's computer by specifying its name and IP address. Ask the remote employee to accept the connection.

3. A junior administrator would like the ability to take full control of a remote computer to perform a service pack upgrade. The computer is currently stored in a locked room in which she does not currently have the key. Which of the following options would ensure she can access the computer with the least amount of effort?
   a. Find someone who has a key to the room and ask them to let her in.
   b. Use Remote Desktop to connect to the server and perform the service pack upgrade.
   c. Configure the computer for Remote Assistance and then send an invitation to her email address.
   d. Contact the help desk and submit a ticket to upgrade the computer at a later date and time.

4. There are 25 Windows 8 computers on the Windows domain. You want to configure them for Remote Management. What is the most efficient way to accomplish this task?
   a. Visit each computer and run the `winrm quickconfig` command.
   b. Visit each computer and configure the Local Group Policy to start the Windows Remote Management service automatically.
   c. Use Remote Desktop to connect to each computer and run the `winrm quickconfig` command.
   d. Configure Windows Remote Management using Group Policy and apply it to the selected computers in the domain.

5. Which of the following best describes what happens if you attempt to connect to another computer using an MMC snap-in without the appropriate level of permissions on the target computer?
   a. The snap-in will not load
   b. The snap-in will load but you will not be able to read information from or modify settings on the target computer.
   c. The snap-in will load but you will have to provide the appropriate credentials to be able to read information from the target computer.
   d. The snap-in will load with read permission only but you will not be able to make any modifications to the target computer.

Matching and Identification

Complete the following exercise by matching the terms with their corresponding definitions.

_______ **a)** Remote Assistance
_______ **b)** WinRS.exe
_______ **c)** Remote Desktop
_______ **d)** Remote Desktop Protocol (RDP)
_______ **e)** Windows Remote Management
_______ **f)** Windows PowerShell
_______ **g)** Microsoft Management Console
_______ **h)** Invitation
_______ **i)** Invoke-Command
_______ **j)** TCP port number 3389

1. Administrative feature that enables users to access computers from remote locations, with no interaction required at the remote computer.
2. A service that enables administrators to execute commands on remote computers using Windows PowerShell or WinRS.exe.
3. Used to execute a command from the Windows 8 command prompt.
4. Used by Remote Assistance for all its network communications.
5. Provides an interface for system administrators to configure and monitor the local and remote systems.
6. Allows an expert/helper to chat and take control of a remote computer.
7. Transmits screen information, keystrokes and mouse movements between two computers.
8. A command line shell and scripting language.
9. The *icm* command is an alias for this cmdlet.
10. Sent by email, file, or chat to an Expert/Helper to get help.

Build a List

1. In order of first to last, specify the correct order of steps to create a Remote Assistance invitation.

_______ **a)** Open the *Windows Control Panel* and click **System and Security > Action Center > Troubleshooting > Get help from a friend**.
_______ **b)** Click **Save this invitation as a file.**
_______ **c)** The Windows Remote Assistance window appears displaying the password you must supply to the helper or expert.
_______ **d)** Click **Invite someone to help you.**
_______ **e)** Specify a name for the invitation file and the location of the folder in which the wizard should create the invitation and then click **Save.**

2. Specify the correct order of steps to run the Remote Desktop Client.

_______ **a)** On the Windows 8 computer, open the charms bar and then click **Search**.
_______ **b)** Click the **Experience** tab.
_______ **c)** Select one of the network connection speeds from the dropdown list or choose the items you want to suppress by clearing their checkboxes.
_______ **d)** In the *Keyboard* box, specify how you want the client to handle the Windows key combinations you press on your local computer.

_________ **e)** Using the controls provided, specify which of the resources on the remote computer you want to bring to your local computer.
_________ **f)** With the Apps option selected, type **remote** and, in the results display, click **Remote Desktop Connection**.
_________ **g)** Click **Connect** to initiate the connection process.
_________ **h)** On the *General* tab, type the name of the host computer you want to access in the Computer text box. Then click the **Display** tab.
_________ **i)** Supply *User Name* and *Password* values to log on to the remote computer, and then click **OK**. A Remote Desktop window appears containing an image of the remote computer's desktop.
_________ **j)** Click the **Local Resources** tab.
_________ **k)** In the *Display configuration* box, use the slider to select the desired size for the image of the host computer's desktop that will appear on the client system.
_________ **l)** In the Colors box, select the desired color depth using the dropdown list.
_________ **m)** Click **Show options**.

3. Specify the correct order of steps to configure Remote Management.
_________ **a)** Open a Command Prompt with Administrator privileges.
_________ **b)** Type **y** and then press **Enter** to continue.
_________ **c)** Type **y** and then press **Enter** to continue.
The command prompts you to create a listener for incoming remote management requests and configure the required firewall **exception**.
_________ **d)** Execute the following command: winrm quickconfig
The command prompts you to start the WinRM service.
_________ **e)** **Close** the *Administrator: Command Prompt* window.

Business Case Scenario

Scenario 13-1: Troubleshooting Remote Assistance

Joe is a new IT Director who is tasked with making sure his Windows 8 computer users can be assisted remotely. On his first day at the company, Joe was told that the Remote Assistance feature was not working for users after a new firewall was installed. What might be causing the problem and how should it be addressed?

14 LESSON

Configuring Shared Resources

70-687 EXAM OBJECTIVE

Objective 4.1 – Configure shared resources. This objective may include but is not limited to configure HomeGroup settings; configure file libraries; configure shared folder permissions; set up and configure SkyDrive; configure Near Field Communication (NFC); and configure shared printers.

Lesson Heading	Exam Objective
Sharing Files and Folders	
Understanding Folder Sharing in Windows 8	
Sharing with Homegroups	Configure HomeGroup settings
Using Libraries	Configure file libraries
Creating a Homegroup	
Joining a Homegroup	
Working with Homegroups	
Sharing the Public Folder	
Sharing a Folder	
Managing Share Permissions	Configure shared folder permissions
Combining Share and NTFS Permissions	
Using Skydrive	Set up and configure SkyDrive
Configuring Near Field Communication	Configure Near Field Communication (NFC)
Working with Printers	
Understanding the Windows Print Architecture	
Adding a Local Printer	
Sharing a Printer	Configure shared printers
Configuring Printer Security	
Accessing a Shared Printer	
Managing Documents	
Managing Printers	

KEY TERMS

homegroups
homegroup networking
libraries
local printer
Near Field Communication (NFC)
print device
print server
printer
printer control language (PCL)
printer driver
SkyDrive

Sharing Files and Folders

THE BOTTOM LINE

Windows 8 is capable of functioning as both a client and a server on a network, meaning that users can access files on other computers, as well as share files and folders on their own computers with other network users.

For network users to be able to access your files, you must first create a network share out of a specific drive or folder. Once you have created a share, users on the network can browse to it in Windows Explorer and access the files there, just as if they were on a local drive.

Understanding Folder Sharing in Windows 8

When compared with versions prior to Windows Vista, Windows 8 provides additional methods for sharing files and folders, as well as additional security mechanisms to protect the computer from intrusion.

Windows 8 provides three basic methods for sharing the files and folders on the computer: any folder sharing, public folder sharing, and homegroup sharing. Table 14-1 lists the capabilities of each sharing method.

The type of sharing method you elect to use depends on the size and formality of the network to which the computer is connected. For home users, homegroup networking is simple to set up and use. For small business networkers, Public folder sharing is often the easiest method, one that users can easily maintain for themselves on a day-to-day basis. For larger networks, Windows domain networks, or any network with more elaborate security requirements, any folder sharing is preferable.

Table 14-1

Windows 8 sharing features

Any Folder Sharing	Public Folder Sharing	Homegroup Sharing
Shares files from any location	Places all shared files in a single location	Shares files from their default library locations
Enables you to set different sharing permissions for individual network users	Uses the same sharing permissions for all network users	Enables you to set the same sharing permissions for all network users or set different sharing permissions for individual users
Access can be limited to network users with a user account and password on your computer	Access can be limited to network users with a user account and password on your computer	Access can be limited to network users with a user account and password on your computer
Individual users can be granted read-only or read/write access to the share	Can be configured as a read-only share or a read/write share	Individual users can be granted read-only or read/write access to the share
Shares files from their original locations	Requires you to copy or move files to be shared to the Public folder	Shares files from their original locations

Sharing with Homegroups

Homegroup networking is a Windows 8 feature that enables computers configured to use the Home network location to share the contents of their respective libraries among themselves.

Using ***homegroups***, Windows 8 users can share their documents, printers, pictures, music, and videos with other Windows 8 users connected to the same home network. A home network has a single read-only homegroup by default, with the individual users selecting what they want to share.

CERTIFICATION READY
Configure HomeGroup Settings
Objective 4.1

Homegroups are relatively limited, when compared to any folder sharing, because you can only share the contents of the libraries in the user's profile. However, compared to Public folder sharing, homegroups don't require users to copy or move files to a Public folder.

In the default homegroup networking configuration, all of the users that join the homegroup have read-only access to all of the libraries the other users have elected to share. However, it is possible for each user to configure the system to provide read/write access, and to share libraries only with specific users.

TAKE NOTE*

Homegroups are designed to share only libraries, but you can extend their capabilities by adding to Windows 8's default libraries. As mentioned in Chapter 1, "Introducing Windows 8," libraries are virtualized folders that enable users to access files from different locations as if they were all in the same place. The Windows 8 libraries point to the standard user profile folders by default, but you can add additional locations to a library as well, and any files at those locations appear in Windows Explorer as part of the library, even though they remain in their original places.

Using Libraries

The redesigned File Explorer interface in Windows 8 retains much from its Windows Explorer predecessors in Windows 7 and Windows Vista,

When you open a File Explorer window in Windows 8, the most immediately identifiable new feature in the default view is the ribbon-style control bar shown in Figure 14-1, much like those in Microsoft Office 2010 and 2013. The left pane retains the Favorites and Libraries folders from earlier versions, as well as the traditional Computer and Network folders.

Figure 14-1

A File Explorer window

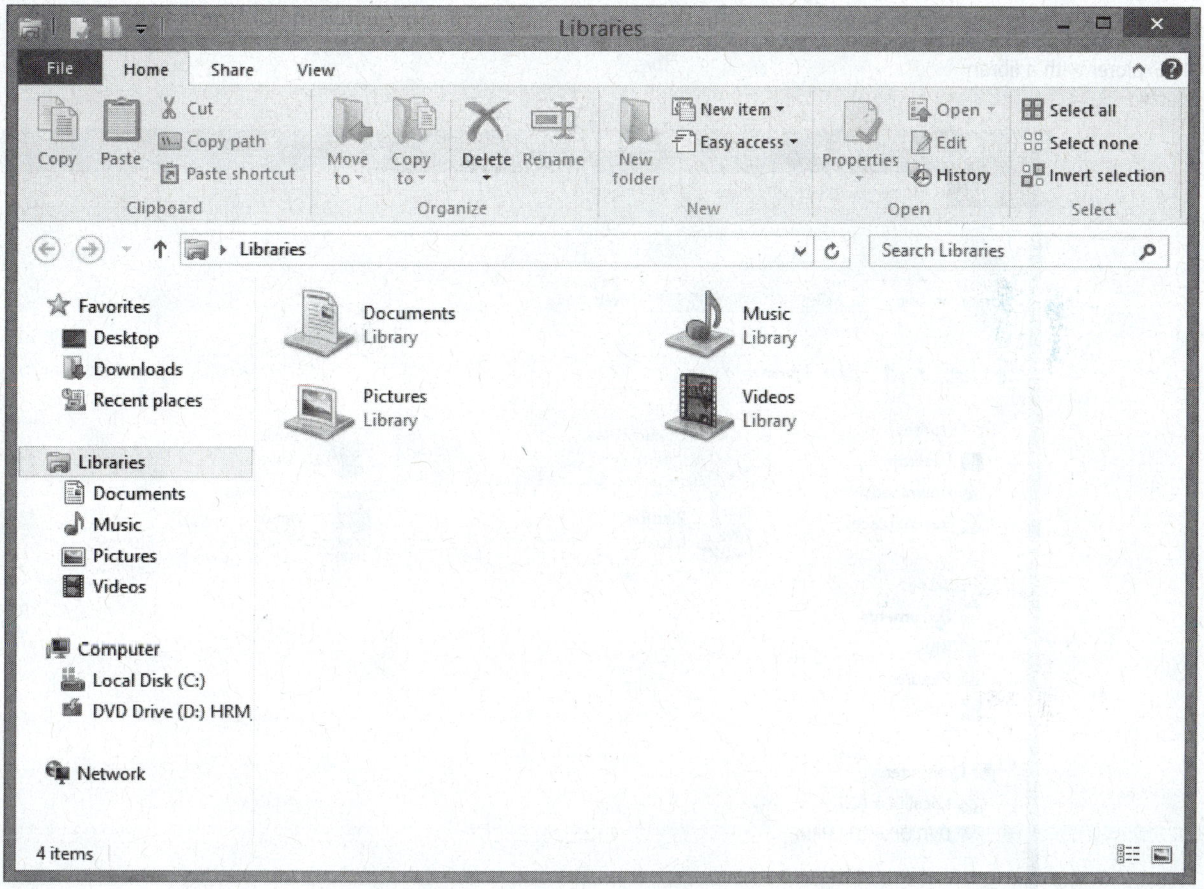

CERTIFICATION READY
Configure file libraries
Objective 4.1

Libraries enable users to aggregate files in multiple locations – and even on multiple computers – into a single folder that makes them appear as though they are all on a local drive. By default, File Explorer has four libraries, called Documents, Music, Pictures, and Videos. Users can also create as many additional libraries as they need.

Each library consists of one or more locations, and each location is a folder on the local or a network computer. For example, the Documents library has two locations: the user's My Documents folder and the Public Documents folder. When you look at the Documents library, you see the files in both locations.

If you add more locations to the library, the files in those locations appear in the library as well. In every library, one of the locations is designated as the save location; this is where files go that the user saves to the library.

To add your own locations to a library, use the following procedure.

ADD LIBRARY LOCATIONS

GET READY. Log on to Windows 8 using an account with Administrator privileges. If you plan to add network folders to the library, make sure that Network Discovery and File and Printer Sharing all turned on. Then perform the following steps:

1. Open **File Explorer** and select the **Libraries** folder.
2. Select one of the four library icons in the right pane.

   A *Manage* menu appears with a *Library Tools* header, as shown in Figure 14-2.

Figure 14-2

File Explorer with a library selected

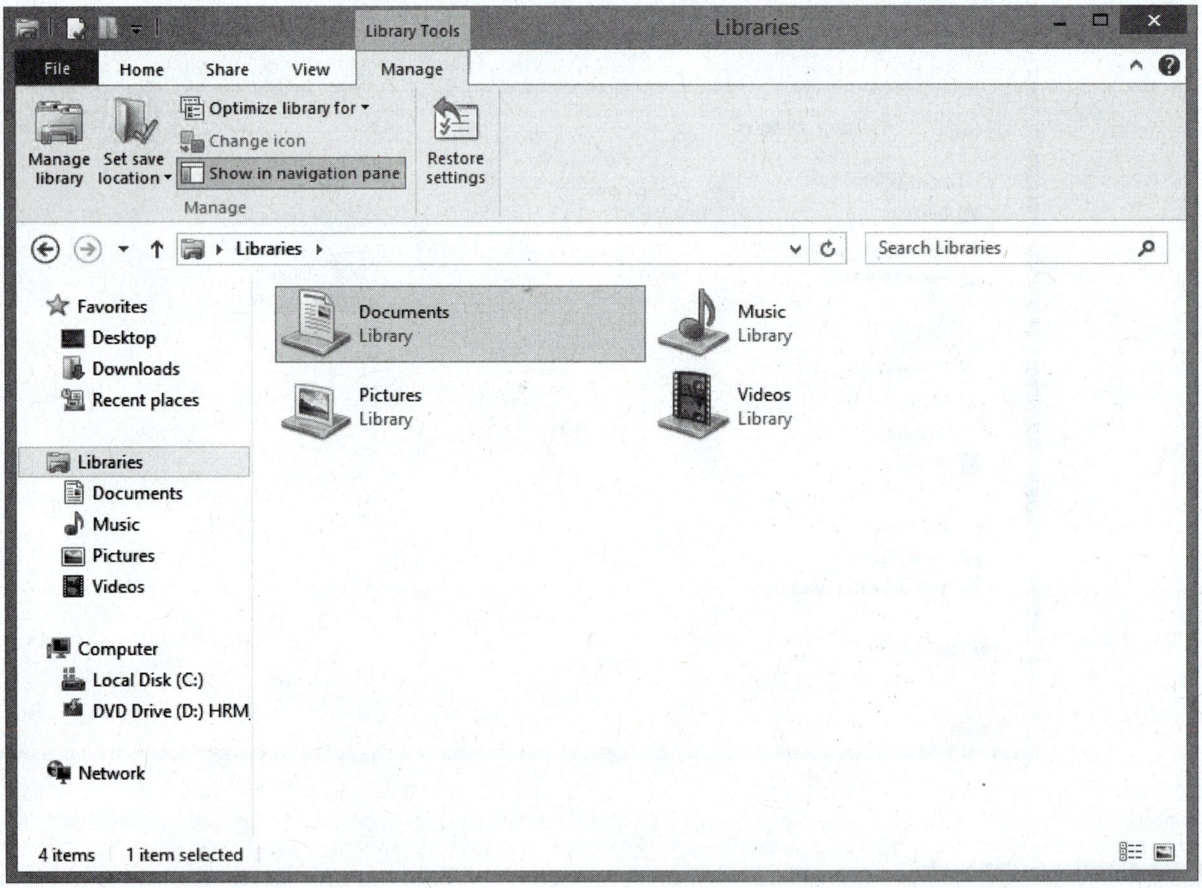

3. Click the **Manage Library** button in the ribbon.

   The Library Locations dialog box appears for the library you selected, as shown in Figure 14-3.

Figure 14-3

The *Library Locations* dialog box

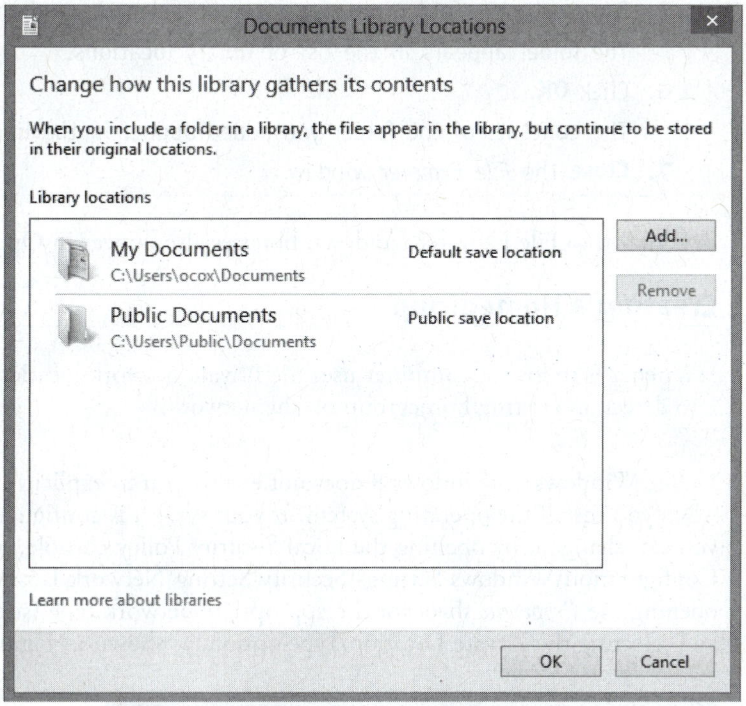

4. Click **Add**.

An Include Folder combo box appears for the library you selected, as shown in Figure 14-4.

Figure 14-4

The *Include Folder* combo box

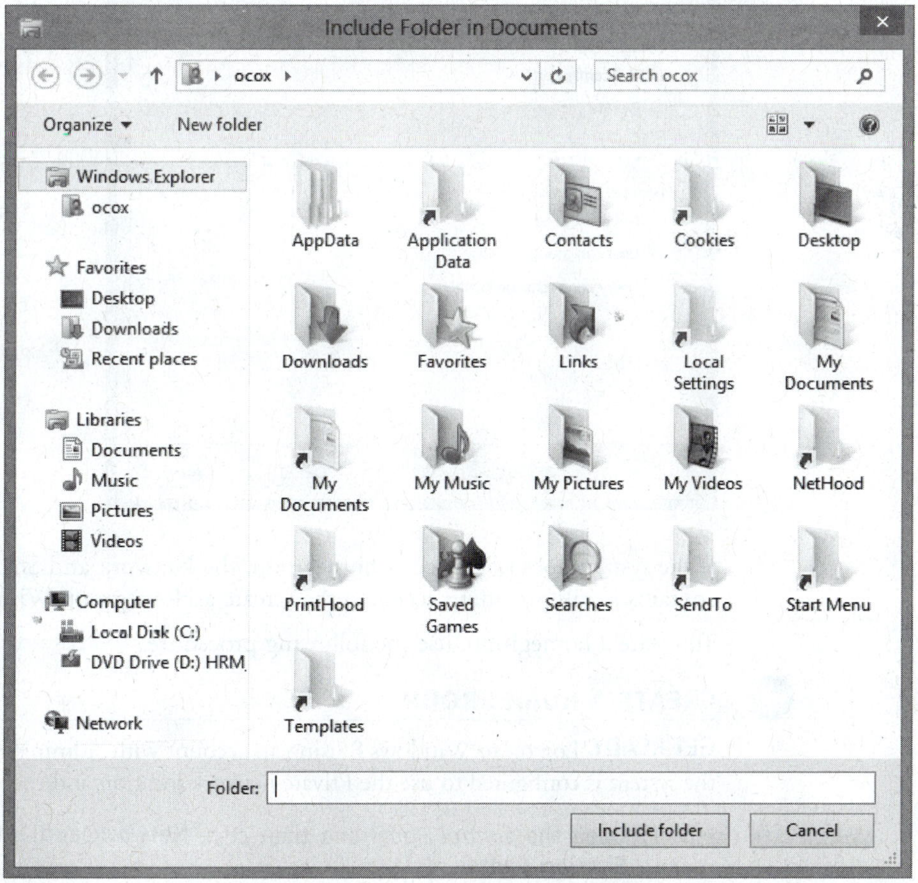

TAKE NOTE*

Any folder you add to a library in Windows 8 must be indexed. If you attempt to added a folder that cannot be indexed, an error message appears.

5. Browse to the folder you want to add, select it, and then click **Include Folder**.

   The folder appears in the list of library locations.

6. Click **OK**.

   The contents of the folder you added appear in the library.

7. **Close** the *File Explorer* window.

In addition to File Explorer windows, libraries also appear in Open and Save As combo boxes.

Creating a Homegroup

When a Windows 8 computer uses the Private network location, the computer attempts to detect an existing homegroup on the network.

Unlike Windows 7, Windows 8 does not enable you to explicitly select a network location when you install the operating system. If your system is configured to use the public location, you can change it by opening the Local Security Policy console, browsing to the Computer Configuration\Windows Settings\Security Setting\Network List Manager Policies folder, opening the *Properties* sheet for the appropriate network type (such as Unidentified Network) and selecting the Private Location Type option, as shown in Figure 14-5.

Figure 14-5

The *Unidentified Network Properties* sheet

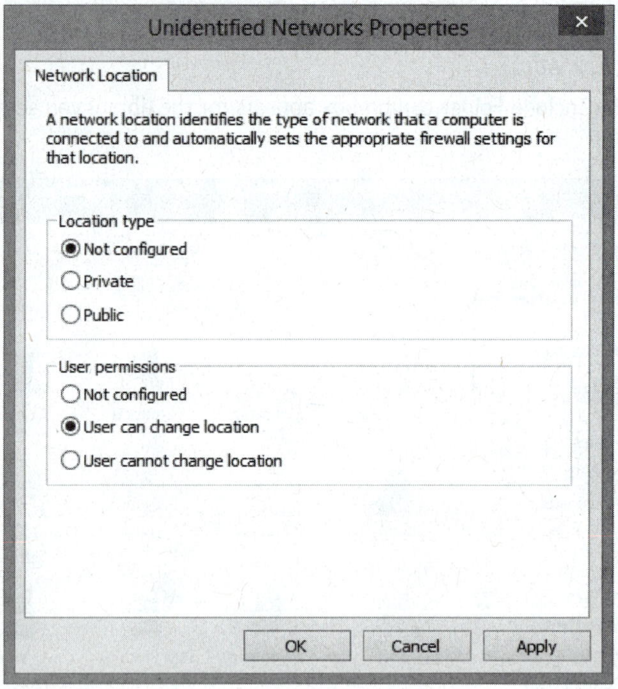

If the system does not detect a homegroup, the Network and Sharing Center control panel contains a link providing access to the Create a Homegroup Wizard.

To create a homegroup, use the following procedure.

CREATE A HOMEGROUP

GET READY. Log on to Windows 8 using an account with Administrator privileges. Make sure that the system is configured to use the Private network location and then perform the following steps:

1. Open the *Control Panel* and then click **Network and Internet > Network and Sharing Center**.

   The *Network and Sharing Center* control panel appears.

2. Click the **HomeGroup** link.

   The HomeGroup control panel appears, as shown in Figure 14-6.

Figure 14-6

The *HomeGroup* control panel, with no HomeGroup installed

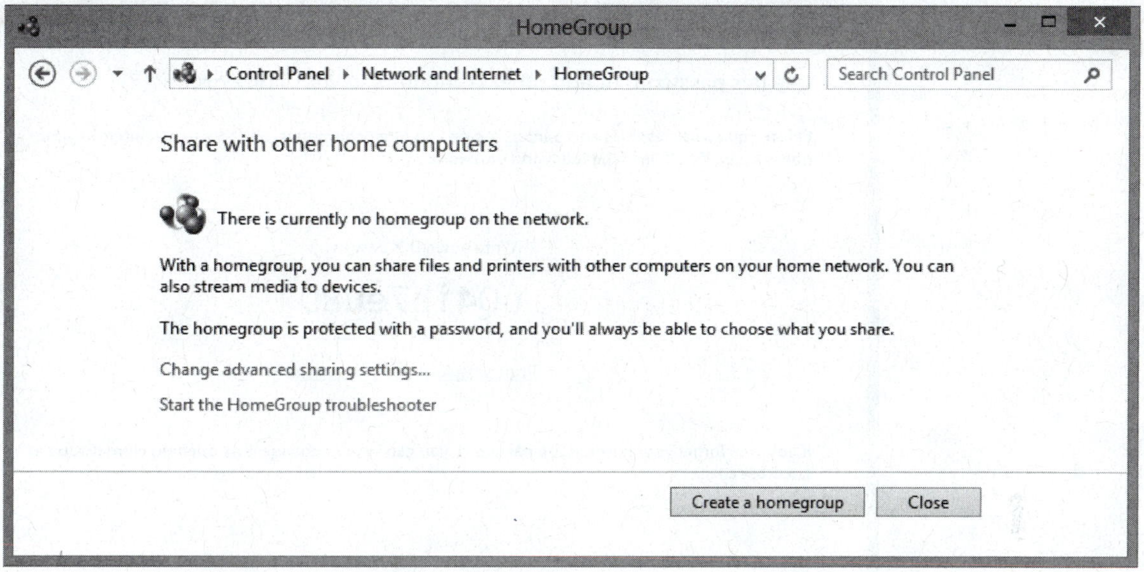

3. Click Create a **HomeGroup**.

   The *Create a HomeGroup* wizard appears.

4. Click **Next**.

   The *Share with other homegroup members* page appears, as shown in Figure 14-7.

Figure 14-7

The *Share with other homegroup members* page

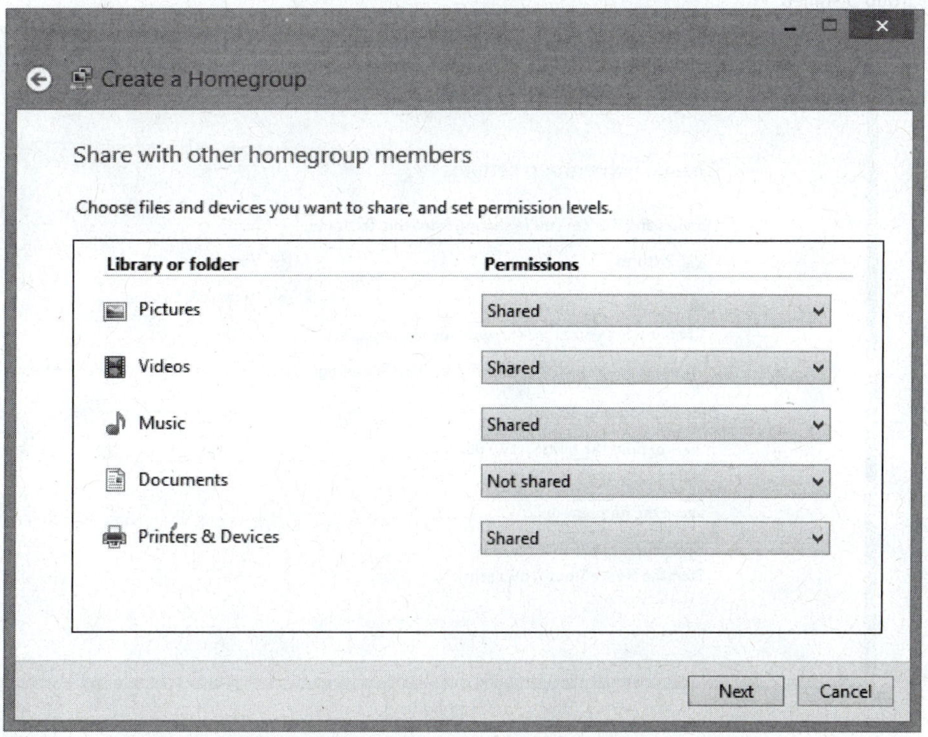

5. Select the libraries that you want to share and then click **Next**.

   The wizard creates the homegroup and assigns it a password. The *Use this password to add other computers to your homegroup* page appears, as shown in Figure 14-8.

Figure 14-8

The *Use this password to add other computers to your homegroup* page

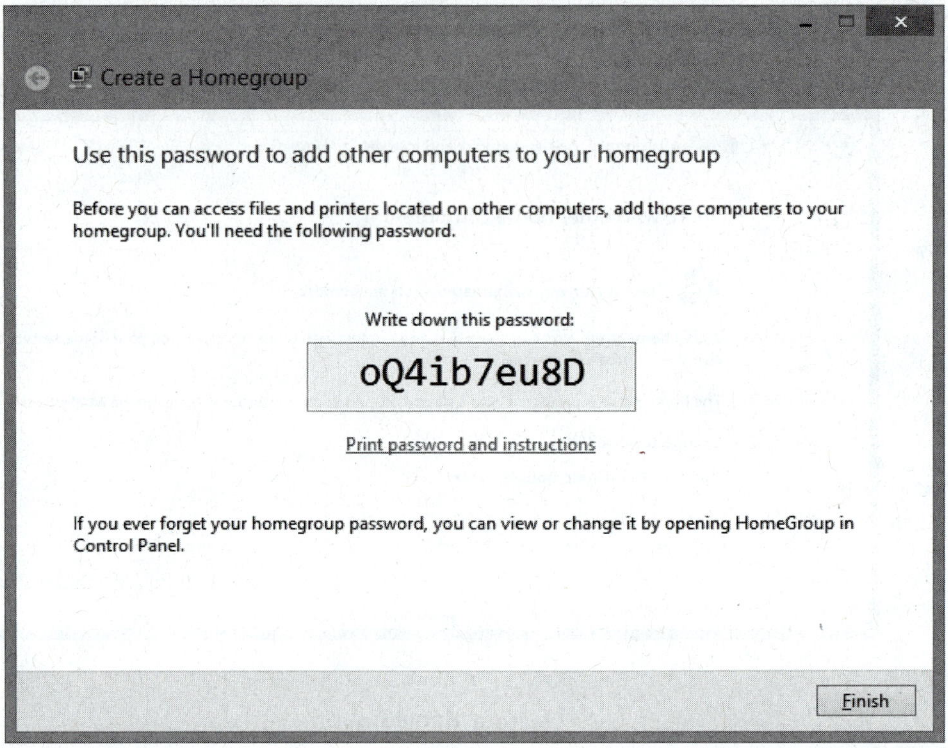

6. Click **Finish**.

   The wizard closes and the HomeGroup control panel changes to reflect its current status, as shown in Figure 14-9.

Figure 14-9

The *HomeGroup* control panel, with a HomeGroup installed

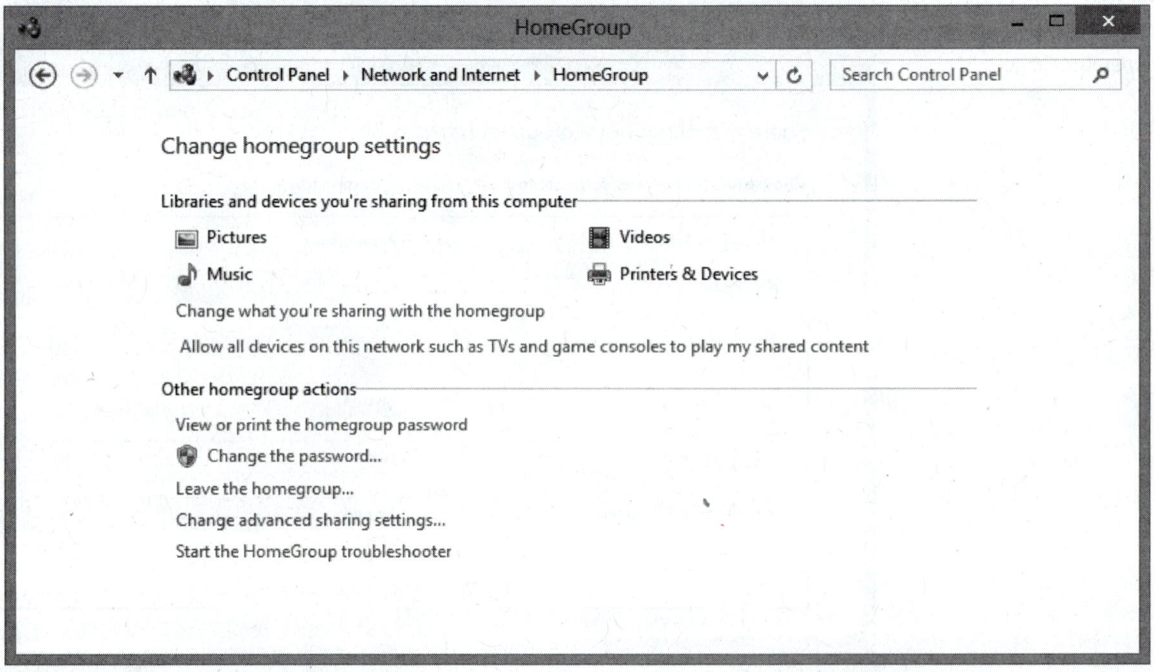

Joining a Homegroup

When a Windows 8 computer using the Private network location does detect a homegroup on the network, the Network and Sharing Center control panel appears with an Available to Join link, as shown in Figure 14-10.

Figure 14-10

The *Network and Sharing Center*, with *Available to join* link

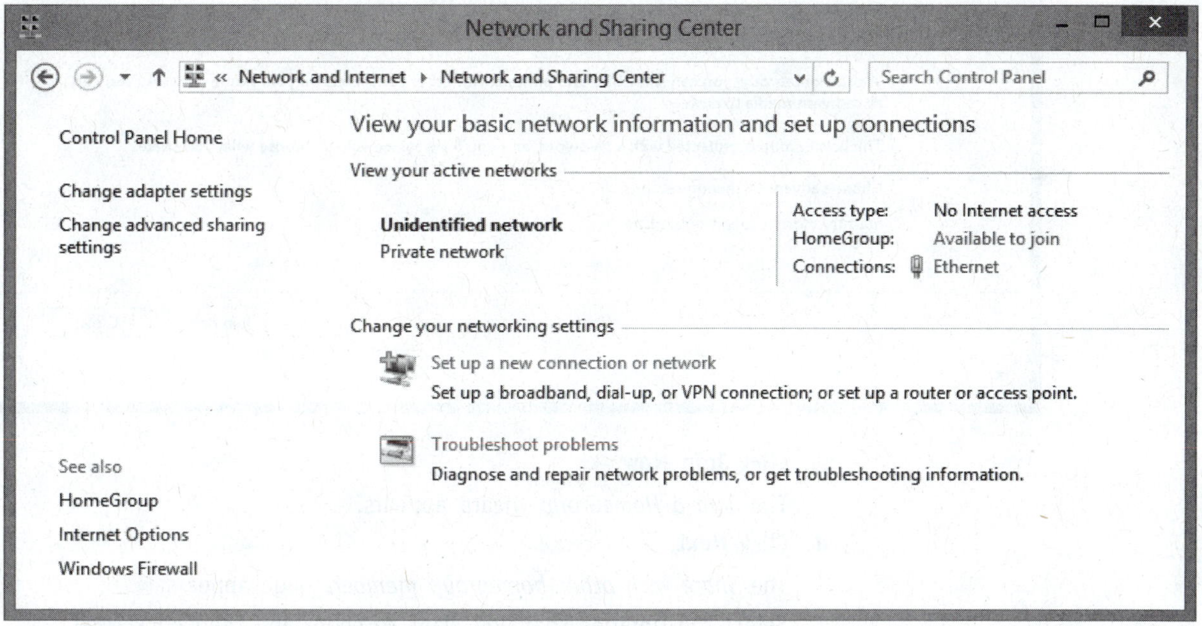

To join an existing homegroup, use the following procedure.

JOIN A HOMEGROUP

GET READY. Log on to Windows 8 using an account with Administrator privileges. Make sure that the system is configured to use the Private network location and then perform the following steps:

1. Open the *Control Panel* and click **Network and Internet > Network and Sharing Center**.

   The *Network and Sharing Center* control panel appears.

2. Click the **HomeGroup** link.

   The HomeGroup control panel appears, as shown in Figure 14-11.

Figure 14-11

The *HomeGroup* control panel, showing the homegroup found on the network

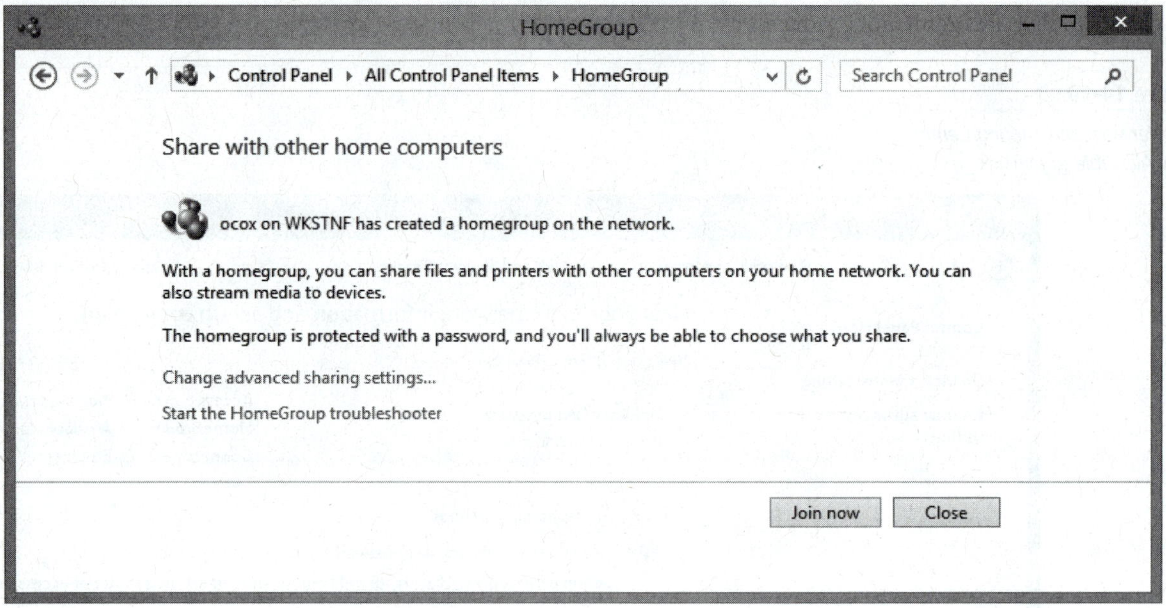

3. Click **Join Now**.

   The *Join a HomeGroup* wizard appears.

4. Click **Next**.

   The *Share with other homegroup members* page appears.

5. Select the libraries that you want to share and then click **Next**.

   The *Type the homegroup password* page appears, as shown in Figure 14-12.

Figure 14-12

The *Type the homegroup password* page

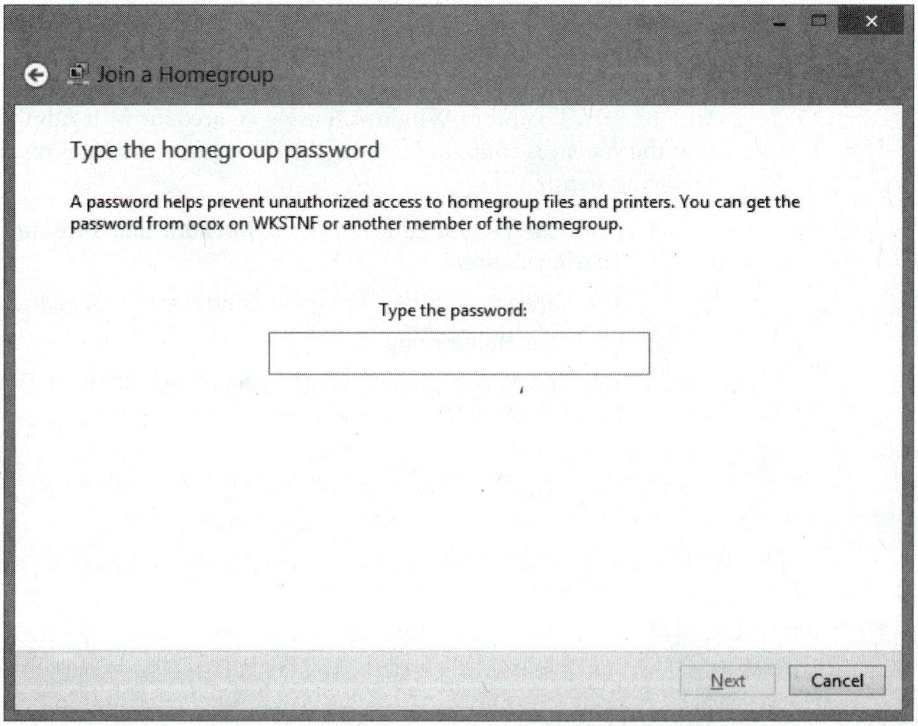

6. In the *Type the password* text box, type the password supplied by the *Create a HomeGroup* wizard and then click **Next**.
7. The *You have joined the homegroup* page appears.
8. Click **Finish**.

   The wizard closes and the HomeGroup control panel changes to reflect its current status.

Working with Homegroups

Once you have joined a computer to a homegroup, the shared libraries of the other computers on the network appear in File Explorer in the Homegroup container, as shown in Figure 14-13.

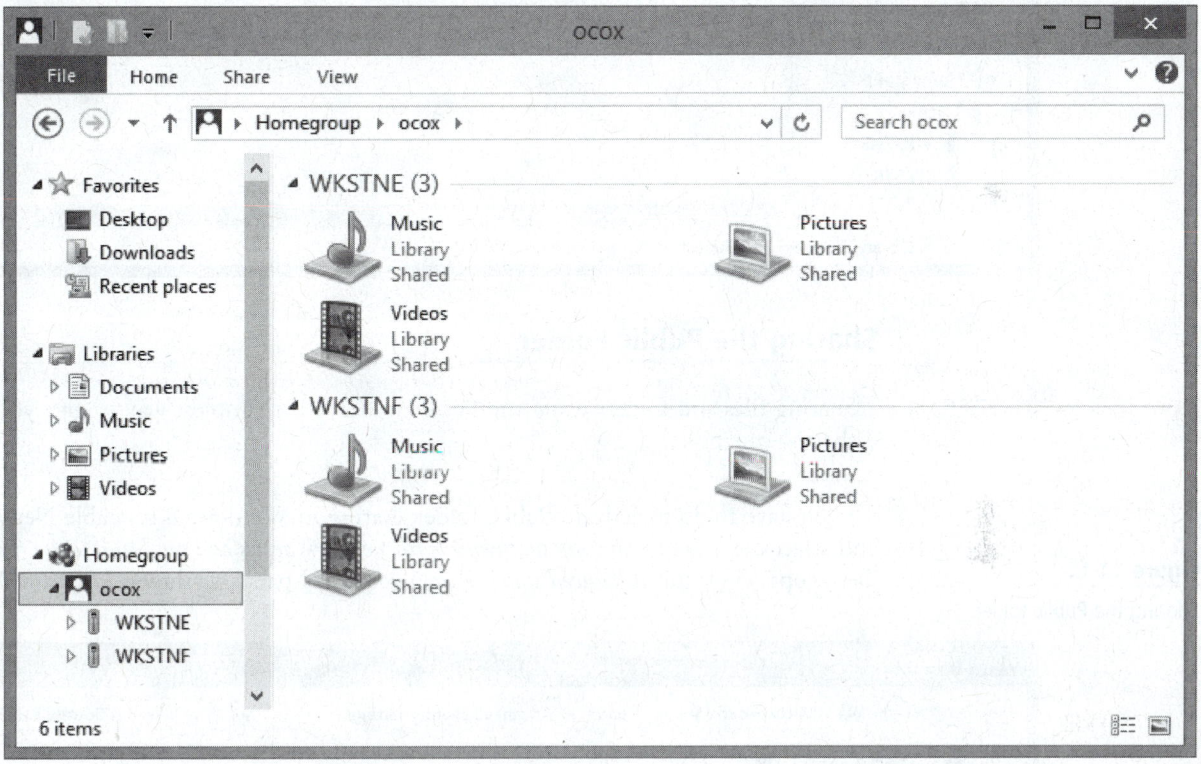

Figure 14-13

Homegroup shares in File Explorer

To modify the default homegroup sharing configuration, you can select one of your shared libraries in File Explorer and click Share in the toolbar, as shown in Figure 14-14. Using the controls that appear in the ribbon, you can change other homegroup users' access to the library from Read to Read/Write. You can also limit access to specific homegroup users, or prevent anyone on the network from accessing that library.

Figure 14-14

Modifying homegroup sharing

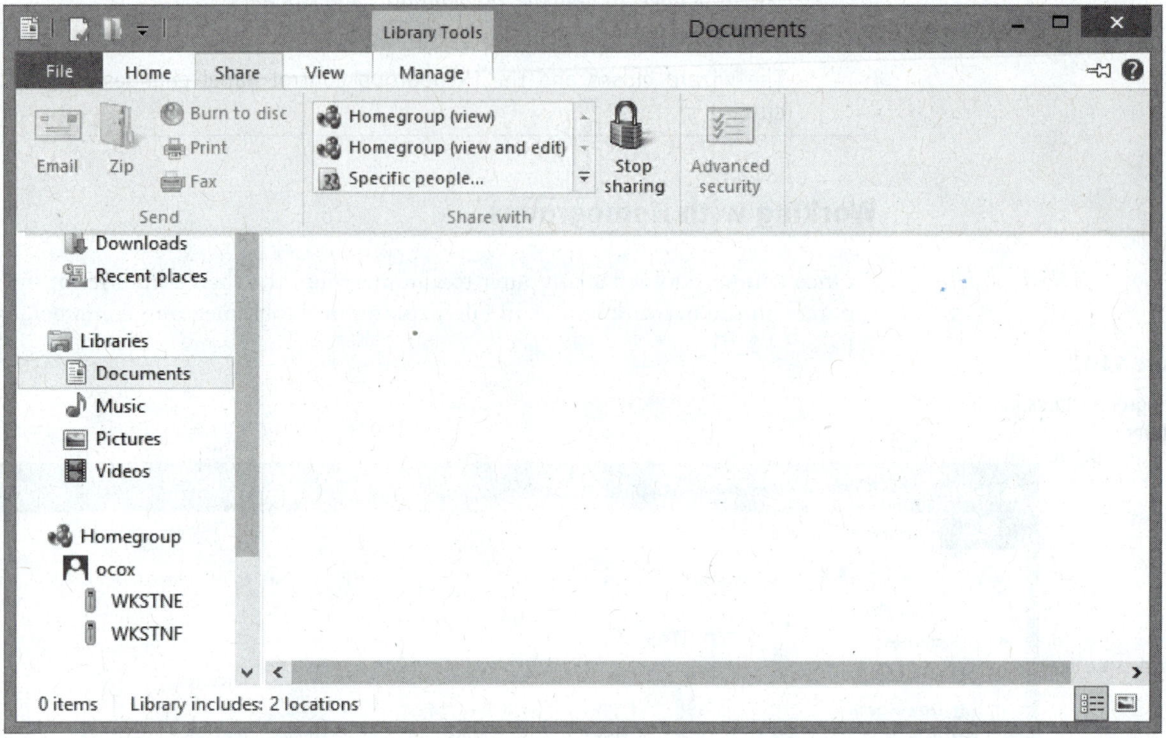

Sharing the Public Folder

Sharing files and folders using the Public folder is the simplest way to give your clients file sharing capability.

All you have to do to activate Public folder sharing in Windows 8 is enable Network Discovery and select the *Turn on sharing so anyone with network access can read and write files in the Public folders* option on the *Advanced sharing settings* control panel, as shown in Figure 14-15.

Figure 14-15

Sharing the Public folder

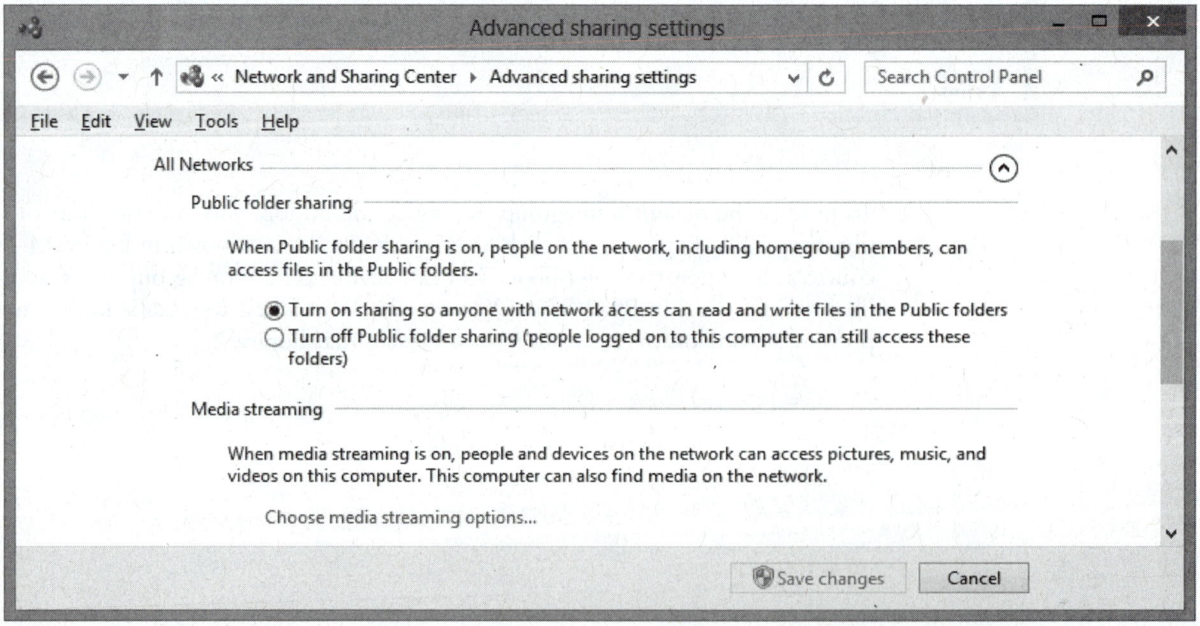

Once you have done this, any files and folders that the user copies to the Public folder are automatically shared. Users on other network computers can browse to the Public share on the client's computer and access any of the files placed there.

If you turn on the password protected sharing option on the same page, only users with accounts on that computer can access the contents of the public folder. Turning off that option provides access to anyone.

Sharing a Folder

The real power and flexibility of Windows 8 file sharing is found in the any folder sharing capability.

With any folder sharing, you have full control over what material on the computer is shared, which users are permitted to access the shared material, and what degree of access each user is granted.

To share a folder on a Windows 8 computer, use the following procedure.

SHARE A FOLDER

GET READY. Log on to Windows 8 using an account with Administrator privileges. Make sure that Network Discovery, File and Printer Sharing, and Password Protected Sharing are all turned on. Then perform the following steps:

1. Open **File Explorer** and expand the **Computer** node and the **Local Disk (C:)** drive.
2. Right-click a folder on the C: drive and, from the context menu, select **Properties**. The folder's *Properties* sheet appears.
3. Click the **Sharing** tab to display the interface shown in Figure 14-16.

Figure 14-16

The Sharing tab of a folder's *Users Properties* sheet

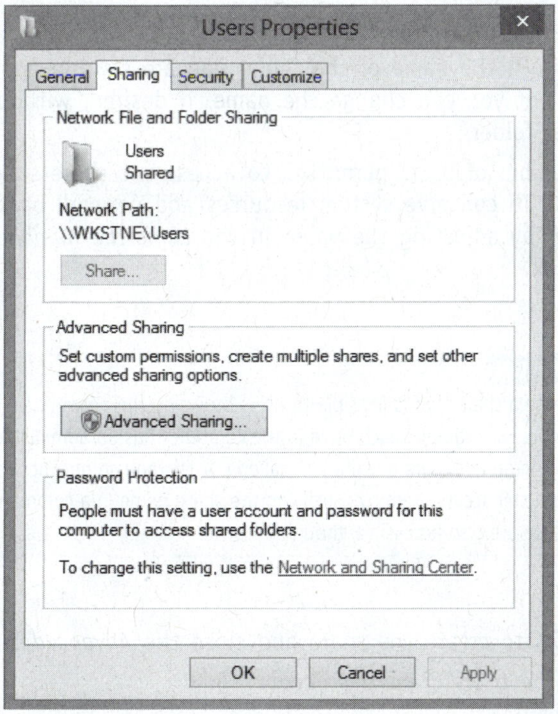

4. Click **Advanced Sharing**.

   The *Advanced Sharing* dialog box appears, as shown in Figure 14-17.

Figure 14-17

The *Advanced Sharing* dialog box

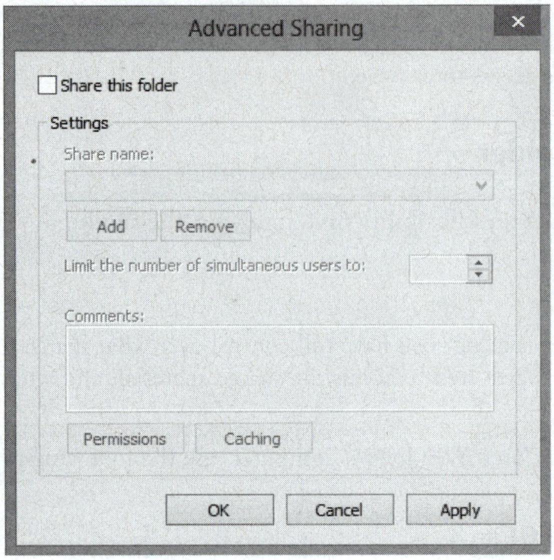

MORE INFORMATION

If you click Share on the Sharing tab, or if you right-click a folder and select Share from the context menu, Windows 8 takes you to the File Sharing Wizard, which is a simplified method for creating a share. The wizard is designed for end users and provides a limited set of features, as well as a means for informing network users that a new share is available. Administrators will usually want to use the Advanced Sharing interface. It is possible to disable the wizard entirely by clearing the Use Sharing Wizard checkbox on the View tab of the Folder Options control panel.

5. Select the **Share this folder** checkbox.

   By default, the name of the folder you are sharing appears as the name of the share, but you can change the name, if desired, without affecting the name of the original folder.

6. The number of users permitted to access the share simultaneously is 20 by default. To conserve system resources and network bandwidth, you can reduce this number by adjusting the value in the *Limit the number of simultaneous users to* spin box.

MORE INFORMATION

It is possible to create a share that is invisible to users browsing the network simply by appending a dollar symbol ($) to the share name. For example, each drive in the computer has an administrative share that the setup program creates during the operating system installation, called C$, D$, and so on. These shares do not appear in File Explorer, but you can still access them by specifying the share name in a command line. Any additional hidden shares that you create are also accessible, though invisible.

7. Click **OK** to create the share and close the *Advanced Sharing* dialog box.
8. **Close** the *Users Properties* sheet.

If you return to File Explorer and browse to the computer in the Network container, you can now see the shared folder there, as shown in Figure 14-18.

Figure 14-18

A File Explorer window displaying a new share

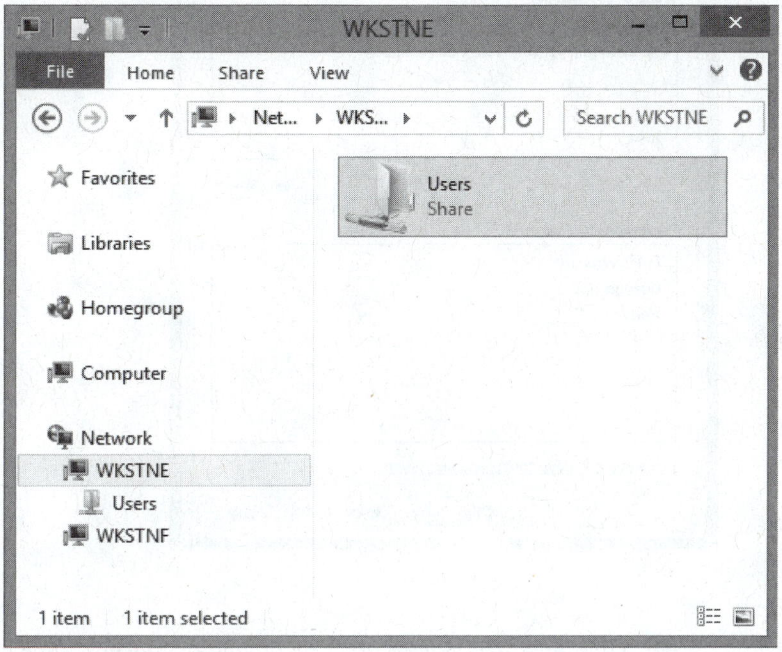

Managing Share Permissions

Windows 8 shares have their own permission system, which is completely independent from the other Windows permission systems.

CERTIFICATION READY
Configure shared folder permissions
Objective 4.1

For network users to access shares on a Windows 8 computer with Password protected sharing enabled, they must have user accounts on the sharing computer (or in a domain to which both computers are joined) and you must grant them the appropriate permissions.

To set share permissions, use the following procedure:

SET SHARE PERMISSIONS

GET READY. Log on to Windows 8 using an account with Administrator privileges. Make sure that Network Discovery, File Sharing, and Password Protected Sharing are all turned on and then perform the following steps:

1. Open **File Explorer** and browse to the folder you shared earlier.
2. Right-click the shared folder and, from the context menu, select **Properties**. The folder's *Properties* sheet appears.
3. Click the **Sharing** tab and then click **Advanced Sharing**.

   The *Advanced Sharing* dialog box appears.
4. Click **Permissions**.

   The *Permissions* dialog box for the folder appears, as shown in Figure 14-19. As with all of the Windows permission systems, the top half of the dialog box lists the security principals that have been granted permissions, and the bottom half displays the permissions granted to the selected principal.

Figure 14-19

The *Permissions for Users* dialog box for a shared folder

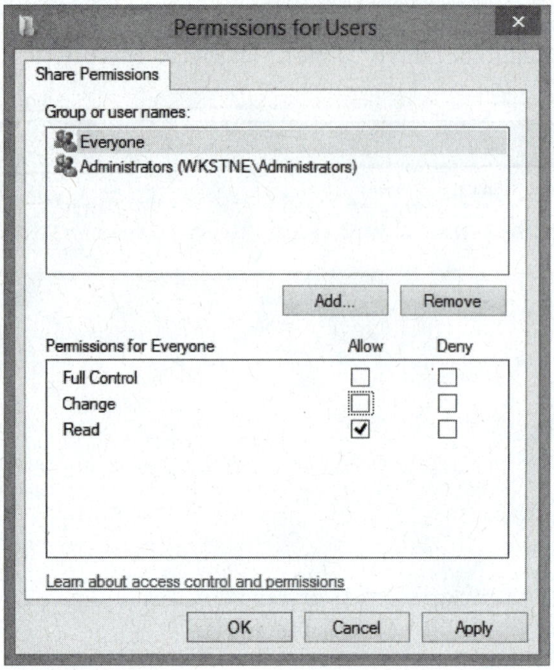

5. Click **Add**. The *Select Users or Groups* dialog box appears.
6. In the *Enter the object names to select* text box, type the name of the security principal you want to add and click **OK**.

   The user or group is added to the *Group or user names* list.
7. In the Permissions list for the user or group, select or clear the checkboxes to **Allow** or **Deny** the user any of the permissions shown in Table 14-2.

Table 14-2

Share Permissions and Their Functions

Share Permission	Allows or Denies Security Principals the Ability to:
Read	• Display folder names, file names, file data, and attributes • Execute program files • Access other folders within the shared folder
Change	• Create folders • Add files to folders • Change data in files • Append data to files • Change file attributes • Delete folders and files • Perform all actions permitted by the Read permission
Full Control	• Change file permissions • Take ownership of files • Perform all tasks allowed by the Change permission

8. Click **OK** to close the *Permissions* dialog box.
9. Click **OK** to close the *Advanced Sharing* dialog box.
10. Click **Close** to close the folder's *Users Properties* sheet.

When assigning share permissions, be aware that they do not combine in the same way that NTFS permissions do. If you grant Alice the Allow Read and Allow Change permissions to the C:\Test Folder share, and at a later time deny her all three permissions to the C:\ share, the Deny permissions prevent her from accessing the any files on the C:\ share, but she can still access the C:\Test Folder share because of the Allow permissions. In other words, the C:\Test Folder share does not inherit the Deny permissions from the C:\ share.

Combining Share and NTFS Permissions

It is crucial for desktop technicians to understand that the NTFS and share permission systems are completely separate from each other, and that for network users to access files on a shared NTFS drive, they must have both the correct NTFS and the correct share permissions.

The share permission system is the simplest of the Windows permission systems, and provides only basic protection for shared network resources. Share permissions provide only three levels of access, compared to the far more complex system of NTFS permissions. Generally speaking, network administrators prefer to use either NTFS or share permissions, but not both.

TAKE NOTE*

The *Effective Access* display in the Advanced Security Settings dialog box shows only the effective NTFS permissions, not the share permissions that might also constrain the user's access.

Share permissions provide limited protection, but this might be sufficient on some small networks. Share permissions are also the only alternative on a computer with FAT32 drives, because the FAT file system does not have its own permission system as NTFS does.

On networks already possessing a well-planned system of NTFS permissions, share permissions are not really necessary. In this case, you can safely grant the Full Control share permission to Everyone, and allow the NTFS permissions to provide security. Adding share permissions to the mix only complicates the administration process, without providing any additional security.

Using SkyDrive

THE BOTTOM LINE

SkyDrive is Microsoft's personal, cloud-based storage service. Every user who applies for a Microsoft account receives free cloud storage. You can use this storage to back up local files, to share files with your other devices, or to share files with other users. SkyDrive is also where Windows 8 stores the personalization settings that you choose to sync using your Microsoft account.

Users can access their SkyDrive storage space is several ways, including the following:

CERTIFICATION READY
Set up and configure SkyDrive
Objective 4.1

- **Through the web** – By browsing to http://skydrive.com and logging on with your Microsoft account, you can access your storage space directly, as shown in Figure 14-20. Using this interface, you can manage your files, perform uploads and downloads, and even open your files in web-based versions of Microsoft Office applications.

Figure 14-20

The Microsoft SkyDrive website

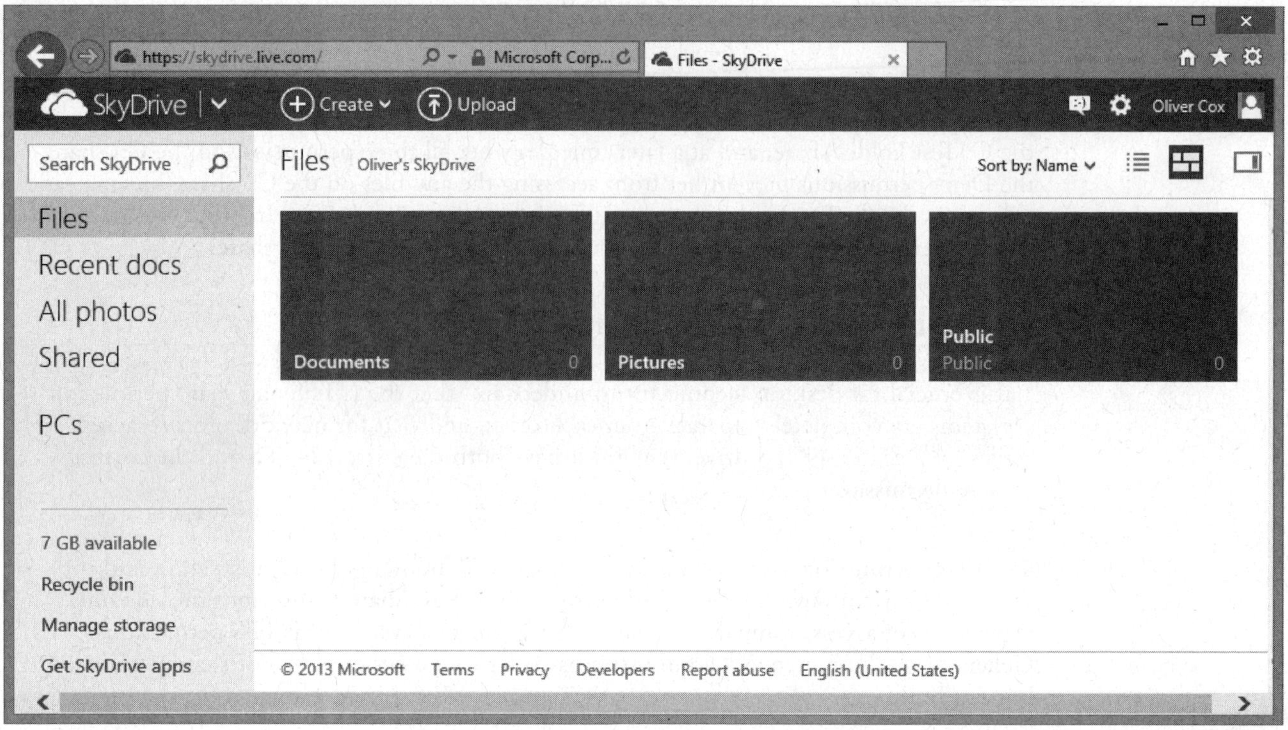

- **Through the SkyDrive desktop app** – When you install the SkyDrive desktop app, it creates a folder in your user profile on the local drive, and installs a program that synchronizes the contents of that folder with your SkyDrive space in the cloud. You simply drop files into your SkyDrive folder and the app automatically uploads them to your storage space. You can install the app on multiple computers, so that they all maintain the latest versions of your files. To manage your storage and control the app, right-click the SkyDrive icon in the notification area, which provides access to the dialog box shown in Figure 14-21.

Figure 14-21

The *Microsoft SkyDrive* dialog box

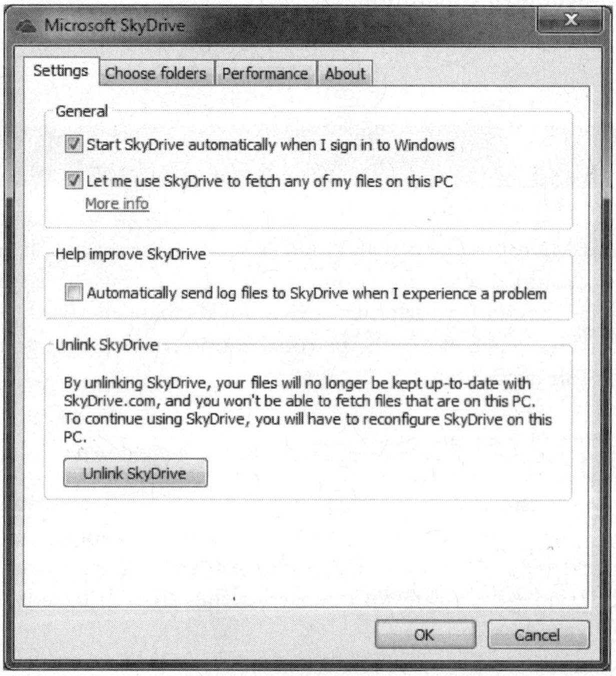

- **Through a desktop application** – Many software developers are incorporating SkyDrive into the storage options for their applications. For example, Microsoft Office 2013 enables you to access files directly from your SkyDrive space, as shown in Figure 14-22, and save revised versions there. When an application is designed to access SkyDrive directly, the synchronization app is not needed.

Figure 14-22

SkyDrive access in Microsoft Office 2013

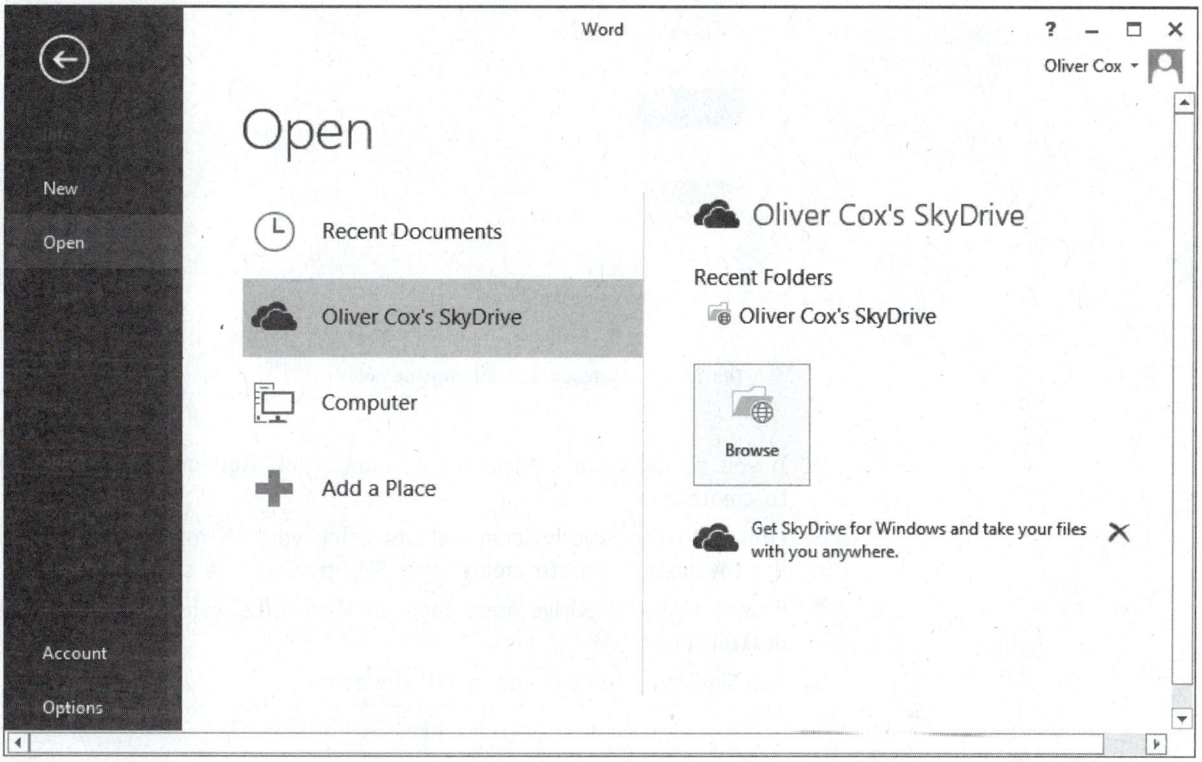

To fully implement SkyDrive on a computer running Windows 8, you must complete the following tasks.

IMPLEMENT SKYDRIVE ON WINDOWS 8

GET READY. Log on to Windows 8 and then perform the following steps:

1. Open **Internet Explorer** and then browse to SkyDrive's website, as shown in Figure 14-23.

Figure 14-23

The SkyDrive.com website

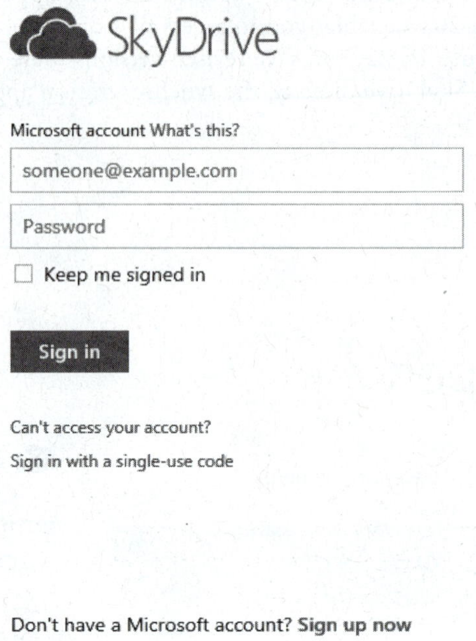

2. If you do not have a Microsoft account, click **Sign up now** and fill out the form to create one.
3. Log on to the Skydrive.com website using your Microsoft account and then following the instructions to create your SkyDrive storage space.
4. Browse to the SkyDrive apps page on Microsoft's website and download the desktop app.
5. Run SkyDriveSetup.exe and install the app.

Configuring Near Field Communication (NFC)

THE BOTTOM LINE

Near field communication (NFC) is a low-speed, close-proximity, radio-based communication technology that is based on existing radio-frequency identification (RFID) standards.

CERTIFICATION READY
Configure Near Field Communication (NFC)
Objective 4.1

Windows 8 includes API support for NFC, but as of this writing, there are no user-configurable settings available in the operating system, nor are there applications or devices on the market that are designed to use the Windows 8 NFC implementation.

NFC is designed for brief transactions, typically between portable devices, or between a portable device and a base station. Envisioned applications include setup transactions for Bluetooth and Wi-Fi networks, small purpose commerce transactions, and brief exchanges of identity credentials, such as business cards and network IDs. As with RFID implementations, the NFC standards include support for transactions between a base station and an unpowered device, called a "tag."

Working with Printers

THE BOTTOM LINE

The printer is one of the most common external devices you find connected to a PC. To manage printers in Windows 8, you work with the Devices and Printers control panel or the Print Management snap-in for Microsoft Management Console (MMC).

Windows 8, like the other Windows versions, provides a great deal of flexibility in its handling and management of printers. As a client, a Windows 8 computer can have a print device directly attached to one of its ports, or it can access a device located elsewhere on the network. Windows 8 can also function as a print server, enabling other users on the network to send print jobs to the computer, which feeds them to a printer. The following sections examine the various printer functions possible with Windows 8.

Understanding the Windows Print Architecture

Printing in the Windows environment involves a number of different roles and components, and the names used to refer to these roles and components can sometimes be confusing. You can avoid confusion by making sure that you understand the terms used for the print components and how they work together.

Printing in Microsoft Windows typically involves the following four components:

- **Print device** – A ***print device*** is the actual hardware that produces hard copy documents on paper or other print media. Windows 8 supports both *local print devices*, which are directly attached to the computer's parallel, serial, Universal Serial Bus (USB), or IEEE 1394 (FireWire) ports, or *network interface print devices*, which are connected to the network, either directly or through another computer.
- **Printer** – In Windows parlance, a ***printer*** is the software interface through which a computer communicates with a print device. Windows 8 supports numerous interfaces, including parallel (LPT), serial (COM), USB, IEEE 1394, Infrared Data Access (IrDA), and Bluetooth ports, and network printing services such as lpr, Internet Printing Protocol (IPP), and standard TCP/IP ports.

TAKE NOTE*

The most common misuse of the Windows printing vocabulary is the confusion of the terms printer and print device. Many sources use the term printer to refer to the printing hardware, but in Windows, the two are not equivalent. For example, you can add a printer to a Windows 8 computer without a physical print device being present. The computer can then host the printer, print server, and printer driver. These three components enable the computer to process the print jobs and store them in a print queue until the print device is actually available.

- **Print server** – A ***print server*** is a computer (or standalone device) that receives print jobs from clients and sends them to print devices that are either locally attached or connected to the network.
- **Printer driver** – A ***printer driver*** is a device driver that converts the print jobs generated by applications into an appropriate string of commands for a specific print device. Printer drivers are designed for a specific print device and provide applications with access to all of the print device's features.

UNDERSTANDING WINDOWS PRINTING

The four printing components work together to process the print jobs produced by Windows applications and turn them into hard copy documents, as shown in Figure 14-24.

Figure 14-24

The Windows print architecture

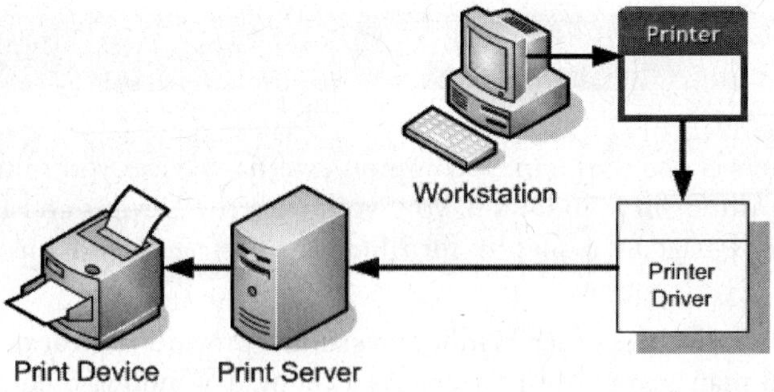

Before you can print documents in Windows, you must install at least one printer. To install a printer in Windows, you must do the following:

- Select a specific manufacturer and model of print device.
- Specify the port (or other interface) the computer will use to access the print device.
- Supply a printer driver specifically created for that print device.

When you print a document in an application, you select the printer that will be the destination for the print job.

The printer is associated with a printer driver that takes the commands generated by the application and converts them into a language understood by the printer, which is called a ***printer control language (PCL)***. PCLs can be standardized, as in the case of the PostScript language, or they can be proprietary languages developed by the print device manager.

The printer driver enables you to configure the print job to use the various capabilities of the print device. These capabilities are typically incorporated into the printer's Properties dialog box, like the one shown in Figure 14-25.

Figure 14-25

A Windows printer's Properties dialog box

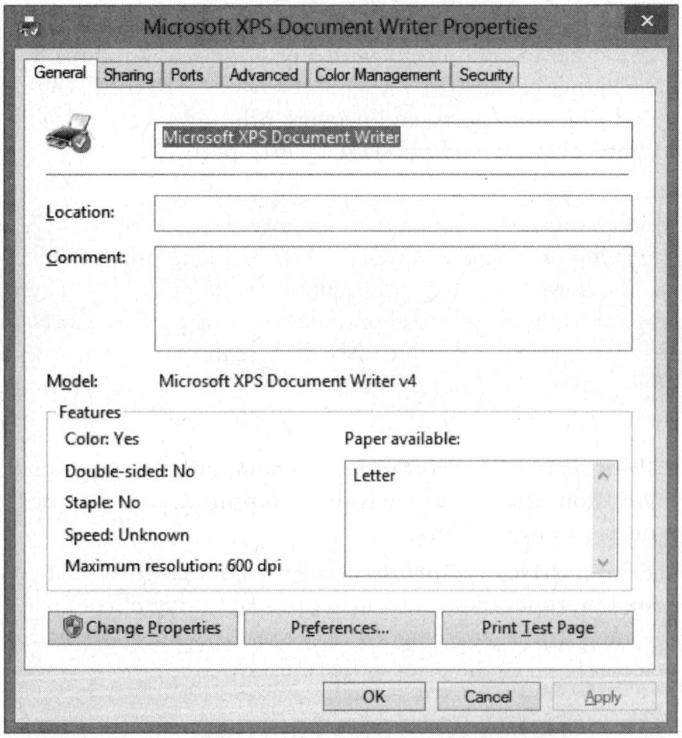

Once the computer converts the print job into the appropriate PCL, it stores the job in a print queue. The print queue then sends the job to the print device when the device is ready to receive it. If there are other jobs waiting to be printed, a new job might wait in the print queue for some time. When the server sends the job to the print device, the device reads the PCL commands and produces the hard copy document.

WINDOWS PRINTING FLEXIBILITY

The flexibility of the Windows print architecture manifests itself in how the roles of these components can be performed by a single computer, or distributed around a network.

When you connect a print device to a standalone Windows 8 computer, for example, the computer supplies the printer, printer driver, and print server functions. However, you can also connect the computer to a local area network (LAN) and share the printer with other users. In this arrangement, the computer with the print device attached to it functions as a print server. The other computers on the network are the print clients.

In this network printing arrangement, each client supplies its own printer and printer driver. As before, the application sends the print jobs to the printer and the printer driver converts the application commands to PCL commands. The client computer then sends the PCL print jobs over the network to the print server on the computer with the attached print device. Finally, the print server sends the jobs to the print device.

This is only the most basic of network printing arrangements. A multitude of possible variations exist to enable you to create a network printing architecture that supports your organization's printing needs. Some of the more advanced possibilities are as follows:

- Print devices do not necessarily have to be connected to computers. Many print devices have integrated network interfaces that enable them to connect directly to the LAN and function as their own print servers. You can also purchase standalone print server devices that connect a print device to a network. In these cases, print devices have their own IP addresses, which clients use to communicate with the devices.
- You can connect a single print server to multiple print devices. This is called a printer pool. On a busy network with many print clients, the print server can distribute large numbers of incoming jobs among several identical print devices to provide timely service. Alternatively, you can connect print devices that support different forms and paper sizes to a single print server, which will distribute jobs with different requirements to the appropriate print devices.
- You can connect multiple print servers to a single print device. By creating multiple print servers, you can configure different priorities, security settings, auditing, and monitoring parameters for different users. For example, you can create a high-priority print server for company executives, while junior users send their jobs to a lower priority server. This ensures that the executives' jobs get printed first, even if the servers are both connected to the same print device.

ADDING A LOCAL PRINTER

The most common configuration for home, small business, or workgroup users is to connect a print device directly to a computer running Windows 8 or another version of Windows, and then add a printer and printer driver. This enables local users to print their own jobs, and it also makes it possible to share the printer with other network users.

To add a local printer to a Windows 8 computer, use the following procedure:

TAKE NOTE*

This procedure is necessary only if the print device is connected (or will be connected) to the computer by a parallel (LPT) port or serial (COM) port interface. This is because these interfaces are not capable of automatically detecting connected devices. If your print device connects to the computer using USB, IEEE 1394, IrDA, Bluetooth, or any other auto-detecting technology, simply connecting the print device will cause the computer to detect it and install it automatically.

ADD A LOCAL PRINTER

GET READY. Log on to Windows 8 using an account with Administrator privileges and then perform the following steps:

1. Open the **Control Panel** and click **Hardware and Sound > Devices and Printers**.

   The Devices and Printers control panel appears, as shown in Figure 14-26.

Figure 14-26

The *Devices and Printers* control panel

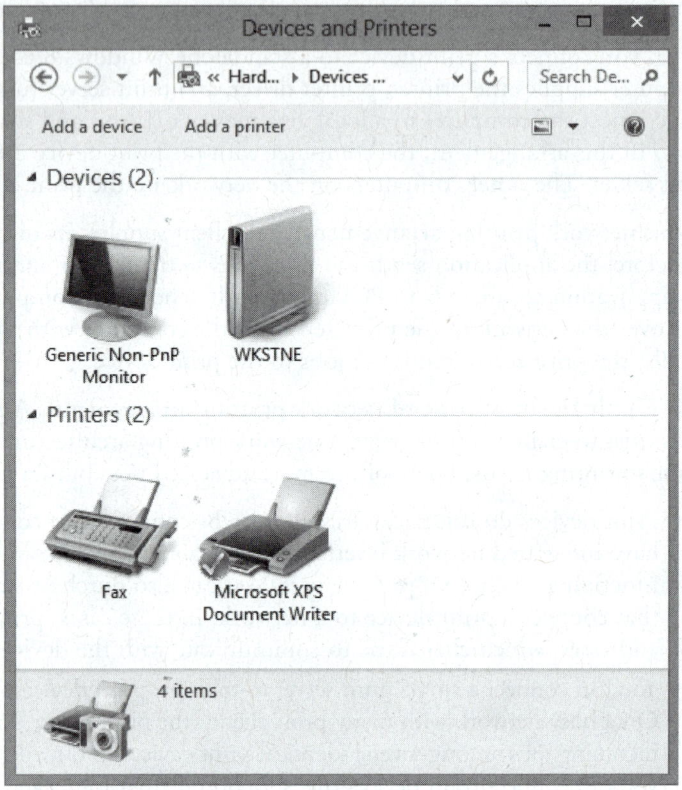

2. Click **Add a printer**.

   The *Add Printer* wizard appears, and begins searching for printers, while displaying the *Searching for available printers* page, as shown in Figure 14-27.

Figure 14-27

The *Searching for available printers* page

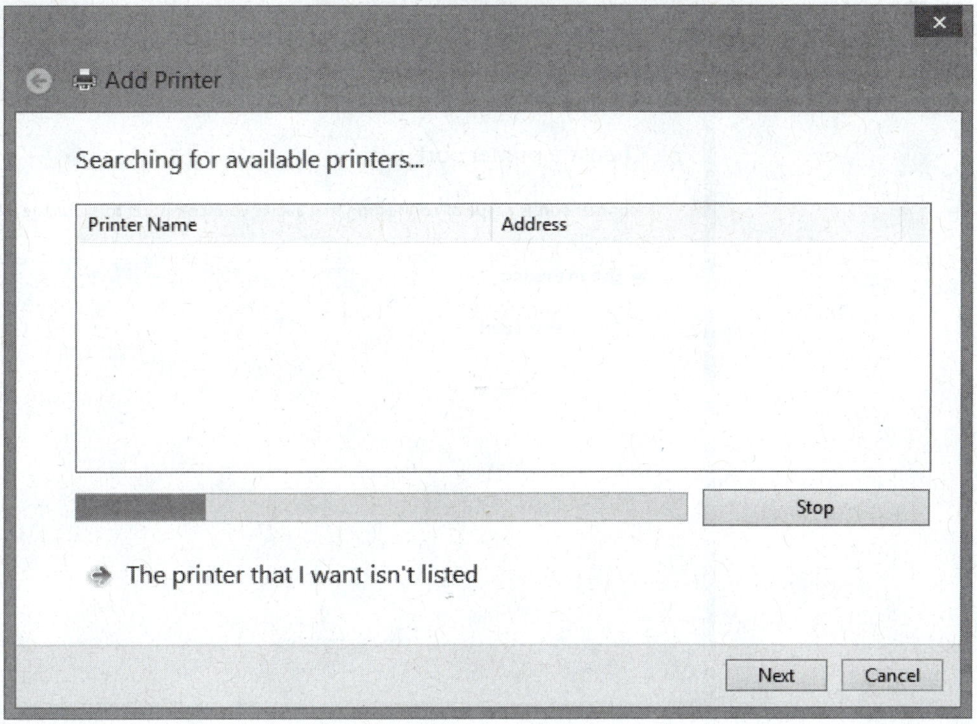

3. When the *No printers were found* page appears, click **Next**, and when the *Find a printer by other options* page appears, click **Next** again (see Figure 14-28).

Figure 14-28

The *Find a printer by other options* page

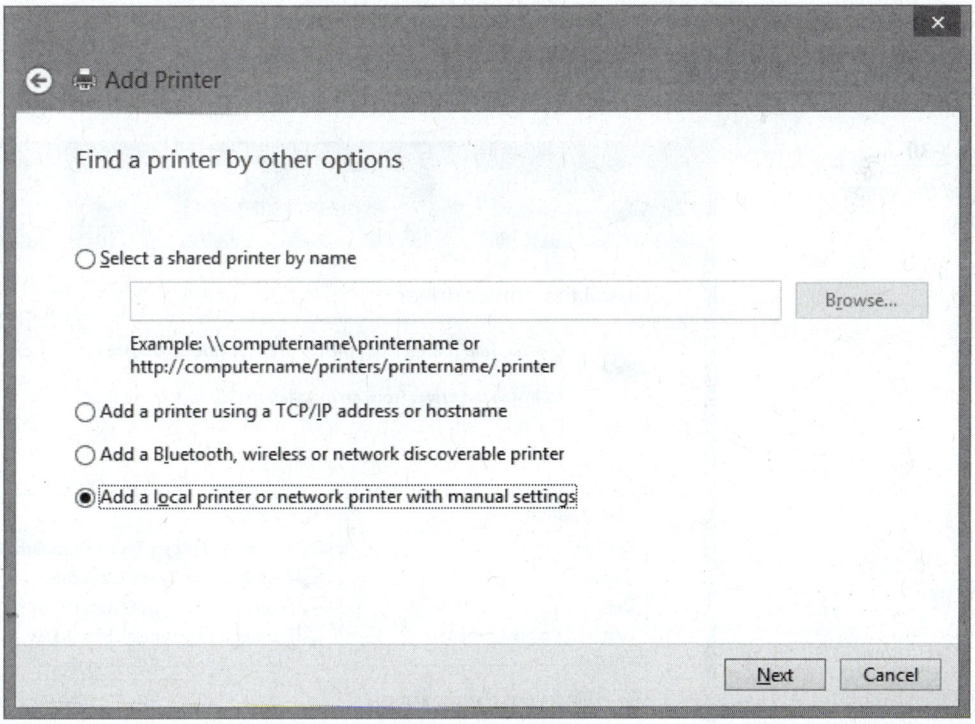

4. Select the *Add a local printer or network printer with manual settings* option and click **Next**.

   The *Choose a printer port* page appears, as shown in Figure 14-29.

Figure 14-29

The *Choose a printer port* page

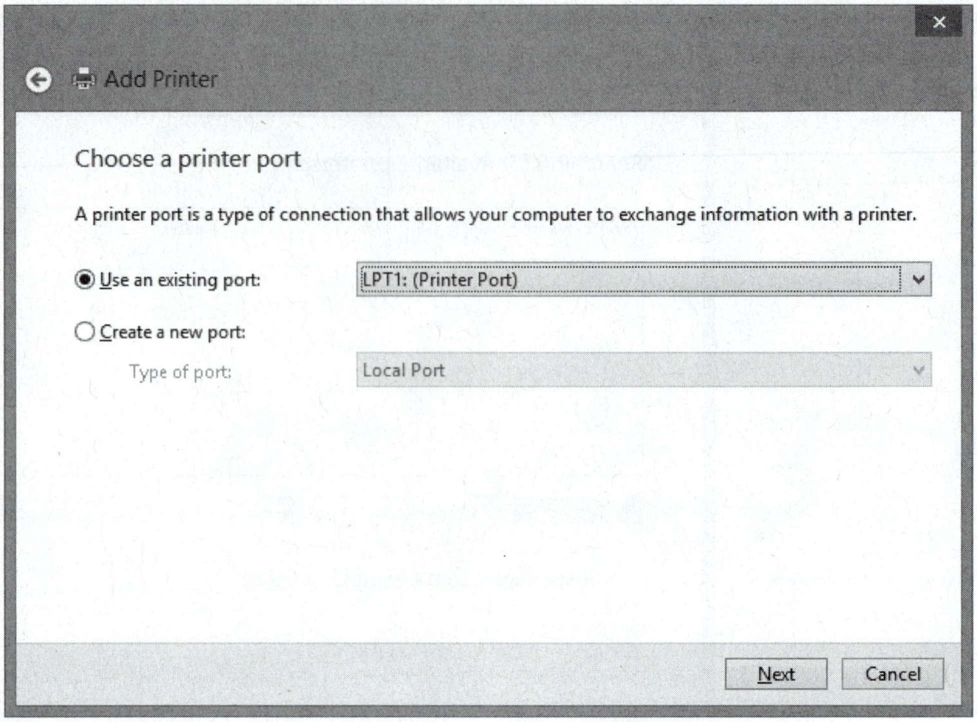

5. Select the **Use an existing port** option and then select the LPT or COM port to which the print device is connected.
6. Click **Next** to continue.

   The *Install the printer driver* page appears, as shown in Figure 14-30.

Figure 14-30

The *Install the printer driver* page

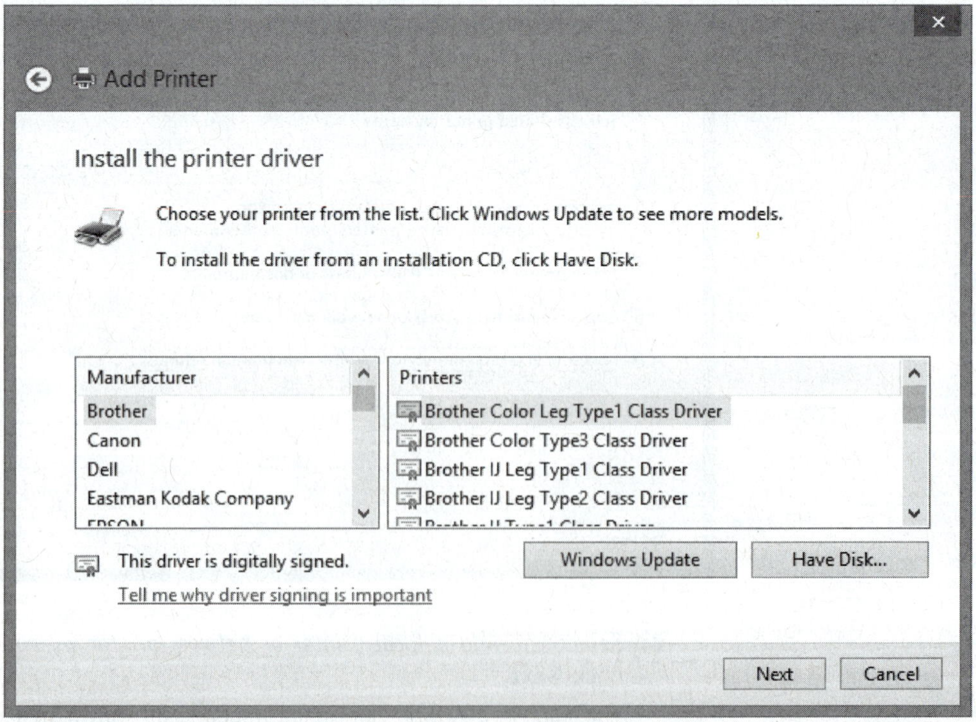

7. In the Manufacturer column, scroll down and select the manufacturer of your print device. Then, in the Printers column, select the specific model of print device you want to install. If your print device does not appear in the list, you must either click **Have Disk**, to supply a driver you downloaded or that came with the print device; or **Windows Update**, to display a selection of drivers available from the Windows Update website.
8. Click **Next** to continue.

   The *Type a printer name* page appears, as shown in Figure 14-31.

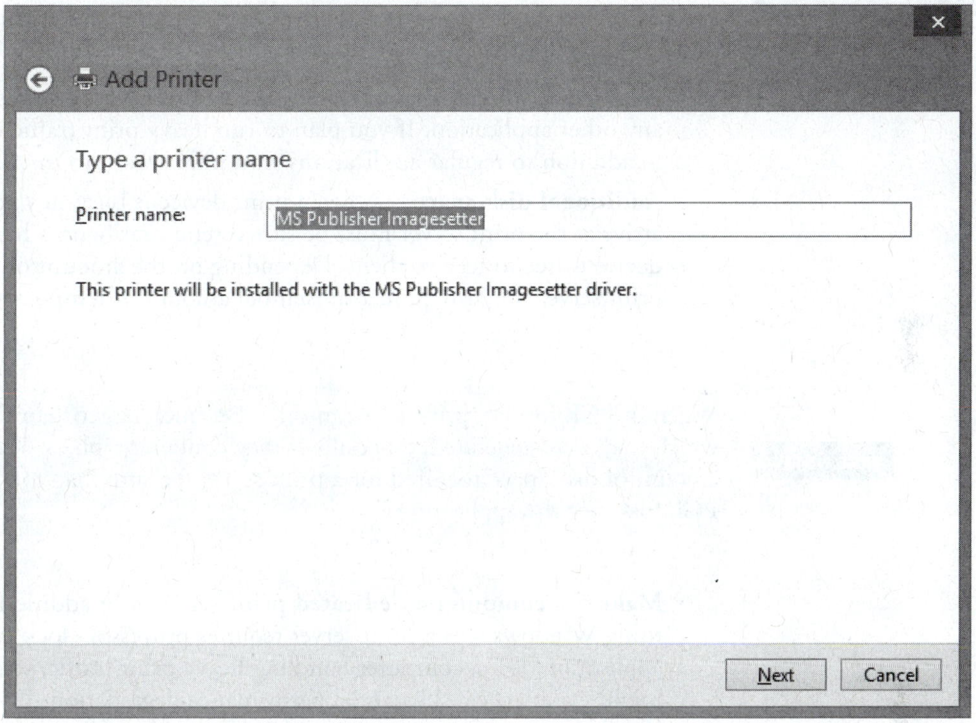

Figure 14-31

The *Type a printer name* page

9. Type a name for the printer in the *Printer name* text box and then click **Next**.

   After a few moments, the *Printer sharing* page appears.
10. Select the **Do not share this printer option** and then click **Next**.
11. The *You've successfully added the printer* page appears. If the printer is connected and ready to use, you can click the *Print a test page* button.
12. Click **Finish**.

    The printer appears in the Devices and Printers control panel.
13. **Close** the *Control Panel* window.

At this point, the printer is ready to receive jobs from applications, but this does not necessarily mean that the print device is ready. As stated earlier, you can complete this entire procedure without the print device being attached to the computer, or turned on, or loaded with paper. Jobs that users send to the printer are processed and remain in the print queue until the print device is available for use.

Sharing a Printer

A ***local printer*** is, of course, available for use by anyone working at the computer to which it is attached. However, you can also share the printer with other users in a homegroup, workgroup, or domain. When you share a printer connected to a Windows 8 computer, you are essentially using Windows 8 as a print server.

CERTIFICATION READY
Configure shared printers
Objective 4.1

Using Windows 8 as a print server can be a simple or a complex matter, depending on how many clients the server has to support and how much printing they do. For a home, small business, or workgroup, in which a handful of users need occasional access to the printer, no special preparation is necessary. However, if the computer must support heavy printer use, any or all of the following hardware upgrades might be needed:

- **Additional system memory** – Processing print jobs requires system memory, just like any other application. If you plan to run heavy print traffic on a Windows 8 computer, in addition to regular applications, you might want to install extra system memory.
- **Additional disk space** – When a print device is busy, any additional print jobs that arrive at the print server must be stored temporarily on a hard drive until the print device is free to receive them. Depending on the amount of print traffic involved, the print server might require a substantial amount of temporary storage for this purpose.

TAKE NOTE*

When in PCL format, print jobs can often be much larger than the document files from which they were generated, especially if they contain graphics. When estimating the amount of disk space required for a print server, be sure that you consider the size of the PCL files, not the application files.

- **Make the computer a dedicated print server** – In addition to memory and disk space, using Windows 8 as a print server requires processor clock cycles, just like any other application. On a computer handling heavy print traffic, standard user applications might experience a substantial performance degradation. If you need a print server to handle heavy traffic, you might want to consider using the computer for print server tasks exclusively and move the user(s) elsewhere.

TAKE NOTE*

If you plan on using a Windows computer as a dedicated print server, Windows 8 might not be your best choice as an operating system. As with all of the workstation versions of Windows, Windows 8 is limited to ten simultaneous network connections, so no more than ten clients can print at any one time. If you need a print server that can handle more than ten connections, you must use a server operating system, such as Windows Server 2012.

To share a printer on a Windows 8 computer, you must enable the appropriate settings in the Network and Sharing Center, just as you have to do to share files and folders. To share printers, the following Sharing and Discovery settings must be turned on:

- Network Discovery
- File and Printer Sharing

In addition, if the Password Protected Sharing setting is turned on, users must be logged on and have appropriate permissions to use the printer.

To share a printer that is already installed on a Windows 8 computer, use the following procedure:

SHARE A PRINTER

GET READY. Log on to Windows 8 using an account with Administrator privileges and then perform the following steps:

1. Open the **Control Panel** and then click **Hardware and Sound > Devices and Printers**.

   The *Devices and Printers* control panel appears.

2. Right-click one of the printer icons in the window and then, from the context menu, select **Printer Properties**.

   The printer's *Properties* sheet appears

3. Click the **Sharing** tab, as shown in Figure 14-32.

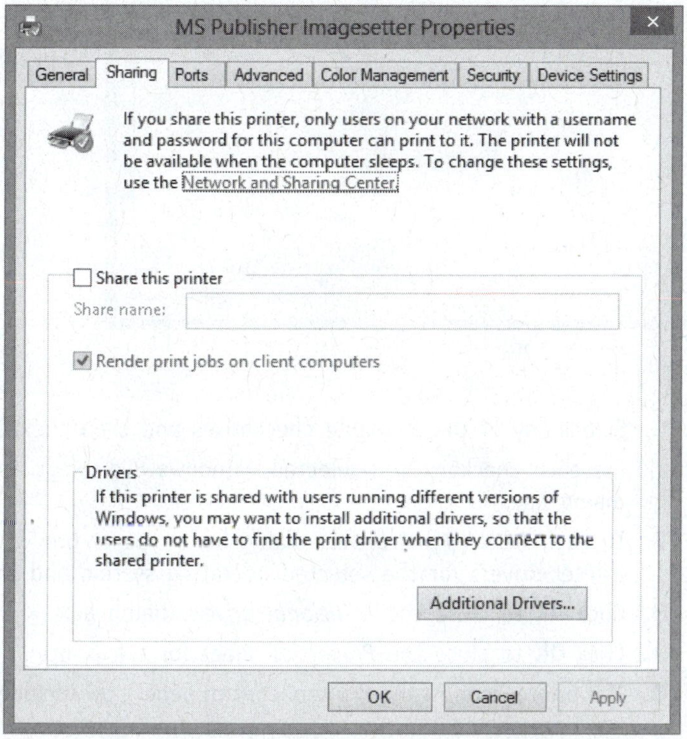

Figure 14-32

The Sharing tab of a printer's *Properties* sheet

4. Select the **Share this printer** checkbox.

   The printer name appears in the Share name text box. You can accept the default name or supply one of your own. Select the *Render print jobs on client computers* checkbox if you want to use the printer drivers on the individual client computers. Leaving this box unchecked will force the print server on the computer hosting the printer to process all of the jobs.

TAKE NOTE*

If the computer is a member of an Active Directory domain, an additional *List printer in the directory* checkbox appears in this dialog box. Selecting this checkbox creates a new printer object in the Active Directory Domain Services database, which enables domain users to locate the printer by searching the directory.

5. Click **Additional Drivers**.

   The Additional Drivers dialog box appears, as shown in Figure 14-33. This dialog box enables you to load printer drivers for other operating system platforms, so that clients installing the printer do not have to locate the drivers themselves.

Figure 14-33

The *Additional Drivers* dialog box

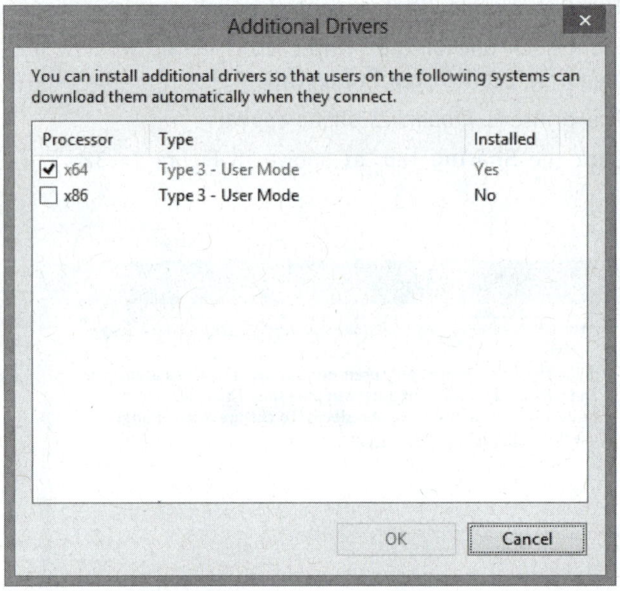

6. Select any of the available checkboxes and then click **OK**.

   For each checkbox you selected, Windows 8 displays an Install Print Drivers dialog box.

7. In each *Install Print Drivers* dialog box, type or browse to the location of the printer drivers for the selected operating system and then click **OK**.
8. Click **OK** to close the *Additional Drivers* dialog box.
9. Click **OK** to close the *Properties* sheet for the printer.
10. The printer icon in the Printers control panel now includes a symbol indicating that it has been shared.

Configuring Printer Security

Just like NTFS files and folders, Windows printers have their own permissions, which enable you to control who has access to the printer and to what degree.

When Password Protected Sharing is turned on in the Windows 8 Network and Sharing Center, users must log on to the computer with a user account that requires a password before they can access a shared printer. In addition, the user account must have the appropriate permissions to use the printer.

Printer permissions are much simpler than NTFS permissions; they basically dictate whether users are allowed to merely use the printer, manage documents submitted to the printer, or manage the properties of the printer itself. To assign permissions for a printer, use the following procedure:

ASSIGN PRINTER PERMISSIONS

GET READY. Log on to Windows 8 using an account with Administrator privileges and then perform the following steps:

1. Open the **Control Panel** and then click **Hardware and Sound > Devices and Printers.**

   The *Devices and Printers* control panel appears.

2. Right-click one of the printer icons in the window and then, from the context menu, select **Printer Properties**.

   The printer's *Properties* sheet appears

3. Click the **Security** tab, as shown in Figure 14-34.

   The top half of the display lists all of the security principals currently possessing permissions to the selected printer. The bottom half lists the permissions held by the selected security principal.

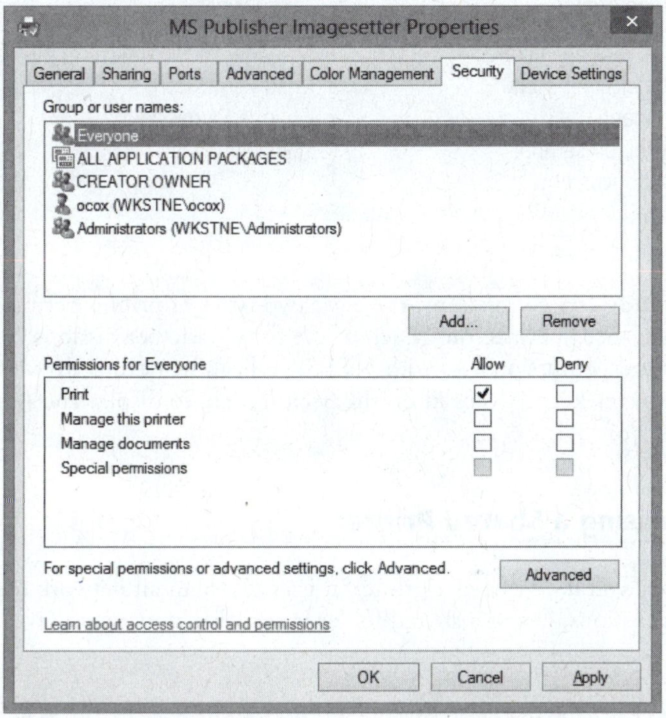

Figure 14-34

The Security tab of a printer's *Properties* sheet

4. Click **Add**.

   The *Select Users or Groups* dialog box appears.

TAKE NOTE*

When you assign permissions on a standalone computer, you select local user and group accounts to be the security principals that receive the permissions. However, if the computer is a member of an Active Directory Domain Services domain, you assign permissions to domain users, groups, and other objects by default.

5. In the *Enter the object names to select* text box, type a user or group name, and then click **OK**.

   The user or group appears in the *Group or user names* list.

6. Select the user or group you added, and select or clear the checkboxes in the bottom half of the display to Allow or Deny the user any of the standard permissions shown in Table 14-3.

7. Click **OK** to close the *Properties* sheet.

Table 14-3

Basic Printer Permissions

PERMISSION	CAPABILITIES	SPECIAL PERMISSIONS	DEFAULT ASSIGNMENTS
Print	• Connect to a printer • Print documents • Pause, resume, restart, and cancel the user's own documents	• Print • Read Permissions	Assigned to the Everyone special identity
Manage This Printer	• Cancel all documents • Share a printer • Change printer properties • Delete a printer • Change printer permissions	• Print • Manage Printers • Read Permissions • Change Permissions • Take Ownership	Assigned to the Administrators group
Manage Documents	• Pause, resume, restart, and cancel all users' documents • Control job settings for all documents	• Manage Documents • Read Permissions • Change Permissions • Take Ownership	Assigned to the Creator Owner special identity

TAKE NOTE* As with NTFS permissions, there are two types of printer permissions: basic permissions and advanced permissions. Each of the three basic permissions consists of a combination of advanced permissions. As with NTFS, you can work directly with the advanced permissions by clicking Advanced on the Security tab, to display the Advanced Security Settings dialog box.

Accessing a Shared Printer

Once you have shared a printer, it is available to all network users with the appropriate permissions, just as a shared folder is available to the network.

To access a shared printer from Windows 8, use the following procedure.

ACCESS A SHARED PRINTER

GET READY. Log on to Windows 8 using any user account and then perform the following steps:

1. Open the **Control Panel** and then click **Hardware and Sound > Devices and Printers**.

   The *Devices and Printers* control panel appears.

2. Click **Add a printer**.

   The *Add Printer Wizard* appears and begins searching the network for shared printers.

3. If the printer you want appears, select it and then click **Next** to install it. If it does not appear, click *The printer that I want isn't listed* to display the *Find a printer by other options* page.

4. Select the proper option to browse for a network printer, enter a printer's IP address or hostname, or add a Bluetooth or wireless printer\UNC name or URL for a printer, or. Then click **Next**.

When you have selected a printer, the *You've successfully added the printer* page appears.

5. Click **Finish**. The printer appears in the *Devices and Printers* control panel.
6. **Close** the *Control Panel* window.

In addition to using the Add Printer wizard, there are several other ways to access shared network printers. If the computer is a member of a homegroup, then all of the printers shared by other members of the same homegroup automatically appear in the Devices and Printers control panel.

When browsing the network in File Explorer, you can see the shared printers for each computer on the network, as shown in Figure 14-35. By right-clicking a printer in any File Explorer window and selecting Connect from the context menu, you can access any printer for which you have the appropriate permissions. Any other Windows 8 mechanism that can display the shared printers on the network provides access to them in the same way.

Figure 14-35

Viewing printers in Windows Explorer

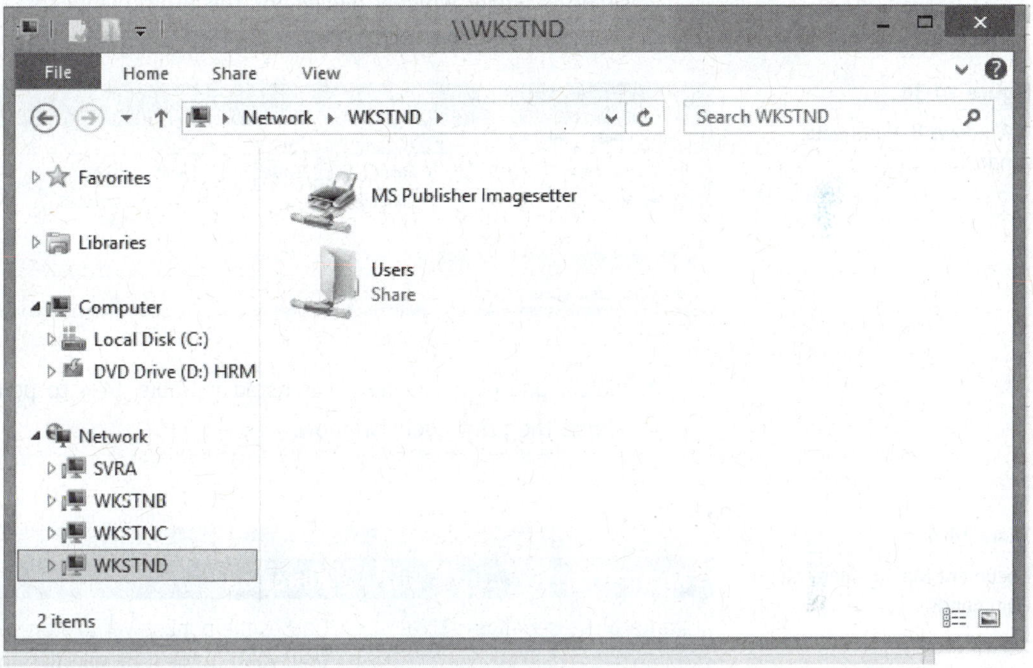

When the computer hosting the printer is a member of an Active Directory Domain Services domain, the ability to locate shared printers is enhanced even further. Opting to list the printer in the Active Directory database creates an object for the printer, and in this object you can specify a lot of information about the print device, including its location and its capabilities.

Recording this information in the printer object makes it possible for users to locate printers by searching the directory for specific characteristics. For example, if a user on a large corporate network needs to find a color duplex printer on the third floor, running a directory search with the appropriate keywords will enable the user to locate the required printer.

Managing Documents

By default, all printers assign the Allow Print permission to the Everyone special identity, which enables all users to access the printer and manage their own documents. Users that possess the Allow Manage Documents permission can manage any users' documents. To manage documents, you open the print queue window for the printer.

Managing documents refers to pausing, resuming, restarting, and cancelling documents that are currently waiting in a print queue. Windows 8 provides a print queue window for every printer, which enables you to view the jobs that are currently waiting to be printed.

To manage documents, use the following procedure:

MANAGE DOCUMENTS

GET READY. Log on to Windows 8 using any user account and then perform the following steps:

1. Open the **Control Panel** and then click **Hardware and Sound > Devices and Printers**.

   The *Devices and Printers* control panel appears.

2. Right-click one of the printer icons and, from the context menu, select **See what's printing**.

   A print queue window named for the printer appears, as shown in Figure 14-36.

Figure 14-36

A Windows 8 print queue window

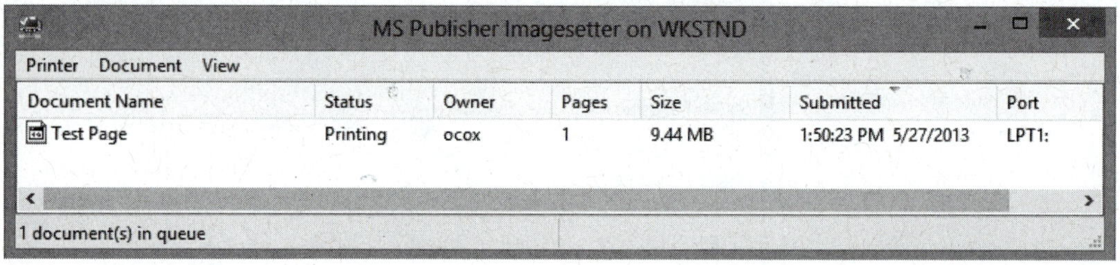

3. Select one of the menu items listed in Table 14-4 to perform the associated function.
4. **Close** the print queue window.

TABLE 14-4

Document Management Menu Commands

MENU ITEM	FUNCTION
Printer > Pause Printing	Causes the print server to stop sending jobs to the print device until you resume it by selecting the same menu item again. All pending jobs remain in the queue.
Printer > Cancel All Documents	Removes all pending jobs from the queue. Jobs that are in progress complete normally.
Printer > Properties	Opens the *Properties* sheet for the printer.
Document > Pause	Pauses the selected document, preventing the print server from sending the job to the print device.
Document > Resume	Causes the print server to resume processing a selected document that has previously been paused.
Document > Restart	Causes the print server to discard the current job and restart printing the selected document from the beginning.
Document > Cancel	Causes the print server to remove the selected document from the queue.
Document > Properties	Opens the *Properties* sheet for the selected job.

TAKE NOTE*

When managing documents, keep in mind that the commands accessible from the print queue window affect only the jobs waiting in the queue, not those currently being processed. For example, a job that is partially transmitted to the print device cannot be completely cancelled. The data already in the print device's memory will be printed, even though the remainder of the job was removed from the queue. To stop a job that is currently printing, you must clear the print device's memory (by power cycling or resetting the unit), as well as clear the job from the queue.

Managing Printers

Users with the Allow Manage Printers permission can go beyond just manipulating queued documents and reconfigure the printer itself. Managing a printer refers to altering the operational parameters that affect all users and controlling access to the printer.

Generally speaking, most of the software-based tasks that fall under the category of managing a printer are those you perform once, while setting up the printer for the first time. Day-to-day printer management is more likely to involve clearing print jams, reloading paper, and changing toner or ribbon cartridges. However, the following sections examine some of the printer configuration tasks that typically are the responsibility of a printer manager.

SETTING PRINTER PRIORITIES

In some cases, you might want to give certain users in your organization priority access to a print device so that when a print device is busy, their jobs are processed before those of other users. To do this, you must create multiple printers, associate them with the same print device, and then modify their priorities, as described in the following procedure:

SET A PRINTER'S PRIORITY

GET READY. Log on to Windows 8 using an account with the Manage Printer permission and then perform the following steps:

1. Open the **Control Panel** and then click **Hardware and Sound > Devices and Printers**.

   The *Devices and Printers* control panel appears.
2. Right-click one of the printer icons in the window and then, from the context menu, select **Printer Properties**.

   The printer's *Properties* sheet appears.
3. Click the **Advanced** tab, as shown in Figure 14-37.

Figure 14-37

The Advanced tab of a printer's *Properties* sheet

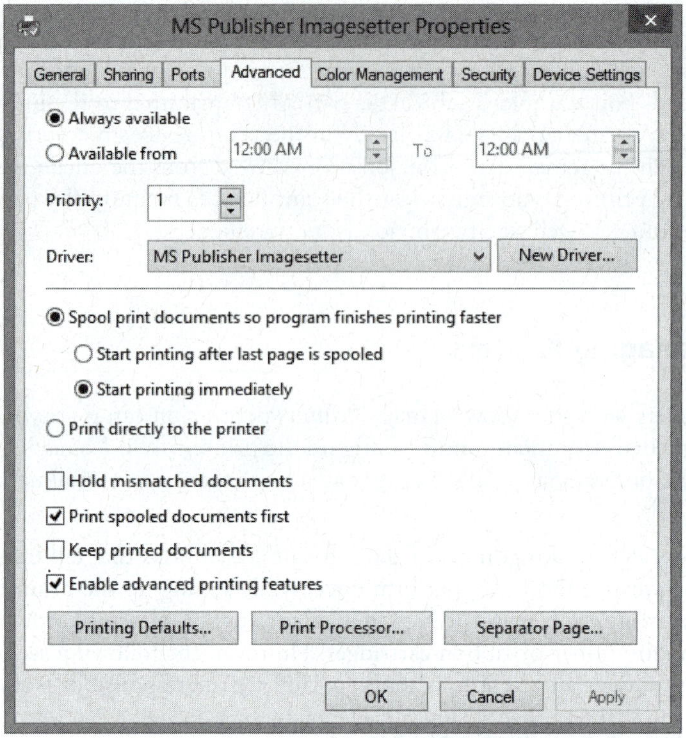

4. Set the *Priority* spin box to a number representing the highest priority you want to set for the printer. Higher numbers represent higher priorities. The highest possible priority is 99.

TAKE NOTE*

The values of the Priority spin box do not have any absolute significance; they are pertinent only in relation to each other. As long as one printer has a higher priority value than another, its print jobs will be processed first. In other words, it doesn't matter if the high-priority value is 9 or 99, as long as the low-priority value is less than 9.

5. Click the **Security** tab.
6. Add the users or groups that you want to provide with high-priority access to the printer and assign them the *Allow Print* permission.
7. Revoke the *Allow Print* permission from the *Everyone* special identity.
8. Click **OK** to close the *Properties* sheet.
9. Create an identical printer using the same printer driver and pointing to the same print device. Leave the *Priority* setting to its default value of *1* and then leave the default permissions in place.
10. Rename the printers, specifying the priority assigned to each one.
11. Inform the privileged users that they should send their jobs to the high-priority printer. All jobs sent to that printer will be processed before those sent to the other, low-priority printer.

SCHEDULING PRINTER ACCESS

Sometimes, you might want to limit certain users' access to a printer to specific times of the day or night. For example, your organization might have a color laser printer that the company's graphic designers use during business hours, but which you permit other employees to use after 5:00 PM. To do this, you associate multiple printers with a single print device, much as you did to set different printer priorities.

After creating two printers, both pointing to the same print device, you configure their scheduling using the following procedure.

CONFIGURE A PRINTER'S SCHEDULE

GET READY. Log on to Windows 8 using an account with the Manage Printer permission and then perform the following steps:

1. Open the **Control Panel** and then click **Hardware and Sound > Devices and Printers**.

   The *Devices and Printers* control panel appears.
2. Right-click one of the printer icons in the window and then, from the context menu, select **Printer Properties**.

   The printer's *Properties* sheet appears.
3. Click the **Advanced** tab.
4. Select the **Available from** radio button and then, in the two spin boxes provided, select the range of hours you want the printer to be available.
5. Click the **Security** tab.
6. Add the users or groups that you want to provide with access to the printer during the hours you selected and grant them the *Allow Print* permission.
7. Revoke the *Allow Print* permission from the *Everyone* special identity.
8. Click **OK** to close the *Properties* sheet.

CREATING A PRINTER POOL

As mentioned earlier, a printer pool is an arrangement that increases the production capability of a single printer by connecting it to multiple print devices. When you create a printer pool, the print server sends each incoming job to the first print device it finds that is not busy. This effectively distributes the jobs among the available print devices, providing users with more rapid service.

To create a printer pool, you must have at least two identical print devices, or at least print devices that use the same printer driver. The print devices must be in the same location, because there is no way to tell which print device will process a given document. You must also connect all of the print devices in the pool to the same print server. If the print server is a Windows 8 computer, you can connect the print devices to any viable ports.

To configure a printer pool, use the following procedure.

CREATE A PRINTER POOL

GET READY. Log on to Windows 8 using an account with the Manage Printer permission and then perform the following steps:

1. Open the **Control Panel** and then click **Hardware and Sound > Devices and Printers**.

   The *Devices and Printers* control panel appears.
2. Right-click one of the printer icons in the window and then, from the context menu, select **Printer Properties**.

   The printer's *Properties* sheet appears.

3. Click the **Ports** tab and then select all of the ports to which the print devices are connected.
4. Select the **Enable printer pooling** checkbox and then click **OK**.

SKILL SUMMARY

IN THIS LESSON, YOU LEARNED:

- Windows 8 provides three basic methods for sharing the files and folders on the computer: any folder sharing, public folder sharing, and homegroup sharing.
- Homegroup networking is a Windows 8 feature that enables computers configured to use the Home network location to share the contents of their respective libraries among themselves.
- Libraries enable users to aggregate files in multiple locations – and even on multiple computers – into a single folder that makes them appear as though they are all on a local drive.
- Sharing files and folders using the Public folder is the simplest way to give your clients file sharing capability.
- Windows 8 has several sets of permissions, which operate independently of each other, including NTFS permissions, share permissions, registry permissions, and Active Directory permissions.
- Share permissions provide rudimentary access control for all of the files on a network share.
- SkyDrive is Microsoft's personal, cloud-based storage service. Every user who applies for a Microsoft account receives seven gigabytes of free cloud storage.
- The printing architecture in Windows is modular, consisting of the print device, a printer, a print server, and a printer driver.
- A local printer is one that supports a print device directly attached to the computer or attached to the network. A network printer connects to a shared printer hosted by another computer.
- To install a printer, you run the Add Printer wizard and specify the printer driver and port to use.
- The print queue window enables you to monitor printers for potential signs of trouble.

Knowledge Assessment

Multiple Choice

Select one or more correct answers for each of the following questions.

1. A user calls the help desk and asks you why she cannot send print jobs to a shared printer that is using Windows 8 as a print server. You determine that the problem is related to the printer permissions. The user cannot send jobs to the printer because she lacks the following permission for the printer.
   a. Print
   b. Manage this Printer
   c. Manage all Printers
   d. Manage Documents

2. To share a folder with network users on a public network, you must first open the Network and Sharing Center and do which of the following? (Choose all that apply.)
   a. Enable DHCP
   b. Turn on Network Discovery
   c. Enable File and Printer Sharing
   d. Create a homegroup

3. In the Windows printing architecture, which of the following are the hardware components. (Choose all that apply.)
   a. Printer
   b. Print driver
   c. Print device
   d. Print server

4. The primary function of a printer driver is to take printer commands generated by applications and convert them into what format?
   a. Printer control language
   b. Print server
   c. Analog
   d. Binary

5. What must you do to create a shared folder called DOCS and hide it from network users?
   a. Append an percent sign to the name (DOCS%)
   b. Append a dollar sign to the name (DOCS$)
   c. Type the name in all lowercase letters (docs)
   d. Append an exclamation point to the name (DOCS!)

6. Share level permissions provide which of the following levels of access? (Choose all that apply.)
   a. Read
   b. Full Control
   c. Change
   d. Modify

7. If a user is granted the share permission Allow READ to a folder named Sales and also has the share permission Allow CHANGE to the same folder as part of her membership in the Finance Group. What is her effective permission to the Sales folder? (Choose all that apply.)
   a. She can create folders, files, and change data in the files in the Sales folder.
   b. She can change file permissions for files in the Sales folder.
   c. She can delete files and folders in the Sales folder.
   d. She can execute any program files located in the Sales folder.

8. Which basic Printer permission is needed to allow a user to cancel all of their documents currently queued on a print device?
   a. Print
   b. Manage this printer
   c. Manage documents
   d. Manage all documents

9. Which of the following methods can be used to access SkyDrive storage space? (Choose all that apply.)
   a. Through the web (http://skydrive.com)
   b. By using the SkyDrive Desktop app
   c. Through an Office 2013 application
   d. By using an FTP client

10. Which type of permissions apply when you are connecting to a resource locally or across the network?
    a. NTFS file permissions only
    b. Share folder permissions
    c. NTFS and Share permissions
    d. NTFS file and folder permissions

Best Answer

Choose the letter that corresponds to the best answer. More than one answer choice may achieve the goal. Select the BEST answer.

1. You are the administrator of a network with several print devices, all of which are hosted by Windows 8 computers. These print devices are shared with all users on the network. One of the print devices is malfunctioning and must be sent out for repair. Which of the following is the most practical way to prevent users from sending jobs to the printer while the print device is unavailable?
   a. Delete the printer on the computer functioning as the print server.
   b. Revoke the Print permission from all of the users.
   c. Modify the printer.
   d. Stop sharing the printer.
2. A folder named Marketing contains each month's sales forecasts. This folder needs to be accessible over the local network so that a subset of the Marketing team (Interns) can have read only access to view the data. Of the following, which would provide the most efficient approach for providing the access needed for those in the Interns group?
   a. Share permission: Full Control (Interns group), NTFS permission: Read (assigned to each Intern's individual user account)
   b. Share permissions: Read (Interns group), NTFS permission: Modify (assigned to each Intern's individual user account)
   c. Share permission: Read (Everyone group), NTFS permission: Read (assigned to the Interns group)
   d. Share permission: Full Control (Interns group), NTFS permission: Read (assigned to the Interns group)
3. There are currently five users on a Windows 8 network. One of the Windows 8 computers is currently configured as a print server. If the number of users is expected to double every 6 months for the next year, what is the best approach to use for to ensure you are able to handle the future growth?
   a. Add additional memory on the Windows 8 print server.
   b. Add additional hard drive space on the Windows 8 print server.
   c. Make the computer a dedicated print server.
   d. Replace the Windows 8 computer with a Windows Server 2012 print server.
4. A new printer has been added to the company network. What is the least amount of privileges you can provide for a junior administrator to allow them to print documents while also being able to pause, resume, restart, and cancel all of their own documents?
   a. Print
   b. Manage This Printer
   c. Manage Documents
   d. Print and Manage Documents

5. Due to tight deadlines, the Executives' print jobs need to have a higher priority than other print jobs on the network. What is the best approach to use to ensure Executives print jobs are always a higher priority than other users while keeping costs down?
   a. Create multiple printers, associate them with different print devices and then assign the Execs Group a priority of 77 and everyone else a priority of 1.
   b. Create multiple printers, associate them with different print devices and then assign the Execs Group a priority of 77 and everyone else a priority of 72.
   c. Purchase a new print device, share it on the network so that only the members of the Execs Group can print to it.
   d. Purchase new print devices for each member of the Execs Group and connect it directly to their computers.

Matching and Identification

Complete the following exercise by matching the terms with their corresponding definitions.

_______ **a)** Homegroups
_______ **b)** SkyDrive
_______ **c)** Local printer
_______ **d)** Libraries
_______ **e)** Printer pool
_______ **f)** Manage this Printer
_______ **g)** Printer control language
_______ **h)** Share permissions
_______ **i)** Printer driver
_______ **j)** Print server

1. A basic printer permission; allows you to cancel all documents and change printer properties.
2. Enable users to aggregate files in multiple locations.
3. Can be standardized (PSL) or can be proprietary languages developed by the print device manager.
4. Microsoft's personal, cloud-based sto rage service.
5. Receives print jobs from clients and sends them to print devices.
6. Provide rudimentary access control for all of the files on a network share.
7. Converts print jobs into commands for a specific print device.
8. Supports a print device directly attached to the computer.
9. Designed to share only libraries.
10. A single print server connected to multiple print devices.

Build a List

1. In order of first to last, specify the correct order of steps to assign printer permissions.

_______ Click the **Security** tab.
_______ Click **Add**. The *Select Users or Groups* dialog box appears.
_______ In the *Enter the object names to select* text box, type a user or group name, and then click **OK**.
_______ Click **OK** to close the *Properties* sheet.
_______ Right-click one of the printer icons in the window and then, from the context menu, select **Printer Properties**.
_______ Select the user or group you added, and select or clear the checkboxes in the bottom half of the display to Allow or Deny the user any of the standard permissions.
_______ Open the **Control Panel** and then click **Hardware and Sound > Devices and Printers**.

2. Specify the correct order of steps to set a printer's priority.
   ________ Right-click one of the printer icons in the window and then, from the context menu, select **Printer Properties**.
   ________ Set the *Priority* spin box to a number representing the highest priority you want to set for the printer. Higher numbers represent higher priorities. The highest possible priority is 99.
   ________ Open the **Control Panel** and then click **Hardware and Sound > Devices and Printers**.
   ________ Click the **Security** tab.
   ________ Click the **Advanced** tab.
   ________ Add the users or groups that you want to provide with high-priority access to the printer and assign them the *Allow Print* permission.
   ________ Create an identical printer using the same printer driver and pointing to the same print device. Leave the *Priority* setting to its default value of *1* and then leave the default permissions in place.
   ________ Rename the printers, specifying the priority assigned to each one.
   ________ Revoke the *Allow Print* permission from the *Everyone* special identity.
   ________ Inform the privileged users that they should send their jobs to the high-priority printer.
   ________ Click **OK** to close the *Properties* sheet.

3. Specify the correct order of steps to add a library location.
   ________ Click the **Manage Library** button in the ribbon.
   ________ Select one of the four library icons in the right pane.
   ________ **Close** the *File Explorer* window.
   ________ Click **OK**. The contents of the folder you added appear in the library.
   ________ Open **File Explorer** and select the **Libraries** folder.
   ________ Browse to the folder you want to add, select it, and then click **Include Folder**.
   ________ Click **OK** to close the *Internet Properties* sheet.
   ________ Click **Add**. An *Include Folder* combo box appears for the library you selected.

Business Case Scenarios

Scenario 14-1: Enhancing Print Performance

You are a desktop support technician for a law firm with a group of ten legal secretaries who provide administrative support to the attorneys. All of the secretaries use a single, shared, high-speed laser printer that is connected to a dedicated Windows 7 print server. The secretaries print multiple copies of large documents on a regular basis, and although the laser printer is fast, it is kept running almost constantly. Sometimes the secretaries have to wait 20 minutes or more after submitting a print job for their documents to reach the top of the queue. The office manager has offered to purchase additional printers for the department. However, the secretaries are accustomed to simply clicking the Print button, and don't like the idea of having to examine multiple print queues to determine which one has the fewest jobs before submitting a document. What can you do to provide the department with a printing solution that will enable the secretaries to utilize additional printers most efficiently?

Scenario 14-2: Understanding Printing Priorities

Jack has the Allow Print, Allow Manage Documents, and Allow Manage Printers permissions to a printer with a priority of 1. Jill has the Allow Print permission to a printer with a priority of 10, connected to the same print device. If Jack and Jill both submit a print job at exactly the same time, whose print job will be processed first?

Configuring File and Folder Access

LESSON 15

70-687 EXAM OBJECTIVE

Objective 4.2 – Configure file and folder access. This objective may include but is not limited to configure NTFS permissions; encrypt files and folders by using EFS; configure disk quotas; and configure object access auditing.

Lesson Heading	Exam Objective
Managing Permissions	
Understanding the Windows Permission Architecture	
Managing NTFS Permissions	Configure NTFS Permissions
Using the Encrypting File System	
Encrypting a Folder with EFS	Encrypt Files and Folders by Using EFS
Determining Whether a File or Folder is Encrypted	
Configuring Disk Quotas	Configure Disk Quotas
Configuring Object Access Auditing	Configure Object Access Auditing

KEY TERMS

access control list (ACL)
access control entries (ACEs)
advanced permissions
Active Directory permissions
auditing
basic permissions
effective access
Encrypting File System (EFS)
New Technology File System (NTFS)
NTFS permissions
NTFS quotas
permissions
Registry permissions
security principal
Share permissions

Managing Permissions

THE BOTTOM LINE

In Lesson 22, "Managing Local Storage," you learn how to prepare hard disk drives so that users can store files on them. To control access to the disks and other resources, Windows 8 uses permissions.

Permissions are privileges granted to specific system entities, such as users, groups, or computers, enabling them to perform a task or access a resource. For example, you can grant a specific user permission to read a file, while denying that same user the permissions needed to modify or delete the file.

Windows 8 has several sets of permissions, which operate independently of each other. As an administrator, you should be familiar with the operation of the following four permission systems:

- ***NTFS permissions*** – Control access to the files and folders stored on disk volumes formatted with the NTFS file system. To access a file, whether on the local system or over a network, a user must have the appropriate NTFS permissions.
- ***Share permissions*** – Control access to files and folders shared over a network. To access a file over a network, a user must have appropriate share permissions and appropriate NTFS permissions.
- ***Registry permissions*** – Control access to specific parts of the Windows registry. An application that modifies registry settings or a user attempting to manually modify the registry must have the appropriate registry permissions.
- ***Active Directory permissions*** – Control access to specific parts of an Active Directory hierarchy. Although Windows 8 cannot host an Active Directory Domain Services domain, desktop technicians might require these permissions when servicing computers that are members of a domain.

All of these permission systems operate independently of each other and can conceivably combine to provide increased protection to a specific resource. For example, Alice might grant Ralph the NTFS permissions needed to access the budget spreadsheet stored on her computer. If Ralph sits down at Alice's computer and logs on as himself, he will be able to access that spreadsheet. However, if Ralph is working at his own computer, he will not be able to access the spreadsheet until Alice creates a share containing the file and until she grants Ralph the proper share permissions.

TAKE NOTE*

Although all of these permissions systems are operating all the time, administrators do not necessarily have to work with them all on a regular basis. In fact, you might not ever have to manually alter a Registry or Active Directory permission. However, many technicians have to work with NTFS and share permissions on a daily basis.

Understanding the Windows Permission Architecture

Permissions protect files, folders, shares, registry keys, and Active Directory objects.

To store permissions, each of these elements has an ***access control list (ACL)***. An ACL is a collection of individual permissions, in the form of ***access control entries (ACEs)***. Each ACE consists of a ***security principal*** (that is, the name of the user, group, or computer being granted the permissions) and the specific permissions assigned to that security principal. When you manage permissions in any of the Windows 8 permission systems, you are actually creating and modifying the ACEs in an ACL.

It is crucial to understand that, in all of the Windows operating systems, permissions are stored as part of the element being protected, not the security principal being granted access. For example, when you grant a user the NTFS permissions needed to access a file, the ACE you create is stored in the file's ACL; it is not part of the user account. You can move the file to a different location, and in most cases, its permissions go with it.

To manage permissions in Windows 8, you use the controls in the Security tab of the element's Properties dialog box, like the one shown in Figure 15-1, with the security principals listed at the top and the permissions associated with them at the bottom. All of the Windows permission systems use the same interface, although the permissions themselves differ.

Figure 15-1

The Security tab of a *User Properties* dialog box

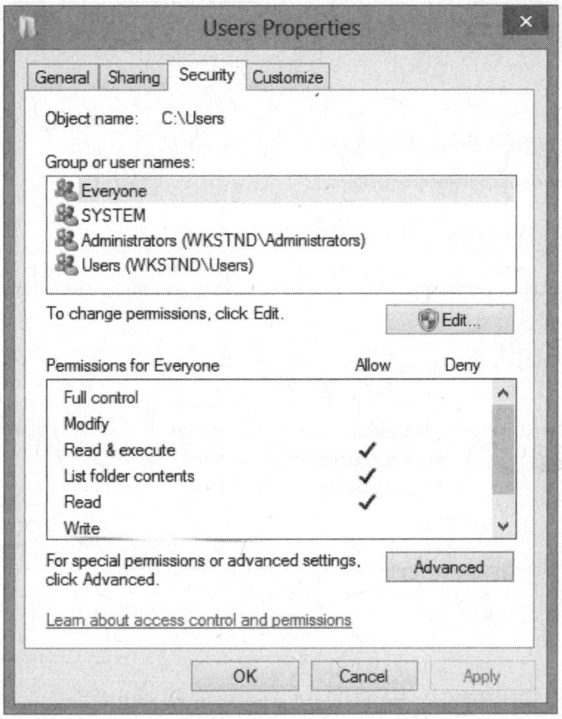

UNDERSTANDING BASIC AND ADVANCED PERMISSIONS

The permissions protecting a particular system element are not like the keys to a lock, which provide either full access or no access at all. Permissions are designed to be granular, enabling you to grant specific degrees of access to security principals.

You can use NTFS permissions to control not only who has access to Alice's spreadsheet, but also the degree to which each user has access. You might grant Ralph permission to read the spreadsheet and also modify it, while Ed can only read it, and Trixie cannot see it at all.

To provide this granularity, each of the Windows permission systems has an assortment of permissions that you can assign to a security principal in any combination. Depending on the permission system you are using, you might have literally dozens of different permissions available for a single system element.

If this is all starting to sound extremely complex, don't worry. Windows provides preconfigured permission combinations that are suitable for most common access control chores. When you open the Properties dialog box for a system element and look at its Security

> **TAKE NOTE***
>
> Prior to Windows 8 and Windows Server 2012, basic and advanced permissions were known as standard and special permissions, respectively.

tab, the permissions you are seeing are called ***basic permissions***. Basic permissions are actually combinations of ***advanced permissions***, which provide the most granular control over the element.

For example, the NTFS permission system has 14 advanced permissions that you can assign to a folder or file. However, there are also six basic permissions, which are various combinations of the 14 advanced permissions. In most cases, you will only have to work with the basic permissions. Many administrators rarely, if ever, work directly with the advanced permissions.

If you do find it necessary to work with advanced permissions directly, Windows makes it possible. When you click the Advanced button on the Security tab of any Properties dialog box, an Advanced Security Settings dialog box appears, as shown in Figure 15-2, which enables you to access the ACEs for the selected system element directly.

Figure 15-2

The *Advanced Security Settings for Users* dialog box

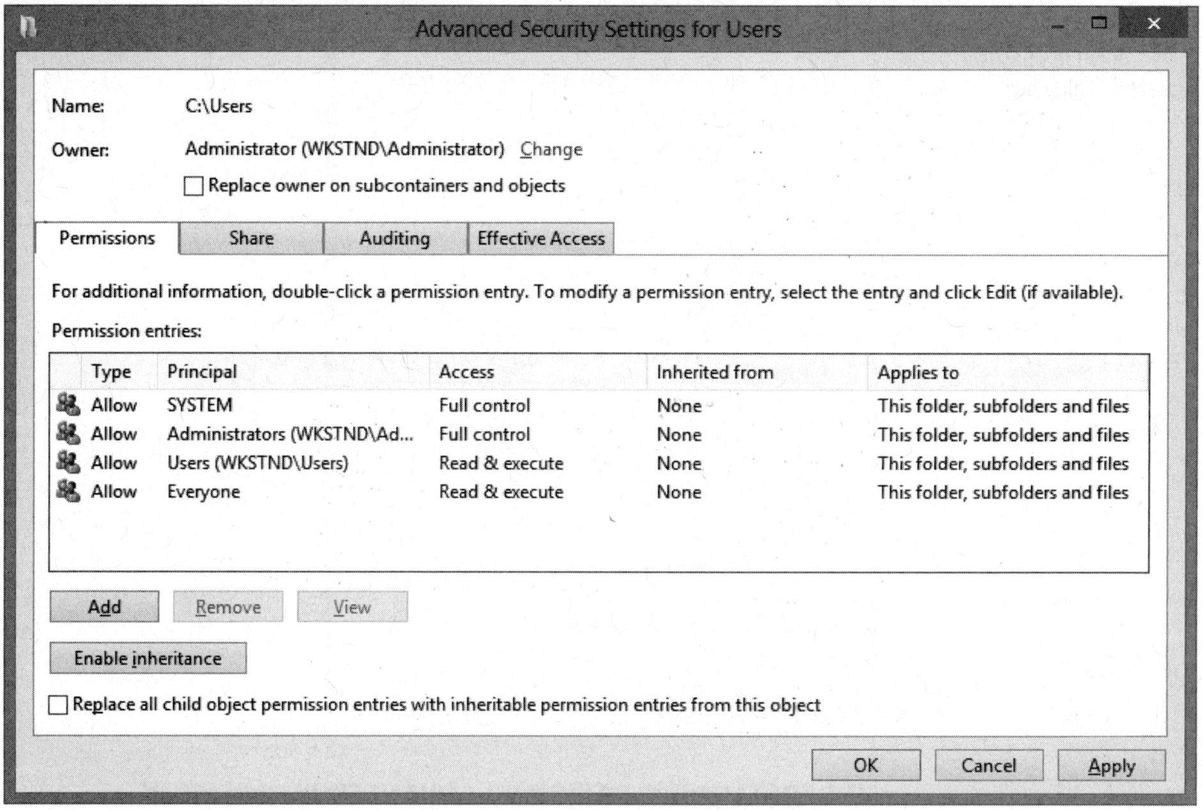

ALLOWING AND DENYING PERMISSIONS

When you assign permissions to a system element, you are, in effect, creating a new ACE in the element's ACL. There are two basic types of ACEs: *Allow* and *Deny*. This makes it possible to approach permission management tasks from two directions:

- **Additive** – Start with no permissions and then grant Allow permissions to individual security principals to provide them with the access they need.
- **Subtractive** – Start by granting all possible Allow permissions to individual security principals, providing them with full control over the system element, and then grant them Deny permissions for the access you don't want them to have.

Most administrators prefer the additive approach, because Windows, by default, attempts to limit access to important system elements. In a properly designed permission hierarchy, the use of Deny permissions is often not needed at all. Many administrators frown on their use, because combining Allow and Deny permissions in the same hierarchy can make it difficult to determine the effective permissions for a specific system element.

INHERITING PERMISSIONS

The most important principle in permission management is that permissions tend to run downwards through a hierarchy. The tendency of permissions to flow downwards through a file system or other hierarchy is called permission inheritance. Permission inheritance means that parent elements pass their permissions down to their subordinate elements.

For example, when you grant Alice Allow permissions to the root of the D: drive, all of the files and subfolders on the D: drive inherit those permissions, and Alice can access them. The principle of inheritance simplifies the permission assignment process enormously. Without it, you would have to grant security principals individual Allow permissions for every file, folder, share, object, and key they need to access. With inheritance, you can grant access to an entire file system by creating one set of Allow permissions.

In most cases, whether they do it consciously or not, system administrators take inheritance into account when they design their file systems and Active Directory trees. The location of a system element in a hierarchy is often based on how the administrators plan to assign permissions. For example, the section of a directory tree shown in Figure 15-3 is intended to be a place where network users can temporarily store files that they want other users to access.

Figure 15-3

A sample xfer directory structure

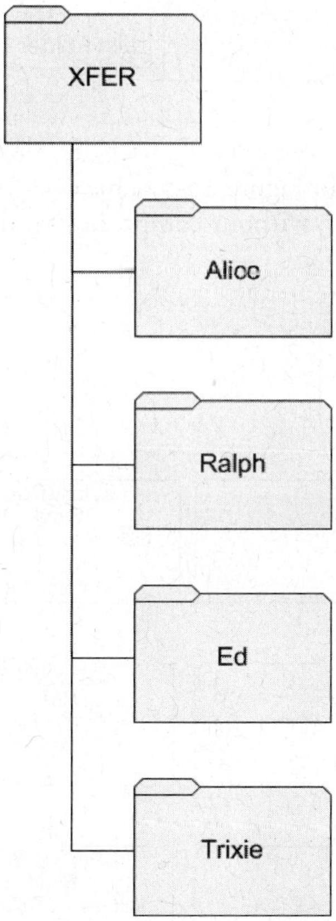

Because the administrator has assigned all users the Allow Read and Allow List Folder Contents basic permissions to the xfer folder, as shown in Figure 15-4, everyone is able to read the files in the xfer directory. Because the assigned permissions run downwards, all of the subfolders beneath xfer inherit those permissions, so all of the users can read the files in all of the subfolders as well.

Figure 15-4

Granting *Allow* permissions to the xfer folder

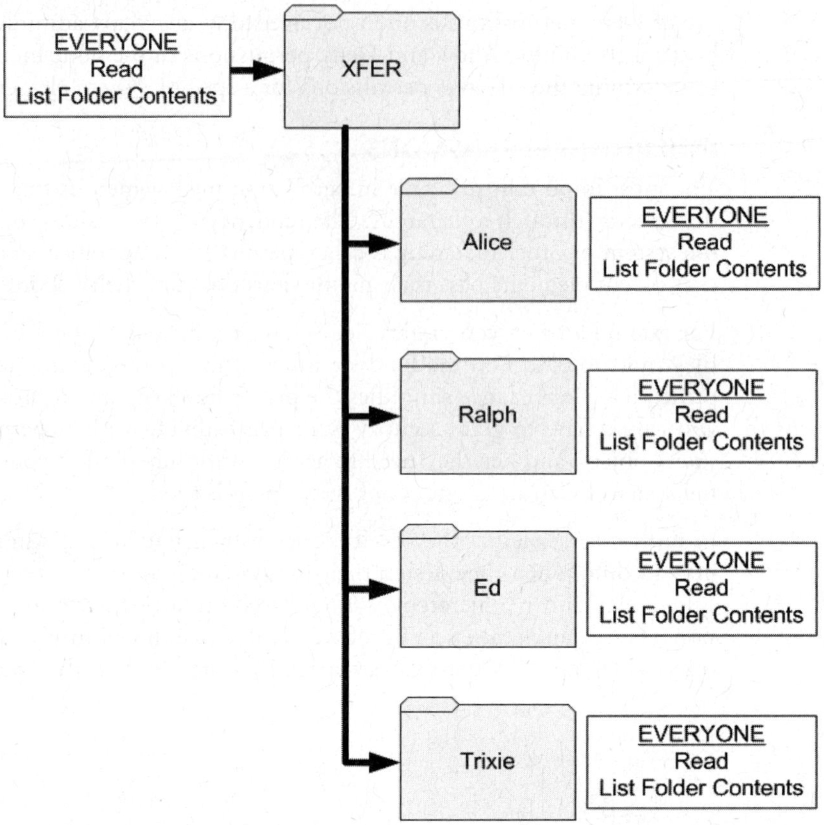

The next step is for the administrator to assign each user the Allow Full Control permission to his or her own subfolder, as shown in Figure 15-5. This enables each user to create, modify, and delete files in his or her own folder, without compromising the security of the other users'

Figure 15-5

Granting *Full Control* to individual user folders

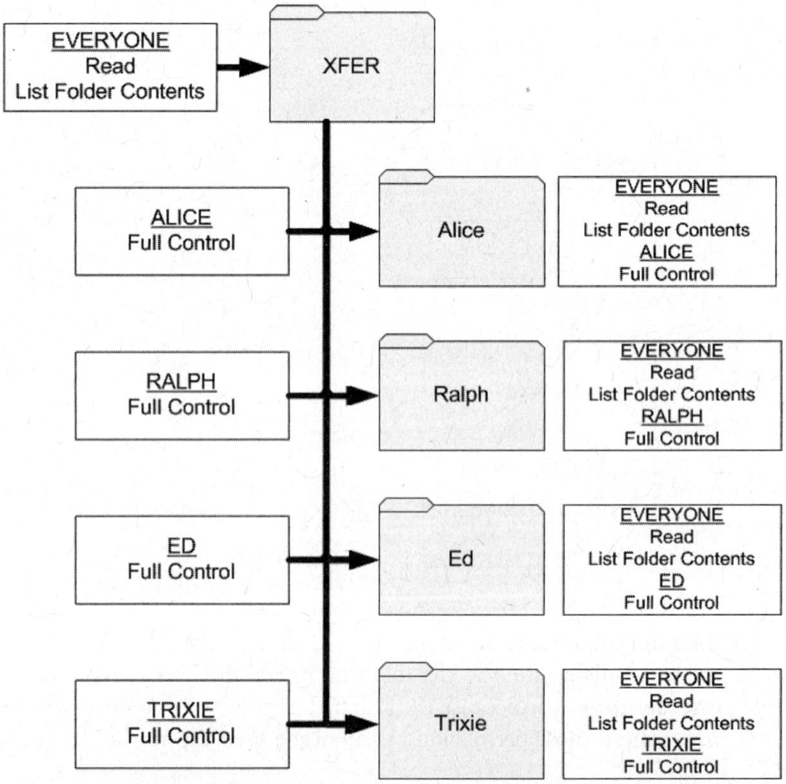

folders. Because the user folders are at the bottom of the hierarchy, there are no subfolders to inherit the Full Control permissions.

There are some situations in which an administrator might want to prevent subordinate elements from inheriting permissions from their parents. There are two ways to do this:

- **Turn off inheritance** – When you assign advanced permissions, you can configure an ACE not to pass its permissions down to its subordinate elements. This effectively blocks the inheritance process.
- **Deny permissions** – When you assign a Deny permission to a system element, it overrides any Allow permissions that the element might have inherited from its parent objects.

COPYING AND MOVING NTFS FILES

NTFS permission inheritance behaves in various ways when you copy and move files and folders to different locations. When you copy NTFS files or folders from one location to another, whether the destination is on the same or a different NTFS volume, the new copy does not take the permissions from its original location with it. Instead, the new copy new inherits permissions from its parent folder at the new location.

When moving files or folders, the behavior is different. If you move files or folders to a new location on the same NTFS volume, their existing permissions move with them. If you move files or folders to a different volume, they leave their existing permissions behind and inherit permissions from the parent folder at the new location.

TAKE NOTE*

It is possible to move NTFS files or folders to a different volume while retaining their existing permissions by using the Robocopy.exe command line utility included with Windows 8.

UNDERSTANDING EFFECTIVE ACCESS

A security principal can receive permissions in many different ways, and it is important for an administrator to understand how these permissions interact. ***Effective access*** is the combination of Allow permissions and Deny permissions that a security principal receives for a given system element, whether explicitly assigned, inherited, or received through a group membership. Because a security principal can receive permissions from so many sources, it is not unusual for those permissions to conflict, so there are rules defining how the permissions combine to form the effective permissions. These rules are as follows:

- **Allow permissions are cumulative** – When a security principal receives Allow permissions from more than one source, the permissions are combined to form the effective permissions. For example, if Alice receives the Allow Read and Allow List Folder Contents permissions for a particular folder by inheriting them from its parent folder, and receives the Allow Write and Allow Modify permissions to the same folder from a group membership, Alice's effective permissions for the folder is the combination of all four permissions. If you then explicitly grant Alice's user account the Allow Full Control permission, this fifth permission is combined with the other four.
- **Deny permissions override Allow permissions** – When a security principal receives Allow permissions, whether explicitly, by inheritance, or from a group, you can override those permissions by granting the principal Deny permissions of the same type. For example, if Alice receives the Allow Read and Allow List Folder Contents permissions for a particular folder by inheritance, and receives the Allow Write and Allow Modify permissions to the same folder from a group membership, explicitly granting her the Deny permissions to that folder prevents her from accessing it in any way.

- **Explicit permissions take precedence over inherited permissions** – When a security principal receives permissions by inheriting them from a parent or from group memberships, you can override those permissions by explicitly assigning contradicting permissions to the security principal itself. For example, if Alice inherits the Deny Full Access permission for a folder, explicitly assigning her user account the Allow Full Access permission to that folder overrides the denial.

Of course, instead of examining and evaluating all of the possible permission sources, you can just open the Advanced Security Settings dialog box, click the Effective Access tab, and select a security principal to display its current effective permissions for the selected file or folder, as shown in Figure 15-6.

Figure 15-6

The Effective Access tab of the *Advanced Security Settings for Test Folder* dialog box

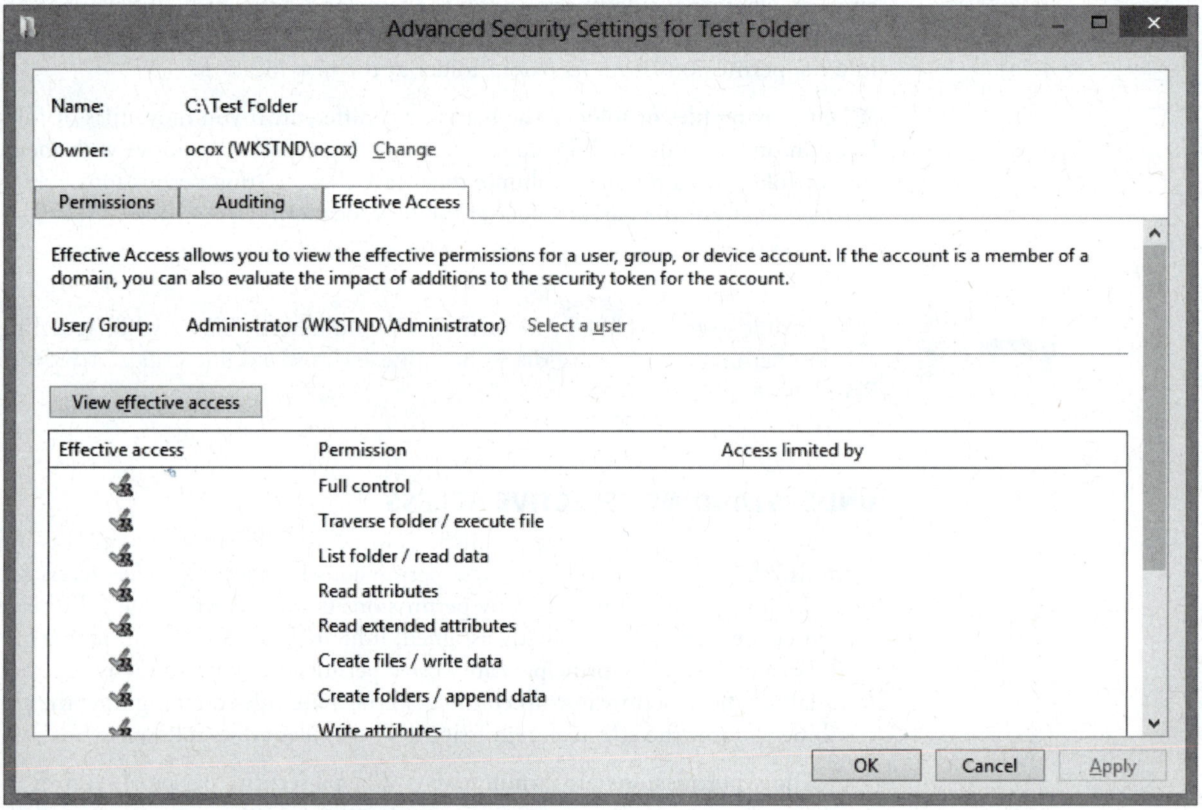

Managing NTFS Permissions

Windows 8 supports two primary file systems, NTFS and FAT, but the majority of Windows installations today use NTFS.

New Technology File System (NTFS), the primary Windows file system, is required to implement various security and administrative features in Windows. NTFS is a journaling file system that can recover from disk errors more readily than the earlier FAT32 file system. It also supports the Unicode character set and long file names (up to 255 characters).

In any Windows network, you can set sharing permissions for drives and folders. On that network, each user can choose to share entire drives or individual folders with the network.

NTFS permissions are available to drives formatted with NTFS. The advantage with NTFS permissions is that they affect local users as well as network users and they are based on the permission granted to each individual user at the Windows logon, regardless of where the user is connecting.

Administrators can use the NTFS utility to provide access control for files and folders, containers and objects on the network as a type of system security. Known as the "Security Descriptor," this information controls what kind of access is allowed for individual users and groups of users.

Along with the additional functionality that NTFS provides comes the potential for complex configurations that can lead to administration headaches. If you don't have a thorough understanding of various permissions and their relationships, it can be difficult to sort out a permission problem when it occurs.

CERTIFICATION READY
Configure NTFS permissions
Objective 4.2

One of the main advantages of NTFS is that it supports permissions, which FAT does not. As described earlier in this lesson, every file and folder on an NTFS drive has an ACL that consists of ACEs, each of which contains a security principal and the permissions assigned to that principal.

MORE INFORMATION

The original 12-bit *file allocation table* file system (now referred to as FAT12) was severely limited in several ways. The FAT12 file system was the source of the 8.3 DOS filename limitation, and it originally imposed a volume size limitation of 32 megabytes. Subsequent enhancements to the file system increased its address space to 16 and eventually 32 bits. The resulting FAT32 file system now supports filenames up to 255 characters long and volumes up to 8 terabytes in size, but it still has no built-in permissions system. However, the versions of Windows supporting FAT32, including Windows 8, impose a FAT32 volume size limit of 32 gigabytes, which is the primary reason why most Windows computers today use NTFS.

In the NTFS permission system, the security principals involved are typically users and groups, which Windows refers to as security identifiers (SIDs). When a user attempts to access an NTFS file or folder, the system reads the user's security access token, which contains the SIDs for the user's account and all of the groups to which the user belongs. The system then compares these SIDs to those stored in the file or folder's ACEs to determine what access the user should have. This process is called authorization.

ASSIGNING BASIC NTFS PERMISSIONS

Most Windows system administrators work with basic NTFS permissions almost exclusively. This is because there is no need to work directly with advanced permissions for most common access control tasks. To assign basic NTFS permissions, use the following procedure:

ASSIGN BASIC NTFS PERMISSIONS

GET READY. Log on to Windows 8 using an account with Administrator privileges, and then perform the following steps:

1. Open the desktop and click the **File Explorer** icon on the taskbar. A *File Explorer* window appears.
2. In the Computer container, right-click the **Local Disk (C:)** drive and then, on the context menu, point to **New** and select **Folder**. Give the folder the name **Test Folder**.
3. Right-click the **Test Folder** folder you created and then, from the context menu, select **Properties**. The *Test Folder Properties* sheet appears.

4. Click the **Security** tab. The top half of the resulting display lists all of the security principals currently possessing permissions to the Test Folder folder. The bottom half lists the permissions held by the selected security principal.
5. Click **Edit**. The *Permissions for Test Folder* dialog box appears, as shown in Figure 15-7. The interface is the same as that of the Security tab on the Properties sheet, except that the permissions are now represented by checkboxes, indicating that you can modify their states.

Figure 15-7

The *Permissions for Test Folder* dialog box

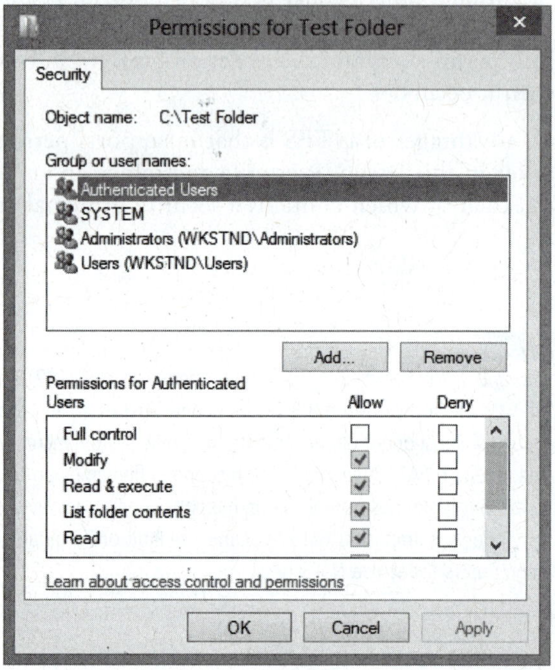

6. Click **Add**. The Select Users or Groups dialog box appears, as shown in Figure 15-8.

Figure 15-8

The *Select Users or Groups* dialog box

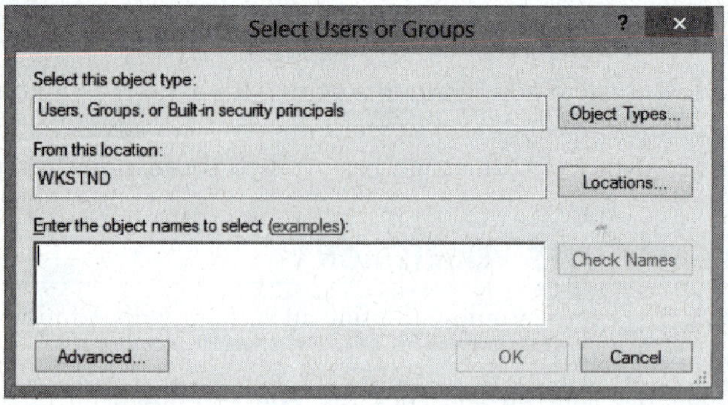

TAKE NOTE*

When you assign permissions on a computer using the Private or Public network location, you select local user and group accounts to be the security principals that receive the permissions. However, if the computer is a member of an Active Directory Domain Services domain, the default is to assign permissions to domain users, groups, and other objects.

7. In the Enter the object names to select text box, type **Guest** and then click **OK**. The Guest user account appears on the *Permissions for Test Folder* dialog box in the Group or user names list, as shown in Figure 15-9.

Figure 15-9

The *Permissions for Test Folder* dialog box, with the Guest user added

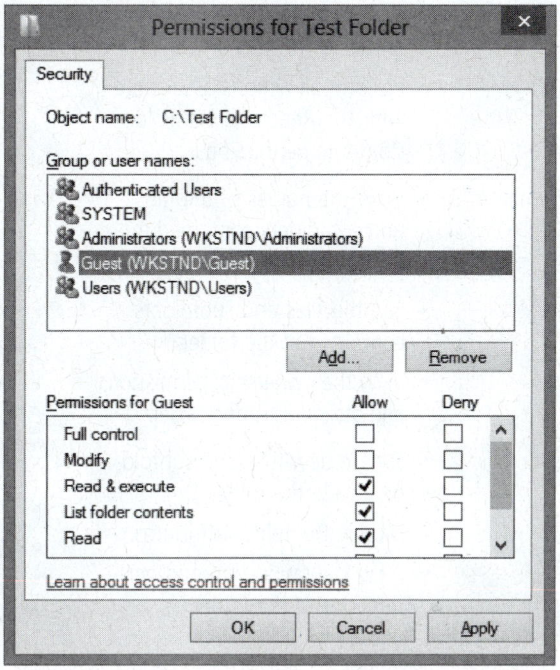

8. Select the **Guest** user and then, in the *Permissions for Guest* box, select or clear the **Allow** checkbox or **Deny** checkbox to allow or deny the user any of the basic permissions shown in Table 15-1.

Table 15-1

NTFS Basic Permissions

Basic Permission	When Applied to a Folder, Enables a Security Principal to:	When Applied to a File, Enables a Security Principal to:
Full Control	• Modify the folder permissions. • Take ownership of the folder. • Delete subfolders and files contained in the folder. • Perform all actions associated with all of the other NTFS folder permissions.	• Modify the file permissions. • Take ownership of the file. • Perform all actions associated with all of the other NTFS file permissions.
Modify	• Delete the folder. • Perform all actions associated with the Write and the Read & Execute permissions.	• Modify the file. • Delete the file. • Perform all actions associated with the Write and the Read & execute permissions.

(continued)

Table 15-1
(continued)

Basic Permission	When Applied to a Folder, Enables a Security Principal to:	When Applied to a File, Enables a Security Principal to:
Read & Execute	• Navigate through restricted folders to reach other files and folders. • Perform all actions associated with the Read and List Folder Contents permissions.	• Perform all actions associated with the Read permission. • Run applications.
List Folder Contents	• View the names of the files and subfolders contained in the folder.	• Not applicable
Read	• See the files and subfolders contained in the folder. • View the ownership, permissions, and attributes of the folder.	• Read the contents of the file. • View the ownership, permissions, and attributes of the file.
Write	• Create new files and subfolders inside the folder. • Modify the folder attributes. • View the ownership and permissions of the folder.	• Overwrite the file. • Modify the file attributes. • View the ownership and permissions of the file.

9. Click **OK** to close the *Permissions for Test Folder* dialog box.
10. Click **OK** to close the Test folder Properties sheet.

TAKE NOTE* Assigning permissions to the single folder you created takes only a moment, but for a folder with a large number of subordinate files and subfolders the process can take a long time because the system must modify the ACL of each folder and file.

ASSIGNING ADVANCED NTFS PERMISSIONS

If you ever have the need to work with advanced NTFS permissions directly, Windows 8 provides the tools to do so. To view and manage the advanced NTFS permissions for a file or folder, use the following procedure.

ASSIGN ADVANCED NTFS PERMISSIONS

GET READY. Log on to Windows 8 using an account with Administrator privileges, and then perform the following steps:

1. Open **File Explorer** and expand the **Local Disk** (C:) drive.
2. Right-click the **Test Folder** folder you created earlier and then, from the context menu, select Properties. The *Test Folder Properties* sheet appears.
3. Click the Security tab, and then click **Advanced**. The *Advanced Security Settings for Test Folder* dialog box appears, as shown in Figure 15-10. This dialog box is as close as the Windows graphical interface can come to displaying the contents of an ACL. Each of the lines in the Permission entries list is essentially an ACE, and includes the following information:

- **Type** – Specifies whether the entry allows or denies the permission.
- **Name** – Specifies the name of the security principal receiving the permission.
- **Permission** – Specifies the name of the basic permission being assigned to the security principal. If the entry is used to assign advanced permissions, the word *Advanced* appears in this field.
- **Inherited From** – Specifies whether the permission is inherited and if so, where it is inherited from.
- **Apply To** – Specifies whether the permission is inherited by subordinate objects and if so, by which ones.

This dialog box also contains the following two controls:

- **Disable inheritance** – A button that enables you to specify whether the file or folder should inherit permissions from parent objects. Clicking it causes a Block Inheritance message box to appear, enabling you to choose whether to convert inherited permissions for the selected object into explicit permissions or remove all of the inherited permissions from the object. If you choose the former, the effective access stays the same, but the file or folder is no longer dependent on the parent for permission inheritance. If you change the permissions on the parent objects, the file or folder remains unaffected.
- **Replace all child object permissions with inheritable permission entries from this object** – Causes subordinate objects to inherit permissions from this file or folder, to the exclusion of all permissions explicitly assigned to the subordinate objects.

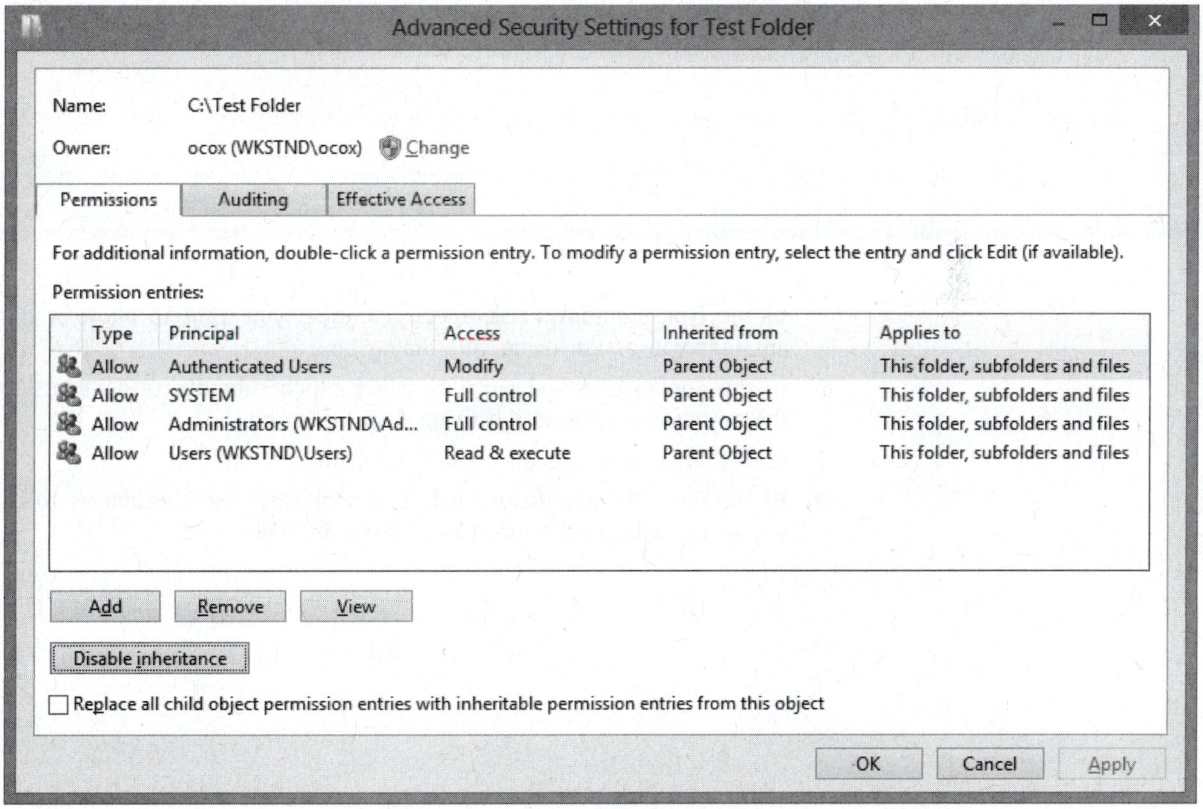

Figure 15-10

The *Advanced Security Settings for Test Folder* dialog box

4. Click **Add**. A *Permission Entry for Test Folder* dialog box appears.
5. Click **Select a principal**. The *Select Users or Groups* dialog box appears.

6. In the *Enter the object names to select text* box, type **Guest,** and then click **OK**. The Guest user appears in the *Permission Entry for Test Folder* dialog box appears, as shown in Figure 15-11.

Figure 15-11

The *Permission Entry for Test Folder* dialog box

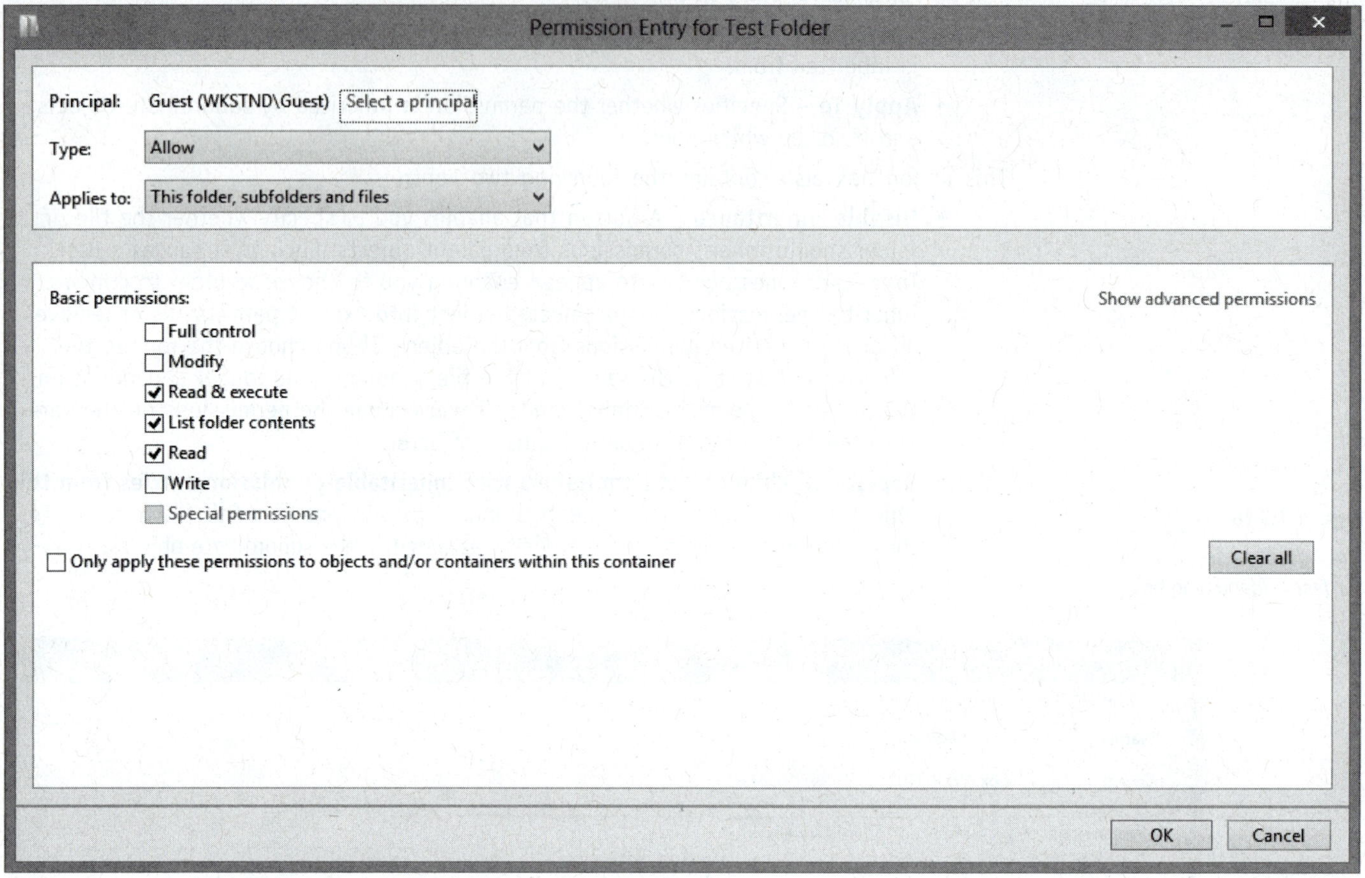

7. In the *Type* drop-down list, specify whether you want to allow or deny the permissions you assign using this dialog box.
8. In the *Applies to* dropdown list, select which subordinate elements should receive the permissions you assign using this dialog box.
9. Click the **Show advanced permissions** link.
10. In the *Advanced permissions* list, select or clear the checkboxes to assign the user any of the advanced permissions shown in Table 15-2.

Table 15-2

NTFS Advanced Permissions

Advanced Permission	Functions
Traverse Folder/Execute File	• The Traverse Folder permission allows or denies security principals the ability to move through folders that they do not have permission to access, so as to reach files or folders that they do have permission to access. This permission applies to folders only. • The Execute File permission allows or denies security principals the ability to run program files. This permission applies to files only.
List Folder/Read Data	• The List Folder permission allows or denies security principals the ability to view the file and subfolder names within a folder. This permission applies to folders only. • The Read Data permission allows or denies security principals the ability to view the contents of a file. This permission applies to files only.
Read Attributes	Allows or denies security principals the ability to view the NTFS attributes of a file or folder.
Read Extended Attributes	Allows or denies security principals the ability to view the extended attributes of a file or folder.
Create Files/Write Data	• The Create Files permission allows or denies security principals the ability to create files within the folder. This permission applies to folders only. • The Write Data permission allows or denies security principals the ability to modify the file and overwrite existing content. This permission applies to files only.
Create Folders/Append Data	• The Create Folders permission allows or denies security principals to create subfolders within a folder. This permission applies to folders only. • The Append Data permission allows or denies security principals the ability to add data to the end of the file but not to modify, delete, or overwrite existing data in the file. This permission applies to files only.
Write Attributes	Allows or denies security principals the ability to modify the NTFS attributes of a file or folder.
Write Extended Attributes	Allows or denies security principals the ability to modify the extended attributes of a file or folder.
Delete Subfolders and Files	Allows or denies security principals the ability to delete subfolders and files, even if the Delete permission has not been granted on the subfolder or file.
Delete	Allows or denies security principals the ability to delete the file or folder.
Read Permissions	Allows or denies security principals the ability to read the permissions for the file or folder.
Change Permissions	Allows or denies security principals the ability to modify the permissions for the file or folder.
Take Ownership	Allows or denies security principals the ability to take ownership of the file or folder.
Synchronize	Allows or denies different threads of multithreaded, multiprocessor programs to wait on the handle for the file or folder and synchronize with another thread that might signal it.

11. Click **OK** to close the *Permission Entry for Test Folder* dialog box.
12. Click **OK** to close the second *Advanced Security Settings for Test Folder* dialog box.
13. Click **OK** to close the first *Advanced Security Settings for Test Folder* dialog box.
14. Click **OK** to close the *Test Folder Properties* sheet.

As mentioned earlier in this lesson, basic permissions are combinations of advanced permissions designed to provide frequently needed access controls. Table 15-3 lists all of the basic permissions, and the advanced permissions that compose them.

Table 15-3

NTFS Basic Permissions and Their Advanced Permission Equivalents

Basic Permission	Advanced Permissions
Read	• List Folder/Read Data • Read Attributes • Read Extended Attributes • Read Permissions • Synchronize
Read & Execute	• List Folder/Read Data • Read Attributes • Read Extended Attributes • Read Permissions • Synchronize • Traverse Folder/Execute File
Modify	• Create Files/Write Data • Create Folders/Append Data • Delete • List Folder/Read Data • Read Attributes • Read Extended Attributes • Read Permissions • Synchronize • Write Attributes • Write Extended Attributes
Write	• Create Files/Write Data • Create Folders/Append Data • Read Permissions • Synchronize • Write Attributes • Write Extended Attributes
List Folder Contents	• List Folder/Read Data • Read Attributes • Read Extended Attributes • Read Permissions • Synchronize • Traverse Folder/Execute File

(continued)

Table 15-3
(continued)

Basic Permission	Advanced Permissions
Full Control	• Change Permissions • Create Files/Write Data • Create Folders/Append Data • Delete • Delete Subfolders and Files • List Folder/Read Data • Read Attributes • Read Extended Attributes • Read Permissions • Synchronize • Take Ownership • Write Attributes • Write Extended Attributes

USING ICACLS.EXE

In addition to configuring NTFS permissions graphically, you can also use the Icacls.exe command line utility. Using Icacls.exe, you can grant or revoke basic or advanced permissions by allowing or denying them to specific security principals. The syntax for granting permissions is as follows:

```
icacls.exe filespec /grant[:r] security_id:(permissions)
[/T][/C][/L][/Q]
```

- ***filespec*** – Specifies the file or folder whose ACL you want to modify.
- **:r** – Causes the assigned permissions to replace any previously assigned ones. Without the :r switch, the program adds the permissions to the existing ones.
- ***security_id*** – Specifies the name or security ID of the user or group to whom you want to assign permissions.
- ***permissions*** – Specifies the permissions you want to assign to the security principal, using the following abbreviations:
    - F (Full Control)
    - M (Modify)
    - RX (Read and Execute)
    - R (Read)
    - W (Write)
- **/T** – Executes the command on all of the files and subfolders contained in the filespec.
- **/C** – Proceeds with the operation despite the occurrence of errors.
- **/L** – Performs the operation on a symbolic link rather than the actual destination.
- **/Q** – Prevents the program from displaying success messages.

MORE INFORMATION

You can also use Icacls.exe to manage advanced permissions. For more information on using Icacls.exe, see Microsoft's TechNet website.

In addition to granting permissions, you can also use the */deny* parameter to assign Deny permissions and the `/remove` parameter to erase permissions from an ACL.

UNDERSTANDING RESOURCE OWNERSHIP

As you study the NTFS permission system, it might occur to you that it seems possible to lock out a file or folder—that is, assign a combination of permissions that permits access to no one at all, leaving the file or folder inaccessible. In fact, this is true.

A user with administrative privileges can revoke his or her own permissions, as well as everyone else's, preventing them from accessing a resource. However, the NTFS permissions system includes a "back door" that prevents these orphaned files and folders from remaining permanently inaccessible.

Every file and folder on an NTFS drive has an owner, and the owner always has the ability to modify the permissions for the file or folder, even if the owner has no permissions him- or herself. By default, the owner of a file or folder is the user account that created it. However, any account possessing the Take Ownership advanced permission (or the Full Control basic permission) can take ownership of the file or folder.

The other purpose for file and folder ownership is to calculate disk quotas. When you set quotas specifying the maximum amount of disk space particular users can consume, Windows calculates a user's current disk consumption by adding up the sizes of all the files and folders that the user owns.

■ Using the Encrypting File System

THE BOTTOM LINE The Encrypting File System (EFS) protects users' data by encrypting and decrypting it on the fly as the user works.

The ***Encrypting File System (EFS)*** is a feature of NTFS that encodes the files on a computer so that even if an intruder can obtain a file, he or she will be unable to read it. The entire system is keyed to a specific user account, using the public and private keys that are the basis of the Windows public key infrastructure (PKI). The user who creates a file is the only person who can read it.

As the user works, EFS encrypts the files he or she creates using a key generated from the user's public key. Data encrypted with this key can be decrypted only by the user's personal encryption certificate, which is generated using his or her private key.

TAKE NOTE* Only the Professional and Enterprise editions of Windows 8 support EFS. The other do not support EFS.

When the user logs on to the computer, the system gains access to the keys that are necessary to encrypt and decrypt the EFS-protected data. To that user, the encryption process is completely invisible, and usually does not have a major impact on system performance. The user creates, accesses, and saves files in the normal manner, unaware that the cryptographic processes are taking place.

If another user logs on to the computer, he or she has no access to the other user's private key, and therefore cannot decrypt the encrypted files. An attacker can conceivably sit down at the computer and try to copy the files off to a flash drive, but he or she will receive an "Access Denied" error message, just as if he or she lacked the appropriate NTFS permissions for the files.

There are two main restrictions when implementing EFS:

- EFS is a feature of the NTFS file system, so you cannot use EFS on FAT drives.
- You cannot use EFS to encrypt files that have already been compressed using NTFS compression.

CERTIFICATION READY
Encrypt files and folders by using EFS
Objective 4.2

Encrypting a Folder with EFS

In Windows 8, you can use File Explorer to encrypt or disable EFS on any individual files or folders, as long as they are on an NTFS drive.

To encrypt a file or folder, use the following procedure.

ENCRYPT A FOLDER

GET READY. Log on to Windows 8, and then to encrypt a folder, perform the following steps:

1. Open **File Explorer**. The File Explorer window appears.
2. Right-click a file or folder and then, from the context menu, select Properties. The **Properties** sheet for the file or folder appears, as shown in Figure 15-12.

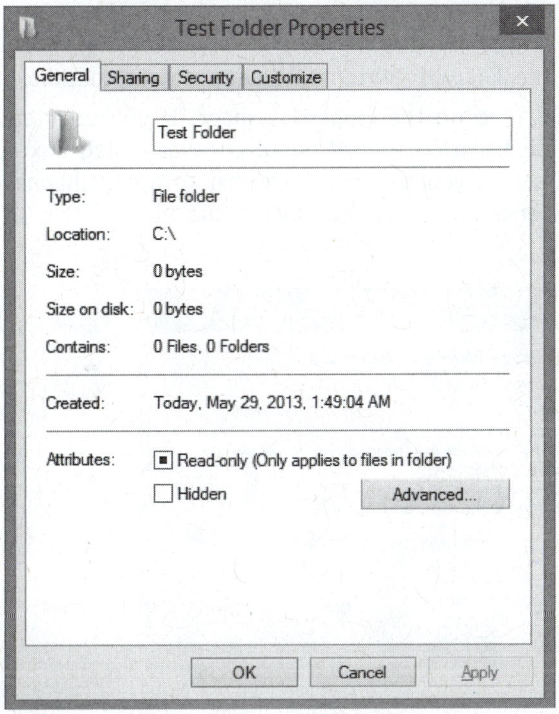

Figure 15-12
A folder's *Properties* sheet

3. On the General tab, click **Advanced**. The *Advanced Attributes* dialog box appears, as shown in Figure 15-13.

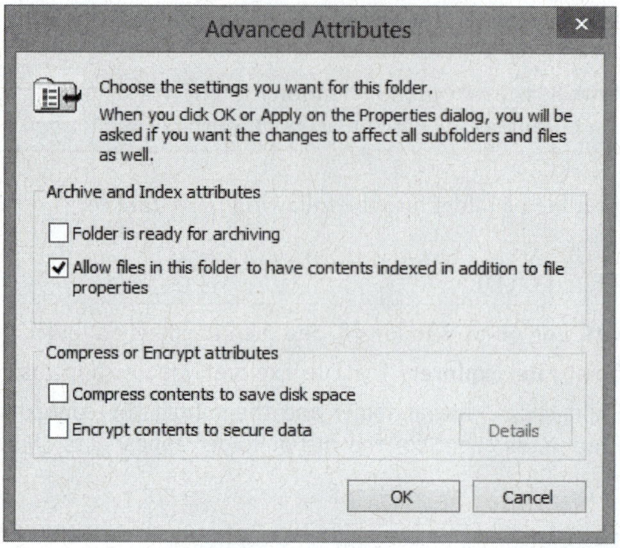

Figure 15-13

The *Advanced Attributes* dialog box

4. Select the **Encrypt contents to secure data** checkbox, and then click **OK**.
5. Click **OK** to close the Properties sheet. If you selected a folder that contains files or subfolders, a *Confirm Attribute Changes* dialog box appears, as shown in Figure 15-14, asking you to choose whether to apply changes to the folder only, or to the folder and all of its subfolders and files.

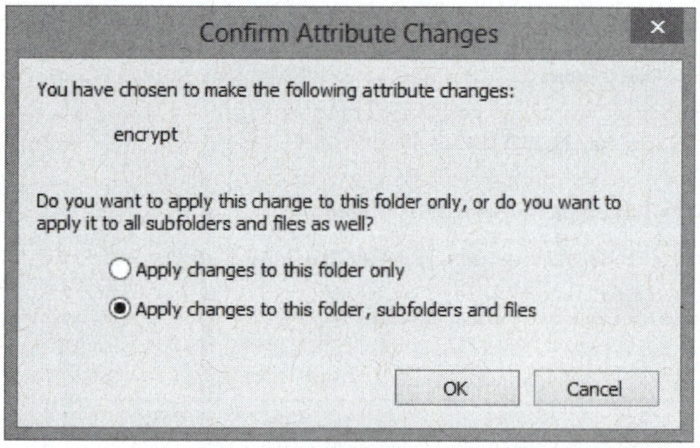

Figure 15-14

A *Confirm Attribute Changes* dialog box

TAKE NOTE* If you elect to apply changes to the selected folder only, EFS does not encrypt any of the files that are currently in the folder. However, any files that you create, copy, or move to the folder after you enable EFS will be encrypted.

6. Select a confirmation option and click **OK**. Depending on how many files and folders there are to be encrypted, the process could take several minutes.

Determining Whether a File or Folder is Encrypted

Administrators commonly receive calls from users who are unable to access their files because they have been encrypted using EFS and the user is unaware of this fact. To resolve the problem, you must first determine whether their files are encrypted or not, and whether the user has the proper NTFS permissions.

File Explorer displays the names of encrypted files in green, by default, but this setting is easily changed in the Folder Options dialog box. To verify that a folder or file is encrypted, use the following procedure:

VIEW THE ENCRYPTION ATTRIBUTE

GET READY. To view the encryption attribute, log on to Windows 8, and then perform the following steps:

1. Open File Explorer. The **File Explorer** window appears.
2. Right-click a file or folder and then, from the context menu, select **Properties**. The Properties sheet for the file or folder appears.
3. On the General tab, click **Advanced**. The *Advanced Attributes* dialog box appears. If the Encrypt contents to secure data checkbox is selected, the file or folder is encrypted.
4. Click **OK** to close the *Advanced Attributes* dialog box.
5. Click **OK** to close the *Properties* sheet.

Configuring Disk Quotas

THE BOTTOM LINE

Managing disk space is a constant concern for server administrators, and one way to prevent users from monopolizing large amount of storage is to implement quotas. Windows 8 supports storage quotas through the NTFS file system. Windows Server also supports a more elaborate quota system as part of File Server Resource Manager. This section discusses only the NTFS implementation.

NTFS quotas enable administrators to set a storage limit for users of a particular volume. Depending on how you configure the quota, users exceeding the limit can be denied disk space, or just receive a warning. The space consumed by individuals users is measured by the size of the files they own or create.

CERTIFICATION READY
Configure disk quotas
Objective 4.2

NTFS quotas a relatively limited in that you can set only a single limit for all of the users of a volume. The feature is also limited in the actions it can take in response to a user exceeding the limit. The quotas in File Server Resource Manager, by contrast, are much more flexible in the nature of the limits you can set and the responses of the program, which can send email notifications, execute commands, and generate reports, as well as log events.

To configure NTFS disk quotas for a volume, use the following procedure.

CONFIGURE DISK QUOTAS

GET READY. To configure disk quotas, log on to Windows 8 using an account with administrative privileges, and then perform the following steps:

1. Click the **File Explorer** icon in the taskbar. The File Explorer window appears.
2. In the Folders list, expand the **Computer** container, right-click a volume and, from the context menu, select **Properties**. The *Properties* sheet for the volume appears.
3. Click the **Quota** tab to display the interface shown in Figure 15-15.

Figure 15-15

The Quota tab of a volume's *Properties* sheet

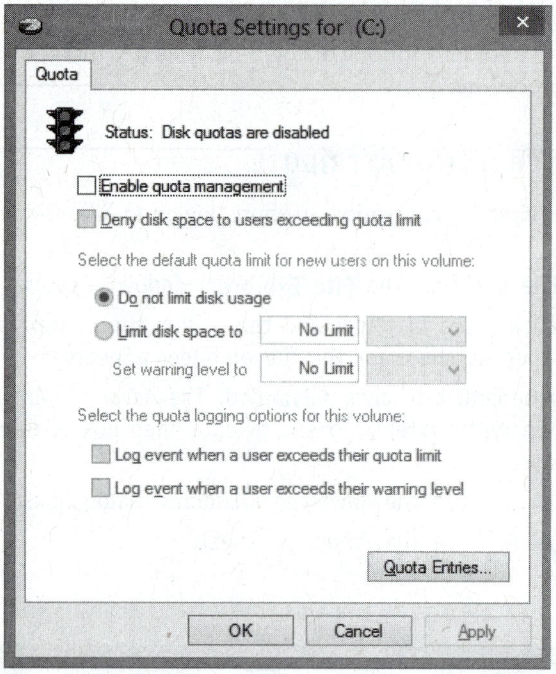

4. Select the **Enable quota management** checkbox to activate the rest of the controls.
5. If you want to prevent users from consuming more than their quota of disk space, select the **Deny disk space to users exceeding quota limit** checkbox.
6. Select the **Limit disk space to** radio button and specify amounts for the quota limit and the warning level.
7. Select the **Log event** checkboxes to control whether users exceeding the specified limits should trigger log entries.
8. Click **OK** to create the quota and close the *Properties* sheet.
9. **Close** Windows Explorer.

Configuring Object Access Auditing

THE BOTTOM LINE

Local Policies enable administrators to set user privileges on the local computer that govern what users can do on the computer and determine if the system should track them in an event log. Tracking events that take place on the local computer, a process referred to as ***auditing***, is an important part of monitoring and managing activities on a computer running Windows 8.

CERTIFICATION READY
Configure object access auditing
Objective 4.2

The Audit Policy section of a Group Policy object (GPO) enables administrators to log successful and failed security events, such as logons and logoffs, account access, and object access. You can use auditing to track both user activities and system activities. Planning to audit requires that you determine the computers to be audited and the types of events you wish to track. Object access auditing enables you to select specific shares, files, and folders for monitoring, as well as any other type of object in the operating system.

When you consider what events to audit, you must decide whether you wish to audit successes or failures, or both. Tracking successful events enables you to determine how often users access network resources. This information can be valuable when planning your resource usage and budgeting for new resources. Tracking failed events can help you determine when security breaches occur or are attempted. The policy settings available for auditing are shown in Figure 15-16.

Figure 15-16

Audit Policies in the Windows 8 Local Computer Policy

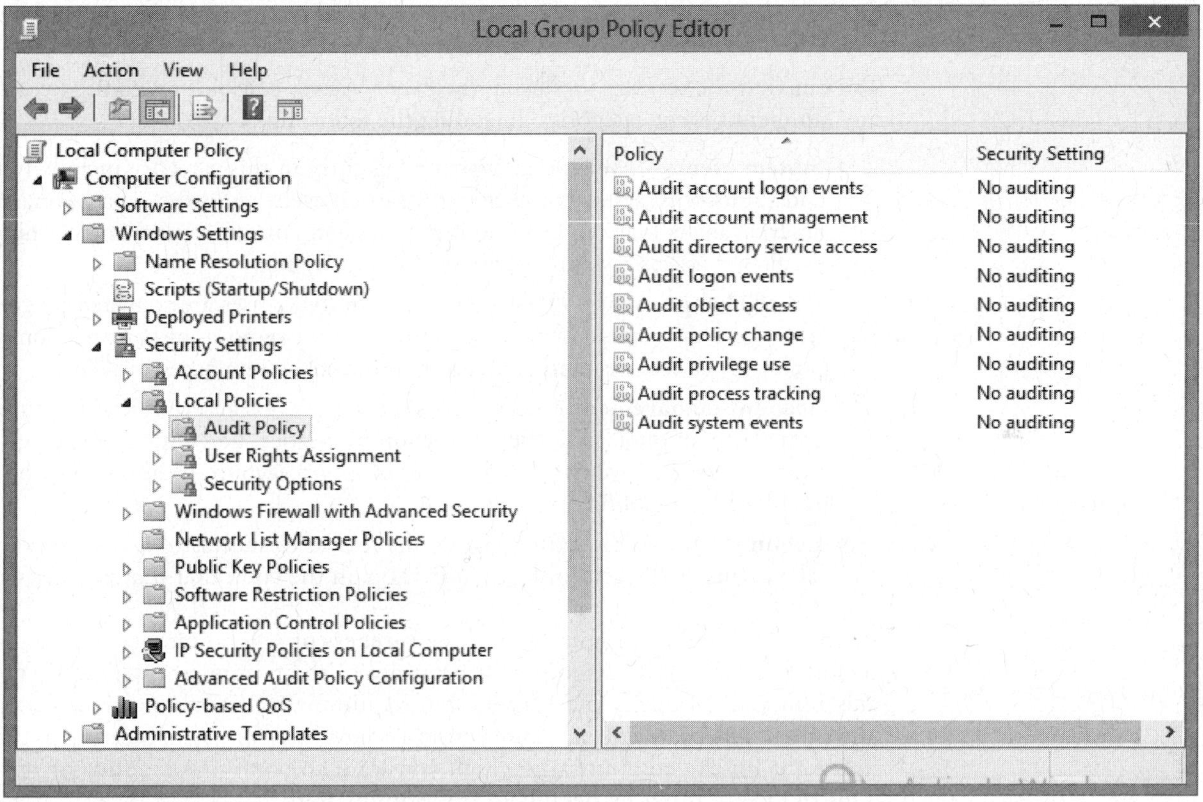

When an audited event occurs, Windows 8 writes an event to the security log on the computer where the event took place. You can then review the audited events in the Event Viewer console.

You must decide which computers, resources, and events you want to audit. It is important to balance the need for auditing against the potential information overload that would be created if you audited every possible type of event. The following guidelines can help you to plan your audit policy:

- **Audit only pertinent items**. Determine the events you want to audit and consider whether it is more important to track successes or failures of these events. You should only plan to audit events that will help you gather network information. When auditing object access, be specific about the type of access you want to track. For example, if you want to audit read access to a file or folder, make sure you audit the read events, not Full Control. Auditing of Full Control would trigger writes to the log for every action on the file or folder. Auditing uses system resources to process and store events. Therefore, auditing unnecessary events will create overhead on your server and make it more difficult to monitor the logs.
- **Archive security logs to provide a documented history**. Keeping a history of event occurrences can provide you with supporting documentation. You can use this documentation to support the need for additional resources based on the usage

of a particular resource. In addition, it provides a history of events that might indicate past security breach attempts. If intruders have administrative privileges, they can clear the log, leaving you without a history of events that document the breach.

- **Configure the size of your security logs carefully**. You need to plan the size of your security logs based on the number of events that you anticipate logging. Event Log Policy settings can be configured under the Computer Configuration\Windows Settings\Security Settings\Event Log node of a GPO.

You can view the security logs using the Event Viewer console and configure it to monitor any number of event categories, including the following:

- **System events** – Events that trigger a log entry in this category include system startups and shutdowns; system time changes; system event resources exhaustion, such as when an event log is filled and can no longer append entries; security log cleaning; or any event that affects system security or the security log.
- **Policy change events** – Policy change audit log entries are triggered by events such as user rights assignment changes, establishment or removal of trust relationships, IPsec policy agent changes, and grants or removals of system access privileges.
- **Account management events** – This setting triggers an event that is written based on changes to account properties and group properties. Log entries written due to this policy setting reflect events related to user or group account creation, deletion, renaming, enabling, or disabling.
- **Logon events** – This setting logs events related to successful user logons on a computer. The events are logged to the Security Log on the computer that processes the request.

Implementation of your plan requires awareness of several factors that can affect the success of your audit policy. You must be aware of the administrative requirements to create and administer a policy plan. Two main requirements are necessary to set up and administer an Audit Policy. First, you must have the Manage Auditing and Security Log user right for the computer on which you want to configure a policy or review a log. This right is granted by default to the Administrators group. However, if you wish to delegate this task to someone else, such as a container administrator, that person must possess the specific right. Second, any files or folders to be audited must be located on NTFS volumes.

Implementation of your plan requires that you specify the categories to be audited and, if necessary, configure objects for auditing. To configure an audit policy, use the following procedure.

CONFIGURE AN AUDIT POLICY

GET READY. To configure an audit policy, log on to Windows 8, using an account with Administrator privileges, and then perform the following steps:

1. Open a Command Prompt window with Administrative Privileges and type **gpedit.msc**. A Local Group Policy Editor console appears.
2. Browse to the Computer Configuration\\Windows Settings\Security Settings\Local Policies node and select **Audit Policy**. The audit policy settings appear in the right pane.
3. Double-click the **Audit object access** setting. The *Properties* sheet for the policy appears, as shown in Figure 15-17.

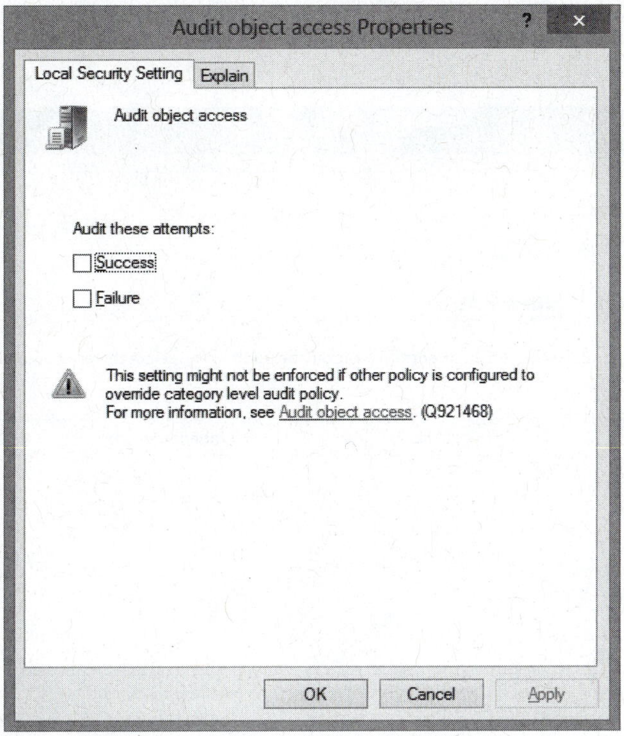

Figure 15-17

The *Properties* sheet for a policy setting

4. Select the appropriate checkbox(es) to audit Success, Failure, or both.
5. Click **OK** to close the setting's Properties sheet.
6. **Close** the *Local Group Policy Editor* console.

You have now configured an audit policy that will enable you to track object accesses. However, configuring objects for auditing is necessary when you have configured the Audit object access policy. This requires additional setup steps, which are described in the following procedure.

CONFIGURE FILES AND FOLDERS FOR AUDITING

GET READY. Log on to a Windows 8 computer, on which you have configured the Audit object access policy, using an account with Administrator privileges. To configure files and folders for auditing, perform the following steps:

1. Open File Explorer, right-click the file or folder you want to audit and, from the context menu, select **Properties**.

   The *Properties* sheet for the file or folder appears.
2. Click the **Security** tab. Then click **Advanced**.

   The *Advanced Security Settings* dialog box appears.
3. Click the **Auditing** tab, as shown in Figure 15-18.

Figure 15-18

The Auditing tab in a folder's *Properties* sheet

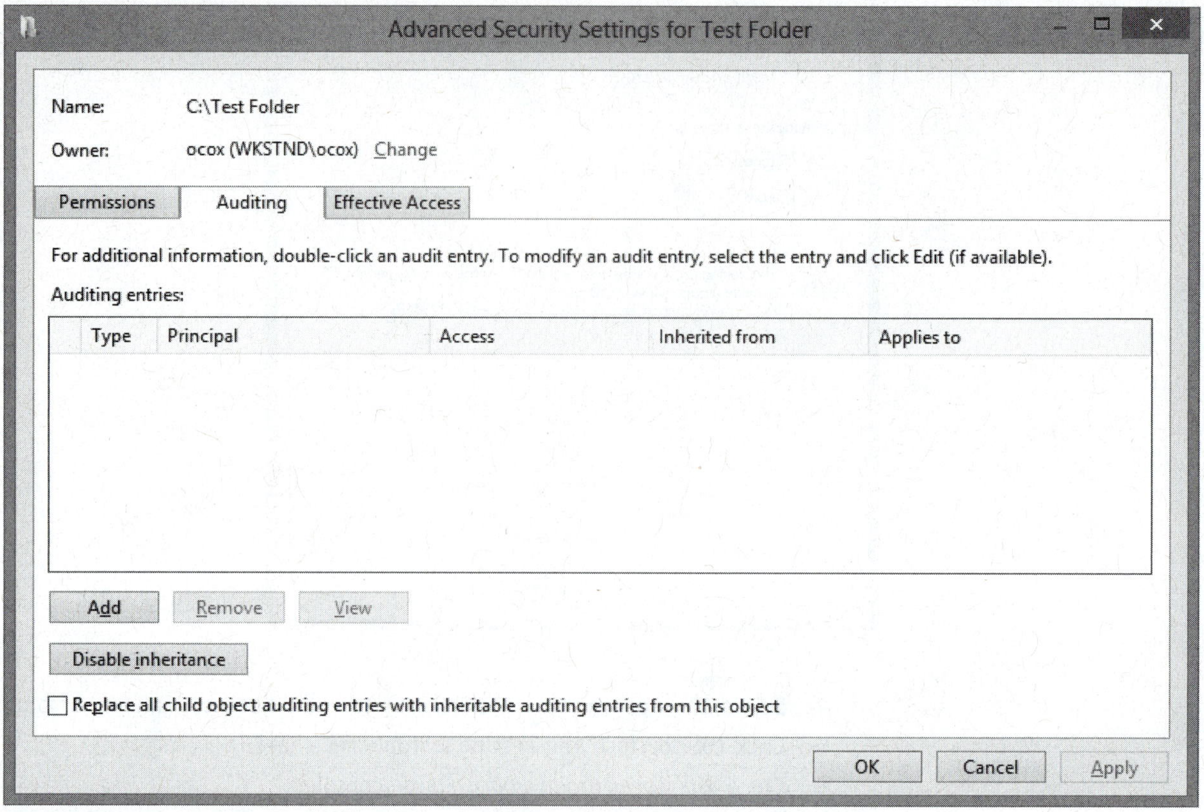

4. Click **Add**.

   The *Auditing Entry* page appears, as shown in Figure 15-19.

Figure 15-19

The *Auditing Entry for Test Folder* page in a folder's Properties sheet

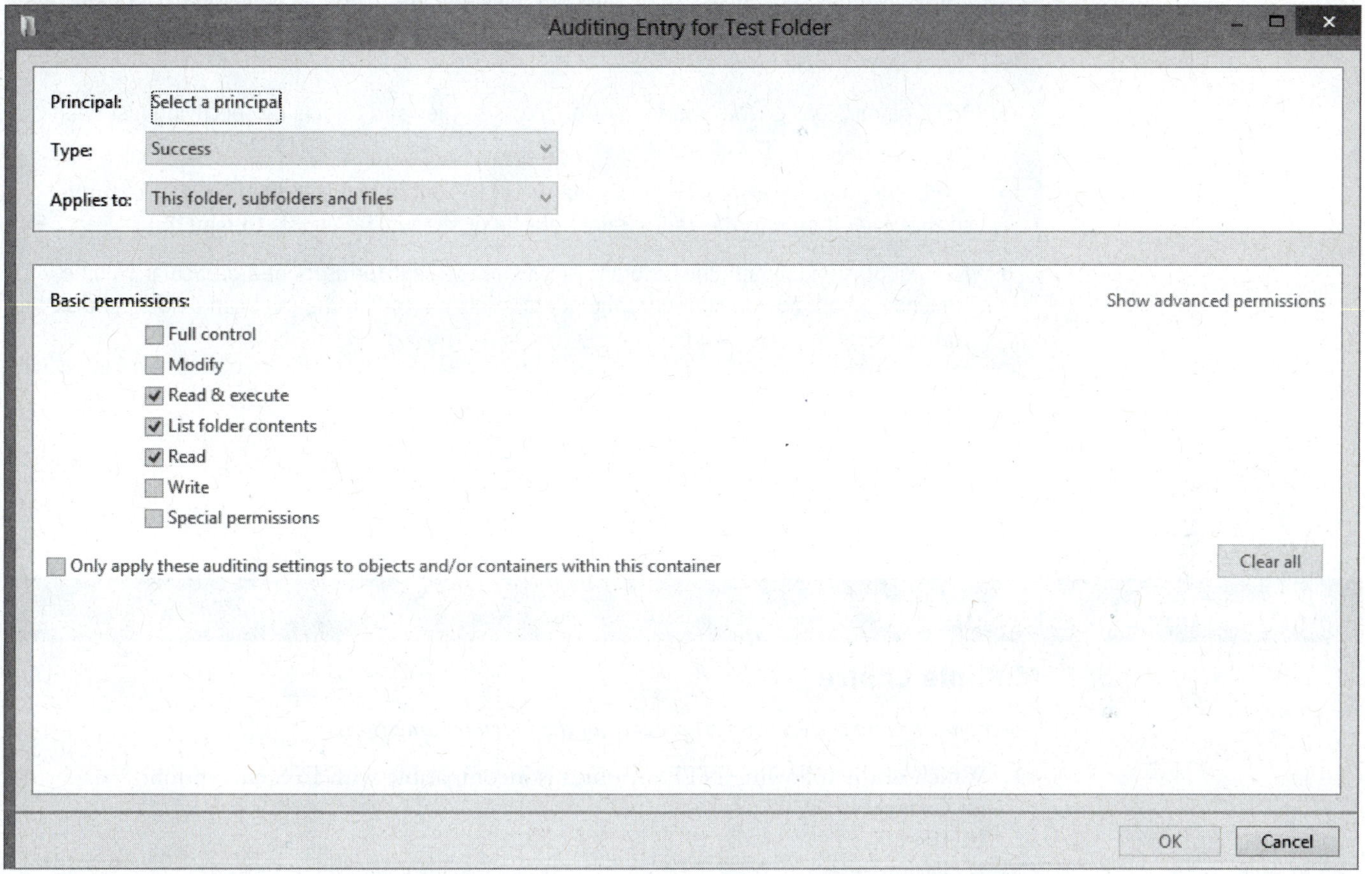

5. Click **Select a Principal**.

   The *Select User, Computer, Service Account, or Group* dialog box appears.

6. Select the users or groups to be audited and then click **OK**.

   The users or groups appear in the *Auditing Entry* dialog box for the object.

7. From the *Type* drop-down list, specify whether you want to audit failures, successes, or both.

8. From the *Applies to* drop-down list, specify which descendent objects should be audited.

9. Select the basic permissions you want to audit for this object and click **OK**. The new Auditing entry appears in the *Advanced Security Settings* dialog box.

10. Create additional auditing entries, if desired, and then click **OK**.

12. Click **OK** to close the object's *Advanced Security Settings* dialog box.

13. Click **OK** to close the object's Properties sheet.

14. **Close** the *File Explorer* window.

You have now configured auditing for files and folders within the Windows 8 operating system. Events corresponding to the settings you have selected will now be recorded in the security log.

SKILL SUMMARY

IN THIS LESSON, YOU LEARNED:

- Windows 8 has several sets of permissions, which operate independently of each other, including NTFS permissions, share permissions, registry permissions, and Active Directory permissions.
- NTFS permissions enable you to control access to files and folders by specifying just what tasks individual users can perform on them.
- The Encrypting File System (EFS) is a feature of NTFS that encodes the files on a computer so that even if an intruder can obtain a file, he or she will be unable to read it.
- NTFS quotas enable administrators to set a storage limit for users of a particular volume. Depending on how you configure the quota, users exceeding the limit can be denied disk space, or just receive a warning.

Knowledge Assessment

Multiple Choice

Select one or more correct answers for each of the following questions.

1. Which of the following NTFS features is incompatible with EFS encryption?
   - **a.** Compression
   - **b.** IPsec
   - **c.** Permissions
   - **d.** Parental controls
2. Which of the following is the best description of a security principal?
   - **a.** The person granting permissions to network users
   - **b.** The network resource receiving permissions
   - **c.** A collection of individual special permissions
   - **d.** An object that assigns permissions
3. Which of the following statements about effective access is not true?
   - **a.** Inherited permissions take precedence over explicit permissions.
   - **b.** Deny permissions always override Allow permissions.
   - **c.** When a security principal receives Allow permissions from multiple groups, the permissions are combined to form the effective access permissions.
   - **d.** Effective access includes both permissions inherited from parents and permissions derived from group memberships.
4. Which of the following statements is not true in reference to resource ownership?
   - **a.** One of the purposes for file and folder ownership is to calculate disk quotas.
   - **b.** Every file and folder on an NTFS driver has an owner.
   - **c.** It is possible for any user possessing the Take Ownership special permission to assume the ownership of a file or folder.
   - **d.** It is possible to lock out a file or folder by assigning a combination of permissions that permits access to no one at all, including the owner of the file or folder.

5. Which of the following statements about permissions are true?
   a. ACLs are composed of ACEs.
   b. Basic permissions are composed of advanced permissions.
   c. All permissions are stored as part of the protected resource.
   d. All of the above.

6. In the NTFS permission system, combinations of advanced permissions are also known as __________ permissions.
   a. special
   b. basic
   c. share
   d. standard

7. When copying and moving files and folders on NTFS volumes, which of the following are accurate statements regarding the results? Select all that apply.
   a. The file's existing permissions are maintained if you move the file to a new location on the same NTFS volume.
   b. The file inherits the permissions from the parent folder if the file is moved to another NTFS volume.
   c. The file inherits the permissions from the parent folder if the file is copied to a new location on the same NTFS volume.
   d. The file's existing permissions are maintained if you copy the file to a new location on the same NTFS volume.

8. Which of the following computers would restrict you from implementing EFS? Select all that apply.
   a. A computer with a hard drive formatted with FAT32 only.
   b. A computer with an NTFS volume that has been compressed.
   c. A computer with an NTFS volume.
   d. A computer with a hard drive formatted with FAT only.

9. When an audited event occurs, Windows 8 writes the event to which log?
   a. Security Log
   b. Application Log
   c. System Log
   d. Setup Log

10. After setting quota limits on an NTFS volume, you want to be able to monitor how much disk space users are consuming while still allowing them to go over the default quota limit you set for them. Which option must *not* be selected for this to work?
   a. Deny disk space to users exceeding quota limit
   b. Enable quota management
   c. Limit disk space to
   d. Log event when a user exceeds their quota limit

Best Answer

Choose the letter that corresponds to the best answer. More than one answer choice may achieve the goal. Select the BEST answer.

1. Which of the following is key reason for assigning permissions when configuring file and share access?
   a. Creates redundancy for file storage, providing a fault-tolerant file archive.
   b. Enables configuring offline files, improving performance.
   c. Improves data security, granting file and share access only to the users who need it.
   d. Assigns ownership to specific users, instilling responsibility and personal accountability.

2. Alice needs NTFS permission system support. She doesn't presently need encryption or compression, but might at a later date. Which file system is the best choice for Alice?
   a. The traditional NTFS file system
   b. The new ReFS file system introduced in Windows Server 2012
   c. The FAT file system
   d. The NFS file system

3. Which of the following sets of permissions is responsible for controlling access to files and folders stored on a local disk volume?
   a. Share permissions
   b. NTFS permissions
   c. Registry permissions
   d. Active Directory permissions

4. Knowing how permissions can be cumulative or override each other is an important factor in understanding what?
   a. Permission inheritance
   b. Explicitly assigned permissions
   c. Permission precedence
   d. Effective access

5. A user wants to be able to provide access to a folder named MyDocs. The MyDocs folder should be accessible over the network but still prevent unauthorized users from accessing the folder and its contents while logged on to the computer locally. The files are not sensitive but only the authorized users should be able to make changes. Which of the following combinations will best meet this need?
   a. Share permissions only
   b. NTFS permissions only
   c. Combined Share and NTFS permissions
   d. Share and NTFS permissions combined with EFS

6. A user has Allow Read and Allow List Folder Contents permissions for a subfolder named Forecasts. The permissions are inherited from the Sales folder. The user also has Allow Write and Allow Modify permission to the Forecasts folder as part of their membership in the SalesTeam group. Which of the following best describes her effective permissions to the Forecasts folder?
   a. Allow Write
   b. Allow Write and Allow Modify
   c. Allow Write, Allow Modify, Allow Read, Allow List Folder Contents
   d. Allow Read and Allow Write

7. There are several sensitive files on your Windows 8 computer stored in a folder named Sales. Inside the Sales folder are several files that provide confidential forecast information. What is the best way to protect those files that you need to access over the network while still protecting them from someone sitting at your computer and attempting to copy the files to a flash drive.
   a. Encrypt the folder using EFS.
   b. Encrypt the folder using EFS and secure the files with NTFS permissions.
   c. Share the folder and secure the files with NTFS permissions.
   d. Share the folder, secure the files with NTFS and use EFS to encrypt the folder and its contents.

Matching and Identification

Complete the following exercise by matching the terms with their corresponding definitions.

_______ **a)** NTFS quotas
_______ **b)** Effective access
_______ **c)** Auditing
_______ **d)** Access control entry (ACE)
_______ **e)** Security principal
_______ **f)** Permissions
_______ **g)** Share permissions
_______ **h)** NTFS permissions
_______ **i)** Permission inheritance
_______ **j)** Security identifier

1. Tracking events that take place on the local computer.
2. The name of a user, group, or computer being granted permission.
3. The combination of Allow permissions and Deny permissions that a security principal receives for a given system element.
4. Enables administrators to set a storage limit for users of a particular volume.
5. Control access to files and folders shared over a network.
6. Used to protect files, folders, shares, registry keys, and Active Directory objects.
7. Consists of the security principal and the specific permission assigned to that security principal.
8. The tendency of permissions to flow downwards through a file system or other hierarchy.
9. Control access to the files and folders stored on disk volumes formatted with the NTFS file system.
10. These are included in the security access token for each user's account and all the groups to which the user belongs.

Build a List

1. In order of first to last, specify the correct order of steps to encrypt a folder.
   _______ Right-click a file or folder and then, from the context menu, select **Properties**.
   _______ Select the **Encrypt contents to secure data** checkbox, and then click **OK**.
   _______ Open **File Explorer**.
   _______ Click **OK** to close the *Properties* sheet. If you selected a folder that contains files or subfolders, a *Confirm Attribute Changes* dialog box appears.
   _______ On the General tab, click **Advanced**.
   _______ Select a confirmation option and click **OK**.

2. In order of first to last, specify the correct order of steps to view the encryption attribute.
   _______ Click **OK** to close the *Properties* sheet.
   _______ On the General tab, click **Advanced**. The *Advanced Attributes* dialog box appears. If the Encrypt contents to secure data checkbox is selected, the file or folder is encrypted.
   _______ Right-click a file or folder and then, from the context menu, select **Properties**.
   _______ Click **OK** to close the *Advanced Attributes* dialog box.
   _______ Open **File Explorer**.

3. In order of first to last, specify the correct order of steps to configure a disk quota.

_________ Click the File Explorer icon in the taskbar.
_________ Select the **Limit disk space to** radio button and specify amounts for the quota limit and the warning level.
_________ Click the Quota tab.
_________ In the Folders list, expand the **Computer** container, right-click a volume and, from the context menu, select Properties.
_________ If you want to prevent users from consuming more than their quota of disk space, select the **Deny disk space to users exceeding quota limit** checkbox.
_________ Select the **Enable quota management** checkbox to activate the rest of the controls.
_________ Select the Log event checkboxes to control whether users exceeding the specified limits should trigger log entries.
_________ Click **OK** to create the quota and close the *Properties* sheet.

■ Business Case Scenarios

Scenario 15-1: Rescuing Orphaned Files

Heidi, a junior desktop technician, approaches her supervisor ashen-faced. A few minutes earlier, the president of the company called the help desk and asked Heidi to give his new assistant the permissions needed to access his personal budget spreadsheet. As she was attempting to assign the permissions, she accidentally deleted the BUDGET_USERS group from the spreadsheet's access control list. Heidi is now terrified because that group was the only entry in the file's ACL. Now no one can access the spreadsheet file, not even the president or the Administrator account. Is there any way to gain access to the file, and if so, how?

Scenario 15-2: Assigning Permissions

Tom works for the help desk for a corporate network and receives a call from a user named Leo, who is requesting access to the files for a new classified project called Trinity. The Trinity files are stored in a shared folder on a file server, which is locked in a secured underground data storage facility in New Mexico. After verifying that the user has the appropriate security clearance for the project, Tom creates a new group on the file server called TRINITY_USERS and adds Leo's user account to that group. Then, he adds the TRINITY_USER group to the access control list for the Trinity folder on the file server, and he assigns the group the following NTFS permissions:

- Allow Modify
- Allow Read & Execute
- Allow List Folder Contents
- Allow Read
- Allow Write

Some time later, Leo calls Tom back to tell him that while he is able to access the Trinity folder and read the files stored there, he has been unable to save changes back to the server. What is the most likely cause of the problem?

Configuring Local Security Settings

LESSON 16

70-687 EXAM OBJECTIVE

Objective 4.3 – Configure local security settings. This objective may include but is not limited to: configure local security policy; configure User Account Control (UAC) behavior; configure SmartScreen Filter; configure Secure Boot.

LESSON HEADING	EXAM OBJECTIVE
Configuring Security for Windows 8	
Configuring Local Security Policies	Configure Local Security Policy
Understanding User Account Control (UAC)	Configure User Account Control (UAC) Behavior
Configuring User Account Control	
Configuring SmartScreen Filters	Configure SmartScreen Filter
Configuring Secure Boot	Configure Secure Boot

KEY TERMS

Admin Approval Mode
Basic Input/Output System (BIOS)
boot loaders
brute force attacks
compatibility support module (CSM)
credential prompt
elevation prompt
local security policies
malware
phishing attacks
Secure Boot
secure desktop
SmartScreen Filter
Unified Extensible Firmware Interface (UEFI)
User Account Control (UAC)
Windows SmartScreen

■ Configuring Security for Windows 8

THE BOTTOM LINE

Home and business computers are prime targets for hackers. These individuals try to steal your personal data, credit card numbers, bank account information, passwords, or even use your computer to attack other computers on the Internet. Understanding and implementing the right features and tools in Windows 8 can ensure your system remains secure.

The Internet provides an excellent resource for discovering the latest statistics regarding the number of computers that are infected with malware, reading news about phishing attacks being at an all-time high, or finding blog posts from someone whose system was compromised or damaged because of weak security settings. In nearly all these situations, the root problem can be tracked to actions initiated by the user either with or without consent.

Malware is software installed on your system without your consent. You might have downloaded and installed a program from a website that you never used before or even installed software from a reputable site that bundled additional software that included the malware.

Phishing attacks are designed to steal your personal identity information and credentials by luring you to a fake website. These types of attacks can come by way of a link in an email message that threatens to suspend your account, offers to fill out an online survey, or by visiting a site that appears to be legitimate. Weak security policies, browsing the Internet, and running programs with administrative credentials when a standard user account would suffice are examples of other security risks. As if those were not enough, you must also protect against attacks that can occur before the operating system has a chance to load.

In this lesson, you learn about the Windows 8 security-centric features and tools to keep your system safe. Although you have the ability to limit the functionality and even disable some of these features and tools, always consider the consequences before doing so.

Configuring Local Security Policies

If you are using a Windows 8 computer that is not a member of an Active Directory domain, you can enhance the security of your system by configuring local security policies.

CERTIFICATION READY
Configure local security policy
Objective 4.3

Local security policies are advanced security settings that you configure to either restrict or allow certain activities on your local computer. The settings can be used to control who can access your computer, whether or not certain actions are recorded in the computer's event logs, and determine the resources users are authorized to access. Security settings configured on the local computer are applied immediately.

There are two primary tools for administering security settings on your Windows 8 computer (see Figure 16-1). The first is the Local Group Policy editor (gpedit.msc) and the other is Local Security Policy (secpol.msc).

Figure 16-1
Reviewing the primary tools for administering security policies

The Local Group Policy editor provides access to all the advanced security settings, including user and software settings, through a single user interface. The Local Security Policy, a subset of the Local Group Policy editor, is focused primarily on security related to registry entries. Because we are focused on security-related settings in this lesson, the Local Security Policy is the tool to explore more in depth.

EXPLORING THE LOCAL SECURITY POLICY

In Windows 8, the Local Security Policy is organized around the following folder structure (see Figure 16-2):

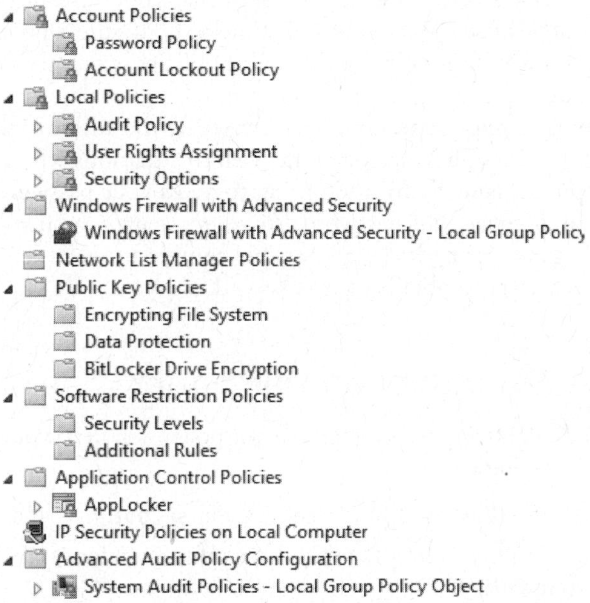

Figure 16-2

Reviewing the folder structure of the Local Security Policy

- **Account Policies:** Password history, age, length, and complexity requirement settings are configured here, and settings on how many invalid logon attempts are allowed before a user is locked out.
- **Local Policies:** Auditing of logins, access of files, and changes to policies are configured with these settings.
- **Windows Firewall with Advanced Security:** Settings here allow you to specify how and when connections between computers are authenticated and to determine which programs or ports are allowed or blocked on the computer.
- **Network List Manager Policies:** Settings here determine how Windows 8 responds when connecting to networks and sets the appropriate firewall settings for that location. You can also control the ability for users to change the network name, location, or its associated icon.
- **Public Key Policies:** Managing certificates and their associated life cycles (enrolling, renewing, expiring, and removing) are configured here.
- **Software Restriction Policies:** Identifying software and controlling its ability to run on the local computer is configured using the settings located here. Software Restriction Policies was originally designed to limit the applications that required administrative access to run. With the introduction of User Account Control (UAC) discussed later in this lesson, and a reduction in the number of applications needing administrative privileges to run, use Application Control Policies instead.
- **Application Control Policies:** Rules can be configured in this section that help administrators control which applications and files users can run. AppLocker was designed to extend the original goals of Software Restriction Policies allowing you to create a list of applications that should be allowed to run. AppLocker can also control package apps, which are those available from the Windows Store.

- **Advanced Audit Policy Configuration:** Settings in this folder allow you to perform a more granular approach to tracking activities. You can select only the behaviors you want to monitor and exclude others. For example, you can use these settings to track whether a specific administrator modified settings or important data file or track a specific user's attempts to access a confidential file.

Now that you have a better understanding of the types of security settings you can configure using the Local Security Policy tool, it is time to configure a policy on your Windows 8 computer and test it. One of the most useful policies is one that restricts the number of times someone can attempt to log in to your computer before they are locked out. Once locked out, the account cannot be used until it is reset by the administrator or until a certain amount of time elapses. This policy setting works well in situations where someone is trying to log in to your computer manually by attempting to guess your password or someone uses a brute force attack to discover your password. ***Brute force attacks***, involve using software that automatically generates and tries all possible combinations of letters, numbers, and special characters to attempt to obtain your password.

CONFIGURE AN ACCOUNT LOCKOUT POLICY

GET READY. To configure an account lockout policy, log in to your Windows 8 computer and perform the following steps:

1. From the Windows 8 Start menu, type **secpol.msc** and then press **Enter**.
2. Under *Security Settings*, expand **Account Policies** and then click **Account Lockout Policy**.
3. In the right pane, double-click **Account lockout threshold**.
4. On the *Local Security Setting* tab, type **3** for the number of invalid logon attempts (see Figure 16-3) and then click **OK**.

   If this parameter is set to 0, the account is never locked out. Values in this field can be between 0 and 999.

Figure 16-3

Setting the number of invalid logon attempts

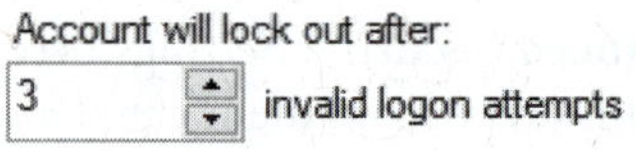

5. When the *Suggested Value Changes* box appears, click **OK**.

   This automatically configures the *Account lockout duration* and the *Reset account lockout counter after* policy settings to 30 minutes. You modify these default settings it the next steps.
6. In the right pane, double-click **Account lockout duration**.
7. On the *Local Security Setting* tab, type **1** for the number of minutes and then click **OK**.

   This security setting determines the number of minutes the account remains locked out before it is automatically unlocked. This is typically set to 30 minutes but is being set to 1 to allow you to test it in the next exercise. If this parameter is set to 0, the account will be locked out until an administration explicitly unlocks it.
8. When the *Suggested Value Changes* box appears, click **OK**.

   This automatically sets the *Reset account lockout counter after* policy to the same setting. Your settings should now match those shown in in Figure 16-4.

Figure 16-4

Confirming the Account Lockout Policy settings are configured

9. Close the *Local Security Policy* window.

TEST AN ACCOUNT LOCKOUT POLICY

GET READY. To test the account lockout policy, perform the following steps:

1. From the Windows 8 Start menu, press the **Windows logo key + w**, type **user accounts**, and then from *Results*, choose **Give others users access to this computer**.
2. Under the *Other users* section, click **Add a user**.
3. At the bottom of the *Add a user* screen, click **Sign in without a Microsoft account**.
4. Click **Local account**.
5. In the *User name* field, type **TiffanyC** and then press the **Tab** key.
6. In the *Password* field, type **P@ssword1** and then press the **Tab** key.
7. In the *Reenter password* field, type **P@ssword1** and then press the **Tab** key.
8. In the *Password hint* field, type **temp password** and then click **Next**.
9. Click **Finish**.
10. To return to the Windows 8 Start menu, press the **Windows logo key**.
11. In the upper-right corner, click the currently logged on user and then select **TiffanyC**.
12. Type an incorrect password for the account and then press **Enter**.
13. When the message *The password is incorrect. Try again*. appears, click **OK**.
14. Perform steps 12 and 13 again until you have exceeded the number of invalid log attempts you set in the account lockout policy (for example, 3).
15. When the message *The referenced account is currently locked out and may not be logged on to* appears, click **OK**.

    Wait for the time to elapse. This is 1 minute based on the setting you configured in the account lockout policy.
16. Type the correct password (for example, **P@ssword1**) and then press **Enter**.
17. In the upper-right corner, click the currently logged on user and then select **Sign out**.

Understanding User Account Control (UAC)

Preventing users from accidentally changing settings on your computer and stopping malware from gaining system-wide access to your system are vulnerabilities that ***User Account Control (UAC)*** can protect against. UAC is a Windows 8 feature that prevents unauthorized changes to your computer.

When a user logs on to Windows 8, the system issues a token, which indicates the user's access level. Whenever the system authorizes the user to perform a particular activity, it consults the token to see whether the user has the required privileges. In previous versions of Windows, standard users received standard user tokens and members of the Administrators group received administrative tokens. Every activity performed by an administrative user was, therefore, authorized using the administrative token.

CERTIFICATION READY
Configure User Account Control (UAC) behavior
Objective 4.3

On a Windows 8 computer running UAC, a standard user still receives a standard user token, but an administrative user receives two tokens: one for standard user access and one for administrative user access. By default, the standard and administrative users both run using the standard user token most of the time.

UNDERSTANDING RECOMMENDED UAC PRACTICES

Despite the introduction of UAC, Microsoft still recommends that all Windows users log on with a standard user account, except when they are logging on for administrative purposes only. As compared to earlier Windows versions, Windows 8 and UAC simplify the process by which standard users can gain administrative access, making the use of standard user accounts less frustrating, even for system administrators.

PERFORMING ADMINISTRATIVE TASKS WITH A STANDARD USER ACCOUNT

When a standard user attempts to perform a task that requires administrative privileges (for example, changing the system time or date), the system displays a ***credential prompt***, as shown in Figure 16-5, requesting that the user supply the name and password for an account with administrative privileges.

Figure 16-5
Receiving a credential prompt

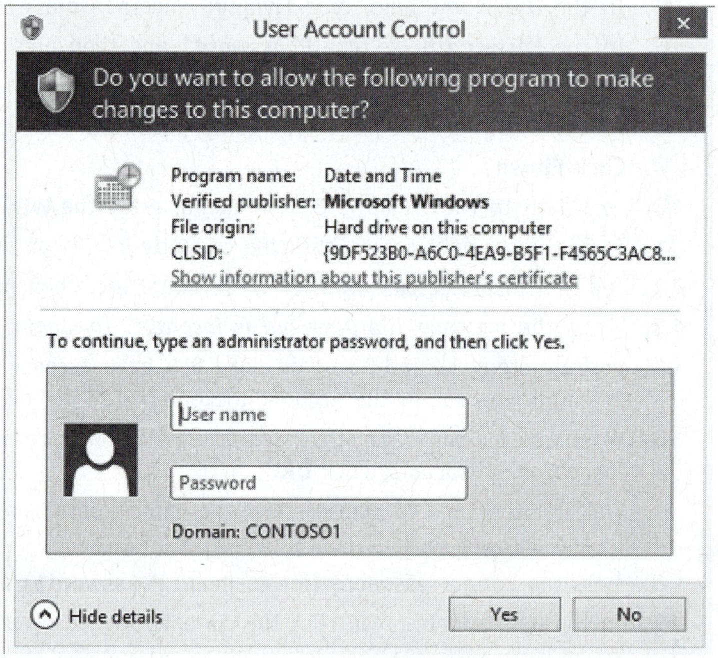

PERFORMING ADMINISTRATIVE TASKS WITH AN ADMINISTRATIVE ACCOUNT

When an administrator attempts to perform a task that requires administrative access, the system switches the account from the standard user token to the administrative token. This is known as ***Admin Approval Mode***.

MORE INFORMATION
The decision to run all users with a standard user token was not one that Microsoft made unilaterally. Part of the process of developing UAC involved working with the software developers both at Microsoft and at third-party companies to minimize the number and type of administrative-level access requests made by applications.

Before the system permits the user to employ the administrative token, it might require the human user to confirm that he or she is actually trying to perform an administrative task (for example, installing an application). To do this, the system generates an elevation prompt. An ***elevation prompt*** is the message box shown in Figure 16-6. This confirmation prevents unauthorized processes, such as those initiated by malware, from accessing the system using administrative privileges.

Figure 16-6

Receiving an elevation prompt

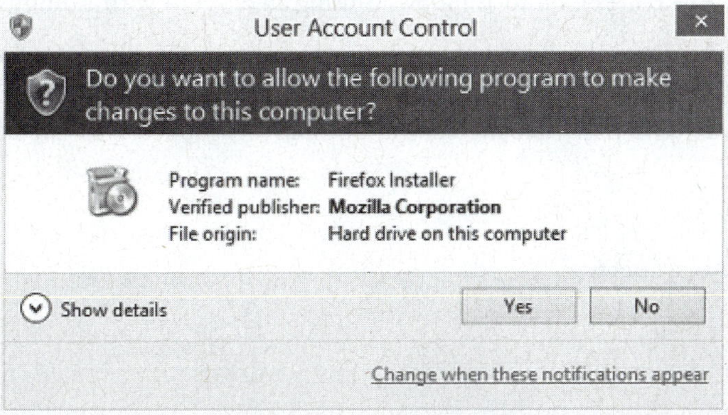

In Windows 8, administrators are faced with elevation prompts far less frequently than in previous versions. In response to complaints from users, Microsoft has modified the default UAC behavior in Windows 8 so that elevation prompts appear only when an application attempts to perform an administrative task.

TAKE NOTE*

The system component that is responsible for recognizing the need for elevated privileges and generating elevation prompts is called the Application Information Service (AIS). AIS is a Windows 8 service that has to be running for UAC to function properly. Disabling this service prevents applications that require administrative access from launching, resulting in Access Denied errors.

USING SECURE DESKTOP

By default, whenever Windows 8 displays an elevation prompt or a credential prompt, it does so using the secure desktop. The ***secure desktop*** is an alternative to the interactive user desktop that Windows normally displays. When Windows 8 generates an elevation or credential prompt, it switches to the secure desktop, suppressing the operation of all other desktop controls and permitting only Windows processes to interact with the prompt. The object of this is to prevent malware from automating a response to the elevation or credential prompt and bypassing the human reply.

WARNING It is still possible for a malware program to imitate the secure desktop and create its own artificial elevation or credential prompt, but an artificial prompt cannot provide the program with genuine access to administrative functions. The only possible danger is that a malware program could use an artificial credential prompt to harvest administrative account names and passwords from unsuspecting users.

Configuring User Account Control

All versions of Windows 8 enable User Account Control by default, but it is possible to configure several of its properties.

In Windows 8, there are four UAC settings available through the Control Panel. To configure UAC through the Control Panel, use the following procedure.

REVIEW UAC SETTINGS

GET READY. Log on to Windows 8 using an account with Administrator privileges.

1. From the Windows 8 Start menu, press the **Windows logo key + w**, type **uac**, and then from *Results*, choose **Change User Account Control settings**.
2. The *User Account Control Settings* box appears as shown in Figure 16-7.

Figure 16-7

Reviewing UAC setting options

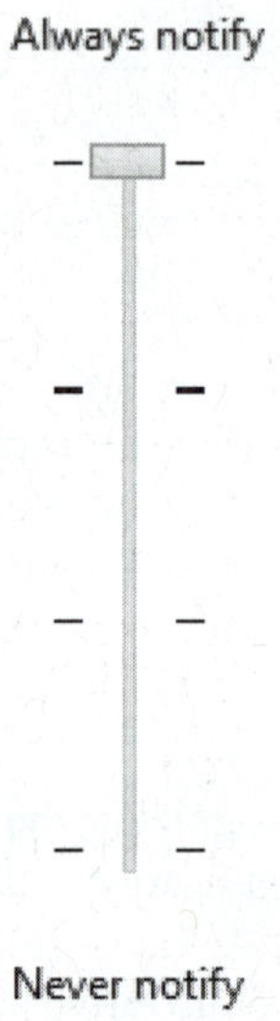

3. Read the current setting and then drag the slider up and down to each setting to review its description.
   - Always notify me
   - Notify me only when apps try to make changes to my computer (default)
   - Notify me only when apps try to make changes to my computer (do not dim my desktop)
   - Never notify me
4. In the *User Account Control Settings* box, click **Cancel**.

In Windows 7, you can fully disable UAC using UAC settings, but with Windows 8 you cannot. Even if you move the slider to *Never notify me*, you are not turning off UAC but just receiving less notifications and running all processes at a medium integrity level. Although it is possible to turn it off via a registry edit on a Windows 8 computer, doing so increases your vulnerability to malware attacks and is not recommended.

Although the UAC controls in Windows 8 are improved, the most granular control over UAC properties is still through Local Security Policy, or on an Active Directory-based network using Group Policy.

To configure UAC properties using Local Security Policy, use the following procedure.

CONFIGURE A UAC POLICY USING THE LOCAL SECURITY POLICY

GET READY. Log on to Windows 8 using an account with Administrator privileges.

1. From the Windows 8 Start menu, type **secpol.msc** and then from *Results*, choose **secpol.msc**.
2. Expand **Local Policies** and then click **Security Options**.
3. Scroll down to the bottom of the policy list until you see the ten policies with the User Account Control prefix, as shown in Figure 16-8. These policy settings are described in detail in Table 16-1.

Table 16-1

UAC Local Security Policy Settings

POLICY SETTING	VALUES AND FUNCTIONS
User Account Control: Admin Approval Mode for the Built-in Administrator account	• When enabled, the built-in Administrator account uses Admin Approval Mode. By default, any operation that requires elevation of privilege prompts the user to approve the operation. • When disabled (default), the built-in Administrator account runs with full administrative privilege.
User Account Control: Allow UIAccess applications to prompt for elevation without using the secure desktop	• When enabled, causes User Interface Accessibility programs to disable the secure desktop when displaying elevation prompts used by a standard user. • When disabled, elevation prompts use the secure desktop, unless the *User Account Control: Switch to the secure desktop when prompting for elevation* policy is enabled.
User Account Control: Behavior of the elevation prompt for administrators in Admin Approval Mode	• When set to *Elevate without prompting*, administrative users are elevated to the administrative token with no consent or credentials from the human user. • When set to *Prompt for credentials on the secure desktop*, administrative users are elevated to the administrative token only after the presentation of a credential prompt on the secure desktop, to which the user must supply a valid administrative account name and password, even if he or she is already logged on using such an account. If valid credentials are entered, the operation continues with the user's highest available privilege. • When set to *Prompt for consent on the secure desktop,* administrative users are elevated to the administrative token only after the presentation of an elevation prompt on the secure desktop and the consent of the human user. The user is prompted to select Permit or Deny. If they select Permit, the operation continues with the user's highest available privilege. • When set to *Prompt for credentials*, administrative users are elevated to the administrative token only after the presentation of a credential prompt to which the user must supply valid administrative account name and password. If valid credentials are entered, the operation continues with the applicable privilege. • When set to *Prompt for consent*, administrative users are elevated to the administrative token only after the presentation of an elevation prompt on the secure desktop and the consent of the human user. The user is prompted to select Permit or Deny. If they select Permit, the operation continues with the user's highest available privilege. • When set to *Prompt for consent for non-Windows binaries (Default),* When an operation for a non-Microsoft application requires elevation of privilege, administrative users are prompted to select either Permit or Deny. If they select Permit, the operation continues with the highest available privilege.

(continued)

Table 16-1

(continued)

Policy Setting	Values and Functions
User Account Control: Behavior of the elevation prompt for standard users	• When set to *Prompt for credentials (default)*, standard users attempting to perform an administrative function receive a credential prompt, to which the user must supply a valid administrative account name and password. • When set to *Automatically deny elevation requests*, suppresses the credential prompt and prevents standard users from being elevated to an administrative token. When an operation requires elevation of privilege, a configurable access denied error message is displayed. • When set to *Prompt for credentials on the secure desktop*, standard users attempting to perform an administrative function receive a credential prompt on the secure desktop, to which the user must supply a valid administrative account name and password.
User Account Control: Detect application installations and prompt for elevation	• When enabled, an attempt to install an application causes standard users to receive credential prompt and administrative users to receive an elevation prompt. The user must supply authentication credentials or consent before the installation can proceed. This is the default setting. • When disabled, elevation and credential prompts are suppressed during application installations, and the installation fails. This setting is for use on enterprise desktops that use an automated installation technology, such as Microsoft System Center Configuration Manager.
User Account Control: Only Elevate executables that are signed and validated	• When enabled, requires successful public key infrastructure (PKI) signature verifications on all interactive applications that request administrative access. Unsigned applications will not run. • When disabled, both signed and unsigned applications run. This is the default setting
User Account Control: Only elevate UIAccess applications that are installed in secure locations	• When enabled, Windows 8 provides access to the protected system user interface only if the executable is located in the \Program Files, \Windows\system32, and \Program Files (x86) folders on the system drive. If the executable is not located in one of these folders, access is denied, despite a positive response to the elevation prompt. This is the default setting. • When disabled, the folder location checks are omitted, so any application can be granted access to the protected system user interface upon successful completion of the elevation prompt.
User Account Control: Run all administrators in Admin Approval Mode	• When enabled, the built-in Administrator account and all other users who are members of the Administrators group can run in Admin Approval Mode. A change in the value of this policy does not take effect until the system is restarted. This is the default setting. • When disabled, the AIS service is disabled and does not automatically start. When the system starts, the Windows Security Center warns the user that operating system security is reduced and provides the ability to activate UAC.
User Account Control: Switch to the secure desktop when prompting for elevation	• When enabled, causes Windows 8 to display all elevation prompts on the secure desktop, which can receive messages only from Windows processes. This is the default setting. • When disabled, causes Windows 8 to display all elevation prompts on the interactive user desktop.
User Account Control: Virtualize file and registry write Failures to per-user locations	• When enabled, allows non-UAC-compliant applications to run by redirecting write requests to protected locations, such as the Program Files and Windows folders or the HKLM\Software registry key, to alternative locations in the registry and file system. This process is called *virtualization*. This is the default setting. • When disabled, virtualization is disabled, and non-UAC-compliant applications attempting to write to protected locations fail to run. This setting is recommended only when the system is running UAC-compliant applications exclusively.

Figure 16-8

Exploring the User Account Control policies

User Account Control: Admin Approval Mode for the Built-in Administrator account	Disabled
User Account Control: Allow UIAccess applications to prompt for elevation without using the secure desktop	Disabled
User Account Control: Behavior of the elevation prompt for administrators in Admin Approval Mode	Prompt for consent for ...
User Account Control: Behavior of the elevation prompt for standard users	Prompt for credentials
User Account Control: Detect application installations and prompt for elevation	Enabled
User Account Control: Only elevate executables that are signed and validated	Disabled
User Account Control: Only elevate UIAccess applications that are installed in secure locations	Enabled
User Account Control: Run all administrators in Admin Approval Mode	Enabled
User Account Control: Switch to the secure desktop when prompting for elevation	Enabled
User Account Control: Virtualize file and registry write failures to per-user locations	Enabled

4. Double-click the **User Account Control: Behavior of the elevation prompt for standard users** policy.
5. On the *Local Security Setting* tab, click the drop-down arrow (see Figure 16-9), choose **Automatically deny elevation requests**, and then click **OK**.

   With this setting enabled, any operation that requires elevation of privilege produces an access denied error for standard users.

Figure 16-9

Configuring security settings

6. Close the Local Security Policy.
7. Press the **Windows logo key** to return to the Windows 8 Start menu.
8. In the upper right corner, click the currently logged on user and then select the user's name (in this example, **TiffanyC**).
9. Type the password (for example, **P@ssword1**) and then press **Enter**.
10. Press the **Windows logo key + r, and in the *Run* box**, type **diskmgmt.msc** and then click **OK**.

    Because TiffanyC is a standard user account, she sees the error message as shown in Figure 16-10.

Figure 16-10

Receiving access denied error message

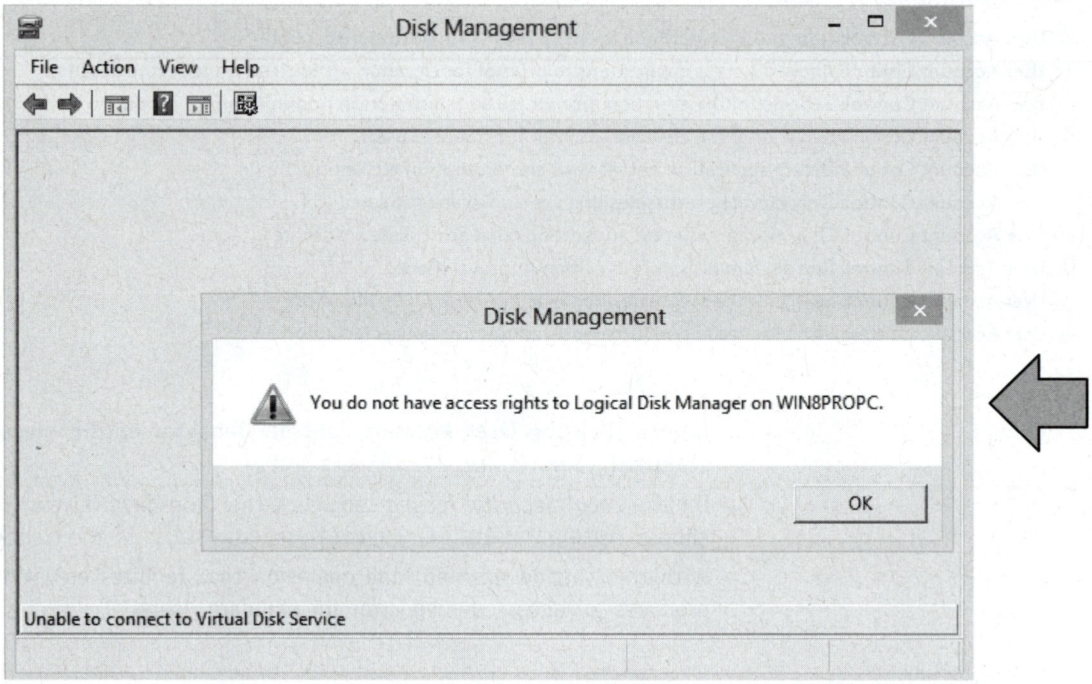

11. Click **OK** and then close the *Disk Management* box.

TAKE NOTE*

If you are working on an Active Directory network, you can configure the same UAC policies for multiple computers simultaneously by creating a Group Policy object, configuring the same policy settings, and applying it to a domain, site, or organizational unit object.

Configuring SmartScreen Filters

When surfing the Internet, you must be able to identify phishing websites, recognize websites known for distributing malicious software, and have a way to protect your computer if you accidentally download a program or file that is known to be unsafe.

SmartScreen Filter is a feature in Internet Explorer designed to keep your computer safe by warning you before you run apps or files from the Internet that are considered to be unsafe. Although it was originally introduced in Internet Explorer 8 to protect against phishing websites while browsing, it is now integrated into Windows 8. If you are running applications other than Internet Explorer that access the Internet, the same technology can protect against unrecognized programs and files that might contain malware. The SmartScreen Filter technology, integrated into the operating system's File Explorer, is called ***Windows SmartScreen.***

Both of these security features work by consulting a dynamic database that includes a list of reported phishing and malware software sites/programs. The list is maintained by Microsoft and updated both manually and through specially designed algorithms.

CERTIFICATION READY
Configure SmartScreen filter
Objective 4.3

While surfing the Internet using Internet Explorer, the SmartScreen Filter works in the background to analyze the webpages you visit and compares them against the dynamic database. If the webpage is considered to be suspicious, a warning message is displayed. You can then provide feedback and determine whether you want to continue. If the site is matched to one in the list, you receive a warning message (see Figure 16-11) indicating the site was blocked for your safety. SmartScreen Filtering is enabled by default but can be disabled (not recommended) from within the Internet Explorer browser.

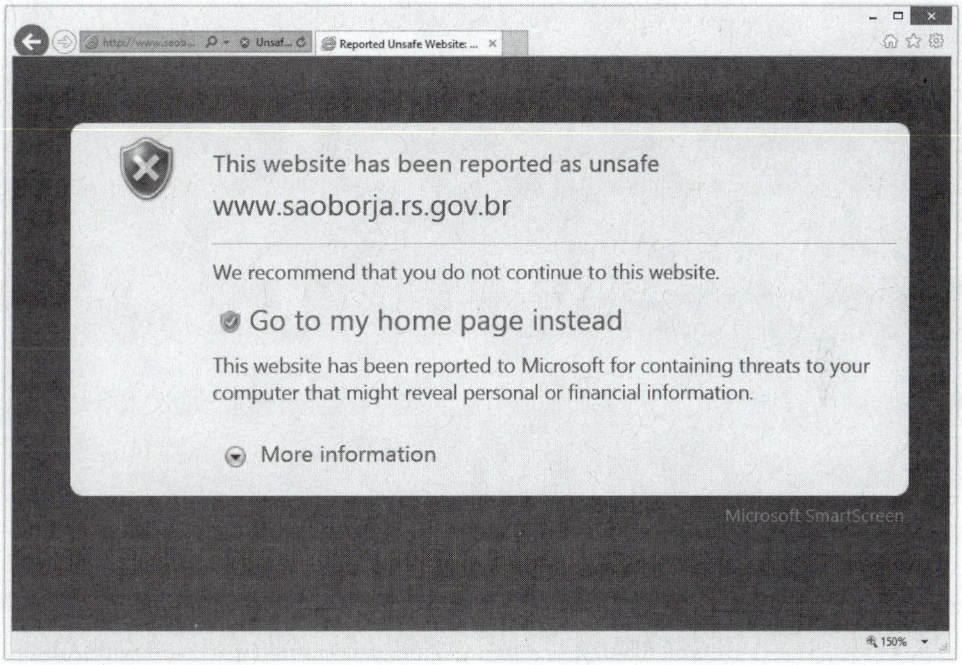

Figure 16-11
Blocking access to unsafe website

Windows SmartScreen checks any program or file that you download from the Internet against a list of known programs. If the program is not recognized in the current database, Windows SmartScreen alerts you (see Figure 16-12). If you click OK, the program is not allowed to run. Clicking the *More info* link provides you with information about the publisher (if one can be identified) and the application name. From there, you can choose to run the program anyway or close the Windows SmartScreen window and the program.

An alert does not always mean the program is malware, just that it is not recognized in the current database list.

Windows SmartScreen settings are managed from within the Action Center.

There are three levels that you can set for Windows SmartScreen:

- Get admin approval before running an unrecognized app from the Internet (recommended). This is the default setting.
- Warn before running an unrecognized app, but don't require administrator approval.
- Don't do anything (turn off Windows SmartScreen).

Figure 16-12

Stopping unrecognized app from starting

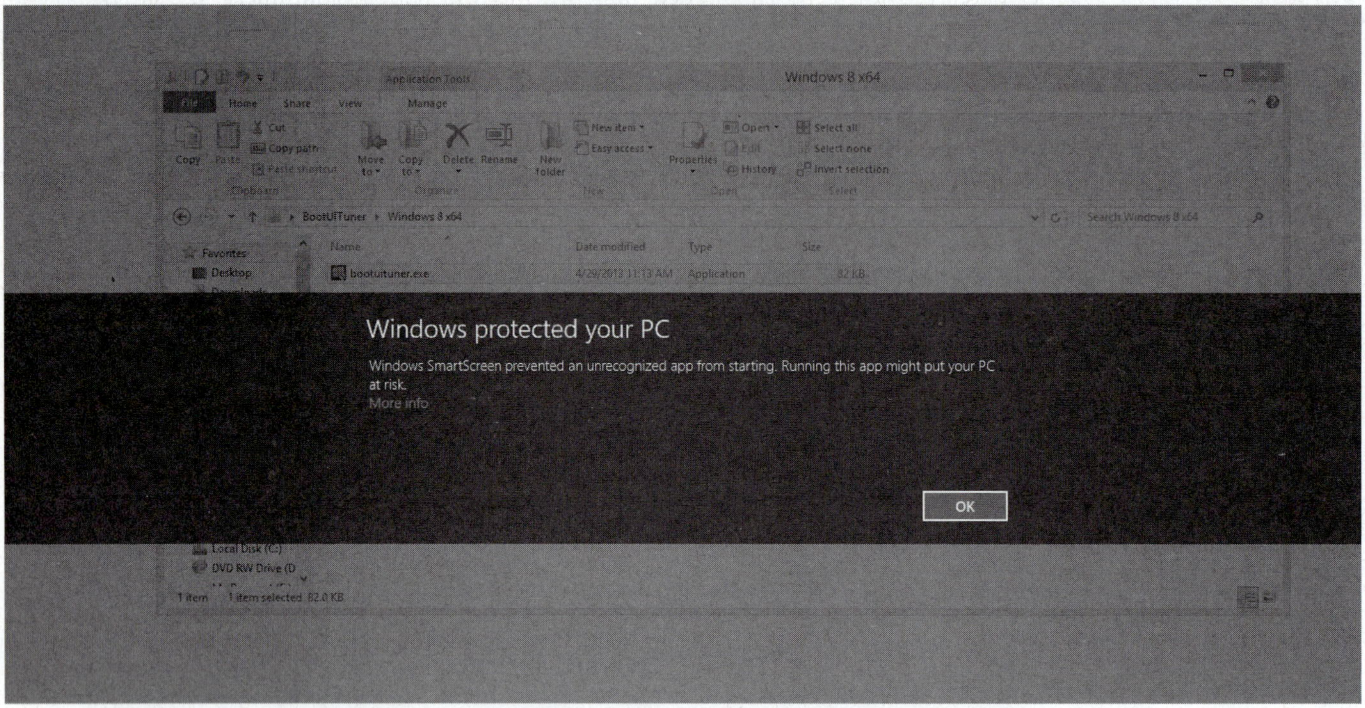

DISABLE/ENABLE SMARTSCREEN FILTER SETTINGS IN INTERNET EXPLORER

GET READY. Log on to Windows 8 using an account with Administrator privileges:

1. From the Windows 8 Start menu, click the **Desktop** tile.
2. On the task bar, click the **Internet Explorer** icon.
3. Press **Alt key + x** and then choose **Safety > Turn off SmartScreen Filter** (see Figure 16-13).

Figure 16-13

Configuring SmartScreen Filter settings

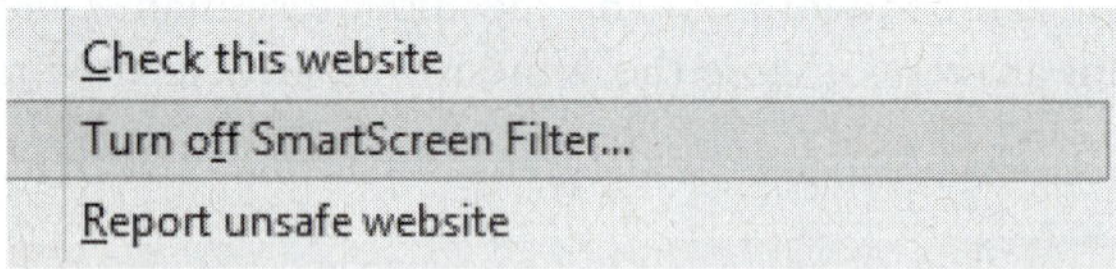

4. In the *Microsoft SmartScreen Filter* window, confirm **Turn off SmartScreen Filter** is selected and then click **OK**.
5. Press the **Alt key + x**, choose **Safety > Turn on SmartScreen Filter**, then click **OK**. This returns Internet Explorer to the recommended setting.
6. Close the *Internet Explorer browser* window.

In the previous steps, you learned how to disable/enable the SmartScreen Filter within Internet Explorer. To control Windows SmartScreen and how it manages unrecognized apps, perform the following steps.

DISABLE/ENABLE WINDOWS SMARTSCREEN IN THE ACTION CENTER

GET READY. Log on to Windows 8 using an account with Administrator privileges:

1. From the Windows 8 Start menu, press the **Windows logo key + w**, type **smart**, and then from *Results*, choose **Change SmartScreen settings**.
2. From the *Action Center*, click **Change Windows SmartScreen settings**.
3. In the *Windows SmartScreen* box, select **Don't do anything (turn off Windows SmartScreen)** and then click **OK**.

   After making this change, you see a warning message under the *Security* section of the Action Center, recommending that you keep Windows SmartScreen enabled.
4. From the *Action Center*, click **Change Windows SmartScreen settings**.
5. In the *Windows SmartScreen* box, select **Get administrator approval before running an unrecognized app from the Internet (recommended)** and then click **OK**.
6. Close the *Action Center* window.

Configuring Secure Boot

During the boot process, your computer is vulnerable to malicious code that can go undetected by the operating system or antimalware software. To protect against this type of vulnerability, you need to make sure that only valid programs and code are allowed to execute while the operating system is loading.

Secure Boot is designed to protect your computer against loading malware when booting. These types of attacks (called *boot loader attacks*) are designed to exploit your computer before the operating system loads. ***Boot loaders*** are responsible for placing the operating system image into memory when the computer is started. If Secure Boot detects a boot loader that is not signed with the appropriate digital signatures, it automatically blocks it. For example, if someone installed a malicious boot loader on a USB drive and then attempted to boot from a Windows 8 computer with Secure Boot enabled, he would receive an error message stating there is a Secure Boot Violation and that an invalid signature was detected. He would not be able to continue further into the boot process.

TAKE NOTE*

If you have a computer with Unitfied Extensible Firmware Interface (UEFI) and Secure Boot and want to boot into another operating system that does not have an approved Microsoft digital signature, you can turn Secure Boot off or check with the manufacturer to see whether it has a key you can add to the UEFI validation routine.

To take advantage of Secure Boot in Windows 8, you need the ***Unified Extensible Firmware Interface (UEFI)***. UEFI is a software technology that is designed as a replacement for the traditional ***Basic Input/Output System (BIOS)*** on today's modern motherboards. BIOS, built-in software stored on a memory chip on the motherboard, is used to identify the hardware in the computer and preform basic functions such as keyboard control and booting. UEFI controls the basic hardware functions and defines the software interface between the operating system and the firmware. UEFI offers several advantages over BIOS including the ability to boot from larger disks (over 2TB), faster boot times, CPU-independent architecture and drivers, and security for the pre-operating system boot environment. BIOS, was never designed for the diversity of hardware in today's computers.

CERTIFICATION READY
Configure Secure Boot
Objective 4.3

In addition to UEFI, you must have an operating system that is signed by the manufacturer. In the case of Windows 8, Microsoft or one of its original equipment manufacturer (OEM) partners would digitally sign the operating system build and then install it with the UEFI/Secure Boot featured enabled on the computer. The digital certificate is stored in the UEFI firmware and because UEFI launches only an operating that has been verified (signed with acceptable digital signatures), malware cannot switch the system to another boot loader.

The process for configuring Secure Boot varies from one system to the next. The type of motherboard, processor, and the version of UEFI firmware used determine whether it works on your specific system.

Here are a few things to keep in mind when considering Secure Boot:

- The motherboard needs to have UEFI firmware (2.3.1 or greater), support booting into native mode (***compatibility support module (CSM)***-disabled), and allow you to enable Secure Boot as a feature. CSM is a module that must be disabled so that the computer can boot only UEFI-based operating systems. It locks down the boot process and turns off the legacy BIOS support.
- If compatibility support module (CSM) was enabled when Windows 8 was initially installed, you have to reinstall the operating system to switch to UEFI. CSM is enabled on most motherboards by default.
- If the Windows 8 system was purchased from a retailer (preinstalled) and carries the Windows 8 logo, it is required to run UEFI.

The following information highlights the basic steps involved in setting up Secure Boot on a clean Windows 8 system. These might or might not match your specific system requirements due to differences in BIOS manufacturers and hardware installed on your computer. The following is only meant to provide a summary overview of the process.

1. Start with no operating system installed and make sure you are running the latest firmware for your specific motherboard.
2. Boot into your BIOS and disable Compatibility Support Module.
3. Change the OS type to Windows 8 UEFI and set the Secure Boot Mode to Standard.
4. Insert your Windows 8 installation disk and reboot the system.
5. Select the unallocated space. The installer creates four partitions for you automatically: a recovery partition, system, MSR (reserved) and a primary.
6. When the Windows 8 Start screen appears, remove the installation media and reboot the system to access UEFI setup.
7. Set the Secure Boot Mode to Custom to load any default security keys.
8. Switch the Secure Boot Mode back to Standard, verify CSM is disabled, and then save and exit. Reboot the computer.
9. When the Windows 8 Start screen appears, open an elevated Windows PowerShell command and verify that Secure Boot is enabled.

VERIFY THAT SECURE BOOT IS ENABLED ON YOUR COMPUTER

GET READY. Log on to Windows 8 using an account with Administrator privileges:

1. From the Windows 8 Start menu, type **powershell** and then from *Results*, choose **Windows Powershell**.
2. Right-click **Windows Powershell** and then from the menu that appears, choose **Run as administrator**.

3. In the *Administrator: Windows PowerShell* window, type **Confirm-SecureBootUEFI** and then press **Enter**.

   If your Windows 8 computer supports Secure Boot and it is enabled, the cmdlet returns the value *True*. If the computer supports Secure Boot and it is disabled, the value *False* is returned. If the computer does not support Secure Boot or is a (BIOS) non-UEFI computer, you see the following message: *Cmdlet not supported on this platform*.

4. Close the PowerShell Window.

SKILL SUMMARY

IN THIS LESSON, YOU LEARNED:

- Local security policies are advanced security settings that you configure to either restrict or allow certain activities on the local computer. When security settings are configured, they are applied immediately.
- There are two primary tools for administering security settings on your Windows 8 computer: Local Group Policy editor and Local Security Policy.
- The Local Security Policy focuses primarily on security settings in the registry and is a subset of the security policies included in the Local Group Policy editor. The settings in the Local Group Policy editor are broader and include additional security settings for users and software.
- The User Account Control (UAC) feature is designed to protect your computer from settings being changed accidentally and stop malware from gaining system-wide access to your system. In Windows 8, you cannot fully disable UAC without resorting to a registry edit, which is not recommended.
- The UAC feature displays two types of prompts. The credential prompt requests a user name and password when a standard user attempts to perform a task that requires administrative privilege. The elevation prompt prevents unauthorized processes, such as those initiated by malware, from accessing the system using administrative privileges.
- Windows 8 switches to a secure desktop when it generates an elevation or credential prompt. This suppresses the operation of all other desktop controls and only permits Windows processes to interact with the prompt.
- The SmartScreen Filter is a feature in Internet Explorer designed to keep you safe by warning you before running apps or programs from the Internet. The SmartScreen Filter technology built into the operating system is called *Windows SmartScreen*. It checks any program or file that you download from the Internet against a list of known programs.
- The SmartScreen Filter is enabled/disabled from within Internet Explorer while Windows SmartScreen is enabled/disabled and configured from within the Windows 8 Control Panel.
- Secure Boot is a feature in Windows 8 that is designed to protect your computer against loading malware when booting.
- Secure Boot requires a Unified Extensible Firmware Interface (UEFI) firmware (2.3.1 or greater), support booting into native mode (compatibility support module disabled), an operating system signed by Microsoft or one of its original equipment manufacturers (OEMs), and hardware that supports the feature (graphics cards, processor, and motherboard).

Knowledge Assessment

Multiple Choice

Select the correct answer for each of the following questions.

1. In which of the following areas of the Local Security Policy would you configure the number of invalid logon attempts that are allowed before a user would be locked out of a Windows 8 computer?
   a. Windows Firewall with Advanced Security
   b. Account Policies
   c. Local Policies
   d. Software Restriction Policies

2. Windows 8 displays a secure desktop under which of the following conditions? (Select all that apply.)
   a. When the user first logs into Windows 8
   b. When an elevation prompt is displayed
   c. When a credential prompt is displayed
   d. When a user opens Internet Explorer with SmartScreen enabled

3. Which of the following is the default configuration for User Account Control (UAC) in Windows 8?
   a. Always notify me
   b. Notify me only when apps try to make changes to my computer
   c. Notify me only when apps try to make changes to my computer (do not dime my desktop)
   d. Never notify me

4. Which of the following is the effect of setting the UAC configuration to *Never notify me* in Windows 8?
   a. It fully disables UAC.
   b. It results in less notifications but does not fully disable UAC.
   c. It allows the processes to run at a medium integrity level.
   d. No notifications will be displayed.

5. Which of the following is the default setting for Windows SmartScreen?
   a. Get admin approval before running an unrecognized app from Internet
   b. Warn before running an unrecognized app, but don't require administrator approval
   c. Don't do anything
   d. Disable Windows Smartscreen

6. Which of the following allows you to access the SmartScreen Filter setting in Internet Explorer?
   a. Press Alt key + x > Safety from the menu that appears.
   b. Press Alt key + y > Safety from the menu that appears.
   c. Press Alt key + x > SmartScreen Filter from the menu that appears.
   d. Press Alt key + y > SmartScreen Filter from the menu that appears.

7. UEFI is a replacement for the traditional Basic Input/Output System. What are some of its key features? (Select all that apply.)
   a. The ability to boot from disks that are over 2TB.
   b. Faster boot times compared to BIOS.
   c. CPU-dependent architecture.
   d. Secure Boot support for pre-operating system boot environments.

8. Which of the following are characteristics of the Secure Boot feature and how it works? (Select all that apply.)
   a. Cannot protect against malware boot loaders.
   b. Requires the boot loaders contain a valid digital signature or it they will be blocked.
   c. Requires the Unified Extensible Firmware Interface (UEFI).
   d. Supported on systems that come preinstalled with the Windows 8 logo.

9. Which of the following must be disabled in the UEFI setup screen to lock down the boot process and turn off legacy BIOS support?
   a. Secure Boot
   b. Compatibility Support Module (CSM)
   c. BIOS
   d. Compliant Support Module (CSM)

10. When an administrator attempts to perform a task that requires administrative access, the system switches the account from the standard user token to the administrative token, which is known as what?
    a. UAC Mode
    b. Credential Approval Mode
    c. Admin Approval Mode
    d. Elevated Approval Mode

Best Answer

Choose the letter that corresponds to the best answer. More than one answer choice may achieve the goal. Select the BEST answer.

1. You would like to prevent users from attempting to guess your password by locking them out after incorrectly typing three incorrect passwords. You would also like to specify which programs are allowed or blocked on the computer. To use a single tool to accomplish the tasks, which of the following would you recommend?
   a. Windows Firewall with Advanced Security
   b. SmartScreen
   c. Local Security Policy (secpol.msc)
   d. UAC

2. To have more granular control over UAC property settings on a Windows 8 computer that is joined to a workgroup, which of the following tools would you recommend?
   a. Group Policy
   b. Local Security Policy
   c. User Account Control Settings via Control Panel
   d. Edit the registry directly

3. To enable Secure Boot on four Windows 8 systems on your network, which of the following systems would most likely allow you to complete this task successfully?
   a. The system that was purchased from a retailer with a Windows 8 logo and the operating system reinstalled.
   b. The Windows 8 system that has UEFI firmware.
   c. The Windows 8 system that was installed with CSM enabled on the motherboard by default.
   d. The Windows 8 system that is running a legacy BIOS.

4. To dual boot a personal Windows 8 computer that has Secure Boot enabled with another operating system, which of the following procedures is the best approach to use in a low security (home setting) environment?
   a. Reinstall Windows 8 and then install the other operating system.
   b. Contact the manufacturer to see whether it has a valid key that can be used with UEFI.

c. Turn Secure Boot off and install the other operating system.
d. Turn Secure Boot off, make a backup of your system, and then install the other system.

5. To configure an account lockout policy that will provide the best protection for your system against failed password attempts while still allowing you to know when someone has attempted to access your system, which of the following settings allows you to accomplish this?
   a. Set the Account lockout threshold to lock out after 3 failed password attempts and the Account lockout duration to 0.
   b. Set the Account lockout threshold to lock out after 10 failed password attempts and the Account lockout duration to 1.
   c. Set the Account lockout threshold to lock out after 20 failed password attempts and the Account lockout duration to 10.
   d. Set the Account lockout threshold to lock out after 100 failed password attempts and the Account lockout duration to 100.

Matching and Identification

1. Match the following terms with their corresponding definitions.
   _______ a) Boot loaders
   _______ b) Malware
   _______ c) Phishing attacks
   _______ d) Secure Boot
   _______ e) User Account Control
   _______ f) Unified Extensible Firmware Interface (UEFI)
   _______ g) Secure desktop
   _______ h) Brute force attack
   _______ i) SmartScreen Filter
   _______ j) Windows SmartScreen
   1. SmartScreen Filter technology integrated into Windows 8 File Explorer
   2. Responsible for placing the operating system image into memory when the computer is started.
   3. A software technology designed to replace the traditional BIOS.
   4. Uses software to automatically generate and try all possible combinations of letters, numbers and special characters to attempt to obtain your password
   5. Software installed on your system without consent.
   6. Prevents unauthorized changes to your computer through the use of elevation and credential prompts.
   7. Feature in Internet Explorer designed to keep you from running apps and files and protects against phishing attacks.
   8. Used when Windows 8 generates an elevation or credential prompt; suppresses operation of all other desktop controls
   9. Protects your computer against loading malware when booting.
   10. Designed to steal your personal identity information and credentials.

Build a List

1. In order of first to last, specify the correct order of steps to disable SmartScreen Filter in Internet Explorer.
   _______ On the task bar, click the **Internet Explorer** icon.
   _______ Close the Internet Explorer browser window.
   _______ From the Windows 8 Start menu, click the **Desktop** tile.
   _______ Press the Alt key + x and then choose **Safety** > **Turn off SmartScreen Filter**.

2. Someone accidentally changed the default setting for UAC to Never notify me. To return the Windows 8 computer to the recommended default setting, specify the correct order of steps to accomplish this task.
   _________ In the *User Account Control Settings* box, move the slider to *Notify me only when apps try to make changes to my computer.*
   _________ Log on to the Windows 8 computer with Administrator privileges.
   _________ Click **OK**.
   _________ From the Windows 8 Start menu, press the Windows logo key + w, type **uac,** and then from Results, choose **Change User Account Control settings**.

3. You have just purchased a new Windows 8 computer from a retail chain. To see whether Secure Boot is enabled, specify the correct order of steps to accomplish this task.
   _________ From the Windows 8 Start menu, type **powershell** and then choose **Windows Powershell** from *Results.*
   _________ Close the PowerShell Window.
   _________ In the *Administrator: Windows PowerShell* window, type **Confirm-SecureBootUEFI** and then press **Enter**.
   _________ Right-click **Windows Powershell** and then choose **Run as administrator** from the menu that appears.

Business Case Scenarios

Scenario 16-1: Protecting Computers from Phishing Attacks

Elliot, the owner of a small research business, is concerned about his employees becoming victims of phishing attacks while they are researching information for his clients. His company recently purchased three new Windows 8 computers and would like to make sure they are configured to protect against these types of attacks. He has already installed and updated the virus definitions on the computers using Windows Defender but is not sure whether he accidentally made changes that might make the computers vulnerable to the attacks. What would you need to do to confirm the appropriate security mechanisms are in place on the new computers?

Scenario 16-2: Troubleshooting Access Denied Errors

One of your users was recently issued a new Windows 8 computer that was configured by a new administrator in your department. The user reports she received an access denied message while trying to view her disk properties using the Disk Management tool. The message was as follows: *You do not have access rights to Logical Disk Manager on Win8Pro.*

You remember the new administrator talking about local security policies and that he had been testing them a few days earlier. You suspect this could be the source of the problem. How would you troubleshoot this?

17 LESSON

Configuring Authentication and Authorization

70-687 EXAM OBJECTIVE

Objective 4.4 – Configure authentication and authorization. This objective may include but is not limited to set up and configure Microsoft Account; manage credentials; configure picture password; configure PIN; configure smart cards; manage certificates; configure biometrics; and configure rights.

LESSON HEADING	EXAM OBJECTIVE
Working with Users and Groups	
Understanding Local and Domain Users	
Understanding Local and Domain Groups	
Creating and Managing Local Users and Groups	
Using the User Accounts Control Settings	Set Up and configure Microsoft Account
Using the Local Users and Groups Snap-in	
Working with Domain Users and Groups	
Authenticating and Authorizing Users	
Working with Passwords	Manage credentials
Using PIN and Picture Passwords	Configure PIN Configure picture password
Using Smart Cards	Configure smart cards
Managing Certificates	Manage certificates
Using Biometrics	Configure biometrics
Elevating Privileges	
Troubleshooting Authentication Issues	
Authorizing Users	Configure rights

KEY TERMS

Active Directory	**domain**	**pass-through authentication**
authentication	**domain controller**	**Personal Identity Verification (PIV)**
authorization	**group**	**user rights**
brute force	**homegroup**	**Windows Biometric Framework**
directory service	**multifactor authentication**	**workgroup**

Working with Users and Groups

THE BOTTOM LINE

The user account is the fundamental unit of identity in the Windows operating systems. In computer terminology, the term *user* has two meanings; it can refer to the human being that is operating the computer, or it can be an operating system element that represents a single human user.

From a programming perspective, a user account is a relatively simple construct, no more than a collection of properties that apply to the human being or other entity that the user account represents. These properties can include information about the user, such as names and contact information, and identifying characteristics, such as passwords.

MORE INFORMATION

Most user accounts represent humans, but Windows also employs user accounts to provide system processes and applications with access to secured resources. These accounts are no different from standard user accounts structurally; the only difference is that they are created and managed automatically by the operating system or an application.

As an operating system element, the user account and its properties are vital components in two of the most important Windows functions:

- ***Authentication*** – The process of verifying that the identity of the person operating the computer is the same as the user account the person is employing to gain access. Typically, to be authenticated, the human user must supply some piece of information associated with the user account, such as a password, demonstrate some personal characteristic, such as a fingerprint, or prove access to an identifying possession, such as a smart card.
- ***Authorization*** – The process of granting an authenticated user a specific degree of access to specific computer or data resources. In Windows, a user account provides access to permissions that grant the human user access to files and folders, printers, and other resources.

The first thing a human user does with a Windows system is authenticate him- or herself, a process typically referred to as logging on. The human user specifies the name of a user account and supplies a password or other identifying token. Once the authentication is successful, the person is known by that user name throughout the Windows session, and the operating system grants access to specific resources using that name.

As the authenticated user begins working with the operating system, the authorization process occurs whenever the user attempts to access certain resources or perform specific tasks. All of the Windows permission systems, including NTFS, share, registry, and ***Active Directory*** permissions, are user-based. The access control list (ACL) for each permission-protected resource contains a list of users and the degree of access each user is granted to the resource.

Another user-based Windows element, completely separate from the permission systems, is called ***user rights***. User rights are specific operating system tasks, such as Shut Down the System or Allow Log On Through Remote Desktop Services, which can only be performed by certain users designated by a system administrator.

A ***group*** is another type of entity that Windows uses to represent a collection of users. System administrators can create groups for any reason and with any name, and then use them just as they would a user account. Any permissions or user rights that an administrator assigns to a group are automatically inherited by all members of the group.

MORE INFORMATION

The concept of group inheritance is one of the fundamental principles of network administration. On all but the smallest networks, administrators typically assign permissions to groups, rather than individual users, and then control access by adjusting group memberships. For example, if a person performing a particular job needs access to a variety of different network resources, it might take an administrator some time to assign all of the rights and permissions that person needs to an individual user account. Later, if that job should be taken over by another person, the administrator has to go through the entire process again twice, once to remove the rights and permissions from the old user's account and once to grant the same rights and permissions to the new user. By creating a group to represent the job, the administrator only has to grant the rights and permissions to the group once. When someone new takes over the job, the administrator only has to remove the departed user from the group and add the new user.

Understanding Local and Domain Users

The concept of users and groups is complicated in Windows because there are two completely separate user account systems: local users and domain users. Which user account system a Windows computer uses depends on whether it is a member of a workgroup or an Active Directory Domain Services domain.

Windows 8 supports three types of networks: homegroups, workgroups, and domains, as described in the following sections.

INTRODUCING THE HOMEGROUP

New in Windows 7, a ***homegroup*** is a simplified networking paradigm that enables users connected to a home network to share the contents of their libraries without the need for creating user accounts and permissions. For more information on creating and using homegroups, see in Lesson 14, "Configuring Shared Resources."

INTRODUCING THE WORKGROUP

A ***workgroup*** is a collection of computers that are all peers. A peer network is one in which every computer can function as both a server, by sharing its resources with other computers, and a client, by accessing the shared resources on other computers.

On a workgroup network, each computer has its own set of users and groups that it uses to control access to its own resources. For example, if you want to use one computer to access resources on all four of the other computers on a five-node workgroup network, you must have a user account on each of those four computers. As you connect to each computer, you are authenticated and authorized by each one. If effect, you are logging on to each computer individually.

TAKE NOTE*

Although it is technically a separate authentication process every time a workgroup computer accesses another computer, this does not necessarily mean that users have to supply account names and passwords each time they connect to another computer. If a user has accounts with the same name and password on multiple workgroup computers, then the authentications occur automatically, with no user intervention. This is called ***pass-through authentication.*** If the passwords for the accounts are different, however, a manual authentication is necessary for each one.

INTRODUCING THE DOMAIN

A ***domain*** is a collection of computers that all utilize a central directory service for authentication and authorization. A ***directory service*** is a collection of logical objects that represent various types of network resources, such as computers, applications, users, and groups. Each object consists of attributes that contain information about the object.

TAKE NOTE*

Do not confuse an Active Directory Domain Services (AD DS) domain with a Domain Name System (DNS) domain. An AD DS domain is a collection of Windows computers and other related objects that are all joined to the Windows directory service. A DNS domain is a collection of Internet host names used by computers that can be running any operating system.

To create a domain, you must have at least one Windows server with the Active Directory Domain Services (AD DS) role installed. This server is called a ***domain controller***. Each of the computers then joins the domain, and is represented by a computer object. In the same way, administrators create user objects that represent human users. In Windows networking, the main difference between a domain and a workgroup is that users log on to the domain once, rather than each computer individually. When users attempt to access network resources, the individual computers hosting the resources send authorization requests to the domain controller, rather than handling the authorizations themselves.

DIFFERENTIATING LOCAL AND DOMAIN USERS

The primary advantage of a domain over a workgroup is that administrators only have to create one user account for each person, while workgroups can require many different user accounts for one person. If, on a workgroup network, a user's password is lost or compromised, someone must change that password on every computer where that user has an account. On a domain, there is only one user account for each person, so only one password change is needed.

Windows 8 computers always have a need for local user accounts, for administrative access to the system, if no other reason. For networking purposes, though, it is typical to use local user accounts or domain user accounts, but not both. Workgroup networks are typically small and informal, with users administering their own computers. Domain networks are usually larger, and have dedicated network administrators responsible for managing user accounts and controlling access to network resources.

Local and domain users are different in several important ways. You use different tools to create and manage the two types of users, and the user accounts themselves are different in composition. As mentioned earlier, a user account consists of attributes, which contain information about the user. Domain users have many more attributes than local users.

As a demonstration of this, Figures 17-1 and 17-2 contain the *Properties* sheets of a Windows 8 local user account and an AD DS domain user account. Notice that the Properties sheet for the local user has only 3 tabs, while the domain user's sheet has 13. This means that the domain user account can store a great deal more information about the user, and can access many more different kinds of network resources.

Figure 17-1

The *Properties* sheet for a local user

Figure 17-2

The *Properties* sheet for a domain user

Table 17-1 lists some of the other differences between local and domain users.

Table 17-1

Frequently Asked Questions About Local and Domain Users

Question	Local Users	Domain Users
What tools do you use to manage the user accounts?	The User Accounts control panel applet or the Local Users and Groups snap-in for Microsoft Management Console (MMC)	The Active Directory Users and Computers MMC snap-in
Where are the user accounts stored?	In the Security Accounts Manager (SAM) on the local computer	On the Active Directory Domain Services domain controllers
What can you access with the user account?	Local computer resources only	All domain and network resources
What restrictions are there on the user name?	Each user name must be unique on the computer	Each user name must be unique in the directory

As an administrator, the type of user accounts you work with depends/. on the nature of your networks you manage and their security requirements. Small businesses are more likely to use workgroup networking, in which case you will be working with local user accounts. Depending on the capabilities of the users, you might have to set up all of the user accounts for all of the computers on the network, or you might be able to show the users how to create accounts on their own computers. Local users are relatively simple to create and manage, and a workgroup network often is a casual affair.

If your client is a medium or large business, it is more likely to be running an AD DS domain, in which case you will be working primarily with domain user accounts. The question of whether to host a Windows domain is a major decision that an organization usually makes when they are designing and installing the network. Hosting a Windows domain is a costly undertaking, both in terms of the additional hardware and software required, and in terms of the time and effort needed for planning and deployment.

INTRODUCING BUILT-IN LOCAL USERS

As mentioned earlier, Windows 8 (like the other Windows workstation operating systems) always has a need for local user accounts. When you perform a standard interactive installation of Windows 8, you are required to create one user account. In addition, the Setup program automatically creates a number of other user accounts.

The following user accounts are built-in on Windows 8:

- **Administrator** – During a typical Windows 8 installation, the Setup program creates an Administrator account and makes it a member of the Administrators group, giving it complete access to all areas of the operating system. However, the Setup program leaves the account in a disabled state and does not assign it a password.
- **New User Account** – During the operating system installation process, the installer must specify the name for a new user account, which the Setup program creates and adds to the Administrators group. This grants the new account full access to the operating system. The installer decides whether to assign a password to this account. Windows 8 uses this account for its initial logons.
- **Guest** – This account is designed for users that require only temporary access to the computer, and who do not need high levels of access. The Guest account is disabled, by default, and is a member only of the Guests group, which provides it with only the most rudimentary access to the system.

In addition to these accounts, Windows 8 also creates a number of system and service accounts, none of which you have to manipulate directly.

TAKE NOTE*

After the Windows 8 installation is completed, you might want to consider enabling the Administrator account and assigning it a strong password. This will provide you with administrative access to the system, even if your main user account becomes compromised.

Understanding Local and Domain Groups

Just as there are local and domain users, there are local and domain groups as well. Whether local or domain, a group is essentially just a collection of users and, in some cases, other groups. As mentioned earlier, by assigning rights and permissions to a group, you assign those rights and permissions to all of its members.

USING LOCAL GROUPS

When compared to domain groups, local groups are quite simple, and are defined more by what they cannot do than what they can do. Local groups are subject to the following restrictions:

- You can only use local groups on the computer where you create them.
- Only local users from the same computer can be members of local groups.
- When the computer is a member of an AD DS domain, local groups can have domain users and domain global groups as members.
- Local groups cannot have other local groups as members. However, they can have domain groups as members.
- You can only assign permissions to local groups when you are controlling access to resources on the local computer.
- You cannot create local groups on a Windows server computer that is functioning as a domain controller.

INTRODUCING BUILT-IN LOCAL GROUPS

Windows 8 includes a number of built-in local groups that are already equipped with the permissions and rights needed to perform certain tasks. You can enable users to perform these tasks simply by adding them to the appropriate group. Table 17-2 lists the Windows 8 built-in local groups and the capabilities they provide to their members.

TAKE NOTE*

Some of the built-in local groups in Windows 8, such as Administrators, Backup Operators, and Remote Desktop Users, are created for the convenience of system administrators so that they can easily grant certain privileges to users. Other groups, such as IIS_USRS and Replicator, are designed to support automated functions that create their own system user accounts. There is no need to manually add users to these groups.

Table 17-2

Windows 8 Built-in Local Groups and Their Capabilities

Built-In Local Group	Group Function
Access Control Assistance Operators	Members can remotely query authorization permissions for resources on this computer.
Administrators	Members have full administrative access to the entire operating system. By default, the Administrator user and the user account created during the operating system installation are both members of this group.
Backup Operators	Members have user rights enabling them to override permissions for the sole purpose of backing up and restoring files, folders, and other operating system elements.
Cryptographic Operators	Members are capable of performing cryptographic operations.
Distributed COM Users	Members are capable of launching, activating, and using distributed COM objects.
Event Log Readers	Members can read the computer's event logs.
Guests	Members have no default user rights. By default, the Guest user account is a member of this group.
Hyper-V Administrators	Members have full control of all Hyper-V features.
IIS_IUSRS	Group used to provide privileges to dedicated Internet Information Services users.
Network Configuration Operators	Members have privileges that enable them to modify the computer's network configuration settings.
Performance Log Users	Members have privileges that enable them to schedule the logging of performance counters, enable trace providers, and collect event traces on this computer, both locally and from remote locations.
Performance Monitor Users	Members have privileges that enable them to monitor performance counter data on the computer, both locally and from remote locations.
Power Users	Members possess no additional capabilities in Windows 8, In previous Windows versions, the Power Users group provided privileges for a limited number of administrative functions, but in Windows 8, the group is included solely for reasons of backwards compatibility.
Remote Desktop Users	Members can log on to the computer from remote locations, using Terminal Services or Remote Desktop.
Remote Management Users	Members can access Windows Management Instrumentation (WMI) resources using management protocols.
Replicator	When the computer is joined to a domain, this group provides the access needed for file replication functions. The only member should be a user account dedicated solely to the replication process.
Users	Members can perform most common tasks, such as running applications, using local and network printers, and locking the server. However, members are prevented from making many system-wide configuration changes, whether they do so accidentally or deliberately.
WinRM RemoteWMIUsers_	Members can access Windows Management Instrumentation (WMI) resources using management protocols.

The built-in local groups in Windows 8, although created by the operating system, are groups like any other. You can modify their properties, change their names, and assign new rights and permissions to them. However, it's a better idea to create your own groups and assign whatever additional rights and permissions you need to them. You can make a single user a member of multiple groups, and the permissions from all of the groups will be combined.

INTRODUCING SPECIAL IDENTITIES

Another type of element in Windows 8 (and all other Windows operating systems) is a special identity, which functions much like a group. A ***special identity*** is essentially a placeholder for a collection of users with a similar characteristic. For example, the Authenticated Users special identity represents all of the users that are logged on to the computer at a given instant. You can assign rights and permissions to a special identity just as you would to a group.

When the access control list (ACL) for a system resource contains a special identity in one of its access control entries (ACEs), the system substitutes the users that conform to the special identity at the moment the ACL is processed.

TAKE NOTE*

It's important to understand that the set of computers represented by a special identity can change from minute to minute. The Authenticated Users special identity changes every time a user logs on or off, for example. When you assign rights and permissions to a special identity, the users who receive those rights and permissions are not those who conform to the special identity at the time you make the assignment, but rather those who conform to the special identity at the time the special identity is read from the ACL.

Table 17-3 lists the special identities included in Windows 8.

Table 17-3

Windows 8 Special Identities and Their Constituents

Special Identity	Function
All Application Packages	Includes all Windows Store apps
Anonymous Logon	Includes all users who have connected to the computer without authenticating
Authenticated Users	Includes all users with a valid local user account whose identities have been authenticated. The Guest user is not included in the Authenticated Users special identity, even if it has a password.
Batch	Includes all users who are currently logged on through a batch facility such as a task scheduler job
Console Logon	Includes all users that are logged on to the computer's physical console
Creator Group	Includes the primary group of the user who created or most recently took ownership of the resource
Creator Owner	Includes only the user who created or most recently took ownership of a resource
Dialup	Includes all users who are currently logged on through a dial-up connection
Everyone	Includes all members of the Authenticated Users special identity plus the Guest user account

(continued)

Table 17-3
(continued)

Special Identity	Function
Interactive	Includes all users who are currently logged on locally or through a Remote Desktop connection
IUSR	Account used to provide anonymous access to webpages through Internet Information Services (IIS)
Local Service	Provides all services configured to run as a local service with the same privileges as the Users group
Network	Includes all users who are currently logged on through a network connection
Network Service	Provides all services configured to run as a network service with the same privileges as the Users group
Owner Rights	Represents the current owner of an object
Remote Interactive Logon	Includes all users who are currently logged on through a Remote Desktop connection
Service	Includes all security principals who have logged on as a service
System	Provides the operating system with all of the privileges it needs to function
Terminal Server User	Includes all users who are currently logged on to a Terminal Services server that is in Terminal Services version 4.0 application compatibility mode
This Organization Certificate	Account used by the default IIS user

Creating and Managing Local Users and Groups

THE BOTTOM LINE

Windows 8 provides two separate interfaces for creating and managing local user accounts: the User Accounts control panel applet and the Local Users and Groups snap-in for the Microsoft Management Console (MMC). Both of these interfaces provide access to the same Security Account Manager (SAM) where the user and group information is stored, so any changes you make using one interface will appear in the other.

Microsoft designed the User accounts control panel applet and the Local Users and Groups snap-in for computer users with different levels of expertise, and they provide different degrees of access to the Security Account Manager, as follows:

- **User Accounts** – Microsoft designed the User accounts control panel applet for relatively inexperienced end users; it provides a simplified interface with extremely limited access to user accounts. With this interface, it is possible to create local user accounts and modify their basic attributes, but you cannot create groups or manage group memberships (except for the Administrators group).
- **Local Users and Groups** – Microsoft includes this MMC snap-in as part of the Computer Management console; it provides full access to local users and groups, as well as all of their attributes. Designed more for the technical specialist or system administrator, this interface is not difficult to use, but it does provide access to controls that beginning users generally do not need.

TAKE NOTE*

Both the User accounts control panel applet and the Local Users and Groups snap-in are capable of working with local users and local groups only. You cannot create and manage domain users and groups using these tools. To work with domain users and groups, you must use a domain tool, such as Active Directory Users and Computers, which is supplied with the server operating system that is hosting the Active Directory Domain Services domain.

Using the User Accounts Control Settings

As described earlier, the first local user account on a Windows 8 computer is the one created during the operating system installation process. The Setup program prompts the installer for an account name, and creates a new user account with administrative privileges. The program also creates the Administrator and Guest accounts, both of which are disabled by default.

When the Windows 8 installation process is completed, the system restarts. Because only one user account is available, the computer automatically logs on using that account. This account has administrative privileges, so at this point you can create additional user accounts or modify the existing ones.

CREATING A NEW USER ACCOUNT

New to Windows 8 is the ability to create a local user account based on an existing Windows Live ID. Windows Live is an Internet-based authentication service that provides users with access to all of their personal data stored in the Microsoft cloud, This includes SkyDrive, a personal storage space in the cloud where users can store their data files and now their Windows operating system configuration settings.

When you create a local user account using a Windows Live ID, you specify your email address and your Windows Live password. Windows 8 uses the information from your Windows Live account to create a local user, and configures Windows 8 to synchronize its configuration elements with the Windows Live service on the Internet. This way, if you log on to another Windows 8 computer using that same account, it will download your desktop configuration, favorites, and other settings from the cloud and reproduce your home configuration on the other machine.

The User accounts control panel applet provides access to existing local accounts, but when creating new accounts, the system transfers you to the *Users* page of the *PC Settings* app. Adding a user through this interface takes you through the same procedure as the new user creation process in the Windows 8 installation.

To create a new user account with the User accounts control panel applet, use the following procedure:

CREATE A NEW USER ACCOUNT

TAKE NOTE*

This procedure is valid only on Windows 8 computers that are part of a workgroup. When you join a computer to an AD DS domain, you can only create new local user accounts with the Local Users and Groups snap-in.

GET READY. Log on to Windows 8 using an account with Administrator privileges and then perform the following steps:

1. On the Start screen, click the **Desktop tile**.

   The Windows Desktop appears.
2. Swipe in from the right edge of the screen or mouse over the top or bottom right corner of the screen to display the charms bar.
3. Click the **Settings** charm.

   The *Settings* bar appears.
4. Click **Control Panel**.

   The *Control Panel* window appears.

5. Click **User Accounts and Family Safety**.

   The *User Accounts and Family Safety* window appears.

6. Click **User Accounts**.

   The *User Accounts* control panel applet appears, as shown in Figure 17-3.

Figure 17-3

The *User Accounts* control panel applet

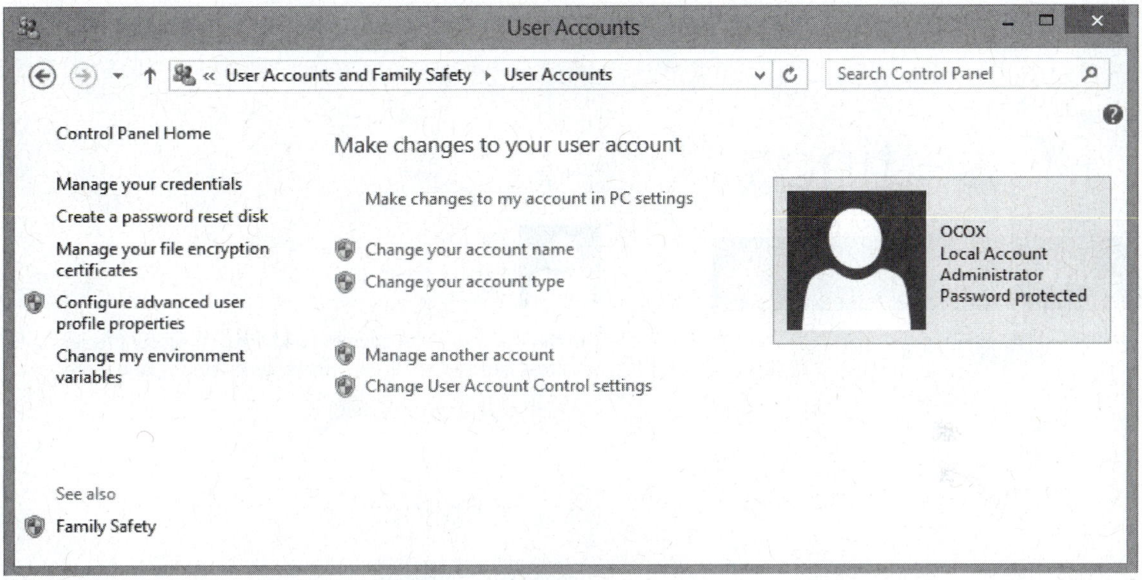

7. Click **Manage another account**.

   The *Choose the user you would like to change* page appears, as shown in Figure 17-4.

Figure 17-4

The *Choose the account you would like to change* page

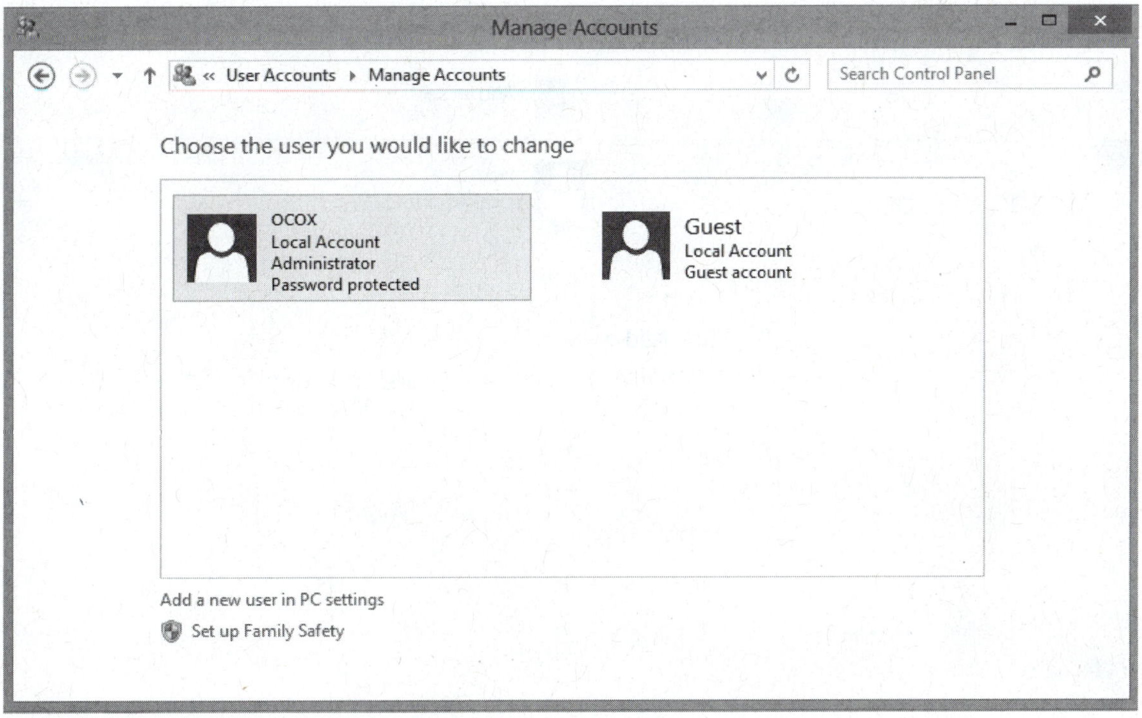

8. Click **Add a new user in PC settings**.

   The *PC Settings* screen appears, displaying the *Users* page, as shown in Figure 17-5.

Figure 17-5

The *Users* page in the *PC Settings* screen

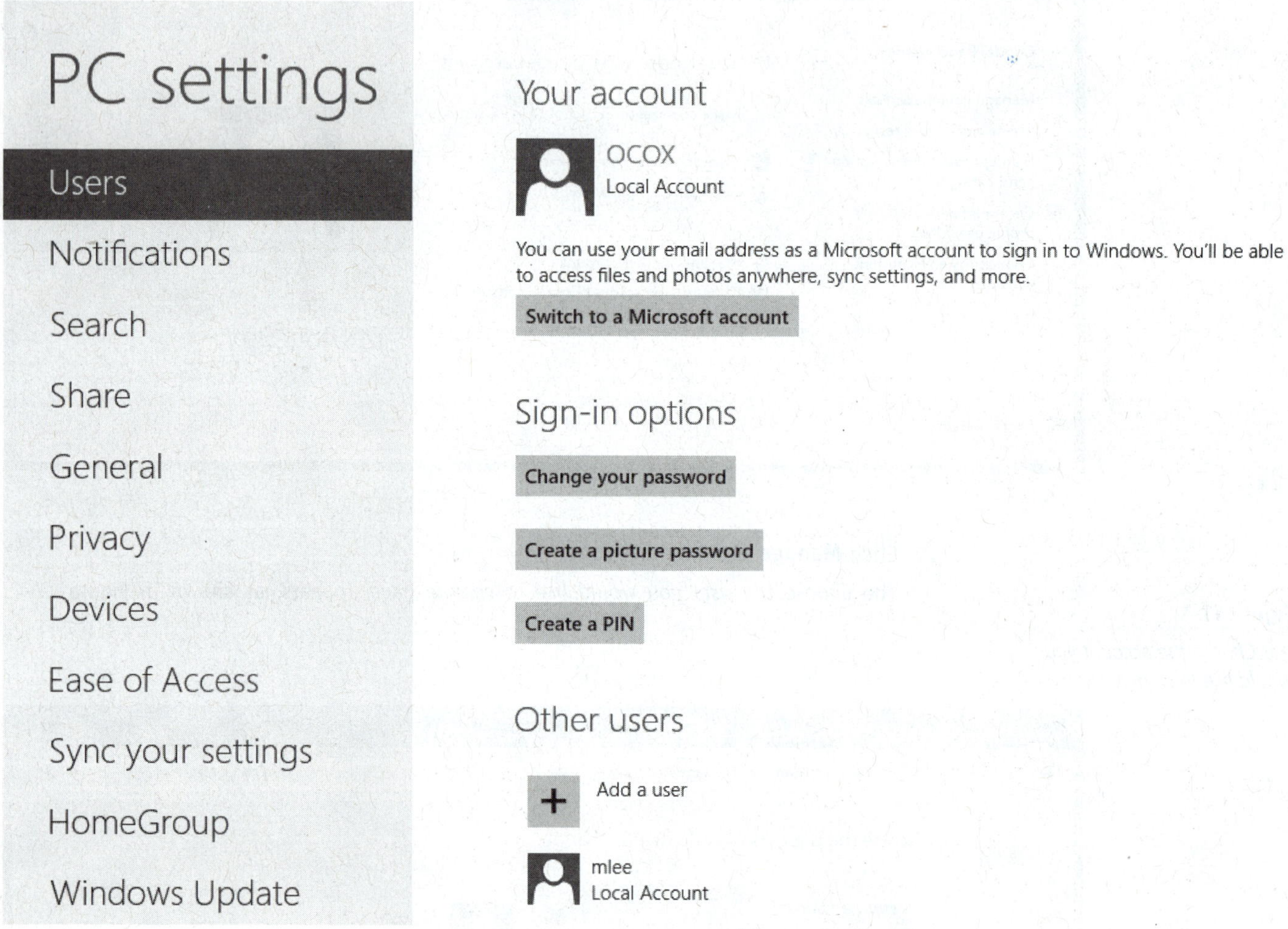

9. Click **Add a user**.

   The *Add a user* screen appears, as shown in Figure 17-6.

Figure 17-6

The *Add a user* screen

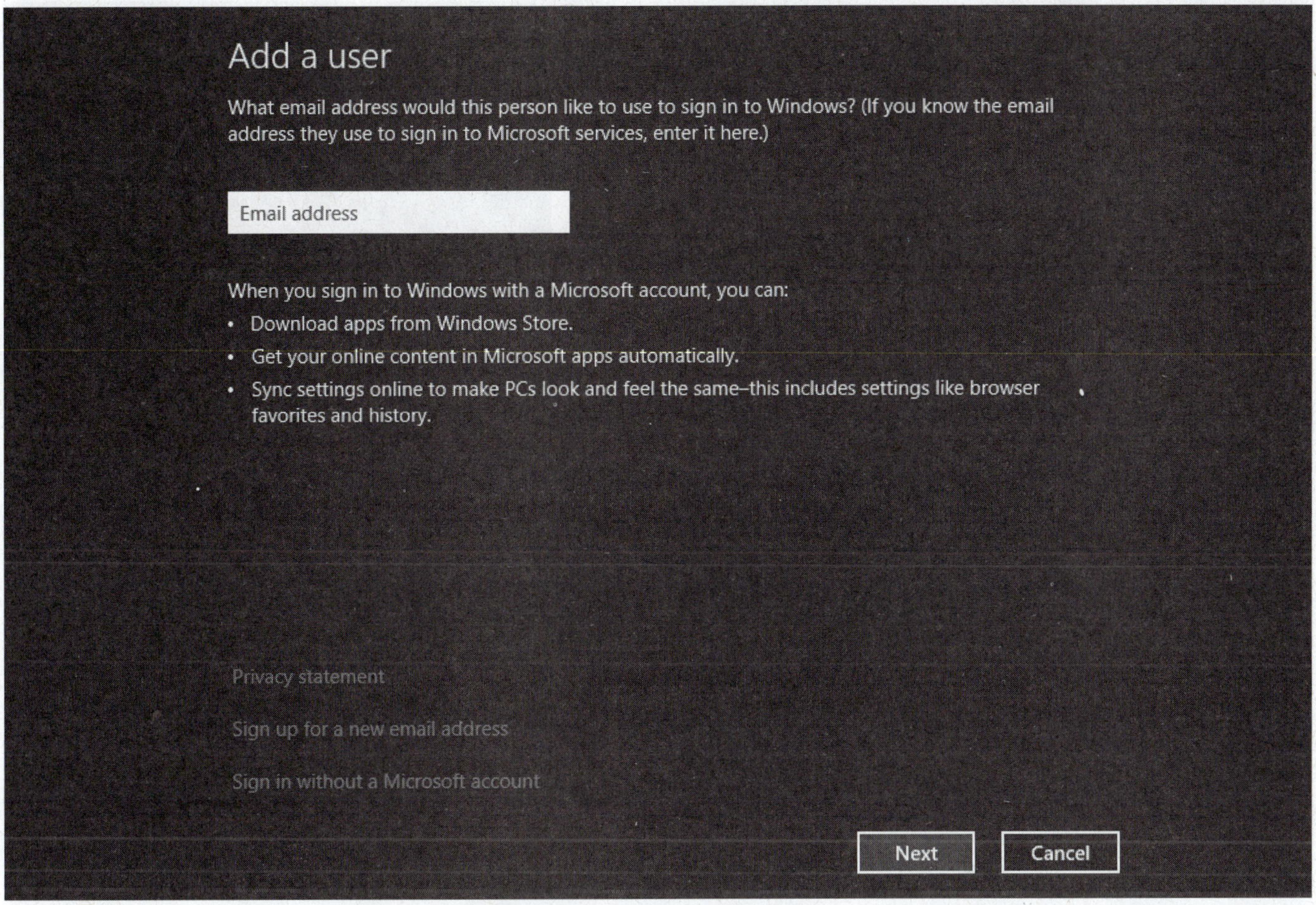

10. Click **Sign in without a Microsoft account**.

    An *Add a user* screen appears, describing the differences between a Microsoft account and a local account.

11. Click **Local account**.

    An *Add a user* form appears, as shown in Figure 17-7.

Figure 17-7

The *Add a user* form

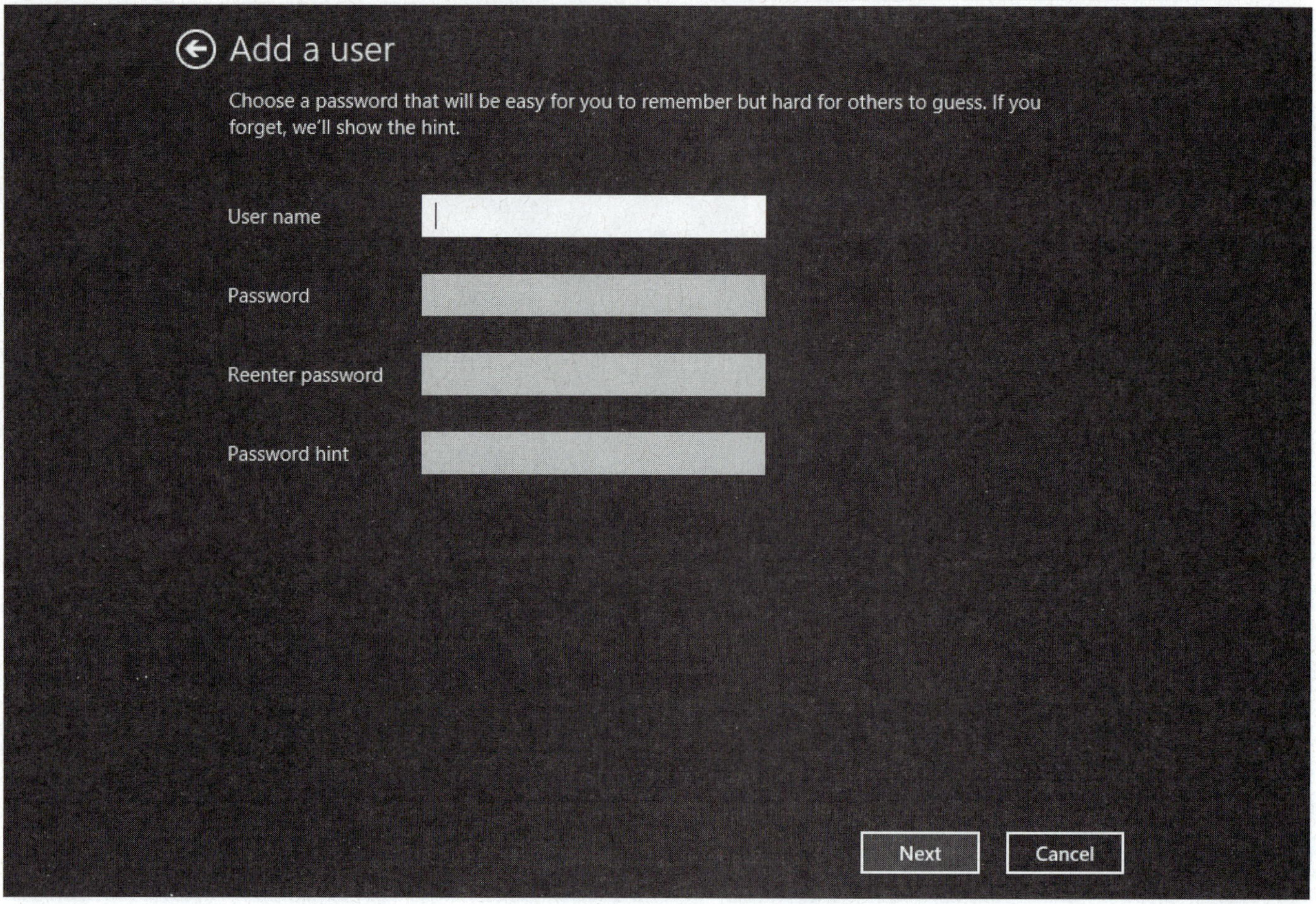

TAKE NOTE*

Recommended network practices call for administrators to use a standardized system for creating user account names. For example, smaller networks often use the first name followed by the first letter of the surname, such as JohnD. For larger networks with a greater chance of name duplication, use of the first initial plus the surname is common, such as JDoe. The purpose of standardizing user names in this way is to enable any administrator to determine the account name for any user.

12. In the *User name* text box, type the new user's account name.
13. In the *Password* and *Reenter password* text boxes, type the password for the new account.
14. In the *Password hint* text box, type a phrase related to the password and click Next. A page appears displaying the new account.
15. Click **Finish**.

The new account appears on the *Users* page of the *PC Settings* screen.

This procedure provides only the most rudimentary access to the user account attributes. Apart from supplying a name for the account, all you can do is specify a password. Local accounts created in this way are Standard users, not Administrators. To modify the account type, you must return to the User accounts control panel applet.

What the User accounts control panel applet refers to as an account type is actually a group membership. Selecting the Standard user option adds the user account to the local Users group, while selecting the Administrator option adds the account to the Administrators group.

MANAGING A USER ACCOUNT

To see the modifications you can make to an existing local user account with the User accounts control panel applet, use the following procedure:

MANAGE USER ACCOUNTS

GET READY. Log on to Windows 8 using an account with Administrator privileges and then perform the following steps:

1. On the Start screen, click the **Desktop tile**.

   The Windows Desktop appears.
2. Swipe in from the right edge of the screen or mouse over the top or bottom right corner of the screen to display the charms bar.
3. Click the **Settings** charm.

   The Settings bar appears.
4. Click **Control Panel**.

   The Control Panel window appears.
5. Click **User Accounts and Family Safety**.

   The *User Accounts and Family Safety* window appears.
6. Click **User Accounts**.

   The *User accounts* control panel applet appears.
7. Click **Manage another account**.

   The *Choose the account you would like to change* page appears.
8. Click one of the existing accounts.

   The *Make changes to [user's] account* page appears, as shown in Figure 17-8.

Figure 17-8

The *Make changes to [user's] account* page

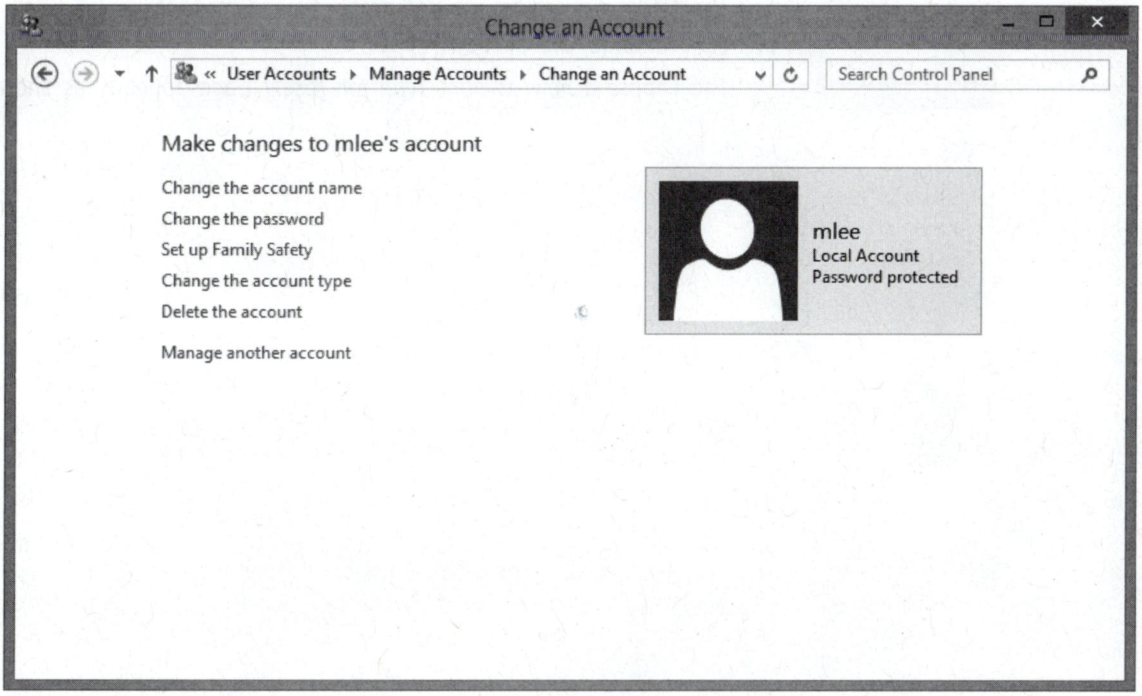

9. Click **Change the account name**.

   The *Type a new account name for [user] account* page appears, as shown in Figure 17-9.

Figure 17-9

The *Type a new account name for [user's] account* page

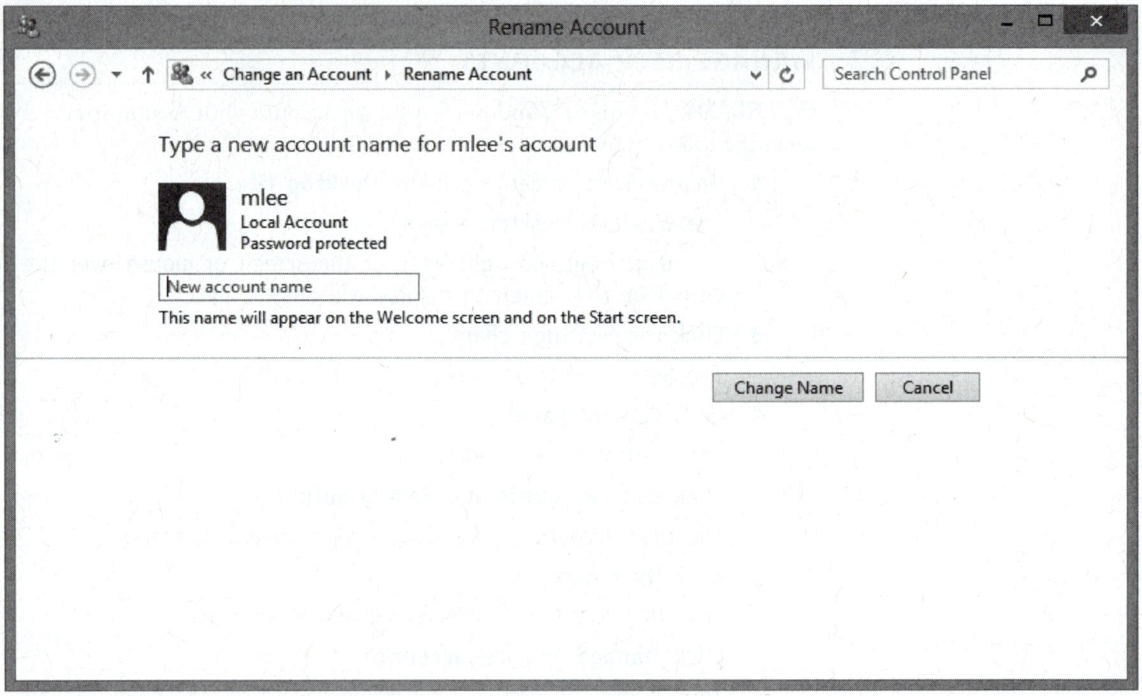

10. Type a new name for the account in the *New account name* text box, and then click **Change Name**.

    The *Make changes to [user's] account* page reappears.

11. Click **Change the account type**.

    The *Choose a new account type for [user]* page appears, as shown in Figure 17-10.

Figure 17-10

The *Choose a new account type for [user]* page

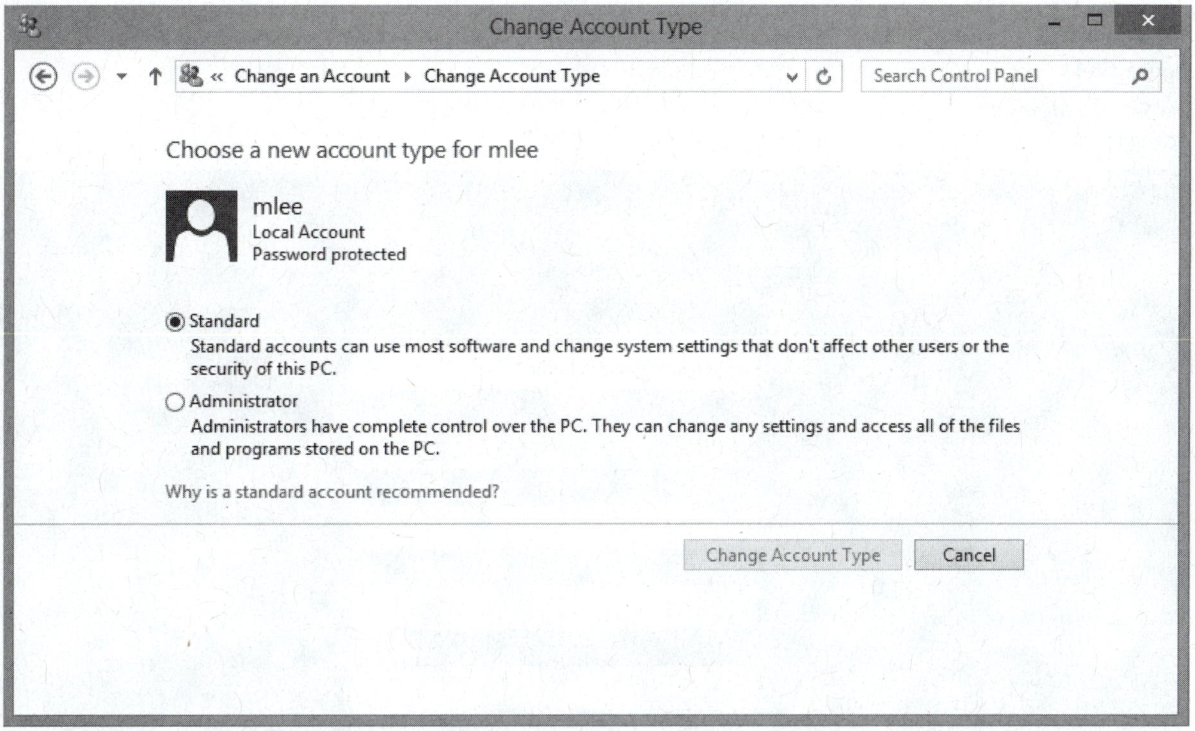

12. Select the **Standard** or **Administrator** radio button, and then click **Change Account Type**.

    The *Make changes to [user's] account* page reappears.

13. Click **Delete the account**.

    The *Do you want to keep [user's] files?* page appears.

14. Click **Delete Files** to delete the user profile, or click **Keep Files** to save it to the desktop.

    The *Are you sure you want to delete [user's] account?* page appears.

15. Click **Delete Account**.

    The *Choose the account you would like to change* page reappears.

16. Close the User accounts control panel applet window.

CREATING A WINDOWS 8 ACCOUNT FROM A MICROSOFT ACCOUNT

CERTIFICATION READY
Set up and configure Microsoft Account
Objective 4.4

If, during the Windows 8 installation, you opt to create your first account by specifying a Microsoft account – formerly called a ***Windows Live ID*** – the procedure is the same as when you supply an email address during the *Add a user* process described earlier.

Windows Live has been around for several years. The service represents Microsoft's attempt to consolidate all of its online services under a single sign-on. If you have ever used Microsoft's Live Messenger application or stored files on SkyDrive, or used any one of Microsoft's other online services, then you probably already have a Microsoft account registered using your email address.

When you specify your email address on the *Add a user* screen, the system searches for a Microsoft account that uses that address, and either prompts you for the account password or, if it fails to find one, displays a *Set up a Microsoft Account* form with which you can create a new account, as shown in Figure 17-11. The system then uses the Microsoft account information to create a new local account on the Windows 8 system.

Figure 17-11

The *Set up a Microsoft Account* page

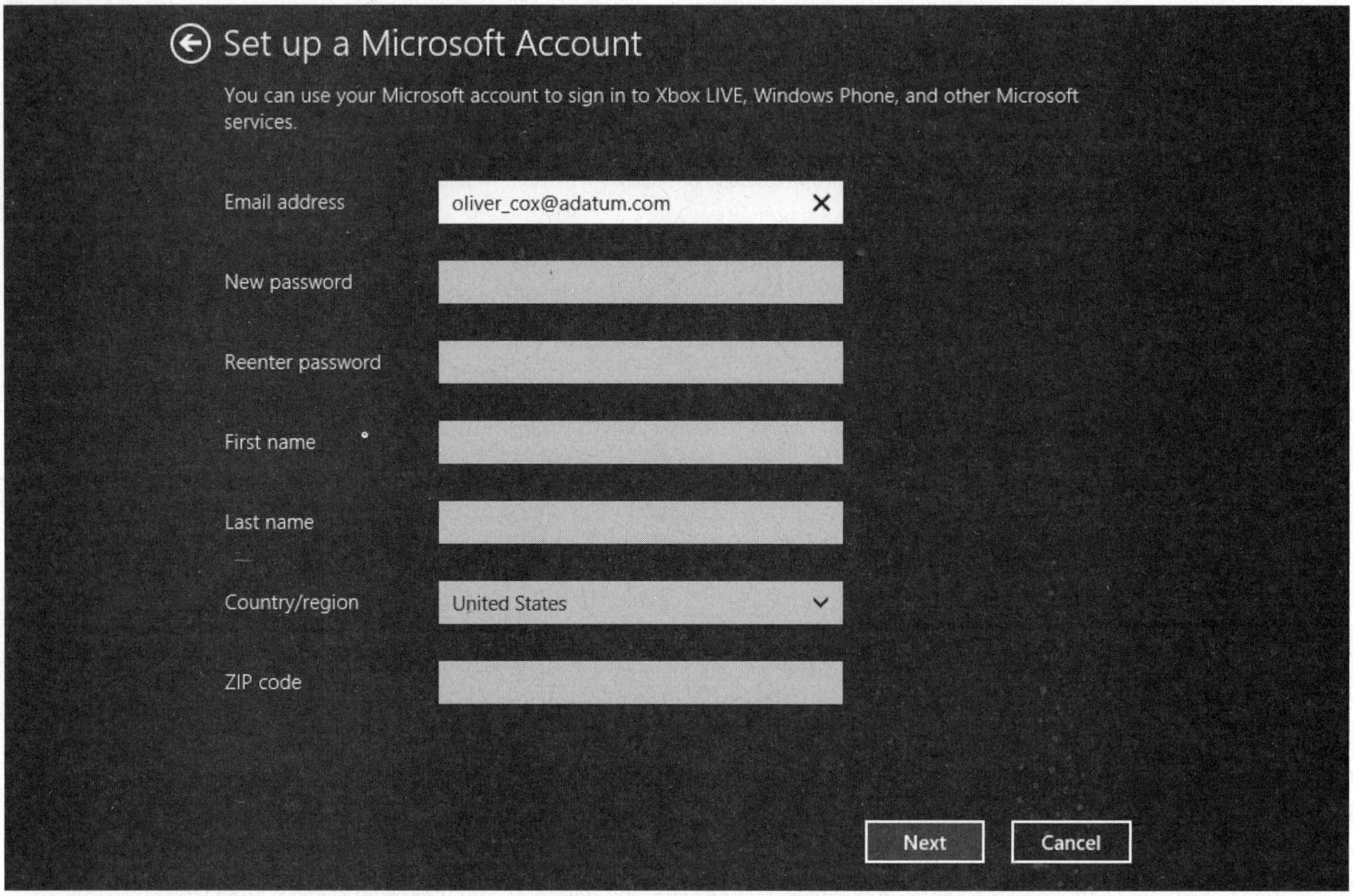

TAKE NOTE*

The sole difference between the local account created during the Windows 8 installation and one that you create later is that the one created during the installation uses the Administrator account type. This is because it is the only functional account on the system and must have full access. Accounts that you create later through the Windows Users control panel are standard user accounts.

With a Microsoft account, you can purchase apps from the Windows Store and synchronize your system settings with other computers by storing them in the cloud. However, this synchronization cannot begin until you verify the use of your Microsoft account for that purpose. Microsoft sends an email message to the address you supplied, confirming that you want to use the account with your specific computer. Once you respond to that email, the connection between your Windows 8 computer and your Microsoft account is fully activated.

Using the Local Users and Groups Snap-in

As you might have noticed in the previous sections, the User accounts control panel applet provides only partial access to local user accounts, and no access to groups other than the Users and Administrators groups. The Local Users and Groups snap-in, on the other hand, provides full access to all of the local user and group accounts on the computer.

By default, the Local Users and Groups snap-in is part of the Computer Management console. However, you can also load the snap-in by itself, or create your own MMC console with any combination of snap-ins you wish.

OPENING THE LOCAL USERS AND GROUPS SNAP-IN

You can open the Local Users and Groups snap-in in one of three basic ways, as follows:

- Open the Control Panel, select **System and Security > Administrative Tools > Computer Management**
- Launch Microsoft Management Console (Mmc.exe), choose **File > Add/Remove Snap-In**, and then select the **Local Users and Groups** snap-in.
- Open the **Run** dialog box and type **Lusrmgr.msc** in the *Open* text box.

Each of these three methods provides access to the same snap-in and the same controls for creating, managing, and deleting local users and groups.

CREATING A LOCAL USER

To create a local user account with the Local Users and Groups snap-in, use the following procedure:

CREATE A NEW USER

GET READY. Log on to Windows 8 using an account with Administrator privileges and then perform the following steps:

1. Open the *Computer Management* console, as shown in Figure 17-12.

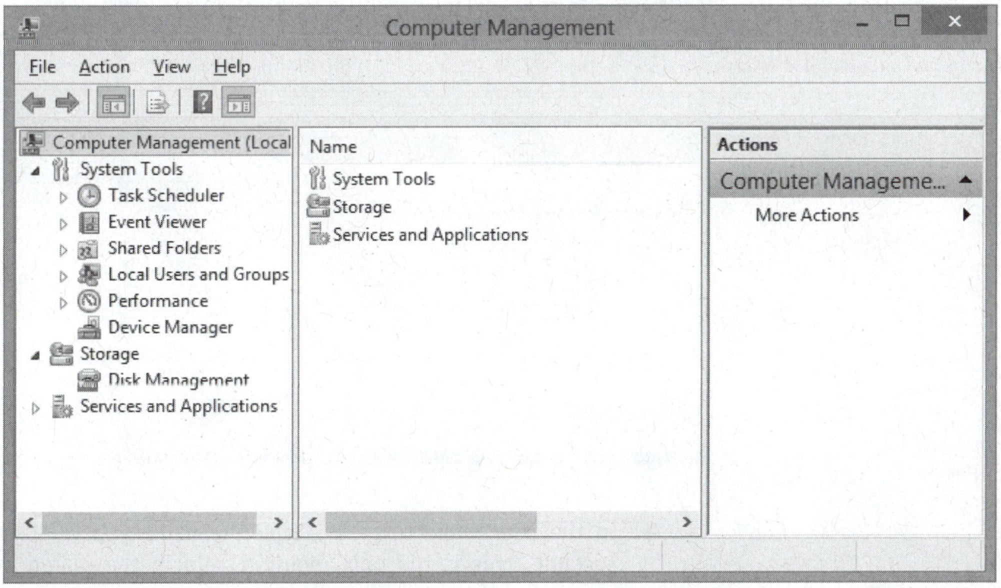

Figure 17-12

The *Computer Management* console

2. In the left pane of the console, expand the *Local Users and Groups* node and click **Users**.

   A list of the current local users appears in the middle pane, as shown in Figure 17-13.

Figure 17-13

The *Local Users and Groups* snap-in

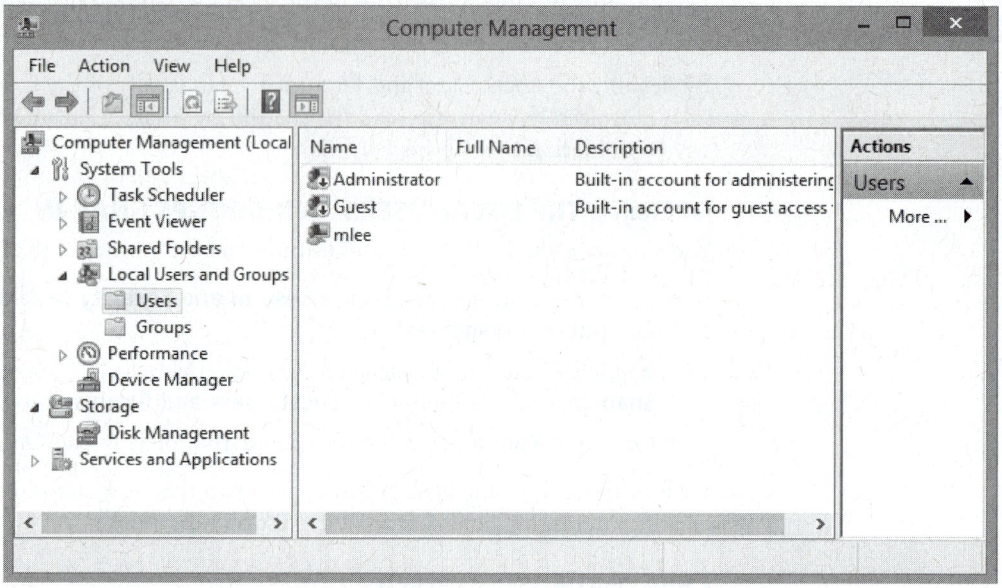

3. Right-click the **Users** folder and, from the context menu, select **New User**.

   The New User dialog box appears, as shown in Figure 17-14.

Figure 17-14

The *New User* dialog box

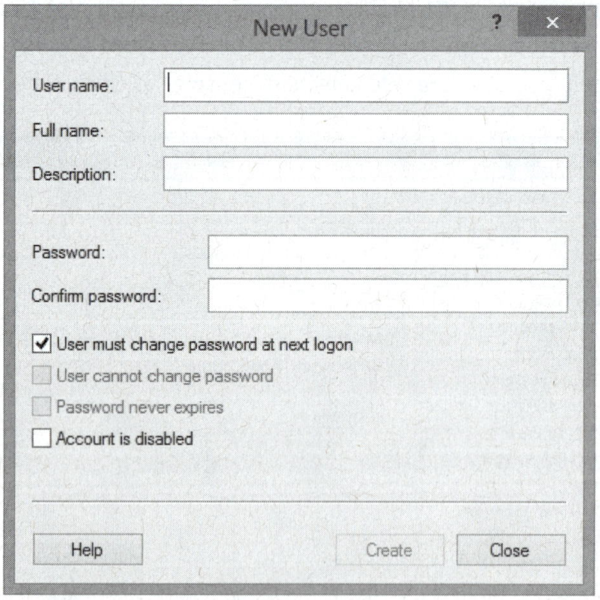

4. In the *User name* text box, type the name you want to assign to the user account. This is the only required field in the dialog box.
5. Specify a *Full name* and a *Description* for the account, if desired.
6. In the *Password* and *Confirm password* text boxes, type a password for the account, if desired.

7. Select or clear the four checkboxes to control the following functions:
   - **User must change password at next logon** – Forces the new user to change the password after logging on for the first time. Select this option if you want to assign an initial password and have users control their own passwords after the first logon. You cannot select this option if you have selected the *Password never expires* checkbox. Selecting this option automatically clears the *User cannot change password* checkbox.
   - **User cannot change password** – Prevents the user from changing the account password. Select this option if you want to retain control over the account password, such as when multiple users are logging on with the same user account. This option is also commonly used to manage service account passwords. You cannot select this option if you have selected the *User must change password at next logon* checkbox.
   - **Password never expires** – Prevents the existing password from ever expiring. This option automatically clears the *User must change password at next logon* checkbox. This option is also commonly used to manage service account passwords.
   - **Account is disabled** – Disables the user account, preventing anyone from using it to log on.
8. Click **Create**.

   The new account is added to the detail pane and the console clears the dialog box, leaving it ready for the creation of another user account.
9. Click **Close**.
10. Close the *Computer Management* console.

MANAGING LOCAL USERS

Local user accounts on a Windows 8 computer are not nearly as complex as domain users, but the Local Users and Groups snap-in provides full access to all of the attributes they do possess. To modify a user's attributes, use the following procedure:

MANAGE A USER

GET READY. Log on to Windows 8 using an account with Administrator privileges and then perform the following steps:

1. Open the *Computer Management* console.
2. In the console's left pane, expand the *Local Users and Groups* subheading, and then click **Users**.

   A list of the current local users appears in the middle pane.
3. Double-click one of the existing user accounts.

   The *Properties* sheet for the user account appears.
4. If desired, modify the contents of the *Full name* and *Description* text boxes.
5. Select or clear any of the following checkboxes:
   - **User must change password at next logon** – Forces the new user to change the password after logging on for the first time. Select this option if you want to assign an initial password and have users control their own passwords after the first logon. You cannot select this option if you have selected the *Password never expires* checkbox. Selecting this option automatically clears the *User cannot change password* checkbox.
   - **User cannot change password** – Prevents the user from changing the account password. Select this option if you want to retain control over the account password, such as when multiple users are logging on with the same user

account. This option is also commonly used to manage service account passwords. You cannot select this option if you have selected the *User must change password at next logon* checkbox.

- **Password never expires** – Prevents the existing password from ever expiring. This option automatically clears the *User must change password at next logon* checkbox. This option is also commonly used to manage service account passwords.
- **Account is disabled** – Disables the user account, preventing anyone from using it to log on.
- **Account is locked out** – When selected, indicates that the account has been disabled because the number of unsuccessful logon attempts specified in the local system policies has been exceeded. Clear the checkbox to unlock the account.

6. Click the **Member Of** tab.

   The interface shown in Figure 17-15 appears.

Figure 17-15

The *Member Of* tab of a user's *Properties* sheet

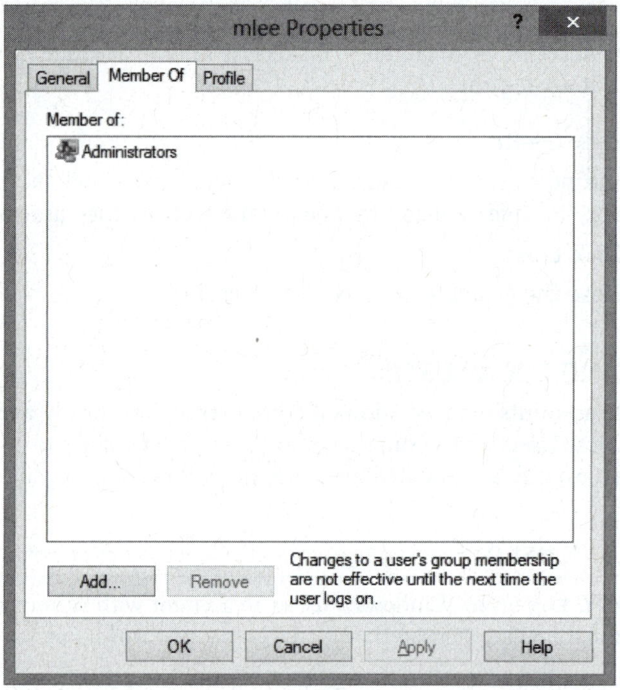

7. To add the user to a group, click the **Add** button.

   The *Select Groups* dialog box appears, as shown in Figure 17-16.

Figure 17-16

The *Select Groups* dialog box

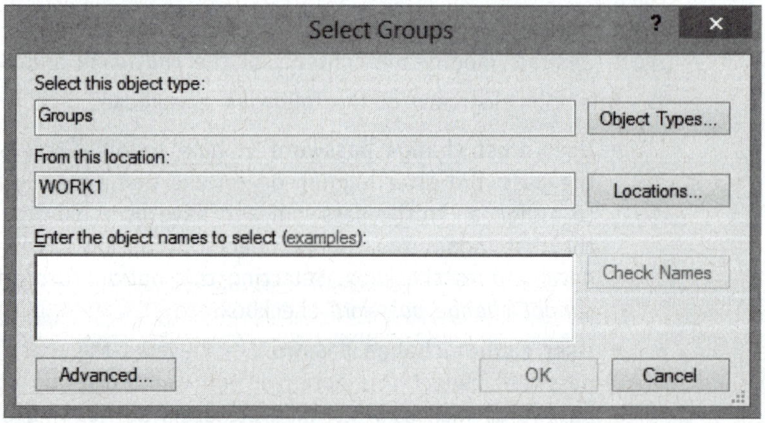

8. Type the name of the local group to which you want to add the user in the text box, and then click **OK**.

   The group is added to the *Member of* list. You can also type part of the group name and click **Check Names** to complete the name or click **Advanced** to search for groups.

9. Click the **Profile** tab.

   The interface shown in Figure 17-17 appears.

Figure 17-17

The *Profile* tab of a user's *Properties* sheet

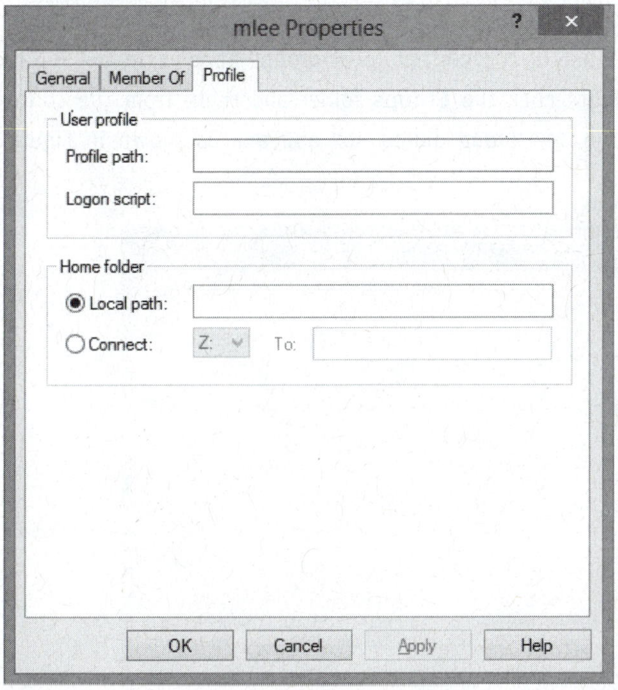

10. Type a path or file name into any of the following four text boxes as needed:
    - **Profile path** – To assign a roaming or mandatory user profile to the account, type the path to the profile stored on a network share using Universal Naming Convention (UNC) notation, as in the example *server**share**folder*.
    - **Logon script** – Type the name of a script that you want to execute whenever the user logs on.
    - **Local path** – To create a home folder for the user on a local drive, specify the path in this text box.
    - **Connect** – To create a home folder for the user on a network drive, select an unused drive letter and type the path to a folder on a network share using Universal Naming Convention (UNC) notation.

X REF

For more information on roaming and mandatory user profiles, see "Understanding User Profiles" later in this lesson.

11. Click **OK** to save your changes and close the *Properties* sheet.
12. Close the *Computer Management* console.

CREATING A LOCAL GROUP

To create a local group with the Local Users and Groups snap-in, use the following procedure:

CREATE A LOCAL GROUP

GET READY. Log on to Windows 8 using an account with Administrator privileges and then perform the following steps:

1. Open the Computer Management console.
2. In the console's scope pane, expand the *Local Users and Groups* node and click **Groups**.

   A list of the current local groups appears in the details pane.
3. Right-click the **Groups** folder and then, from the context menu, select **New Group**.

   The *New Group* dialog box appears, as shown in Figure 17-18.

Figure 17-18

The *New Group* dialog box

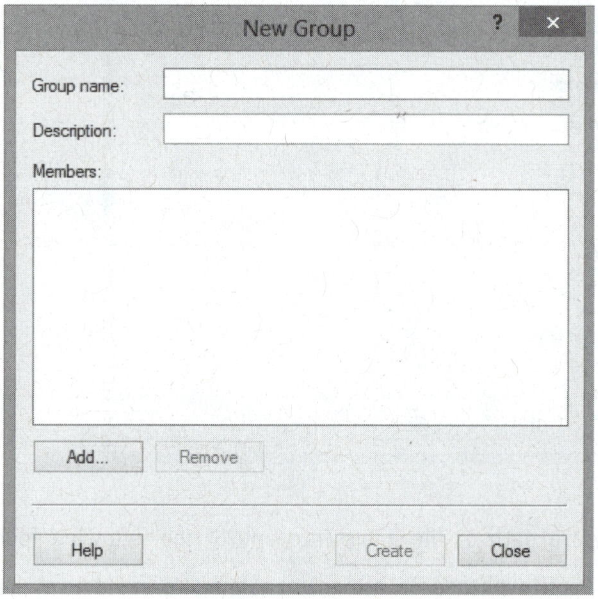

4. In the *Group name* text box, type the name you want to assign to the group. This is the only required field in the dialog box.
5. If desired, specify a *Description* for the group.
6. Click the **Add** button.

   The *Select Users* dialog box appears.
7. Type the names of the users that you want to add to the group, separated by semicolons, in the text box, and then click **OK**.

   The users are added to the Members list. You can also type part of a user name and click **Check Names** to complete the name or click **Advanced** to search for users.
8. Click **Create** to create the group and populate it with the user(s) you specified. The console then clears the dialog box, leaving it ready for the creation of another group.
9. Click **Close**.
10. Close the Computer Management console.

Windows 8 includes features that can provide users with a more convenient password experience, and also compel them to obey network password selection and maintenance policies that minimize these potential weaknesses. Some of these features are discussed in the following sections.

CONFIGURING PASSWORD POLICIES

Windows 8 supports a number of Group Policy settings that administrators can use to enforce password security practices on individual computers or on Active Directory Domain Services (AD DS) networks. By enforcing these password practices, you can ensure that your systems remain secure, even though the end users are responsible for their own passwords.

To configure password policies using Local Security Policy, use the following procedure.

CONFIGURE PASSWORD POLICIES

GET READY. Log on to Windows 8 using an account with Administrator privileges and then perform the following steps:

1. On the Start screen, click the **Desktop tile**.

   The *Windows Desktop* appears.
2. Swipe in from the right edge of the screen or mouse over the top or bottom right corner of the screen to display the charms bar.
3. Click the **Settings** charm. The *Settings* bar appears.
4. Click **Control Panel**.

   The *Control Panel* window appears.
5. Click **System and Security > Administrative Tools**.

   The *Administrative Tools* window appears.
6. Double-click **Local Security Policy**.

   The *Local Security Policy* console appears, as shown in Figure 17-19.

Figure 17-19

The *Local Security Policy* console

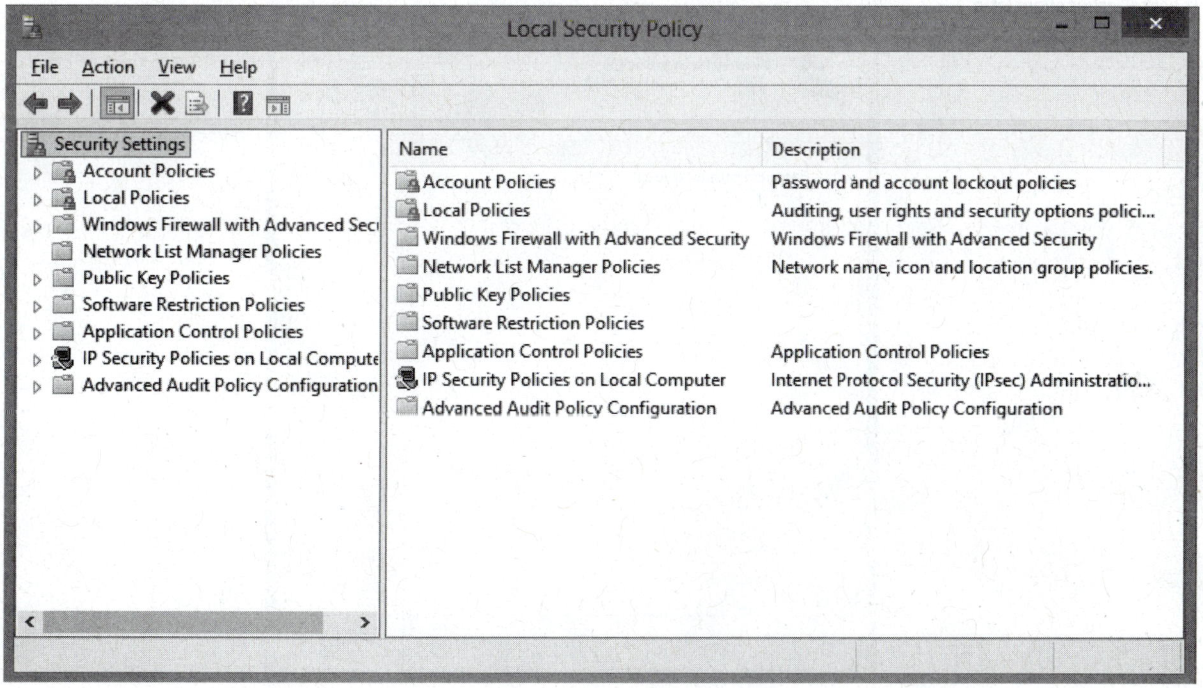

7. Expand the *Account Policies* header and then click **Password Policy**.

A list of password policies appears in the right pane, as shown in Figure 17-20.

Figure 17-20

Password Policies in the *Local Security Policy* console

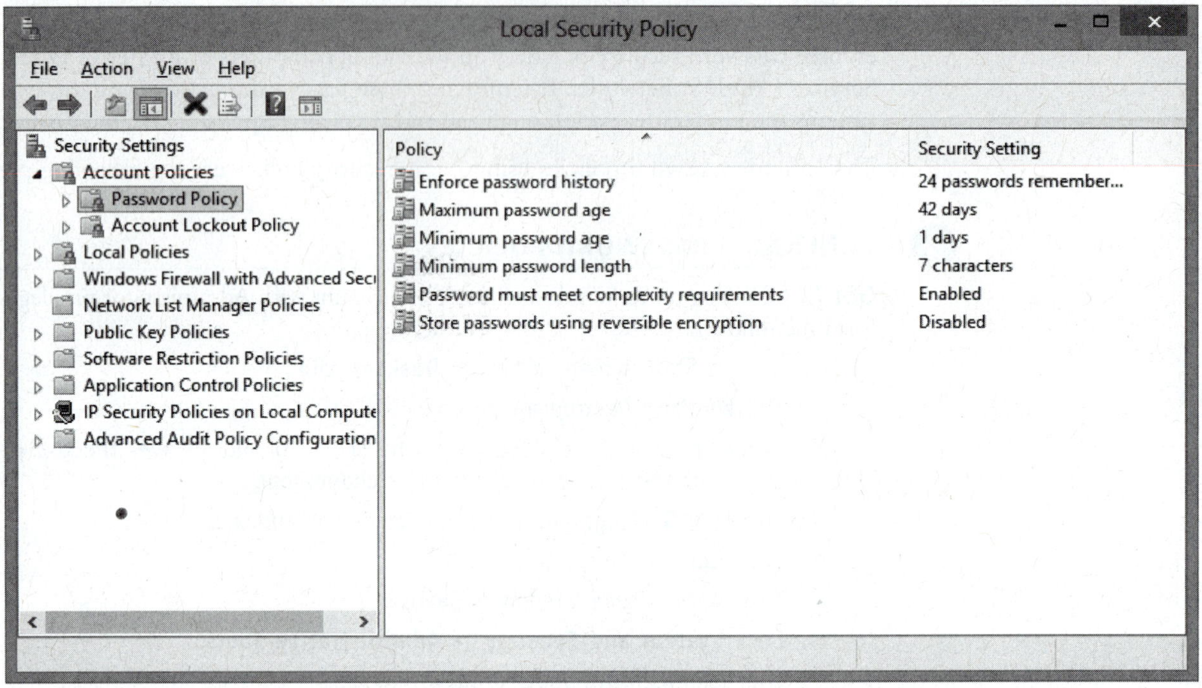

8. Double-click one of the password policies described in Table 17-4.

The *Properties* sheet for the policy appears, as shown in Figure 17-21.

Figure 17-21

The *Properties* sheet of a password policy

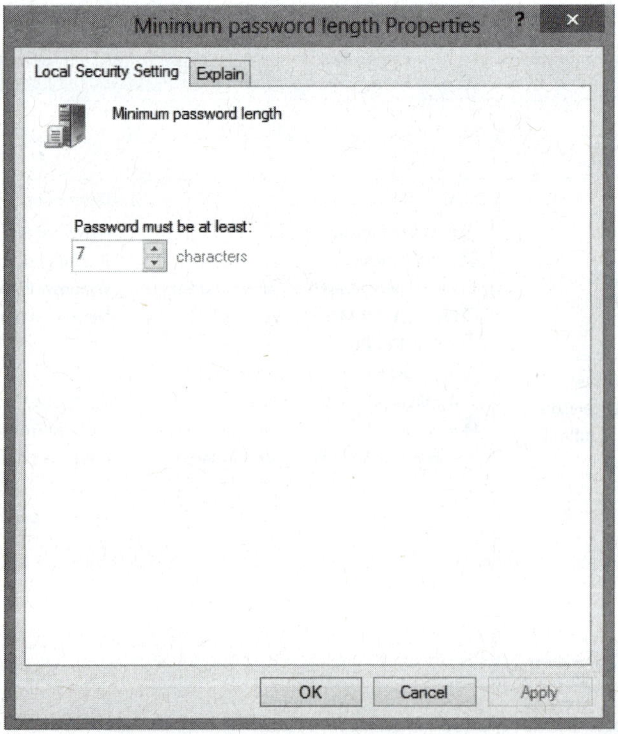

Table 17-4

Windows Password Policy Settings

Password Policy Settings	Values and Function
Enforce Password History	Specifies the number of unique passwords that users have to supply before Windows 8 permits them to reuse an old password. Possible values range from 0 to 24. The default value is 0.
Maximum Password Age	Specifies how long a single password can be used before Windows 8 forces the user to change it. Possible values range from 0 to 999. A value of 0 causes the password never to expire. The default value is 42 days.
Minimum Password Age	Specifies how long a single password must be used before Windows 8 permits the user to change it. Possible values range from 0 to 998. The default value is 0 days, which enables the user to change the password immediately.
Minimum Password Length	Specifies the minimum number of characters Windows 8 permits in user-supplied passwords. Possible values range from 0 to 14. The default value is 0, which means that no password is required.
Password Must Meet Complexity Requirements	When enabled, indicates that passwords supplied by users must be at least six characters long, with no duplication of any part of the user's account name; and must include characters from at least three of the following four categories: uppercase letters, lowercase letters, numbers, and symbols. By default, this policy is disabled.
Store Passwords Using Reversible Encryption	When enabled, causes Windows 8 to store user account passwords using a less effective encryption algorithm.This policy is designed to support authentication protocols that require access to the user's password, such as the Challenge Handshake Authentication Protocol (CHAP). From a security perspective, this policy is functionally equivalent to using plaintext passwords. The default value is disabled.

9. Configure the policy by setting a value using the spin box, radio button, or other control, and then click **OK**.

   The *Properties* sheet closes.

10. Repeat Steps 5 and 6 to configure other policies, if desired.
11. Close the *Local Security Policy* console and the *Administrative Tools* window.

In an enterprise network environment, administrators generally prefer to configure these settings using AD DS Group Policy, so they can distribute them to large numbers of workstations simultaneously. To configure password policies on an AD DS network, you must run the Group Policy Management Editor console and create a Group Policy object, which you then link to a domain, site, or organizational unit object in your AD DS tree. The password policies in a GPO are located in the Computer Configuration\Policies\Windows Settings\Security Settings\Account Policies\Password Policies node, as shown in Figure 17-22. The policy settings themselves are exactly the same.

Figure 17-22

Password Policies in an AD DS Group Policy object

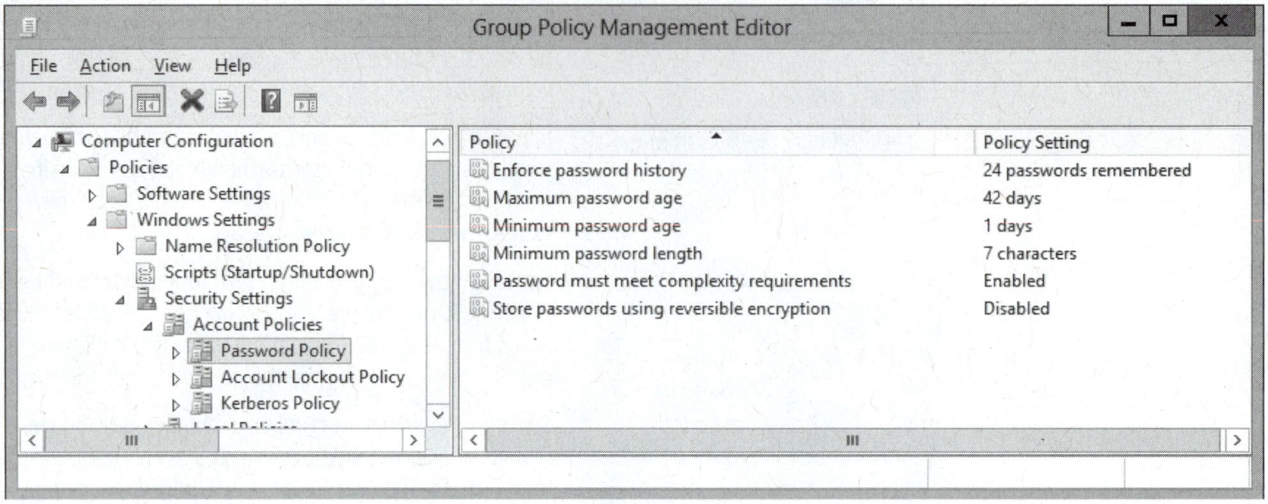

TAKE NOTE* The Group Policy Management Editor console is supplied with the Windows Server operating systems and installed automatically on AD DS domain controllers. To manage AD DS Group Policy settings on a Windows 8 workstation, you must download and install the Remote Server Administration Tools for Windows 8 package.

CONFIGURING ACCOUNT LOCKOUT POLICIES

It is possible to penetrate any password-protected resource, given enough time and an unlimited number of access attempts. The brute force approach to password penetration is supported by programs designed to try thousands of different character combinations in an attempt to find the one that matches the password.

Windows 8 can protect against brute force password penetration techniques by limiting the number of unsuccessful logon attempts allowed by each user account. When a potential infiltrator exceeds the number of allowed attempts, the system locks the account for a set period of time. To impose these limits, you can use Local Security Policy for standalone computers, or Group Policy for AD DS networks.

To set account lockout parameters using Local Security Policy, use the following procedure.

CONFIGURE ACCOUNT LOCKOUT POLICIES

GET READY. Log on to Windows 8 using an account with Administrator privileges:

1. Open Control Panel, and then click **System and Security > Administrative Tools**.

   The *Administrative Tools* window appears.

2. Double-click **Local Security Policy**.

   The *Local Security Policy* console appears.

3. Expand the Account Policies header, and then click **Account Lockout Policy**.

   A list of policies appears in the right pane, as shown in Figure 17-23.

Figure 17-23

Account Lockout Policy in the *Local Security Policy* console

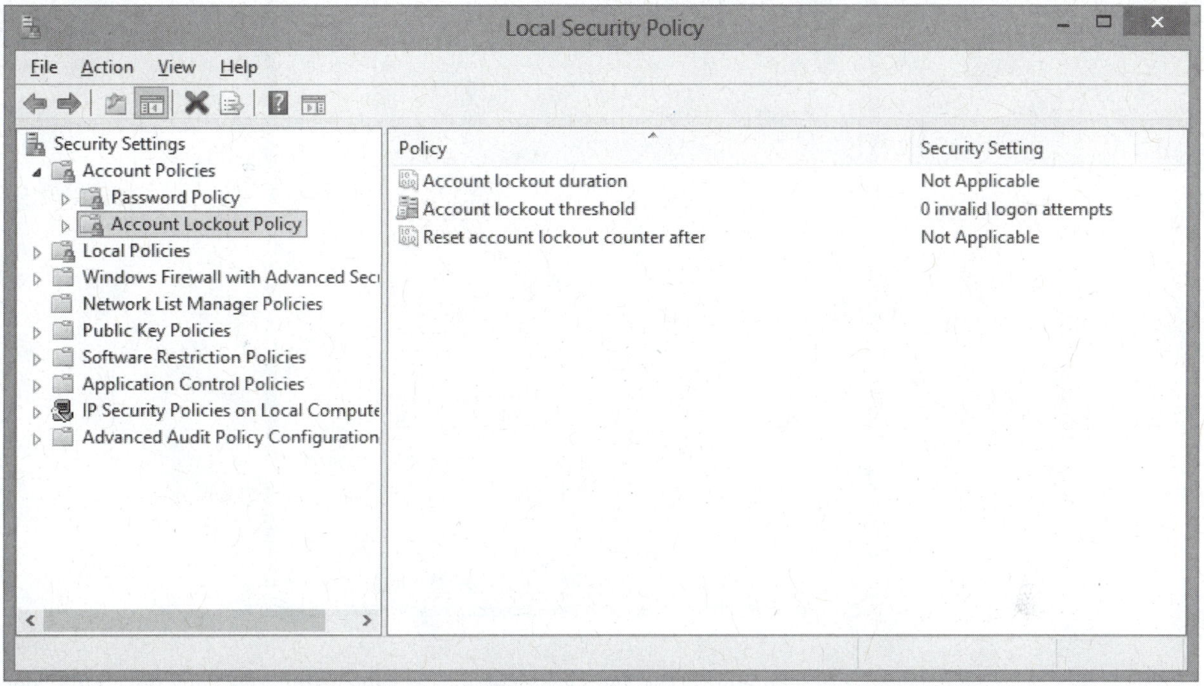

4. Double-click one of the policies described in Table 17-5.

   The *Properties* sheet for the policy appears, as shown in Figure 17-24.

Table 17-5

Windows Account Lockout Policy Settings

Account Lockout Policy Setting	Values and Function
Account Lockout Duration	Determines the period of time that must pass after a lockout before Windows 8 automatically unlocks a user's account. The policy is not set by default, as it is viable only in conjunction with the Account Lockout Threshold policy. Possible values range from 0 to 99999 minutes (about 10 weeks). A low setting (5 to 15 minutes) is usually sufficient to reduce attacks significantly without unreasonably affecting legitimate users who are mistakenly locked out. A value of 0 requires an administrator to unlock the account manually. When the Account Lockout Threshold policy is activated, this policy is activated as well and set to a default value of 30 minutes.
Account Lockout Threshold	Specifies the number of invalid logon attempts that will trigger an account lockout. Possible values range from 0 to 999. A value that is too low (as few as three, for example) may cause lockouts due to normal user error during logon. A value of 0 prevents accounts from ever being locked out. The default value is 0.
Reset Account Lockout Counter After	Specifies the period of time that must pass after an invalid logon attempt before the lockout counter resets to zero. Possible values range from 1 to 99999 minutes, and must be less than or equal to the account lockout duration. When the Account Lockout Threshold policy is activated, this policy is activated as well and set to a default value of 30.

Figure 17-24

The *Properties* sheet of an account lockout policy

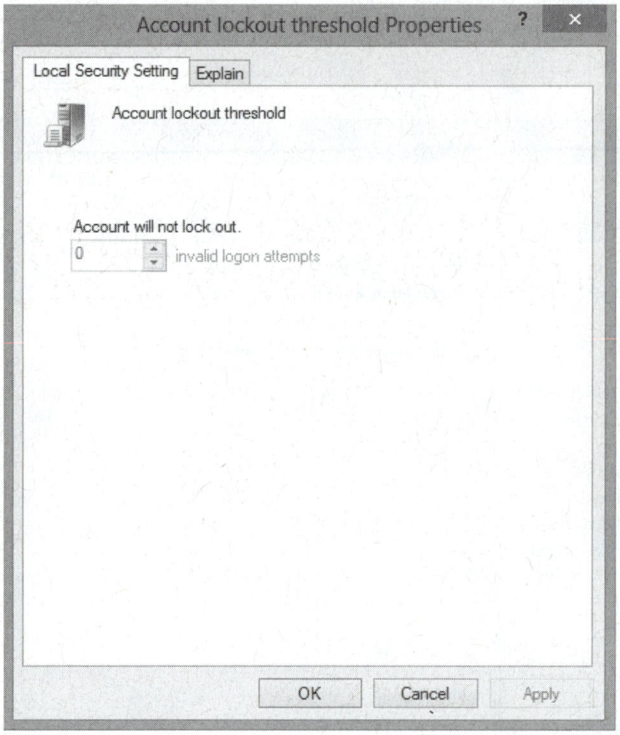

5. Configure the policy by setting a value using the spin box, radio button, or other control, and then click **OK**.

   The *Properties* sheet closes.

6. Repeat Steps 5 and 6 to configure other policies, if desired.
7. Close the *Local Security Policy* console and the *Administrative Tools* window.

TAKE NOTE*

As with password policies, you can also deploy account lockout policies on an AD DS network using Group Policy.

USING CREDENTIAL MANAGER

CERTIFICATION READY
Manage credentials
Objective 4.4

Users and administrators alike often become frustrated when forced to re-enter passwords whenever they have to access a protected resource. This is one reason why Microsoft modified the default behavior of User Account Control beginning in Windows 7 to eliminate elevation prompts for administrative operating system tasks.

Credential Manager is a Windows 8 tool that stores the user names and passwords people supply to servers and web sites in a protected area called the Windows Vault. When a user selects the *Remember my credentials* checkbox while authenticating in Windows Explorer, Internet Explorer, or Remote Desktop Connection, as shown in Figure 17-25, the system adds the credentials to the Windows Vault.

Figure 17-25

The *Remember my credentials* control

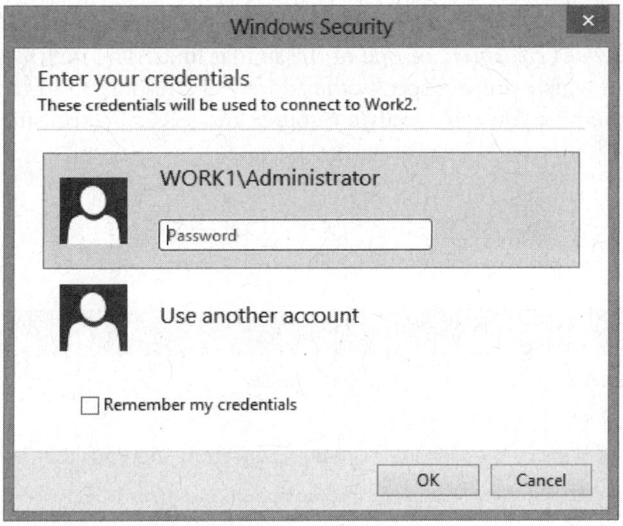

From the Credential Manager window in Control Panel, you can see the resources for which the Windows Vault contains credentials, as shown in Figure 17-26, although you cannot view the passwords themselves.

Figure 17-26

The *Credential Manager* window

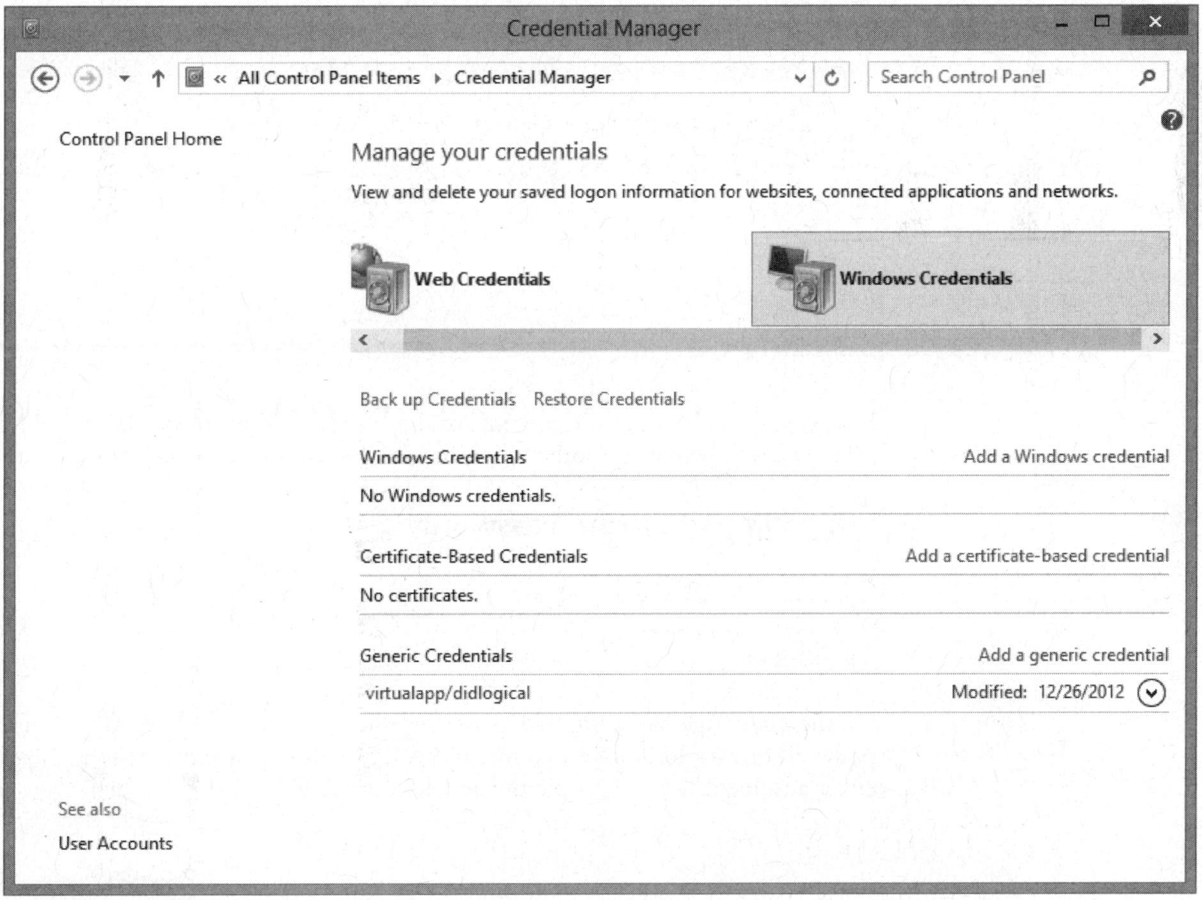

It is also possible to add credentials directly to the vault using Credential Manager, by clicking *Add a Windows credential*, or one of the similar links. The interface shown in Figure 17-27 then appears, in which you can specify the address of a resource and the credentials that go with it. In the same way, you can specify a resource and select a certificate from the computer's store.

Figure 17-27

The *Add a Windows Credential* window

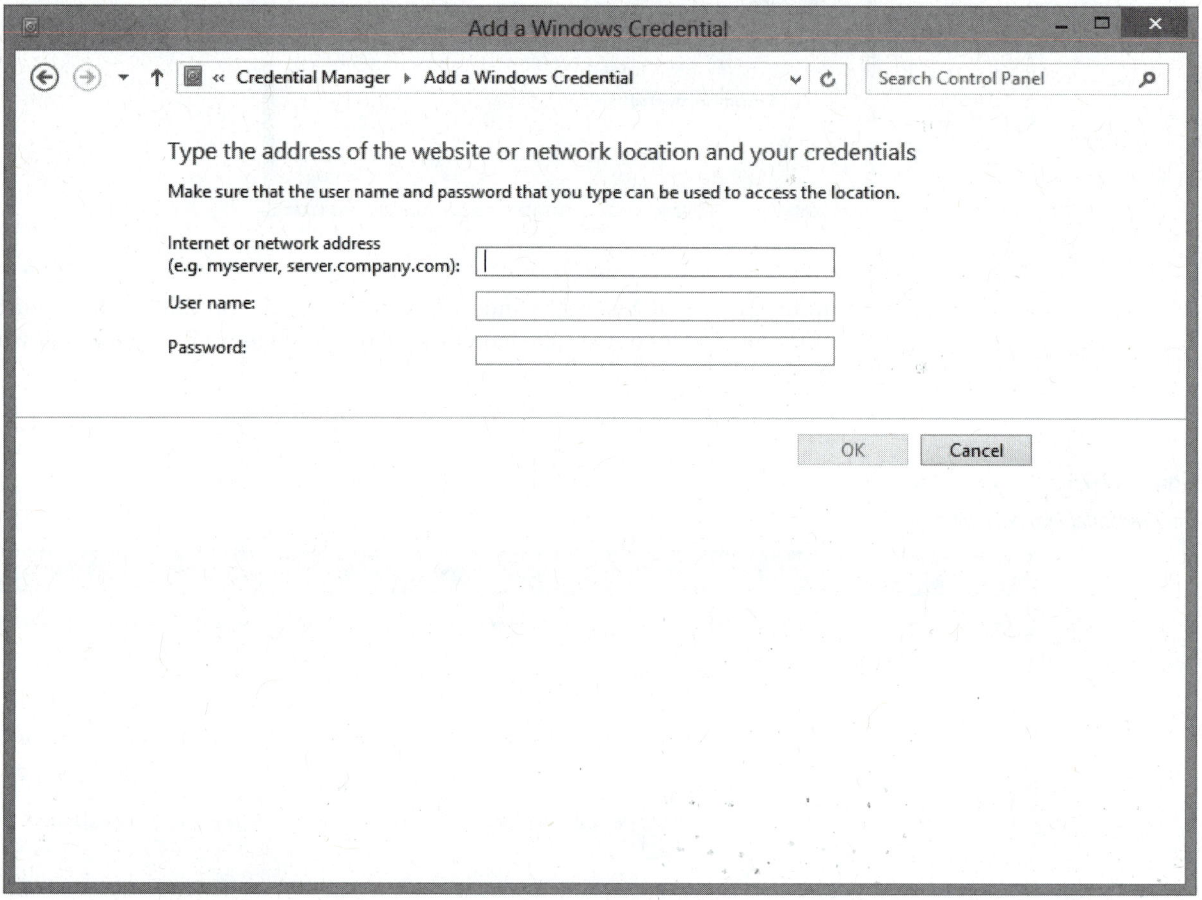

Finally, you can back up the contents of the Windows Vault from Credential Manager and restore it to the same or another computer, to protect the credentials or migrate them.

Using PIN and Picture Passwords

Windows 8 introduces two new options for password processing, designed to simplify the logon process and take advantage of the touch interfaces provided in tablets and smartphones.

On the *Users* page of the *PC Settings* screen, shown in Figure 17-28, you can change the password of your local user account, and you can also replace the password entirely, with either a numerical PIN or a picture and a sequence of gestures.

Figure 17-28

The *Users* page of the *PC Settings* screen

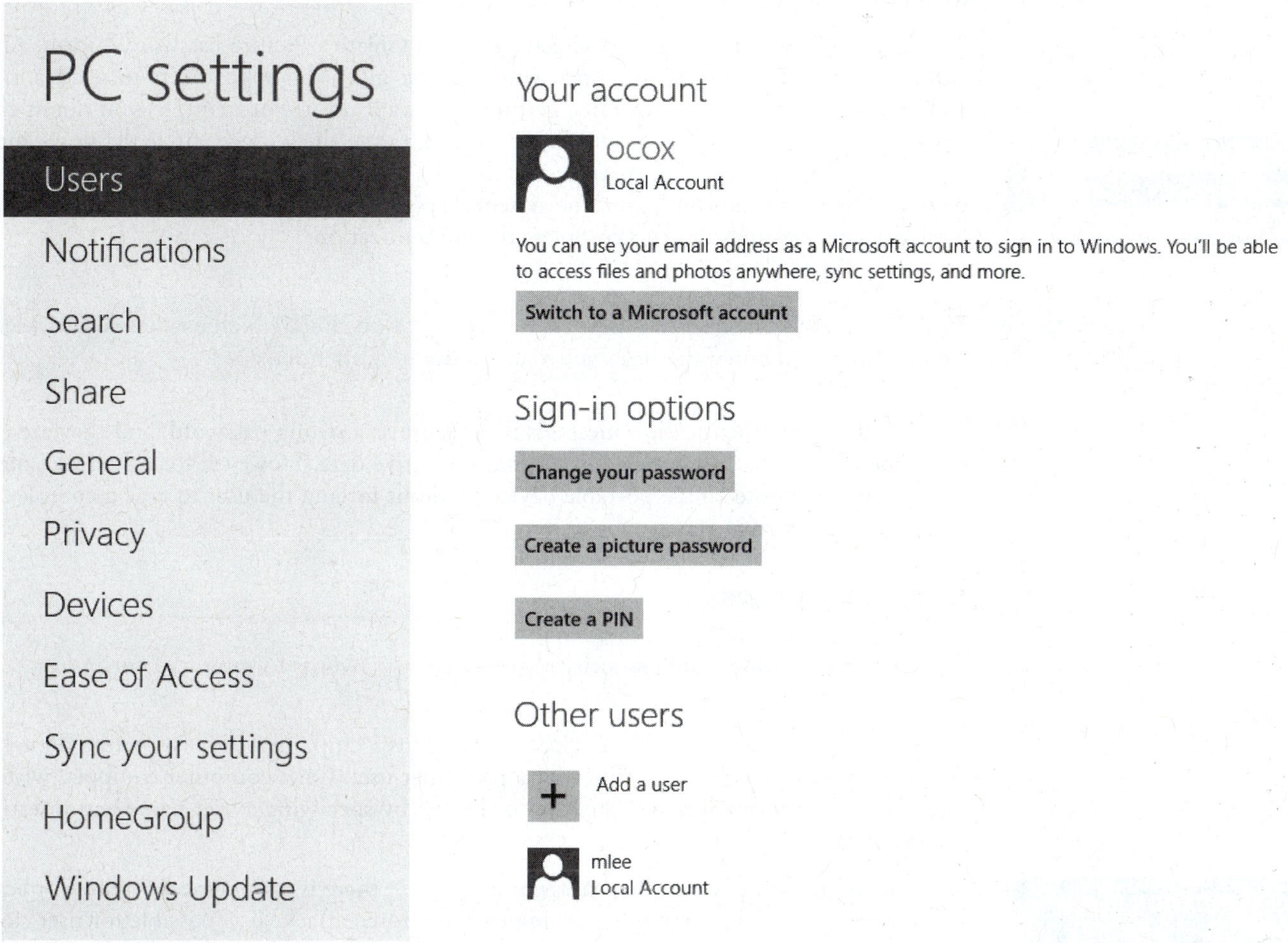

CERTIFICATION READY
Configure PIN
Objective 4.4

A PIN password is a four-digit number that a user can employ to log on in place of a password. PIN passwords are designed for use on portable devices with small screens, on which it is easier to display and use a numerical keypad than a full virtual keyboard.

When you click the Create a PIN button, you must first re-authenticate with your account password, and then the system displays a Create a PIN screen, as shown in Figure 17-29, on which you enter and verify the four-digit PIN you want to use. The next time you log on, the system prompts you for your PIN instead of your password.

Figure 17-29

The *Create a PIN* screen

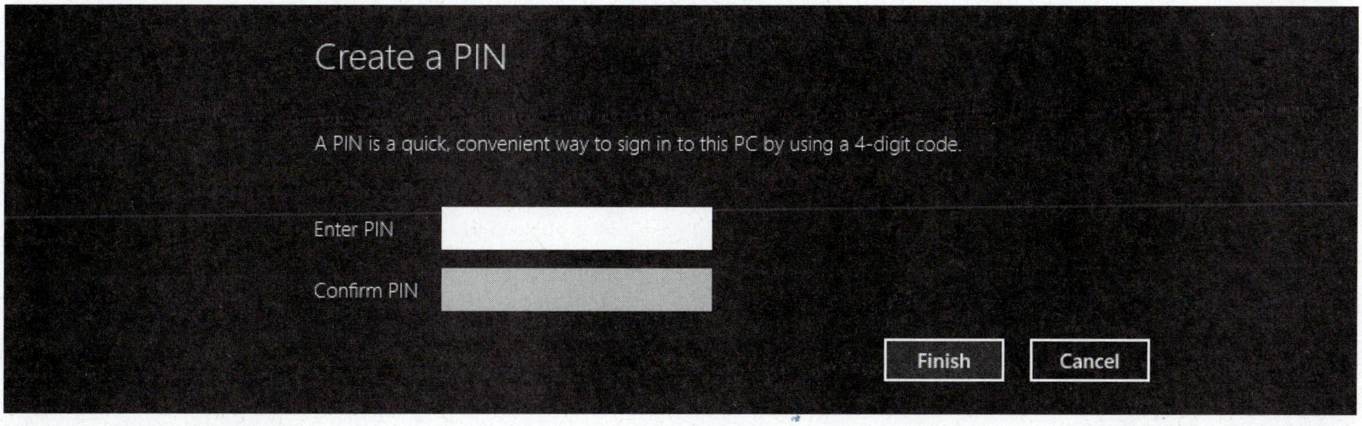

Picture passwords are designed to take advantage of touch interfaces by replacing the standard alphanumeric password with a picture. Instead of typing in a password, the user must duplicate a sequence of three gestures – taps, circles, or lines – on the picture, using the touch screen.

CERTIFICATION READY
Configure picture password
Objective 4.4

The *Users* page on the *PC Settings* screen also has a Create a Picture Password button. After authenticating with your standard password, you are given the opportunity to select a picture, and draw whatever sequence of three gestures you want on it. For example, you might choose a photograph of a person's face, and for your gestures tap the left eye, circle the nose, and draw a line along the mouth. After performing the gestures twice, the system saves the pattern. The next time you logon, the system displays your selected picture, and you must draw the same gestures on it to complete the authentication.

TAKE NOTE* The Windows 8 Logon screen includes a Logon Options link, which enables you to select which of the configured methods you want to use to authenticate.

Neither of these authentication methods is as secure as a strong password, and they are not recommended for use on devices that contain sensitive data. However, for casual use, they are a simple way of protecting a portable device, without forcing the user to type a complex password on a tiny, virtual keyboard.

Using Smart Cards

Smart cards provide a high-security alternative to passwords for user authentication.

A smart card is a credit card-like device that contains a chip, on which is stored a digital certificate that serves as an identifier for a particular user. On a computer equipped with a card reader, a user can authenticate him- or herself by specifying a user name and inserting the smart card.

CERTIFICATION READY
Configure smart cards
Objective 4.4

Smart cards are more secure than passwords, because there is no practical way to duplicate the information they contain by guessing or brute force attack. It is possible for users to have their smart cards lost or stolen, but in most cases, they know when this occurs and can report the loss. An administrator can then revoke the certificate on the card, rendering it invalid and useless.

Windows has supported smart card authentication for some time, but until Windows 7, you had to install a third-party device driver along with the card reader hardware. By including support for the ***Personal Identity Verification (PIV)*** standard, published by the National Institute of Standards and Technology (NIST), Windows 8 can now obtain drivers for PIV smart cards from Windows Update, or use a PIV minidriver included with the operating system.

For organizations that are committed to the use of smart cards for authentication, there are two smart card-related Group Policy settings that Windows 8 supports. These settings, located in the Computer Configuration\Policies\Windows Settings\Security Settings\Local Policies\Security Options node, are as follows:

- **Interactive Logon: Require Smart Card** – Configures Windows 8 to allow only smart card user authentications.

- **Interactive Logon: Smart Card Removal Behavior** – Specifies how Windows 8 should behave when a user removes the smart card from the reader while logged on to the computer. The possible values are as follows:
  - **No action** – Enables the user to remove the smart card without affecting the session. This is the default setting.
  - **Lock Workstation** – Disables the workstation while leaving the session open until the user reinserts the smart card. This enables the user to leave the workstation temporarily without leaving the smart card and without having to log off.
  - **Force Logoff** – Causes the workstation to log the user off as soon as the smart card is removed.
  - **Disconnect if a Remote Desktop Services session** – Disconnects the computer from the Remote Desktop Services server without logging the user off from the session. The user can then resume the session by reinserting the smart card at the same or another computer.

Managing Certificates

Windows 8 uses digital certificates for a variety of authentication tasks, internally, on the local network, and on the Internet. Every user account has a certificate store containing a variety of certificates obtained by various means.

Windows 8 creates some certificates itself, such as the self-signed certificate it uses for the Encrypting File System. Others it downloads from other computers, such as servers on the Internet. In most cases, activities involving certificates are invisible to the user. Windows 8 obtains most of the certificates it needs automatically and stores them for future use.

CERTIFICATION READY
Manage certificates
Objective 4.4

However, it is possible for users to manage their certificate stores directly, including creating backups of certificates for disaster recovery or migration purposes. Windows 8 includes a Certificates snap-in for MMC that provides access to the certificate store, but the snap-in is not accessible from the Start menu or the Control Panel.

To access the Certificates snap-in, click the **Search** charm, select **Settings**, and type **cert** in the search box. In the Results list, click **Manage user certificates** to load the snap-in and point it at the current user account, as shown in Figure 17-30.

Figure 17-30
The *Certificates* snap-in

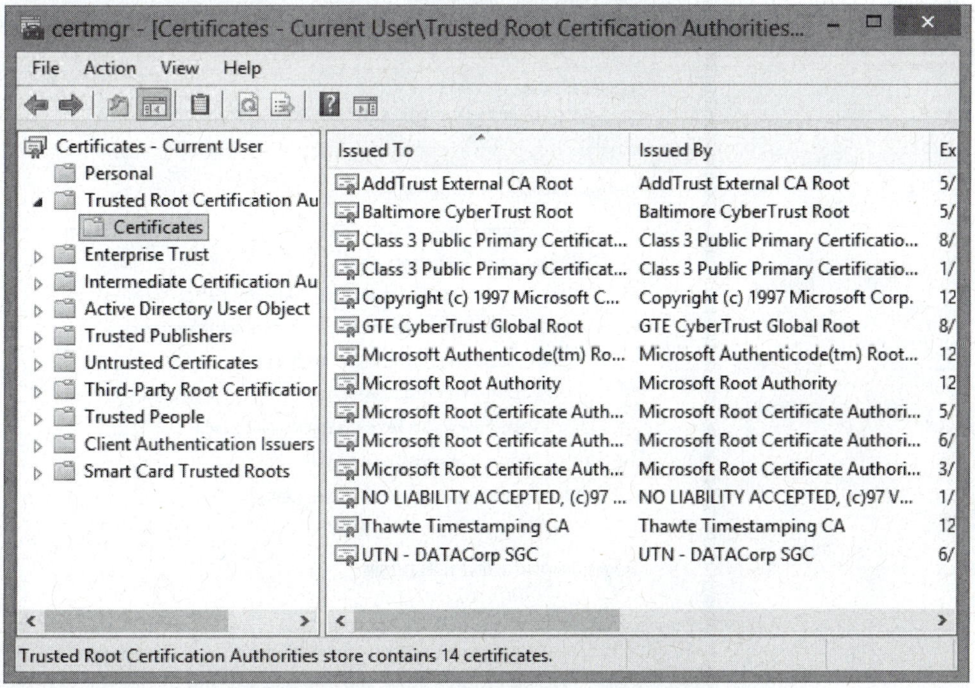

Double-clicking one of the certificates in the store displays a Certificate dialog box like the one shown in Figure 17-31. This dialog box contains information about the certificate and the data stored in it.

Figure 17-31

A *Certificate* dialog box

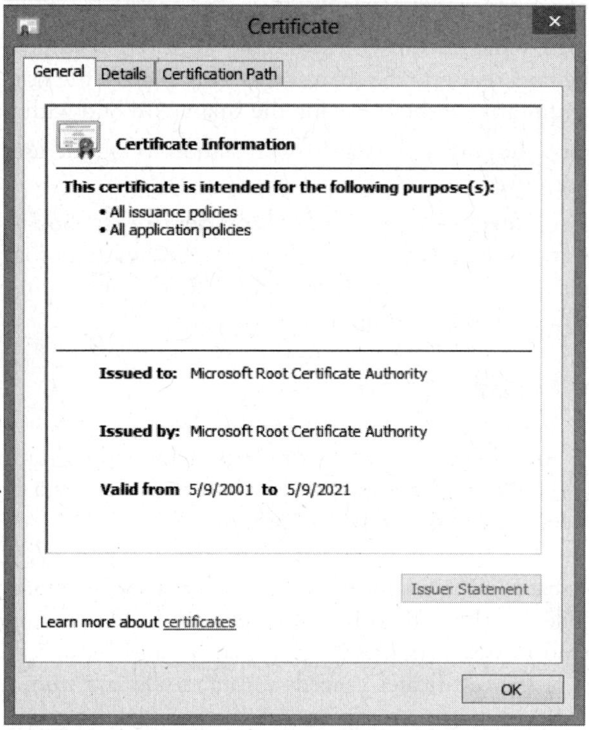

To back up a certificate to a file, right-click it in the snap-in and, in the context menu, select All Tasks > Export, to launch the Certificate Export Wizard. This wizard prompts you to select a format for the file, as shown in Figure 17-32, and the location where you want to save it.

Figure 17-32

The *Export File Format* page in the *Certificate Export Wizard*

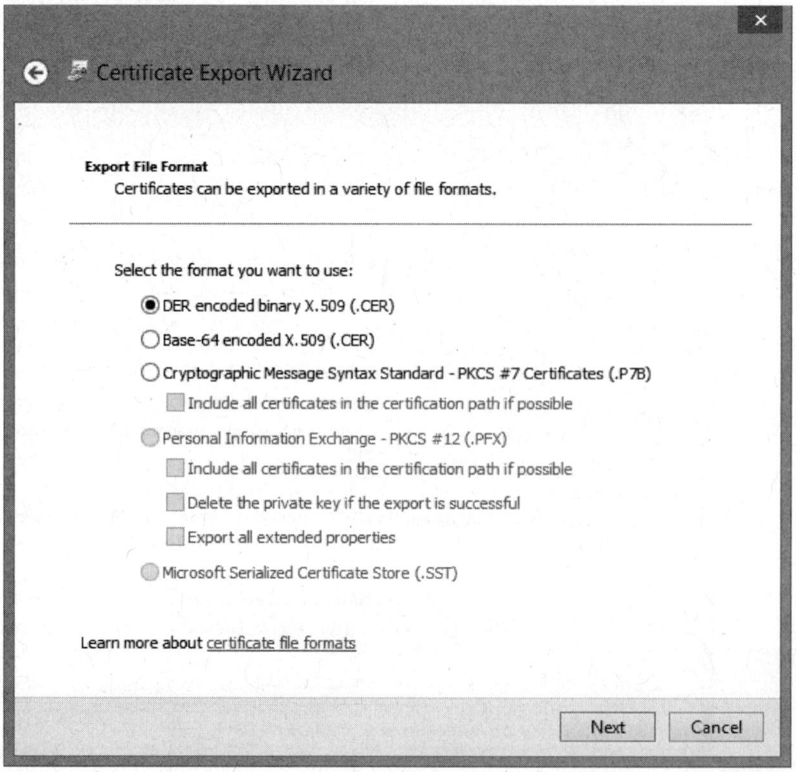

Using Biometrics

Biometric authentication uses a scan of a physical characteristic to confirm the identity of a user.

Biometric authentication is theoretically more secure than a token-based or secret-based authentication method, because the identifying characteristic is difficult or impossible to duplicate. Even the grisly stories of severed body parts being used to fool biometric scanners are (hopefully) fictitious, as the technology exists to confirm that a finger or other appendage is still connected to a living body.

CERTIFICATION READY
Configure biometrics
Objective 4.4

There are a great many third-party biometric authentication solutions available, most of which take the form of finger print scanners for laptop computers. Prior to Windows 7, the operating system included no support for biometric devices at all, and required the third-party vendor to supply a complete software solution along with the hardware. However, Windows 8 now includes a new component called the ***Windows Biometric Framework***, which provides a core biometric functionality and a Biometric Device control panel.

Even with the Windows Biometric Framework, however, the reliability of these technologies and the security they provide can vary widely. Most biometric solutions include a secondary authentication method, such as a password or a smart card, for when the biometric scan fails. Others are multifactor solutions, requiring both a biometric scan and another form of authentication.

Elevating Privileges

Ever since the Windows Vista release, Microsoft has made a concerted effort to persuade users not to log on to Windows for their everyday tasks using an administrative account. This practice not only makes accidental configuration changes more possible, it also increases the likelihood of intrusion by malevolent attackers.

The preferred mechanism for performing tasks that require administrative privileges is to use the Run As feature to execute a program using another account. Shortcuts in the Start menu have a *Run as administrator* option in their context menus, which causes standard users to receive a credential prompt and administrators to receive an elevation prompt, according to the system's normal User Account Control (UAC) practices.

It is also possible to use the Runas.exe command line program to execute an application using any other account. The syntax for the Runas.exe program is as follows:

```
runas [/user:domain\user] [/profile] [/noprofile] [/savecred]
[/smartcard] [/env] [/netonly] [/trustlevel] [/showtrustlevels]
"program.exe /parameter"
```

- **/user:*domain**user*** – Specifies the account that Runas.exe should use to execute the program. The account can be specified in the form *domain\user* or *user@domain*. The *domain* variable can also be the name of a standalone workstation and *user* a local user account.
- **/profile** – Causes the Runas.exe program to load the profile of the account specified by the / user parameter. This is the default value.
- **/noprofile** – Prevents the Runas.exe program from loading the profile of the account specified by the /user parameter. Without the profile, the program cannot access the EFS-encrypted files belonging to the account specified by the /user parameter.
- **/savecred** – Causes the Runas.exe program to save the credentials for the account specified by the /user parameter in the Windows Vault or, in the case of a previously-saved account, to use the credentials saved in the vault.
- **/smartcard** – Specifies that the credentials for the account specified by the \user parameter will be supplied using a smart card.

- **/env** – Causes the Runas.exe program to use the current environment, rather than the one of the account specified by the /user parameter.
- **/netonly** – Specifies that the credentials of the account specified by the /user variable are for remote access only.
- "***program.exe/parameter***" – Specifies the name of the application that Runas.exe should run with elevated privileges, along with any of the application's necessary command line parameters.

A typical example of a Runas command line would appear as follows:

```
runas /user:example\administrator "notepad.exe \script.vbs"
```

When you run the command, the program prompts for the password to the Administrator account, loads the user profile for the account, executes Notepad.exe, and then loads the Script.vbs file.

Troubleshooting Authentication Issues

> The most common problem related to authentication experienced by Windows 8 users is password loss. There is no way for a user or an administrator to read a password from a user account on a Windows system, whether it is stored in the Security Account Manager (SAM), the Windows Vault, or an AD DS domain controller.

When a user loses a Windows 8 account password, there is no way to reclaim it; the only solution is to reset (that is, change) the password. There are two ways of doing this: either the user resets his or her own password or an administrator resets it.

To reset your own password, you must supply the old one first. If you cannot do this, because you have lost or forgotten the old password, the only solution is to use a password reset disk. The password reset disk supplies the old password for you, enabling you to reset the password to a new value.

The problem with this solution is that you must have created a password reset disk before losing your password. In the User accounts control panel applet, the *Make changes to your user account* page for each user has a link that enables the user to run the Forgotten Password Wizard and create a password reset disk, using a floppy disk or a USB flash drive.

When a user loses his or her password, and does not have a password reset disk, the only alternative is for an administrator to reset the password, using either the Local Users and Groups snap-in or the Manage Accounts page of the User accounts control panel applet. Administrators can reset passwords without having to supply the old password first.

The problem, however, is that an administrative reset causes the user to lose access to all EFS-encrypted files, all certificates in the user's personal certificate store, and all passwords stored in the Windows Vault. These passwords might be recoverable from a backup of the Windows Vault or the EFS key, but it would be a lot easier if the user had created a password reset disk in the first place.

Authorizing Users

> Authentication confirms a user's identity. Authorization grants the user access to certain resources.

A successful authentication confirms that a user is who he or she purports to be, but logging on successfully does not guarantee access to system resources. Some authenticated users have full access to the system, while others might have nearly none. The difference between the two is the resources that they are authorized to access.

USING PERMISSIONS

The most commonly-used mechanisms for authorizing users in Windows 8 are the NTFS, share, and registry permission systems. By adjusting permissions in the protected resources, administrators can specify who should have access to them and what degree of access users should receive.

For more information on managing permissions, see Lesson 14, "Configuring Shared Resources" and Lesson 15, "Configuring File and Folder Access."

CONFIGURING USER RIGHTS

CERTIFICATION READY
Configure rights
Objective 4.4

Some people confuse the concept of user permissions with that of user rights; in Windows 8, these are two different concepts. In Windows 8, ***user rights*** are policies that define specific operating system functions. For example, in order to sit down at a Windows 8 computer and log on, users must not only have accounts, they also must possess the *Allow log on locally* user right.

Administrators can assign user rights to individual users, but as with permissions, this is rare. The more practical alternative is to assign user rights to groups and them add individual users to the groups as needed.

In fact, Windows 8 does this for you, by default. The built-in local groups on a computer running Windows 8 receive their special capabilities through default user rights assignments. For example, the Remote Desktop Users group has been assigned the *Allow log on through Remote Desktop Services* user right.

To assign user rights to users or groups, you can open the Local Security Policy snap-in on a Windows 8 workstation and browse to Security Settings\Local Policies\User Rights Assignment, as shown in Figure 17-33. In an AD DS environment, you open a GPO and browse to the Computer Configuration\Policies\Windows Settings\Security Settings\Local Policies\User Rights Assignment node. In both interfaces, there are 44 user rights assignments that you can grant to local or domain users and groups.

Figure 17-33

The *User Rights Assignment* node in the *Local Security Policy* snap-in

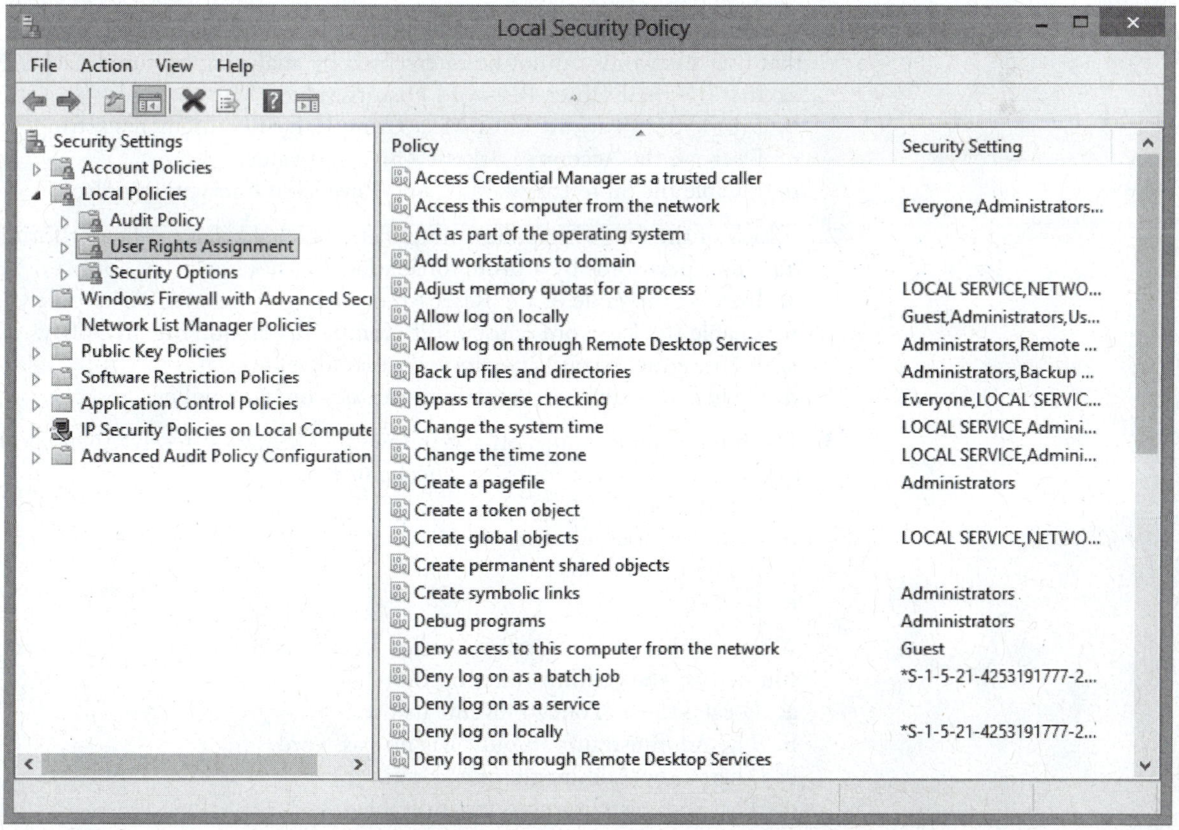

SKILL SUMMARY

IN THIS LESSON, YOU LEARNED:

- The user account is the fundamental unit of identity in the Windows operating systems.
- A group is an identifying token that Windows uses to represent a collection of users.
- A workgroup is a collection of computers that are all peers. A peer network is one in which every computer can function as both a server, by sharing its resources with other computers, and a client, by accessing the shared resources on other computers.
- A domain is a collection of computers that all utilize a central directory service for authentication and authorization.
- Windows 8 provides two separate interfaces for creating and managing local user accounts: the User Accounts (or user Accounts and Family Safety) control panel and the Local Users and Group snap-in for the Microsoft Management Console (MMC).
- Windows 8 supports a number of Group Policy settings that administrators can use to enforce password security practices on individual computers or on Active Directory Domain Services (AD DS) networks.
- Credential Manager is a Windows 8 tool that stores the user names and passwords people supply to servers and web sites in a protected area called the Windows Vault.

■ Knowledge Assessment

Multiple Choice

Select one or more correct answers for each of the following questions.

1. Which of the following account lockout policy modifications could you make to ensure that user passwords cannot be intercepted by analyzing captured packets?
   a. Increase the Enforce Password History value.
   b. Enable the Password Must Meet Complexity Requirements setting.
   c. Decrease the Account Lockout Threshold value.
   d. Disable the Store Passwords Using Reversible Encryption policy.
2. Which of the following policy modifications would make it harder for intruders to penetrate user passwords by a brute force attack? (Choose all that apply.)
   a. Increase the value of the Reset Account Logon Counter After policy.
   b. Enable the Password Must Meet Complexity Requirements policy.
   c. Increase the Account Lockout Threshold value.
   d. Reduce the value of the Minimum Password Age policy.
3. The built-in local groups on a Windows 8 workstation receive their special capabilities through which of the following mechanisms?
   a. Security options
   b. Windows firewall rules
   c. NTFS permissions
   d. User rights
4. When you log on to a newly-installed Windows 8 computer for the first time, why can you not use the Administrator account?
   a. Local Security Policy prevents its use.
   b. The Administrator account has no password.
   c. There is no Administrator account.
   d. The Administrator account is disabled.

5. Which of the following statements is true?
   a. The User accounts control panel applet can create local users and local groups only.
   b. The User accounts control panel applet can create local and domain users.
   c. The User accounts control panel applet can create local users only.
   d. The User accounts control panel applet can create local users, local groups, domain users, and domain groups.
6. This Windows element contains a list of users for each permission-protected resource and the degree of access each user has to the resource.
   a. Access control list (ACL)
   b. Authorization control list (ACL)
   c. Authentication control list (ACL)
   d. Access control entry (ACE)
7. Your Windows 8 computer is currently a member of a workgroup that includes four other Windows 8 computers. If you want to access resources on all four of these computers, you must have a user account on how many of them?
   a. 1
   b. 5
   c. 4
   d. 2
8. Which of the following statements are true regarding domain and local user accounts? (Choose all that apply.)
   a. Local user accounts are stored in the Security Account Manager (SAM) database.
   b. Domain accounts can access local computer resources only.
   c. Local user accounts are created using the Active Directory Users and Computers MMC snap-in.
   d. Domain user accounts must be unique within the directory.
9. You have set the Account Lockout Duration policy setting to 15 and the Account Lockout Threshold to 3. What would be the result? (Choose all that apply.)
   a. A user will have to wait 15 minutes before Windows 8 automatically unlocks their account.
   b. The Administrator will have to unlock the user's account manually.
   c. A user will be allowed 3 invalid logon attempts before they are locked out.
   d. The user may get locked out due to normal user error during logon.
10. Which of the following provides you with the strongest level of password protection on a computer that contains sensitive data?
    a. PIN
    b. Picture Password
    c. A password created using 7 alphabetical characters.
    d. A password created using 7 characters including upper case, lower case, numerical characters and symbols.

Best Answer

Choose the letter that corresponds to the best answer. More than one answer choice may achieve the goal. Select the BEST answer.

1. You would like to implement an identification method that would provide the best security when it comes to protecting sensitive information on your network. Which of the following would you recommend?
   a. PIN + Smart Card.
   b. Use 7 character passwords that are a combination of numbers, characters, and symbols.
   c. Use 8 character passwords that use alphanumeric characters.
   d. Use picture passwords.

2. You have a resource that you want to make available to only selected users on your domain-based network. Which of the following would provide the most efficient method of assigning and managing access to the resource as users join and leave the company?
   a. Assign permissions for the resource to each individual user's account.
   b. Assign permissions for the resource to a group that contains the selected users' accounts.
   c. Assign permission for the resource to the Authenticated Users group
   d. Assign permission for the resource to the Everyone group.

3. You would like to configure an Account Lockout Threshold policy that will protect your system from brute force attacks while still preventing lockouts from normal user error. Which value would you recommend for the Account Lockout Threshold setting?
   a. 1
   b. 2
   c. 3
   d. 5

4. A user lost their password and requested that an administrator reset it for them. Of the options listed below for resetting the password, which would have the least impact on the user assuming they have EFS-encrypted files on their computer?
   a. Using a password reset disk.
   b. Restoring from a backup of the Windows Vault.
   c. Using a backup of the user's EFS key.
   d. Resetting the user's password via the Local Users and Groups snap-in.

5. You want to configure an account lockout policy that will provide the best protection for your system against failed password attempts while still allowing you to know when someone has attempted to access your system. Which setting will allow you to accomplish this?
   a. Set the Account lockout threshold to lock out after 5 failed password attempts and the Account lockout duration to 0.
   b. Set the Account lockout threshold to lock out after 10 failed password attempts and the Account lockout duration to 1.
   c. Set the Account lockout threshold to lock out after 20 failed password attempts and the Account lockout duration to 10.
   d. Set the Account lockout threshold to lock out after 100 failed password attempts and the Account lockout duration to 100.

Matching and Identification

Complete the following exercise by matching the terms with their corresponding definitions.

_______ **a)** Authentication
_______ **b)** Account Lockout Threshold
_______ **c)** Windows Biometric Framework
_______ **d)** User rights
_______ **e)** Authorization
_______ **f)** Group
_______ **g)** Workgroup
_______ **h)** Directory service
_______ **i)** Multifactor authentication
_______ **j)** Personal Identity Verification (PIV)

1. Allows Windows 8 to obtain drivers for smart cards from Windows Update or use a mini driver included with the operating system.
2. Specifies the number of invalid logon attempts that will trigger an account lockout.
3. The process of granting an authenticated user a specific degree of access to specific data resources.

4. The process of verifying that the identity of the person operating the computer is the same as the user account the person is employing to gain access.
5. Provides a core biometric functionality and a Biometric Device control panel.
6. Collection of computers that are all peers.
7. Policies that define specific operating system functions (e.g., allow log on locally).
8. Involves using more than one identification method.
9. Collection of logical objects that represent various types of network resources.
10. Used to represent a collection of users.

Build a List

1. In order of first to last, specify the correct order of steps create a Local Group.
   _________ Open the Computer Management console.
   _________ Right-click the **Groups** folder and then, from the context menu, select **New Group**.
   _________ Specify a Description for the group.
   _________ Type the names of the users that you want to add to the group, separated by semi colons, in the text box, and then click **OK.**
   _________ Click **Create** to create the group and populate it with the user(s) you specified.
   _________ Close the Computer Management console.
   _________ In the Group name text box, type the name you want to assign to the group.
   _________ Click the **Add** button.
   _________ In the console's scope pane, expand the Local Users and Groups node and click **Groups.**
   _________ Click **Close.**

2. Specify the correct order of steps to back up an existing Windows 8 certificate.
   _________ Right-click the certificate you want to backup and choose **All Tasks > Export** certificate.
   _________ Click the **Search** charm, choose **Settings** and then type **cert** in the search box.
   _________ Select the *file format* you want to use.
   _________ In the *Results* list, click **Manage user certificates** to load the snap-in.
   _________ Type a *name* for the file, browse to the location where you want to store the file and then click **Finish**.

3. You want to configure an Account Lockout Policy. Specify the correct order of steps to accomplish the task.
   _________ Open Control Panel and then click **System and Security > Administrative Tools**.
   _________ Double-click the policy you want to configure to open its' Properties sheet.
   _________ Expand the Account Policies header, and then click **Account Lockout Policy.**
   _________ Double-click **Local Security Policy**.
   _________ Configure the policy by setting a value using the spin box, radio button, or other control and then click **OK.**
   _________ Close the Local Security Policy console and the Administrative Tools window.

Business Case Scenarios

Scenario 17-1: Using Password and Account Lockout Policies

You are working on a corporate network owned by a company with several government contracts to develop classified technology. You have been assigned the task to create a set of password and account policy settings that meet the following criteria:

- Users must change passwords every four weeks and cannot reuse the same passwords for one year.
- User passwords must be at least 12 characters long, case sensitive, and consist of letters numbers and symbols.
- Users are allowed no more than three unsuccessful logon attempts before the account is permanently locked down until released by an administrator.

In the following table, enter the values for the policies that will meet these requirements.

Policy Setting	Value
Enforce Password History	
Maximum Password Age	
Minimum Password Age	
Minimum Password Length	
Password Must Meet Complexity Requirements	
Store Passwords Using Reversible Encryption	
Account Lockout Threshold	
Account Lockout Duration	
Reset Account Lockout Counter After	

Scenario 17-2: Recovering a Lost Password

A junior administrator has just informed you that a user on your network has lost their password. She would like to reset the password for the user. What advice would you provide her?

Configuring Remote Connections

LESSON 18

70-687 EXAM OBJECTIVE

Objective 5.1 – Configure remote connections. This objective may include but is not limited to configure remote authentication; establish VPN connections and authentication; enable VPN reconnect; manage broadband connections; and configure Remote Desktop settings.

LESSON HEADING	EXAM OBJECTIVE
Using BranchCache	
Understanding Network Infrastructure Requirements	
Understanding BranchCache Communications	
Understanding Content Information Versions	
Configuring BranchCache Settings	
Using Remote Network Connections	
Understanding Virtual Private Networking	
Authenticating Remote Users	Configure Remote Authentication Establish VPN connections and authentication
Creating a VPN Connection	Establish VPN Connections and Authentication Enable VPN Reconnect
Creating a Broadband Connection	Manage Broadband Connections
Using Remote Desktop	Configure Remote Desktop Settings
Using DirectAccess	

KEY TERMS

BranchCache
DirectAccess
distributed cache mode
Extensible Authentication Protocol (EAP)
hosted cache mode
Internet Key Exchange, Version 2 (IKEv2)
Layer 2 Tunneling Protocol (L2TP)
Microsoft Challenge Handshake Authentication Protocol
Point-to-Point Protocol (PPP)
Point-to-Point Tunneling Protocol (PPTP)
Protected Extensible Authentication Protocol (PEAP)
Secure Password (EAP-MSCHAPv2),
Secure Socket Tunneling Protocol (SSTP)
tunneling
virtual private network (VPN)
VPN Reconnect

■ Using BranchCache

THE BOTTOM LINE

BranchCache is a feature in Windows 8 and Windows Server 2012 that enables networks with computers at remote locations to conserve bandwidth by storing frequently-accessed files on local drives.

Caching is a process in which computers copy frequently-used data to an intermediate storage medium so they can satisfy subsequent requests for the same data more quickly or less expensively. For example, virtually all computers have an area of high-speed memory between the system processor and the main system memory that functions as a cache. Repeated requests for the same data can be satisfied more quickly from the cache memory than the slower main memory. BranchCache works in much the same way, except that it is a disk storage cache that reduces the traffic between branch office computers and a server at another site.

Wide area network (WAN) connections between offices are slower and more expensive than the local area network (LAN) connections within an office. When a computer in a branch office requires a file stored on a server at the main office, the server must transmit the file over a WAN connection. If twenty computers at the branch office require that same file, the server must transmit it twenty times, using twenty times the WAN bandwidth.

BranchCache is a feature that can store a copy of the file on a computer (or computers) at the branch office site, so that the server only has to transmit the files over the WAN connection once. All of the subsequent requests access the file from the cache on the local network.

Understanding Network Infrastructure Requirements

To use BranchCache, you must have a server running Windows Server 2008 R2 or Windows Server 2012 at the main office and computers running Windows Server 2008 R2, Windows Server 2012, Windows 7, or Windows 8 at the branch office.

BranchCache was first introduced in the Windows Server 2008 R2 Enterprise, Datacenter, and Itanium editions and the Windows 7 Enterprise and Ultimate editions, and is now also available in Windows 8 Enterprise and Windows Server 2012; only computers running these operating systems can use it. The content server that stores the data initially must be running Windows Server 2008 R2 or Windows Server 2012. The workstations at the branch office that access the data must be running Windows 7 or Windows 8.

BranchCache is a client/server application that supports two operational modes, as follows:

- ***Distributed cache mode*** – Each Windows workstation on the branch office network caches data from the content server on its local drive and shares that cached data with other local workstations.
- ***Hosted cache mode*** – Windows workstations on the branch office network cache data from the content server on a branch office server, enabling other workstations to access the cached data from there.

Obviously, the major difference between the two modes is the need for a second, branch-office server in hosted cache mode, which makes the caching process more efficient, but which adds to the expense of the implementation. In distributed cache mode, each workstation is responsible for maintaining its own cache and processing cache requests from the other workstations on the local network.

Understanding BranchCache Communications

BranchCache clients and servers exchange relatively small messages among themselves, to coordinate their caching activities.

BranchCache supports file requests using Server Message Blocks (SMB), the standard Windows file sharing protocol, Hypertext Transfer Protocol (HTTP), the standard protocol for web communications, and the Background Intelligent Transfer Service (BITS). The BranchCache communications process is as follows:

TAKE NOTE*

Only Windows 8 Enterprise includes BranchCache support for the SMB, HTTP, and BITS protocols. The BranchCache implementation in Windows 8 Pro supports only BITS traffic.

1. **Client request (BranchCache)** – A branch office workstation requests a file from the content server, and identifies itself as a BranchCache client.
2. **Server reply (metadata)** – The server replies to the client, not with the requested file, but with a message containing metadata that describes the file. The metadata is much smaller than the requested file itself, reducing the amount of WAN bandwidth consumed.
3. **Client cache check** – Using the metadata supplied by the server, the client sends messages to the local caching computers, asking if the requested file is available locally.
4. **Caching computer reply** – In hosted cache mode, the local caching server replies to the client, indicating whether the requested file is available in its cache. In distributed cache mode, caching workstations only reply in the positive. If the client workstation receives no replies, it assumes that the requested file is not cached locally.
5. **Client request (non-BranchCache)** – The client issues another file request, this time without the BranchCache identifier, and sends it either to a local caching computer or the content server.
6. **Server reply (data)** – The computer receiving the request replies by sending all or part of the requested file to the client.
7. **Client data cache** – On receiving the requested file, the client clients caches it for use by other branch office workstations. In hosted cache mode, the client caches the file on the branch office server. In distributed cache mode, the client caches the file on its own local disk.

As a result of this process, the traffic transmitted over the WAN consists primarily of small messages containing client requests and metadata replies, as well as one single copy of every requested file.

It is critical to understand that BranchCache is a read-only caching application. The metadata messages described here occurs only when branch office clients are requesting files from the content server, not when they are writing modified files back to the server. BranchCache does not support write caching, which is a far more complicated process, because the systems must account for the possibility of conflicts between multiple versions of the same file.

Understanding Content Information Versions

The BranchCache implementation in Windows 8 and Windows Server 2012 differs slightly from the original release in the way that it handles cached files.

Any BranchCache implementation that includes one or more computers running Windows Server 2008 R2 or Windows 7 in any role is said to use content information version 1, or V1. If all of the computers involved in the BranchCache transactions are running Windows Server 2012 or Windows 8, the implementation can use content information version 2, or V2.

BranchCache V1 uses large, fixed length file segments, while V2 uses smaller segments of variable length. This difference affects the frequency at which cached files must be refreshed from the content server. When a user modifies a file on a V1 content server, all of the segments from the location of the change to the end of the file are invalidated. The next time a branch office client requests that file from the cache, the content server must transmit all of the segments from the change forward over the WAN.

In a V2 implementation, the smaller, variable length segments enable files to tolerate changes more easily. Instead of transmitting all of the segments from the change to the end of the file, the content server can, in many cases, transmit the changed segments only. This reduces WAN traffic and increases the efficiency of the cache.

The *Hash Version support for BranchCache* policy setting, shown in Figure 18-1, enables you to specify whether your installation should generate hashes for the server data files that are compatible with V1, V2, or both.

Figure 18-1

The *Hash Version support for BranchCache* policy setting

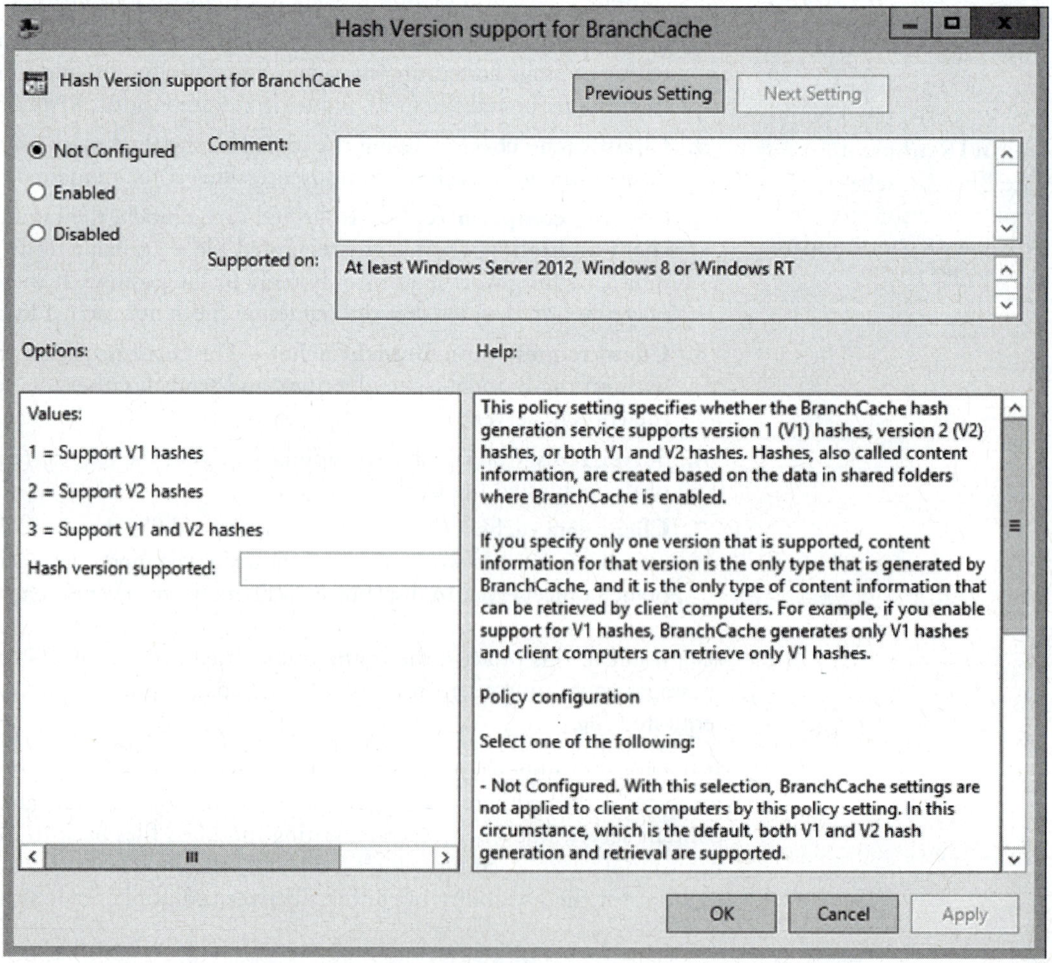

Configuring BranchCache Settings

To implement BranchCache on your network, you must install the appropriate modules on your server(s) and configure Group Policy settings on both servers and clients.

BranchCache requires a minimum of one content server and one or more branch office workstations. You can install additional content servers at any location that serves files to branch offices.

At the branch office, a typical BranchCache installation in distributed cache mode can support up to 50 workstations. To use hosted cache mode, you must have a branch office server at each location where there are branch office workstations.

CONFIGURING A CONTENT SERVER

To use BranchCache on your network, your files must be stored on a content server running either Windows Server 2008 R2 or Windows Server 2012. To support SMB requests, the server must have the BranchCache for Network Files role service installed in the File Services role. To support HTTP and BITS requests, you must install the BranchCache feature.

Once you have installed the required BranchCache modules, you must configure a Group Policy setting called Hash Publication for BranchCache. This setting is located in the Computer Configuration\Policies\Administrative Templates\Network\Lanman Server node of a Group Policy object (GPO) or in Local Computer Policy.

The Hash Publication for BranchCache setting, shown in Figure 18-2, enables the server to respond to file requests from BranchCache clients with metadata instead of the files themselves.

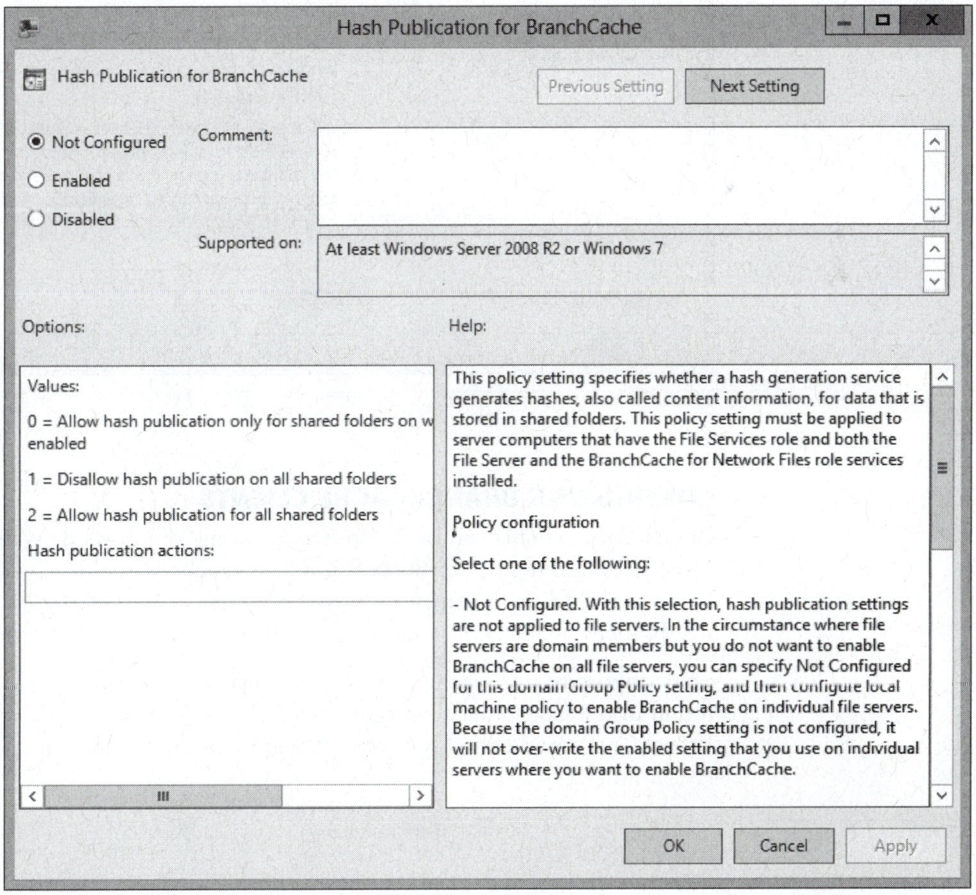

Figure 18-2

The *Hash Publication for BranchCache* setting in Group Policy

In this setting, you can stipulate that the server publish hash metadata for all of its shared files or for only the shares you select.

If you select the *Allow hash publication only for shared folders on which BranchCache is enabled* option, you must configure each share for which you want to enable BranchCache by opening the share's Properties sheet in the Windows Server 2012 Server Manager console, as shown in Figure 18-3, or the Windows Server 2008 R2 Share and Storage Management console, and selecting an appropriate option.

Figure 18-3

A share's *Properties* sheet in Windows Server 2012 Server Manager

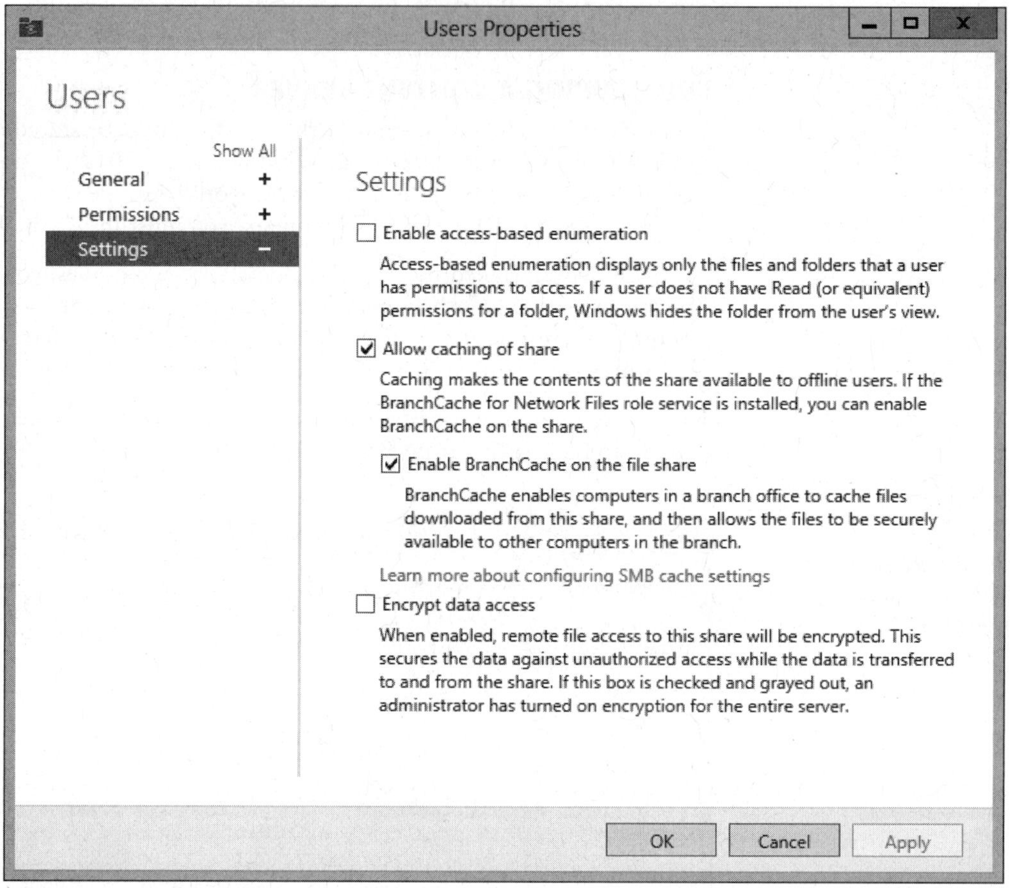

CONFIGURING BRANCHCACHE CLIENTS

BranchCache clients can be computers running Windows 8, Windows 7, Windows Server 2012, or Windows Server 2008 R2. BranchCache is enabled by default in Windows 8 and Windows 7. To use a computer running Windows Server 2012 or Windows Server 2008 R2 as a BranchCache client, you must install the BranchCache feature.

To configure BranchCache clients, you must configure the appropriate Group Policy settings, found in the Computer Configuration\Policies\Administrative Templates\Network\BranchCache node of a GPO or in Local Computer Policy, as shown in Figure 18-4.

Figure 18-4

The *BranchCache* settings in Group Policy

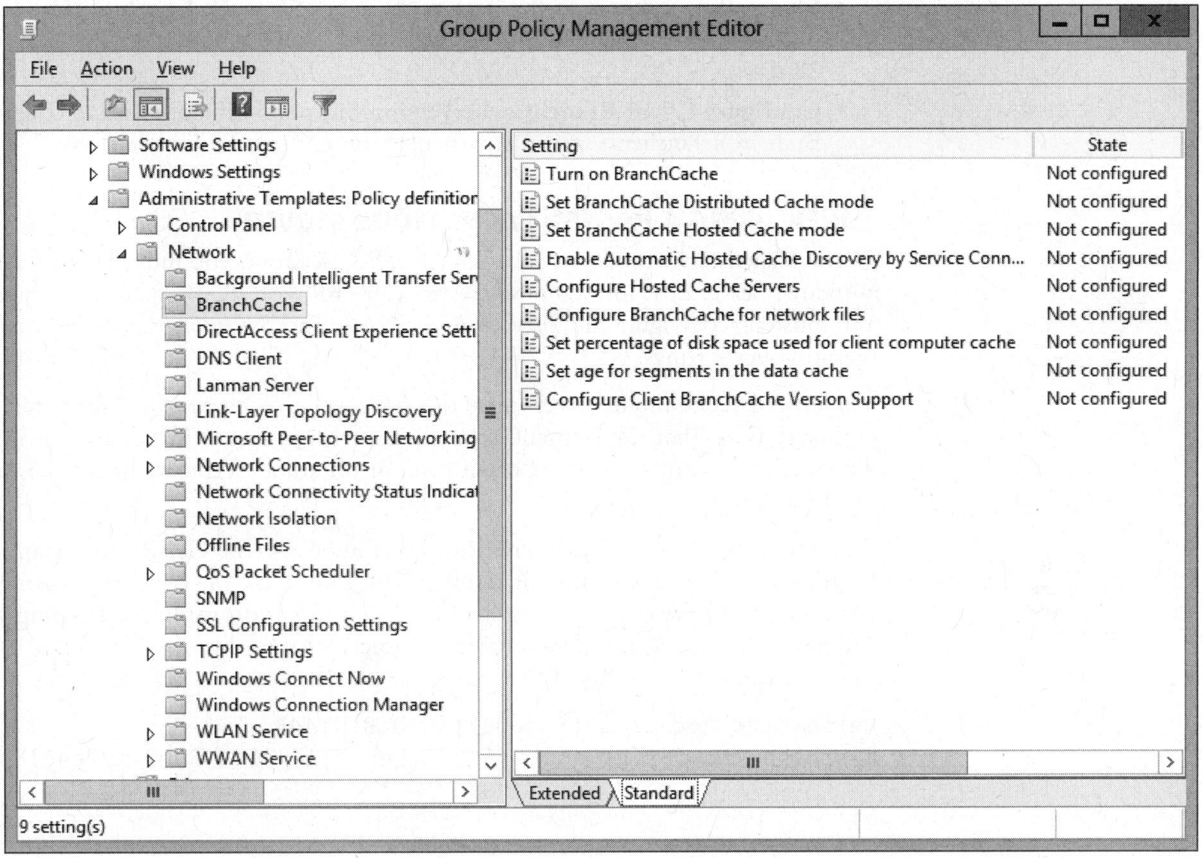

The BranchCache Group Policy settings are as follows:

- **Turn on BranchCache** – Enables BranchCache on the client computer. Enabling this setting along with either *Set BranchCache Distributed Cache mode* or *Set BranchCache Hosted Cache mode* configures the client to use one of those operational modes. Enabling this setting without either one of the mode settings configures the client to cache server data on its local drive only, without accessing caches on other computers.
- **Set BranchCache Distributed Cache mode** – When enabled along with the *Turn on BranchCache* setting, configures the client to function in distributed cache mode.
- **Set BranchCache Hosted Cache mode** – When enabled along with the *Turn on BranchCache* setting, configures the client to function in hosted cache mode. In the *Enter the location of the hosted cache* field, you must specify the address of the computer that will function as the hosted cache server on the branch office network.
- **Enable Automatic Hosted Cache Discovery by Service Connection Point** – Enables BranchCache clients to automatically locate hosted cache servers by searching Active Directory Domain Services.
- **Configure Hosted Cache Servers** – Specifies the names of the hosted cache servers available to BranchCache clients
- **Configure BranchCache for network files** – When enabled, this setting controls the round trip network latency value that BranchCache uses to differentiate local from remote servers. The default setting is 80 ms. When you decrease the value, the client caches more files; increasing the value causes it to cache fewer files.

- **Set percentage of disk space used for client computer cache** – When enabled, this setting specifies the maximum amount of total disk space that the computer should devote to the BranchCache cache. The default value is 5 percent.
- **Set age for segments in the data cache** – Specifies the length of time (in days) that segments remain viable in the BranchCache data cache. The default value is 28 days.
- **Configure Client BranchCache Version Support** – Enables you to configure all BranchCache clients to run a particular content information version.

CONFIGURING A HOSTED CACHE MODE SERVER

To use hosted cache mode on your branch office network, you must have a server running Windows Server 2012 or Windows Server 2008 R2 with the BranchCache feature installed. You must also configure the *Turn on BranchCache* and *Set BranchCache Hosted Cache mode* Group Policy settings.

The hosted cache mode server must also have a digital certificate issued by a certification authority (CA) that the BranchCache clients trust. You can install an internal CA on the network and use it to issue the certificate, or obtain a certificate from a commercial, third-party CA.

Once you have obtained the certificate, you must use the Certificates snap-in on the hosted cache server to import it. Finally, you must link the certificate to the BranchCache service by opening an elevated command prompt and typing the following command, replacing the thumbprint variable with the thumbprint value from the certificate you imported.

```
netsh http add sslcert ipport=0.0.0.0:443
certhash=thumbprint appid={d673f5ee-a714-454d-8de2-492e4c1bd8f8}
```

■ Using Remote Network Connections

THE BOTTOM LINE

Windows supports two types of remote client connections: dial-up, which typically uses standard asynchronous modems and telephone lines, and virtual private networking, which uses the Internet as the medium connecting the client to the remote access server. In addition, Windows 8 includes support for a new type of remote connection called DirectAccess, which eliminates the need to manually establish a connection to a remote server.

While new technologies such as BranchCache aid technical specialists in maintaining permanent or semi-permanent links between remote sites, they do not address the other type of remote user: the traveling or telecommuting worker that must connect to the company network from a remote site. These workers do not have permanent connections, so they cannot log on to the network in the usual manner. However, Windows provides a number of remote solutions that enable these users to access network resources from any location with a telephone line or an Internet connection.

Remote network access is a client/server application, so administrators must plan and implement a server infrastructure at the network site before Windows clients can connect to it. The first step in planning a Remote Access solution for an enterprise network is to decide which connection type you plan to use. To use dial-up connections, you must equip your servers with at least one modem and telephone line. For a single-user connection, as for an administrator dialing in from home, a standard off-the-shelf modem is suitable. For multiple connections, there are modular rack-mounted modems available that enable you to connect dozens of users at once, if necessary.

In today's networking world, however, hardware and telephone costs and the near-ubiquity of high-speed Internet connections have caused dial-up remote connections to be almost entirely replaced by virtual private network (VPN) connections.

Understanding Virtual Private Networking

Virtual private network connections violate standard networking concepts to provide security for private connections transmitted over the public Internet.

A dial-up connection is a dedicated link between the two modems that remains in place during the entire session, as shown in Figure 18-5. The client and the server establish a ***Point-to-Point Protocol (PPP)*** connection, during which the server authenticates the client and the computers negotiate a set of communication parameters they have in common. PPP takes the place of the Ethernet protocol at the data-link layer, by encapsulating the datagrams created by the Internet Protocol (IP) at the network layer, to prepare them for their transmission. PPP is much simpler than Ethernet because the two computers are using a dedicated connection, and there is no need to address each packet to a particular destination, as they must do on a local area network (LAN).

Figure 18-5

A dial-up remote access connection

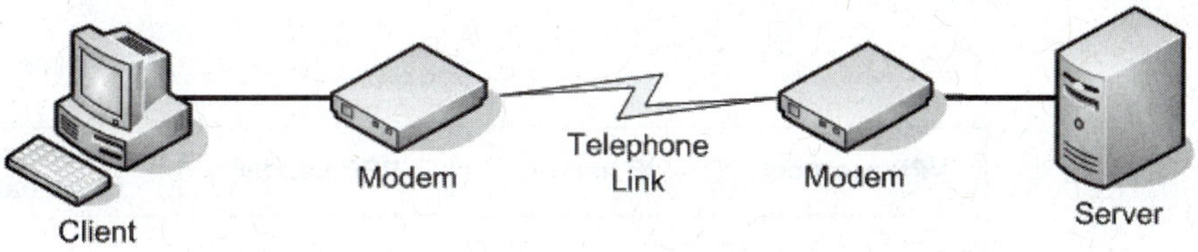

In a ***virtual private network (VPN)*** connection, the remote client and the remote access server are both connected to the Internet, using local service providers, as shown in Figure 18-6. This eliminates the expense of long distance telephone charges common to dial-up connections, as well as the additional hardware expense, since both computers most likely have Internet connections already. The client establishes a connection to the server using the Internet as a network medium and, after authentication, the server grants the client access to the network.

Figure 18-6

A VPN remote access connection

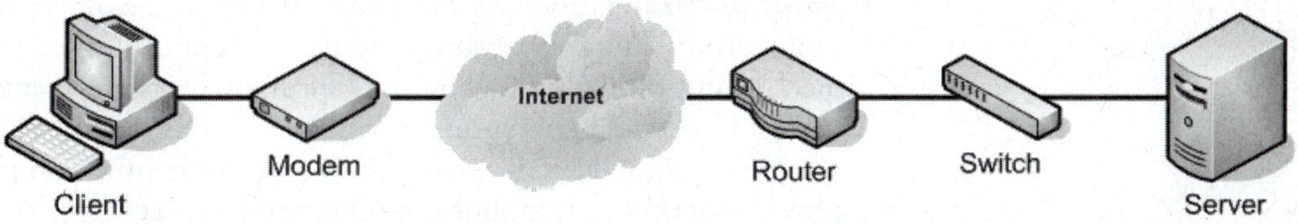

While it is theoretically possible for someone to tap into the telephone line used by a dial-up connection, intercept the analog signals exchanged by the two modems, convert them into digital data packets, and access the data, it is not likely to occur and remote connections are almost never compromised in this manner. Therefore, the data transmitted during a dial-up connection is considered to be relatively secure.

A VPN is another matter, however, because the client and the server transmit their data over the Internet, which makes the data packets accessible to anyone with the equipment needed to capture them. For this reason, VPN clients and servers use a specialized protocol when establishing a connection, which encapsulates their data packets inside another packet, a process called ***tunneling***. The VPN protocol establishes a virtual connection, or tunnel, between the client and the server, which encrypts data encapsulated inside.

In the tunneling process, the two computers establish a PPP connection, just as they would in a dial-up connection, but instead of transmitting the PPP packets over the Internet as they are, they encapsulate the packets again using one of the VPN protocols supported by the Windows operating systems. As shown in Figure 18-7, the original PPP data packet generated by the computer consists of an network layer IP datagram, encapsulated within a data-link layer PPP frame. The system then encapsulates the entire frame in another IP datagram, which the VPN protocol encrypts and encapsulates one more time, for transmission over the network.

Figure 18-7

VPN protocol encapsulation

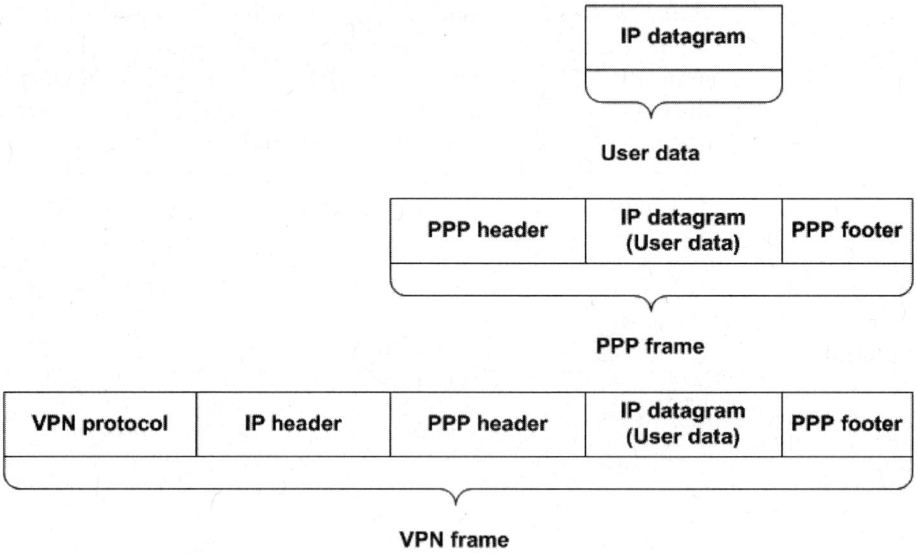

Having a data-link layer frame inside an network layer datagram is a violation of the Open System Interconnection (OSI) reference model's most basic principles, but this is what makes tunneling an effective carrier mechanism for private data transmitted over a public network. Intruders can intercept the transmitted packets, but they cannot decrypt the inner PPP frame, which prevents them from obtaining any of the information inside

The VPN protocols that Windows 8 supports are as follows:

- ***Point-to-Point Tunneling Protocol (PPTP)*** – The oldest and least secure of the VPN protocols, PPTP takes advantage of the authentication, compression, and encryption mechanisms of PPP, tunneling the PPP frame within a Generic Routing Encapsulation (GRE) header and encrypting it with Microsoft Point-to-Point Encryption (MPPE), using encryption keys generated during the authentication process. PPTP therefore can provide data protection, but not other services, such as packet origin identification or data integrity checking. For authentication, PPTP supports only the ***Microsoft Challenge Handshake Authentication Protocol*** version 1 (MS-CHAP v1), Microsoft Challenge Handshake Authentication Protocol version 2 (MS-CHAP v2), ***Extensible Authentication Protocol*** **(EAP), or** ***Protected Extensible Authentication Protocol (PEAP).*** Although it can use them (with EAP), one of the advantages of PPTP is that it does not require the use of certificates. In most cases, organizations use PPTP as a fall-back protocol for clients running non-Windows operating systems.

- ***Layer 2 Tunneling Protocol (L2TP)*** – L2TP relies on the IP security extensions (IPsec) for encryption, and as a result performs a double encapsulation. The system adds an L2DP header to the PPP frame and packages it with the User Datagram Protocol (UDP). Then it encapsulates the UDP datagram with the IPsec Encapsulating Security Payload (ESP) protocol, encrypting the contents using the Data Encryption Standard (DES) or Triple DES (3DES) algorithm, with encryption keys generated during IPsec's Internet Key Exchange (IKE) negotiation process. L2TP/IPsec can use certificates or preshared keys for authentication, although administrators typically use the latter only for testing. The end result is that the L2TP/IPsec combination provides a more complete set of services than PPTP, including packet origin identification, data integrity checking, and replay protection. For VPN connections involving Windows clients, L2TP/IPsec is the preferred protocol.
- ***Secure Socket Tunneling Protocol (SSTP)*** – Introduced in Windows Server 2008 and supported only by clients running Windows Vista SP1 or later, SSTP encapsulates PPP traffic using the Secure Sockets Layer (SSL) protocol supported by virtually all Web servers. The advantage of this is that administrators do not have to open an additional external firewall port in the server, as SSTP uses the same TCP port 443 as Secure Sockets Layer (SSL). SSTP uses certificates for authentication, with the EAP-TLS authentication protocol, and in addition to data encryption, provides integrity checking and enhanced key negotiation services.
- ***Internet Key Exchange, Version 2 (IKEv2)*** – First introduced in Windows 7 and Windows Server 2008 R2, IKEv2 uses TCP port 500 and provides support for IPv6 and the new VPN Reconnect feature, as well as authentication by EAP, using PEAP, EAP-MSCHAPv2, or smart cards. IKEv2 does not support the older authentication mechanisms, however, such as PAP and CHAP. By default, Windows 8 computers use IKEv2 when attempting to connect to remote access servers, only falling back to the other protocols when the server does not support it as well.

Authenticating Remote Users

Windows remote access connections use an authentication system that is entirely separate from the Kerberos authentication system that clients on the local network use. However, authentication is even more important for remote access clients than for local ones, because of the increased likelihood of intrusion.

CERTIFICATION READY
Configure remote authentication
Objective 5.1

CERTIFICATION READY
Establish VPN connections and authentication
Objective 5.1

All remote access connections, whether dial-up or VPN, use PPP to package their data, and the PPP connection establishment process includes a sequence in which the client and the server negotiate the use of a specific authentication protocol. In this sequence, each computer sends a list of the authentication protocols it supports to the other, and the two then agree to use the strongest protocol they have in common.

In Windows 8, you configure the authentication method a VPN connection uses on the Security tab of the connection's Properties sheet, as shown in Figure 18-8. The options are as follows:

- **Use Extensible Authentication Protocol (EAP)** – EAP is a shell protocol that provides a framework for the use of various types of authentication mechanisms. The primary advantage of EAP is that it enables a computer to use mechanisms other than passwords for authentication, including public key certificates and smart cards, as well as providing an extensible environment for third-party authentication mechanisms. Windows 8 supports three types of EAP-based authentication Protected EAP (PEAP), ***Secure Password (EAP-MSCHAPv2)***, and Smart Card or other certificate. EAP-MSCHAPv2, the default selection for new connections and the strongest password-based mechanism in Windows 8, requires a certificate only at the server. The Smart Card or other certificates option requires the clients, as well as the server, to have a certificate, stored either on a smart card or in the computer's certificate store.

- **Allow these protocols** – Provides support for the Password Authentication Protocol (PAP), Challenge Handshake Authentication Protocol (CHAP), and Microsoft Challenge Handshake Authentication Protocol Version 2 (MSCHAPv2), which are included to provide support for downlevel clients. These protocols apply only to PPTP, L2TP, and SSTP connections; IKEv2 connections must use EAP-MSCHAPv2 or a certificate.

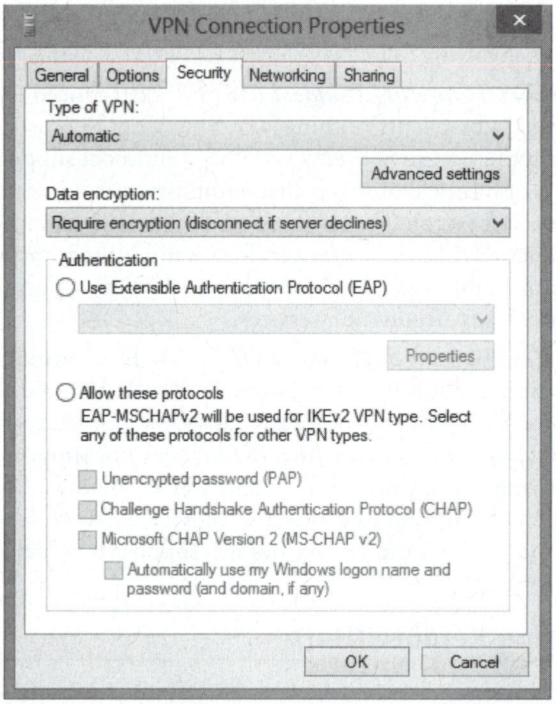

Figure 18-8

The *Security* tab of a connection's *Properties* sheet

Creating a VPN Connection

To connect a computer running Windows 8 to a remote access server, you must create a new VPN or dial-up connection.

CERTIFICATION READY
Establish VPN connections and authentication
Objective 5.1

In Windows 8, the Network Connections window contains a connection for every network interface adapter installed in the computer. The Windows installation program creates these connections automatically, but to connect to a dial-up or VPN server, you must create additional connections manually.

To create a VPN connection, use the following procedure.

CREATE A VPN CONNECTION

GET READY. Log on to Windows 8 using an account with administrative privileges and then perform the following steps:

1. Open the Windows control Panel and then click **Network and Internet > Network and Sharing Center**.

   The *Network and Sharing Center* control panel appears.

2. Click **Set up a new connection or network**.

   The *Set Up a Connection or Network* wizard appears, displaying the *Choose a connection option* page, as shown in Figure 18-9.

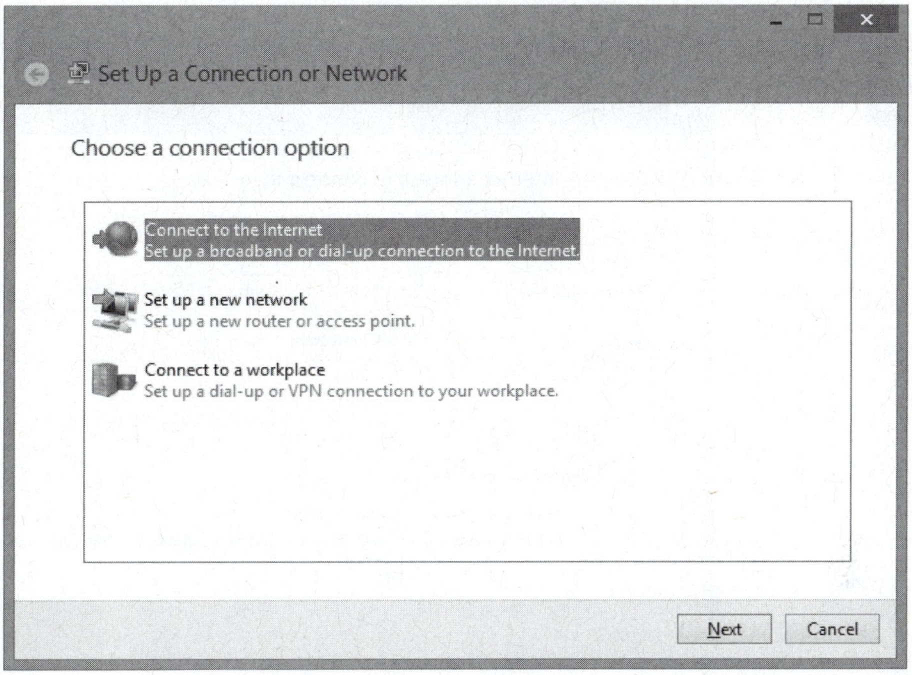

Figure 18-9

The *Choose a connection option* page

3. Click **Connect to a workplace** and then click **Next**.

   The *How do you want to connect?* page appears, as shown in Figure 18-10.

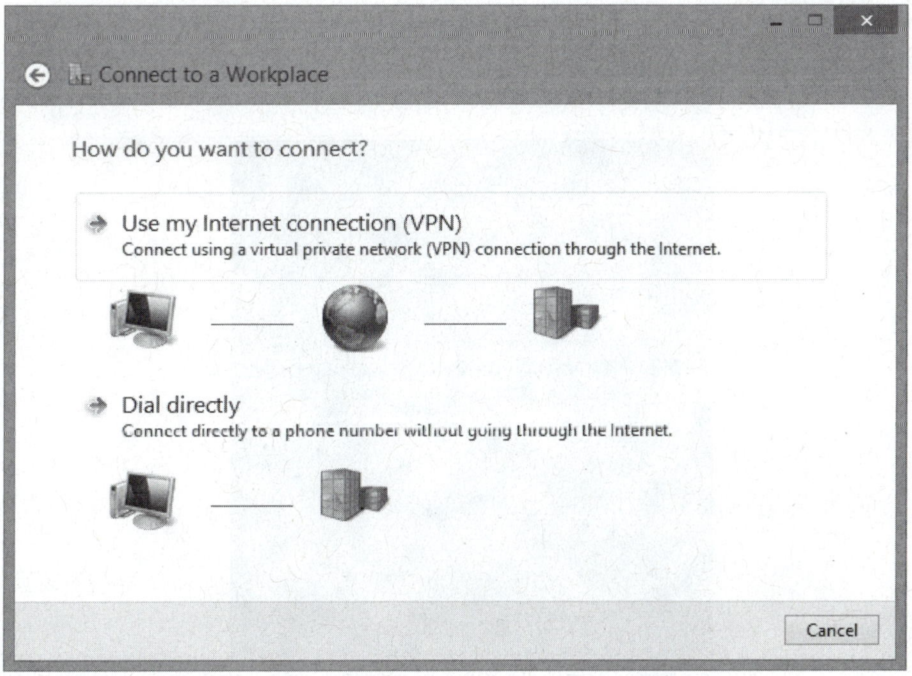

Figure 18-10

The *How do you want to connect?* page

4. Click **Use my Internet connection (VPN)**.

   The *Type the Internet address to connect to* page appears, as shown in Figure 18-11.

Figure 18-11

The *Type the Internet address to connect to* page

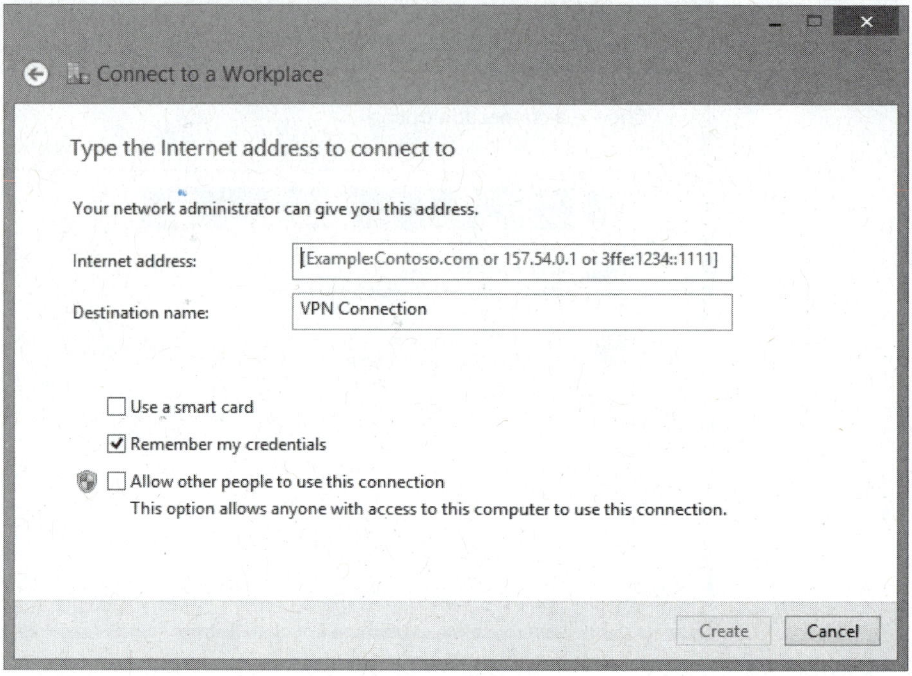

TAKE NOTE*

The process of configuring a dial-up connection is essentially similar to that of creating a VPN connection, except that for a dial-up, you must specify a phone number to call and configure other dialing criteria.

5. In the *Internet address* text box, type the fully-qualified domain name or IP address of the remote server to which you want to connect.
6. In the *Destination name* text box, type a descriptive name for the connection.
7. Click **Create**.

   The connection you created appears in the Networks display in the right fly-out pane, as shown in Figure 18-12.

Figure 18-12

The Networks pane

Once you have created the connection, you can open the Network Connections window, right-click the icon and select Properties to display the connection's Properties sheet. From here, you can reconfigure the options you just set in the wizard, plus configure all of the other settings for the connection, such as the VPN and authentication protocols it should use.

To activate the connection, you select it in the Networks display, and a Network Authentication pane appears, as shown in Figure 18-13. After supplying credentials appropriate for the VPN server, the system establishes the connection between the two.

Figure 18-13

The *Network Authentication* pane

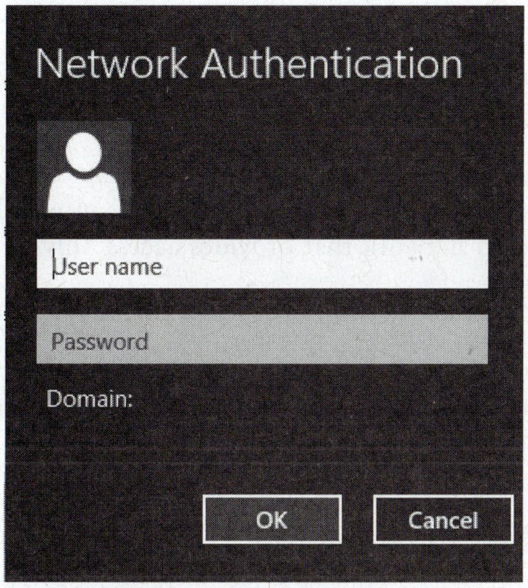

USING VPN RECONNECT

CERTIFICATION READY
Enable VPN reconnect
Objective 5.1

When a VPN connection is interrupted for any reason, it has always been necessary for the user to manually re-establish the connection. In recent years, the growing use of wireless Internet connections in public places has made this more of a problem. When a connection is interrupted, or a user moves from one access point to another, reconnecting to a VPN server can be an irritating chore.

Windows 8 includes a feature called ***VPN Reconnect***, based on the IKEv2 Mobility and Multihoming (MOBIKE) protocol, which enables a computer to reconnect to a VPN server automatically, after an interruption as long as eight hours. VPN only works with connections that use the IKEv2 protocol, which means that the client must be running Windows 8 and the remote access server must be running Windows Server 2008 R2.

To configure VPN Reconnect, you open the Properties sheet for a VPN connection, click the Security tab, and click Advanced settings. In the Advanced Properties dialog box that appears, click the IKEv2 tab and select the Mobility checkbox, as shown in Figure 18-14. The default network outage time is 30 minutes, but you can configure it to be as short as 5 minutes or as long as 8 hours.

Figure 18-14

Enabling VPN Reconnect

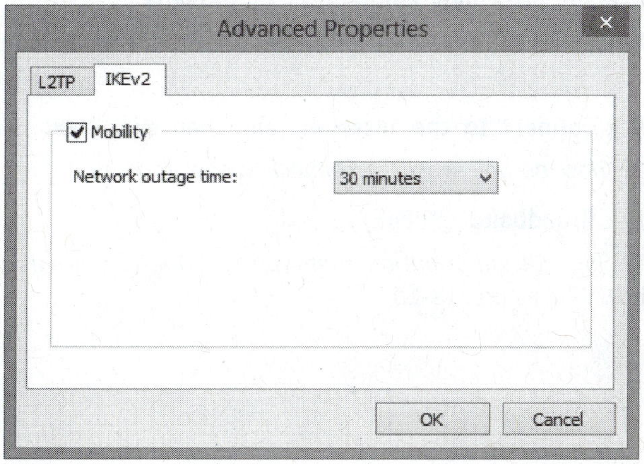

UNDERSTANDING NETWORK ACCESS PROTECTION

Network Access Protection (NAP) is a component of the Network Policy and Access Services role in Windows Server 2012, Windows Server 2008 R2, and Windows Server 2008, which is designed to prevent potentially dangerous clients – local or remote – from connecting to the network. Server administrators can configure NAP with security health validators (SHVs) that ensure that all clients meet a minimum set of criteria before allowing them to connect. The criteria can include any or all of the following:

- Up-to-date anti-virus protection
- Up-to-date anti-spyware protection
- Installation of the latest Windows updates
- A properly functioning firewall

If a client does not meet all of the required criteria in the SHV, the NAP server can simply deny it access, or it can begin a process of remediation, in which the client is essentially quarantined to an isolated network that provides access only to the resources it needs to bring it into compliance.

These resources can include Windows Server Update Services (WSUS) and a server to provide updates for malware protection. It is also possible for administrators to configure Windows 8 clients to perform remediative actions themselves in this situation, such as turning on Windows Firewall or running Windows Update.

Creating a Broadband Connection

While many Internet Service Providers (ISPs) offer broadband services that provide "always on" connections to the Internet, some still offer metered connections that require users to log on and log off. Windows 8 provides wizard options that enable you to create a broadband connection that you can activate and deactivate at will.

To create a broadband connection to the Internet, use the following procedure.

CERTIFICATION READY
Manage broadband connections
Objective 5.1

CREATE A BROADBAND CONNECTION

GET READY. Connect your computer to the modem or other hardware providing access to your ISP's network and log on to Windows 8 using an account with administrative privileges. Then perform the following steps:

1. Open the Windows control Panel and then click **Network and Internet > Network and Sharing Center**.

   The *Network and Sharing Center* control panel appears.

2. Click **Set up a new connection or network**.

   The *Set Up a Connection or Network* wizard appears, displaying the *Choose a connection option* page.

3. Click **Connect to the Internet**, and then click **Next**.

   The *How do you want to connect?* page appears.

4. Click **Broadband (PPPoE)**.

   The *Type the information from your Internet Service Provider (ISP)* page appears, as shown in Figure 18-15.

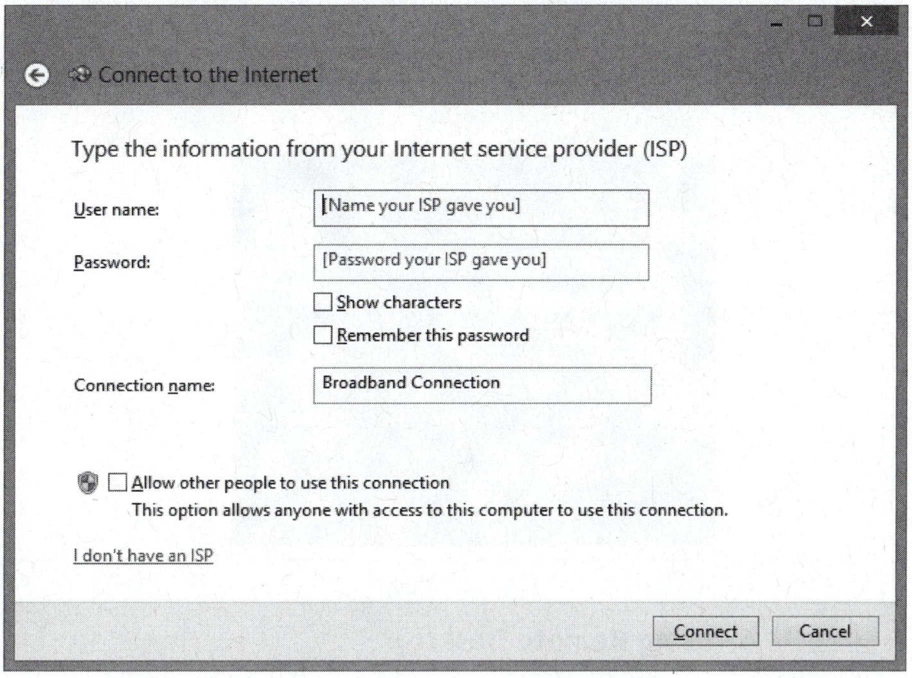

Figure 18-15

The *Type the information from your Internet Service Provider (ISP)* page

5. In the *User name* and *Password* text boxes, type the credentials provided by your ISP.
6. In the *Connection name* text box, type a descriptive name for the connection.
7. Click **Connect**.

   The wizard attempts to connect to the ISP's network and creates the connection. A *The connection to the Internet is ready to use* page appears, as shown in Figure 18-16.

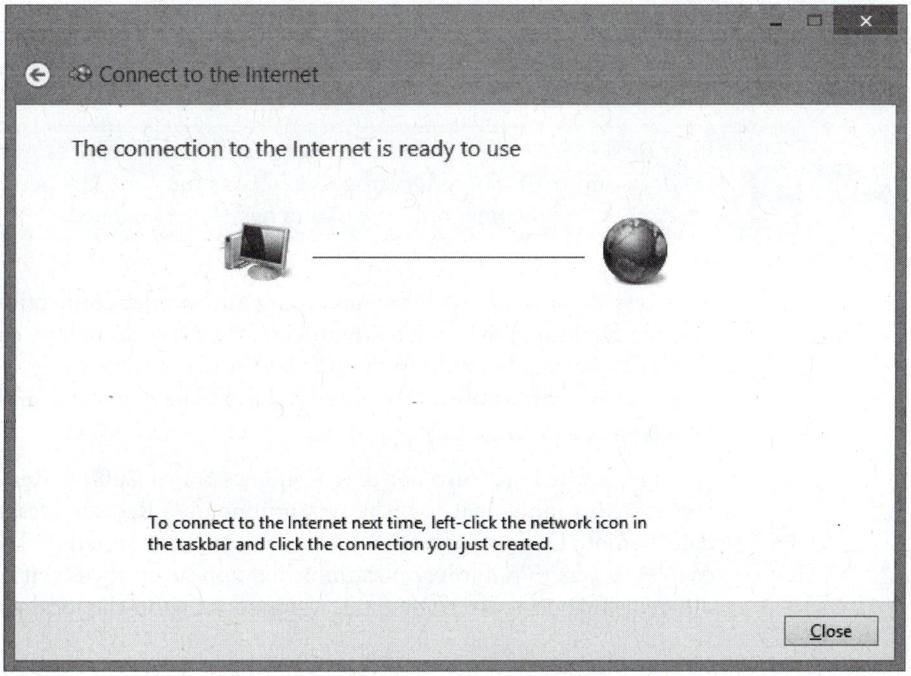

Figure 18-16

The *The connection to the Internet is ready to use* page

8. Click **Close**.

The wizard adds the connection you created to the Networks display in the right fly-out pane, as shown in Figure 18-17.

Figure 18-17
The Networks display

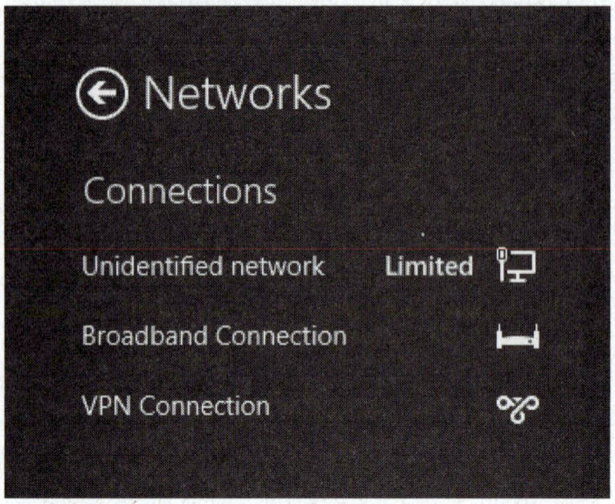

Using Remote Desktop

In Lesson 13, you learned how you can use Remote Desktop to connect to computers on the network and administer them from any location. It is also possible to use this Remote Desktop technology to provide clients with access to network computers and individual applications, even when the clients are at a remote location.

CERTIFICATION READY
Configure Remote Desktop settings
Objective 5.1

Windows Server 2012 includes a role called Remote Desktop Services, which provides clients with access to server resources in a variety of ways. The Remote Desktop Session Host role service functions much like the Remote Desktop Services service in Windows 8, except that it can provide multiple (licensed) users with access to the server desktop.

To provide remote clients with this type of access, using their standard Internet connections, there is a role service called Remote Desktop Gateway. Users at remote sites can use the standard Remote Desktop Connection client included with Windows 8 to connect to the gateway, and the gateway provides access to the Remote Desktop server.

TAKE NOTE*

Prior to Windows Server 2008 R2, Remote Desktop Services was known as Terminal Services, and the Remote Desktop Gateway as the Terminal Services Gateway. The services are essentially the same; only the names have been changed.

To access Remote Desktop Services using an Internet connection, you must open the Remote Desktop Connection client, click the Options arrow, click the Advanced tab, and then click Settings to display the RD Server Gateway Settings dialog box. Here, you specify the name or address of the Remote Desktop Gateway server and specify how you intend to log on.

Another new feature introduced in Windows Server 2008 is RemoteApp, which enables clients to access individual applications running on a Remote Desktop server. Unlike the standard Remote Desktop session, which creates a full-featured desktop at the client, RemoteApp enables servers to publish applications that appear on the client in separate windows, no different in appearance from applications running on the local computer.

Using DirectAccess

DirectAccess is a feature in Windows 8 and Windows Server 2012 that enables remote users to automatically connect to the company network whenever they have Internet access.

For many end-users, the entire concept of network computing is difficult to comprehend. There are people who don't know which resources are on their local drives and which are on network servers, and what's more, they don't care. They just want to be able to turn the machine on and know that it will work.

This issue can be particularly vexing for users that are traveling or working from home, and don't have immediate access to technical support. A VPN connection can provide them with access to the company network, but they have to remember to initiate the connection first. And if the connection should fail while they are working, they have to re-establish it, a process that can take several minutes each time a failure occurs.

Windows 8 and Windows Server 2012 include a remote access solution called DirectAccess, which addresses these problems by enabling clients to remain connected to their host networks whenever they have access to the Internet, reconnecting automatically whenever it is necessary.

DIRECTACCESS BENEFITS

Designed as a replacement for VPNs, DirectAccess eliminates the need for client users to manually establish wide area connections to their networks. As soon as the client computer accesses the Internet, the system automatically initiates the connection to the network. If the client becomes disconnected from the Internet, such as when the user wanders out of range of a WiFi hot spot, DirectAccess re-establishes the network connection as soon as the client regains access to the Internet.

DirectAccess provides many other benefits to users and administrators, including the following:

- **Bidirectional** – Network administrators can initiate connections to client computers, to install updates and perform maintenance tasks.
- **Encrypted** – All intranet traffic between DirectAccess clients and servers is encrypted using the IPsec protocols.
- **Authenticated** – DirectAccess clients perform both a computer authentication and a user authentication, and support the use of smart cards or biometric devices, such as fingerprint scanners.
- **Authorized** – Administrators can grant DirectAccess clients full intranet access or limit them to specific resources.
- **Verified** – Administrators can use Network Access Protection (NAP) and Network Policy Server (NPS) to screen clients for the latest updates before allowing them access to the network.

UNDERSTANDING THE DIRECTACCESS INFRASTRUCTURE

DirectAccess is all but invisible to the client, but the cost of this invisibility is a relatively complicated communications process and a long list of back end infrastructure requirements. Chief among these requirements is that DirectAccess is only supported by Windows 7, in its Enterprise and Ultimate editions, Windows 8 Enterprise, Windows Server 2012, and Windows Server 2008 R2.

The DirectAccess implementation in Windows 8 and Windows Server 2012 includes a number of improvements over the Windows 7/Windows Server 2008 R2 version, including the ability for DirectAccess to coexist on the same server with the Routing and Remote

Access Service (RRAS) that provides VPN server services. In Windows Server 2008 R2, you must deploy the two services on different computers, because their traffic models conflict. Windows Server 2012 also includes a Getting Started Wizard that simplifies the deployment of DirectAccess, and eliminates some of the more complicated requirements. DirectAccess and IPv6.

DirectAccess is also heavily reliant on IPv6, the new version of the Internet Protocol that expands the IP address space from 32 bits to 128 bits. Because IPv6 addresses are globally routable, a DirectAccess client can use the same address wherever it happens to be in the world.

IPv6 is not yet deployed universally, however. Many networks still rely on IPv4, most notably the Internet. Therefore, DirectAccess also relies on a variety of transition technologies that enable IPv4 networks to carry IPv6 traffic. These technologies are as follows:

- **6to4** – Provides IPv6 connectivity over IPv4 networks for hosts with public IP addresses.
- **Teredo** – Provides IPv6 connectivity over IPv4 networks for hosts with private IP addresses behind a Network Address Translation (NAT) router.
- **IP-HTTPS** – Provides Secure Sockets Layer (SSL) tunneling as a backup for systems that cannot use 6to4 or Teredo.
- **Intra-Site Automatic Tunnel Addressing Protocol (ISATAP)** – Provides IPv6 connectivity for IPv4 intranets.
- **Network Address Translation–Protocol Translation (NAT-PT)** – A hardware device that enables DirectAccess clients to access IPv4 applications.

DirectAccess and IPsec

IPsec is a collection of IP extensions that provide additional security for network communications. DirectAccess relies on IPsec for authentication of users and computers and for encryption of the data exchanged by clients and servers.

IPsec uses tunneling to protect communications between computers connecting over a private network. During the DirectAccess connection process, the client uses one IPsec tunnel to access the DNS server and AD DS domain controller on the host network. Then the systems negotiate the creation of a second tunnel that provides the client with access to the other resources on the network.

IPsec consists of two protocols, Authenticated Header (AH) and Encapsulating Security Payload (ESP), and two operational modes, transport mode and tunnel mode. Windows 8, Windows 7, Windows Server 2012, and Windows Server 2008 R2 both include full support for IPsec, but if other servers on your network do not, DirectAccess has ways to work around that limitation.

The way in which the host network uses IPsec is dependent on the access model you elect to use. If all of the servers on your network support IPv6, then DirectAccess clients can establish connections that go through the DirectAccess server and all the way to their application servers, using IPsec in transport mode. This is called the end-to-end access model, as shown in Figure 18-18.

Figure 18-18

DirectAccess: the end-to-end access model

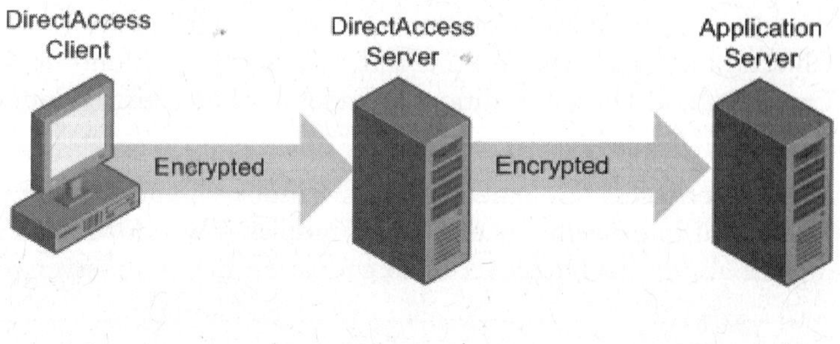

To keep IPsec traffic off of the company intranet, you can use the end-to-edge access model, as shown in Figure 18-19. In this model, DirectAccess clients establish tunnel mode connections to an IPsec gateway server (which might or might not be the same computer functioning as the DirectAccess server). The gateway server then forwards the traffic to the applications servers in the intranet.

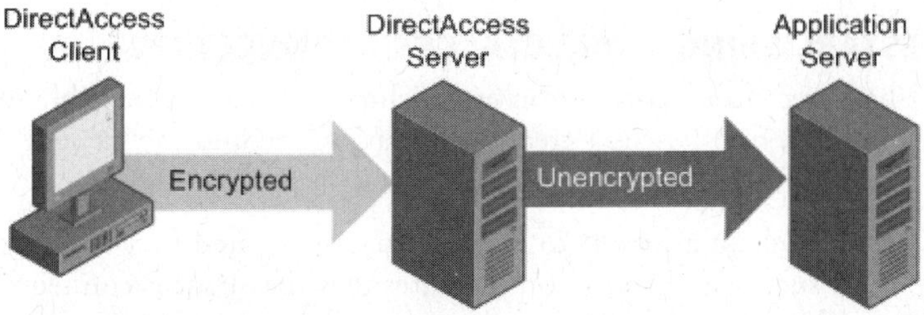

Figure 18-19

DirectAccess: the end-to-edge access model

A third model, called modified end-to-edge, adds an additional IPsec tunnel that goes all the way to the application server, as shown in Figure 18-20, enabling clients to perform another authentication directly with the application server.

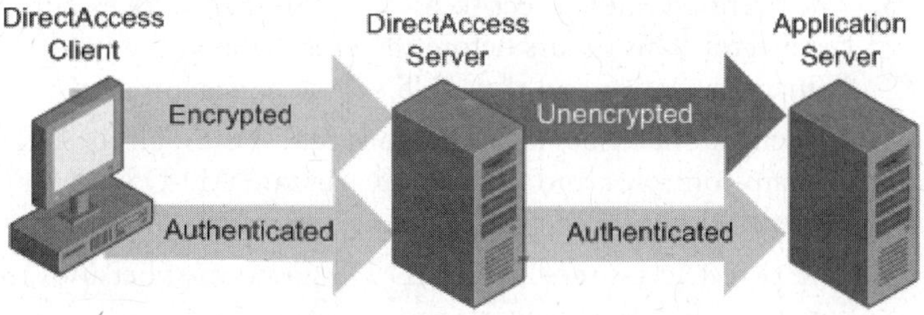

Figure 18-20

DirectAccess: the modified end-to-edge access model

DirectAccess Server Requirements

The primary access point for DirectAccess clients on the host network is a DirectAccess server, which you create by installing the Remote Access role with the DirectAccess and VPN (RAS) role service using Server Manager. The DirectAccess server must be running Windows Server 2012, and must also have the following:

- Membership in an AD DS domain
- At least one network interface adapter installed
- A direct connection to the Internet (that does not use NAT or a similar technology)
- A direct connection to the company intranet
- The Group Policy Management feature installed

In addition to the DirectAccess server, the host network must also have the following:

- An AD DS domain with at least one domain controller running Windows Server 2012
- Optionally, a Windows server functioning as an enterprise root or enterprise subordinate certification authority
- An AD DS security group containing the computer objects for all of the DirectAccess clients as members, so that they can receive Group Policy settings
- A network detection server that hosts a web site on the company intranet, which clients use to confirm their connections
- Transition technologies that enable clients to use IPv6 to access the DirectAccess server, the AD DS domain controller, and the application servers they need
- Firewall exceptions that enable the clients to access all of the servers they need, using the appropriate protocols

DirectAccess Client Requirements

DirectAccess clients must be running Windows 8 Enterprise, Windows 7 Enterprise or Ultimate, Windows Server 2012, or Windows Server 2008 R2, and they must be joined to the same domain as the DirectAccess server. You must deploy the client computers on the company network first, so they can join the domain and receive certificates and Group Policy settings, before you send them out into the field.

ESTABLISHING A DIRECTACCESS CONNECTION

The DirectAccess connection establishment process is invisible to the user on the client computer, but there is a great deal going on behind the scenes. The individual steps of the connection process are as follows:

1. The client attempts to connect to a designated network detection server on the intranet. A successful connection indicates that the client is connected to the host network locally. If the client fails to connect to the server, then the DirectAccess connection establishment process begins.
2. The client connects to the DirectAccess server on the host network using IPv6. If a connection using IPv6 natively is not possible, the systems fall back to 6to4, Toredo, or, if necessary, IP-HTTPS.
3. The client and the DirectAccess server authenticate each other using their computer certificates. This occurs before the user logon and provides the client with access to the domain controller and the DNS server on the intranet.
4. The client establishes a second connection through the DirectAccess server to the domain controller and performs a standard AD DS user authentication, using NTLMv2 credentials and the Kerberos V5 authentication protocol.
5. The DirectAccess server uses AD DS group memberships to authorize the client computer and user to access the intranet.
6. If required, the client submits a health certificate to a Network Policy Server (NPS) on the host network, to verify its compliance with existing policies.
7. The client begins to access application servers and other resources in the intranet, using the DirectAccess server as a gateway.

CONFIGURING DIRECTACCESS

The process of installing and configuring DirectAccess is much simpler in Windows Server 2012, requiring only that you install the Remote Access role and run a simple configuration wizard. In the wizard, you only have to supply the public name or IPv4 address of the DirectAccess server. The wizard then configures the server and creates the Group Policy settings needed to configure the DirectAccess clients. The process is much less complicated than in Windows Server 2008 R2.

There is no separate installation procedure for the clients; you simply have to ensure that they receive the Group Policy settings.

When you initiate the DirectAccess Setup process, the console performs a prerequisite check and displays any errors that you must resolve before the procedure can continue, as shown in Figure 18-21.

Figure 18-21

The DirectAccess prerequisite check

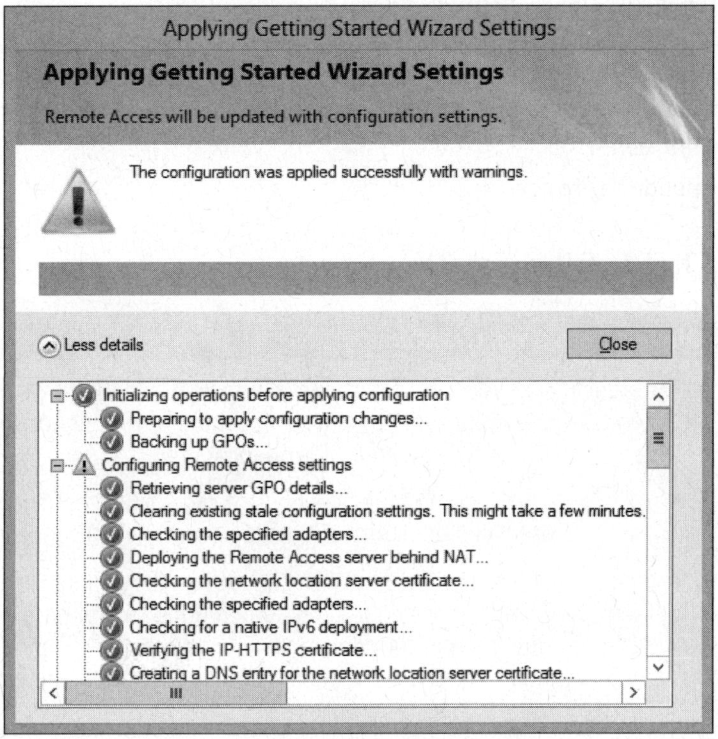

When you have met all the prerequisites, and the wizard has finished running, the service starts and the computer launches the Remote Access Management Console, shown in Figure 18-22, a new tool for managing and monitoring RAS connections.

Figure 18-22

The *Remote Access Management Console*

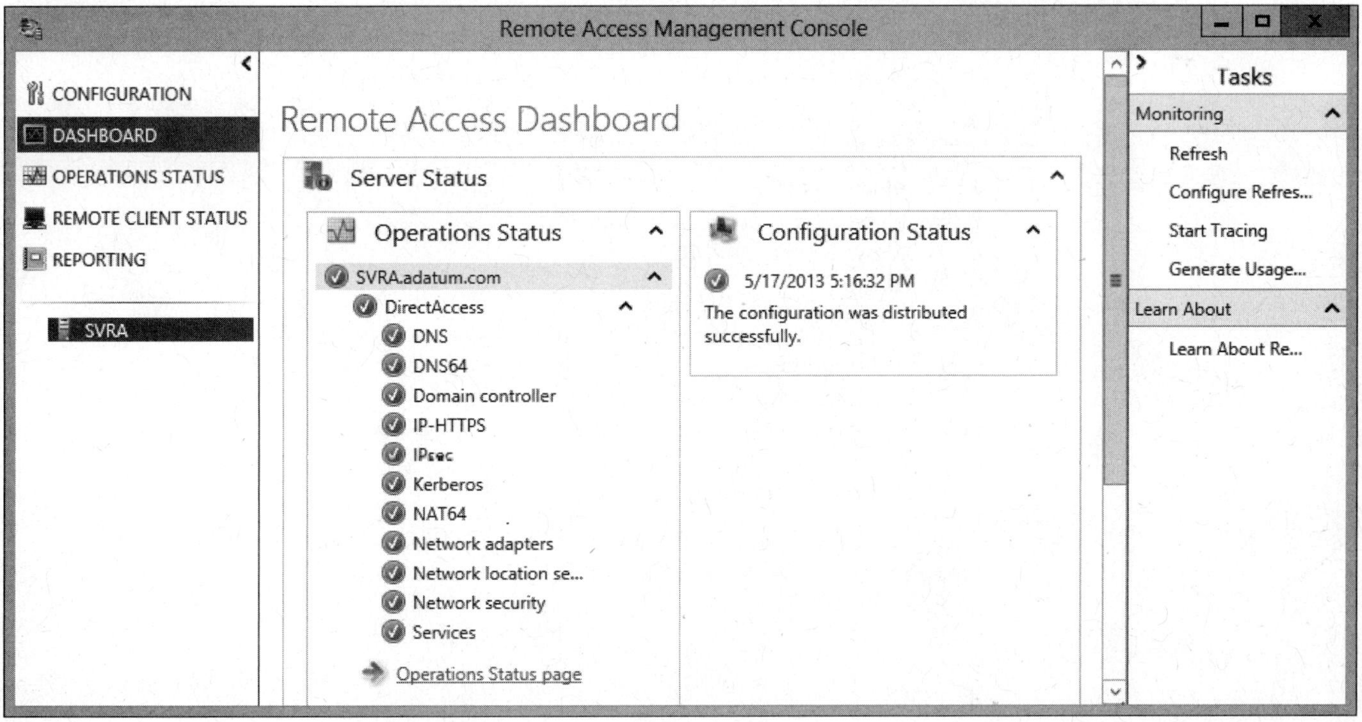

While the clients do not have to be connected to the intranet as you perform the server setup, you must connect them at some time afterwards, so they can receive the Group Policy settings that the setup process creates. To force a Group Policy update on a client, you can either restart the system or open a Command Prompt window, type the following command, and press Enter:

```
gpupdate/force
```

SKILL SUMMARY

IN THIS LESSON, YOU LEARNED:

- BranchCache is a new feature in Windows 8 and Windows Server 2008 R2 that enables networks with computers at remote locations to conserve bandwidth by storing frequently-accessed files on local drives.
- Windows 7 includes remote access client capabilities that enable users to connect to a network using dial-up or virtual private network (VPN) connections.
- In a virtual private network (VPN) connection, the remote client and the remote access server are both connected to the Internet, using local service providers. The client establishes a connection to the server using the Internet as a network medium and, after authentication, the server grants the client access to the network.
- Windows 7 and Windows Server 2008 R2 include a new remote access solution called DirectAccess, which enables clients to remain connected to their host networks whenever they have access to the Internet.

■ Knowledge Assessment

Multiple Choice

Select one or more correct answers for each of the following questions.

1. Which of the following operating systems cannot use BranchCache? (Choose all that apply.)
   a. Windows Vista
   b. Windows Server 2008
   c. Windows Server 2008 R2
   d. Windows 7
2. BranchCache is a client/server application that supports which of the following two operational modes?
   a. Content Server cache mode
   b. Workstation cache mode
   c. Distributed cache mode
   d. Hosted cache mode
3. Which of the following is the most secure password-based authentication protocol supported by the VPN client in Windows 7?
   a. EAP (PEAP)
   b. EAP-MSCHAPv2
   c. CHAP
   d. POP

4. Which of the following IPv6/IPv4 transition technologies takes the form of a hardware device?
   a. ISATAP
   b. 6to4
   c. NAT-PT
   d. Teredo
5. What is the main advantage of using DirectAccess over VPN connections? (Choose all that apply.)
   a. Users don't have to manually connect to the remote network.
   b. DirectAccess uses IPv4 rather than IPv6.
   c. DirectAccess supports more operating systems than VPNs.
   d. DirectAccess connections are unidirectional.
6. Which of the following is not a prerequisite for a DirectAccess server?
   a. Membership in an AD DS domain
   b. Two network interface adapters
   c. Two consecutive, public IPv4 addresses
   d. A NAT connection to the Internet
7. Which of the following protocols does a dial-up client use to connect to a remote access server?
   a. PPTP
   b. L2TP
   c. PPP
   d. IPsec

Best Answer

Choose the letter that corresponds to the best answer. More than one answer choice may achieve the goal. Select the BEST answer.

1. Which of the following is the best remote access solution for users that have a minimal understanding of how networks operate?
   a. Dial-up access
   b. Metered broadband
   c. Virtual private network
   d. DirectAccess
2. Which of the following is the best remote access solution for network administrators who are looking for the simplest possible client configuration procedure?
   a. Dial-up access
   b. Metered broadband
   c. Virtual private network
   d. DirectAccess
3. Which of the following is the best remote access solution for network administrators who are servicing clients that will be traveling in a country that blocks all access to the Internet?
   a. Dial-up access
   b. Metered broadband
   c. Virtual private network
   d. DirectAccess

Build a List

1. Place the following steps of the DirectAccess connection establishment process in the correct order:
   _________ a) Client and DirectAccess server authenticate each other.
   _________ b) Client fails to connect to network detection server.
   _________ c) Client establishes a connection through the DirectAccess server to a domain controller.
   _________ d) Client begins to access application servers and other resources on the intranet.
   _________ e) DirectAccess server authorizes the client using AD DS group memberships.
   _________ f) Client performs Active Directory Domain Services authentication.
   _________ g) Client connects to DirectAccess server.

■ Business Case Scenario

Scenario 18-1: Deploying BranchCache

Ralph is an IT director who is trying to reduce the enormous WAN costs incurred by his network. Towards this end, he is using BranchCache in hosted cache mode in each of his company's five branch offices. Workers in the branches must frequently access case log files stored on servers at the company headquarters, update them with new information, and save them back to the server.

The content servers at the headquarters are all running Windows Server 2012 and the BranchCache clients are a mixture of Windows 7 and Windows 8. Each branch office also has a hosted cache server running Windows Server 2008 R2.

After installing the required roles and features on the servers, and after configuring the appropriate Group Policy settings, Ralph has only noticed a slight reduction in WAN traffic. Describe two ways that Ralph can modify the installation to reduce the WAN traffic further.

Configuring Mobility Options

LESSON 19

70-687 EXAM OBJECTIVE

Objective 5.2 – Configure mobility options. This objective may include but is not limited to configure power policies; configure offline file policies; configure sync options; configure Wi-Fi direct; and configure Windows to Go.

Lesson Heading	Exam Objective
Using Windows Mobility Controls	
Opening Windows Mobility Center	
Configuring Mobile Display Options	
Configuring Presentation Settings	
Configuring Power Options	Configure Power Policies
Synchronizing Data	Configure Offline File Policies Configure Sync Options
Using Wi-Fi Direct	Configure Wi-Fi Direct
Configuring Windows To Go	Configure Windows To Go

KEY TERMS

Offline Files
Sync Center
transparent caching
Windows Mobility Center
Wi-Fi Direct

■ Using Windows Mobility Controls

THE BOTTOM LINE

As the computer market continues its trend towards smaller, more portable devices, the Windows Mobility Center becomes an increasingly important tool to many more users, providing convenient access to Windows 8's most frequently used mobile configuration settings.

Windows 8 includes a number of special tools designed specifically for mobile PCs, including smartphones, tablets, and all classes of laptop computers. Some of these tools take advantage of features that are unique to mobile computers, whereas others simply consolidate frequently used settings into a single interface.

Opening Windows Mobility Center

Windows Mobility Center provides users with quick access to the configuration settings most commonly adjusted by mobile computer users.

Windows Mobility Center is a shell application. It performs no special functions of its own; it simply provides a central point of access for many of the configuration settings that mobile computer users need frequently. These settings are located in various Control Panel applets, but placing them in a single window enables users to make adjustments quickly and easily. This is particularly beneficial to business users that give presentations with their portable computers.

To open the Windows Mobility Center on a Windows 8 mobile computer, open the Control Panel and click Hardware and Sound > Windows Mobility Center to display the window shown in Figure 19-1. You can also press the WIN+X key combination and select Mobility Center from the context menu that appears.

Figure 19-1

The Windows Mobility Center

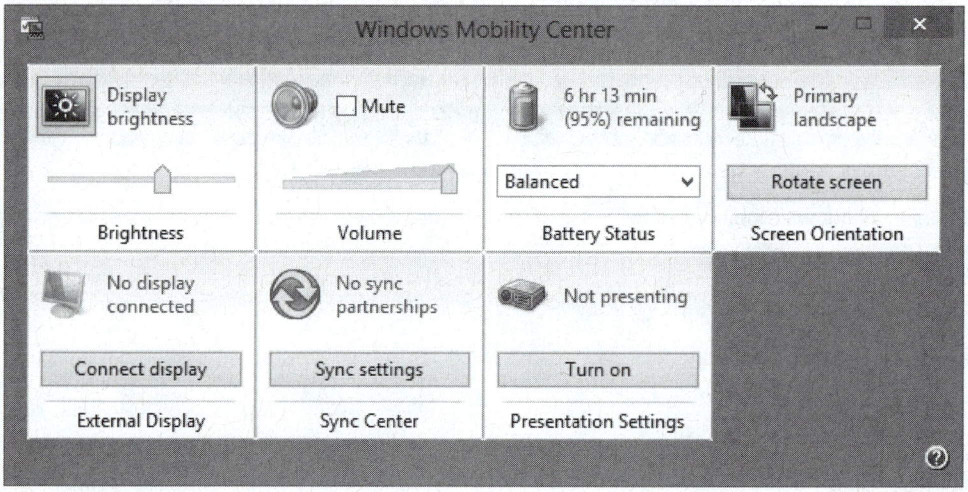

TAKE NOTE*

Windows 8 identifies mobile devices during the operating system installation and configures them to display the Windows Mobility Center and the controls specific to the hardware in the machine. Therefore, the Windows Mobility Center icon will not appear in a desktop computer's Control Panel.

The Windows Mobility Center window is divided into as many as eight tiles. The tiles that appear and the controls in them depend on the type of computer you are using, its hardware components, and the software supplied by the computer's manufacturer. You can modify configuration settings by using the controls that appear in the Windows Mobility Center window or by clicking the icon in one of the tiles to open the corresponding Control Panel applet.

The eight tiles that can appear in the Windows Mobility Center are as follows:

- **Brightness** – Enables the user to adjust the brightness of the computer's display.
- **Volume** – Enables the user to adjust the volume of the computer's speakers, or mute them completely.
- **Battery Status** – Displays the computer's current power status (AC or battery) and the battery's charge, as well as enabling the user to select one of the computer's power plans.
- **Wireless Network** – Displays the status of the computer's wireless network connection and enables the user to turn the wireless network adapter on or off.
- **Screen Orientation** – On a tablet PC, enables the user to toggle the computer's display orientation between portrait and landscape.
- **External Display** – Enables the user to connect an external display to the computer and modify the display settings.
- **Sync Center** – Enables the user to set up a sync partnership, start a sync event, or monitor the status of a sync event in progress.

TAKE NOTE*

Original equipment manufacturers (OEMs) can also modify the default Windows Mobility Center display, to add their own tiles controlling model-specific hardware and software features.

- **Presentation Settings** – When turned on, prevents presentations from being interrupted by screen savers, alarms, and attempts to put the computer to sleep. This tile also enables the user to adjust the settings most often used during a presentation, such as the screen saver, the speaker volume, and the desktop background.

Configuring Mobile Display Options

To accommodate presentation audiences and other situations, mobile users are likely to adjust their display settings more frequently than desktop users.

One of the biggest benefits of mobile computing is the ability to collaborate with other users, bringing your data and your applications with you. Many portable computers have the capability to connect an external display device, making it possible for a group of users to view the desktop without having to crowd around a single small screen. Many people use this external display capability to give lectures, presentations, or demonstrations, using a variety of external display technologies.

Desktop technicians should be familiar with the computer capabilities, configuration settings, and controls used to manage the display options, as discussed in the following settings.

CONNECTING AN EXTERNAL DISPLAY

In most cases, the ability to connect an external display to a portable computer depends on the system's hardware and software. Many portables include an external video port, such as a VGA (Video Graphics Array), DVI (Digital Visual Interface), S-Video, High-Definition Multimedia Interface (HDMI), or DisplayPort connector, which enables you to attach an external display to the computer, and video drivers that enable you to configure the properties of each display separately.

At its simplest, an external display can be a standard desktop monitor—analog or digital, LCD or CRT—connected to the portable device and configured to mirror the image on the device's own display. If the computer has an HDMI, DisplayPort, or S-Video jack, it is also possible to connect a similarly equipped television set. The user can then work with the computer in the normal manner, and a small group of observers can follow the user's action on the external monitor. However, for more elaborate presentations or large audiences, many users employ a display projector, which is a device that uses computer display technology to project an image on a large screen or wall.

Installing the hardware is simply a matter of connecting the external display to the computer using whatever port is provided. VGA and DVI ports are designed for computer monitors. CRTs and lower-end LCD monitors use the standard 15-pin VGA port, while many LCD monitors use the 29-pin DVI connector. However, some DVI monitors come with an adapter that enables you to plug them into a computer with only a VGA port. Many of the small form-factor portable computers now on the market, such as tablets and ultrabooks, are equipped with HDMI or DisplayPort connectors, which are smaller than DVI and VGA connectors and can carry audio as well as video signals.

Portable computers that have a port for an external monitor typically have a video adapter that is capable of supporting two display configurations. This adapter, plus the device driver that goes with it, enables you to configure the displays using different resolutions, if necessary, and to choose how to use the two displays.

CONFIGURING MULTIPLE DISPLAYS

Windows 8 provides two ways to control the second display. Typically, when you plug a second display into a port, and the system is able to detect it, the current display is mirrored on the secondary device. To modify this default configuration, you can open the Windows Mobility Center and, in the Display tile, click or tap the Disconnect Display button. This causes a fly-out Second Screen menu to appear on the right side of the screen, as shown in Figure 19-2.

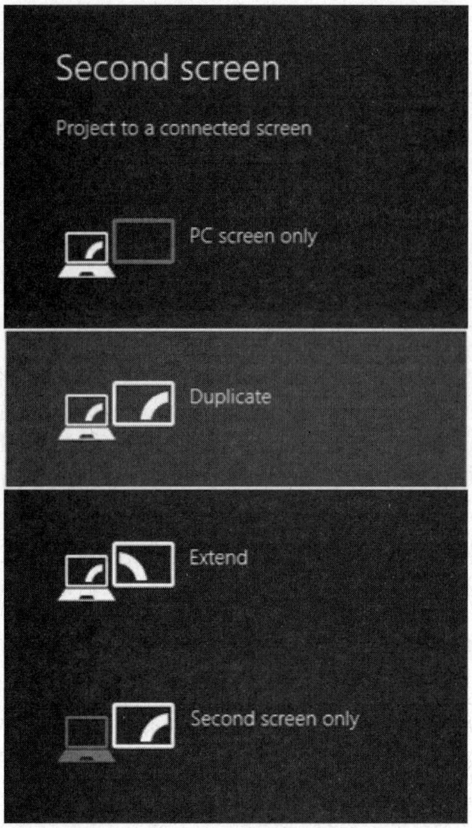

Figure 19-2

The *Second Screen* menu

From this menu, you can select whether the system should use one display or the other, mirror the same content on both displays, or extend the interface to encompass both displays. With these options, the user can allow an audience to see the same content he or she is seeing on the device, or play a video or slide show on the secondary display while reading from notes or other documents shown on the primary.

The other method for controlling the displays is to open the Display control panel and click **Adjust resolution** to open the Screen Resolution dialog box, as shown in Figure 19-3. You can also open this dialog box by clicking or tapping the icon in the Display tile of the Windows Mobility Center.

Figure 19-3

Mirrored displays in the *Screen Resolution* dialog box

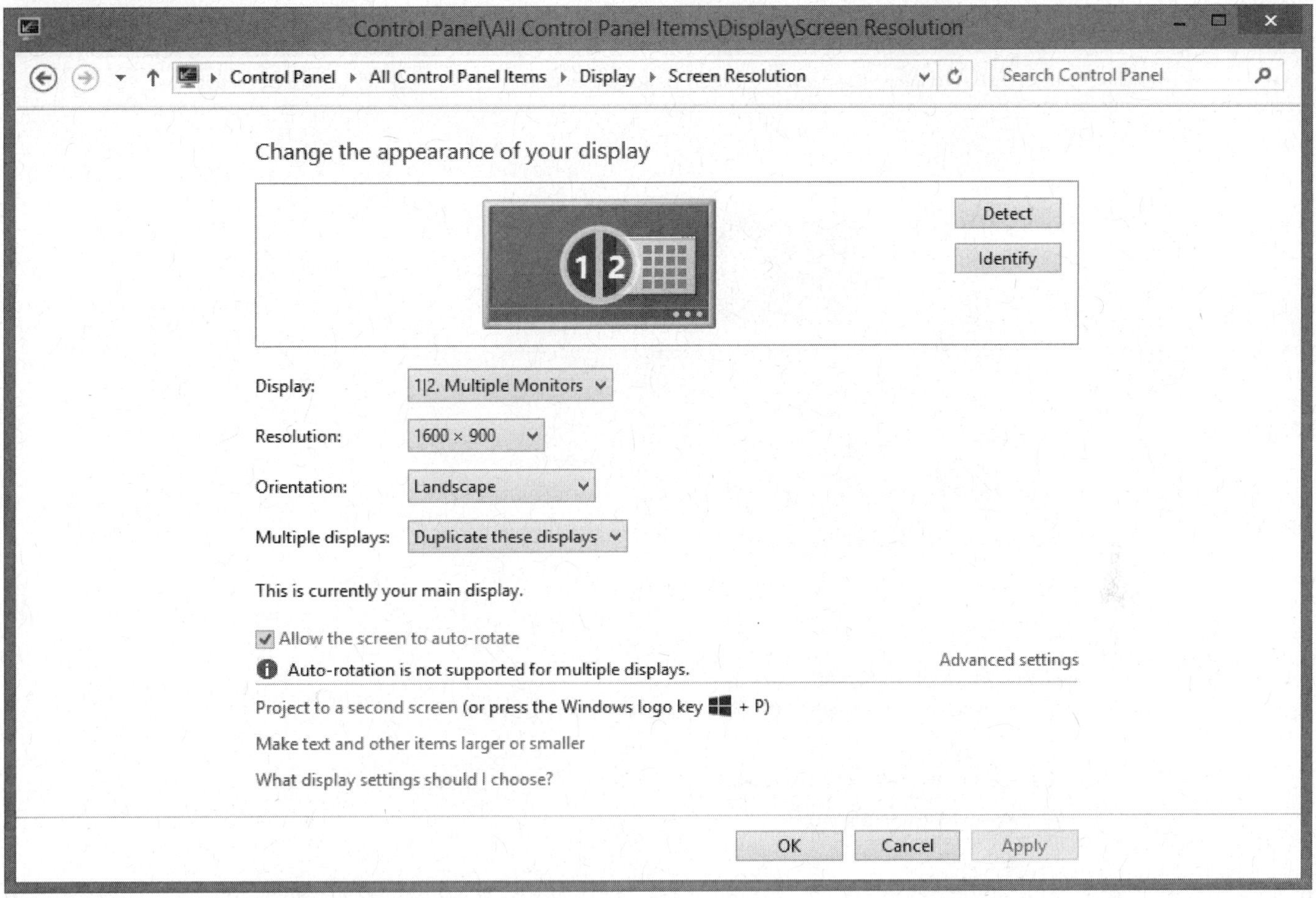

When the system is configured to mirror the displays, they must use the same resolution, and other settings, so any changes you make to the display configuration apply to both. However, if you opt to extend the screen to the second display, using either the Second Screen menu or by selecting Extend these displays in the Multiple Monitors drop down list of the Screen Resolution dialog box, the two displays appear as separate entities, as shown in Figure 19-4.

Figure 19-4

An extended display in the *Screen Resolution* dialog box

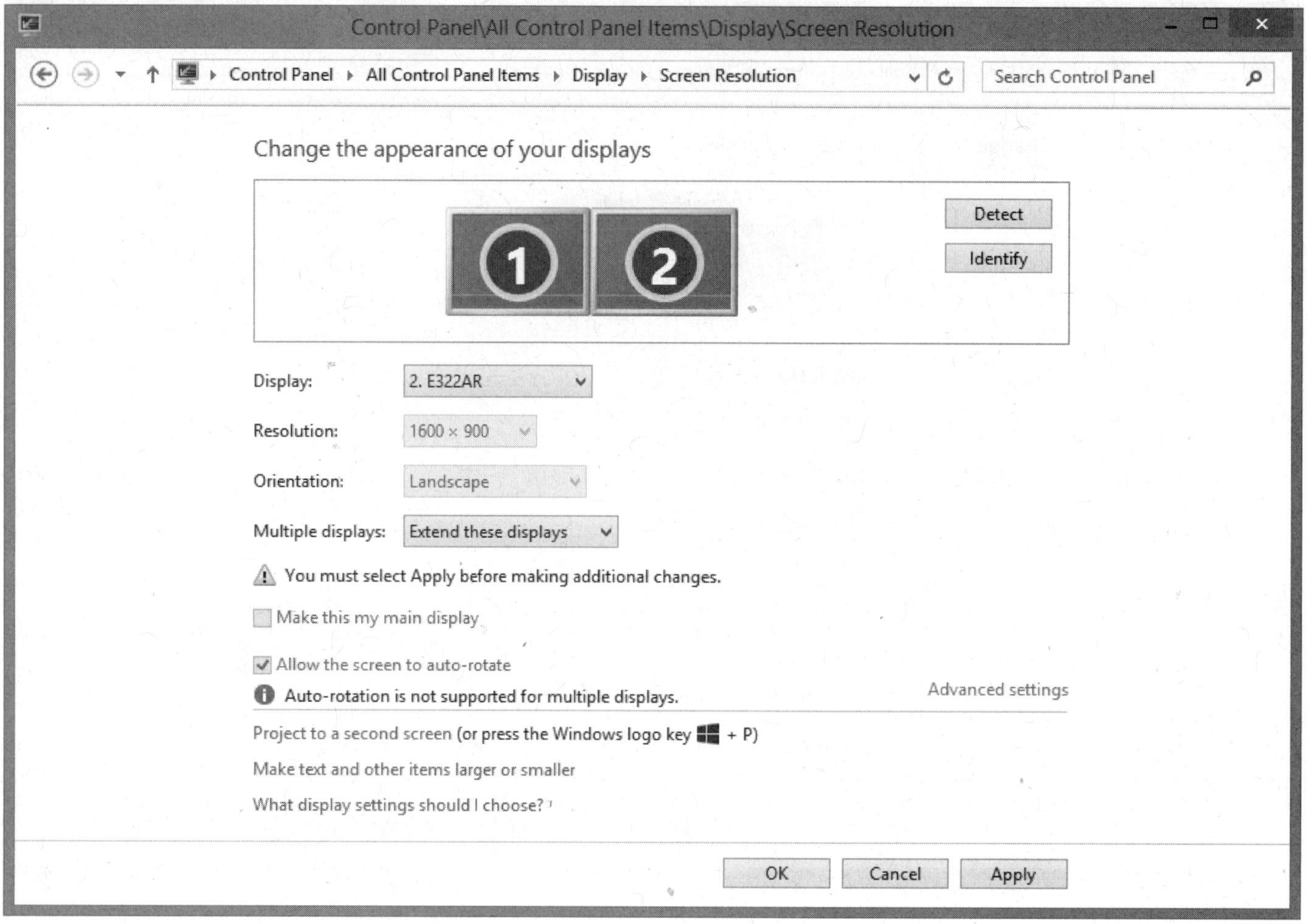

In this arrangement, you can configure the displays independently. When you select one of the displays, by clicking or tapping one of the numbered icons, or by selecting from the Display drop down list, you can specify a resolution and orientation that will apply to the selected display only.

USING A DISPLAY PROJECTOR

For presentations to larger audiences, many portable computer users prefer to use a display projector as an external display, instead of a standard monitor. A display projector is a device that works much like a monitor, except that instead of creating an image on an LED, LCD, or plasma display, it projects a live image of the computer's desktop onto a screen.

Most display projectors can connect to a computer's video port, just like a regular monitor. Some have HDMI or DisplayPort connects that provide access to an audio system as well. Some of the more advanced (and expensive) models can even connect directly to a network, either wired or wireless, enabling any computer on the network to send its desktop display to the projector.

Unlike external monitors, projectors are designed to mirror the computer's desktop, not extend it. Portable computers with external monitor ports typically have some sort of keyboard mechanism that enables you to select whether the computer should send the desktop to the internal display, the projector, or both. However, Windows 8 simplifies this selection process by displaying a dialog box when you connect a projector, asking you which display(s) you want to use.

Network projectors are a different situation, because they do not connect directly to the video display adapter, and they are not automatically detectible by Windows 8. Instead of simply directing the monitor signal out through a port, the computer uses the Remote Desktop Protocol (RDP) to transmit the monitor signals over the network to the projector device, which has an embedded Windows operating system built into it.

One of the first obstacles to using a network projector with Windows 8 is that Windows Firewall, by default, blocks the port used for RDP traffic. To simplify the process of configuring the necessary firewall exceptions and locating the projector on the network, Windows 8 provides the Connect to a Network Projector wizard.

Unlike Windows 7, the Connect to a Network Projector Wizard is not installed with Windows 8 by default. It is instead provided as a feature, which you must add before you can run it.

To install and run the Connect to a Network Projector Wizard, use the following procedure.

INSTALL AND RUN THE CONNECT TO A NETWORK PROJECTOR WIZARD

GET READY. Connect the projector to the network and configure it according to the manufacturer's instructions. Then, log on to Windows 8 and perform the following steps:

1. Open the Control Panel and click or tap **Programs > Programs and Features > Turn Windows features on or off**.

   The *Windows Features* dialog box appears.

2. Select the *Network Projection* checkbox and then click **OK**.

   The system installs the selected feature.

3. Click **Close**.

4. On the **Start** screen, click or tap the **Connect to a Network Projector** tile.

   The Connect to a Network Projector Wizard appears, displaying the *Windows Firewall is blocking the network projector from communicating with your computer* page, as shown in Figure 19-5.

Figure 19-5

The *Windows Firewall is blocking the network projector from communicating with your computer* page

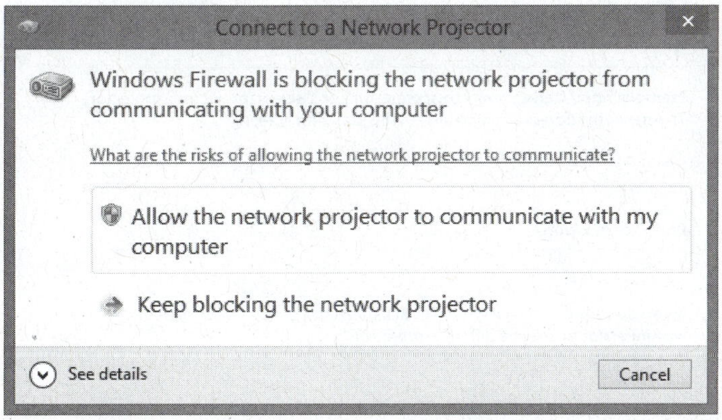

5. Click **Allow the network projector to communicate with my computer** to create exceptions in the Windows Firewall that will permit communications with the projector.

   The *How do you want to connect to a network projector?* page appears, as shown in Figure 19-6.

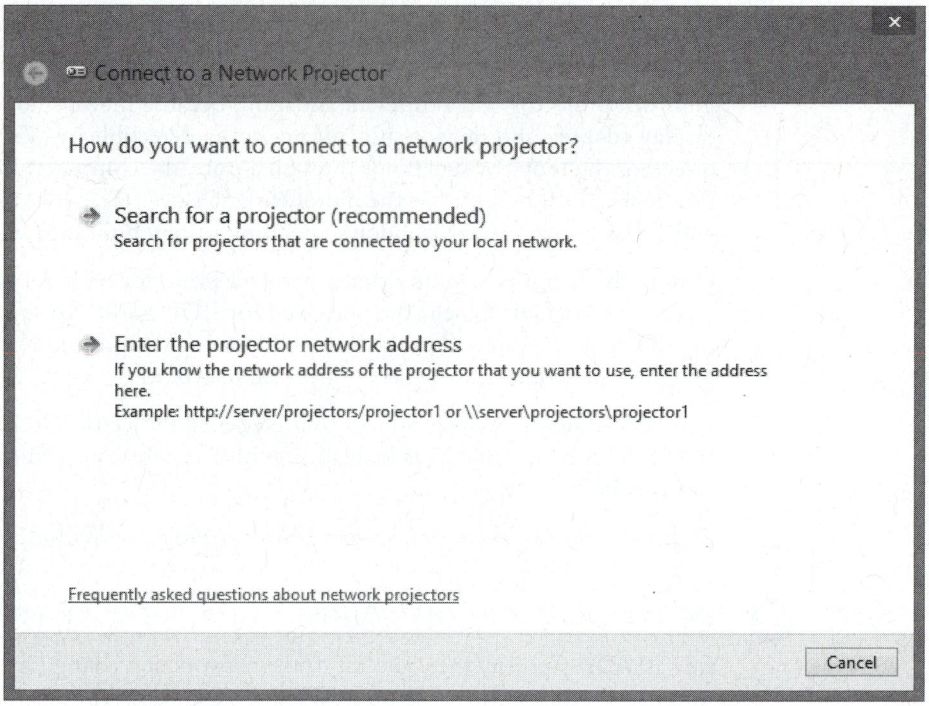

Figure 19-6

The *How do you want to connect to a network projector?* page

6. Click **Search for a projector (recommended)**.

   The wizard searches for a projector on the network and prompts you for a password if one is required.

7. You can also click **Enter the projector network address** to display the *Enter the network address of a network projector* page, as shown in Figure 19-7, in which you can manually supply the printer's network address and password.

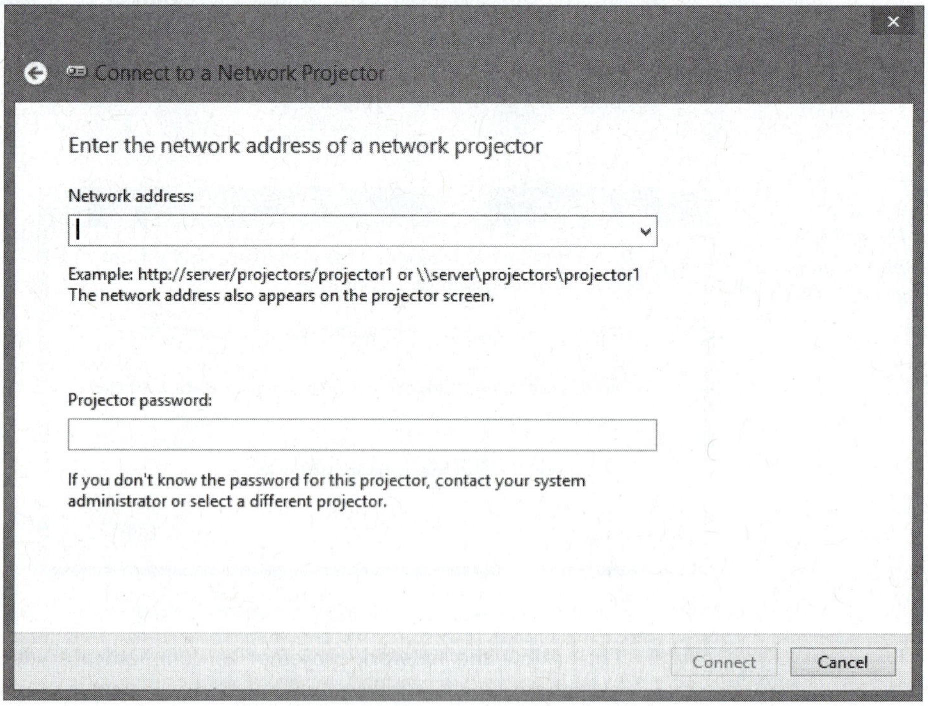

Figure 19-7

The *Enter the network address of a network projector* page

8. Click **Connect** to establish the connection to the projector.

Configuring Presentation Settings

The Presentation Settings dialog box provides quick access to the most common adjustments performed by presenters.

The designers of Windows 8 have attempted to anticipate the needs of many types of computer users. For people that use their mobile computers to give presentations to an audience, few things are more unwelcome than an unexpected system event, such as an error message or a screen saver kicking in. Depending on the audience and the type of presentation, the result of problems like these can range from simple embarrassment to lost sales.

Windows 8 includes a dialog box that bundles together the configuration settings that users most often adjust before giving a presentation, and makes it possible to activate all of the settings with a single switch.

To configure the presentation settings for a computer, use the following procedure.

CONFIGURE PRESENTATION SETTINGS

GET READY. Log on to Windows 8 using an account with administrative privileges and then perform the following steps:

1. Open **Windows Mobility Center** and then click the icon in the **Presentation Settings** tile.

   The Presentation Settings dialog box appears, as shown in Figure 19-8.

Figure 19-8

The *Presentation Settings* dialog box

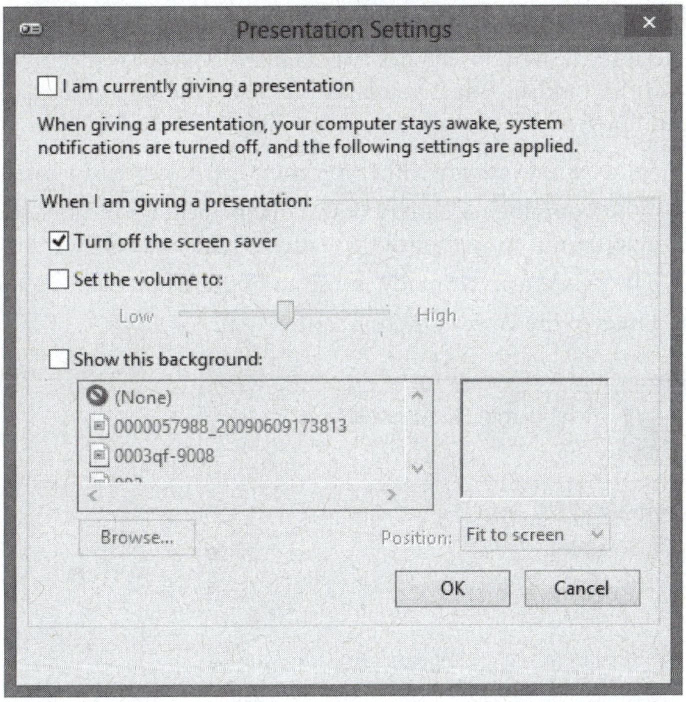

2. Use the controls to turn off the screen saver, adjust the speaker volume, or display an alternate desktop background when the Presentation Settings feature is activated.
3. Click **OK** to save your settings.

In addition to the settings in the dialog box, activating the Presentation Settings feature prevents the computer from displaying system notification messages or going to sleep. To activate the Presentation Settings feature, use one of the following procedures:

- Open the Presentation Settings dialog box, select the *I am currently giving a presentation* checkbox, and click **OK**.
- Open Windows Mobility Center and in the Presentation Settings tile, click **Turn on**.

Configuring Power Options

Windows 8 enables you to fine-tune the power consumption of a mobile computer by configuring individual components to operate at lower power levels.

CERTIFICATION READY
Configure power policies
Objective 5.2

Power conservation is a critical issue for portable computer users who rely on batteries, particularly when using the computer for a presentation or other business critical function. Running out of power in the middle of a demonstration could be disastrous, so it is important for users to be aware of the computer's power level and its power consumption.

To conserve battery power as much as possible, virtually all portable devices made today include the hardware and firmware elements needed to dynamically adjust the power consumption of individual components. Some computer components, such as processors and LCD panels, can operate at various power levels, while other devices can be shut down completely when not in use. Windows 8 includes extensive controls called power plans that enable you to create power usage profiles for a portable computer and assign different profiles depending on whether the computer is plugged in to an AC power source or running on batteries.

MONITORING BATTERY POWER

By default, the Windows 8 desktop contains a power icon in the notification area on the right side of the Taskbar. When you click that icon, the system displays a tile like that in Figure 19-9, which contains the following:

- An icon indicating whether the computer is currently using AC or battery power
- When running on battery power, the percentage of the battery charge remaining and the amount of time left until the battery is drained
- The power plan currently in use and options to select an alternative power plan
- Links to the Power Options control panel

Figure 19-9
The *Power* tile in the notification area

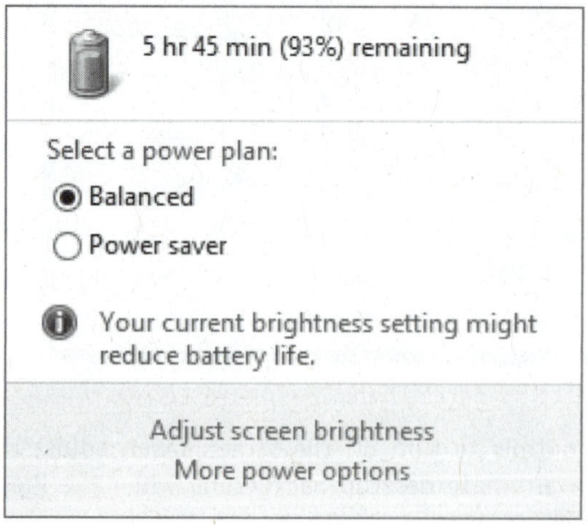

You can also right-click the icon to open the Windows Mobility Center or the Power Options control panel.

WORKING WITH POWER PLANS

Power management is the process of balancing conservation versus performance. Windows 8 includes extensive power management capabilities, including support for the Advanced Configuration and Power Interface (ACPI) and the ability to configure power settings in three ways, using graphical control panel settings, Group Policy, or the command prompt.

TAKE NOTE*

The Power Options control panel does not display the High Performance plan by default. You must click the *Show additional plans* down arrow for it to appear.

The Power Options control panel is the primary interactive power configuration interface. From this control panel you can select the power plan that the computer should use; modify the settings for the default power plans; and create new, custom power plans of your own.

A power plan is a combination of power management settings that provides a balance between power consumption and system performance. Windows 8 includes three default power plans: Balanced (recommended), Power saver, and High performance, as shown in Figure 19-10.

Figure 19-10

The *Power Options* control panel

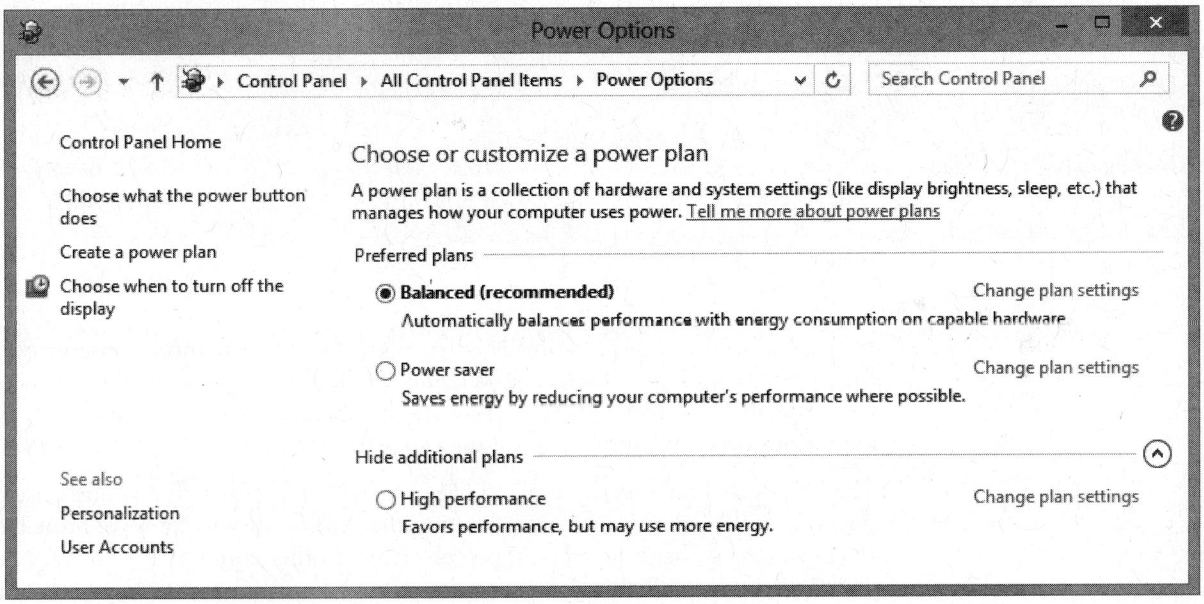

To select one of the default power plans, you can use any of the following procedures.

- Open the Windows Mobility Center and, in the Battery Status tile, select one of the plans from the dropdown list.
- Open the Control Panel and click or tap **Hardware and Sound** > **Power Options**, and select the radio button for the desired plan.
- Click the power icon in the notification area, and then select one of the plans from the menu that appears.

On portable systems, each power plan consists of two sets of settings, one for when the computer is plugged into an AC power source and one for when the computer is running on battery power. Table 19-1 lists some of the primary settings for each of the power plans.

Table 19-1

Default Power Plan Settings

Power Setting	Power Saver	Balanced	High Performance
Wireless adapter power saving mode	Maximum Power Saving (battery) Maximum Performance (AC)	Medium Power Saving (battery) Maximum Performance (AC)	Maximum Performance (battery) Maximum Performance (AC)
Dim the display	1 minutes (battery) 2 minutes (AC)	2 minutes (battery) 5 minutes (AC)	5 minutes (battery) 10 minutes (AC)
Turn off the display	2 minutes (battery) 5 minutes (AC)	5 minutes (battery) 10 minutes (AC)	10 minutes (battery) 15 minutes (AC)
Put the computer to sleep	10 minutes (battery) 15 minutes (AC)	45 minutes (battery) Never (AC)	Never (battery) Never (AC)
Adjust plan brightness	40% (battery) 100% (AC)	50% (battery) 100% (AC)	100% (battery) 100% (AC)
Turn off hard disk	5 minutes (battery) 20 minutes (AC)	10 minutes (battery) 20 minutes (AC)	20 minutes (battery) 20 minutes (AC)
Minimum processor state	5% (battery) 5% (AC)	5% (battery) 5% (AC)	5% (battery) 100% (AC)
System cooling policy	Passive (battery) Passive (AC)	Passive (battery) Active (AC)	Active (battery) Active (AC)
Maximum processor state	100% (battery) 100% (AC)	70% (battery) 100% (AC)	100% (battery) 100% (AC)

As you can see from the data in the table, all of the plans are more conservative when the computer is running on battery power, and the differences between the plan settings are incremental. There is, however, no way for the operating system to know exactly what effect the various power settings will have on a specific computer.

The LCD panel on a laptop with a large, widescreen display will obviously use more power than one with a smaller display, so turning the display off will conserve more battery power. In the same way, hard disk drives, processors, and other components can vary greatly in their power consumption levels. It is up to the user to determine what effect each of the power plans has on a specific computer.

Using the Power Options control panel, you can modify any of the individual settings in a power plan, or you can create a new power plan of your own. To create a custom power plan, use the following procedure:

CREATE A CUSTOM POWER PLAN

GET READY. Log on to Windows 8 using an account with administrative privileges and then perform the following steps:

1. Open the Control Panel and then click or tap **Hardware and Sound > Power Options**.

   The *Power Options* control panel appears.

2. Click **Create a Power Plan**.

   The *Create a Power Plan* wizard appears, as shown in Figure 19-11.

Figure 19-11

The *Create a Power Plan* wizard

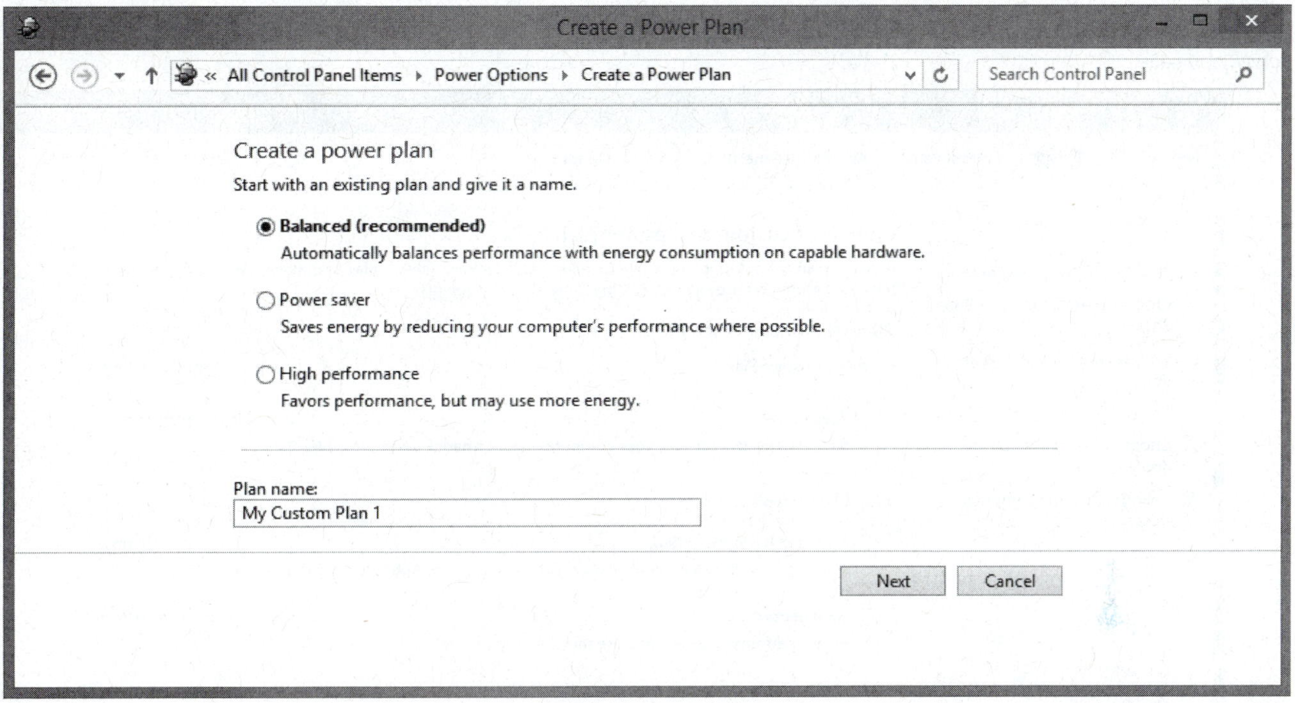

3. Select the radio button for the default power plan that will be the basis for your new plan.
4. Type a name for your power plan in the *Plan name* text box and then click **Next**.

   The *Change settings for the plan* page appears, as shown in Figure 19-12.

Figure 19-12

The *Change settings for the plan* page

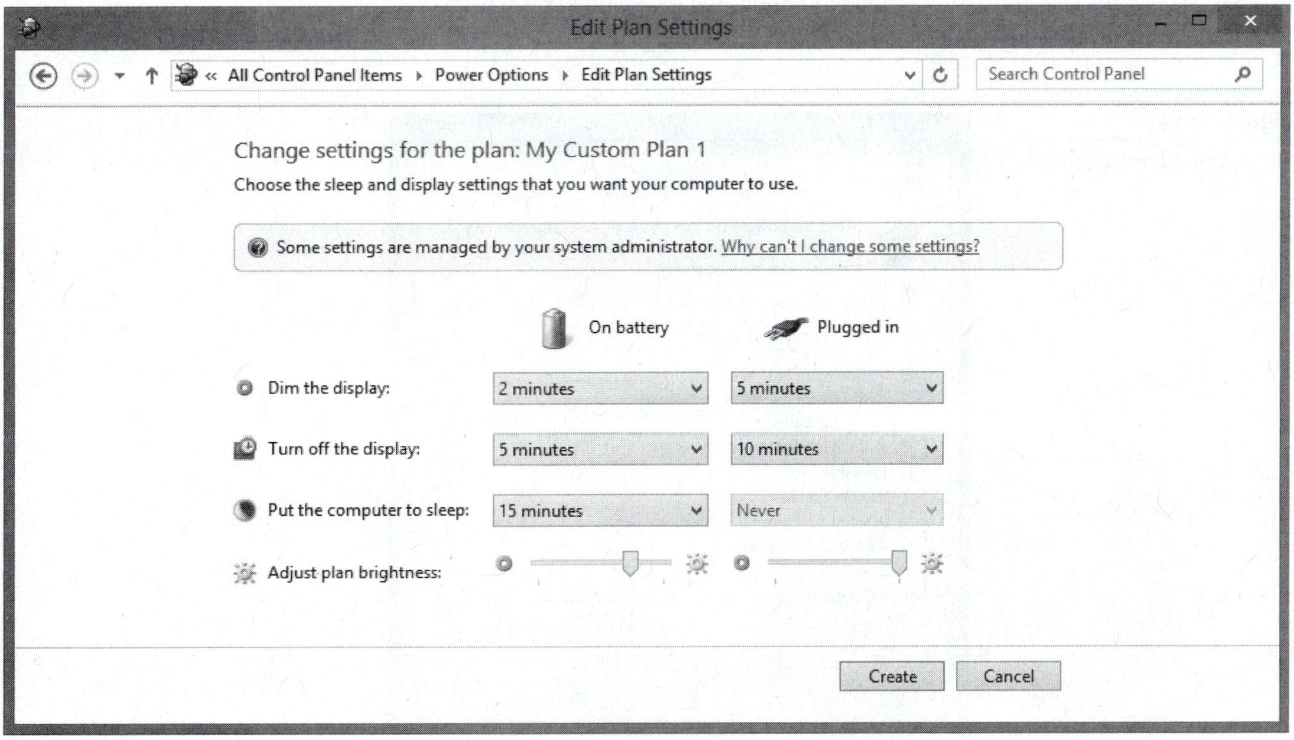

5. Modify the display and sleep settings as desired for the *On battery* and *Plugged in* power states and then click **Create**.

   The *Choose or customize a power plan* page appears, with the new plan you created listed as one of the options, as shown in Figure 19-13.

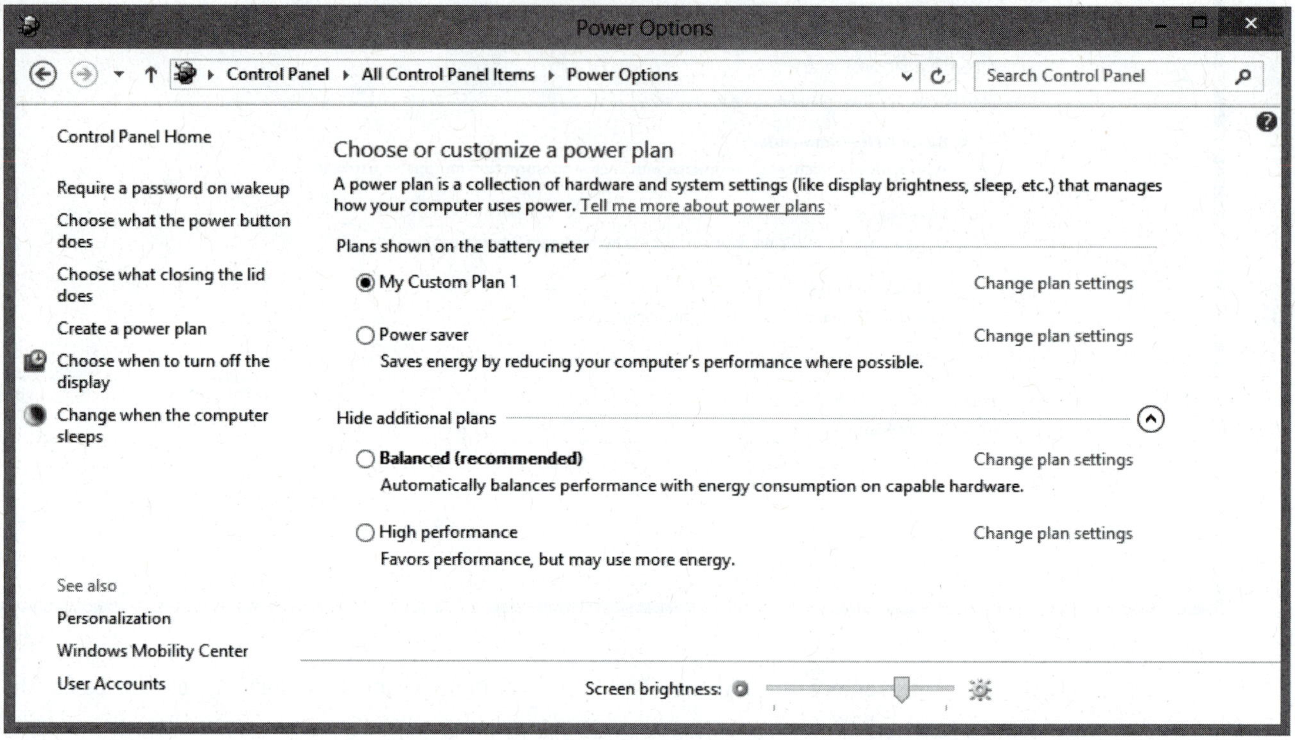

Figure 19-13

The *Choose or customize a power plan* page

6. Click the **Change plan settings** link for the plan you created.

   The *Change settings for the plan* page appears again.

7. Click **Change advanced power settings**.

   The *Advanced settings* page appears, as shown in Figure 19-14.

Figure 19-14

The *Advanced settings* page

8. Modify any of the settings as desired and then click **OK**.
9. Click **Save Changes** to close the *Change settings for the plan* page.

CONFIGURING POWER POLICIES

It is also possible for administrators to configure workstation power options using Group Policy. The Computer Configuration\Policies\Administrative Templates\System\Power Management container in every GPO, as shown in Figure 19-15, contains settings that duplicate all of the controls in the Power Options control panel.

Figure 19-15

Power Management settings in a GPO

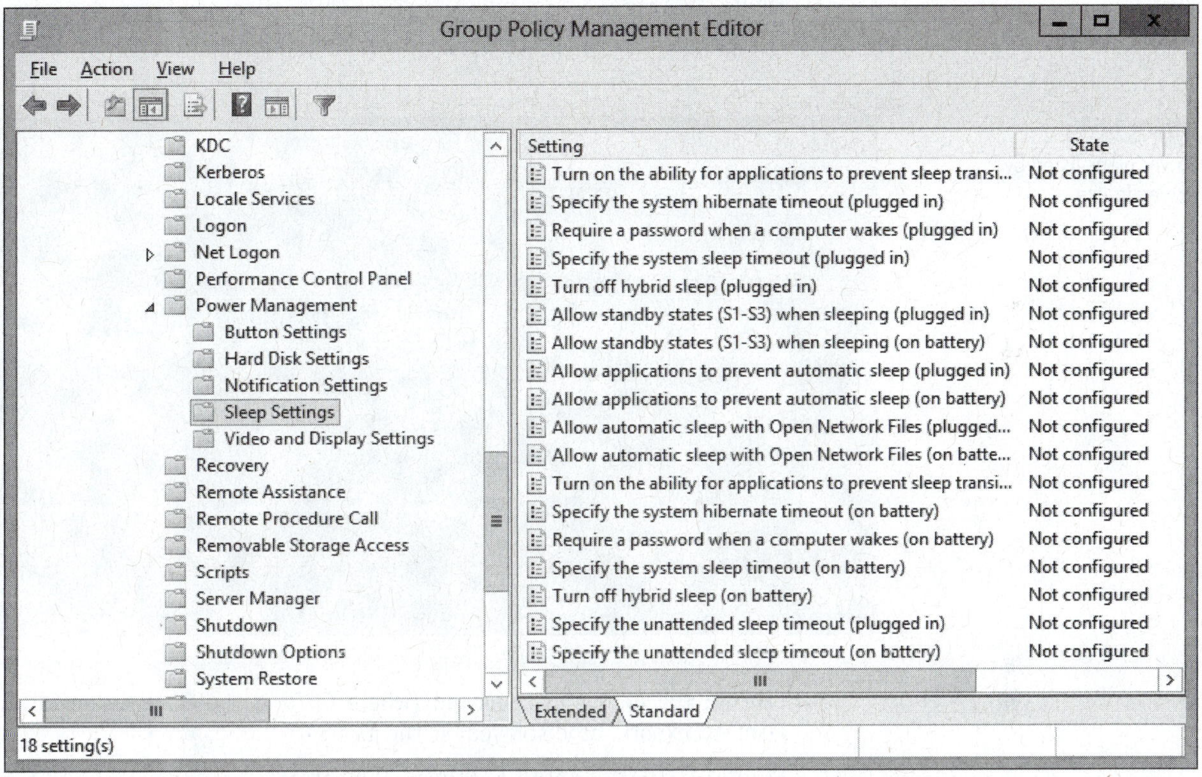

There are a few Power Management settings in Group Policy that you cannot configure through the Control Panel. In the Sleep Settings container, the following six settings appear:

- Allow applications to prevent automatic sleep (plugged in)
- Allow applications to prevent automatic sleep (on battery)
- Allow automatic sleep with Open Network Files (plugged in)
- Allow automatic sleep with Open Network Files (on battery)
- Turn on the ability for applications to prevent sleep transition (plugged in)
- Turn on the ability for applications to prevent sleep transition (on battery)

These settings enable you to control whether a workstation can go to sleep when applications are active or network files open.

USING POWERCFG.EXE

Powercfg.exe is the command line program for the Windows 8 power management system. As the most comprehensive power management interface, Powercfg.exe can configure settings that are not available from the Control Panel or in Group Policy.

One of the most valuable capabilities of Powercfg.exe is the ability to export entire power management plans to a file, and then import them on another computer.

To export a power plan, use the following procedure.

EXPORT A POWER PLAN

GET READY. Log on to Windows 8 using an account with administrative privileges and then perform the following steps:

1. Open a Command Prompt window with administrative privileges.
2. In the Command Prompt window, execute the **powercfg.exe –list** command (see Figure 19-16).

   The program displays the power plans on the computer.

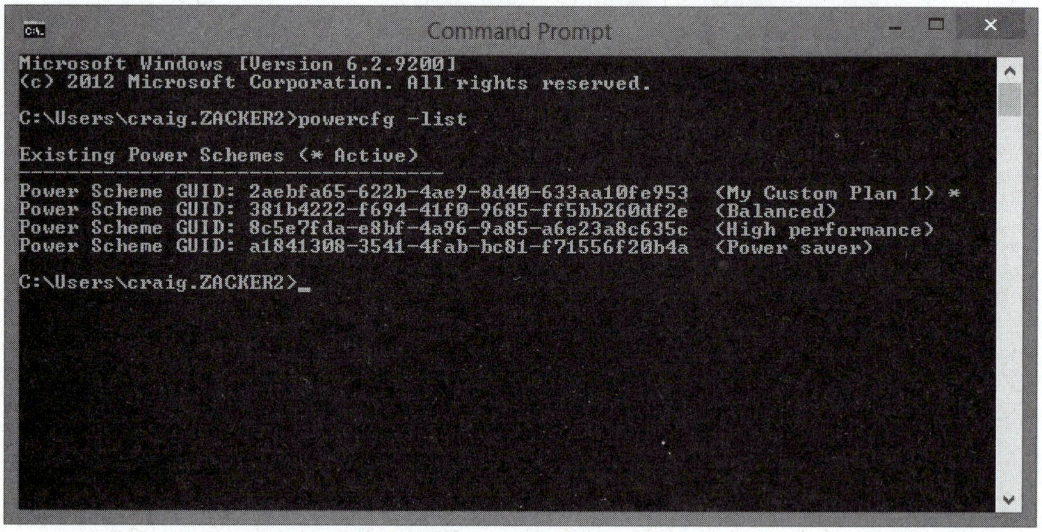

Figure 19-16
Power plans listed by Powercfg.exe

3. Execute the following command (where *GUID* is the GUID value for the plan you want to export, as displayed in the list):

   `powercfg.exe -export power.pow GUID`
4. **Close** the *Command Prompt* window.

After transferring the file to another computer, you can import it using the following command.
`powercfg.exe -import power.pow`

Synchronizing Data

Mobile devices enable users to take their data with them wherever they go, but this creates a version control problem.

Mobile computer users often connect to a network when they are in the office, and then take their computers with them when they go home or travel on business. Once the computer disconnects from the network, however, access to the network drives and the files they contain is interrupted. Fortunately, Windows 8 includes the ability to store copies of network files on the local drive for use when the computer is disconnected. This feature is called Offline Files. Windows 8 also makes it possible to maintain copies of files on handheld devices, such as smartphones and PDAs running Windows Phone.

The key to this offline files capability is the synchronization process that occurs when the computer or other device reconnects to the network. Simply copying the files to the mobile device is not enough. Users would have to remember to copy their revised documents back to the network drive after reconnecting. Synchronization is a process in which Windows 8 compares the offline version of a file with the network version, and makes sure that the most recent revisions are present in both places.

Windows 8 supports two types of synchronization, as follows:

- **One-way synchronization** – Data moves in one direction only, from the source to the destination. The system replicates any changes users make to the source files to the destination, but changes to the destination files are not replicated to the source. This is recommended for scenarios such as synchronizing music files on a computer with a portable music player.
- **Two-way synchronization** – Data moves in both directions. Changes users make to either copy of the files are replicated to the other system. In the event that both copies have changed, the system prompts the user to resolve the conflict by selecting one of the two versions. This is recommended for scenarios such as copying network-based document files to a mobile system for offline use.

The following sections describe the tools and procedures you can use to ensure that mobile computers synchronize their data reliably.

USING OFFLINE FILES

CERTIFICATION READY
Configure offline file policies
Objective 5.2

Offline Files is a form of fault tolerance that individual users can employ to maintain access to their server files, even in the event of a network service failure. Windows 8 workstations copy server-based folders that users designate for offline use to the local drive, and the users work with the copies, which remain accessible whether the computer is connected to the network or not.

If the network connection fails, or the user disconnects a portable computer, access to the offline files continues uninterrupted. When the computer reconnects to the network, a synchronization procedure occurs that replicates the files between server and workstation in whichever direction is necessary. If there is a version conflict, such as when users have modified both copies of a file, the system prompts the user to specify which copy to retain.

To synchronize a Windows 8 computer with a network folder you simply browse to the folder using File Explorer, right-click the folder name, and select Always Available Offline from the context menu. Windows 8 then establishes the partnership and copies the contents of the selected folder to the local hard drive.

Although it is an effective fault tolerance mechanism, primary control of offline files rests with the user, which makes it a less suitable solution for an enterprise network than other measures, such as File Redirection.

Configuring Share Caching

Administrators can configure shares to prevent users from saving offline copies. When you create a share using the Advanced Sharing dialog box, clicking Caching opens the Offline Settings dialog box, as shown in Figure 19-17. Here you can specify which files and programs users are permitted to select for storage in the Offline Files cache.

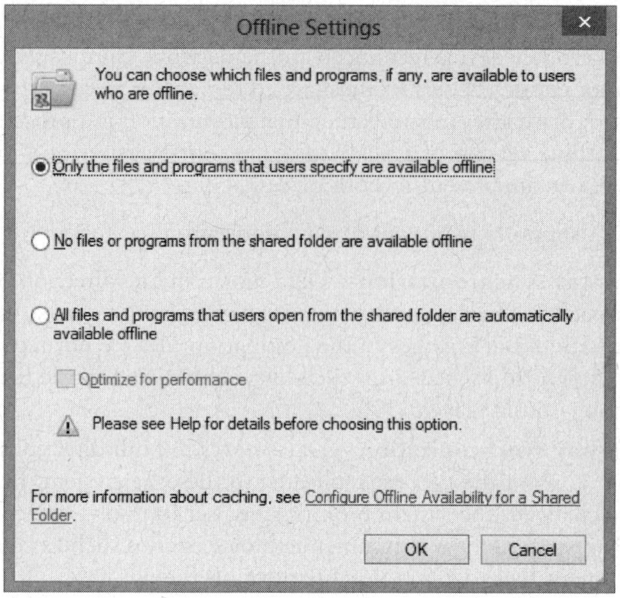

Figure 19-17

The *Offline Settings* dialog box

Configuring Offline File Policies

Administrators can use Group Policy to configure Offline Files behavior on Windows 8 workstations. The Computer Configuration\Policies\Administrative Templates\Network\Offline Files container in every Group Policy object (GPO) has 28 policy settings, as shown in Figure 19-18.

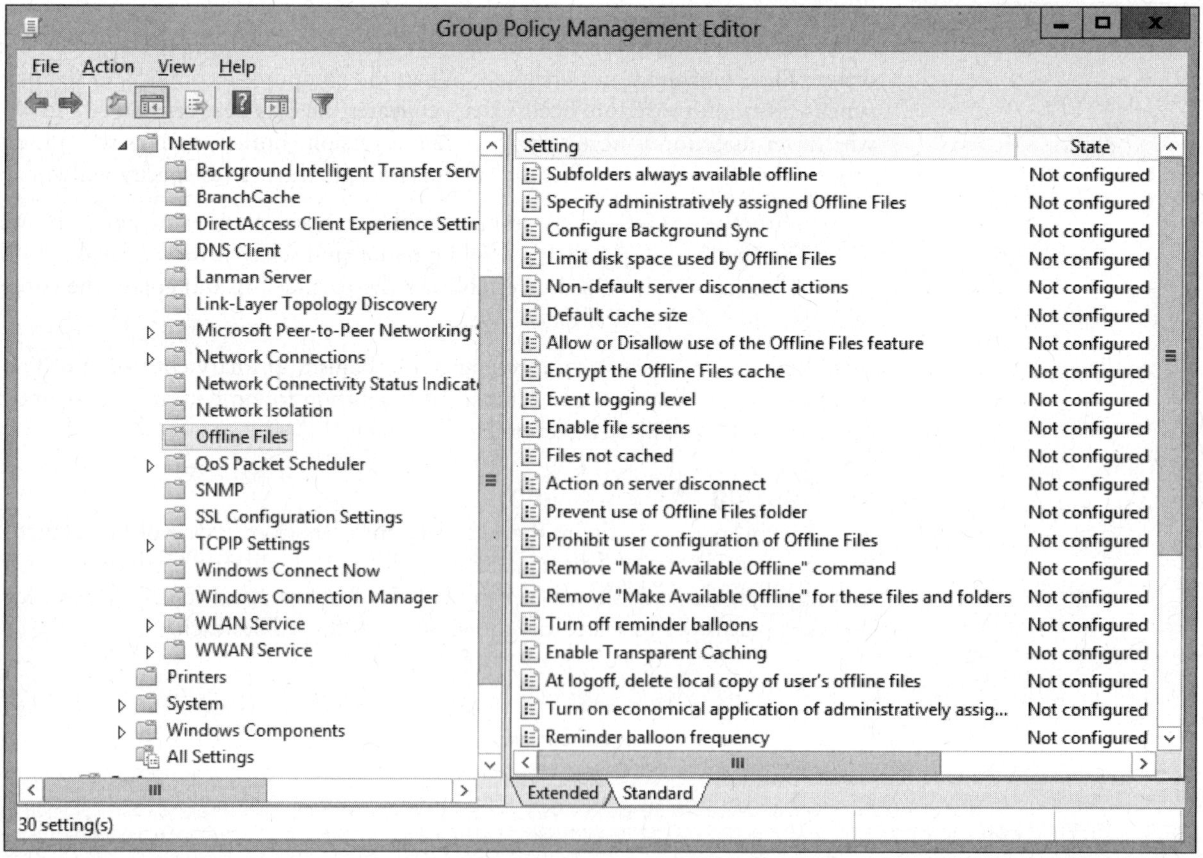

Figure 19-18

The *Offline Files* Group Policy settings

Using these settings, administrators can control whether workstations are permitted to use offline files, how much disk space to allocate to the offline files cache, whether to encrypt the contents of the cache, and when synchronization events should occur.

Using Transparent Caching

The Enable Transparent Caching policy setting, shown in Figure 19-19, causes Windows 8 to save copies of files users access from remote servers on a local drive, whether or not the files are configured as offline files. Unlike offline files, the cached files do not remain available when the computer is disconnected from the network, but they do provide the users with faster repeat access, while conserving network bandwidth.

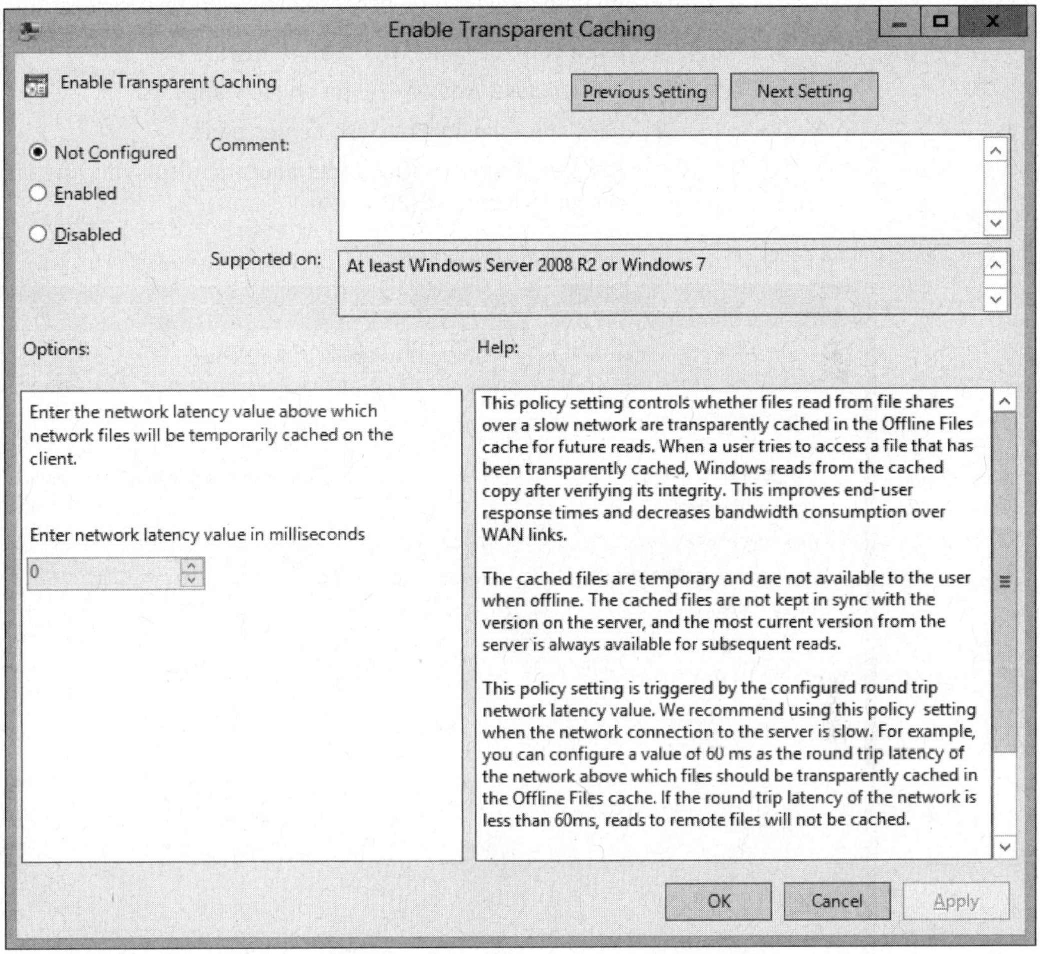

Figure 19-19

The *Enable Transparent Caching* policy setting

Transparent caching is functionally similar to the BranchCache feature discussed in Lesson 18, "Configuring Remote Connections," except that each Windows 8 workstation has exclusive use of its own cache; it does not share the cached files with other clients.

Windows 8 decides whether to cache a file based on the network latency value for the connection between the workstation and the server. Transparent caching is designed primarily for clients and servers connected by relatively slow wide area network (WAN) connections. The network latency value is the round time transmission time between the client and the server. The default value for the policy setting is 32,000 milliseconds, or 32 seconds.

USING SYNC CENTER

Sync Center is an application that functions as a central control panel for all of a Windows 8 computer's synchronization partnerships, including those with network drives and mobile

CERTIFICATION READY
Configure sync options
Objective 5.2

devices. Sync partnerships are pairs of folders or devices that are configured to synchronize their data on a regular basis. You can use Sync Center to establish synchronization partnerships, schedule synchronizations, monitor synchronization events, and manage synchronization conflicts.

Once you have established the partnership, you can configure its synchronization schedule. To configure a sync partnership, use the following procedure.

CONFIGURE A SYNC PARTNERSHIP

GET READY. Log on to Windows 8 using an account with administrative privileges, create a sync partnership with a folder on a network drive, and then perform the following steps:

1. Open **Control Panel** and click **Hardware and Sound > Windows Mobility Center**.

   The *Windows Mobility Center* window appears.

2. Click the icon in the *Sync Center* pane.

   The *Sync Center* control panel appears, displaying the *View sync partnerships* page, as shown in Figure 19-20.

Figure 19-20

The *Sync Center* control panel

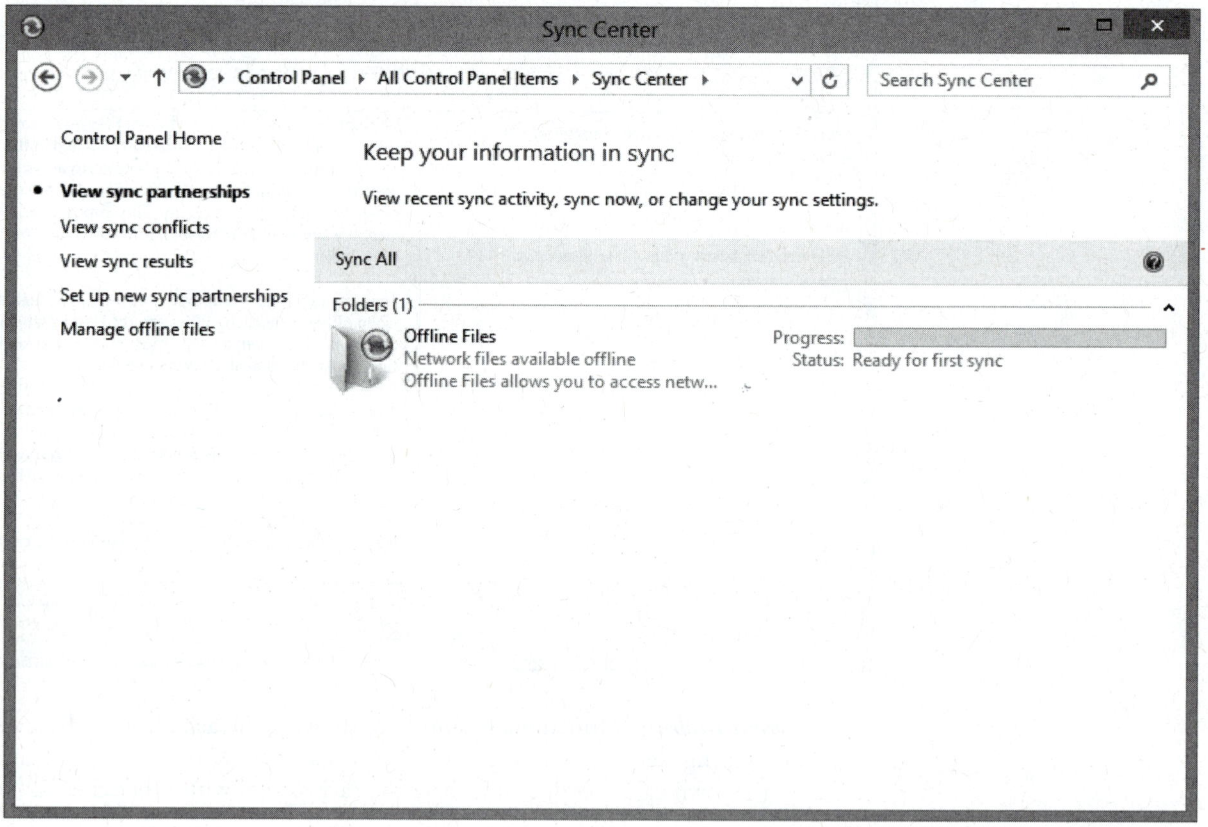

3. Select the **Offline Files** partnership and then click **Schedule**.

   The *Offline Files Sync Schedule* wizard appears, displaying the *Which items do you want to sync on this schedule?* page, as shown in Figure 19-21.

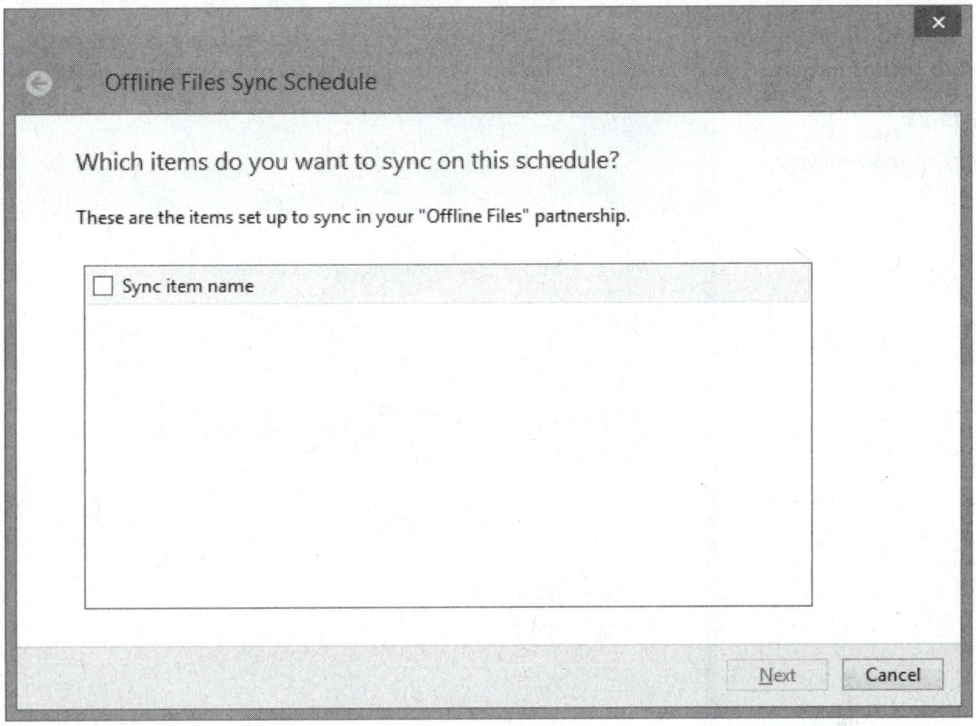

Figure 19-21

The *Which items do you want to sync on this schedule?* page

4. Select the network folder whose synchronization you want to schedule and then click **Next**.

   The *When do you want this sync to begin?* page appears, as shown in Figure 19-22.

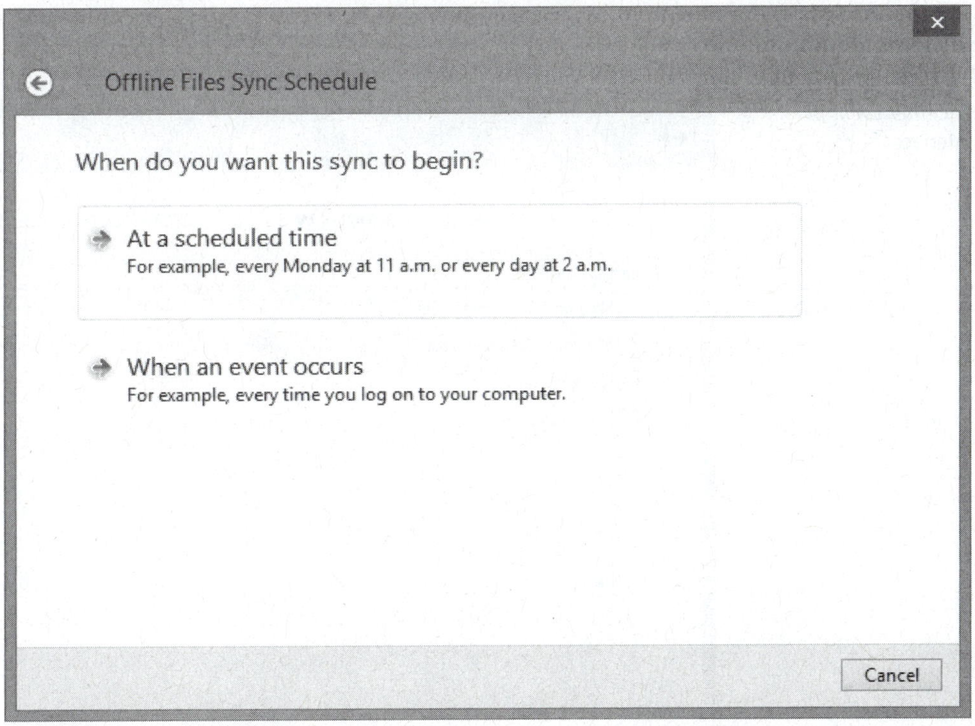

Figure 19-22

The *When do you want this sync to begin?* page

5. Select one of the following options, configure its properties, and then click **Next**.
   - **At a scheduled time** – Using the interface shown in Figure 19-23, specify a date and time for the synchronization and a repeat interval. You can also click

More Options to specify conditions under which the scheduled synchronization should or should not occur.

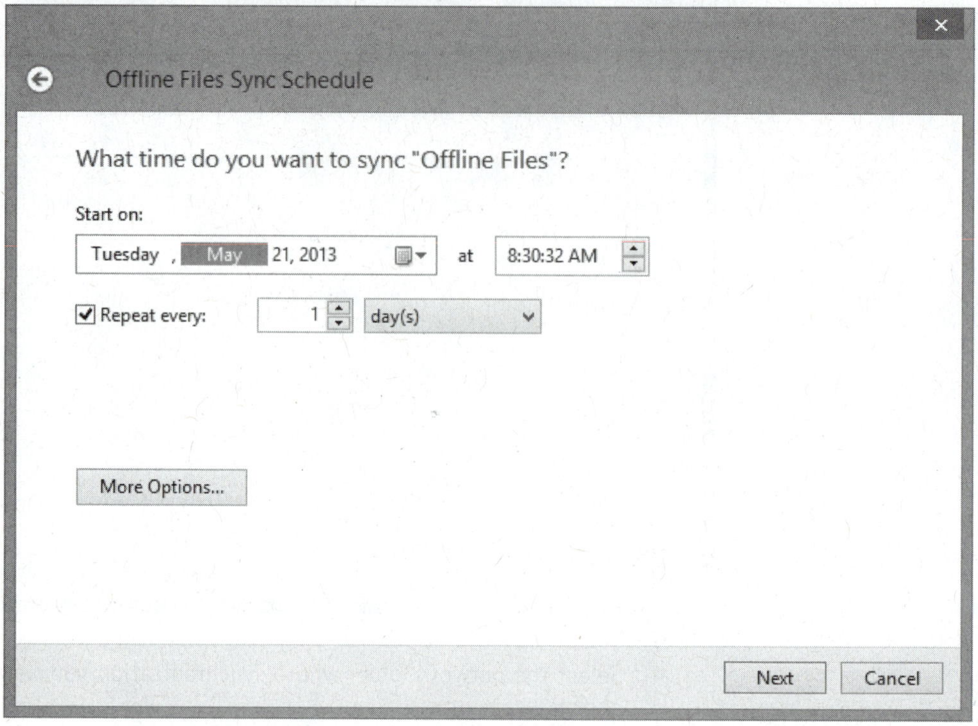

Figure 19-23

The *Sync Center Scheduled time* interface

- **When an event occurs** – Using the interface shown in Figure 19-24, select an event or action that you want to trigger a synchronization, such as logging on to Windows or when the system has been idle for specified amount of time.

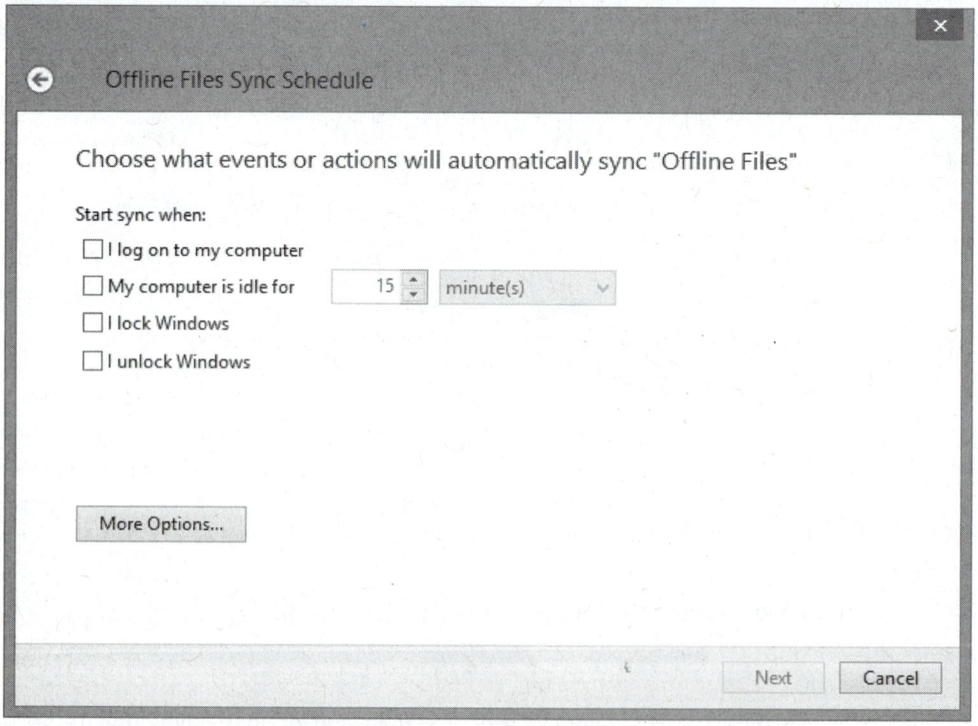

Figure 19-24

The *Sync Center Event or Action* interface

6. Specify a name for the schedule and then click **Save Schedule**.

CONFIGURING SYNC OPTIONS

The Offline Files and Sync Center features have been part of Windows for several versions, but Windows 8 introduces a new option: the ability to sync settings across -multiple Windows 8 systems.

When you specify a Microsoft account during the initial Windows 8 operating system setup, you are able to store your computer settings with the account on the Internet. These settings can include colors, backgrounds, desktop configuration, ease of access and language preferences, application settings, browser favorites, and even passwords. When you log on from another computer running Windows 8 using the same Microsoft account, you can download the settings you stored, effectively syncing your environment among multiple computers.

To control what settings the system should sync, open the Charms bar, click **Settings**, and then click **Change PC Settings**. On the PC Settings screen, click **Sync your settings**, as shown in Figure 19-25. From this page, you can toggle the sync function and select the individual settings that you want to sync to your Microsoft account.

Figure 19-25

The *Sync your settings* screen

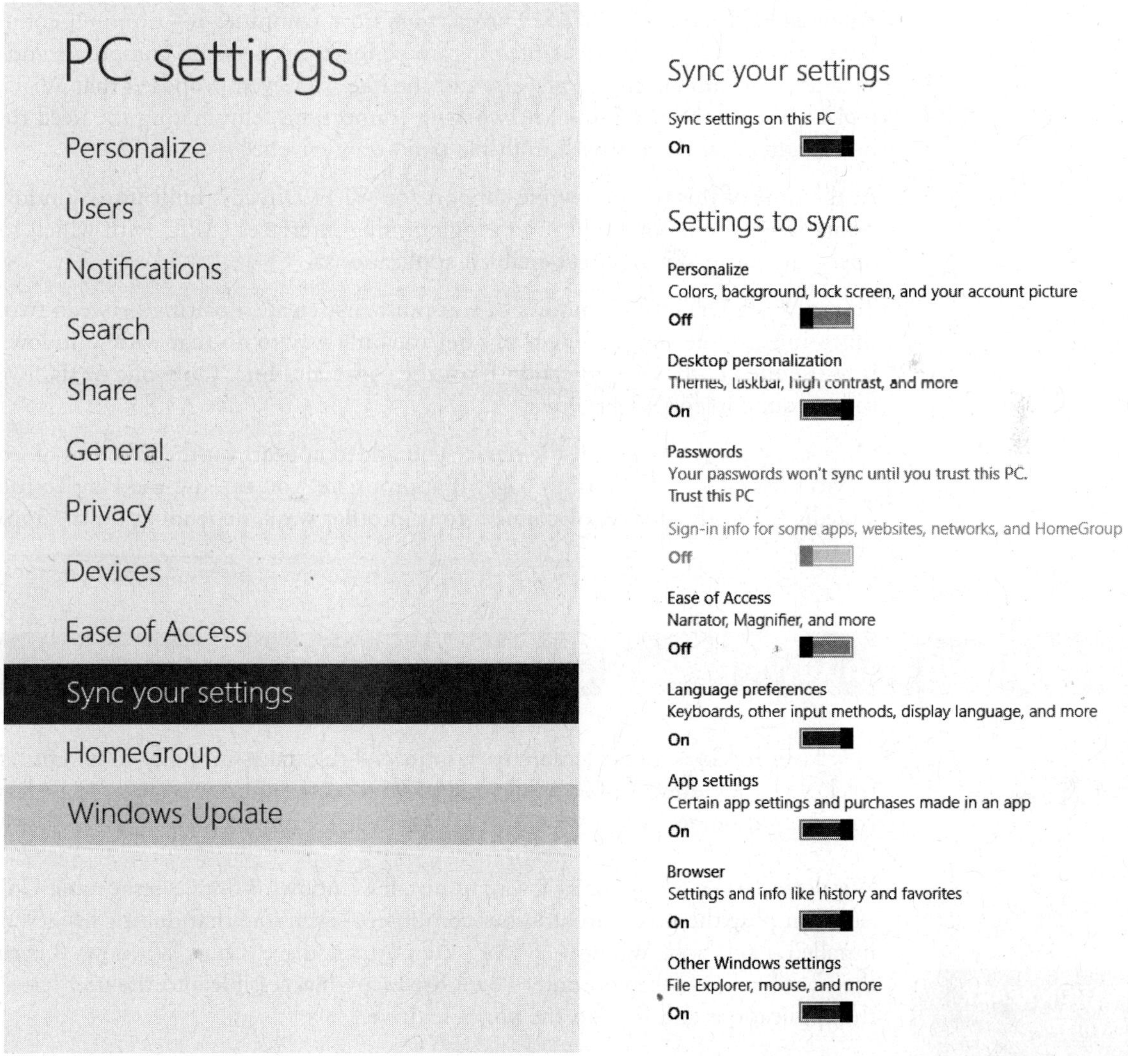

Before Windows 8 will actually sync your settings, you must designate the computer as trusted by responding to an email message that the computer sends to your Microsoft account. This confirms that you are in control both of the computer and the account.

Using Wi-Fi Direct

THE BOTTOM LINE

Wireless networking based on the IEEE 802.11 standards supports two communications modes: ad hoc and infrastructure.

CERTIFICATION READY
Configure Wi-Fi Direct
Objective 5.2

Most Wi-Fi networks are based on the infrastructure model, in which the wireless devices all connect to a central access point, which enables them to communicate with each other. Many of the broadband routers intended for the home and small business markets include a Wi-Fi access point, which provides network access to all wireless devices within proximity of the router.

An ad hoc wireless network, by contrast, consists of only two devices, which connect directly to each other, without the need for an intermediate access point. ***Wi-Fi Direct*** is a new Microsoft implementation of ad hoc wireless networking, which enables a computer running Windows 8 to establish a connection to another wireless device.

Potential applications for Wi-Fi Direct range from computer-to-computer connections, for file transfers and even media streaming, to connections between computers and other devices, such as smartphones, music players, and the like. It is even proposed that Wi-Fi Direct could replace Bluetooth for personal networking connections, eliminating the need to equip computers and other devices with multiple radio transceivers.

At the time of this writing, while support for Wi-Fi Direct is built into Windows 8, it exists primarily as a series of application programming interfaces (APIs) with which software developers can create Wi-Fi Direct-enabled applications.

To use Wi-Fi Direct in Windows 8, you must first create a pairing between two devices, much in the same way as Bluetooth, but the only way to do that with Windows 8 native tools is to use the Netsh.exe application from the command line. Only one of the two devices has to have support for Wi-Fi Direct.

Once the devices are paired, the device you added appears on the Windows 8 computer in the Devices list on the PC Settings page. If appropriate, you can use the Play To function to push a media file to the device, or connect to it in other ways, depending on the application you are using.

Configuring Windows To Go

THE BOTTOM LINE

Windows To Go is a new feature in Windows 8 that takes mobility to an entirely new level. With Windows To Go, you can take your workstation with you, while leaving your computer at home.

Windows To Go is essentially a way to install Windows 8 onto a removable USB drive. You can then plug the drive into another computer – even one that doesn't have Windows 8 installed – and boot Windows 8 from the portable drive. Once Windows 8 is running from the portable drive, the computer's own drives are inaccessible and the user has access to all of the applications and files on the portable drive.

CERTIFICATION READY
Configure Windows To Go
Objective 5.2

For more information on how to configure Windows To Go, see Lesson 2, "Installing Windows 8.".

SKILL SUMMARY

IN THIS LESSON, YOU LEARNED:

- Windows Mobility Center is a shell application that provides a central point of access for many of the configuration settings that mobile computer users need frequently.
- Most laptop computers have the capability to connect an external display device, making it possible for a group of users to view the desktop without having to crowd around a single screen.
- To conserve battery power as much as possible, virtually all laptops include the hardware and firmware elements needed to dynamically adjust the power consumption of individual components.
- Windows 8 includes a dialog box that bundles together the configuration settings that users most often adjust before giving a presentation and make it possible to activate all of the settings with a single switch.
- Windows 8 includes the ability to store copies of network files on the local drive, for use when the computer is disconnected.
- Sync Center is an application that functions as a central control panel for all of a Windows 8 computer's synchronization partnerships, including those with network drives and mobile devices.

Knowledge Assessment

Multiple Choice

Select one or more correct answers for each of the following questions.

1. Which of the following Second Screen settings must you select to create a display on two monitors using a different resolution for each one?
   a. PC screen only
   b. Duplicate
   c. Extend
   d. Second screen only

2. Which of the following tools can you use to import and export power management plans in Windows 8?
   a. Powercfg.exe and Group Policy
   b. The Power Options control panel only
   c. Powercg.exe only
   d. The Power Options control panel and Group Policy

3. Transparent caching saves temporary copies of files based on which of the following criteria?
   a. Number of requests for the file
   b. User time limits
   c. File size
   d. Network roundtrip latency

4. Which of the following Windows 8 utilities can you use to create a Wi-Fi Direct device pair?
   a. Nslookup.exe
   b. Netsh.exe
   c. Net.exe
   d. Netstat.exe

5. Which of the following commands will display the power profiles on a computer running Windows 8, along with their GUIDs?
   a. `powercfg.exe`
   b. `powercfg.exe -GUID`
   c. `powercfg.exe -list`
   d. `powercfg.exe -profile`

6. Which of the following settings is affected by default when you turn on the Windows 8 Presentation Settings option?
   a. Screen saver
   b. Volume
   c. Sleep
   d. Background

7. Which of the following tasks must you complete before you can sync your passwords and settings with other computers running Windows 8? (Choose all that apply.)
   a. Create a local user account.
   b. Log on using a Microsoft account.
   c. Join an Active Directory Domain Services domain.
   d. Verify that your computer is trusted.

8. The Windows 8 Mobility Center Window is divided into as many as eight tiles. Which tile would be accessed to configure settings that control attempts to put the computer to sleep?
   a. Sync Center
   b. Screen Orientation
   c. Presentation Settings
   d. External Display

9. Which of the following are ways that you can use to configure how Windows 8 works with multiple displays? Select all that apply.
   a. Windows Mobility Center > Display Tile > click the disconnect Display button.
   b. Open the Display control panel and click Adjust resolution
   c. Windows Mobility Center > Sync Center
   d. Windows Mobility Center > Screen Orientation

10. Wi-Fi Direct is a new Microsoft implementation for what type of wireless networking?
   a. Infrastructure model wireless networks
   b. Ad hoc wireless networks
   c. Workgroup-based networks
   d. Domain-based networks

Best Answer

Choose the letter that corresponds to the best answer. More than one answer choice may achieve the goal. Select the BEST answer.

1. Several new Windows 8 mobile computers have been purchased. Unfortunately, there is no way for the operating system to know exactly what effect the default power settings will have on a specific computer. What is the best approach to use to ensure you maintain a balance between power consumption and system performance on these new systems?
   a. Select the Power Saver Power Plan.
   b. Select the Balanced Power Plan.
   c. Select the High Performance Power Plan.
   d. Test each of the default Power Plans and then create a custom plan to meet your specific needs.

2. Which of the following is the best approach to use when connecting a new Windows 8 mobile computer to a network projector while avoiding problems with the Windows Firewall?
   a. Install the software that comes with the network projector and configure your Windows 8 Firewall settings manually.
   b. Install the Connect to a Network Projector Wizard feature and disable your Windows Firewall.
   c. Install the Connect to a Network Projector Wizard feature and let it determine the appropriate exceptions for the Windows Firewall.
   d. Install the Connect to a Network Projector Wizard feature.

3. Of the following tools, which provides you with the most comprehensive power management interface for configuring power policies?
   a. Control Panel
   b. Group Policy
   c. Windows Mobility Center
   d. Powercfg.exe

4. The company would like to provide users with access to their files while using their mobile devices. They want to conserve bandwidth and provide users with faster repeat access to the files while still allowing them to access the files when disconnected from the network. Which technology best fits this need?
   a. Transparent caching combined with offline files and two-way synchronization
   b. Share caching
   c. Transparent caching combined with offline files
   d. Share caching with offline files

5. The company wants to implement Windows 8 features that will support users who copy network-based document files to a mobile system. These features should ensure that if two users are working on the same file offline, when they reconnect, they have the option of resolving the conflict between the two versions. Which of the following features would best support that goal?
   a. Offline files with two-way synchronization
   b. Offline files with one-way synchronization
   c. Transparent caching, offline files and one-way synchronization
   d. Transparent caching, offline files and two-way synchronization

Matching and Identification

Complete the following exercise by matching the terms with their corresponding definitions.

_______ a) Windows Mobility Center
_______ b) Offline files
_______ c) Sync Center
_______ d) Wi-Fi Direct
_______ e) Transparent caching
_______ f) One-way synchronization
_______ g) Two-way synchronization
_______ h) Infrastructure model
_______ i) Ad hoc wireless networking
_______ j) Windows To Go

1. Designed for clients connected by relatively slow WAN connections.
2. Data moves from source to destination only.
3. A shell application that provides central point of access for mobile configuration settings.
4. Wireless devices connection to a central access point.
5. Allows you to install Windows 8 on a removable USB drive.
6. Allows users to access server files even in the event of network service failure.

7. Changes users make to either copy of a file is replicated to the other system. Data moves in both directions.
8. Microsoft implementation of ad hoc wireless networking.
9. Consists of only two wireless devices that connect directly to each other.
10. Functions as a central control panel for synchronization partnerships.

Build a List

1. In order of first to last, specify the correct order of steps to create a custom Power Plan.
   ________ Click **Create a power plan**.
   ________ Type a name for your power plan in the *Plan name* text box and then click **Next**.
   ________ Select the radio button for the default power plan that will be the basis for your new plan.
   ________ Click **Change advanced power settings**,
   ________ Click the **Change plan settings** link for the plan you created.
   ________ Modify the display and sleep settings as desired for the *On battery* and *Plugged in* power states and then click **Create**.
   ________ Modify any of the settings as desired and then click **OK**.
   ________ Click **Save Changes** to close the *Change settings for the plan* page.
   ________ Open the **Control Panel** and then click or tap **Hardware and Sound > Power Options**.
2. Specify the correct order of steps to configure a sync partnership.
   ________ Select the network folder whose synchronization you want to schedule and then click **Next**.
   ________ Open **Control Panel** and click **Hardware and Sound > Windows Mobility Center**.
   ________ Click the icon in the Sync Center pane**.** The *Sync Center* control panel appears, displaying the *View sync partnerships* page
   ________ Select the **Offline Files** partnership and then click **Schedule**.
   ________ Select one of the following options, configure its properties, and (**at a scheduled time or when an event occurs**, then click **Next**
   ________ Specify a name for the schedule and then click **Save Schedule**.
3. Specify the correct order of steps to export a Power Plan.
   ________ **Close** the *Command Prompt* window.
   ________ In the Command Prompt window, execute the **powercfg.exe –list** command.
   ________ Open a Command Prompt window with administrative privileges**.**
   ________ Execute the following command (where *GUID* is the GUID value for the plan you want to export, as displayed in the list **powercfg.exe -export power.pow** GUID.

■ Business Case Scenarios

Scenario 19-1: Troubleshooting Network Projectors

A new network projector has recently been added to the company's network. A Windows 8 computer was connected to the network projector last week and several training presentations were given successfully. For some reason, another Windows 8 computer that is being used for training presentations this week cannot access the projector. What could be causing the problem?

Scenario 19-2: Configuring Multiple Displays

A user connected a second display to their mobile computer. The current display was then mirrored on the secondary device. The user would like to extend their current display instead of mirroring it. Can this be accomplished? If so, explain how it would be done.

Configuring Security for Mobile Devices

LESSON 20

70-687 EXAM OBJECTIVE

Objective 5.3 – Configure security for mobile devices. This objective may include but is not limited to configure BitLocker and BitLocker To Go policies; configure startup key storage; configure remote wipe; and configure location settings (GPS).

Lesson Heading	Exam Objective
Securing Your Mobile Devices	
Configuring BitLocker	Configure BitLocker and BitLocker To Go policies
Understanding BitLocker Requirements	Configure Startup key storage
Enabling BitLocker on Operating System Drives	
Configuring BitLocker To Go	Configure BitLocker and BitLocker To Go
Using Data Recovery Agents	
Configuring Remote Wipe	Configure Remote Wipe
Using Windows Intune to Perform Remote Wipes	
Managing Location Settings	Configure Location Settings (GPS)
Using Windows Location Provider (WLP)	
Using Personally Identifiable Information (PII)	

KEY TERMS

Active Directory Certificate Services (ADCS)
BitLocker Drive Encryption
BitLocker To Go
certificates
certification authorities
Data Recovery Agent (DRA)
Encrypting File System (EFS)
Exchange ActiveSync
hardware-based encryption
location settings
Network Unlock
New Technology File System (NTFS)
Personal Identification Number (PIN)
Personally Identifiable Information (PII)
recovery key
remote wipe
Secure Digital (SD) cards
software-based encryption
startup key
Trusted Platform Module (TPM)
Windows Location Provider (WLP)

Securing Your Mobile Devices

THE BOTTOM LINE

As more employees use mobile devices to get their work done, administrators will need to ensure they have the technology and security in place to protect against the lost/theft of those devices while at the same time protecting against the accidental release of Personally Identifiable Information (PII) through location-aware apps.

With an increasing number of employees bringing their smartphones, tablets, and laptop devices into corporate network environments, balancing access with protection is critical for today's network administrators. Rather than focusing on banning the devices, you should educate users on how to keep their mobile devices secure, set security policies, and make sure you have the technology in place to manage them. There are a variety of threats to mobile devices. These include theft, loss, intercepting the wireless communications, and malicious software to name just a few.

In this lesson, you learn about the features in Windows 8 that can be used to prevent the loss of sensitive information when a computer/device is lost or stolen, policies that can be configured to protect your system, and how to keep your computer's boot environment safe from modification. You also learn how to configure Windows 8 to control whether or not you want to reveal your location to Windows Apps.

Configuring BitLocker

BitLocker Drive Encryption is designed to protect the sensitive data stored on your hard drives even in situations where they are stolen and moved to another computer.

Encrypting File System (EFS) enables users to protect specific files and folders, so that no one else can access them. ***BitLocker Drive Encryption***, on the other hand, is a feature available in Windows 8 Professional, Windows 8 Enterprise, and in all editions of Windows Server 2012. It makes it possible to protect files by encrypting an entire volume or drive.

BitLocker Drive Encryption is designed to protect against brute force attacks to gain access to the drive or situations where someone tries to install and access the drive from another computer. This feature can be used to further enhance security by checking the integrity of boot files when a ***Trusted Platform Module (TPM)*** chip is available on your system. The TPM is a dedicated cryptographic processor chip that the system uses to store the BitLocker encryption keys.

CERTIFICATION READY
Configure BitLocker and BitLocker To Go policies
Objective 5.3

Although Windows 7 required you to configure BitLocker after the operating system was installed, Windows 8 supports the ability to enable BitLocker before you deploy the operating system. It also introduces two new options for encrypting your disk:

- **Encrypt used disk space only** – This option encrypts only the part of your drive that currently has data stored on it.
- **Encrypt the entire drive** – This option encrypts the full volume and offers more security. It encrypts areas of the disk that contain data that has been deleted but may still be retrievable from the drive.

You can configure Group Policy to specify the type of encryption option you want to use on each type of drive: fixed data drives, operating system drives, and removable data drives. If you do not configure and link a Group Policy Object (GPO), users will be able to choose the encryption type they want to use after BitLocker is enabled on their drive.

In Windows 8, you must be a member of the administrators group to configure BitLocker, but non-administrative users can change the BitLocker ***Personal Identification Number (PIN)*** or password for the operating system and fixed data volumes by default. The PIN is any 4–20 digit number you choose that is stored on your computer and must be entered each time you start the system. Although this can reduce help desk calls, you should consider either disabling this option through Group Policy or configure a policy that forces users to create complex passwords that are not easily guessed.

BitLocker supports manufacturer drives that provide ***hardware-based encryption*** capabilities. Although ***software-based encryption*** relies on the computer's resources and processor to encrypt data, hardware-based encryption uses its own dedicated processor that is located on the encrypted drive.

Windows Server 2012 includes a new BitLocker feature called ***Network Unlock***. This feature automatically unlocks an operating system volume at reboot if the computer is connected to a domain. Prior to the introduction of this feature, users needed to enter their PIN. For administrators, Network Unlock allows them to perform unattended installations and software upgrades without visiting each machine and unlocking it after a reboot.

Unlike EFS, BitLocker is not designed to protect files for specific users, so that other users cannot access them. Instead, BitLocker protects entire volumes and drives from being compromised by unauthorized persons. For example, if someone alters the server's boot components after stealing the hard drive and installing it into another computer, BitLocker will lock the protected volumes, preventing access. When the system boots successfully under normal conditions, the BitLocker volumes are accessible to anyone.

BitLocker is not designed to replace EFS or NTFS permissions. You must still protect your files and folders using these standard Windows 8 tools. Instead of being a replacement, consider BitLocker an additional layer of security and protection for your Windows 8 and Windows Server 2012 systems.

Understanding BitLocker Requirements

To use BitLocker, you need to understand how startup and recovery keys are used and what to do if you lose them.

The first time you enable BitLocker on a drive, you create a ***startup key***. The startup key is used to encrypt/decrypt the drive. It can be stored on a USB drive or on a TPM chip. If the key is stored on a USB drive, you must insert the drive each time you start the computer and then enter the key.

If the startup key is stored on a TPM chip that has a system BIOS that is compatible with its use, the key is automatically retrieved for you during startup.

TAKE NOTE*

The TPM chip enables BitLocker to enhance security by checking the validity of not only the encrypted volume, but your boot files, boot manager, and operating system files to make sure they have not been tampered with while the operating system was offline.

CERTIFICATION READY
Configure startup key storage
Objective 5.3

An alternative to the startup key is to use a PIN. The startup key or PIN can be changed through the BitLocker Drive Encryption control panel application after BitLocker is enabled. You can also make additional copies of the startup key to use in case the original is lost.

If you lose the startup key, move the drive to another system, or the system is compromised, you will need to use a ***recovery key*** to gain access to the drive. The recovery key is a 48-digit number that can be stored on a USB drive, a folder on another drive, or be printed out. If the recovery key is saved to a USB drive, it will also include a machine-readable version that can be read by just inserting the drive; otherwise, you need to type in the number to recover the system.

TAKE NOTE*

You can determine whether you have a TPM chip by pressing the *Windows logo key* + *R* and typing `tpm.msc`. This opens the Trusted Platform Module (TPM) console on a Windows 8 computer. If the TPM chip does not appear in the console, you should also check to make sure it is enabled through the computer's BIOS.

BitLocker has five authentication methods to choose from during startup to provide additional protection for your encrypted data. These methods, in descending order from most to least secure, are as follows:

- **TPM + startup PIN + startup key** – The system stores the BitLocker volume encryption key on the TPM chip, but an administrator must supply a PIN and insert a USB flash drive containing a startup key before the system can unlock the BitLocker volume and complete the system boot sequence.
- **TPM + startup key** – The system stores the BitLocker volume encryption key on the TPM chip, but an administrator must insert a USB flash drive containing a startup key before the system can unlock the BitLocker volume and complete the system boot sequence.
- **TPM + startup PIN** – The system stores the BitLocker volume encryption key on the TPM chip, but an administrator must supply a PIN before the system can unlock the BitLocker volume and complete the system boot sequence.
- **Startup key only** – The BitLocker configuration process stores a startup key on a USB flash drive, which the administrator must insert each time the system boots. This mode does not require the server to have a TPM chip, but it must have a system BIOS that supports access to the USB flash drive before the operating system loads.
- **TPM only** – The system stores the BitLocker volume encryption key on the TPM chip, and accesses it automatically when the chip has determined that the boot environment is unmodified. This unlocks the protected volume and the computer continues to boot. No administrative interaction is required during the system boot sequence.

Enabling BitLocker on Operating System Drives

Enabling BitLocker to protect your operating system drive requires that your system meet certain requirements.

When you encrypt the drive where the Windows operating system is installed, BitLocker must store the startup key on a separate piece of hardware. The key can be stored on a TPM version 1.2 (or later) microchip or on a removable USB flash drive.

When you start a computer with a TPM that has BitLocker enabled, the TPM will check the operating system to make sure it has not been tampered with while the operating system was offline. If it detects any tampering with the boot files or drive, it will lock the system partition until a recovery key is entered to unlock it.

To support BitLocker Drive Encryption on the drive that contains your operating system, you need the following:

- **Two partitions** – BitLocker holds files needed to start your computer on one partition. This is called the *system partition* and needs to be a minimum of 100 MB in size. This partition is not encrypted. The second partition, encrypted by BitLocker, holds the operating system. This allows BitLocker to protect the operating system and the information in the encrypted drive and to perform its pre-startup authentication steps and verify system integrity.

- ***New Technology File System (NTFS)*** – The partitions must be formatted with NTFS to support the BitLocker feature. NTFS is a file system used to store and retrieve files on hard disks. It also provides improvements over older file systems (FAT, FAT32) in the areas of security and performance.
- **TPM Compatible BIOS** – Your BIOS must be compatible with TPM version 1.2 or 2.0; otherwise, the BIOS firmware must be able to read from a USB drive that contains the startup key on boot to enable BitLocker on an operating system drive. BitLocker needs the startup key from either the TPM or the USB flash drive before it can unlock the protected drive. If a USB drive is used on a non-TPM system, BitLocker will not be able to verify the integrity of the system.

If you attempt to enable BitLocker using the BitLocker Drive Encryption control panel for your operating system drive on a computer that does not have a compatible TPM, you will receive a message that states, "This device can't use a Trusted Platform Module." When this happens, you need to configure the *Allow BitLocker without a compatible TPM* option in the *Require additional authentication at startup* policy for operating system volumes before you can enable BitLocker.

To configure this policy for a single computer, use the Local Group Policy editor (gpedit.msc) from the Windows 8 machine. To apply this policy across your domain, use the Group Policy Management console (gpmc.msc).

Using the Group Policy Management console, you find the *Require additional authentication at startup* setting in the following location (see Figure 20-1):

Computer Configuration > Policies > Administrative Templates > Windows Components > BitLocker Drive Encryption > Operating System Drives

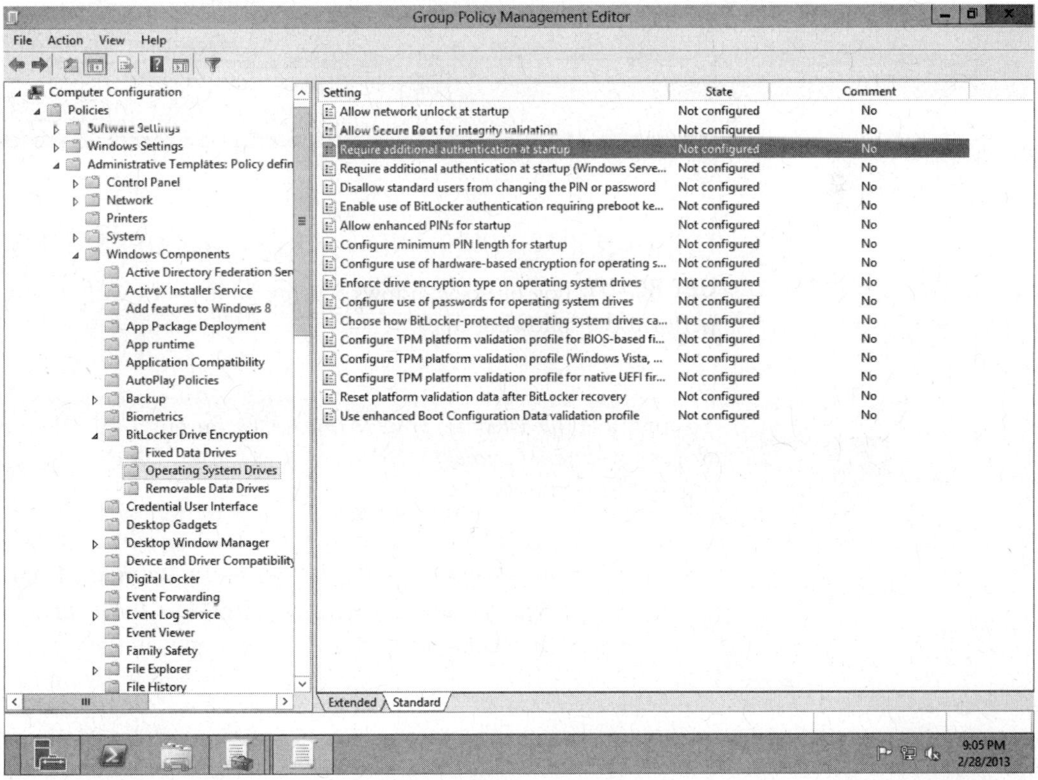

Figure 20-1

Selecting the *Require additional authentication at startup* Group Policy setting

From there, select *Allow BitLocker without a compatible TPM*, as shown in Figure 20-2.

Figure 20-2

Configuring BitLocker to run a startup key and a startup PIN

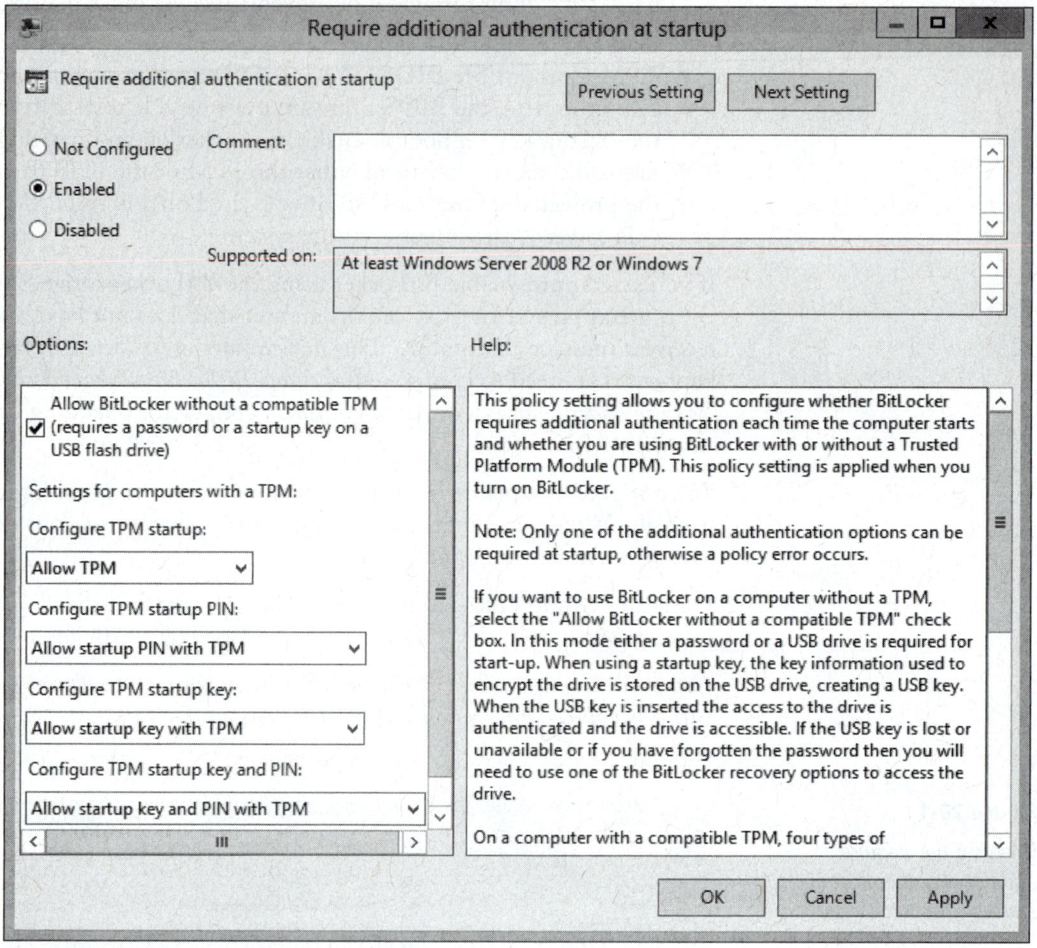

TURN ON BITLOCKER AND ENCRYPT THE OPERATING SYSTEM DRIVE

GET READY. Log on to Windows 8 using an account with administrative privileges and then perform the following steps:

TAKE NOTE*

To complete this exercise, your Windows 8 computer must be on a domain where the *Require additional authentication at startup* Group Policy option has been configured as discussed previously.

1. Select the **Windows logo key + R**. In the *Run* dialog box, type **control**.
2. Select **System and Security > BitLocker Drive Encryption**. The BitLocker Drive Encryption control panel application appears, as shown in Figure 20-3.

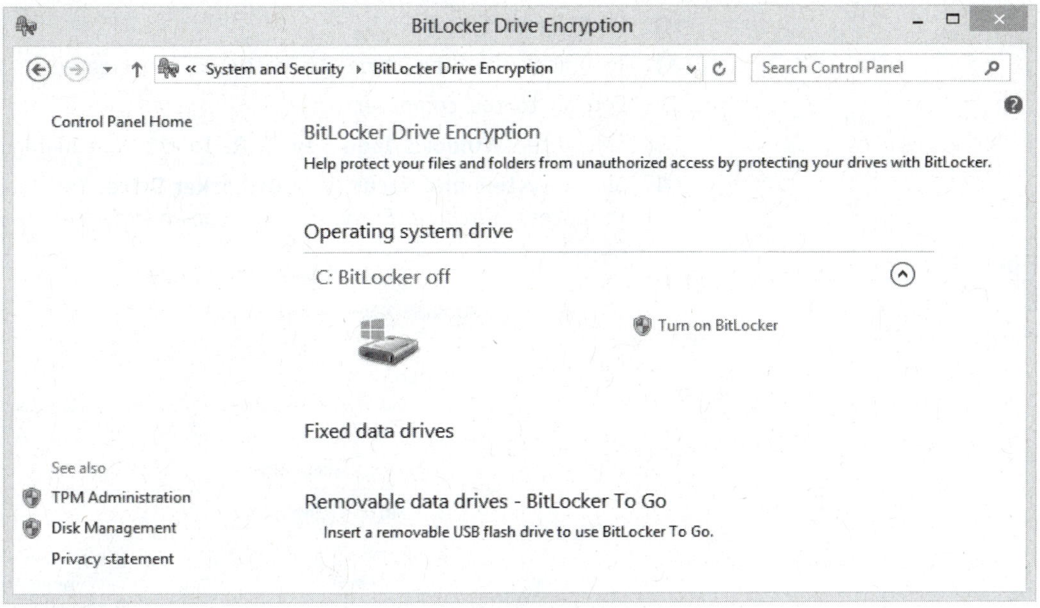

Figure 20-3

Reviewing the BitLocker Drive Encryption control panel

TAKE NOTE*

While performing step 6, you should save the key in additional locations such as a folder on another computer or print out the key to have it in more than one location before you click **Next.**

3. For the drive that contains your operating system, click **Turn on BitLocker**.
4. When prompted to choose how you will unlock your drive at startup, click **Enter a password**.
5. Type a password, reenter it to confirm it, and then click **Next** to continue.
6. When prompted to back up your recovery key, click **Save to a USB flash drive**.
7. Insert your USB device, select it from the list provided, and then click **Save**.
8. After saving your recovery key, click **Next**.
9. Make sure the **Run BitLocker system check** is selected and then click **Continue** (see Figure 20-4).

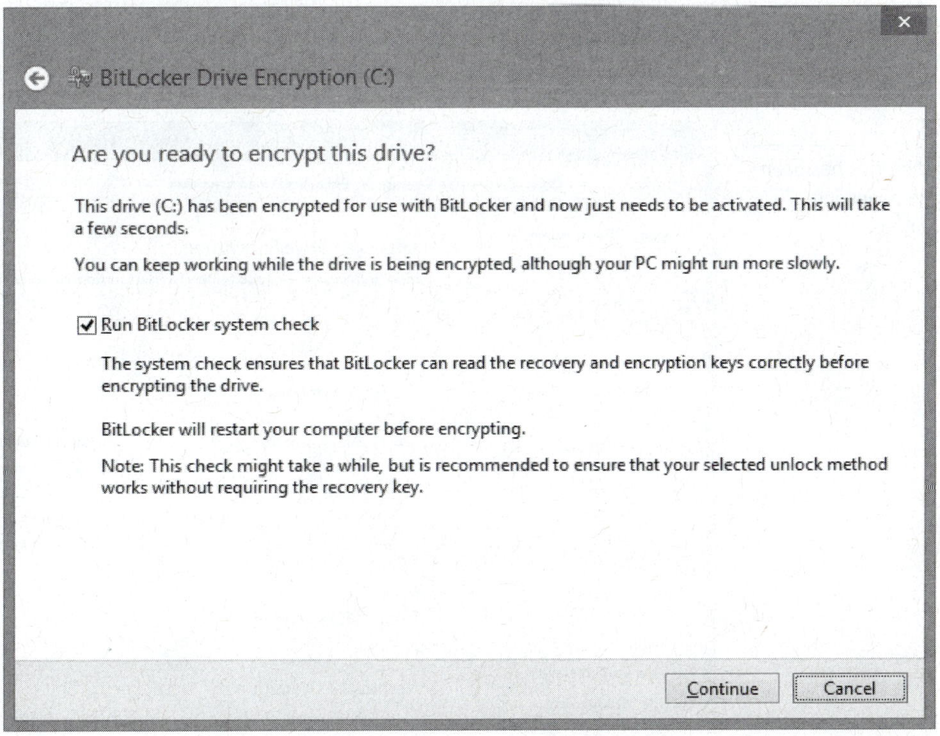

Figure 20-4

Confirming Run BitLocker system check is enabled

10. Click **Restart Now**.
11. To unlock the drive, type the password you created in step 4 and then press **Enter**.
12. Log on to the computer.
13. Select the **Windows logo key + R**. In the *Run* dialog box, type **control**.
14. Select **System and Security > BitLocker Drive**. You should now see the encryption is in process (*BitLocker Encrypting*), as shown in Figure 20-5.

Figure 20-5

Reviewing the status of the encryption process

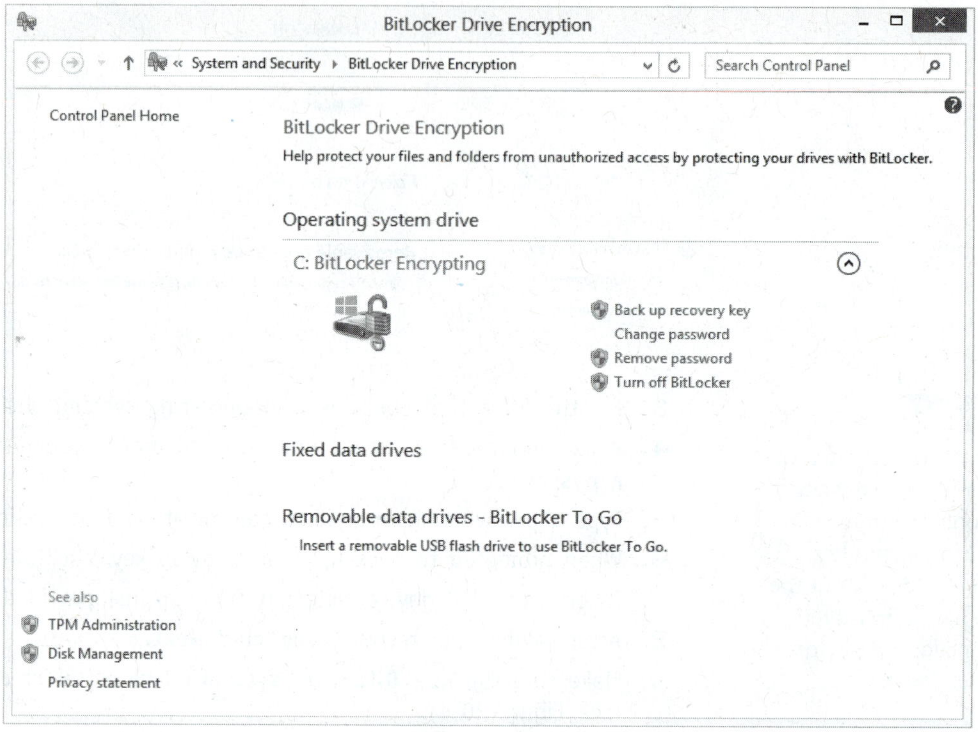

Once the encryption process is complete, the status will change to BitLocker on, and you will see additional options appear in the control panel (see Figure 20-6).

Figure 20-6

Confirming the drive has been encrypted and reviewing additional options

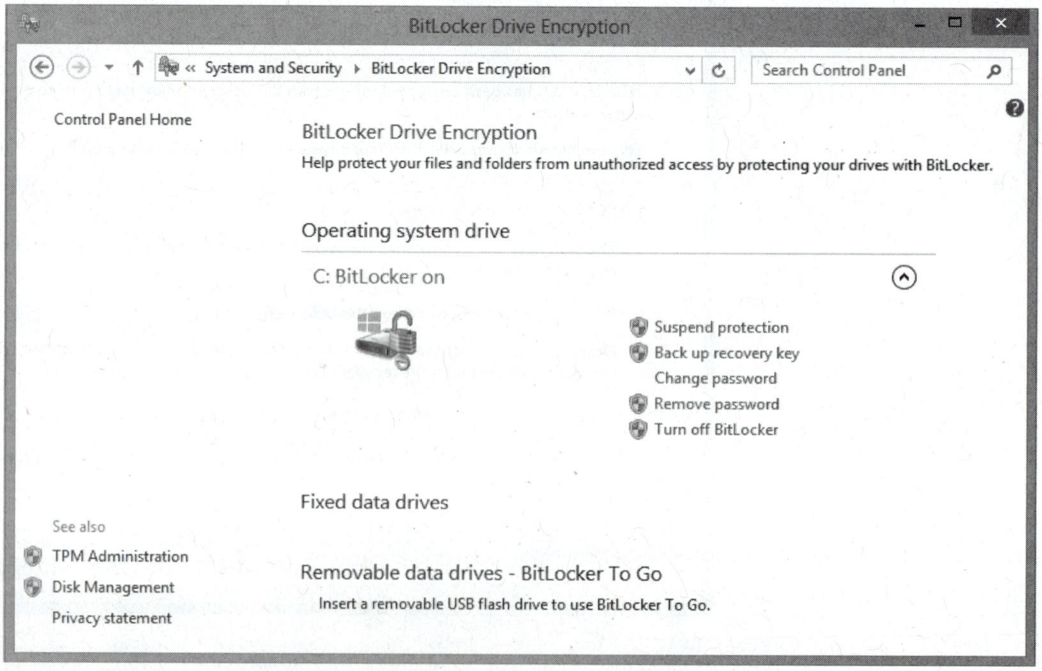

These options are as follows:

- **Suspend protection** – Use this option if you want to temporarily suspend BitLocker. This allows you to install new software, update your PC's firmware, hardware, or operating system. After the system is rebooted, BitLocker automatically re-enables itself on the drive.
- **Back up recovery key** – This option allows you to save your recovery key to a USB flash drive, save to a file, or print out the key.
- **Change password** – This option allows you to change the startup password after confirming your old password.
- **Remove password** – If you select this option, you will be prompted to add another unlocking method before removing the current option.
- **Turn off BitLocker** – This option turns off BitLocker on the drive.

Configuring BitLocker To Go

BitLocker To Go is a feature in Windows 8 that allows you to take advantage of BitLocker Encryption to protect your removable USB devices (flash drives and external hard disks).

BitLocker To Go is BitLocker Drive Encryption on removable data drives. This includes ***Secure Digital (SD) cards***, USB flash drives, and external hard disk drives. These drives can be formatted with NTFS, FAT16, FAT32, or exFAT file systems. SD cards are nonvolatile memory cards used in mobile phones, digital cameras, and tablet computers (e.g., Microsoft's Surface RT).

CERTIFICATION READY
Configure BitLocker and BitLocker To Go policies
Objective 5.3

Once encrypted, you need to use a password or a smart card with PIN to unlock the drive. If needed, an administrator can configure the drive to be automatically unlocked on a computer for a specific user.

BitLocker To Go enables you to use the encrypted device on other computers without performing an involved recovery process. Because the system is not using the removable drive as a boot device, a TPM chip is not required.

To use BitLocker To Go, insert the removable drive and open the BitLocker Drive Encryption control panel application. The device appears in the interface, with a *Turn on BitLocker* link (see Figure 20-7) just like that of the computer's hard disk drive.

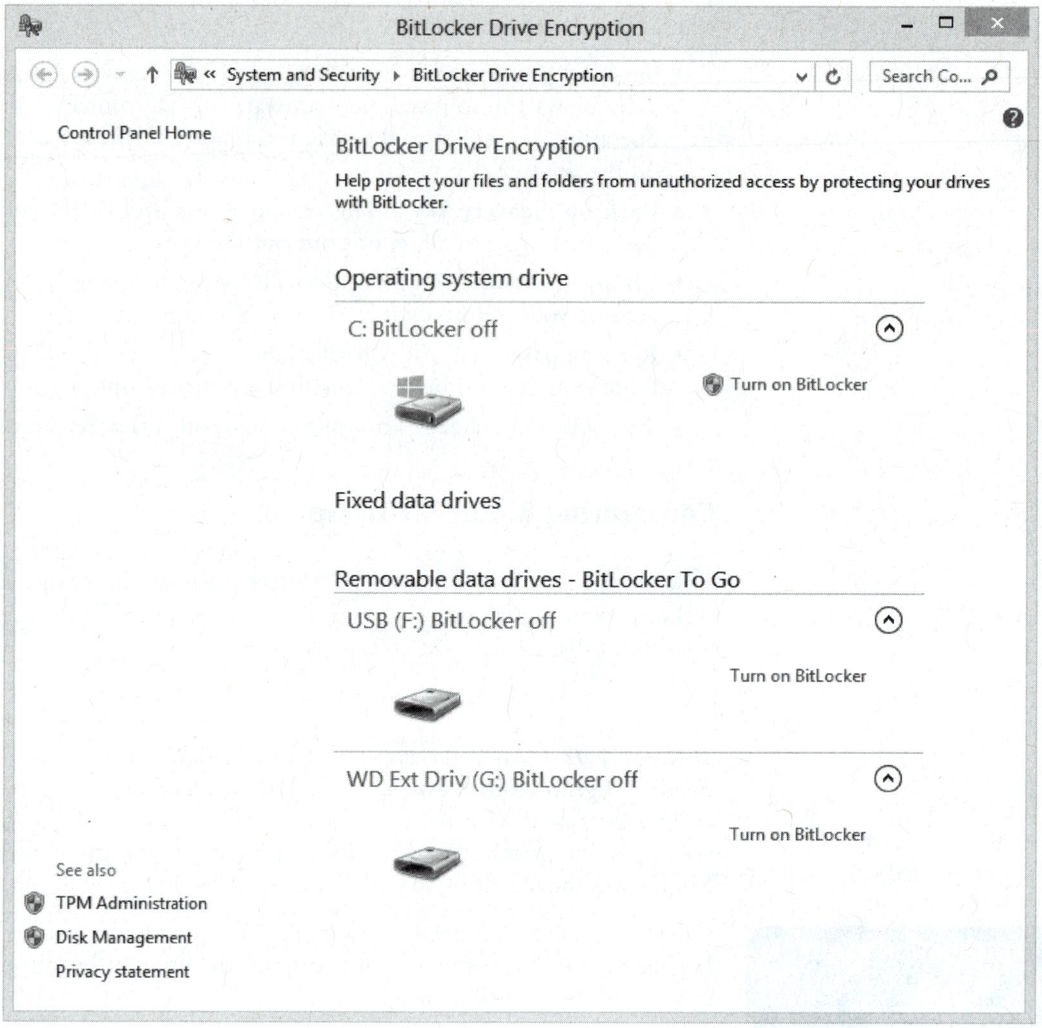

Figure 20-7
Reviewing removable data drives

ENABLE BITLOCKER TO GO ON A REMOVABLE DRIVE

GET READY. To enable BitLocker To Go on a removable drive, perform the following steps:

1. Press the **Windows logo key + R**. In the *Run* dialog box, type **control** and then click **OK**.
2. Select **System and Security > BitLocker Drive Encryption**.
3. Click **Turn on BitLocker** for the removable drive you want to protect.
4. Choose how you want to unlock the drive. The options include using a password or using a smart card to unlock the drive.
5. Choose where to back up the recovery key. The options include saving to your Microsoft account, saving to a file, or printing the recovery key.
6. Choose how much of the drive to encrypt. The options include used disk space only or the entire drive.
7. Start encrypting the drive.

CONTROLLING BITLOCKER TO GO BEHAVIOR

To control BitLocker To Go behavior for Windows 8 computers in a domain, you need to use the Group Policy Management console to create a policy, link it to the appropriate organizational unit (OU) in the Active Directory domain, and then edit the *Removable Data Drives* section of the policy (see Figure 20-8).

Figure 20-8

Reviewing the BitLocker removable data drives Group Policy settings

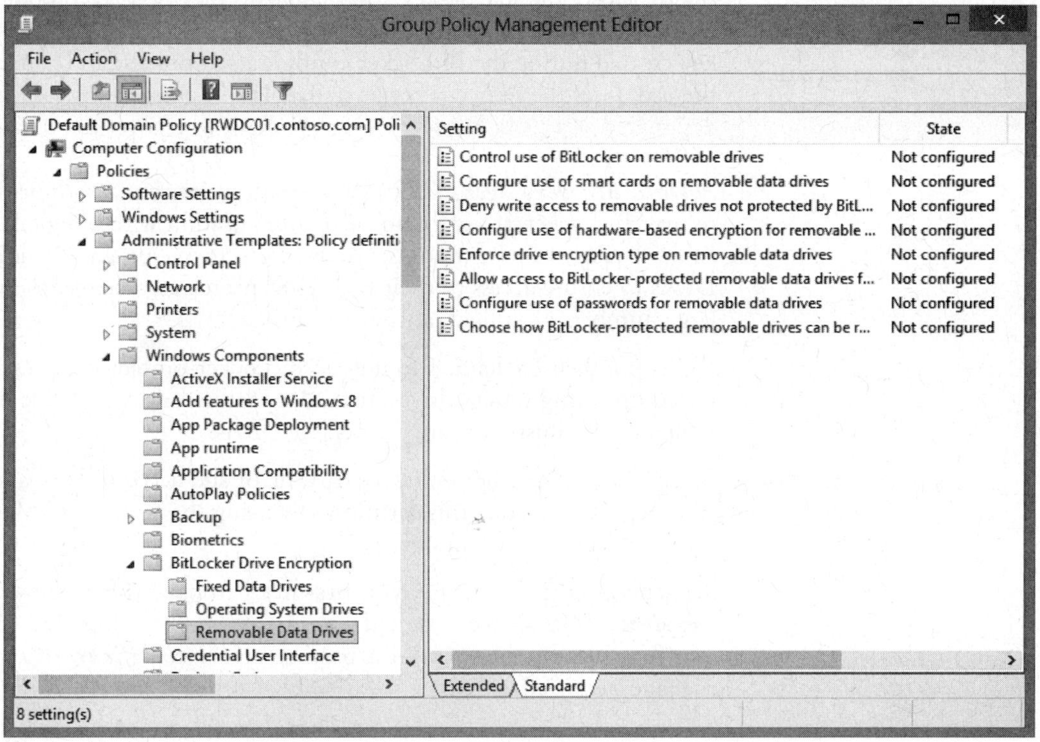

These policy settings are as follows:

- **Control use of BitLocker on removable drives** – Specifies whether users are permitted to add BitLocker encryption to removable drives and whether they can remove BitLocker from drives that are already encrypted.
- **Configure use of smart cards on removable data drives** – Specifies whether users can or must use a smart card to access a removable drive.
- **Deny write access to removable drives not protected by BitLocker** – Prevents users from saving data to removable drives that are not encrypted using BitLocker.
- **Configure use of hardware-based encryption for removable data drives** – Specifies options that control whether BitLocker software-based encryption is used instead of hardware-based encryption on computers that do not support hardware-based encryption. It also allows you to specify which encryption algorithms can be used with hardware-based encryption.
- **Allow access to BitLocker-protected removable data drives from earlier versions of Windows** – Specifies whether FAT-formatted removable BitLocker drives are accessible from previous Windows versions.
- **Configure use of passwords for removable data drives** – Specifies whether removable BitLocker drives must be password-protected.
- **Choose how BitLocker-protected removable drives can be recovered** – Specifies whether DRAs can access the data on removable BitLocker drives.

Using Data Recovery Agents

THE BOTTOM LINE

If a user loses the startup key and/or startup PIN needed to boot a system with BitLocker enabled, the system enters recovery mode. In this mode, the user can supply the recovery key created during the BitLocker configuration process and gain access to the system. If the user loses the recovery key as well, it is still possible for someone, who has been designated as a Data Recovery Agent (DRA), to recover the data on the drive.

A ***Data Recovery Agent (DRA)*** is a user account that an administrator has authorized to recover BitLocker drives for an entire organization with a digital certificate on a smart card. In most cases, administrators of Active Directory Domain Services (AD DS) networks use DRAs to ensure access to their BitLocker-protected systems, to avoid having to maintain large numbers of individual keys and PINs.

DRAs use their credentials to unlock BitLocker-protected drives and recover BitLocker protected operating system drives, fixed data drives, and removable data drives. In a domain, Domain Administrators are the default DRAs.

To designate a specific user as a DRA, he or she needs to have a personal encryption certificate. You can generate this certificate by using the Certificate Manager (certmgr.msc) console on the Windows 8 client device.

To generate the certificate, you first need to have the ***Active Directory Certificate Services (ADCS)*** role installed on a server in your domain. ADCS provides the certificate infrastructure and is used to create ***certification authorities*** that issue and manage ***certificates***.

INSTALL ACTIVE DIRECTORY CERTIFICATE SERVICES

GET READY. To install the Active Directory Certificate Services role on an existing domain controller, perform the following steps:

1. Log on to a Windows Server 2012 domain controller with administrative credentials.
2. Server Manager should open automatically. If not, click the **Server Manager** icon from the task bar.
3. Click **Manage > Add Roles and Features**.
4. Click **Next** to start the *Add Roles and Features Wizard*.
5. Click **Next** to accept the default setting *Role-based or feature-based installation*.
6. From the Server pool, click your domain controller click **Next**.
7. Select **Active Directory Certificate Services** and then click **Add Features** to include the management tools.
8. Click **Next** to continue.
9. Click **Next** to continue on the *Select features* screen.
10. After reading the information provided on the *Active Directory Certificate Services* screen, click **Next**.
11. Confirm that **Certification Authority** is checked and click **Next**.
12. On the *Select role services* screen, select *Restart the destination server automatically if required* and then click **Yes** to allow automatic restarts.
13. Click **Install** to begin the installation of the ADCS role.
14. Click **Close** when the installation has completed.

15. Click the Red Flag that appears at the top of the Server Manager Dashboard and then click **Configure Active Directory Certificate Services** to complete the post-deployment configuration.
16. Click **Next** to accept the default credentials *CONTOSO\Administrator* on the *Specify credentials to configure role services* screen.
17. On the *Select Role Services to configure* screen, select **Certification Authority** and click **Next**.
18. On the *Specify the setup type of the CA* screen, click **Next** to accept the default setting **Enterprise CA**.
19. On the *Specify the type of the CA* screen, click **Next** to accept the default setting **Root CA**.
20. On the *Specify the type of the private key* screen, click **Next** to accept the default setting **Create a new private key**.
21. On the *Specify the cryptographic options* screen, click **Next** to accept the default setting.
22. On the *Specify the name of the CA* screen, click **Next** to accept the default settings.
23. On the *Specify the validity period* screen, click **Next** to accept the default settings.
24. On the *Specify the database locations* screen, click **Next** to accept the default settings.
25. Click **Configure** and then **Close** when the configuration succeeds.

CREATE A PERSONAL ENCRYPTION CERTIFICATE FOR A USER

GET READY. To create a personal encryption certificate, perform the following steps:

1. Log on to a Windows 8 client that is a member of the domain with the account you want to use as a DRA.
2. Select the **Windows logo key + R**.
3. In the *Run* dialog box, type **certmgr.msc**.
4. Expand the Personal Folder and right-click **Certificates**.
5. Click **All Tasks > Request New Certificate**.
6. When the *Certificate Enrollment* wizard appears, click **Next**.
7. Make sure *Active Directory Enrollment Policy* is highlighted and click **Next** to continue.
8. On the *Request Certificates* screen, select **Basic EFS** and click **Enroll**.
9. Click **Finish** after being informed the certificate has been enrolled and installed on the computer.
10. Double-click the certificate and select the **Details** tab.
11. Click the **Copy to File** button. When the *Certificate Export Wizard* dialog box appears, click **Next**.
12. Leave the *No, do not export the private key* option selected and click **Next**.
13. Verify that the *DER encoded binary X.509 (.cer)* format is selected and click **Next**.
14. On the *File to Export* page, click **Browse** to display the *Save as* dialog box.
15. In the *File name*, type **BitLocker**. In the *Save as type*, verify that *DER Encoded Binary X.509 (.cer)* is selected and click **Save**.

16. Make a note of the location of your certificate in the *File to Export* dialog box and click **Next** to continue. You use this in the exercise that follows. The default location is C:\Users*username*\Documents\BitLocker.cer where *username* is the name you are currently logged in with.
17. Click **Finish** to complete the *Certificate Export Wizard*.
18. Click **OK** to close the dialog box that states, "The export was successful."
19. Close any open dialog boxes.
20. Log off the computer.

Once you configure the DRA with the proper certificate, you need to add them to the Public Key Policies\BitLocker Drive Encryption in the Group Policy Management console. You also need to enable and configure the *Provide the unique identifiers for your organization* policy setting to associate a unique identifier to a new drive that is enabled with BitLocker. The identified files are a string that uniquely identifies the business unit or organization. BitLocker manages and updates only DRAs when an identification field is present on a drive and is identical to the value configured on the computer.

CONFIGURE THE UNIQUE COMPANY IDENTIFIER AND ADD THE DRA AGENT TO THE BITLOCKER ENCRYPTION POLICY

GET READY. To configure the unique company identifier and add the DRA to the BitLocker Drive Encryption policy, perform the following steps:

1. Log on (with domain administrative credentials) to the same Windows 8 client you used to create the BitLocker.cer file in the previous exercise.

TAKE NOTE* This computer must have the Remote Server Administration Tools (RSAT) installed to gain access to the Group Policy Management console.

2. Press the **Windows logo key + R**.
3. In the *Run* dialog box, type **gpmc.msc**.
4. Right-click the **Group Policy Objects** folder and select **New**.
5. Type **BitLocker DRA** for the new GPO's name and click **OK**.
6. Expand the Group Policy Objects folder, right-click the BitLocker DRA GPO, and select **Edit**.
7. Expand **Computer Configuration > Policies > Windows Settings > Security Settings > Public Key Policies**.
8. Right-click the **BitLocker Drive Encryption** folder and select **Add Data Recovery Agent**.
9. Click **Next** when the *Add Recovery Agent Wizard* appears.
10. Click the **Browse Folders** button and navigate to C:\Users\username\MyDocuments folder. Select the **BitLocker.cer** file and then click **Open**.
11. Click **Next** after adding the certificate and then click **Finish**.
12. Expand the **Administrative Templates > Windows Components** section of the policy and then click **BitLocker Drive Encryption**.
13. Double-click **Provide the unique identifiers for your organization**.
14. Select **Enabled** and enter **Contoso** for both the fields as shown in Figure 20-9 and then click **OK**.

You have now completed the appropriate policies for BitLocker DRAs.

Figure 20-9

Providing unique identifiers for your organization

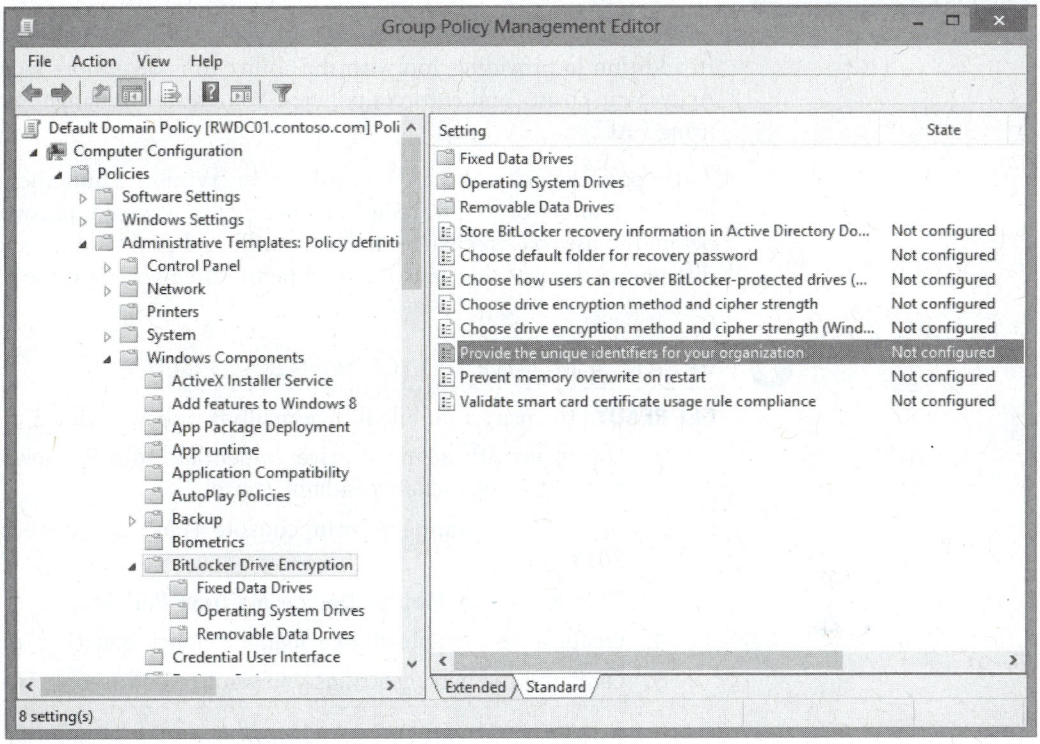

By default, BitLocker identification fields are associated with BitLocker-protected drives when you enable BitLocker on a drive. If you set up this policy after encrypting a drive, you need to log on to the computer where you want to assign the identification field, open an elevated command prompt, and then type the following:

```
Manage-bde -SetIdentifer <drive letter>
```

Replace `<drive letter>` with the letter of the BitLocker-protected drive. The `-SetIdentifer` uses the value you entered in the *Provide the unique identifiers for your organization* Group Policy setting.

■ Configuring Remote Wipe

THE BOTTOM LINE

Theft and loss of mobile devices is a common occurrence in today's world. Having the ability to reset these devices to their factory settings ensures sensitive information doesn't fall into the wrong hands.

There are two things you should prepare for when working with mobile devices:

- The device will contain data that is considered sensitive at some point in time.
- The device might eventually be lost or stolen.

Fortunately, Windows 8 devices support a feature called ***remote wipe***. When you remote wipe a device, you are issuing a remote wipe command from a central location to reset the device back to its factory default settings. Exchange Server and Windows Intune both provide remote wipe features.

CERTIFICATION READY
Configure remote wipe
Objective 5.3

Exchange Server 2013 provides access to the feature through the Exchange Admin Center (EAC) using ***Exchange ActiveSync***. Exchange ActiveSync is a protocol that is designed to not only synchronize email, contacts, calendars, and tasks but also provide the ability to perform mobile device management.

In addition to providing you with the ability to issue remote wipe commands, Exchange ActiveSync creates and enforces policies. You create Exchange ActiveSync mailbox policies using EAC.

These policies spell out the password and encryption requirements, the minimum password lengths, number of sign-in failures before device is wiped, password lifetime (number of days before the user has to change the password), and password recycle count settings (number of different passwords that must be used before the user can reuse a password).

CREATE A MOBILE DEVICE MAILBOX POLICY

GET READY. To create a mobile device mailbox policy, perform the following steps:

1. Log in in with administrative credentials to a Windows 8 computer that has access to the Exchange Admin console.
2. Open the **Exchange Admin** console (EAC) to connect to your Exchange 2013 server.
3. Click **Mobile > Mobile Device Mailbox Policies**.
4. Create a new mobile device mailbox policy and then give it a name.
5. Configure the policy settings you want to enforce.

PERFORM A REMOTE WIPE USING THE EAC

GET READY. To perform a remote wipe using the Exchange Admin console (EAC), perform the following steps:

1. Log in with administrative credentials to a Windows 8 computer that has access to the Exchange Administrative console.
2. Open the **Exchange Administrative** console (EAC) to connect to your Exchange 2013 server.
3. Navigate to **Recipients > Mailboxes**.
4. Select the user, and under *Mobile devices*, choose **View details**.
5. On the *Mobile Device Details* page, select the lost mobile device and then click **Wipe Data**.
6. Click **Save**.

PERFORM A REMOTE WIPE FROM THE MICROSOFT OUTLOOK WEB APP

GET READY. Users can perform a remote wipe of their own device from the Microsoft Outlook Web App by performing the following steps:

1. Open **Internet Explorer** and type your Outlook Web App web address: **https://<exchangeserver>/OWA**.
2. Log in using your domain credentials
3. Click **Options**.
4. Click **Phone**.
5. Click **Wipe Device**.

Using Windows Intune to Perform Remote Wipes

Windows Intune, Microsoft's cloud-based management solution, allows you to work through Exchange ActiveSync or directly through Windows Intune to manage your mobile devices and perform a remote wipe.

This can be accomplished directly through the Windows Intune administrator console or by allowing users to wipe their own device through their Windows Intune company portal.

PERFORM A REMOTE WIPE VIA THE WINDOWS INTUNE ADMINISTRATOR

GET READY. To perform a remote wipe via the Windows Intune administrator console, follow these steps:

1. Open the **Windows Intune administrator** console.
2. In the *Workspace Shortcuts* pane, click **Groups**.
3. In the navigation pane, click **All Users**, click the user of the device you want to wipe, and then click **View Properties**.
4. Click the **Devices** tab and then click the name of the device you want to wipe.
5. Click **Retire/Wipe**.
6. Select the **Wipe the device before retiring** check box and then click **Yes**.

Managing Location Settings

THE BOTTOM LINE

Using the Windows Location Provider, Windows apps can target content that is relevant to your current location. In situations where you do not want to expose personal information, you need to disable the feature.

CERTIFICATION READY
Configure location settings (GPS)
Objective 5.3

Are you looking to pay the lowest price for that next tank of gas, read the local news, find out what the local weather forecast is, or locate an Italian restaurant nearby? If so, using ***location settings*** on your Windows 8 device provides the answers you seek. Location settings are used by some Windows apps and desktop apps to provide you with information that is specific to your current location.

Using Windows Location Provider (PLP)

Location aware apps use the built-in ***Windows Location Provider (WLP)*** to gain access to location data. The WLP is responsible for generating the geographic data that tells the app the geographic location of your computer/device. It accomplishes this by using Wi-Fi triangulation or IP address resolution.

Wi-Fi triangulation involves using information provided by the Wi-Fi Access point. A Wi-Fi Access point transmits a signal every 100 milliseconds that includes information about its identity, signal strength, media access control (MAC) address (e.g., unique serial number for that piece of hardware), and its received signal strength indicator (a measure of the strength of the signal at the time it is received by a mobile device). This information is used by the WLP to calculate location information. If Wi-Fi is not available, the WLP uses IP address resolution to establish location information.

As an administrator, you can disable access to the location settings for all users through the Control Panel, Local Group Policy (gpedit.msc), or by using the Group Policy Management console (gpmc.msc). This is done by disabling the Windows Location Platform in the Windows 8 control panel.

DISABLE WINDOWS LOCATION PLATFORM USING THE WINDOWS 8 CONTROL PANEL

GET READY. To disable Windows Location Platform using the Windows 8 Control Panel, log in to Windows 8 using administrative credentials and then perform the following steps:

1. Press the **Windows logo key + R**.
2. Type **control** and then click **Enter**.
3. Click the **Hardware and Sound** category.
4. Click **Location Settings** (see Figure 20-10).

Figure 20-10

Reviewing the location settings

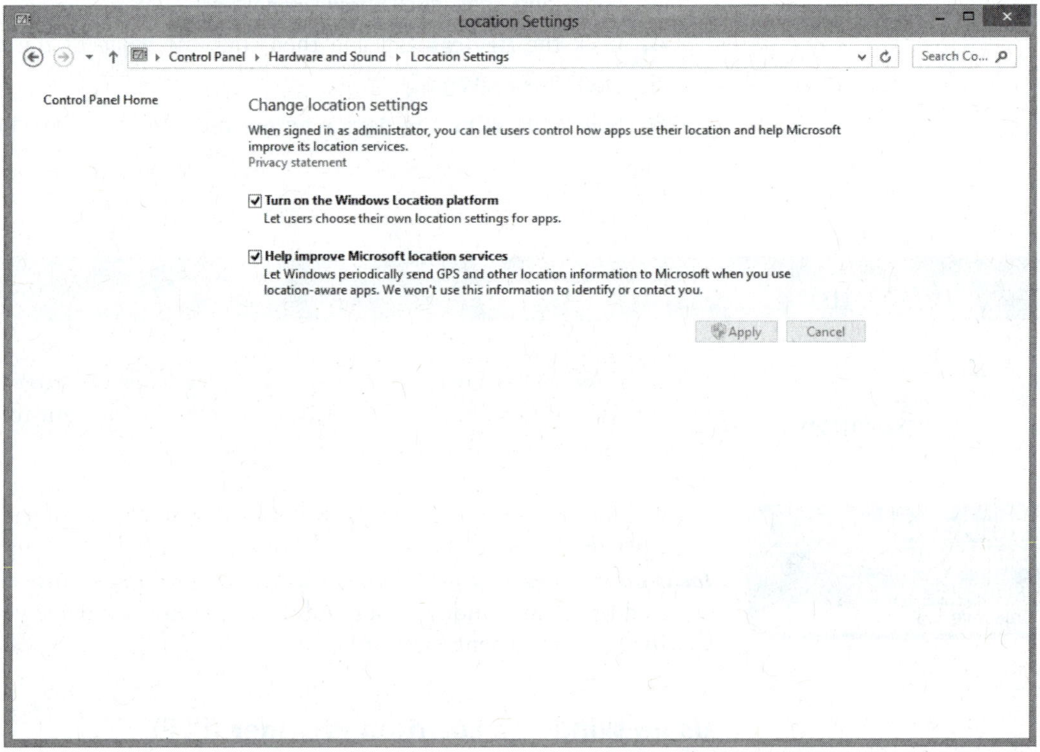

The *Turn on the Windows Location platform* option is enabled by default, which means users can configure the apps they choose to use the location services.

5. Deselect **Turn on the Windows Location platform** and then click **Apply**.

TAKE NOTE* The option to help improve Microsoft location services, if enabled, sends location details to Microsoft to help improve the overall feature.

The Local Group Policy editor (gpedit.msc) can also be used to disable the Windows Location Provider, as shown in the next exercise.

DISABLE WINDOWS LOCATION PROVIDER USING THE LOCAL GROUP POLICY EDITOR

GET READY. To disable the Windows Location Provider using the Local Group Policy editor, log on as an administrator and then perform the following steps:

1. Press the **Windows logo key + R**.
2. In the *Run* dialog box, type **gpedit.msc**.
3. Click **Computer Configuration > Administrative Templates > Windows Components > Location and Sensors > Windows Location Provider**.
4. Double-click **Turn off Windows Location Provider policy** and then click **Enabled**.

DISABLE WINDOWS LOCATION PROVIDER ON ALL WINDOWS 8 DEVICES

GET READY. To disable the Windows Location Provider on all Window 8 devices in your enterprise, perform the following steps:

1. Log on to a Windows 8 computer with domain administrative credentials that has the Remote Server Administration Tools (RSAT) installed or log in directly to a domain controller.
2. Press the **Windows logo key + R**.
3. In the *Run* dialog box, type **gpmc.msc**.
4. Right-click the **Group Policy Objects** container and choose **New**.
5. Type a name for the GPO and then click **OK**.
6. Right-click the GPO and choose **Edit**.
7. Click **Computer Configuration > Policies > Administrative Templates > Windows Components > Location and Sensors > Windows Location Provider**.
8. Double-click the **Turn off Windows Location Provider** policy and then click **Enabled**.

Using Personally Identifiable Information (PII)

To leave the Windows Location enabled, the concept of ***Personally Identifiable Information (PII)*** comes into play. PII is information that can be used to uniquely identify, contact, or locate you and has been a major focus of lawmakers in the U.S. and other countries.

The Privacy Act of 2005 was designed to limit the display, purchase, or sale of PII without the person's consent. Basically, this means the user of the Windows 8 device, in the example, must give permission for the app to use the location even if the administrator has enabled the Windows Location Provider on the device.

The first time a Windows app or desktop app tries to access location data, the user is prompted with a question, "Can <app> access your location?" Clicking *Yes* provides consent. If you do not give consent when initially opening the app, you can do so later from within the application.

Users can disable the location feature for all Apps by performing the steps in the following exercise.

DISABLE THE LOCATION FEATURE

GET READY. To disable the location feature for all Apps, users can perform the following steps while logged in to their Windows 8 device under their Microsoft account:

1. Move the mouse to the top-right side of the screen and, on the Charms bar, click **Settings**.
2. Click **Change PC Settings**.
3. Click **Privacy**.
4. Move the slider to the left to turn off the *Let Apps use my location* option.

PROVIDE PII CONSENT FROM WITHIN A WINDOWS APP

GET READY. To provide PII consent from within a Windows app, log on to Windows 8 using your Microsoft account and then perform the following steps:

1. Press the **Windows logo key** to access the Windows 8 Start menu.
2. Click the **Weather** tile.
3. Move the mouse to the upper-right top area of the screen and, from the Charms bar that appears, click **Settings**.
4. Click **Permissions**.
5. Move the Location slider to the right to turn on *Windows Location* (see Figure 20-11).

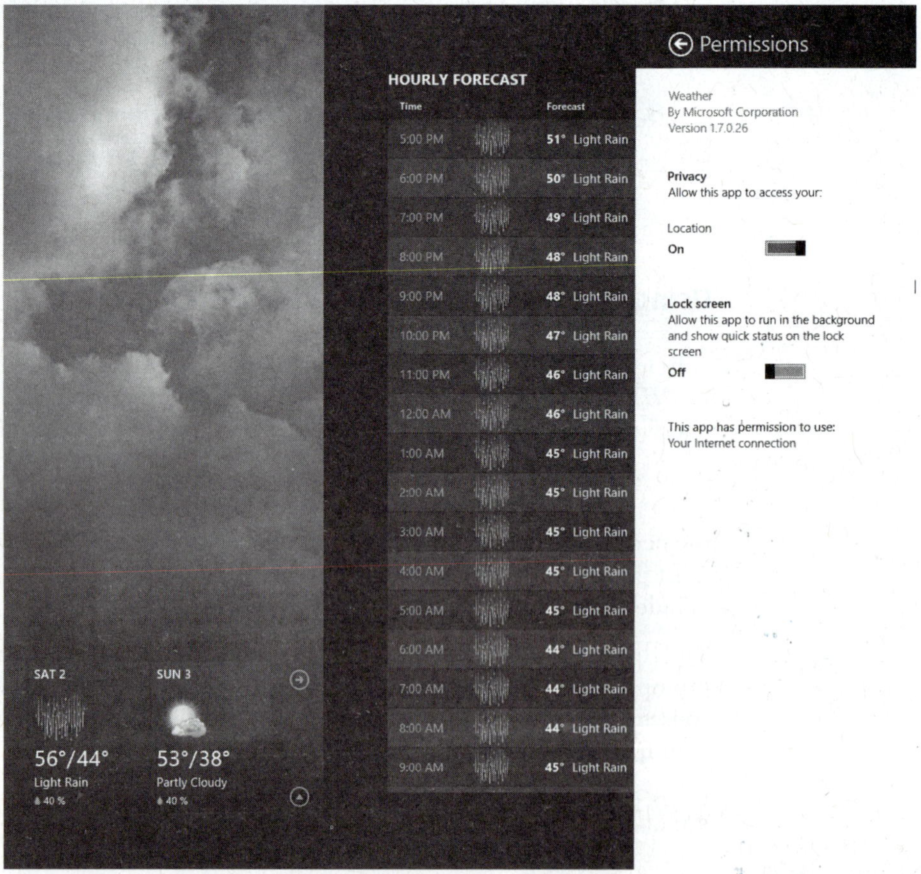

Figure 20-11

Enabling the Windows Location setting from within the Weather app

SKILL SUMMARY

IN THIS LESSON, YOU LEARNED:

- BitLocker Drive Encryption and BitLocker To Go are features available in Windows 8 to protect your drive and volumes using encryption.
- BitLocker Drive Encryption can be used to encrypt used disk space only or the entire drive.
- BitLocker Drive Encryption can be used with fixed data drives, operating system drives, and removable drives.
- There are five authentication methods that can be used to provide additional protection for your encrypted drive: TPM+startup PIN+startup key, TPM+startup key, TPM+startup PIN, startup key only, and TPM only.
- To support BitLocker Drive Encryption on the drive that contains the operating system, you need two partitions, formatted with NTFS, a TPM compatible BIOS or BIOS firmware that supports booting from a USB flash drive.
- The Local Group Policy editor can be used to manage BitLocker policies on a local machine whereas the Group Policy Management console is used to create policies that are enforced across the entire organization.
- BitLocker To Go is BitLocker Drive Encryption for removable data drives. To unlock removable data drives, you need to use either a password or a smart card with a PIN.
- Recovery keys are used when BitLocker startup keys will not unlock the drive. In situations where you lose both, a Data Recovery Agent can be used to ensure access to the system.
- Remote wipe allows you to return a mobile system to its default settings in case of loss or theft. You can use it with Exchange ActiveSync or Windows Intune. Both offers remote wipe options for the administrator and for the users to remote wipe their own device.
- Location settings are used by Windows apps and desktop apps to provide you with information that is specific to your current location.
- Location settings can be disabled on a global basis using a Group Policy Object but in situations where they are enabled, users must still consent to the app using their current location. This is due to laws designed to limit the display, purchase, or sale of Personally Identifiable Information (PII) without the user's consent.

Knowledge Assessment

Multiple Choice

Select the correct answer for each of the following questions.

1. Which of the following can be used to protect files after someone has successfully booted into a shared Windows 8 computer and logged in using an authorized user account? (Select all that apply.)
   - **a.** BitLocker Drive Encryption
   - **b.** BitLocker To Go
   - **c.** NTFS
   - **d.** EFS

2. What is a 4–20 digit number that you create when enabling BitLocker, which must be entered each time you start your system? (Select all that apply.)
   a. Startup key
   b. PIN
   c. Recovery key
   d. PII
3. Which of the following tools can be used by end users to perform a remote wipe of their mobile device?
   a. Microsoft Outlook Web app
   b. Exchange Admin console
   c. Windows Intune company portal
   d. Windows Intune Administrator console
4. What is the component responsible for generating the geographic data that tells the Windows app the location of your device?
   a. Exchange ActiveSync
   b. NTFS
   c. Windows Location Provider
   d. App Location Provider
5. The built-in Windows Location Provider uses which of the following to generate the geographic data for Windows apps?
   a. GPS triangulation
   b. IP address resolution
   c. Wi-Fi triangulation
   d. PING
6. Which of the following is the information that can be used to uniquely identify, contact, or locate you?
   a. PIN
   b. PII
   c. NTFS
   d. EFS
7. To support BitLocker Drive Encryption on the drive that contains your operating system, you need which of the following?
   a. Two partitions
   b. EFS
   c. TPM Compatible BIOS or BIOS firmware that can read from a USB drive on startup
   d. NTFS
8. Which of the following is the least secure authentication method?
   a. TPM only
   b. TPM + startup key
   c. TPM + startup PIN
   d. TPM + startup PIN + startup key
9. Which key is used to encrypt/decrypt the drive and must be entered each time you boot your computer?
   a. Startup key
   b. Recovery key
   c. Personal key
   d. TPM key
10. What user account can be authorized to recover BitLocker drives for an entire organization?
    a. Domain administrator
    b. Enterprise administrator
    c. Data recovery assistance
    d. Data Recovery Agent

Best Answer

Choose the letter that corresponds to the best answer. More than one answer choice may achieve the goal. Select the BEST answer.

1. It is a Sunday afternoon and after arriving home from lunch with a friend, you discover your Windows 8 mobile device was stolen. It was configured to connect to your company's Active Directory domain. What is the quickest way to protect sensitive information on the device?
   a. Enable BitLocker Drive Encryption.
   b. Contact your company's network administrator.
   c. Call the police and report the theft.
   d. Connect using your Outlook Web app from another device and perform a remote wipe on your device.
2. With BitLocker To Go enabled on a data volume for additional protection, to disable it because there is no longer any sensitive data stored on the volume, what tool would you use?
   a. Local Group Policy editor
   b. Group Policy Management console
   c. Control Panel > Manage BitLocker
   d. Delete and reformat the volume
3. To use BitLocker to encrypt the drive that contains your operating system, which of the following drives supports this goal?
   a. 50 MB boot partition
   b. 50 MB system partition
   c. 200 MB boot partition
   d. 200 MB system partition
4. Which of the following represents the most secure authentication option?
   a. TPM only
   b. Startup key only
   c. TPM + startup key
   d. TPM + startup PIN
5. To disable the locating settings for all users in your Active Directory domain, which option allows you to do this with the least administrative effort?
   a. gpedit.msc
   b. gpmc.msc
   c. Windows 8 Control panel
   d. Windows Store

Matching and Identification

1. Match the following terms with their corresponding definitions.
   _________ **a)** Recovery key
   _________ **b)** Exchange ActiveSync
   _________ **c)** BitLocker To Go
   _________ **d)** BitLocker Drive Encryption
   _________ **e)** Data Recovery Agent
   _________ **f)** location settings
   _________ **g)** Personal Identification Number (PIN)
   _________ **h)** Personally Identifiable Information (PII)
   _________ **i)** Remote wipe
   _________ **j)** Trusted Platform Module (TPM)

   1. Encryption feature designed to protect removable USB devices.
   2. Authorized to recover BitLocker drives for an entire organization.
   3. A 48-digit number used when you lose/forget your startup key.
   4. A command that resets the device back to its factory default settings.

5. A 4–20 digit number you create and enter each time you start.
6. A protocol designed that supports perform mobile device management.
7. Used by some Windows apps to provide you with information that is specific to your current location.
8. Information that can be used to uniquely identify, contact, or locate you.
9. Dedicated cryptographic processor chip that the system uses to store BitLocker Drive Encryption keys.
10. Used to encrypt entire volumes and drives.

Build a List

1. In order of first to last, specify the six steps used to encrypt a removable drive using BitLocker To Go.
   _______ Type BitLocker Drive Encryption from the Windows 8 start menu and select it from the results list.
   _______ Choose how you want to unlock the drive.
   _______ Start encrypting the drive.
   _______ Choose where to back up the recovery key.
   _______ Select Turn on BitLocker for the removable drive.
   _______ Choose how much of the drive to encrypt.

2. To disable the access to the location settings for all users on a Windows 8 computer, specify the correct order of steps required to disable the location settings for all users via the Windows 8 Control panel.
   _______ Select the Windows log key + R.
   _______ Select the Hardware and Sound category.
   _______ Type "control panel" and press Enter.
   _______ Select Location settings.
   _______ Log in to the Windows 8 device with administrative credentials.

3. In order of first to last, specify the tasks required to provide PII consent from within a Windows App.
   _______ Move the mouse to the upper right top area of the screen and select Settings from the Charms bar that appears.
   _______ Move the Location slider to the right to turn on Windows Location.
   _______ Click the Weather tile.
   _______ Select Permission.
   _______ Press the Windows logo key to access the Windows 8 Start menu.

Business Case Scenarios

Scenario 20-1: Encrypting an Operating System Drive

Amanda Killingsworth is the network administrator for a small company that upgraded its Windows 7 mobile devices to Windows 8 for its sales staff. It also upgraded its Exchange server to Exchange Server 2013 and can use the Microsoft Outlook Web app. The sales staff travels a lot for the company and has in the past, left the devices at the airport. In a few cases, the devices have been stolen. What recommendations would you make to protect the sensitive data based on what you know about the network?

Scenario 20-2: Troubleshooting BitLocker Drive Encryption

You attempt to enable BitLocker Drive Encryption to protect the operating system drive on a Windows 8 computer but are unable to complete the process. What could be contributing to the problem?

LESSON 21

Configuring and Managing Updates

70-687 EXAM OBJECTIVE

Objective 6.1 – Configure and manage updates. This objective may include but is not limited to configure update settings; configure Windows Update policies; manage update history; roll back updates; and update Windows Store applications.

LESSON HEADING	EXAM OBJECTIVE
Configuring Update Settings	
Checking for Updates	Configure Update Settings
Changing Update Settings	
Hiding and Restoring Updates	
Configuring Windows Update Policies	
Configuring Local Computer Policies and Microsoft Domain Group Policies to Manage Updates	Configure Windows Update Policies
Managing Update History	
Viewing Update History	Manage Update History
Rolling Back Updates	Roll Back Updates
Updating Windows Store Applications	Update Windows Store applications

KEY TERMS

critical updates
group policies
important updates
Microsoft Updates
optional updates
recommended updates
security updates
service packs
update settings
update history

Configuring Update Settings

THE BOTTOM LINE

Microsoft routinely issues patches, service packs, and drivers to Microsoft software products in the form of Microsoft and Windows Updates. Through end-user interaction or system administration, personal and enterprise computers running Microsoft operating systems, signed drivers, and applications are patched and secured against the latest vulnerabilities, security risks, and threats.

Many users ask "Why do I need to run updates on my computer?" The answer is, to protect, secure, improve, and enhance the end users' experience. Throughout the lifetime of Microsoft operating systems, signed drivers, and applications, new vulnerabilities are found, exploited, and used against end users. If a vulnerability is found in the "wild" or reverse engineered by a malicious user, that user could potentially gain unauthorized access to manipulate a user's computer. To combat these vulnerabilities, new patches are released routinely allowing users to download, install, and protect their systems.

The second Tuesday of every month, sometimes known as "Patch Tuesday," is typically release day for all tested and signed patches from Microsoft. Microsoft is not strictly limited to issuing patches on the second Tuesday alone; for instance, if a zero-day exploit is found, an update may be released as soon as possible. Along with Patch Tuesday, the day after is often considered "Exploit Wednesday." The day after patches are released, malicious users have been known to reverse engineer the patch, find the exploit it fixes, and then prepare an attack for users that have not yet patched their systems. This is important to remember when going through this lesson. Allowing updates to download and install automatically can save a lot of headaches for the end user.

Windows Updates not only helps protect your computers, they also fix minor to major problems found throughout the lifetime of the operation system. Updates are released throughout the lifetime of an operating system and application. This means, eventually Microsoft no longer supports an operating system and application and can no longer guarantee they are safe from malicious actions. The only solution is then to upgrade the operating system or application to the latest version.

Checking for Updates

It is important to routinely check for updates, and to also ensure that updates are-configured for automatic download and installation for all your Microsoft products. Keeping your system up-to-date with the latest patches keeps you secured and protected from the latest threats.

To protect a Windows 8 operating system, ***Microsoft Updates*** can be downloaded and installed from the Control Panel by the end users. This provides the end user the ability to control when updates are downloaded and installed depending on the use of the computer, speed of the network, or phase of update testing.

When performing the installation of Windows 8, the end user is allowed to customize the installation options. The choices for customization are Automatically install important and recommended updates, Automatically install important updates, or Don't set up Windows Update (not recommended), as shown in Figure 21-1.

Figure 21-1
Configuring automatic updates during Windows 8 installation

CERTIFICATION READY
Configure update settings
Objective 6.1

There are several categories of updates provided by Microsoft; each category prioritizes the updates based on importance and recommended use by the end user.

- ***Important updates*** can be configured to be installed automatically and typically included updates that fix or improve security, privacy, and reliability within the OS or application.
- ***Recommended updates*** can be configured to install automatically and typically take care of non-critical problems that might enhance end-user usability with the software.
- ***Optional updates*** must be installed manually and might include updates, drivers, and software not typically installed with the operating systems.
- ***Security updates***, rated as critical, important, moderate or low, are released to fix product-specific security-related vulnerabilities that might affect end-user or enterprise systems.
- ***Critical updates*** fix critical, non-security related "bugs."
- ***Service packs*** are a cumulative package of updates and patches released for a system or application over a period of time.

The option to check for other Microsoft products also exists. By clicking the *Find out more* link as shown in Figure 21-2, the end user is redirected to an external Microsoft site where a Terms of Use agreement must be agreed to and the Microsoft Update service will be installed. The Microsoft Update service searches for additional updates for other Microsoft products like Office, SQL Server, Exchange Server, Visual Studio, and so on. Once installed, the end user is returned to the Windows Update in Control Panel to continue checking for, downloading, and installing the latest updates.

Figure 21-2

Checking for updates to other Microsoft products

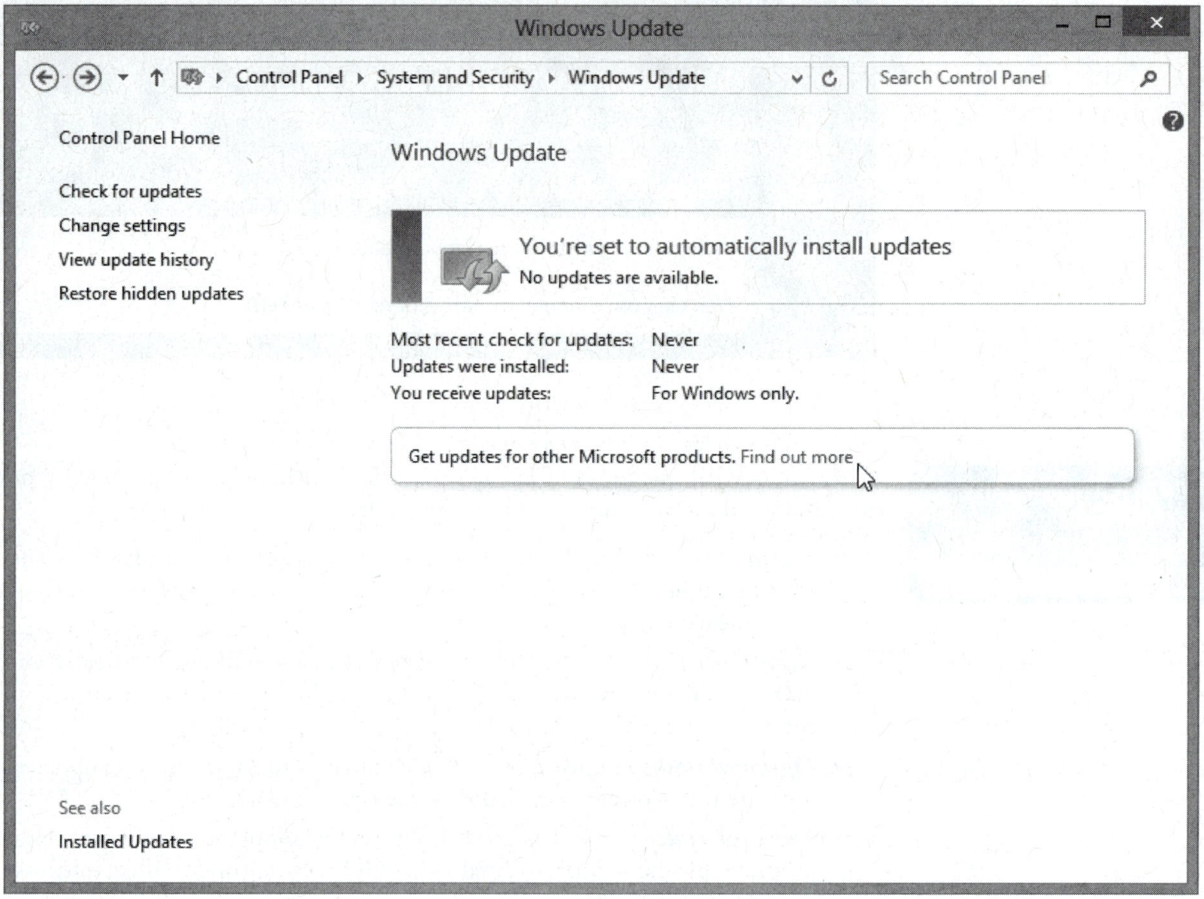

Changing Update Settings

Update settings are configurable to allow for immediate download and installation of important and recommended updates.

For users that require different download and installation options, ***update settings*** are configurable based on the end-user requirements.

Important updates can be downloaded and applied by selecting one of the following selections.

- **Install updates automatically (recommended)** – When configured, Windows update will automatically download and install all of the important updates on the system.
- **Download updates but let me choose whether to install them** – When configured, Windows Update will automatically download important updates, and notify the end user that it is ready for installation. For users in a heavy production environment where downloads can happen in the background, but resources must be fully allocated to production tasks, the installation can take place at user discretion.
- **Check for updates but let me choose whether to download and install them** – When configured, Windows Update will not automatically download or install updates. The user will be notified of available download. Once the user downloads the updates, he will then be notified again when the recently downloaded updates are ready for install.

TAKE NOTE*

If update settings are configured by your system administrator, some options may be disabled for end-user configuration.

- **Never check for updates (not recommended)** – When configured, Windows update will never automatically check for updates or notify the user. All update checks must be initiated by the end user. The user must then follow up with the download and installation tasks to perform all updates.

Recommended updates can also be installed the same way important updates are installed, which allows a more streamlined approach to downloading and installing all updates automatically.

Updates for other Microsoft products can also be installed when you update Windows as shown in Figure 21-3.

Figure 21-3

Modifying update settings

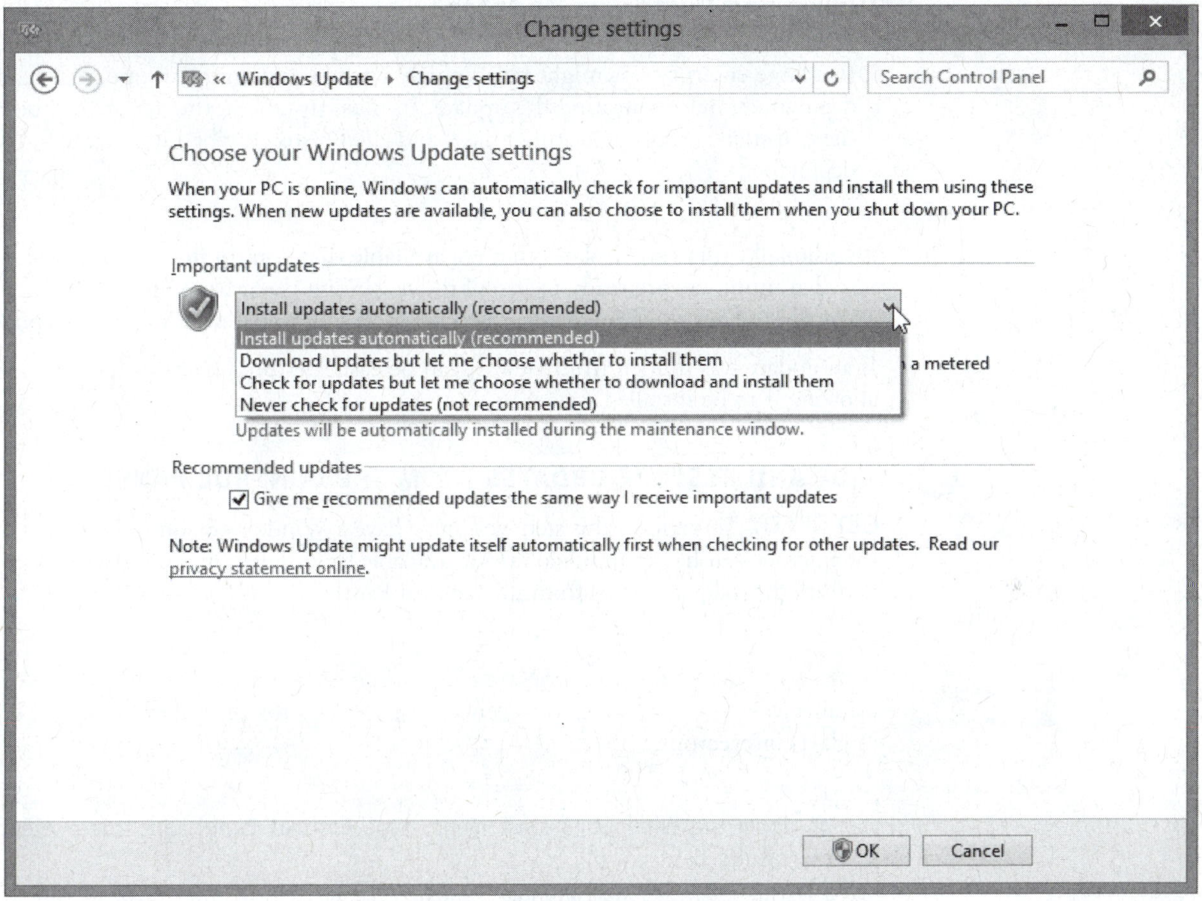

CHANGE UPDATE SETTINGS FROM THE CONTROL PANEL

GET READY. Logged into a Windows 8 machine, perform the following actions to change the updates settings from the Control Panel:

TAKE NOTE*

If the Windows 8 computer you are configuring is on a domain that has implemented an intranet Windows update server, using group policies for Automatic Updates, some selections might be greyed out.

1. From the Windows 8 start menu, type **Control Panel** and then select it from the results list.

   The *Control Panel* window appears.

2. Within the *Control Panel* window, click **System and Security**.
3. To display the *Windows Update configuration* window, click **Windows Update**.
4. Click **Change settings**. The *Choose your Windows Update settings* window appears.
5. From the drop-down selection under important updates, select **Install updates automatically (recommended)**.
6. Verify the **Give me recommended updates the same way I receive important updates** and **Give me updates for other Microsoft products when I update Windows** selection boxes are checked.
7. Click **OK**.

Hiding and Restoring Updates

In a large enterprise, it might be acceptable to test and verify an update is ready for mass deployment before pushing the update. In most instances, the update can be hidden from the end user during the testing phase, and then restored when it is ready for system wide deployment.

Occasionally, there are updates that are available that you do not want to be reminded of, or installed, until you are ready to install them. Hiding them from view eliminates the need to manually remove the update when you are installing updates in Windows Update.

If an update was hidden from view, it can be easily restored from its hidden view status, allowing it to be installed.

HIDE AND RESTORE UPDATES FROM THE CONTROL PANEL

GET READY. To perform this step, you must have a Windows 8 computer that is connected to the Internet that has an optional update available for installation. To hide and restore an update, perform the following steps from the Control Panel:

TAKE NOTE* If the Windows 8 computer you are configuring is on a domain that has implemented an intranet Windows update server, using group policies for Automatic Updates, some selections might be greyed out.

1. From the Windows 8 start menu, type **Control Panel**, and then select it from the results list.

   The *Control Panel* window appears.
2. Within the *Control Panel* window, click **System and Security**.
3. Click **Windows Update** to display the *Windows Update* configuration window.
4. If no updates are displayed for download, click **Check for updates**, and then select the link indicating an **optional update is available**.

   The *Select updates to install* window appears.
5. Right-click the update you want to hide and then select **Hide update** as shown in Figure 21-4.

   The update is now gray and hidden from future update selections.

Figure 21-4

Hiding unwanted updates

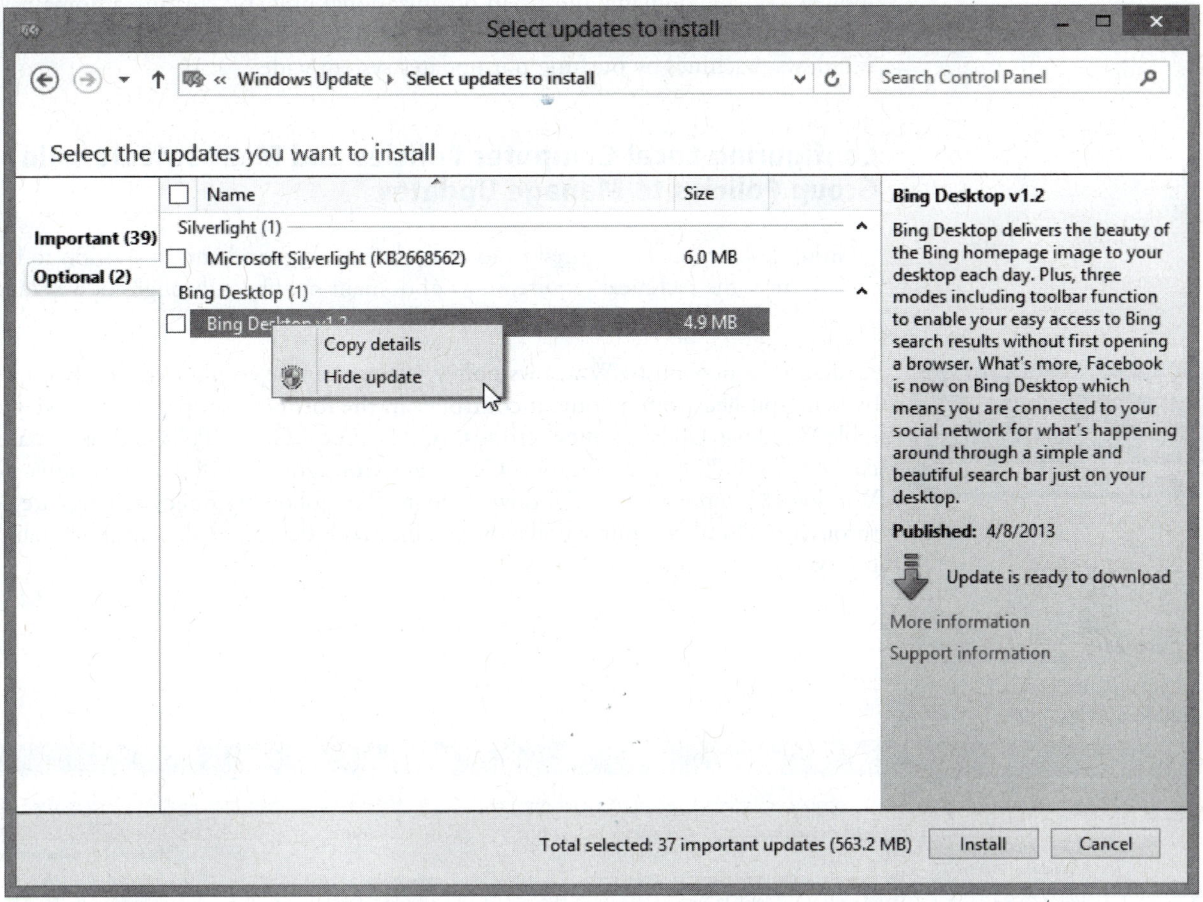

6. In the breadcrumb path at the top of the window, click **Windows Update**.

   You are now returned to the *Windows Update* window.

7. From the left side of the window, click on **Restore hidden updates**.

   The *Restore hidden updates* window appears.

8. Check the check box next to the update you want to unhide and then click the **Restore** button.

   The updates now are restored and available for installation once again. You are returned to the *Windows Update* window.

9. Close the *Windows Update* window.

Configuring Windows Update Policies

THE BOTTOM LINE

Since Windows 2000, system administrators have been able to configure Windows Update throughout the enterprise by configuring Group Policies. By using a domain member server with the Windows Server Update Service (WSUS) role, or System Center Configuration Manager (ConfigMgr) installed, administrators can deploy updates to domain computers without any end-user intervention. This allows managed update administration through a single console.

Microsoft ***group policies*** can be configured on a local machine by editing the Local Group Policy editor of that machine. In an enterprise environment, group policies are created and applied to a site, domain, and/or an organizational unit. By creating a domain-wide group policy, system administrators are then able to manage and secure all domain joined Microsoft Windows machines by pushing out updates system wide.

Configuring Local Computer Policies and Microsoft Domain Group Policies to Manage Updates

> Group policies are configured to force update settings and administration to be identical, or to meet the technical requirements of domain members throughout a Windows domain.

CERTIFICATION READY
Configure Windows Update policies
Objective 6.1

As described previously, Windows policy settings can be configured locally on a machine or by being pushed from a domain controller in the form of group policy. To view the configurable Windows Update policy settings, run the Local Group Policy editor on a computer and navigate to the following location Computer Configuration > Administrative Templates > Windows Components > Windows Update. The following policy settings are configurable through the local computer policy of a Windows 8 device, or through a domain's group policy as shown in Figure 21-5.

Figure 21-5

Navigating to Windows Update policies

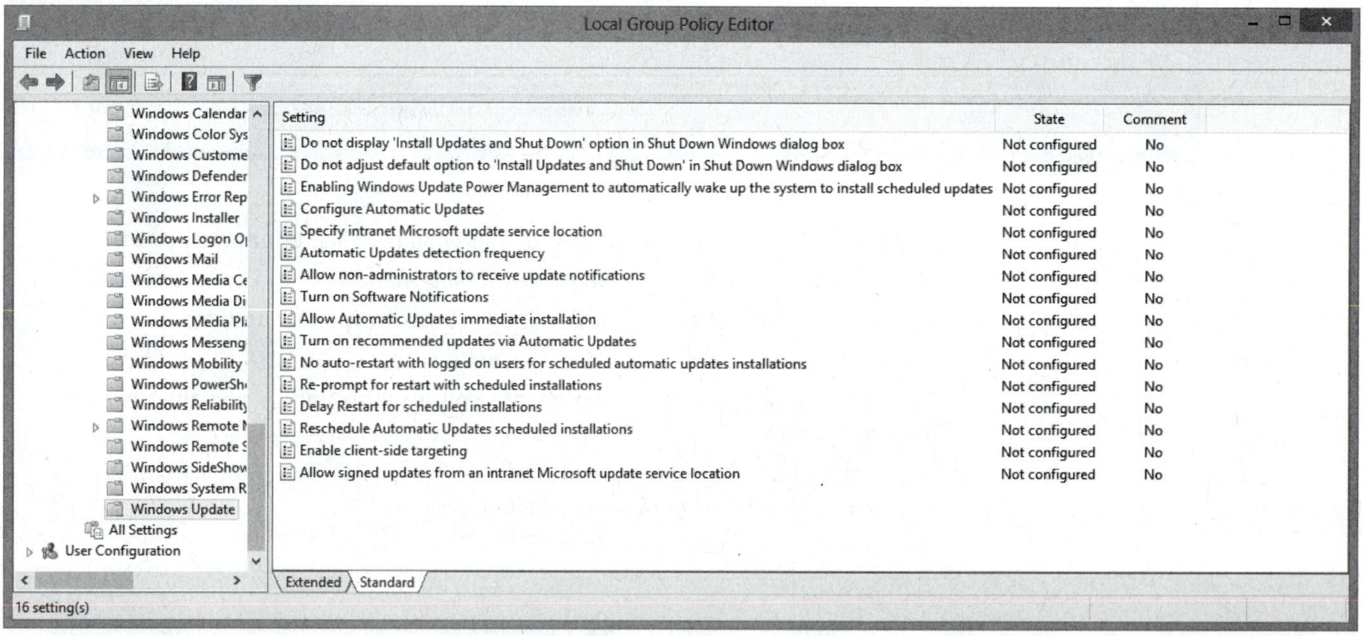

Each policy provides additional details regarding each policy, how it reacts when enabled, disabled, or not configured. It is critical to understand the client reaction to the configuration prior to configuring any Windows Update policy as any misconfiguration or unintended setting change can result in unforeseen downtime and possible data loss. If Windows Update policies are configured in an enterprise environment, understand the consequences of forced system restarts, application installations, and driver updates deployed to managed devices during production hours.

CONFIGURING THE INSTALL UPDATES AND SHUT DOWN DIALOG BOX POLICY

The *Do not display 'Install Updates and Shut Down' option in Shut Down Windows dialog box* removes, or keeps in place the *Install Updates and Shut Down* option when shutting down the system.

The following options are configurable within this policy setting:

- **Enabled** – When enabled, the *Install Updates and Shut Down* selection is removed from the *Shut Down Windows* dialog box, even when updates are available for installation on the system.
- **Disabled** – When disabled, if updates are available for installation on the system, the *Install Updates and Shut Down* selection is available to choose in the *Shut Down Windows* dialog box.
- **Not Configured** – When not configured, if updates are available for installation on the system, the *Install Updates and Shut Down* selection is available to choose in the *Shut Down Windows* dialog box.

CONFIGURING THE DEFAULT OPTION TO INSTALL UPDATES AND SHUT DOWN DIALOG BOX POLICY

The *Do not adjust default option to 'Install Updates and Shut Downs' in Shut Down Windows dialog box* policy allows the end users to maintain their default shut down selection when shutting down from the *Shut Down Windows* dialog box.

The following options are configurable within this policy setting:

- **Enabled** – When enabled, the user's last shut down selection (Log Off, Shut Down, Restart, Hibernate, and so on) remains the default selection when the next system shut down is initiated from the *Shut Down Windows* dialog box.
- **Disabled** – When disabled, the *Install Updates and Shut Down* selection is made the default selection when the next system shut down is initiated from the *Shut Down Windows* dialog box.
- **Not Configured** – When not configured, the *Install Updates and Shut Down* selection is made the default selection when the next system shut down is initiated from the *Shut Down Windows* dialog box.

This policy has no effect if the *Do not display 'Install Updates and Shut Down' option in Shut Down Windows dialog box* is enabled.

CONFIGURING THE WAKE UP TO INSTALL SCHEDULED UPDATES POLICY

Windows machines that are in hibernation can be configured to wake from hibernation, install updates, and return to hibernation once the update installations have completed. The Enabling Windows Update Power Management to automatically wake up the system to install scheduled updates policy can wake the system up to perform scheduled updates.

The following options are configurable within this policy setting:

- **Enabled** – When enabled, Windows Update will wake up a system that is hibernating, using the Windows Power Management feature, to install updates that are scheduled for installation.
- **Disabled** – When disabled, Windows Update will not wake up a system that is hibernating to install scheduled updates.
- **Not Configured** – When not configured, Windows Update will not wake up a system that is hibernating to install scheduled updates.

If a hibernating system is running on battery power on wake up, updates will not be installed. Instead, the system will automatically return to hibernation after two minutes.

Windows Update brings only a computer out of hibernation if there are updates to be installed.

CONFIGURING THE AUTOMATIC UPDATES POLICY

One of the required policies for system wide control of Automatic Updates, the Configure Automatic Updates policy sets the method of downloading and installing Automatic Updates.

The following options are configurable within this policy setting:

- **Enabled** – When enabled, one of the following, additional options must be configured.
- **Notify for download and notify for install** – Requires user intervention to both download and install available updates. When updates are made available for download, the end-user is notified. The end-user must then initiate the download of available updates. Once the updates have been downloaded, Windows Update will again, notify the end-user and require that they initiate the installation of the recently downloaded updates. This option requires the most user interaction and may leave critical systems at risk if updates are not installed on a regular schedule.
- **Auto download and notify for install** – Configured as the default setting, Windows Update will automatically download updates in the background without user intervention. Once the updates have been downloaded and are ready for installation the user will be notified that there are updates ready for installation. The user is then given the opportunity to select and install the queued updates.
- **Auto download and schedule install** – Requires the least amount of end-user interaction and administrative effort, this selection allows a system administrator to fully automate update installation by download and installing the updates in the background. If no schedule is selected updates will automatically be installed every day at 3:00 Am.
    - **Scheduled install day:**
        - 0 – Every day
        - 1 – Every Sunday
        - 2 – Every Monday
        - 3 – Every Tuesday
        - 4 – Every Wednesday
        - 5 – Every Thursday
        - 6 – Every Friday
        - 7 – Every Saturday
    - ***Scheduled install time*** – Defined by hour, the selection list ranges from 00:00–23:00.

TAKE NOTE*

Scheduling for Windows 8 and Windows RT devices are not affected by this defined schedule and must be configured in the following policy: Computer Configuration > Administrative Templates > Windows Components > Maintenance Scheduler > Automatic Maintenance Activation Boundary. If a schedule is not defined in either location, Windows 8 and Windows RT devices will install updates every day at 3:00 Am.

- **Allow local admin to choose setting** – Local administrators to the system are allowed to choose their own download and installation setting; they will not be allowed to disable Automatic Updates.

- **Disabled** – When disabled, all update downloads and installations require the end user to manually initiate the process.
- **Not Configured** – When not configured, the end user can configure Automatic Updates from within the Control Panel.

CONFIGURING THE INTRANET MICROSOFT UPDATE SERVICE LOCATION POLICY

The Specify intranet Microsoft update service location policy allows the system administrator to configure devices meeting the scope of the policy to receive updates from the intranet WSUS or SCCM server.

The following options are configurable within this policy setting:

- **Enabled** – When enabled, the device within the scope of the policy will detect and download selected updates from the configured intranet update service WSUS or SCCM server. Additionally, the Set the intranet update service for detecting updates option and the Set the intranet statistics server option require the fully qualified domain name (FQDN) and the port of the WSUS or SCCM server issuing the updates.
- **Disabled** – When disabled, clients will receive their updates from the Internet, not from an intranet server.
- **Not Configured** – When not configured, clients will receive their updates from the Internet, not from an intranet server.

TAKE NOTE* If the Configure Automatic Updates policy is not enabled and applied to the devices that this policy applies to, they will not be affected by this policy.

CONFIGURING THE AUTOMATIC UPDATES DETECTION FREQUENCY POLICY

The Automatic Updates detection frequency policy controls how often the system will check for new updates to download and install.

The following options are configurable within this policy setting:

- **Enabled** – When enabled, Windows will check for updates at a configured time interval between 1 and 22 hours. The wait time uses the interval selected minus 0% to 20% of the hours configured.
- **Disabled** – When disabled, Windows will use the default interval of 22 hours.
- **Not Configured** – When not configured, Windows will use the default interval of 22 hours.

TAKE NOTE* If the Configure Automatic Updates policy is not enabled and applied to the devices that this policy applies to, they will not be affected by this policy.

CONFIGURING THE NON-ADMINISTRATOR UPDATE NOTIFICATION POLICY

Enabled by default on Windows 8 devices, the Allow non-administrators to receive update notifications policy allows non-administrators on non-Windows 8 devices to receive update notifications.

The following options are configurable within this policy setting:

- **Enabled** – When enabled, non-administrators will receive update notifications and are allowed to install the updates in which a notification was received.

- **Disabled** – When disabled, only users with elevated permissions will receive notifications and be able to install updates.
- **Not Configured** – When not configured, systems running Windows 7 and Windows 8 are already permitting non-administrators to be notified and to install updates.

TAKE NOTE* If the Configure Automatic Updates policy is not enabled and applied to the devices that this policy applies to, they will not be affected by this policy.

CONFIGURING THE SOFTWARE NOTIFICATIONS POLICY

The Turn on Software Notifications policy notifies the end user of pending optional or featured updates are waiting for download or installation.

The following options are configurable within this policy setting:

- **Enabled** – When enabled, users will receive notifications when optional or featured software applications are available from Microsoft.
- **Disabled** – When disabled, users will not receive notifications when optional or featured software applications are available from Microsoft.
- **Not Configured** – When not configured, users will not receive notifications when optional or featured software applications are available from Microsoft.

TAKE NOTE* If the Configure Automatic Updates policy is not enabled and applied to the devices that this policy applies to, they will not be affected by this policy.

CONFIGURING THE IMMEDIATE INSTALLATION OF AUTOMATIC UPDATES POLICY

The Allow Automatic Updates immediate installation policy triggers the system to install updates once they have been downloaded and prepared for installation.

The following options are configurable within this policy setting:

- **Enabled** – When enabled, Automatic Updates will be installed once they have been downloaded and queued for installation.
- **Disabled** – When disabled, Automatic Updates will not be installed immediately.
- **Not Configured** – When not configured, Automatic Updates will not be installed immediately.

TAKE NOTE* If the Configure Automatic Updates policy is not enabled and applied to the devices that this policy applies to, they will not be affected by this policy.

CONFIGURING THE RECOMMENDED UPDATES THROUGH AUTOMATIC UPDATES POLICY

The Turn on recommended updates via Automatic Updates policy allows automatic installation of both important and recommended updates.

The following options are configurable within this policy setting:

- **Enabled** – When enabled, recommended updates and important updates will be received and installed.
- **Disabled** – When disabled, only important updates will be received and installed.
- **Not Configured** – When not configured, only important updates will be received and installed.

CONFIGURING THE NO AUTO-RESTART WITH LOGGED ON USERS POLICY

Configuring the No auto-restart with logged on users for scheduled automatic updates installations policy prevents a system from rebooting immediately after an update has installed if a user is logged in.

The following options are configurable within this policy setting:

- **Enabled** – When enabled, systems that have recently download and installed Automatic Updates, requiring a restart, will not be forced to restart immediately after installation. Automatic Updates will notify the end user to restart when convenient.
- **Disabled** – When disabled, systems that have recently downloaded and installed Automatic Updates, requiring a restart, will notify the end user that the system will restart in 5 minutes.
- **Not Configured** – When not configured, systems that have recently downloaded and installed Automatic Updates, requiring a restart, will notify the end user that the system will restart in 5 minutes.

WARNING If this is set to Disabled or Not Configured, systems users are logged into will be restarted 5 minutes after the installation. They might lose unsaved data if the computer restarts without their knowledge.

CONFIGURING THE RE-PROMPT FOR RESTART WITH SCHEDULED UPDATES POLICY

The Re-prompt for restart with scheduled installations policy, re-prompts users to restart at a specified interval. If the end user postpones a restart after automatic updates have been installed, the re-prompt for restart policy will notify the end user at the time specified.

The following options are configurable within this policy setting:

- **Enabled** – When enabled and an installation has been postponed, will notify the end user to restart at the specified minute interval. The interval range must be between 1–1440 minutes.
- **Disabled** – When disabled, and an installation has been postponed, will notify the end user to restart after 10 minutes.
- **Not Configured** – When not configured, and an installation has been postponed, will notify the end user to restart after 10 minutes.

TAKE NOTE* If the Configure Automatic Updates policy is not enabled and applied to the devices that this policy applies to, they will not be affected by this policy.

TAKE NOTE* If the Configure Automatic Updates policy is not enabled and applied to the devices that this policy applies to, they will not be affected by this policy.

CONFIGURING THE DELAY RESTART FOR SCHEDULED INSTALLATIONS POLICY

An administrator may modify the Delay Restart for scheduled installations policy to allow additional time for the user to finish work before the restart is initiated.

The following options are configurable within this policy setting:

- **Enabled** – When enabled, a scheduled restart will occur after the specified minutes are reached. The minimum time allowed is 1 minute and the maximum time allowed is 30 minutes.
- **Disabled:** When disabled, a schedule restart will occur after 15 minutes.
- **Not Configured:** When not configured, a schedule restart will occur after 15 minutes.

TAKE NOTE* If the Configure Automatic Updates policy is not enabled and applied to the devices that this policy applies to, they will not be affected by this policy.

CONFIGURING THE RESCHEDULE AUTOMATIC UPDATES SCHEDULED INSTALLATIONS POLICY

If a scheduled Automatic Update was not performed, the amount of time to wait for the next attempt at installation can be rescheduled to happen at next startup. This is configured through the Reschedule Automatic Updates scheduled installations policy.

The following options are configurable within this policy setting:

- **Enabled** – When enabled, once the wait time configured is reached, a scheduled installation will take place to install the updates that were missed earlier. The minimum time allowed is 1 minute and the maximum time allowed is 60 minutes.
- **Disabled** – When disabled, missed scheduled updates will be installed at the next scheduled update.
- **Not Configured** – When not configured, missed scheduled updates will be installed one minute after the computer has restarted.

TAKE NOTE* If the Configure Automatic Updates policy is not enabled and applied to the devices that this policy applies to, they will not be affected by this policy.

CONFIGURING THE ENABLE CLIENT-SIDE TARGETING POLICY

By configuring multiple group policies, multiple group names can be sent to the intranet Microsoft update servers. These groups are configured in the "Enable client-side targeting" policy.

Separate target groups for Windows servers: a target group for Windows desktops, and a target group for Windows laptops. Allowing the intranet Windows update server administrator the ability to deploy, choose selected updates, and/or delay updates based on specified target group.

TAKE NOTE* If the Specify intranet Microsoft update service location policy is not enabled and applied to the devices that this policy applies to, they will not be affected by this policy.

The following options are configurable within this policy setting:

- **Enabled** – When enabled, the configured target group will be sent to the intranet Microsoft update server. The Microsoft update server can then be configured to deploy updates to the specified group.
- **Disabled** – When disabled, no target group information is sent to the intranet Microsoft update server.
- **Not Configured** – When not configured, no target group information is sent to the intranet Microsoft update server.

CONFIGURING THE ALLOW SIGNED UPDATES FROM AN INTRANET MICROSOFT UPDATE SERVICE LOCATION POLICY

Microsoft, by default, allows only the installation of updates that are signed by Microsoft. By configuring the Allowed signed updates from an intranet Microsoft update service location policy, an administrator can permit trusted updates from being installed that are not signed by Microsoft.

The following options are configurable within this policy setting:

- **Enabled** – When enabled, Automatic Updates from non-Microsoft companies, which are received from the intranet Windows Update server, will be accepted if they are signed by a certificate found within the Trusted Publishers certificate store. Updates signed by Microsoft will also be installed.
- **Disabled** – When disabled, only Automatic Updates delivered from the intranet Microsoft update server, that are signed by Microsoft, will be installed.
- **Not Configured** – When not configured, only Automatic Updates delivered from the intranet Microsoft update server, which are signed by Microsoft, will be installed.

CONFIGURE THE DO NOT DISPLAY INSTALL UPDATES AND SHUT DOWN POLICY

GET READY. To configure local group policies from a Windows 8 machine, perform the following actions:

1. From the Windows 8 start menu, type **gpedit.msc** and then select it from the results list.

   The *Local Group Policy Editor* window appears.
2. Navigate through the Local Computer Policy tree on the left to the following location: **Computer Configuration > Administrative Templates > Windows Components > Windows Update**.
3. Double-click on **Do not display 'Install Updates and Shut Down' option in Shut Down Windows dialog box**.

   The *Do not display 'Install Updates and Shut Down' option in Shut Down Windows dialog box* appears.
4. Verify that the *Do not display 'Install Updates and Shut Down'* option in *Shut Down Windows* dialog box state is set to **Enabled**.
5. Close the *Local Group Policy Editor* window.

Managing Update History

THE BOTTOM LINE

Microsoft routinely issues patches, service packs, and drivers to Microsoft software products in the form of Microsoft and Windows Updates.

Through end-user interaction or system administration settings, personal and enterprise computers as well as Microsoft signed devices are patched and secured against the latest vulnerabilities, security risks, and threats.

Viewing Update History

All updates that are installed on the Windows 8 system can be viewed, sorted by Name, Status, Importance, and Date installed from within the Control Panel.

CERTIFICATION READY
Manage update history
Objective 6.1

All installed updates are listed within the View ***update history*** windows within Windows Update. Viewing the update history can assist in troubleshooting failed updates, finding an update that could potentially be causing problems, or even help when verifying a required patch is installed prior to some software installations.

The View update history window also provides detailed information about what the installed update fixes, or what security risks are patched with a specific update.

REVIEW THE UPDATE HISTORY

GET READY. Perform the following actions to review the update history of your Windows 8 system:

1. From the Windows 8 start menu, type **Control Panel** and then select it from the results list.

   The *Control Panel* window appears.
2. Within the *Control Panel* window, click **System and Security**.
3. Click **Windows Update** to display the *Windows Update configuration* window.

TAKE NOTE*

If the Windows 8 computer you are configuring is on a domain that has implemented an intranet Windows update server, using group policies for Automatic Updates, some selections might be greyed out.

4. Click **View update history**.

   The *View update history* window appears.

5. Review the update history of your Windows 8 computer, and then notice the update Name, Status, Importance, and Date installed. These columns are also sortable.

6. Double-click on an update.

   The *Windows Update* window appears providing additional details about the update.

7. Note the window contents and links provided about the update.

8. Click **Close**.

9. Click **OK** to close the *View update history* window.

10. Close the *Windows Update* window.

Rolling Back Updates

THE BOTTOM LINE

Microsoft updates are routinely tested before they are deployed to the mass market of Windows users. Unfortunately, there are times that a Windows update is release that might cause conflict with a third-party application or program installed on the system. Rolling back updates allows the end user to uninstall a previously installed update to the point before its original installation.

Take into consideration a web application that was written when Internet Explorer 6 was the preferred Internet browser. Now think of the company that wrote the web application has not made any significant updates to the application to take advantage of the latest releases of Internet Explorer.

If an end user installs the Internet Explorer 10 from Windows Update, the web application that she uses might become unusable due to the inadequacies of the third-party web application.

It would now be required of the web application developer to fix the web application for compatibility, and to take advantage of the security features of the latest version of Internet Explorer.

Until the third-party web application is fixed, the end user will need to roll back her Internet Explorer 10 update to Internet Explorer 9, where the web application formerly worked.

CERTIFICATION READY
Roll back updates
Objective 6.1

You can perform any of the following tasks to roll back an update to get a system back to its original state before an update caused an issue:

- Performing a system restore of the system to a time before the problem update was installed.
- Manually uninstalling an update to remove roll back the newest version of an update to the prior version of the update. Uninstalling an update might also return a system back to an operable state if a recently released update has created issues within the system.
- As indicated previously, you can view updates based on their installation date. If a system was working properly before updates were installed, it is beneficial to review the latest installed updates and begin troubleshooting update problems by uninstalling the most recently installed updates as listed.

TAKE NOTE*

If an update is installed that was configured to be automatically installed, additional configuration might need to be considered to prevent the update from being reinstalled during the next scheduled update.

UNINSTALL AN INSTALLED UPDATE

GET READY. For lab purposes, you may choose any update you want to uninstall. To uninstall an installed update, perform the following actions:

TAKE NOTE*

If the Windows 8 computer you are configuring is on a domain that has implemented an intranet Windows update server, using group policies for Automatic Updates, some selections might be grayed out.

1. From the Windows 8 start menu, type **Control Panel**, and then select it from the results list.

   The *Control Panel* window appears.
2. Within the *Control Panel* window, click **System and Security**.
3. Click **Windows Update** to display the *Windows Update configuration* window.
4. From the bottom left corner of the window, click **Installed Updates**.

   The *Installed Updates* window appears.
5. Select the update you want to uninstall, and from the toolbar above the list, click **Uninstall**.

   The *Uninstall* dialog box appears.
6. Click **Uninstall**.
7. You might be prompted to reboot your machine after the update uninstall has completed. If prompted, you can click **Yes** to reboot or **No** to reboot at a later time.

TAKE NOTE*

You can also uninstall an update by right-clicking the update and selecting *Uninstall*.

Updating Windows Store Applications

THE BOTTOM LINE

Windows Store Applications (Apps) are not updated through Windows Update. Because Windows Store Apps are user-based applications, updates for these apps are performed through the Windows Store.

Windows Store Apps are downloaded and installed by using the Windows Store. Any apps that have been purchased, downloaded, and installed in the Windows Store can be updated only through the Microsoft Store.

CERTIFICATION READY
Update Windows Store applications
Objective 6.1

Viewing the settings within the Microsoft Store, there is an option to *Automatically download updates for my apps* as shown in Figure 21-6. Leaving this set to the default option of Yes allows the Microsoft Store to download updates. End users must then manually initiate the installation of the app through the Microsoft Store.

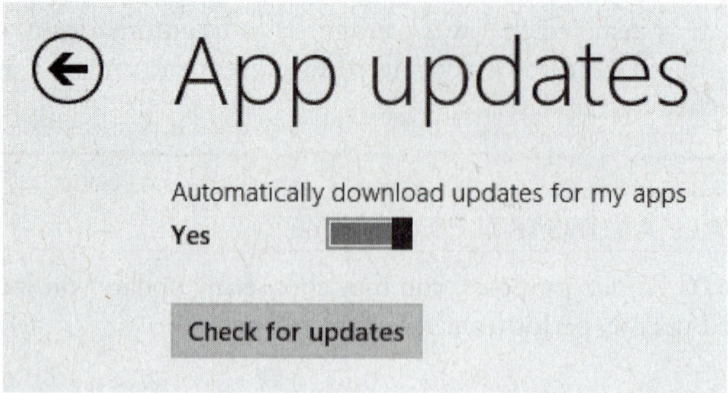

Figure 21-6

Configuring automatic downloading of updates to Windows Store apps

At the time of this writing, automatic installation of updates through the Windows Store app was not available.

UPDATE WINDOWS STORE APPS

GET READY. To update Windows Store applications, perform the following actions:

1. From the Windows 8 start menu, type **Store** and then select it from the results list.

   The Store app connects and appears.

2. In the upper-right corner of the Windows Store, click **Updates (XX)**, where *XX* is the number of updates available for installation.

   The App updates panel appears.

3. View the available updates, and then choose the updates you want to install or click the **Select all** icon.

4. Once you have selected the updates to install, click the **Install** icon as shown in Figure 21-7.

   The Installing apps pane appears providing the progress of the updates being performed. When all updates have completed, click the back arrow icon.

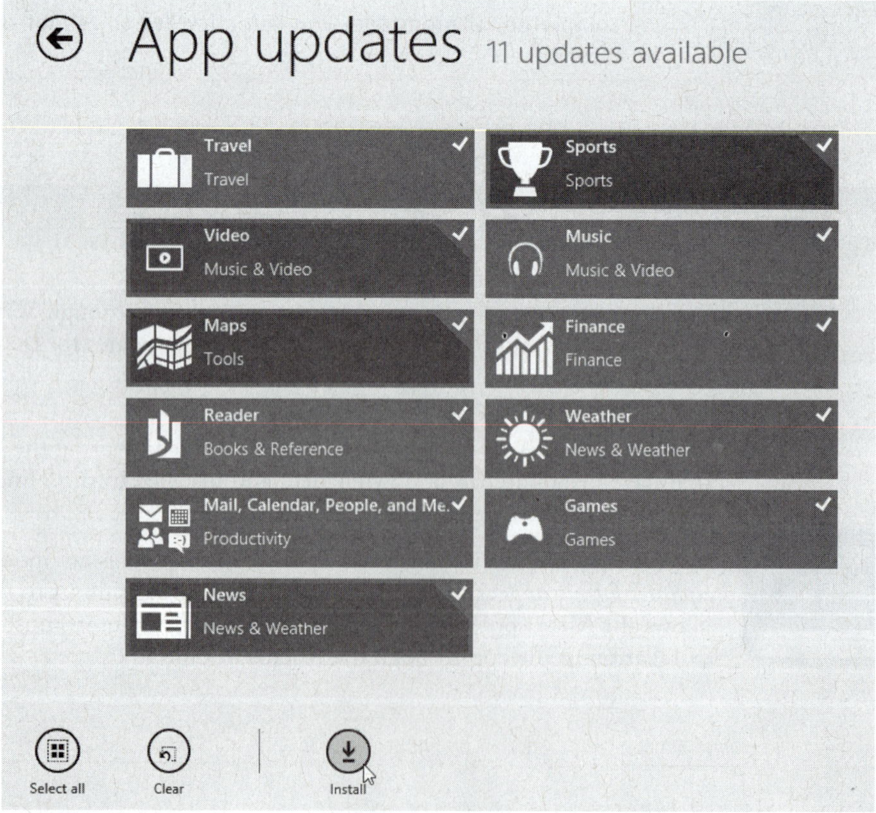

Figure 21-7

Updating Windows Store Apps

5. If all updates have been installed, you will no longer see the Updates link in the upper-right corner of the Store window.
6. Close the Store.

SKILL SUMMARY

IN THIS LESSON, YOU LEARNED:

- Updates are performed on a system to enhance, improve, secure, and protect end users from threats.
- It is important to keep a system up-to-date with the lastest patches, service packs, and updates. Automatic udpates can be configured to allow minimal user intertaction when updates are downloaded and installed.
- Updates can be manually hidden from view and prevented from being downloaded onto a system.
- The download, installation, timing, and user interaction regarding updates can be configured in the Local Computer Policy or by using Domain Group Policies.
- Configuring Windows policies allows for updates to be managed from a central location.
- Windows updates can be scheduled for installation to meet the needs of the end user, small business, or enterprise.
- Recently installed updates are listed along with a status, date of installation, and more detailed information of the updated and what it has affected.
- Windows Updates can be easily uninstalled or rolled back to a previous state if a recently installed update is causing problems. This can also be beneficial when troubleshooting a system instability after updates were recently installed.
- Windows Store Apps can be updated through the Windows Store.

Knowledge Assessment

Multiple Choice

Select the correct answer for each of the following questions.

1. When a user attempts to restart the machine, the default option in the Start Menu is to Install Updates and Shut Down. What can you change to allow the user's last selection to be the default?
   a. Taskbar
   b. Power Options
   c. Group Policy
   d. Start Menu Properties
2. Users report that when they were busy working on a time-sensitive project, their computer issued a warning that it would be restarted in five minutes to complete an update installation. They are unable to cancel the warning and must save their work and reboot. You need to prevent users' computers from rebooting when the computer is in use. What policy setting will you modify?
   a. Allow users to cancel Windows Update restart initiation.
   b. Client-side targeting.

c. Delay Restart for scheduled installations.
d. No auto-restart with logged on users for scheduled automatic updates installations.

3. Microsoft Store application updates are downloaded and installed from what location?
   a. Windows Update
   b. Microsoft Update
   c. App Update
   d. Microsoft Store
4. To ensure that all computers can receive Automatic Updates even if they are in hibernation, what policy will you change?
   a. Enabling Windows Update Power Management to automatically wake up the system to install scheduled updates.
   b. Configure Automatic Updates.
   c. Automatic Updates detection frequency.
   d. Allow Automatic Updates immediate installation.
5. To prevent an update from appearing in the Updates ready to install list on the three computers in your office, which policy will you change?
   a. Do not display 'Install Updates and Shut Down' option in Shut Down Windows dialog box.
   b. Allow non-administrators to receive update notifications.
   c. Manually hide the updates.
   d. Uncheck the update from the list of available updates.
6. After running Windows Updates, a critical application no longer runs properly. You have found the update that is the culprit. What will be your next troubleshooting step? The solution must minimize the amount of system downtime.
   a. Uninstall recently installed updates.
   b. Perform a system rollback.
   c. Perform a system restore.
   d. Hide recently installed updates.
7. To receive recommended updates the same way you receive important updates, where in the Windows Update settings will allow this option?
   a. View update history.
   b. Properties.
   c. Change settings.
   d. Check online for updates from Microsoft Update.
8. Where will you view the success or failure status of installed updates?
   a. View update history
   b. Installed Updates
   c. Microsoft Store
   d. Check for updates
9. What is the recommended Windows Update setting for downloading and installing updates?
   a. Download updates but let me choose whether to install them.
   b. Check for updates but let me choose whether to download and install them.
   c. Never check for updates.
   d. Install updates automatically.
10. These updates must be selected and installed manually from Windows Updates.
    a. Featured updates
    b. Optional updates
    c. Recommended updates
    d. Important updates

Best Answer

Choose the letter that corresponds to the best answer. More than one answer choice may achieve the goal. Select the BEST answer.

1. Which policy setting allows select updates to be applied to a specific group of computers?
   a. Local Group Policy editor
   b. Client Side Targeting
   c. Group Policy editor
   d. Windows Domain Groups
2. Users are not receiving notifications that updates are available for download or install. What will you configure?
   a. Give me recommended updates the same way I receive important updates
   b. Grant the user elevated privileges
   c. Configure Automatic Updates
   d. Allow non-administrators to receive update notifications
3. Where can you quickly view the details of an update and the applications it affects?
   a. View update history
   b. Installed Updates
   c. Add/Remove Programs
   d. TechNet
4. You would like to put off an update until you are ready to install it at a later time. What can you configure?
   a. Hide update
   b. Ignore update
   c. Remove update from list
   d. Roll back update
5. Windows Server Update Service (WSUS) and System Center Configuration Manager (SCCM) are considered which of the following Microsoft update service locations?
   a. Internet
   b. Intranet
   c. Server-side target
   d. Client-site target

Matching and Identification

1. Match the following terms with their corresponding definitions.
   _______ a) Critical updates
   _______ b) Group policies
   _______ c) Important updates
   _______ d) Microsoft updates
   _______ e) Optional updates
   _______ f) Recommended updates
   _______ g) Security updates
   _______ h) Service packs
   _______ i) Update settings
   _______ j) Update history
   1. A cumulative collection of updates released over a period of time.
   2. All updates that have been installed on the system, sortable by status, importance and date installed.
   3. Requiring additional components, these updates include Office products.
   4. Improves security, privacy, and reliability within the OS or application.

5. Rated as critical, important, moderate, or low, these are released to fix product-specific security related vulnerabilities that might affect end-user or enterprise systems
6. These are used to configure a large group of computers to receive the same updates.
7. Modifying these will change the download and notification settings.
8. Takes care of non-critical problems that might enhance end-user usability with the software.
9. These updates and features must be manually installed.
10. Fix non-security related bugs.

Build a List

1. In order of first to last, specify the order of precedence for downloading and installing updates for other Microsoft Products.
   _______ Accept the Terms of Use.
   _______ Open System and Security.
   _______ Click Install.
   _______ Open Windows Update.
   _______ Click Find out more.
   _______ Open Control Panel.
2. Navigate to the Windows Update Policies.
   _______ Expand Administrative Templates.
   _______ Open Local Group Policy Editor.
   _______ Expand Windows Components.
   _______ Expand Computer Configuration.
   _______ Select Windows Update.
3. Uninstall a recently installed update.
   _______ Open Installed Updates.
   _______ Open System and Security.
   _______ Open Windows Update.
   _______ Open Control Panel.
   _______ Select the update for uninstallation.
   _______ Right-click and select Uninstall.

Business Case Scenarios

Scenario 21-1: Configuring Updates for an Enterprise

You have been hired on as a consultant for a local call center that has a local datacenter with 25 fully redundant, virtualized Windows Server 2012 servers, 200 phone operators on staff, and 125 desktops running Windows 8 Enterprise. The call center runs 24 hours a day, 7 days per week. You have been tasked with finding a solution to update all 150 systems without noticeable downtime. What solution and policies will be included in the plan of action to configure updates for this enterprise? Can any other solutions be used?

Scenario 21-2: Securing a Multi-Client Environment

A small company hires you on as a consultant to assist in securing its mixed Windows client environment. There are 5 computers with Windows 2000 Professional, 10 with Windows XP, and 10 with Windows 8. You have already recommended the systems have an up-to-date antivirus installed and firewalls be enabled. What are the other concerns with its current client configurations?

Managing Local Storage

LESSON 22

70-687 EXAM OBJECTIVE

Objective 6.2 – Manage local storage. This objective may include but is not limited to manage disk volumes; manage storage spaces; and manage file system fragmentation.

Lesson Heading	Exam Objective
Working with Disks	
Understanding Partition Styles	
Understanding Disk Types	
Understanding Volume Types	
Understanding File Systems	
Using the Disk Management Snap-in	Manage Disk Volumes
Using Storage Spaces	Manage Storage Spaces
Using Diskpart.exe	
Using Disk Tools	Manage File System Fragmentation

KEY TERMS

basic disk
Diskpart.exe
dynamic disk
exFAT
FAT
FAT32
GUID (globally unique identifier) partition table (GPT)
master boot record (MBR)
mirrored volume
simple volume
spanned volume
striped volume

Working with Disks

THE BOTTOM LINE

Hard disks are nearly always the primary storage medium in a computer running Windows 8, but in many cases, administrators must prepare a hard disk to store data by performing certain tasks before the computer can use it. After you prepare the hard disk, you can keep the data stored on the disk secure with tools and features provided by Windows 8.

When you install Windows 8 on a computer, the setup program automatically performs all of the preparation tasks for the hard disks in the computer. However, adding another disk is a common upgrade, and after you install the hardware, you must perform the following tasks before the user can begin storing data on it:

- **Select a partitioning style** – In Windows 8, two hard disk partition styles are available for both x86- and x64-based computers. The ***master boot record (MBR)*** partition style has been around as long as Windows, and is still the default partition style. ***GUID (globally unique identifier) partition table (GPT)*** has been around for a while also, but no x86 version of Windows prior to Vista supports it. (Windows XP Professional x64 Edition does support GPT.) You must choose one of these partition styles for a drive; you cannot use both.
- **Select a disk type** – Two disk types are available in Windows 8: basic disks and dynamic disks. Both the MBR and the GPT partition styles support basic and dynamic disks. You cannot use both types on the same disk drive. You have to decide which is best for the computer.
- **Divide the disk into partitions or volumes** – Although many professionals use the terms partition and volume interchangeably, it is correct to refer to creating partitions on basic disks, and volumes on dynamic disks.
- **Format the volumes with a file system** – Because of the high capacities of the hard drives on the market today, NTFS is the preferred file system for Windows 8. However, the FAT (File Allocation Table) file system is also available, in the form of FAT32 and exFAT.

The following sections examine these tasks in more detail.

Understanding Partition Styles

The term partition style refers to the method that Windows operating systems use to organize partitions on the disk.

There are two hard disk partition styles that you can use in Windows 8:

- **MBR** – This is the default partition style for x86-based and x64-based computers.
- **GPT** – First introduced in Windows Vista, you can now use the GPT partition style on x86-, as well as x64-based, Windows 8 computers.

Before Windows Vista, all x86-based computers used the MBR partition style only. Computers based on the x64 platform used either the MBR or GPT partition style, as long as the GPT disk was not the boot disk.

MBR uses a partition table to point to the locations of the partitions on the disk. Windows selected this style automatically on x86-based workstation computers because, prior to Windows Vista, this was the only style available to them. The MBR disk partitioning style supports volumes up to 2 terabytes in size, and up to either four primary partitions or three primary partitions and one extended partition. Data critical to platform operations is stored in hidden (unpartitioned) sectors.

Table 22-1 lists the Windows operating systems that can use either the MBR or the GPT partition style for their disks:

Table 22-1

Windows Operating Systems Supporting MBR and GPT Partition Styles

Operating System	x86-based	x64-based	IA-64-based
Windows XP	No	Yes	Yes
Windows Server 2003 SP1 (or later)	Yes	Yes	Yes
Windows Vista	Yes	Yes	N/A
Windows Server 2008	Yes	Yes	Yes
Windows 8	Yes	Yes	N/A
Windows Server 2008 R2	No	Yes	Yes
Windows Server 2012	N/A	Yes	N/A

Keep in mind, however, that unless the computer's architecture provides support for an Extensible Firmware Interface (EFI)-based boot partition, it is not possible to boot from GPT disks. In this case, the operating system must reside on an MBR disk, and GPT must reside on an entirely separate, non-bootable disk, used for data storage only.

One of the ways that GPT differs from MBR is that data critical to platform operation is stored in partitions rather than in hidden sectors. Additionally, GPT partitioned disks use redundant primary and backup partition tables for improved integrity. Although GPT specifications permit an unlimited number of partitions, the Windows implementation is restricted to 128 partitions per disk. The GPT disk partitioning style supports volumes up to 18 exabytes in size (1 exabyte = 1 billion gigabytes, or 2^{60} bytes).

MORE INFORMATION

As far as the Windows 8 disk management tools are concerned, there is no difference between creating partitions or volumes in MBR and in GPT. You create partitions and volumes for both by using the same tools in the same ways.

Table 22-2 compares some of the characteristics of the MBR and GPT partition styles.

Table 22-2

MBR and GPT Partition Style Comparison

Master Boot Record (MBR)	GUID Partition Table (GPT)
Supports up to four primary partitions or three primary partitions and one extended partition, with unlimited logical drives on the extended partition.	Supports up to 128 primary partitions.
Supports volumes up to 2 terabytes in size.	Supports volumes up to 18 exabytes in size.
Data critical to platform operations is stored in hidden (unpartitioned) sectors.	Data critical to platform operation is stored in partitions rather than in hidden sectors.
Replication and CRC are not features of MBR's partition table.	Replication and cyclical redundancy check (CRC)protection of the partition table provide increased reliability.

Understanding Disk Types

Windows 8 supports two disk types: basic disks and dynamic disks.

Most Windows computers use basic disks, because they are the easiest to manage. A ***basic disk*** uses primary partitions, extended partitions, and logical drives to organize data. A primary partition appears to the operating system as though it is a physically separate disk and can host an operating system. A primary partition that hosts an operating system is marked as the *active partition.*

During the Windows 8 operating system installation, the setup program creates a *system partition* and a *boot partition.* The system partition contains hardware-related files that the computer uses to start. The boot partition contains the operating system files, which are stored in the Windows folder. In Windows 8, the system partition is the active partition, which the computer uses when starting.

When you use the Disk Management snap-in to work with basic disks using the MBR partition style, you can create up to three primary partitions. The fourth partition you create must be an extended partition, after which you can create as many logical drives as you need from the space in the extended partition. You can format and assign drive letters to logical drives, but they cannot host an operating system. Table 22-3 compares some of the characteristics of primary and extended partitions.

Table 22-3

Comparison of Primary and Extended Partitions

Primary Partitions	Extended Partitions
A primary partition functions as if it is a physically separate disk and can host an operating system.	Extended partitions cannot host an operating system.
A primary partition can be marked as an active partition. You can have only one active partition per hard disk. The system BIOS looks to the active partition for the boot files it uses to start the operating system.	You cannot mark an extended partition as an active partition.
You can create up to four primary partitions or three primary partitions and one extended partition.	A basic disk can contain only one extended partition, but an unlimited number of logical partitions.
You format each primary partition and assign a unique drive letter.	You do not format the extended partition itself, but the logical drives it contains. You assign a unique drive letter to each of the logical drives.

When you use DiskPart, a command-line utility included with Windows 8, to manage a basic disk, you can create up to four primary partitions or three primary partitions and one extended partition.

TAKE NOTE*

The DiskPart command-line utility contains a superset of the commands that the Disk Management snap-in supports. In other words, DiskPart can do everything Disk Management can do, and more.

The Disk Management snap-in prohibits you from unintentionally performing actions that may result in data loss. DiskPart does not have the built-in protections that Disk Management possesses, and so does not prohibit you from performing such actions. For this reason, Microsoft recommends that only advanced personnel use DiskPart and that they use it infrequently and with due caution, because unlike Disk Management, DiskPart provides absolute control over partitions and volumes.

The alternative to using a basic disk is to convert it to a ***dynamic disk***. The process of converting a basic disk to a dynamic disk creates a single partition that occupies the entire disk. You can then create an unlimited number of volumes out of the space in that partition. The advantage of using dynamic disks is that they support several different types of volumes, as described in the next section.

Understanding Volume Types

Dynamic disks can support five types of volumes: simple, spanned, striped, mirrored, and RAID-5 (Redundant Array of Independent Disks, level 5). Windows 8 only supports four of these volume types, however: simple, spanned, striped, and mirrored.

A dynamic disk is able to contain an unlimited number of volumes that function like primary partitions on a basic disk. However, you cannot access a dynamic disk from any operating system instance other than the one that converted it from basic to dynamic, which means you cannot use dynamic disks on multiboot systems.

When you create a volume on a dynamic disk in Windows 8, you can choose from the following four volume types:

- ***Simple volume*** – Consists of space from a single disk. Once you have created a simple volume, you can later extend it to multiple disks to create a spanned or striped volume, as long as it is not a system volume or boot volume. Windows 8 supports simple volumes on both basic and dynamic disks.
- ***Spanned volume*** – Consists of space from at least two, to a maximum of 32, physical disks, all of which must be dynamic disks. A spanned volume is essentially a method for combining the space from multiple dynamic disks into a single large volume. Windows 8 writes to the spanned volume by filling all of the space on the first disk, and then filling each of the additional disks in turn. You can extend a spanned volume at any time by adding additional disk space. Creating a spanned volume does not increase the read/write performance, nor does it provide fault tolerance. In fact, if a single physical disk in the spanned volume fails, all of the data in the entire volume is lost.
- ***Striped volume*** – Consists of space from at least two, to a maximum of 32, physical disks, all of which must be dynamic disks. The difference between a striped volume and a spanned volume is that in a striped volume, the system writes data one stripe at a time to each successive disk in the volume. Striping provides improved performance because each disk drive in the array has time to seek the location of its next stripe while the other drives are writing. Striped volumes do not provide fault tolerance, and you cannot extend them after creation. If a single physical disk in the striped volume fails, all of the data in the entire volume is lost.
- ***Mirrored volume*** – Consists of an equal amount of space from two disks, both of which must be dynamic disks. In a mirrored volume, each disk holds an identical copy of the data written to the volume as a fault tolerance measure. If one disk fails, the data remains accessible from the second disk. Because of the data redundancy, a mirrored volume only provides half as much storage space as any of the other volume types.

TAKE NOTE*

The disk volume limitations described here are those of Windows 8 itself. It is also possible to implement these disk technologies using third party hardware and software products that have their own capabilities and limitations. For example, while Windows 8 does not support software RAID-5, there are many disk adapter products on the market that enable you to create RAID volumes of various types on computers running Windows 8.

The type of disk configuration you choose for a Windows 8 computer depends on the user's needs. While standalone systems for home or small business users might benefit from striped, spanned, or mirrored volumes, for most Windows 8 workstations in an enterprise environment, basic disks are adequate. If the client's computer stores data that requires additional performance or protection against failure, dynamic disks can fill the bill.

Understanding File Systems

To organize and store data or programs on a hard drive, you must install a file system. A file system is the underlying disk drive structure that enables you to store information on your computer. You install file systems by formatting a partition or volume on the hard disk.

In Windows 8, there are two basic file system options to choose from: NTFS and FAT. ***NTFS*** is the preferred file system for Windows 8, its main benefits being improved support for larger hard drives and better security in the form of encryption and permissions that restrict access by unauthorized users.

Because the FAT file systems lack the security that NTFS provides, any user who gains access to your computer can read any file without restriction. Additionally, most of the various FAT file systems have disk size limitations that render them impractical.

The FAT file systems that Windows 8 supports are as follows:

- ***FAT*** – The original 16-bit FAT file system for hard disks, also known as FAT16, is limited to partitions no larger than 4 GB, which makes it virtually useless for today's computers.
- ***FAT32*** – Using the 32-bit version of FAT, called FAT32, Windows 8 can create partitions up to 32 GB in size, with individual files up to 4 GB. Although these limits at one time seemed outlandishly large, they make FAT32 an impractical file system solution on computers today. The 32 GB maximum partition size is a deliberate restriction in Windows 8, not an inherent limitation of FAT32. In fact, Windows 8 can access FAT32 partitions up to 2 TB in size; it just can't create them. This limitation is intended to prevent Windows performance degradation caused by large FAT32 partitions.
- ***exFAT*** – Introduced in Windows Vista SP1, the Extended File Allocation Table (exFAT) file system, also known as FAT64, is a 64-bit FAT implementation that is intended primarily for large USB flash drives. The theoretical limitations of exFAT are partitions and files of up to 64 zettabytes in size. (1 zettabyte equals 1 billion terabytes or 10^{21} bytes.) The recommended maximum size for an exFAT partition in Windows 8 is 512 TB. The exFAT file system does not support the encryption and permission features found in NTFS, and is therefore not recommended for use on Windows 8 hard disks.

When you create or format a partition or volume using the Disk Management snap-in, the interface displays only the file system options that are available to you, based on the size of the partition or volume. Because of these size limitations, the only viable reason for using any of the FAT file systems on Windows 8 hard disks is the need to multiboot the computer with an operating system that does not support NTFS.

Using the Disk Management Snap-in

Disk Management is the primary Windows 8 graphical utility for creating and manipulating hard disk partitions and volumes.

Disk Management is a Microsoft Management Console (MMC) snap-in that you use to perform disk-related tasks, such as the following:

- Initializing disks.
- Selecting a partition style.
- Converting basic disks to dynamic disks.

TAKE NOTE*

You can also use command-line utilities, such as the DiskPart.exe program, to perform Disk Management tasks.

- Creating partitions and volumes.
- Extending, shrinking, and deleting volumes.
- Formatting partitions and volumes.
- Assigning and changing driver letters and paths.
- Examining and managing physical disk properties, such as disk quotas, folder sharing and error-checking.

To access the Disk Management Snap-in, use the following procedure.

OPEN THE DISK MANAGEMENT SNAP-IN

GET READY. Log on to Windows 8 using an account with Administrator privileges, and then perform the following steps:

1. Open the Control Panel window.
2. Click **System and Security**, and then, in the *Administrative Tools* category, click **Create and Format Hard Disk Partitions**.

   The Disk Management window appears, as shown in Figure 22-1.

Figure 22-1

The *Disk Management* window

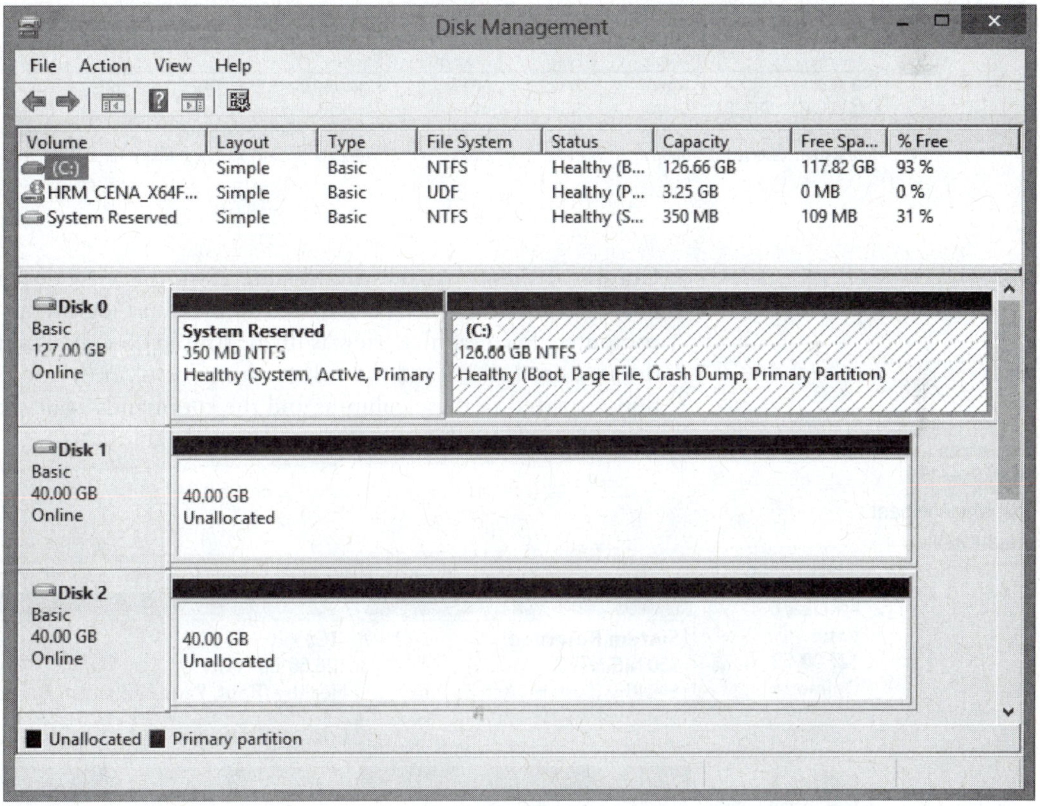

The Disk Management console is divided into two customizable panes: the Top view and the Bottom view, which display disk and volume information, respectively. Although Disk Management can display only two views at any one time, three views are available:

- **Disk List** – As shown in Figure 22-2, this view provides a summary about the physical drives in the computer. This information includes the disk number; disk type, such as basic or DVD; disk capacity; size of unallocated space; the status of the disk device, such as online, offline, or no media; the device interface, such as small computer system interface (SCSI) and integrated device electronics (IDE); and the partition style, such as MBR or GPT.

Figure 22-2

Disk Management's Disk List view

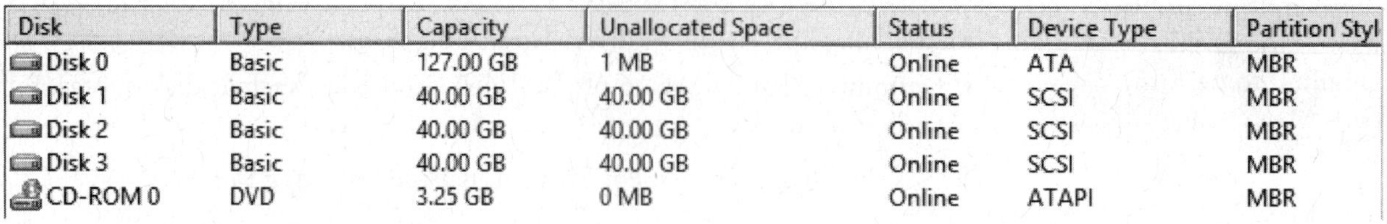

Disk	Type	Capacity	Unallocated Space	Status	Device Type	Partition Styl
Disk 0	Basic	127.00 GB	1 MB	Online	ATA	MBR
Disk 1	Basic	40.00 GB	40.00 GB	Online	SCSI	MBR
Disk 2	Basic	40.00 GB	40.00 GB	Online	SCSI	MBR
Disk 3	Basic	40.00 GB	40.00 GB	Online	SCSI	MBR
CD-ROM 0	DVD	3.25 GB	0 MB	Online	ATAPI	MBR

- **Volume List** – As shown in Figure 22-3, this view provides a more detailed summary of all the drives on the computer. This information includes the volume name; the volume layout, such as simple; the disk type, such as basic or dynamic; the file system in use, such as NTFS or CDFS; the hard disk status, such as healthy, failed, or formatting; the disk capacity and available free space; the percentage of the hard disk that is free; whether the hard disk is fault tolerant; and the disk overhead percentage.

Figure 22-3

Disk Management's Volume List view

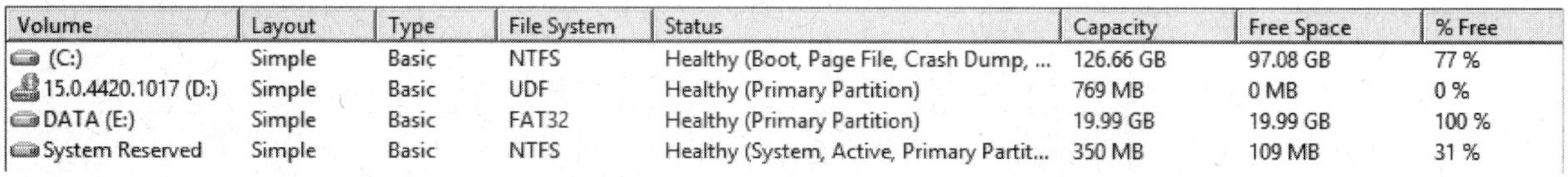

Volume	Layout	Type	File System	Status	Capacity	Free Space	% Free
(C:)	Simple	Basic	NTFS	Healthy (Boot, Page File, Crash Dump, ...	126.66 GB	97.08 GB	77 %
15.0.4420.1017 (D:)	Simple	Basic	UDF	Healthy (Primary Partition)	769 MB	0 MB	0 %
DATA (E:)	Simple	Basic	FAT32	Healthy (Primary Partition)	19.99 GB	19.99 GB	100 %
System Reserved	Simple	Basic	NTFS	Healthy (System, Active, Primary Partit...	350 MB	109 MB	31 %

- **Graphical View** – As shown in Figure 22-4, this view displays a graphical representation of all the physical disks, partitions, volumes, and logical drives available on the computer. The graphical view is divided into two columns: the disk status column (located on the left) and the volume status column (located on the right). The information displayed in these columns and the commands available in the context menu produced by right-clicking them, are shown in Table 22-4.

Figure 22-4

Disk Management's Graphical View

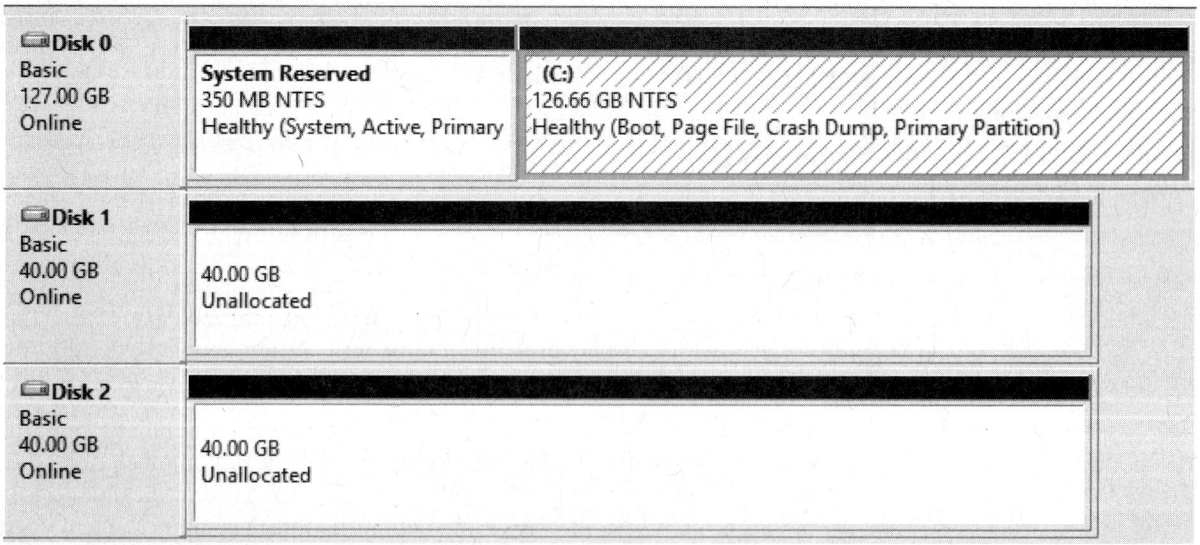

Table 22-4

Disk Management Graphical View Information

	Disk Status Column	Volume Status Column
Information displayed	• Disk number • Disk type • Disk capacity • Disk status	• Volume name • Volume size • File system • Volume status
Context menu commands	• Convert a basic disk to a dynamic disk • Convert an MBR disk to a GPT disk • Create a new spanned, striped, or mirrored volume • Take the disk offline • Open the disk's Properties sheet	For a mounted partition or volume: • Mark a basic disk as active • Change the drive letter and paths • Format the partition or volume • Extend the volume • Shrink the volume • Add a mirror • Delete the volume • Open the volume's Properties sheet For unallocated space: • Create a new simple volume • Create a new spanned volume • Create a new striped volume • Create a new mirrored volume • Open the disk's Properties sheet

By default, the Top view pane depicts the Volume List view, and the Bottom view pane depicts the Graphical View. You can change the views of both the Top view and Bottom view to suit your purposes by clicking the View menu, selecting either Top or Bottom, and then selecting the desired view. You can hide the Bottom view by clicking the Hidden menu option.

TAKE NOTE*

You can circumvent using Control Panel to access the Disk Management console by using the Windows 8 Search feature, or by opening a File Explorer window, right-clicking Computer, and then selecting Manage from the context menu. In the Computer Management console that appears, select Disk Management. You can also press the WIN1X key combination and select Disk Management from the resulting context menu.

VIEWING PHYSICAL DISK PROPERTIES

To view and configure certain properties and settings for the physical disk, right-click the disk status column in Disk Management's graphical view and then select Properties from the context menu. A *Properties* sheet appears as shown in Figure 22-5, with the General tab active.

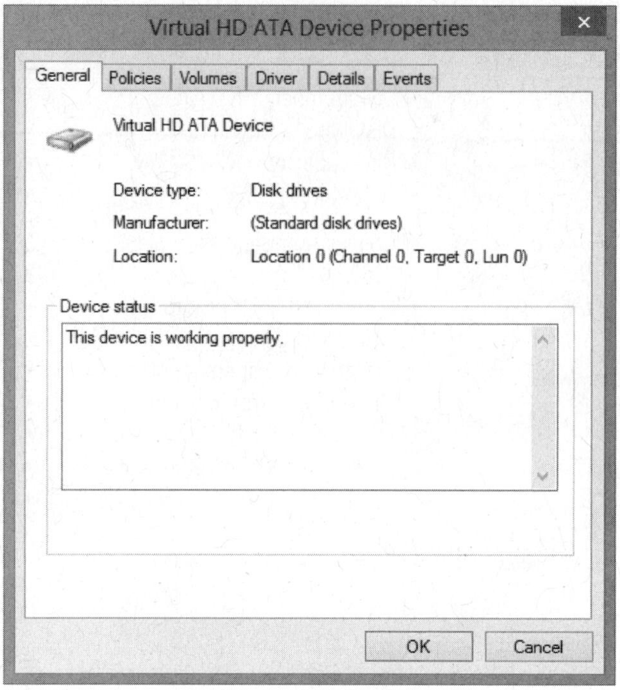

Figure 22-5

The General tab on a disk's *Properties* sheet

TAKE NOTE*

You can open a disk's *Properties* sheet by right-clicking a drive in the Disk List view, and then clicking Properties.

The disk's Properties sheet contains the following tabs:

- General lists the device type, drive manufacturer, device status, and physical location of the device, including the bus number or the SCSI identifier
- Policies provides control over the disk's write-cache buffer, which can improve system performance while increasing the danger of data loss in the event of a power failure.
- Volumes lists the volumes contained on the disk, as well as the disk number, disk type, status, partition style, capacity, unallocated space, and reserved space. If you highlight a volume in the Volumes list, you can click the Properties button to display the *Properties* sheet for the partition or volume.
- Driver displays driver details, and enables you to update, roll back, disable, and uninstall the driver for this device.
- Details displays a Property drop-down list that enables you to display extensive information about the disk.
- Events lists the most recent system events concerning the disk and provides access to the Event Viewer console.

VIEWING PARTITION OR VOLUME PROPERTIES

To view or configure the properties of a partition or volume, right-click the volume status column in Disk Management's Graphical View and then select Properties from the context menu. The volume's *Properties* sheet appears, as shown in Figure 22-6.

Figure 22-6

The General tab on a volume's *Properties* sheet

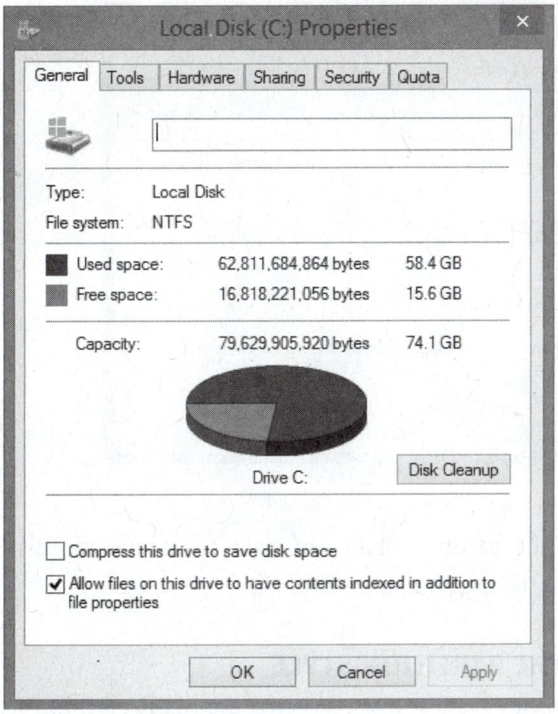

TAKE NOTE*

You can also open a volume's *Properties* sheet by right-clicking a drive in the Volume List view and selecting Properties from the context menu.

The *Properties* sheet for a partition or volume contains the following tabs:

- **General** – Lists the volume label, type of disk, file system, used space, free space, and provides a graphical representation of the total disk capacity. For drives formatted with the NTFS file system, you can choose to compress the drive and to have the Indexing Service index the disk for faster file searching. Additionally, you can run the Disk Cleanup tool to delete unnecessary files, clearing up disk space.
- **Tools** – Enables you to check the partition or volume for errors and fragmentation, and to back up files on the volume.
- **Hardware** – Enables you to view properties for all of the disk drives on the computer, including their manufacturers, bus locations, and device status.
- **Sharing** – Enables you to share the drive or specific folder(s) on the drive, set permissions for the share, and specify the type of caching for the share.
- **Security** – Enables you to set NTFS permissions to secure files and folders by assigning permissions that allow or deny users or groups to perform specific actions on that object. (Appears only on NTFS drives).
- **Quota** – Enables you to configure disk quota management on the computer, which limits the amount of disk space a user can consume. You must format the disk with the NTFS file system in order for this tab to be available.

ADDING A NEW DISK

To add a new secondary disk, shut down your computer and install or attach the new physical disk per the manufacturer's instructions. Use the following procedure to initialize the new disk:

ADD A NEW DISK

GET READY. Log on to Windows 8 using an account with Administrator privileges, and then perform the following steps:

1. Open the **Disk Management** snap-in.

   If the disk does not have a disk signature, the console automatically displays the *Initialize Disk* dialog box, as shown in Figure 22-7.

Figure 22-7

The *Initialize Disk* dialog box

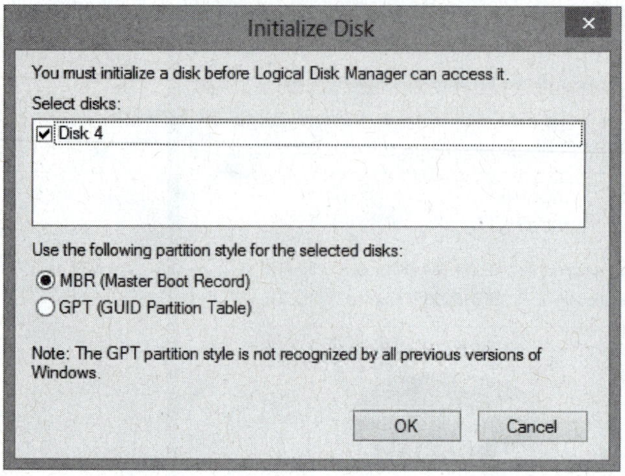

2. Select the partition style you want to use for the disk and then click **OK**. The disk is ready to be partitioned.

CHANGING THE PARTITION STYLE

Disk Management has most likely selected the MBR partition style by default. You can quickly check which partition style the hard disk is assigned by right-clicking the disk status column in the Graphical view. If the context menu contains the Convert to GPT Disk menu item, the disk is using the MBR partition style.

You can also check the volume's information by opening the *Properties* sheet for disk and clicking the Volumes tab, as shown in Figure 22-8. This tab displays information such as disk type, disk status and partition style.

Figure 22-8

The Volumes tab of a disk's *Properties* sheet

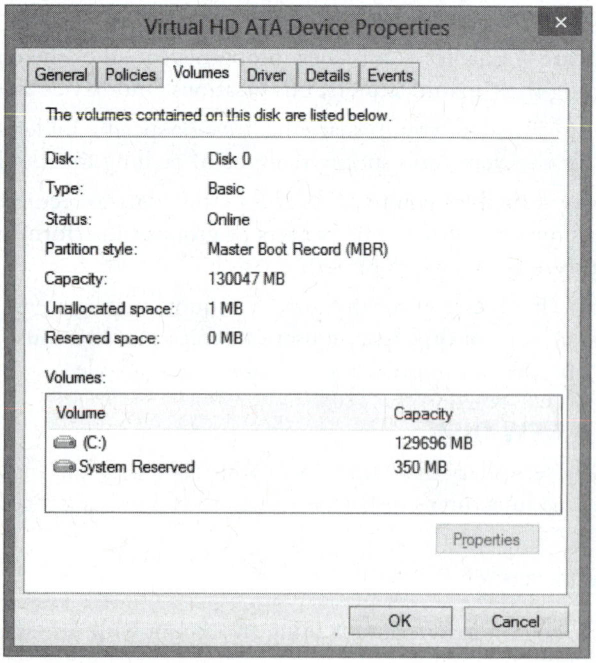

To convert the partition style for a disk, use the following procedure:

CONVERT THE DISK PARTITION STYLE

GET READY. Log on to Windows 8 using an account with Administrator privileges, and then perform the following steps:

WARNING Converting the disk partition style is a destructive process. You can only perform the conversion on an unallocated disk, so if the disk you want to convert contains data, you must back up the disk, verify the back up, and then delete all existing partitions or volumes, before you begin the process.

1. Open the **Disk Management** snap-in.
2. In *Disk List* view, right-click the disk you need to convert and, from the context menu, select **Convert to GPT Disk** or **Convert to MBR Disk**.

   The system then proceeds with the conversion. The length of time this process takes depends on the size of the hard disk.

CONVERTING A BASIC DISK TO A DYNAMIC DISK

When you create a striped, spanned, or mirrored volume on a basic disk, the Disk Management snap-in automatically converts the basic disk (and any additional disks needed to create the volume) to a dynamic one. Therefore, it usually is not necessary to manually convert disks yourself. However, you can convert a basic disk to a dynamic disk at any time, without affecting the data stored on it. Before you convert a basic disk to a dynamic disk, you must be aware of the following conditions:

- Make sure that you have enough hard disk space available for the conversion. The basic-to-dynamic conversion will fail if the hard drive does not have at least 1 MB of free space at the end of the disk. The Disk Management console reserves this free space when creating partitions and volumes, but you cannot presume that other disk management tools you might use will also preserve that space.
- You should not convert a basic disk to a dynamic disk if you are multibooting the computer. If you convert to a dynamic disk, you will not be able to start installed operating systems from any volume on the disk, except the current boot volume.
- You cannot convert removable media to dynamic disks. You can configure them only as basic disks with primary partitions.
- You cannot convert drives that use an allocation unit size (sector size) greater than 512 bytes unless you reformat the drive with a smaller sector size before the conversion.
- Once you change a basic disk to a dynamic disk, the only way you can change it back again is to back up the entire disk and delete the dynamic disk volumes. When you delete the last volume, the dynamic disk automatically reverts back to a basic disk.

To manually convert a basic disk to a dynamic disk, use the following procedure:

CONVERT A BASIC DISK TO A DYNAMIC DISK

GET READY. Log on to Windows 8 using an account with Administrator privileges, and then perform the following steps:

1. Open the **Disk Management** snap-in.
2. In *Disk List* view, right-click the basic disk that you want to convert and, from the context menu, select **Convert to Dynamic Disk**.

   The Convert to Dynamic Disk dialog box appears, as shown in Figure 22-9.

Figure 22-9

The *Convert to Dynamic Disk* dialog box

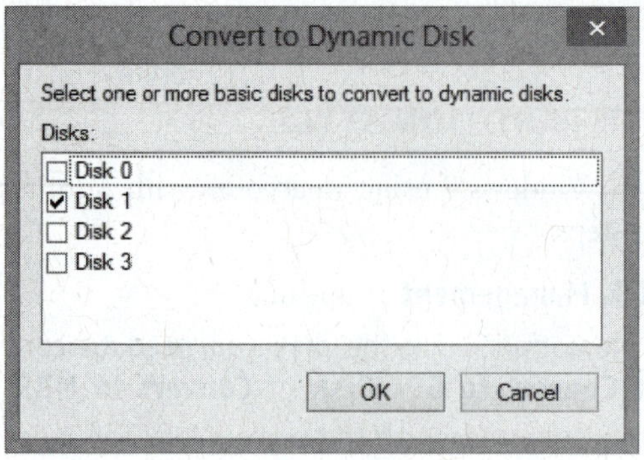

3. Select the checkboxes for the disks you want to convert and then click **OK**.

   If the disks you selected do not contain formatted partitions, clicking **OK** immediately converts the disks, and you do not need to follow the remaining steps.

   If the disks you are converting to dynamic disks do have formatted partitions, clicking **OK** displays the Disks to Convert dialog box, as shown in Figure 22-10, which means that you need to follow the remaining steps to complete the disk conversion.

Figure 22-10

The *Disks to Convert* dialog box

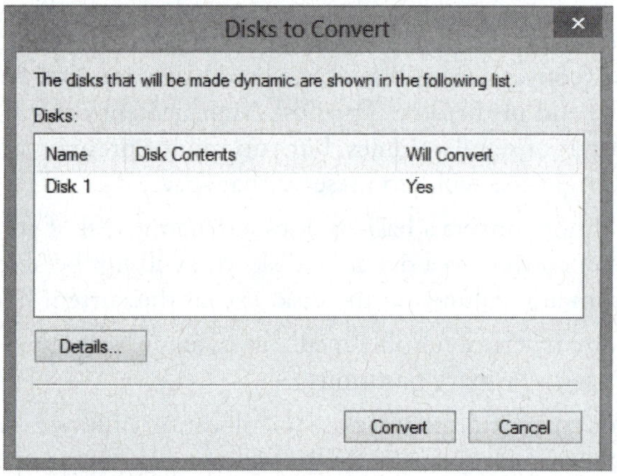

4. The *Disks to Convert* dialog box lists the disks you chose for conversion for your confirmation. In the *Will Convert* column, check the value. It should be set to *Yes* for each of the disks that you are converting. If any of the disks have the value *No*, they might not meet Windows conversion criteria.
5. Click **Details**.

   The Convert Details dialog box appears, as shown in Figure 22-11. This dialog box lists the partitions on the selected drives that Disk Management will convert.

Figure 22-11

The *Convert Details* dialog box

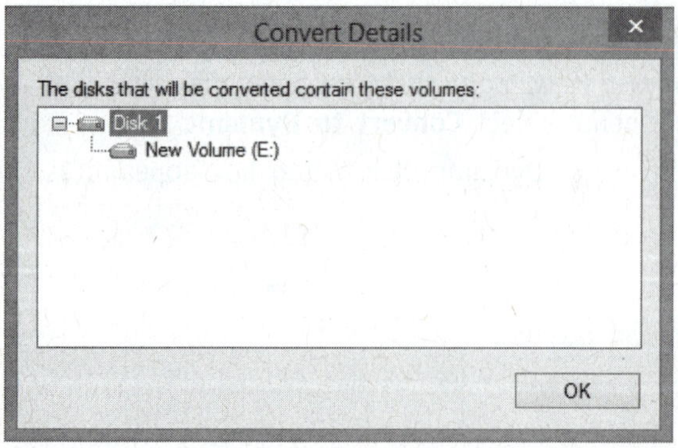

6. When you are ready to continue with the conversion, click **OK**.
7. On the *Disks to Convert* dialog box, click **Convert** to start the conversion.

   A Disk Management information box appears, as shown in Figure 22-12, to warn you that once you convert the disks to dynamic disks, you will not be able to boot installed operating system from any volume other than the current boot volume.

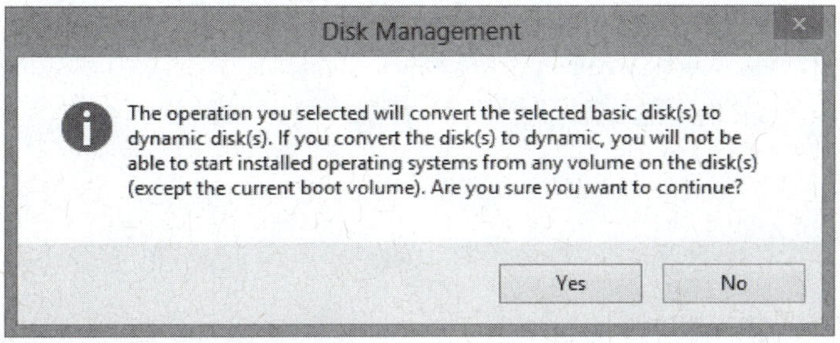

Figure 22-12

A *Disk Management* information box

8. Click **Yes** to continue.

   Disk Management completes the conversion. If a selected drive contains the boot partition, the system partition, or a partition that is in use, Disk Management prompts you to restart the computer.

When you convert from a basic disk to a dynamic disk, Disk Management performs the following tasks.

- Basic disk partitions are converted to dynamic disk volumes of equal size.
- Basic disk primary partitions and logical drives in the extended partition are converted to simple volumes.
- Any free space in a basic disk extended partition is marked as unallocated.

CREATING PARTITIONS AND VOLUMES

The Disk Management console creates both partitions and volumes with one set of dialog boxes and wizards. To create a new partition on a basic disk, or a new volume on a dynamic disk, use the following procedure:

TAKE NOTE*

Technically speaking, the Disk Management snap-in creates partitions on basic disks and volumes on dynamic disks. However, in recent Windows versions, including Windows 8, the interface tends to use the terms interchangeably. In most instances, the snap-in refers to volumes on both basic and dynamic disks, but it still uses the term partition when referring to formatting and making a partition active.

CREATE A VOLUME

CERTIFICATION READY
Manage disk volumes
Objective 6.2

GET READY. Log on to Windows 8 using an account with Administrator privileges, and then perform the following steps:

1. Open the **Disk Management** snap-in.
2. In the *Graphical* view, right-click the unallocated area on the volume status column for the disk on which you want to create a volume and, from the context menu, select **New Simple Volume**.

   The *New Simple Volume Wizard* appears.
3. Click **Next** to bypass the Welcome page.

   The Specify Volume Size page appears, as shown in Figure 22-13.

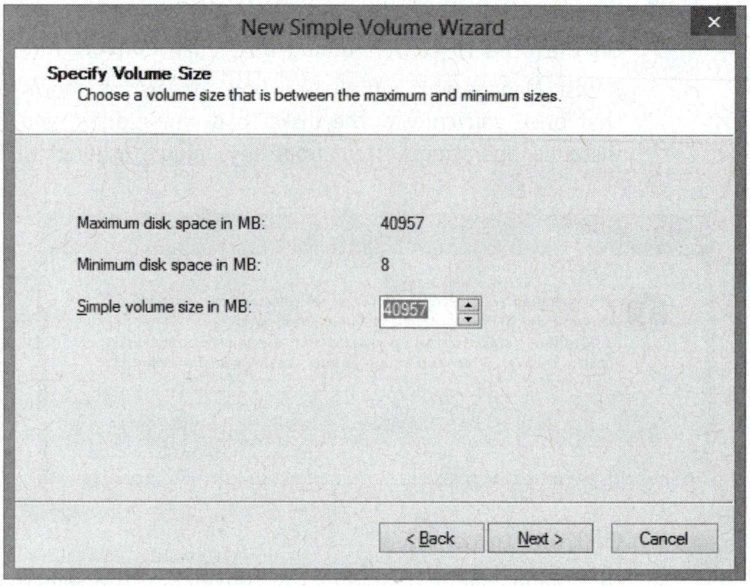

Figure 22-13

The *Specify Volume Size* page

4. In the *Simple Volume Size in MB* spin box, specify the size for the new volume, within the maximum and minimum limits stated on the page, and then click **Next**.

   The *Assign Drive Letter or Path* page appears, as shown in Figure 22-14.

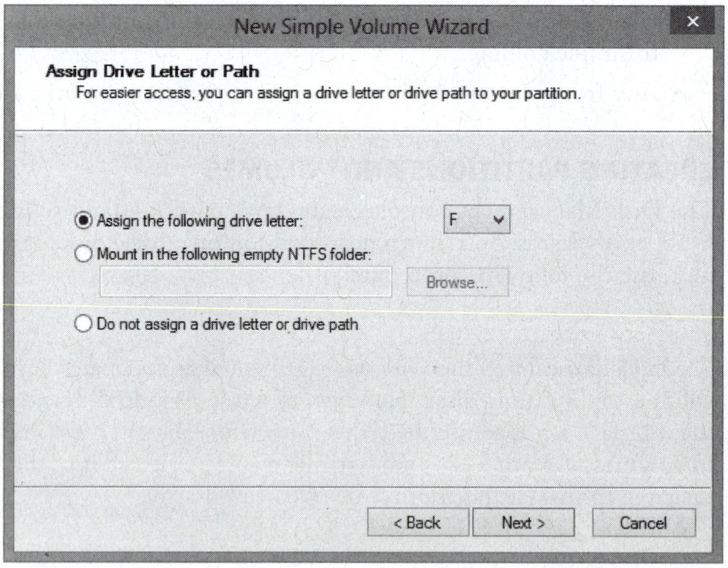

Figure 22-14

The *Assign Drive Letter or Path* page

5. Configure one of the following three options and then click **Next**.

   The Format Partition page appears, as shown in Figure 22-15.

   - ***Assign the following drive letter*** – If you select this option, click the associated drop-down list for a list of available drive letters, and then select the desired letter you want to assign to the drive.
   - ***Mount in the following empty NTFS folder*** – If you select this option, you are required to either type the path to an existing NTFS folder, or click Browse to search for or create a new folder. The entire contents of the new drive will appear in the folder you specify.

- ***Do not assign a drive letter or drive path*** – Select this option if you want to create the partition, but are not ready to use it yet. When you do not assign a volume a drive letter or path, the drive is left unmounted and inaccessible. When you want to mount the drive for use, assign a drive letter or path to it.

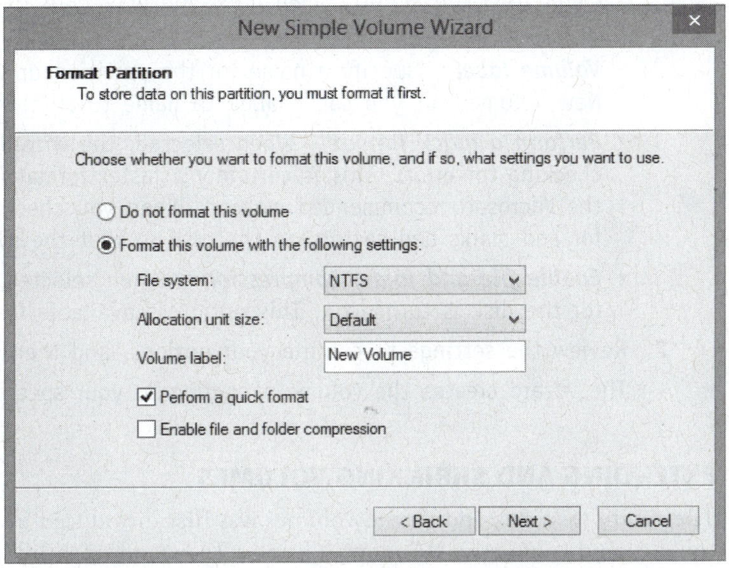

Figure 22-15

The *Format Partition* page

6. Specify whether and how the wizard should format the volume. If you do not want to format the volume at this time, select the **Do not format this volume** option. If you do want to format the volume, select the **Format this volume with the following settings** option and then configure the associated options, which are as follows. Then click **Next**.

   The *Completing the New Simple Volume Wizard* page appears, as shown in Figure 22-16.

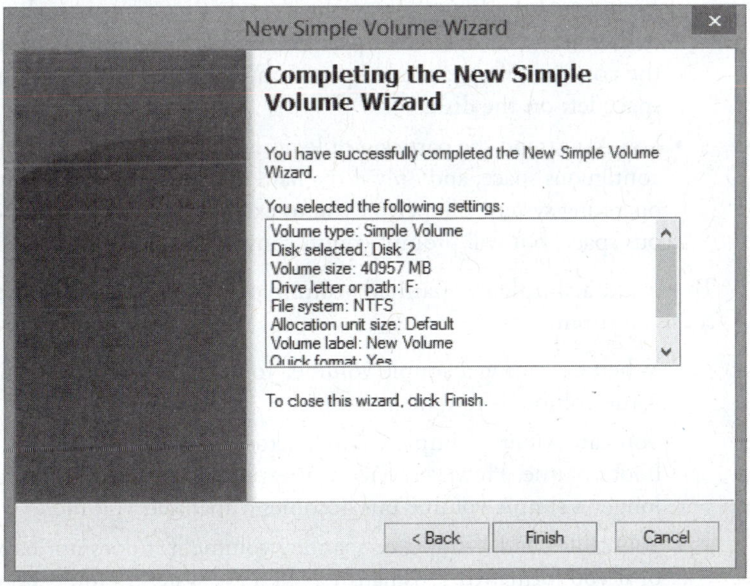

Figure 22-16

The *Completing the New Simple Volume Wizard* page

- ***File system*** – Select the desired file system: NTFS, FAT, FAT32, or exFAT. The options that appear in the drop-down list are based on the size of the partition or volume you are creating.

- ***Allocation unit size*** – Specify the file system's cluster size. The cluster size specifies the size of the basic unit that the system will use to allocate disk space. The system calculates the default allocation unit size based on the size of the volume. You can override this value by clicking on the associated drop-down list and then selecting one of the values in the list. For example, if your client uses consistently small files, you may want to set the allocation unit size to a smaller cluster size.
- ***Volume label*** – Specify a name for the partition or volume. The default name is New Volume, but you can change to name to anything you want.
- ***Perform a quick format*** – When selected, the wizard formats the disk without checking for errors. This is certainly a faster formatting method, but it is not the Microsoft recommended method. When you check for errors, the system looks for and marks bad sectors on the disk so that the system will not use them.
- ***Enable file and folder compression*** – When selected, file and folder compression for the disk is turned on. This option is available for the NTFS file system only.

7. Review the settings to confirm your options, and then click **Finish**.

   The wizard creates the volume according to your specifications.

EXTENDING AND SHRINKING VOLUMES

The ability to shrink and extend volumes was first introduced in Windows Vista. (And you could extend volumes in Windows XP, too.) To extend or shrink a partition or volume, you simply right-click a partition or volume and select Extend Volume or Shrink Volume from the context menu, or from the Action menu.

TAKE NOTE*

You must be a member of the Backup Operator or the Administrators group to extend or shrink any partition or volume.

Windows 8 extends existing primary partitions, logical drives, and simple volumes by expanding them into adjacent unallocated space on the same disk. When you extend a simple volume across multiple disks, the simple volume becomes a spanned volume. You cannot extend striped volumes.

To extend a partition on a basic disk, the system must meet the following requirements:

- A basic partition must be either unformatted or formatted with the NTFS file system.
- If you extend a logical drive, the console first consumes the contiguous free space remaining in the extended partition. If you attempt to extend the logical drive beyond the confines of its extended partition, the extended partition expands to any unallocated space left on the disk.
- You can extend the partition of logical drives, boot volumes, or system volumes only into contiguous space, and only if the hard disk can be upgraded into a dynamic disk. The operating system will permit you to extend other types of basic volumes into noncontiguous space, but will prompt you to convert the basic disk to a dynamic disk.

To extend a simple or spanned volume on a dynamic disk, the system must meet these requirements:

- When extending a simple volume, you can only use the available space on the same disk, if the volume is to remain simple.
- You can extend a simple volume across additional disks if it is not a system volume or a boot volume. However, once you expand a simple volume to another disk, it is no longer a simple volume but becomes a spanned volume.
- You can extend a simple or spanned volume if it does not have a file system (a raw volume) or if you formatted it using the NTFS file system. (You cannot extend FAT volumes.)

When shrinking partitions or volumes, the Disk Management console frees up space at the end of the volume, relocating the existing volume's files, if necessary. The console then converts that free space to new unallocated space on the disk. To shrink a basic disk partition or any kind of dynamic disk volume except for a striped volume, the system must meet the following requirements.

- The existing partition or volume must not be full and must contain the specified amount of available free space for shrinking.
- The partition or volume must not be a raw partition (one without a file system). Shrinking a raw partition that contains data mighty destroy the data.
- You can shrink a partition or volume only if you formatted it using the NTFS file system. (You cannot shrink FAT volumes.)

CREATING SPANNED, STRIPED, AND MIRRORED VOLUMES

Spanned, striped, or mirrored volumes require dynamic disks. When you create a spanned, striped, or mirrored volume, you create a single dynamic volume that extends across multiple physical disks.

To create a spanned, striped, or mirrored volume, use the following procedure:

CREATE A SPANNED OR STRIPED VOLUME

GET READY. Log on to Windows 8 using an account with Administrator privileges, and then perform the following steps:

1. Open the **Disk Management** snap-in.
2. In the *Graphical* view, right-click an unallocated area on a disk and, from the context menu, select **New Spanned Volume**, **New Striped Volume**, or **New Mirrored Volume**.
   A wizard appears, named for the volume type.
3. Click **Next** to bypass the *Welcome* page.
   The *Select Disks* page appears.
4. On the *Select Disks* page, under the *Available standard* list box, select each disk you want to use in the volume and then click **Add**. For a spanned or striped volume, you can add up to 31 additional disks; for a mirrored volume, you can add only one.
5. Specify the space you want to use on each disk by selecting the disk in the Selected standard list box, and then, using the *Select The Amount Of Space In MB* spin box, specify the amount of disk space that you want to include in the volume. For spanned or striped volumes, you can use different amounts of space on each drive. For mirrored volumes, you must use the same amount of space on both disks. Then click **Next**.
   The *Assign Drive Letter or Path* page appears.
6. Specify whether you want to assign a drive letter or path and then click **Next**.
   The *Format Partition* page appears.
7. Specify whether or how you want to format the volume and then click **Next**.
   The *Completing* page appears.
8. Review the settings to confirm your options, and then click **Finish**. If one or more of the disks you selected is a basic disk, a *Disk Management* message box appears, informing you that the wizard will convert the basic disk(s) to dynamic disk(s). Click **Yes** to continue.
   The wizard creates the volume according to your specifications.

Once the wizard has created the volume, it appears in the Graphical view with a single color on each of the disks contributing to the volume space, as shown in Figure 22-17.

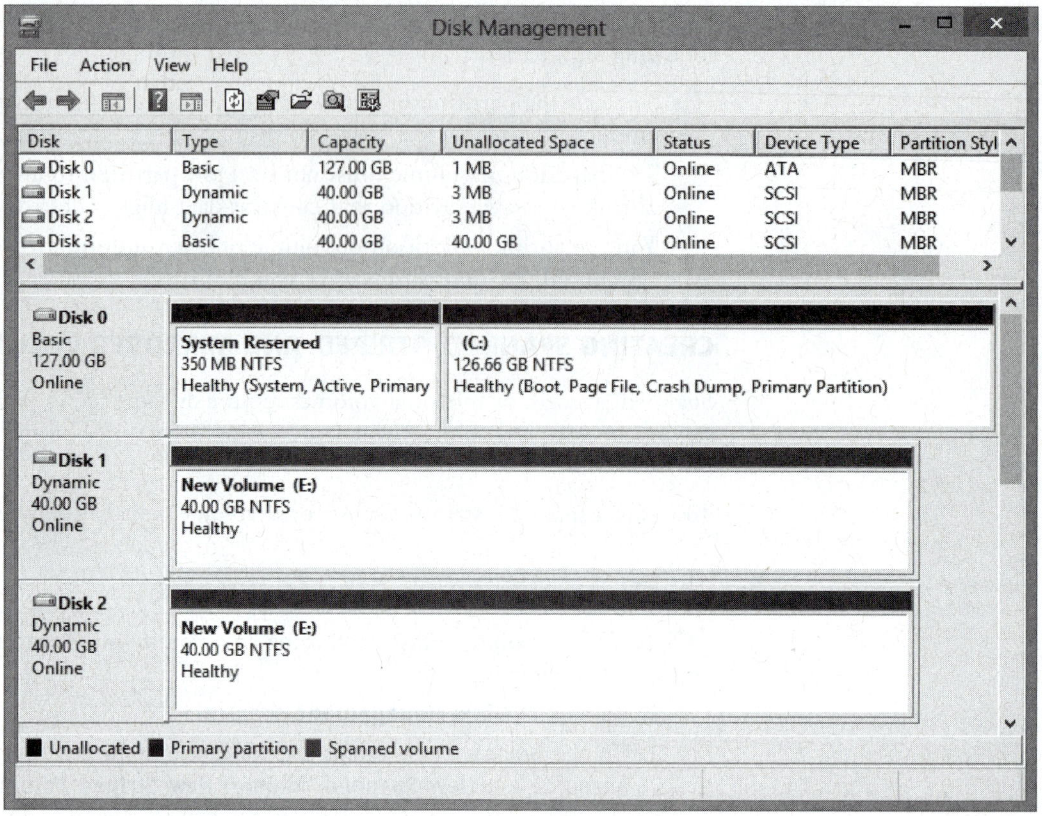

Figure 22-17

A spanned volume in the *Disk Management* snap-in

TAKE NOTE*

Windows Server 2012, in addition to simple, spanned, striped, and mirrored volumes, also supports RAID-5 volumes. RAID 5 stripes data and parity blocks across three or more disks, making sure that a block and its parity information are never stored on the same disk. Parity is a bit-level fault tolerance mechanism that enables the system to reconstruct the data from any one of the disks in the array that fails.

Using Storage Spaces

Windows 8 includes a new disk virtualization technology called ***Storage Spaces***, which enables a computer to concatenate storage space from individual physical disks and use that space to create a virtual disk.

CERTIFICATION READY
Manage storage spaces
Objective 6.2

This type of virtualization is a feature often found in SAN and NAS technologies, which require a substantial investment in specialized hardware and administrative skill. Storage Space provides similar capabilities, using standard direct-attached disk drives or simple external arrays.

Storage Spaces uses unallocated disk space to create storage pools. A ***storage pool*** can span multiple drives invisibly, providing an accumulated storage resource that you can expand or reduce as needed by adding disks to or removing them from the pool.

When you create a storage pool, it appears to the operating system as a single volume, called a storage space, even if it consists of many physical disks. Storage spaces can also provide fault tolerance by using the physical disks in the storage pool to hold mirrored or parity data.

Storage spaces can also be thinly provisioned, meaning that while you specify a maximum size for the disk, it starts out small and grows as you add data to it. You can therefore create a virtual disk with a maximum size that is larger than that of your storage space.

For example, if you plan to allocate a maximum of 10 TB for your database files, you can create a thin 10 TB storage pool, even if you only have physical disks totaling 2 TB. The application using the volume will function normally, gradually adding data until the storage pool is nearly consumed, at which point the system notifies you to add more space to the pool. You can then install more physical storage and add it to the pool, gradually expanding it until it can support the entire 10 TB required by the disk.

To create and manage storage spaces, you use the Storage Spaces control panel, as in the following procedure.

CREATE A STORAGE POOL

GET READY. Log on to Windows 8 using an account with Administrator privileges, and then perform the following steps:

1. Click **Control Panel > System & Security > Storage Spaces**.

   The Storage Spaces control panel appears, as shown in Figure 22-18.

Figure 22-18

The *Storage Spaces* control panel

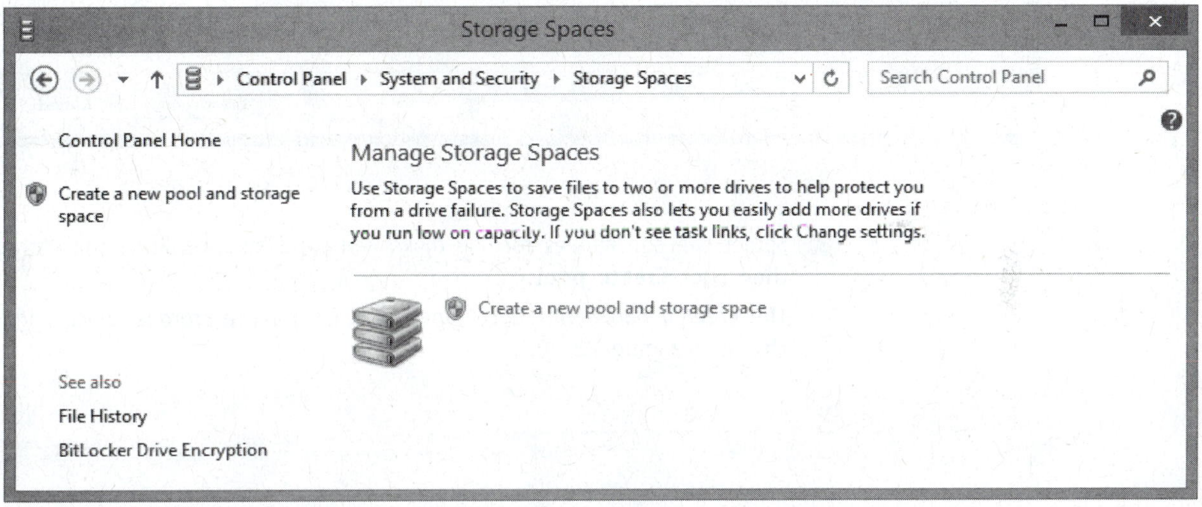

2. Click **Create a new pool and storage space**.

   The *Create a Storage Pool Wizard* appears, displaying the *Select drives to create a storage pool* page, as shown in Figure 22-19.

Figure 22-19

The *Select drives to create a storage pool* page

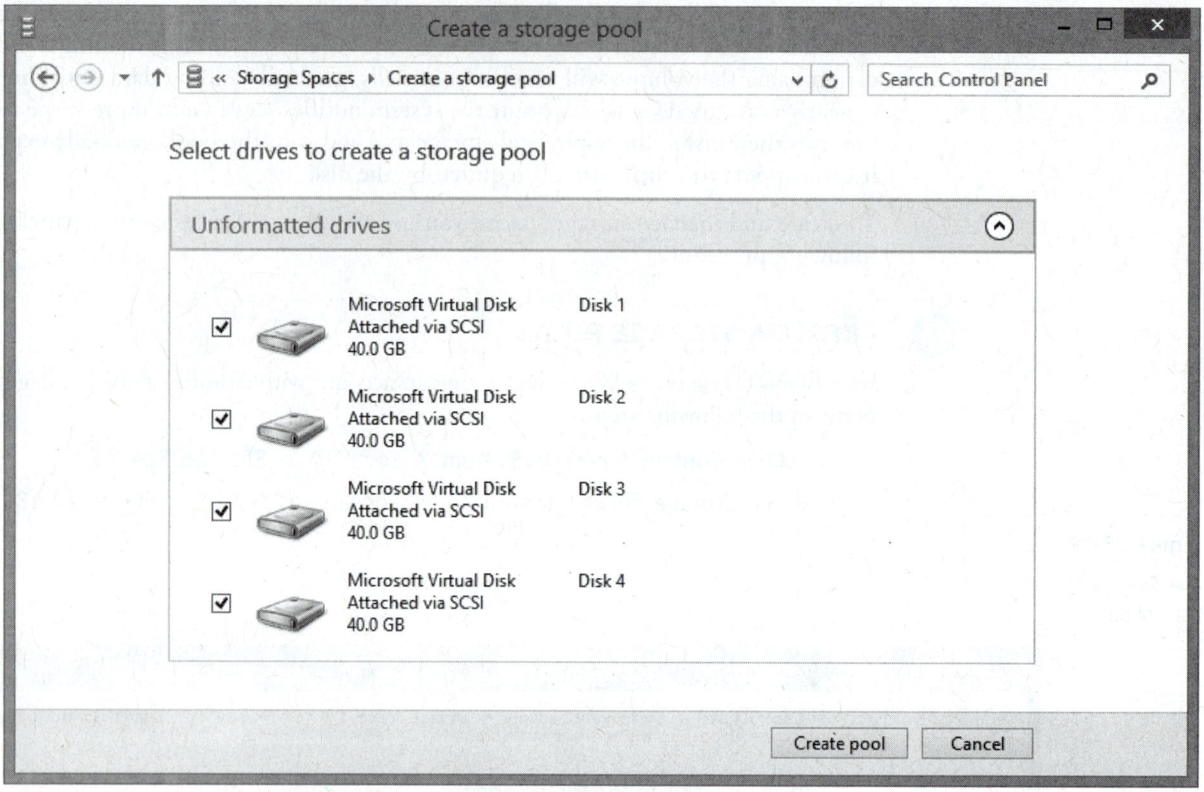

3. Select the checkboxes for the disks you want to include in the storage pool and then click **Create pool**.

   The *Enter a name, resiliency type, and size for the storage space* page appears, as shown in Figure 22-20.

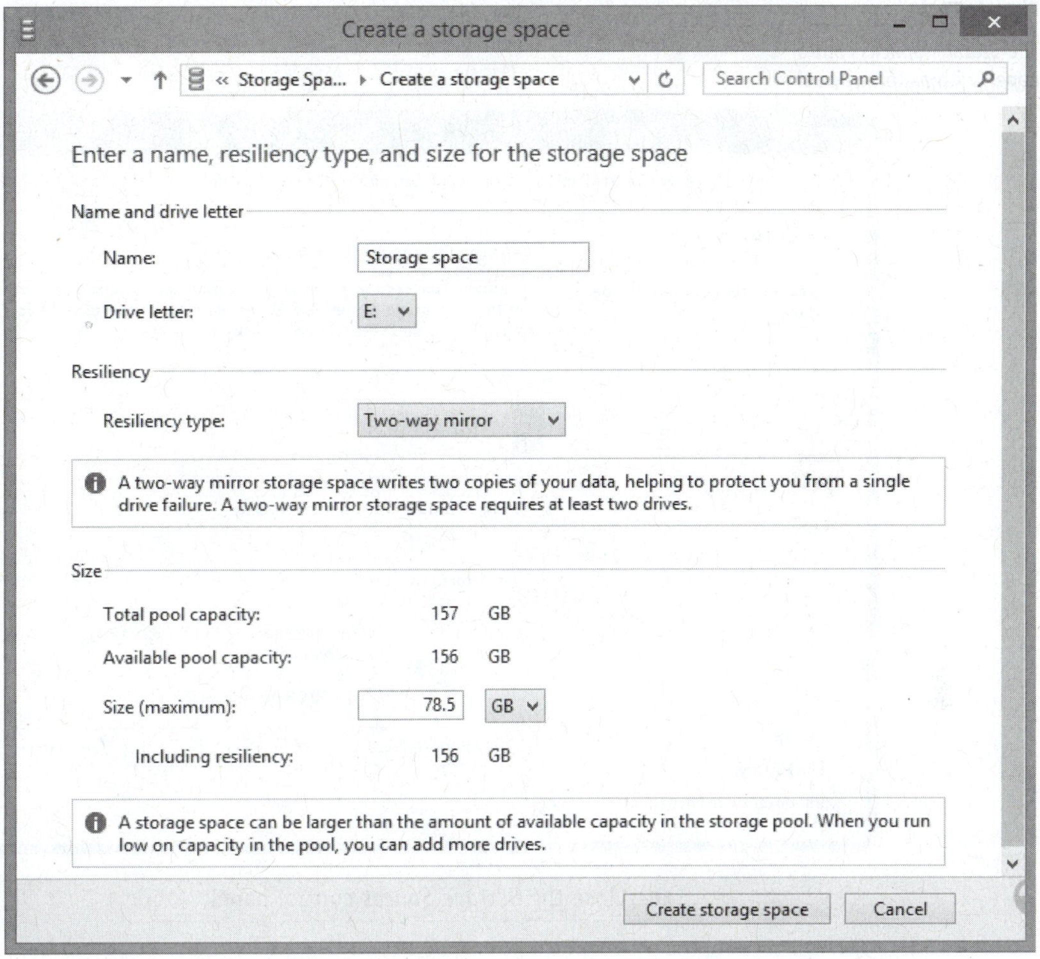

Figure 22-20

The *Enter a name, resiliency type, and size for the storage space* page

TAKE NOTE*

The physical disks you select for inclusion in a storage pool must be wholly dedicated to that purpose. Creating the pool destroys any data currently stored on the selected disks.

4. In the *Name* text box, specify the volume name that will identify the pool in File Explorer and other applications.
5. In the *Drive letter* drop-down list, select the drive letter the pool will use.
6. In the *Resiliency type* drop-down list, choose one of the following options:
   - **Simple (no resiliency)** – No redundant data is stored. If a physical disk fails, its data is lost.
   - **Two-way mirror** – Two copies of every file are stored on different physical disks, so that if a disk fails, all of its files remain available. The resulting size of the storage space is one-half of the total size of the physical disks in the pool.
   - **Three-way mirror** – Three copies of every file are stored on different physical disks, so that if two disks fail, all of the files remain available. The resulting size of the storage space is one-third of the total size of the physical disks in the pool
   - **Parity** – Data is stored on two disks, while parity information is stored onthe third. This yields a larger storage space than mirroring, while providing tolerance for a failed disk drive. Parity is the most processor-intensive of the resiliency options.
7. In the *Size (maximum)* text box, specify the ultimate maximum size of the storage space (which can be larger than the currently available physical disk space).
8. Click **Create storage space**.

   The storage space and the pool appear in the Storage Spaces control panel, as shown in Figure 22-21.

Figure 22-21

The *Storage Spaces* control panel, with a storage pool

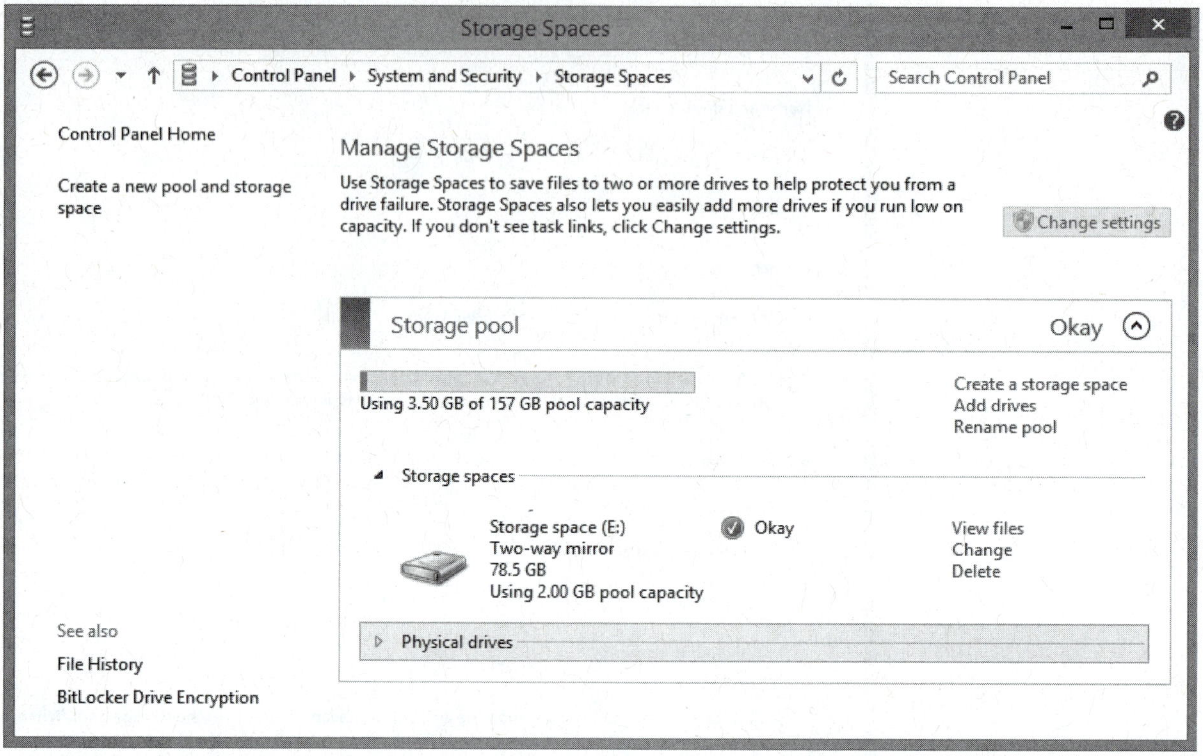

9. Close the *Storage Spaces* control panel.

The storage space is now ready for use an appears like a regular volume in File Explorer, the Disk Management snap-in, and other applications.

MORE INFORMATION

Parity is a mathematical algorithm that some disk storage technologies use to provide data redundancy in their disk write operations. To calculate the parity information for a drive array, the system takes the values for the same data bit at a specific location on each drive in the array and adds them together to determine whether the total is odd or even. The system then uses the resulting total to calculate a value for a parity bit corresponding to those data bits. The system then repeats the process for every bit location on the drives. If one drive is lost due to a hardware failure, the system can restore each lost data bit by calculating its value using the remaining data bits and the parity bit.

For example, in an array with five disks, suppose the first four disks have the values 1, 1, 0, and 1 for their first bit. The total of the four bits is 3, an odd number, so the system sets the first bit of the fifth disk, the parity disk, to 0, indicating an odd result for the total of the bits on the other four disks. Suppose then that one disk fails. If the parity disk fails, no actual data is lost, so data I/O can proceed normally. If one of the four data disks is lost, the total of the first bits in the remaining three disks will be either odd or even. If the total is even, because we know the parity bit is odd, the bit in the missing disk must have been a 1. If the total is odd, the bit in the missing disk must have been a 0. After the failed disk hardware is replaced, the system can use this information to reconstruct the lost data.

Using Diskpart.exe

In addition to the graphical interface in the Disk Management snap-in, Windows 8 also includes a command line tool called ***Diskpart.exe***, which you can use to manage disks.

Diskpart.exe is a powerful utility that can perform any task the Disk Management snap-in can and more. For example, Diskpart enables you to create a fourth primary partition on a basic disk, rather than an extended partition and a logical disk.

Diskpart.exe has two operational modes, a script mode and an interactive mode. If you choose to create Diskpart scripts, you can run them from the command prompt using the following syntax:

```
Diskpart.exe /s scriptname
```

When you run Diskpart.exe from the Windows 8 command prompt without any parameters, a DISKPART> prompt appears, from which you execute additional commands. The typical working method is to shift the focus of the program to the specific object you want to manage, and then execute commands on that object.

For example, the `list disk` command displays a list of the disk drives in the system, as shown in Figure 22-22. The `select disk 1` command then shifts the focus to Disk 1. Any disk-specific commands you execute the program will now apply to Disk 1. The `create partition primary size=10000` command therefore creates a new 10 GB primary partition on Disk 1.

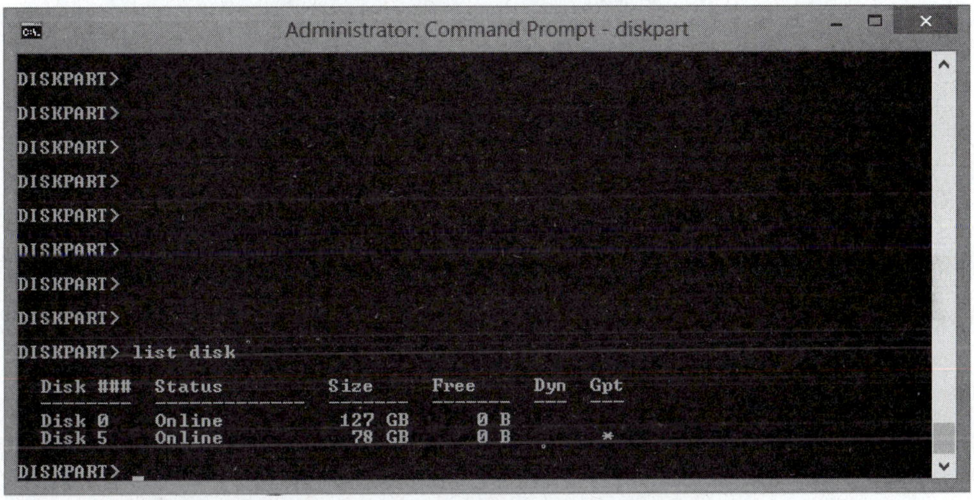

Figure 22-22
Shifting object focus in Diskpart.exe

TAKE NOTE*
Unlike the Disk Management snap-in, the Diskpart.exe program is particular about disk terminology. When you are working with a basic disk, for example, you can only create partitions, not volumes, unless you convert the basic disk to a dynamic disk first.

Using Disk Tools

Windows 8 provides a selection of tools that you can use to free up disk space, defragment volumes, and check disks for errors. These tools are simple and safe enough for most end-users and still powerful enough for administrators.

The Windows 8 disk tools are all accessible from each volume's Properties sheet. You can therefore access the tools from any File Explorer window or from the Disk Management snap-in.

USING DISK CLEANUP

When a disk starts to run low on storage space, it is often possible to reclaim space occupied by unnecessary files, such as temporary files, setup logs, and files in the Recycle Bin. Windows 8 refers to the process of deleting these files as cleaning up a disk.

To clean up a Windows 8 volume, use the following procedure.

CLEAN UP A VOLUME

GET READY. Log on to Windows 8 using an account with Administrator privileges and then perform the following steps:

1. Open the **Disk Management** snap-in.
2. In the *Graphical* view, right-click a volume and, from the context menu, select **Properties**.

   The Properties sheet for the volume appears.
3. On the *General* tab, click **Disk Cleanup**. After a scan of the volume, the Disk Cleanup dialog box appears, as shown in Figure 22-23.

   The dialog box lists the types of files that are available for cleanup and specifies the amount of disk space you can reclaim.

Figure 22-23

The *Disk Cleanup* dialog box

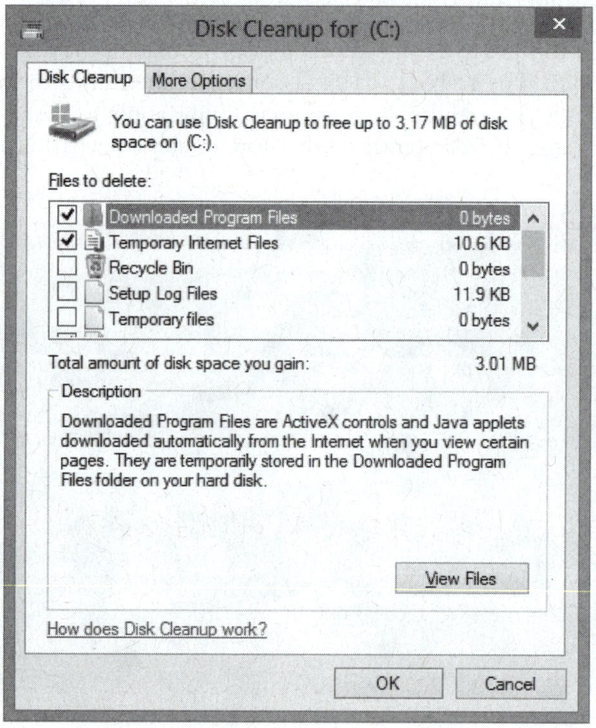

4. Select the checkboxes for the files you want to delete and then click **OK**.

   A *Disk Cleanup* message box appears.
5. Click **Delete Files** to confirm that you want to delete the selected files.

   Disk Cleanup deletes the selected files.
6. Click **OK** to close the volume's *Properties* sheet.

Once you delete files using the Disk Cleanup tool, you cannot reclaim them from the Recycle Bin.

CERTIFICATION READY
Manage file system fragmentation
Objective 6.2

DEFRAGMENTING DISKS

Hard disk drives write data in clusters, units of a standard size designated when you format the disk. Initially, when you save a file to a hard disk, the drive writes it to contiguous clusters, that is, a sequence of clusters that are all next to each other. Over time, however, as files are written and rewritten to the disk, the contiguous spaces grow smaller, and the drive is forced to split files into clusters located at different places on the disk. This process is called fragmentation.

Fragmentation reduces the efficiency of the disk because it forces the drive to relocate its heads many times to read a single file. The effect is the same as if you were forced to read a book with pages not in numerical order. You would spend a lot of time looking for each page and less time actually reading.

Windows 8 includes a tool that enables you to defragment your volumes by recopying fragmented files to contiguous space on the disk. The Disk Defragmentation tool in Windows 8 is changed substantially from the one in Windows Vista.

WARNING It is strongly recommended that you perform a full backup of your volumes before you defragment them. While the Windows 8 Disk Defragmenter is a reliable tool, defragmentation is a hardware-intensive process, and drive failures can conceivably occur.

To defragment a volume, use the following procedure.

DEFRAGMENT A VOLUME

GET READY. Log on to Windows 8 using an account with Administrator privileges and then perform the following steps

1. Open the **Disk Management** snap-in.
2. In the *Graphical* view, right-click a volume and, from the context menu, select **Properties**.

   The *Properties* sheet for the volume appears.
3. Click the **Tools** tab.
4. Click **Optimize**.

   The *Optimize Drives* dialog box appears, as shown in Figure 22-24.

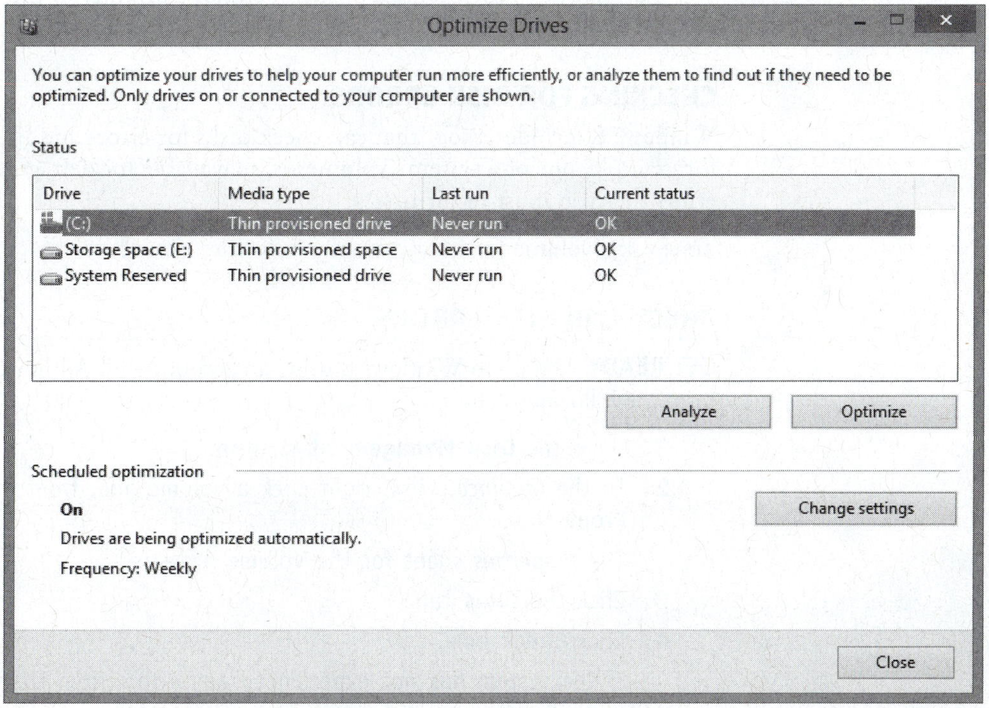

Figure 22-24

The *Optimize Drives* dialog box

5. In the *Current Status* box, select the volume you want to work with and then click **Analyze Disk**.

   The *Current Status* box displays the percent of the volume that is fragmented.

6. In the *Current Status* box, select the volume you want to work with and then click **Analyze Disk**.

   The Disk Defragmenter manipulates the files on the volume to eliminate as much fragmentation as possible. When the process is completed, the *Current Status* box displays the new fragmentation percentage for the volume.

7. Click **Close** to close the *Optimize Drives* dialog box.
8. Click **OK** to close the volume's *Properties* dialog box.

The time required for the defragmentation process depends on the size of the volume, the number of files stored there, the amount of free space, and the degree to which the volume is fragmented. The process can easily take several hours. In addition to the graphical interface, it is also possible to defragment disks from the command prompt, using the Defrag.exe program. This enables you to incorporate defragmentation into scripts. The syntax for the command line interface is as follows:

```
Defrag.exe volume [/C][/E
volumes][/A][/X][/T][/H][/M][/U][/V]
```

- `volume` – Specifies the drive letter or mount point of the volume to defragment.
- `/C` – Defragments all local volumes on the computer.
- E *volumes* – Defragments all local volumes on the computer except those you specify.
- `/A` – Displays a fragmentation analysis for the volume without performing a defragmentation.
- `/X` – Consolidates the free space on the volume.
- `/T` – Tracks the operation currently in progress.
- `/H` – Runs the operation at normal priority, instead of the default low priority.
- `/M` – Defragments multiple volumes simultaneously.
- `/U` – Displays the progress of the operation currently in progress.
- `/V` – Displays information in verbose mode, with additional detail and statistics.

CHECKING FOR DISK ERRORS

Windows 8 includes a tool that can check disks for errors and, in many cases, repair them. If, for example, one of a system's volumes is unavailable for defragmentation, it could be due to errors that you must repair first.

To check a volume for errors, use the following procedure.

CHECK FOR DISK ERRORS

GET READY. Log on to Windows 8 using an account with Administrator privileges and then perform the following steps:

1. Open the **Disk Management** snap-in.
2. In the *Graphical* view, right-click a volume and, from the context menu, select **Properties**.

   The *Properties* sheet for the volume appears.

3. Click the **Tools** tab.
4. Click **Check now**.

   If the system has not experienced any errors from that drive, a *You don't need to scan this drive* page appears.

5. Click **Scan drive**.

   The system scans the selected disk and generates a result page like that shown in Figure 22-25.

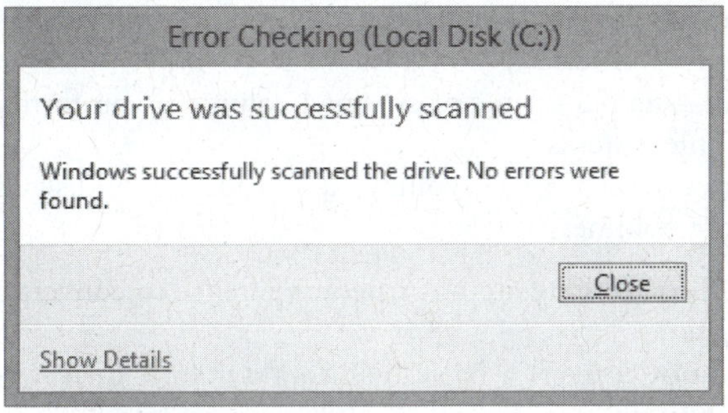

Figure 22-25
The *Error Checking* message box

6. Click **Close**.

You can also use the Chkdsk.exe utility to check for disk errors from the command prompt. For example, to check the C: drive for errors, search for bad sectors, and fix any errors found, you can use the following command:

```
Chkdsk.exe C: /f /r
```

SKILL SUMMARY

IN THIS LESSON, YOU LEARNED:

- There are two hard disk partition styles that you can use in Windows 8: MBR and GPT.
- Windows 8 supports two disk types: basic disks and dynamic disks.
- Basic disks can have up to four partitions: three primary partitions and the fourth usually being an extended partition, on which you can create multiple logical drives.
- Windows 8 supports four types of dynamic volumes: simple, spanned, striped, and mirrored.
- You use the Disk Management snap-in for MMC to manage disks.
- Windows 8 includes a new disk virtualization technology called Storage Spaces, which enables a server to concatenate storage space from individual physical disks and allocate it to create virtual disks of any size.

Knowledge Assessment

Multiple Choice

Select one or more correct answers for each of the following questions.

1. Which of the following statements are true of striped volumes? (Choose all that apply.)
   a. Striped volumes provide enhanced performance over simple volumes.
   b. Striped volumes provide greater fault tolerance than simple volumes.
   c. You can extend striped volumes after creation.
   d. If a single physical disk in the striped volume fails, all of the data in the entire volume is lost.

2. Which of the following are requirements for extending a volume on a dynamic disk? (Choose all that apply.)
   a. If you want to extend a simple volume, you can use only the available space on the same disk, if the volume is to remain simple.
   b. The volume must have a file system before you can extend a simple or spanned volume.
   c. You can extend a simple or spanned volume if you formatted it using the FAT or FAT32 file systems.
   d. You can extend a simple volume across additional disks if it is not a system volume or a boot volume.

3. Which of the following are not true in reference to converting a basic disk to a dynamic disk?
   a. You cannot convert a basic disk to a dynamic disk if you need to dual boot the computer.
   b. You cannot convert drives with volumes that use an allocation unit size greater than 512 bytes.
   c. A boot partition or system partition on a basic disk cannot be extended into a striped or spanned volume, even if you convert the disk to a dynamic disk.
   d. The conversion will fail if the hard drive does not have at least 1 MB of free space at the end of the disk.

4. Which of the following volume types supported by Windows 8 do not provide fault tolerance? (Choose all that apply)
   a. Striped
   b. Spanned
   c. Mirrored
   d. None of the above

5. Which of the following are true statements regarding Storage Spaces? Select all that apply.
   a. Uses unallocated disk space to create storage pools
   b. Appears as a single volume called a storage volume
   c. Can be thinly provisioned
   d. Appears as a single volume called a provisioned volume

6. Which of the following commands is used to switch the focus from disk 1 to disk 2 using the Diskpart.exe tool?
   a. list disk
   b. select disk 2
   c. select disk 1 > 2
   d. diskpart.exe /select disk 1

7. Which of the following can impact the time it takes to complete the defragmentation process? Select all that apply.
   a. Volume size
   b. Number of files stored on a volume
   c. Amount of free space
   d. Degree to which the volume is fragmented

8. What are the maximum number of partitions available on a basic disk?
   a. 1 primary and 1 extended
   b. 2 primary and 1 extended
   c. 3 primary and 1 extended
   d. 4 primary and 1 extended

9. Which of the following are true statements regarding disks in Windows 8? Select all that apply.
   a. Boot partition contains the operating system files
   b. System partition contains the operating files
   c. System partition is the active partition
   d. Boot partition is the active partition

10. Which of the following operating systems support MBR and GPT partition styles? Select all that apply.
    a. Windows 8 x86-based
    b. Windows XP x64-based
    c. Windows XP x86-based
    d. Windows Server 2012 x64-based

Best Answer

Choose the letter that corresponds to the best answer. More than one answer choice may achieve the goal. Select the BEST answer.

1. Which of the following resiliency options provides the most protection to a storage space?
   a. Simple
   b. Two-way mirror
   c. Three-way mirror
   d. Parity

2. In Windows 8, there are four volume types to choose from. If the goal is to take advantage of dynamic disk features, protect the computer against single disk failure and the loss of storage space is not a major concern, which volume type would best fit the need?
   a. Striped volume
   b. Mirrored volume
   c. Spanned volume.
   d. Simple volume.

3. Windows 8 supports FAT, FAT32, exFAT, and NTFS file systems. Which of the following best reflects a viable reason to use a FAT file system instead of NTFS?
   a. The need to share files over the network
   b. The need to create partitions up to 32GB in size
   c. The need to use diagnostic utilities that only run on FAT systems.
   d. To support a multi-boot system with a non-Windows operating system

4. A user would like to perform basic disk maintenance on their computer. Of the tools available, which is likely to cause the most damage if used in the hands of a novice?
   a. Disk Management console
   b. Disk Cleanup
   c. Chkdsk.exe
   d. Diskpart.exe

5. A user indicates they would like to convert their basic disk to a dynamic disk to take advantage of the simple, striped, spanned, and volume mirror capabilities. Of the disks listed, which is most likely to support the conversion from basic to dynamic with the least amount of administrative effort?
   a. 1 MB free space at end of disk, non-multi-boot system, allocation unit size 512.
   b. 1 MB free space at end of disk, non-multi-boot system, allocation unit size >512
   c. 5 MB free space at end of disk, multi-boot system, allocation unit size 512
   d. 5 MB free space at end of disk, multi-boot system, allocation unit size >512

6. In Windows 8, Storage Spaces uses unallocated space to create storage pools. While creating a new storage pool, the option to select the type of resiliency must be chosen. If you have five hard disks in the pool, what resiliency type would provide the best choice in regard to protecting against disk failure?
   a. Simple
   b. Two-way mirror
   c. Three-way mirror
   d. Parity

Matching and Identification

Complete the following exercise by matching the terms with their corresponding definitions.

_______ a) Passphrase
_______ b) Location-aware printing
_______ c) Mobile broadband network
_______ d) Adhoc mode
_______ e) Infrastructure mode
_______ f) Denial of service
_______ g) WEP
_______ h) Shared secret
_______ i) WPA2-Enterprise
_______ j) WPA2-Personal

1. Configures wireless adapter to connect through a WAP.
2. Prevents legitimate users from communicating with a WAP.
3. Words and characters used to authenticate a wireless connection.
4. A security setting used to encrypt network traffic before it is sent in WEP.
5. Also known as WPA-PSK or pre-shared key mode.
6. Feature that allows you to set default printer for each network you connect to.
7. Wireless security protocol that uses a shared key to encrypt traffic.
8. Configures wireless adapter to connect to other wireless computers bypassing the WAP.
9. Also known as WPA-802.1x or WPA-RADIUS.
10. Provide high-speed access through portable devices; requires data plan.

Build a List

1. Order the steps to create a storage pool.
   _______ Select a fault tolerance option for the storage space.
   _______ Create the storage pool.
   _______ Launch The Create a Storage Pool Wizard.
   _______ Specify a name for the storage space.
   _______ Open the Storage Spaces control panel.
   _______ Create the storage space.
   _______ Select the disks to add to the storage pool.
   _______ Select a drive letter for the storage space.
2. In order of first to last, specify the correct order of steps to convert a basic disk to a dynamic disk.
   _______ In *Disk List* view, right-click the basic disk that you want to convert and, from the context menu, select **Convert to Dynamic Disk**.
   _______ Select the checkboxes for the disks you want to convert and then click **OK**.
   _______ Click **Details**. The *Convert Details* dialog box appears,
   _______ Click **Yes** to continue. Disk Management completes the conversion.
   _______ On the *Disks to Convert* dialog box, click **Convert** to start the conversion.
   _______ When you are ready to continue with the conversion, click **OK**.

_________ The *Disks to Convert* dialog box lists the disks you chose for conversion for your confirmation.
_________ Open the **Disk Management** snap-in.

3. Specify the correct order of steps to create a spanned or striped volume.
_________ Click **Next** to bypass the *Welcome* page.
_________ Specify the space you want to use on each disk by selecting the disk in the Selected standard list box, and then, using the *Select The Amount Of Space In MB* spin box, specify the amount of disk space that you want to include in the volume. Click Next.
_________ On the *Select Disks* page, under the *Available standard* list box, select each disk you want to use in the volume and then click **Add**.
_________ In the *Graphical* view, right-click an unallocated area on a disk and, from the context menu, select **New Spanned Volume**, **New Striped Volume**, or **New Mirrored Volume**.
_________ Open the **Disk Management** snap-in.
_________ Review the settings to confirm your options, and then click **Finish**. If one or more of the disks you selected is a basic disk, a *Disk Management* message box appears, informing you that the wizard will convert the basic disk(s) to dynamic disk(s). Click **Yes** to continue.
_________ Specify whether or how you want to format the volume and then click **Next**. The *Completing* page appears.
_________ Specify whether you want to assign a drive letter or path and then click **Next**. The *Format Partition* page appears.

4. Specify the correct order of steps to create a volume.
_________ Specify whether and how the wizard should format the volume.
_________ Open the **Disk Management** snap-in.
_________ Configure one of the following three options (Assign the following drive letter, Mount in the following empty folder, or Do not assign a drive letter or drive path) and then click **Next**.
_________ In the *Graphical* view, right-click the unallocated area on the volume status column for the disk on which you want to create a volume and, from the context menu, select **New Simple Volume**.
_________ In the *Simple Volume Size in MB* spin box, specify the size for the new volume, within the maximum and minimum limits stated on the page, and then click **Next**.
_________ Review the settings to confirm your options, and then click **Finish**.
_________ Click **Next** to bypass the Welcome page. The *Specify Volume Size* page appears.

Business Case Scenarios

Scenario 22-1: Creating Volumes on Dynamic Disks

Maria has 3 hard disks on her computer. Using the Disk Management tool, she created a striped volume. What are advantages and disadvantages of her choice of volume type?

Scenario 22-2: Converting Disk Partition Styles

Elliot, the junior administrator for the company, is currently reviewing a Windows 8 x86 system. After opening Disk Management and right-clicking the disk status column in the Graphical view, he notices the context menu contains the *Convert to GTP Disk* menu item. What does this mean and what are the implications of performing the conversion?

23 LESSON

Monitoring System Performance

70-687 EXAM OBJECTIVE

Objective 6.3 – Monitor system performance. This objective may include but is not limited to configure and analyze event logs; configure event subscriptions; monitor system resources; configure Task Manager; optimize the desktop environment; configure indexing options; and optimize networking performance.

Lesson Heading	Exam Objective
Monitoring and Diagnosing Performance	Configure and Analyze Event Logs Configure Event Subscriptions
The Comprehensive List of Performance Tools	
Using Event Viewer	Monitor System Resources
Using the Performance Monitor Console	
Using Reliability Monitor	
Managing Performance	
Working with Processes	
Using Task Manager	Configure Task Manager
Using Resource Monitor	
Viewing Advanced System Details in System Information	Optimize the Desktop Environment
Viewing System Configuration Details	
Adjusting Performance Settings	
Configuring Index Settings	Configure Indexing Options
Modifying Power Settings	
Troubleshooting Windows 8	
Using the Windows Memory Diagnostic Tool	Optimize Networking Performance
Using the Windows Network Diagnostic Tool	
Viewing Problem Reports	

KEY TERMS

affinity
baseline
base score
bottleneck
channel
Clear-Eventlog
collectors
custom view
data collector set
diacritic
events
Fast Boot
Get-WinEvent
instance
intelligent network
log
performance counters
performance object
process trees
Reliability Access Component Agent (RACAgent)
Reliability Monitor
sources
subscriptions
System Configuration tool (msconfig.exe)
System Information tool (msinfo32.exe)
Windows Experience Index

Monitoring and Diagnosing Performance

THE BOTTOM LINE

For a computer to perform well, all of its components must be individually efficient. Windows 8 includes a variety of tools that enable you to locate components whose performance is below par.

A computer's level of performance is based on a combination of factors, any of which can function as a bottleneck that slows down the entire system. For example, a Windows 8 computer might have an extremely fast processor, but if it is lacking in memory, it will have to page data to the swap file on the hard drive more often, slowing down the system. In the same way, a computer might have a fast processor and plenty of memory, but if its hard drive is slow, the faster components can't run at peak efficiency.

TAKE NOTE*

Windows 8 includes an array of tools for monitoring and managing system performance that may be used by either standard users or administrators, as well as tool specifically designed for use by account holders with specific administrative rights. Further, the enhanced security of Windows 8 requires that some operations may only be performed using the local administrative account.

Windows Management Instrumentation (WMI) is an interface to managed resources in Windows 7 that administrators can use to create scripts to configure performance parameters, among many other things. WMI classes describe the properties of managed resources in Windows 8 and the actions that WMI can use to manage those resources. Administrators can create WMI scripts using Microsoft Visual Basic, Jscript, or any language supported by the Windows Scripting Host (WSH) engine.

Windows 8 also includes Windows PowerShell 3.0, which has been enhanced to enable greater system diagnostic, management, and configuration capabilities.

CERTIFICATION READY
Configure and analyze event logs
Objective 6.3

Hardware problems are not the only cause of performance degradations. Software incompatibilities and resource depletion can also affect performance. In essence, the task of optimizing the performance of a Windows 8 computer consists of locating the bottlenecks and eliminating them. This might require a hardware upgrade or a reexamination of the

CERTIFICATION READY
Configure event subscriptions
Objective 6.3

computer's suitability to its role. Whatever the solution, the first step in determining what factors are negatively affecting the computer's performance is to quantify that performance and monitor its fluctuations.

The following sections examine some of the tools provided by Windows 8, which enable you to gather information about the computer's ongoing performance levels.

Using Event Viewer

Beginning in Windows Vista, the Event Viewer console has been enhanced to provide easier access to a more comprehensive array of event logs.

Software developers commonly use logs as a means of tracking the activities of particular algorithms, routines, and applications. A ***log*** is a list of events, which can track the activity of the software, document errors, and provide analytical information to administrators. Logs are traditionally text files, but the Windows operating systems have long used a graphical application called *Event Viewer* to display the log information gathered by the operating system.

Windows has maintained the same three basic logs throughout several versions: a System log, a Security log, and an Application log. Recent versions have added a Setup log, and servers performing certain roles have additional logs, such as those tracking DNS and File Replication activities. The format of these logs has remained consistent, although the Event Viewer has undergone some changes. In Windows Server 2003 and Windows XP, Event Viewer first took the form of an MMC snap-in, rather than an independent application.

In Windows Vista and Windows Server 2008, Microsoft gave the Windows event engine its most comprehensive overhaul in many years. Windows Eventing 6.0 includes the following enhancements:

- A three pane display: Log List | Event Viewer | Actions.
- A new, XML-based log format.
- The addition of a Setup log documenting the operating system's installation and configuration history.
- New logs for key applications and services, including DFS Replication and the Key Management Service.
- Individual logs for Windows components.
- Enhanced querying capabilities that simplify the process of locating specific events, including the creation of Custom Views that may be saved, exported, or imported.
- The ability to create subscriptions that enable administrators to collect and store specific types of events from other computers on the network.

LAUNCHING THE EVENT VIEWER CONSOLE

The primary function of the Windows Eventing engine is to record information about system activities as they occur and package that information in individual units called ***events***. The application you use to view the events is an MMC snap-in called *Event Viewer*. As with all MMC snap-ins, you can launch the Event Viewer console in a variety of ways, including the following:

- WinKey + w > search for **ev** and then select View Event Logs
- Start Screen > type View Event Logs
    - Note the View Event Logs is a *Settings* result
- Start Screen > type MMC and then add the Event Viewer snap-in.

- Start Screen > Control Panel > System and Security > Administrative Tools > Event Viewer
- Start Screen > type eventvwr.exe
- Open the Computer Management console and then expand the Event Viewer node

USING THE OVERVIEW AND SUMMARY DISPLAY

When the Event Viewer console appears, you see the Overview and Summary display shown in Figure 23-1.

Figure 23-1

The *Overview and Summary* screen in the *Event Viewer* console

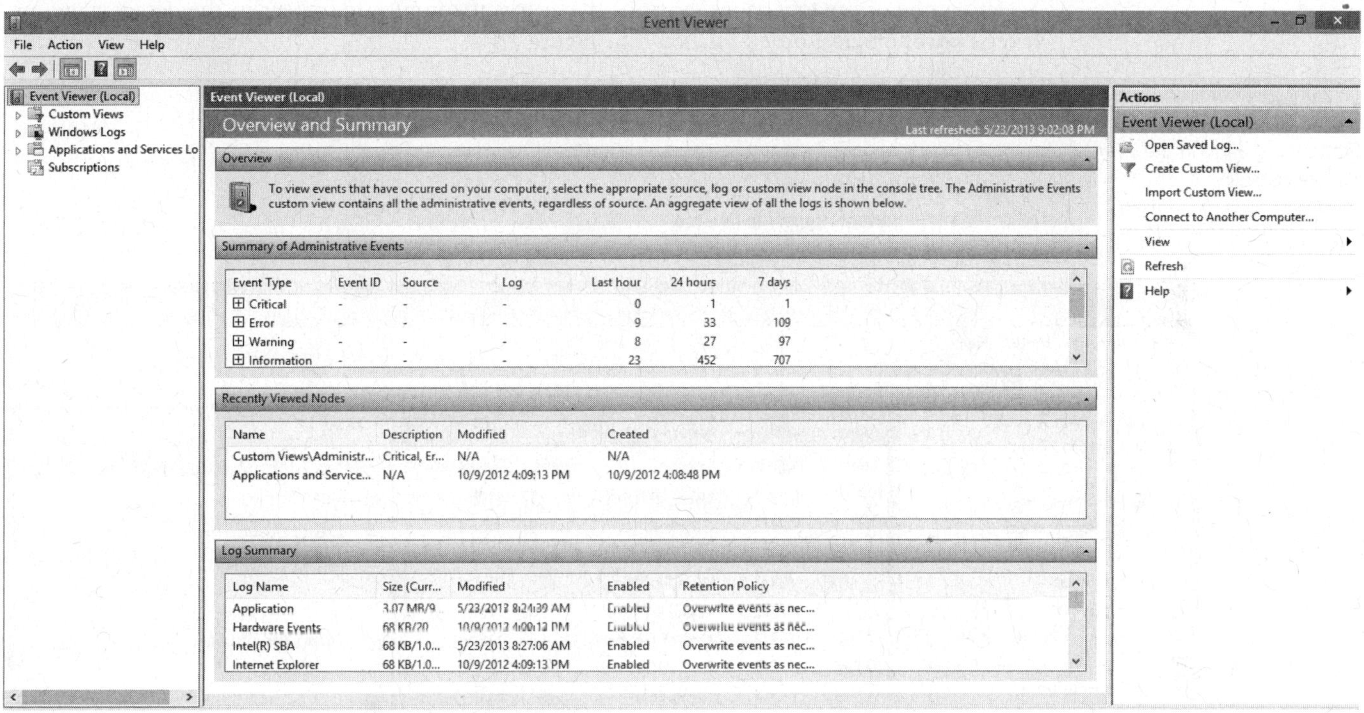

The Summary of Administrative Events displays the total number of events recorded in the last hour, day, and week, sorted by event type. This panel serves as a source for a quick diagnostic or performance check of your system health. When you expand an event type, the list is broken down by event ID.

When you double-click one of the event IDs, the console creates a filtered custom view that displays only the events having that ID.

VIEWING WINDOWS LOGS

When you expand the Windows Logs folder, you see the following logs:

- **Application** – Contains information about specific programs running on the computer, as determined by the application developer.
- **Security** – Contains information about security-related events, such as failed logons, attempts to access protected resources, and success or failure of audited events. The events recorded in this log are determined by audit policies, which you can enable using either local computer policies or Group Policy.
- **Setup** – Contains information about the operating system installation and setup history.

- **System** – Contains information about events generated by the operating system, such as services and device drivers. For example, a failure of a service to start or a driver to load during system startup is recorded in the System log.
- **Forwarded Events** – Contains events received from other computers on the network via subscriptions.

TAKE NOTE*

The Administrative Events log under Custom Views is the fastest means to identify potential system or performance problems that may be recorded from the more than 200 logs available for review in Windows 8.

Selecting one of the logs causes a list of the events it contains to appear in the details pane, in reverse chronological order, as shown in Figure 23-2.

Figure 23-2

Contents of a log in the *Event Viewer* console

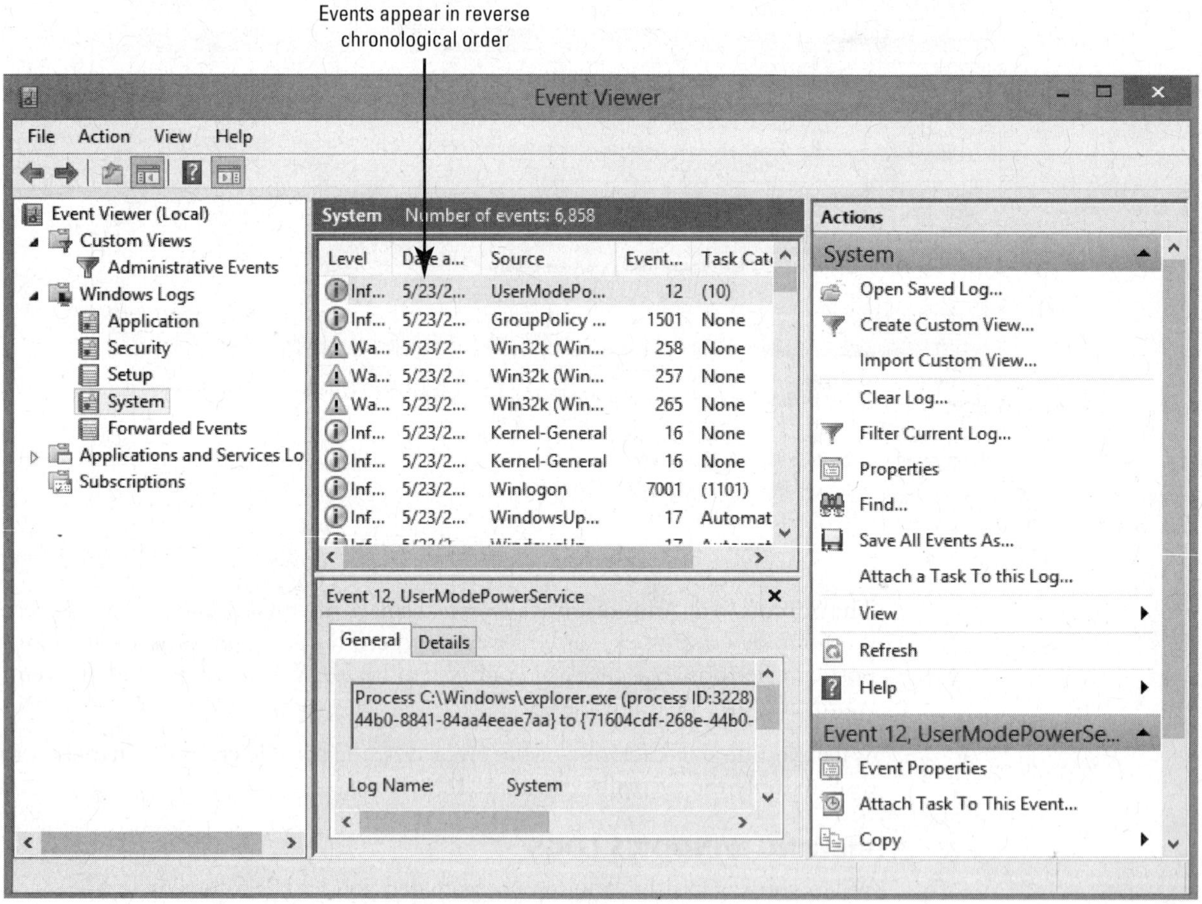

The Windows event logs contain different types of events, which are identified by icons. The five event types are as follows:

- **Information** – An event that describes a change in the state of a component or process as part of a normal operation.
- **Error** – An event that warns of a problem that is not likely to affect the performance of the component or process where the problem occurred, but that could affect the performance of other components or processes on the system.

- **Warning** – An event that warns of a service degradation or an occurrence that can potentially cause a service degradation in the near future, unless you take steps to prevent it.
- **Critical** – An event that warns that an incident resulting in a catastrophic loss of functionality or data in a component or process has occurred.
- **Verbose** – Provides verbose status, such as progress or success messages.

When you select one of the events in the list of events, its properties appear in the preview pane at the bottom of the list. You can also double-click an event to display a separate Event Properties dialog box.

VIEWING COMPONENT LOGS

The Event Viewer console contains a great deal of information, and one of the traditional problems for system administrators and desktop technicians is finding the events they need in a large mixture of results. Windows Eventing 6.0 includes several innovations that can help in this regard.

One of these innovations is the addition of component-specific logs that enable you to examine the events for a particular operating system component or application. Any component that is capable of recording events in the System log or Application log can also record events in a separate log dedicated solely to that component.

The Event Viewer console comes preconfigured with a large collection of component logs for Windows 8. When you expand the Applications and Services Logs folder, you see logs for Windows applications, such as Internet Explorer. You might also see other vendor-specific logs and log folders depending on the OEM and installed system components. When you further expand the Microsoft and its child Windows folder, you will discover more than 200 folders that contain logs for specific Windows components, as shown in Figure 23-3. Each of these components has its own separate log, called a ***channel***.

Figure 23-3

Windows component logs in the *Event Viewer* console

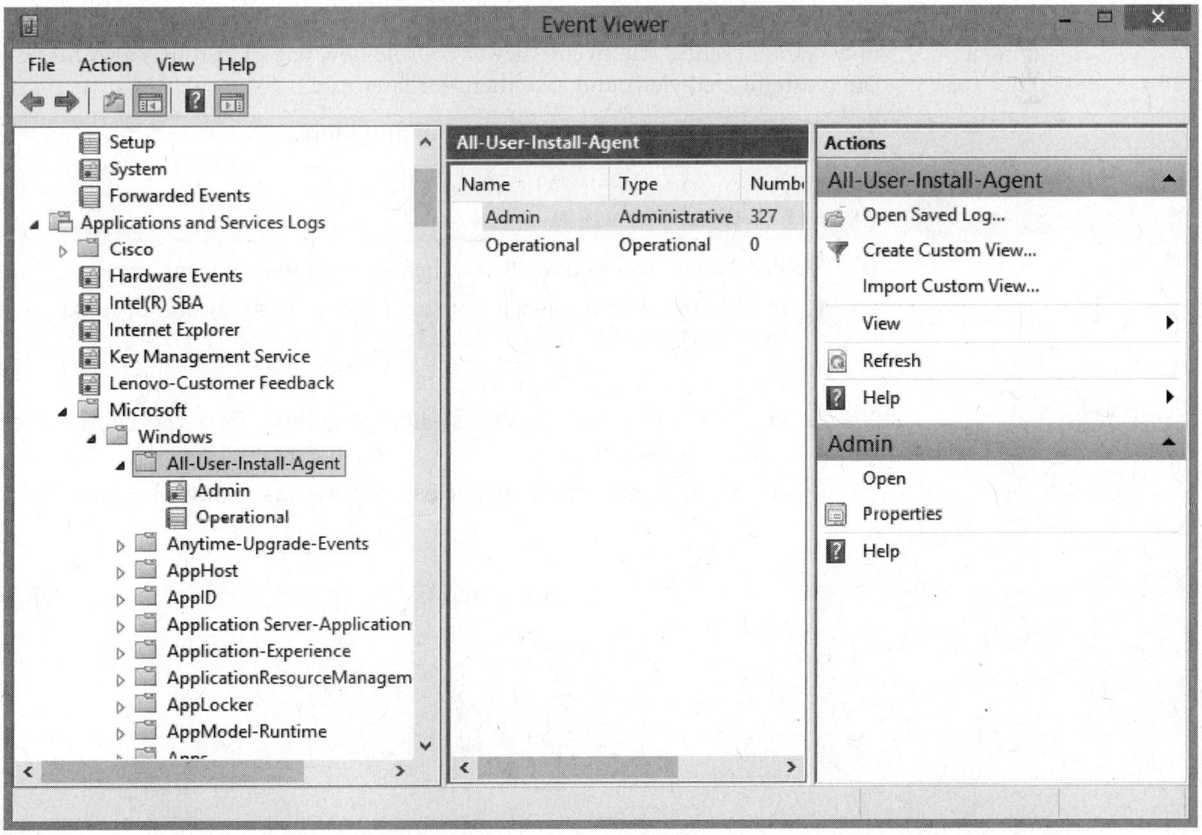

In many cases, the events in the component logs are non-administrative, meaning that they are not indicative of problems or errors. The components continue to save the administrative events to the System log or Application log. The events in the component logs are:

- **Admin** – Information, warning, error, and critical event status.
- **Operational** – Operational status and configuration issues that might lead to problem cause identification.
- **Analytical and Debug** – These component logs are intended more for use in troubleshooting long-term problems and for software developers seeking debugging information. They need to be enabled by selecting the View > Show Analytical and Debug logs in the Action pane of the Event Viewer.

SCHEDULING A TASK TO RUN IN RESPONSE TO AN EVENT

Event Viewer offers the opportunity to associate an event with the Task Scheduler. Navigate to the Event Viewer log, which contains an event that you want to monitor. Select the event and right-click to Attach Task to This Event.

Identify the event source by providing the Log File, Source, and Event ID. You can then associate one of three Actions with the event:

- Start a Program.
- Send an email.
- Display a Message.

You can perform all three Actions by repeating the process and selecting each action during one pass through the process.

CREATING CUSTOM VIEWS

Another means of locating and isolating information about specific events is to use custom views. A ***custom view*** is essentially a filtered version of a particular log, configured to display only certain events. The Event Viewer console now has a Custom Views folder in which you can create filtered views and save them for later use.

To create a custom view, use the following procedure.

CREATE A CUSTOM VIEW

GET READY. Log on to Windows 8 and then perform the following steps:

1. In the Start screen, launch **Control Panel > System and Security > Administrative Tools > Event Viewer**.

   The *Event Viewer* console appears.

2. Right-click the **Custom Views** folder and then, from the context menu, select **Create Custom View**.

   The *Create Custom View* dialog box appears, as shown in Figure 23-4.

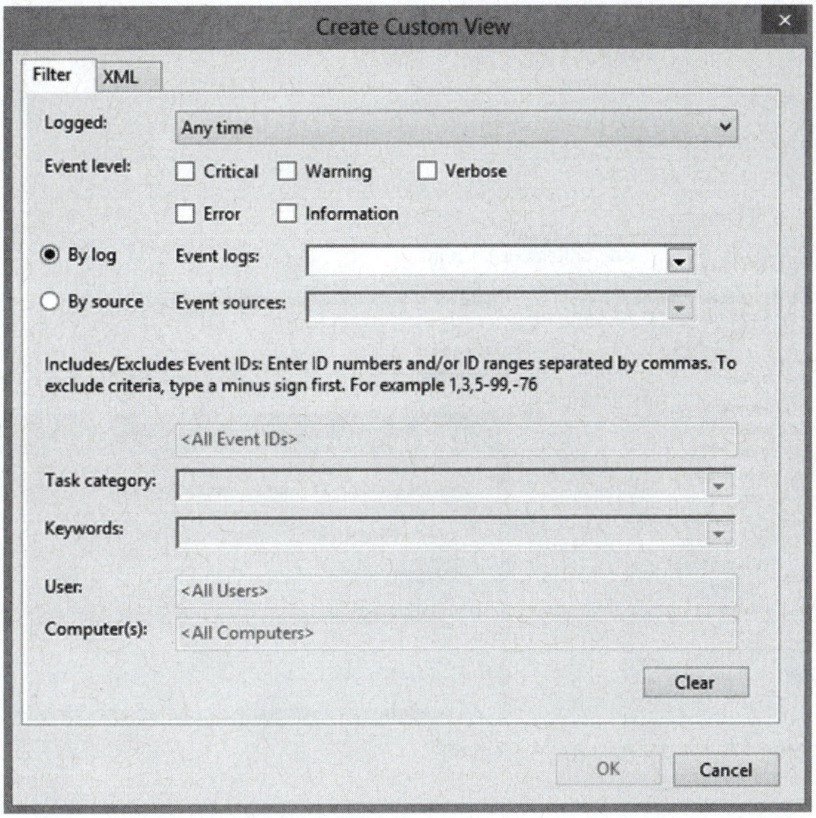

Figure 23-4
The *Create Custom View* dialog box

3. From the *Logged* drop-down list, select the time interval from which you want to display events.
4. In the *Event level* area, select the check boxes for the types of events you want to display.
5. From the *By log* drop-down list, select the log(s) from which you want to display events. Alternatively, from the *By source* list, select the source(s) from which you want to display events.
6. Optionally, you can specify event ID numbers, task categories, keywords, and user credentials to narrow your search.
7. Click **OK**.

   The *Save Filter to Custom View* dialog box appears.
8. In the *Name* text box, type a name for the view, a description if desired, and select the folder in which you want to create your custom view.
9. Click **OK**.

   The console adds your view to the folder you selected and displays the view in the detail pane.

SUBSCRIBING TO EVENTS

The Event Viewer console can provide an enormous amount of information about a Windows 8 computer. For a technical specialist supporting hundreds of workstations, quickly isolating relevant information can be a challenge. Using the Microsoft Management console and adding the Event View snap-in, rather than selecting the local computer, you can select to remotely manage another computer's Event Viewer. The Event Viewer snap-in selection offers the options shown in Figure 23-5.

Figure 23-5

The *Event Viewer* snap-in

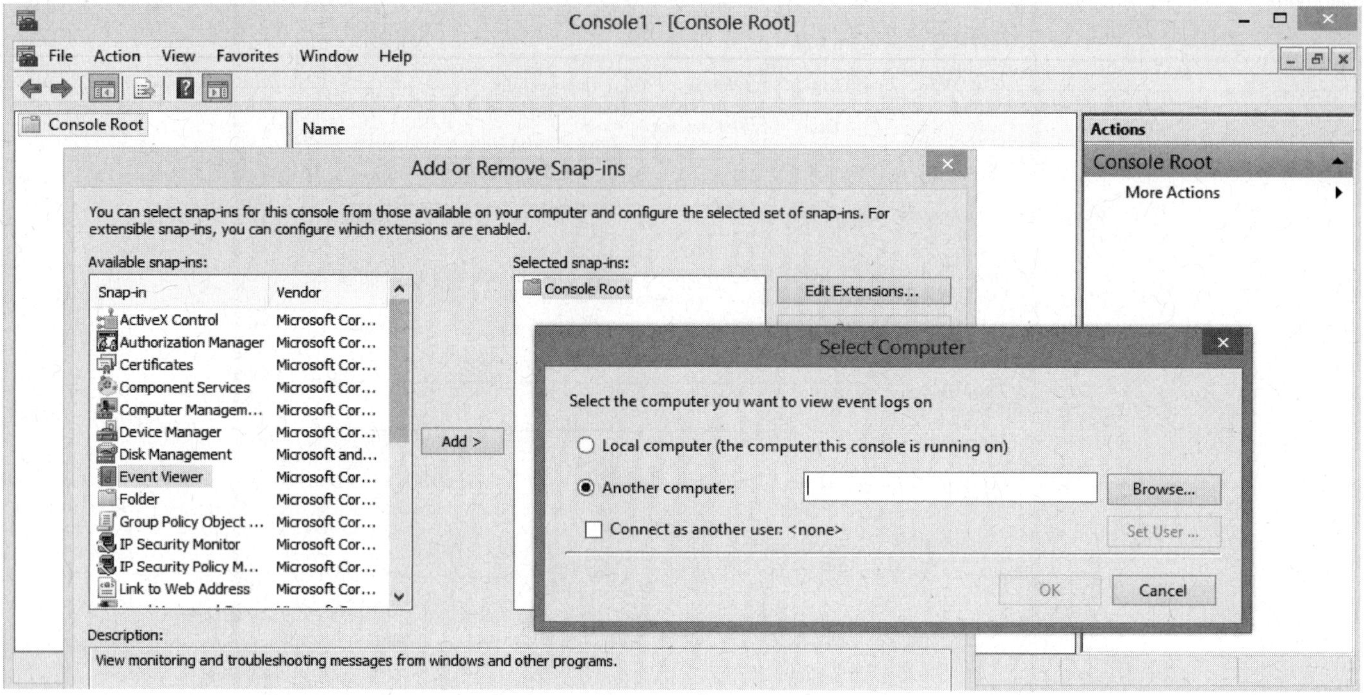

You can use the Event Viewer console on one computer to connect to another computer and display its logs. Although this saves some travel time, it is hardly practical to check logs for hundreds of computers on a regular basis.

The Windows 8 Event Viewer console provides a better solution for enterprise administrators in the form of subscriptions. ***Subscriptions*** enable administrators to receive events from other computers (called ***sources***) in the Event Viewer console on their own computers (called ***collectors***). Windows Eventing supports two types of subscriptions, as follows:

- **Collector initiated** – The collector computer retrieves events from the source computer. This type of subscription is intended for smaller networks, because you must configure each of the computers manually.
- **Source computer initiated** – The source computer sends events to the collector computer. Designed for larger networks, this type of subscription uses Group Policy settings to configure the source computers. Another advantage is the creation of a subscription that can be used to add computers at a later time (for example, as new systems are added to the domain).

TAKE NOTE*

To launch an elevated command prompt in Windows 8, use the WinKey to access the Start Screen. Type **cmd**. Select the **Command Prompt** and right-click to select **Run as Administrator** from the bottom panel.

You create subscriptions in the local Event Viewer console. Before you can configure a subscription and event collection, you must configure both the source and collector systems to run the appropriate services required for remote communication and administration. Source computers require a service called *Windows Remote Management* and collectors need the Windows Event Collector service. To configure the computers, use the following procedures.

On the collector computer:

- To start and autoconfigure the Windows Event Collector Service, open an elevated command prompt, type the following command, and then press *Enter*:
- `wecutil qc`

On each source computer:

- To enable the Windows Remote feature, open an elevated command prompt, type the following command, and then press *Enter*:
- `winrm quickconfig`
- Open the Computer Management console and, in the Local Users and Groups snap-in, add the computer account for the collector to the local Administrators group. (Alternately, you can add an Active Directory Users and Computers group that will be granted remote computer access.)
- Services launched using the command prompt sequence can be set for manual start in the Services console. To affect a more permanent solution, the following elements should be configured either manually or through Group Policy:
    - Using System Properties > Remote, set the source computer to allow remote connections using the appropriate connection service.
    - Either through System Properties > Remote > Select Users or through the Computer Management Console > Local Users and Groups, add the computer or users to be granted access to the local administrators group.
    - Using Computer Manager Console > Services, set the Event Collector and Remote services to automatic or automatic (Delayed) start.
    - Configure the Basic Windows Firewall or Firewall with Advanced Security via Group Policy to enable the Remote Event Log Management application on the source computer and the Windows Event Collector (port 5985) on the collector system.

TAKE NOTE*

Event log subscriptions use the Hypertext Transfer Protocol (HTTP), or optionally, the Secure Hypertext Transfer Protocol (HTTPS), for communications. These are the same protocols used by Internet web servers and browsers, so most computers are configured to allow them through their firewalls. However, if you experience communication problems, make sure that the firewalls on the collector and all source computers are configured to allow traffic on TCP port 80 for HTTP or TCP port 443 for HTTPS in addition to specific firewall rules enabling the relevant remote applications.

Once you complete these tasks, you can proceed to create a subscription in the Event Viewer console on the collector computer, using the following procedure.

CREATE AN EVENT SUBSCRIPTION

GET READY. Log on to the Windows 8 computer you have configured as the collector and then perform the following steps:

1. In the Start screen, launch **Control Panel > System and Security > Administrative Tools > Event Viewer**.

   The *Event Viewer* console appears.

2. Right-click the **Subscriptions** node and, from the context menu, select **Create Subscription**.

   The Subscription Properties dialog box appears, as shown in Figure 23-6.

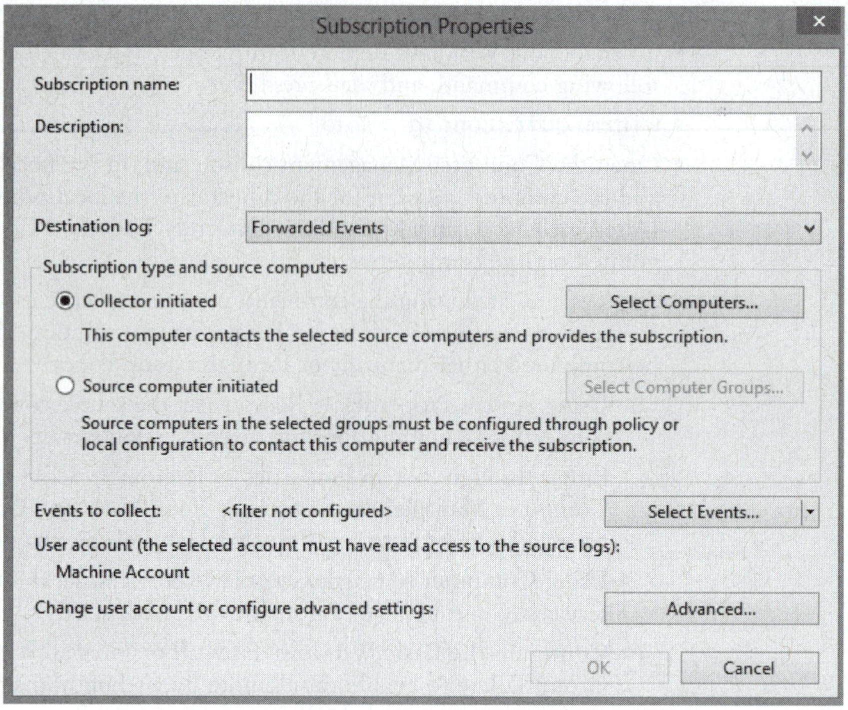

Figure 23-6

The *Subscription Properties* dialog box

3. In the *Subscription Name* text box, type a name for the subscription.
4. Select one of the following subscription type options:
   - **Collector initiated** – If you choose this option, you must click **Select Computers** to display the *Computers* dialog box, in which you must specify the name of all the source computers from which you want to receive events.
   - **Source computer initiated** – If you choose this option, you must click **Select Computer** groups to display the *Computer Groups* dialog box, in which you can specify the names of source computers or the names of security groups into which you will add the computers from which you want to receive events.
5. Click **Select Events**. The *Query Filter* dialog box appears.
6. Use the controls to select the events you want the source computers to forward and then click **OK**.
7. Click **Advanced** to set delivery optimization settings or use **HTTPS** for additional security.
8. Click **OK** to create the subscription.

After creating a source computer initiated subscription, you must configure the source computers to forward their events by configuring a Group Policy setting called *Configure Target Subscription Manager*. This setting is found in the Computer Configuration\Policies\Administrative Templates\Windows Components\Event Forwarding folder of all local and AD DS GPOs.

USING WINDOWS POWERSHELL 3.0 TO ENUMERATE EVENT LOGS

Windows 8 offers you the option to use Windows PowerShell 3.0 to manage event logs using the ***Get-WinEvent*** and ***Clear-Eventlog*** cmdlets. Launch Windows PowerShell 3.0 from the Start Screen.

A simple Windows PowerShell script to view Event Viewer logs follows:

```
Clear-Host

Get-WinEvent -Listlog * | Format-Table LogName
```

CERTIFICATION READY
Monitor system resources
Objective 6.3

You may also use the –LogName parameter rather than the –Listlog parameter. To learn more about the Get-WinEvent cmdlet, you can type the following Windows PowerShell command:

```
Get-Help Get-WinEvent
```

USING PERFORMANCE INFORMATION AND TOOLS

The System control panel provides a system rating called the ***Windows Experience Index***, which quantifies the capabilities of a Windows 8 computer by breaking it down into categories and assigning each one a rating.

One key function of this rating is to help users determine system ability to run features like the Windows Aero user experience. However, the underlying technology of this tool has other uses as well.

To view the Windows 8 Experience Index, use the following procedure.

VIEW AND RUN THE WINDOWS EXPERIENCE INDEX ASSESSMENT

GET READY. Log on to Windows 8 and then perform the following steps:

1. At the Start Screen, type **Windows Experience Index**.
2. Click the Settings search parameter and then click **Use tools to improve performance**. (Alternatively, type **Control Panel** and then view all control panel items by selecting the small icon view. Then select **Performance Information and Tools**.)

   The Performance Information and Tools panel appears, as shown in Figure 23-7.

Figure 23-7

Performance Information and Tools panel

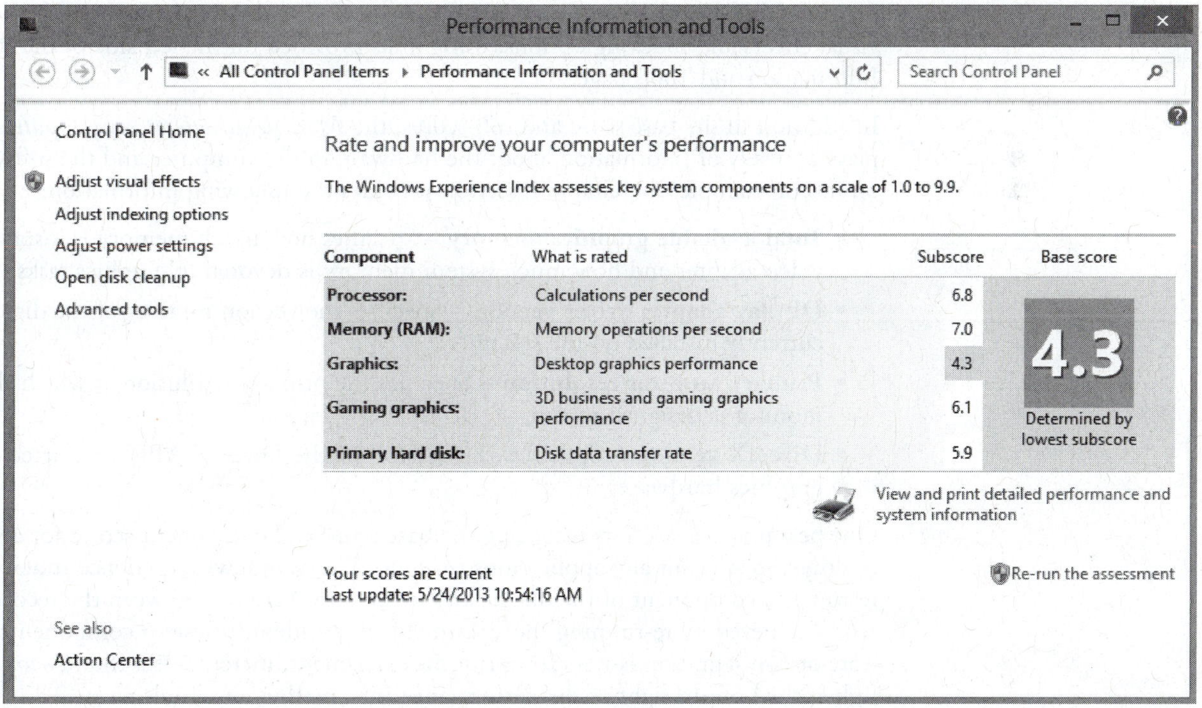

3. Click the **View and print detailed performance and system information** link.

   The *Performance Information and Tools - More details about my computer* window appears.

The *Performance Information and Tools* window breaks down the computer into the following five components:

- Processor
- Memory (RAM)
- Graphics
- Gaming graphics
- Primary hard disk

The tool assigns to each of these areas a numerical score that gauges its performance. The overall system performance rating for the computer, known as the ***base score***, is the lowest of the component scores. The lowest performing component on the computer provides the ***bottleneck*** score that in turn dictates the systems overall performance level. In the same way, that one component can prevent the computer from running Windows Aero, it can also represent a general degradation of performance created by other causes.

TAKE NOTE*

The score range for Windows 8 is now 1.0 to 9.9, expanding the score range of 1.0 to 7.9 offered in Windows 7. As one result, ratings for identical hardware might result in lower bottleneck and base scores in Windows 8. The rating range is a change in the metrics scale. Also, scores below 2.0 were considered sub-scores in Windows 7; scores of 3.0 or lower are considered sub-scores in Windows 8.

One of the best ways to improve the performance of your computer is to try to raise the system's base score. This might require a hardware upgrade, such as installing additional memory, replacing a graphics adapter, or installing a faster hard drive. However, there are often less invasive (and less expensive) ways to improve performance. Examples include modifying visual effects and indexing options, using links provided on the left side of the Performance Information and Tools page.

In addition to the base score and sub-scores, the *More details about my computer* window displays a variety of information about the hardware in the computer and the software running on it. For example, the Graphics section provides the following information:

- **Total available graphics memory** – Specifies how much memory is installed on the video adapter and how much system memory is devoted to graphics tasks.
- **Display adapter driver version** – Specifies the version number of the display driver currently installed on the system.
- **Primary monitor resolution** – Specifies the primary resolution at which the computer's monitor is designed to run.
- **DirectX version** – Specifies the version of the DirectX APIs supported by the graphics hardware.

One best practice suggests recording the base score and component scores for a system while healthy and without any applications running. The Windows Experience Index might then be re-run as a component of the diagnostics procedure. Variance between the recorded score and scores achieved by re-running the assessment might identify system components with hardware or configuration issues. To re-run the assessment, merely select the *Re-run this assessment* link at the bottom right of the Performance Information and Tools page.

The Comprehensive List of Performance Tools

Although each of the Performance Tools provided with Windows 8 can be launched individually, most of the performance, configuration, and diagnostics tools can be found on a single Control Panel list.

1. At the Start Screen, type *Control Panel* and view all control panel items by selecting the small icon view.
2. Then select *Performance Information and Tools.* This is the same panel that displays the Windows Experience Index.
3. From the list of links on the left, select *Advanced Tools.* The *Advanced Tools* panel appears.

The list of tools includes the Windows Experience Index, Event Viewer, Performance Monitor, Resource Monitor, Task Manager, System Information (MSInfo32.exe), System Properties > Advanced, Disk Defragmenter, and the General System Health report.

Using the Performance Monitor Console

A computer's performance level is constantly changing as it performs different combinations of tasks. Monitoring the performance of the various components over a period of time is the only way to get a true picture of the system's capabilities.

Although the Performance Information and Tools page provides a snapshot of your computer's performance at a single moment in time, the Performance Monitor console enables you to view much of the same information, but on a continuous, real-time basis. Like Event Viewer, the Performance Monitor console is an MMC snap-in that you can launch in a variety of ways, including the following:

- On the Start Screen, type *Control Panel.* Select *Control Panel* > *System and Security* > *Administrative Tools* > *Performance Monitor.*
- On the Start Screen, type *MMC.* Add the Performance Monitor snap-in.
- On the Start Screen, type *Perfmon.* Select the *Perfmon.exe* tile.
- Open the Computer Management console by right-clicking on *Computer* either within Windows Explorer or from the Start Screen, and then selecting *Performance.*

The Performance Monitor will launch.

Performance Monitor provides a high-level system summary on the landing page, and it can measure and display hundreds of different statistics (called ***performance counters***) in a variety of ways. Performance Monitor can display a real-time graph that approximates an oscilloscope, capture information for later graphic display, or analyze and present data in an interpreted, formatted report. You can either use pre-built diagnostic and performance measurements, or create a custom evaluation set of your own.

When you expand the Performance Monitor option in the left tools pane, the detail pane displays a real-time line graph for the % Processor Time performance counter.

ADDING COUNTERS

The performance counter that appears in Performance Monitor by default is a useful gauge of the computer's performance, but the snap-in includes hundreds of other counters that you can add to the display. To add counters to the Performance Monitor display, click the *Add* button in the toolbar, or press *Ctrl+I* to display the Add Counters dialog box.

TAKE NOTE*

Hovering over the green Add button suggests the use of the *Ctrl+N* hotkey. Extensive hotkey remapping in Windows 8 is not always reflected appropriately in the pop-up notations generated by mouse-over. When uncertain, use the mouse to click on desired toolbar functions.

TAKE NOTE* Unlike most MMC snap-ins, Performance Monitor does not insert its most commonly used functions into the MMC console's Action menu. The only methods for accessing Performance Monitor functions are the toolbar buttons, hotkey combinations, and the context menu that appears when you right-click the display.

In this dialog box, specify the following four pieces of information to add a counter to the display:

- ***Computer*** – The name of the computer you want to monitor with the selected counter. Unlike most MMC snap-ins, you cannot redirect the entire focus of Performance Monitor to another computer on the network. Instead, you specify a computer name for each counter you add to the display. This enables you to create a display showing counters for various computers on the network, such as a single graph of processor activity for all of your workstations.

TAKE NOTE* You must have remote permissions, the appropriate remote service features started, and the related firewall ports enabled on both the source and collector systems to remotely gather Performance Monitor information.

- ***Performance object*** – A category representing a specific hardware or software component in the computer. Click the down arrow on a performance object to display a selection of performance counters related to that component.
- **Performance counter** – A statistic representing a specific aspect of the selected performance object's activities.
- ***Instance*** – An element representing a specific occurrence of the selected performance counter. For example, on a computer with two network interface adapters, each counter in the Network Interface performance object would have two instances, one for each adapter, enabling you to track the performance of the two adapters individually. Some counters also have instances such as Total or Average, enabling you to track the performance of all instances combined or the median value of all instances.

Once you select a computer name, a performance object, a performance counter in that object, and an instance of that counter, click Add to add the counter to the Added Counters list. The dialog box remains open so that you can add more counters. Click *OK* when you are finished to update the graph with your selected counters.

TAKE NOTE* Select the *Show description* check box to display a detailed explanation of the selected performance counter.

The performance objects, performance counters, and instances that appear in the *Add Counters* dialog box depend on the computer's hardware configuration, the software installed on the computer, and the computer's role on the network.

MODIFYING THE GRAPH VIEW

Once you select multiple performance objects and add them to the active Performance Monitor, the tool will display a real-time graph similar to Figure 23-8.

Figure 23-8

Performance Monitor real-time display

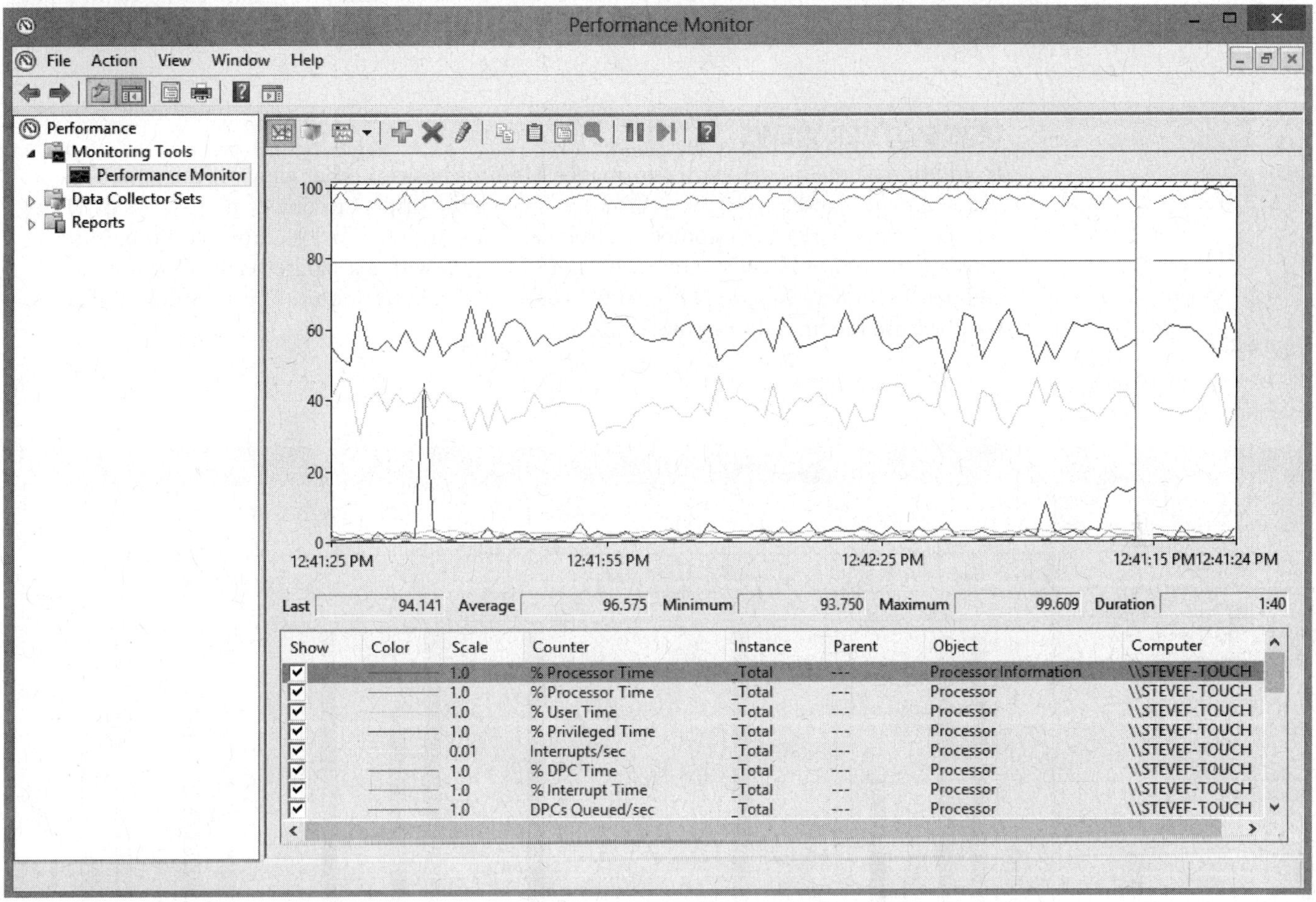

The legend beneath the Performance Monitor graph specifies the line color for the counter, the scale of values for the counter, and other identifying information. When you select a counter in the legend, its current values appear in numerical form at the bottom of the graph. Click the *Highlight* button in the toolbar (or press *Ctrl+ H*) to change the selected counter to a broad line that is easier to distinguish in the graph.

If your computer is otherwise idle, you will probably notice that the line in the default graph is hovering near the bottom of the scale, making it difficult to see its value. You can address this problem by modifying the scale of the graph's Y (that is, vertical) axis. Click the *Properties* button in the toolbar (or press *Ctrl+ Q*) to display the Performance Monitor Properties sheet and then click the *Graph* tab. In the *Vertical scale* box, you can reduce the maximum value for the Y axis, thereby using more of the graph to display the counter data.

Within the General tab of the Performance Monitor Properties sheet you can also modify the sample rate of the graph. By default, the graph updates the counter values every one second, but you can increase this value to display data for a longer period of time on a single page of the graph. This can make it easier to detect long-term trends in counter values.

TAKE NOTE*

The *Performance Monitor Properties* sheet contains several other controls that you can use to modify the appearance of the graph. For example, on the Graph tab, you can add axis titles and gridlines, and in the Appearance tab, you can control the graph's background and select a different text font.

USING OTHER VIEWS

In addition to the line graph, Performance Monitor has two other views of the same data: a histogram view and a report view. You can change the display to one of these views by clicking the *Change Graph Type* toolbar button. You can also use *Ctrl+ G* to scroll through the three report views. The histogram view is a bar graph with a separate vertical bar for each counter, as shown in Figure 23-9. In this view, it is easier to monitor large numbers of counters, because the lines do not overlap.

Figure 23-9

The *Performance Monitor* histogram view

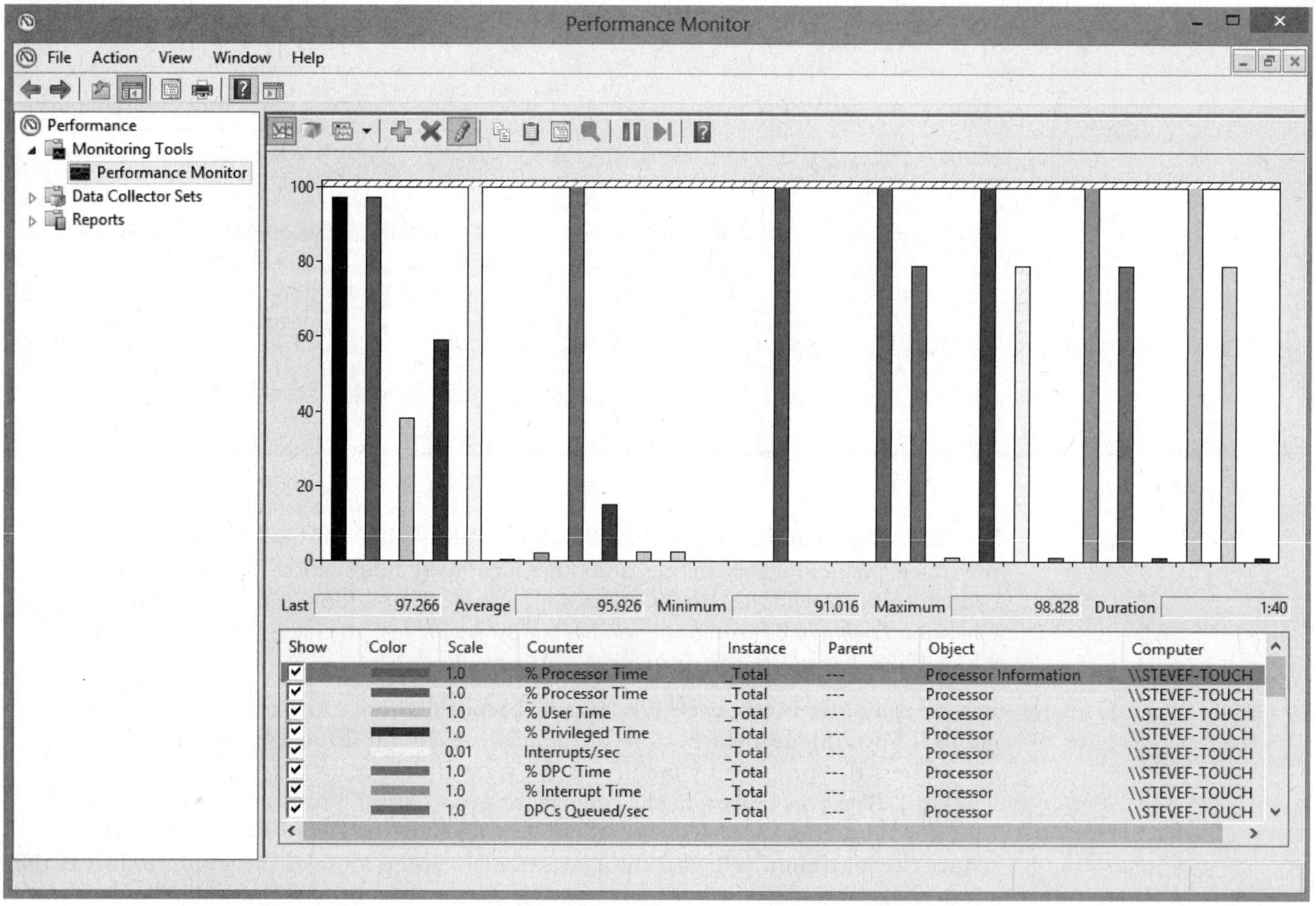

The report view (see Figure 23-10) displays the numerical value for each of the performance counters.

Figure 23-10

The *Performance Monitor* report view

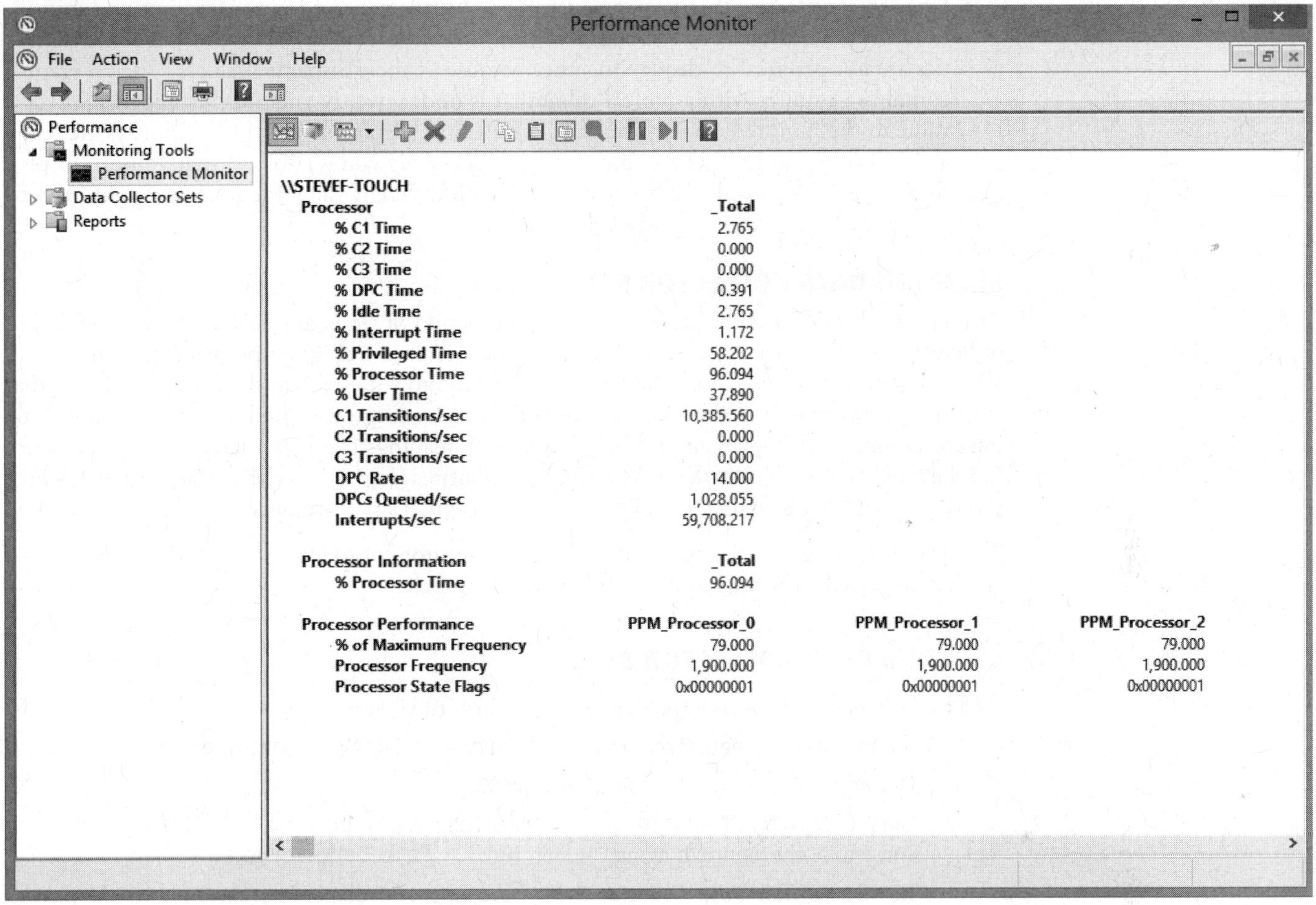

As with the line graph, the histogram and report views both update their counter values at the interval specified in the General tab of the *Performance Monitor Properties* sheet. The main drawback of these two views, however, is that they do not display a history of the counter values, only the current value. Each new sampling overwrites the previous one in the display, unlike the line graph, which displays the previous values as well.

CREATING AN EFFECTIVE DISPLAY

In most cases, when users first discover Performance Monitor, they see the dozens of available performance objects and proceed to create a line graph containing dozens of different counters. In most cases, the result is a graph that is hopelessly crowded and incoherent. The number of counters that you can display effectively depends on the size of your monitor and the resolution of your video display.

Consider the following tips when selecting counters:

- **Limit the number of counters** – Too many counters make the graph more difficult to understand. To display a large number of statistics, you can display multiple windows in the console and select different counters in each window, or use the histogram or report view to display a large number of counters in a more compact form.
- **Modify the counter display properties** – Depending on the size and capabilities of your monitor, the default colors and line widths that System Monitor uses in its graph might

make it difficult to distinguish counters from each other. In the Data tab in the Performance Monitor Properties sheet, you can modify the color, style, and width of each counter's line in the graph to make it easier to distinguish.

- **Choose counters with comparable values** – Performance Monitor imposes no limitations on the combinations of counters you can select for a single graph, but some statistics are not practical to display together because of their disparate values. When a graph contains a counter with a typical value that is under twenty and another counter with a value in the hundreds, it is difficult to arrange the display so that both counters are readable. Choose counters with values that are reasonably comparable so that you can display them legibly. If you must display counters with different value ranges, you might prefer to use the report view instead of the graph view.

CREATING DATA COLLECTOR SETS

Performance bottlenecks can develop over a long period of time, and it can often be difficult to detect them by observing a server's performance levels at a singular point in time. It is always a good idea to use tools like Performance Monitor to establish the operational baseline levels for a workstation. A ***baseline*** is simply a set of readings, captured under normal operating conditions, which you can save and compare to readings taken at a later time. By comparing the baseline readings to the workstation's current readings at regular intervals, you might possibly detect trends that eventually affect the computer's performance.

To capture counter statistics in the Performance Monitor console for later review, you must create a ***data collector set***, using the following procedure.

CREATE A DATA COLLECTOR SET

GET READY. Log on to Windows 8 and then perform the following steps:

1. On the Start Screen, type **Perfmon** and then click the **Perfmon.exe** tile.

   The *Performance Monitor* console appears.

2. Expand the **Data Collector Sets** folder. Then right-click the **User Defined** folder and, from the context menu, select **New > Data Collector Set**.

   The *Create New Data Collector Set* wizard appears, displaying the *How would you like to create this new data collector set?* page.

3. In the *Name* text box, type a name for the data collector set. Then, select the **Create manually (Advanced)** option and then click **Next**.

   The *What type of data do you want to include?* page appears.

4. Select the **Performance counter** check box and then click **Next**.

   The *Which performance counters would you like to log?* page appears.

5. Click **Add**. The standard *Add Counters* dialog box appears. Select the counters you want to log in the usual manner and then click **OK**.

   The counters appear in the *Performance counters* box.

TAKE NOTE* You can also use the *Create New Data Collector Set* wizard to create performance counter alerts, which monitor the values of specific counters and perform a task, such as sending an email to an administrator, when the counters reach a specific value.

TAKE NOTE* The default location is %systemdrive%\Perflogs\Admin\ .)

6. Select the interval at which you want the system to collect samples and then click **Next**. The *Where would you like the data to be saved?* page appears.

7. Type the name of or browse to the folder where you want to store the data collector set and then click **Next**.

   The *Create the data collector set?* page appears.

8. If the account you are currently using does not have the privileges needed to gather the log information, click **Change** to display a *Performance Monitor* dialog box in which you can supply alternative credentials.
9. Select one of the following options:
   - **Open properties for this data collector set** – Saves the data collector set to the specified location and opens its Properties sheet, as shown in Figure 23-11, for further modifications.
   - **Start this data collector set now** – Saves the data collector set to the specified location and starts collecting data immediately.
   - **Save and close** – Saves the data collector set to the specified location and closes the wizard.

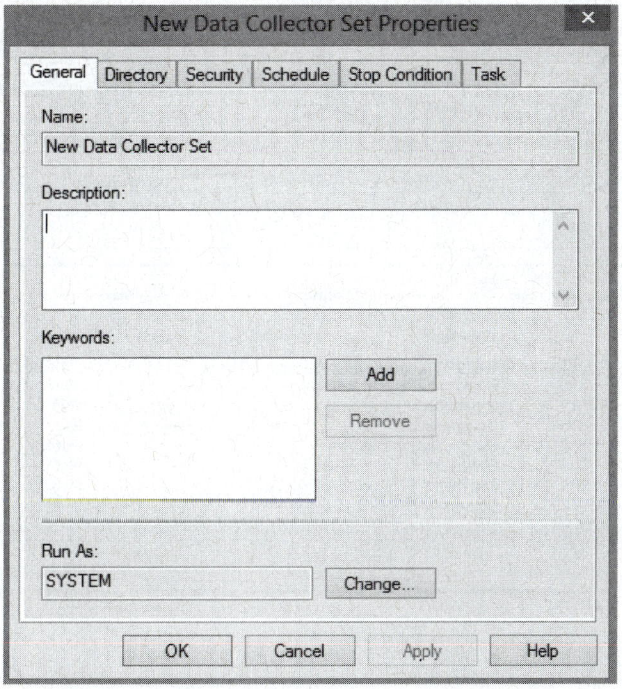

Figure 23-11

The *Properties* sheet for a data collector set

10. Click **Finish**. The new data collector set appears in the *User Defined* folder.
11. Select the new data collector set and then click **Start** in the toolbar.

    The console begins collecting data until you click **Stop**.

Once you capture data using the collector set, you can display the data by double-clicking the *Performance Monitor* file in the folder you specified during its creation. This opens a Performance Monitor window containing a graph of the collected data, as shown in Figure 23-12, instead of real-time activity.

Figure 23-12

Performance Monitor information collected using a data collector set

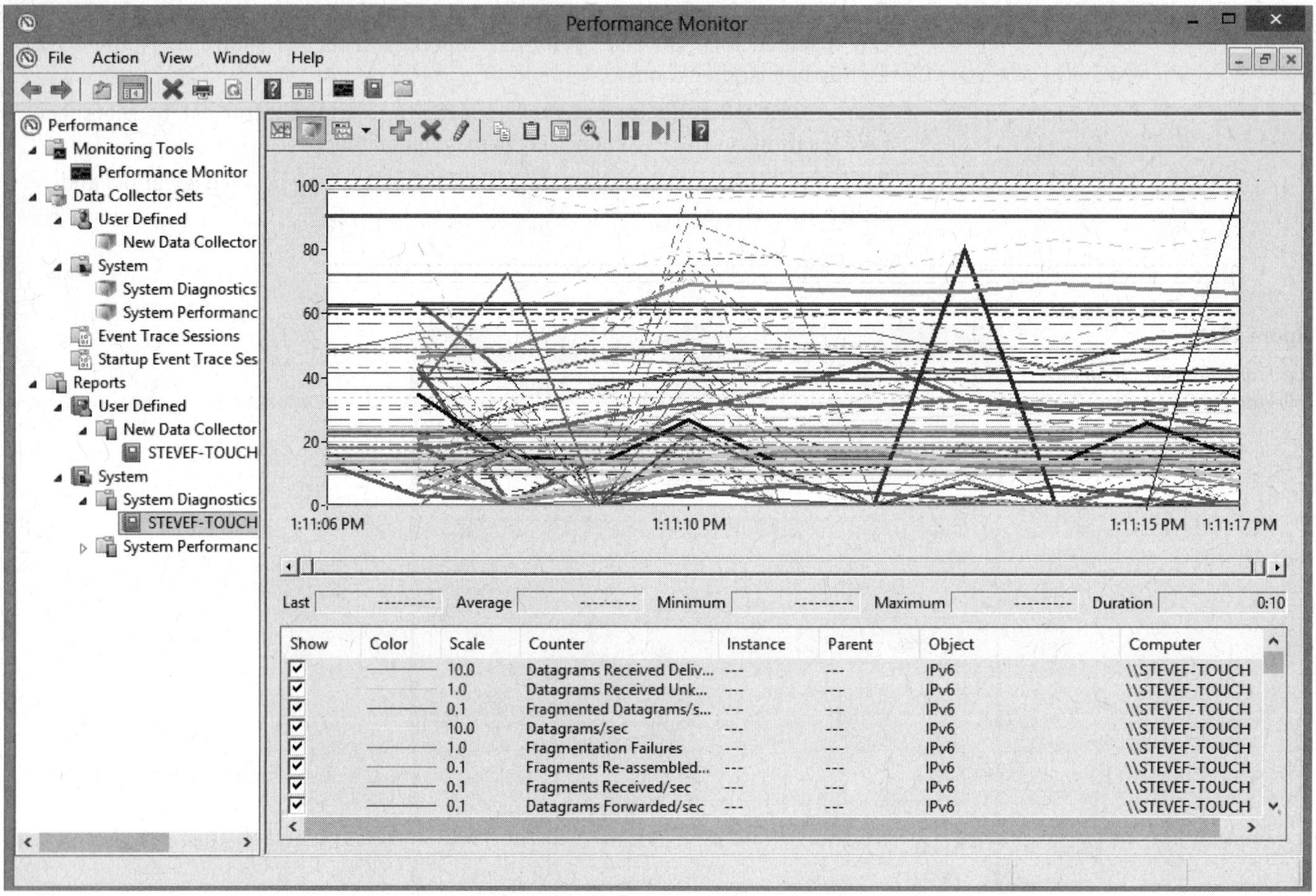

You can also choose to look at formatted report generated by an analysis of the results, or the folder containing all of the XML components generating during the report generation period. To access these alternatives, right-click on the report or select *View* from the toolbar. An example of an auto-generated report is provided in Figure 23-13.

Figure 23-13

Performance Monitor—Report generated from a data collector set

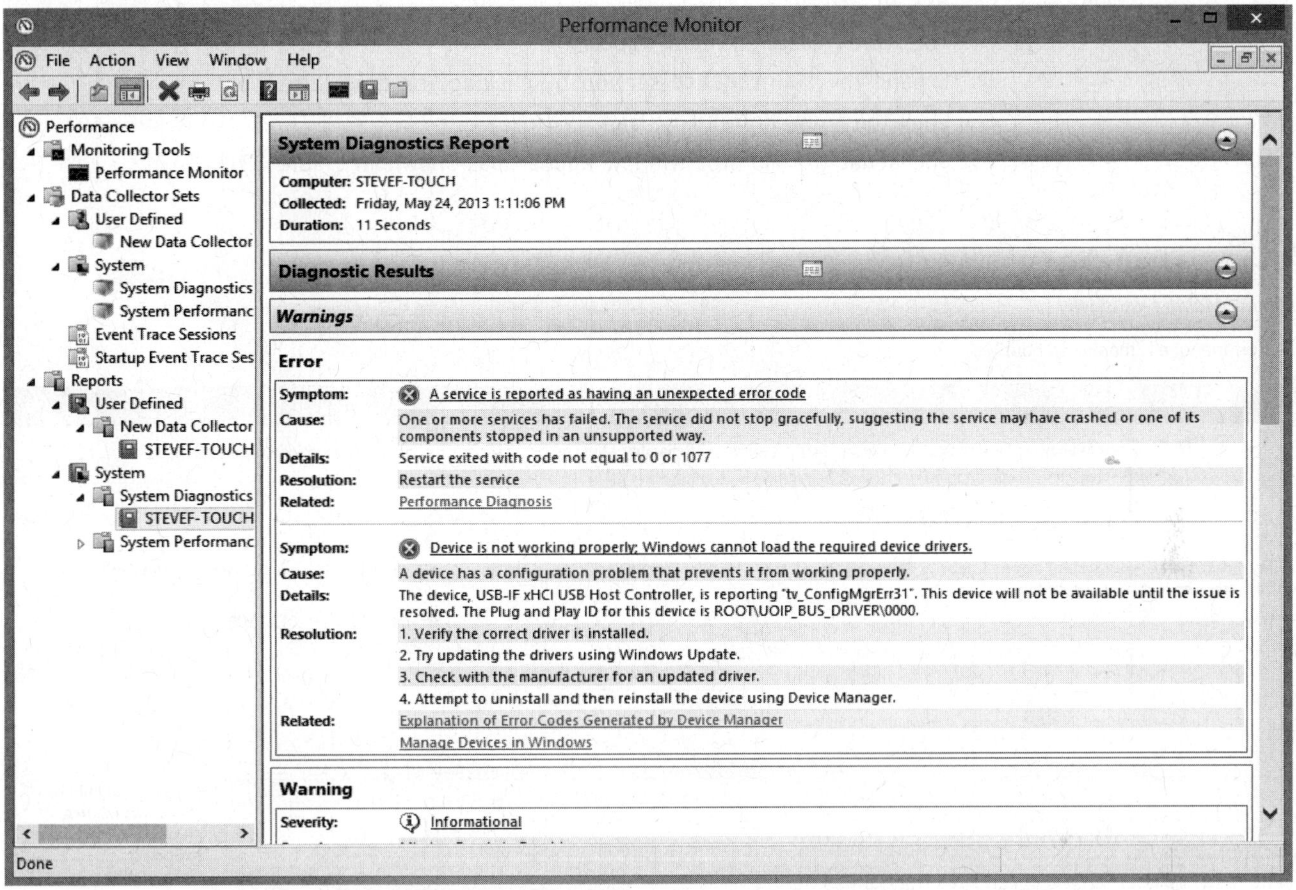

By repeating this process at a later time and comparing the information in the two data collector sets, you can often detect performance trends that indicate the presence of bottlenecks.

CREATING A SYSTEM DIAGNOSTICS REPORT

In addition to its user-configurable capabilities, Performance Monitor also includes preset system diagnostics, system performance, Event Trace Session, and Startup Event Session collector sets. The System Diagnostic and System Performance collector set can be found by expanding the Data Collector Sets\System node, selecting a report, and then clicking the *Start* button in the toolbar.

After allowing the program about 60 seconds to gather data, browse to the Reports\System\System Diagnostics node to view the report. The same View options exist for pre-configured reports as for user-generated collector sets.

Using Reliability Monitor

Reliability Monitor is a stability-tracking tool that extends the capabilities of the Event Viewer and Windows Experience Index enhancing both baseline comparison and problem resolution. The Reliability Monitor can be launched several ways:

- From the Start Screen, type *Reliability Monitor.*
- From the Start Screen open *Control Panel > System and Security > Action Center > Maintenance > View Reliability History.*

To practice accessing Reliability Monitor, use the following procedure.

OPEN RELIABILITY MONITOR

GET READY. Log on to Windows 8 and then perform the following steps:

1. From the *Start* screen, launch **Control Panel > System and Security > Action Center**.

   The *Action Center* window appears.
2. Expand the **Maintenance** section by clicking the down arrow button.
3. Click the **View Reliability History** link.

   The Reliability Monitor window appears, as shown in Figure 23-14.

Figure 23-14

The *Reliability Monitor* window

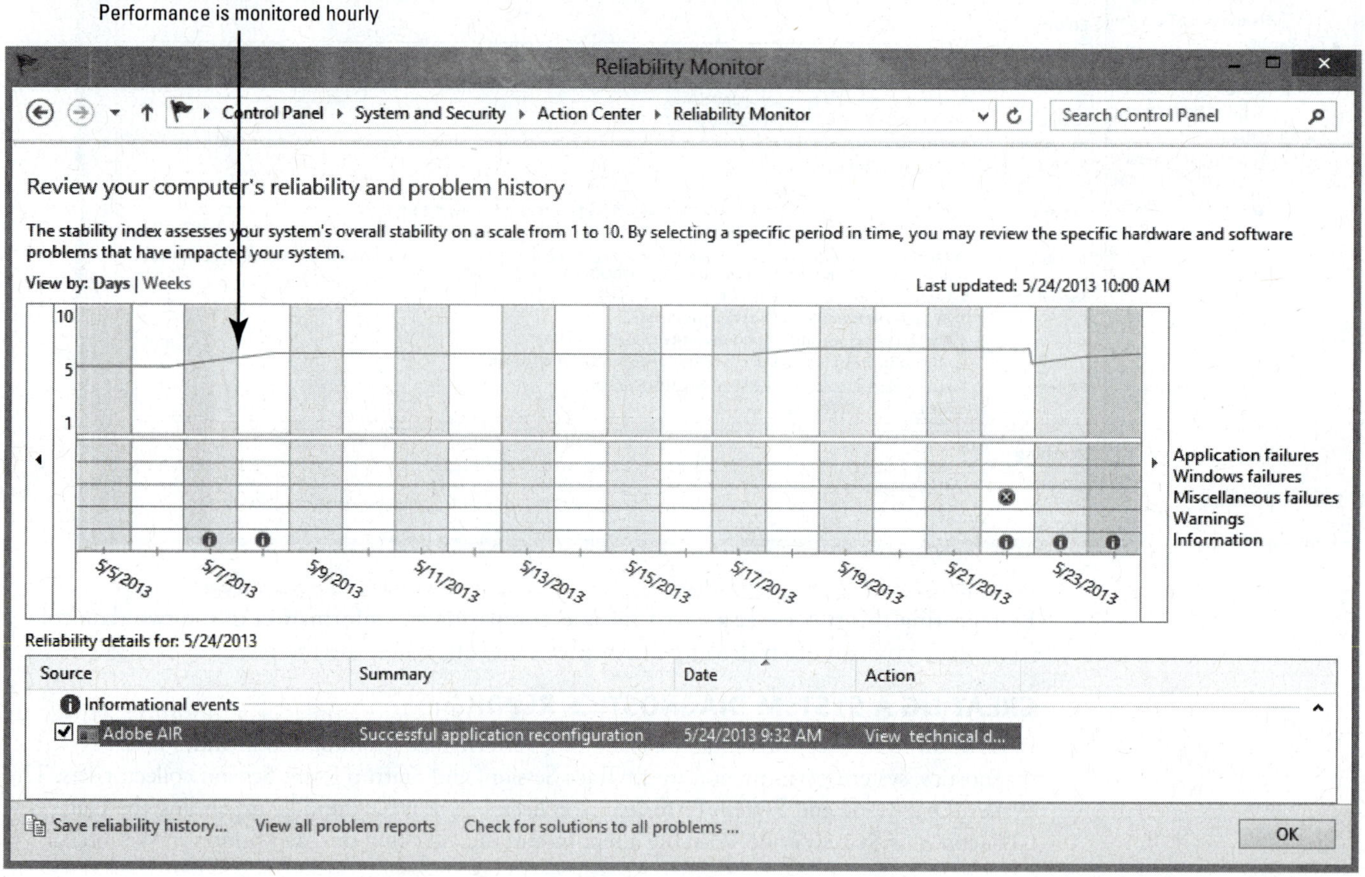

Reliability Monitor gathers information using a hidden scheduled task called ***Reliability Access Component Agent (RACAgent)***. The agent collects data from the event logs every hour and updates the Reliability Monitor display every 24 hours. The stability index is a number from 0 to 10 (with 0 representing the least and 10 the most stability) that is calculated using information about the following types of events:

- **Software (Un)Installs** – Includes software installations, uninstallations, updates, and configurations for the operating system, applications, and device drivers.
- **Application Failures** – Includes application hangs, crashes, and terminations of non-responding applications.

- **Hardware Failures** – Includes disk and memory failures.
- **Windows Failures** – Includes boot failures, operating system crashes, and sleep failures.
- **Miscellaneous Failures** – Includes unrequested system shutdowns.
- **System Clock Changes** – Includes all significant clock time changes. This entry appears only when a significant clock time change has occurred recently.

Pertinent events appear in the System Stability Chart as data points. Clicking one of the points displays information about it in the System Stability Report.

The Reliability Monitor snap-in doesn't actually do anything except present event log information in a different way. It is not possible to configure the snap-in or alter the criteria it uses to evaluate a computer's reliability. If you ever notice that the stability index has decreased, you should check the events listed below the data point of instability. These events, or those listed on immediately preceding dates might be the cause for the value decline. Evaluate the nature of the event report to decide whether more detailed event log or additional performance diagnostic tools may be used to identify or resolve the issue.

TAKE NOTE *

Reliability Monitor is an excellent first stop during system troubleshooting. Using the timeline, and viewing changes to the stability baseline along with associated event entries, you might be able to identify when issues began or were introduced. This can enable you to develop a diagnostic plan or identify an appropriate Restore Point for system recovery.

You also have the ability to Save the reliability history, View problem reports submitted from the system to Microsoft, or Check for solutions to all problems by clicking on one of the links at the bottom of the *Reliability Monitor* panel.

Managing Performance

THE BOTTOM LINE

Windows 8 incorporates and enhances the performance monitoring and measurement tools introduced with Windows Vista and expanded in Windows 7.

Monitoring and diagnosing system performance is of little use unless you optimize settings or correct e system issues. The following section provides an overview of Windows 8 performance management and configuration tools.

Working with Processes

The ability to monitor and manage processes is an important part of Windows 8 maintenance, and Microsoft provides a variety of tools that simplify configuration identification, modification, or automated correction. Task Manager remains one of the most significant tools for active system management, and is one of the tools most notably enhanced in Windows 8.

Every application and service running on a Windows 8 computer, including those that are part of the operating system, generate processes, individual tasks that contribute to the overall performance of the system. When performance degrades, the most common method of troubleshooting is to examine the processes running on the computer and the system resources they are consuming. Task Manager remains the most prominent process analysis tool.

One of the challenges historically associated with use of the Task Manager has been the ability to identify process relationships called ***process trees***. The revised layout and presentation of Task Manager now groups processes together according to the process tree of which they are a member, and further groups the trees together based on the services or application features that they provide.

Because enhanced tools like Performance Monitor require advanced skillsets and elevated permissions, Task Manager is the tool most often recommended to the standard user for symptom or cause identification. The Task Manager interface has been enhanced to both the effort of the standard user and the expanded needs of the system technician or help desk administrator.

Using Task Manager

Task Manager has been updated in Windows 8 to expand the ability to monitor, diagnose, and enhance system performance.

CERTIFICATION READY
Configure Task Manager
Objective 6.3

To access Task Manager, use one of the following procedures.

- As always, you can use CTL+ALT+DEL and select Task Manager from the list of available options. This is not an ideal recommendation for the standard user, because repeating the key set reboots the computer.
- Microsoft has added a more user-friendly hot-key combination, CTL+SHIFT-ESC, that performs the same function.
- You can right-click the taskbar when on the desktop and select *Task manager*.
- From the Start Screen, type *Taskmgr*, although only *ta* are actually required to raise the Task Manager tile.
- Task Manager is also available from Comprehensive list of Performance Tools identified previously in this chapter.

Let's try to open Task Manager as efficiently as possible.

OPEN TASK MANAGER

GET READY. Log on to Windows 8 and then perform the following steps:

1. Tap the **Windows** key to get to the Start screen.
2. Type **ta** and then click the **Task Manager** tile.
   The *Task Manager* opens.
3. Click the **more details** option at the bottom of the panel to access the full features of the Windows 8 Task Manager.

TAKE NOTE*
You might see no or only a few applications running. This is typically all that the standard user needs to identify or end task.

USING WINDOWS TASK MANAGER

The enhanced Windows Task manager has some useful tabs:

- **Processes** – Actually process trees, listed in groups that identify the process group or application with which they are associated, that can be expanded as in Figure 23-15 to reveal all the processes within the group. Note that each Service Host set is also clearly identified.

Figure 23-15

The *Processes* tab

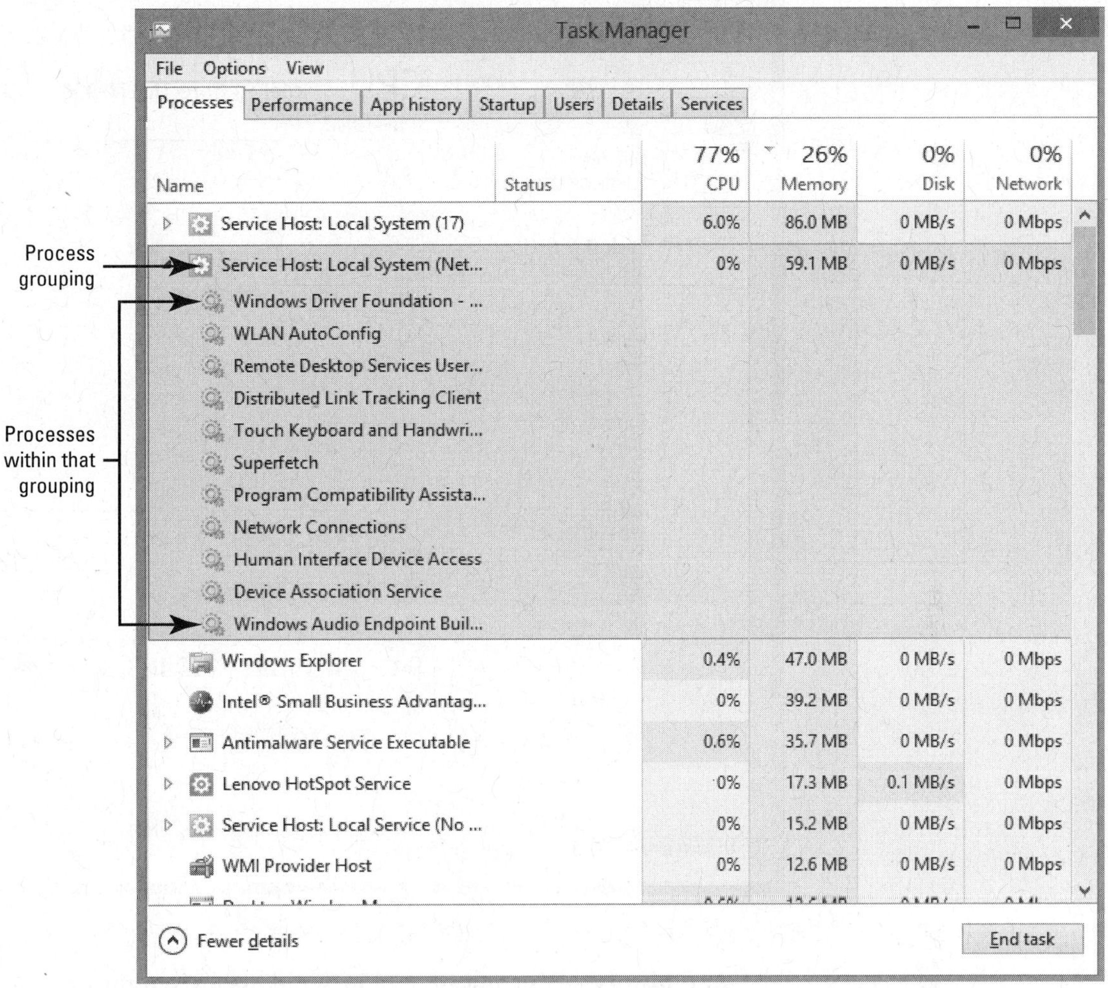

- **Performance** – Real-time performance for system components including CPU, Memory, each disk volume, Bluetooth, Wi-Fi, and each Network Interface card. By clicking on the component in the left panel, real-time graphics are displayed at the top of the right panel along with configuration and statistical information in report format at the bottom of the right panel. A snapshot of Task manager CPU performance information is presented in Figure 23-16.

Figure 23-16

The *Performance* tab

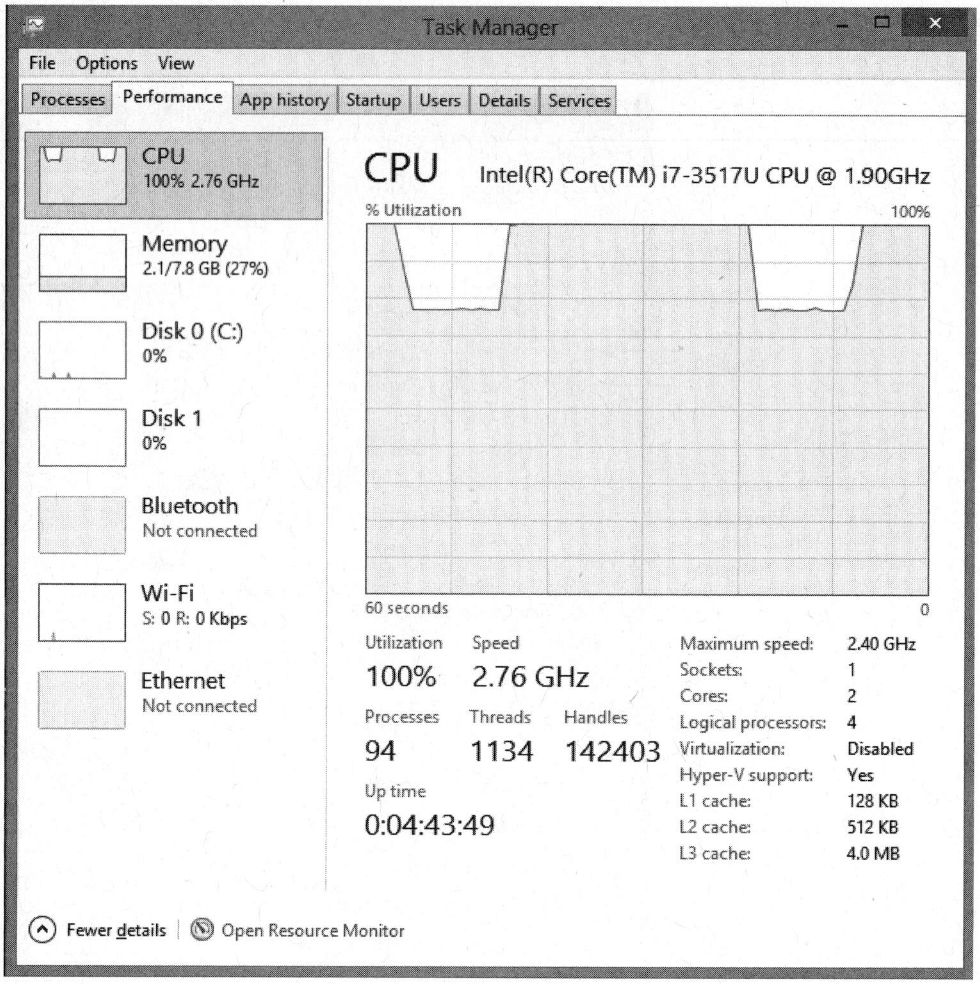

- **App history** – A significant tool in Windows 8 given the expansion of Cloud connectivity and the use of Metro/Modern applications. The App History tile provides CPU time, Network utilization, Metered Network Utilization, and Metro Tile updates information for all applications installed and enabled on the system, whether they are currently in use when the Task Manager is launched or not. This information is beneficial when attempting to determine the system load created by active Metro applications. Note the link on the top of the tab panel that allows you to Delete Usage History to start a new analysis after making system configuration changes. An example of Task Manager App History information is provided in Figure 23-17.

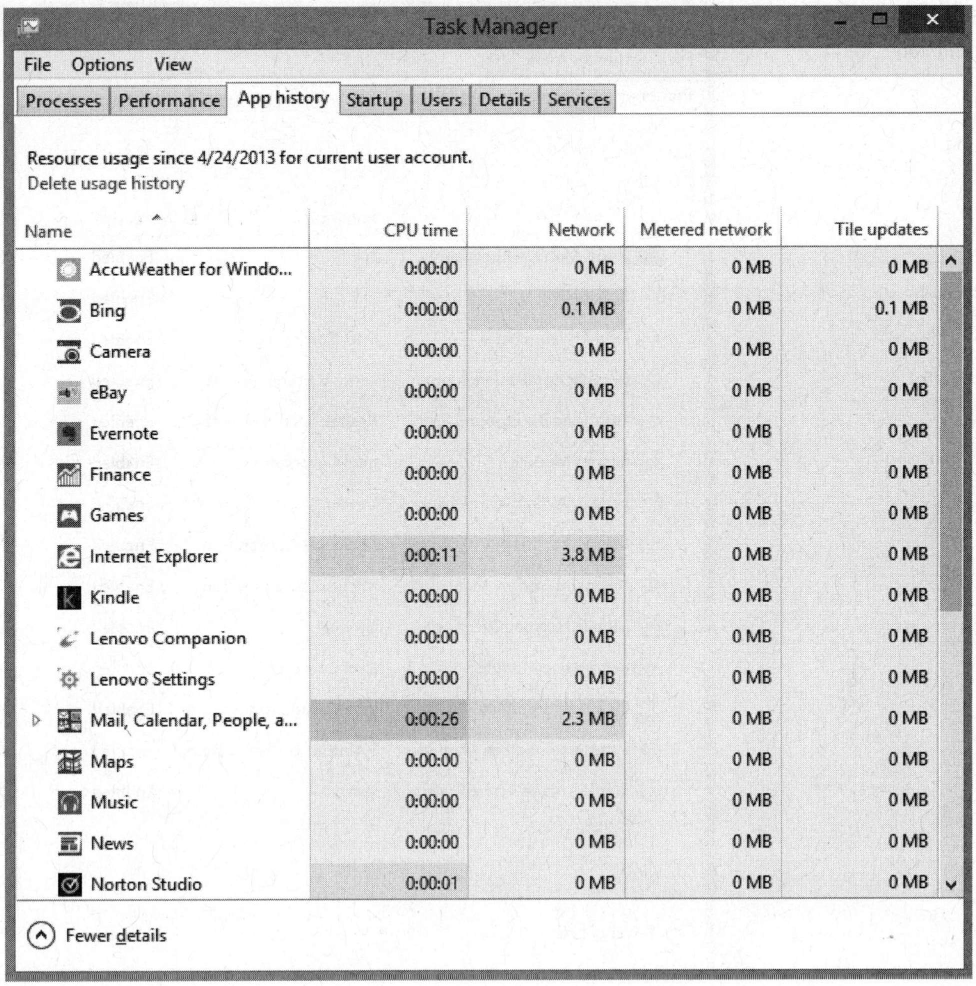

Figure 23-17

The *App history* tab

- **Startup** – The Startup tab identifies all the system components that are launched upon system start. Applications with multiple components can be expanded to review the subcomponents or multiple instances. You can each highlight and right-click on an application to disable its launch at startup, or select an application and use the Disable/ Enable toggle button at the bottom right of the panel. An example of the Startup tab is provided in Figure 23-18.

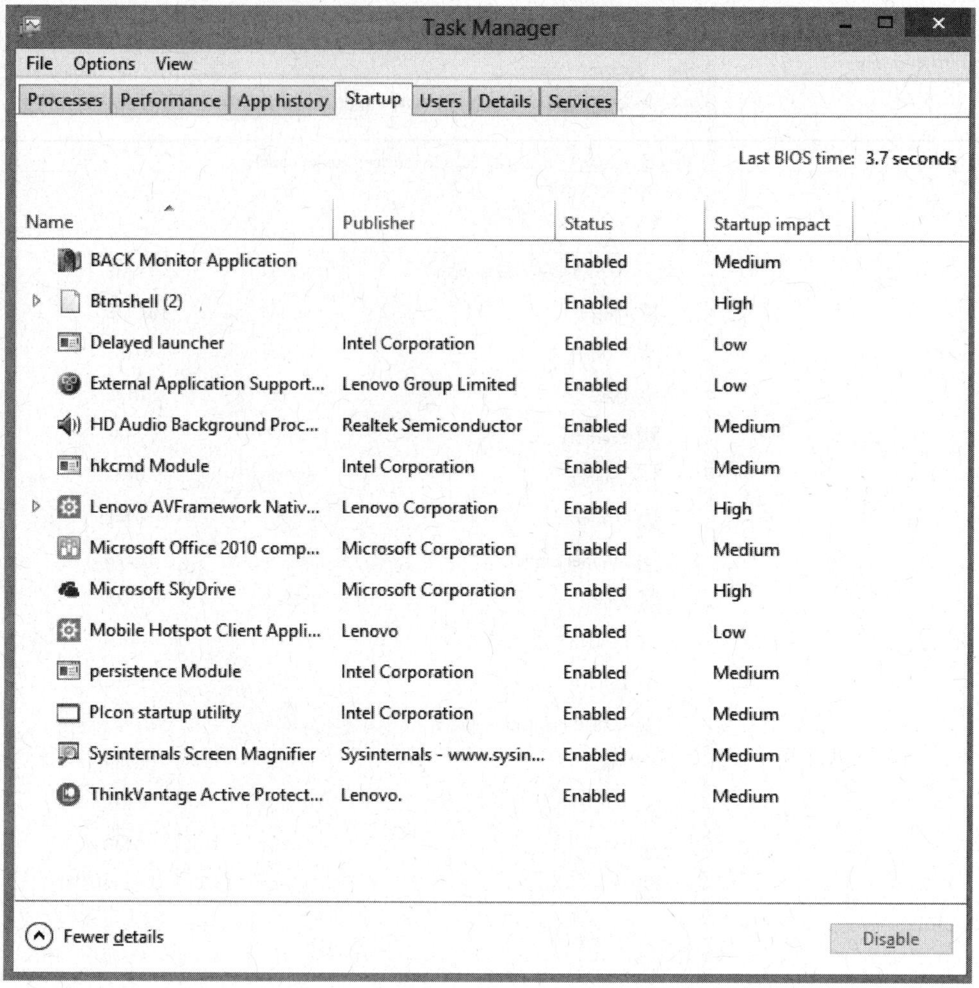

Figure 23-18

The *Startup* tab

- **Users** – The Users tab identifies all users locally or remotely connected to the system. The example shown in Figure 23-19 expands the active user, identifying the active processes for the selected user. After selecting a specific user, you can disconnect the session by using the *Disconnect* button at the bottom of the panel. The active user will be prompted for confirmation before the Disconnect request is completed. This prevents the active user from accidentally disconnecting himself or remote support personnel.

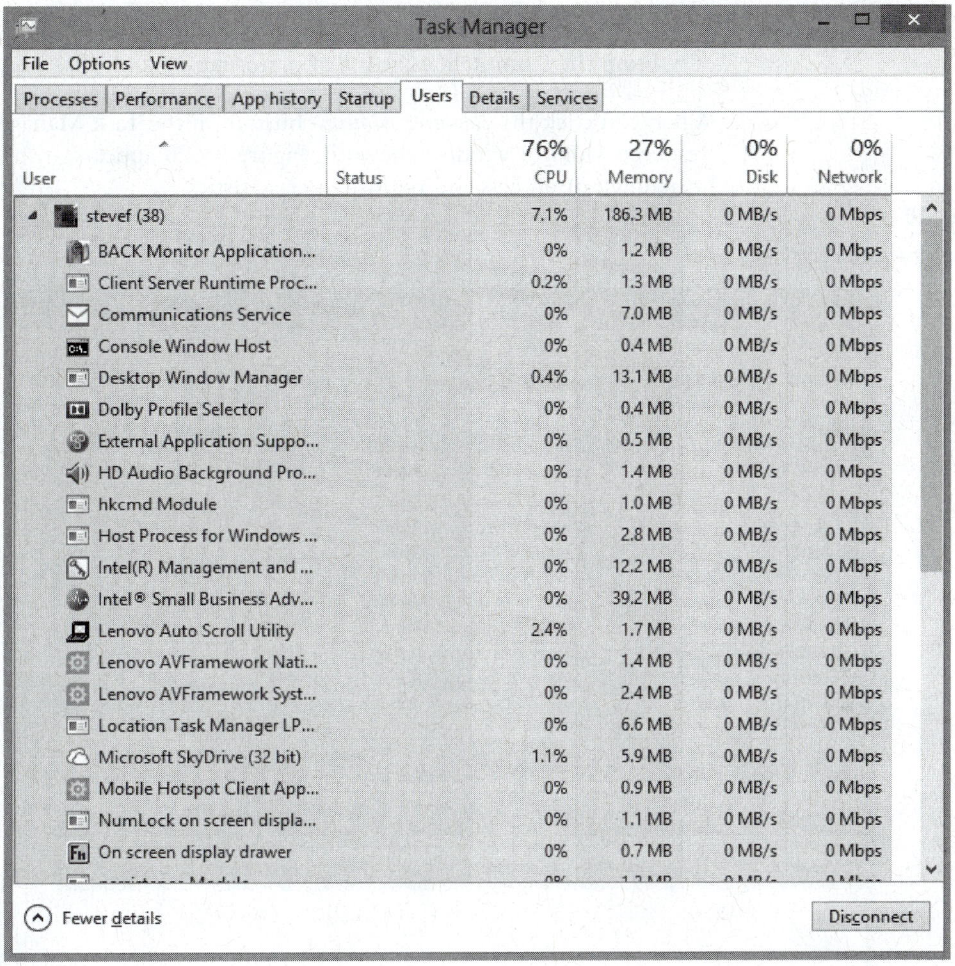

Figure 23-19

The *Users* tab

- **Details** – The Details tab provides the information once presented within the Task Manager processes tab, albeit with an updated format. Right-clicking on a process enables configuration of the process, including End Task, End process tree, Set Priority, Set Affinity, Analyze wait chain, UAC virtualization, Create Dump File, Open File location, Search online, Properties, and Go To Services. These options enable diagnostic or performance enhancement settings. The Set ***Affinity*** capability enables a process to be assigned to one or more specific processors in a multi-processor or multi-core system to affect customized processing capabilities.
- **Services** – The Services tab displays all of the enabled services for the current instance of the Windows 8 system. Right-click enables the user to stop or start services, though not the ability to configure service properties. There is a link at the bottom of the panel that enables a user with elevated privileges to launch the Services Management snap-in if there is a need to modify service start properties.

Using Resource Monitor

Resource Monitor is a Performance tool that extends the capabilities of the Task Manager.

The Resource Monitor can be launched several ways.

- From within Task Manager, select the *Performance* tab, click the *Open Resource Monitor* link at the bottom of the panel.
- From the Start Screen, open *Control Panel > System and Security > Administrative Tools > Resource Monitor.*

- On the Start Screen or within the Search box, type *perfmon.exe /res* and select the tile.
- From the Comprehensive list of performance tools discussed previously in this chapter.

When you click the *Resource Monitor* button on the Task Manager's Performance tab, the Resource Monitor window shown in Figure 23-20 appears, displaying a more comprehensive breakdown of process and performance statistics.

Figure 23-20

The *Resource Monitor* window

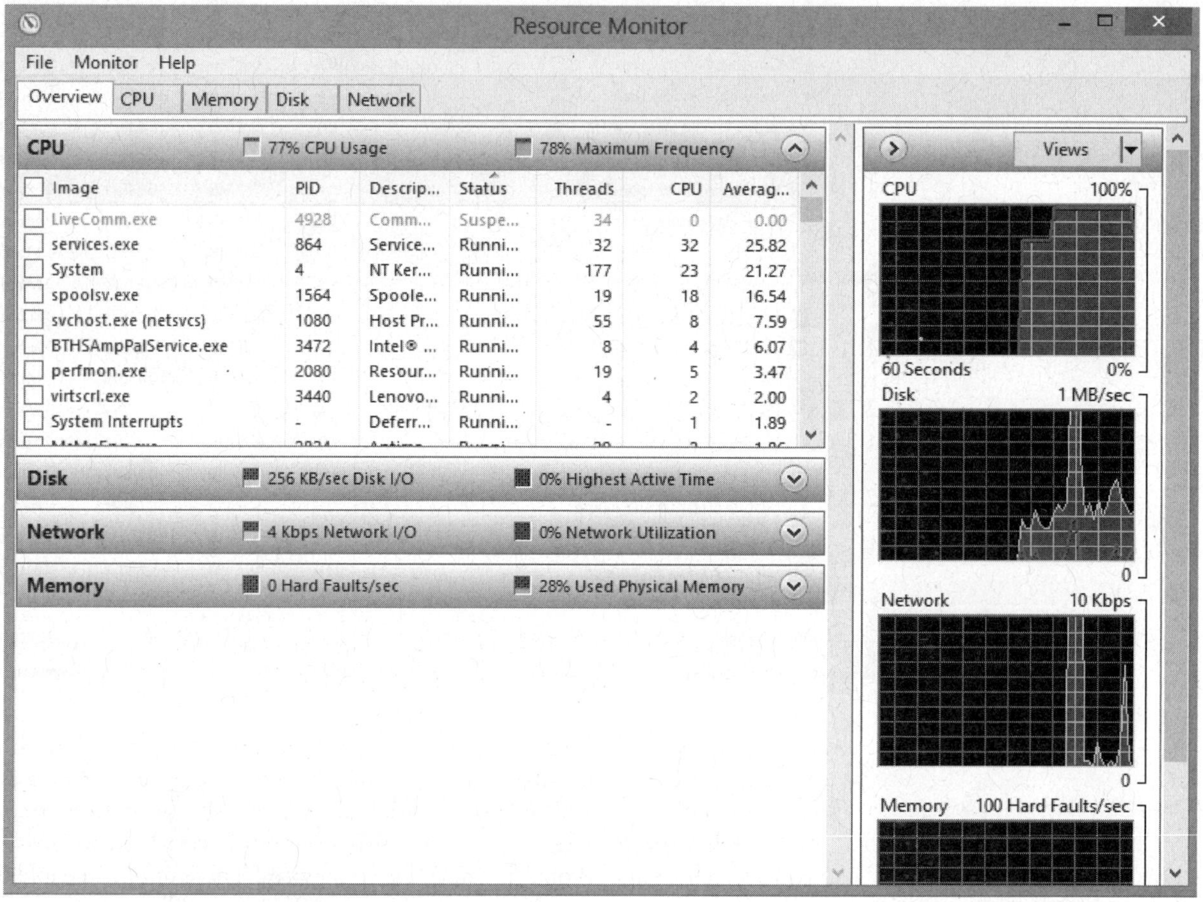

On the Overview tab, there are four real-time line graphs (CPU, Disk, Network, and Memory) that display information about the main system hardware components. Each of the four components also has a separate, expandable section listed below the Overview tab that display more detailed information in text form, such as the resources used by individual applications and processes. Table 23-1 lists the statistics displayed by the graphs and the text sections for each component. Clicking the CPU, Memory, Disk or Network tabs provides even greater analytical detail relative to the hardware component selected. All information is associated with the process using the hardware component. Within each tab, the column headers can be used to hierarchically sort the information in ascending or descending order.

Further, you can use the check box to the left of each process to select one or more processes for more specific analysis. Once one or more processes are selected, both the graphical and numerical analysis information focuses solely on the selected process. The check box next to the image header can be used to select or deselect the entire process list. Selections made in the Overview tab are carried into the other tabs to simplify the task of researching system performance or analyzing process dependencies.

Table 23-1

Resource Monitor Overview Statistics

Component	Line Graph Statistics	Text Statistics
CPU	CPU Usage (%) Maximum Frequency (%)	Image – The executable using CPU resources PID – The Process ID of the application Description – The application using CPU resources Status – The current operational status of the application Threads – The number of active threads generated by the application CPU – The number of CPU cycles currently being used by the application Average CPU – The percentage of the total CPU capacity being used by the application
Disk	Total current disk I/O rate (in KB/sec) Highest Active Time (%)	Image – The application using disk resources PID – The Process ID of the application File – The file currently being read or written by the application Read – The speed of the current read operation (in bytes/second) Write – The speed of the current write operation (in bytes/second) Total – The speed of the combined read and write operations (in bytes/second) I/O Priority – The priority of the I/O task currently being performed by the application Response Time – The interval between the issuance of a command to the disk and its response (in milliseconds)
Network	Current total network I/O (in Kb/sec) Network Utilization (%)	Image – The application using network resources PID – The Process ID of the application Address – The network address or computer name of the system with which the computer is communicating Send – The speed of the current network send operation (in bytes/second) Receive – The speed of the current network receive operation (in bytes/second) Total – The combined bandwidth of the current network send and receive processes (in bytes/second)
Memory	Current hard faults per second Percentage of physical memory currently in use (%)	Image – The application using memory resources PID – The Process ID of the application Hard Faults Per Second – The number of hard faults currently being generated by the application Commit – The amount of memory (in KB) committed by the application Working Set – The amount of physical memory (in KB) currently being used by the application Shareable – The amount of memory (in KB) being used by the application that it can share with other applications Private – The amount of memory (in KB) being used by the application that it cannot share with other applications

Examining the resources utilized by specific applications and processes over time can help you to determine ways to improve the performance of a computer. For example, if all of the system's physical memory is frequently being utilized, then the system is probably slowed by large amount of paging to disk. Increasing the amount of physical memory or reducing the application load will probably improve the overall performance level of the computer.

TAKE NOTE*

The Network tab and related sub-sections operate much like a Network analyzer. On this page, it is possible to monitor active network traffic, connections, listening services and ports, and performance. When testing network, firewall, or connection security settings, Resource monitor is an extremely powerful aid.

Given the emphasis on security layering that includes components like services hardening, Group Policy enforcement, and firewall capabilities, the use of Resource Monitor assists with analysis and testing of multiple security components. The Network tab of the Resources monitor, in particular, is useful for identifying active TCP/IP connections including process IDs, local and remote address and port, listening ports, and associated network traffic.

Viewing Advanced System Details in System Information

The ***System Information tool (msinfo32.exe)*** is designed to gather and display detailed system information to aid with system analysis and troubleshooting.

The Advanced System Information tool is listed in the Comprehensive Performance tool list mentioned earlier in this chapter. You can also launch it by typing *msinfo32.exe* on the Start Screen. This tool is beneficial to system diagnostics and configuration because it allows a single location to view comprehensive hardware, software, and configuration information. Three subsections (Hardware resources, Components, and Software Environment) can each be expanded to provide additional information. There is also a *Find What* search box at the bottom of the panel enabling less experienced users to search for specific items or device settings.

CERTIFICATION READY
Optimize the desktop environment
Objective 6.3

msinfo32 does not support the configuration of system elements. As such, it is an excellent tool, which a standard user might be directed when providing telephone support to obtain both basic and detailed system information without the need for elevated privileges.

Viewing System Configuration Details

The ***System Configuration tool (Msconfig.exe)*** is designed to support system boot and startup options without the need to use the Boot Control Database, recovery environment, or BCDEdit. You can use this tool to configure custom and diagnostic boot settings so that the user or technician does not have to tap the F8 key during boot.

Tapping the F8 key to access the recovery environment in Windows 8 can be problematic. Fast boot and system load processes, accelerated by UEFI-based systems, can make it near impossible to interrupt a boot process to enter the Recovery Environment. If the user or technician does not possess an independent boot media, like a Windows PE recovery disk or memory device, then the MSConfig tool provides a means to set the system to reboot into the alternate recovery diagnostic environments.

When you start the System Configuration tool, you see the General tab, in which you can temporarily set the system's default startup sequence to a diagnostic or selective mode. These modes can help you to identify programs loading at startup that are slowing the system down.

The Boot tab (see Figure 23-21) enables you to manage the boot mode for the system, including selection of alternate boot partitions on a multi-boot system, and the various Windows RE and Safe Mode boot options typically access through the F8 key. The Services tab allows you to enable or disable selected system Services for diagnostic purposes without making permanent changes through the Services Manager snap-in. In Windows 8, the Startup tab prompts the user to Open Task manager to manage or alter processes and applications launched at system start.

Figure 23-21

The *Boot* tab in the *System Configuration* tool

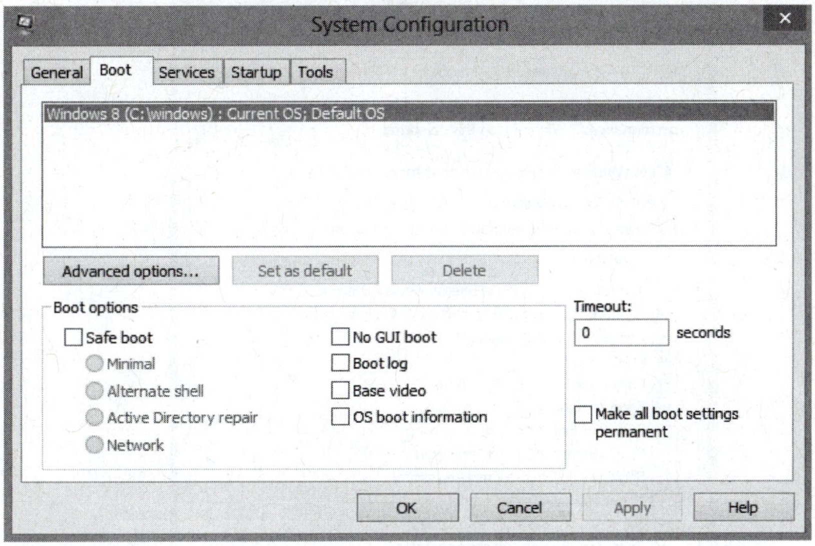

The Tools tab, as shown in Figure 23-22, provides another comprehensive list of system management tools to aid system administrators more efficiently manage system performance.

Figure 23-22

The *Tools* tab in the *System Configuration* tool

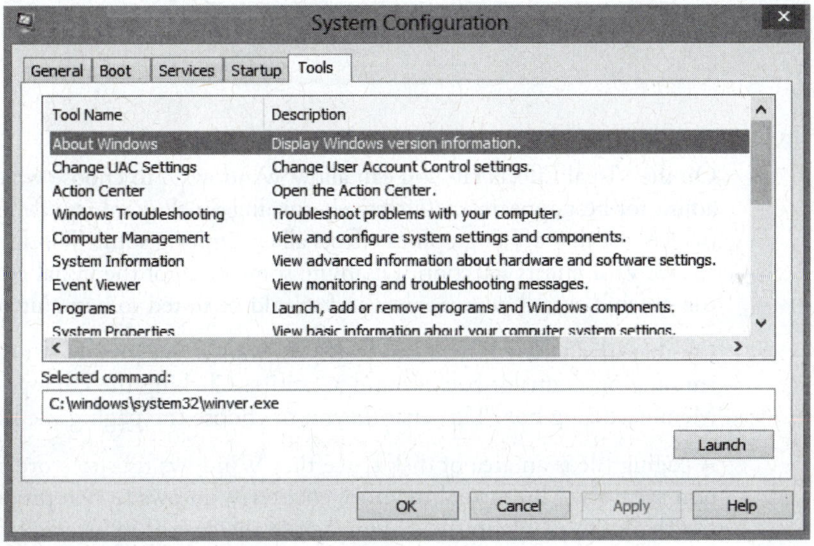

Adjusting Performance Settings

TAKE NOTE*

MSConfig can be launched from within the Windows 8 Recovery Environment. This allows reconfiguration of the boot process while performing diagnostic or recovery work.

Adjusting advanced performance settings in Windows 8 is perhaps more important than in previous Windows operating systems. The graphics requirements and virtual memory (pagefile.sys) size can dramatically impact Windows 8 performance.

You can navigate to the Performance Options dialog box (see Figure 23-23) in several ways, all of which require elevated privilege.

- Use the *Adjust Visual Appearance* link on the Performance Information and Tools panel.
- On the Start Screen, type *Adjust Visual*, and then from the Settings search set select *Adjust the appearance and performance of Windows.*
- Right-click on *Computer*, select *Properties*, select the *Change Settings* link on the right side of the System Panel, which now takes you directly to the Performance Options panel.

Figure 23-23

The *Performance Options* dialog box

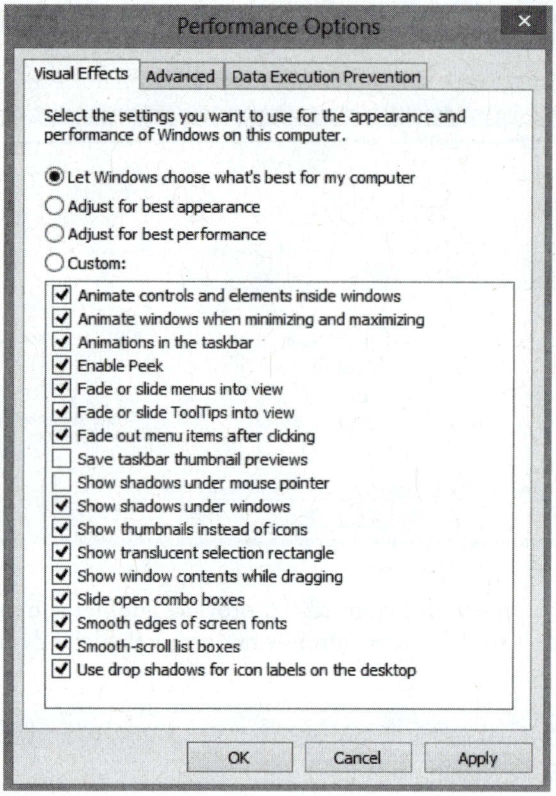

On the Visual Effects tab you can allow Windows 8 to choose what's best for your system, adjust for best appearance (effectively turning on all graphics effects), adjust for best performance (turning off all graphics effects albeit limiting some Windows 8 functionality), or customize your effects selection. Disabling some or all of the visual effects can significantly enhance the system's overall performance and should be tested to best suit your Windows 8 preferences.

On the Advanced tab, you can configure the system processor to allocate more resources to running programs or background activities. Clicking the Change button opens the Virtual Memory dialog box. This enables you to choose the paging file size.

A paging file is an area of disk space that Windows uses to store data that overflows from system memory. This virtual memory enables Windows to run programs that utilize more memory than is available in the system, but at the cost of reduced performance. This is because memory I/O is inherently faster than disk I/O.

In most cases, you should allow Windows 8 to automatically manage the paging file size. On a workstation in which memory is the performance bottleneck, you might be able to tweak performance by increasing the size of the paging file. Microsoft recommends you maintain sufficient available, contiguous drive space on your OS drive to support a virtual memory file twice the size of installed RAM.

Configuring Index Settings

The Performance Information and Tools panel also offers the Adjust Indexing Options link. This option does not require elevated privilege.

CERTIFICATION READY
Configure indexing options
Objective 6.3

The Indexing Options panel (see Figure 23-24) enables you to modify indexed locations, and to launch an automated troubleshooter by selecting the *Troubleshoot search and indexing* link.

Figure 23-24

The *Indexing Options* panel

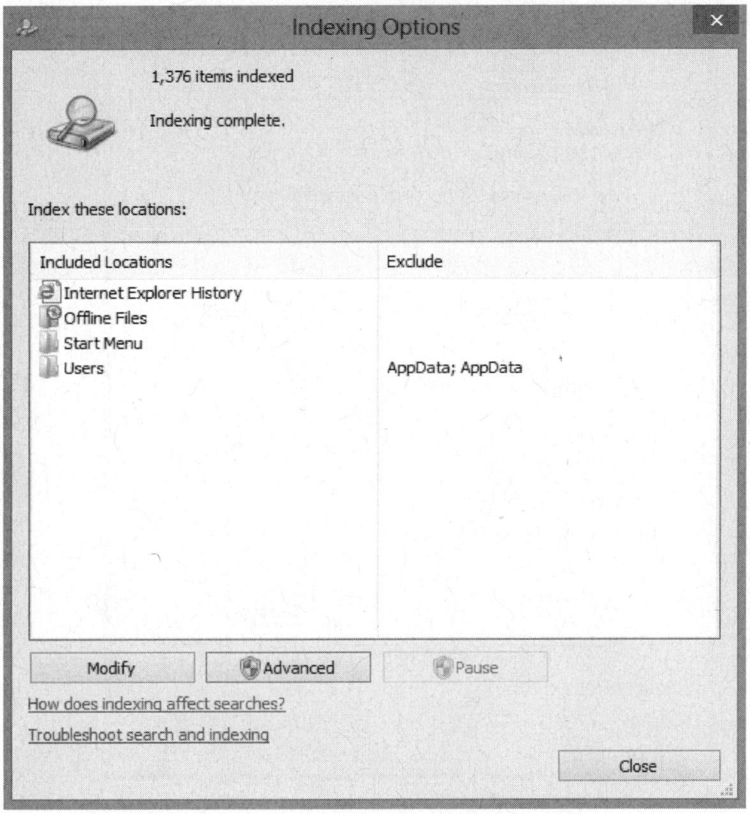

The Advanced Options button launches a sub-panel (see Figure 23-25). Advanced options include the following:

- The ability to index encrypted files, although only when they are opened by the file owner or an account with equivalent permissions and access to the file encryption key (FEK).
- Treating similar words with diacritics as similar words. A ***diacritic*** is a vowel or consonant utilizing accent marks that may alter pronunciation or interpretation within select language sets. The default is for diacritic indexing to be disabled. Enabling diacritics can enhance search for some language sets although it might decrease performance and will decidedly increase the index file size.
- Delete and rebuild the index. This can enhance system performance if the index becomes excessively large over time. An index file rebuild might require days to complete, and will dramatically limit the ability of Windows 8 auto-search features until the index file is fully rebuilt. Caution should be exercised when selecting this option.
- Relocate the index file. This option enables you to relocate the index file to an alternate drive, although the drive must be available during system operation so networked and removable drive locations should not be selected. This might be an excellent option to aid performance if your system provides a separate solid state storage medium.

Figure 23-25

The *Advanced Options* dialog box

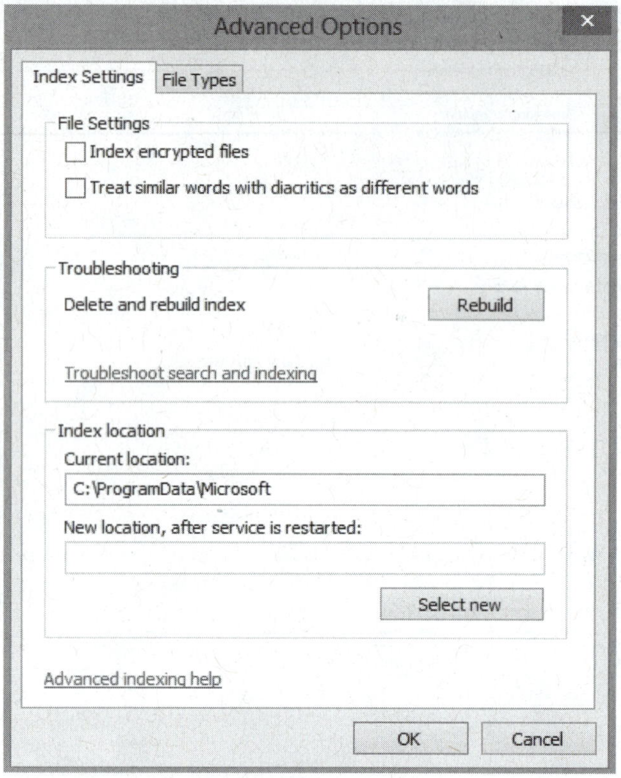

Modifying Power Settings

Power settings in Windows 8 have a direct effect on system performance, particularly due to the new Fast Boot option. Power settings enable you to throttle various system components to optimize their power utilization.

Fast Boot uses a modified hiberfil.sys that contains only the essential kernel an driver elements of the operating system. This enables both visibly and measurably faster boot times. Changing your power settings can save battery life for portable devices, power consumption for the environmentally conscious, and the performance of boot processes. Plan and test your power settings in Windows 8 before committing power option changes.

Adjust power settings is also accessed from the Performance Information and Tools panel. The Power Options panel enables you to select a pre-configured power plan for Windows 8, to modify a default power configuration, or to create a custom plan using one of the templates as a starting point. Given ecological awareness, the full range of power options are available to both mobile and desktop devices, although default settings are system generated based upon detection of platform characteristics.

■ Troubleshooting Windows 8

THE BOTTOM LINE

Configuration and diagnostics tools are of little importance unless system technicians can use the information to enhance system performance and repair problems. Windows 8 continues the evolution of Microsoft automated problem detection, repair and reporting features introduced with the Windows Vista platform.

Standard diagnostic tools are now available both from within the Recovery Environment and Windows 8 Operating System environment.

Windows 8 includes automated troubleshooters that enable standard users to diagnose and repair many common system problems. Some of the troubleshooters require elevated rights to correct a problem, though will minimally diagnose and report symptoms or root cause that enable technical support personnel to focus quickly upon appropriate courses of action. Windows 8 also deploys with Windows PowerShell 3.0, expanding the range of possible diagnostic and repair solutions.

Using the Windows Memory Diagnostic Tool

The Windows 8 memory diagnostic tool conducts extensive memory testing upon system reboot.

The Windows 8 memory diagnostic tool can detect, and based upon installed RAM features sometimes affect repair of system memory. Because of the comprehensive nature of the tool, it can be run only upon system reboot or from the Recovery Environment. To launch the Memory Diagnostic, follow the ensuing procedure:

- On the Start Screen, type memory and from the Settings search results, select Diagnose your computer's memory problems.
- Select Control Panel > System and Security > Administrative Tools > Windows Memory Diagnostic.
- Select the Memory Diagnostic after booting into the Windows 8 Recovery environment.

The Windows Memory Diagnostic tool provides an environment similar to BIOS/CMOS configuration, wherein only arrow, tab, function, and return keys enable navigation. The Windows Memory Diagnostic scheduler panel offers the ability to restart the system immediately and check for problems, or to schedule the tool for execution upon the next system restart.

CERTIFICATION READY
Optimize networking performance
Objective 6.3

Using the Windows Network Diagnostic Tool

The Windows Network Diagnostic tool is one of several automated troubleshooting tools built into Windows 8 to enable user-generated network diagnostics and repair capability.

The Windows Network Diagnostic tool is an expansion of the basic network troubleshooting capabilities built into Windows 7. Windows 8 uses an ***intelligent network*** management system to detect, monitor, control, and attempt to automatically connect or repair both wired and wireless network connections. The Windows 8 Network Diagnostics tool automatically launches if network connectivity issues are encountered during system operation. Alternately, you can click on the red "X" that appears on broken network connections or network connected drives to launch the tool. You can also manually launch the tool to run diagnostics at any time.

- From the Start Screen, select *Control Panel > Network and Internet > Network and Sharing Center > Troubleshoot Problems.* This launches the list of Network and Internet troubleshooters shown in Figure 23-26.

Figure 23-26

The *Windows Network Diagnostic* Tool

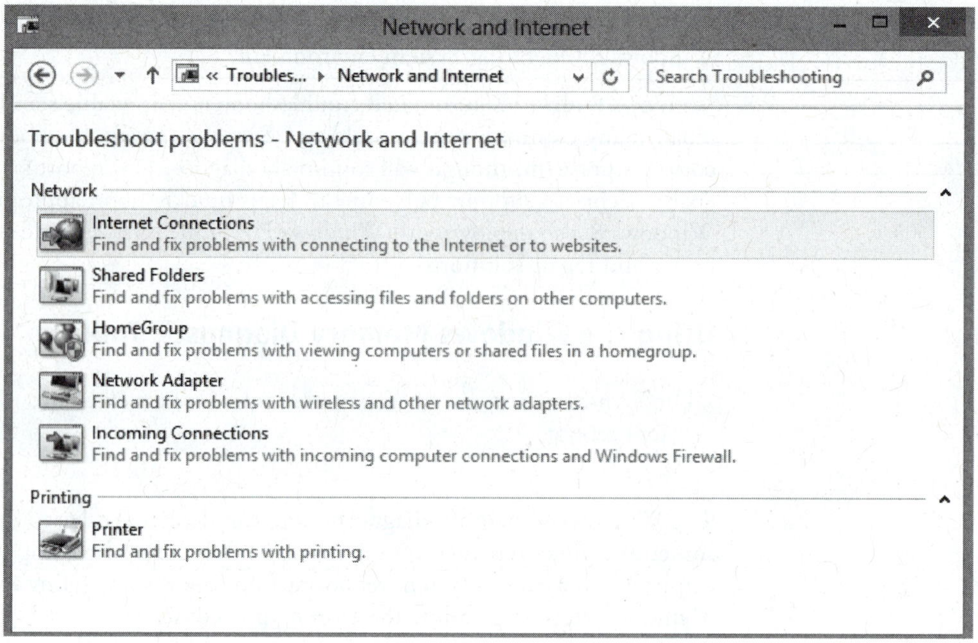

- From the Start Screen, type *Internet Connection* and then from the Settings search results, select *Find and fix networking and connection problems.* The Internet Connections diagnostic Wizard appears. Note that selected advanced options identifies that some repairs will require elevated permissions.

Viewing Problem Reports

Action Center provides access to many of the user-enabled performance and diagnostic tools discussed in this chapter. Additionally, Action Center enables access to any problems reported to Microsoft during automated testing scenarios as well as recommended solutions Microsoft can provide based upon Problem Reporting history.

The Action Center panel in Figure 23-27 can be accessed

- by selecting the Action Center pennant from the taskbar on the Desktop,
- from the Start Screen, by typing and selecting *Action Center*, or
- from *Control Panel* > *System and Security* > *Action Center.*

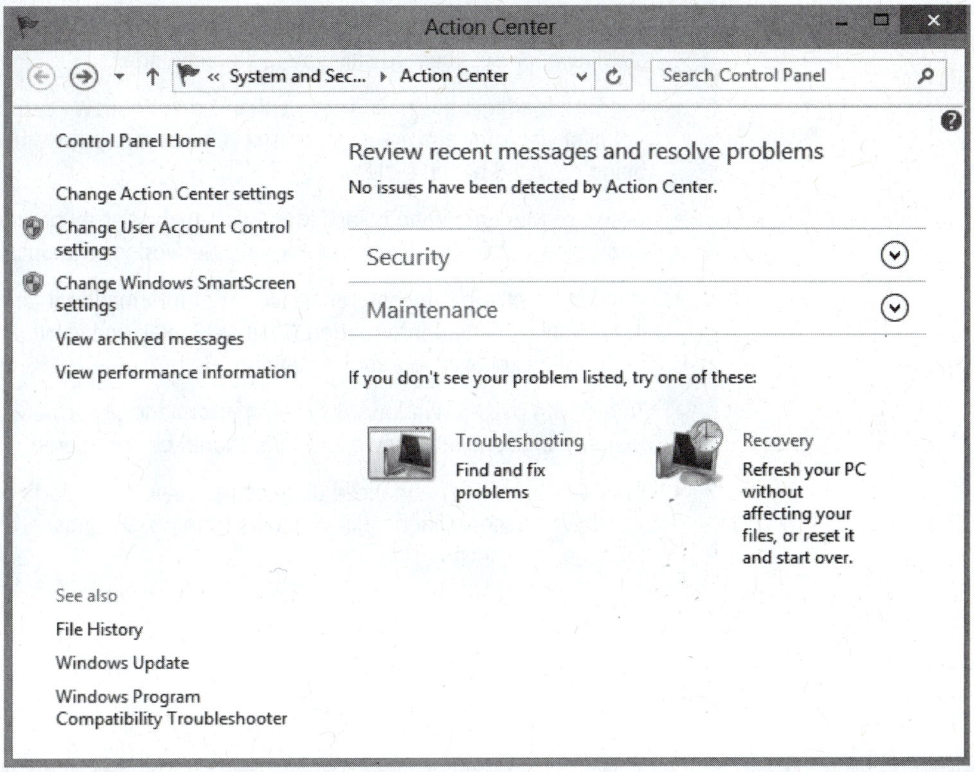

Figure 23-27

The *Action Center* panel

From the Action Center panel, you can perform the following:

- Select *View Performance Information* to access the Performance Information and Tools panel.
- Select *Troubleshooting* to access a list of Windows 8 troubleshooters, including Programs, Hardware and Sound, Network and Internet, and System and Security diagnostics tools.
- Select *View Archived Messages* to view messages associated with problem reports automatically sent to Microsoft. Should a problem be reported to Microsoft, and a possible resolution be available from Microsoft, clicking on the report provides instructions for problem resolution or redirection to a Microsoft site proving potential Knowledge Base patches or updates. From this panel, you can also select *Change Action Center Settings.*

From within Action Center, you can also select *Change Action Center settings* and from among the options at the bottom of the panel select *Problem Reporting Settings* to set preferences for forwarding Troubleshooter problem reports to Microsoft.

SKILL SUMMARY

IN THIS LESSON, YOU LEARNED:

- Windows uses a graphical application called *Event Viewer* to display the log information gathered by the operating system.
- The Performance Information and Tools page provides a snapshot of your computer's performance at a single moment in time called the *Windows Experience Index*, and access to a range of tools designed to assist with the configuration or diagnosis of system performance.
- The Performance Monitor enables you to view real-time, detailed system information, filter the information for problem isolation, or capture the data for later analysis. Performance Monitor provides line graphs, histograms, or interpretive reports to aid in results analysis.

(continued)

- Reliability Monitor automatically tracks events that can have a negative effect on system stability and uses them to calculate a stability index.
- The Task Manager has been vastly enhanced in Windows 8, providing both aggregate and detailed views for processes, process sets, hardware, software, and network resources being provided by the system.
- Resource Monitor expands Task Manager capabilities by providing more detailed analysis and graphics for CPU, Memory, Disk, and Network operations.
- Windows 8 provides a comprehensive set of informational and configuration tools including advanced system information (MSInfo32.exe), and startup configuration details (MSConfig.exe) available to the standard user.
- To aid with overall Windows 8 system performance, specific visual performance, virtual memory, indexing, and power settings should be considered.
- Windows 8 provides enhanced diagnostic, repair and reporting tools including the Windows Memory Diagnostic, Windows Network Diagnostic, and Problem Reporting and Solutions tool sets.

Knowledge Assessment

Multiple Choice

Select the correct answer for each of the following questions.

1. Which of the following terms best describes the hundreds of statistics that Performance Monitor can display?
   - **a.** Performance objects
   - **b.** Performance counters
   - **c.** Instances
   - **d.** Histograms
2. Which of the following is NOT one of the graphs found in Resource Monitor?
   - **a.** CPU
   - **b.** Disk
   - **c.** Display
   - **d.** Memory
3. Which of the following Event Viewer logs contains no events until you configure auditing policies?
   - **a.** Application
   - **b.** Security
   - **c.** Setup
   - **d.** System
4. When setting Visual Effects, which of the following is NOT an option offered by the interface?
   - **a.** Best Appearance
   - **b.** Custom
   - **c.** Fast Boot
   - **d.** Let Windows choose

5. In Event Viewer, what is the term used for the Windows component logs in the Applications and Services Logs folder?
   a. Instances
   b. Events
   c. Subscriptions
   d. Channels
6. In Task Manager, which tab enables you to set processor affinity?
   a. Performance
   b. Processes
   c. App History
   d. Details
7. Which of the following tools allows you to view configuration settings without making changes?
   a. MSConfig
   b. Task manager
   c. MSInfo32
   d. Windows Experience Index
8. In an event-forwarding situation, the source computers must have which of the following services running?
   a. Windows Event Collector
   b. Secure Hypertext Transfer Protocol
   c. Background Intelligent Transfer Service
   d. Windows Remote Management
9. A user has reported a history of system issues. Which tool would be the best researching the problem?
   a. Event Viewer
   b. Reliability Monitor
   c. Resource Monitor
   d. Task Manager
10. Which of the following is the primary function of the System Configuration tool?
    a. To configure and troubleshoot the Windows 7 startup process.
    b. To configure display and virtual memory settings.
    c. To configure services.
    d. To monitor CPU, Disk, Network, and Memory activity in real time.

Best Answer

Choose the letter that corresponds to the best answer. More than one answer choice may achieve the goal. Select the BEST answer.

1. Which of the following approaches would provide the best and most efficient method of analyzing event logs on twenty Windows 8 computers located on the same network?
   a. Use Event Viewer on each computer to analyze its logs.
   b. Use Event Viewer and create a custom view on each computer to analyze its logs.
   c. Use the Microsoft Management console and add the Event Viewer snap-in for each of the 20 computers.
   d. Create Subscriptions in the Event Viewer on the administrator's computer.

2. There are four computers that have recently been upgraded to Windows 8. You want to select one of them to test a new 3D gaming application that is being designed by the company. On the basis of Windows Experience Index subscores, which computer would best support this endeavor?
   a. 5.9 base score, with gaming graphics subscore of 6.1
   b. 6.0 base score, with gaming graphics subscore of 6.3
   c. 3.9 base score, with gaming graphics subscore of 6.2
   d. 5.5 base score, with gaming graphics subscore of 6.4

3. A standard user wants to be able to monitor the processes running on their computer. Of the tools listed, which would work best while keeping in mind elevated permission and skill sets needed to setup and gather the required information?
   a. Performance Monitor
   b. Reliability Monitor snap-in
   c. Task Manager
   d. Resource Monitor

4. A Windows 8 computer is not providing the high level of performance a user expected. The user indicates the hard drive light is blinking a lot when they are working on the computer. Which of the following would represent the most cost effective approach to solve this type of problem?
   a. Increase the physical memory.
   b. Increase the physical memory and add a larger hard disk.
   c. Increase the physical memory and install a faster processor.
   d. Install a faster processor.

5. A help desk employee needs to collect hardware, component and software information from standard users while providing phone support. Which is the best tool for collecting this type of information quickly?
   a. Task Manager
   b. System Information Tool
   c. Performance Monitor
   d. Resource Monitor

Matching and Identification

1. Match the following terms with their corresponding definitions.
   _______ a) Diacritic
   _______ b) Affinity
   _______ c) Performance counter
   _______ d) Windows Experience Index
   _______ e) Data collector set
   _______ f) Collector
   _______ g) Performance object
   _______ h) Reliability Monitor
   _______ i) Events
   _______ j) Process tree
   1. Stability tracking tool
   2. Captured activity for process ID units
   3. Process relationship
   4. Processor association
   5. Captures performance counter data
   6. Performance Monitor statistic
   7. Recipient of forwarded events
   8. Vocabulary accent
   9. Windows performance rating
   10. Performance Monitor category

Build a List

1. In order of first to last, specify the correct order of steps to view the Windows Experience Index Assessment on a Windows 8 computer.
   _______ Click the **Settings search parameter** and then click **Use tools to improve performance**.
   _______ Click the **View and print detailed performance and system information** link.
   _______ At the Start Screen, type **Windows Experience Index**.

2. Specify the correct order of steps to create a custom view in Event Viewer.
   _______ From the *Logged* drop-down list, select the time interval from which you want to display events.
   _______ From the *By log* drop-down list, select the log(s) from which you want to display events.
   _______ In the *Event level* area, select the check boxes for the types of events you want to display.
   _______ Right-click the **Custom Views** folder and then, from the context menu, select **Create Custom View**.
   _______ In the Start screen, launch **Control Panel > System and Security > Administrative Tools > Event Viewer**.
   _______ Click **OK**. The console adds your view to the folder you selected and displays the view in the detail pane.
   _______ In the *Name* text box, type a name for the view, a description if desired, and select the folder in which you want to create your custom view.
   _______ Click **OK**. The *Save Filter to Custom View* dialog box appears.

3. Specify the correct order of steps to create an event subscription.
   _______ Click **OK** to create the subscription.
   _______ Use the controls to select the events you want the source computers to forward and then click **OK**.
   _______ In the Start screen, launch **Control Panel > System and Security > Administrative Tools > Event Viewer**.
   _______ Click **Select Events**. The *Query Filter* dialog box appears.
   _______ Right-click the **Subscriptions** node and, from the context menu, select **Create Subscription**.
   _______ Select one of the following subscription type options: **Collector initiated** or **Source computer initiated**.
   _______ Click **Advanced** to set delivery optimization settings or use **HTTPS** for additional security.
   _______ In the *Subscription Name* text box, type a name for the subscription.

■ Business Case Scenarios

Scenario 23-1: Using the Window Network Diagnostic Tool

A standard user is experiencing Internet connectivity issues. You have advised the user to run the Windows Network Diagnostic tool to repair the problem, to no effect. Diagnostics identify problems resolving host names and accessing specific services on remote computers. Explain what might be limiting the automated repairs associated with the Windows Network Diagnostic tool.

Scenario 23-2: Setting Up an Event Collector

A remote engineering system fails intermittently. The helpdesk attempts to create an event collector to monitor specific incidents occurring on the remote system, The remote system is visible across the network, and you confirm that you can telnet to the system. An event subscription exists in the collector computer; the remote system recently rebooted, yet there are no events in the Forwarded Events log. Explain some of the steps that you might take to affect a working solution.

Configuring Backup

LESSON 24

70-687 EXAM OBJECTIVE

Objective 7.1 – Configure backup. This objective may include but is not limited to: back up files, folders, and full system; schedule backups; and create a system recovery disk.

Lesson Heading	Exam Objective
Configuring Data Protection	
Using Windows 7 File Recovery	Back up files, folders, and Full system Schedule backups
Creating a Windows 8 Recovery Drive	Create a system recovery disk

KEY TERMS

incremental backup
system image backup
system repair disk
virtual hard disk (VHDX)
Windows 7 File Recovery
Windows Recovery Environment (Windows RE)

Configuring Data Protection

THE BOTTOM LINE

Protecting data from accidental loss or deliberate destruction is a critical element of workstation administration, whether you are working in an enterprise, small business, or residential setting. To do this, you must create system backups at regular intervals.

Larger, and even some medium-sized, organizations have network-based backup systems that enable multiple workstations to transmit their data to a backup device on the network, such as a disk array or a magnetic tape drive. Depending on the amount of data involved and the type of storage device, these network backup solutions can easily cost tens of thousands of dollars for hardware and software.

For standalone systems or small networks, Windows 8 includes backup tools that you can use to protect your data by copying it to a network drive, another hard disk drive, a USB flash drive, or a series of writable CDs or DVDs. Windows 8 also includes a variety of other tools that you can use to recover from data loss or other system disasters.

MORE INFORMATION

The ever-increasing speeds and capacities of hard disk drives, along with their ever-decreasing prices per gigabyte, have led to their use as the primary backup medium for home users and small networks in recent years. Even more significant than speed and capacity, however, is the ubiquity of the high speed external interfaces, such as Universal Serial Bus (USB) , IEEE 1394 (FireWire), and External SATA (eSATA), in today's computers.

Internal hard disk drives can be good for backups. They are fast; they hold a lot of data, and they are inexpensive. However, internal drives are not easily removable, and for backups to be truly secure, it should be possible to store a copy at another location, such as a bank vault. The high-speed interfaces now included with every computer address this issue, though.

External hard drives, which are basically standard hard disk drives in a simple housing with a USB, FireWire, and/or eSATA interface and a power supply, are wildly popular products on the home and small business computing markets. Although usable for any storage purpose, they are particularly suitable for backups, because you can easily detach them from the computer and take them offsite, either as part of a regular backup regiment, or in the event of an emergency, such as a natural disaster or fire.

Individual, external hard drives can serve as an inexpensive and effective backup medium for a single computer or even a small network, but are generally not practical for high-capacity servers and enterprise networks. In these cases, a drive array with removable hard disks would be more suitable, such as a network attached storage (NAS) device or a storage area network (SAN) array.

For long-term data archiving, hard disk drives are a somewhat less suitable choice. Compared with magnetic tapes or optical disks, hard disks are quite fragile, and it is probably not economically feasible to leave entire hard drives in storage for long periods of time. USB flash drives, however, are inexpensive and both easily portable and storable, and they are available in ever-increasing capacities (up to 64 GB, as of this writing), which make them viable candidates for backup media.

Using Windows 7 File Recovery

The Windows 7 File Recovery control panel enables users to easily set up a repeating regimen of backup jobs using a wizard-based interface.

The backup program included with Windows seems to change significantly with every version of the operating system. The backup program included with Windows XP was capable of getting the job done, but the software was limited in the types of backup devices it could use, and scheduling repeated backup jobs was difficult.

In Windows Vista, creating a repeating backup job is a simple matter of running the wizard, selecting the files to back up, and selecting the medium to store the backups. However, the Vista backup program backs up only document files, not application or operating system files, and there is no way to avoid the wizard and manually create a job. To perform a full backup of the entire system, you must use Complete PC, a separate utility.

The Windows 7 Backup and Restore program integrates the wizard-based file and folder backup and the system image backup capabilities into one program. In Windows 8, this Backup and Restore program is deprecated in favor of the File History application.

MORE INFORMATION

For more information on using the Windows 8 File History application, see Lesson 26, "Configure File Recovery Operations."

However, Windows 8 still includes Backup and Restore—now renamed as ***Windows 7 File Recovery***—primarily to support users upgrading from Windows 7 who have existing system backups and scheduled jobs. The program will be omitted entirely from future versions of Windows.

TAKE NOTE* To discourage the use of Windows 7 File Recovery by new Windows 8 users, Microsoft has removed all links to the program except for the one in the Control Panel. In addition, you cannot access Windows 7 File Recovery through the Control Panel's category view. You must either select the large icons or small icons view, or search the Control Panel for Windows 7 File Recovery.

CERTIFICATION READY
Back up files, folders, and full system
Objective 7.1

CREATING A BACKUP JOB

To create a backup job with the Windows 7 File Recovery program, use the following procedure.

CREATE A BACKUP JOB

GET READY. Log on to Windows 8 using an account with administrative privileges and then perform the following steps:

1. Open the **Control Panel** and then, in the *View by* drop-down list, click **Large icons**.

   The Control Panel interface displays individual icons for each of the available applications.

2. Click **Windows 7 File Recovery**.

   The Windows 7 File Recovery control panel appears, as shown in Figure 24-1.

Figure 24-1
The *Windows 7 File Recovery* control panel

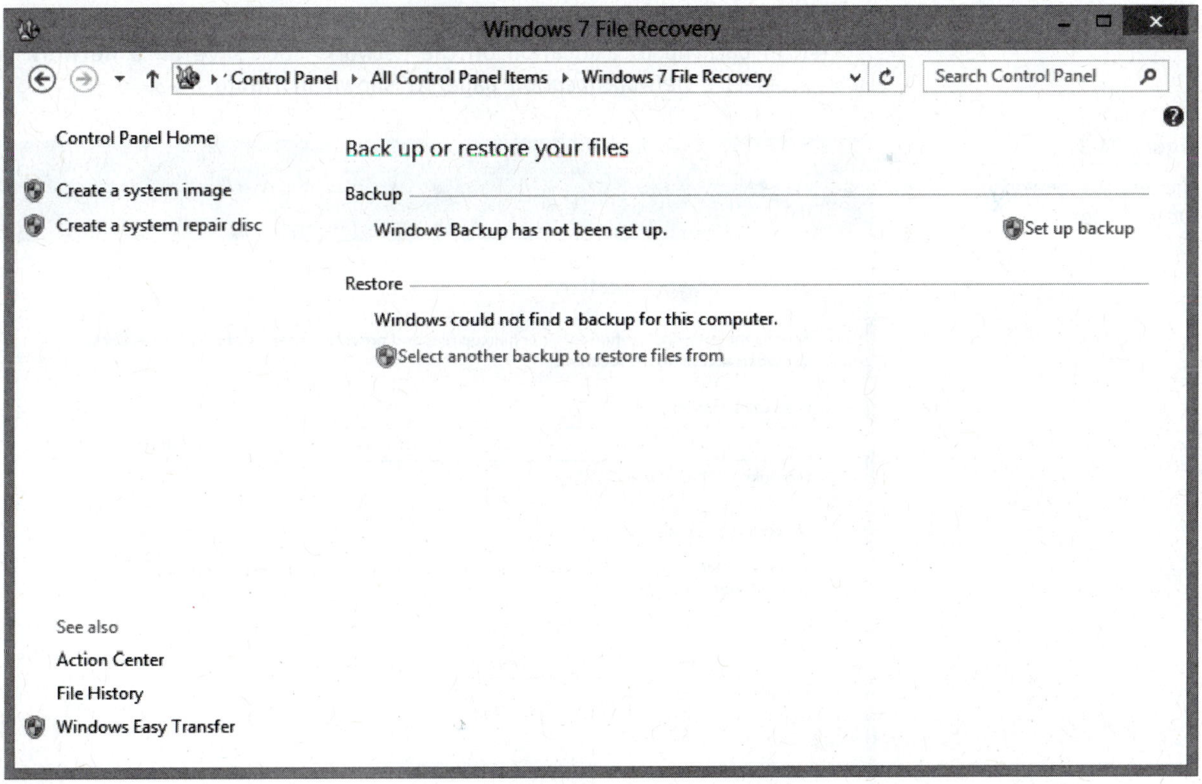

3. Click **Set up backup**.

   The program starts and the *Select where you want to save your backup* page appears, as shown in Figure 24-2.

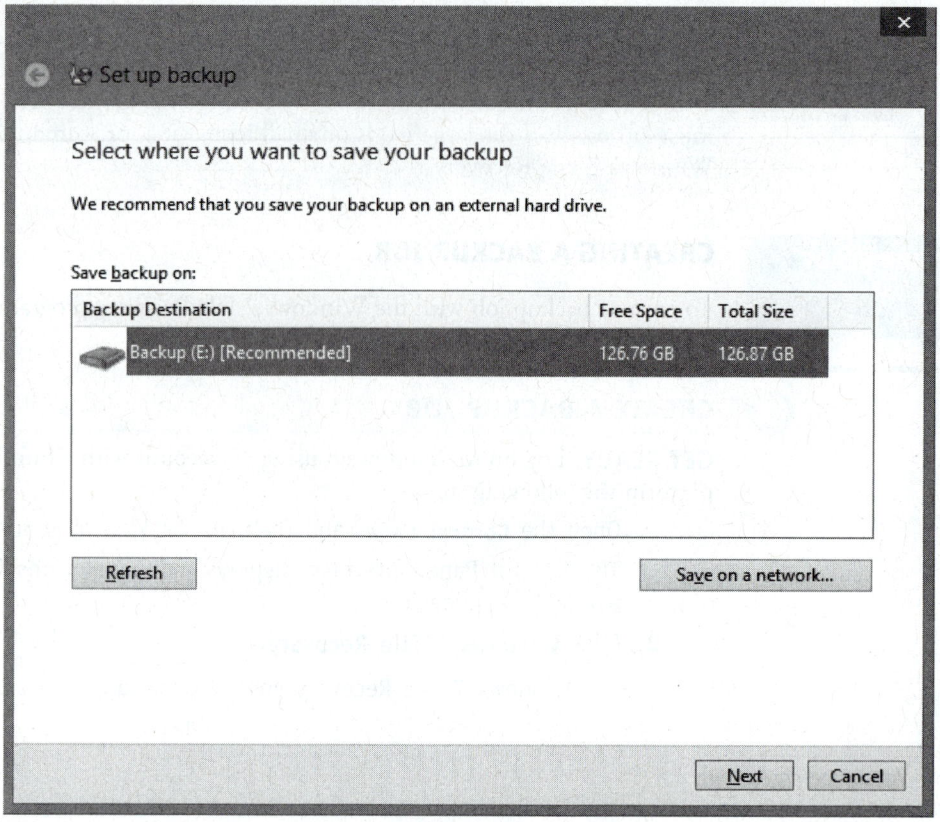

Figure 24-2

The *Select where you want to save your backup* page

4. To back up to a location on the network, click **Save on a network** to display the *Select a network location* page, as shown in Figure 24-3.

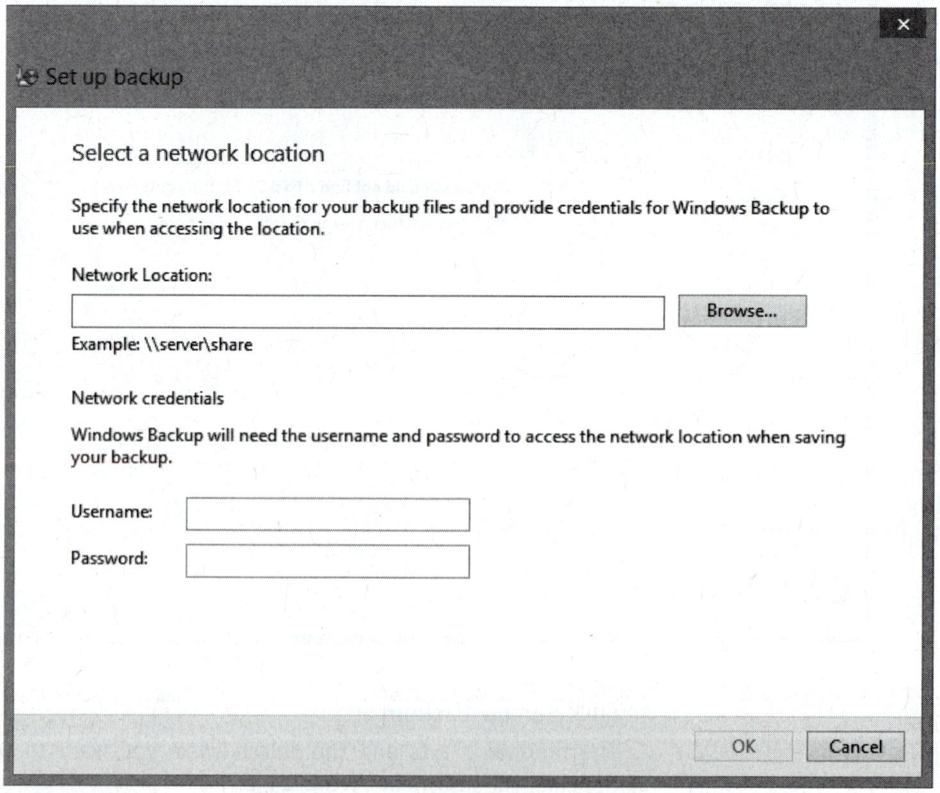

Figure 24-3

The *Select a network location* page

On this page, you supply the path to the network share you want to use and the credentials needed to access it. When you click OK, the wizard adds the network location to the *Save backup on* list.

TAKE NOTE* Windows 7 File Recovery supports the use of internal and external hard disks, USB flash drives, writable DVD-ROM and CD-ROM drives, and network locations, subject to the limitations shown in Table 24-1.

5. Select one of the destinations in the *Save backup on* list and then click **Next**. The *What do you want to back up?* page appears, as shown in Figure 24-4.

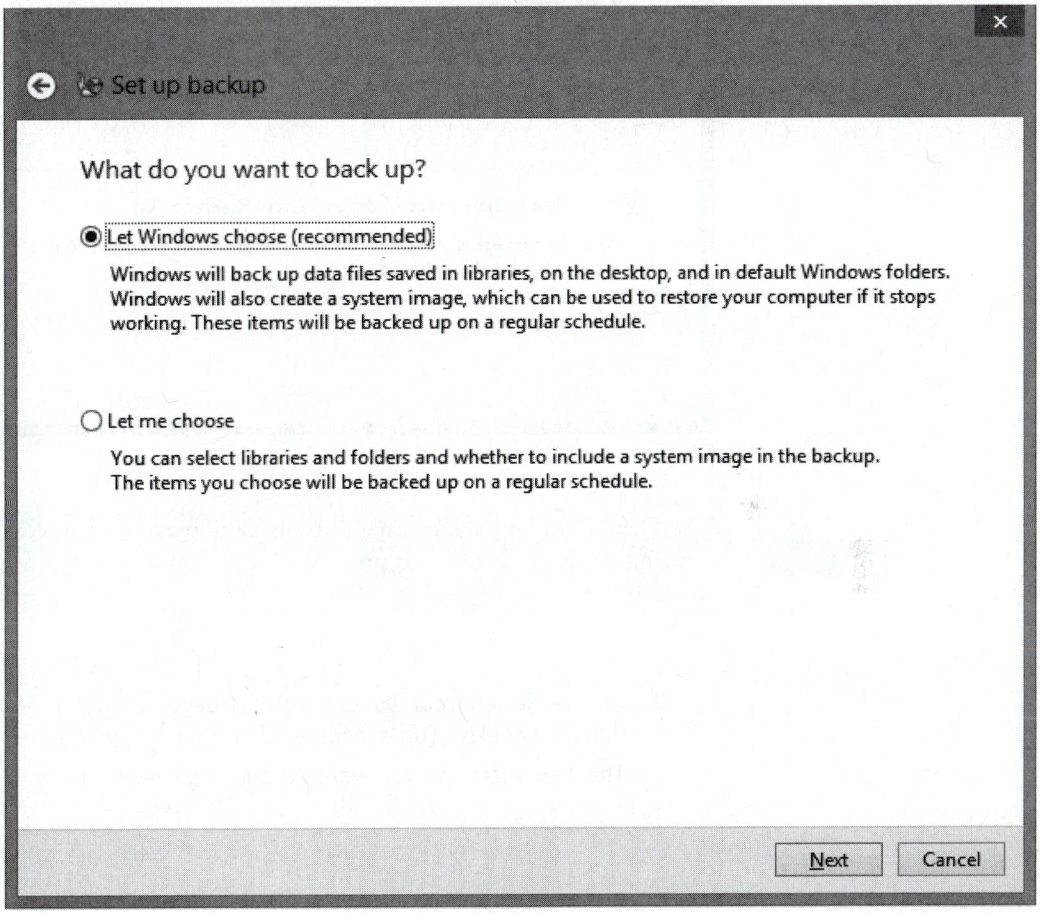

Figure 24-4

The *What do you want to back up?* page

6. Select one of the following options and then click **Next**.
   The *Review your backup settings* page appears.
   - *Let Windows choose (recommended)* backs up files in libraries and in the default windows folders. This setting also creates a system image backup.
   - *Let me choose* displays a second *What do you want to back up?* page, as shown in Figure 24-5, on which you can select the files and folders you want to back up. You can also opt to perform a system image backup as well.

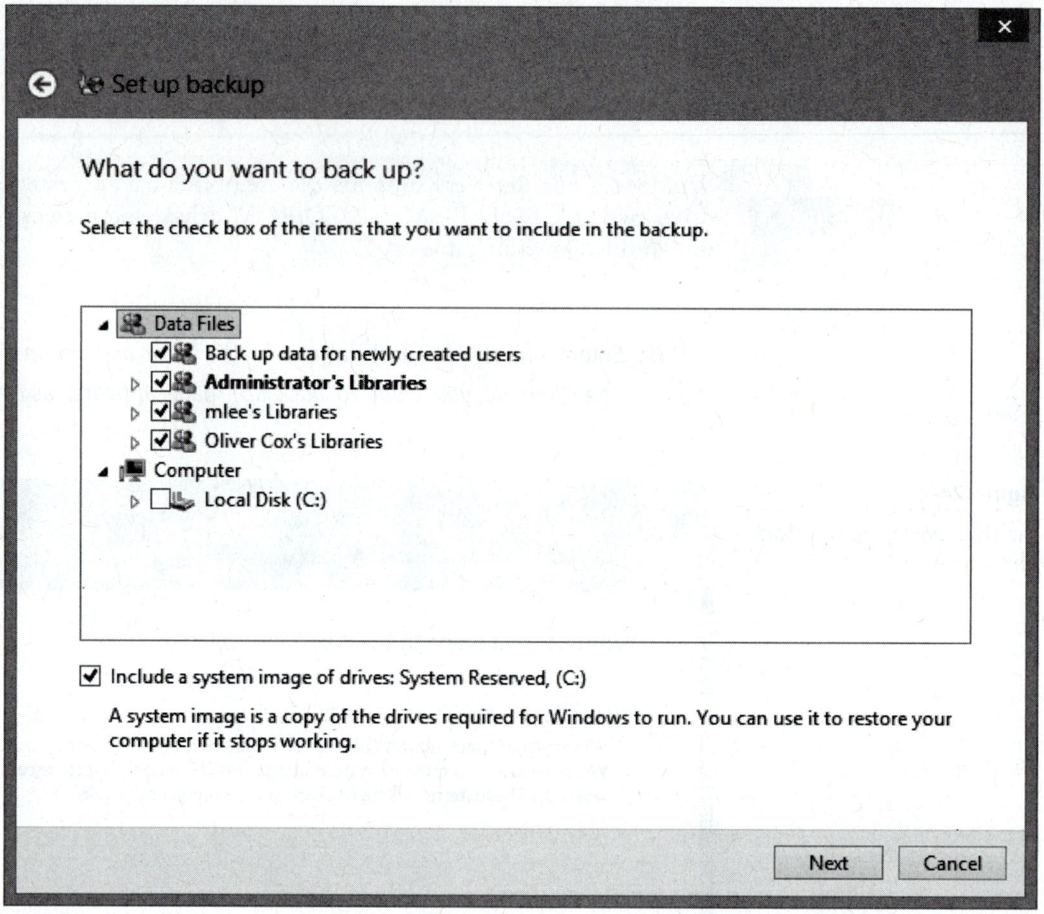

Figure 24-5

The second *What do you want to back up?* page

TAKE NOTE*

The file and folder backup capability in Windows 7 File Recovery cannot back up system and application files. To protect the entire system drive, you must perform a system image backup.

7. On the *Review your backup settings* page, shown in Figure 24-6, to change the default (weekly) job schedule, click **Change schedule**.

   The *How often do you want to back up?* page appears, as shown in Figure 24-7.

Figure 24-6

The *Review your backup settings* page

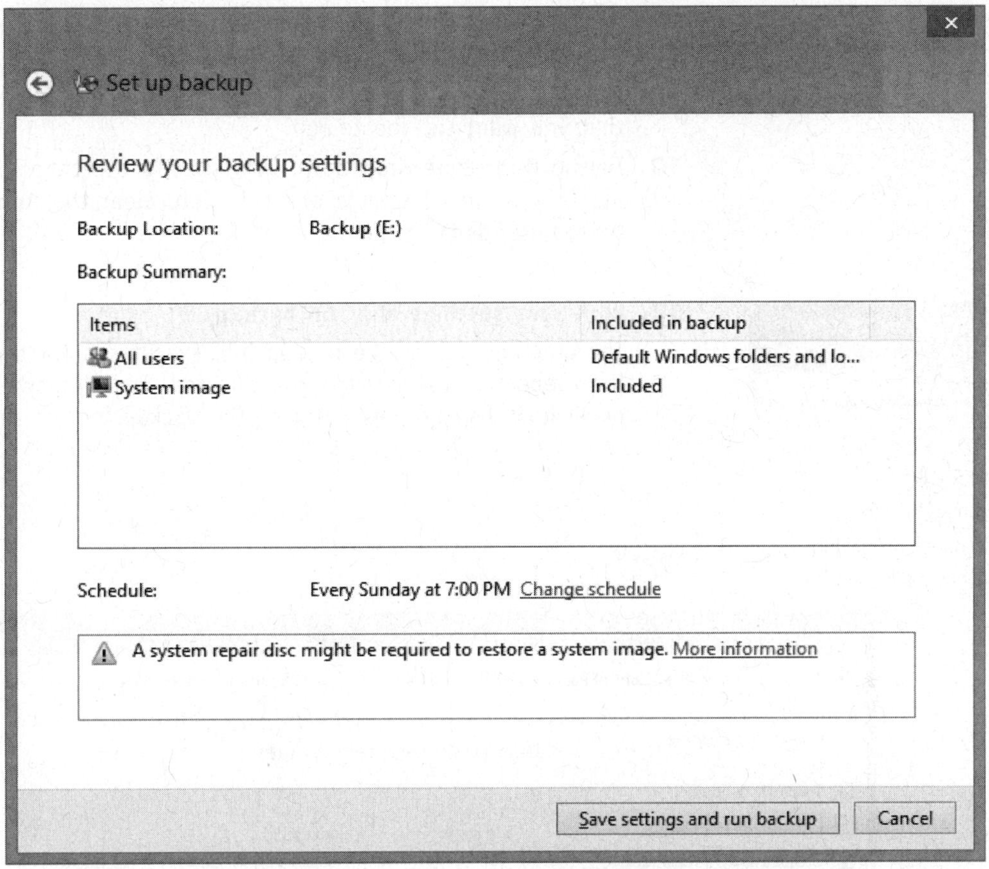

Figure 24-7

The *How often do you want to back up?* page

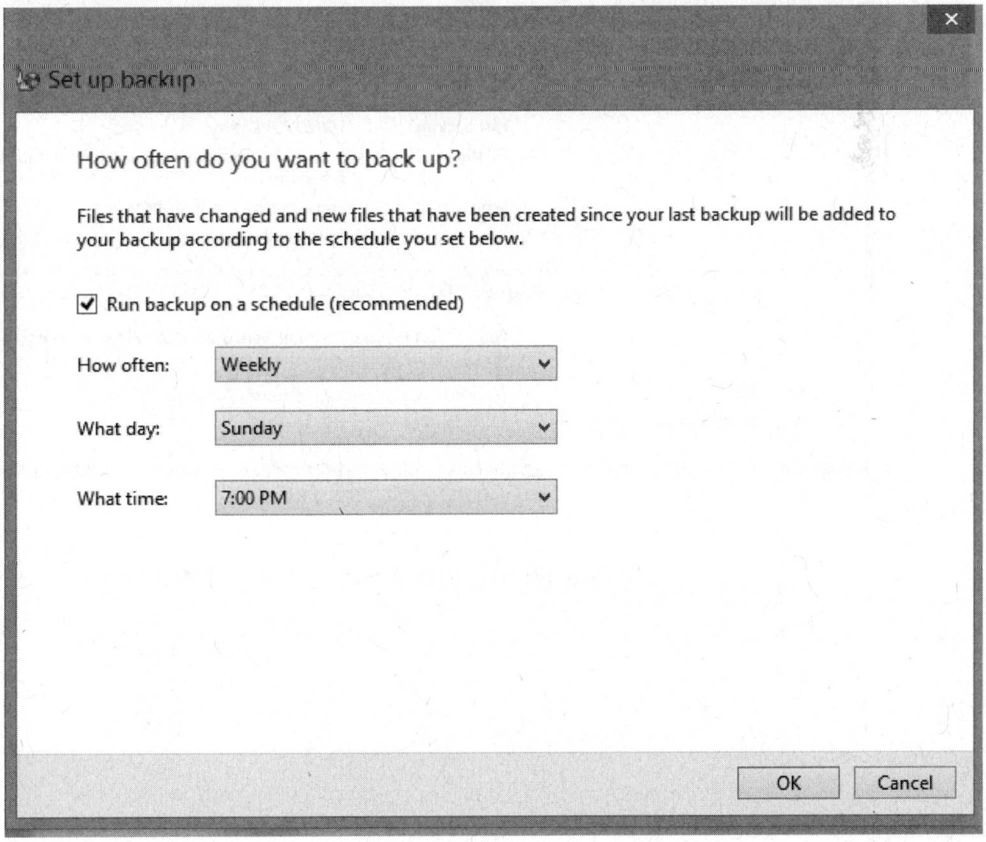

8. In the *How often* drop-down list, specify whether you want the job to run daily, weekly, or monthly.
9. In the *What day* drop-down list, specify the day of the week or the monthly date that you want the job to run.
10. In the *What time* drop down list, specify the time of day that you want the job to run. To perform a one-time job, clear the **Run backup on a schedule (recommended)** checkbox.
11. Click **OK**.
12. Click **Save settings and run backup**.

    The program creates the backup job, executes it for the first time, and schedules it to repeat at the interval you selected. The Windows 7 File Recovery control panel now displays the status of the backup job, as shown in Figure 24-8.

CERTIFICATION READY
Schedule backups
Objective 7.1

Figure 24-8

The *Backup and Restore control* panel, displaying the backup job status

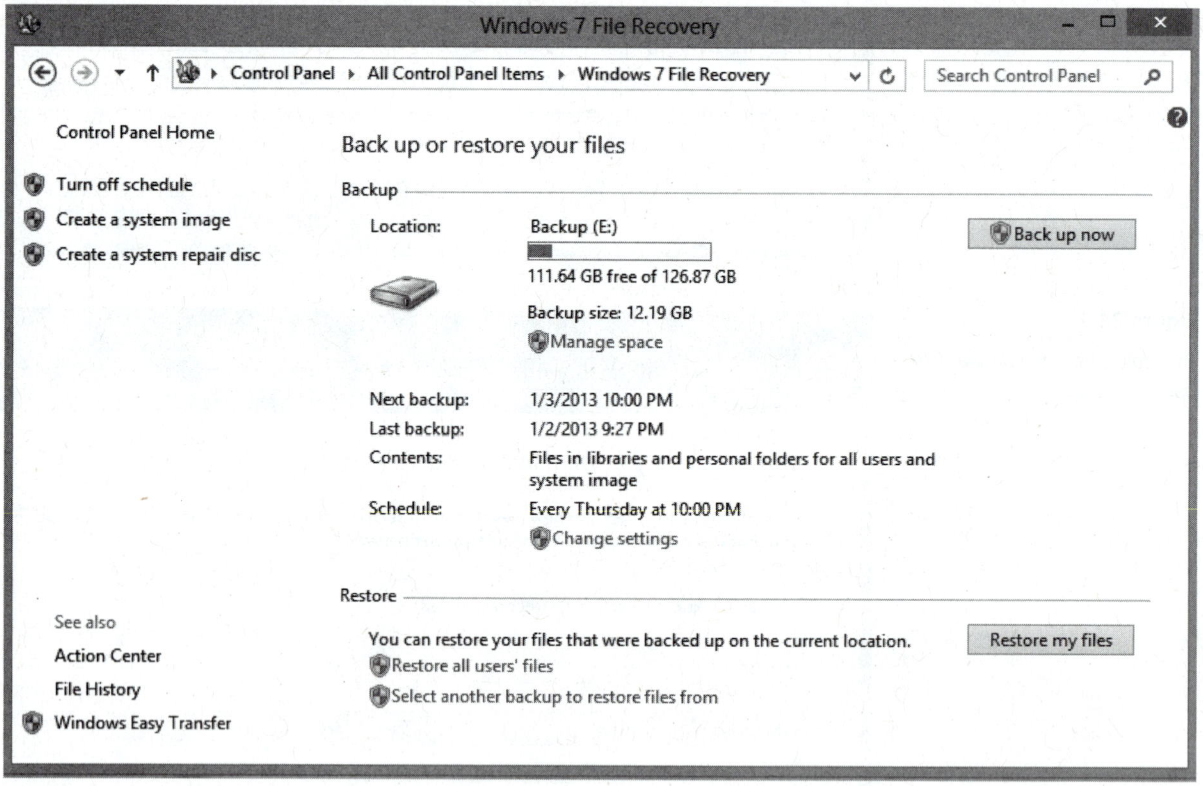

13. **Close** the *Windows 7 File Recovery* control panel.

Table 24-1

Backup Devices Supported in Windows 7 File Recovery

Device	Windows 8 Editions Supported	Backups Supported
Internal hard disks	All editions	Files/folders and system images
External hard disks	All editions	Files/folders and system images
DVD-ROMs	All editions	Files/folders and unscheduled system images
CD-ROMs	All editions	Files/folders and unscheduled system images
USB flash drives	All editions	Files/folders only
Network locations	Windows 8 Pro and Enterprise	Files/folders and system images

The file and folder backup process stores the selected files in compressed archives with a .zip extension, minimizing the amount of storage space consumed on the backup medium. Windows 7 File Recovery also conserves space, as well as time, by performing incremental backups automatically.

An ***incremental backup*** is a type of job that backs up only the files that have changed since the last backup was performed. Windows 7 File Recovery saves multiple versions of each file that changes, but it does not back up multiple copies of unchanged files. It is possible to restore previous versions of modified files; the program only deletes older versions when the backup medium runs out of space.

Because Windows 7 File Recovery is designed for use with random access storage devices, it always provides the latest version of every file when performing a restore, unless you specifically select an older version.

RESTORING FILES

Once you have completed a file and folder backup job, you can restore specific files from that job at any time. To perform a restore, use the following procedure.

RESTORE FILES

GET READY. Log on to Windows 8 using an account with administrative privileges and then perform the following steps:

1. Open the **Control Panel** and then, in the *View by* drop-down list, click **Large icons**.

   The *Control Panel* interface displays individual icons for each of the available applications.

2. Click **Windows 7 File Recovery**.

   The *Windows 7 File Recovery* control panel appears.

3. Click **Restore my files**.

   The *Browse or search your backup for files and folders to restore* page appears, as shown in Figure 24-9.

Figure 24-9

The *Browse or search your backup for files and folders to restore* page

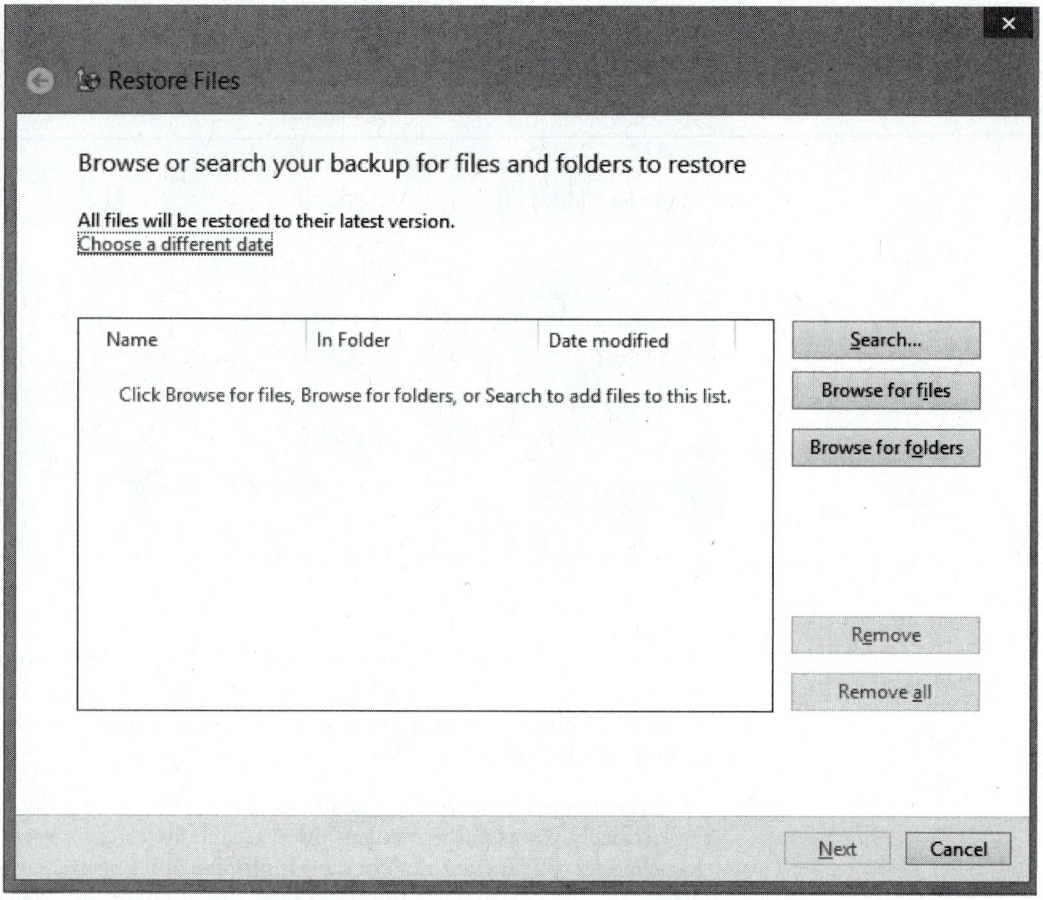

4. Click **Browse for files**.

The *Browse the backup for files* combo box appears, as shown in Figure 24-10.

Figure 24-10

The *Browse the backup for files* combo box

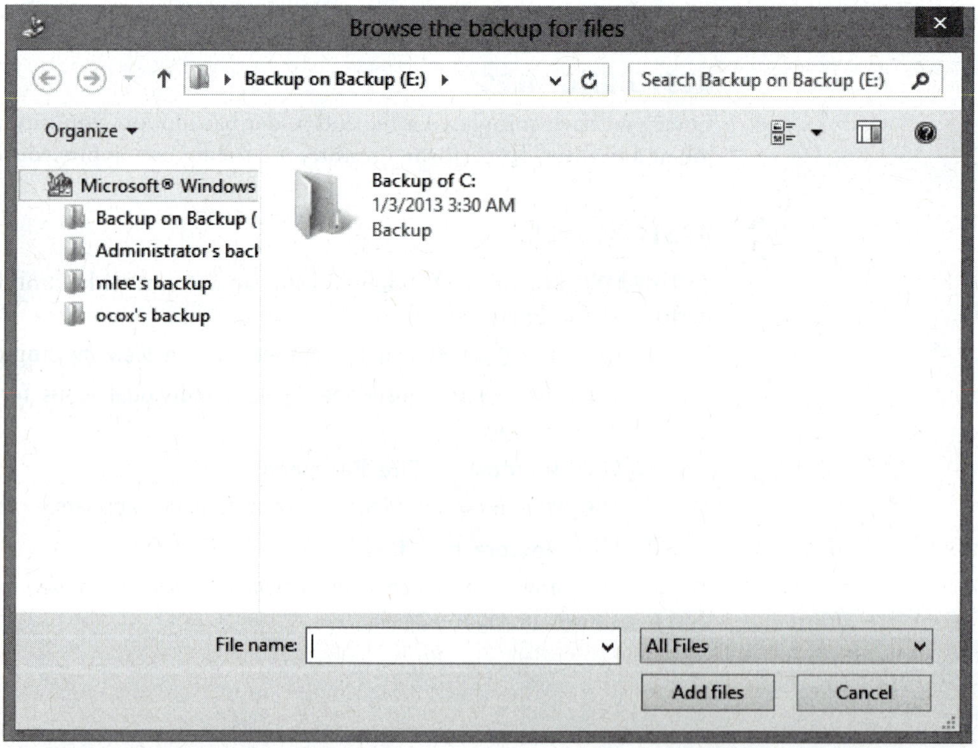

5. Browse to and select the files you want to restore and then click **Add files**.

   The files appear on the *Browse or search your backup for files and folders to restore* page.

6. Click **Next**.

   The *Where do you want to restore your files?* page appears, as shown in Figure 24-11.

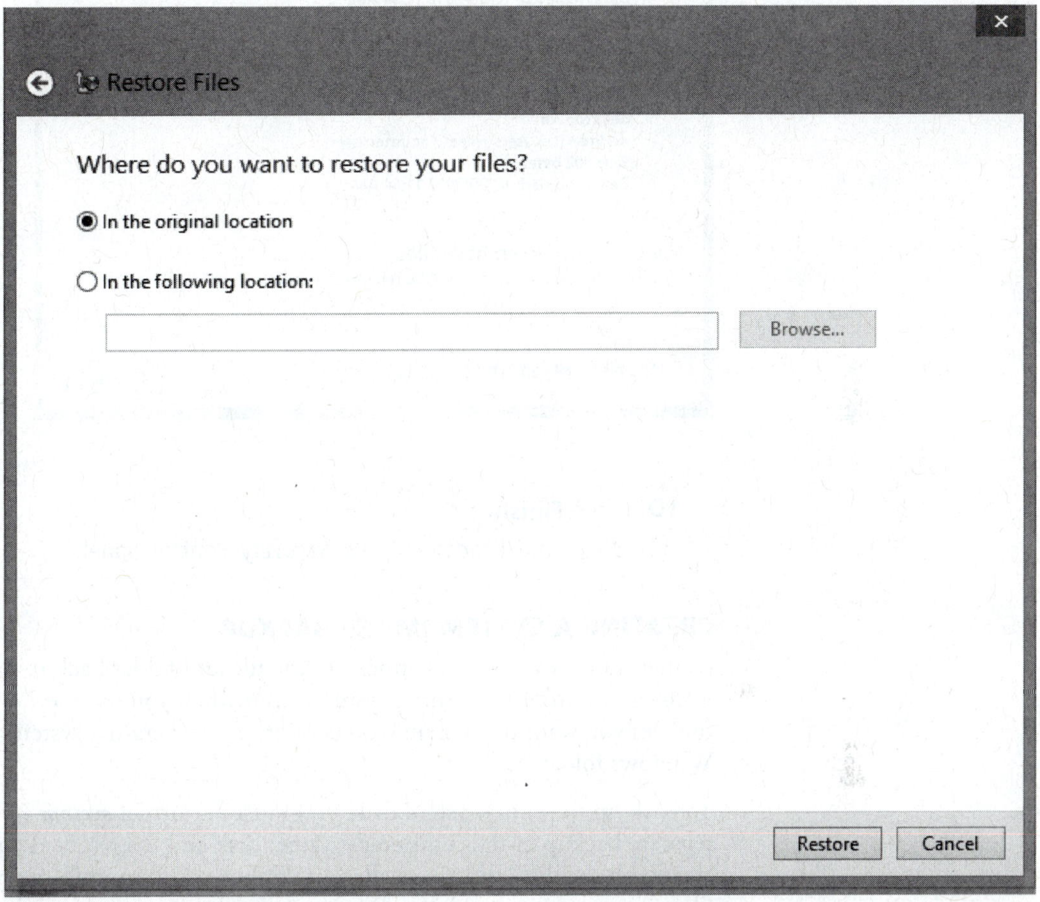

Figure 24-11

The *Where do you want to restore your files?* page

7. Leave the default **In the original location** option selected or select **In the following location** and then type or browse to the destination for the restore.

8. Click **Restore**.

   The program restores the selected files. If files of the same name exist at the destination, the Copy File dialog box appears, as shown in Figure 24-12.

9. Select one of the file copy options to continue.

   The *Your files have been restored* page appears.

Figure 24-12

The *Copy File* dialog box

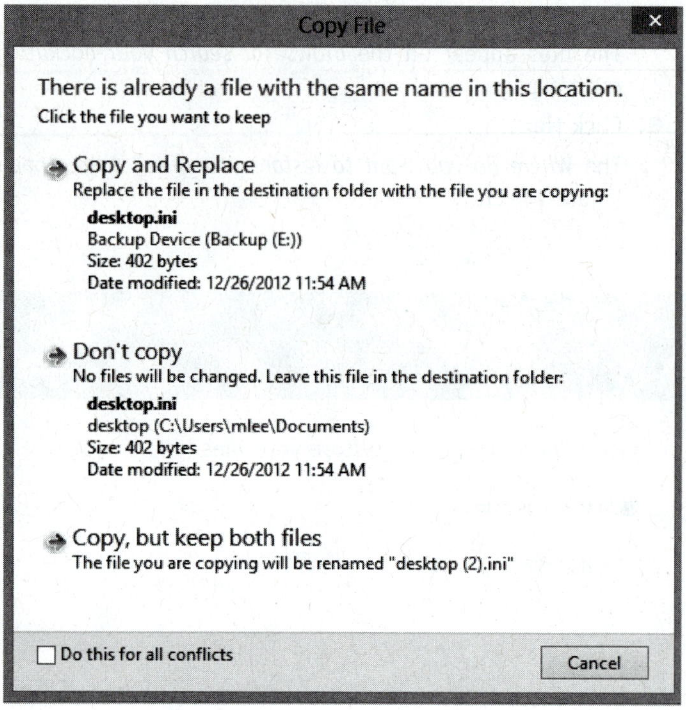

10. Click **Finish**.
11. **Close** the *Windows 7 File Recovery* control panel.

CREATING A SYSTEM IMAGE BACKUP

As mentioned earlier, you cannot use the file and folder backup capability in Windows 7 File Recovery to protect the entire system. Even when you use the *Let me choose* option and select the files you want to back up, you cannot select operating system files, such as those in the Windows folder.

To back up the entire system disk, you must perform a ***system image backup***, which is a separate backup of the computer's system disk and the reserved partition that Windows 8 creates on the disk during installation. Unlike the file and folder backup, which simply copies files to a compressed archive, a system image backup saves each block of the selected targets to a ***virtual hard disk (VHDX)*** file on the backup device.

You can create a system image backup as part of your regular scheduled backup job, or you can create one separately on demand, but you cannot schedule a system image backup through the Windows 7 File Recovery control panel. You can, however, schedule a job from the command prompt, using the Wbadmin.exe utility.

To perform a system image backup, use the following procedure.

CREATE A SYSTEM IMAGE BACKUP

GET READY. Log on to Windows 8 using an account with administrative privileges and then perform the following steps:

1. Open the **Control Panel** and then, in the *View by* drop-down list, click **Large icons**.

   The *Control Panel* interface displays individual icons for each of the available applications.

2. Click **Windows 7 File Recovery**.

   The Windows 7 File Recovery control panel appears.

3. Click **Create a system image**.

   The *Where do you want to save the backup?* page appears, as shown in Figure 24-13.

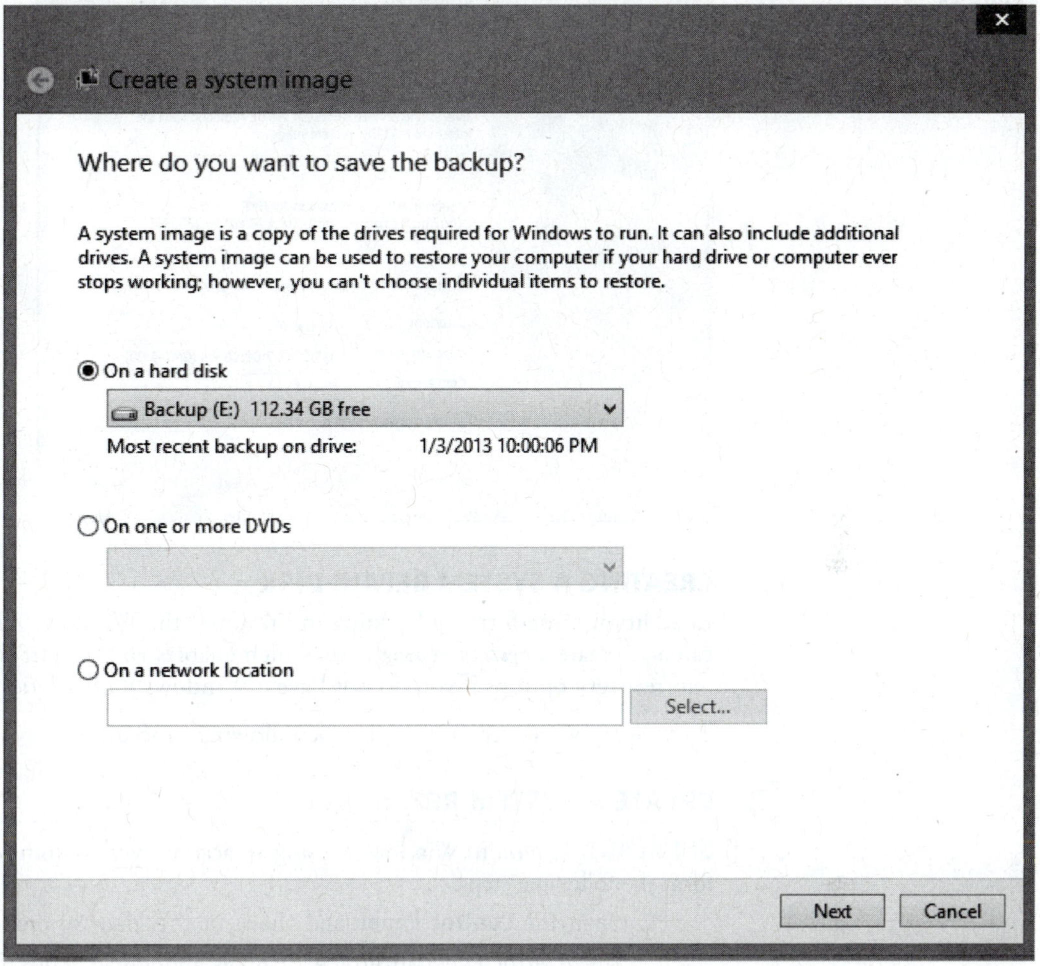

Figure 24-13

The *Where do you want to save the backup?* page

4. Select one of the destination options (hard disk, DVD, network), and the device where you want to save the backup, and then click **Next**.

   The *Confirm your backup settings* page appears.

5. Click **Start backup**.

   The backup job starts.

6. **Close** the *Windows 7 File Recovery* control panel.

As with file and folder backups, system image backups use incremental jobs by default. However, the incrementals in this type of job simply replace the older versions of files with new ones. The program does not retain copies of older versions.

To restore the computer from a system image backup, you must boot the system into the ***Windows Recovery Environment (Windows RE)***. You can do this in either of the following ways:

- Start the computer using a Windows 8 installation disk and, after selecting your language settings, choose Repair Your Computer. Then select Troubleshoot > Advanced Options > System Image Recovery.
- Restart the computer using the Advanced Startup Options and select Troubleshoot > Advanced Options > System Image Recovery.

In either case, you will have to specify a logon account. Next, you will have to specify the location of the backup, as shown in Figure 24-14. You will be able to restore the image to the computer.

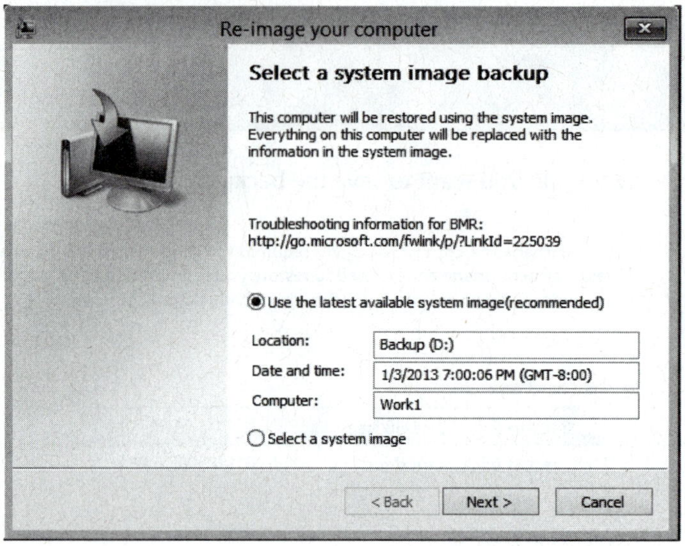

Figure 24-14

Specify the location of the backup

CREATING A SYSTEM REPAIR DISK

In addition to performing backups and restores, the Windows 7 File Recovery control panel can also create a ***system repair disk***, which enables you to start the computer and access system recovery options if you do not have a Windows 8 installation disk or a recovery partition.

To create a system repair disk, use the following procedure.

CREATE A SYSTEM REPAIR DISK

GET READY. Log on to Windows 8 using an account with administrative privileges and then perform the following steps:

1. Open the **Control Panel** and then, in the *View by* drop-down list, click *Large icons*.

   The *Control Panel* interface displays individual icons for each of the available applications.

2. Click **Windows 7 File Recovery**.

   The *Windows 7 File Recovery* control panel appears.

3. Click **Create a system repair disc**.

   The *Create a system repair disc* dialog box appears, as shown in Figure 24-15.

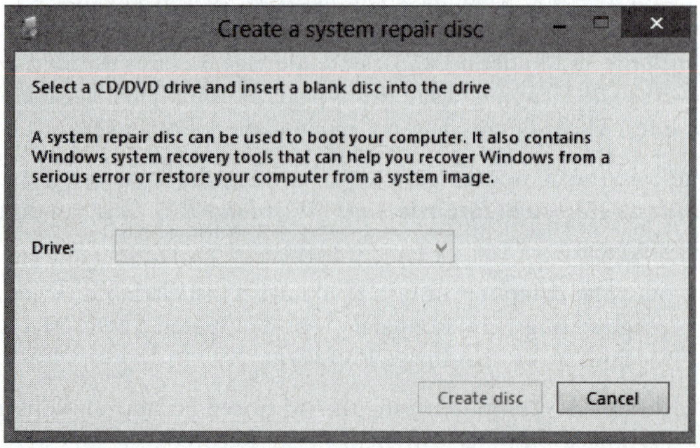

Figure 24-15

The *Create a system repair disc* dialog box

4. Insert a blank DVD-ROM disk into your DVD burner.
5. In the *Drive* drop-down list, select the drive letter corresponding to your DVD burner and then click **Create disc**.

   The system creates the system repair disk and displays a *Using the system repair disc* page.
6. Click **Close**.
7. **Close** the *Windows 7 File Recovery* control panel.

Store the system repair disk in a safe place, in case you experience a system failure. To use the disk, you simply insert the disk in the drive and boot the system. Windows 7 then displays system recovery options.

Creating a Windows 8 Recovery Drive

When working with Windows 8 recovery tools, be sure to note that the system repair disk you can create in the Windows 7 File Recovery control panel is not the same thing as the recovery drive you create in the Recovery control panel.

To create a system repair disk, you must use a writable DVD-ROM or CD-ROM disk, and the disk only provides access to the Windows Recovery Environment tools. When you create a recovery drive in Windows 8, you can use a USB flash drive or a DVD-ROM/CD-ROM.

CERTIFICATION READY
Create a system recovery disk
Objective 7.1

In addition, if your computer is an original equipment manufacturer (OEM) product that includes a recovery partition containing the Windows 8 installation files, you can create a recovery drive that includes those files, enabling you to use the disk to perform a complete reset of the computer,

MORE INFORMATION
For more information on resetting and restoring a Windows 8 PC, see Lesson 25, "Configure System Recovery Options."

To create a Windows 8 recovery drive, use the following procedure.

CREATE A RECOVERY DRIVE

GET READY. Log on to Windows 8 using an account with administrative privileges and then perform the following steps:

1. Open the **Control Panel** and, in the *View by* drop-down list, click **Large icons**.

   The Control Panel interface displays individual icons for each of the available applications.
2. Click **Recovery**.

   The Recovery control panel appears, as shown in Figure 24-16.

Figure 24-16

The *Recovery* control panel

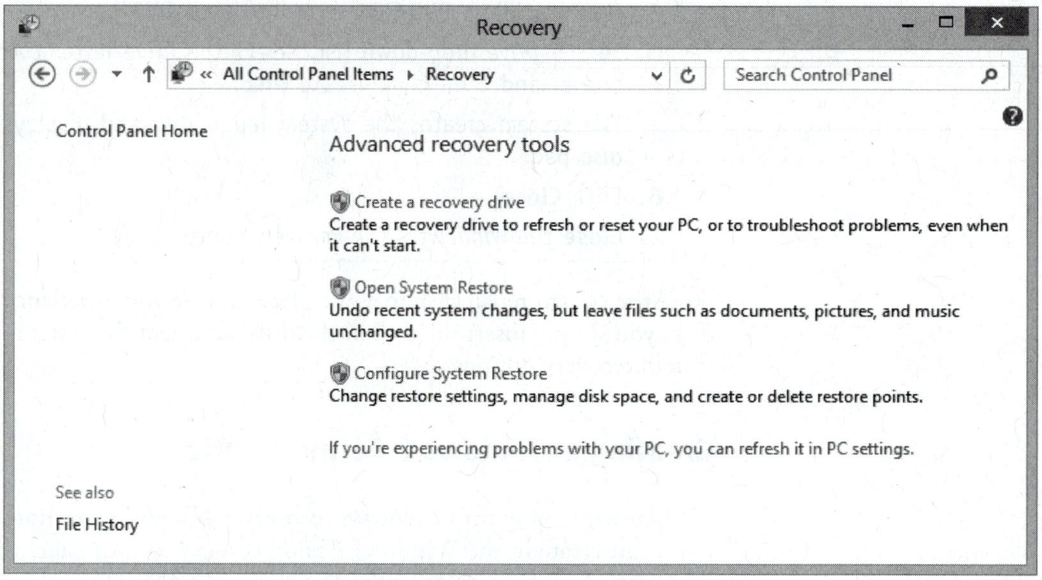

3. Click **Create a recovery drive**.

   The *Recovery Drive* wizard appears, displaying the *Create a recovery drive* page, as shown in Figure 24-17.

Figure 24-17

The *Create a recovery drive* page

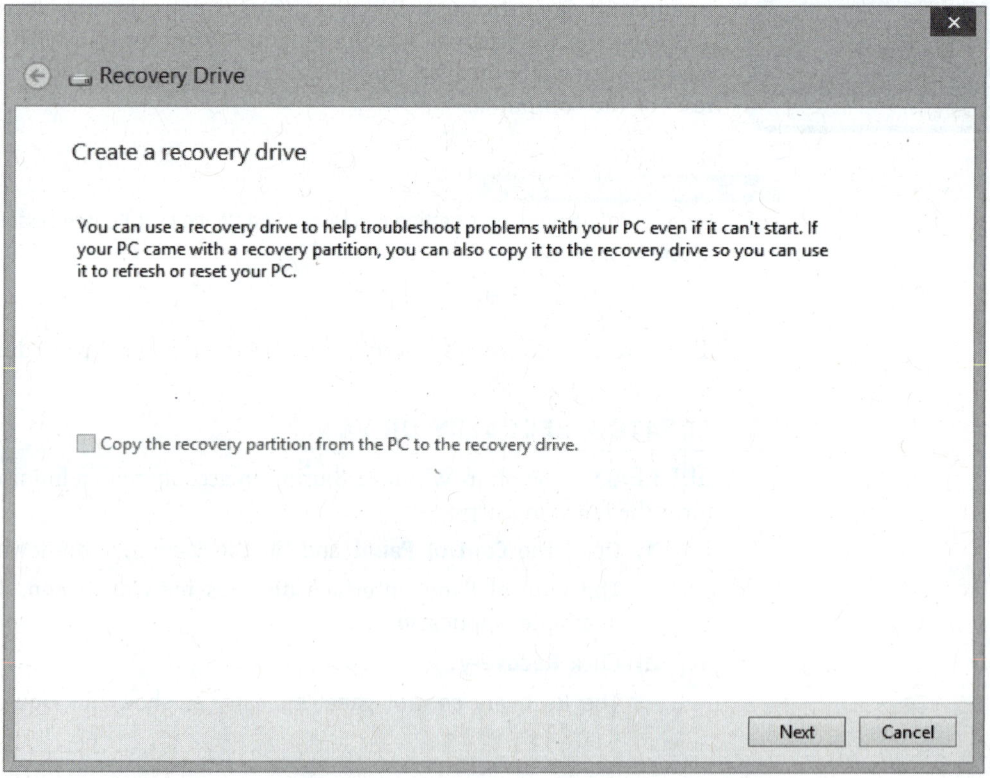

4. To create a USB recovery drive, insert a flash drive with a capacity of at least 256 MB into a USB slot.
5. If your computer has a recovery partition that you want to include on the recovery drive, select the *Copy the recovery partition from the PC to the recovery drive* checkbox and then click **Next**.

   The *Select the USB flash drive* page appears, as shown in Figure 24-18.

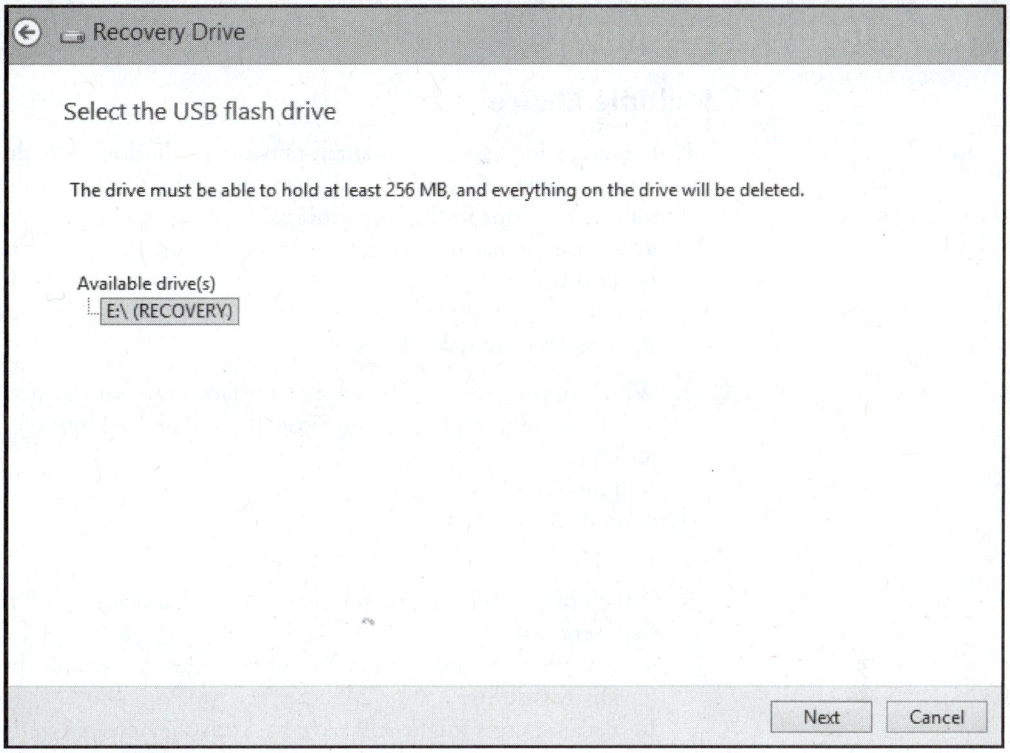

Figure 24-18
The *Select the USB flash drive* page

6. From the *Available drives* list, select the USB drive you want to use and then click **Next**.

   The *Create the recovery drive* page appears.

7. Click **Create**.

   The wizard creates the recovery drive and the *The recovery drive is ready* page appears.

8. Click **Finish**.

9. **Close** the *Recovery* control panel.

SKILL SUMMARY

IN THIS LESSON, YOU LEARNED:

- The Windows 7 Backup and Restore program integrates the Windows Vista wizard-based file and folder backup and the system image backup capabilities into one program. In Windows 8, this Backup and Restore program is deprecated in favor of the File History application.
- The file and folder backup process stores the selected files in compressed archives with a .zip extension, minimizing the amount of storage space consumed on the backup medium.
- You cannot use the file and folder backup capability in Windows 7 File Recovery to protect the entire system.
- To back up the entire system disk, you must perform a system image backup, which is a separate backup of the computer's system disk and the reserved partition that Windows 8 creates on the disk during installation. A system image backup saves each block of the selected targets to a virtual hard disk (VHDX) file on the backup device.
- The Windows 7 File Recovery control panel can also create a system repair disk, which enables you to start the computer and access system recovery options if you do not have a Windows 8 installation disk or a recovery partition.

Knowledge Assessment

Multiple Choice

1. For standalone systems or small networks, Windows 8 includes backup tools that you can use to protect your data. Which of the following devices do the Windows 8 backup tools not permit for backup storage?
   a. An online backup service
   b. Another hard disk drive
   c. A USB flash drive
   d. A series of writable CDs or DVDs

2. Which of the following is not an interface that you can use to connect a removable hard disk to a computer for the purpose of creating backups?
   a. USB
   b. FireWire
   c. eSATA
   d. VHDX

3. Which of the following is the reason why Windows 8 still includes the Windows 7 File Recovery utility ?
   a. Because there are certain Windows 8 files that cannot be backed up by the new File History utility.
   b. Because users might still have backups they created with Windows 7 that they want to restore.
   c. Because Windows 7 File Recovery provides more comprehensive backup capabilities than any of the Windows 8 backup mechanisms.
   d. Because the name of the Windows 7 File Recovery utility is copyrighted and cannot be changed.

4. Which of the following types of backup targets is not supported by Windows 7 File Recovery in all of the Windows 8 editions?
   a. CD-ROMs
   b. DVD-ROMs
   c. Network drives
   d. USB flash drives

5. Which of the following must you do to restore a system image file created on a Windows 8 computer?
   a. Boot the system to the Windows Recovery Environment
   b. Use the Windows 7 File Recovery utility
   c. Create a restore partition on the computer's hard disk
   d. Burn the system image file to a bootable disk or flash drive

6. How many scheduled backup jobs can the Windows 7 File Recovery utility support at once?
   a. 0
   b. 1
   c. 4
   d. Unlimited

7. What is the primary advantage of backing up system images to a virtual hard disk (VHDX) format?
   a. The VHDX format provides greater compression than other formats.
   b. You can mount a VHDX file as a drive on a Hyper-V server.
   c. The VHDX format is faster than other formats.
   d. You can restore a VHDX system image using the Windows 8 File History application.

Best Answer

Choose the letter that corresponds to the best answer. More than one answer choice may achieve the goal. Select the BEST answer.

1. What is the best reason why Windows 8 includes the Windows 7 File Recovery utility?
   - **a.** To provide individual file backup capabilities.
   - **b.** To provide restore job scheduling capabilities.
   - **c.** To provide restore capabilities to those who have backup media they created in Windows 7.
   - **d.** To provide system image backup capabilities.

Matching and Identification

1. Match the following terms with their corresponding definitions.

_______ **a)** Windows 7 File Recovery
_______ **b)** System image backup
_______ **c)** File History
_______ **d)** Sirtual hard disk (VHDX)
_______ **e)** Incremental backup
_______ **f)** Windows Recovery Environment (Windows RE)
_______ **g)** System repair disk
_______ **h)** Network attached storage
_______ **i)** Complete PC
_______ **j)** Storage area network

1. A backup of every file changed since the last backup.
2. Format used for system image backups.
3. Windows Vista backup utility.
4. Required to restore a system image backup.
5. A LAN dedicated to storage devices.
6. New Windows 8 backup utility.
7. A bit-by-bit backup of an entire disk.
8. Formerly known as Backup and Restore.
9. Standalone storage server.
10. Provides access to damaged system.

Build a List

1. Place the following steps for scheduling a backup job in Windows 7 File Recovery in the proper order.

_______ **a)** Click **Save settings** and run backup.
_______ **b)** Click **Save** on a network.
_______ **c)** Click **Change schedule**.
_______ **d)** Supply the path to the network share.
_______ **e)** Specify the day of the week or the monthly date that you want the job to run.
_______ **f)** Supply credentials to access the share.
_______ **g)** Specify the time of day that you want the job to run.
_______ **h)** Click **Set up backup**.
_______ **i)** Select what you want to back up.
_______ **j)** Launch *Windows 7 File Recovery*.
_______ **k)** Specify whether you want the job to run daily, weekly, or monthly.

Business Case Scenario

Scenario 24-1: Performing Windows 8 Backups

Ralph has been backing up a client's Windows 7 computers using the Backup and Restore utility supplied with that operating system. He uses removable hard disks to perform regularly scheduled backups of the data files on the computers, as well as system image backups at the same time.

Ralph recently installed some new computers with Windows 8, and was delighted to discover that the new operating system includes Windows 7 File Recovery, a renamed version of the backup software he has been using for years. Ralph decides to discontinue his data file backups. However, he still wants to perform scheduled system image backups on his new computers every week.

What must Ralph do to implement this backup regimen?

Configuring System Recovery Options

LESSON 25

70-687 EXAM OBJECTIVE

Objective 7.2 – Configure system recovery options. This objective may include but is not limited to: configure startup settings; configure System Restore; determine when to choose Last Known Good Configuration; perform a complete restore; perform a driver rollback; and perform a push button refresh or reset.

Lesson Heading	Exam Objective
Performing System Recovery of Windows 8	
Understanding the Windows 8 Startup Process	Configure Startup Settings
Troubleshooting Startup Failures	
Configuring System Restore Points	Configure System Restore
Using the Last Known Good Configuration	Determine when to choose Last Known Good Configuration
Performing a Complete Restore	Perform a Complete Restore
Performing Driver Rollbacks	Perform a Driver Rollback
Exploring PC Refresh and PC Reset	Perform a Push Button Refresh or Reset

KEY TERMS

Boot Configuration Data (BCD)
driver roll back
Last Known Good Configuration (LKGC)
PC Refresh
PC Reset
power-on self-test (POST)
recimg.exe
registry
restore points
system image
System Restore
Windows Boot Loader

Performing System Recovery of Windows 8

THE BOTTOM LINE

The ability to isolate problems, select the right tool(s) to resolve them and return a system to a functional state quickly is a key skill that all administrators need.

You just completed a new install of an application, updated a device driver for an existing piece of hardware, or removed a service that you think you no longer needed. In most situations, all will go well and you can expect Windows 8 to perform as expected. At some point in the future, at the most inopportune time, your Windows 8 system will start to boot but for one reason or another it will not work the way you expect it to. When this happens, you will need to have the tools and experience to return the system to a functional state as quickly as possible.

The key to learning how to effectively troubleshoot your system starts with having a basic understanding of the startup process. Once you know what is supposed to happen when a Windows 8 system boots normally, you will gain the insight you need to isolate the problem, determine the appropriate tool to use, and eventually repair the system.

In this lesson, you learn about the tools available with Windows 8 and how they can help you return your Windows 8 system to a functional state.

Understanding the Windows 8 Startup Process

Understanding what happens from the point that you turn on the power to your Windows 8 client computer until you log on and see the desktop will help you isolate and troubleshoot problems quickly.

The Windows 8 startup process consists of the following phases:

1. ***Power-on self-test (POST)* phase** – When you first turn the computer on, it loads the BIOS or Extensible Firmware Interface (EFI) and runs a hardware self-test procedure that detects the devices installed in the system and configures the using settings stored in non-volatile memory. After the main POST, any devices with their own BIOS firmware (such as video display adapters) can run their own self-test procedures. On BIOS-equipped computers, the system reads the BIOS settings to determine which hardware device it should use to boot the computer. When booting from a hard disk, the system loads the master boot record (MBR) from the disk and locates the active (bootable) partition. The system then loads and runs a stub program called Bootmgr, which switches the processor from real mode to protected mode and loads the Windows Boot Manager application. EFI computers have their own built-in boot manager, which Windows 8 configures to run the same Windows Boot Manager application, eliminating the need for the interim disk location steps. POST passes control to the operating system loader also known as the Windows Boot Manager.

CERTIFICATION READY
Configure startup settings
Objective 7.2

2. **Windows Boot Manager phase** – The system reads the ***Boot Configuration Data (BCD)*** file, which contains the system's boot menu information and provides the user with access to the boot menu. If there are multiple operating systems installed, the boot menu appears as shown in Figure 25-1, providing the user with 30 seconds to select one of the operating systems before it loads the default. The Windows Boot Manager then starts the Windows Boot Loader.

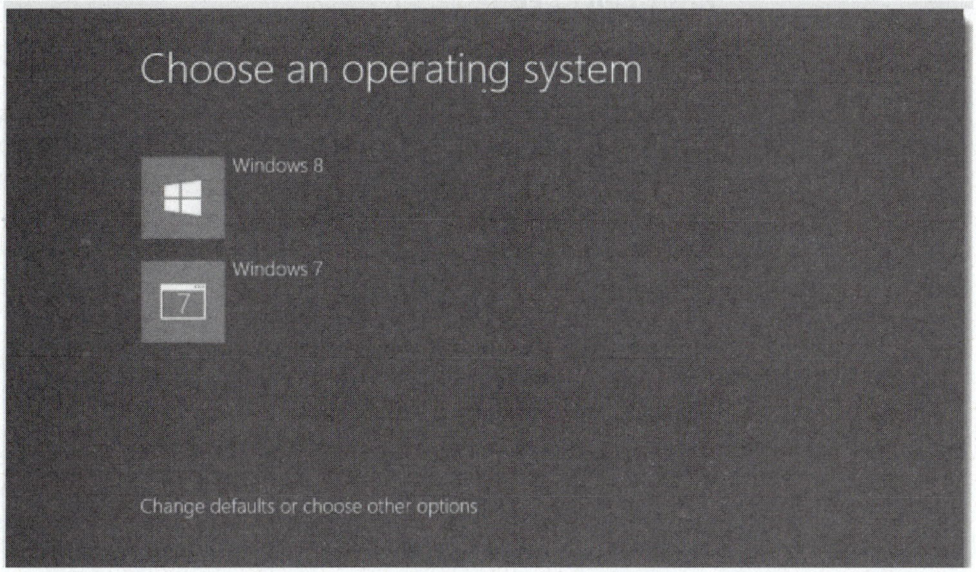

Figure 25-1

Reviewing the Windows 8 boot menu with multiple operating systems installed

3. ***Windows Boot Loader* phase** – The system initiates the memory paging process and loads various operating system elements into memory, such as the Windows kernel, the hardware abstraction layer (HAL), the system registry hive, and boot class device drivers, but it does not actually run them. The Windows Boot Loader then passes control to the operating system kernel.
4. **Kernel loading phase** – The system runs the Windows Executive (consisting of the Windows kernel and the HAL), which processes the registry hive and initializes the drivers and services specified there. The kernel then starts the Session Manager, which loads the kernel-mode part of the Win32 subsystem, causing the system to switch from text mode to graphics mode. Then the kernel loads the user-mode portion of Win32, which provides applications with indirect, protected access to the system hardware. At this time, the system also performs delayed rename operations resulting from system updates that must replace files that were in use when the update was installed. Finally, the kernel creates additional virtual memory paging files and starts the Windows Logon Manager.
5. **Logon phase** – The system loads the Service Control Manager (SCM) and the Local Security Authority (LSA), and then presents the logon user interface (LogonUI). The interface passes the credentials supplied by the user to the LSA for authentication, and the SCM loads the Plug and Play services and drivers that are configured for auto loading. If the authentication is successful, the Logon Manager launches Userinit.exe, which is responsible for applying group policy settings, creating user environment variables and running the programs in the Startup group, and then loads the Windows File Explorer shell, which provides the Windows desktop.

Troubleshooting Startup Failures

A computer that will not start can be very frustrating and impacts a user's ability to get work done. Understanding what happens during startup can help you isolate the problem and select/use the right tool to get the computer back online.

The symptoms of a startup failure differ depend on where in the process the failure occurs. Therefore, the first step to take when a Windows 8 computer fails to start is to determine exactly where in the startup sequence the problem occurs.

POST FAILURES

One of the most fundamental questions a troubleshooter can ask is whether a problem is being caused by a hardware or a software failure. If a computer fails to make it through the POST successfully, the problem is unquestionably hardware-related. In most cases, the BIOS will display an error message or produce a series of beeps identifying the exact problem that is causing the failure. Consult the BIOS documentation for more information on its error messages and/or beep codes.

MORE INFORMATION

Some BIOS programs enable you to select between a "quick" POST or an extended "diagnostic" sequence. At the first sign of a hardware problem, you should switch to the diagnostic mode to gather as much information as possible about the problem.

INITIAL STARTUP FAILURES

A failure during the POST phase typically results in a "Non-system disk or disk error," which means that there is an issue with the BIOS configuration, the storage subsystem, or the file system. Startup failures that occur before the progress bar appears are typically caused by one of the following problems:

- **Incorrect BIOS Settings** – If the boot settings in the BIOS are misconfigured, the system might be attempting to boot from the wrong device. For example, if the BIOS is configured to boot from the CD or DVD drive, and there is no bootable disk in the drive, the computer will be unable to start.
- **Hardware faults** – If anyone has recently worked inside the computer's case, you might want to begin by checking the hard drive's power and data connections. Also, if there is an internal problem with the hard disk, such as corruption of the MBR, the system might not be able to locate the active partition.
- **Missing startup files** – If some of the required startup files are missing or damaged, the computer will fail to boot. This could be due to the installation of another operating system, accidental deletion of system files, or data corruption on the hard disk.
- **Data corruption** – Corrupted data on a disk drive can be the result of a hardware fault, environmental factors (such as magnetic fields), or some form of malware.

Resolving these problems can require the replacement of a hardware component, but in many cases you can repair them using the specialized recovery tools provided with Windows 8, as discussed later in this lesson.

DRIVER AND SERVICE FAILURES

When a startup failure occurs before the logon user interface appears, the problem could be hardware-related, but it is most likely due to an issue with one of the drivers or services that the kernel is attempting to load. Resolving the problem is a matter of determining which of the drivers or services is at fault.

To locate the offending driver or service, you must first attempt to get the computer started by using the Safe Mode. Then you can examine the event logs, enable the boot log, and run the System Information tool to gather information on what is affecting the startup sequence. Finally, use Device Manager or the Services console to disable the offending drivers or services. Once you are able to get the computer started in normal mode, you can begin to examine the problematic driver or service, perhaps replacing them with an updated version or rolling back to a previous one.

LOGON FAILURES

When the startup process fails after the user has supplied logon credentials, the problem is most likely due to one of the applications running from the Startup group. To troubleshoot this type of problem, you would need to boot into Safe Mode.

In Windows 8, booting into Safe Mode (discussed in "Using the Last Known Configuration" section of this lesson) and troubleshooting applications in the Startup group involves the following steps.

TROUBLESHOOT LOGON FAILURES

GET READY. Log into the Windows 8 client computer with administrative privileges on the computer and then perform the following steps:

1. Press the **Windows logo key + r**.
2. In the *Run* dialog box, type **taskmgr** and then click **OK**.
3. Click the **Startup** tab.
4. Right-click the application(s) that you think might be causing the problem and choose **Disable** from the menu that appears.
5. Restart the computer.

Repeat steps 1-5 to isolate the offending application. Once discovered, you can attempt to reconfigure, upgrade, or uninstall it until the problem is eliminated.

Configuring System Restore Points

Installing a new program or driver can sometimes make Windows 8 crash or function in a way you never expected. If this happens, you will want to return the PC's system files and programs to a time when things were working while not affecting your personal documents or other data.

Windows 8 ***System Restore*** is a recovery option for your computer that saves information about your drives, registry settings, programs, and files in the form of ***restore points***. You use the restore points to return these items to an earlier state without impacting your personal files. You should create restore points prior to performing any major system event such as the installation of a program.

CERTIFICATION READY
Configure System Restore
Objective 7.2

Windows 8, by default, automatically creates restore points every seven days if you have not created one during that time period. You can also create restore points manually anytime you choose.

CREATE A SYSTEM RESTORE POINT

GET READY. To create a system restore, perform the following steps:

1. Log into the Windows 8 client computer with local Administrative privileges.
2. Press the **Windows logo key + w** and then type **System Restore**.
3. In the *Results* list, click **Create a restore point**.
4. On the *System Protection* tab, click **Configure** and confirm the option *Turn on system protection* is selected.
5. Under *Disk Space Usage*, drag the slider to set the maximum disk space you want to use for system protection (Figure 25-2), click **Apply** and then click **OK**.

   As the amount of drive space is filled up, restore points will be deleted to make room for new ones.

TAKE NOTE*
You can also access System Restore via the Control Panel > System and Security > System Protection

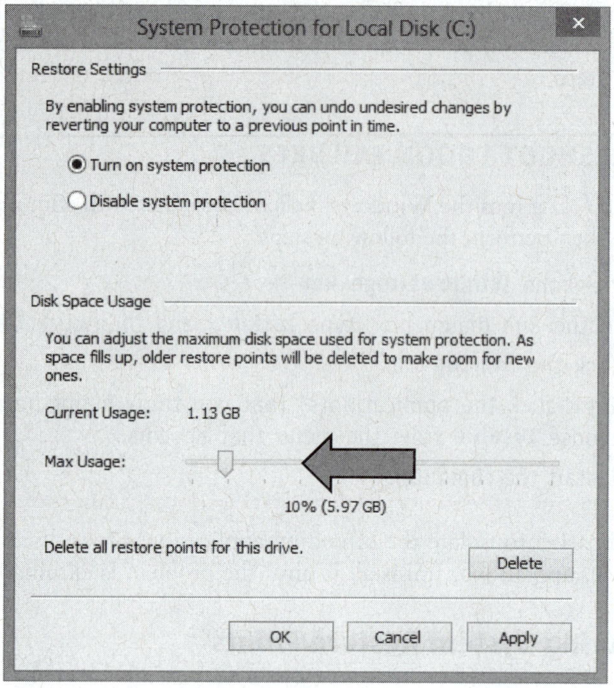

Figure 25-2
Setting *Disk Space Usage*

6. Click **Create** to create a new restore point.
7. Type a description for the restore point in the dialog box.
8. Click **Create**.
9. Click **Close** when notified the restore point was created successfully.
10. Click **OK** to close the *System Properties* dialog box.

PERFORM A SYSTEM RESTORE

GET READY. To perform a system restore, perform the following steps:

1. Log into the Windows 8 client computer with local Administrative privileges.
2. Press the **Windows logo key + w** and then type **System Restore**.
3. In the *Results* list, click **Create a restore point**.
4. Click **System Restore** from the *System Protection* tab.
5. Click **Next** to start the *System Restore* wizard.

   System restore does not affect your documents, pictures, or other personal data. Recently installed programs and drivers may be uninstalled.
6. Choose the restore point (Figure 25-3) and click **Scan for affected programs**.

   After the scan is completed, you can see programs and drivers that will be deleted and programs and drivers that might be restored.

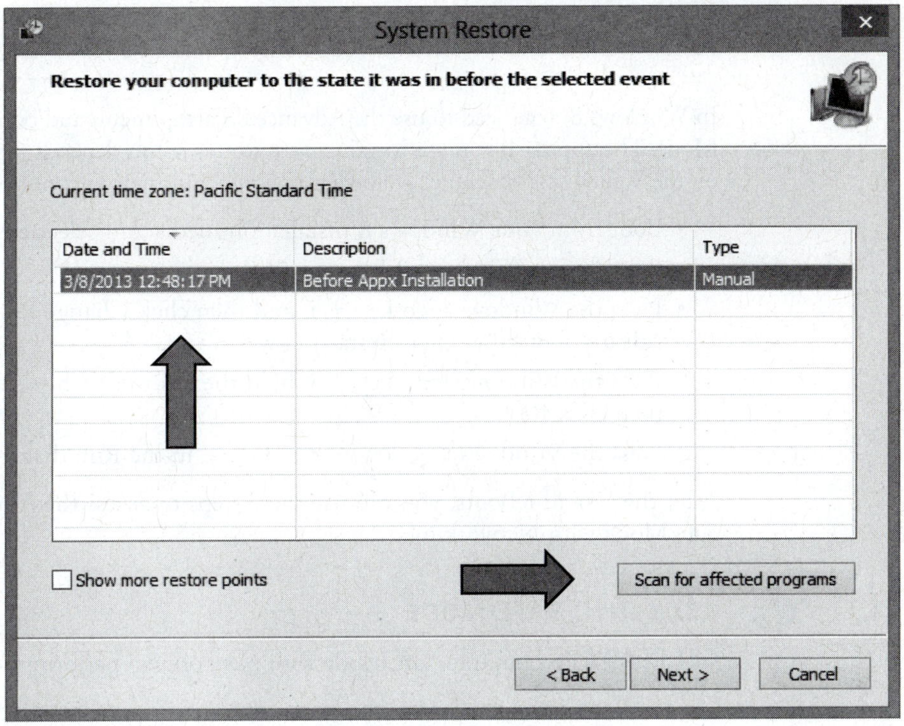

Figure 25-3
Selecting a restore point

7. Review and click **Close** and then click **Next**.
8. Confirm your restore point and click **Finish**.

   Note: If you changed your Windows password, you should also create a password reset disk. This can be done by pressing the **Windows logo key + Q** and searching for *Create a password reset* disk.
9. Click **Yes** to begin the system restore process.

   Windows restarts the computer, restores your files and settings, restore the registry, and removes temp files as part of the restore process.
10. Log back into the Windows 8 client computer when the restore process is completed.

Using the Last Known Good Configuration

After installing a new device driver or disabling a critical service, you may run into trouble getting into your Windows 8 system. Although Windows 8 no longer uses the Last Known Good Configuration, you can still access the Advanced Startup menu to enter Safe Mode and repair the system.

The ***Last Known Good Configuration (LKGC)*** option, found in Windows 7 and earlier operating systems by pressing F8, is no longer available in Windows 8. The LKGC was a recovery option used to restore ***registry*** and driver settings that were in place the last time your system started successfully. The registry is a database in Windows that stores information on services, installed programs and their settings, user profiles, and system hardware. When a Windows system shuts down successfully, certain settings in regard to services and device drivers are recorded in the registry.

CERTIFICATION READY
Determine when to choose Last Known Good Configuration
Objective 7.2

The LKGC was used in situations for which you installed a new device driver that caused your system not to boot or you disabled a driver or critical service by accident that was needed by Windows. It would not be used to repair deleted system files or in cases where you are able to boot into Windows and the system froze after you logged in. In the latter case, Windows will have already overwritten the LKGC backup.

MORE INFORMATION

The Last Known Good Configuration can be accessed in Windows Server 2012 by pressing the F8 key during startup

In Windows 8, you need to use the Advanced Startup menu and boot the computer into Safe Mode. The approach you use to gain access to this menu depends upon how much access you have on the Windows 8 machine. Following is a quick summary of your options for accessing the menu:

- Boot from your Windows 8 installation media and select Repair Your Computer option.
- Boot from a Windows 8 Recovery drive.
- Press the Windows logo key + i and then click Change PC Settings > General. Under Advanced Startup, click Restart Now.
- Press the Windows logo key + i, hold the Shift key while selecting the Power icon, and then click Restart.
- Press the Windows logo key + r and then, in the Run dialog box, type shutdown /r /o.

After the system reboots, you can use these steps to access the Advanced menu and boot into Safe Mode with Networking:

BOOT INTO SAFE MODE

GET READY. To boot into Safe Mode with Networking, perform the following steps:

1. Boot into your computer from your Windows 8 installation media and select **Repair Your Computer**.
2. On the *Choose an option* screen, click the **Troubleshoot** tile.
3. On the *Troubleshoot* screen, click the **Advanced options** tile.
4. On the *Advanced options* screen, click the **Startup Settings** tile.
5. On the *Startup Settings* screen, click **Restart**.
6. Choose **#5-Enable Safe Mode with Networking** as shown in Figure 25-4.

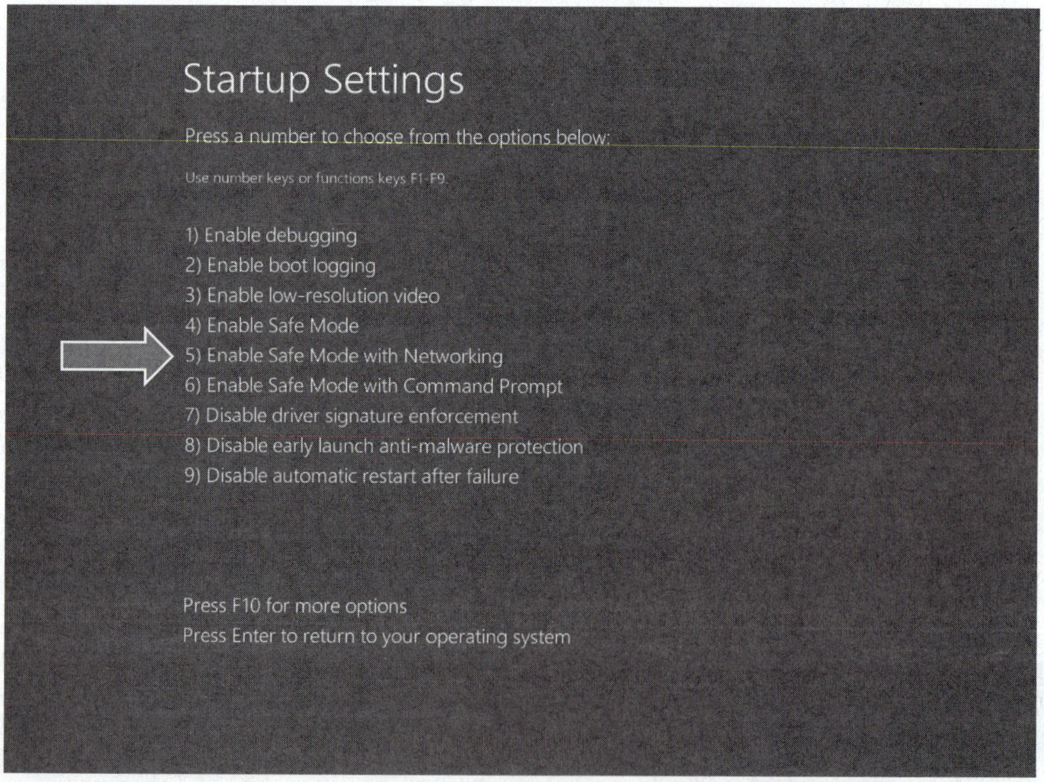

Figure 25-4

Enabling Safe Mode with Networking

7. Log into the Windows 8 client computer with your administrator credentials and password. The words *Safe Mode* should now appear in all four corners of your screen.

From this point, you can uninstall drivers, restart services or make other changes to troubleshoot and get your system running again.

Performing a Complete Restore

If you experience a crash of your Windows 8 system and your hard drive is no longer functional, you can perform a complete restore from a system image you have prepared previously.

To prepare for a complete restore, you will need to create a ***system image*** of your computer. The system image is an exact copy of the drives required for Windows to run. This includes the Windows 8 operating system, system settings, programs and files. When you restore from an image, it is a complete restore; therefore, you will not be able to choose individual items.

CERTIFICATION READY
Perform a complete restore
Objective 7.2

The option to create a system image can be found in the Control Panel\Windows 7 File Recovery. A system image can be stored on a hard disk formatted with NTFS, on one or more DVDs or on a network location.

CREATE A WINDOWS 8 SYSTEM IMAGE

GET READY. To create a Windows 8 system image, perform the following steps:

TAKE NOTE*
You will need to create a shared folder on another computer in your domain to store the image and must have access to the Windows 8 installation media to complete this exercise.

1. Log into the Windows 8 client computer with local Administrative privileges.
2. Press the **Windows logo key + w** and then type **Windows 7 File Recovery**.
3. In the *Results* list, choose **Windows 7 File Recovery**.
4. Click Create a system image.
5. Select the option **On a network location** as shown in Figure 25-5 and then click **Select**.

Figure 25-5

Selecting a network location to save the system image to

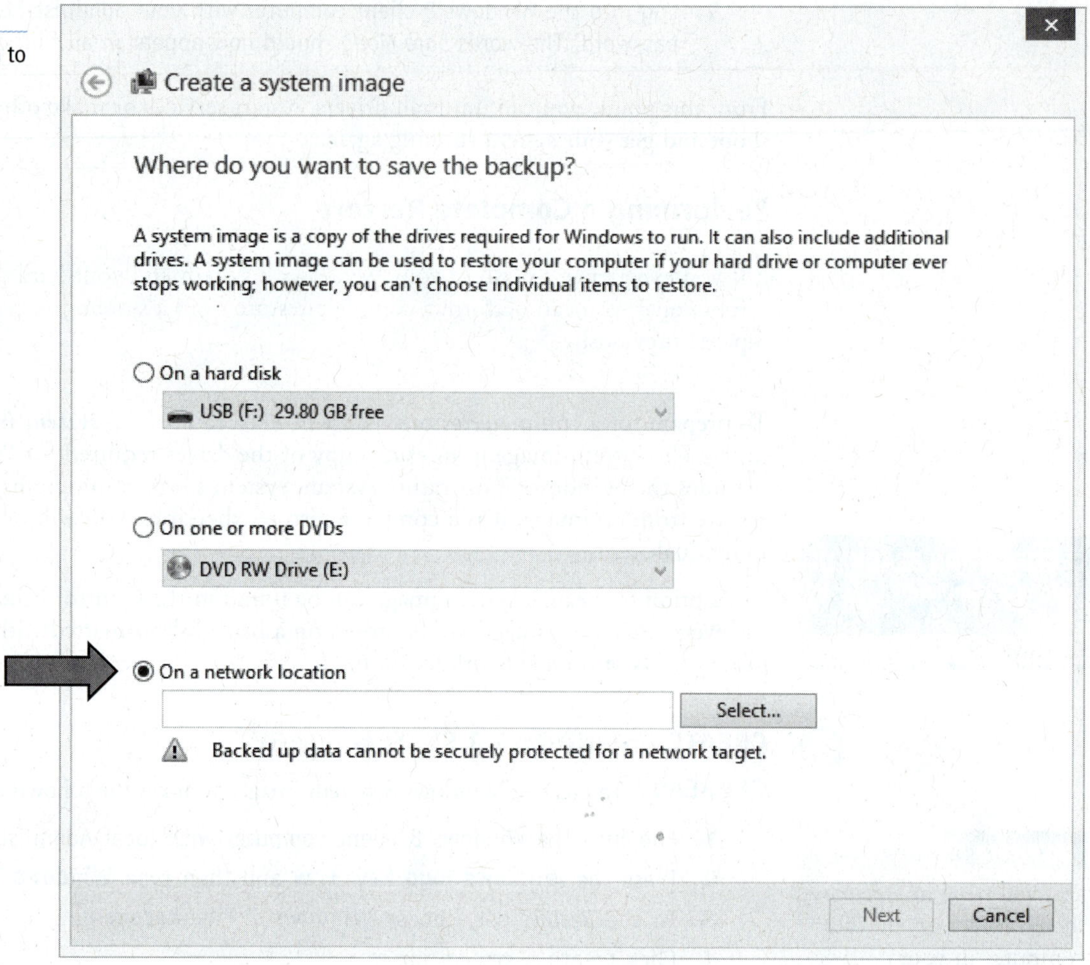

6. On the *Select a network location* screen, click **Browse** and navigate to the network location where you want to store the system image and click **OK**.
7. Under *Network credentials*, type a user name and password that can access the share and then click **OK**.
8. Click **Next** to continue.
9. Confirm your backup settings and click **Start backup** as shown in Figure 25-6.

   Windows 8 saves the system image backup to the location you specified under a folder named

   WindowsImageBackup\\<*computername*> where *computername* is the name of the computer you are running the backup from.

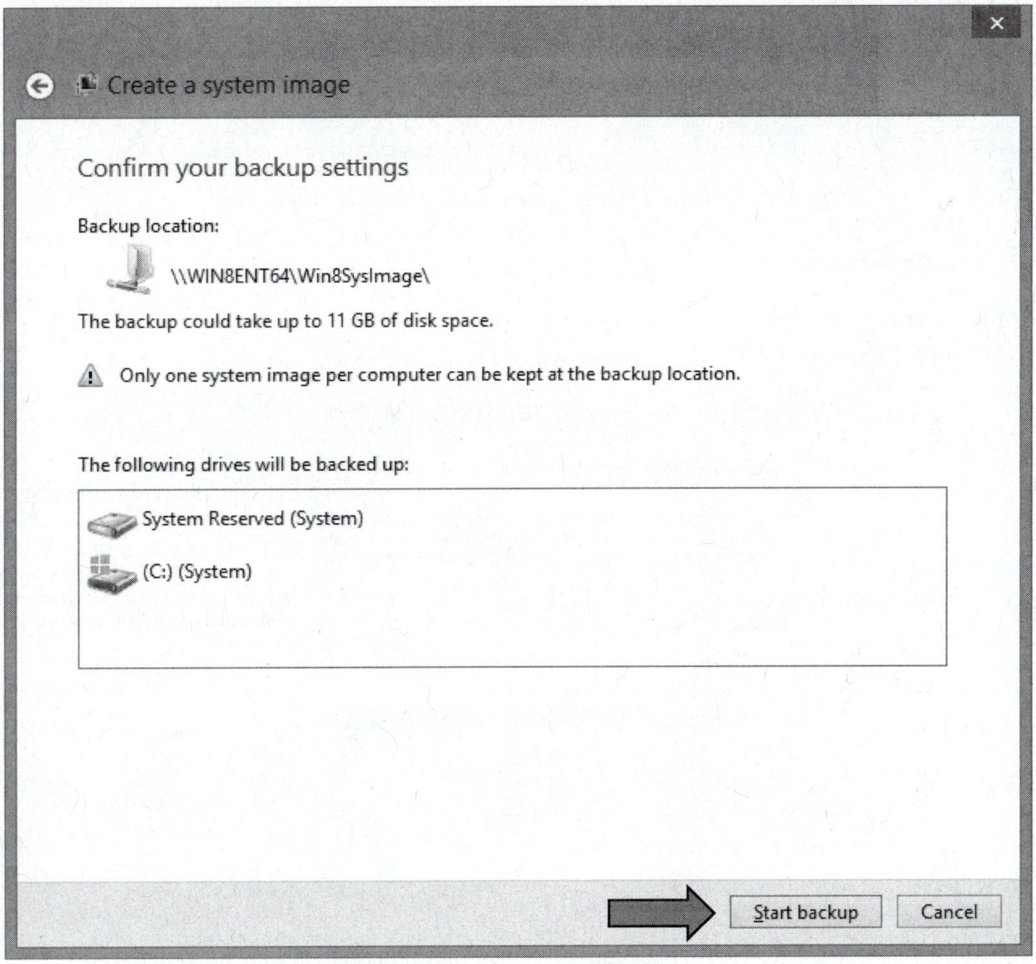

Figure 25-6

Starting the backup of the Windows 8 system image

10. When prompted to create a system repair disc, click **No**.

> **MORE INFORMATION**
> A system repair disc is not required if you have access to a Windows 8 installation disc. If you do not have one available, you will need to create the disc at this time; otherwise, continue to Step 14

11. Select a CD/DVD drive, insert a blank disc and click **Create disc**.
12. Read the message about using the system repair disc (Figure 25-7) and then click **Close**.

Figure 25-7

Reviewing the system repair disc message

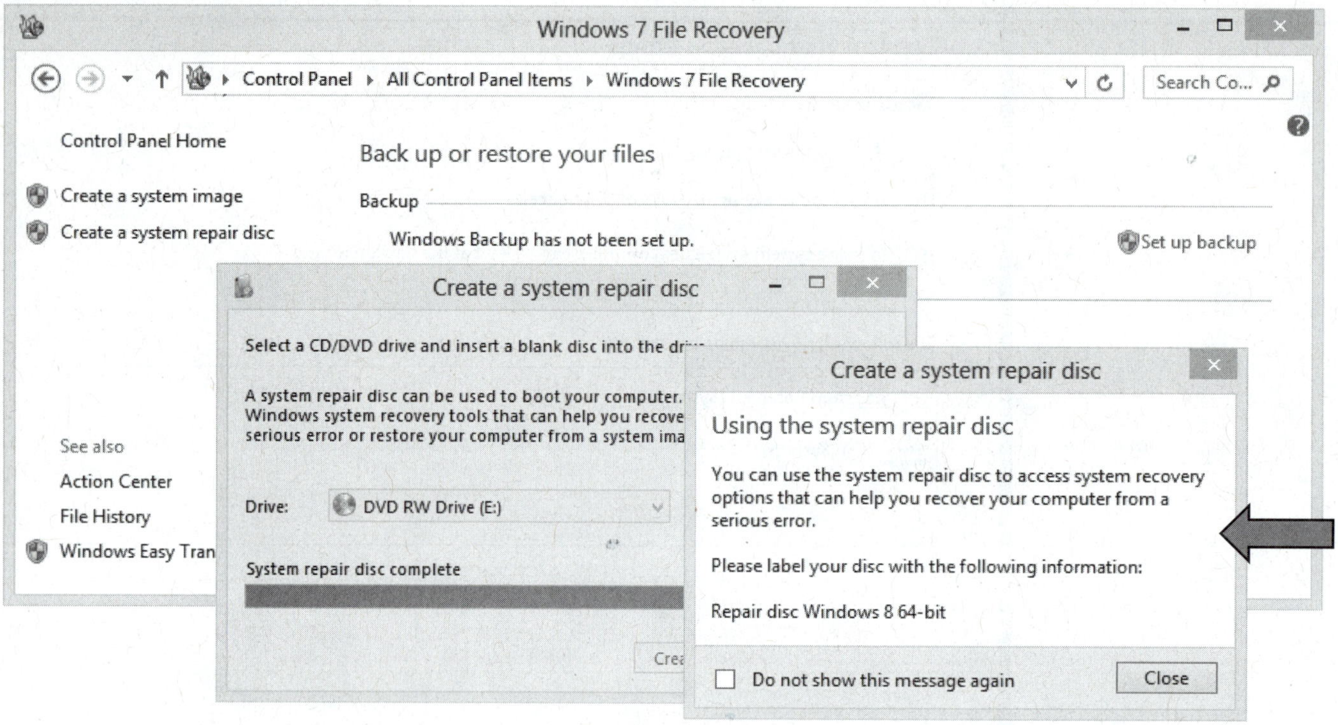

13. Label the disc as indicated in the previous step.
14. When the backup reports it has completed successfully, click **Close**.

CREATE A SYSTEM REPAIR DISC (OPTIONAL)

GET READY. To create a Windows 8 system repair disc, log into the Windows 8 client computer with administrative credentials and then perform the following steps:

1. Press the **Windows logo key + w** and then type **Windows 7 File Recovery**.
2. In the *Results* list, choose **Windows 7 File Recovery**.
3. Click **Create a system repair disc**.
4. Select the CD or DVD drive, insert a blank disc and then click **Create disc**.
5. In the *Using the system repair disc* dialog box that appears, read the information provided about labeling the disc and then click **Close**.
6. After the message *System repair disc complete* appears, click **OK**.
7. Eject and label the disc as directed in Step 6 and store it in a safe place.

PERFORM A COMPLETE SYSTEM RESTORE

GET READY. To perform a complete system restore of Windows 8, perform the following steps:

1. Insert the System repair disc you created for the Windows 8 computer.
2. Restart the Windows 8 computer and when you see the "*Press any key to boot from CD or DVD...*" press **Enter**.

3. On the *Choose your keyboard layout* screen, select **U.S**.
4. On the *Choose an option* screen, click the **Troubleshoot** tile.
5. On the *Troubleshoot* screen, click the **Advanced options** tile.
6. On the *Advanced options* screen click the **System Image Recovery** tile.
7. Select **Windows 8** as the target operating system.
8. When the message *Windows cannot find a system image on this computer* appears, click **Cancel**.
9. Click **Next** to continue.
10. Click the **Advanced** button and then choose **Search for a system image on the network** as shown in Figure 25-8.

Figure 25-8

Searching for Windows image on network

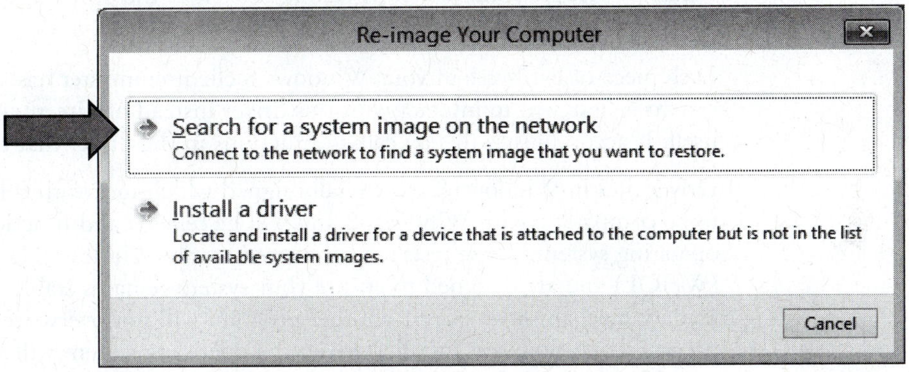

11. When prompted to connect to the network, click **Yes**.
12. Specify the path to the system image and then click **OK**.

    This is the location you backed it up to in the earlier exercise.
13. Type the *user name* and *password* of an account that has access to the share and then click **OK**.
14. Choose the image to restore as shown in Figure 25-9 and then click **Next**.

Figure 25-9

Selecting the Windows image to restore

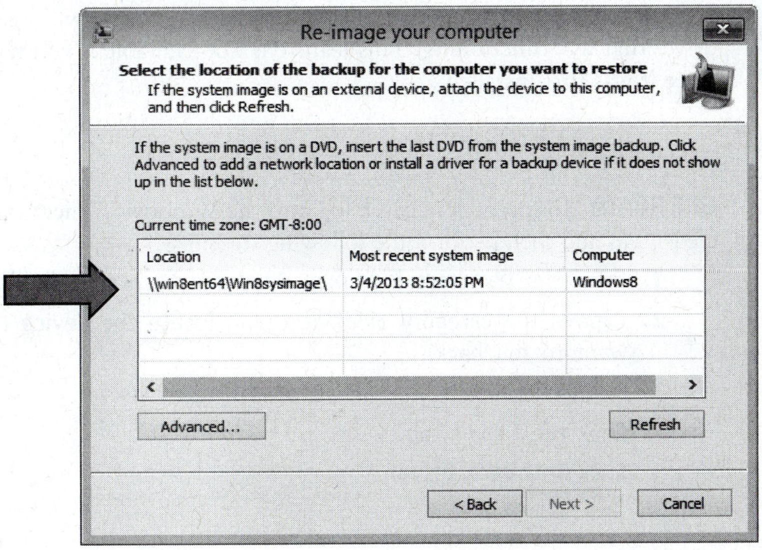

15. Select the date and time of the image you want to restore and then click **Next**.
16. Click **Format and repartition disks** and then click **Next**.
17. Click **Finish** to start the restore.
18. Read the message that states all disks to be restored will be formatted and replaced with the layout and data in the system image and then click **Yes**.
19. Log into the Windows 8 client computer after the system is restored to confirm functionality.

Performing Driver Rollbacks

When installing a device driver for a new piece of hardware or updating and existing driver, you may discover your system is no longer functioning properly. If this occurs, you can quickly recover your system by rolling it back to the previous device driver.

Each piece of hardware in your Windows 8 client computer has a device driver. The operating system is designed to interact with this driver instead of directly with the hardware device itself. It accomplishes this by calling functions in the driver that carries out a specific action.

Driver files in Windows 8 are digitally signed which means they have been tested and verified to be compatible with Windows 8 and will be reliable and function appropriately with the operating system. These tests are conducted by the Windows Hardware Quality Labs (WHQL) and are designed to ensure your system remains stable. This signature is also used as a safety mechanism to ensure another program will not overwrite it during its installation process. Each time you install a driver, the operating system will check for the digital signature. If it does not find one, a message will be generated allowing you to ignore or exit out of the install process.

The Local Group Policy editor (gpedit.msc) or the Group Policy Management console (gpmc.msc) can be used to create a policy that determines how the Windows 8 system will respond when a user tries to install a device driver that is not digitally signed. The following options can be configured with a policy:

- **Block** – Directs the system to refuse to install unsigned files.
- **Ignore** – Directs the system to proceed with the install even if the driver is unsigned.
- **Warn** – Notifies the user that the driver files are not digitally signed and will let them decide if they want to proceed with the installation of the unsigned files.

CERTIFICATION READY
Perform a driver rollback
Objective 7.2

Driver roll back is a recovery feature in Windows 8 that will let you reinstall the last device driver that was functioning. This feature is not available if you have not updated the driver since it was first installed.

ROLL BACK A DRIVER

GET READY. To roll back a driver, log into the Windows 8 client computer with administrative credentials and then perform the following steps:

1. Press the **Windows logo key + w** and then type **Device Manager**.
2. Expand the category of devices and locate the device that uses the driver you want to roll back.
3. Right-click the device and choose **Properties**.
4. Click the **Driver** tab.
5. Click **Roll Back Driver**.

ROLL BACK A DEVICE DRIVER

GET READY. To roll back a device driver, log into the Windows 8 client computer with local Administrative privileges and then perform the following steps:

1. Press the **Windows logo key + w** and then type **Device Manager**.
2. Expand **Network Adapters**.
3. Right-click the adapter and choose **Update Driver Software**.
4. Click **Browse my computer for driver software**.
5. Click **Let me pick from a list of device drivers on my computer**.
6. On the *Select Network Adapter* screen, uncheck **Show compatible hardware**.
7. Choose a different network adapter and click **Next**. For example, Marvel 3COM 3C2000-T Gigabit Adapter.
8. When you receive the *Update Driver Warning* message, click **Yes**.
9. Click **Close** and then restart the computer.
10. Open **Device Manager** and locate the network adapter you updated the driver for. It should have a yellow warning symbol with an exclamation point.
11. Right-click the adapter and choose **Properties**.
12. Click the **Driver** tab and then click **Roll Back Driver**.
13. When prompted to roll back the driver, click **Yes** and then click **Close**.

Exploring PC Refresh and PC Reset

Over time as you add/remove applications and make changes to your system, you may find it no longer functions quite as well as it used to. If this happens, you can use the PC Reset and PC Refresh options to return your system to a functioning state.

A ***PC Reset*** is used when you need to return your PC back to the original state it was in when you purchased it or first set it up. This will remove any custom settings you have made, erase your personal data and remove traditional as well as Windows apps from the computer. This is basically a full reinstall of the Windows 8 operating system minus the need to answer the setup questions.

CERTIFICATION READY
Perform a push button refresh or reset
Objective 7.2

If you want to take a less intrusive approach, you would perform a ***PC Refresh***. A PC Refresh allows you to keep your personal data, your Windows Store apps, and basic settings (mapped drives, drive letter assignments), personalization settings, BitLocker or BitLocker To Go and wireless settings. A PC Refresh does not keep your PC settings, file associations, display settings or traditional applications. If you have traditional applications installed (from disk or a website), an HTML file will be placed on your desktop following a PC Refresh. This will contain information about the traditional application's name along with a link that will take you to the manufacturer's website to download and reinstall it.

PERFORM A PC RESET

GET READY. To perform a PC Reset on Windows 8 client computer, log into the Windows 8 client computer with local Administrative privileges and then the following steps:

1. Press the **Windows logo key + w** and then type **Remove**.
2. In the *Results* list, choose **Remove everything and reinstall Windows**.
3. On the *Reset your PC* screen, click **Next**.
4. Click **Just remove my files** as shown in Figure 25-10.

Figure 25-10

Removing files

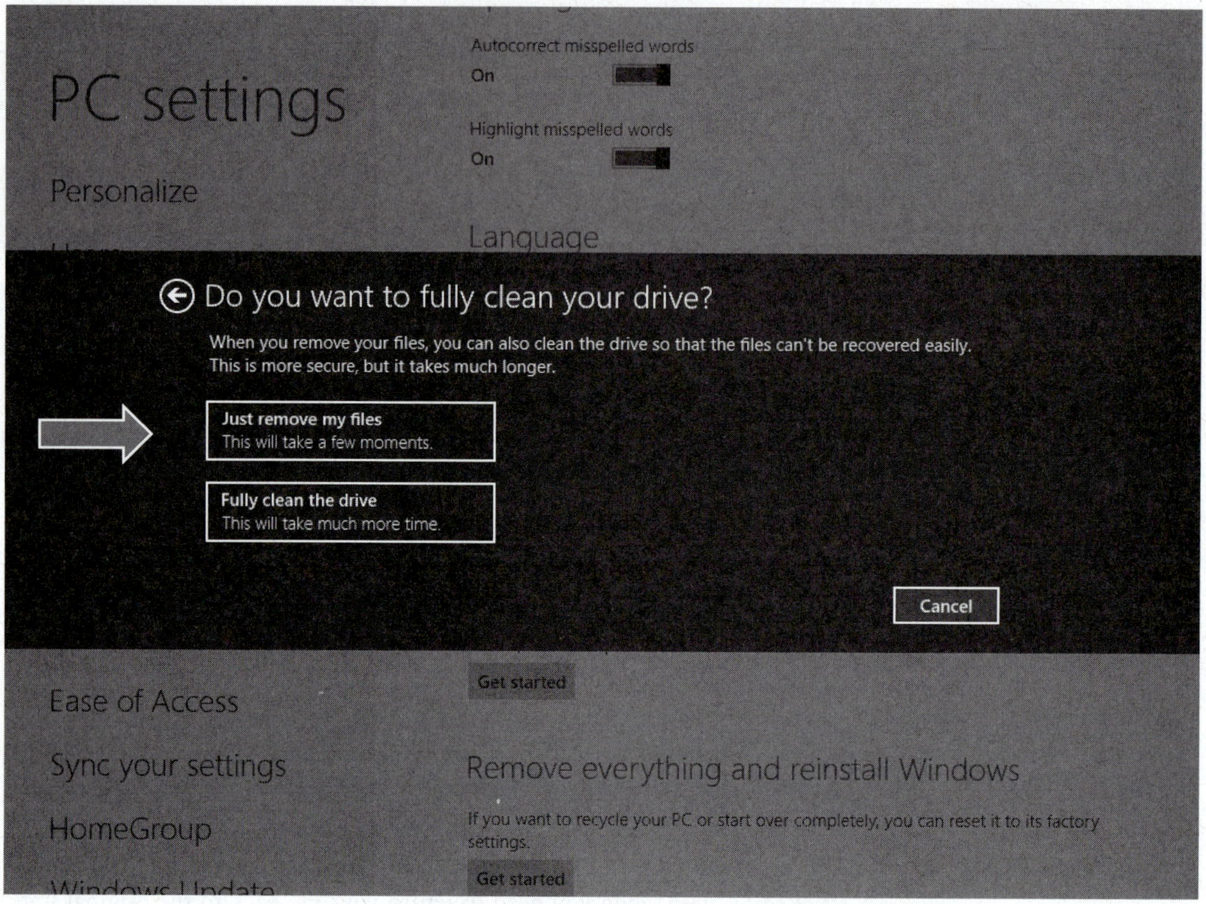

MORE INFORMATION

This process formats the drive; if the drive contains sensitive information, select fully clean the drive. This will write random patterns to each sector on the drive adding an additional level of protection.

5. On the *Ready to reset your PC* screen, read the information provided and then click **Reset**.
6. Read and select **I accept the license terms for using Windows,** and then click **Accept**.
7. Select a color scheme, type a name for your PC, and then click **Next**.
8. Select **Use express settings**.
9. Type your email address as a Microsoft Account and then click **Next**.
10. Type a password for your Microsoft Account and then click **Next**.
11. Type a phone number and an alternate email address, and then click **Next**.
12. Log into the Windows 8 client computer.

PERFORM A PC REFRESH

GET READY. To perform a PC Refresh on a Windows 8 client computer, Log into the Windows 8 client computer with local administrative privileges and then perform the following steps:

1. Press the **Windows logo key + w** and then type **Refresh**.
2. In the *Results* list, choose **Refresh your PC**.
3. Review the summary screen and then select **Next**.
4. Click **Refresh** and the system will restart.
5. If prompted, click **Yes** to turn on sharing and connect to devices.
6. Press the **Windows logo key** to toggle back to your desktop.
7. Double-click the **Removed Apps** link.
8. Review the lists of traditional apps that will need to be reinstalled as shown in Figure 25-11.

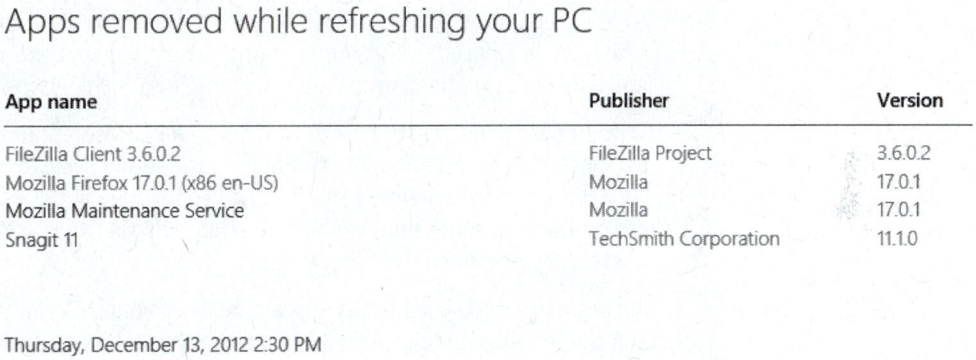

Figure 25-11

Reviewing *Apps removed while refreshing your PC*

MORE INFORMATION

Clicking on an app name will take you to the manufacturer's website where you can download and reinstall the app.

9. Reinstall any applications that you need.
10. Delete the **Removed Apps** link when you are done.

If you want to keep your settings and traditional applications, you can use a utility called ***recimg.exe.*** Recimg.exe captures an image of your PC, after you install the applications and make any personal customizations, and stores it in a folder you specify. The next time you perform a PC Refresh, the image is used and your settings and traditional apps are retained.

SKILL SUMMARY

IN THIS LESSON, YOU LEARNED:

- The Windows 8 Startup procees consists of the following phases: Power-on self test (POST), Windows Boot Manager, Windows Boot Loader, Kernel loading phase, and a logon phase.
- When a failure occurs during POST it means there is a problem with the BIOS configuration, storage subsystem, or file system.
- When a failure occurs just before the user logs on, the problem is most likely hardware related and associated with one of the drivers or services.
- When a failure occurs after you log in, the problem is most likely related to applications in the Startup group.

(continued)

- Windows 8 System Restore is a recovery option that that saves information about your drives, registry settings, programs and files in the form of restore points. These restore points are created automatically every 7 days but you can create the manually as well.
- The Last Known Good Configuration is available in Windows Server 2012 but is no longer available in Windows 8. You will need to boot into Safe Mode instead.
- To perform a complete system restore, you will need to create a system image. The system image is an exact copy of the drives required to run Windows 8. The option to create a system image is found in the Control Panel under Windows 7 File Recovery. You will need either a System Repair disc or your Windows installation media to restore the system image.
- When installing a device driver for a new piece of hardware, you have the option to perform a driver roll back. This reinstalls the last device driver that was functioning. The feature is not available if you have not updated the driver since it was first installed.
- A PC Reset is used when you need to return your PC back to the original state it was in when you purchased it. This removes any custom settings, erases your personal data and removes both traditional and Windows apps from the computer.
- A PC Refresh is less destructive compared to a PC Reset. It allows you to keep your personal data, your Windows Store apps, basic settings, custom personalization settings, your BitLocker and wireless settings. Once completed, an HTML file is placed on the desktop that provides links to the manufacturer's site to assist you in downloading and reinstalling your traditional applications.
- Recimg.exe can be used to capture an image of your PC after you have installed Windows and traditional applications and customized the system to your liking. The image is placed in a folder you specify and the next time you run a PC Refresh, the image will be used and your settings and traditional apps retained.

Knowledge Assessment

Multiple Choice

Select one or more correct answers for each of the following questions.

1. During which phase is the Boot Configuration Data (BCD) file read during startup?
- **a.** Windows Boot Loader phase
- **b.** Windows Boot Manager phase
- **c.** Hardware Abstraction Layer (HAL) phase
- **d.** POST phase

2. If a computer fails to make it through the POST successfully, the problem is related to what?
- **a.** Software related
- **b.** Hardware related
- **c.** Application related
- **d.** Permissions related

3. Which of the following are true regarding system restore points? (Choose all that apply.)
   a. Create them on a monthly basis.
   b. Create them prior to performing a major system event.
   c. Windows 8 creates them every 7 days if one has not been created during that time period.
   d. Windows 8 creates them every 3 days if one has not been created during that time period.
4. You want to boot into Safe Mode on Windows 8. Which of the following could you use? (Choose all that apply.)
   a. **Windows logo key + I > Change PC Settings > General > Click Restart Now** under Advanced Startup
   b. Press **F8** during startup
   c. Press **F9** during startup
   d. Type **shutdown /r /o** in the Run dialog box.
5. Which of the following tools would you use to create a system image that can be used for PC Refresh?
   a. Windows 8 File Recovery
   b. Windows 7 File Recovery
   c. Reimg.exe
   d. Recimg.exe
6. Which of the following can be used to restore a system image created using the Windows 7 File Recovery option? (Choose all that apply.)
   a. Recimg.exe
   b. Windows 8 installation media
   c. Windows 8 System repair disc
   d. Windows 8 System recover disc
7. You want to create a policy that can be used to control the installation of unsigned drivers on Windows 8 client computers in your domain. Which of the following are options you can set? (Choose all that apply.)
   a. Warn
   b. Ignore
   c. Block
   d. Alert
8. Which option would you recommend to make sure your Windows 8 traditional applications are not lost during a restore?
   a. PC Reset
   b. PC Refresh with recimg.exe
   c. PC Reset with recimg.exe
   d. PC Refresh with recoverimg.exe
9. Which of the following will create an HTML file on your desktop that contains links to traditional applications where they can be downloaded?
   a. PC Reset
   b. Recimg.exe
   c. PC Refresh
   d. PC Reset with recimg.exe
10. What entity is responsible for making sure driver files for Windows 8 are compatible with the operating system and will not impact the stability of the operating system?
    a. Microsoft
    b. Windows Hardware Quality Labs
    c. Windows Software Quality Labs
    d. Windows Quality Driver Labs

Best Answer

Choose the letter that corresponds to the best answer. More than one answer choice may achieve the goal. Select the BEST answer.

1. A user calls the help desk and indicates their Windows 8 computer is failing right after they enter their logon credentials. Other complaints from users indicate the problem is related to a new program that is in the Startup Group. Which option is the best approach to use to resolve the problem in the most efficient way?
   a. Use a system restore point to return the system to a previous point in time that it was functioning.
   b. Perform a Complete Restore.
   c. Boot into Safe Mode and use the Task Manager to disable the new program.
   d. PC Reset.

2. A user wants to be able to restore traditional applications on their Windows 8 client computer should a problem occur in the future. Which combination of tools should be used for this task that will make the process as simple as possible and require the least amount of administrative effort?
   a. Create an image with Windows 7 File Recovery and use a Windows 8 media disc.
   b. Run Recimg.exe and use PC Refresh to restore.
   c. Run Windows 7 File Recovery only.
   d. Run Recimg.exe only.

3. A user is unable to log into their Windows 8 client computer. Which option could be used to gain access as quickly as possible to begin the troubleshooting process?
   a. Boot from a Windows 8 Recovery drive.
   b. Select the **Windows logo key + I**.
   c. Select the **Windows logo key + R** and type **shutdown /r /o**.
   d. Restart and press **F8**.

4. A user makes major changes to their Windows 8 client computer every two days. How frequently should they create a system restore point?
   a. Every 2 days.
   b. Let Windows 8 create it automatically based on its default schedule.
   c. Every 5 days.
   d. Every day.

5. A PC Refresh has just been completed on a user's Windows 8 client computer. What is the best way to reinstall traditional applications that were removed from the computer during the refresh?
   a. Refer to your notes on what was original installed on the computer.
   b. Contact your system administrator to see if they can provide a software inventory of what was on the system prior to the refresh.
   c. Refer to the HTML file on the desktop that was created as part of the refresh process.
   d. Ask the user of the computer what was original installed on their system.

Matching and Identification

Complete the following exercise by matching the terms with their corresponding definitions.

_______ **a)** Recimg.exe
_______ **b)** PC Reset
_______ **c)** PC Refresh
_______ **d)** Restore point
_______ **e)** Last Known Good Configuration
_______ **f)** POST

________ g) Driver Rollback
________ h) Windows Boot Loader phase
________ i) Registry
________ j) Windows Boot Manager phase

1. The Boot Configuration Data (BCD) file is read during this phase of startup.
2. Hardware self-test procedure is run during this phase of startup.
3. Used in combination with PC Refresh to restore your settings and traditional applications.
4. Should be created prior to performing any major system event. Allow you to return to a point in time.
5. Used to return your system to the state it was in when you purchased it or first set it up.
6. A database used by Windows to store information on services, installed programs and their settings, user profiles and system hardware.
7. Windows kernel, HAL, and the system registry hive are loaded during this phase of startup.
8. Creates an HTML file on your desktop after it completes the restore process
9. This feature is no longer available in Windows 8.
10. Allows you to reinstall the last device driver that was functioning.

Build a List

1. In order of first to last, specify the six steps used to roll back a device driver:
   ________ Press the **Windows logo key + w** and then type **Device Manager**.
   ________ Right-click the device and then choose **Properties**.
   ________ Log into the Windows 8 client computer with administrative credentials
   ________ Expand the category of devices and locate the device that uses the driver you want to roll back.
   ________ Click the **Drivers** tab.
   ________ Click **Roll Back Driver**.

2. List the steps, in the correct order, used to create a Windows 8 System Repair disc.
   ________ Press the **Windows logo key + w** and then type **Windows 7 File Recovery**.
   ________ Select the CD/DVD drive, insert a blank disc and then click **Create disc**.
   ________ In the *Results* list, choose **Windows 7 File Recovery**.
   ________ In the Using the system repair disc dialog box that appears, read the information provided about labeling the disc and then click **Close**.
   ________ Click **Create a system repair disc**.
   ________ Log into the Windows 8 client computer with administrative credentials
   ________ After the message *System repair disc complete* appears, click **OK**.
   ________ Eject and label the disc and store it in a safe place

3. In order of first to last, specify the steps needed to boot into Safe Mode with Networking.
   ________ On the *Choose an option* screen, click the **Troubleshoot** tile.
   ________ On the *Advanced options* screen, click the **Startup Settings** tile.
   ________ On the *Startup Settings* screen, click **Restart**.
   ________ On the *Troubleshoot* screen, click the **Advanced options** tile.
   ________ Choose **#5-Enable Safe Mode with Networking**.
   ________ Log into the Windows 8 client computer with your administrator credentials and password. The word *Safe Mode* should appear in all four corners of your screen.
   ________ Boot into your computer from your Windows 8 installation media and select **Repair Your Computer**.

Business Case Scenarios

Scenario 25-1: Troubleshooting a Device Driver Roll Back

A Windows 8 client computer is having problems with an HP LaserJet printer. The device driver is rolled back to see if this resolves the problem. After accessing the properties for the device, the option to roll back the device is greyed out. What could be causing this problem?

Scenario 25-2: Restoring the Missing Apps

Tom receives a call while working on the help desk from a Windows 8 user. The user informs Tom that Elliot, one of the junior administrators, just repaired his computer but he can no longer find some of the applications that were once installed on the computer. After talking to the junior administrator, Tom discovers that Elliot used the PC Refresh option. How should Tom respond to the user?

Configuring File Recovery Options

LESSON 26

70-687 EXAM OBJECTIVE

Objective 7.3 – Configure file recovery options. This objective may include but is not limited to: configure file restore points; restore previous versions of files and folders; configure File History.

Technology Skill	Objective Domain
Overview of Windows 8 File Recovery Options	
Configuring File History	Configure File History
Restoring Files and Folders	Restore previous versions of files and folders
Configuring File Restore Points	Configure file restore points

KEY TERMS

File History **restore point** **volume shadow snapshot**

Overview of Windows 8 File Recovery Options

THE BOTTOM LINE

The capability to recover files and folders when they become corrupt or accidentally deleted has been available in versions of Windows for some time. Windows 8, however, provides two main methods for recovering files and folders. Neither of these methods is intended to be a replacement for an enterprise-wide backup solution; however, they are quick, convenient, and useful for small-scale use.

The primary method of file recovery for use on a Windows 8 client machine is the Windows 8 ***File History*** feature. The alternative, Windows 7 File recovery feature, is provided as the replacement for Windows Backup. The Windows 7 File recovery feature allows for files backed up on previous versions of Windows to be recovered to Windows 8 and the facility to back up files in a more traditional manner. It is important to note that these features are not intended to be run together. If File History is switched on, then Windows 7 File Recovery cannot be used until it is switched off.

MORE INFORMATION

Since Windows Server 2003, Windows users have used ***volume shadow snapshots*** of their files to save and recover historic data. This feature was also available in Windows XP, Vista, and all versions of Windows 7, and was called Previous Versions. In Windows 8, it is renamed File History.

Configure File History

File History is available on all versions of Windows 8 and simply requires switching on and configuring.

CERTIFICATION READY
Configure File History
Objective 7.3

File History is the primary feature Windows 8 uses to ensure that accidental deletion or corruption does not permanently prevent you from accessing files. In addition, it is possible to retrieve a version created at an earlier point in time. If you make changes that you need to remove, File History allows you to restore the previous version of a file, either to its original location, thereby overwriting the original, or to an alternative folder.

CONFIGURE FILE HISTORY

GET READY. Log on to the Windows 8 computer with administrative privileges. To configure the File History feature, perform the following steps:

1. From the Start screen, type **File History**, and then click **Settings**. Figure 26-1 shows the File History options on the Search Results screen.

Figure 26-1

Enabling File History—Search Results screen

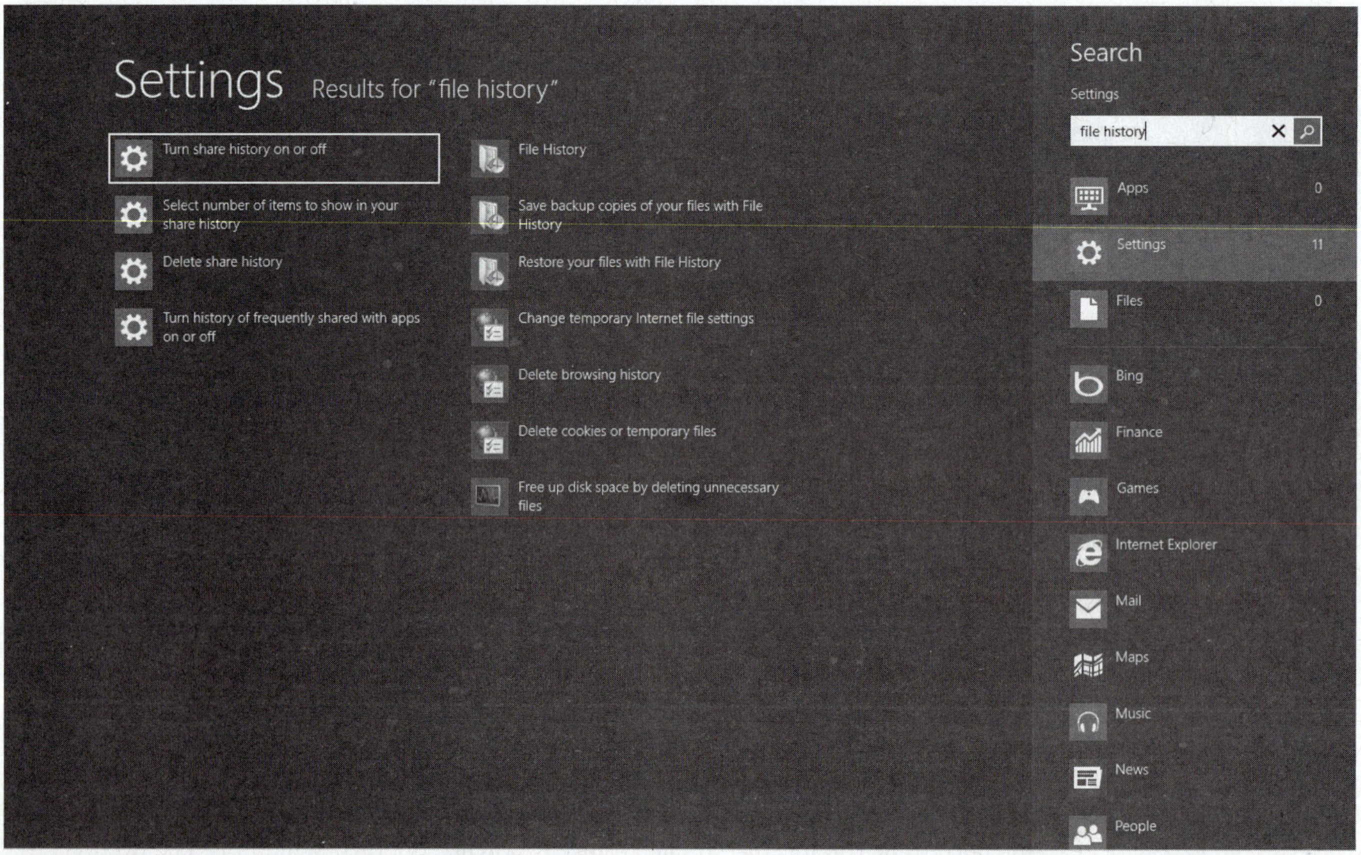

2. Click **File History** and the File History section of the Control Panel opens on the desktop. Figure 26-2 shows that File History is off by default and recommends an external drive is used.

Figure 26-2

Enabling File History—Control Panel options

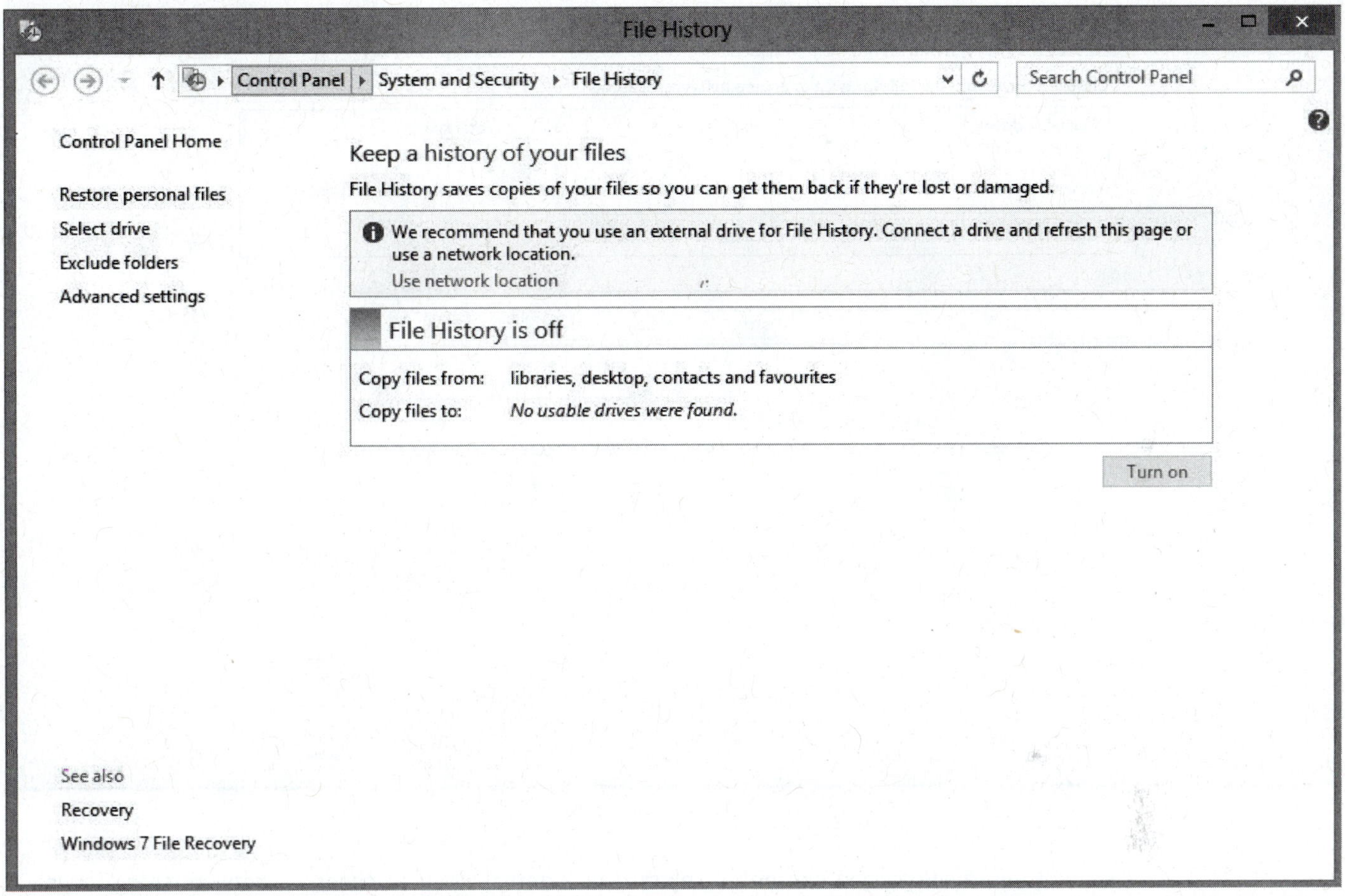

3. Click **Select Drive** and the Select a File History Drive window opens. If there are no external drives connected to the computer, the only available option, as shown in Figure 26-3, is Add a Network Location.

Figure 26-3

Enabling File History—
selecting a File History drive

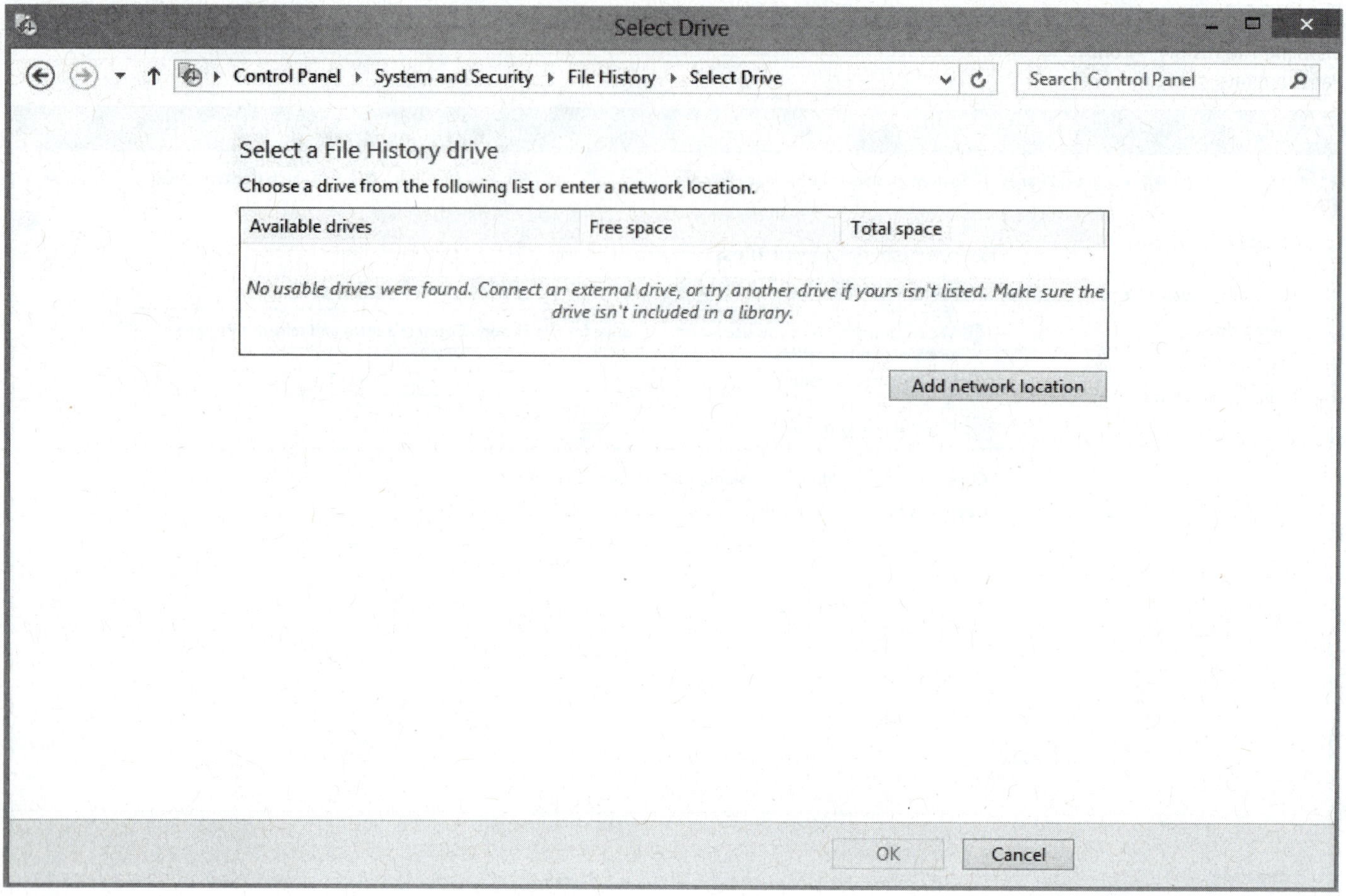

4. Go ahead and either select your external drive or choose a network share to use as your File History Drive and Click **OK**

5. Having chosen your File History Drive, the next step is to configure the advanced settings. Click **Advanced Settings**. The available options are shown below in Figure 26-4.

MORE INFORMATION

The Advanced settings window allows the selection of three important options: how often the copies are saved (from 10 minutes to once a day, default is hourly); what percentage of your own internal drive is reserved for using as a cache when the File History drive is offline; (default is 5% with options between 2% and 20%); and how long the saved versions are kept (default is Forever with the option range from Until space is needed to 2 years). In addition, this window allows the user to join a Homegroup and recommend the File History drive to other users, clean up older versions of the File History, and view File History event logs.

Figure 26-4

Enabling File History—Advanced settings

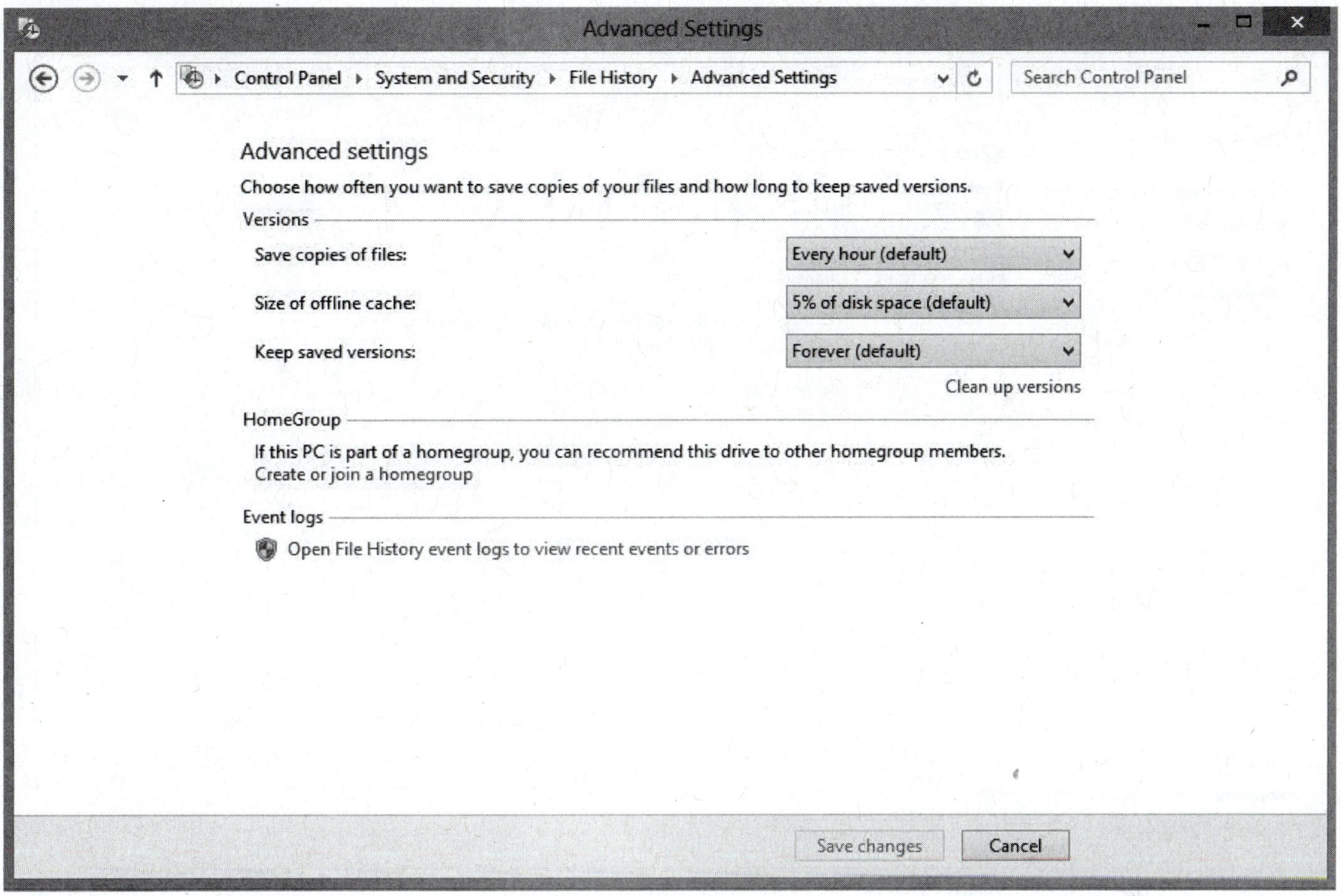

6. Having set your advanced options, the next step is to exclude any files and folders that you do not want to save. Click **Exclude Folders**.

   Here, you can add folders to an exclusion list to prevent them being saved on your File History drive.

7. Click **Save Changes** or cancel.

   Your File History settings are now complete.

8. Click **Turn On**.

   File History now runs at the specified intervals set in advanced settings. To run on demand, return to this window and click **Run Now**. Figure 26-5 shows the File History in a configured and operational state.

Figure 26-5

Enabling File History—operational state

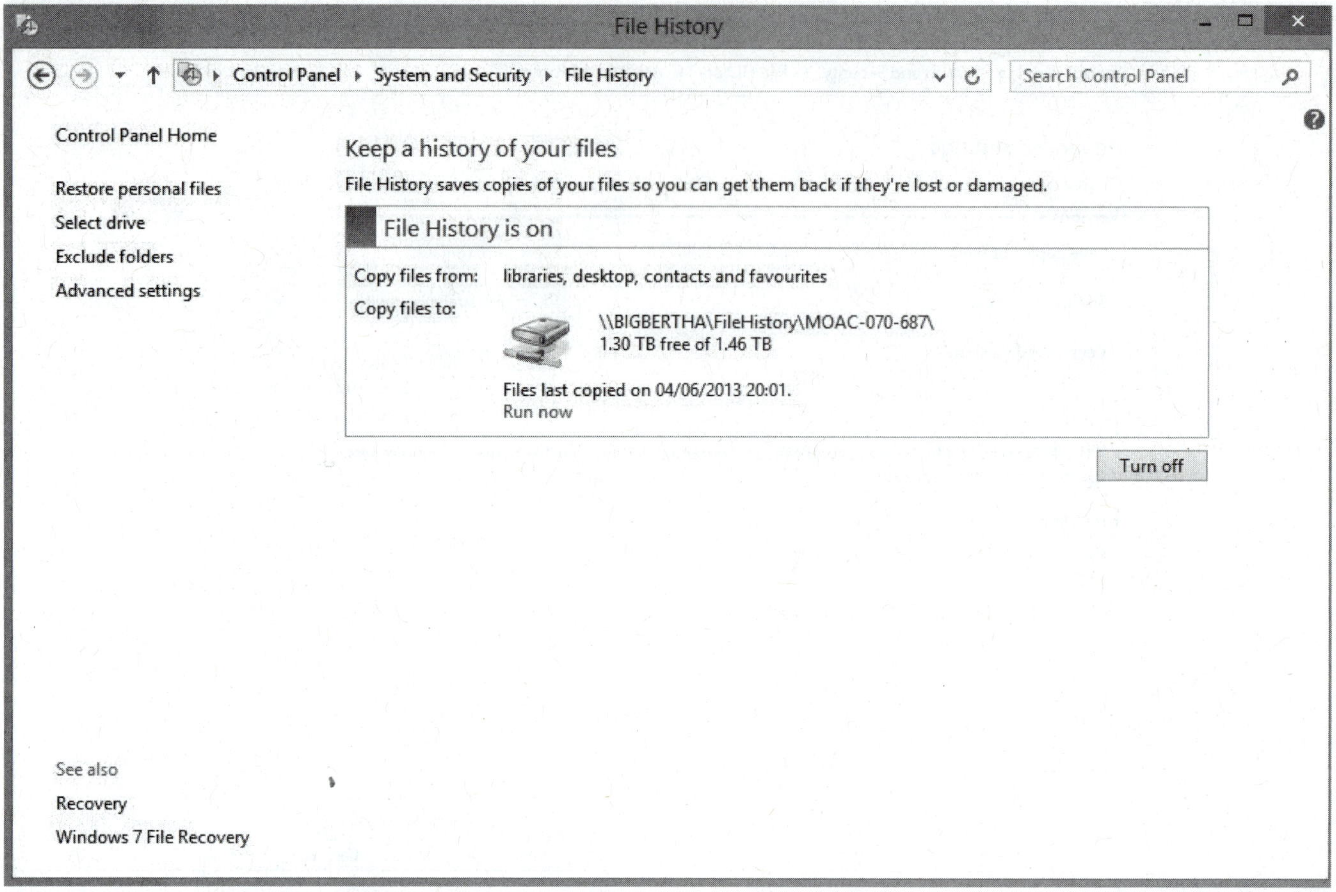

TAKE NOTE*

The Windows 8 File History feature replaces Windows Backup available in previous versions of Windows. If a user prefers to use a traditional backup utility, the Windows 7 program is still available by clicking on Windows 7 File Recovery on the File History screen.

Restoring Files and Folders

Having configured File History, all your previous versions are now available to recover should they become corrupted or should you accidentally delete them.

CERTIFICATION READY
Restore previous versions of files and folders
Objective 7.3

A noted, File History allows you to preserve a number of versions of your files and folders so that you can restore them at a later time. This replaces the need to have a dedicated backup program or utility. Once you have identified the need to restore files from a previous point in time, the Restore files and folders section of File History allows the safe recovery of those important files and folders, which may have become lost or corrupt.

RESTORE FILES AND FOLDERS

GET READY. Log on to the Windows 8 computer with administrative privileges. To restore files and folders from your File History drive, perform the following steps:

1. From the Start screen, type **Restore**, and then click **Settings**. Figure 26-6 shows the Restore options on the Search screen results.

Figure 26-6

Restoring Files and folders—Search screen results

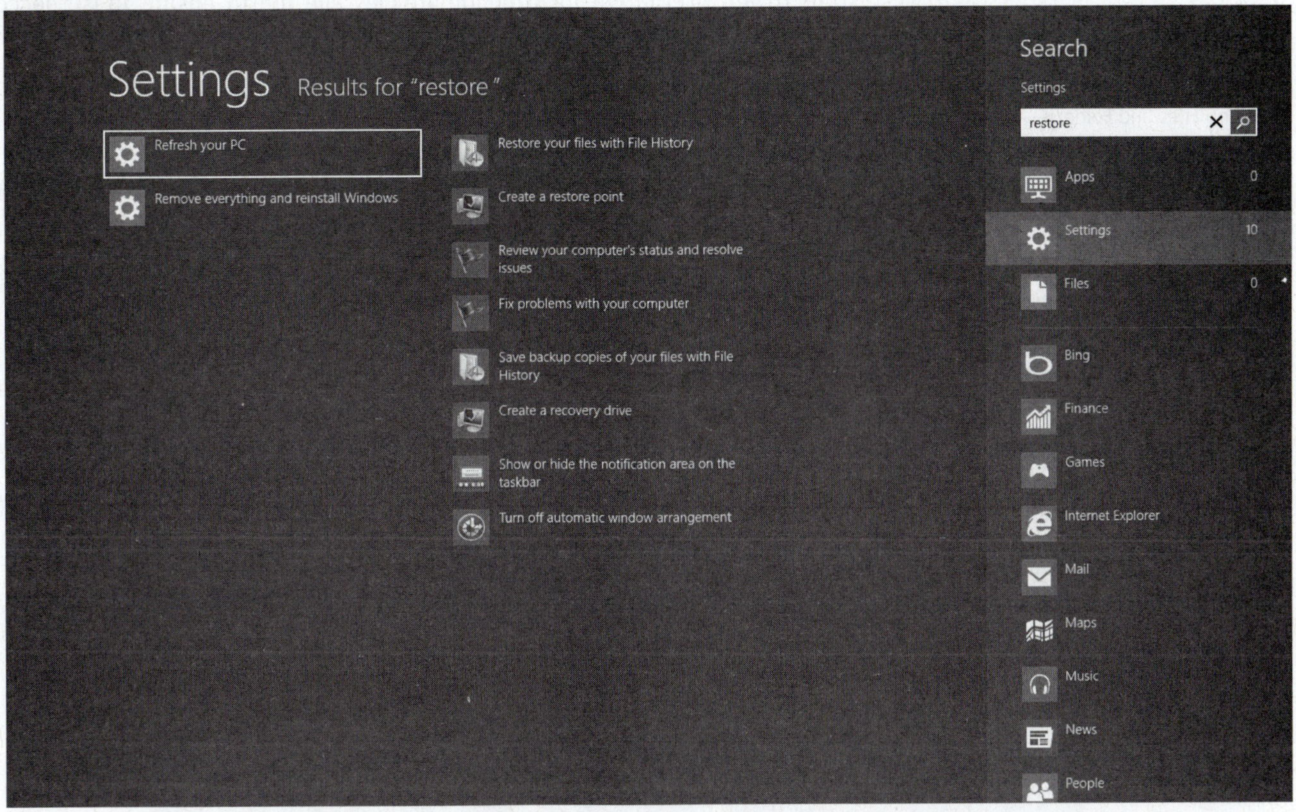

2. Click **Restore your files with File History** and the File History Home screen opens on the Windows 8 desktop. Figure 26-7 shows the File History Home screen and the files and folders that are available to restore.

Figure 26-7

Restoring Files and Folders—File History Home Screen

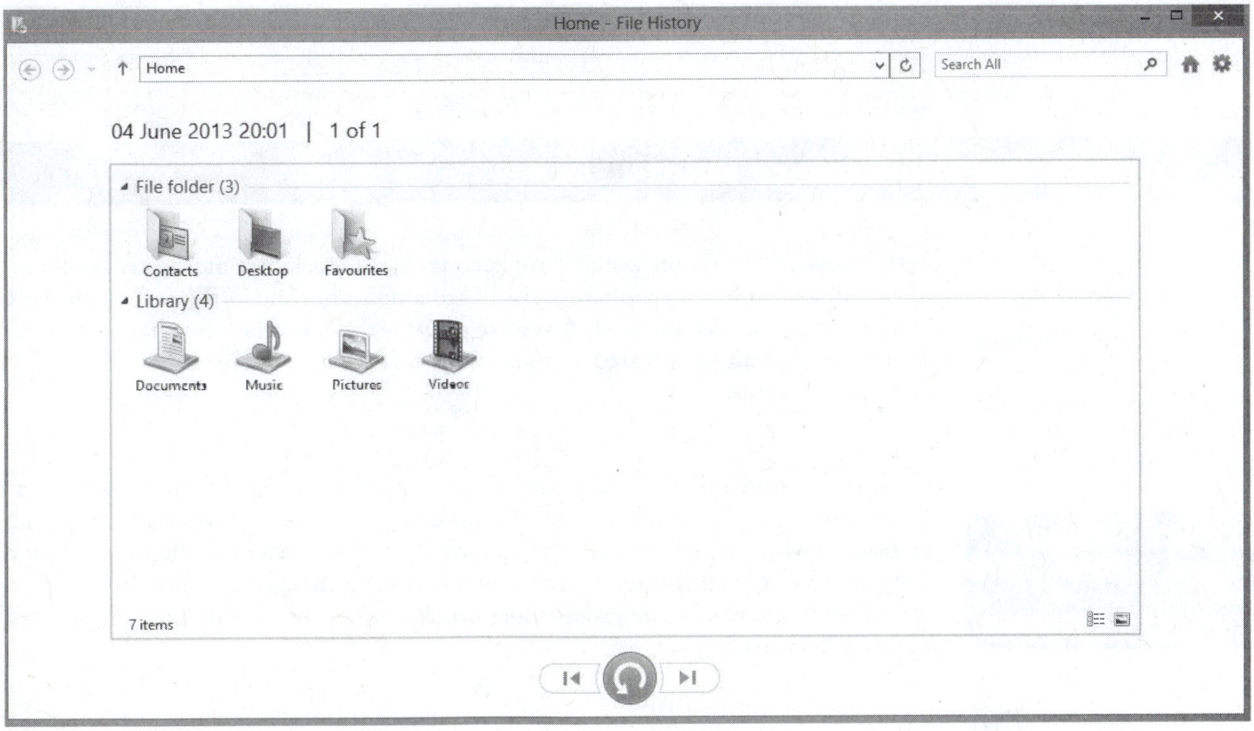

Click the relevant file or folder to restore and then click on the Green Button in the middle of the bottom of the window. This restores the chosen files and folders to their original locations. If you right-click the file or folder, you can restore to an alternative location or preview the file to ensure it is the correct version before restoring it. Figure 26-8 shows an example of the File Preview window.

Figure 26-8

Restoring Files and Folders—File Preview

Configuring File Restore Points

THE BOTTOM LINE

System restore and restore points have been around for a long time. System restore is a feature that enables a user to return his PC to a point in time in the past when the system was working as it was intended. A ***restore point*** is the bookmark for that point in time. Some restore points are created automatically; it is possible to create and configure your own restore points.

CERTIFICATION READY
Configure file restore points
Objective 7.3

The use of restore points is a key part of ensuring that your Windows 8 system files may be restored to a previous point in time. A restore point enables you to select a date and time to go back to when restoring a file. This doesn't revert your system to the time before you may have installed some software or when you might have changed a device driver or just made a restore point manually. The process does not recover or replace any files or folders. That is the role of File History.

CONFIGURE FILE RESTORE POINTS

GET READY. Log on to the Windows 8 computer with administrative privileges. To configure a file restore point, perform the following steps:

1. From the Start screen, type **Restore Point**, and then click **Settings**. Figure 26-9 shows the Restore Point options on the Search Results screen.

Figure 26-9

Configuring restore points—Search Results screen

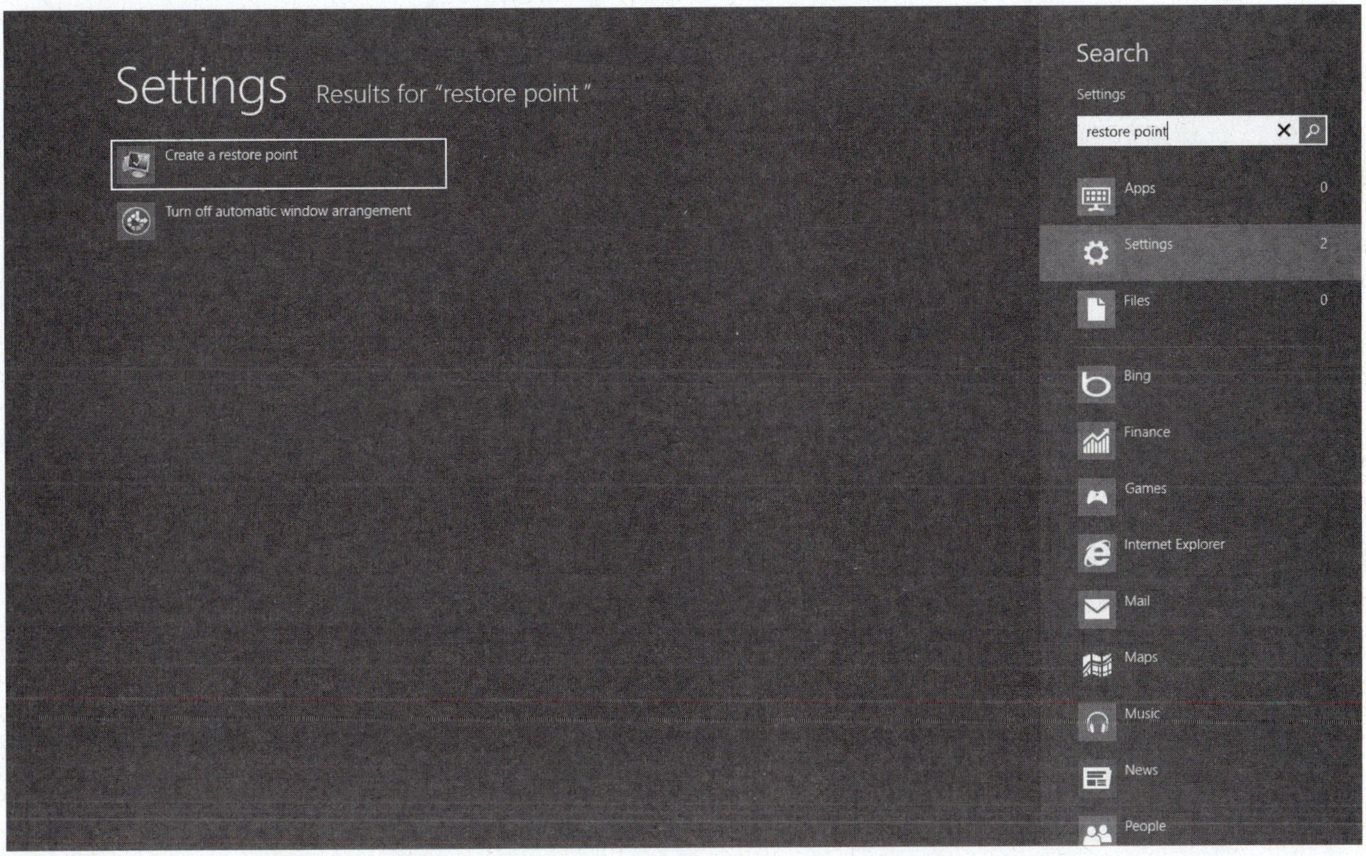

2. Click Create and enter a title for the restore point. Figure 26-10 shows the Restore Point Creation dialog in System protection. Click Create again.

   The restore point is created.

Figure 26-10

Configuring a restore point

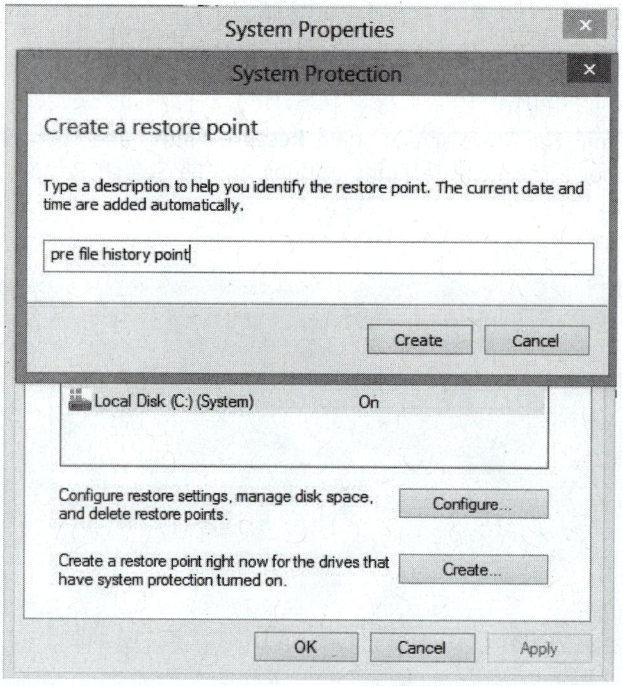

Once system protection has been turned on, several configuration items can be set. The first is that you can select the percentage of the hard disk that will be used to hold system protection information. System protection uses Volume shadow service snapshots to keep important files safe from corruption or deletion. It is also possible to delete restore points to free up space for new ones.

Having configured the system restore points, it is then possible from the system protection window to restore the system to a previous point in time. This is not the same as the modern application interface for refreshing and resetting your PC.

SKILL SUMMARY

IN THIS LESSON, YOU LEARNED:

- How to enable the File History feature on Windows 8 using the Start screen and Control Panel.
- How to configure a File History drive on Windows 8.
- How to configure an excluded folder for File History on Windows 8.
- How to configure advanced settings for File History on Windows 8.
- How to restore Files and Folders using the File History home screen on Windows 8.
- How to preview files prior to restoring them using the File History Home screen on Windows 8.
- How to configure a file restore point using System protection on Windows 8.

Knowledge Assessment

Multiple Choice

1. Where is the File History stored if the File History drive is offline?
   a. Nowhere. File History is off.
   b. On a network share
   c. On a different external drive
   d. System drive cache
2. Which is the default retention period for File History files and folders?
   a. 1 year
   b. 1 month
   c. Forever
   d. 2 years
3. How do you advertise a File History drive to other computer users?
   a. Email
   b. Network share
   c. HomeGroup
   d. File transfer
4. Which is the built-in alternative solution to Windows 8 File History?
   a. File Backup
   b. NTBackup.exe
   c. Windows Server Backup
   d. Windows 7 File recovery
5. To prepare a PC to recover to a previous point in time, what do you start?
   a. Restore a backup.
   b. Recover Windows 7 files.
   c. Enable system protection.
   d. Create a restore point.

Best Answer

Choose the letter that corresponds to the best answer. More than one answer choice may achieve the goal. Select the BEST answer.

1. Which of the following should be used as a File History drive?
   a. External hard disk
   b. USB Flash drive
   c. Network share
   d. Internal hard disk
2. Which method should be used to preserve files and folders in Windows?
   a. Windows 7 File Recovery
   b. System Protection
   c. Previous versions
   d. File History
3. What percentage of your system drive should be reserved for an offline cache (when the File History drive is not available)?
   a. 1%
   b. 10%
   c. 20%
   d. 5%

Matching and Identification

1. Identify which of the following tasks you can accomplish with File History in Windows 8.
   ________ Create a recovery disk
   ________ NTBackup.exe
   ________ Create a File History Drive
   ________ Backup the system state
   ________ Restore Files and Folders
   ________ Preview a file
   ________ Create file restore points

Build a list

1. Specify the correct order of steps necessary to create a Local Group recover files using file history. (Not all steps will be used.)
   ________ Enter Restore files at the start screen.
   ________ Choose settings.
   ________ Run Windows 7 File recovery.
   ________ Select the relevant files.
   ________ Create a File History drive.
   ________ Restore files.
   ________ Select Restore my files.

■ Business Case Scenarios

Scenario 26-1: Choosing How to Preserve Files

To ensure that a user does not lose her important documents and files on a Windows 8 PC, what should you choose to do?

Scenario 26-2: Choosing a Way of Recovering the System

To ensure a user can revert his PC back to a particular point in time, what would you recommend?

Scenario 26-3: Recovering Files

A Windows 8 user needs help. The user has encountered file corruption in some important work documents. How would you assist him?

Appendix A

Exam 70-687 Configuring Windows 8

Exam Objective	Objective Number	Lesson Number
Install and Upgrade to Windows 8		
Evaluate Hardware Readiness and Compatibility	1.1	1
Install Windows 8	1.2	2
Migrate and Configure User Data	1.3	3
Configure Hardware and Applications		
Configure Devices and Device Drivers	2.1	4
Install and Configure Desktop Applications	2.2	5
Install and Configure Windows Store Applications	2.3	6
Control Access to Local Hardware and Applications	2.4	7
Configure Internet Explorer	2.5	8
Configure Hyper-V	2.6	9
Configure Network Connectivity		
Configure IP Settings	3.1	10
Configure Networking Settings	3.2	11
Configure and Maintain Network Security	3.3	12
Configure Remote Management	3.4	13
Configure Access to Resources		
Configure Shared Resources	4.1	14
Configure File and Folder Access	4.2	15
Configure Local Security Settings	4.3	16
Configure Authentication and Authorization	4.4	17
Configure Remote Access and Mobility		
Configure Remote Connections	5.1	18
Configure Mobility Options	5.2	19
Configure Security for Mobile Devices	5.3	20
Monitor and Maintain Windows Clients		
Configure and Manage Updates	6.1	21
Manage Local Storage	6.2	22
Monitor System Performance	6.3	23
Configure Backup and Recovery Options		
Configure Backup	7.1	24
Configure System Recovery Options	7.2	25
Configure File Recovery Options	7.3	26

Index

Note: Page numbers followed by f and t indicates figure and table respectively.

E

L

M

N

R

T

U

V

W

Configuring Windows 8®
Exam 70-687

Lab Manual

Craig Zacker
Patrick Regan

WILEY

EXECUTIVE EDITOR	John Kane
EDITORIAL ASSISTANT	Allison Winkle
DIRECTOR OF SALES	Mitchell Beaton
EXECUTIVE MARKETING MANAGER	Chris Ruel
SENIOR PRODUCTION & MANUFACTURING MANAGER	Janis Soo
ASSOCIATE PRODUCTION MANAGER	Joel Balbin
PRODUCTION EDITOR	Eugenia Lee

www.wiley.com/college/microsoft or
call the MOAC Toll-Free Number: 888-764-7001 (U.S. & Canada only)

ISBN 978-1-118-55080-9

Printed in the United States of America

10 9 8 7 6 5 4 3 2 1

BRIEF CONTENTS

CONTENTS

LAB 1
EVALUATING HARDWARE READINESS AND CAPABILITY

THIS LAB CONTAINS THE FOLLOWING EXERCISES AND ACTIVITIES:

Exercise 1.1	Evaluating Your Machine
Exercise 1.2	Running the Upgrade Assistant
Lab Challenge	Reviewing Your Upgrade Options

BEFORE YOU BEGIN

The lab environment consists of student workstations connected to a local area network, along with a server that functions as the domain controller for a domain called adatum.com. The computers required for this lab are listed in Table 1-1.

Table 1-1
Computers Required for Lab 1

Computer	*Operating System*	*Computer Name*
Server	Windows Server 2012	SVR-DC-A
Client	Windows 7 Enterprise	WKSTN-MBR-D

In addition to the computers, you will also need the software listed in Table 1-2 to complete Lab 1.

Table 1-2
Software Required for Lab 1

Software	***Location***
Windows 8 Upgrade Assistant (Windows8-UpgradeAssistant.exe)	\\SVR-DC-A\software
Lab 1 student worksheet	Lab01_worksheet.docx (provided by instructor)

Working with Lab Worksheets

Each lab in this manual requires that you answer questions, shoot screen shots, and perform other activities that you will document in a worksheet named for the lab, such as Lab01_worksheet.docx. You will find these worksheets on the book companion site. It is recommended that you use a USB flash drive to store your worksheets so you can submit them to your instructor for review. As you perform the exercises in each lab, open the appropriate worksheet file, type the required information, and then save the file to your flash drive.

SCENARIO

After completing this lab, you will be able to:

- Use basic tools to evaluate your PC's hardware
- Run the Upgrade Assistant to determine if your machine can be upgraded to Windows 8

Estimated lab time: 35 minutes

Exercise 1.1	Evaluating Your Machine
Overview	In this exercise, you will use several built-in tools to view the current Windows version and hardware.
Mindset	Before you install or deploy Windows to a machine, you need identify what hardware the machine has and if that hardware meets the minimum requirements for Windows 8. An enterprise organization may have a software component that can perform inventory. However, you must still identify the hardware of a computer using the built-in tools that are included with Windows 8.
Completion time	10 minutes

1. On **WKSTN-MBR-D**, log on using the **adatum\administrator** account and the **Pa$$w0rd** password.
2. Click **Start**, then right-click **Computer** and choose **Properties**.

Question 1	*What version and edition of Windows are you using? Is it a 32-bit or 64-bit version of Windows*

Question 2	*How much memory does your system have?*

3. Close the *System* window.

4. Click the **Start** > **All Programs** > **Accessories** > **System Tools** > **System Information** (see Figure 1-1).

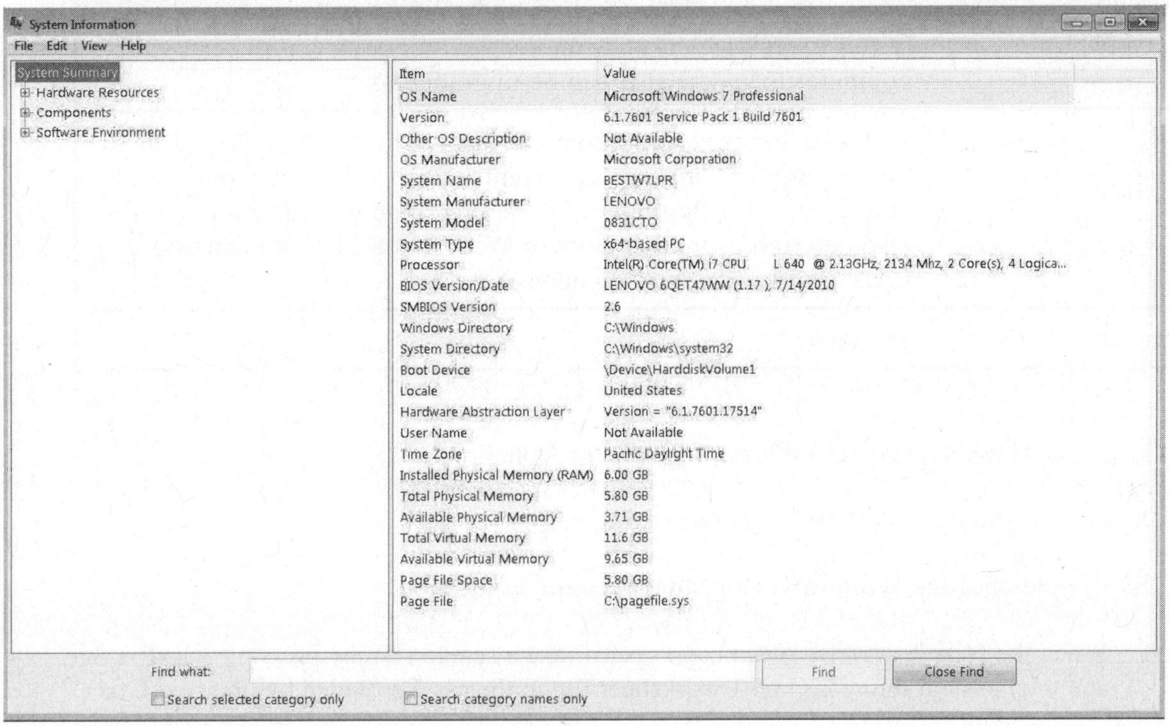

Figure 1-1
The System Information window

Question 3	*Which version are you using?*

Question 4	*Which processor or processors do you have?*

5. Close the *System Information* window.

6. On the Taskbar, click the **Windows Explorer** icon.

7. Click **Computer**.

Question 5	*How much disk space do you have on your C drive?*

End of exercise. Leave the computer logged into WKSTN-MBR-C for the next exercise.

Exercise 1.2	Running the Upgrade Assistant
Overview	In this exercise, you will run the upgrade assistant to scan your computer to see what it can be upgraded to.
Mindset	To make things easier for an end-user, Microsoft has developed the Windows 8 Upgrade Assistant, which scans the computer to determine if the computer can be upgraded to Windows 8 and also determines the versions of Windows 8 that you can upgrade to based on your upgrade needs.
Completion time	15 minutes

1. On the Taskbar, click the **Windows Explorer** icon.

2. Navigate to the **SVR-DC-A\software** folder.

3. Double-click the **Windows8-UpgradeAssistant** application.

4. When the *Here's what we found* page opens, take a screen shot by pressing **Alt+Prt Scr** and then paste it into your Lab 1 worksheet file in the page provided by pressing **Ctrl+V**.

5. Click **See compatibility details**.

Question 6	*Which items do you need to review?*

6. Click **Close**.

7. Click **Next**.

8. Log off of **WKSTN-MBR-C**.

Lab Challenge	Review Your Upgrade options
Overview	During this exercise, you will perform a written exercise to ensure that you understand the available installation and upgrade options.
Mindset	Prior to installing or deploying Windows, you must look at the hardware that you want to use and determine if the computer can handle Windows 8. If the hardware cannot, you will need to determine if you want to upgrade the current hardware, or replace the computer.
Completion time	10 minutes

For this written exercise, answer the following questions based on the given scenario.

1. You are visiting a client that has a computer running Windows 7. However, you do not know the specifications for the computer. What tool or option can you use to quickly view the computer name, domain name, processor information, installed memory, if the system is 32-bit or 64-bit, the edition of Windows, and if Windows 7 includes a service pack or not?

2. You are purchasing a computer with Windows 8. You need to be able to add the computer to an Active Directory Domain. You will need to be able to access shared folders and printers on the network, and you need to share your printer to other users. You will need to be able to run a virtual machine running Windows XP on the computer. You will also need to install Office 2013. What is the least expensive edition of Windows 8 that you will need?

3. What is the maximum number of processors that Windows 8 Professional can support?

4. You have a computer that has a Intel quad-core processor. Can you run Windows 8 Professional and will Windows be able to use all four cores?

5. You have an application that will require 8 GB of memory. What is the least expensive edition and version of Windows 8 that you can use for this application to run?

6. You want Windows 8 to use BranchCache. What is the least expensive edition of Windows 8 that you can use?

7. You have a computer running Windows 7 Professional. Which version of Windows can you perform an in-place upgrade to?

8. You have Windows Vista. You want to upgrade to Windows 8 while keeping all of the applications. How should you upgrade the system?

End of lab.

LAB 2
INSTALLING WINDOWS 8

THIS LAB CONTAINS THE FOLLOWING EXERCISES AND ACTIVITIES:

Exercise 2.1 Performing a Clean Windows 8 Installation

Exercise 2.2 Joining a Domain

Lab Challenge Upgrading Windows 7 to Windows 8

BEFORE YOU BEGIN

The lab environment consists of computers connected to a local area network. The computers required for this lab are listed in Table 2-1.

Table 2-1
Computers Required for Lab 2

Computer	***Operating System***	***Computer Name***
Server	Windows Server 2012	SVR-DC-A
New workstation	Bare Metal	WKSTN-MBR-B
Workstation for upgrade	Windows 7 Enterprise	WKSTN-MBR-D

In addition to the computers, you will also need the software listed in Table 2-2 to complete Lab 2.

Table 2-2
Software Required for Lab 2

Software	***Location***
Installation disk for Windows 8 Enterprise	Mounted on WKSTN-MBR-B
Installation disk for Windows 8 Enterprise	Mounted on WKSTN-MBR-D
Lab 2 student worksheet	Lab02_worksheet.docx (provided by instructor)

Working with Lab Worksheets

Each lab in this manual requires that you answer questions, create screenshots, and perform other activities that you will document in a worksheet named for the lab, such as Lab02_worksheet.docx. You will find these worksheets on the book companion site. It is recommended that you use a USB flash drive to store your worksheets so you can submit them to your instructor for review. As you perform the exercises in each lab, open the appropriate worksheet file, type the required information, and then save the file to your flash drive.

SCENARIO

After completing this lab, you will be able to:

- Perform a clean Windows 8 installation on a bare metal computer
- Join a Windows 8 workstation to an Active Directory Domain Services domain
- Upgrade a Windows 7 workstation to Windows 8

Estimated lab time: 60 minutes

Exercise 2.1	Performing a Clean Windows 8 Installation
Overview	In this exercise, you will install Windows 8 on a new computer that has no previously installed operating system.
Mindset	In many cases, organizations purchase computers without operating systems installed—sometimes called bare metal workstations—either because they have an existing license agreement or because they intend to purchase the operating system (OS) through a different channel. In these cases, you perform what is known as a clean operating system installation, which is a procedure that creates a new server with the default operating system settings.
Completion time	30 minutes

1. Select the **WKSTN-MBR-B** computer, on which the Windows 8 installation disk is mounted and loaded. The *Windows Setup* page appears.

2. Accept the default values for the *Language to install* setting, the *Time and currency format* setting, and the *Keyboard or input method* setting by clicking **Next**. Another *Windows Setup* page appears.

3. Click the **Install now** button. The *License terms* page appears.

4. Select *I accept the license terms* and then click **Next**. The *Which type of installation do you want?* page appears.

5. Click **Custom: Install Windows only (advanced)**. The *Where do you want to install Windows?* page appears (see Figure 2-1).

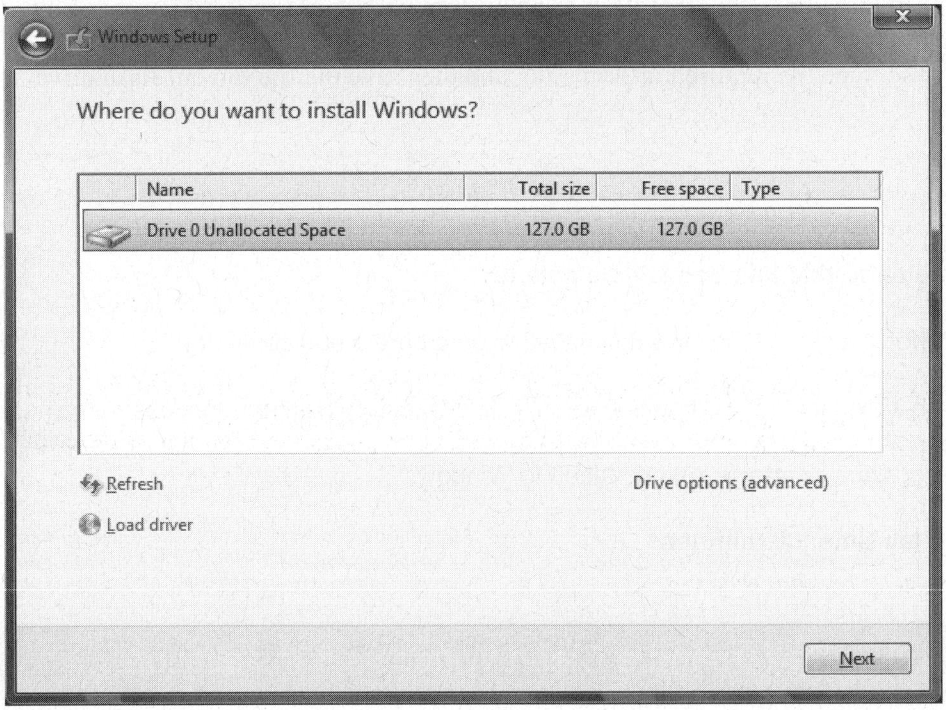

Figure 2-1
The *Where do you want to install Windows?* page

6. Leave **Drive 0 Unallocated Space** selected and then click **Next**. The *Installing Windows* page appears as the system installs Windows 8.

Question 1	*What should you do if the drive on which you want to install Windows 8 already has a partition on it containing an operating system and data you do not need?*

Question 2	*What should you do if the* Where do you want to install Windows? *page appears, but it does not list any drives or partitions?*

7. After several minutes and a system restart, the *Personalize* page appears.

8. In the *PC name* textbox, type **WKSTN-MBR-B** and then click **Next**. The *Settings* page appears.

9. Click **Use express settings**. The *Sign in to your PC* page appears.

10. Click **Sign in without a Microsoft account**. Another *Sign in to your PC page* appears.

11. Click **Local account**. The next *Sign in to your PC page* appears (see Figure 2-2).

12. Take a screen shot of the *Sign in to your PC page* by pressing **Alt+Prt Scr** and then paste it into your Lab 2 worksheet file in the page provided by pressing **Ctrl+V**.

13. In the *User name* text box, type **ocox**. In the *Password* text box and in the *Reenter password* text box, type **Pa$$w0rd**. In the *Password hint* text box, type **ocox** and then click Finish. After a brief introduction to Windows 8, the Start screen appears.

End of exercise. Leave all windows open for the next exercise.

Exercise 2.2	Joining a Domain
Overview	In this exercise, you will join your newly installed Windows 8 workstation to your network's Active Directory Domain Services domain.
Mindset	To function in an enterprise environment, Windows 8 workstations typically must be part of an Active Directory domain. An administrator must join the workstation to the domain by supplying appropriate credentials.
Completion time	10 minutes

1. Click the **Desktop** tile, mouse over the lower-left corner of the desktop and then right-click the **Start** screen thumbnail that appears there. Then, from the context menu that appears, click **Control Panel**. The *Control Panel* window appears.

2. Click **Network** and **Internet** > **Network and Sharing Center**. The *Network and Sharing Center* window appears.

3. Click **Change adapter settings**. The *Network Connections* window appears.

4. Right-click the **Ethernet** connection and choose **Properties**. The *Ethernet Properties* sheet appears.

5. Double-click **Internet Protocol Version 4 (TCP/IPv4)**. The *Internet Protocol Version 4 (TCP/IPv4) Properties* sheet appears.

6. Select the **Use the following IP address** option and then type values in the following text boxes:

   - *IP address:* **10.0.0.2**
   - *Subnet mask:* **255.255.255.0**

7. Select the **Use the following DNS server addresses** option and then type a value in the following text box:

   - *Preferred DNS server:* **10.0.0.1**

8. Click **OK** to close the *Internet Protocol Version 4 (TCP/IPv4) Properties* sheet.

9. Click **OK** to close the *Ethernet Properties* sheet.

10. Close the *Network Connections* window. Click the Control Panel Home link in the left pane.

11. In *Control Panel*, click **System and Security > System**. The *System* control panel appears.

12. Click **Change settings**. The *System Properties* sheet appears.

13. Click **Change**. The *Computer Name/Domain Changes* dialog box appears (see Figure 2-2).

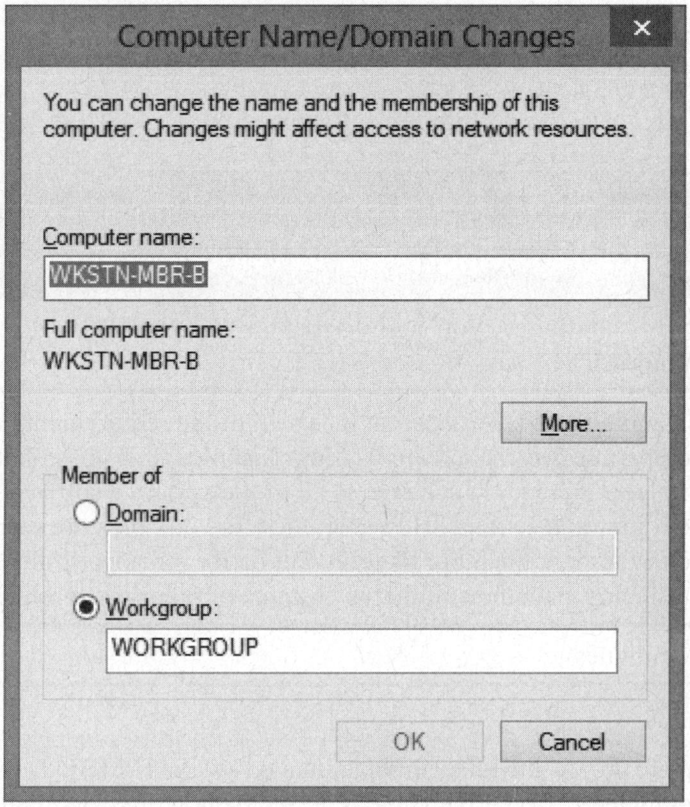

Figure 2-2
The *Computer Name/Domain Changes* dialog box

14. Select the **Domain** option, type **adatum.com** in the text box, and then click **OK**. A *Windows Security* dialog box appears.

Question 3	*What is the primary reason for the joining to a domain to fail at this point?*

15. Authenticate with a *User name* of **Administrator** and a *Password* of **Pa$$w0rd** and then click **OK**. A message box appears, welcoming you to the domain.

16. Take a screen shot of the message box by pressing **Alt+Prt Scr** and then paste it into your Lab 2 worksheet file in the page provided by pressing **Ctrl+V**.

17. Click **OK**. Another message box appears, prompting you to restart the computer.

18. Click **OK**.

19. Click **Close** to close the *System Properties* dialog box.

20. A *You must restart your computer to apply these changes* message box appears.

21. Click **Restart Now**. The computer restarts.

End of exercise.

Lab Challenge	Upgrading Windows 7 to Windows 8
Overview	In this challenge, you will upgrade a Windows 7 workstation to Windows 8.
Mindset	Assuming that a workstation meets all of the requirements and has compatible drivers and applications installed, it is possible to perform an in-place upgrade, which retains all of the system's software, data, and configuration settings. However, the more complex the workstation configuration, the more likely it will be for incompatibilities to arise, producing an end result that is unstable or otherwise problematic.
Completion time	20 minutes

In this challenge, you are provided with a computer named WKSTN-MBR-D that is running Windows 7. In the computer's DVD drive, there is an installation disk for Windows 8 Enterprise, which you must use to upgrade the operating system from Windows 7 to Windows 8. To complete the challenge, complete the following tasks:

1. Windows 7, as configured on WKSTN-MBR-D, is running Internet Information Services. Before you begin the upgrade process, demonstrate that IIS is running by taking a screen shot of the IIS default website. Press **Alt+Prt Scr** and then paste it into your Lab 2 worksheet file in the page provided by pressing **Ctrl+V**.

2. Upgrade the workstation to Windows 8, documenting the process by listing the basic steps you performed.

Note	*The length of time required for the Windows 8 upgrade process can be 20 minutes or more, depending on the number and type of applications, files, and configuration settings on the computer at the outset.*

3. Demonstrate that IIS is still running on the upgraded workstation by taking a screen shot of the new IIS default website. Press **Alt+Prt Scr** and then paste it into your Lab 2 worksheet file in the page provided by pressing **Ctrl+V**.

4. Answer the following questions:

   a. Under what conditions would the Upgrade option be unavailable to you during the Windows 8 installation process?

   b. The compatibility notes that appear during this exercise are recommendations; they do not prevent you from performing the upgrade. However, in a real-world upgrade situation, this might not be the case. Give an example of a compatibility note that will stop the upgrade process and force you to take action before restarting the installation.

End of lab.

LAB 3
MIGRATING AND CONFIGURING USER DATA

THIS LAB CONTAINS THE FOLLOWING EXERCISES AND ACTIVITIES:

Exercise 3.1 Collecting User Profile Data

Exercise 3.2 Importing User Profile Data

Lab Challenge Migrating User Profiles Over the Network

BEFORE YOU BEGIN

The lab environment consists of computers connected to a local area network. The computers required for this lab are listed in Table 3-1.

Table 3-1
Computers Required for Lab 3

Computer	*Operating System*	*Computer Name*
Server	Windows Server 2012	SVR-DC-A
Workstation	Windows 8 Enterprise	WKSTN-MBR-B
Workstation	Windows 7 Enterprise	WKSTN-MBR-C

In addition to the computers, you will also require the software listed in Table 3-2 to complete Lab 3.

Table 3-2
Software Required for Lab 3

Software	*Location*
Lab 3 student worksheet	Lab03_worksheet.docx (provided by instructor)

Working with Lab Worksheets

Each lab in this manual requires that you answer questions, create screenshots, and perform other activities that you will document in a worksheet named for the lab, such as Lab03_worksheet.docx. You will find these worksheets on the book companion site. It is recommended that you use a USB flash drive to store your worksheets so you can submit them to your instructor for review. As you perform the exercises in each lab, open the appropriate worksheet file, type the required information, and then save the file to your flash drive.

SCENARIO

After completing this lab, you will be able to:

- Collect user profile data using Windows Easy Transfer
- Import user profile data
- Migrate user profiles over the network

Estimated lab time: 60 minutes

Exercise 3.1	Collecting User Profile Data
Overview	In this exercise, you will create users on a Windows 7 workstation and then run the Windows Easy Transfer program to collect the user profile data that you will migrate to Windows 8.
Mindset	Windows Easy Transfer enables you to save user profile data to a file on a network share or a removable medium and then import it to another computer. You can use this method to perform either a side-by-side migration or a wipe-and-load migration.
Completion time	20 minutes

1. On **WKSTN-MBR-C**, log in as local user Admin with the Pa$$w0rd password and then click **Start** > **Control Panel** > **System and Security** > **Administrative Tools**. The *Administrative Tools* control panel appears.

2. Double-click **Computer Management**. The *Computer Management* console appears.

3. Expand the **Local Users and Groups** node and then click the **Users** container.

4. Right-click the **Users** container and, from the context menu, click **New User**. The *New User* dialog box appears.

5. In the *User Name* text box, type **Alice**. In the *Password* text box and the *Confirm password* text box, type **Pa$$w0rd**.

6. Clear the **User must change password at next logon** check box and then click **Create**. The system creates the user account and then presents a blank new *User* dialog box.

7. Repeat steps 5 and 6 to create three additional user accounts named **Ralph**, **Ed**, and **Trixie**.

8. Click **Close**. The four new accounts appear in the *Users* container.

9. Click the Start icon and in the **Shut down** menu, click **Log off**.

10. Log on using the –.**\Alice** account you just created and the **Pa$$w0rd** password.

11. Repeat the previous two steps to log off and log on again, first using the **Ralph** account and then using the **Ed** account (using **Pa$$w0rd** as the password).

12. Log off the workstation.

13. Log on using the **adatum\Administrator** account and the **Pa$$w0rd** password.

14. Click **Start**. In the *Search programs and files* text box, type **Windows Easy Transfer** and then press **Enter**.

15. The *Windows Easy Transfer Wizard* appears, displaying the *Welcome to Windows Easy Transfer* page.

16. Click **Next**. The *What do you want to use to transfer items to your new computer?* page appears.

17. Click **An external hard disk or USB flash drive**. The *Which computer are you using now?* page appears.

18. Click **This is my old computer**. The program scans the computer for files and settings it can transfer and then displays the results in the *Choose what to transfer from this computer* page (see Figure 3-1).

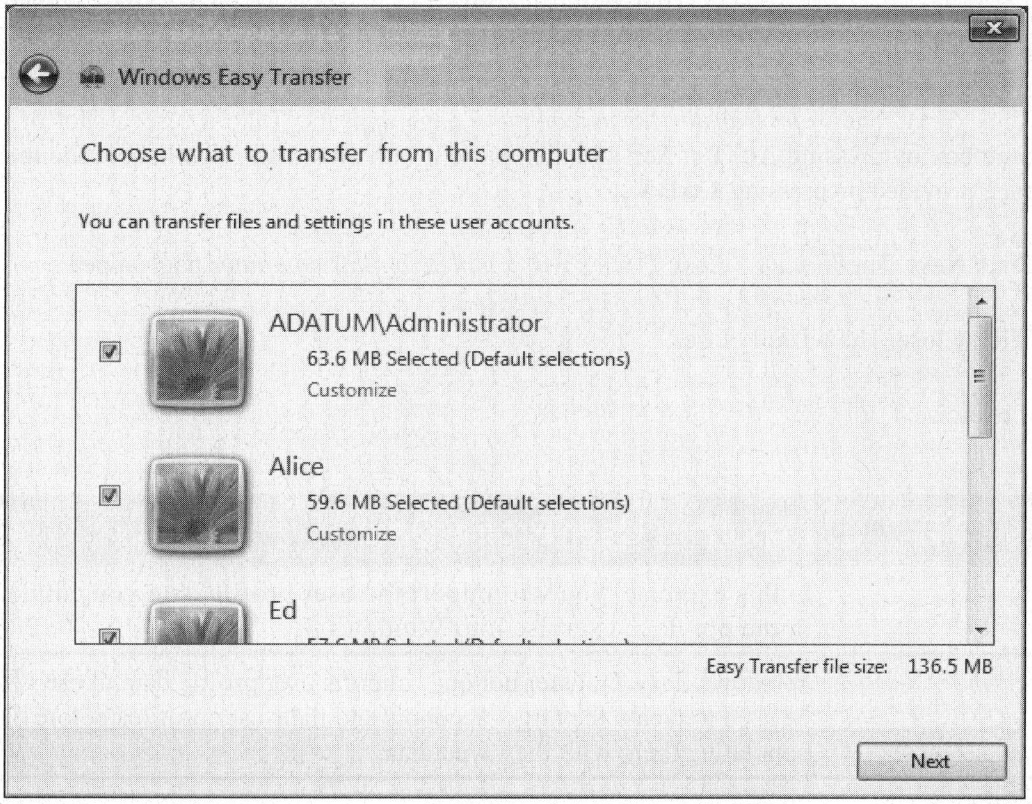

Figure 3-1
The *Choose what to transfer from this computer* page

Question 1	*Of the four users you created in this exercise, which have user profiles that are available for transfer?*

19. Leave the checkboxes selected for all of the available accounts as well as the *Shared Items* object and then click **Next**. The *Save your files and settings for transfer* page appears.

Question 2	*Why aren't the user profiles for all of the accounts you created available for transfer?*

20. In the *Password* text box and the *Confirm Password* text box, type **Pa$$w0rd** and then click **Save**. The *Save your Easy Transfer file* combo box appears.

21. In the *File Name* text box, type **svr-dc-a\downloads\Windows Easy Transfer - Items from old computer** and then click **Save**. The wizard saves the selected profiles to the lab server and then displays a *These files and settings have been saved for your transfer* page.

22. Click **Next**. The *Your transfer file is complete* page appears. Take a screen shot of the page box by pressing **Alt+Prt Scr** and then paste it into your Lab 3 worksheet file in the page provided by pressing **Ctrl+V**.

23. Click **Next**. The *Windows Easy Transfer is complete on this computer* page appears.

24. Click **Close**. The wizard closes.

End of exercise.

Exercise 3.2	Importing User Profile Data
Overview	In this exercise, you will import the user profile data you collected in the previous exercise into Windows 8.
Mindset	Windows Easy Transfer not only imports user profile data, it can also be used to create the target accounts and their user profiles before populating them with the saved data.
Completion time	20 minutes

1. On **WKSTN-MBR-B**, log on using the **adatum\Administrator** account and the **Pa$$w0rd** password.

2. At the *Start* screen, type **Windows Easy Transfer**. The *Apps Results* screen appears.

3. Click **Windows Easy Transfer**. The *Windows Easy Transfer Wizard* appears, displaying the *Welcome to Windows Easy Transfer* page.

4. Click **Next**. The *What do you want to use to transfer items to your new computer?* page appears.

5. Click *An external hard disk or USB flash drive*. The *Which PC are you using now?* page appears.

6. Click **This is my new PC**. The *Has Windows Easy Transfer already saved your files from your old computer to an external hard disk or USB flash drive?* page appears.

7. Click **Yes**. The *Open an Easy Transfer file* combo box appears.

8. In the *File Name* text box, type **\\svr-dc-a\downloads\Windows Easy Transfer - Items from old computer** and then click **Open**. The *Enter the password you used to help protect your transfer file and start the transfer* page appears.

9. In the text box, type **Pa$$w0rd** and then click **Next**. The wizard opens the file and then displays the *Choose what to transfer to this PC* page (see Figure 3-2).

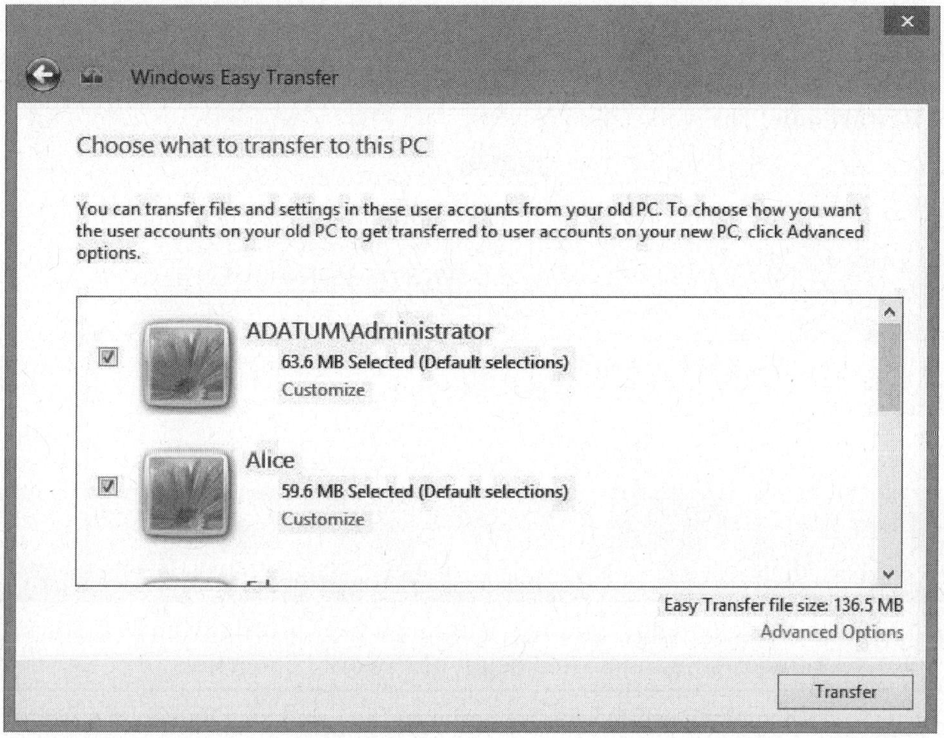

Figure 3-2
The *Choose what to transfer to this PC* page

10. Select all of the available items and then click **Advanced Options**. The *Advanced Options* dialog box appears.

11. For the **Alice** user account, select **Create User** in the appropriate drop-down menu. The *Create New User* dialog box appears.

12. In the *User Name* text box, type **Alice**. In the *Password* text box and the *Confirm password* text box, type **Pas$$w0rd** and then click **Create**.
13. Repeat steps 11 and 12 for the **Ed** user account and the **Ralph** user account. Click **Save**.
14. Click **Transfer**. The wizard transfers the settings you saved from the Windows 7 workstation to your Windows 8 workstation and then displays the *Your transfer is complete* page.
15. Click **See what was transferred**. The *Windows Easy Transfer Reports* window appears.
16. Take a screen shot of the *Windows Easy Transfer Reports* window by pressing **Alt+Prt Scr** and then paste it into your Lab 3 worksheet file in the page provided by pressing **Ctrl+V**.
17. Close the *Windows Easy Transfer Reports* window.
18. Click **Close**. A *Restart your PC to complete your transfer* dialog box appears.
19. Click **Restart now**. The workstation restarts.

Question 3	*The Windows Easy Transfer application does not migrate passwords. Why then, when you attempt to log on to WKSTN-MBR-B using the* ***WKSTN-MBR-B\Alice*** *account and the password* ***Pa$$w0rd****, does the logon succeed?*

End of exercise.

Lab Challenge	Migrating User Profiles Over the Network
Overview	In this challenge, you will migrate a user profile from Windows 7 to Windows 8 in real time using a network connection.
Mindset	When two workstations are active at the same time and connected to the same network, you can use Windows Easy Transfer to migrate user profiles directly between them without having to save the profile information to a file.
Completion time	20 minutes

A user wants to transfer user profiles from a Windows 7 workstation to a Windows 8 workstation, but these two computers are connected to the network at the same time. To complete this challenge, you must create a user profile for the Trixie account you created on WKSTN-MBR-C and transfer it directly to the WKSTN-MBR-B workstation using the network. Then complete the following tasks:

1. Write out the steps you performed to complete the challenge.

2. Take a screen shot of the *Go to your new computer and enter your Windows Easy Transfer key* page on the Windows 7 workstation by pressing **Alt+Prt Scr** and then paste it into your Lab 3 worksheet file in the page provided by pressing **Ctrl+V**.

3. Take a screen shot of the *Enter your Windows Easy Transfer key* page on the Windows 8 workstation by pressing **Alt+Prt Scr** and then paste it into your Lab 3 worksheet file in the page provided by pressing **Ctrl+V**.

End of lab.

LAB 4
CONFIGURING DEVICES AND DEVICE DRIVERS

THIS LAB CONTAINS THE FOLLOWING EXERCISES AND ACTIVITIES:

Exercise 4.1	Troubleshooting Devices with Device Manager
Exercise 4.2	Updating Device Drivers
Exercise 4.3	Rolling Back Drivers
Lab Challenge	Accessing Advanced Boot Options

BEFORE YOU BEGIN

The lab environment consists of student workstations connected to a local area network, along with a server that functions as the domain controller for a domain called adatum.com. The computers required for this lab are listed in Table 4-1.

Table 4-1
Computers Required for Lab 4

Computer	***Operating System***	***Computer Name***
Server	Windows Server 2012	SVR-DC-A
Client	Windows 8 Enterprise	WKSTN-MBR-B

In addition to the computers, you will also need the software listed in Table 4-2 to complete Lab 4.

Table 4-2
Software required for Lab 4

Software	***Location***
Lab 4 student worksheet	Lab04_worksheet.docx (provided by instructor)

Working with Lab Worksheets

Each lab in this manual requires that you answer questions, shoot screen shots, and perform other activities that you will document in a worksheet named for the lab, such as Lab04_worksheet.docx. You will find these worksheets on the book companion site. It is recommended that you use a USB flash drive to store your worksheets so you can submit them to your instructor for review. As you perform the exercises in each lab, open the appropriate worksheet file, fill in the required information, and then save the file to your flash drive.

SCENARIO

After completing this lab, you will be able to:

- View and manage devices with Device Manager
- Update a driver with Device Manager
- Rollback a driver with Device Manager

Estimated lab time: 50 minutes

Exercise 4.1	Troubleshooting Devices with Device Manager
Overview	In this exercise, you will use Device Manager to troubleshoot problems with devices and device drivers.
Mindset	While a hardware problem can be a physical failure of the device, often the problem is caused by not having the proper device driver loaded. To view hardware that Windows sees, to view the drivers that are loaded for the hardware devices, and to manage the hardware devices and drivers, you would use Device Manager.
Completion time	20 minutes

1. On WKSTN-MBR-B, log on using the **adatum\Administrator** account and the **Pa$$w0rd** password. When the Start menu appears, click the Desktop tile.

2. Mouse over the lower-left corner of the desktop and right-click the **Start** screen thumbnail that appears there. Click **Device Manager**.

Question 1	*Are there any errors or unknown devices?*

3. Expand the **Ports (COM and LPT)** node (see Figure 4-1).

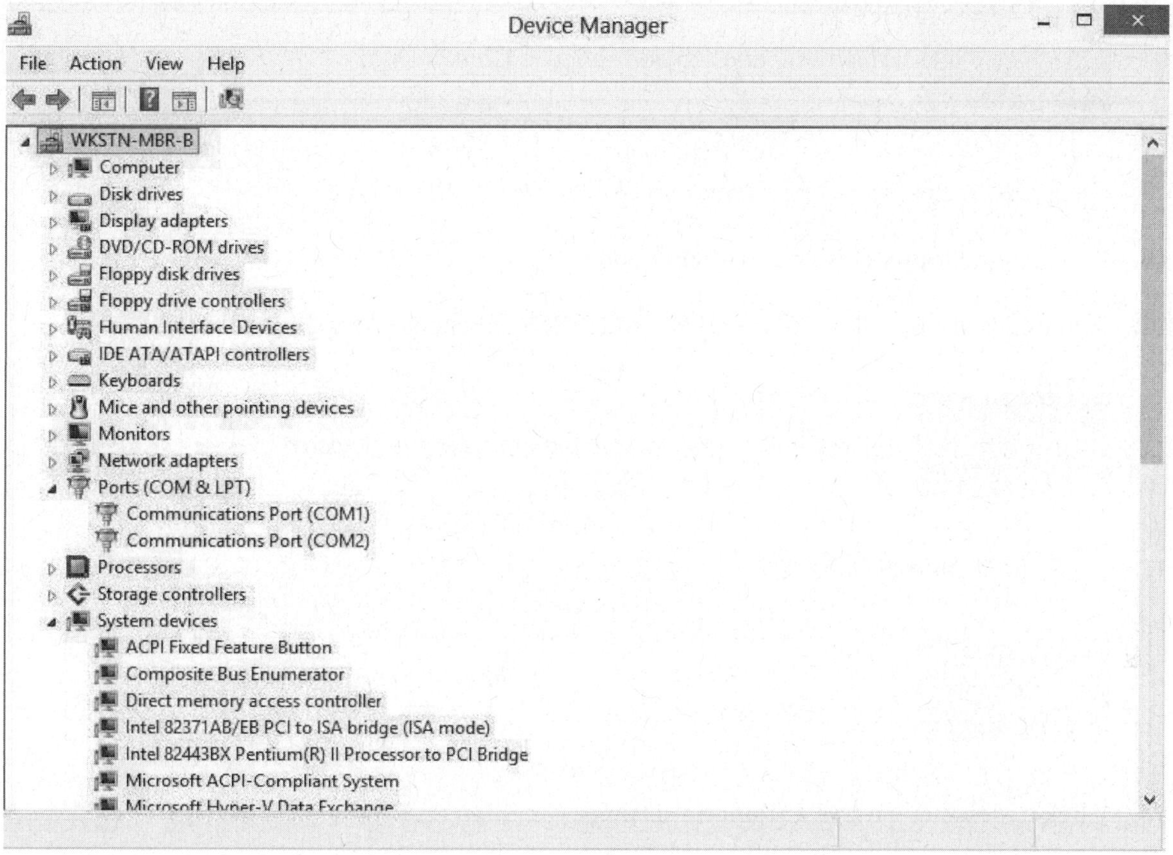

Figure 4-1
The Device Manager window

4. Right-click **Communications Port (COM2)** and choose **Disable**.

5. When you are prompted to confirm if you want to disable the device, click **Yes**.

Question 2	*Which icon represents a disabled device?*

6. Right-click the **Communications Port (COM2)** and choose **Enable**.

7. Right-click the **Communications Port (COM2)** and choose **Properties**.

Question 3	*In the General tab, what is the status of the device?*

8. Click the **Resources** tab.

Question 4	*Which IRQ and I/O port range is Com2 using?*

9. Click **OK** to close the *Communications Port (COM2)* dialog box.
10. Expand the **Floppy drive controllers** node.
11. Right-click the **Standard floppy disk controller** and choose **Properties**.

Question 5	*In the General tab, what is the status of the device?*

12. Click the **Resources** tab.

Question 6	*Which IRQ, DMA and I/O port ranges does the Standard floppy disk controller use?*

13. Click to deselect the **Use automatic settings**.

Note:	*Today, it would be extremely rare that you will ever have to manually configure these settings. This is for demonstration purposes only.*

14. Change *Setting based on* to **Basic configuration 0002**.
15. Double-click the **IRQ**. When the *Edit Interrupt Request* dialog box opens, change *Value* to **05**. Click **OK** to close the *Edit Interrupt Request* dialog box.
16. Click **OK** to close the *Standard floppy disk controller Properties* dialog box.
17. When you are prompted to confirm if you want to continue, click **Yes**.
18. When you are prompted to restart the computer, click **No**.

Question 7	*Which icon does the Standard floppy disk controller have now?*

19. Double-click **Standard floppy disk controller**.

Question 8	*What is the device status now?*

20. Click the Resources tab, take a screen shot of the *Resources* tab on the *Device Manager Standard floppy disk controller Properties* dialog box by pressing **Alt+Prt Scr** and then paste it into your Lab 4 worksheet file in the page provided by pressing **Ctrl+V**.
21. Click **Set Configuration Manually**.
22. Click to select **Use automatic settings**.
23. Click **OK** to close the *Standard floppy disk controller Properties* dialog box.
24. When you are prompted to restart the computer, click **Yes**.

End of exercise. Wait for WKSTN-MBR-B to reboot for the next exercise.

Exercise 4.2	Updating Device Drivers
Overview	In this exercise, you will update device drivers with Device Manager.
Mindset	There are multiple reasons why vendors may update a driver. They may need to fix an issue, allow the driver to run more efficiently, or additional capability or functionality. For whatever reason, you will update a driver.
Completion time	15 minutes

1. Log into **WKSTN-MBR-B** as **adatum\administrator** with the **Pa$$w0rd** password. When the Start menu opens, click the **Desktop** tile.
2. Mouse over the lower-left corner of the desktop and right-click the **Start** screen thumbnail that appears there. Click **Device Manager**.
3. Right-click **WKSTN-MBR-B** and choose **Scan for hardware changes**.
4. Expand the **Ports (COM and LPT)** node and then click **Communications Port (COM2) port**.
5. Right-click **Communications Port (COM2) port** and then click **Update Driver Software**.
6. When the *How do you want to search for driver software?* page opens, click **Search automatically for updated driver software**.

Question 9	*Which driver did it find and what does it say about the driver?*

7. Click **Close** to close the *Update Driver Software – Communications Port (COM2)* dialog box.

8. Right-click **Communications port (COM2)** and choose **Properties**.

9. Click the **Driver** tab (see Figure 4-2).

Figure 4-2
The *Driver* tab

Question 10	*Which driver version is Communication Port (COM2) using?*

10. Click **Update Driver**.

11. On the *How do you want to search for driver software?* page, click **Browse my computer for driver software**.

12. On the *Browse for driver software on your computer* page, click **Let me pick from a list of device drivers on my computer**.

13. On the *Select the device driver you want to install for this hardware* page, click to deselect the **Show compatible hardware**.

Note:	*Normally, you would not want to use other drivers that are not compatible. This is for demonstration purposes only.*

14. For the *Manufacturer* setting, click **Trimble** and then click **Trimble PCMICA GPS Adapter (Rev. B)**. Click **Next**.

15. When an update driver warning message appears, click **Yes**.

16. When the driver has been installed, click **Close.**

17. Take a screen shot of the *Trimble PMCIA GPS Adapter (Rev. B) (COM2) Properties* dialog box by pressing **Alt+Prt Scr** and then paste it into your Lab 4 worksheet file in the page provided by pressing **Ctrl+V**.

18. Click **Close** to close the *Trimble PCMCIA GPS Adapter (Rev. B) (COM2) Properties* dialog box.

End of exercise. Leave the Device Manager open for the next exercise.

Exercise 4.3	Rolling Back Drivers
Overview	In this exercise, you will use Device Manager to rollback a driver.
Mindset	From time to time, you will encounter problems when you upgrade a driver. So you will need to know how to roll back the driver.
Completion time	5 minutes

1. On **WKSTN-MBR-B**, using **Device Manager**, right-click the **Trimble PCMICA GPS Adapter (Rev B) (COM2)** and choose **Properties**.

2. Click the **Driver** tab (see Figure 4-3).

Figure 4-3
The *Driver* tab

3. Click **Roll Back Driver**.

4. When you are prompted to confirm if you would like to roll back to the previously installed driver software, click **Yes**.

5. Take a screen shot of the *Communications Port (COM2) Properties* dialog box by pressing **Alt+Prt Scr** and then paste it into your Lab 4 worksheet file in the page provided by pressing **Ctrl+V**.

6. Click **Close** to close the *Communications Port (COM2) Properties* dialog box.

End of exercise. You can close the Device Manager and leave the computer logged on for the lab challenge.

Lab Challenge	Accessing Advanced Boot Options
Overview	In this exercise, you will disable driver signature enforcement.
Mindset	On occasion, you may need to install a driver that you trust but has not been signed by the vendor. You can disable driver signature enforcement by modifying the Startup Settings.
Completion time	10 minutes

1. On **WKSTN-MBR-B**, mouse over the lower-right corner of the screen, and when the fly-out menu appears, click the **Settings** charm. The *Settings* menu appears.
2. Click **Change PC Settings**. The *PC Settings* menu appears.
3. Click **General**. The *General* menu appears.
4. Scroll down to the bottom. Under *Advanced Startup*, select **Restart Now**.
5. When the system restarts and the *Choose an option* page appears, click **Troubleshoot**. See Figure 4-4.

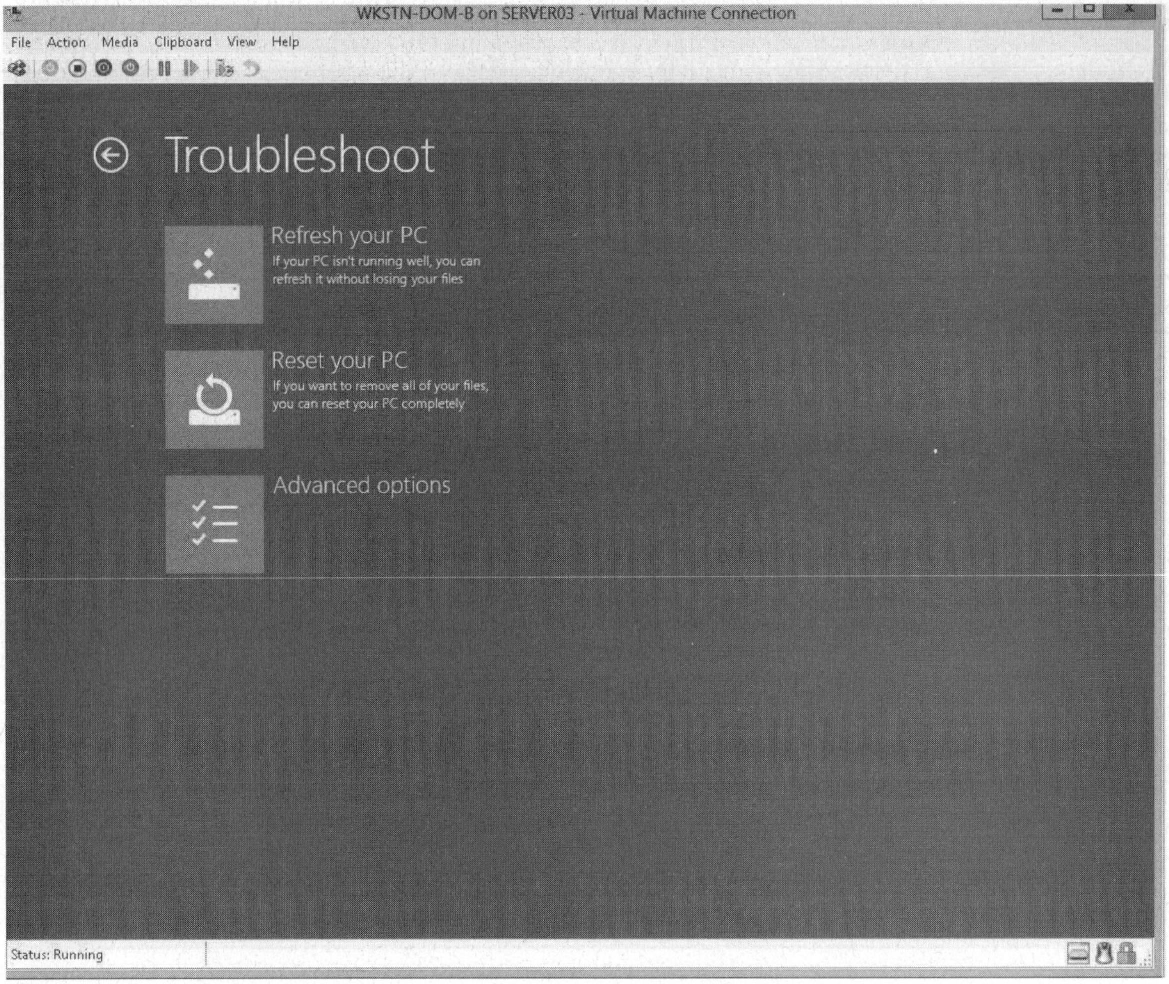

Figure 4-4
The Windows 8 Troubleshoot menu

6. On the *Troubleshoot* menu, click **Advanced Options**.
7. Click **Startup Settings**.
8. On the *Startup Settings* page, click **Restart**.
9. When the *Startup Settings* page appears, press **7** to disable driver signature enforcement. The system starts, loading all drivers, whether signed or not and whether altered or not.

End of lab.

LAB 5
INSTALLING AND CONFIGURING DESKTOP APPLICATIONS

THIS LAB CONTAINS THE FOLLOWING EXERCISES AND ACTIVITIES:

Exercise 5.1	Setting File Associations
Exercise 5.2	Setting Compatibility Modes
Lab Challenge	Modifying File Associations

BEFORE YOU BEGIN

The lab environment consists of computers connected to a local area network. The computers required for this lab are listed in Table 5-1.

Table 5-1
Computers Required for Lab 5

Computer	***Operating System***	***Computer Name***
Server	Windows Server 2012	SVR-DC-A
Workstation	Windows 8 Enterprise	WKSTN-MBR-B
Workstation	Windows 8 Enterprise	WKSTN-MBR-C

In addition to the computers, you will also need the software listed in Table 5-2 to complete Lab 5.

Table 5-2
Software Required for Lab 5

Software	*Location*
Lab 5 student worksheet	Lab05_worksheet.docx (provided by instructor)

Working with Lab Worksheets

Each lab in this manual requires that you answer questions, create screenshots, and perform other activities that you will document in a worksheet named for the lab, such as Lab05_worksheet.docx. You will find these worksheets on the book companion site. It is recommended that you use a USB flash drive to store your worksheets so you can submit them to your instructor for review. As you perform the exercises in each lab, open the appropriate worksheet file using Word, type the required information, and then save the file to your flash drive.

SCENARIO

After completing this lab, you will be able to:

- Set Windows 8 file associations
- Set compatibility modes
- Modify file associations

Estimated lab time: 60 minutes

Exercise 5.1	Setting File Associations
Overview	In this exercise, you will demonstrate how you can use file associations to control which application loads when you execute a file of a particular type.
Mindset	Windows 8 uses file types to associate data files with specific applications. File can also appear as file name extensions.
Completion time	20 minutes

1. On **WKSTN-MBR-C**, log on using the **adatum\Student** account and the **Pa$$w0rd** password.

2. Click the **Desktop** tile. The *Desktop* appears.

3. In the taskbar, click the **File Explorer** icon. The *File Explorer* window appears.

4. Expand the **Computer** container and then select the **Local Disk (C:)** drive.

5. In the *Search Local Disk (C:)* box, type **jpg** and wait as the program searches the disk for JPG files.

6. Scroll down in the results list and double-click the **IMG104** file. The file opens in Photo.

7. Mouse over the lower-left corner of the window, right-click the **Start** screen thumbnail, and, from the context menu that appears, click **Control Panel**. The *Control Panel* window appears.

8. Click **Programs > Default Programs > Associate a file type or protocol with a program**. The *Associate a file type or protocol with a specific program* control panel appears (see Figure 5-1).

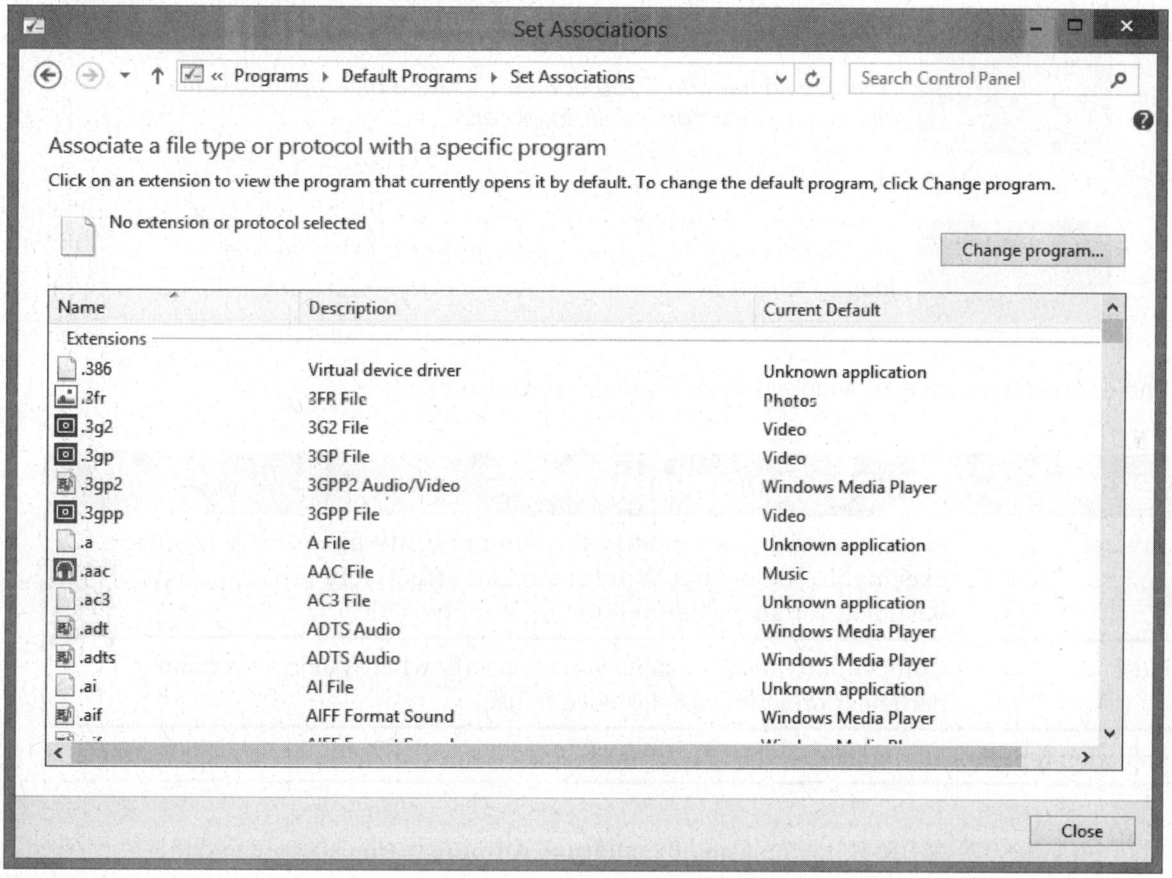

Figure 5-1
The Associate a file type or protocol with a specific program control panel

9. Scroll down in the list and select the **.jpg** file name extension.

Question 1	*What program is currently associated with the .jpg file name extension?*

10. Click **Change program**. The *How do you want to open this type of file (.jpg)?* dialog box appears.

11. Click **Windows Photo Viewer**. The default file association for the .jpg extension changes to *Windows Photo Viewer*.

12. Switch back to the *File Explorer* window and then double-click the **IMG104** file again. The image appears again, but now in the *Windows Photo Viewer* application.

13. Take a screen shot of the *Windows Photo Viewer* window by pressing **Alt+Prt Scr** and then paste it into your Lab 5 worksheet file in the page provided by pressing **Ctrl+V**.

Question 2	*What would happen if you double-clicked a different JPEG file with a .jpg extension in File Explorer?*

Question 3	*What would happen if you double-clicked a JPEG file with a .jpeg extension?*

End of exercise. Leave all windows open for the next exercise.

Exercise 5.2	Setting Compatibility Modes
Overview	In this exercise, you modify the compatibility mode for a specific executable file so that Windows 8 can effectively run a program designed for an earlier version of Windows.
Mindset	Compatibility modes enable you to specify what Windows version a particular program was designed to use.
Completion time	20 minutes

1. On **WKSTN-MBR-B**, log on using the **adatum\Administrator** account and the **Pa$$w0rd** password.

2. On the *Start* screen, click the **Desktop** tile. The *Desktop* appears.

3. On the taskbar, click the **File Explorer** button. The *File Explorer* window appears.

4. Expand the **Network** container and browse to the **\\SVR-DC-A\Downloads** folder.

5. Copy the **WinXP-SOL** folder to the **C:\Users\Administrator\Downloads** folder on **WKSTN-MBR-B**.

6. In the **C:\Users\Administrator\Downloads\WinXP-SOL** folder, right-click the **Sol** file and, from the context menu, choose **Properties**. The *sol Properties* sheet appears.

7. Click the *Compatibility* tab (see Figure 5-2).

Figure 5-2
The Compatibility tab of the sol Properties sheet

8. Select the **Run this program in compatibility mode for** check box and, in the drop-down list, click **Windows XP (Service Pack 3)**.

Question 4	*What can you do if you are unsure which version of Windows you should specify in the compatibility settings?*

9. Click **OK**.

10. In *File Explorer*, double-click the **Sol** file. The *Solitaire* game screen appears.

11. Take a screen shot of the *Solitaire* window by pressing **Alt+Prt Scr** and then paste it into your Lab 5 worksheet file in the page provided by pressing **Ctrl+V**.

End of exercise. Leave all windows open for the next exercise.

Lab Challenge	Modifying File Associations
Overview	Windows 8 often provides more than one way to complete a given task. In this challenge, you must discover an alternate way to complete a task you performed earlier in this lab.
Mindset	Windows 8 uses its modern interface to provide alternative ways of performing tasks usually found in the Control Panel.
Completion time	20 minutes

To complete this challenge, you must once again change the default file association for JPEG files with a .jpg extension. However, this time, you cannot use the Default Programs control panel. Change the default file association to the Paint program and, in doing so, complete the following tasks:

1. List the steps you took to complete the task.

2. Take a screen shot of the interface you used to change the default file association by pressing Alt+Prt Scr and then paste it into your Lab 5 worksheet file in the page provided by pressing Ctrl+V.

End of lab.

LAB 6
INSTALLING AND CONFIGURING WINDOWS STORE APPLICATIONS

THIS LAB CONTAINS THE FOLLOWING EXERCISES AND ACTIVITIES:

Exercise 6.1 Using Group Policy to Restrict Access to the Windows Store

Exercise 6.2 Disabling Automatic Download Updates of the Windows Store

Lab Challenge Blocking Automatic Updates from Within the Windows Store App

BEFORE YOU BEGIN

The lab environment consists of student workstations connected to a local area network, along with a server that functions as the domain controller for a domain called adatum.com. The computers required for this lab are listed in Table 6-1.

Table 6-1
Computers Required for Lab 6

Computer	*Operating System*	*Computer Name*
Server	Windows Server 2012	SVR-DC-A
Client	Windows 8 Enterprise	WKSTN-MBR-B
Client	Windows 7 Enterprise	WKSTN-MBR-C

In addition to the computers, you will also need the software listed in Table 6-2 to complete Lab 6.

Table 6-2
Software Required for Lab 6

Software	***Location***
Administrative Templates for Windows 8 and Windows Server 2012 (Windows8-Server2012ADMX-RTM.msi)	\\SVC-DC-A\Downloads
Lab 6 student worksheet	Lab06_worksheet.docx (provided by instructor)

Working with Lab Worksheets

Each lab in this manual requires that you answer questions, shoot screen shots, and perform other activities that you will document in a worksheet named for the lab, such as Lab06_worksheet.docx. You will find these worksheets on the book companion site. It is recommended that you use a USB flash drive to store your worksheets so you can submit them to your instructor for review. As you perform the exercises in each lab, open the appropriate worksheet file, type the required information, and then save the file to your flash drive.

SCENARIO

After completing this lab, you will be able to:

- Restrict access to the Windows Store
- Disable Automatic Download Updates of the Store
- Block automatic updates from within the Windows Store app

Estimated lab time: 35 minutes

Exercise 6.1	Using Group Policy to Restrict Access to the Windows Store
Overview	In this exercise, you will install the Windows 8/Windows Server 2012 Administrative Templates and then use GPOs to restrict access to the Windows Store.
Mindset	To maintain security within an organization, you may choose to restrict users from using the Store to download and install applications.
Completion time	20 minutes

1. On **SVR-DC-A**, log on using the **adatum\administrator** account and the **Pa$$w0rd** password.

2. Open **File Explorer** and navigate to the **\\SVR-DC-A\Downloads** folder.

3. Double-click the **Windows8-Server2012ADMX-RTM.msi** file. When you are prompted to confirm that you want to run this file, click **Run**.

4. When the *Administrative Templates for Windows Server 2012 Setup Wizard* opens, click **Next**.

5. On the *License Agreement* page, click **I Agree** and then click **Next**.

6. On the *Select Installation folder* page, click **Everyone**.

Question 1	*What is the default installation folder?*

7. Click **Next**.

8. On the *Confirm Installation* page, click **Next**.

9. When the installation is complete, click **Close**.

10. Using **File Explorer**, open the **C:\Program Files (x86)\Microsoft Group Policy\Windows Server2012** folder. Right-click the **PolicyDefinitions** folder and choose **Copy**.

11. Using **File Explorer**, open **\\SVR-DC-A\sysvol\adatum.com\Policies** (see Figure 6-1).

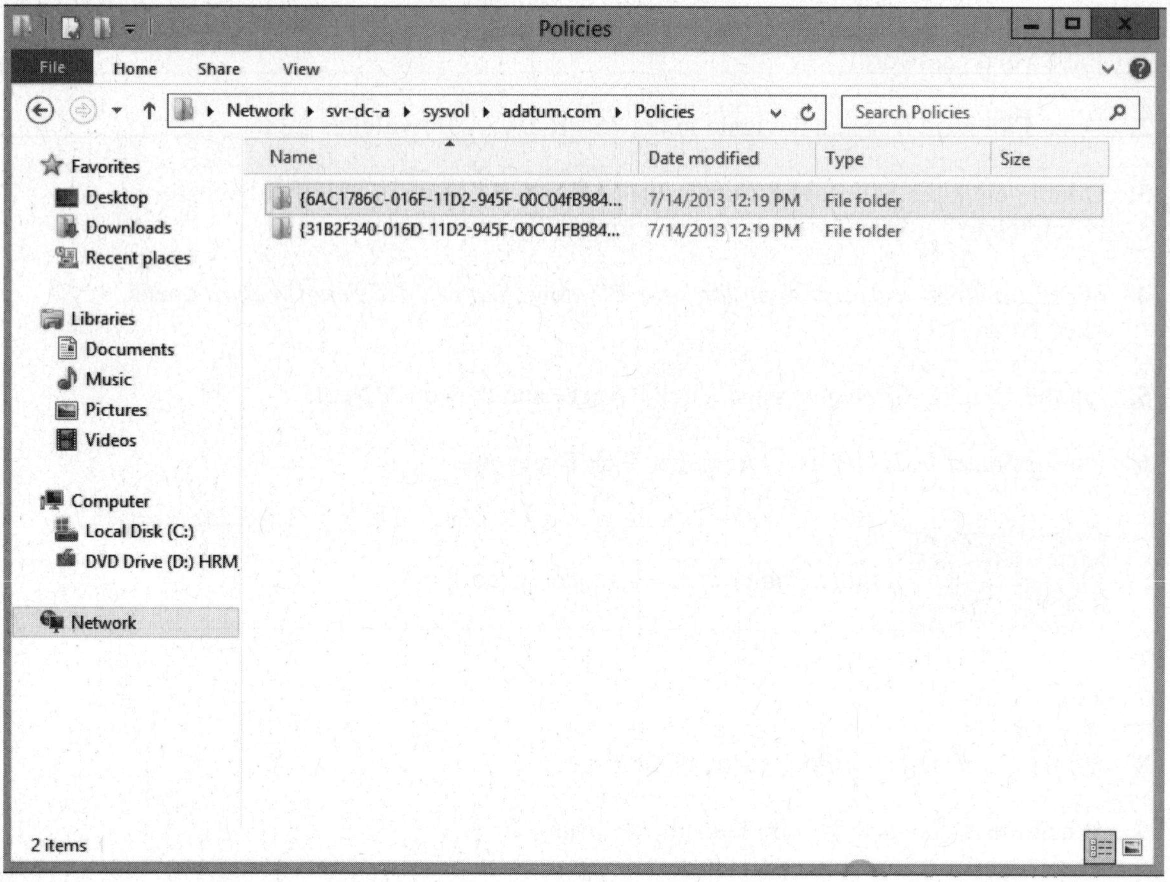

Figure 6-1
The Policies folder on a domain controller

12. In the *Policies* folder, right-click the empty white space and choose **Paste**.

13. Using **Server Manager**, click **Tools** > **Group Policy Management**.

14. When *Group Policy Management* opens, expand the **Forest: adatum.com** node, expand the **Domains** node, and then expand **adatum.com**.

15. Right-click the **Default Domain Policy** and choose **Edit**.

16. When the *Group Policy Management Editor* opens, navigate to **Computer Configuration** > **Policies** > **Administrative Templates** > **Windows Components** > **Store**.

17. Double-click the **Turn off the Store application setting**. The *Turn off the Store application* dialog displays. Click **Enabled**.

18. Press **Ctrl+Prt Scr** to take a screen shot that captures both the *Turn off the Store application* dialog box and the *Group Policy Management Editor* window. Press **Ctrl+V** to paste the image on the page provided in the Lab 6 worksheet file.

19. Click **OK** to close the *Turn off the Store application* dialog box. The next time the group policy settings are replicated to the client, the store will be disabled.

End of exercise. Leave the Group Policy Management Editor open for the next exercise.

Exercise 6.2	Disabling Automatic Download Updates of the Windows Store
Overview	In this exercise, you will use a GPO to disable the automatic downloading of updates from the Windows store.
Mindset	Sometimes, updates can cause unforeseen problems. To avoid some of these problems, you can stop applications from downloading and installing updates for Windows Store applications.
Completion time	10 minutes

1. On **SVR-DC-A**, using **Group Policy Management Editor**, navigate to **Computer Configuration > Policies > Administrative Templates > Windows Components > Store** (see Figure 6-2).

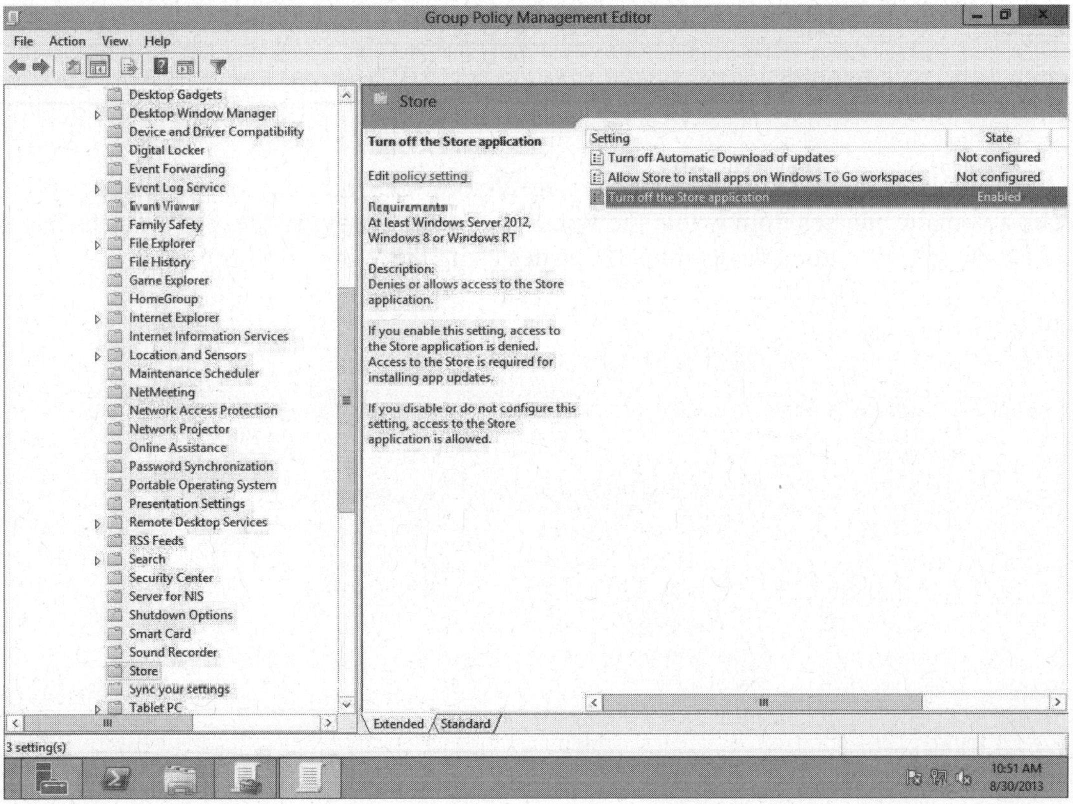

Figure 6-2
A GPO showing the *Store* node

2. Double-click **Turn off Automatic Download of updates**.

3. For the policy setting, select **Enabled**.

4. Press **Ctrl+Prt Scr** to take a screen shot of the *Turn off Automatic Download of updates* dialog box and the *Group Policy Management Editor* window. Press **Ctrl+V** to paste the image on the page provided in the Lab 6 worksheet file.

5. Click **OK** to close the *Turn off Automatic Download of updates* dialog box.

6. Close **Group Policy Management Editor** and then close **Group Policy Management**.

End of exercise.

Lab Challenge	Blocking Automatic Updates from within the Windows Store App
Overview	In this lab challenge, you will demonstrate how to disable automatic download updates using the Windows Store App.
Mindset	You have a local computer that is sensitive and you do not want to deploy any updates or changes to the system unless you manually update or change the system.
Completion time	5 minutes

As a local administrator for the computer running Windows 8, you want to demonstrate how to block automatic updates from within the Windows Store App by writing out the steps that it would take to disable automatic downloads updates using the Windows Store app.

End of lab.

LAB 7
CONTROLLING ACCESS TO LOCAL HARDWARE AND APPLICATIONS

THIS LAB CONTAINS THE FOLLOWING EXERCISES AND ACTIVITIES:

BEFORE YOU BEGIN

The lab environment consists of student workstations connected to a local area network, along with a server that functions as the domain controller for a domain called adatum.com. The computers required for this lab are listed in Table 7-1.

Table 7-1
Computers Required for Lab 7

Computer	*Operating System*	*Computer Name*
Server	Windows Server 2012	SVR-DC-A
Client	Windows 8 Enterprise	WKSTN-MBR-B

In addition to the computers, you will also need the software listed in Table 7-2 to complete Lab 7.

Table 7-2
Software Required for Lab 7

Software	*Location*
Remote Server Administration Tools for Windows 8 (Windows6.2-KB2693643-x64.msu)	\\SVR-DC-A\Downloads
Lab 7 student worksheet	Lab07_worksheet.docx (provided by instructor)

Working with Lab Worksheets

Each lab in this manual requires that you answer questions, shoot screen shots, and perform other activities that you will document in a worksheet named for the lab, such as Lab07_worksheet.docx. You will find these worksheets on the book companion site. It is recommended that you use a USB flash drive to store your worksheets so you can submit them to your instructor for review. As you perform the exercises in each lab, open the appropriate worksheet file, type the required information, and then save the file to your flash drive.

SCENARIO

After completing this lab, you will be able to:

- Install the Remote Server Administration Tools on a computer running Windows 8
- Configure a Removable Storage Access Policy
- Use AppLocker to restrict software applications for a user

Estimated lab time: 60 minutes

Exercise 7.1	Installing Remote Server Administration Tools
Overview	In this exercise, you will install the Remote Server Administration Tools on a computer running Windows 8 so that you can use Active Directory tools and other administrative tools on a Windows 8 workstation.
Mindset	Since users work from their client computers, it is always convenient to have the Remote Server Administration Tools available on the administrator's client computer.
Completion time	20 minutes

1. On **WKSTN-MBR-B**, log on using the **adatum\Administrator** account and the **Pa$$w0rd** password.

2. Click the **Desktop** tile.

3. On the Taskbar, click the **File Explorer** icon.

4. When *File Explorer* opens, open the **\\SVR-DC-A\downloads** folder (see Figure 7-1).

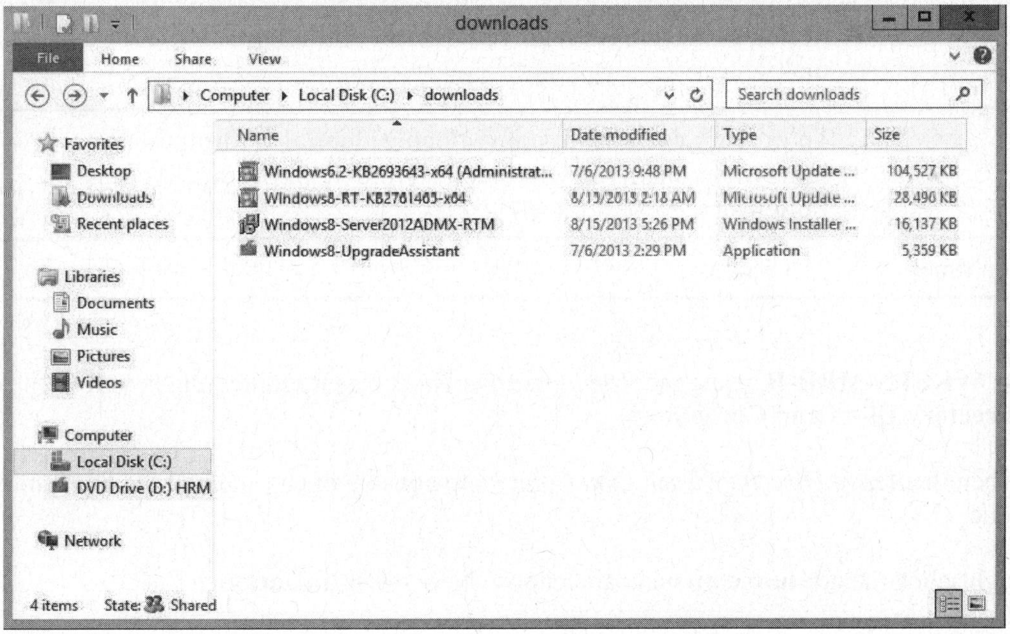

Figure 7-1
The *Downloads* folder

5. Double-click the **Windows6.2-KB2693643-x64.msu** file.

6. If you are prompted to install this file, click **Open**. When you are prompted to install the Windows software update, click **Yes**.

7. On the *Read these license terms* page, click **I Accept**.

8. If you are prompted to restart the computer, click **Restart Now**.

9. If you need to restart, then after rebooting, log back in to **WKSTN-MBR-B** as **adatum\Administrator** using the **Pa$$w0rd** password.

10. Scroll to the right and then click the **Administrative Tools** tile.

Question 1	*Which two tools are used to administer users for Active Directory?*

11. Take a screen shot of the *Administrative Tools* window by pressing **Alt+Prt Scr** and then paste the resulting image into the Lab 7 worksheet file in the page provided by pressing **Ctrl+V**.

End of exercise. Leave the system logged in for the next exercise.

Exercise 7.2	Configuring Removable Storage Access Policies
Overview	In this exercise, you will restrict the ability to write to an optical disk.
Mindset	To prevent users from copying confidential information to a removable disk, you can create Removable Storage Access Policies.
Completion time	15 minutes

1. On **WKSTN-MBR-B**, using the *Administrative Tools* folder, double-click **Active Directory Users and Computers**.

2. When the *Active Directory Users and Computers* console opens, expand the **adatum.com** node.

3. Right-click the **adatum.com** node and choose **New** > **Organizational Unit**.

4. When the *New Object – Organizational Unit* dialog box displays, in the *Name* text box, type **Restricted**.

5. Click **OK** to close the *New Object – Organizational Unit* dialog box.

6. Close **Active Directory Users and Computers**.

7. Go back to the *Administrative Tools* folder and double-click **Group Policy Management**.

8. When the *Group Policy Management* console opens, expand the **Forest: adatum.com** node, expand the **Domains** node, expand the **adatum.com** node, and then expand the **Group Policy Objects** node (see Figure 7-2).

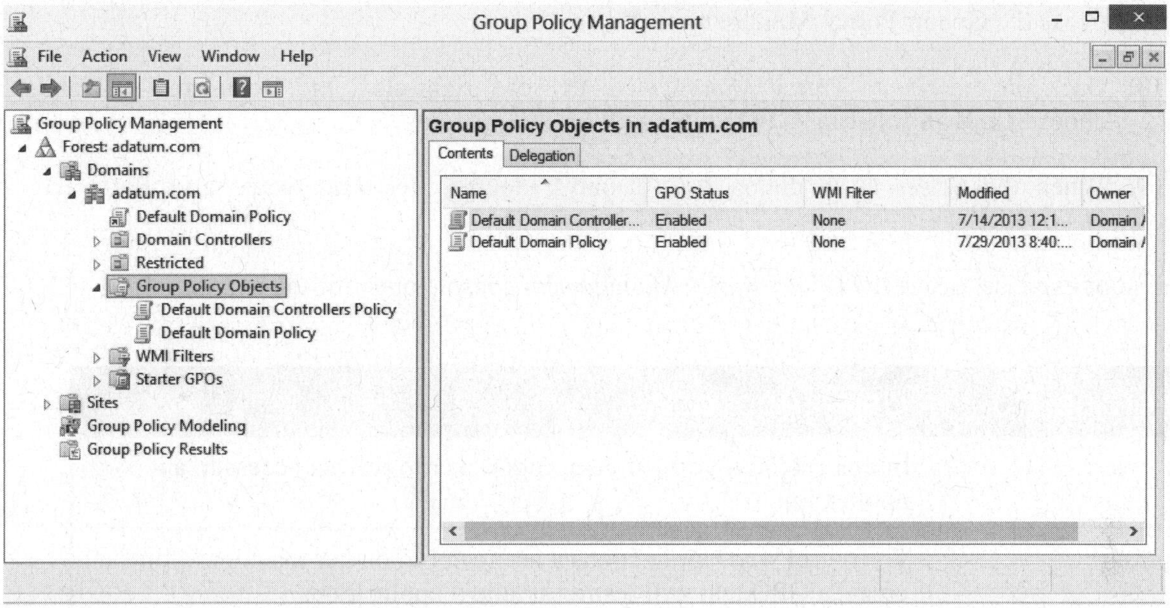

Figure 7-2
The *Group Policy Objects* node

9. Right-click **Group Policy Objects** and choose **New**.

10. When the *New GPO* window displays, in the *Name* text box, type **Hardware and Software Restrictions**, and then click **OK**.

11. Right-click the **Hardware and Software Restrictions** GPO and choose **Edit**.

12. When the *Group Policy Management Editor* window opens, under the **User Configuration** node, expand the **Policies** node, expand the **Administrative Templates**, expand the **System** node, and then click the **Removable Storage Access** node.

Question 2	*Which policy setting prevents writing to a USB device?*

13. To stop writing to writable optical disk, in the right pane, double-click **CD and DVD: Deny Write access**.

14. When the *CD and DVD: Deny write access* dialog box displays, click the **Enabled** option.

15. Click **OK** to close the *CD and DVD: Deny write access* dialog box.

16. Take a screen shot of the *Group Policy Management Editor* window by pressing **Alt+Prt Scr** and then paste the resulting image into the Lab 7 worksheet file in the page provided by pressing **Ctrl+V**.

17. Close the **Group Policy Management Editor**.

18. Back on the *Group Policy Management* console, right-click the **Restricted** OU and choose **Link an Existing GPO**.

19. When the *Select GPO* dialog box displays, double-click **Hardware and Software Restrictions**.

End of exercise. Leave the *Group Policy Management* console open for the next exercise.

Exercise 7.3	Using AppLocker
Overview	In this exercise, you will use AppLocker to restrict access to an application.
Mindset	To control what applications a user can run on her machine, you can create a GPO that will restrict or allow applications.
Completion time	15 minutes

1. On **WKSTN-MBR-B**, using the *Group Policy Management* console, under the Group Policy Objects node, right-click the **Hardware and Software Restricted** GPO and then choose click **Edit**.

2. When the *Group Policy Management Editor* console displays, browse to the **Computer Configuration\Policies\Windows Settings\Security Settings\Application Control Policies** container and then click the **AppLocker** node.

3. Expand the **AppLocker** container and then click the **Executable Rules** node (see Figure 7-3).

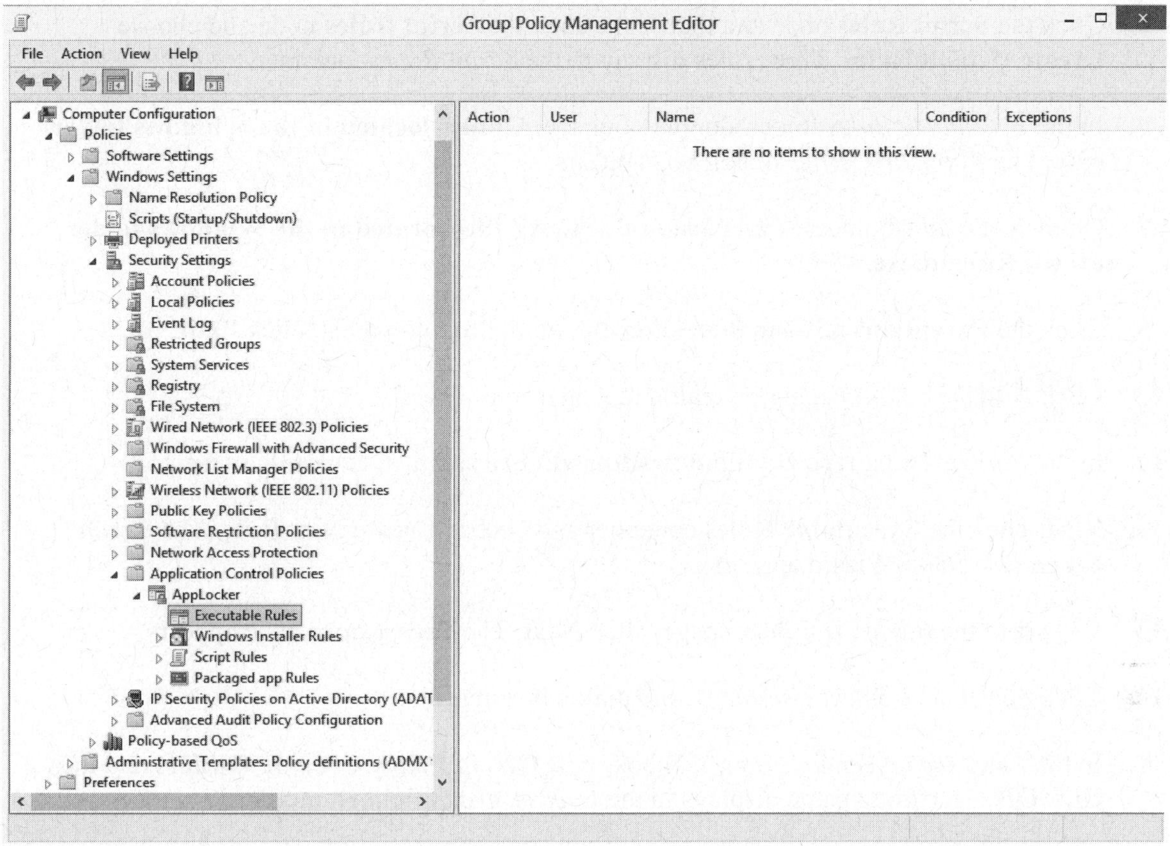

Figure 7-3
A GPO that shows the AppLocker Executable Rules node

4. Right-click the **Executable Rules** node and choose **Create Default Rules**. Three rules display in the *Executable Rules* container.

Question 3	*Based on the default rules that appear in the Executable Rules folder, which programs can a typical user run on a Windows 8 workstation? Which programs can members of the Administrators group run?*

5. Click the **Windows Installer Rules** node and then right-click the **Windows Installer Rules** node and choose **Create Default Rules**. Three rules display in the *Windows Installer Rules* container.

Question 4	*Based on the default rules that appear in the Windows Installer Rules folder, which Windows Installer files can a typical user run on a Windows 8 workstation? Which Windows Installer files can members of the Administrators group run?*

6. Click the **Script Rules** node and then right-click the **Script Rules** node and choose **Create Default Rules**. Three rules display in the *Script Rules* container.

7. In the *Executable Rules* folder, double-click the **All files located in the Windows folder rule**. The *Allow Properties* dialog box appears.

8. On the *General* tab, modify the *Name* value to **All files located in the Windows folder except Regedit.exe**.

9. Click the **Exceptions** tab, and in the *Add exception* drop-down list, click **Path**.

10. Click **Add**. The *Path Exception* dialog box appears.

11. In the *Path* text box, type **C:\Windows\Regedit.exe** and then click **OK** twice.

12. Right-click the **Executable Rules** container and choose **Create New Rule**. The *Create Executable Rules* Wizard appears.

13. To bypass the *Before You Begin* page, click **Next**. The *Permissions* page appears.

14. Click **Select**. The *Select User or Group* dialog box appears.

15. In the *Enter the object name to select* box, type **Group Policy Creator Owners** and then click **OK**. The group name displays in the *User or group* field on the *Permissions* page.

16. Click **Next**. The *Conditions* page appears.

17. Select the **Path** option and then click **Next**. The *Path* page appears.

18. In the *Path* text box, type **C:\Windows\Regedit.exe** and then click **Create**. The new rule displays in the *Executable Rules* container.

Question 5	*Why is it necessary to create the additional rule for the Group Policy Creator Owners group?*

19. Take a screen shot of the *Group Policy Management Editor* console displaying the contents of the *Executable Rules* container by pressing **Alt+Prt Scr** and then paste the resulting image into the Lab 7 worksheet file in the page provided by pressing **Ctrl+V**.

End of exercise. Leave the Group Policy Management console and Group Policy Editor for the Hardware and Software Restricted GPO open for the next exercise.

Lab Challenge	Creating an AppLocker Rule Based on File Hash
Overview	In this exercise, you will create a rule that will deny users from running the Math Input Panel (mip.exe) based on the file hash.
Mindset	Sometimes, when administrators block a file based on a specific path, some users will try to install or copy a file to a different folder and run the program from there. You can block a file based on file hash, which will stop the program from running no matter where it is being executed from.
Completion time	10 minutes

During this exercise, you will create an AppLocker rule that will deny users from running the Math Input Panel based on file hash. The Math Input Panel file is located at C:\Program Files\Common\microsoft shared\ink\mip.exe. Write out the procedure you used to configure the settings, and then take a screen shot of the container where the settings are located by pressing **Alt+Prt Scr** and then paste the resulting image into the Lab 7 worksheet file in the page provided by pressing **Ctrl+V**.

End of lab.

LAB 8
CONFIGURING INTERNET EXPLORER

THIS LAB CONTAINS THE FOLLOWING EXERCISES AND ACTIVITIES:

Exercise 8.1	Configuring Internet Explorer
Exercise 8.2	Testing Internet Explorer Policies
Lab Challenge	Suppressing Compatibility Warnings

BEFORE YOU BEGIN

The lab environment consists of student workstations connected to a local area network, along with a server that functions as the domain controller for a domain called adatum.com. The computers required for this lab are listed in Table 8-1.

Table 8-1
Computers Required for Lab 8

Computer	*Operating System*	*Computer Name*
Server	Windows Server 2012	SVR-DC-A
Client	Windows 8 Enterprise	WKSTN-MBR-B

In addition to the computers, you will also need the software listed in Table 8-2 to complete Lab 8.

Table 8-2
Software Required for Lab 8

Software	*Location*
Lab 8 student worksheet	Lab08_worksheet.docx (provided by instructor)

Working with Lab Worksheets

Each lab in this manual requires that you answer questions, shoot screen shots, and perform other activities that you will document in a worksheet named for the lab, such as Lab08_worksheet.docx. You will find these worksheets on the book companion site. It is recommended that you use a USB flash drive to store your worksheets so you can submit them to your instructor for review. As you perform the exercises in each lab, open the appropriate worksheet file, type the required information, and then save the file to your flash drive.

SCENARIO

After completing this lab, you will be able to:

- Configure Internet Explorer settings using Group Policy.
- Test Internet Explorer policies
- Suppress compatibility warnings

Estimated lab time: 50 minutes

Exercise 8.1	Configuring Internet Explorer
Overview	In this exercise, you will configure Internet Explorer using Group Policy.
Mindset	As an administrator, you need to ensure that Internet Explorer is configured based on the policy of your organization. To configure IE for the entire organization, you can use Group Policy.
Completion time	20 minutes

1. On **WKSTN-MBR-B**, log on using the **adatum\administrator** account and the **Pa$$w0rd** password.
2. On the **Start** screen, scroll to the right, click **Administrative Tools,** and then double-click **Group Policy Management**.
3. When the *Group Policy Management* console displays, expand **Forest:adatum.com**, expand **Domains**, expand **adatum.com**, expand the **Restricted** OU, and then click the **Hardware and Software Restriction** GPO.
4. Right-click the **Hardware and Software Restrictions** GPO and choose **Edit**. The *Group Policy Management Editor* console appears.
5. Browse to the **User Configuration\Policies\Administrative Templates\Windows Components\Internet Explorer** container (see figure 8-1).

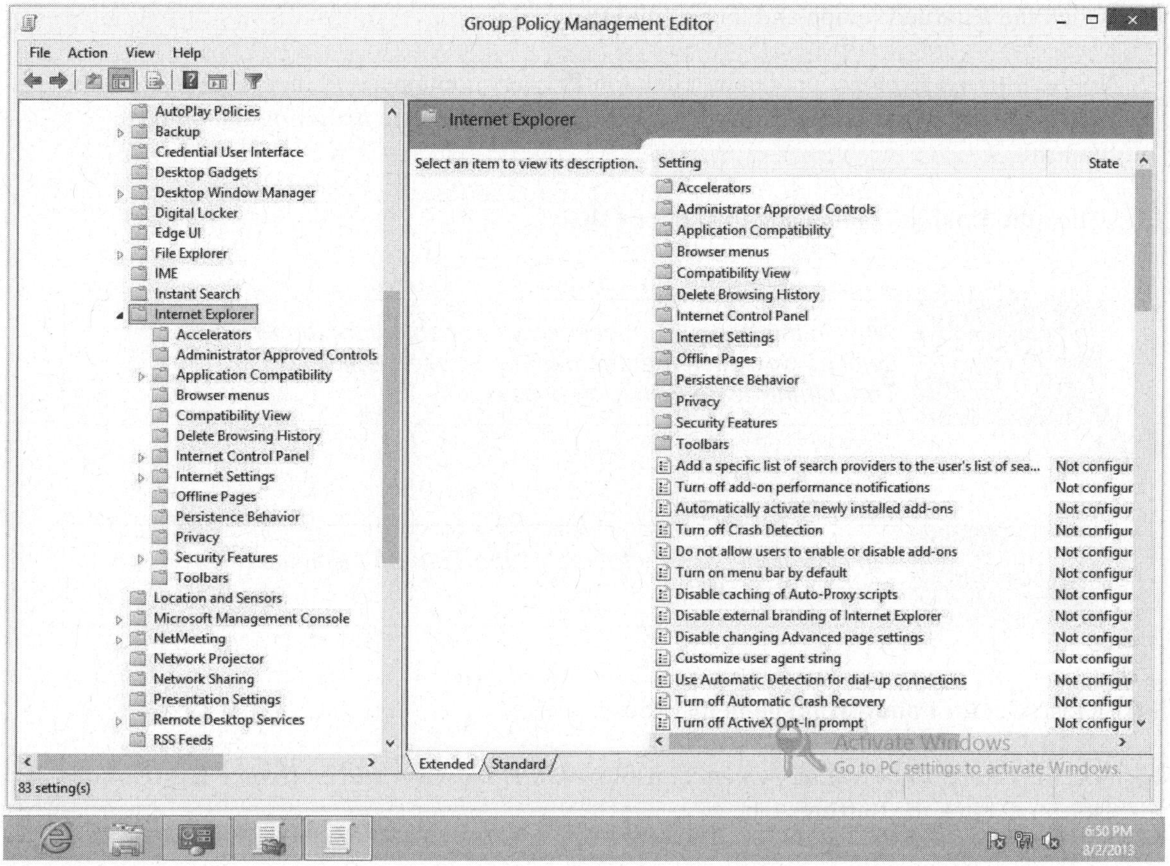

Figure 8-1
The Internet Explorer GPO settings

6. Double-click the **Do not allow users to enable or disable add-ons** policy. The *Do not allow users to enable or disable add-ons* dialog box appears.

7. Click **Enabled** and then click **OK**.

8. In the *Internet Explorer* container, select the **Compatibility View** container and then double-click the **Turn on Internet Explorer 7 Standards Mode for local intranet** policy. The *Turn on Internet Explorer 7 Standards Mode for local intranet* dialog box appears.

9. Select **Disabled** and then click **OK**.

Question 1	*Why is it necessary to disable the Turn on Internet Explorer Standards Mode for Local Intranet policy?*

10. In the *Internet Explorer* container, click the **Delete Browsing History** container and then double-click the **Prevent deleting web sites that the user has visited** policy. The *Prevent deleting web sites that the user has visited* dialog box appears.

11. Click the **Enabled** option and then click **OK**.

12. In the *Internet Explorer* container, click the **Privacy** container and then double-click the **Turn off InPrivate Browsing** policy. The *Turn off InPrivate Browsing* dialog box appears.

13. Click the **Enabled** option and then click **OK**.

Question 2	*Why, in this case, is it necessary to enable both the Prevent deleting web sites that the user has visited policy and the Turn off InPrivate Browsing policy?*

Question 3	*Why isn't it necessary to enable the Turn off InPrivate Filtering as well?*

14. Close **Group Policy Management Editor**.

15. On the *Group Policy Management* console, with **Hardware and Software Restrictions** selected, click the **Settings** tab.

16. Under *User Configuration*, click **Administrative Templates**.

17. Take a screen shot of the *Group Policy Management* console displaying all of the policy settings you configured in this exercise by pressing **Alt+Prt Scr** and then paste the resulting image into the Lab 8 worksheet file in the page provided by pressing **Ctrl+V**.

18. Close the **Group Policy Management** console.

End of exercise. Leave the console open and the computer logged on for the next exercise.

Exercise 8.2	Testing Internet Explorer Policies
Overview	In this exercise, you will confirm the Internet Explorer settings that are configured with a GPO are deployed to a client computer.
Mindset	When troubleshooting problems, you will need to ensure that settings that you configure with a GPO are actually deployed to the clients.
Completion time	20 minutes

1. On **WKSTN-MBR-B**, Using the **Administrative Tools** folder, double-click **Active Directory Users and Computers**.
2. Right-click the **Restricted** OU and choose **New > User**.
3. When the *New Object – User* dialog box displays, type the following information and then click **Next**:

   First name: **User**

   Last name: **1**

   User logon name: **User1**
4. In the *Password* box and in the *Confirm Password* box, type **Pa$$w0rd**. Deselect **User must change password at next logon** and then select **Password never expires**. Click **Next**.
5. When the wizard is complete, click **Finish**.
6. Close **Active Directory Users and Computers**.
7. Log off as **adatum\administrator**.
8. Log on as **adatum\user1** with the **Pa$$w0rd** password.
9. Click the **Desktop** tile.
10. Log off as **adatum\user1**.
11. Logon as **adatum\administrator** with the **Pa$$w0rd** password.
12. Open the **Administrative Tools** folder and double-click **Group Policy Management**.
13. Click the **Group Policy Results** node (see Figure 8-2).

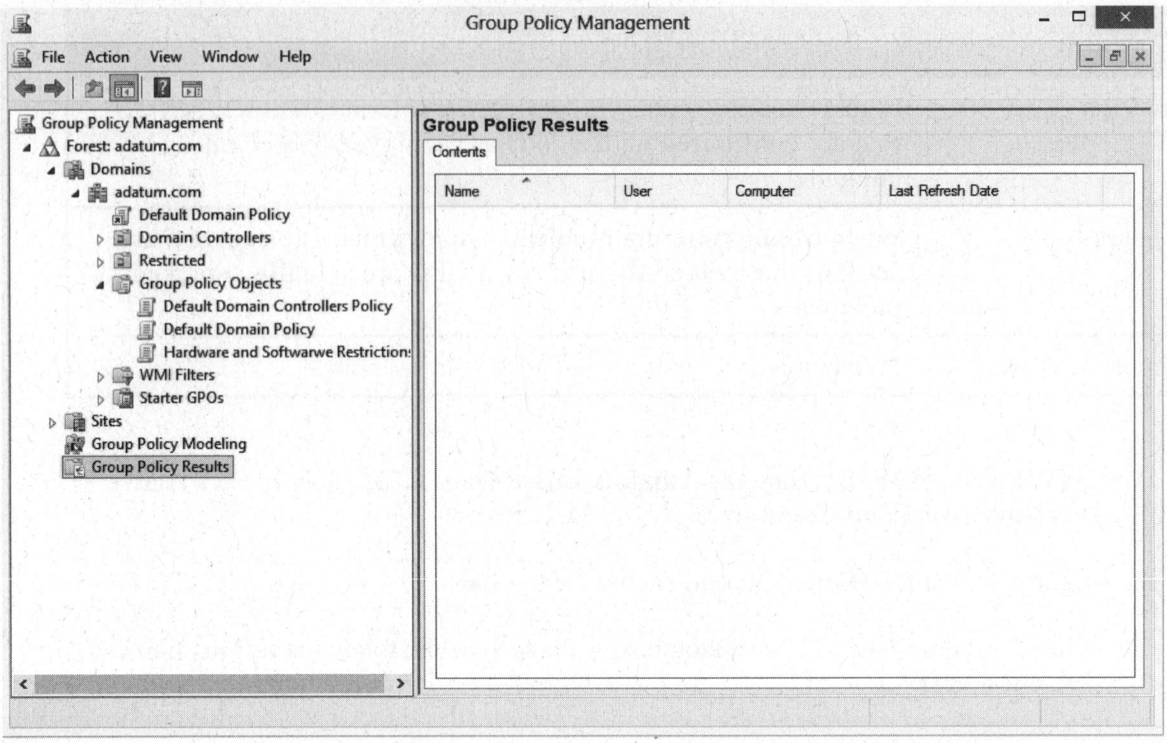

Figure 8-2
Opening the Group Policy Results node

14. Right-click the **Group Policy Results** node and choose **Group Policy Results Wizard**.

15. When the *Group Policy Results Wizard* starts, click **Next**.

16. On the *Computer Selection* page, click **Next**.

17. On the *User Selection* page, click to select the **Select a specific user** and then click **Adatum\User1**. Click **Next**.

18. On the *Summary of Selections* page, click **Next**.

19. When the wizard is complete, click **Finish**.

20. With **user1** on **WKSTN-MBR-B** selected, in the right pane, click the **Details** tab.

21. Examine the options to verify that User 1 is receiving the IE settings that you just set by clicking **show** next to **User Details, Settings, and Policies**.

22. Expand **show** next to **Windows Components/Internet Explorer** and **Windows Components/Internet Explorer/Compatibility View**.

23. Take a screen shot of the *Group Policy Management* console showing the Internet Explorer policy settings displayed with the Group Policy Results by pressing **Alt+Prt Scr** and then paste the resulting image into the Lab 8 worksheet file in the page provided by pressing **Ctrl+V**.

Question 4	*If you have confirmed GPO settings are configured correctly, and the GPO is assigned to the correct container, which command can be used to ensure that the GPO settings is deployed to the user immediately?*

24. Close **Group Policy Management Editor**.

End of exercise. Leave the Group Policy Management console open for the lab Challenge.

Lab Challenge	Suppressing Compatibility Warnings
Overview	To complete this challenge, you must demonstrate how to suppress the compatibility warnings.
Mindset	The Windows 8 users at Contoso, Ltd. are restricted to a predefined set of applications, all of which have been recently updated and carefully tested for compatibility. To prevent users from attempting to run down-level applications, you have been instructed to disable the Windows 7 compatibility mode controls using Group Policy.
Completion time	10 minutes

To complete this challenge, you must locate and configure the appropriate Group Policy settings to accomplish these goals in the GPO you created in Exercise 8.1. Write out the procedure you used to configure the settings, and then take a screen shot of the container where the settings are located by pressing **Alt+Prt Scr** and then paste the resulting image into the Lab 8 worksheet file in the page provided by pressing **Ctrl+V**.

End of lab.

LAB 9
CONFIGURING HYPER-V

THIS LAB CONTAINS THE FOLLOWING EXERCISES AND ACTIVITIES:

Exercise 9.1 Installing Client Hyper-V

Exercise 9.2 Creating a Virtual Machine Using Hyper-V Manager

Exercise 9.3 Configuring Virtual Machine Settings

Lab Challenge Expanding a Virtual Hard Disk

BEFORE YOU BEGIN

The lab environment consists of computers connected to a local area network. The computers required for this lab are listed in Table 9-1.

Table 9-1
Computers Required for Lab 9

Computer	*Operating System*	*Computer Name*
Server	Windows Server 2012	SVR-DC-A
Client	Windows 8 Enterprise	WKSTN-MBR-B

In addition to the computers, you will also require the software listed in Table 9-2 to complete Lab 9.

Table 9-2
Software Required for Lab 9

Software	*Location*
Windows 8 installation ISO	\\SVR-DC-A\Software\.
Lab 9 student worksheet	Lab09_worksheet.docx (provided by instructor)

Working with Lab Worksheets

Each lab in this manual requires that you answer questions, create screen shots, and then perform other activities that you will document in a worksheet named for the lab, such as Lab09_worksheet.docx. You will find these worksheets on the book companion site. It is recommended that you use a USB flash drive to store your worksheets so you can submit them to your instructor for review. As you perform the exercises in each lab, open the appropriate worksheet file, type the required information, and then save the file to your flash drive.

SCENARIO

After completing this lab, you will be able to:

- Install and configure Hyper-V
- Create a virtual machine in Hyper-V
- Take a snapshot of a virtual machine and then delete a snapshot of a virtual machine

Estimated lab time: 45 minutes

Exercise 9.1	Installing Client Hyper-V
Overview	In this exercise, you will install Hyper-V on a computer running Windows 8.
Mindset	Sometimes an older application will not work on Windows 8, even though you use the Compatibility Troubleshooter. One solution is to install Hyper-V on the client computer, create a virtual machine, and then install Windows XP on the virtual machine. You can then install and run the application on the virtual machine.
Completion time	15 minutes

1. On **WKSTN-MBR-B**, log on using the **adatum\administrator** account and the **Pa$$w0rd** password. Click the **Desktop** tile.

2. Mouse over the lower-left corner of the desktop and right-click the Start screen thumbnail that appears there. Then click **Command Prompt (Admin)**.

3. Since Windows 8 is running as a virtual machine, you will need to install Hyper-V using the DISM command. Therefore, execute the following command:

```
dism /online /enable-feature /featurename:Microsoft-Hyper-
V-All
```

4. When prompted to reboot the computer, type **Y**.

5. Log into WKSTN-MBR-B as **adatum\administrator** using the **Pa$$w0rd** password.

6. Click the **Desktop** tile.

7. Mouse over the lower-left corner of the desktop and right-click the Start screen thumbnail that appears there. Then click **Control Panel**.

8. Click **Programs**, and then in the *Programs* window, click **Turn Windows Features on or off**.

9. In the *Windows Features* window, expand **Hyper-V** and then expand **Hyper-V Management Tools**.

10. Take a screen shot of the *Windows Features* window by pressing **Alt+Prt Scr** and then paste it into your Lab 9 worksheet file in the page provided by pressing **Ctrl+V**.

11. Click **OK** to close the *Windows Features* window.

12. Close the *Programs and Features* window.

13. Mouse over the lower-left corner of the desktop and click the Start screen thumbnail that appears there. When the *Start* screen displays, scroll to the right and then click **Hyper-V Manager**.

14. When *Hyper-V Manager* opens, right-click **WKSTN-MBR-B** and then click **Virtual Switch Manager**.

15. When the *Virtual Switch Manager* appears (see Figure 9-1) in the right pane, where it prompts you do identify the type of virtual switch that you want to create, click **Internal**.

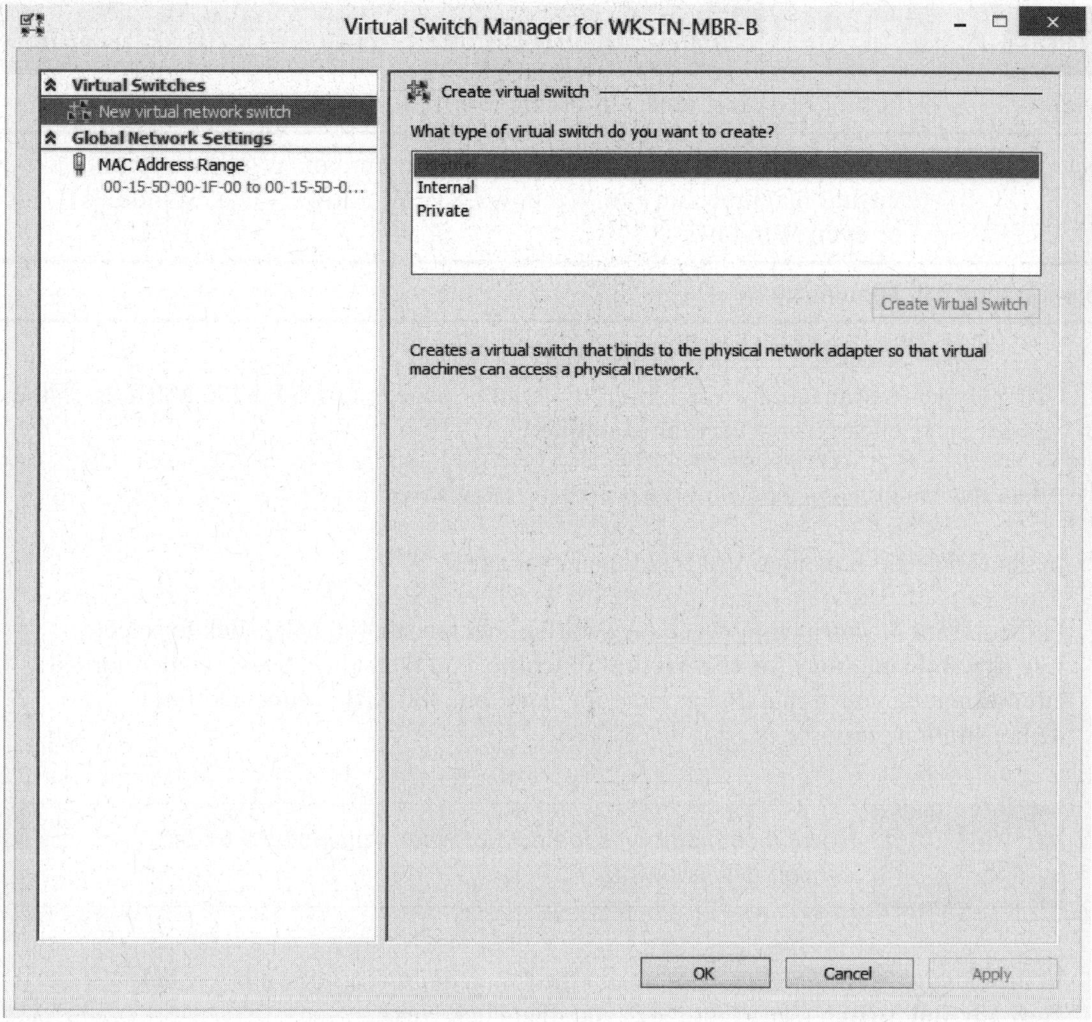

Figure 9-1
The Virtual Switch Manager

Question 1	*Which type of virtual switch would you select if you want the VM to connect to the Internet?*

16. Click **Create Virtual Switch**.

17. Click **OK** to close the *Virtual Switch Manager*.

End of exercise. Leave the computer on for the next exercise.

Exercise 9.2	Creating a Virtual Machine Using Hyper-V Manager
Overview	In this exercise, you will create a virtual machine in Hyper-V.
Mindset	Hyper-V allows you to run a virtual machine on Windows 8. The virtual machine can run Windows XP, Windows Vista, Windows 7, or even Windows 8.
Completion time	10 minutes

1. Using Hyper-V Manager, on the *Hyper-V Manager* page, click **WKSTN-MBR-B**. In the *Actions* pane, click **New** > **Virtual Machine.**

2. When the *New Virtual Machine Wizard* starts, click **Next.**

3. In the *Name* text box, type **VM1** and then click **Next.**

4. In the *Assign Memory* window, change startup memory to 480 MB, click to select **Use dynamic memory for this virtual machine**, and then click **Next**. (Under normal circumstances, you would assign more memory, but 480 MB is adequate for demonstration purposes.)

Question 2	*How much memory is the default when you install a 64-bit version of windows 8?*

5. In the *Configure Networking* window, in the *Connection* drop-down box, click **New Virtual Switch** (see Figure 9-2) and then click **Next.**

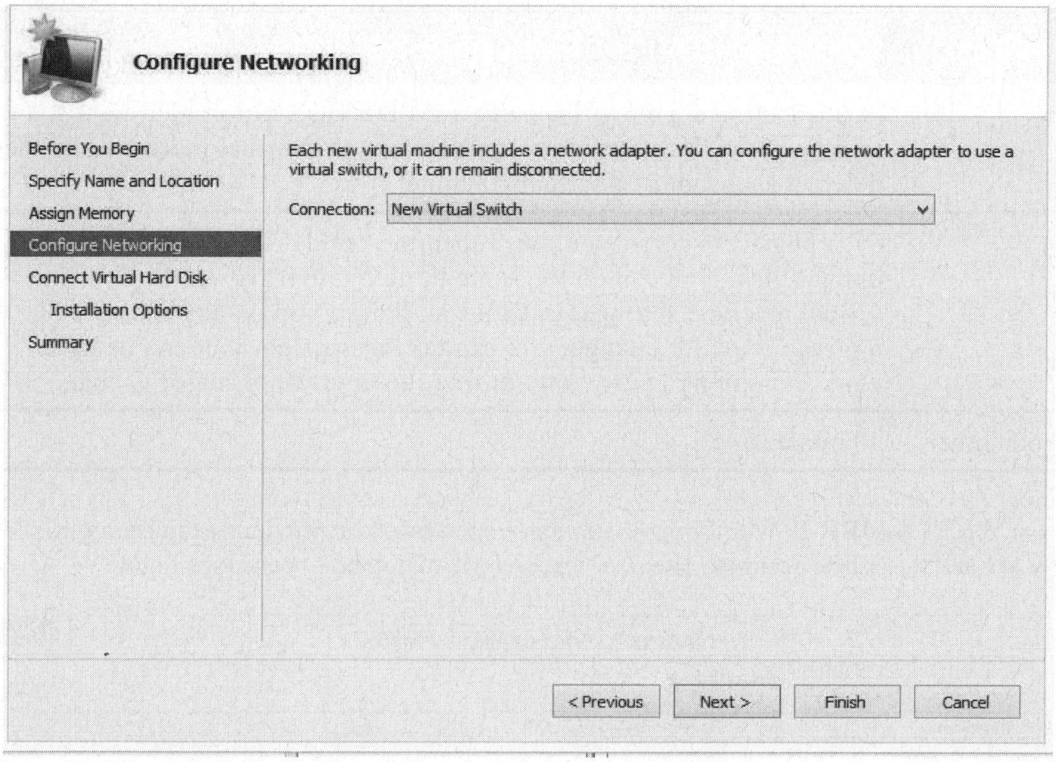

Figure 9-2
The *Configure Networking* page

6. In the *Connect Virtual Hard Disk* window, click to select **Create a virtual hard disk**, and then specify **5** GB for the size. Click **Next**. (Again, you would not normally use a small hard drive, but this setting is adequate for demonstration purposes.)

7. On the *Installation Options* page, click to select **Install an operating system later** and then click **Next**.

8. In the *Completing the New Virtual Machine Wizard* window, click **Finish**. Once completed, the new virtual machine appears in the Virtual Machines list of the Hyper-V Manager.

9. Take a screen shot of the *Hyper-V Manager* console showing the newly created VM by pressing **Alt+Prt Scr** and then paste it into your Lab 9 worksheet file in the page provided by pressing **Ctrl+V**.

Note	*Since we are running Hyper-V on a virtual machine, we will not be able to run virtual machines.*

End of exercise. Leave Hyper-V Manager open for the next exercise.

Exercise 9.3	Configuring Virtual Machine Settings
Overview	In this exercise, you will specify a DVD to use within a virtual machine. You will also create a snapshot of a virtual machine and then delete a snapshot of a virtual machine.
Mindset	On a physical server, you must open the optical drive and insert an optical disk. You can do the same thing on a virtual server by using the virtual machine settings. In addition, before you do any type of upgrade or major change, you can take a snapshot that can be used when something goes wrong during the upgrade or major change.
Completion time	10 minutes

1. On **WKSTN-MBR-B**, with *Hyper-V Manager* open from the previous exercise, right-click **VM1** and then click **Settings**. The *Settings for VM1* dialog box opens (see Figure 9-3).

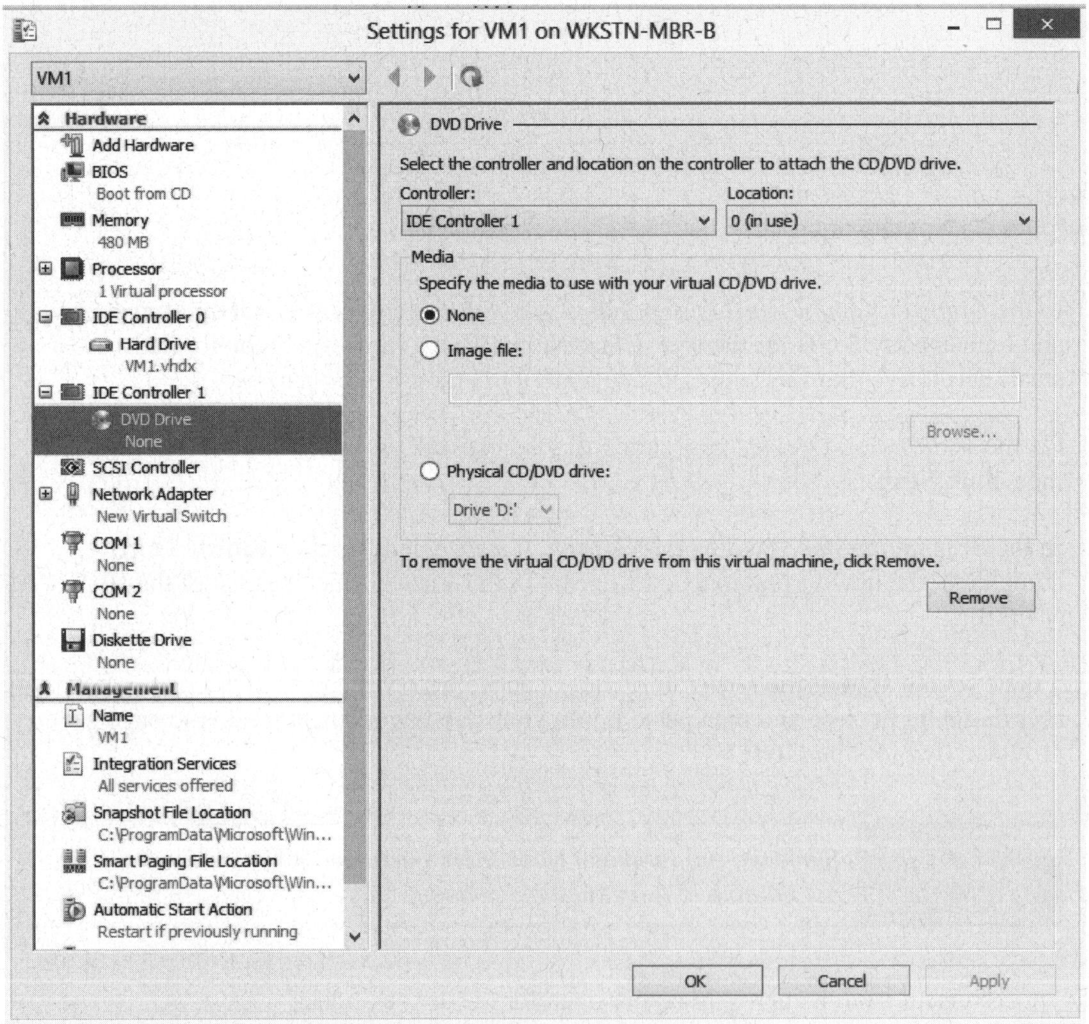

Figure 9-3
The VM settings dialog box

2. In the *Hardware* pane, under the *IDE Controller 1* section, click **DVD Drive**. On the right pane, click **Image file** and then click **Browse**.

3. In the *File name* text box, type **SVR-DC-A\Software**, click **Open**, and then double-click the Windows 8 image file.

4. Take a screen shot of the *Settings* window by pressing **Alt+Prt Scr** and then paste it into your Lab 9 worksheet file in the page provided by pressing **Ctrl+V**.

5. Click **OK** to close the *Settings* window.

6. To take a snapshot, right-click **VM1** and choose **Snapshot**.

Question 3	*What are snapshots used for?*

7. To delete the snapshot, right-click the **VM1** snapshot choose **Delete Snapshot**. When you are prompted to confirm if you want to delete the selected snapshot, click **Delete**.

End of exercise. Leave Hyper-V Manager open for the challenge lab.

Lab Challenge	Expanding a Virtual Hard Disk
Overview	In this challenge, you will expand the virtual hard drive for VM1 from 5 GB to 6 GB.
Mindset	As you install applications and add data files, you sometimes have to expand the drive.
Completion time	10 minutes

To complete this challenge, you have a virtual machine on your computer running Windows 8. Since the C drive is filling up, you need to first expand the C drive of the virtual machine from 5 GB to 6 GB. Write out the procedure to expand the drive and then take a snapshot of the *Expand Virtual Hard Disk* page by pressing **Alt+Prt Scr** and then paste the resulting image into the Lab 9 worksheet file in the page provided by pressing **Ctrl+V**.

End of lab.

LAB 10 CONFIGURING IP SETTINGS

THIS LAB CONTAINS THE FOLLOWING EXERCISES AND ACTIVITIES:

Exercise 10.1 Manually Configuring TCP/IP

Exercise 10.2 Creating and Managing a DHCP Scope

Exercise 10.3 Testing Network Connections

Lab Challenge Configuring IP at the Command Prompt

BEFORE YOU BEGIN

The lab environment consists of student workstations connected to a local area network, along with a server that functions as the domain controller for a domain called adatum.com. The computers required for this lab are listed in Table 10-1.

Table 10-1
Computers Required for Lab 10

Computer	*Operating System*	*Computer Name*
Server	Windows Server 2012	SVR-DC-A
Client	Windows 8 Enterprise	WKSTN-MBR-B

In addition to the computers, you will also need the software listed in Table 10-2 to complete Lab 10.

Table 10-2
Software required for Lab 10

Software	***Location***
Lab 10 student worksheet	Lab10_worksheet.docx (provided by instructor)

Working with Lab Worksheets

Each lab in this manual requires that you answer questions, shoot screen shots, and perform other activities that you will document in a worksheet named for the lab, such as Lab10_worksheet.docx. You will find these worksheets on the book companion site. It is recommended that you use a USB flash drive to store your worksheets so you can submit them to your instructor for review. As you perform the exercises in each lab, open the appropriate worksheet file, type the required information, and then save the file to your flash drive.

SCENARIO

After completing this lab, you will be able to:

- Manually configure IPv4 Configuration on a computer running Windows 8
- Create and configure a DHCP scope
- Use basic IP configuration troubleshooting tools

Estimated lab time: 55 minutes

Exercise 10.1	Manually Configuring TCP/IP
Overview	In this exercise, you will configure the IP configuration of a computer running Windows 8.
Mindset	As an administrator, you will have to configure the IP settings for workstations and servers.
Completion time	20 minutes

1. On **WKSTN-MBR-B**, log on using the **adatum\Administrator** account and the **Pa$$w0rd** password. Click the Desktop tile.

2. Mouse over the lower-left corner of the desktop and right-click the **Start** screen thumbnail that appears there. Then, from the context menu that appears, click **Command Prompt (Admin)**.

3. When the command prompt displays, execute the following command:

```
ipconfig
```

Question 1	*What is the IPv4 address and subnet mask assigned to the computer?*

Question 2	*What is the IPv6 address?*

4. On the *Taskbar*, right-click the **Network Status** icon and choose **Open Network and Sharing Center**.

5. When the *Network and Sharing Center* window displays, click **Change adapter settings**.

6. Right-click the **Ethernet** adapter and choose **Properties**.

7. In the *Ethernet Properties* dialog box, scroll down and double-click **Internet Protocol Version 4 (TCP/IPv4)**.

8. In the *Internet Protocol Version 4 (TCP/IPv4) Properties* dialog box, click to select the **Obtain an IP address automatically** option and the **Obtain DNS server address automatically** option.

9. Click **OK** to close the *Internet Protocol Version 4 (TCP/IPv4) Properties* dialog box and then click **OK** to close the *Ethernet Properties* dialog box.

10. At the command prompt, execute the following command:

```
ipconfig /all
```

Question 3	*By looking at the response from ipconfig, what is the address of the DHCP server that assigned the IPv4 address to this computer?*

11. Close the *Command Prompt* window.

12. Back at the *Network Connections* window, right-click the **Ethernet connection** and choose **Status**.

13. In the *Ethernet Status* dialog box, click **Details**. This should display the same information you saw with the ipconfig /all command. Click **Close** to close the *Network Connection Details* dialog box.

14. In the *Ethernet Status* dialog box, click **Properties**.

15. In the *Ethernet Properties* dialog box (see Figure 10-1), scroll down and double-click **Internet Protocol Version 4 (TCP/IPv4)**.

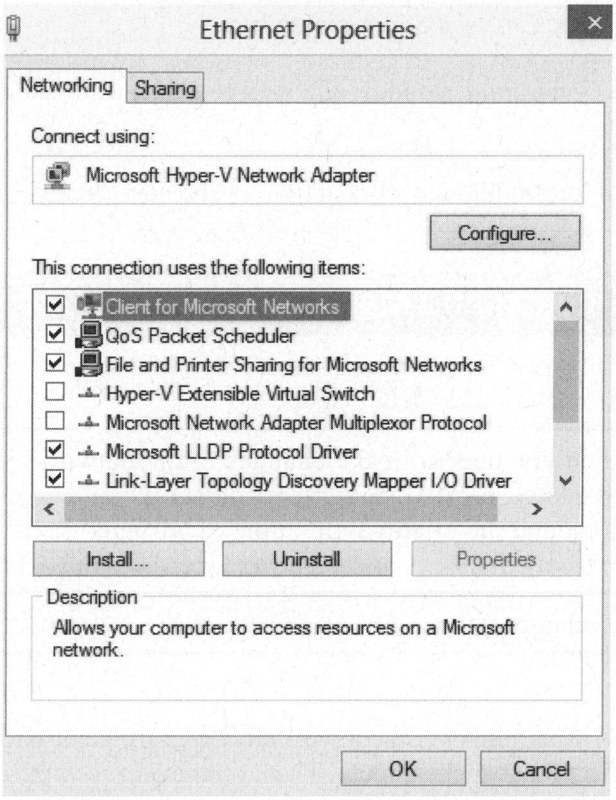

Figure 10-1
The *Ethernet Properties* dialog box

16. When the *Internet Protocol Version 4 (TCP/IPv4) Properties* dialog box displays, click **Use the following IP address**.

17. Type the following information:

    IP address: **10.0.0.2**

    Subnet mask: **255.255.255.0**

    Default gateway: **10.0.0.20**

18. Click to select the **Use the following DNS server addresses**.

19. For the *Preferred DNS server* setting, type **10.0.0.1**.

20. Take a screen shot of the *Internet Protocol Version 4 (TCP/IPv4) Properties* dialog box by pressing **Alt+Prt Scr** and then paste it into your Lab 10 worksheet file in the page provided by pressing **Ctrl+V**.

21. Click **OK** to close the *Internet Protocol Version 4 (TCP/IPv4) Properties* sheet.

22. Click **OK** to close the *Ethernet Properties* dialog box.

23. Click **Close** to close the *Ethernet Status* dialog box.

24. Close the *Network Connections* window and then close the *Network and Sharing Center* windows.

End of exercise. Remain logged into the workstation for the next exercise.

Exercise 10.2	Creating and Managing a DHCP Scope
Overview	In this exercise, you will create a DHCP scope and look at the parameters of a DHCP scope.
Mindset	When you need to make changes to the network, including changing the addresses of DNS servers and such, you can change the DHCP scope and the clients will automatically get the IP configuration automatically.
Completion time	15 minutes

1. On **WKSTN-MBR-B**, mouse over the lower-left corner of the desktop and click the **Start** screen thumbnail that appears there. Then, on the *Start* screen, click **Administrative Tools**.

2. Double-click **DHCP**.

3. When the *DHCP* console displays, right-click **DHCP** and choose **Add Server**.

4. In the *This server* text box, type **10.0.0.1** and then click **OK**.

5. Expand the **svr-dc-a node**, expand the **IPv4** node, and then expand the **Scope [10.0.0.0] Main Scope** node (see Figure 10-2).

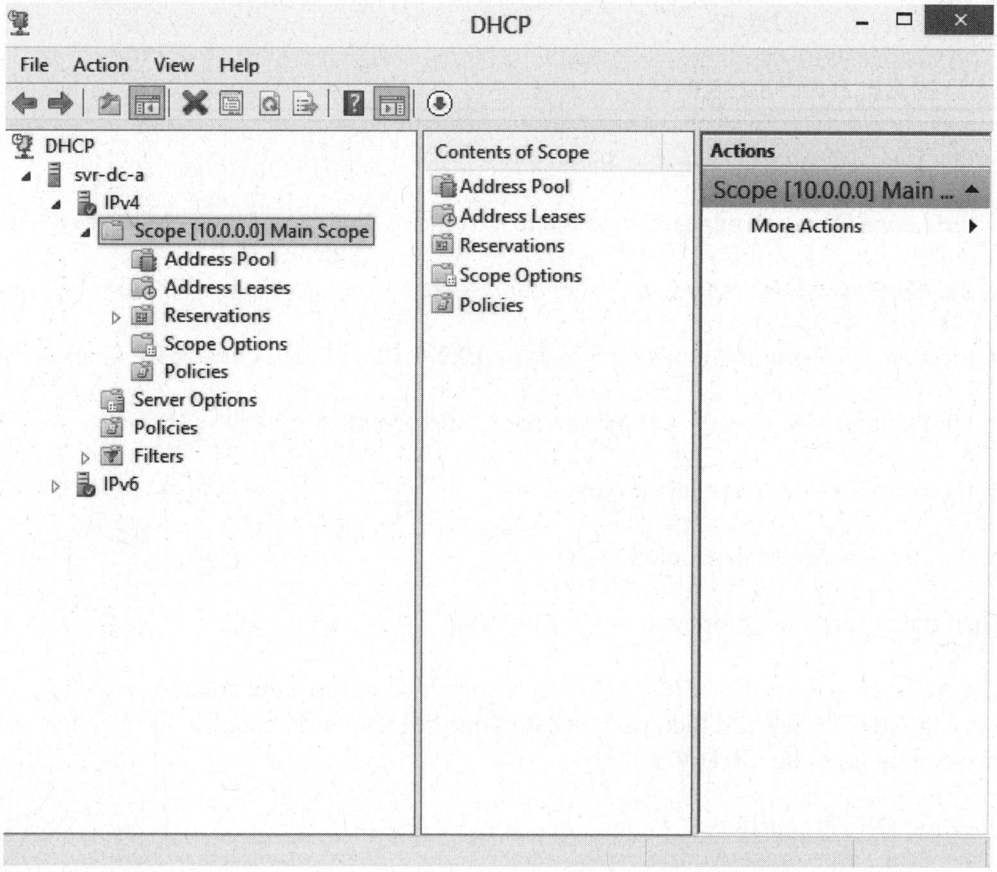

Figure 10-2
Expanding the *Scope* node

6. Right-click the **Scope [10.0.0.0] Main Scope** and choose **Properties**.

Question 4	*What is the start and end IP addresses being assigned?*

7. Click **OK** to close the *Scope [10.0.0.0] Main Scope Properties* dialog box.

8. Click **Address Leases** to view the current leases assigned.

9. To create a new DHCP scope, right-click **IPv4** and choose **New Scope**.

10. When the *New Scope* Wizard displays, click **Next**.

11. On the *Scope Name* page, in the *Name* text box, type **Test** and then click **Next**.

12. On the *IP Address Range* page, type the following information and then click **Next**:

    Start IP address: **10.2.0.30**

End IP address: **10.2.0.40**

Subnet mask: **255.255.255.0**

13. On the *Add Exclusions and Delay* page, click **Next**.
14. On the *Lease Duration* page, change the lease time to **3** days and then click **Next**.
15. On the *Configure DHCP Options* page, click **Next**.
16. On the *Router (Default Gateway)* page, type **10.2.0.20** and then click **Add**. Click **Next**.
17. On the *Domain Name and DNS Servers* page, click **Next**.
18. On the *WINS Servers* page, click **Next**.
19. On the *Activate Scope* page, click **Next**.
20. When the wizard has completed, click **Finish**.
21. Take a screen shot of the *DHCP* console dialog showing the new created scope by pressing **Alt+Prt Scr** and then paste it into your Lab 10 worksheet file in the page provided by pressing **Ctrl+V**.
22. Close the *DHCP* console.

End of exercise. Leave the computer logged in for the next exercise.

Exercise 10.3	Testing Network Connections
Overview	In this exercise, you will test the network connection and network connectivity between computers. You will also use nslookup to get the IP address of a host.
Mindset	Network connection problems occur; they are usually caused by physical problems (such as when a cable is not connected) or by an IP configuration problem (such as having the wrong subnet mask or default gateway). As an administrator, you need to know how to troubleshoot such problems.
Completion time	10 minutes

1. On **WKSTN-MBR-B**, mouse over the lower-left corner of the desktop and right-click the **Start** screen thumbnail that appears there. Then, from the context menu that appears, click **Command Prompt (Admin)**.
2. At the command prompt, type **ping 127.0.0.1** (see Figure 10-3) and then press **Enter**.

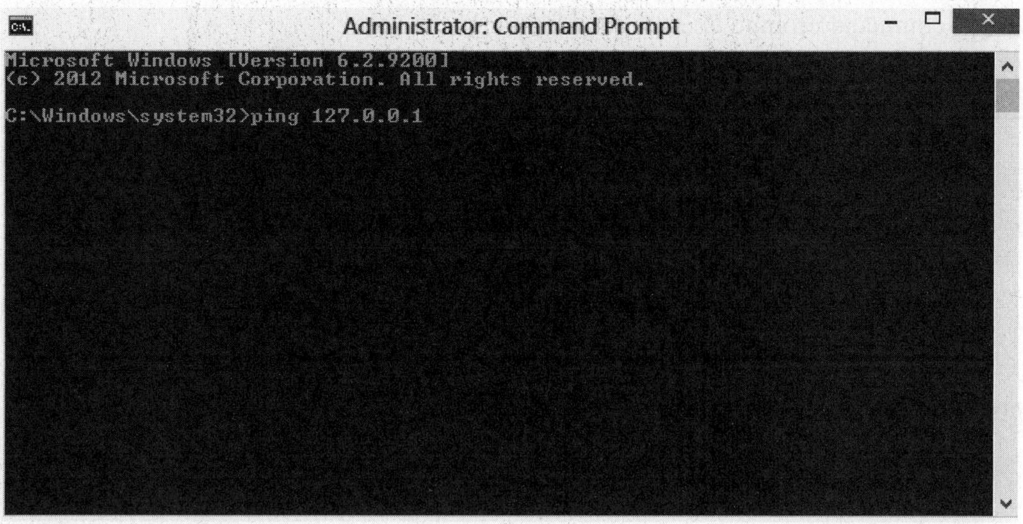

Figure 10-3
Executing the ping command

Question 5	*What is the result of executing ping 127.0.0.1?*

Question 6	*What does this result prove about the computer's network connectivity?*

Question 7	*What would be the result if you unplugged your computer's network cable before executing the ping 127.0.0.1 command?*

3. At the command prompt, type **ping SVR-DC-A** and then press **Enter**.

Question 8	*What is the result of executing ping SVR-DC-A and what does it prove?*

Question 9	*What is the IP address of SVR-DC-A?*

4. At the command prompt, execute the following command:

   nslookup SVR-DC-A

Question 10	*What is the IP address of SVR-DC-A?*

5. Take a screen shot of the *Administrator Command Prompt* window by pressing **Alt+Prt Scr** and then paste it into your Lab 10 worksheet file in the page provided by pressing **Ctrl+V**.

6. Close the *Command Prompt* window.

End of exercise. Close any open windows before you begin the next exercise.

Lab Challenge	Configuring IP at the Command Prompt
Overview	In this exercise, you will perform a written exercise to demonstrate configuring IP settings using commands.
Mindset	As an administrator, you may want create scripts, which contain commands that you would execute to configure Windows. Some of these commands may include configuring IP.
Completion time	10 minutes

For this written exercise, answer the following questions.

1. Which command is used to configure the following?

   IP Address: 10.2.0.50

   Subnet mask: 255.255.255.0

   Default Gateway: 10.2.0.20

2. Which command is used to configure the primary DNS server as 10.0.0.50?
3. Which command would you set the computer to use DHCP?

End of lab.

LAB 11
CONFIGURING NETWORK SETTINGS

THIS LAB CONTAINS THE FOLLOWING EXERCISES AND ACTIVITIES:

Exercise 11.1 Configuring Network Adapter Settings

Lab Challenge Configuring Wireless Network Settings

BEFORE YOU BEGIN

The lab environment consists of student workstations connected to a local area network, along with a server that functions as the domain controller for a domain called adatum.com. The computers required for this lab are listed in Table 11-1.

Table 11-1
Computers Required for Lab 11

Computer	*Operating System*	*Computer Name*
Server	Windows Server 2012	SVR-DC-A
Client	Windows 8 Enterprise	WKSTN-MBR-B

In addition to the computers, you will also need the software listed in Table 11-2 to complete Lab 11.

Table 11-2
Software Required for Lab 11

Software	*Location*
Lab 11 student worksheet	Lab11_worksheet.docx (provided by instructor)

Working with Lab Worksheets

Each lab in this manual requires that you answer questions, shoot screen shots, and perform other activities that you will document in a worksheet named for the lab, such as Lab11_worksheet.docx. You will find these worksheets on the book companion site. It is recommended that you use a USB flash drive to store your worksheets so you can submit them to your instructor for review. As you perform the exercises in each lab, open the appropriate worksheet file, type the required information, and then save the file to your flash drive.

SCENARIO

After completing this lab, you will be able to:

- Configure network adapter settings
- Manage adapters using the Network Connections window

Estimated lab time: 40 minutes

Exercise 11.1	Configuring Network Adapter Settings
Overview	In this exercise, you will configure network adapters and their properties.
Mindset	While the common settings are configured directly using the Network and Sharing Center, you can configure additional settings using Network Connections window and the network adapter properties.
Completion time	20 minutes

1. On **WKSTN-MBR-B**, log on using the **adatum\administrator** account and the **Pa$$w0rd** password. Click the **Desktop** tile.
2. On the *Taskbar*, right-click the network connection icon and choose **Open Network and Sharing Center**.
3. In the *Network and Sharing Center* (see Figure 11-1), click **Change adapter settings**.

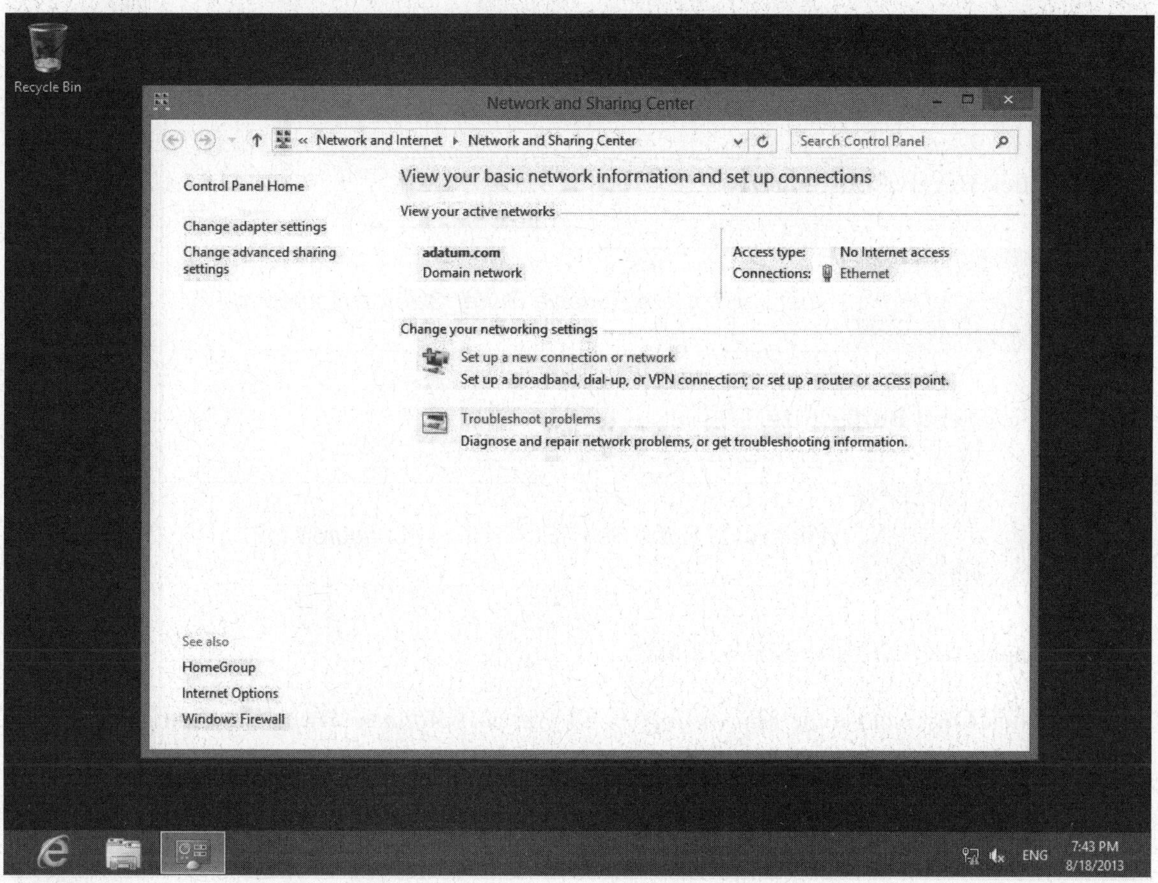

Figure 11-1
The *Network and Sharing Center*

4. In the *Network Connections* dialog box, right-click **Ethernet** and choose **Disable**.

5. With Ethernet already selected, click the **Enable this network device** button.

6. Right-click the **Ethernet** adapter and choose **Properties**. The Ethernet Properties dialog box opens.

Question 1	*What type of adapter is it the adapter using?*

7. Click the **Configure** button.

8. When the *Microsoft Hyper-V Network Adapter Properties* dialog box opens, click the **Advanced** tab.

9. Click **Jumbo Packet**.

Question 2	*What value is the Jumbo Packet configured to?*

10. Click **Receive Buffer Size**.

Question 3	*What value is the Receive Buffer Size configured to?*

11. Click **Send Buffer Size**.

Question 4	*What value is the Send Buffer Size configured to?*

12. Change **Send Buffer Size** to **2 MB**.

13. Click **OK** to close the *Microsoft Hyper-V Network Adapter Properties* dialog box.

14. The BCM5708C NetExtemeII GigE is an adapter that you may find on a physical computer, not on a virtual machine. Look at the *Broadcom BCM5708C NetXtreme II GigE* dialog box shown in Figure 11-2.

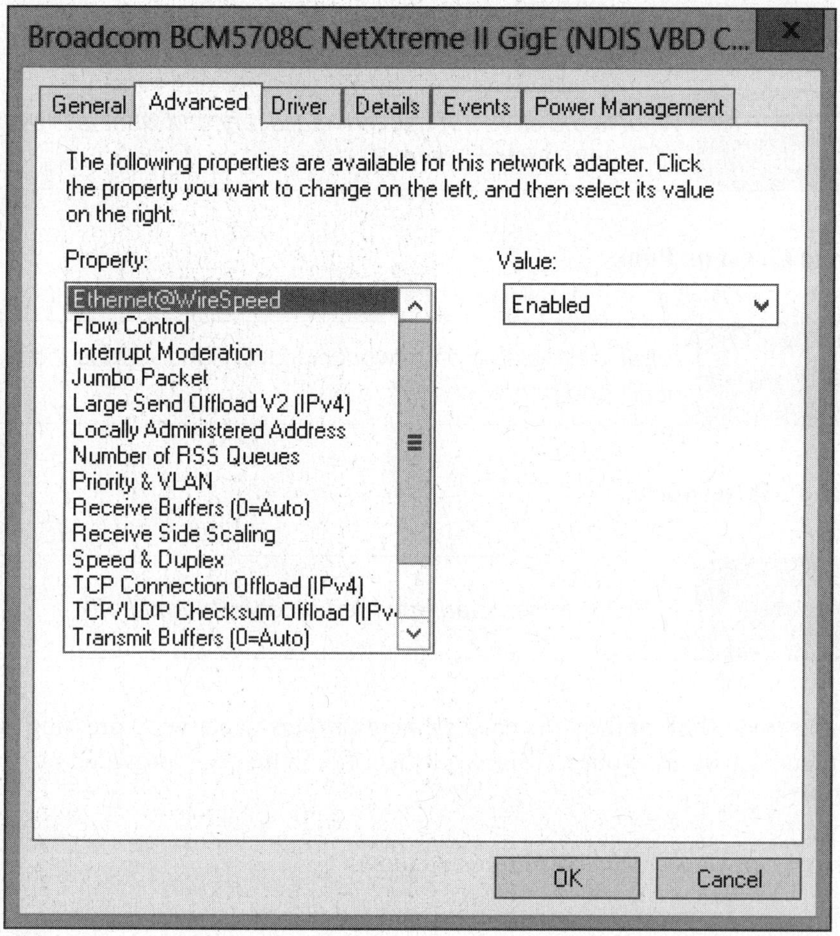

Figure 11-2
Broadcom adapter properties

Question 5	*You have a 1 Gbps adapter and you want to reduce the speed to 100 Mbps. Which settings would you select from Figure 11-2 to reduce the speed and which value would you select?*

15. In the *Network and Sharing Center* window, click **Change advanced sharing settings**.

Question 6	*What is the current profile?*

Question 7	*What is the status of network discovery and what is the status of file and printer sharing?*

16. Expand **Private**.

Question 8	*What is the status of network discovery and what is the status of file and printer sharing?*

17. Expand **Guest or Public**.

Question 9	*What is the status of network discovery and what is the status of file and printer sharing?*

18. Expand **All Networks**.

Question 10	*Is Public folder sharing turned on or is it turned off?*

19. Take a screen shot of the *Advanced sharing settings* window by pressing **Alt+Prt Scr** and then paste it into your Lab 11 worksheet file in the page provided by pressing **Ctrl+V**.

20. Close the *Advanced sharing settings* window.

Lab Challenge	Configuring Wireless Network Adapter Settings
Overview	In this lab challenge, you will identify the settings that are unique to wireless network adapters.
Mindset	Because the physical security capabilities of standard Ethernet networks do not apply, wireless networks must have additional security mechanisms.

To complete this challenge, specify how each of the following elements (see Figure 11-3 and Figure 11-4) contribute to the security of the network.

1. Connect even if the network is not broadcasting its name
2. Security type
3. Encryption type
4. Network security key

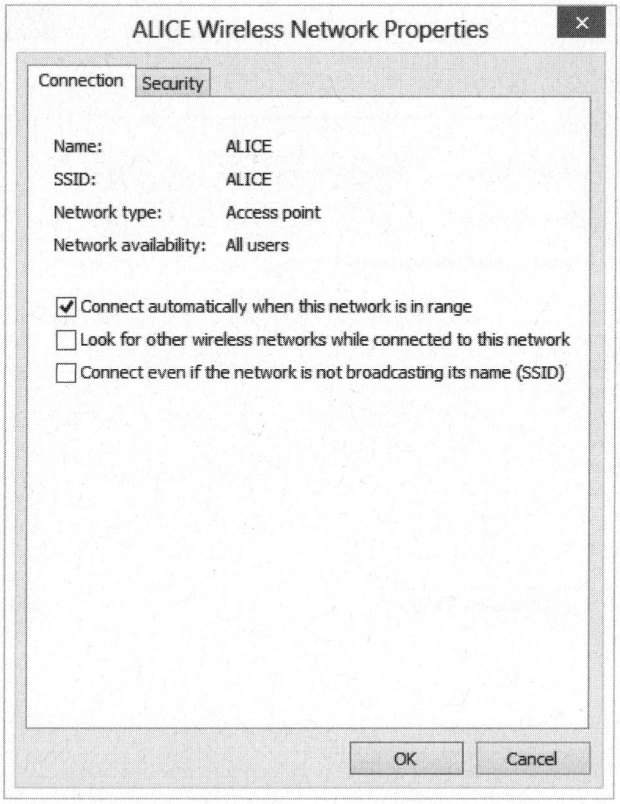

Figure 11-3
Wireless adapter properties

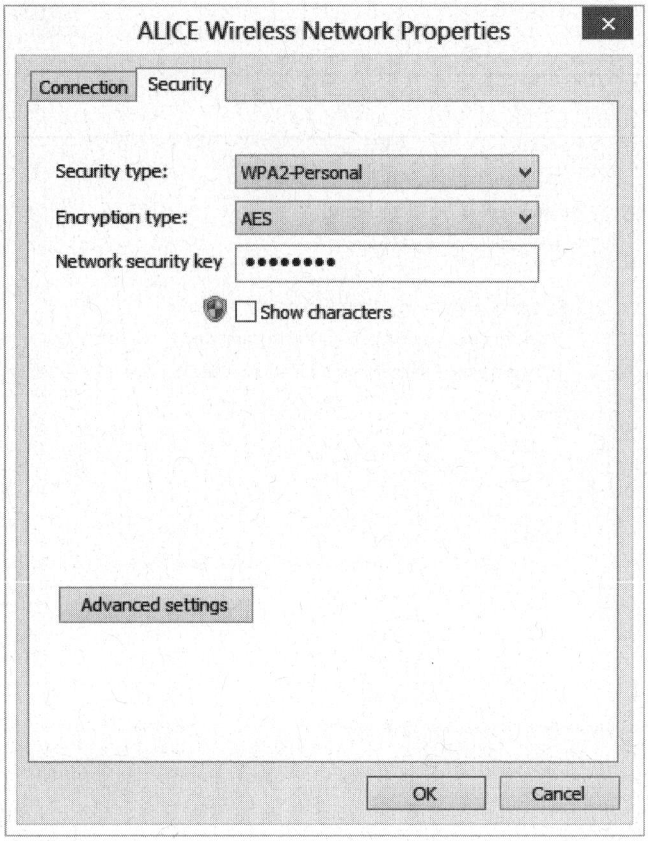

Figure 11-4
Wireless security properties

End of lab.

LAB 12
CONFIGURING AND MAINTAINING NETWORK SECURITY

THIS LAB CONTAINS THE FOLLOWING EXERCISES AND ACTIVITIES:

Exercise 12.1 Installing Internet Information Server

Exercise 12.2 Testing IIS Connectivity

Exercise 12.3 Allowing a Program Through the Firewall

Lab Challenge Creating Windows Firewall Rules

BEFORE YOU BEGIN

The lab environment consists of computers connected to a local area network. The computers required for this lab are listed in Table 12-1.

Table 12-1
Computers Required for Lab 12

Computer	***Operating System***	***Computer Name***
Server	Windows Server 2012	SVR-DC-A
Workstation	Windows 8 Enterprise	WKSTN-MBR-B
Workstation	Windows 8 Enterprise	WKSTN-MBR-C

In addition to the computers, you will also need the software listed in Table 12-2 to complete Lab 12.

Table 12-2
Software Required for Lab 12

Software	***Location***
Lab 12 student worksheet	Lab12_worksheet.docx (provided by instructor)

Working with Lab Worksheets

Each lab in this manual requires that you answer questions, create screenshots, and perform other activities that you will document in a worksheet named for the lab, such as Lab12_worksheet.docx. You will find these worksheets on the book companion site. It is recommended that you use a USB flash drive to store your worksheets, so you can submit them to your instructor for review. As you perform the exercises in each lab, open the appropriate worksheet file, type the required information, and then save the file to your flash drive.

SCENARIO

After completing this lab, you will be able to:

- Configure Windows Firewall
- Create Windows Firewall rules

Estimated lab time: 60 minutes

Exercise 12.1	Installing Internet Information Server
Overview	Because this is only a test deployment, you will be using a Windows 8 computer to function as the web server. In this exercise, you will install Internet Information Services on your workstation and then configure it to host two websites.
Mindset	Internet Information Services enables you to configure websites to use specific port numbers. This makes it possible to test the functionality of Windows Firewall.
Completion time	15 minutes

1. On **WKSTN-MBR-B**, log on using the **adatum\Administrator** account and the **Pa$$w0rd** password.

2. On the *Start* screen, click the **Desktop** tile. The *Desktop* appears.

3. Mouse over the lower-right corner of the window and, when the Charms bar appears, click **Settings**.

4. On the *Settings* menu, click **Control Panel**. The *Control Panel* window appears.

5. Click **Programs** > **Programs and Features**. The *Uninstall or change a program* window appears.

6. Click **Turn Windows features on or off**. The *Windows Features* dialog box appears.

7. Browse to the *Internet Information Services\World Wide Web Services* folder, as shown in Figure 12-1.

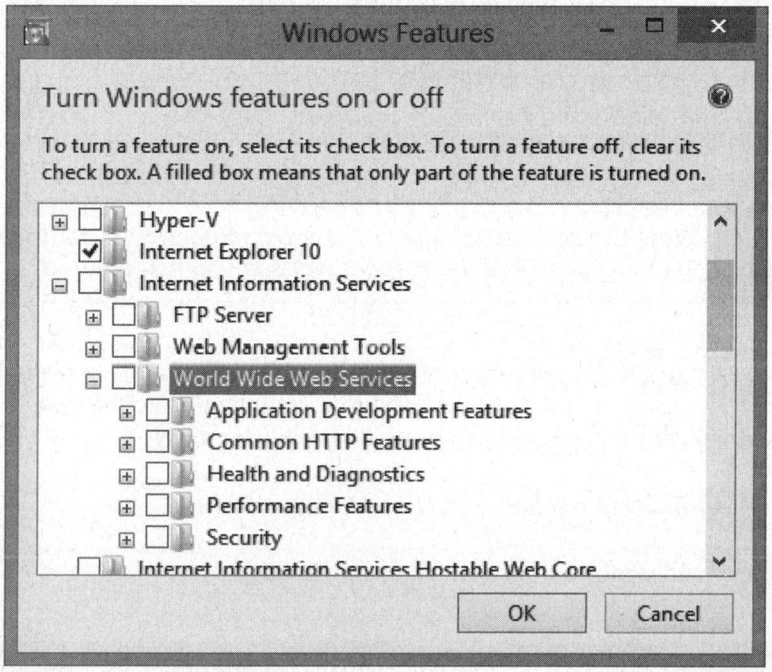

Figure 12-1
The World Wide Web Services folder in the *Windows Features* dialog box

8. Select the **Common HTTP Features** check box, the **Health and Diagnostics** check box, and the **Security** check box.

9. Expand the **Web Management Tools** folder, select the **IIS Management Console** check box, and then click **OK**. Windows 8 installs the selected components.

10. Close the **Windows Features** control panel window.

11. In the *Programs and Features* address bar, click **Control Panel** and then click **System and Security > Administrative Tools**. The *Administrative Tools* window appears.

12. Double-click **Internet Information Services (IIS) Manager**. The *Internet Information Services (IIS) Manager* console appears.

13. An *Internet Information Services (IIS) Manager* message box appears, prompting you to confirm if you want to stay connected.

14. Click **No**.

15. Expand the **WKSTN-MBR-B** container and then expand the **Sites** folder.

16. Right-click the **Sites** folder and, from the context menu, choose **Add Website**. The *Add Website* dialog box appears.

17. In the *Site* name text box, type **Intranet**.

18. In the *Physical* path text box, type **c:\inetpub\wwwroot**.

19. Change the value in the *Port* text box to **4444**.

20. Click **OK**. The new Intranet website appears in the *Sites* folder.

Question 1	*What URLs could you use in your computer's browser to test the functionality of the intranet website you just created?*

21. Take a screen shot of the *Internet Information Services (IIS) Manager* console, showing the new site you created, by pressing **Alt+Prt Scr**, and then paste the resulting image into the Lab 12 worksheet file in the page provided by pressing **Ctrl+V**.

22. Close the *Internet Information Services (IIS) Manager* console.

End of exercise. Leave all windows open for the next exercise.

Exercise 12.2	Testing IIS Connectivity
Overview	In this exercise, you will test the functionality of the web server you just installed.
Mindset	The way to test the functionality of a web server is to attempt to connect to it.
Completion time	15 minutes

1. On the **WKSTN-MBR-B** desktop, click the **Internet Explorer** button in the taskbar. An *Internet Explorer* window appears.

2. In the *Address* box, type **http://127.0.0.1** and then press **Enter**.

Question 2	*What is the result, and what does the result indicate?*

3. Test the Intranet website by using the URLs you specified in Exercise 12-1, Question 1.

Question 3	*What is the result, and what does it indicate?*

4. On **WKSTN-MBR-C**, log on using the **adatum\Administrator** account and the **Pa$$w0rd** password.

5. Click the **Desktop** tile and then open **Internet Explorer**. Try to access the IIS web server running on your WKSTN-MBR-B workstation by typing **http://wkstn-mbr-b** in the *Address* box and pressing **Enter**.

Question 4	*What is the result?*

6. Now, try to connect to the Intranet website from **WKSTN-MBR-C**.

Question 5	*What is the result?*

Question 6	*List three possible reasons as to why you might be unable to connect to your computer's web server using a browser on another computer.*

7. Back on the **WKSTN-MBR-B** workstation, in the *System and Security* control panel, click **Windows Firewall**. The *Windows Firewall* control panel appears (see Figure 12-2).

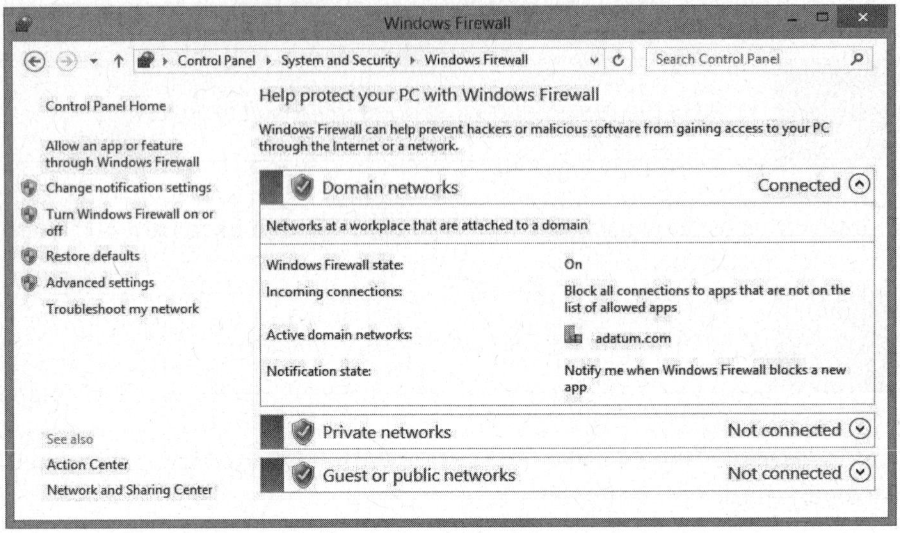

Figure 12-2
The Windows Firewall control panel

8. Below the *Control Panel Home* link on the left of the screen, click **Turn Windows Firewall on or off**. The *Customize settings for each type of network* window appears.

9. Under *Domain network settings*, select the **Turn off Windows Firewall (not recommended)** option.

10. Take a screen shot of the *Customize settings for each type of network* window, showing the setting you just modified, by pressing **Alt+Prt Scr**, and then paste the resulting image into the Lab 12 worksheet file in the page provided by pressing **Ctrl+V**. Click **OK**.

11. Back on **WKSTN-MBR-C**, try again to access both of the sites on the web server using Internet Explorer.

Question 7	*What are the results, and what do the results indicate?*

Question 8	*What other test could you perform to prove that it was your computer's firewall that was blocking the connection and not the firewall on the computer you are using as a client?*

12. Clear the Internet Explorer cache on **WKSTN-MBR-C** test client computer by clicking **Tools > Internet Options**. The *Internet Options* dialog box appears.

13. Under *Browsing History*, click the **Delete** button. The *Delete Browsing History* dialog box appears.

14. Click **Delete**. Then click **OK** to close the *Internet Options* dialog box.

Question 9	*Why is it necessary to clear the cache before you retest the web server connections?*

15. Back on **WKSTN-MBR-B**, in the *Windows Firewall* control panel, click **Turn Windows Firewall on or off** to open the *Customize settings for each type of network* window again, and then turn the **Domain network settings** Windows Firewall back on. Click **OK** to close the window.

Question 10	*Why can you not simply leave Windows Firewall turned off when you deploy an actual web server?*

End of exercise. Leave all windows open for the next exercise.

Exercise 12.3	Allowing a Program Through the Firewall
Overview	Windows Firewall is preventing clients from connecting to your web server. To enable client access, you will use the Windows Firewall control panel to allow access to the web server.
Mindset	The Windows Firewall control panel provides access to basic functions of the firewall, but for complete control, you must use the Windows Firewall with Advanced Security console, which you'll see in the Lab Challenge.
Completion time	10 minutes

1. On **WKSTN-MBR-B**, in the *Windows Firewall* control panel, click **Allow an app or feature through Windows Firewall**. The *Allow apps to communicate through Windows Firewall* window appears (see Figure 12-3).

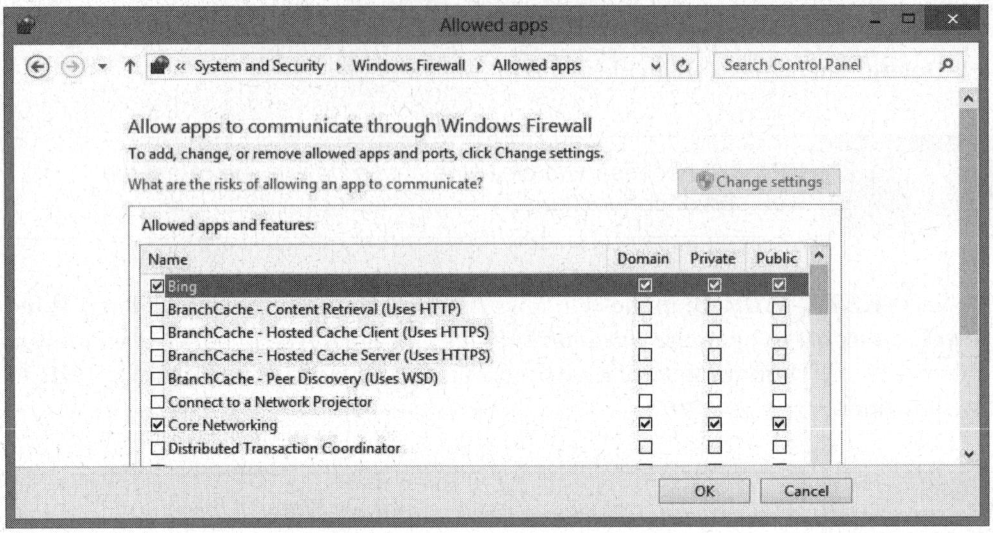

Figure 12-3
The *Allow apps to communicate through Windows Firewall* window

2. Scroll down the *Allowed apps and features* list and, in the *Domain* column, select the **World Wide Web Services (HTTP)** check box and then click **OK**.

3. On **WKSTN-MBR-C**, try again to connect to the default website at **http://wkstn-mbr-b**.

Question 11	*Why are you now able to connect to the website from the client?*

4. Now, try to connect to the Intranet website.

Question 12	*Why are you unable to connect to the intranet site from the client?*

5. On **WKSTN-MBR-B**, open the **Allow an app or feature through Windows Firewall** window again and clear the **World Wide Web Services (HTTP)** check box. Then click **OK**.

End of exercise. Leave all windows open for the next exercise.

Lab Challenge	Creating Windows Firewall Rules
Overview	The port you opened in Exercise 12.3 enables clients to access the default website hosted by your web server, but not the Intranet website. In this challenge, you must configure your web server to allow traffic to the Intranet website.
Mindset	Windows 8 often provides more than one way to complete a given task. The Windows Firewall control panel provides a relatively simple interface to the firewall, but it is not a comprehensive one, as we saw in the previous Exercise.
Completion time	20 minutes

To complete this challenge, you must use the Windows Firewall With Advanced Security console to configure WKSTN-MBR-B to allow traffic to both the default website and the Intranet website you created in Exercise 12.1.

To complete the challenge, perform the following tasks:

1. List the steps you took to complete the task.
2. Take a screen shot of the interface you used to create the firewall rules by pressing **Alt+Prt Scr** and then paste it into your Lab 12 worksheet file in the page provided by pressing **Ctrl+V**.
3. Answer the following questions.

Question 13	*Why are there two separate rules for the World Wide Web Services in the Inbound Rules container?*

Question 14	*How would the opening of the port you performed in Exercise 12.3 affect the World Wide Web Services (HTTP Traffic-In) rules in the Inbound Rules container?*

Question 15	*How would the rule creation procedure you just performed differ if you wanted to restrict client access to the intranet website to computers on the local network only?*

End of lab.

LAB 13
CONFIGURING REMOTE MANAGEMENT

THIS LAB CONTAINS THE FOLLOWING EXERCISES AND ACTIVITIES:

Exercise 13.1	Configuring Remote Desktop Client
Exercise 13.2	Connecting to a Remote Workstation
Lab Exercise	Using Windows Remote Management

BEFORE YOU BEGIN

The lab environment consists of computers connected to a local area network. The computers required for this lab are listed in Table 13-1.

Table 13-1
Computers Required for Lab 13

Computer	***Operating System***	***Computer Name***
Server	Windows Server 2012	SVR-DC-A
Workstation	Windows 8 Enterprise	WKSTN-MBR-B
Workstation	Windows 8 Enterprise	WKSTN-MBR-C

In addition to the computers, you will also need the software listed in Table 13-2 to complete Lab 13.

Table 13-2
Software Required for Lab 13

Software	*Location*
Lab 13 student worksheet	Lab13_worksheet.docx (provided by instructor)

Working with Lab Worksheets

Each lab in this manual requires that you answer questions, create screenshots, and perform other activities that you will document in a worksheet named for the lab, such as Lab13_worksheet.docx. You will find these worksheets on the book companion site. It is recommended that you use a USB flash drive to store your worksheets so you can submit them to your instructor for review. As you perform the exercises in each lab, open the appropriate worksheet file, type the required information, and then save the file to your flash drive.

SCENARIO

After completing this lab, you will be able to:

- Configure Remote Desktop Client
- Connect to another system using Remote Desktop Client

Estimated lab time: 35 minutes

Exercise 13.1	Configuring Remote Desktop Client
Overview	Before you can test the Remote Desktop Client program, both of the Windows 8 computers involved must be configured to allow secured connections to occur. In this exercise, you will configure the Remote Access settings on your workstations.
Mindset	By default, Windows 8 disables the operating system's ability to receive incoming Remote Desktop client requests.
Completion time	10 minutes

1. On **WKSTN-MBR-B**, log on using the **adatum\Administrator** account and the **Pa$$w0rd** password.

2. On the *Start* page, type **Control Panel**.

3. Click the **Control Panel** tile. The *Control Panel* window appears.

4. Click **System and Security > System**. The *System* control panel appears.

5. Click **Remote settings**. The *System Properties* sheet appears with the Remote tab selected (see Figure 13-1).

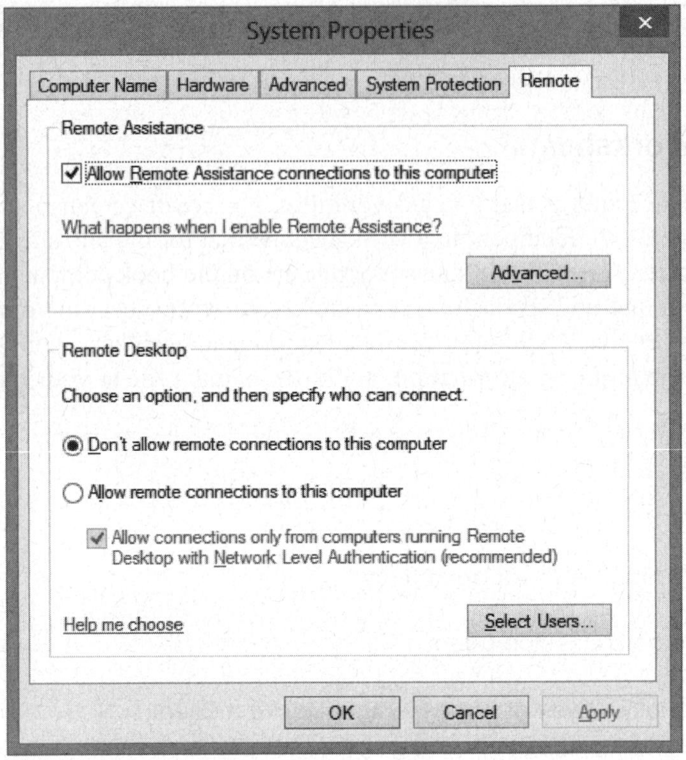

Figure 13-1
The *System Properties* sheet

6. Leave the **Allow Remote Assistance connections to this computer** check box selected and, in the Remote Desktop area, select the **Allow remote connections to this computer** option and then click **Advanced**. The *Remote Assistance Settings* dialog box appears.

7. Make sure that the **Allow this computer to be controlled remotely** check box is selected and then configure **Set the maximum amount of time invitations can remain open** to **24 Hours** (see Figure 13-2).

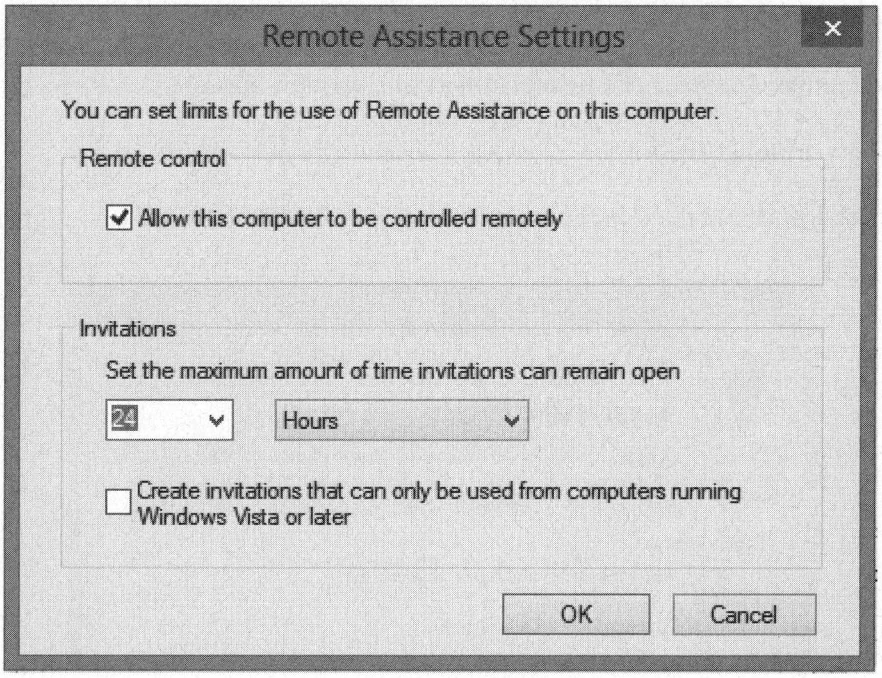

Figure 13-2
The *Remote Assistance Settings* sheet

8. Click **OK**.

Question 1	*When using Remote Assistance, why might it be necessary to impose a time limit on the invitation?*

9. Click **OK** to close the *System Properties* dialog box.

End of exercise. Close all windows and log off of the computer.

Exercise 13.2	Connecting to a Remote Workstation
Overview	In this exercise, you will connect to another computer and control it from a remote location.
Mindset	The Remote Desktop feature in Windows 8 does not require a user to be present at the remote computer.
Completion time	15 minutes

1. On **WKSTN-MBR-C**, log on using the **adatum\Administrator** account and the **Pa$$w0rd** password.

2. Mouse over the lower-right corner of the window and, when the Charms bar appears, click **Search**.

3. In the *Search* box, type **Remote** and, in the results list, click the **Remote Desktop Connection** tile. The *Remote Desktop Connection* window appears.

4. Click **Show options**. The *Remote Desktop Connection* window expands.

5. On the *General* tab, in the *Computer* text box, type **WKSTN-MBR-B** (see Figure 13-3).

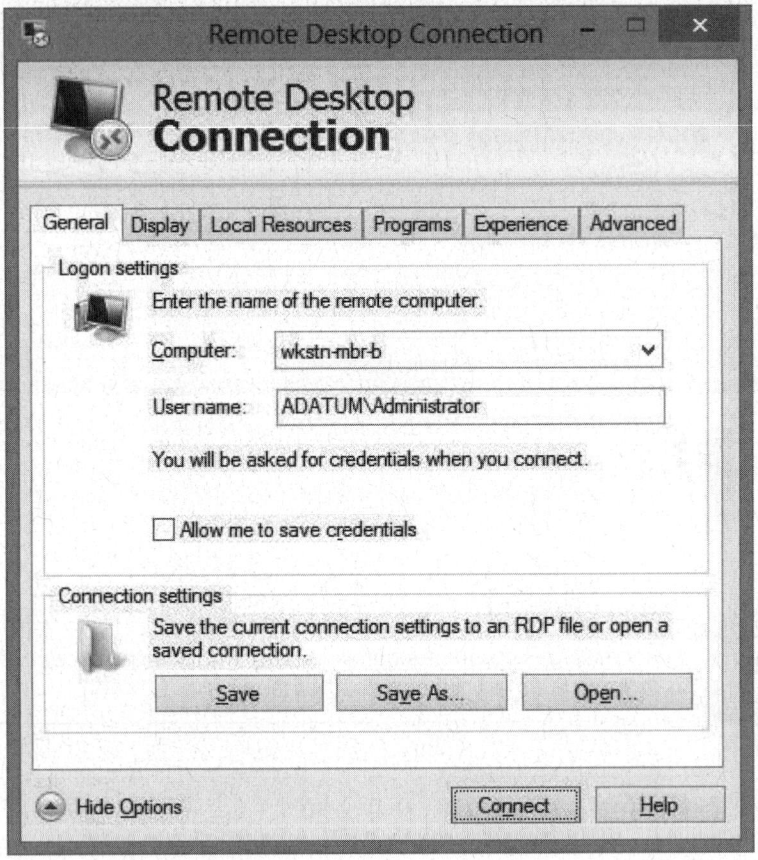

Figure 13-3
The expanded *Remote Desktop Connection* window

6. Click the **Display** tab.

7. Set the **Display Configuration** slider to **800 by 600** pixels.

8. Click the **Local Resources** tab.

9. Clear the **Printers** check box and then click **More**. The *Local devices and resources* dialog box appears.

10. Select the **Drives** check box and then click **OK**.

11. Click the **Experience** tab.

12. From the *Choose your connection speed to optimize performance* drop-down list, select **LAN (10 Mbps or Higher)**.

13. Click **Connect**. A *Remote Desktop Connection* message box appears, prompting you to confirm that you trust the remote computer.

14. Select the *Don't ask me again for connections to this computer* check box and then click **Connect**.

15. Type the **Pa$$w0rd** password for the **adatum\Administrator** account and then click **OK**.

16. A *WKSTN-MBR-B — Remote Desktop Connection* window appears, showing an image of the remote computer's desktop.

17. Take a screen shot of the *WKSTN-MBR-B — Remote Desktop Connection* window by pressing **Alt+Prt Scr** and then paste the resulting image into the Lab 13 worksheet file in the page provided by pressing **Ctrl+V**.

18. In the *WKSTN-MBR-B — Remote Desktop Connection* window, mouse over the lower-right corner of the window and, when the Charms bar appears, click **Search**.

19. In the *Search* box, type **Notepad**. In the results list, click the **Notepad** tile. The *Notepad* window appears.

Question 2	*On which computer is the Notepad program actually running?*

20. In the *Notepad* window, click **File** > **Open**. The *Open* combo box appears.

Question 3	*When you browse the Local Disk (C:) drive in the Open combo box, which computer's C: drive are you actually looking at?*

21. In the *Open* combo box, select the **Computer** container and then scroll down to display the **WKSTN-MBR-C** disks.

22. Take a screen shot of the *WKSTN-MBR-B — Remote Desktop Connection* window, showing the *WKSTN-MBR-C* disks in the *Open* combo box, by pressing **Alt+Prt Scr** and then paste the resulting image into the Lab 13 worksheet file in the page provided by pressing **Ctrl+V**.

Question 4	*Why Is it possible to access the host computer's – that is, the WKSTN-MBR-C computer's – various drives while working in the WKSTN-MBR-B Remote Desktop Connection window?*

23. Click **Cancel** to close the *Open* combo box.

Question 5	*During a Remote Desktop session, what would happen if you opened the Network Connections window on the remote computer and configured the network adapter to use a different IP address? Explain the result.*

24. Close the *Notepad* window.

25. Close the *WKSTN-MBR-B — Remote Desktop Connection* window. A *Remote Desktop Connection* message box appears, informing you that this will disconnect the Remote Desktop session.

26. Click **OK**. The *WKSTN-MBR-B — Remote Desktop Connection* window closes.

End of exercise. Close all windows and log off of the computer.

Lab Challenge	Using Windows Remote Management
Overview	In this exercise, you will configure a Windows 8 workstation to accept commands issued remotely from other computers.
Mindset	Windows Remote Management is a service that enables administrators to execute command-line programs on a remote computer by running a remote shell program called Winrs.exe.
Completion time	10 minutes

To complete this challenge, you must write out the complete procedure for enabling Windows Remote Management and executing a command that uses the adatum\Administrator account to create a local user account for a user called Mark Lee (**mlee**) with the **Pa$$w0rd** password on the remote workstation. After writing out the procedure, execute it on your workstation and take a screen shot showing the creation of the user account.

End of lab.

LAB 14
CONFIGURING SHARED RESOURCES

THIS LAB CONTAINS THE FOLLOWING EXERCISES AND ACTIVITIES:

Exercise 14.1	Sharing a Folder
Exercise 14.2	Sharing a Printer
Lab Challenge	Creating a Homegroup

BEFORE YOU BEGIN

The lab environment consists of computers connected to a local area network in a workgroup configuration. The computers required for this lab are listed in Table 14-1.

Table 14-1
Computers Required for Lab 14

Computer	*Operating System*	*Computer Name*
Server	Windows Server 2012	SVR-WKGRP-A
Workstation	Windows 8 Enterprise	WKSTN-WKGRP-B
Workstation	Windows 8 Enterprise	WKSTN-WKGRP-C

In addition to the computers, you will also need the software listed in Table 14-2 to complete Lab 14.

Table 14-2
Software Required for Lab 14

Software	***Location***
Lab 14 student worksheet	Lab14_worksheet.docx (provided by instructor)

Working with Lab Worksheets

Each lab in this manual requires that you answer questions, create screenshots, and perform other activities that you will document in a worksheet named for the lab, such as Lab14_worksheet.docx. You will find these worksheets on the book companion site. It is recommended that you use a USB flash drive to store your worksheets so you can submit them to your instructor for review. As you perform the exercises in each lab, open the appropriate worksheet file, type the required information, and then save the file to your flash drive.

SCENARIO

After completing this lab, you will be able to:

- Share folders and printers
- Create a homegroup

Estimated lab time: 60 minutes

Exercise 14.1	Sharing a Folder
Overview	In this exercise, you will share a folder on a Windows 8 workstation and control access to it using share permissions.
Mindset	Share permissions enable you to control access to shared resources, but only when users access the resources over the network.
Completion time	20 minutes

1. On **WKSTN-WKGRP-B**, log on using the **wkstn-wrkgrp-b\ocox** account and the **Pa$$w0rd** password.
2. On the Start screen, click the **Desktop** tile. The *Desktop* appears.
3. On the Taskbar, click the **File Explorer** icon. The *File Explorer* window appears.
4. Browse to the *C:\Users\ocox* folder.
5. Right-click the **My Documents** folder and choose **Properties**. The *My Documents Properties* sheet appears.

6. Click the **Sharing** tab and then click **Advanced Sharing**. The *Advanced Sharing* dialog box appears (see Figure 14-1).

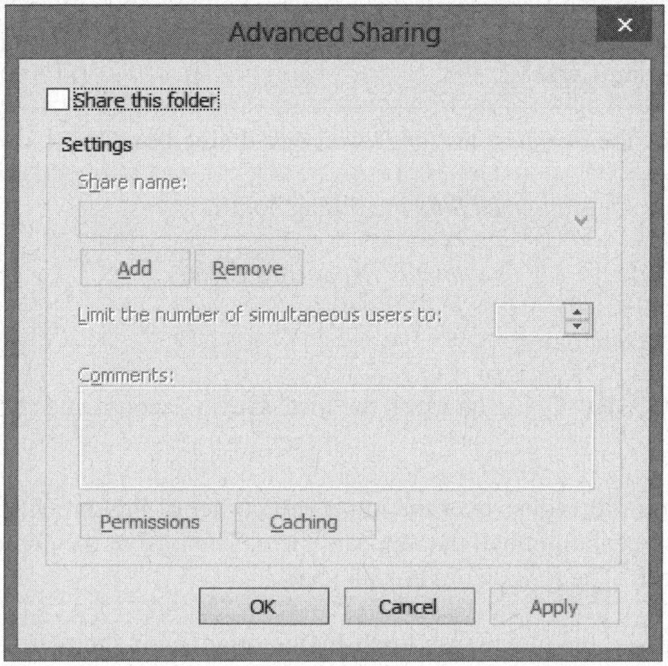

Figure 14-1
The Advanced Sharing dialog box

7. Select the **Share this folder** check box. The *Documents* default value appears in the *Share name* text box.

8. Click **Permissions**. The *Permissions for Documents* dialog box appears.

9. Select the **Everyone** special identity and, in the *Allow* column, clear all of the check boxes.

10. Click **Add**. The *Select Users or Groups* dialog box appears.

11. In the *Enter the object names to select* box, type **Administrators** and then click **OK**. The Administrators group appears in the *Group or user names* list in the *Permissions for Documents* dialog box.

12. Select the **Administrators** group and then, in the *Permissions for Administrators* box, in the *Allow* column, select the **Full Control** check box. This action also selects the **Change** check box.

13. Using the same technique, add the **Users** group to the *Group or user names* list and then assign it the **Allow Change** permission and **Allow Read** permission.

14. In the *Group or user names* list, add the **Guest** user account to and then assign it the **Allow Read** permission only.

15. Take a screen shot of the *Permissions for Documents* dialog box by pressing **Alt+Prt Scr**, and then paste the resulting image into the Lab 14 worksheet file in the page provided by pressing **Ctrl+V**.

16. Click **OK** to close the *Permissions for Documents* dialog box.

17. Click **OK** to close the *Advanced Sharing* dialog box.

18. Click **Close** to close the *My Documents Properties* sheet.

19. Log off of the workstation.

20. On **WKSTN-WKGRP-C**, log on using the local **Guest** account and the **Pa$$w0rd** password.

21. Click the **Desktop** tile, mouse over the lower-left corner of the screen, and then right-click the **Start** screen thumbnail that appears there. Then, from the context menu that appears, click **Run**. The *Run* dialog box appears.

22. In the *Open* text box, type **\\wkstn-wkgrp-b\Documents** and then click **OK**. A Network Error window appears, informing you that you do not have permission to access *\\wkstn-wkgrp-b\Documents*.

23. Take a screen shot of the *Network Error* window by pressing **Alt+Prt Scr**, and then paste the resulting image into the Lab 14 worksheet file in the page provided by pressing **Ctrl+V**.

Question 1	*Why are you unable to access the share using the Guest account, despite having granted the user the Allow Read permission?*

Question 2	*Would the Guest user be able to access the share if you granted it the Allow Full Control share permission, rather than the Allow Read permission?*

24. Log off **WKSTN-WKGRP-C** and then log on again using the **wkstn-wkgrp-c\ocox** account and the **Pa$$w0rd** password.

25. Click the **Desktop** tile, mouse over the lower-left corner of the desktop, and then right-click the **Start** screen thumbnail that appears there. Then, from the context menu that appears, click **Run**. The *Run* dialog box appears.

26. In the *Open* text box, type **wkstn-wkgrp-b\Documents** and then click **OK**. An *Explorer* window appears, displaying the contents of the support folder.

Question 3	*Why are you able to access the share, despite having logged on using the ocox account on WKSTN-WKGRP-C, not WKSTN-WKGRP-B?*

End of exercise. Close any open windows before you begin the next exercise.

Exercise 14.2	Sharing a Printer
Overview	In this exercise, you will create a new printer and share it with network users.
Mindset	Printers have a separate system of shares and share permissions that enable you to control access to the physical print device.
Completion time	20 minutes

1. On **WKSTN-MBR-B**, log on using the **wkstn-wrkgrp-b\ocox** account and the **Pa$$w0rd** password.

2. On the Start screen, click the **Desktop** tile. The Desktop appears.

3. Mouse over the lower-left corner of the desktop and right-click the **Start** screen thumbnail that appears there. Then, from the context menu that appears, click **Control Panel**. The *Control Panel* appears.

4. Click **Hardware and Sound > Devices and Printers**. The *Devices and Printers* control panel appears (see Figure 14-2).

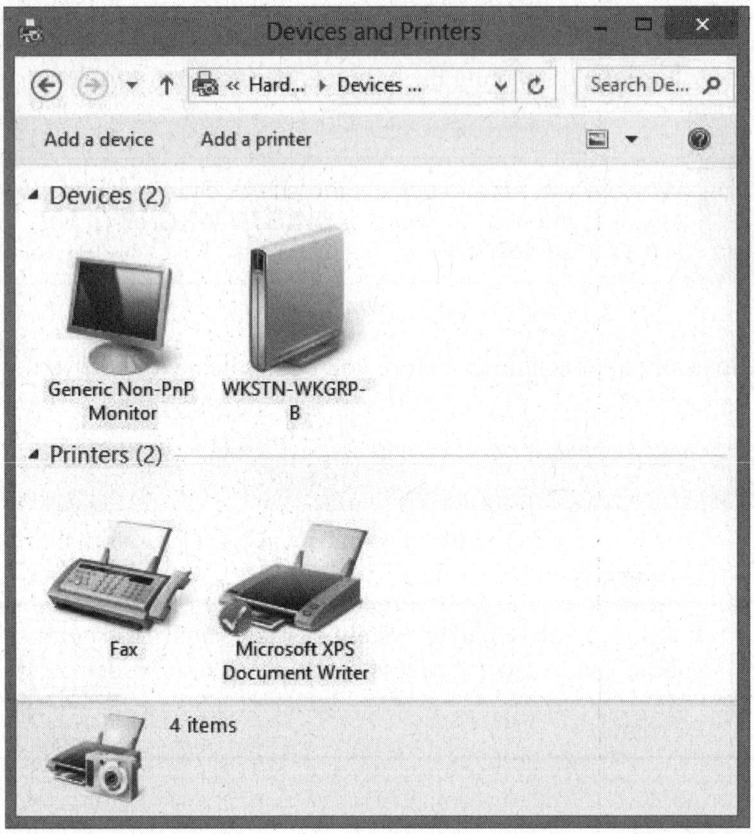

Figure 14-2
The Devices and Printers control panel

5. Click **Add a printer**. The *Add Printer Wizard* appears and searches for attached print devices. When it finds none, a *No printers were found* message appears.

6. Click **The printer that I want isn't listed**. The *Find a printer by other options* page appears.

7. Select **Add a local printer or network printer with manual settings** and then click **Next**. The *Choose a printer port* page appears.

8. Leaving the **Use an existing port** option selected, click **LPT2: (Printer Port)** from the drop-down list and then click **Next**. The *Install the printer driver* page appears.

Question 4	*Why doesn't Windows 8 attempt to automatically detect a printer connected to the computer?*

9. In the *Manufacturer* column, click **Generic**. In the *Printers* column, click **MS Publisher Color Printer** and then click **Next**. The *Type a printer name* page appears.

10. In the *Printer Name* text box, type **MS Color** and then click **Next**. The wizard installs the driver and the *Printer Sharing* page appears.

11. Select the *Do not share this printer* option and then click **Next**. The *You've Successfully Added MS Color* page appears.

12. Click **Finish**. The *MS Color* icon appears in the *Devices and Printers* control panel.

13. Take a screen shot of the *Devices and Printers* control panel displaying the new printer icon you created by pressing **Alt+Prt Scr**, and then paste the resulting image into the Lab 14 worksheet file in the page provided by pressing **Ctrl+V**.

14. Right-click the **MS Color** icon and choose **Printer properties**. The *MS Color Properties* sheet appears.

15. Click the **Sharing** tab (see Figure 14-3).

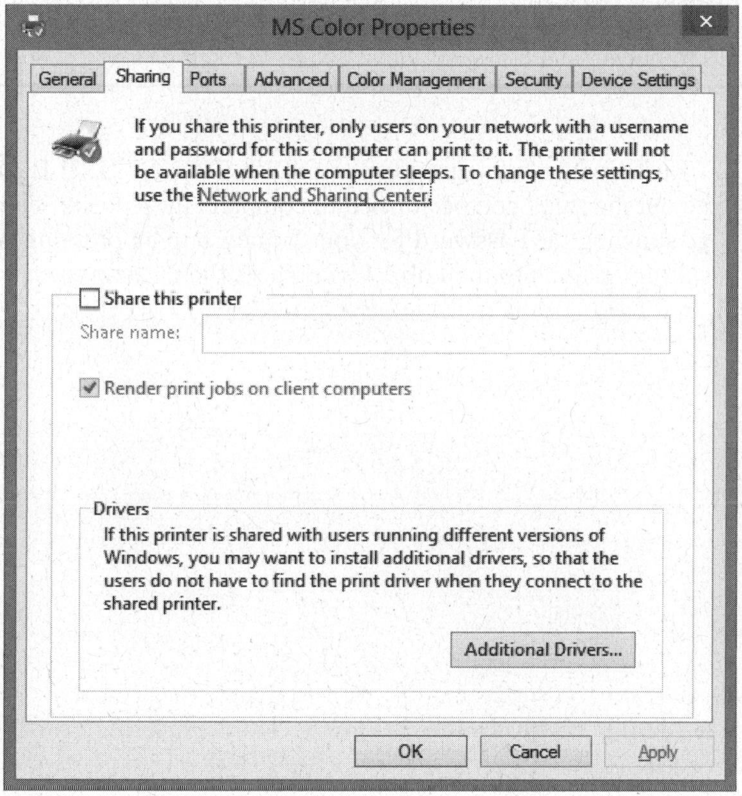

Figure 14-3
The Sharing tab of a printer's Properties sheet

16. Select the **Share this printer** check box. Leave the **Render print jobs on client computers** check box selected and then click **OK**.

Question 5	*How can you tell whether the printer has been shared?*

End of exercise. Close any open windows before you begin the next exercise.

Lab Challenge	Creating a Homegroup
Overview	Homegroup networking is a Windows 8 feature that enables computers configured to use the Private network location to share the contents of their respective libraries among themselves.
Mindset	Homegroups simplify the process of sharing files among workgroup network users.
Completion time	20 minutes

In this challenge, you must create a homegroup and join WKSTN-WKGRP-B and WKSTN-WKGRP-C to it. Write out the steps you performed to complete these tasks. Then take a screen shot of the page showing the password for your homegroup by pressing **Alt+Prt Scr** and then paste the resulting image into the Lab 14 worksheet file in the page provided by pressing **Ctrl+V**.

End of lab.

LAB 15
CONFIGURING FILE AND FOLDER ACCESS

THIS LAB CONTAINS THE FOLLOWING EXERCISES AND ACTIVITIES:

Exercise 15.1	Configuring NTFS Permissions
Exercise 15.2	Configuring NTFS Quotas
Exercise 15.3	Configuring Auditing
Lab Challenge	Viewing Audit Data

BEFORE YOU BEGIN

The lab environment consists of computers connected to a local area network. The computers required for this lab are listed in Table 15-1.

Table 15-1
Computers Required for Lab 15

Computer	*Operating System*	*Computer Name*
Server	Windows Server 2012	SVR-DC-A
Workstation	Windows 8 Enterprise	WKSTN-MBR-B
Workstation	Windows 8 Enterprise	WKSTN-MBR-C

In addition to the computers, you will also require the software listed in Table 15-2 to complete Lab 15.

Table 15-2
Software Required for Lab 15

Software	*Location*
Lab 15 student worksheet	Lab15_worksheet.docx (provided by instructor)

Working with Lab Worksheets

Each lab in this manual requires that you answer questions, create screenshots, and perform other activities that you will document in a worksheet named for the lab, such as Lab15_worksheet.docx. You will find these worksheets on the book companion site. It is recommended that you use a USB flash drive to store your worksheets so you can submit them to your instructor for review. As you perform the exercises in each lab, open the appropriate worksheet file, type the required information, and then save the file to your flash drive.

SCENARIO

After completing this lab, you will be able to:

- Configure NTFS permissions and quotas
- Configure Auditing
- Audit Windows activities

Estimated lab time: 60 minutes

Exercise 15.1	Configuring NTFS Permissions
Overview	To enable users to access the files on a Windows 8 computer, they must have the appropriate NTFS permissions. In this exercise, you will configure the permissions to enable the Student user to access a shared folder.
Mindset	Users need NTFS permissions to access files on an NTFS disk, whether they are sitting at the console or accessing the disk over the network.
Completion time	20 minutes

1. On **WKSTN-MBR-B**, log on using the **adatum\Administrator** account and the **Pa$$w0rd** password.

2. Click the **Desktop** tile. The *Desktop* appears.

3. Click the **File Explorer** button on the Taskbar. The *File Explorer* window appears.

4. In *File Explorer*, create a new folder on the *C:* drive named **C:\Users\Documents**.

5. Browse to the **C:\Windows\Logs** folder and copy its contents to the **C:\Users\Documents** folder you created.

6. Right-click the **Documents** folder you created and, from the context menu, choose **Properties**. The *Documents Properties* sheet appears.

7. Click the **Sharing** tab and then click **Advanced Sharing**. The *Advanced Sharing* dialog box appears.

8. Select the *Share this folder* check box and then click **Permissions**. The *Permissions for Documents* dialog box appears.

9. Ensure that *Everyone* is highlighted, select the **Allow Full Control** check box, and then click **OK**.

10. Click **OK** to close the *Advanced Sharing* dialog box.

11. On the *Documents Properties* sheet, click the **Security** tab and then click **Edit**. The *Permissions for Documents* dialog box appears (see Figure 15-1).

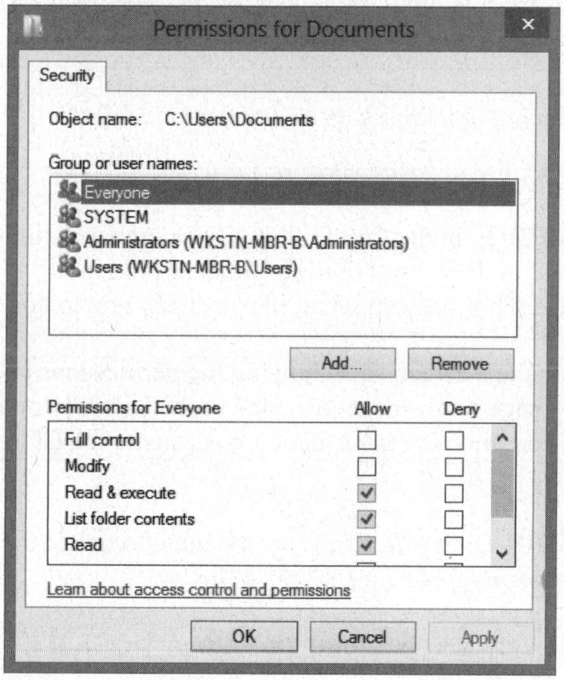

Figure 15-1
The *Permissions for Documents* dialog box

12. Click **Add**. The *Select Users, Computers, Service Accounts, or Groups* dialog box appears.

13. In the *Enter the object names to select* box, type **Student** and then click **OK**. The Student user appears in the *Group or user names* list in the *Permissions for support* dialog box.

14. Click **Apply**.

Question 1	*What permissions are assigned to the Student user by default?*

15. On **WKSTN-MBR-C**, log on using the **adatum\Student** account and the **Pa$$w0rd** password. Wait for the Student profile to complete.

16. Click the **Desktop** tile. The *Desktop* appears.

17. Click the **File Explorer** button on the Taskbar. The *File Explorer* window appears.

18. Expand the **Network** container and browse to the *\\WKSTN-MBR-B\Users\Documents* folder.

19. Right-click the SettingSync subfolder in the *Documents* folder and choose **Delete**. Click Yes to delete. Click Cancel to close the Folder Access Denied message.

Question 2	*Why are you unable to delete the subfolder?*

20. Back on **WKSTN-MBR-B**, in the *Permissions for Documents* dialog box, select the **Student** user and then, in the *Permissions for Student* box, in the *Allow* column, select the **Modify** check box. This also causes the *Write* check box to be selected.

21. Press **Alt+Prt Scr** to take a screen shot showing the permissions you added. Press **Ctrl+V** to paste the image on the page provided in the Lab 15 worksheet file. Click **OK** to close the *Permissions for Documents* dialog box, then click Close to close the Documents Properties.

22. Back on **WKSTN-MBR-C**, in *File Explorer*, try again to delete the SettingSync subfolder in the *Documents* folder.

End of exercise. Leave all windows open for the next exercise.

Exercise 15.2	Configuring NTFS Quotas
Overview	In this exercise, you will configure a disk to limit a user's storage space to 1 MB.
Mindset	NTFS quotas enable you to regulate the amount of disk space utilized by individual users.
Completion time	10 minutes

1. On the **WKSTN-MBR-B** workstation, in *File Explorer,* right-click the **Local Disk (C:)** container and choose **Properties**. The *Local Disk (C:) Properties* sheet appears.

2. Click the **Quota** tab (see Figure 15-2).

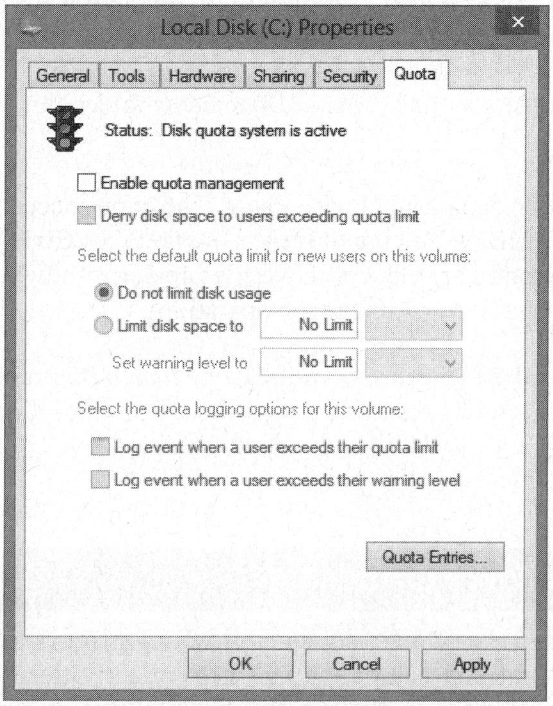

Figure 15-2
The *Quota* tab of a disk's Properties sheet

Question 3	*Why does the Quota tab only appear in the Properties sheet for volumes?*

3. Select the **Enable quota management** check box and the **Deny disk space to users exceeding quota limit** check box.

4. Click **Quota Entries**. The *Quota Entries for C:* dialog box appears.

5. From the *Quota* menu, click **New Quota Entry**. The *Select Users* dialog box appears.

6. In the *Enter the object names to select* text box, type **Student** and then click **OK**. The *Add New Quota Entry* dialog box appears.

7. Select the **Limit disk space to** option, specify **1 MB** for the limit, and then click **OK**. The Student user appears in the *Quota Entries* list. Observe that the percent used is 0. The folders currently in the Documents folder were copied there by the Domain Administrator and will not count against the Student quota. Close the Quota Entries window, click OK to close Local Disk (C:) Properties, then click OK to enable the quota system now.

8. On **WKSTN-MBR-C**, in *File Explorer*, browse to the same WKSTN-MBR-B share, **C:\Users\Documents,** that you accessed in Exercise 15.1.

9. Select all of the subfolders in the *C:\Users\Documents* folder. Right-click the selection and choose **Copy**.

10. Right-click the selection again and choose **Paste**. The copy succeeded because the added folders are less than 1 MB, within the Student's quota. Press **Ctrl+V** to copy the folders again. A Copy Item prompt to delete or move files appears, showing that there is not enough disk space available to complete the operation.

11. Press **Alt+Prt Scr** to take a screen shot of the *Copy Item* box. Press **Ctrl+V** to paste the image on the page provided in the Lab 15 worksheet file. Click **Cancel** to close the box.

End of exercise. Leave all windows open for the next exercise.

Exercise 15.3	Configuring Auditing
Overview	To complete this exercise, you will configure a Windows 8 workstation to audit specific system activities.
Mindset	In an enterprise environment, administrators typically use Active Directory-based Group Policy to configure auditing.
Completion time	20 minutes

1. On **WKSTN-MBR-B**, mouse over the lower-right corner of the window and, when the Charms bar appears, click **Search**.

2. Type **Administrative Tools** and then click **Settings**. Then click the **Administrative Tools** tile. The *Administrative Tools* window appears.

3. Double-click **Local Security Policy**. The *Local Security Policy* window appears.

4. Browse to the **Security Settings\Local Policies\Audit Policy** folder. The audit policies appear in the right pane.

5. Double-click the **Audit account logon events** policy. The *Audit account logon events Properties* sheet appears.

6. Select the **Failure** check box, clear the **Success** check box, and then click **OK**.

Question 4	*Why, in this case, is the auditing of event failures more useful than the auditing of successes?*

7. Double-click the **Audit object access** policy. The *Audit object access Properties* sheet appears.

8. Select the **Failure** check box, select the **Success** check box, and then click **OK**.

9. Press **Alt+Prt Scr** to take a screen shot showing the policies you configured. Press **Ctrl+V** to paste the image on the page provided in the Lab 15 worksheet file.

10. In *File Explorer*, browse to the **C:** drive on the local computer.

11. Right-click the **C:\Windows** folder and choose **Properties**. The *Windows Properties* sheet appears.

12. Click the **Security** tab and then click **Advanced**. The *Advanced Security Settings for Windows* dialog box appears.

13. Click the **Auditing** tab (see Figure 15-3).

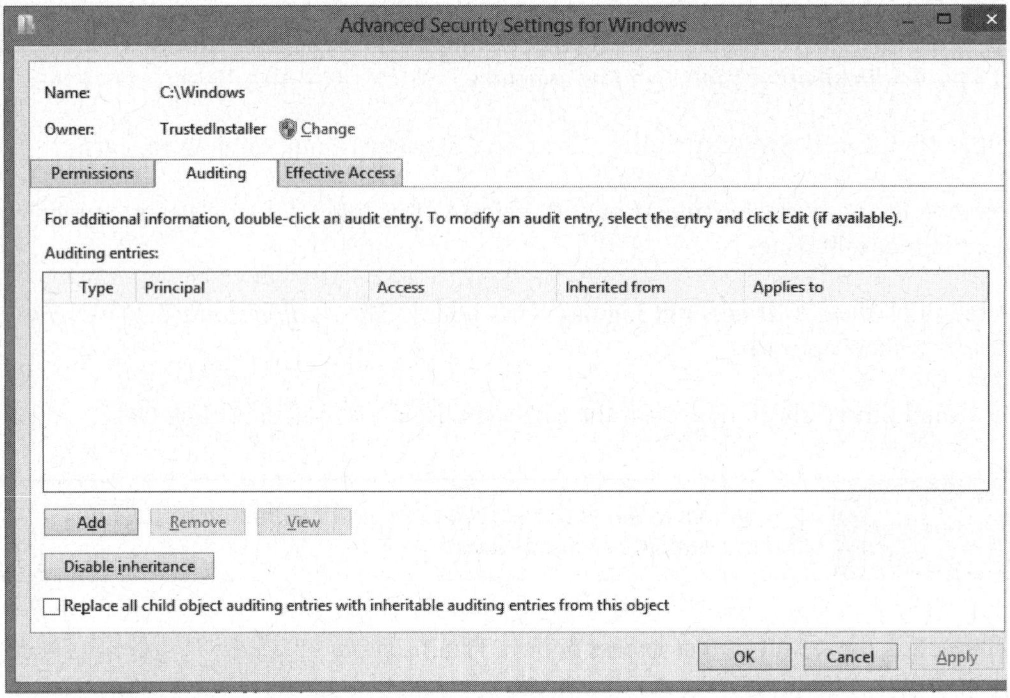

Figure 15-3
The *Advanced Security Settings for Windows* dialog box

14. Click **Add**. The *Auditing Entry for Windows* dialog box appears.

15. Click **Select a Principal**. The *Select User, Computer, Service Account, or Group* dialog box appears.

16. In the *Enter the object name to select* text box, type **Administrator** and then click **OK**.

17. Select the **Full Control** check box and then click **OK**.

18. Click **OK** to close the *Advanced Security Settings for Windows* dialog box, bypassing any error messages that appear.

19. Click **OK** to close the *Windows Properties* sheet.

20. Open an administrative Command Prompt window and type **gpupdate/force** to update the system's Group Policy settings.

End of exercise. Close all windows except Administrative Tools.

Lab Challenge	Viewing Auditing Data
Overview	To complete this exercise, you must demonstrate that your SVR-MBR-B computer is actually gathering the auditing data you configured its policies to gather.
Mindset	How do you display auditing data?
Completion time	10 minutes

To complete this challenge, display the auditing data you configured your server to gather in Exercise 15.3. Press **Alt+Prt Scr** to take a screen shot showing a sample of the data you gathered. Press **Ctrl+V** to paste the image on the page provided in the Lab 15 worksheet file.

End of lab.

LAB 16
CONFIGURING LOCAL SECURITY SETTINGS

THIS LAB CONTAINS THE FOLLOWING EXERCISES AND ACTIVITIES:

Exercise 16.1 Configuring Security Policy

Exercise 16.2 Configuring User Account Control Behavior

Exercise 16.3 Configuring Smart Screen Filter

Lab Challenge Configuring Secure Boot

BEFORE YOU BEGIN

The lab environment consists of computers connected to a local area network. The computers required for this lab are listed in Table 16-1.

Table 16-1
Computers Required for Lab 16

Computer	*Operating System*	*Computer Name*
Server	Windows Server 2012	SVR-DC-A
Client	Windows 7 Enterprise	WKSTN-MBR-C

In addition to the computers, you will also need the software listed in Table 16-2 to complete Lab 16.

Table 16-2
Software Required for Lab 16

Software	*Location*
Lab 16 student worksheet	Lab16_worksheet.docx (provided by instructor)

Working with Lab Worksheets

Each lab in this manual requires that you answer questions, shoot screen shots, and perform other activities that you will document in a worksheet named for the lab, such as Lab16_worksheet.docx. You will find these worksheets on the book companion site. It is recommended that you use a USB flash drive to store your worksheets, so you can submit them to your instructor for review. As you perform the exercises in each lab, open the appropriate worksheet file, type the required information, and then save the file to your flash drive.

SCENARIO

After completing this lab, you will be able to:

- Configure the local security policy including account and password policy
- Configure UAC
- Enable and disable SmartScreen Filter

Estimated lab time: 80 minutes

Exercise 16.1	Configuring Security Policy
Overview	In this exercise, you will modify the Default Domain Policy to set the account and password policy.
Mindset	To help ensure that users are using secure passwords, that passwords are changed regularly, and that a hacker does not keep trying different passwords, you can configure the account and password policy.
Completion time	40 minutes

1. On **SVR-DC-A**, log in using the **adatum\administrator** account and the **Pa$$w0rd** password.
2. When *Server Manager* opens, click **Tools** > **Active Directory Users and Computers**.
3. Right-click **Users OU**, click **New**, and then click **User**.

4. When the *New Object – User* dialog box opens (see Figure 16-1), type the following information, and then click **Next**.

   First name: **Tiffany**

   Last Name: **Columb**

   User logon name: **TiffanyC**

5. On the *Password* page (see Figure 16-1), type the following information and then click **Next**.

   Password: **P@ssword1**

   Confirm password: **P@ssword1**

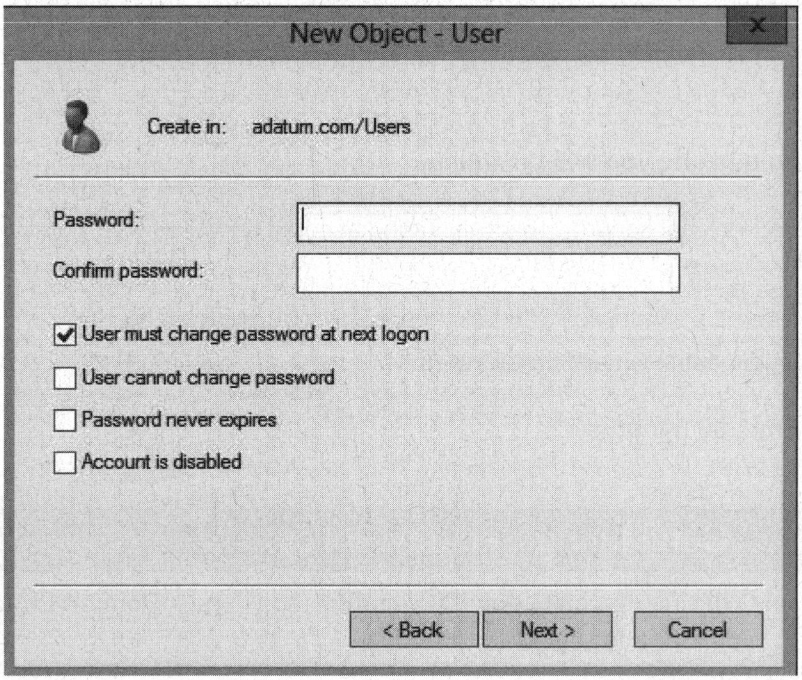

Figure 16-1
Configuring password settings

6. Click to deselect **User must change password at next logon**.

7. Click to select **Password never expires**. Click **Next**.

8. Click **Finish**.

9. When Server Manager appears, click **Tools > Group Policy Management**.

10. Navigate to **Forest:adatum.com>Domains>adatum.com**, expand the **adatum.com** domain, and then right-click **Default Domain Policy** and choose **Edit**.

11. When the *Group Policy Management Editor* opens, expand **Computer Configuration**, expand **Policies**, expand **Windows Settings**, expand **Security Settings**, expand **Account Policies**, and then click **Password Policy**.

Question 1	*What is the Minimum Password length?*

Question 2	*What is the maximum password age?*

12. Click the **Account Lockout Policy** node.

Question 3	*What is the Account lockout threshold?*

13. In the right pane, double-click **Account lockout threshold**.

14. On the *Local Security Setting* tab, type **3** for the number of invalid logon attempts and then click **OK**.

15. When the *Suggested Value Changes* box appears, answer Questions 4 and 5, then click **OK**.

Question 4	*What is the Account lockout duration?*

Question 5	*What is the reset account lockout counter after set to?*

16. In the right pane, double-click **Account lockout duration** (see Figure 16-2).

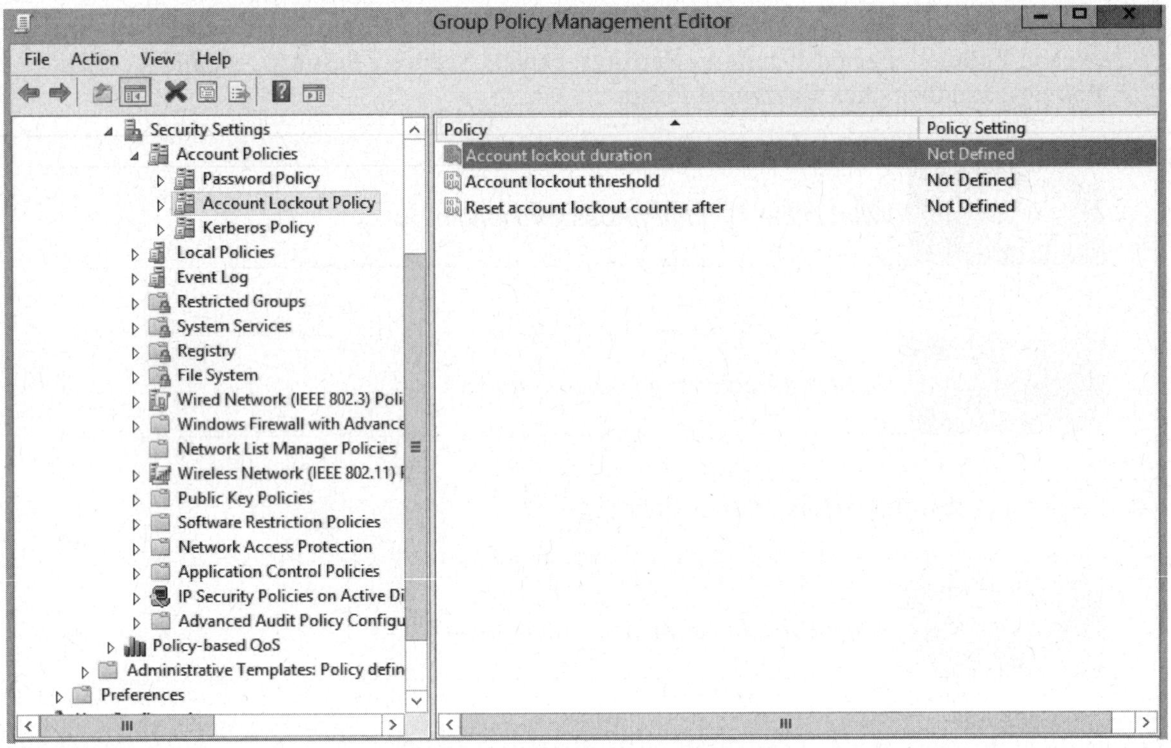

Figure 16-2
Setting the account lockout duration

17. On the *Security Policy Setting* tab, type **3** for the number of minutes and then click **OK**.

18. When the *Suggested Value Changes* box appears, click **OK**.

19. Take a screen shot of the *Policy and Policy Setting* pane by pressing **Alt+Prt Scr** and then paste it into your Lab 16 worksheet file in the page provided by pressing **Ctrl+V**.

20. To simulate a lockout, you are going to login with the TiffanyC account with the wrong password by logging in to **WKSTN-MBR-C** as **adatum\TiffanyC** with the **Password** password. Attempt this same password three more times.

Question 6	*What error message did you get?*

21. Click **OK**.

22. Go back to **SVR-DC-A**. Using **Active Directory Users and Computers**, double-click the **Tiffany Columb** account.

23. When the *Properties* dialog box opens, click the **Account** tab.

24. Click to select **Unlock account** and then click **OK**.

25. Go back to WKSTN-MBR-C and log in as **adatum\TiffanyC** with the **Password** password. Log in three more times until the account is locked again.

26. Wait three minutes. Then log in as **adatum\TiffanyC** with the **Pa$$w0rd** password.

27. In the upper-right corner, click the currently logged-on user and then click **Sign out**.

28. Go back to **SVR-DC-A** and go back to the **Group Policy Management Editor**.

29. Double-click the **Account lockout threshold** option.

30. When the *Account lockout threshold Properties* dialog box opens, change the value to **0** and then click **OK**.

31. When the *Suggested Value Changes* dialog box opens, click **OK**.

32. Close the **Group Policy Management Editor** and then close **Group Policy Management**.

33. Close **Active Directory Users and Computers**.

End of exercise. Leave the SVR-DC-A logged in for the next exercise.

Exercise 16.2	Configuring User Account Control Behavior
Overview	In this exercise, you will configure the UAC on a workstation, and then modify the local security policy to control the UAC settings.
Mindset	The User Account Control helps protect the system by preventing programs from performing unauthorized actions, However, sometimes you will need to modify the User Account Control settings so that your programs will run properly.
Completion time	20 minutes

1. Log in to **WKSTN-MBR-C** as **adatum\TiffanyC**.

2. Click the **Desktop** tile.

3. Mouse over the lower-left corner of the desktop and right-click the **Start** screen thumbnail that appears there. Then click **Control Panel**.

4. Using the *Control Panel*, in the *Search Control Panel* text box, type **UAC**

5. Under *Action Center*, click **Change user Account Control settings**.

6. Notice that the screen dims. In the *User Account Control* dialog box, type the following:

   User name: **adatum\administrator**

Password: **Pa$$w0rd**

Click Yes.

Question 7	*On the User Account Control Settings page, what was the default UAC setting?*

7. On the *User Account Control Settings* page (see Figure 16-3), click and drag the slider down to the **Always notify me (and do not dim my desktop) when:** setting, and then click **OK**.

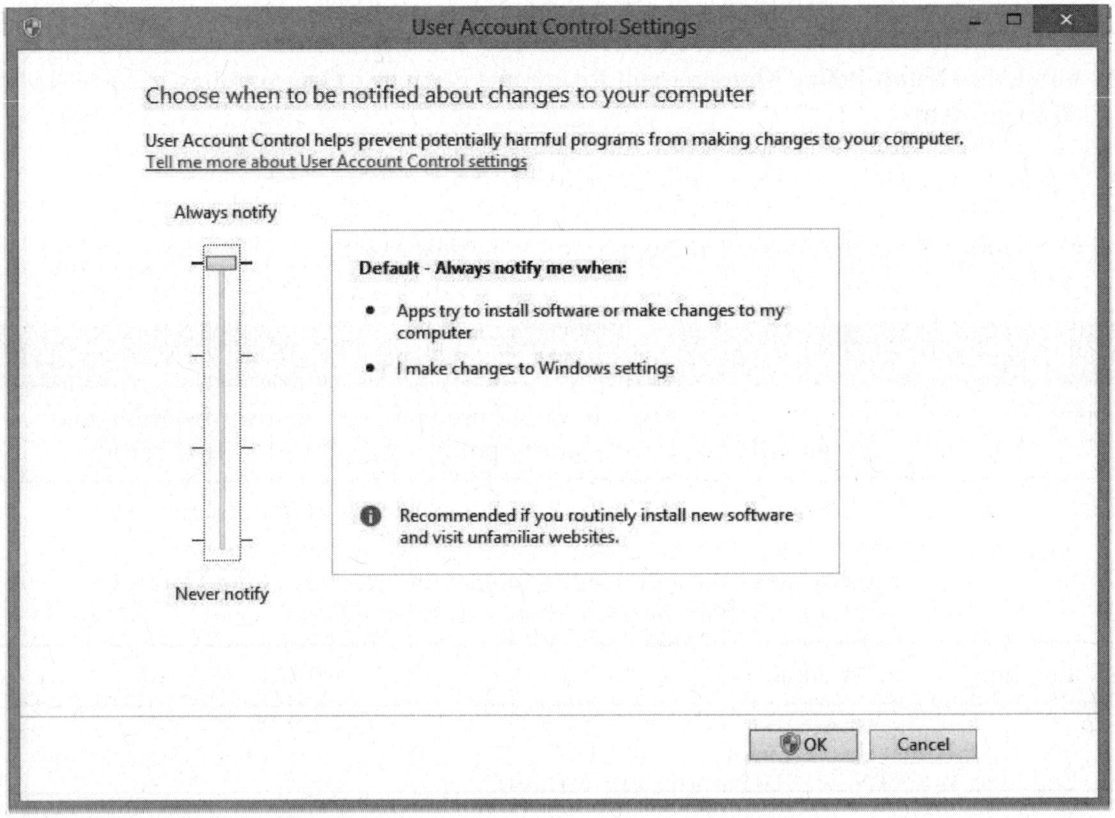

Figure 16-3
The *User Account Control Settings* page

8. In the *User Account Control* dialog box, type the following:

   User name: **adatum\administrator**

   Password: **Pa$$w0rd**

9. In the *UAC - Control Panel*, click the **Change User Account Control settings** option again. Notice that the screen does not dim this time.

10. At the *User Account Control* dialog box, type the following and then click **Yes**:

User name: **adatum\administrator**

Password: **Pa$$w0rd**

11. Slide the slider back to **Default - Always notify me when:,** and then click **OK**.

12. In the *User Account Control* dialog box, type the following and then click **Yes**:

User name: **adatum\administrator**

Password: **Pa$$w0rd**

13. Log off as **adatum\TiffanyC**.

14. Log on as **adatum\administrator** with the **Pa$$w0rd** password.

15. In the *Start* screen, type **secpol.msc** and press **Enter**.

16. When the *Local Security Policy* console opens, expand **Local Policies** and then click **Security Options**.

17. Scroll down to the bottom of the policy list until you see the 10 policies with the User Account Control prefix.

18. Double-click the **User Account Control: Behavior of the elevation prompt for standard users** policy.

19. On the *Local Security Setting* tab, click the drop-down arrow, choose **Automatically deny elevation requests**, and then click **OK**.

20. Take a screen shot of the *Local Security Policy* console by pressing **Alt+Prt Scr** and then paste it into your Lab 16 worksheet file in the page provided by pressing **Ctrl+V**.

21. Close the **Local Security Policy**.

22. Log off as **adatum\administrator**.

23. Log on as **adatum\TiffanyC** with the **Pa$$w0rd** password.

24. On the *Start* screen, type **diskmgmt.msc** and then press **Enter**.

Question 8	*What error message is displayed?*

25. Click **OK** to close the *Disk Management* dialog box.

26. Close **Disk Management**.

27. Log off as TiffanyC.

End of exercise. Leave the computers running for the next exercise.

Exercise 16.3	Configuring SmartScreen Filter
Overview	In this exercise, you will enable and then disable the SmartScreen filter in Internet Explorer.
Mindset	To help maintain the security on organization's computers, SmartScreen Filters is designed to keep your computer safe by warning you before you run apps or files from the Internet that are considered to be unsafe.
Completion time	10 minutes

1. Log in to **WKSTN-MBR-C** as **adatum\administrator** with the **Pa$$w0rd** password.
2. From the *Windows 8 Start* screen, click the **Desktop** tile.
3. On the task bar, click the **Internet Explorer** icon.
4. Press **Alt+X** and then click **Safety > Turn off SmartScreen Filter**.
5. In the *Microsoft SmartScreen Filter* window (see Figure 16-4), confirm *Turn off SmartScreen Filter* is selected and then click **OK**.

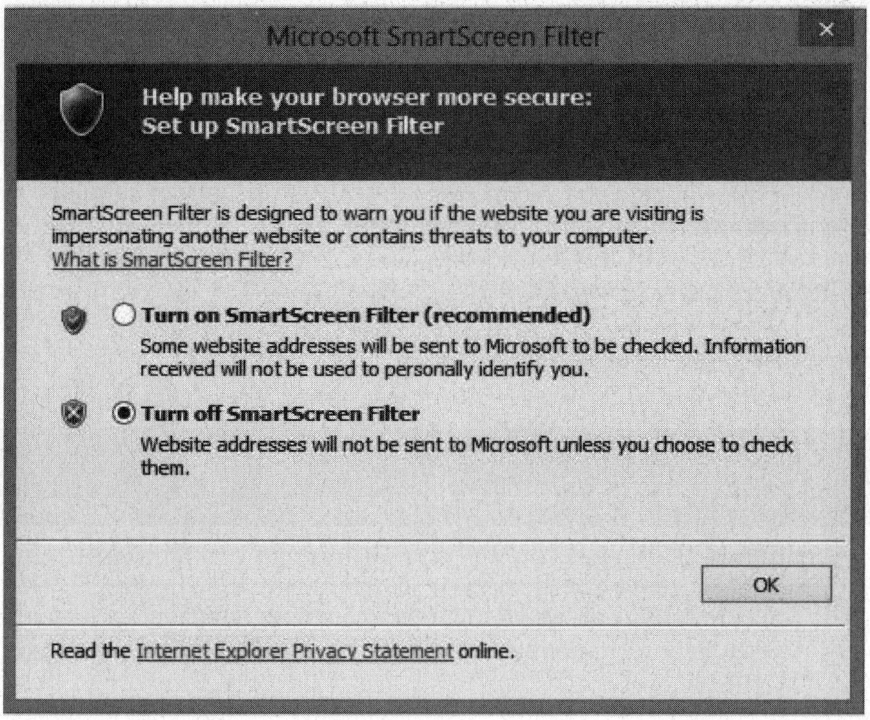

Figure 16-4
The *Microsoft SmartScreen Filter* dialog box

6. Press the **Alt+X**, click **Safety > Turn on SmartScreen Filter**, and then click **OK**.
7. Close the *Internet Explorer* browser window.
8. Mouse over the lower-left corner of the desktop and click the **Start** screen thumbnail that appears there to open the *Start Menu*.
9. Type **Control Panel** and then press **Enter**.
10. When the *Control Panel* opens, in the *Search Control Panel* text box, type **Change SmartScreen settings**.

Question 9	*Where is the Change SmartScreen settings found in the Control Panel?*

11. Click **Change SmartScreen settings**.
12. In the *Windows SmartScreen* box, select **Don't do anything (turn off Windows SmartScreen)** and then click **OK**.
13. After making this change, a warning message displays under the *Security* section, recommending that you keep Windows SmartScreen enabled.

14. Take a screen shot of the *Action Center* by pressing **Alt+Prt Scr** and then paste it into your Lab 16 worksheet file in the page provided by pressing **Ctrl+V**.

15. In the left pane of the *Action Center*, click **Change Windows SmartScreen settings**.

16. In the *Windows SmartScreen* box, select **Get administrator approval before running an unrecognized app from the Internet (recommended)** and then click **OK**.

17. Close the *Action Center* window.

End of exercise. Leave the computers running for the next exercise.

Lab Challenge	Configuring Secure Boot
Overview	In this challenge, you will demonstrate how to configure Secure Boot.
Mindset	Secure Boot is designed to protect your computer against loading malware when booting systems that have the Unified Extensible Firmware Interface (UEFI).
Completion time	10 minutes

To protect the boot process from malware, you can use SecureBoot. Therefore, during this lab challenge, you will write out the steps used to enable Secure Boot Mode. Since SecureBoot requires UEFI, this is only a written exercise.

End of lab.

LAB 17 CONFIGURING AUTHENTICATION AND AUTHORIZATION

THIS LAB CONTAINS THE FOLLOWING EXERCISES AND ACTIVITIES:

Exercise 17.1	Creating Local Users
Exercise 17.2	Managing Credentials
Lab Challenge	Assigning User Rights

BEFORE YOU BEGIN

The lab environment consists of computers connected to a local area network in a workgroup configuration. The computers required for this lab are listed in Table 17-1.

Table 17-1
Computers Required for Lab 17

Computer	*Operating System*	*Computer Name*
Server	Windows Server 2012	SVR-WKGRP-A
Workstation	Windows 8 Enterprise	WKSTN-WKGRP-B
Workstation	Windows 8 Enterprise	WKSTN-WKGRP-C

In addition to the computers, you will also need the software listed in Table 17-2 to complete Lab 17.

Table 17-2
Software Required for Lab 17

Software	*Location*
Lab 17 student worksheet	Lab17_worksheet.docx (provided by instructor)

Working with Lab Worksheets

Each lab in this manual requires that you answer questions, create screenshots, and perform other activities that you will document in a worksheet named for the lab, such as Lab17_worksheet.docx. You will find these worksheets on the book companion site. It is recommended that you use a USB flash drive to store your worksheets so you can submit them to your instructor for review. As you perform the exercises in each lab, open the appropriate worksheet file, type the required information, and then save the file to your flash drive.

SCENARIO

After completing this lab, you will be able to:

- Create local users and groups
- Configure user rights
- Manage credentials

Estimated lab time: 50 minutes

Exercise 17.1	Creating Local Users
Overview	In this exercise, you will create new local user accounts with the controls provided in the Windows 8 PC Settings screen.
Mindset	In a workgroup environment, users must have separate accounts on every computer they access.
Completion time	15 minutes

1. On WKSTN-MBR-B, log on using the **wkstn-wrkgrp-b\ocox** account and the **Pa$$w0rd** password.

2. Mouse over the lower right corner of the **Start** screen and, when the Charms bar appears, click **Settings > Change PC Settings**. The *PC Settings* screen appears.

3. Click **Users**. The *Users* page appears (see Figure 17-1).

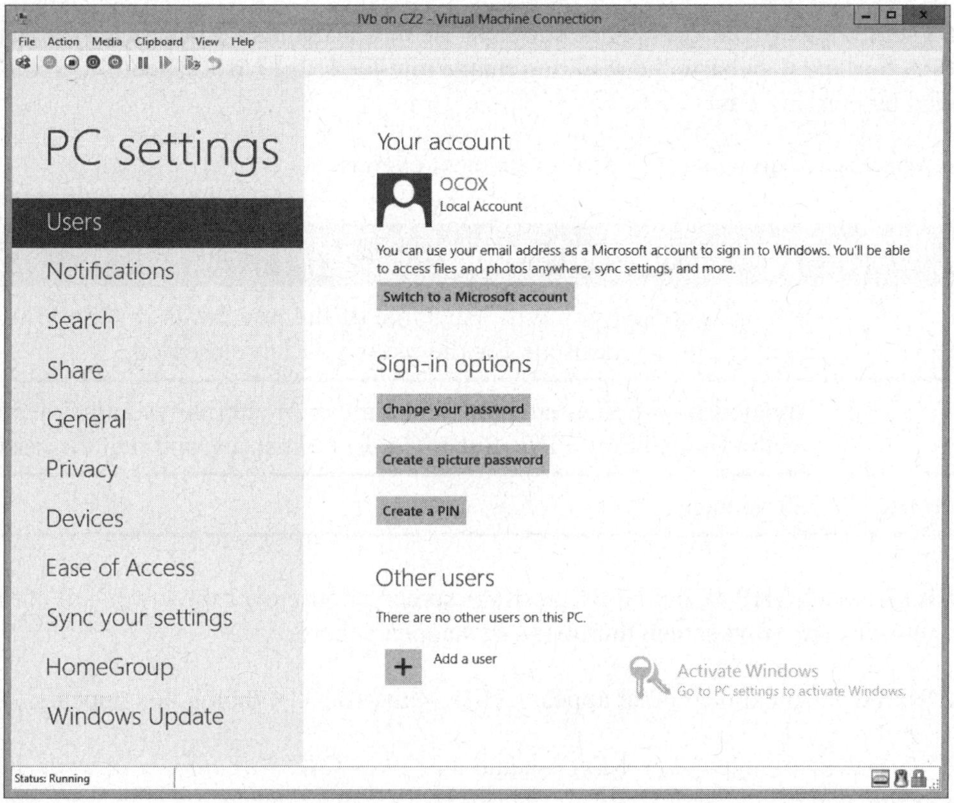

Figure 17-1
The *Users* page of the PC Settings *screen*

4. Click **Add a user**. The *Add a user* screen appears.

5. In the *User name* text box, type **JKotas**.

6. In the *Password* text box and the *Reenter password* text box, type **Pa$$w0rd**.

7. In the *Password hint* text box, type **hint** and then click **Next**. The system creates the user account.

8. Click **Finish**. The new account is added to the *Users* page.

Question 1	*What happens in Windows 8 when you try to create a user through the traditional method, using the User Control Panel?*

9. Repeat steps 4 to 8 to create two more users with the names **TAllen** and **AKol**, using the same password and password hint values shared in Step 6 and Step 7.

10. Take a screen shot of the *Users* page showing the new accounts you created by pressing **Ctrl+Prt Scr** and then paste the resulting image into the Lab 17 worksheet file in the page provided by pressing **Ctrl+V**.

End of exercise. Leave all windows open for the next exercise.

Exercise 17.2	Managing Credentials
Overview	In this exercise, you will use some of the new tools in Windows 8 to manage the credentials for the users you have created.
Mindset	Windows 8 provides support for a number of alternative authentication methods, including PINs, Smart Cards, biometrics, and picture passwords.
Completion time	20 minutes

1. On **WKSTN-WKGRP-B**, on the **PC Settings** screen, mouse over the lower-left corner and right-click the **Start** screen thumbnail that appears there.

2. Then, from the context menu that appears, click **Run**. The *Run* dialog box appears.

3. In the *Open* text box, type **\\svr-wkgrp-a** and then click **OK**. A *Windows Security* dialog box appears, requesting credentials for the server SVR-WKGRP-A.

4. Click **Cancel**.

Question 2	*Why are you unable to connect to SVR-WKGRP-A without supplying credentials?*

5. Mouse over the lower-left corner of the desktop and right-click the **Start** screen thumbnail that appears there. Then, from the context menu that appears, click **Control Panel**. The *Control Panel* appears.

6. Click **User Accounts and Family Safety > Credential Manager**. The *Credential Manager* control panel applet appears, as shown in Figure 17-2.

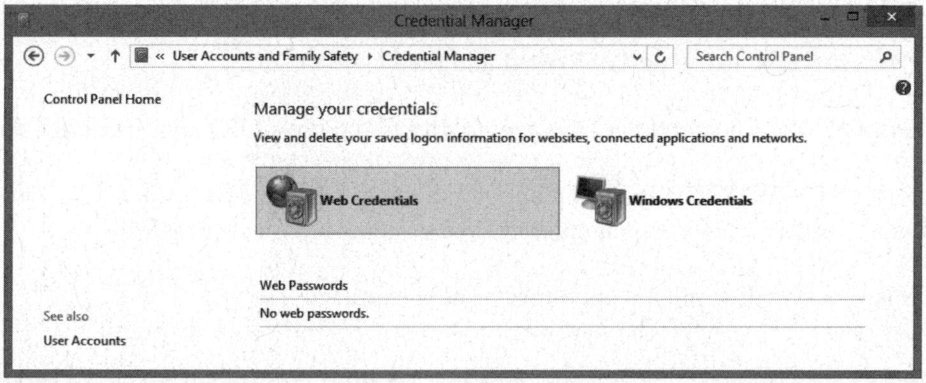

Figure 17-2
The *Credential Manager* control panel

7. Click **Windows Credentials** and then click **Add a Windows credential**. The *Add a Windows Credential* dialog box appears.

8. In the *Internet or network address* text box, type **\\SVR-WKGRP-A**.

9. In the *User name* text box, type **Administrator**.

10. In the *Password* text box, type **Pa$$w0rd** and then click **OK**. The credential appears in the *Windows Credentials* list.

11. Take a screen shot of the *Windows Credentials* control panel showing the new credential you entered by pressing **Ctrl+Prt Scr** and then paste the resulting image into the Lab 17 worksheet file in the page provided by pressing **Ctrl+V**.

12. Close the Credential Manager window, then open the **Run** dialog box again and try to connect to the **\\SVR-WKGRP-A** server. This time, the *File Explorer* window appears, displaying the shares on the remote computer.

Question 3	*Why are you now able to connect to SVR-WKGRP-A without supplying credentials?*

13. Log off **WKSTN-WKGRP-B** and log on again using the **JKotas** account you created and the **Pa$$w0rd** password.

14. Mouse over the lower right corner of the **Start** screen and, when the Charm bar appears, click **Settings > Change PC Settings**. The *PC Settings* screen appears.

15. Click **Users**. The *Users* page appears.

16. Click **Create a PIN**. A *Create a PIN* screen appears, prompting you to confirm your password.

17. In the *Password* text box, type **Pa$$w0rd** and then click **OK**.

18. In the *Enter PIN* text box and the *Confirm PIN* text box, type **1234** and then click **Finish**.

19. Log off **WKSTN-WKGRP-B** and then log on again using the **JKotas** account you created and the PIN **1234** you just entered. The system logs on successfully.

End of exercise. Leave all windows open for the next exercise.

Lab Challenge	Assigning User Rights
Overview	In this challenge, you will add a selection of user rights assignments to the ones that already exist.
Mindset	User rights provide specific users or groups with the ability to perform specific tasks on a computer running Windows 8.
Completion time	15 minutes

Your organization has created a new job role called the director, and your job is to provide the new directors with the user rights they need to perform their jobs. To complete this challenge, you must create the Directors group and add the three user accounts you created in Exercise 17.1 to that group. Then you must grant the Directors group the following user rights to your local system, without interfering with any of the existing rights:

- Deny logon locally
- Enable computer and user accounts to be trusted for delegation
- Force shutdown from a remote system
- Manage auditing and security log
- Shut down the system

Write out the basic steps you had to perform to accomplish the challenge and then shoot a screen shot showing the user rights you configured. Then press **Ctrl+V** to paste the image on the page provided in the Lab 17 worksheet file.

End of lab.

LAB 18 CONFIGURING REMOTE CONNECTIONS

THIS LAB CONTAINS THE FOLLOWING EXERCISES AND ACTIVITIES:

BEFORE YOU BEGIN

The lab environment consists of computers connected to a local area network in an Active Directory Domain Services configuration. The computers required for this lab are listed in Table 18-1.

Table 18-1
Computers Required for Lab 18

Computer	*Operating System*	*Computer Name*
Server	Windows Server 2012	SVR-DC-A
Workstation	Windows 8 Enterprise	WKSTN-MBR-B

In addition to the computers, you will also need the software listed in Table 18-2 to complete Lab 18.

Table 18-2
Software Required for Lab 18

Software	*Location*
Lab 18 student worksheet	Lab18_worksheet.docx (provided by instructor)

Working with Lab Worksheets

Each lab in this manual requires that you answer questions, create screenshots, and perform other activities that you will document in a worksheet named for the lab, such as Lab18_worksheet.docx. You will find these worksheets on the book companion site. It is recommended that you use a USB flash drive to store your worksheets so you can submit them to your instructor for review. As you perform the exercises in each lab, open the appropriate worksheet file, type the required information, and then save the file to your flash drive.

SCENARIO

After completing this lab, you will be able to:

- Configure a VPN connection
- Establish a VPN connection

Estimated lab time: 40 minutes

Exercise 18.1	Configuring a VPN Connection
Overview	In this exercise, you will create a connection that enables the workstation to connect to your server using virtual private networking.
Mindset	VPNs use tunneling to create secure connections across a public network.
Completion time	20 minutes

1. On **WKSTN-MBR-B**, log on using the **adatum\Administrator** account and the **Pa$$w0rd** password.
2. Click the **Desktop** tile. The *Desktop* appears.
3. Mouse over the lower-left corner of the desktop and right-click the **Start** screen thumbnail that appears there. Then, from the context menu that appears, click **Control Panel**. The *Control Panel* window appears.
4. Click **Network and Internet > Network and Sharing Center**. The *Network and Sharing Center* control panel appears (see Figure 18-1).

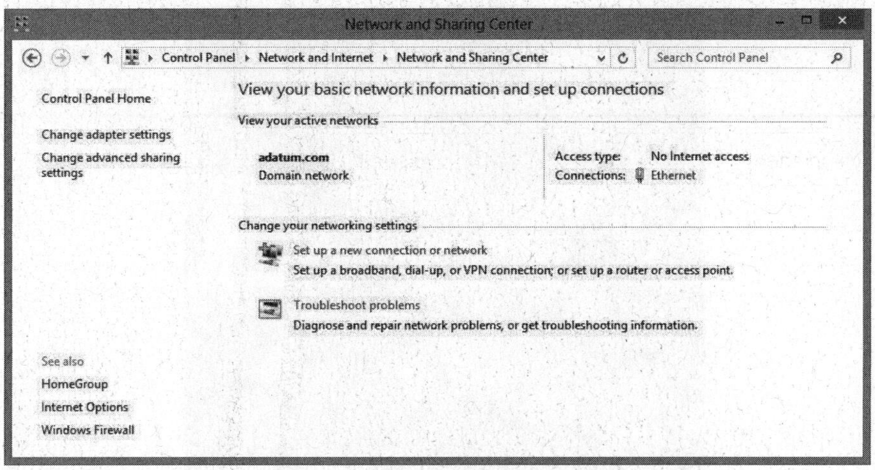

Figure 18-1
The *Network and Sharing Center* control panel

5. Click **Set up a new connection or network**. The *Set Up a Connection or Network Wizard* appears, displaying the *Choose a connection option* page.

6. Select **Connect to a workplace** and then click **Next**. The *How do you want to connect?* page appears.

7. Click **Use my Internet connection (VPN)**. The *Do you want to set up an Internet connection before continuing?* page appears.

NOTE	*For the purposes of this lab, the network does need not be connected to the Internet.*

8. Click **I'll set up an Internet connection later**. The *Type the Internet address to connect to* page appears.

9. In the *Internet address* text box, type **SVR-DC-A.adatum.com**.

10. In the *Destination name* text box, type **VPN Server Connection**.

11. Select the **Allow other people to use this connection** check box.

12. Take a screen shot of the *Connect to a Workplace* Wizard showing the page you just configured by pressing **Alt+Prt Scr**, and then paste the resulting image into the Lab 18 worksheet file in the page provided by pressing **Ctrl+V**.

13. Click **Create**. The wizard creates the connection and adds it to the *Connections* list on the fly-out menu (see Figure 18-2).

Figure 18-2
The *Connections* list in the Windows 8 fly-out menu

Question 1	*How many connections are there in the Network Connections window?*

14. On the fly-out menu, right-click **VPN Server Connection** and choose **View connection properties**. The *VPN Server Connection Properties* sheet appears.

15. Click the **Security** tab and then take a screen shot of the *VPN Server Connection Properties* sheet by pressing **Alt+Prt Scr**. Then paste the resulting image into the Lab 18 worksheet file in the page provided by pressing **Ctrl+V**.

16. Click the **Options** tab.

17. From the *Idle time before hanging up* drop-down list, select **5 minutes**.

18. Click **OK** to close the *VPN Server Connection Properties* sheet.

End of exercise. Leave all windows open for the next exercise.

Exercise 18.2	Connecting to a VPN Server
Overview	In this exercise, you will use the connection you created earlier to connect to your SVR-DC-A server using virtual private networking.
Mindset	During the connection establishment process, the two computers involved in a VPN connection authenticate each other and select a VPN protocol.
Completion time	10 minutes

1. On the Windows 8 desktop, click the network icon in the notification area (located at the lower-right corner of the screen). The *Networks* flyout menu appears.

2. Click **VPN Server Connection** and then click **Connect**. A *Network Authentication* tile appears (see Figure 18-3).

Figure 18-3
The *Network Authentication* dialog box

3. In the *User name* text box, type **Administrator**. In the *Password* text box, type **Pa$$w0rd**. Then click **OK**. The workstation connects to the VPN server and the connection appears in the *Networks* list with a *Connected* indicator.

4. Right-click the **VPN Server Connection** link and click the View network status option. The *VPN Server Connection Status* dialog box appears.

5. Click the **Details** tab (not the Details button).

Question 2	*Which VPN protocol is the connection using?*

Question 3	*Which authentication protocol is the VPN connection using?*

6. Take a screen shot of the *VPN Server Connection Status* dialog box by pressing **Alt+Prt Scr** and then paste the resulting image into the Lab 18 worksheet file in the page provided by pressing **Ctrl+V**.

End of exercise. Close any open windows before you begin the next exercise.

Lab Challenge	Testing VPN Protocols
Overview	By default, the Windows 8 VPN client is configured to select a VPN type automatically. In this challenge, you configure the client to use each of its supported VPN types to then determine which ones are currently supported by your VPN server.
Mindset	Windows VPN clients and servers each supports a variety of connection protocols with different authentication requirements and levels of security.
Completion time	10 minutes

To complete this challenge, open the Properties sheet for the VPN connection you created in Exercise 18.1, click the Security tab, and then select each of the four specific Type of VPN values in turn, attempting to connect to the server with each one. Record your results in Table 18-3 on your worksheet.

Table 18-3
Connection Results for VPN Protocols

Type of VPN	*Result message*
Point-to-Point Tunneling Protocol	
Layer 2 Tunneling Protocol with IPsec (L2TP/IPSec)	
Secure Socket Tunneling Protocol (SSTP)	
IKEv2	

End of lab.

LAB 19 CONFIGURING MOBILITY OPTIONS

THIS LAB CONTAINS THE FOLLOWING EXERCISES AND ACTIVITIES:

Exercise 19.1 Configuring Power Options

Exercise 19.2 Creating a Custom Power Plan

Lab Challenge Using Powercfg.exe

BEFORE YOU BEGIN

The lab environment consists of computers connected to a local area network in an Active Directory Domain Services configuration. The computers required for this lab are listed in Table 19-1.

Table 19-1
Computers Required for Lab 19

Computer	*Operating System*	*Computer Name*
Server	Windows Server 2012	SVR-DC-A
Workstation	Windows 8 Enterprise	WKSTN-MBR-B
Workstation	Windows 8 Enterprise	WKSTN-MBR-C

In addition to the computers, you will also need the software listed in Table 19-2 to complete Lab 19.

Table 19-2
Software Required for Lab 19

Software	*Location*
Lab 19 student worksheet	Lab19_worksheet.docx (provided by instructor)

Working with Lab Worksheets

Each lab in this manual requires that you answer questions, create screenshots, and perform other activities that you will document in a worksheet named for the lab, such as Lab19_worksheet.docx. You will find these worksheets on the book companion site. It is recommended that you use a USB flash drive to store your worksheets so you can submit them to your instructor for review. As you perform the exercises in each lab, open the appropriate worksheet file, type the required information in Word, and then save the file to your flash drive.

SCENARIO

After completing this lab, you will be able to:

- Configure power options
- Create a custom power plan
- Use powercfg.exe

Estimated lab time: 50 minutes

Exercise 19.1	Configuring Power Options
Overview	In this exercise, you will examine the power settings used in the default power plans provided in Windows.
Mindset	Windows 8 provides a range of settings that you can use to conserve power.
Completion time	20 minutes

1. On **WKSTN-MBR-B**, log on using the **adatum\Administrator** account and the **Pa$$w0rd** password.

2. Click the **Desktop** tile. The *Desktop* appears.

3. Mouse over the lower-left corner of the desktop and right-click the **Start** screen thumbnail that appears there. Then, from the context menu that appears, click **Control Panel**. The *Control Panel* window appears.

4. Click **Hardware and Sound > Power Options**. The *Power Options* control panel appears (see Figure 19-1).

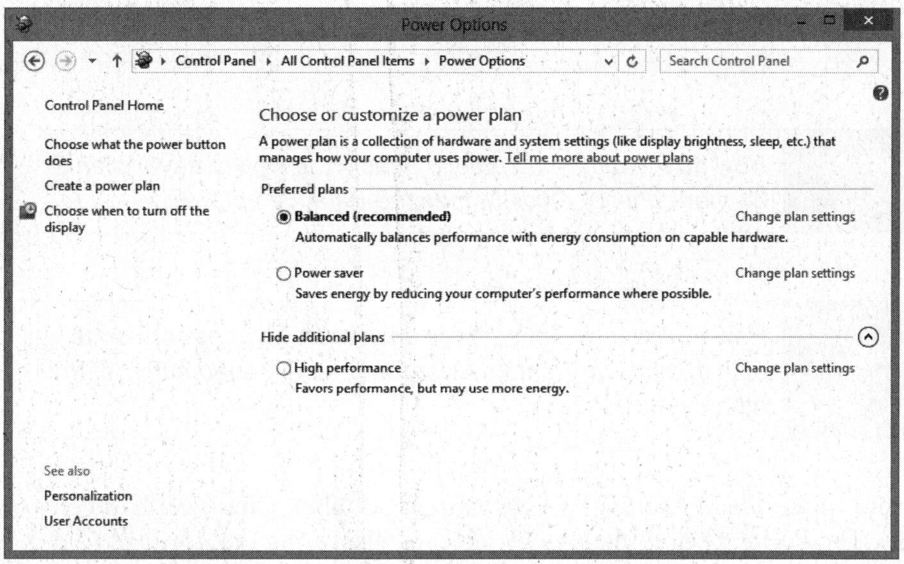

Figure 19-1
The *Power Options* control panel

5. Click the **Show additional plans** down-arrow.

Question 1	*How many power plans are available for your selection in the Power Options control panel?*

6. In the Balanced plan option, click the **Change plan settings** link. The *Change settings for the plan: Balanced* page appears.

7. In cell Table 19-3, enter the value for the *Turn off the display* setting.

8. Click **Cancel**.

9. Click the **Change plan settings** link for the *Power saver* plan and then enter the values for the *Turn off the display* setting into the appropriate cells of Table 19-3. Click Cancel.

10. Click the **Change plan settings** link for the *High performance* plan and then type the values for the *Turn off the display* setting into the appropriate cells of Table 19-3. Click Cancel.

Table 19-3
Default Windows 8 Power Configuration Settings

Setting	*Balanced*	*Power Saver*	*High Performance*
Turn off the display			

Question 2	*How do the different settings enable the Power saver plan to be more energy efficient than the Balanced plan?*

Question 3	*How do the different settings enable the High performance plan to achieve greater performance levels than either of the other two plans?*

11. In any one of the *Change settings for the plan* pages, click **Change advanced power settings**. The *Power Options* dialog box appears, displaying the *Advanced Settings* tab.

12. Take a screen shot of the *Power Options* dialog box by pressing **Alt+Prt Scr** and then paste the resulting image into the Lab 19 worksheet file in the page provided by pressing **Ctrl+V**.

13. Using the drop-down list to change power plans, examine the values for the advanced power settings and type them in Table 19-4.

Table 19-4
Default Windows 7 Advanced Power Configuration Settings

Setting	*Balanced*	*Power Saver*	*High Performance*
Turn off hard disk after			
Internet Explorer \ JavaScript Timer Frequency			
Desktop background settings \ Slide show			
Wireless Adapter Settings \ Power Saving Mode			
Sleep \ Allow wake timers			
USB settings \ USB selective suspend setting			

Power buttons and lid \ Power button action			
PCI Express \ Link State Power Management			
Processor power management \ System cooling policy			
Display \ Turn off display after			
Display \ Enable adaptive brightness			
Multimedia settings \ When sharing media			
Multimedia settings \ When playing video			

Question 4	*Which of the settings on the Advanced settings tab enables the Power saver plan to conserve more energy than the other two plans?*

14. Click **OK** to close the *Power Options* dialog box.

End of exercise. Leave all windows open for the next exercise.

Exercise 19.2	Creating a Custom Power Plan
Overview	In this exercise, you will create power plans for your company's desktop and laptop workstations.
Mindset	Desktop and portable computers have different power requirements and therefore require separate power plans.
Completion time	20 minutes

1. On **WKSTN-MBR-B**, in the *Power Options* control panel, click **Create a power plan**. The *Create a Power Plan* Wizard appears (see Figure 19-2).

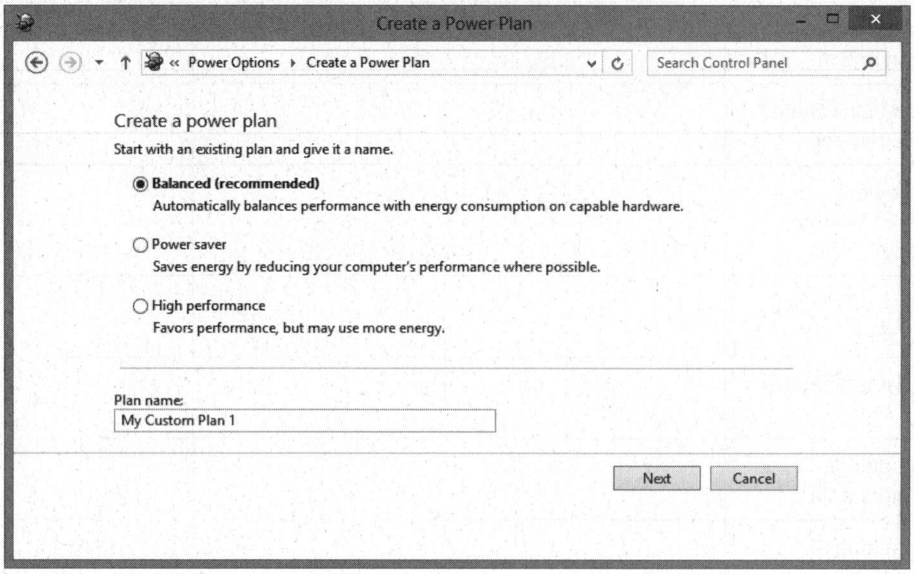

Figure 19-2
The *Create a Power Plan* Wizard

2. Leave the *Balanced (recommended)* option selected and, in the *Plan name* text box, type **Adatum Desktops** and then click **Next**. The *Change settings for the plan: Adatum Desktops* page appears.

3. In the *Turn off the display* drop-down list, select **15 minutes**.

4. Click **Create**. The *Adatum Desktops* plan appears in the *Power Options* control panel.

5. Repeat steps 2 thru 4 to create another power plan called **Adatum Laptops** with the *Turn off the display* setting set to **5 minutes**.

6. Take a screen shot of the *Power Options* control panel, showing the power plans you created, by pressing **Alt+Prt Scr** and then paste the resulting image into the Lab 19 worksheet file in the page provided by pressing **Ctrl+V**.

7. Click the **Change plan settings** link for the *Adatum Desktops* plan. The *Change settings for the plan: Adatum Desktops* page appears.

8. Click **Change advanced power settings**. The *Power Options* dialog box appears, displaying the *Advanced Settings* tab.

9. Make sure that *Adatum Desktops* is selected in the drop-down list and then configure the following settings:

   - Turn off hard disk after: 15 minutes
   - PCI Express \ Link State Power Management: Maximum power savings

- Processor power management \ System cooling policy: Active
- Multimedia settings \ When playing video: Optimize power savings

10. Click **OK** to close the *Power Options* dialog box.

11. Click **Cancel** to close the *Change settings for the plan: Adatum Desktops* page.

12. Open the *Change settings for the plan: Adatum Laptops* page and then click **Change advanced power settings**. The *Power Options* dialog box appears, displaying the *Advanced Settings* tab.

13. Make sure that *Adatum Laptops* is selected in the drop-down list and then configure the following settings:

    - Turn off hard disk after: 5 minutes
    - Wireless adapter settings \ Power saving mode: Maximum power saving
    - PCI Express \ Link State Power Management: Maximum power savings
    - Processor power management \ System cooling policy: Passive
    - Multimedia settings \ When playing video: Optimize power savings

14. Click **OK** to close the *Power Options* dialog box.

Question 5	*Why does the Adatum Laptops power plan have a setting to maximize wireless adapter power savings, which the Adatum Desktops plan does not?*

15. Close the *Power Options* control panel.

End of exercise. Leave all windows open for the next exercise.

Lab Challenge	Using Powercfg.exe
Overview	Now that you have created power plans for your company's desktop and laptop computers, you must determine how to transfer those plans to other computers.
Mindset	You can use the Powercfg.exe command-line utility to export your power plans from your WKSTN-MBR-B workstation and import them on WKSTN-MBR-C.
Completion time	10 minutes

In this challenge, you will use the Powercfg.exe command-line utility to export your power plans from your WKSTN-MBR-B workstation and import them on WKSTN-MBR-C.

To complete the challenge, you must perform the following tasks:

1. Use the Powercfg.exe utility to display the 32-character GUID values for the power plans you created in Exercise 19.2, and then copy the GUID values into Table 19-5.

Table 19-5
Custom Power Plan GUIDs

Power Plan Name	*32-character GUID*
Adatum Desktops	
Adatum Laptops	

2. Write the commands needed to export the power plans you created on WKSTN-MBR-B to files, copy the files to the Downloads share on SVR-DC-A, and then import the power plans on WKSTN-MBR-C.

3. Execute the commands on the two workstations and take screen shots of each by pressing **Alt+Prt Scr** and then paste the two resulting images into the Lab 19 worksheet file in the page provided by pressing **Ctrl+V**.

End of lab.

LAB 20
CONFIGURING SECURITY FOR MOBILE DEVICES

THIS LAB CONTAINS THE FOLLOWING EXERCISES AND ACTIVITIES:

Exercise 20.1 Configuring BitLocker

Exercise 20.2 Creating a Data Recovery Agent (DRA)

Exercise 20.3 Disabling the Windows Location Provider

Lab Challenge Performing a Remote Wipe using the Exchange Admin Center (EAC)

BEFORE YOU BEGIN

The lab environment consists of student workstations connected to a local area network, along with a server that functions as the domain controller for a domain called adatum.com. The computers required for this lab are listed in Table 20-1.

Table 20-1
Computers Required for Lab 20

Computer	*Operating System*	*Computer Name*
Server (VM 1)	Windows Server 2012	SVR-DC-A
Client (VM 3)	Windows 7 Enterprise	WKSTN-MBR-C

In addition to the computers, you will also need the software listed in Table 20-2 to complete Lab 20.

Table 20-2
Software Required for Lab 20

Software	*Location*
Lab 20 student worksheet	Lab20_worksheet.docx (provided by instructor)

Working with Lab Worksheets

Each lab in this manual requires that you answer questions, shoot screen shots, and perform other activities that you will document in a worksheet named for the lab, such as Lab20_worksheet.docx. You will find these worksheets on the book companion site. It is recommended that you use a USB flash drive to store your worksheets so you can submit them to your instructor for review. As you perform the exercises in each lab, open the appropriate worksheet file, type the required information, and then save the file to your flash drive.

SCENARIO

After completing this lab, you will be able to:

- Enable and configure BitLocker
- Install the Certificate Authority
- Request a certificate from a Certificate Authority
- Disable the Windows Location Provider
- Create a Data Recovery Agent (DRA) for EFS
- Perform a Remote Wipe using the Exchange Admin Center (EAC)

Estimated lab time: 70 minutes

Exercise 20.1	Configuring BitLocker
Overview	In this exercise, you will enable BitLocker for the volume containing the operating system.
Completion time	20 minutes

1. On **WKSTN-MBR-C**, log on using the **adatum\administrator** account and the **Pa$$w0rd** password.

2. On the *Start* screen, type **gpedit.msc**, and then press **Enter**.

3. When the Local Group Policy Editor opens, navigate to **\Computer Configuration\Administrative Templates\Windows Components\BitLocker Drive Encryption\Operating System Drives** and then double-click **Require additional authentication at startup**.

4. When the *Require additional authentication at startup* dialog box opens, click **Enabled**.

5. Take a screen shot of the local policy setting by pressing **Alt+Prt Scr** and then paste it into your Lab 20 worksheet file in the page provided by pressing **Ctrl+V**.

6. Click **OK** to close the *Require additional authentication at startup* dialog box.

7. Close **Local Group Policy Editor**.

8. Mouse over the lower-left corner of the desktop and right-click the **Start** screen thumbnail that appears there. Then, from the context menu that appears, click **Control Panel**.

9. When the *Control Panel* opens, click **System and Security > BitLocker Drive Encryption**. The *BitLocker Drive Encryption* control panel application appears (see Figure 20-1).

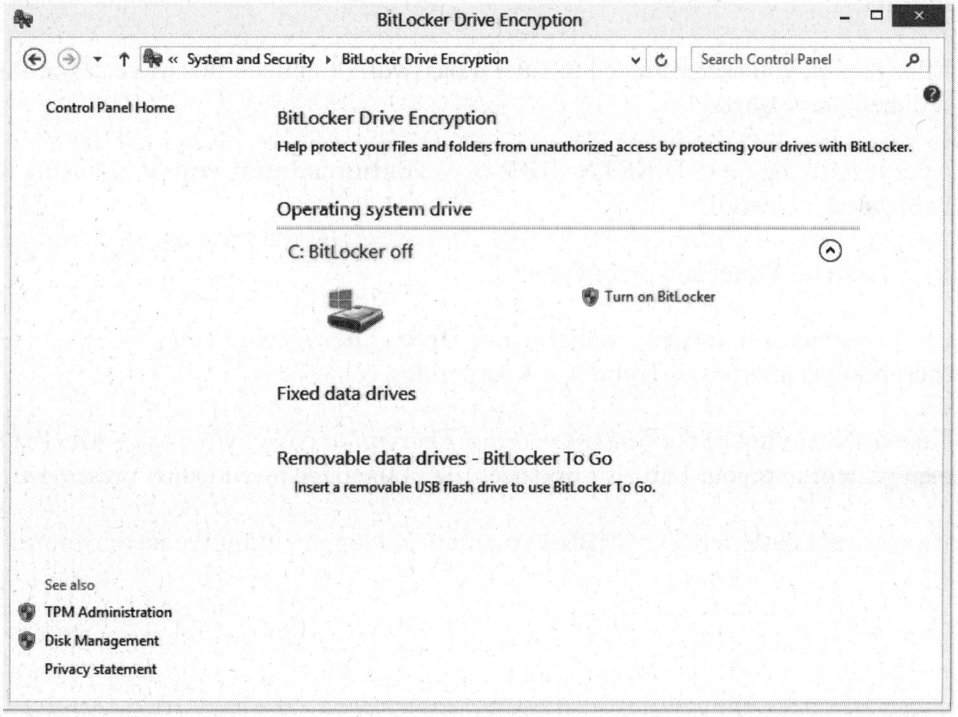

Figure 20-1
The *BitLocker Drive Encryption* page

10. For the *C* drive, click **Turn on BitLocker**.

11. When prompted to choose how you will unlock your drive at startup, click **Enter a password**.

Question 1	*Why is it necessary to use a password to unlock the drive?*

12. In the *Enter your password* text box and in the *Reenter your password* text box, type **Pa$$w0rd** and then click **Next**.

13. When prompted to back up your recovery key, click **Save to a file**

14. Type **SVR-DC-A\Downloads**\ in front of the filename, and then press the **Enter**. Click **Save**.

15. Back on the *How do you want to back up your recovery key?* page, click **Next**.

16. On the *Choose how much of your drive to encrypt* page, click **Next**. On the *Are you ready to encrypt this drive?* page, with *Run BitLocker system check* selected, click **Continue**.

17. Move mouse to lower right corner and select **Settings**. Click **Power** and then click **Restart**.

18. After reboot, you are prompted to enter a password to unlock this drive. Type **Pa$$w0rd** and then press **Enter**.

19. After restart, log on to **WKSTN-MBR-C** as **adatum\administrator** and using the **Pa$$w0rd** password.

20. Type **Control Panel** and press **Enter**.

21. Click **System and Security > BitLocker Drive Encryption**. You should now see the encryption is in process (BitLocker Encrypting).

22. Take a screen shot of the *BitLocker Drive Encryption* page by pressing **Alt+Prt Scr** and then paste it into your Lab 20 worksheet file in the page provided by pressing **Ctrl+V**.

End of exercise. Leave WKSTN-MBR-C running and logged in for the next exercise.

Exercise 20.2	Creating a Data Recovery Agent (DRA)
Overview	In this exercise, you will create an EFS data recovery agent that can be used to recover documents that are protected with EFS.
Mindset	When a user forgets his or her password to unlock a drive that is protected by BitLocker or when a user has left the company and the account has been deleted, a Data Recovery Agent (DRA) can be used to recover the encrypted disk.
Completion time	30 minutes

First, you must install a Certificate Authority by performing the following steps:

1. On **SVR-DC-A**, log on using the **adatum\administrator** account and the **Pa$$w0rd** password.
2. When *Server Manager* opens, click **Manage > Add Roles and Features**.
3. Click **Next** to start the *Add Roles and Features* Wizard.
4. Click **Next** to accept the *Role-based or feature-based installation* default setting.
5. From the *Server* pool, click your domain controller and then click **Next**.
6. On the *Select server roles* page, click to select **Active Directory Certificate Services** and then click **Add Features** to include the management tools.
7. Click **Next** to continue.
8. Click **Next** to continue on the *Select features* screen.
9. After reading the information provided on the *Active Directory Certificate Services* screen, click **Next**.
10. Confirm that *Certification Authority* is checked and then click **Next**.
11. On the *Confirm installation selections* screen, select **Restart the destination server automatically if required** and then click **Yes** to allow automatic restarts.
12. Click **Install** to begin the installation of the AD CS role.
13. When the installation has completed, click **Close**.
14. Click the yellow triangle with black exclamation point that appears at the top of the *Server Manager Dashboard* (see Figure 20-2), and then click **Configure Active Directory Certificate Services on the destination server** to complete the post-deployment configuration.

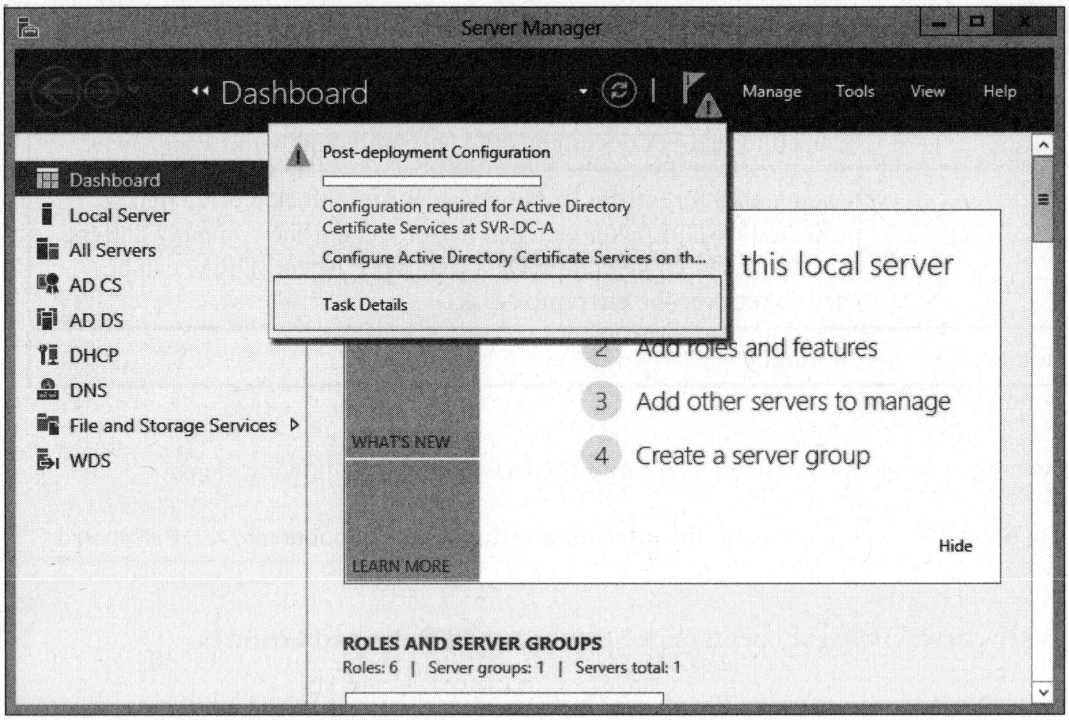

Figure 20-2
The *Post-deployment Configuration* dialog box.

15. On the *Specify credentials to configure role services* screen, click **Next** to accept the default credentials (**ADATUM\Administrator**).

16. On the *Select Role Services to configure* screen, select **Certification Authority** and then click **Next**.

17. On the *Specify the setup type of the CA* screen, click **Next** to accept the *Enterprise CA* default setting.

18. On the *Specify the type of the CA* screen, click **Next** to accept the *Root CA* default setting.

19. On the *Specify the type of the private key* screen, click **Next** to accept the *Create a new private key* default setting.

20. On the *Specify the cryptographic options* screen, click **Next** to accept the default settings.

21. On the *Specify the name of the CA* screen, click **Next** to accept the default settings.

22. On the *Specify the validity period* screen, change the validity period to **10** years. Click **Next** to accept the default settings.

23. On the *Specify the database locations* screen, click **Next** to accept the default settings.

24. Click **Configure**. When the configuration succeeds, click **Close**.

Next, you must request a Digital Certificate by performing the following steps:

1. On **WKSTN-MBR-C**, mouse over the lower-left corner of the desktop and right-click the **Start** screen thumbnail that appears there. Click **Run**.
2. In the *Run* dialog box, type **certmgr.msc**.
3. Click the **Personal Folder**, then right-click the **Personal Folder**, and click **All Tasks > Request New Certificate**.
4. When the *Certificate Enrollment* Wizard appears, click **Next**.
5. Make sure *Active Directory Enrollment Policy* is highlighted and then click **Next** to continue.
6. On the *Request Certificates* screen, select **Basic EFS** and then click **Enroll**.
7. After you are informed the certificate has been enrolled and installed on the computer, click **Finish**.
8. Expand the *Personal* folder, click **Certificates,** and then double-click the **Administrator** certificate.
9. When the *Certificate* dialog box opens, click the **Details** tab.
10. Click the **Copy to File** button. When the *Certificate Export* Wizard dialog box appears, click **Next**.
11. Leave the *No, do not export the private key* option selected and then click **Next**.
12. Verify that the *DER encoded binary X.509 (.CER)* format is selected and then click **Next**.
13. On the *File to Export* page, click **Browse** to display the *Save as* dialog box.
14. In the *File name* text box, type **BitLocker**. In the *Save as type* option, verify that *DER Encoded Binary X.509 (.cer)* is selected and then click **Save**.

Question 2	*What is the path of the certificate export?*

15. Back on the *File to Export* page, click **Next**.

16. Click **Finish** to complete the *Certificate Export* Wizard.

17. Take a screen shot of the *The export was successful* dialog box by pressing **Alt+Prt Scr** and then paste it into your Lab 20 worksheet file in the page provided by pressing **Ctrl+V**.

18. When the *The export was successful* dialog box displays, click **OK**.

19. Close any open dialog boxes.

20. Close the *certmgr* console.

21. Log off of **SVR-DC-A**.

End of exercise. Leave WKSTN-MBR-C running and logged in for the next exercise.

Exercise 20.3	Disabling the Windows Location Provider (WLP)
Overview	In this exercise, you will disable the Windows Location Provider (WLP) for a computer running Windows 8, and then modify a policy to perform the same action.
Mindset	The Windows Location Provider (WLP) is used by applications to gain access to location data. If you do not want to establish location information, you can disable the WLP.
Completion time	10 minutes

1. On **WKSTN-DOM-C**, mouse over the lower-left corner of the desktop and right-click the **Start** screen thumbnail that appears there. Click **Control Panel**.

2. When the *Control Panel* is open, click the **Hardware and Sound** category.

3. Click **Location Settings**.

Question 3	*What does Windows Location Provider use to determine geographic location?*

4. Deselect **Turn on the Windows Location platform** and then click **Apply**.

5. Take a screen shot of the *Location Settings* page by pressing **Alt+Prt Scr** and then paste it into your Lab 20 worksheet file in the page provided by pressing **Ctrl+V**.

6. Close the **Control Panel**.

7. Mouse over the lower-left corner of the desktop and right-click the **Start** screen thumbnail that appears there. Click **Run**.

8. In the *Run* dialog box, type **gpedit.msc**.

9. Click **Computer Configuration > Administrative Templates > Windows Components > Location and Sensors > Windows Location Provider** (see Figure 20-3).

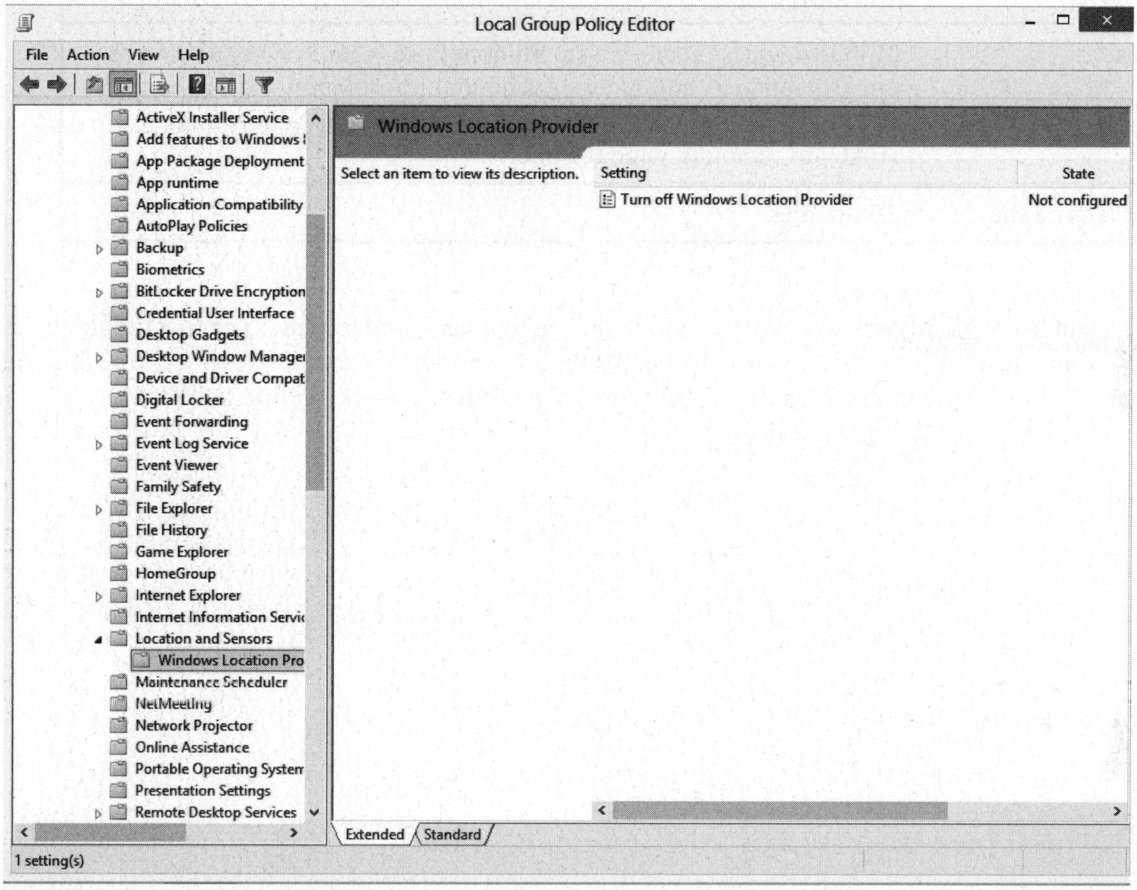

Figure 20-3
The *Windows Location Provider* page

10. Double-click **Turn off Windows Location Provider** and then click **Enabled**.

11. Take a screen shot of the *Turn off Location Provider* dialog box by pressing **Alt+Prt Scr** and then paste it into your Lab 20 worksheet file in the page provided by pressing **Ctrl+V**.

12. Click **OK** to close the *Turn off Windows Location Provider* dialog box.

13. Close **Local Group Policy Editor**.

14. Log off of **WKSTN-MBR-C**.

End of exercise. Close all windows before you start the next exercise.

Lab Challenge	Performing a Remote Wipe using the Exchange Admin Center (EAC)
Overview	In this challenge, you will demonstrate how to perform a remote wipe using the Exchange Admin Center (EAC)
Mindset	Mobile devices (such as a smartphone) use Active Sync to retrieve emails, contacts, and other confidential information. If the phone has become lost or stolen, you can use the Exchange Admin Center (EAC) to remotely wipe the phone.
Completion time	10 minutes

You can use EAC to remotely wipe a mobile device that uses ActiveSync to connect to the Exchange environment. In this exercise, you will specify the steps to wipe a mobile device. Since this exercise would require an Exchange environment connected to the network or Internet as well as a mobile device, this is only a written exercise.

End of lab.

LAB 21
CONFIGURING AND MANAGING UPDATES

THIS LAB CONTAINS THE FOLLOWING EXERCISES AND ACTIVITIES:

BEFORE YOU BEGIN

The lab environment consists of student workstations connected to a local area network, along with a server that functions as the domain controller for a domain called adatum.com. The computers required for this lab are listed in Table 21-1.

Table 21-1
Computers Required for Lab 21

Computer	*Operating System*	*Computer Name*
Server	Windows Server 2012	SVR-DC-A
Client	Windows 8 Enterprise	WKSTN-MBR-B

In addition to the computers, you will also need the software listed in Table 21-2 to complete Lab 21.

Table 21-2
Software Required for Lab 21

Software	*Location*
A patch for Internet Explorer 10 (Windows8-RT-KB2761465-x64)	\\svr-dc-a\downloads
Lab 21 student worksheet	Lab21_worksheet.docx (provided by instructor)

Working with Lab Worksheets

Each lab in this manual requires that you answer questions, shoot screen shots, and perform other activities that you will document in a worksheet named for the lab, such as Lab21_worksheet.docx. You will find these worksheets on the book companion site. It is recommended that you use a USB flash drive to store your worksheets so you can submit them to your instructor for review. As you perform the exercises in each lab, open the appropriate worksheet file, type the required information, and then save the file to your flash drive.

SCENARIO

After completing this lab, you will be able to:

- Configure Windows updates
- Install and uninstall an update
- Configure Windows updates using a local policy

Estimated lab time: 55 minutes

Exercise 21.1	Changing Update Settings from the Control Panel
Overview	In this exercise, you will use the Control Panel to configure Windows updates.
Mindset	Unless you use Group Policy (which is often the solution used within larger organizations) to manage Windows updates, you must use the Control Panel to manage Windows update settings.
Completion time	10 minutes

1. On **WKSTN-MBR-B**, log using the **adatum\administrator** account and the **Pa$$w0rd** password.

2. Type **Control Panel** and then select it from the results list.

3. Within the *Control Panel* window, click **System and Security**.

4. To display the *Windows Update* configuration window, click **Windows Update**.

5. On the *Windows Update* page (see Figure 21-1), click **Change settings**. The *Choose your Windows Update settings* window displays.

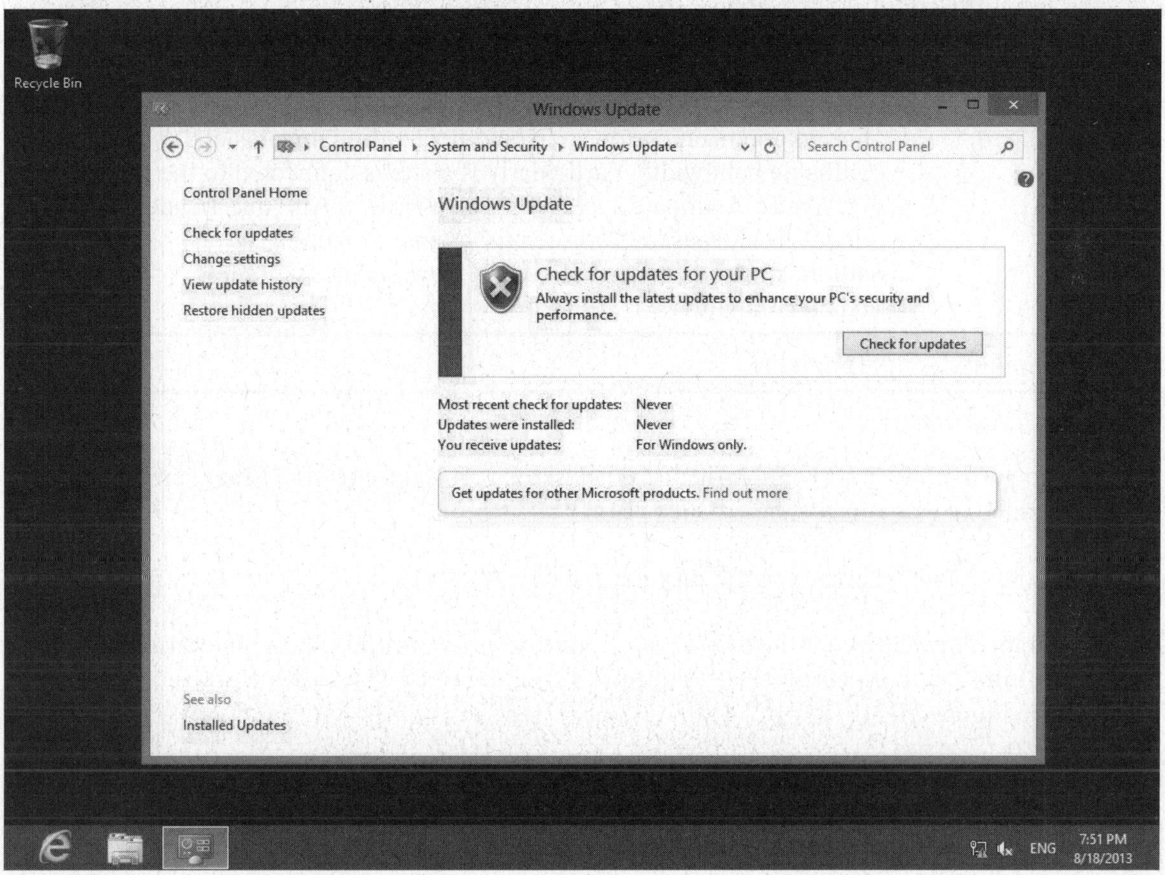

Figure 21-1
The *Windows Update* page

6. Under *Important updates*, click the drop-down and choose **Download updates but let me chose whether to install them**.

Question 1	*Which settings are available for Important updates?*

7. Verify the **Give me recommended updates the same way I receive important updates** option is selected.

8. Take a screen shot of the *Change settings* window by pressing **Alt+Prt Scr** and then paste it into your Lab 21 worksheet file in the page provided by pressing **Ctrl+V**.

9. Click **Cancel** and then close **Windows Update**.

End of exercise. Leave WKSTN-MBR-B running and logged in for the next exercise.

Exercise 21.2	Configuring Windows Update Policies
Overview	In this exercise, you will use Local Group Policy to configure Windows update settings.
Mindset	For an organization, one person downloading updates could waste valuable bandwidth, particularly if a site is connected to the Internet or Windows Update server through a slow WAN link. In addition, updates can cause unforeseen problems. Therefore, as an administrator, you need to control how updates get deployed to client computers.
Completion time	15 minutes

1. Mouse over the lower-left corner of the desktop and right-click the **Start** screen thumbnail that appears there. Click **Run**.

2. In the *Open* text box, type **gpedit.msc** and then click **OK**.

3. On the *Local Group Policy Editor* page, navigate to **Computer Configuration > Administrative Templates > Windows Components > Windows Update** (see Figure 21-2).

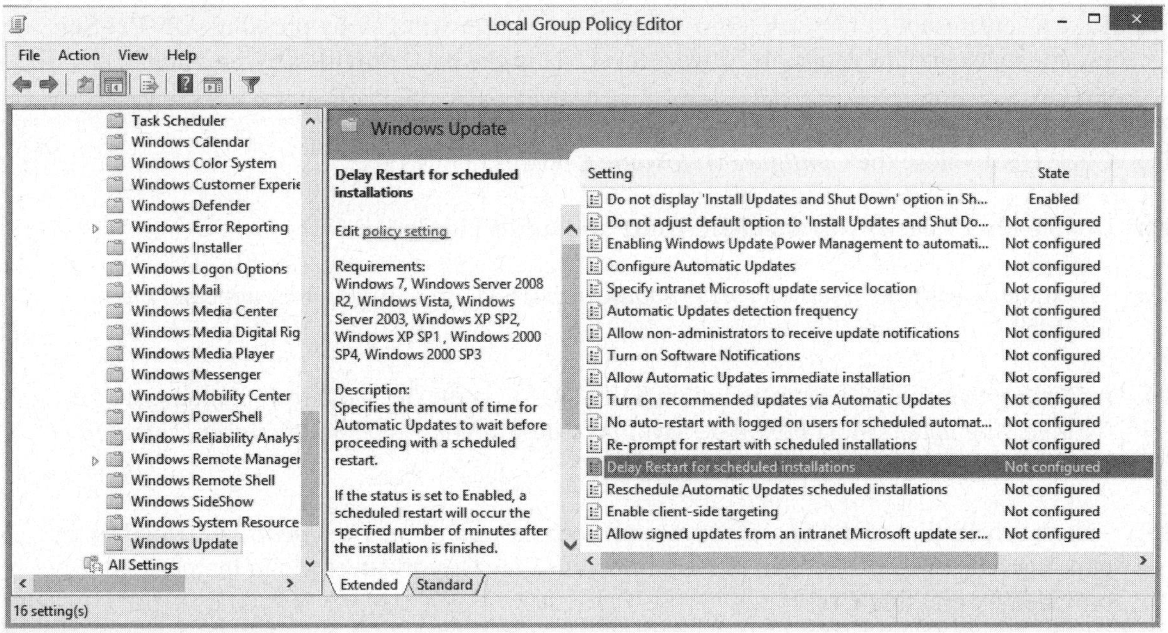

Figure 21-2
Windows Update settings

4. Double-click the **Do not display 'Install Updates and Shut Down' option in Shut Down Windows dialog box**.

5. When the *Do not display 'Install Updates and Shut Down' option in Shut Down Windows dialog box* appears, click **Enabled**.

6. Click **OK** to close the **Do not display 'Install Updates and Shut Down' option in Shut Down Windows** dialog box.

7. Double-click **Configure Automatic Updates**.

8. When the *Configure Automatic Updates* dialog box opens, click **Enabled**.

Question 2	*Which default Configure automatic updating setting is selected?*

Question 3	*By default, when are updates installed?*

9. Change the scheduled install day to **7 - Every Saturday**.

10. Take a screen shot of the *Configure Automatic Updates* window by pressing **Alt+Prt Scr** and then paste it into your Lab 21 worksheet file in the page provided by pressing **Ctrl+V**.

11. Click **OK** to close the *Configure Automatic Updates* dialog box.

12. Double-click **Specify intranet Microsoft update service location**.

13. When the *Specify intranet Microsoft update service location* dialog box appears, click **Enabled**.

14. Assuming that WSUS was installed on SVR-DC-A, in the *Set the intranet update service for detecting updates* text box, type **http://svr-dc-a:8530**. In the *Set the inranet statistics server* text box, type **http://svr-dc-a:8530**.

15. Take a screen shot of the *Specify intranet Microsoft update service location* dialog box by pressing **Alt+Prt Scr** and then paste it into your Lab 21 worksheet file in the page provided by pressing **Ctrl+V**.

16. Click **OK** to close the *Specify intranet Microsoft update service location* dialog box.

17. Double-click **Delay Restart for Scheduled installations**.

18. In the *Delay Restart for scheduled installations* dialog box, click **Enabled**.

19. For the restart (minutes), specify **30** minutes.

Question 4	*If the* Delay Restart for scheduled installations *is not defined, what is the default delay?*

20. Click **OK** to close the *Delay Restart for scheduled installations* dialog box.

21. Close **Local Group Policy Editor**.

End of exercise. Leave WKSTN-MBR-B running and logged in for the next exercise.

Exercise 21.3	Uninstalling an Installed Update
Overview	In this exercise, you will install an update, and then remove the update.
Mindset	If you have a problem with an update and you cannot find an easy solution to fix the problem, you might need to remove the update.
Completion time	20 minutes

1. On **WKSTN-MBR-B**, click the **File Explorer** icon on the Taskbar to open *File Explorer*.

2. Using *File Explorer*, open the **\\SVR-DC-A\Downloads** folder.

3. To install a patch for Internet Explorer 10, double-click **Windows8-RT-KB2761465-x64**.

4. When you are prompted to install the update, click **Yes**.

5. When the update is installed, click **Restart Now**.

6. Log into WKSTN-MBR-B as **adatum\administrator** using **Pa$$w0rd**.

7. Type **Control Panel** and then press **Enter**.

8. When the *Control Panel* opens, click **System and Security > Windows Update**.

Question 5	*If you hide an update that you know you want to install, which option is clicked to view the update?*

9. Click **View update history**.

10. On the *View update history* page, click **Installed Updates**. The updates are listed as shown in Figure 21-3.

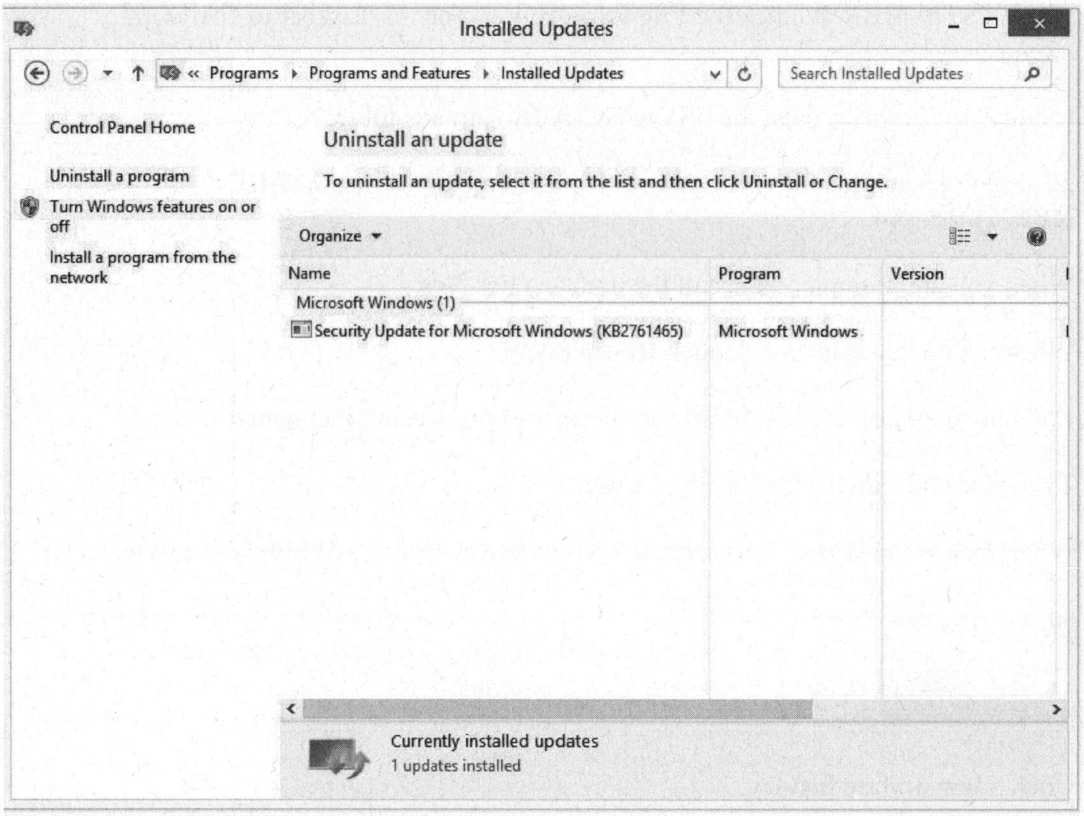

Figure 21-3
The *Installed Updates* page

11. Click **Security Update for Microsoft Windows (KB2761465)** and then click **Uninstall**.

12. When you are prompted to confirm that you want to uninstall this update, click **Yes**.

13. When you are prompted to Restart the computer, take a screen shot by pressing **Alt+Prt Scr** and then paste it into your Lab 21 worksheet file in the page provided by pressing **Ctrl+V**.

14. Click **Restart Now**.

End of exercise. Leave Windows running for the next exercise.

Lab Challenge	Configuring the Do Not Display Install Updates and Shutdown Policy
Overview	During this exercise, you will configure Local Group Policy from a computer running Windows 8.
Mindset	For organizations that manage the updates deployed to users, an administrator might choose not to display that install updates are available to be installed when the computer is being shut down.
Completion time	10 minutes

To complete this challenge, you must have a virtual machine on your computer running Windows 8. You will write out the procedure to configure the *Do not display 'Install Updates and Shut Down' option in Shut Down Windows dialog box* and then take a snapshot of the *Do not display 'Install Updates and Shut Down' option in Shut Down Windows dialog box* page by pressing **Alt+Prt Scr** and then paste the resulting image into the Lab 21 worksheet file in the page provided by pressing **Ctrl+V**.

End of lab.

LAB 22
MANAGING LOCAL STORAGE

THIS LAB CONTAINS THE FOLLOWING EXERCISES AND ACTIVITIES:

Exercise 22.1	Working with Basic Partitions
Exercise 22.2	Working with Dynamic Partitions
Lab Challenge	Managing Storage Spaces

BEFORE YOU BEGIN

The lab environment consists of computers connected to a local area network. The computers required for this lab are listed in Table 22-1.

Table 22-1
Computers Required for Lab 22

Computer	*Operating System*	*Computer Name*
Server	Windows Server 2012	SVR-DC-A
Workstation	Windows 8 Enterprise	WKSTN-MBR-B
Workstation	Windows 8 Enterprise	WKSTN-MBR-C

Aside from its system disk, the WKSTN-MBR-C workstation will require two additional disk drives, holding 20 GB each.

In addition to the computers, you will also need the software listed in Table 22-2 to complete Lab 22.

Table 22-2
Software Required for Lab 22

Software	***Location***
Lab 22 student worksheet	Lab22_worksheet.docx (provided by instructor)

Working with Lab Worksheets

Each lab in this manual requires that you answer questions, create screenshots, and perform other activities that you will document in a worksheet named for the lab, such as Lab22_worksheet.docx. You will find these worksheets on the book companion site. It is recommended that you use a USB flash drive to store your worksheets so you can submit them to your instructor for review. As you perform the exercises in each lab, open the appropriate worksheet file, type the required information, and then save the file to your flash drive.

SCENARIO

After completing this lab, you will be able to:

- Create and manipulate volumes on a basic disk
- Create and manipulate volumes on a dynamic disk
- Create and manipulate storage spaces

Estimated lab time: 40 minutes

Exercise 22.1	Working with Basic Partitions
Overview	In this exercise, you will create and manipulate partitions on a basic disk.
Mindset	Basic disks enable you to create simple volumes and then extend or shrink them as needed.
Completion time	10 minutes

1. On **WKSTN-MBR-C**, log on using the **adatum\Administrator** account and the **Pa$$w0rd** password.

2. On the **Start** screen, click the **Desktop** tile. The *Desktop* appears.

3. Mouse over the lower-left corner of the desktop, right-click the **Start** screen thumbnail and, from the context menu, choose **Disk Management**. The *Disk Management* snap-in appears (see Figure 22-1).

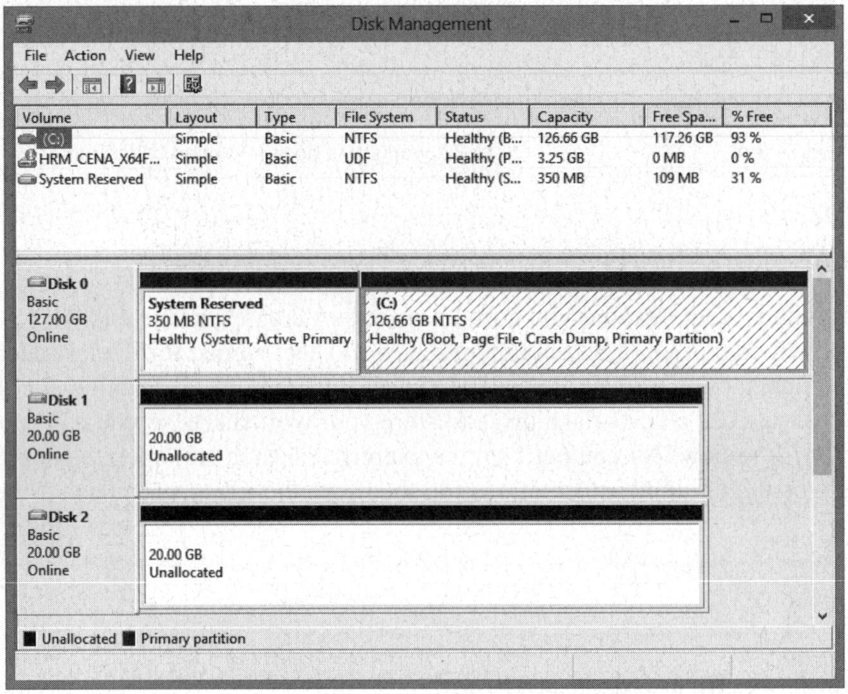

Figure 22-1
The *Disk Management* snap-in

4. Click **OK** to initialize *Disk1* and *Disk2*. Based on the information in the Disk Management snap-in, fill out the information in Table 22-1 on your lab worksheet.

Table 22-1
Disk information

	Disk 0	*Disk 1*	*Disk 2*
Disk type (basic or dynamic)			
Total disk size			
Number and type of partitions			
Amount of unallocated space			

5. In the graphical display of the snap-in, in the *Disk 1* information, right-click the Unallocated area and choose **New Simple Volume**. The *New Simple Volume* Wizard appears.

6. Click **Next** to bypass the *Welcome* page. The *Specify Volume Size* page appears.

7. In the *Simple Volume Size In MB* text box, type **2000** and then click **Next**. The *Assign Drive Letter Or Path* page appears.

8. Leave the *Assign the following drive letter* option selected, choose drive letter **X** from the drop-down list, and then click **Next**. The *Format Partition* page appears.

9. Leave the *Format this volume with the following settings* option selected and then configure the next three parameters as follows:

    - *File System:* **FAT32**
    - *Allocation Unit Size:* **Default**
    - *Volume Label:* **Part1**

10. Leave the *Perform a quick format* check box selected and then click **Next**. The *Completing The New Simple Volume Wizard* page appears.

11. Click **Finish**. The new volume appears in the *Disk Management* window.

12. Take a screen shot of the *Disk Management* window that shows the simple volume you created by pressing **Ctrl+Prt Scr** and then paste the resulting image into the Lab 22 worksheet file in the page provided by pressing **Ctrl+V**.

End of exercise. Leave all windows open for the next exercise.

Exercise 22.2	Working with Dynamic Partitions
Overview	In this exercise, you will create a spanned volume that utilizes space from two physical hard disks.
Mindset	A spanned volume enables you to combine the space from two or more disks into a single entity.
Completion time	10 minutes

1. On **WKSTN-MBR-C**, in the *Disk Management* snap-in, in the graphical display, right-click the **Disk 1** box and choose **Convert To Dynamic Disk**. The *Convert To Dynamic Disk* dialog box appears.

2. Leave the default Disk 1 check box selected and then click **OK**. The *Disks to Convert* dialog box appears (see Figure 22-2).

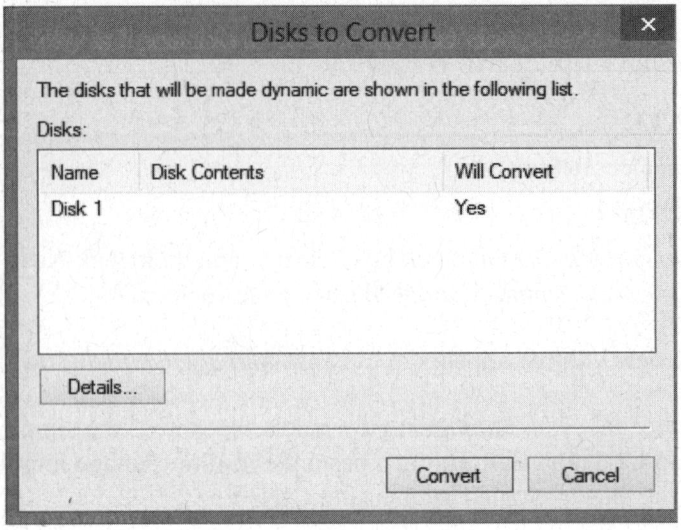

Figure 22-2
The *Disks to Convert* dialog box

3. Click **Convert**. A *Disk Management* message box appears, warning you that after you convert the disk to a dynamic disk, you will not be able to start installed operating systems from any volume other than the current boot volume.

4. Click **Yes** to continue. The program performs the disk conversion.

Question 1	*What has happened to the primary partition you created earlier in this lab?*

Question 2	*After you converted the basic disk to a dynamic disk, how many partitions can be found on the disk? How do you know?*

5. Right-click the **Part1** volume and study the context menu.

Question 3	*Why is the option to extend the volume grayed out?*

6. Right-click the unallocated space on **Disk1** and choose **New Spanned Volume**. The *New Spanned Volume* Wizard appears, displaying the *Welcome* page.

7. Click **Next**. The *Select Disks* page appears.

8. In the *Available* box, select **Disk2** and then click **Add**. *Disk2* moves to the *Selected* box.

9. Using the *Select the amount of space in MB* spin-box, configure *Disk1* and *Disk2* to contribute all of their available disk space to the spanned volume and then click **Next**. The *Assign Drive Letter or Path* page appears.

10. Select the drive letter **Z** and then click **Next**. The *Format Volume* page appears.

11. Leave the *Format this volume with the following settings* option selected and then configure the next three parameters as follows:

    - *File System:* **NTFS**
    - *Allocation Unit Size:* **Default**
    - *Volume Label:* **Part2**

12. Select the *Perform a quick format* check box and click then click **Next**. The *Completing The New Spanned Volume Wizard* page appears.

13. Click **Finish**. Click Yes to convert Disk 2 to dynamic. The wizard creates the volume.

14. Take a screen shot of the *Disk Management* window that shows the spanned volume you created by pressing **Ctrl+Prt Scr** and then paste the resulting image into the Lab 22 worksheet file in the page provided by pressing **Ctrl+V**.

End of exercise. Leave all windows open for the next exercise.

Lab Challenge	Managing Storage Spaces
Overview	In this challenge, you will use storage spaces to create a fault tolerant storage pool on a workstation running Windows 8
Mindset	Windows 8 includes a new storage virtualization technology called Storage Spaces, which enables a computer to use storage space from individual physical disks to create a virtual disk.
Completion time	20 minutes

To complete this challenge, you must delete the volumes you created on Disk1 and Disk2 of WKSTN-MBR-C and then use those disks to create a storage pool and a storage space with the following parameters:

- *Name:* **Databases**
- *Drive Letter:* **P**
- *Resiliency type:* **Two-way mirror**
- *Maximum size:* **80 GB**

Write out the steps you followed to complete the challenge and then show the pool you created by using **Ctrl+Prt Scr** to take screen shots of the *Create a storage pool* dialog box, the *Create a storage space* dialog box, and the *Disk Management* window. Then paste the resulting images into the Lab 22 worksheet file in the page provided by pressing **Ctrl+V**.

End of lab.

LAB 23
MONITORING SYSTEM PERFORMANCE

THIS LAB CONTAINS THE FOLLOWING EXERCISES AND ACTIVITIES:

Exercise 23.1	Using Event Viewer
Exercise 23.2	Using Task Manager
Exercise 23.3	Using Performance Monitor Console
Exercise 23.4	Using Resource Monitor
Lab Challenge	Using Reliability Monitor

BEFORE YOU BEGIN

The lab environment consists of student workstations connected to a local area network, along with a server that functions as the domain controller for a domain called adatum.com. The computers required for this lab are listed in Table 23-1.

Table 23-1
Computers Required for Lab 23

Computer	*Operating System*	*Computer Name*
Server	Windows Server 2012	SVR-DC-A
Client	Windows 8 Enterprise	WKSTN-MBR-B

In addition to the computers, you will also need the software listed in Table 23-2 to complete Lab 23.

Table 23-2
Software Required for Lab 23

Software	***Location***
Lab 23 student worksheet	Lab23_worksheet.docx (provided by instructor)

Working with Lab Worksheets

Each lab in this manual requires that you answer questions, shoot screen shots, and perform other activities that you will document in a worksheet named for the lab, such as Lab23_worksheet.docx. You will find these worksheets on the book companion site. It is recommended that you use a USB flash drive to store your worksheets, so you can submit them to your instructor for review. As you perform the exercises in each lab, open the appropriate worksheet file, type the required information, and then save the file to your flash drive.

SCENARIO

After completing this lab, you will be able to:

- View Windows logs using Event Viewer
- View performance using Task Manager, Resource Manager, and Performance Monitor
- Use Reliability Monitor for potential problems

Estimated lab time: 80 minutes

Exercise 23.1	Using Event Viewer
Overview	In this exercise, you will use the Event Viewer to look at the current Windows logs and to create a filter so that you can reduce the number of entries.
Mindset	The Event Viewer is used to view the warnings and errors for Windows.
Completion time	10 minutes

1. On **WKSTN-MBR-B**, log on using the **Adatum\administrator** account and the **Pa$$w0rd** password.
2. Type **Administrative Tools** and then press **Enter**.
3. When the *Administrative Tools* window opens, double-click **Event Viewer**.

4. Expand the **Windows Logs** folder and then click the **System** log (see Figure 23-1). The contents of the log appear in the detail pane.

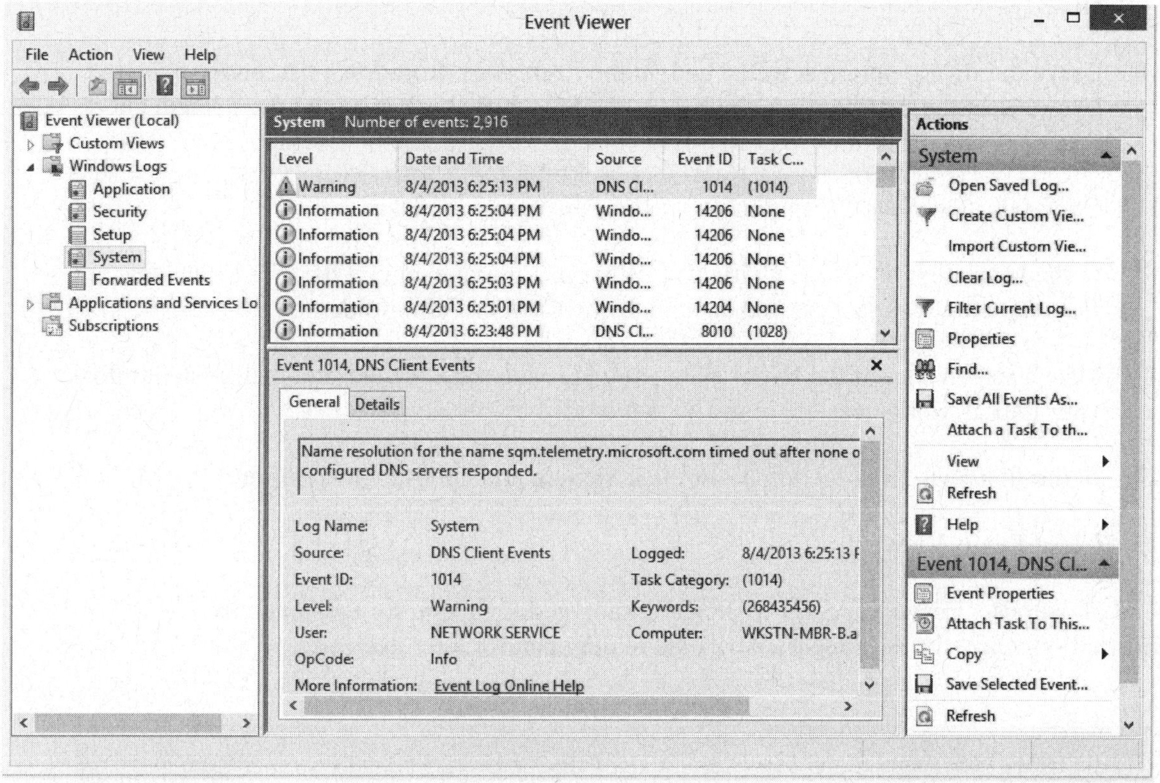

Figure 23-1
The *Event Viewer* page

Question 1	*How many events appear in the System log?*

5. Click the **Action** menu and choose **Filter Current Log**. The *Filter Current Log* dialog box appears.

6. In the *Event Level* area, select the **Critical** check box and then select the **Warning** check box. Click **OK**.

Question 2	*How many events appear in the System log now?*

7. Click **Action** > **Create Custom View**. The *Create Custom View* dialog box appears.

8. In the *Logged* drop-down list, click **Last 7 days**.

9. In the *Event Level* area, click the **Critical** check box and then select the **Warning** check box.

10. Leave the *By log* option selected and, in the *Event logs* drop-down list, under *Windows Logs*, select the **Application** check box, the **Security** check box, and the **System** check box.

11. Click **OK**. The *Save Filter to Custom View* dialog box appears.

12. In the *Name* text box, type **Critical & Warning** and then click **OK**. The *Critical & Warning* view you just created appears in the *Custom Views* folder.

13. Take a screen shot of the Event Viewer by pressing **Alt+Prt Scr** and then paste it into your Lab 23 worksheet file in the page provided by pressing **Ctrl+V**.

14. In the *Windows Logs* section, right-click **System** and choose **Clear Filter**.

15. Close **Event Viewer**.

End of exercise. Leave WKSTN-MBR-B running and logged in for the next exercise. In addition, leave the Administrative Tools folder open for later exercises.

Exercise 23.2	Using Task Manager
Overview	In this exercise, you will use the Task Manager to look at the basic performance of the system and to view the current processes running on Windows.
Mindset	Use the Task Manager when you need to quickly determine how well your machine is performing or when you need to stop a process that will not stop on its own.
Completion time	20 minutes

1. On **WKSTN-MBR-B**, right-click the **Taskbar** and choose **Task Manager**.

Question 3	*Which applications are running?*

Question 4	*Which tabs are shown?*

2. Click **More Details**. *Task Manager* expands (see Figure 23-2).

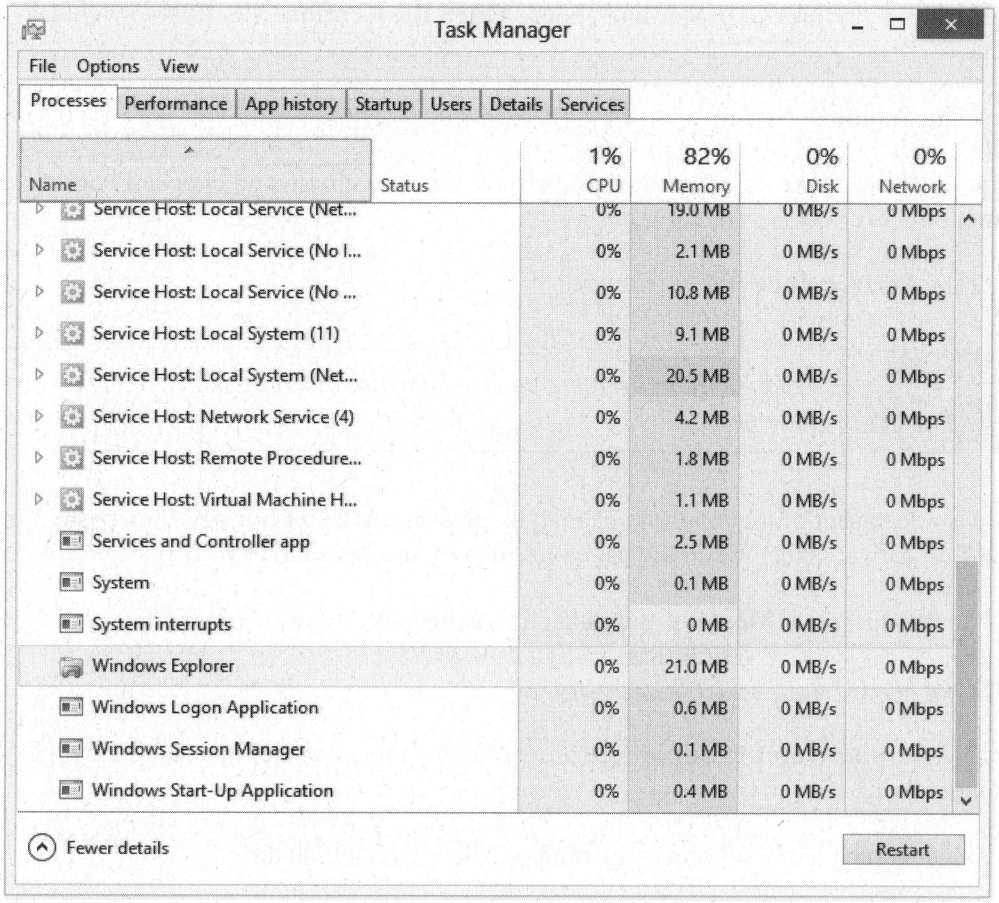

Figure 23-2
The *Task Manager* page

Question 5	*Which tabs are shown?*

3. Mouse over the lower-left corner of the desktop and click the **Start** screen thumbnail that appears there. Type **wordpad** and then press **Enter**.

Question 6	*In the Apps section, which process is used for WordPad?*

4. On the *Task Manager* page, click **Fewer details**.

5. Right-click **Windows Wordpad Application** and choose **End Task**.

6. Click **More details**.

7. Right-click **Windows Explorer** and choose **Open file location**. The *Windows* folder opens.

8. Close the **Windows** folder.

9. Right-click the ***Name*** column title at the top of the first column and choose **Process name**.

10. Click the **Performance** tab.

Question 7	*Which primary systems can be monitored with Task Manager?*

11. Take a screen shot of the *Performance* tab by pressing **Alt+Prt Scr** and then paste it into your Lab 23 worksheet file in the page provided by pressing **Ctrl+V**.

12. In the left pane, click **Memory** and then click **Ethernet** to view each option.

13. Click the **Users** tab.

14. Expand **Administrator** to display the programs and processes being executed by the administrator.

15. To see a detailed list of all processes running, click the **Details** tab.

16. To display additional columns, right-click the **Name** column title and choose **Select columns**.

17. When the *Select columns* dialog box opens, click to select the **Session ID** column and select the **Threads** column. Click **OK**.

18. To sort by components that make up the most memory, click the **Memory (private work set)** title.

19. From time to time, a program or action might cause Windows Explorer to stop functioning. In these cases, you can use Task Manager to stop and restart Explorer. Therefore, find and right-click **explorer.exe** and then choose **End task**.

20. When you are prompted to end *explorer.exe*, click **End process**.

21. Click **File** > **Run new task**.

22. When the *Create new task* dialog box, in the *Open* text box, type **explorer** and then click **OK**.

23. To view the current services, click the **Services** tab.

24. Close **Task Manager**.

End of exercise. Close any open windows before you begin the next exercise.

Exercise 23.3	Using Performance Monitor Console
Overview	In this exercise, you will open the Performance Monitor to take a closer look at system performance.
Mindset	The Task Manager gives you a quick view of system performance, but you can use Performance Monitor to probe a bit deeper (including the use of performance counters).
Completion time	30 minutes

To monitor various performance counters, perform the following steps:

1. On **WKSTN-MBR-B**, using **Administrative Tools**, double-click **Performance Monitor**.

2. Browse to and click **Monitoring Tools\Performance Monitor** (see Figure 23-3).

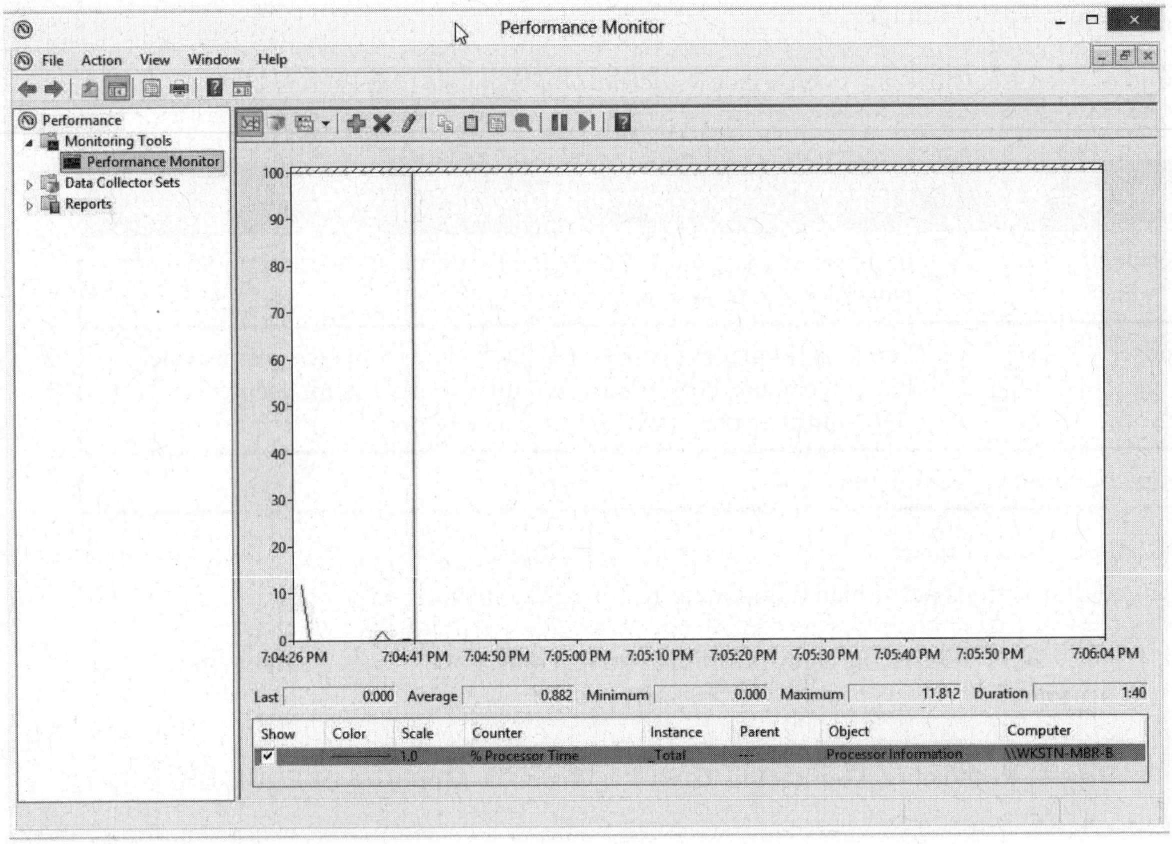

Figure 23-3
The *Performance Monitor* page

3. At the bottom of the screen, click **% Processor Time**. To remove the counter, click the **Delete** (red X) button at the top of the Window.

4. Click the **Add** (green plus (+) sign) button on the Toolbar. The *Add Counters* dialog box appears.

5. Under *Available counters*, expand **Processor**, click **% Processor Time**, and then click **Show description**. Read the description for *% Processor Time.*

6. Click **Add**. *% Processor Time* should show up in the *Added counters* section.

7. Under *Available Counters*, expand the **Server Work Queues** and then click the **Queue Length** counter. Under *Instances of selected objects*, click **0**. Then click **Add**.

8. Add the following counters:

   - *System:* **Processor Queue Length**
   - *Memory:* **Page Faults/Sec**
   - *Memory:* **Pages/Sec**
   - *PhysicalDisk (_Total):* **Current Disk Queue Length**

9. Click **OK** to close the *Add Counters* dialog box.

10. Mouse over the lower-left corner of the desktop, right-click the **Start** screen thumbnail that appears there, and then click **Command Prompt (Admin)**.

11. At the command prompt, execute the following command:

    ```
    dir c:\ /s
    ```

    You should see a spike in CPU usage.

12. At the top of the graph, you see a Toolbar with 13 buttons. Click the down arrow of the **Change graph type** (third button) and then click **Histogram bar**.

13. Change the graph type to **Report**.

14. Change back to the **Line graph**.

15. Click the **Properties** button (the fifth button from the end) on the Toolbar. The *Performance Monitor Properties* sheet appears. Notice the counters that you have selected.

16. Click **Processor (_Total)\%Processor Time**.

17. Change the width to heaviest line width. Change the color to **Red**.

18. Click the **Graph** tab.

19. In the *Vertical scale* box, change the value of the *Maximum* field to **200** and then click **OK**.

20. Close the *Administrator: Command Prompt* window.

To create and use a Data Collector Set, perform the following steps:

1. On **WKSTN-MBR-B**, in the left pane, expand **Data Collector Sets**.

2. Right-click the **User Defined** folder, choose **New** and then click **Data Collector Set**. In the *Name:* text box type **MyDCS1**.

3. Click **Create manually (Advanced)** and then click **Next**.

4. Select **Performance Counter** and then click **Next**.

5. To add counters, click **Add**.

6. Under *Available Counters*, expand the *Processor* node by clicking the down arrow next to *Processor*. Scroll down and click **%Processor Time**. Click **Add**.

7. Add the following counters.

   - *Server Work Queues:* **Queue Length counter**
   - *System:* **Processor Queue Length**
   - *Memory:* **Page Faults/Sec**
   - *Memory:* **Pages/Sec**
   - *PhysicalDisk (_Total):* **Current Disk Queue Length**

8. Click **OK** and then click **Next**.

9. Click **Finish**.

10. Right-click **MyDCS1** and choose **Start**.

11. Let it run for at least two minutes.

12. Right-click **MyDCS1** and choose **Stop**.

13. Open **File Explorer** and navigate to **c:\PerfLogs\Admin\MyDCS1**. Then open the folder that was just created.

14. Double-click **DataCollector01.blg**. The *Performance Monitor* graph opens.

Question 8	*Now that the DCS has been created, what advantages does the MyDCS1 have?*

15. Take a screen shot of the *Performance Monitor* window by pressing **Alt+Prt Scr** and then paste it into your Lab 23 worksheet file in the page provided by pressing **Ctrl+V**.

16. Close the **Performance Monitor** graph and then close the **MyDCS1** folder.

17. Close **Performance Monitor**.

End of exercise. Leave the *Administrator Tools* window open. You can close any other open windows before you begin the next exercise.

Exercise 23.4	Using Resource Monitor
Overview	In this exercise, you will use Resource Monitor to determine which processes are using the primary computer resources.
Mindset	The Resource Monitor extends the capabilities of the Task Manager.
Completion time	10 minutes

1. On **WKSTN-MBR-B**, using the *Administrative Tools*, double-click **Resource Monitor**.

Question 9	*Which primary systems can be monitored with Resource Monitor?*

2. On the *Resource Monitor* page (see Figure 23-4), click the **CPU** tab.

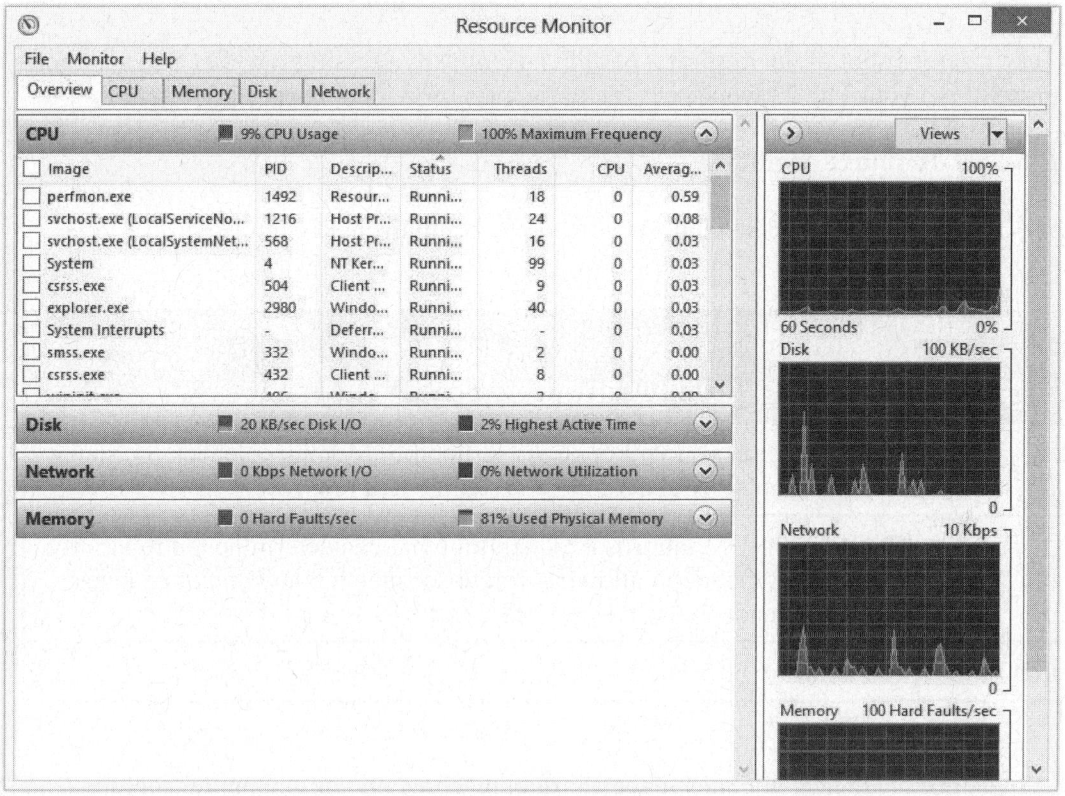

Figure 23-4
The *Resource Monitor* page

3. To sort the processes alphabetically, click the **Image** title at the top of the first column in the *Processes* section.

4. Click the **Memory** tab.

Question 10	*Which process is using the most memory?*

5. Click the **Disk** tab.

Question 11	*Which process is using the disk the most?*

6. Click the **Network** tab and then expand **Listening Ports**.

Question 12	*Which image is listening on port 53?*

7. Take a screen shot of the *Resource Monitor* window by pressing **Alt+Prt Scr** and then paste it into your Lab 23 worksheet file in the page provided by pressing **Ctrl+V**.

8. Close the **Resource Monitor**.

End of exercise. Close any open windows before you begin the next exercise.

Lab Challenge	Using Reliability Monitor
Overview	In this exercise, you will open the Reliability Monitor to check the status of the computer by generating a system health report.
Mindset	The Reliability Monitor is a hidden tool that can determine the reliability of a system, including allowing you to see whether any recent changes have been made to the system itself
Completion time	10 minutes

To complete this challenge, you must have a virtual machine on your computer running Windows 8. You will write out the procedure to open Reliability Monitor and generate a system health report. Then you will take a snapshot of the *Resource and Performance Monitor System Diagnostics Report* page by pressing **Alt+Prt Scr** and then paste the resulting image into the Lab 23 worksheet file in the page provided by pressing **Ctrl+V**.

End of lab.

LAB 24
CONFIGURING BACKUPS

THIS LAB CONTAINS THE FOLLOWING EXERCISES AND ACTIVITIES:

Exercise 24.1 Creating a Custom Backup Job

Exercise 24.2 Performing an Incremental Backup Job

Lab Challenge Scheduling a Backup Job

BEFORE YOU BEGIN

The lab environment consists of computers connected to a local area network in an Active Directory Domain Services configuration. The computers required for this lab are listed in Table 24-1.

Table 24-1
Computers Required for Lab 24

Computer	***Operating System***	***Computer Name***
Server	Windows Server 2012	SVR-DC-A
Workstation	Windows 8 Enterprise	WKSTN-MBR-B
Workstation	Windows 8 Enterprise	WKSTN-MBR-C

In addition to the computers, you will also need the software listed in Table 24-2 to complete Lab 24.

Table 24-2
Software Required for Lab 24

Software	*Location*
Lab 24 student worksheet	Lab24_worksheet.docx (provided by instructor)

Working with Lab Worksheets

Each lab in this manual requires that you answer questions, create screenshots, and perform other activities that you will document in a worksheet named for the lab, such as Lab24_worksheet.docx. You will find these worksheets on the book companion site. It is recommended that you use a USB flash drive to store your worksheets so you can submit them to your instructor for review. As you perform the exercises in each lab, open the appropriate worksheet file, type the required information, and then save the file to your flash drive.

SCENARIO

After completing this lab, you will be able to:

- Create backup jobs
- Understand incremental backup jobs
- Create a backup schedule

Estimated lab time: 45 minutes

Exercise 24.1	Creating a Custom Backup Job
Overview	In this exercise, you will use the Windows 7 File Recovery program to back up files on a Windows 8 computer.
Mindset	Windows 8 includes the backup program from Windows 7 to support users with existing backups made with the previous operating system version.
Completion time	20 minutes

1. On **WKSTN-MBR-C**, log on using the **adatum\Administrator** account and the **Pa$$w0rd** password.

2. Click the **Desktop** tile. The *Desktop* appears.

3. Mouse over the lower-left corner of the desktop and right-click the **Start** screen thumbnail that appears there. Then, from the context menu that appears, click **Disk Management**. The *Disk Management* window appears.

4. On Disk 1, right-click the unallocated space and choose **New Simple Volume**. The *New Simple Volume* Wizard appears.

5. Follow the instructions in the wizard to create an NTFS volume from all of the unallocated disk space using the drive letter **X:** and the volume name **Backup**.

6. Close the *Disk Management* window.

7. Mouse over the lower-left corner of the desktop and right-click the **Start** screen thumbnail that appears there. Then, from the context menu that appears, click **Control Panel**. The *Control Panel* window appears.

8. In the *View by* drop-down list, click **Large icons**. The *Control Panel* interface displays individual icons for each of the available applications.

9. Click **Windows 7 File Recovery**. The *Windows 7 File Recovery* control panel appears (see Figure 24-1).

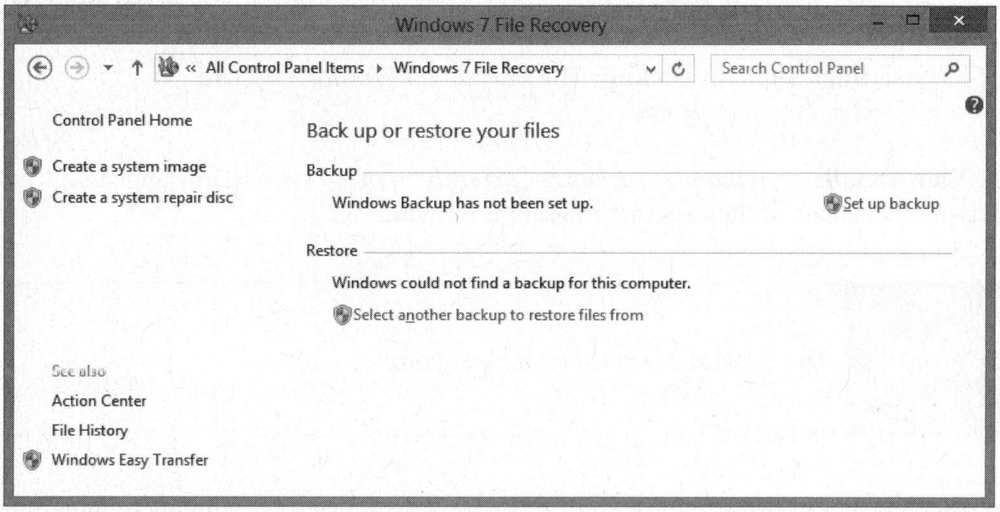

Figure 24-1
The *Windows 7 File Recovery* control panel

10. Click **Set up backup**. The *Set Up Backup* Wizard appears, displaying the *Select where you want to save your backup* page.

11. Select the **Backup (X:)** partition and then click Next. The *What do you want to back up?* page appears.

Question 1	*Why doesn't the system drive (C:) appear on the* Select where you want to save your backup *page?*

12. Select the **Let me choose** option and then click **Next**. The *What do you want to back up?* page appears.

13. Expand the **Local Disk (C:)** container.

Question 2	*Why doesn't the Windows folder appear under the Local Disk (C:) drive?*

14. Select the **Local Disk (C:)** check box and then clear the **Include a system image of drives: System Reserved, (C:)** check box. Click **Next**. The *Review your backup settings* page appears.

15. Click **Change Schedule**. The *How often do you want to back up?* page appears.

16. Clear the **Run backup on a schedule (recommended)** check box and then click **OK**. The schedule indicator on the *Review your backup settings* page changes to *On demand.*

17. Take a screen shot of the *Review your backup settings* page by pressing **Alt+Prt Scr** and then paste the resulting image into the Lab 24 worksheet file in the page provided by pressing **Ctrl+V**.

18. Click **Save settings and run backup**. The *Backup and Restore* Wizard now shows the backup in progress.

19. Click **View Details**. A *Windows Backup is currently in progress* window appears, displaying the names of the files the program is copying.

NOTE	*The backup process can take several minutes.*

20. Take a screen shot of the *Windows Backup is currently in progress* window by pressing **Alt+Prt Scr** and then paste the resulting image into the Lab 24 worksheet file in the page provided by pressing **Ctrl+V**.

21. Click **Close**.

Question 3	*What is the size of the backup, as indicated on the Backup and Restore control panel?*

22. Close the *Windows 7 File Recovery* control panel.

End of exercise. Close all open windows before the next exercise.

Exercise 24.2	Performing an Incremental Backup Job
Overview	In this exercise, you will create a new file on the computer and repeat the backup job you performed in Exercise 24.1 to demonstrate how incremental backup jobs work.
Mindset	An incremental backup job only saves the files that have changed since the last backup. This saves time and storage space on the backup medium.
Completion time	15 minutes

1. On **WKSTN-MBR-C**, mouse over the lower-left corner of the desktop and right-click the **Start** screen thumbnail that appears there.

2. On the **Start** screen, type **Notepad**. Then, in the results area, click the *Notepad* tile. A *Notepad* window appears (see Figure 24-2).

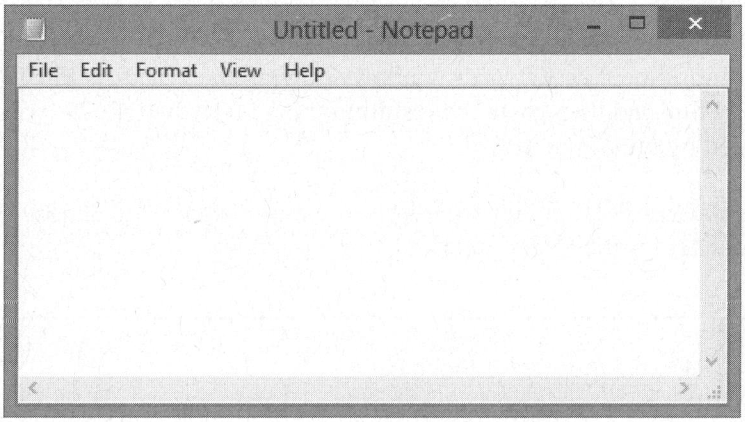

Figure 24-2
A *Notepad* window

3. Type any text in the Notepad window and then click **File > Save As**. The *Save As* combo box appears.

4. In the *File name* text box, type **c:\newfile.txt** and then click **Save**. Notepad creates the new file at the root of the C: drive.

5. Open the **Windows 7 File Recovery** control panel, just as you did in Exercise 24.1.

Question 4	*How is the Windows 7 control panel interface different from when you opened it the first time?*

6. Click **Back up now**. The program repeats the backup job you configured earlier.

Question 5	*How does the time required for this backup compare with that for the same job the first time you ran it?*

7. Switch to the **Notepad** window.

8. Modify the text you typed in the *Notepad* window and then click **File** > **Save**.

9. Switch back to the **Windows 7 File Recovery** control panel and then click **Back up now** again. The program performs a third backup.

10. On the Taskbar, click the **File Explorer** button. A *File Explorer* window appears.

11. Browse to the **Backup (X:)** drive, expand the **WKSTN-MBR-C** container and expand the folder beginning with **Backup Set** (including the date).

Question 6	*How many Backup Files folders are there beneath the Backup Set folder?*

12. Take a screen shot of the *File Explorer* window showing the *Backup Files* folders, by pressing **Alt+Prt Scr** and then paste the resulting image into the Lab 24 worksheet file in the page provided by pressing **Ctrl+V**.

13. Right-click the **Backup Files** folder with the earliest timestamp and choose **Properties**. The *Properties* sheet for the folder appears.

Question 7	*What is the size of the folder?*

14. Click **OK** to close the *Properties* sheet.

15. Open the *Properties* sheet for the second and third *Backup Files* folders.

Question 8	*Why are these Backup Files folders so much smaller than the first one?*

16. Click **OK** to close the Properties sheet.

End of exercise. Leave all windows open for the next exercise.

Lab Challenge	Scheduling a Backup Job
Overview	Performing a single backup job provides only limited protection against hardware failure. To fully protect your data, you must back up regularly. Windows 8 enables you to schedule backup jobs to run at specified intervals.
Mindset	Creating a regularly scheduled backup strategy is an essential part of Windows 8 administration.
Completion time	10 minutes

To complete this challenge, you must create a job that backs up your workstation's entire system (C:) drive to the X: drive every Friday at 11:00 PM. Write out the procedure for creating the job and take a screen shot of the *Review your backup settings* page by pressing **Alt+Prt Scr** and then paste the resulting image into the Lab 24 worksheet file in the page provided by pressing **Ctrl+V**.

End of lab.

LAB 25
CONFIGURING SYSTEM RECOVERY OPTIONS

THIS LAB CONTAINS THE FOLLOWING EXERCISES AND ACTIVITIES:

Exercise 25.1	Creating and Reverting to a System Restore Point
Exercise 25.2	Using Windows Safe Mode
Exercise 25.3	Performing a File Restore from Backup
Lab Challenge	Performing a PC Reset

BEFORE YOU BEGIN

The lab environment consists of student workstations connected to a local area network, along with a server that functions as the domain controller for a domain called adatum.com. The computers required for this lab are listed in Table 25-1.

Table 25-1
Computers Required for Lab 25

Computer	*Operating System*	*Computer Name*
Server	Windows Server 2012	SVR-DC-A
Client	Windows 8 Enterprise	WKSTN-MBR-B
Client	Windows 7 Enterprise	WKSTN-MBR-C

In addition to the computers, you will also need the software listed in Table 25-2 to complete Lab 25.

Table 25-2
Software Required for Lab 25

Software	***Location***
Lab 25 student worksheet	Lab25_worksheet.docx (provided by instructor)

Working with Lab Worksheets

Each lab in this manual requires that you answer questions, shoot screen shots, and perform other activities that you will document in a worksheet named for the lab, such as Lab25_worksheet.docx. You will find these worksheets on the book companion site. It is recommended that you use a USB flash drive to store your worksheets so you can submit them to your instructor for review. As you perform the exercises in each lab, open the appropriate worksheet file, type the required information, and then save the file to your flash drive.

SCENARIO

After completing this lab, you will be able to:

- Create and revert to a system restore point
- Boot Windows into Safe Mode
- Backup and restore files using Windows 7 Backup

Estimated lab time: 70 minutes

Exercise 25.1	Creating and Reverting to a System Restore Point
Overview	In this exercise, you will create a restore point that can be used to roll back the system files and programs to a previously saved restore point.
Mindset	Sometimes when you install or upgrade a program, Windows or the program does not run properly. If you have a restore point, you can recover from these problems by rolling back to the previous point.
Completion time	15 minutes

1. On **WKSTN-MBR-B**, log on using the **adatum\administrator** account and the **Pa$$w0rd** password.

2. Type **Control Panel** and then click the **Control Panel** icon.

3. In the *Search Control Panel* text box, type **Create a Restore point** and then press **Enter**. When the *Create a restore point* option is displayed, click **Create a restore point**.

Question 1	*Which drive is listed in the Protection Settings box?*

4. In the *System Properties* dialog box (see Figure 25-1), click **Configure**.

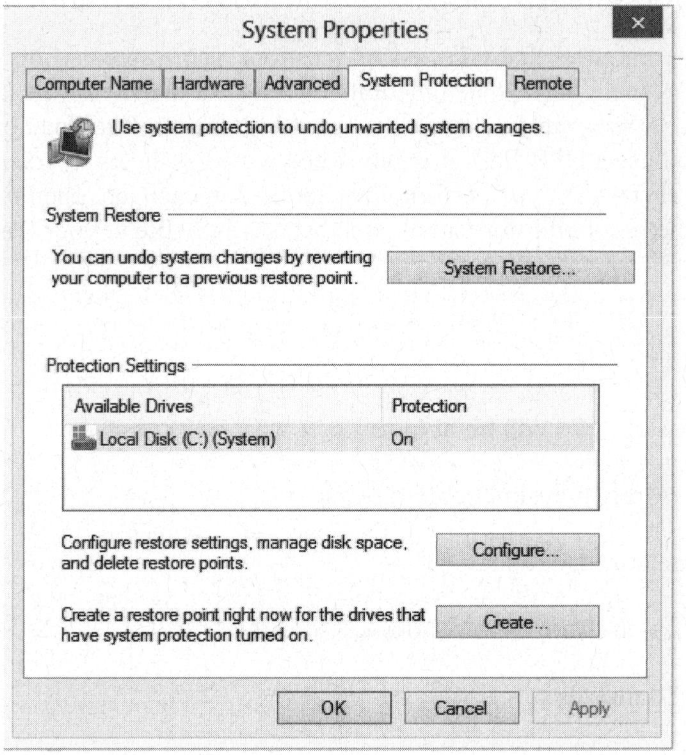

Figure 25-1
The *System Properties* page

5. When the *System Protection for Local Disk (C:)* dialog box opens, click to select **Turn on system protection**. Then slide *Max Usage:* to **10%**.

6. Click **OK** to close the *System Protection for Local Disk (C:)* dialog box.

7. To create a restore point, click **Create**.

8. In the *System Protection* dialog box, in the *Description* text box, type **Test** and then click **Create**.

9. When the restore point is created, take a screen shot of the *System Protection* dialog box by pressing **Alt+Prt Scr** and then paste it into your Lab 25 worksheet file in the page provided by pressing **Ctrl+V**.

10. Click **Close**.

11. In the *System Properties* dialog box, click **System Restore**.
12. When the *System Restore* Wizard opens, click **Next**.
13. Click the **Test** restore point that you just made and then click **Next**.
14. In the *Confirm your restore point* dialog box, click **Finish**.
15. When presented with a warning message indicating that system restore cannot be interrupted, click **Yes** to continue.
16. After WKSTN-MBR-B reboots, log on as **adatum\administrator** using the **Pa$$w0rd** password.
17. Click the **Desktop** tile.
18. The system restore is completed. Take a screen shot of the *System Restore* dialog box by pressing **Alt+Prt Scr** and then paste it into your Lab 25 worksheet file in the page provided by pressing **Ctrl+V**.
19. Click **Close** to close the *System Restore* dialog box.

End of exercise. Leave WKSTN-MBR-B running and logged in for the next exercise.

Exercise 25.2	Using Windows Safe Mode
Overview	In this exercise, you will boot to Safe Mode and look at the various tools that are available in Safe Mode that can be used to troubleshoot Windows.
Mindset	Safe Mode is a troubleshooting option used for Windows that launches Windows with basic files and drivers.
Completion time	20 minutes

1. Mouse over the lower-left corner of the desktop and right-click the **Start** screen thumbnail that appears there. Then, from the context menu that appears, click **Command Prompt (Admin)**.
2. At the command prompt, execute the following command:

   shutdown /r /o

3. When prompted to shut down the system, click **Close**. The system will shut down in less than a minute.
4. Click the **Troubleshoot** tile.
5. Click the **Advanced options** tile.

6. Click **Startup Settings**.

7. Select **Restart**.

8. When the *Startup Settings* options show (see Figure 25-2), press **4** on the keyboard.

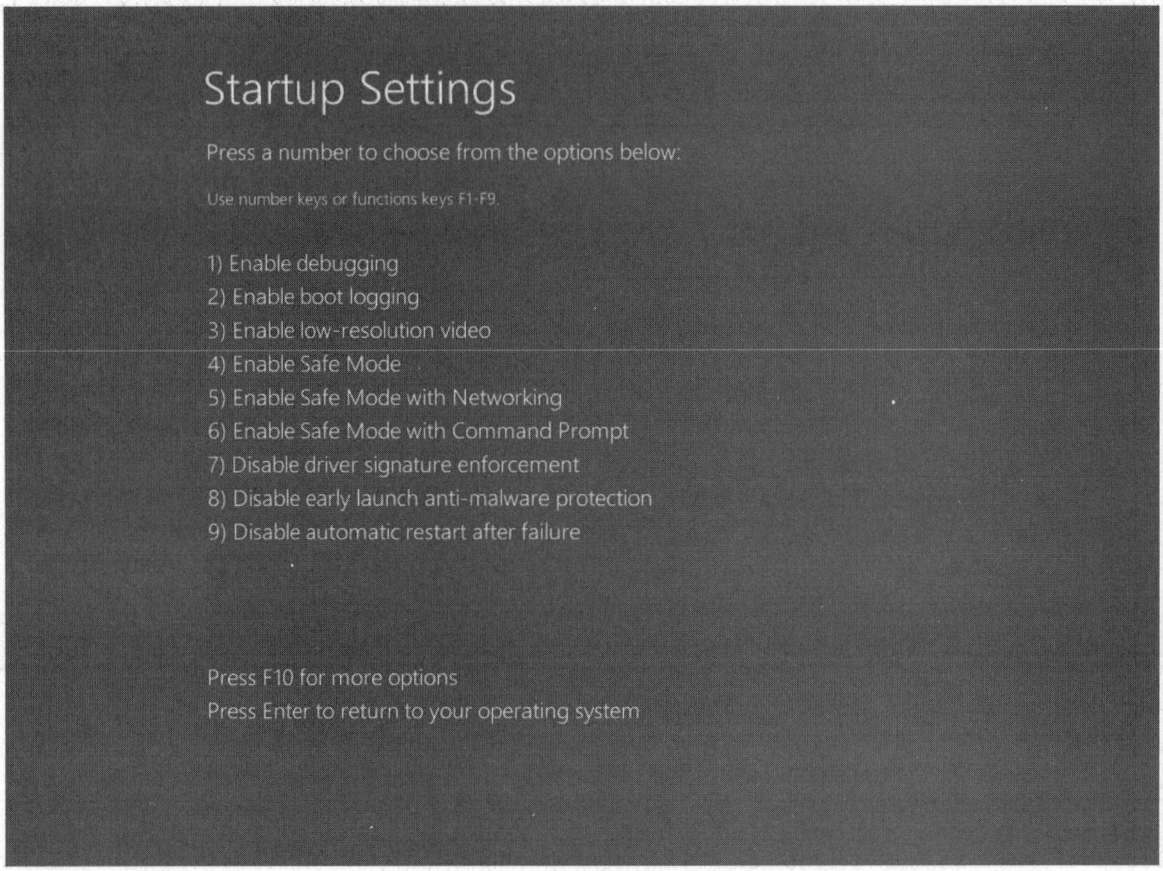

Figure 25-2
The *Startup Settings* page

9. After WKSTN-MBR-B boots, log in as **adatum\administrator** using the **Pa$$w0rd** password.

10. Close the **Windows Help and Support** window.

11. Mouse over the lower-left corner of the desktop and click the **Start** screen thumbnail that appears there. Then, on the *Start* page, type **msconfig** and then click the **msconfig** tile.

12. Take a screen shot of the *General* tab by pressing **Alt+Prt Scr** and then paste it into your Lab 25 worksheet file in the page provided by pressing **Ctrl+V**.

13. Click the **Boot** tab.

Question 2	*What is the boot entry that is shown?*

14. Click the **Services** tab.

Question 3	*How many services are running? (Click the Status column to sort the Running vs Stopped entries to make it easier to count the Running entries).*

15. Click to select **Hide all Microsoft services**.

Question 4	*How many non-Microsoft services do you have?*

16. Click **OK** to close the *System Configuration* window.

17. Mouse over the lower-left corner of the desktop and click the **Start** screen thumbnail that appears there. Then, on the screen, type **compmgmt.msc** and then click the **compmgmt tile**.

Question 5	*Which program was opened by typing compmgmt?*

18. Click **Event Viewer > Windows Logs** and then review the *System* log and the *Application* log. (If you were actually experiencing a problem, you would look for events that would help you troubleshoot the problem.)

19. Close the **Computer Management** console.

20. Use **File Explorer** to navigate to the **C:\Windows** folder and locate the **ntbtlog.txt** file.

21. Open the **ntbtlog.txt** file to view its contents.

22. Take a screen shot of the *ntbtlog* file by pressing **Alt+Prt Scr** and then paste it into your Lab 25 worksheet file in the page provided by pressing **Ctrl+V**.

23. Close the **ntbtlog.txt** file.

24. Move the mouse pointer to the bottom-right corner to display the Charms bar. Then click **Settings > Power > Restart** to restart the computer.

End of exercise.

Exercise 25.3	Performing a File Restore from Backup
Overview	In this exercise, you will back up some files and then restore one of those files using the Windows 7 Backup program.
Mindset	When you are having computer problems and all other troubleshooting efforts fail to reveal the issue, you can restore from a backup (assuming you took the precaution of taking a backup).
Completion time	25 minutes

1. On **SVR-DC-A**, log in using the **Adatum\administrator** account and the **Pa$$w0rd** password.
2. On the *Taskbar*, click **File Explorer**.
3. Create a **C:\Data** folder.
4. Right-click the **C:\Data** folder and choose **Properties**.
5. In the *Data Properties* dialog box, click the **Sharing** tab.
6. Click the **Advanced Sharing** button.
7. In the *Advanced Sharing* dialog box, click to select **Share this folder**.
8. Click the **Permissions** button.
9. Click to select **Allow Full Control Permission** for the *Everyone* group.
10. Click **OK** to close the *Permissions for Data* dialog box.
11. Click **OK** to close the *Advanced Sharing* dialog box.
12. Click **Close** to close the *Data Properties* dialog box.
13. Log into WKSTN-MBR-B as **contoso\administrator** using the **Pa$$w0rd** password. Click the **Desktop** tile.
14. Mouse over the lower-left corner of the desktop and right-click the **Start** screen thumbnail that appears there. Then, from the context menu that appears, click the **Control Panel** option.
15. In the *Search Control Panel* text box, type **Windows 7 File Recovery** and click **Windows 7 File Recovery** link. The Windows 7 File Recovery page appears (see Figure 25-3).

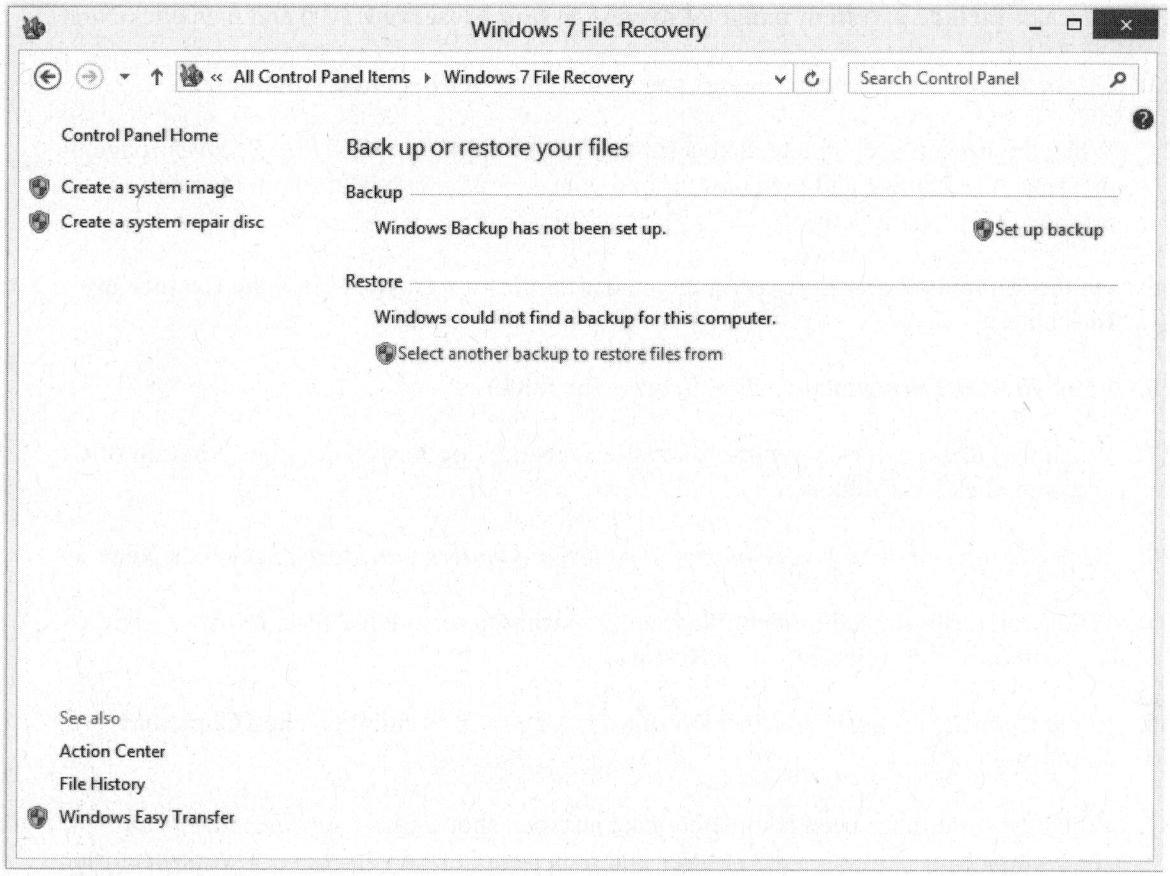

Figure 25-3
The *Windows 7 File Recovery* page

16. Click **Set up backup**.

17. On the *Set up backup* page, click **Save on a network**.

18. When the *Set up backup* page opens, ... In the *Network location* text box, type **\\svr-dc-a\data**.

19. In the *Username* text box, type **adatum\administrator**. In the *Password* text box, type **Pa$$w0rd**. Click **OK**.

20. On the *Set up backup* page, ensure **\\SVR-DC-A\data** is selected and then click **Next**.

21. On the *What do you want to back up?* page, select the **Let me choose** option and then click **Next**.

Question 6	*By default, which items are selected for backup?*

22. Deselect **Include a system image of drives: System Reserved, (C:)** and then click **Next**.

23. On the *Review your backup settings* page, click **Save settings and run backup**.

24. When the backup is complete, take a screen shot of the *Windows 7 File Recovery* page by pressing **Alt+Prt Scr** and then paste it into your Lab 25 worksheet file in the page provided by pressing **Ctrl+V**.

25. On the *Windows 7 File Recovery* page, under the *Restore* section, click the **Restore my files** button.

26. In the *Restore Files* window, click **Browse for folders**.

27. When the *Browse the backup for folders or drives* dialog box opens, click **Backup of C:** and then click **Add folder**.

28. On the *Browse or search your backup for files and folders to restore* page, click **Next**.

29. When you are prompted to identify where you want to restore the files, *In the original location* is already selected. Click **Restore**.

30. In the *Copy file* dialog box, select **Do this for all conflicts** and then click **Copy and Replace**.

31. When the restore has been completed, take a screen shot of the *Your files have been restored* page by pressing **Alt+Prt Scr** and then paste it into your Lab 25 worksheet file in the page provided by pressing **Ctrl+V**.

32. Click **Finish**.

33. Close **Windows 7 File Recovery**.

End of exercise. Leave Windows open for the next exercise.

Lab Challenge	Performing a PC Reset
Overview	In this exercise, you will demonstrate how to perform a PC reset.
Mindset	A PC reset allows you reset the computer to its factory settings, removing all of your personal files and apps. A PC refresh allows you to reset the computer without affecting your files.
Completion time	10 minutes

During this exercise, you will specify the steps to perform a PC reset. This exercise is a written exercise.

End of lab.

LAB 26
CONFIGURING FILE RECOVERY OPTIONS

THIS LAB CONTAINS THE FOLLOWING EXERCISES AND ACTIVITIES:

Exercise 26.1 Using File History

Lab Challenge Configuring the Advanced Settings of File History

BEFORE YOU BEGIN

The lab environment consists of student workstations connected to a local area network, along with a server that functions as the domain controller for a domain called adatum.com. The computers required for this lab are listed in Table 26-1.

Table 26-1
Computers required for Lab 26

Computer	***Operating System***	***Computer Name***
Server	Windows Server 2012	SVR-DC-A
Client	Windows 8 Enterprise	WKSTN-MBR-B

In addition to the computers, you will also need the software listed in Table 26-2 to complete Lab 26.

Table 26-2
Software Required for Lab 26

Software	***Location***
Lab 26 student worksheet	Lab26_worksheet.docx (provided by instructor)

Working with Lab Worksheets

Each lab in this manual requires that you answer questions, shoot screen shots, and perform other activities that you will document in a worksheet named for the lab, such as Lab26_worksheet.docx. You will find these worksheets on the book companion site. It is recommended that you use a USB flash drive to store your worksheets so you can submit them to your instructor for review. As you perform the exercises in each lab, open the appropriate worksheet file, type the required information, and then save the file to your flash drive.

SCENARIO

After completing this lab, you will be able to:

- Restore a file that is saved in File History
- Configure the advanced settings of File History

Estimated lab time: 30 minutes

Exercise 26.1	Using File History
Overview	In this exercise, you will restore a file that is saved in File History.
Mindset	File History is an alternative to Windows 7 File Recovery. It allows for files backed up on previous versions of Windows to be recovered.
Completion time	20 minutes

1. On **WKSTN-MBR-B**, log on using the **adatum\administrator** account and the **Pa$$w0rd** password. Click the **Desktop** tile.

2. Right-click the **Desktop** and choose **New > Text Document**. Name the document **Test**.

3. Mouse over the lower-left corner of the desktop and right-click the **Start** screen thumbnail that appears there. Then, from the context menu that appears, click the **Control Panel** icon.

4. Click **System and Security** and then click **File History**.

Question 1	*According to what's shown on-screen, which feature must be disabled before you can use File History?*

5. Click **Configure Windows 7 Backup**.

6. On the *Windows 7 File Recovery* page, click **Turn off schedule**.

7. On the *Windows 7 File Recovery* page, click the back arrow.

8. On the *File History* page (see Figure 26-1), click **Use network location**.

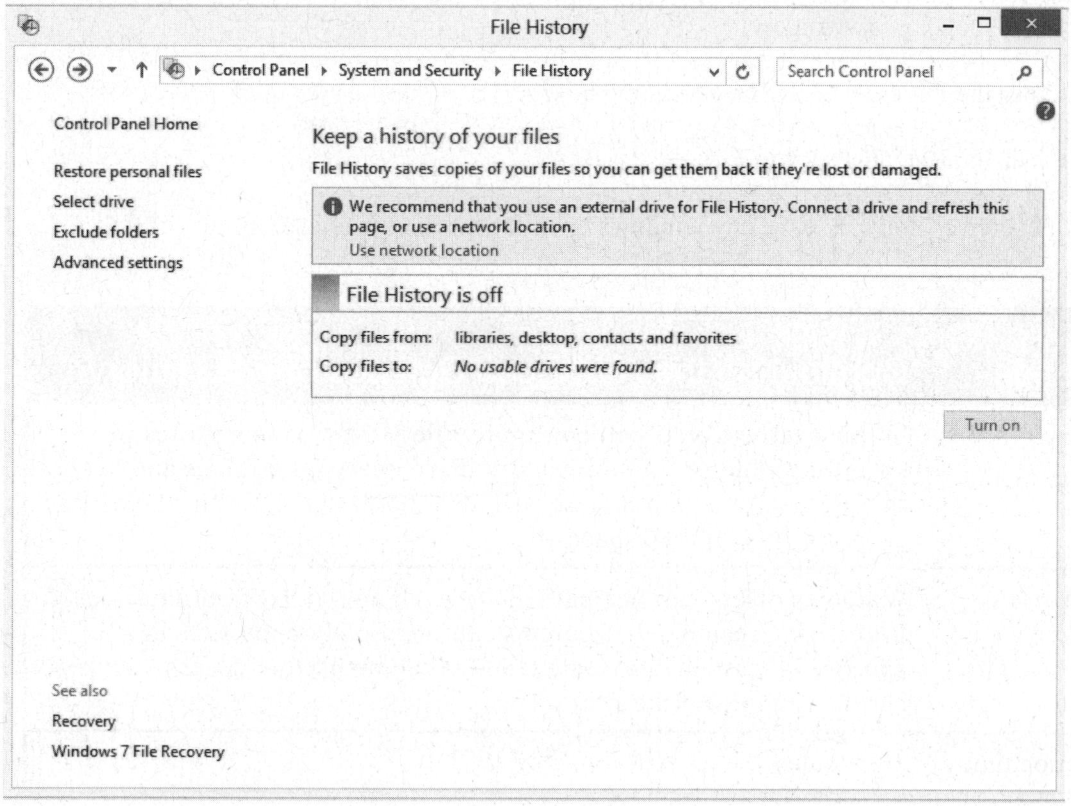

Figure 26-1
The *File History* page

9. On the *Select Drive* page, click **Add network location**.

10. In the *Select Folder* dialog box, in the *Folder* text box, type **SVR-DC-A\Data** and then click **Select Folder**.

11. On the *Select Drive* page, click **OK**.

12. On the *File History* page, click **Turn on**.

13. Click **Run now**.

14. Take a screen shot of the *File History* window by pressing **Alt+Prt Scr** and then paste it into your Lab 26 worksheet file in the page provided by pressing **Ctrl+V**.

15. In the left pane, click **Restore personal files**.

16. On the *Home - File History* window, double-click **Desktop**.

17. Click **Test** and then click the **Restore to original location** button (green button) at the bottom of the window.

18. In the *Replace or Skip Files* dialog box, click **Replace this file in the destination**.

19. **Close** the *Desktop* window.

20. **Close** the *Desktop - File History* dialog box.

21. **Close** the *File History* window.

End of exercise. You can leave any windows open for the next exercise.

Lab Challenge	Configuring the Advanced Settings of File History
Overview	In this exercise, you will configure File History to copy files in specified folders to a File History drive every 30 minutes and keep the files for one month. You will also increase the size of the offline cache to 10% of disk space.
Mindset	Windows offers various methods to back up and recover data files. File History can be configured to automatically copy files to a specified location. Then File History can be used to access an earlier versions of the files.
Completion time	10 minutes

To complete this challenge, you must have a virtual machine on your computer running Windows 8. You will write out the procedure to configure the Advanced Settings of File History. Then you will take a snapshot of the *File History Advanced Settings* page by pressing **Alt+Prt Scr** and then paste the resulting image into the Lab 26 worksheet file in the page provided by pressing **Ctrl+V**.

End of lab.